SAINT THOMAS AQUINAS

SUMMA THEOLOGIAE
SUPPLEMENTUM, 1–68

Translated by Fr. Laurence Shapcote, OP

SUMMA THEOLOGIAE

Volume 21
Latin/English Edition of the Works of St. Thomas Aquinas

AQUINAS INSTITUTE | EMMAUS ACADEMIC
GREEN BAY, WI | STEUBENVILLE, OH

We would like to thank Kevin Bergdorf, Patricia Lynch, Josh and Holly Harnisch, Fr. Brian McMaster, Dr. Brian Cutter, and the Studentate Community of the Dominican Province of St. Albert the Great, USA, for their support. This series is dedicated to Marcus Berquist, Rose Johanna Trumbull, John and Mary Deignan, Thomas and Eleanor Sullivan, Ann C. Arcidi, the Very Rev. Romanus Cessario, OP, STM, and Fr. John T. Feeney and his sister Mary.

Published with the ecclesiastical approval of
The Most Reverend David L. Ricken, DD, JCL
Bishop of Green Bay
Given on July 16, 2017

PUBLISHER'S CATALOGING-IN-PUBLICATION DATA

Thomas Aquinas, St., 1225?–1274
  Summa Theologiae Supplementum, 1–68 / Saint Thomas Aquinas; edited by The Aquinas Institute;
  translated by Fr. Laurence Shapcote, OP
  p. 544 cm.
  ISBN 978-1-62340-020-0

1. Thomas, Aquinas, Saint, 1225?–1274 — Summa theologiae — Supplementum — 1-68. 2. Catholic Church — Doctrines— Early works to 1800. 3. Theology, Doctrinal — Early works to 1800. I. Title. II. Series

BX1749.T512 2015
230′.2--dc23   2015947391

Notes on the Text

Latin Text of St. Thomas

The Latin text used in this volume is based on the Leonine Edition, transcribed and revised by The Aquinas Institute.

English Translation of St. Thomas

The English translation of the Summa Theologiae was prepared by Fr. Laurence Shapcote, OP (1864-1947), of the English Dominican Province. It has been edited and revised by The Aquinas Institute.

The Aquinas Institute requests your assistance in the continued perfection of these texts.
If you discover any errors, please send us a note by email: editor@theaquinasinstitute.org

DEDICATED WITH LOVE TO
OUR LADY OF MT. CARMEL

Contents

SUMMA THEOLOGIAE
SUPPLEMENTUM, 1-68

QUESTION 1

CONTRITION

Deinde considerandum est de singulis partibus poenitentiae: et primo, de contritione; secundo, de confessione; tertio, de satisfactione.

De contritione autem consideranda sunt quinque: primo, quid sit; secundo, de quo esse debeat; tertio, quanta esse debeat; quarto, de duratione ipsius; quinto, de effectu ipsius.

Circa primum quaeruntur tria.

Primo: utrum convenienter definiatur.

Secundo: utrum contritio sit actus virtutis.

Tertio: utrum attritio possit fieri contritio.

We must now consider each single part of penance: (1) Contrition; (2) Confession; (3) Satisfaction.

The consideration about contrition will be fivefold: (1) What it is; (2) What it should be about; (3) How great it should be; (4) Of its duration; (5) Of its effect.

Under the first head there are three points of inquiry:

(1) Whether contrition is suitably defined?

(2) Whether it is an act of virtue?

(3) Whether attrition can become contrition?

Article 1

Whether Contrition Is an Assumed Sorrow for Sins With the Purpose of Confessing and Making Satisfaction?

AD PRIMUM SIC PROCEDITUR. Videtur quod contritio non sit *dolor pro peccatis assumptus cum proposito confitendi et satisfaciendi*, ut quidam definiunt. Quia, sicut Augustinus dicit, in libro *de Civ. Dei, dolor est de his quae nobis nolentibus accidunt*. Sed peccata non sunt huiusmodi. Ergo contritio non est *dolor pro peccatis*.

PRAETEREA, contritio nobis a Deo datur. Sed quod datur, non assumitur. Ergo contritio non est dolor *assumptus*.

PRAETEREA, satisfactio et confessio sunt necessaria ad hoc quod poena remittatur quae in contritione remissa non fuit. Sed quandoque tota poena in contritione remittitur. Ergo non est necessarium semper quod contritus habeat *propositum confitendi et satisfaciendi*.

SED CONTRA est ipsa definitio.

RESPONDEO dicendum quod *initium omnis peccati est superbia*, per quam homo, sensui suo inhaerens, a mandatis divinis recedit. Et ideo oportet quod illud quod destruit peccatum, hominem a proprio sensu discedere faciat. Ille autem qui in suo sensu perseverat, *rigidus et durus* per similitudinem vocatur: unde et frangi dicitur aliquis quando a suo sensu divellitur. Sed inter *fractionem* et *comminutionem* sive *contritionem* in rebus materialibus, unde haec nomina ad spiritualia transferuntur, hoc interest, ut dicitur in IV *Meteor.*, quod frangi dicuntur aliqua *quando in magnas partes dividuntur*, sed comminui vel conteri *quando ad partes minimas reducitur* hoc quod in se solidum erat. Et quia ad dimissionem

OBJECTION 1: It would seem that contrition is not *an assumed sorrow for sins, together with the purpose of confessing them and of making satisfaction for them*, as some define it. For, as Augustine states (*The City of God* 14.6), *sorrow is for those things that happen against our will*. But this does not apply to sin. Therefore, contrition is not *sorrow for sins*.

OBJ. 2: Further, contrition is given us by God. But what is given is not assumed. Therefore, contrition is not an *assumed* sorrow.

OBJ. 3: Further, satisfaction and confession are necessary for the remission of the punishment which was not remitted by contrition. But sometimes the whole punishment is remitted in contrition. Therefore, it is not always necessary for the contrite person to have the *purpose of confessing and of making satisfaction*.

ON THE CONTRARY, There is the definition itself.

I ANSWER THAT, As stated in Sirach 10:15, *pride is the beginning of all sin*, because thereby man clings to his own judgment, and strays from the divine commandments. Consequently, that which destroys sin must make man give up his own judgment. Now, he that persists in his own judgment is called metaphorically *rigid* and *hard*: wherefore anyone is said to be broken when he is torn from his own judgment. But in material things, whence these expressions are transferred to spiritual things, there is a difference between *breaking* and *crushing* or *contrition*, as stated in *Meteorology* 4, in that we speak of breaking *when a thing is sundered into large parts*, but of crushing or contrition when that which was in itself solid *is reduced to minute particles*.

1

peccati requiritur quod homo totaliter affectum peccati dimittat, per quem quandam continuitatem et soliditatem in sensu suo habebat, ideo actus ille quo peccatum dimittitur *contritio* dicitur per similitudinem.

In qua quidem contritione plura possunt considerari: scilicet ipsa substantia actus, modus agendi, principium, et effectus. Et secundum hoc, de contritione inveniuntur diversae definitiones traditae.

Quantum enim ad ipsam substantiam actus, datur praedicta definitio. Et quia actus contritionis est actus virtutis; et est pars poenitentiae sacramenti: ideo manifestatur in praedicta definitione, inquantum est actus virtutis, in hoc quod ponitur genus ipsius, scilicet *dolor*, et obiectum, in hoc quod dicit *pro peccatis*: et electio, quae requiritur ad actum virtutis, in hoc quod dicit *assumptus*. Sed inquantum est pars sacramenti, per hoc quod tangitur ordo ipsius ad alias partes, cum dicit, *cum proposito confitendi* etc.

Alia etiam definitio invenitur quae definit contritionem secundum quod est actus virtutis tantum: sed additur ad praedictam definitionem differentia contrahens ipsam ad specialem virtutem, scilicet poenitentiam. Dicit enim quod poenitentia est *dolor voluntarius pro peccato puniens quod dolet se commisisse.* In hoc enim quod additur *punitio*, ad specialem virtutem contrahitur.

Alia autem definitio invenitur Isidori, quae talis est: *contritio est compunctio et humilitas mentis, cum lacrimis, veniens de recordatione peccati et timore iudicii.* Et haec quidem tangit rationem hominis, in hoc quod dicit *humilitas mentis*: quia, sicut per superbiam aliquis in suo sensu redditur rigidus, ita per hoc quod a suo sensu contritus recedit, humiliatur. Tangit etiam modum exteriorem, in hoc quod dicit *cum lacrimis*; et principium contritionis, in hoc quod dicit, *veniens de recordatione peccati*, etc.

Alia sumitur ex verbis Augustini, qui tangit effectum contritionis, quae est: *contritio est dolor remittens peccatum.*

Alia sumitur ex verbis Gregorii, quae talis est: *contritio est humilitas spiritus, annihilans peccatum, inter spem et timorem.* Et haec tangit rationem nominis, in hoc quod dicit quod *contritio est humilitas spiritus*; et effectus eius, in hoc quod dicit, *annihilans peccatum*; et originem, in hoc quod dicit, *inter spem et timorem.* Nec solum ponit causam principalem, quae est timor: sed etiam quae est spes, sine qua timor desperationem facere posset.

AD PRIMUM ergo dicendum quod, quamvis peccata, quando acciderunt, voluntaria fuerunt; tamen, quando de eis conterimur, voluntaria non sunt. Et ideo *nobis nolentibus acciderunt*, non quidem secundum volunta-

And since, for the remission of sin, it is necessary that man should put aside entirely his attachment to sin, which implies a certain state of continuity and solidity in his mind, therefore it is that the act through which sin is cast aside is called *contrition* metaphorically.

In this contrition several things are to be observed: namely, the very substance of the act, the way of acting, its origin, and its effect. In respect of this, we find that contrition has been defined in various ways.

For as regards the substance of the act, we have the definition given above. And since the act of contrition is both an act of virtue, and a part of the sacrament of penance, its nature as an act of virtue is explained in this definition by mentioning its genus, viz. *sorrow*; its object, by the words *for sins*; and the act of choice which is necessary for an act of virtue, by the word *assumed*: while, as a part of the sacrament, it is made manifest by pointing out its relation to the other parts in the words, *together with the purpose of confessing and of making satisfaction.*

There is another definition which defines contrition only as an act of virtue; but at the same time including the difference which confines it to a special virtue, viz. penance, for it is thus expressed: *contrition is voluntary sorrow for sin whereby man punishes in himself that which he grieves to have done*, because the addition of the word *punishes* confines the definition to a special virtue.

Another definition is given by Isidore (*On the Highest Good* 2.12) as follows: *contrition is a tearful sorrow and humility of mind, arising from remembrance of sin and fear of the judgment.* Here we have an allusion to the derivation of the word when it is said that it is *humility of the mind*, because, as pride makes the mind rigid, so is a man humbled when contrition leads him to give up his mind. Also, the external manner is indicated by the word *tearful*, and the origin of contrition by the words, *arising from remembrance of sin*, etc.

Another definition is taken from the words of Augustine (*Expositions of the Psalms*), and indicates the effect of contrition. It runs thus: *contrition is the sorrow which takes away sin.*

Yet another is gathered from the words of Gregory as follows: *contrition is humility of the soul, crushing sin between hope and fear* (*Morals on Job* 33.11). Here the derivation is indicated by saying that contrition is *humility of the soul*; the effect, by the words *crushing sin*; and the origin, by the words, *between hope and fear.* Indeed, it includes not only the principal cause, which is fear, but also its joint cause, which is hope, without which fear might lead to despair.

REPLY OBJ. 1: Although sins, when committed, were voluntary, yet when we are contrite for them, they are no longer voluntary, so that *they occur against our will*; not indeed in respect of the will that we had when we consented

tem quam tunc habuimus cum ea volebamus, sed secundum illam quam nunc habemus, qua vellemus quod nunquam fuissent.

AD SECUNDUM dicendum quod contritio est a Deo solo quantum ad formam qua informatur: sed quantum ad substantiam actus, ex libero arbitrio et a Deo, qui operatur in omnibus operibus et naturae et voluntatis.

AD TERTIUM dicendum quod, quamvis tota poena possit per contritionem dimitti, tamen adhuc necessaria est confessio et satisfactio. Tum quia homo non potest esse certus de sua contritione quod fuerit ad totum tollendum sufficiens. Tum etiam quia confessio et satisfactio sunt in praecepto. Unde transgressor constitueretur si non confiteretur et non satisfaceret.

to them, but in respect of that which we have now, so as to wish they had never been.

REPLY OBJ. 2: Contrition is from God alone as to the form that informs it, but as to the substance of the act, it is from the free-will and from God, who operates in all works both of nature and of will.

REPLY OBJ. 3: Although the entire punishment may be remitted by contrition, yet confession and satisfaction are still necessary, both because man cannot be sure that his contrition was sufficient to take away all, and because confession and satisfaction are a matter of precept: wherefore he becomes a transgressor who confesses not and makes not satisfaction.

Article 2

Whether Contrition Is an Act of Virtue?

AD SECUNDUM SIC PROCEDITUR. Videtur quod contritio non sit actus virtutis. Passiones enim non sunt actus virtutum: quia *eis non laudamur nec vituperamur*, ut dicitur II *Ethic.* Sed dolor est passio. Cum ergo contritio sit dolor, videtur quod non sit actus virtutis.

PRAETEREA, sicut contritio dicitur a *terendo*, ita et attritio. Sed attritio non est actus virtutis: ut ab omnibus dicitur. Ergo neque contritio.

SED CONTRA, nihil est meritorium nisi actus virtutis. Sed contritio est actus quidam meritorius. Ergo est actus virtutis.

RESPONDEO dicendum quod contritio secundum proprietatem nominis sui non significat actum virtutis, sed potius quandam corporalem passionem: sed hic non quaeritur sic de contritione, sed de eo ad quod significandum hoc nomen per similitudinem adaptatur. Sicut enim inflatio propriae voluntatis ad malum faciendum importat, quantum est de se, malum ex genere; ita illius voluntatis annihilatio et comminutio quaedam de se importat bonum ex genere, quia hoc est detestari propriam voluntatem qua peccatum est commissum. Et ideo contritio, quae hoc significat, importat aliquam rectitudinem voluntatis. Et propter hoc est actus virtutis: illius scilicet cuius est peccatum praeteritum detestari et destruere, scilicet poenitentiae, ut patet ex his quae in 14 distinctione dicta sunt.

AD PRIMUM ergo dicendum quod in contritione est duplex dolor de peccato. Unus in parte sensitiva, qui passio est. Et hic non est essentialiter contritio, prout est actus virtutis, sed magis effectus eius. Sicut enim poenitentiae virtus exteriorem poenam suo corpori infligit ad recompensandam offensam quae in Deum commissa est officio membrorum; ita etiam et ipsi concupiscibi-

OBJECTION 1: It would seem that contrition is not an act of virtue. For passions are not acts of virtue, since *they bring us neither praise nor blame* (*Ethics* 2.5). But sorrow is a passion. Therefore, as contrition is sorrow, it seems that it is not an act of virtue.

OBJ. 2: Further, as contrition is so called from its being a *crushing*, so is attrition. Now all agree in saying that attrition is not an act of virtue. Neither, therefore, is contrition an act of virtue.

ON THE CONTRARY, Nothing but an act of virtue is meritorious. But contrition is a meritorious act. Therefore, it is an act of virtue.

I ANSWER THAT, Contrition as to the literal signification of the word does not denote an act of virtue, but a corporeal passion. But the question in point does not refer to contrition in this sense, but to that which the word is employed to signify by way of metaphor. For just as the inflation of one's own will unto wrong-doing implies, in itself, a generic evil, so the utter undoing and crushing of that same will implies something generically good, for this is to detest one's own will whereby sin was committed. Wherefore contrition, which signifies this, implies rectitude of the will; and so it is the act of that virtue to which it belongs to detest and destroy past sins, the act, namely, of penance, as is evident from what was said above (*Sentences* IV, D. 14, Q. 1: Q. 85, A. 2–3).

REPLY OBJ. 1: Contrition includes a twofold sorrow for sin. One is in the sensitive part, and is a passion. This does not belong essentially to contrition as an act of virtue, but is rather its effect. For just as the virtue of penance inflicts outward punishment on the body, in order to compensate for the offense done to God through the instrumentality of the bodily members, so does it inflict on the concupiscible

li poenam infert doloris peccati, quia ipsa etiam ad peccata cooperabatur. Sed tamen hic dolor potest pertinere ad contritionem inquantum est pars sacramenti: quia sacramenta non solum in interioribus actibus, sed etiam in exterioribus et in rebus sensibilibus nata sunt esse.

Alius dolor est in voluntate, qui nihil aliud est quam displicentia alicuius mali: secundum quod affectus voluntatis nominantur per nomina passionum, ut in Tertio, distinctione 26, dictum est. Et sic contritio est dolor per essentiam, et est actus virtutis poenitentiae.

AD SECUNDUM dicendum quod attritio dicit accessum ad perfectam contritionem: Unde in corporalibus dicuntur *attrita* quae aliquo modo diminuta sunt, sed non perfecte; sed *contritio* dicitur quando omnes partes tritae sunt simul per divisionem ad minima. Et ideo significat attritio in spiritualibus quandam displicentiam de peccatis commissis, sed non perfectam: contritio autem perfectam.

part of the soul a punishment, viz. the aforesaid sorrow, because the concupiscible also cooperated in the sinful deeds. Nevertheless, this sorrow may belong to contrition taken as part of the sacrament, since the nature of a sacrament is such that it consists not only of internal but also of external acts and sensible things.

The other sorrow is in the will, and is nothing else save displeasure for some evil, for the emotions of the will are named after the passions, as stated above (*Sentences* III, D. 26, Q. 1, A. 5; I, Q. 22, A. 3). Accordingly, contrition is essentially a kind of sorrow, and is an act of the virtue of penance.

REPLY OBJ. 2: Attrition denotes approach to perfect contrition, wherefore in corporeal matters, things are said to be *attrite*, when they are worn away to a certain extent, but not altogether crushed to pieces; while they are said to be *contrite*, when all the parts are crushed minutely. Wherefore, in spiritual matters, attrition signifies a certain but not a perfect displeasure for sins committed, whereas contrition denotes perfect displeasure.

Article 3
Whether Attrition Can Become Contrition?

AD TERTIAM SIC PROCEDITUR. Videtur quod attritio possit fieri contritio. Differt enim attritio a contritione sicut formatum ab informi. Sed fides informis fit formata. Ergo attritio potest fieri contritio.

PRAETEREA, materia recipit perfectionem remota privatione. Sed dolor se habet ad gratiam sicut materia ad formam: quia gratia informat dolorem. Ergo dolor qui prius erat informis culpa existente, quae est privatio gratiae, remota culpa recipiet perfectionem informationis a gratia. Et sic idem quod prius.

SED CONTRA, quorum principia sunt diversa omnino, eorum non potest fieri unum id quod est alterum. Sed attritionis principium est timor servilis, contritionis autem timor filialis. Ergo attritio non potest fieri contritio.

RESPONDEO dicendum quod super hoc est duplex opinio. Quidam dicunt quod attritio fit contritio, sicut fides informis fit formata. Sed hoc, ut videtur, non potest esse. Quia, quamvis habitus fidei informis fiat formatus, tamen nunquam actus fidei informis fit actus fidei formatae: quia actus ille informis transit et non manet veniente caritate. Attritio autem et contritio non dicunt habitum, sed actum tantum. Habitus autem virtutum infusarum qui voluntatem respiciunt, non possunt esse informes: cum caritatem consequantur, ut in Tertio Libro dictum est. Unde, antequam gratia infundatur, non est habitus a quo actus contritionis postea elicitur. Et sic nul-

OBJECTION 1: It would seem that attrition can become contrition. For contrition differs from attrition, as living from dead. Now dead faith becomes living. Therefore, attrition can become contrition.

OBJ. 2: Further, matter receives perfection when privation is removed. Now sorrow is to grace as matter to form, because grace informs sorrow. Therefore, the sorrow that was previously unformed while guilt remained receives perfection through being informed by grace: and so the same conclusion follows as above.

ON THE CONTRARY, Things which are caused by principles altogether diverse cannot be changed, one into the other. Now the principle of attrition is servile fear, while filial fear is the cause of contrition. Therefore, attrition cannot become contrition.

I ANSWER THAT, There are two opinions on this question: for some say that attrition may become contrition, even as lifeless faith becomes living faith. But seemingly this is impossible; since, although the habit of lifeless faith becomes living, yet never does an act of lifeless faith become an act of living faith, because the lifeless act passes away and remains no more, as soon as charity comes. Now attrition and contrition do not denote a habit, but an act only: and those habits of infused virtue which regard the will cannot be lifeless, since they result from charity, as stated above (*Sentences* III, D. 27, Q. 2, A. 4; I, Q. 65, A. 4). Hence, until grace is infused, there is no habit by which afterwards the

lo modo attritio potest fieri contritio. Et hoc alia opinio dicit.

AD PRIMUM ergo dicendum quod non est simile de fide et contritione, ut dictum est.

AD SECUNDUM dicendum quod, remota privatione a materia quae manet perfectione adveniente, formatur materia illa. Sed dolor ille qui erat informis, non manet caritate adveniente. Et ideo formari non potest.

Vel dicendum quod materia essentialiter non habet originem a forma: sicut actus habet originem ab habitu quo formatur. Unde non est inconveniens materiam informari aliqua forma de novo qua prius non informabatur. Sed hoc de actu est impossibile: sicut impossibile est quod aliquid idem numero oriatur a principio a quo prius non oriebatur; quia res semel tantum in esse procedit.

act of contrition may be elicited; so that attrition can in no way become contrition: and this is the other opinion.

REPLY OBJ. 1: There is no comparison between faith and contrition, as stated above.

REPLY OBJ. 2: When the privation is removed from matter, the matter is formed if it remains when the perfection comes. But the sorrow which was lifeless does not remain when charity comes, wherefore it cannot be formed.

It may also be replied that matter does not take its origin from the form essentially, as an act takes its origin from the habit which informs it. Wherefore nothing hinders matter being informed anew by some form whereby it was not informed previously: whereas this cannot be said of an act, even as it is impossible for the identically same thing to arise from a cause wherefrom it did not arise before, since a thing is brought into being but once.

QUESTION 2

THE OBJECT OF CONTRITION

Deinde considerandum est de obiecto contritionis.
Circa quod quaeruntur sex.
Primo: utrum debeat homo conteri de poenis.

Secundo: utrum de peccato originali.
Tertio: utrum de omni actuali commisso.
Quarto: utrum de peccato actuali committendo.
Quinto: utrum de peccato alieno.
Sexto: utrum de singulis peccatis mortalibus.

We must now consider the object of contrition.
Under this head there are six points of inquiry:
(1) Whether a man should be contrite on account of his punishment?
(2) Whether on account of original sin?
(3) Whether for every actual sin he has committed?
(4) Whether for actual sins he will commit?
(5) Whether for the sins of others?
(6) Whether for each single mortal sin?

Article 1

*Whether a Man Should Be Contrite on Account of the
Punishment, and Not Only on Account of His Sin?*

AD PRIMUM SIC PROCEDITUR. Videtur quod homo debeat conteri de poenis, et non solum de culpa. Augustinus enim, in libro *de Poenitentia*, dicit: *nemo vitam aeternam desiderat nisi eum huius vitae mortalis poeniteat*. Sed mortalitas vitae quaedam poena est. Ergo debet poenitens etiam de poenis conteri.

PRAETEREA, supra habitum est, ex verbis Augustini, quod poenitens debet dolere ex hoc quod *virtute se privavit*. Sed privatio virtutis quaedam poena est. Ergo contritio est dolor etiam de poenis.

SED CONTRA, nullus tenet illud de quo dolet. Sed poenitens, secundum suum nomen, *poenam tenet*. Ergo non dolet de poena. Et sic contritio, quae est dolor poenitentialis, non est de poena.

RESPONDEO dicendum quod contritio importat; ut dictum est, alicuius duri et integri comminutionem. Haec autem integritas et duritia invenitur in malo culpae: quia voluntas, quae est ipsius causa, in eo qui male agit, in suis terminis stat nec praecepto legis cedit. Et ideo huius mali displicentia contritio per similitudinem dicitur. Haec autem similitudo non potest adaptari ad malum poenae: quia poena simpliciter dicit diminutionem. Et ideo de malis poenae potest esse dolor, sed non contritio.

AD PRIMUM ergo dicendum quod poenitentia, secundum Augustinum, debet esse de hac mortali vita, non ratione ipsius mortalitatis (nisi poenitentia large di-

OBJECTION 1: It would seem that man should be contrite on account of the punishment, and not only on account of his sin. For Augustine says in *On Penance* 50: *no man desires life everlasting unless he repent of this mortal life.* But the mortality of this life is a punishment. Therefore, the penitent should be contrite on account of his punishments also.

OBJ. 2: Further, the Master says (*Sentences* IV, D. 16), quoting Augustine (*On True and False Penance*), that the penitent should be sorry for *having deprived himself of virtue.* But privation of virtue is a punishment. Therefore, contrition is sorrow for punishments also.

ON THE CONTRARY, No one holds to that for which he is sorry. But a penitent, by the very signification of the word, is *one who holds to his punishment.* Therefore, he is not sorry on account of his punishment, so that contrition which is penitential sorrow is not on account of punishment.

I ANSWER THAT, As stated above (Q. 1, A. 1), contrition implies the crushing of something hard and whole. Now this wholeness and hardness is found in the evil of fault, since the will, which is the cause thereof in the evil-doer, sticks to its own ground, and refuses to yield to the precept of the law, wherefore displeasure at such an evil is called metaphorically 'contrition.' But this metaphor cannot be applied to evil of punishment, because punishment simply denotes a lessening, so that it is possible to have sorrow for punishment but not contrition.

REPLY OBJ. 1: According to St. Augustine, penance should be on account of this mortal life, not by reason of its mortality (unless penance be taken broadly for every kind

catur omnis dolor), sed ratione peccatorum, ad quae ex infirmitate huius vitae deducimur.

AD SECUNDUM dicendum quod ille dolor quo quis dolet ex amissione virtutis per peccatum, non est essentialiter ipsa contritio, sed est principium eius: sicut enim aliquis movetur ad appetendum aliquid propter bonum quod inde expectat, ita movetur ad dolendum de aliquo propter malum quod inde consecutus est.

of sorrow), but by reason of sins, to which we are prone on account of the weakness of this life.

REPLY OBJ. 2: Sorrow for the loss of virtue through sin is not essentially the same as contrition, but is its principle. For just as we are moved to desire a thing on account of the good we expect to derive from it, so are we moved to be sorry for something on account of the evil accruing to us therefrom.

Article 2

Whether Contrition Should Be on Account of Original Sin?

AD SECUNDUM SIC PROCEDITUR. Videtur quod contritio esse debeat de originali. De peccato enim actuali conteri debemus, non ratione actus inquantum est ens quoddam, sed ratione deformitatis: quia actus secundum suam substantiam bonum quoddam est, et a Deo. Sed peccatum originale habet deformitatem, sicut et actuale. Ergo de eo etiam conteri debemus.

PRAETEREA, per peccatum originale homo fuit a Deo aversus: quia poena eius erat carentia divinae visionis. Sed cuilibet debet displicere se fuisse a Deo aversum. Ergo homo debet habere displicentiam peccati originalis. Et sic debet de eo conteri.

SED CONTRA, medicina debet esse proportionata morbo. Sed peccatum originale sine nostra voluntate contractum est. Ergo non requiritur quod per actum voluntatis, qui est contritio, ab ipso purgemur.

RESPONDEO dicendum quod contritio, ut dictum est, est dolor respiciens et quodammodo comminuens voluntatis duritiem. Et ideo solum de illis peccatis potest esse quae ex duritia nostrae voluntatis in nos proveniunt. Et quia peccatum originale nostra voluntate non est inductum, sed ex vitiatae naturae origine contractum, ideo de ipso non potest esse contritio, proprie loquendo: sed displicentia potest esse de eo, vel dolor.

AD PRIMUM ergo dicendum quod contritio non est de peccato ratione substantiae actus tantum, quia ex hoc non habet rationem mali: neque iterum ratione deformitatis tantum, quia deformitas de se non dicit rationem culpae, sed quandoque importat poenam. Debet autem de peccato esse contritio inquantum importat utramque deformitatem ex actu voluntatis provenientem. Et hoc non est in peccato originali. Et ideo de eo non est contritio.

ET SIMILITER dicendum ad secundum: quia aversio voluntatis est illa cui debetur contritio.

OBJECTION 1: It would seem that contrition should be on account of original sin. For we ought to be contrite on account of actual sin not by reason of the act, considered as a kind of being, but by reason of its deformity, since the act, regarded in its substance, is a good, and is from God. Now original sin has a deformity, even as actual sin has. Therefore, we should be contrite on its account also.

OBJ. 2: Further, by original sin man has been turned away from God, since in punishment thereof he was to be deprived of seeing God. But every man should be displeased at having been turned away from God. Therefore, man should be displeased at original sin; and so he ought to have contrition for it.

ON THE CONTRARY, The medicine should be proportionate to the disease. Now, we contracted original sin without willing to do so. Therefore, it is not necessary that we should be cleansed from it by an act of the will, such as contrition is.

I ANSWER THAT, Contrition is sorrow respecting and, so to speak, crushing the hardness of the will, as stated above (Q. 1, A. 1). Consequently, it can regard those sins only which result in us through the hardness of our will. And as original sin was not brought upon us by our own will, but contracted from the origin of our infected nature, it follows that, properly speaking, we cannot have contrition on its account, but only displeasure or sorrow.

REPLY OBJ. 1: Contrition is for sin not by reason of the mere substance of the act, because it does not derive the character of evil therefrom; nor again by reason of its deformity alone, because deformity, of itself, does not include the notion of guilt, and sometimes denotes a punishment. But contrition ought to be on account of sin as implying deformity resulting from an act of the will; and this does not apply to original sin, so that contrition does not apply to it.

THE SAME ANSWER applies to the second objection, because contrition is due to aversion of the will.

Article 3

Whether We Should Have Contrition for Every Actual Sin?

AD TERTIAM SIC PROCEDITUR. Videtur quod non de omni actuali peccato commisso a nobis debeamus conteri. Quia *contraria contrariis curantur*. Sed quaedam peccata per tristitiam committuntur: sicut acedia et invidia. Ergo medicina eorum non debet esse tristitia, quae est contritio, sed gaudium.

PRAETEREA, contritio est actus voluntatis, qui non potest esse de eo quod cognitioni non subiacet. Sed quaedam peccata sunt quae in cognitione non habemus, sicut oblita. Ergo de eis non potest esse contritio.

PRAETEREA, per voluntariam contritionem delentur illa quae per voluntatem committuntur. Sed ignorantia voluntarium tollit: ut patet per Philosophum, III *Ethic.* Ergo de his quae per ignorantiam accidunt, non debet esse contritio.

PRAETEREA, de illo peccato non debet esse contritio quod per contritionem non tollitur. Sed quaedam peccata non tolluntur per contritionem: sicut venialia, quae adhuc post contritionis gratiam manent. Ergo non de omnibus peccatis praeteritis debet esse contritio.

SED CONTRA poenitentia est medicina contra omnia peccata actualia. Sed poenitentia non est aliquorum quorum non sit contritio, quae est prima pars eius. Ergo et de omnibus peccatis debet esse contritio.

PRAETEREA, nullum peccatum dimittitur nisi quis iustificetur. Sed ad iustificationem requiritur contritio, ut prius dictum est. Ergo de quolibet peccato conteri oportet.

RESPONDEO dicendum quod omnis actualis culpa ex hoc contingit quod voluntas legi Dei non cedit, vel eam transgrediendo, vel omittendo, vel praeter eam agendo. Et quia durum est quod habet potentiam ut non facile patiatur, ideo in omni actuali peccato duritia quaedam est. Et propter hoc, si debeat peccatum curari, oportet quod per contritionem comminuentem remittatur.

AD PRIMUM ergo dicendum quod, sicut ex dictis patet, contritio opponitur peccato ex parte illa qua ex electione voluntatis procedit non sequentis imperium divinae legis, non autem ex parte eius quod est in peccato materiale: et hoc est illud super quod cadit electio. Cadit autem voluntatis electio non solum super actus aliarum virium, quibus voluntas ad suum finem utitur, sed etiam super actum proprium ipsius: voluntas enim vult se velle aliquid. Et sic electio voluntatis cadit super dolorem illum seu tristitiam quae invenitur in peccato invidiae et huiusmodi, sive dolor ille sit in sensu sive in ipsa voluntate. Et ideo illis peccatis contritionis dolor opponitur.

AD SECUNDUM dicendum quod oblivio de aliquo potest esse dupliciter. Aut ita quod totaliter a memoria

OBJECTION 1: It would seem that we have no need to have contrition for every actual sin we have committed. For *contraries are healed by their contraries.* Now some sins are committed through sorrow, e.g., sloth and envy. Therefore, their remedy should not be sorrow, such as contrition is, but joy.

OBJ. 2: Further, contrition is an act of the will, which cannot refer to that which is not known. But there are sins of which we have no knowledge, such as those we have forgotten. Therefore, we cannot have contrition for them.

OBJ. 3: Further, by voluntary contrition those sins are blotted out which we committed voluntarily. But ignorance takes away voluntariness, as the Philosopher declares (*Ethics* 3.1). Therefore, contrition need not cover things which have occurred through ignorance.

OBJ. 4: Further, we need not be contrite for a sin which is not removed by contrition. Now some sins are not removed by contrition, such as venial sins, which remain after the grace of contrition. Therefore, there is no need to have contrition for all one's past sins.

ON THE CONTRARY, Penance is a remedy for all actual sins. But penance cannot regard some sins without contrition regarding them also, for it is the first part of penance. Therefore, contrition should be for all one's past sins.

FURTHER, No sin is forgiven a man unless he be justified. But justification requires contrition, as stated above (Q. 1, A. 1; Q. 113). Therefore, it is necessary to have contrition for all one's sins.

I ANSWER THAT, Every actual sin is caused by our will not yielding to God's law, either by transgressing it, or by omitting it, or by acting beside it: and since a hard thing is one that is disposed not to give way easily, hence it is that a certain hardness of the will is to be found in every actual sin. Wherefore, if a sin is to be remedied, it needs to be taken away by contrition which crushes it.

REPLY OBJ. 1: As clearly shown above (A. 2), contrition is opposed to sin insofar as it proceeds from the choice of the will that had failed to obey the command of God's law, and not as regards the material part of sin: and it is on this that the choice of the will falls. Now the will's choice falls not only on the acts of the other powers, which the will uses for its own end, but also on the will's own proper act: for the will wills to will something. Accordingly, the will's choice falls on that pain or sadness which is to be found in the sin of envy and the like, whether such pain be in the senses or in the will itself. Consequently, the sorrow of contrition is opposed to those sins.

REPLY OBJ. 2: One may forget a thing in two ways: either so that it escapes the memory altogether, and then one

exciderit: et tunc non potest aliquis inquirere illud. Aut ita quod partim a memoria exciderit et partim maneat: sicut cum recolo me aliquid audivisse in generali, sed nescio quid in speciali. Et tunc requiro in memoria ad recognoscendum.

Et secundum hoc, etiam aliquod peccatum potest esse oblitum dupliciter. Aut ita quod in generali memoria maneat, sed non in speciali. Et tunc debet recogitare homo ad inveniendum peccatum: quia de quolibet peccato mortali tenetur homo specialiter conteri. Si autem invenire non possit, sufficit de eo conteri secundum quod in notitia tenet. Et debet homo non solum de peccato, sed de oblivione eius dolere, quae ex negligentia contingit.

Si autem peccatum omnino ex memoria excidit, tunc ex impotentia faciendi excusatur a debito, et sufficit generalis contritio de omni eo in quo Deum offendit. Sed quando impotentia tollitur, sicut cum ad memoriam revocatur peccatum, tunc tenetur homo specialiter conteri. Sicut etiam est de paupere qui non potest solvere quod debet: excusatur, et tamen tenetur cum primo poterit.

AD TERTIUM dicendum quod, si ignorantia, omnino tolleret voluntatem male agendi, excusaret, et non esset peccatum. Sed quandoque non totaliter tollit voluntatem: et tunc a toto non excusat, sed a tanto. Et ideo de peccato per ignorantiam commisso debet homo conteri.

AD QUARTUM dicendum quod post contritionem de mortali potest remanere veniale, sed non post contritionem de veniali. Et ideo de venialibus etiam debet esse contritio, eo modo quo et poenitentia, sicut supra dictum est.

cannot search for it; or so that it escapes from the memory in part, and in part remains, as when I remember having heard something in general, but know not what it was in particular, and then I search my memory in order to discover it.

Accordingly, a sin also may be forgotten in two ways, either so as to remain in a general, but not in a particular remembrance, and then a man is bound to bethink himself in order to discover the sin, because he is bound to have contrition for each individual mortal sin. And if he is unable to discover it, after applying himself with due care, it is enough that he be contrite for it, according as it stands in his knowledge, and indeed he should grieve not only for the sin, but also for having forgotten it, because this is owing to his neglect.

If, however, the sin has escaped from his memory altogether, then he is excused from his duty through being unable to fulfill it, and it is enough that he be contrite in general for everything wherein he has offended God. But when this inability is removed, as when the sin is recalled to his memory, then he is bound to have contrition for that sin in particular, even as a poor man, who cannot pay a debt, is excused, and yet is bound to pay as soon as he can.

REPLY OBJ. 3: If ignorance were to remove altogether the will to do evil, it would excuse, and there would be no sin: but sometimes it does not remove the will altogether, and then it does not altogether excuse, but only to a certain extent; therefore, a man is bound to be contrite for a sin committed through ignorance.

REPLY OBJ. 4: A venial sin can remain after contrition for a mortal sin, but not after contrition for the venial sin: wherefore contrition should also cover venial sins even as penance does, as stated above (*Sentences* IV, D. 16, Q. 2, A. 2, qu. 2; III, Q. 87, A. 1).

Article 4

Whether a Man is Bound to Have Contrition for His Future Sins?

AD QUARTUM SIC PROCEDITUR. Videtur quod etiam de peccatis futuris aliquis debet conteri. Contritio enim est actus liberi arbitrii. Sed liberum arbitrium magis se extendit ad futura quam ad praeterita: quia electio, quae est actus liberi arbitrii, est de contingentibus futuris, ut dicitur III *Ethic.* Ergo contritio magis est de peccatis futuris quam de praeteritis.

PRAETEREA, peccatum aggravatur ex consequenti effectu. Unde Hieronymus dicit quod poena Arii nondum est terminata, quia adhuc est possibile aliquos per eius haeresim ruere. Et similiter est de illo qui iudicatur homicida si letaliter percussit, etiam antequam percussus moriatur. Sed in illo intermedio debet peccator

OBJECTION 1: It would seem that a man is bound to have contrition for his future sins also. For contrition is an act of the free-will: and the free-will extends to the future rather than to the past, since choice, which is an act of the free-will, is about future contingents, as stated in *Ethics* 3. Therefore, contrition is about future sins rather than about past sins.

OBJ. 2: Further, sin is aggravated by the result that ensues from it: wherefore Jerome says that the punishment of Arius is not yet ended, for it is yet possible for some to be ruined through his heresy, by reason of whose ruin his punishment would be increased: and the same applies to a man who is judged guilty of murder if he has committed a mur-

conteri de peccato. Ergo non solum secundum quod habet quantitatem ex praeterito actu, sed etiam secundum quod habet quantitatem ex futuro. Et sic contritio respicit futurum.

SED CONTRA, contritio est pars poenitentiae. Sed poenitentia semper respicit praeterita. Ergo et contritio.

RESPONDEO dicendum quod in omnibus motoribus et mobilibus ordinatis ita est quod motor inferior habet motum proprium, et, praeter hoc, sequitur in aliquo motum superioris motoris: sicut patet in motu planetarum, qui, praeter motus proprios, sequuntur motum primi orbis. In omnibus autem virtutibus moralibus motor est ipsa prudentia, quae dicitur *auriga virtutum*. Et ideo quaelibet virtus moralis cum motu proprio habet aliquid de motu prudentiae. Et ideo, cum poenitentia sit quaedam virtus moralis, quia est pars iustitiae, cum actu proprio consequitur prudentiae motum.

Proprius autem actus eius est in obiectum proprium, quod est peccatum commissum. Et ideo actus eius principalis, scilicet contritio, secundum suam speciem respicit tantum peccatum praeteritum. Sed ex consequenti respicit peccatum futurum, secundum quod habet aliquid de actu prudentiae adiunctum.

Et tamen in illud futurum secundum rationem propriae speciei non movetur. Et propter hoc, ille qui conteritur dolet de peccato praeterito, et cavet futurum: sed non dicitur esse contritio de peccato futuro, sed magis cautio, quae est pars prudentiae contritioni adiuncta.

AD PRIMUM ergo dicendum quod liberum arbitrium dicitur esse de contingentibus futuris secundum quod est de actibus: sed non secundum quod est de obiectis actuum. Quia homo potest cogitare ex libero arbitrio de rebus praeteritis et necessariis: sed tamen ipse actus cogitationis, secundum quod sub libero arbitrio cadit, contingens futurum est. Et sic etiam actus contritionis contingens futurum est secundum quod sub libero arbitrio cadit: sed obiectum eius potest esse praeteritum.

AD SECUNDUM dicendum quod ille effectus consequens qui peccatum aggravat, iam in actu praecessit velut in causa. Et ideo, quando commissum est, totam suam quantitatem habuit, et ex effectu consequente non accessit ei aliquid quoad culpae rationem. Quamvis accrescat quoad poenam accidentalem: secundum quod plures habebit rationes dolendi in inferno de pluribus malis ex suo peccato consecutis. Et sic loquitur Hieronymus. Unde non oportet quod contritio sit nisi de peccatis praeteritis.

derous assault, even before his victim dies. Now the sinner ought to be contrite during that intervening time. Therefore, the degree of his contrition ought to be proportionate not only to his past act, but also to its eventual result: and consequently contrition regards the future.

ON THE CONTRARY, Contrition is a part of penance. But penance always regards the past: therefore, contrition does also.

I ANSWER THAT, In every series of things moving and moved ordained to one another, we find that the inferior mover has its proper movement, and besides this, it follows in some respect the movement of the superior mover: this is seen in the movement of the planets, which, in addition to their proper movements, follow the movement of the first heaven. Now, in all the moral virtues, the first mover is prudence, which is called the *charioteer of the virtues*. Consequently, each moral virtue, in addition to its proper movement, has something of the movement of prudence: and therefore, since penance is a moral virtue, as it is a part of justice, in addition to its own act it acquires the movement of prudence.

Now its proper movement is towards its proper object, which is a sin committed. Therefore, its proper and principal act, viz. contrition, essentially regards past sins alone; but, inasmuch as it acquires something of the act of prudence, it regards future sins indirectly, although it is not essentially moved towards those future sins.

For this reason, he that is contrite is sorry for his past sins and is cautious of future sins. Yet we do not speak of contrition for future sins, but of greater caution, which is a part of prudence conjoined to contrition.

REPLY OBJ. 1: The free-will is said to regard future contingents insofar as it is concerned with acts, but not with the object of acts: because of his own free-will a man can think about past and necessary things, and yet the very act of thinking, insofar as it is subject to the free-will, is a future contingent. Hence the act the contrition also is a future contingent, insofar as it is subject to the free-will; and yet its object can be something past.

REPLY OBJ. 2: The consequent result which aggravates a sin was already present in the act as in its cause; wherefore when the sin was committed, its degree of gravity was already complete, and no further guilt accrued to it when the result took place. Nevertheless, some accidental punishment accrues to it, in the respect of which the damned will have more reasons of regret for the more evils that have resulted from their sins. It is in this sense that Jerome speaks. Hence there is not need for contrition to be for other than past sins.

Article 5

Whether a Man Ought to Have Contrition for Another's Sin?

Ad quintum sic proceditur. Videtur quod homo debeat conteri de peccato alieno. Non enim petit aliquis indulgentiam nisi de peccato de quo contritus est. Sed de peccatis alienis indulgentia petitur in Psalmo: *ab alienis parce servo tuo.* Ergo debet homo conteri de peccatis alienis.

Praeterea, homo ex caritate debet diligere proximum *sicut seipsum.* Sed propter dilectionem sui et de malis suis dolet et bona desiderat. Ergo, cum teneamur proximo desiderare bona gratiae sicut et nobis, videtur quod debeamus de culpis eius dolere sicut et de nostris. Sed contritio nihil est quam dolor de peccatis. Ergo homo debet conteri de peccatis alienis.

Sed contra, contritio est actus poenitentiae virtutis. Sed nullus poenitet nisi de his quae ipse fecit. Ergo nullus conteritur de peccatis alienis.

Respondeo dicendum quod illud idem conteritur quod prius durum et integrum fuit. Unde oportet quod contritio pro peccato sit in eodem, in quo peccati duritia praecessit. Et sic de alienis peccatis non est contritio.

Ad primum ergo dicendum quod ab alienis peccatis sibi parci Propheta precatur, inquantum ex consortio: peccatorum aliquis per consensum aliquam immunditiam contrahit: cum scriptum sit: *cum perverso perverteris.*

Ad secundum dicendum quod de peccatis aliorum dolere debemus, non tamen oportet quod de eis conteramur: quia non omnis dolor de peccato praeterito est contritio, ut ex dictis patet.

Objection 1: It would seem that a man ought to have contrition for another's sin. For one should not ask forgiveness for a sin unless one is contrite for it. Now forgiveness is asked for another's sin in Psalm 18:13: *from those of others spare your servant.* Therefore, a man ought to be contrite for another's sins.

Obj. 2: Further, man is bound, ought of charity, to love his neighbor *as himself.* Now, through love of himself, he both grieves for his ills, and desires good things. Therefore, since we are bound to desire the goods of grace for our neighbor as for ourselves, it seems that we ought to grieve for his sins, even as for our own. But contrition is nothing else than sorrow for sins. Therefore, man should be contrite for the sins of others.

On the contrary, Contrition is an act of the virtue of penance. But no one repents save for what he has done himself. Therefore, no one is contrite for others' sins.

I answer that, The same thing is crushed which hitherto was hard and whole. Hence contrition for sin must be in the same subject in which the hardness of sin was hitherto: so that there is no contrition for the sins of others.

Reply Obj. 1: The prophet prays to be spared from the sins of others, insofar as, through fellowship with sinners, a man contracts a stain by consenting to their sins; thus it is written: *with the perverse you will be perverted* (Ps 17:27).

Reply Obj. 2: We ought to grieve for the sins of others, but not to have contrition for them, because not all sorrow for past sins is contrition, as is evident for what has been said already.

Article 6

Whether It Is Necessary to Have Contrition for Each Mortal Sin?

Ad sextum sic proceditur. Videtur quod non requiratur de singulis peccatis mortalibus contritio. Est enim motus contritionis in iustificatione in instanti. Sed in instanti non potest homo recogitare singula peccata. Ergo non oportet quod sit contritio de singulis.

Praeterea, contritio debet esse de peccatis secundum quod avertunt a Deo: quia conversio ad creaturam sine aversione a Deo contritionem non requirit. Sed omnia peccata mortalia in aversione conveniunt. Ergo contra omnia sufficit una contritio.

Praeterea, plus conveniunt peccata mortalia, actualia ad invicem quam actuale et originale. Sed unus

Objection 1: It would seem that it is not necessary to have contrition for each mortal sin. For the movement of contrition in justification is instantaneous, whereas a man cannot think of every mortal sin in an instant. Therefore, it is not necessary to have contrition for each mortal sin.

Obj. 2: Further, contrition should be for sins inasmuch as they turn us away from God, because we need not be contrite for turning to creatures without turning away from God. Now all mortal sins agree in turning us away from God. Therefore, one contrition for all is sufficient.

Obj. 3: Further, mortal sins have more in common with one another than do actual and original sin. Now one bap-

baptismus delet omnia actualia et originale. Ergo una contritio generalis delet omnia peccata mortalia.

SED CONTRA: Diversorum morborum diversae sunt medicinae: quia *non sanat oculum quod sanat calcaneum*, ut dicit Hieronymus. Sed contritio est medicina singularis contra unum tantum mortale. Ergo non sufficit una communis de omnibus.

PRAETEREA, contritio explicatur per confessionem. Sed oportet singula peccata mortalia confiteri. Ergo et de singulis conteri.

RESPONDEO dicendum quod contritio potest considerari dupliciter: scilicet quantum ad sui principium; et quantum ad terminum. Et dico principium contritionis cogitationem qua quis cogitat de peccato et dolet, etsi non dolore contritionis, saltem dolore attritionis. Terminus autem contritionis est quando dolor ille iam gratia informatur. Quantum ergo ad principium contritionis, oportet quod sit de singulis peccatis quae quis in memoria habet. Sed quantum ad terminum sufficit quod sit una communis de omnibus: tunc enim ille motus agit in vi omnium dispositionum praecedentium.

ET PER HOC patet responsio ad primum.

AD SECUNDUM dicendum quod, quamvis omnia mortalia conveniant in aversione, tamen differunt in causa et modo aversionis, et quantitate elongationis a Deo. Et hoc est secundum diversitatem conversionis.

AD TERTIUM dicendum quod baptismus agit in virtute meriti Christi, quod habuit infinitam virtutem ad delendum omnia peccata: et propterea unus sufficit contra omnia. Sed in contritione cum merito Christi requiritur actus noster. Et ideo oportet quod singulis peccatis respondeat singillatim: cum non habeat infinitam virtutem ad contritionem.

Vel dicendum quod baptismus est spiritualis generatio: sed poenitentia, quantum ad contritionem et alias sui partes, est spiritualis quaedam sanatio per modum cuiusdam alterationis. Patet autem in generatione corporali alicuius, quae est cum corruptione, quod una generatione removentur omnia accidentia contraria rei generatae, quae erant accidentia rei corruptae. Sed in alteratione removetur tantum unum accidens, contrarium accidenti ad quod terminatur alteratio. Et similiter unus baptismus simul delet omnia peccata, novam vitam inducendo. Sed poenitentia non delet omnia peccata nisi ad singula feratur. Et ideo oportet de singulis conteri et confiteri.

tism blots out all sins both actual and original. Therefore, one general contrition blots out all mortal sins.

ON THE CONTRARY, For diverse diseases there are diverse remedies, since *what heals the eye will not heal the foot*, as Jerome says (*On the Gospel of Mark* 9.28). But contrition is the special remedy for one mortal sin. Therefore, one general contrition for all mortal sins does not suffice.

FURTHER, Contrition is expressed by confession. But it is necessary to confess each mortal sin. Therefore, it is necessary to have contrition for each mortal sin.

I ANSWER THAT, Contrition may be considered in two ways: as to its origin, and as to its term. By origin of contrition I mean the process of thought when a man thinks of his sin and is sorry for it, even if without the sorrow of contrition, but with only that of attrition. The term of contrition is when that sorrow is already informed by grace. Accordingly, as regards the origin of contrition, a man needs to be contrite for each sin that he calls to mind; but as regards its term, it suffices for him to have one general contrition for all, because then the movement of his contrition acts in virtue of all his preceding dispositions.

THIS SUFFICES for the reply to the first objection.

REPLY OBJ. 2: Although all mortal sins agree in turning man away from God, yet they differ in the cause and mode of aversion, and in the degree of separation from God; and this regards the different ways in which they turn us to creatures.

REPLY OBJ. 3: Baptism acts in virtue of Christ's merit, which had infinite power for the blotting out of all sins; and so for all sins one baptism suffices. But in contrition, in addition to the merit of Christ, an act of ours is requisite, which must, therefore, correspond to each sin, since it has not infinite power for contrition.

It may also be replied that baptism is a spiritual generation; whereas penance, as regards contrition and its other parts, is a kind of spiritual healing by way of some alteration. Now it is evident in the generation of a body, accompanied by corruption of another body, that all the accidents contrary to the thing generated, and which were the accidents of the thing corrupted, are removed by the one generation: whereas in alteration, only that accident is removed which was contrary to the accident which is the term of the alteration. In like manner, one baptism blots out all sins together and introduces a new life; whereas penance does not blot out each sin unless it be directed to each. For this reason it is necessary to be contrite for, and to confess, each sin.

QUESTION 3

THE DEGREE OF CONTRITION

Deinde considerandum est de quantitate contritionis.

Circa quod quaeruntur tria.

Primo: utrum contritio sit maior dolor qui esse possit in natura.

Secundo: utrum possit esse nimis magnus dolor.

Tertio: utrum debeat esse maior dolor de uno peccato quam de alio.

We must now consider the degree of contrition.

Under this head there are three points of inquiry:

(1) Whether contrition is the greatest possible sorrow in the world?

(2) Whether the sorrow of contrition can be too great?

(3) Whether sorrow for one sin ought to be greater than for another?

Article 1

Whether Contrition Is the Greatest Possible Sorrow in the World?

AD PRIMUM SIC PROCEDITUR. Videtur quod contritio non sit maior dolor qui esse possit in natura. Dolor enim est sensus laesionis. Sed aliquae laesiones magis sentiuntur quam laesio peccati: sicut laesio vulneris. Ergo non est maximus dolor contritio.

PRAETEREA, ex effectu sumimus iudicium de causa. Sed effectus doloris sunt lacrimae. Cum ergo aliquando contritus non emittat lacrimas corporales de peccatis, quas tamen emittit de morte amici, vel de percussione, vel aliquo huiusmodi; videtur quod contritio non sit dolor maximus.

PRAETEREA, quanto aliquid plus habet de admixtione contrarii, tanto est minus intensum. Sed contritionis dolor habet multum de gaudio admixtum: quia contritus gaudet de liberatione, de spe veniae, et de multis huiusmodi. Ergo dolor suus est minimus.

PRAETEREA, dolor contritionis displicentia quaedam est. Sed multa sunt quae magis displicent contrito quam peccata praeterita: non enim vellet poenam inferni sustinere potius quam peccare, nec iterum sustinuisse omnes poenas temporales, aut etiam sustinere; alias pauci invenirentur contriti. Ergo dolor contritionis non est maximus.

SED CONTRA: Secundum Augustinum omnis dolor in amore fundatur. Sed amor caritatis, in quo fundatur dolor contritionis, est maximus. Ergo dolor contritionis est maximus.

PRAETEREA, dolor est de malo. Ergo de magis malo debet esse maior dolor. Sed culpa est magis malum quam poena. Ergo dolor de culpa, qui est contritio, excedit omnem alium dolorem.

OBJECTION 1: It would seem that contrition is not the greatest possible sorrow in the world. For sorrow is the sensation of hurt. But some hurts are more keenly felt than the hurt of sin, for instance, the hurt of a wound. Therefore, contrition is not the greatest sorrow.

OBJ. 2: Further, we judge of a cause according to its effect. Now the effect of sorrow is tears. Since, therefore, sometimes a contrite person does not shed outward tears for his sins, whereas he weeps for the death of a friend, or for a blow, or the like, it seems that contrition is not the greatest sorrow.

OBJ. 3: Further, the more a thing is mingled with its contrary, the less its intensity. But the sorrow of contrition has a considerable admixture of joy because the contrite man rejoices in his delivery, in the hope of pardon, and in many like things. Therefore, his sorrow is very slight.

OBJ. 4: Further, the sorrow of contrition is a kind of displeasure. But there are many things more displeasing to the contrite than their past sins; for they would not prefer to suffer the pains of hell rather than to sin, nor to have suffered, nor yet to suffer all manner of temporal punishment; else few would be found contrite. Therefore, the sorrow of contrition is not the greatest.

ON THE CONTRARY, According to Augustine (*The City of God* 14.7–9), all sorrow is based on love. Now the love of charity, on which the sorrow of contrition is based, is the greatest love. Therefore, the sorrow of contrition is the greatest sorrow.

FURTHER, Sorrow is for evil. Therefore, the greater the evil, the greater the sorrow. But the fault is a greater evil than its punishment. Therefore, contrition, which is sorrow for fault, surpasses all other sorrow.

15

Respondeo dicendum quod in contritione est duplex dolor. Unus in ipsa voluntate, quae est essentialiter ipsa contritio: quae nihil aliud est quam displicentia praeteriti peccati. Et talis dolor in contritione excedit omnes alios dolores. Quia quantum aliquid placet, tantum contrarium eius displicet. Finis autem super omnia placet: cum omnia propter ipsum desiderentur. Et ideo peccatum, quod a fine ultimo avertit, super omnia displicere debet.

Alius dolor est in parte sensitiva, qui causatur ex primo dolore: vel ex necessitate naturae, secundum quod vires inferiores sequuntur motum superiorum; vel ex electione, secundum quod homo poenitens in seipso hunc dolorem excitat ut de peccatis doleat. Et neutro modo oportet quod sit maximus dolor. Quia vires inferiores moventur vehementius ab obiectis propriis quam ex redundantia superiorum virium. Et ideo, quanto operatio superiorum virium est propinquior obiectis inferiorum, tanto magis sequuntur earum motum. Et ideo maior dolor est in sensitiva parte ex laesione sensibili quam sit ille qui in ipsa redundat ex ratione. Et similiter maior qui redundat ex ratione de corporalibus deliberante, quam qui redundat ex ratione considerante spiritualia.

Unde dolor in sensitiva parte ex displicentia rationis proveniens de peccato non est maior dolor aliis doloribus qui in ipsa sunt. Et similiter nec dolor qui est voluntarie assumptus. Tum quia non obedit affectus inferior superiori ad nutum, ut tanta; passio sequatur in inferiori appetitu qualem ordinat superior. Tum etiam quia passiones a ratione assumuntur in actibus virtutum secundum mensuram quandam: quam quandoque dolor qui est sine virtute, non servat, sed excedit.

Ad primum ergo dicendum quod, sicut dolor sensibilis est de sensu laesionis, ita dolor interior est de cognitione alicuius nocivi. Et ideo, quamvis laesio peccati secundum exteriorem sensum non percipiatur, tamen percipitur esse maxima secundum sensum interiorem rationis.

Ad secundum dicendum quod corporales immutationes immediate consequuntur ad passiones sensitivae partis, et eis mediantibus ad affectiones appetitivae superioris. Et inde est quod ex dolore sensibili, vel etiam sensibili vicino, citius defluunt lacrimae corporales quam de dolore spirituali contritionis.

Ad tertium dicendum quod gaudium illud quod poenitens de dolore habet, non minuit displicentiam, quia ei non contrariatur, sed auget: secundum quod *omnis operatio augetur per propriam delectationem*, ut dicitur in X *Ethic.*; sicut qui delectatur in addiscendo ali-

I answer that, As stated above (Q. 1, A. 2), there is a twofold sorrow in contrition: one is in the will, and is the very essence of contrition, being nothing else than displeasure at past sin, and this sorrow in contrition surpasses all other sorrows. For the more pleasing a thing is, the more displeasing is its contrary. Now the last end is above all things pleasing: wherefore sin, which turns us away from the last end, should be, above all things, displeasing.

The other sorrow is in the sensitive part, and is caused by the former sorrow either from natural necessity, insofar as the lower powers follow the movements of the higher, or from choice, insofar as a penitent excites in himself this sorrow for his sins. In neither of these ways is such sorrow of necessity the greatest, because the lower powers are more deeply moved by their own objects than through redundance from the higher powers. Wherefore the nearer the operation of the higher powers approaches to the objects of the lower powers, the more do the latter follow the movement of the former. Consequently, there is greater pain in the sensitive part on account of a sensible hurt, than that which redounds into the sensitive part from the reason; and likewise, that which redounds from the reason when it deliberates on corporeal things is greater than that which redounds from the reason in considering spiritual things.

Therefore, the sorrow which results in the sensitive part from the reason's displeasure at sin is not greater than the other sorrows of which that same part is the subject: and likewise, neither is the sorrow which is assumed voluntarily greater than other sorrows—both because the lower appetite does not obey the higher appetite infallibly, as though in the lower appetite there should arise a passion of such intensity and of such a kind as the higher appetite might ordain—and because the passions are employed by the reason, in acts of virtue, according to a certain measure, which the sorrow that is without virtue sometimes does not observe, but exceeds.

Reply Obj. 1: Just as sensible sorrow is on account of the sensation of hurt, so interior sorrow is on account of the thought of something hurtful. Therefore, although the hurt of sin is not perceived by the external sense, yet it is perceived to be the most grievous hurt by the interior sense or reason.

Reply Obj. 2: Affections of the body are the immediate result of the sensitive passions and, through them, of the emotions of the higher appetite. Hence it is that bodily tears flow more quickly from sensible sorrow, or even from a thing that hurts the senses, than from the spiritual sorrow of contrition.

Reply Obj. 3: The joy which a penitent has for his sorrow does not lessen his displeasure (for it is not contrary to it), but increases it, according as *every operation is increased by the delight which it causes*, as stated in *Ethics* 10.5. Thus he who delights in learning a science, learns the better,

quam scientiam, melius addiscit. Et similiter qui gaudet de displicentia, vehementius displicentiam habet. Sed bene potest esse quod illud gaudium temperat dolorem ex ratione in partem sensitivam resultantem.

Ad quartum dicendum quod quantitas displicentiae de aliqua re debet esse secundum quantitatem malitiae ipsius. Malitia autem in culpa mortali mensuratur ex eo in quem peccatur, inquantum est ei indigna; et ex eo qui peccat, inquantum est ei nociva. Et quia homo debet magis Deum quam seipsum diligere, ideo plus debet odire culpam inquantum est offensa Dei, quam, inquantum est nociva sibi.

Est autem nociva sibi principaliter inquantum separat ipsum a Deo. Et ex hac parte ipsa separatio a Deo, quae poena quaedam est, magis debet displicere quam ipsa culpa inquantum hoc nocumentum inducit, quia quod propter alterum oditur, minus oditur: sed minus quam culpa inquantum est offensa in Deum.

Inter omnes autem poenas attenditur ordo malitiae secundum quantitatem nocumenti. Et ideo, cum hoc sit maximum nocumentum quo maximum bonum privatur, erit inter poenas maxima separatio a Deo.

Est etiam alia quantitas malitiae accidentalis, quam oportet in displicentia attendere secundum rationem praesentis et praeteriti: quia quod praeteritum est, iam non est; unde habet minus de ratione et malitiae et bonitatis. Et inde est quod plus refugit homo sustinere aliquid mali in praesenti vel futuro quam horreat de praeterito. Unde nec aliqua passio animae directe respondet praeterito, sicut dolor respondet praesenti malo, et timor futuro. Et propter hoc de duobus malis praeteritis illud magis abhorret animus cuius maior effectus in praesenti remanet vel in futurum timetur, etiam si in praeterito minus fuerit. Et quia effectus praecedentis culpae non ita percipitur quandoque sicut effectus praeteritae poenae, tum quia culpa perfectius sanatur quam quaedam poena, tum quia defectus corporalis magis est manifestus quam spiritualis; ideo homo, etiam bene dispositus, quandoque magis in se percipit horrorem praecedentis poenae quam praecedentis culpae, quamvis magis esset paratus pati eandem poenam quam committere eandem culpam.

Est etiam considerandum in comparatione culpae et poenae quod quaedam poenae habent inseparabiliter coniunctam Dei offensam, sicut separatio a Deo; quaedam etiam addunt perpetuitatem, sicut poena inferni. Ergo poena illa quae offensam annexam habet, eodem modo cavenda est sicut etiam culpa. Sed illa quae perpetuitatem addit, est magis quam culpa simpliciter fugienda. Si tamen ab eis separetur ratio offensae et consideretur tantum ratio poenae, minus habent de malitia quam

and, in like manner, he who rejoices in his displeasure, is the more intensely displeased. But it may well happen that this joy tempers the sorrow that results from the reason in the sensitive part.

Reply Obj. 4: The degree of displeasure at a thing should be proportionate to the degree of its malice. Now the malice of mortal sin is measured from him against whom it is committed, inasmuch as it is offensive to him; and from him who sins, inasmuch as it is hurtful to him. And, since man should love God more than himself, therefore he should hate sin as an offense against God more than as being hurtful to himself.

Now it is hurtful to him chiefly because it separates him from God; and in this respect the separation from God which is a punishment, should be more displeasing than the sin itself, as causing this hurt (since what is hated on account of something else is less hated), but less than the sin, as an offense against God.

Again, among all the punishments of malice a certain order is observed according to the degree of the hurt. Consequently, since this is the greatest hurt, inasmuch as it consists in privation of the greatest good, the greatest of all punishments will be separation from God.

Again, with regard to this displeasure, it is necessary to observe that there is also an accidental degree of malice, in respect of the present and the past; since what is past is no more, and thereby it has less of the character of malice or goodness. Hence it is that a man shrinks from suffering an evil at the present, or at some future time, more than he shudders at the past evil: wherefore also, no passion of the soul corresponds directly to the past, as sorrow corresponds to present evil, and fear to future evil. Consequently, of two past evils, the mind shrinks the more from that one which still produces a greater effect at the present time, or which, it fears, will produce a greater effect in the future, although in the past it was the lesser evil. And, since the effect of the past sin is sometimes not so keenly felt as the effect of the past punishment, both because sin is more perfectly remedied than punishment, and because bodily defect is more manifest than spiritual defect, therefore even a man who is well disposed sometimes feels a greater abhorrence of his past punishment than of his past sin, although he would be ready to suffer the same punishment over again rather than commit the same sin.

We must also observe, in comparing sin with punishment, that some punishments are inseparable from offense of God, e.g., separation from God; and some also are everlasting, e.g., the punishment of hell. Therefore, the punishment to which is connected offense of God is to be shunned in the same way as sin; whereas that which is everlasting is simply to be shunned more than sin. If, however, we separate from these punishments the notion of offense, and consider only the notion of punishment, they have the

culpa inquantum est offensa Dei. Et propter hoc minus debent displicere.

Sciendum est etiam quod, quamvis talis debeat esse contriti dispositio, non tamen de his tentandus est. Quia affectus suos homo non de facili mensurare potest: et quandoque illud quod minus displicet videtur magis displicere, quia est propinquius nocumento sensibili, quod magis est nobis notum.

character of malice less than sin has as an offense against God: and for this reason should cause less displeasure.

We must, however, take note that, although the contrite should be thus disposed, yet he should not be questioned about his feelings, because man cannot easily measure them. Sometimes that which displeases least seems to displease most, through being more closely connected with some sensible hurt, which is more known to us.

Article 2

Whether the Sorrow of Contrition Can Be Too Great?

AD SECUNDUM SIC PROCEDITUR. Videtur quod non possit esse nimis magnus contritionis dolor. Nullus enim dolor potest esse immoderatior quam ille qui proprium subiectum destruit. Sed dolor contritionis, si est tantus quod mortem vel corruptionem corporis inducit, est laudabilis: dicit enim Anselmus: *utinam sic impinguentur viscera animae meae ut medullae corporis mei exsiccentur*; et Augustinus dicit *se esse dignum oculos caecare plorando*. Ergo dolor contritionis non potest esse nimius.

PRAETEREA, dolor contritionis ex amore caritatis procedit. Sed amor caritatis non potest esse nimius. Ergo nec dolor contritionis.

SED CONTRA, omnis virtus moralis corrumpitur per superabundantiam et defectum. Sed contritio est actus virtutis moralis, scilicet poenitentiae: cum sit pars iustitiae. Ergo potest esse superfluus dolor de peccatis.

RESPONDEO dicendum quod contritio ex parte doloris qui est in ratione, scilicet displicentiae, quo peccatum displicet inquantum est offensa Dei, non potest esse nimia: sicut nec amor caritatis, quo intenso talis displicentia intenditur, non potest esse nimius. Sed quantum ad dolorem sensibilem potest esse nimia: sicut etiam exterior corporis afflictio potest esse nimia. In his autem omnibus debet accipi pro mensura conservatio subiecti, et bonae habitudinis sufficientis ad ea quae agenda incumbunt. Et propter hoc dicitur, Rom. 12: *rationabile obsequium vestrum*.

AD PRIMUM ergo dicendum quod Anselmus desiderabat ex pinguedine devotionis medullas corporales exsiccari, non quantum ad humorem naturalem, sed quantum ad desideria et concupiscentias corporales.

Augustinus autem, quamvis dignum se cognosceret amissione exteriorum oculorum propter peccatum, quia quilibet peccator non solum aeterna, sed etiam temporali morte dignus est; non tamen volebat sibi oculos caecare.

AD SECUNDUM dicendum quod ratio illa procedit de dolore qui est in ratione.

OBJECTION 1: It would seem that the sorrow of contrition cannot be too great. For no sorrow can be more immoderate than that which destroys its own subject. But the sorrow of contrition, if it be so great as to cause death or corruption of the body, is praiseworthy. For Anselm says: *would that such were the exuberance of my inmost soul, as to dry up the marrow of my body* (*Prayers* 52), and Augustine confesses that *he deserves to blind his eyes with tears*. Therefore, the sorrow of contrition cannot be too great.

OBJ. 2: Further, the sorrow of contrition results from the love of charity. But the love of charity cannot be too great. Neither, therefore, can the sorrow of contrition be too great.

ON THE CONTRARY, Every moral virtue is destroyed by excess and deficiency. But contrition is an act of a moral virtue, viz. penance, since it is a part of justice. Therefore, sorrow for sins can be too great.

I ANSWER THAT, Contrition as regards the sorrow in the reason, i.e., the displeasure whereby the sin is displeasing through being an offense against God, cannot be too great; even as neither can the love of charity be too great, for when this is increased the aforesaid displeasure is increased also. But, as regards the sensible sorrow, contrition may be too great, even as outward affliction of the body may be too great. In all these things the rule should be the safeguarding of the subject, and of that general well-being which suffices for the fulfillment of one's duties; hence it is written: *present your bodies . . . a reasonable sacrifice* (Rom 12:1).

REPLY OBJ. 1: Anselm desired the marrow of his body to be dried up by the exuberance of his devotion not as regards the natural humor, but as to his bodily desires and concupiscences.

And, although Augustine acknowledged that he deserved to lose the use of his bodily eyes on account of his sins, because every sinner deserves not only eternal, but also temporal death, yet he did not wish his eyes to be blinded.

REPLY OBJ. 2: This objection considers the sorrow which is in the reason.

Tertia autem procedit de dolore sensitivae partis.

The third, however, considers the sorrow of the sensitive part.

Article 3

Whether Sorrow for One Sin Should Be Greater than for Another?

Ad tertium sic proceditur. Videtur quod non debeat esse maior dolor de uno peccato quam de alio. Hieronymus enim collaudat Paulam in hoc quod *minima peccata sicut magna plangebat*. Ergo non est magis dolendum de uno quam de alio.

Praeterea, motus contritionis est subitus. Sed non potest esse unus motus intensior simul et remissior. Ergo contritio non debet esse maior de uno quam de alio peccato.

Praeterea, de peccato praecipue est contritio secundum quod a Deo avertit. Sed in aversione omnia peccata mortalia conveniunt: quia omnia tollunt gratiam, qua anima Deo coniungitur. Ergo de omnibus peccatis mortalibus aequalis debet esse contritio.

Sed contra: Deut. 25 dicitur: *secundum mensuram peccati erit et plagarum modus*. Sed contritioni de peccatis plagae commensurantur: quia contritio habet propositum satisfaciendi annexum. Ergo contritio magis debet esse de uno peccato quam de alio.

Praeterea, de hoc debet homo conteri quod debuit vitare. Sed homo debuit magis vitare unum peccatum quam aliud quia gravius est, si necessitas alterum faciendi incumberet. Ergo et similiter debet de uno, scilicet graviori, magis quam de alio dolere.

Respondeo dicendum quod de contritione dupliciter possumus loqui. Uno modo, secundum quod singillatim singulis peccatis respondet. Et sic, quantum ad dolorem superioris affectus, requiritur quod de maiori peccato quis doleat magis: quia ratio doloris est magis in uno quam in alio, scilicet offensa Dei; ex magis enim inordinato actu Deus magis offenditur. Similiter etiam, cum maiori culpae maior poena debeatur, etiam dolor sensitivae partis, secundum quod pro peccato ex electione assumitur quasi poena peccati, debet esse maior die maiori peccato. Secundum autem quod ex impressione superioris appetitus nascitur in inferiori, attenditur quantitas doloris secundum dispositionem partis inferioris ad recipiendam impressionem a superiori, et non secundum quantitatem peccati.

Alio modo potest accipi contritio secundum quod est simul de omnibus: sicut in actu iustificationis. Et haec quidem contritio vel ex singulorum consideratione peccatorum procedit: et sic, quamvis sit actus unus, tamen

Objection 1: It would seem that sorrow for one sin need not be greater than for another. For Jerome (*Epistle to Paula and Eustochium* 108) commends Paula because *she deplored her slightest sins as much as great ones*. Therefore, one need not be more sorry for one sin than for another.

Obj. 2: Further, the movement of contrition is instantaneous. Now one instantaneous movement cannot be at the same time more intense and more remiss. Therefore, contrition for one sin need not be greater than for another.

Obj. 3: Further, contrition is for sin chiefly as turning us away from God. But all mortal sins agree in turning us away from God, since they all deprive us of grace whereby the soul is united to God. Therefore, we should have equal contrition for all mortal sins.

On the contrary, It is written: *according to the measure of the sin shall the measure also of the stripes be* (Deut 25:2). Now, in contrition, the stripes are measured according to the sins, because to contrition is united the purpose of making satisfaction. Therefore, contrition should be for one sin more than for another.

Further, Man should be contrite for that which he ought to have avoided. But he ought to avoid one sin more than another, if that sin is more grievous, and it be necessary to do one or the other. Therefore, in like manner he ought to be more sorry for one, viz. the more grievous, than for the other.

I answer that, We may speak of contrition in two ways: first, insofar as it corresponds to each single sin, and thus, as regards the sorrow in the higher appetite, a man ought to be more sorry for a more grievous sin, because there is more reason for sorrow, viz. the offense against God, in such a sin than in another, since the more inordinate the act is, the more it offends God. In like manner, since the greater sin deserves a greater punishment, the sorrow also of the sensitive part, insofar as it is voluntarily undergone for sin as the punishment thereof, ought to be greater where the sin is greater. But insofar as the emotions of the lower appetite result from the impression of the higher appetite, the degree of sorrow depends on the disposition of the lower faculty to the reception of impressions from the higher faculty, and not on the greatness of the sin.

Second, contrition may be taken insofar as it is directed to all one's sins together, as in the act of justification. Such contrition arises either from the consideration of each single sin, and thus, although it is but one act, yet the distinc-

distinctio peccatorum virtute manet in ipso. Vel ad minus habet propositum de singulis cogitandi annexum. Et sic etiam habitualiter est magis de uno quam de alio.

Ad primum ergo dicendum quod Paula non laudatur de hoc quod de omnibus peccatis doleret aequaliter: sed quia de parvis peccatis tantum dolebat ac si essent magna, per comparationem ad alios qui de peccatis dolent. Sed ipsa multo amplius de maioribus doluisset.

Ad secundum dicendum quod in illo contritionis motu subitaneo, quamvis non actualiter distinctio intensionis respondens diversis peccatis inveniri posset, tamen invenitur ibi eo modo sicut dictum est. Et etiam alio modo, secundum quod singula peccata ordinem habent ad illud de quo in illa contritione generali contrito dolendum occurrit, scilicet offensa Dei. Qui enim aliquod totum diligit, potentia diligit etiam partes eius, quamvis non actu: et hoc modo, secundum quod habent ordinem ad totum, quasdam plus, quasdam minus; sicut qui aliquam communitatem diligit, virtute singulos diligit plus et minus secundum eorum ordinem in bono communi. Et similiter qui dolet de hoc quod Deum offendit, de diversis implicite dolet diversimode, secundum quod plus vel minus per ea Deum offendit.

Ad tertium dicendum quod, quamvis quodlibet peccatum mortale a Deo avertat et gratiam tollat, tamen quoddam plus elongat quam aliud, inquantum habet maiorem dissonantiam ex sua inordinatione ad ordinem divinae bonitatis quam aliud.

tion of the sins remains virtually therein; or, at least, it includes the purpose of thinking of each sin; and in this way too it is habitually more for one than for another.

Reply Obj. 1: Paula is commended, not for deploring all her sins equally, but because she grieved for her slight sins as much as though they were grave sins, in comparison with other persons who grieve for their sins: but for graver sins she would have grieved much more.

Reply Obj. 2: In that instantaneous movement of contrition, although it is not possible to find an actually distinct intensity in respect of each individual sin, yet it is found in the way explained above; and also in another way, insofar as in this general contrition each individual sin is related to that particular motive of sorrow which occurs to the contrite person, viz. the offense against God. For he who loves a whole loves its parts potentially, although not actually, and accordingly he loves some parts more and some less, in proportion to their relation to the whole; thus he who loves a community virtually loves each one more or less according to their respective relations to the common good. In like manner, he who is sorry for having offended God grieves implicitly for his different sins in different ways, according as by them he offended God more or less.

Reply Obj. 3: Although each mortal sin turns us away from God and deprives us of his grace, yet some remove us further away than others, inasmuch as through their inordinateness they become more out of harmony with the order of the divine goodness than others do.

QUESTION 4

THE TIME FOR CONTRITION

Deinde considerandum est de tempore contritionis. Circa quod tria quaeruntur.

Primo: utrum tota vita haec sit contritionis tempus.

Secundo: utrum expediat continue; de peccato dolere.

Tertio: utrum post hanc vitam animae de peccatis conterantur.

We must now consider the time for contrition. Under this head there are three points of inquiry:

(1) Whether the whole of this life is the time for contrition?

(2) Whether it is expedient to grieve continually for our sins?

(3) Whether souls grieve for their sins even after this life?

Article 1

Whether the Whole of This Life Is the Time for Contrition?

AD PRIMUM SIC PROCEDITUR. Videtur quod non tota haec vita sit contritionis tempus. Sicut enim de peccato commisso debet esse dolor, ita et pudor. Sed non per totam vitam durat pudor de peccato: quia, sicut dicit Ambrosius, *non habet quod erubescat cui peccatum dimissum est.* Ergo, videtur quod nec contritio, quae est dolor de peccato.

PRAETEREA, I Ioan. 4, dicitur quod *perfecta caritas foras mittit timorem, quia timor poenam habet.* Sed dolor etiam poenam habet. Ergo in statu perfectae caritatis non potest dolor contritionis manere.

PRAETEREA, de praeterito non posset esse dolor, qui proprie est de malo praesenti, nisi secundum quod aliquid de peccato praeterito in praesenti manet. Sed quandoque pervenitur ad aliquem statum in hac vita in quo nihil de peccato praeterito manet, neque dispositio, neque culpa, neque reatus aliquis. Ergo non oportet ulterius de illo peccato dolere.

PRAETEREA, Rom. 8, dicitur quod *diligentibus Deum omnia cooperantur in bonum*: etiam peccata, ut dicit Glossa. Ergo non oportet, post remissionem peccati, quod de ipso doleat.

PRAETEREA, contritio est pars poenitentiae contra satisfactionem divisa. Sed non oportet semper satisfacere. Ergo nec semper conteri de peccato.

SED CONTRA: Augustinus, in libro *de Poenitentia*, dicit quod, *ubi dolor finitur, deficit poenitentia: ubi deficit poenitentia, nihil relinquitur de venia.* Ergo videtur, cum oporteat veniam concessam non perdere, quod oporteat semper de peccato dolere.

OBJECTION 1: It would seem that the time for contrition is not the whole of this life. For as we should be sorry for a sin committed, so should we be ashamed of it. But shame for sin does not last all one's life, for Ambrose says that *he whose sin is forgiven has nothing to be ashamed of* (*On Penance* 2). Therefore, it seems that neither should contrition last all one's life, since it is sorrow for sin.

OBJ. 2: Further, it is written that *perfect charity casts out fear, because fear has pain* (1 John 4:18). But sorrow also has pain. Therefore, the sorrow of contrition cannot remain in the state of perfect charity.

OBJ. 3: Further, there cannot be any sorrow for the past (since it is, properly speaking, about a present evil) except insofar as something of the past sin remains in the present time. Now, in this life, sometimes one attains to a state in which nothing remains of a past sin, neither disposition, nor guilt, nor any debt of punishment. Therefore, there is no need to grieve any more for that sin.

OBJ. 4: Further, it is written that *to them that love God all things work together unto good* (Rom 8:28), even sins, as a Gloss declares (Augustine, *On Rebuke and Grace*). Therefore, there is no need for them to grieve for sin after it has been forgiven.

OBJ. 5: Further, contrition is a part of penance condivided with satisfaction. But there is no need for continual satisfaction. Therefore, contrition for sin need not be continual.

ON THE CONTRARY, Augustine in *On True and False Penance* says that *when sorrow ceases, penance fails, and when penance fails, no pardon remains.* Therefore, since one ought not to lose the forgiveness which has been granted, it seems that one should always grieve for one's sins.

21

PRAETEREA, Eccli. 5, dicitur: *de propitiatu peccatorum noli esse sine metu.* Ergo homo semper debet dolere, ad peccatorum propitiationem habendam.

RESPONDEO dicendum quod in contritione est duplex dolor: unus rationis, qui est detestatio peccati a se commissi; alius sensitivae partis, qui ex isto consequitur., Et quantum ad utrumque, contritionis tempus est totius vitae praesentis status. Quandiu enim est aliquis in statu viae, detestatur incommoda quibus a perventione ad terminum viae impeditur vel retardatur. Unde, cum propter peccatum praeteritum viae nostrae cursus in Deum retardetur, quia tempus illud quod erat deputatum ad currendum recuperari non potest; oportet quod in vitae huius tempore status contritionis maneat quantum ad peccati detestationem. Similiter etiam quantum ad sensibilem dolorem, qui ut poena a voluntate assumitur. Quia enim homo poenam aeternam peccando meruit, et contra aeternum Deum peccavit, debet, poena aeterna in temporalem mutata, saltem dolor in *aeterno hominis*, idest statu huius vitae, manere. Et propter hoc dicit Hugo de Sancto Victore quod *Deus, absolvens hominem a culpa et poena aeterna, ligat eum vinculo perpetuae detestationis peccati.*

AD PRIMUM ergo dicendum quod erubescentia respicit peccatum solum inquantum habet turpitudinem. Et ideo, postquam peccatum quantum ad culpam remissum, est, non manet pudori locus. Manet autem dolori, qui non solum de culpa est inquantum habet turpitudinem, sed etiam inquantum habet nocumentum annexum.

AD SECUNDUM dicendum quod timor servilis, quem caritas foras mittit, oppositionem habet ad caritatem ratione suae servitutis, qua poenam respicit. Sed dolor contritionis ex caritate causatur, ut dictum est. Et ideo non est simile.

AD TERTIUM dicendum quod, quamvis per poenitentiam peccator redeat ad gratiam pristinam et immunitatem a reatu poenae, nunquam tamen redit ad pristinam dignitatem innocentiae. Et ideo semper ex praeterito peccato aliquid in ipso manet.

AD QUARTUM dicendum quod, sicut non debet homo *facere mala ut veniant bona*, ita non debet gaudere de malis quia ex eis occasionaliter proveniunt bona, divina providentia agente: quia illorum bonorum peccata causa non fuerunt, sed magis impedimenta. Sed divina providentia ea causavit: et de ea debet homo gaudere, de praeteritis autem dolere.

AD QUINTUM dicendum quod satisfactio attenditur secundum poenam taxatam, quae pro peccatis iniungi debet. Et ideo potest terminari, ut non oporteat ulterius satisfacere. Haec autem poena praecipue proportionatur culpae ex parte conversionis, ex qua finitatem habet: sed dolor contritionis respondet culpae ex parte aversionis,

FURTHER, It is written: *be not without fear about sin forgiven* (Sir 5:5). Therefore, man should always grieve, that his sins may be forgiven him.

I ANSWER THAT, As stated above (Q. 3, A. 1), there is a twofold sorrow in contrition: one is in the reason, and is detestation of the sin committed; the other is in the sensitive part, and results from the former: and as regards both, the time for contrition is the whole of the present state of life. For as long as one is a wayfarer, one detests the obstacles which retard or hinder one from reaching the end of the way. Hence, since past sin retards the course of our life towards God (because the time which was given to us for the course cannot be recovered), it follows that the state of contrition remains during the whole of this lifetime as regards the detestation of sin. The same is to be said of the sensible sorrow, which is assumed by the will as a punishment: for since man, by sinning, deserved everlasting punishment, and sinned against the eternal God, the everlasting punishment being commuted into a temporal one, sorrow ought to remain during the whole of *man's eternity*, i.e., during the whole of the state of this life. For this reason Hugh of St. Victor says that *when God absolves a man from eternal guilt and punishment, he binds him with a chain of eternal detestation of sin.*

REPLY OBJ. 1: Shame regards sin only as a disgraceful act; therefore, after sin has been taken away as to its guilt, there is no further motive for shame, but there does remain a motive of sorrow, which is for the guilt not only as being something disgraceful, but also as having a hurt connected with it.

REPLY OBJ. 2: Servile fear, which charity casts out, is opposed to charity by reason of its servility, because it regards the punishment. But the sorrow of contrition results from charity, as stated above (Q. 3). Therefore, it is not similar.

REPLY OBJ. 3: Although by penance the sinner returns to his former state of grace and immunity from the debt of punishment, yet he never returns to his former dignity of innocence, and so something always remains from his past sin.

REPLY OBJ. 4: Just as a man ought not *to do evil that good may come of it*, so he ought not to rejoice in evil for the reason that good may perchance come from it through the agency of divine grace or providence, because his sins did not cause but hindered those goods. Rather, it was divine providence that was their cause, and in this man should rejoice, whereas he should grieve for his sins.

REPLY OBJ. 5: Satisfaction depends on the punishment appointed, which should be enjoined for sins; hence it can come to an end, so that there be no further need of satisfaction. But that punishment is proportionate to sin chiefly on the part of its adherence to a creature whence it derives its finiteness. On the other hand, the sorrow of contrition

ex qua habet quandam infinitatem. Et ita vera contritio semper debet manere. Nec est inconveniens si, remoto posteriori, manet prius.

corresponds to sin on the part of the aversion, whence it derives a certain infinity. Therefore, contrition ought to continue always. Neither is it unreasonable if that which precedes remains when that which follows is taken away.

Article 2

Whether It Is Expedient to Grieve for Sin Continually?

AD SECUNDUM SIC PROCEDITUR. Videtur quod non expediat continue de peccato dolere. Expedit enim quandoque gaudere, ut patet Philip. 4: super illud, *gaudete in Domino semper*, dicit Glossa quod *necessarium est gaudere*. Sed non est possibile gaudere simul et dolere. Ergo non expedit continue de peccato dolere.

PRAETEREA, illud quod est de se malum et fugiendum, non est assumendum nisi quatenus est necessarium ut medicina ad aliquid: sicut patet de ustione et sectione vulneris. Sed tristitia de se mala est: unde dicitur Eccli. 30, *tristitiam longe expelle a te*, et subditur causa, *multos enim occidit tristitia, et non est utilitas in illa*. Hoc etiam Philosophus dicit expresse in VII *Ethic.* et X. Ergo non debet amplius dolere de peccato nisi quatenus sufficit ad peccatum delendum. Sed statim post primam contritionis tristitiam peccatum deletum est. Ergo non expedit ulterius dolere.

PRAETEREA, Bernardus dicit: *dolor bonus est si continuus non sit mel enim absynthio est admiscendum*. Ergo videtur quod non expedit continue dolere.

SED CONTRA est quod Augustinus dicit: *semper doleat poenitens, et de dolore gaudeat*.

PRAETEREA, actus in quibus consistit beatitudo, expedit semper continuare quantum, possibile est. Sed huiusmodi est dolor de peccato: quod patet Matth. 5, *beati qui lugent*. Ergo expedit dolorem continuare quantum possibile est.

RESPONDEO dicendum quod haec est conditio in actibus virtutum inventa, quod non potest in eis accipi *superfluum* et *diminutum*: ut in II *Ethic.* probatur. Unde, cum contritio, quantum ad id quod est displicentia quaedam iri appetitu rationis, sit actus poenitentiae virtutis, nunquam potest ibi esse superfluum, sicut nec quantum ad intensionem, ita nec quantum ad durationem: nisi secundum quod actus unius virtutis impedit actum alterius magis necessarium pro tempore illo. Unde, quantumcumque homo continue in actu huius displicentiae esse possit, melius est: dummodo actibus aliarum virtutum vacet suo tempore, secundum quod oportet.

OBJECTION 1: It would seem that it is not expedient to grieve for sin continually. For it is sometimes expedient to rejoice, as is evident from the Gloss on Philippians 4:4, *rejoice in the Lord always*, which says that *it is necessary to rejoice*. Now it is not possible to rejoice and grieve at the same time. Therefore, it is not expedient to grieve for sin continually.

OBJ. 2: Further, that which, in itself, is an evil and a thing to be avoided should not be taken upon oneself, except insofar as it is necessary as a remedy against something, as in the case of burning or cutting a wound. Now, sorrow is in itself an evil; wherefore it is written: *drive away sadness far from you*, and the reason is given: *for sadness has killed many, and there is no profit in it* (Sir 30:24–25). Moreover, the Philosopher says the same (*Ethics* 7.13–14; 10.5). Therefore, one should not grieve for sin any longer than suffices for the sin to be blotted out. Now, sin is immediately blotted out after the first sorrow of contrition. Therefore, it is not expedient to grieve any longer.

OBJ. 3: Further, Bernard says: *sorrow is a good thing, if it is not continual; for honey should be mingled with wormwood* (*Sermons on the Song of Songs*). Therefore, it seems that it is inexpedient to grieve continually.

ON THE CONTRARY, Augustine says: *the penitent should always grieve, and rejoice in his grief* (*On True and False Penance*).

FURTHER, It is expedient always to continue, as far as it is possible, those acts in which beatitude consists. Now such is sorrow for sin, as is shown by the words, *blessed are they that mourn* (Matt 5:5). Therefore, it is expedient for sorrow to be as continual as possible.

I ANSWER THAT, We find this condition in the acts of the virtues, that in them *excess* and *defect* are not possible, as is proved in *Ethics* 2.6–7. Wherefore, since contrition, so far as it is a kind of displeasure seated in the rational appetite, is an act of the virtue of penance, there can never be excess in it, either as to its intensity or as to its duration, except insofar as the act of one virtue hinders the act of another which is more urgent for the time being. Consequently, the more continually a man can perform acts of this displeasure, the better it is, provided he exercises the acts of other virtues when and how he ought to.

Sed passiones possunt habere superfluum et diminutum, et quantum ad intensionem, et quantum ad durationem. Et ideo, sicut passio doloris quam voluntas assumit, debet esse moderate intensa, ita debet moderate durare: ne, si nimis duret, homo in desperationem et pusillanimitatem et huiusmodi vitia labatur.

AD PRIMUM ergo dicendum quod gaudium saeculi impeditur per dolorem contritionis: non autem gaudium quod de Deo est, quia habet ipsum dolorem pro materia.

AD SECUNDUM dicendum quod Ecclesiasticus de tristitia saeculi loquitur. Et Philosophus loquitur de tristitia quae est passio: qua moderate utendum est, secundum quod expedit ad finem ad quem assumitur.

AD TERTIUM dicendum quod Bernardus loquitur de dolore qui est passio.

On the other hand, passions can have excess and defect, both in intensity and in duration. Wherefore, as the passion of sorrow, which the will takes upon itself, ought to be moderately intense, so ought it to be of moderate duration, lest, if it should last too long, man fall into despair, cowardice, and such like vices.

REPLY OBJ. 1: The sorrow of contrition is a hindrance to worldly joy, but not to the joy which is about God, and which has sorrow itself for object.

REPLY OBJ. 2: The words of Ecclesiasticus refer to worldly joy: and the Philosopher is referring to sorrow as a passion, of which we should make moderate use according as the end, for which it is assumed, demands.

REPLY OBJ. 3: Bernard is speaking of sorrow as a passion.

Article 3

Whether Our Souls Are Contrite for Sins Even After This Life?

AD TERTIUM SIC PROCEDITUR. Videtur quod etiam post hanc vitam animae de peccatis conterantur. Amor enim caritatis displicentiam de peccato causat. Sed post hanc vitam manet in aliquibus caritas, et quantum ad actum et quantum ad habitum: *quia caritas nunquam excidit*, ut dicitur I Cor. 13. Ergo manet displicentia de peccato commisso, quae essentialiter est contritio.

PRAETEREA, magis est dolendum de culpa quam de poena. Sed animae in purgatorio dolent de poena sensibili et de dilatione gloriae. Ergo multo magis dolent de culpa ab eis commissa.

PRAETEREA, poena purgatorii est satisfactoria de peccato. Sed satisfactio habet efficaciam ex vi contritionis. Ergo contritio manet post hanc vitam.

SED CONTRA: Contritio est pars poenitentiae sacramenti. Sed sacramenta non manent post hanc vitam. Ergo nec contritio.

PRAETEREA, contritio potest esse tanta quod delet et culpam et poenam. Si ergo animae in purgatorio conteri possent, posset vi contritionis earum reatus poenae eis dimitti, et omnino a poena sensibili liberari: quod est falsum.

RESPONDEO dicendum quod in contritione tria consideranda sunt: primum est contritionis, genus, quod est dolor; secundum est contritionis forma, quia est actus virtutis gratia informatus; tertium est contritionis efficacia, quia est meritorius, et sacramentalis, et quodammodo satisfactorius. Animae igitur post hanc vitam quae in patria surit, contritionem habere non possunt: quia carent dolore, propter gaudii plenitudinem. Illae vero quae sunt in inferno, carent contritione: quia, etsi dolorem ha-

OBJECTION 1: It would seem that our souls are contrite for sins even after this life. For the love of charity causes displeasure at sin. Now, after this life, charity remains in some both as to its act and as to its habit, since *charity never falls away* (1 Cor 13:8). Therefore, the displeasure at the sin committed, which is the essence of contrition, remains.

OBJ. 2: Further, we should grieve more for sin than for punishment. But the souls in purgatory grieve for their sensible punishment and for the delay of glory. Much more, therefore, do they grieve for the sins they committed.

OBJ. 3: Further, the pain of purgatory satisfies for sin. But satisfaction derives its efficacy from the power of contrition. Therefore, contrition remains after this life.

ON THE CONTRARY, Contrition is a part of the sacrament of penance. But the sacraments do not endure after this life. Neither, therefore, does contrition.

FURTHER, Contrition can be so great as to blot out both guilt and punishment. If, therefore, the souls in purgatory could have contrition, it would be possible for their debt of punishment to be remitted through the power of their contrition so that they would be delivered from their sensible pain, which is false.

I ANSWER THAT, Three things are to be observed in contrition: first, its genus, which is sorrow; second, its form, for it is an act of virtue informed by charity; third, its efficacy, for it is a meritorious and sacramental act, and, to a certain extent, satisfactory. Accordingly, after this life, those souls which dwell in the heavenly country cannot have contrition, because they are void of sorrow by reason of the fullness of their joy: those which are in hell have no contrition, for although they have sorrow, they lack the grace

beant, deficit tamen eis gratia dolorem informans. Sed illi qui in purgatorio sunt, habent dolorem de peccatis gratia informatum, sed non meritorium: quia non sunt in statu merendi. In hac autem vita omnia tria praedicta inveniri possunt.

Ad primum ergo dicendum quod caritas non causat istum dolorem nisi in illis qui doloris capaces sunt. Sed plenitudo gaudii a beatis omnem capacitatem doloris excludit. Et ideo, quamvis caritatem habeant, tamen contritione carent.

Ad secundum dicendum quod animae in purgatorio dolent de peccatis: sed ille dolor non est contritio, quia deest ei contritionis efficacia.

Ad tertium dicendum quod poena illa quam animae in purgatorio sustinent, non potest proprie dici satisfactio, quia satisfactio opus meritorium requirit: sed largo modo dicitur satisfactio poenae debitae solutio.

which informs sorrow; while those which are in purgatory have a sorrow for their sins that is informed by grace, yet it is not meritorious, for they are not in the state of meriting. In this life, however, all these three can be found.

Reply Obj. 1: Charity does not cause this sorrow save in those who are capable of it; but the fullness of joy in the blessed excludes all capability of sorrow from them: wherefore, though they have charity, they have no contrition.

Reply Obj. 2: The souls in purgatory grieve for their sins, but their sorrow is not contrition, because it lacks the efficacy of contrition.

Reply Obj. 3: The pain which the souls suffer in purgatory, cannot, properly speaking, be called satisfaction, because satisfaction demands a meritorious work; yet, in a broad sense, the payment of the punishment due may be called satisfaction.

QUESTION 5

THE EFFECT OF CONTRITION

Deinde considerandum est de effectu contritionis. Circa quod tria quaeruntur.

Primo: utrum peccati remissio sit contritionis effectus.

Secundo: utrum contritio possit totaliter tollere reatum poenae.

Tertio: utrum parva contritio sufficiat ad deletionem magnorum peccatorum.

We must now consider the effect of contrition. Under this head there are three points of inquiry:

(1) Whether the remission of sin is the effect of contrition?

(2) Whether contrition can take away the debt of punishment entirely?

(3) Whether slight contrition suffices to blot out great sins?

Article 1

Whether the Forgiveness of Sin Is the Effect of Contrition?

AD PRIMUM SIC PROCEDITUR. Videtur quod peccati remissio non sit contritionis effectus. Solus enim Deus peccata remittit. Sed contritionis nos sumus aliqualiter causa: quia actus noster est. Ergo contritio non est causa remissionis culpae.

PRAETEREA, contritio est actus virtutis. Sed virtus sequitur culpae remissionem: quia virtus et culpa non sunt simul in anima. Ergo contritio non est causa remissionis culpae.

PRAETEREA, nihil impedit a perceptione Eucharistiae nisi culpa. Sed contritus ante confessionem non debet accedere ad Eucharistiam. Ergo nondum est consecutus remissionem culpae.

SED CONTRA est quod dicitur in Glossa, super illud Psalmi, *sacrificium Deo spiritus contribulatus,* etc.: *contritio cordis est sacrificium in quo peccata solvuntur.*

PRAETEREA, *virtus et vitium eisdem causis corrumpuntur et generantur,* ut dicitur in II *Ethic.* Sed per inordinatum amorem cordis peccatum committitur: ergo per dolorem ex amore caritatis ordinato causatum peccatum solvitur. Et sic peccatum contritio delet.

RESPONDEO dicendum quod contritio potest dupliciter considerari: vel inquantum est pars sacramenti; vel inquantum est actus virtutis. Et utroque modo est causa remissionis peccati, sed diversimode. Quia, inquantum est pars sacramenti, primo operatur ad remissionem peccati instrumentaliter: sicut et de aliis sacramentis in I distinctione patuit. Inquantum autem est actus virtutis, sic est quasi causa materialis remissionis peccati: eo quod dispositio est quasi necessitas ad iustificationem; dispositio autem reducitur ad causam materialem, si accipiatur dispositio quae disponit materiam ad re-

OBJECTION 1: It would seem that the forgiveness of sin is not the effect of contrition. For God alone forgives sins. But we are somewhat the cause of contrition, since it is an act of our own. Therefore, contrition is not the cause of forgiveness.

OBJ. 2: Further, contrition is an act of virtue. Now virtue follows the forgiveness of sin: because virtue and sin are not together in the soul. Therefore, contrition is not the cause of the forgiveness of sin.

OBJ. 3: Further, nothing but sin is an obstacle to receiving the Eucharist. But the contrite should not go to Communion before going to confession. Therefore, they have not yet received the forgiveness of their sins.

ON THE CONTRARY, A Gloss on Psalm 50:19: *a sacrifice to God is an afflicted spirit*, says, *a hearty contrition is the sacrifice by which sins are loosed.*

FURTHER, *Virtue and vice are engendered and corrupted by the same causes*, as stated in *Ethics* 2.1–2. Now sin is committed through the heart's inordinate love. Therefore, it is destroyed by sorrow caused by the heart's ordinate love; and consequently contrition blots out sin.

I ANSWER THAT, Contrition can be considered in two ways: either as part of a sacrament, or as an act of virtue, and in either case it is the cause of the forgiveness of sin, but not in the same way. Because, as part of a sacrament, it operates primarily as an instrument for the forgiveness of sin, as is evident with regard to the other sacraments (*Sentences* IV, D. 1, Q. 1, A. 4; III, Q. 62, A. 1); while, as an act of virtue, it is the quasi-material cause of sin's forgiveness. For a disposition is, as it were, a necessary condition for justification, and a disposition is reduced to a material cause, if it be taken to denote that which disposes matter to receive

cipiendum. Secus autem est de dispositione agentis ad agendum: quia illa reducitur ad genus causae efficientis.

AD PRIMUM ergo dicendum quod solus Deus est causa efficiens principalis remissionis peccati: sed causa dispositiva potest etiam esse ex nobis. Et similiter etiam causa sacramentalis: quia formae sacramentorum verba sunt a nobis prolata, quae habent virtutem instrumentalem gratiam inducendi, qua peccata remittuntur.

AD SECUNDUM dicendum quod peccati remissio uno modo praecedit virtutem et gratiae infusionem, et alio modo sequitur. Et secundum hoc quod sequitur, actus a virtute elicitus potest esse causa aliqua remissionis peccati.

AD TERTIUM dicendum quod dispensatio Eucharistiae pertinet ad ministros Ecclesiae. Et ideo ante remissionem peccati per ministros Ecclesiae non debet aliquis ad Eucharistiam accedere, quamvis sit sibi culpa quoad Deum remissa.

something. It is otherwise in the case of an agent's disposition to act, because this is reduced to the genus of efficient cause.

REPLY OBJ. 1: God alone is the principal efficient cause of the forgiveness of sin: but the dispositive cause can be from us also, and likewise the sacramental cause, since the sacramental forms are words uttered by us, having an instrumental power of conferring grace whereby sins are forgiven.

REPLY OBJ. 2: In one way, the forgiveness of sin precedes virtue and the infusion of grace, and follows in another: and insofar as it follows, the act elicited by the virtue can be a cause of the forgiveness of sin.

REPLY OBJ. 3: The dispensation of the Eucharist belongs to the ministers of the Church: wherefore a man should not go to Communion until his sin has been forgiven through the ministers of the Church, although his sin may be forgiven him before God.

Article 2

Whether Contrition Can Take Away the Debt of Punishment Entirely?

AD SECUNDUM SIC PROCEDITUR. Videtur quod contritio non possit totaliter tollere reatum poenae. Quia satisfactio et confessio ordinantur ad liberationem a reatu poenae. Sed nullus ita perfecte conteritur quin oporteat eum confiteri et satisfacere. Ergo contritio nunquam est tanta quod totaliter deleat reatum totum.

PRAETEREA, in poenitentia oportet esse quaedam recompensatio poenae ad culpam. Sed aliqua culpa per membra corporis exercetur. Ergo, cum oporteat ad debitam poenae recompensationem ut *per quae peccat quis, per haec et torqueatur*, videtur quod nunquam possit poena talis peccati per contritionem absolvi.

PRAETEREA, dolor contritionis est finitus. Sed pro aliquo peccato, scilicet mortali, debetur poena infinita. Ergo nunquam potest esse tanta contritio quod totam poenam deleat.

SED CONTRA est quod Deus plus affectum cordis acceptat quam etiam exteriorem actum. Sed per exteriores actus absolvitur homo a poena et culpa. Ergo et similiter per cordis affectum, qui est contritio.

PRAETEREA, exemplum huius de Latrone habetur, cui dictum est, *hodie mecum eris in Paradiso*, propter unicum poenitentiae actum.

OBJECTION 1: It would seem that contrition cannot take away the debt of punishment entirely. For satisfaction and confession are ordained for man's deliverance from the debt of punishment. Now no man is so perfectly contrite as not to be bound to confession and satisfaction. Therefore, contrition is never so great as to blot out the entire debt of punishment.

OBJ. 2: Further, in penance the punishment should in some way compensate for the sin. Now some sins are accomplished by members of the body. Therefore, since it is for the due compensation for sin that *by what things a man sins, by the same also he is tormented* (Wis 11:17), it seems that the punishment for such sins can never be remitted by contrition.

OBJ. 3: Further, the sorrow of contrition is finite. Now an infinite punishment is due for some, namely mortal, sins. Therefore, contrition can never be so great as to remit the whole punishment.

ON THE CONTRARY, The affections of the heart are more acceptable to God than external acts. Now man is absolved from both punishment and guilt by means of external actions, and therefore he is also by means of the heart's affections, such as contrition.

FURTHER, We have an example of this in the thief, to whom it was said: *this day you will be with me in paradise* (Luke 23:43) on account of his one act of repentance.

Utrum autem totus reatus per contritionem semper tollatur, supra, dist. 14, quaesitum est, ubi hoc ipsum de poenitentia quaerebatur.

RESPONDEO dicendum quod intensio contritionis potest attendi dupliciter. Uno modo, ex parte caritatis, quae displicentiam causat. Et sic contingit tantum intendi paritatem in actu quod contritio inde sequens merebitur non solum culpae amotionem, sed etiam absolutionem ab omni poena. Alio modo, ex parte doloris sensibilis, quem voluntas in contritione excitat. Et quia illa etiam poena quaedam est, tantum potest intendi quod sufficiat ad deletionem culpae et poenae.

AD PRIMUM ergo dicendum quod aliquis non potest esse certus quod contritio sua sit sufficiens ad deletionem poenae et culpae. Et ideo tenetur confiteri et satisfacere: maxime cum contritio vera non fuerit nisi propositum confitendi habuisset annexum. Quod debet ad effectum reduci, etiam propter praeceptum quod est de confessione datum.

AD SECUNDUM dicendum quod, sicut gaudium interius redundat etiam ad exteriores corporis partes, ita etiam dolor interior ad exteriora membra derivatur. Unde dicitur Prov. 17: *spiritus tristis exsiccat ossa*.

AD TERTIUM dicendum quod dolor contritionis, quamvis sit finitus quantum ad intensionem, sicut etiam poena peccato mortali debita finita est, habet tamen infinitam virtutem ex caritate, qua informatur. Et secundum hoc potest valere ad deletionem culpae et poenae.

As to whether the whole debt of punishment is always taken away by contrition, this question has already been considered above (*Sentences* IV, D. 14, Q. 2, A. 1–2; III, Q. 86, A. 4), where the same question was raised with regard to penance.

I ANSWER THAT, The intensity of contrition may be regarded in two ways. First, on the part of charity, which causes the displeasure, and in this way it may happen that the act of charity is so intense that the contrition resulting therefrom merits not only the removal of guilt, but also the remission of all punishment. Second, on the part of the sensible sorrow, which the will excites in contrition: and since this sorrow is also a kind of punishment, it may be so intense as to suffice for the remission of both guilt and punishment.

REPLY OBJ. 1: A man cannot be sure that his contrition suffices for the remission of both punishment and guilt: wherefore he is bound to confess and to make satisfaction, especially since his contrition would not be true contrition unless he had the purpose of confessing united to it. This purpose must also be carried into effect, on account of the precept given concerning confession.

REPLY OBJ. 2: Just as inward joy redounds into the outward parts of the body, so does interior sorrow show itself in the exterior members; hence it is written: *a sorrowful spirit dries up the bones* (Prov 17:22).

REPLY OBJ. 3: Although the sorrow of contrition is finite in its intensity, even as the punishment due for mortal sin is finite, yet it derives infinite power from charity, whereby it is informed, and so it avails for the remission of both guilt and punishment.

Article 3

Whether Slight Contrition Suffices to Blot Out Great Sins?

AD TERTIUM SIC PROCEDITUR. Videtur quod contritio parva non sufficiat ad deletionem magnorum peccatorum. Quia contritio est medicina peccati. Sed corporalis medicina quae sanat corporalem morbum minorem, non sufficit ad sanandum maiorem. Ergo minima contritio non sufficit ad delendum maxima peccata.

PRAETEREA, supra dictum est quod oportet de maioribus peccatis magis conteri. Sed contritio non delet peccatum nisi sit secundum quod oportet. Ergo minima contritio non delet omnia peccata.

SED CONTRA, quaelibet gratia gratum faciens delet omnem culpam mortalem, quae simul stare cum ea non

OBJECTION 1: It would seem that slight contrition does not suffice to blot out great sins. For contrition is the remedy for sin. Now a bodily remedy that heals a lesser bodily infirmity does not suffice to heal a greater. Therefore, the least contrition does not suffice to blot out very great sins.

OBJ. 2: Further, it was stated above (Q. 3, A. 3) that for greater sins one ought to have greater contrition. Now, contrition does not blot out sin unless it fulfills the requisite conditions. Therefore, the least contrition does not blot out all sins.

ON THE CONTRARY, Every sanctifying grace blots out every mortal sin, because it is incompatible therewith. Now

potest. Sed quaelibet contritio est gratia gratum faciente informata. Ergo, quantumcumque sit parva, delet omnem culpam.

RESPONDEO dicendum quod contritio, ut saepe dictum est, habet duplicem dolorem. Unum rationis, qui est displicentia peccati commissi. Et hic potest esse adeo parvus quod non sufficiet ad rationem contritionis, ut si minus displiceret ei peccatum quam debeat displicere separatio a fine: sicut etiam amor potest esse ita remissus quod non sufficit ad rationem caritatis. Alium dolorem habet in sensu. Et parvitas huius non impedit rationem contritionis: quia non se habet essentialiter ad contritionem, sed quasi ex accidenti ei adiungitur. Et iterum non est in potestate nostra.

Sic ergo dicendum quod, quantumcumque parvus sit dolor dummodo ad contritionis rationem sufficiat, omnem culpam delet.

AD PRIMUM ergo dicendum quod medicinae spirituales habent efficaciam infinitam ex virtute infinita quae in eis operatur. Et ideo illa medicina quae sufficit ad curationem parvi peccati, sufficit etiam ad curationem magni: sicut patet de baptismo, quo et magna et parva solvuntur. Et similiter est de contritione: dummodo ad rationem contritionis pertingat.

AD SECUNDUM dicendum quod hoc sequitur ex necessitate, quod unus homo plus doleat de maiori peccato quam de minori, secundum quod magis repugnat amori, qui dolorem causat. Sed si unus alius haberet tantum de dolore pro maiori quantum ipse habet de minori, sufficeret ad remissionem culpae.

every contrition is informed by sanctifying grace. Therefore, however slight it be, it blots out all sins.

I ANSWER THAT, As we have often said (Q. 1, A. 2; Q. 3, A. 1; Q. 4, A. 1), contrition includes a twofold sorrow. One is in the reason, and is displeasure at the sin committed. This can be so slight as not to suffice for real contrition, e.g., if a sin were less displeasing to a man than separation from his last end ought to be; just as love can be so slack as not to suffice for real charity. The other sorrow is in the senses, and the slightness of this is no hindrance to real contrition, because it does not, of itself, belong essentially to contrition, but is connected with it accidentally: nor again is it under our control.

Accordingly, we must say that sorrow, however slight it be, provided it suffice for true contrition, blots out all sin.

REPLY OBJ. 1: Spiritual remedies derive infinite efficacy from the infinite power which operates in them: wherefore the remedy which suffices for healing a slight sin suffices also to heal a great sin. This is seen in baptism which looses great and small: and the same applies to contrition provided it fulfill the necessary conditions.

REPLY OBJ. 2: It follows of necessity that a man grieves more for a greater sin than for a lesser, according as it is more repugnant to the love which causes his sorrow. But if one has the same degree of sorrow for a greater sin as another has for a lesser, this would suffice for the remission of the sin.

QUESTION 6

THE NECESSITY OF CONFESSION

Deinde considerandum est de confessione. De qua sex sunt consideranda: primo, de confessionis necessitate; secundo, de eius quidditate; tertio, de ipsius ministro; quarto, de qualitate eius; quinto; de eius effectu; sexto, de eius sigillo.

Circa primum quaeruntur sex.

Primo: utrum confessio sit necessaria ad salutem.

Secundo: utrum confessio sit de iure naturali.

Tertio: utrum omnes ad confessionem teneantur.

Quarto: utrum aliquis possit confiteri peccatum quod non habet.

Quinto: utrum statim homines peccatum confiteri teneantur.

Sexto: utrum possit cum aliquo dispensari ne homini confiteatur.

We must now consider confession, about which there are six points for our consideration: (1) The necessity of confession; (2) Its nature; (3) Its minister; (4) Its quality; (5) Its effect; (6) The seal of confession.

Under the first head there are six points of inquiry:

(1) Whether confession is necessary for salvation?

(2) Whether confession is according to the natural law?

(3) Whether all are bound to confession?

(4) Whether it is lawful to confess a sin of which one is not guilty?

(5) Whether one is bound to confess at once?

(6) Whether one can be dispensed from confessing to another man?

Article 1

Whether Confession Is Necessary for Salvation?

AD PRIMUM SIC PROCEDITUR. Videtur quod confessio non sit necessaria ad salutem. Sacramentum enim poenitentiae propter remissionem culpae ordinatum est. Sed culpa per gratiae infusionem sufficienter remittitur. Ergo ad poenitentiam de peccato agendam non est necessaria confessio.

PRAETEREA, aliquibus est peccatum remissum sine hoc quod confessi legantur: sicut patet de Petro et Magdalena, et de Paulo. Sed non est minoris efficaciae gratia remittens peccatum nunc quam tunc fuerit. Ergo nec nunc de necessitate salutis est quod homo confiteatur.

PRAETEREA, peccatum quod ex alio contractum est, ex alio debet habere medicinam. Ergo peccatum actuale, quod ex proprio motu quilibet commisit, oportet ex seipso tantum habere medicinam. Sed contra tale peccatum ordinatur poenitentia. Ergo confessio non est de necessitate poenitentiae.

PRAETEREA, confessio ad hoc exigitur in iudicio ut secundum quantitatem culpae poena infligatur. Sed homo potest poenam sibi ipsi infligere maiorem quam etiam ab alio sibi infligatur. Ergo videtur quod confessio non sit de necessitate salutis.

SED CONTRA: Boetius, in libro *de Consolatione*: *si operam medicantis expectas, oportet quod morbum detegas*. Sed de necessitate salutis est quod homo de pecca-

OBJECTION 1: It would seem that confession is not necessary for salvation. For the sacrament of penance is ordained for the sake of the remission of sin. But sin is sufficiently remitted by the infusion of grace. Therefore, confession is not necessary in order to do penance for one's sins.

OBJ. 2: Further, we read of some being forgiven their sins without confession, e.g., Peter, Mary Magdalene, and Paul. But the grace that remits sins is not less efficacious now than it was then. Therefore, neither is it necessary for salvation now that man should confess.

OBJ. 3: Further, a sin which is contracted from another should receive its remedy from another. Therefore, actual sin, which a man has committed through his own act, must take its remedy from the man himself. Now penance is ordained against such sins. Therefore, confession is not necessary for salvation.

OBJ. 4: Further, confession is necessary for a judicial sentence, in order that punishment may be inflicted in proportion to the offense. Now a man is able to inflict on himself a greater punishment than even that which might be inflicted on him by another. Therefore, it seems that confession is not necessary for salvation.

ON THE CONTRARY, Boethius says (*Consolation of Philosophy*, 1): *if you want the physician to be of assistance to you, you must make your disease known to him*. But it is nec-

tis medicinam accipiat. Ergo et de necessitate salutis est quod morbum per confessionem detegat.

PRAETEREA, in iudicio saeculari non est idem iudex et reus. Sed iudicium spirituale est ordinatius. Ergo peccator, qui est reus, non debet esse sui ipsius iudex, sed ab alio iudicari. Et ita oportet quod ei confiteatur.

RESPONDEO dicendum quod passio Christi, sine cuius virtute nec originale nec actuale peccatum dimittitur, in nobis operatur per sacramentorum susceptionem, quae ex ipsa efficaciam habent. Et ideo ad culpae remissionem, et actualis et originalis, requiritur sacramentum Ecclesiae, vel actu susceptum; vel saltem, voto, quando articulus necessitatis, non contemptus, sacramentum excludit. Et per consequens illa sacramenta quae ordinantur contra culpam, cum qua salus esse non potest, sunt de necessitate salutis. Et ideo, sicut baptismus, quo deletur originale, est de necessitate salutis, ita et poenitentiae sacramentum. Sicut autem aliquis per hoc quod baptismum petit se ministris Ecclesiae subiicit, ad quos pertinet dispensatio sacramenti; ita etiam per hoc quod confitetur peccatum suum se ministro Ecclesiae subiicit, ut per sacramentum poenitentiae, ab eo dispensatum, remissionem consequatur. Qui congruum remedium adhibere non potest nisi peccatum cognoscat: quod fit per confessionem peccantis. Et ideo confessio est de necessitate salutis eius qui in peccatum actuale mortale cecidit.

AD PRIMUM ergo dicendum quod gratiae infusio sufficit ad culpae remissionem, sed post culpam remissam adhuc est peccator debitor poenae temporalis. Sed ad gratiae infusionem consequendam ordinata sunt gratiae sacramenta: ante quorum susceptionem vel actu vel proposito aliquis gratiam non consequitur, sicut in baptismo patet. Et similiter est de confessione. Et ulterius per confessionis erubescentiam; et vim clavium, quibus se confitens subiicit; et satisfactionem iniunctam, quam sacerdos moderatur secundum qualitatem criminum sibi per confessionem innotescentium; poena temporalis expiatur.

Sed tamen ex hoc quod operatur confessio ad poenae remissionem, non habet quod sit de necessitate salutis. Quia poena ista est temporalis, ad quam post culpae remissionem aliquis remanet ligatus: unde sine hoc quod in praesenti via expiaretur, esset via salutis. Sed habet quod sit de necessitate salutis ex hoc quod ad remissionem culpae modo praedicto operatur.

AD SECUNDUM dicendum quod, etsi non legatur eorum confessio, potuit tamen fieri: *multa enim facta sunt quae non sunt scripta.* Et praeterea Christus habet pote-

essary for salvation that man should take medicine for his sins. Therefore, it is necessary for salvation that man should make his disease known by means of confession.

FURTHER, In a civil court the judge is distinct from the accused. Therefore, the sinner who is the accused ought not to be his own judge, but should be judged by another and consequently ought to confess to him.

I ANSWER THAT, Christ's Passion, without the power of which neither original nor actual sin is remitted, produces its effect in us through the reception of the sacraments, which derive their efficacy from it. Therefore, for the remission of both actual and original sin a sacrament of the Church is necessary, received either actually, or at least in desire, when a man fails to receive the sacrament actually through an unavoidable obstacle, and not through contempt. Consequently, those sacraments which are ordained as remedies for sin (which is incompatible with salvation) are necessary for salvation: and so just as baptism, whereby original sin is blotted out, is necessary for salvation, so also is the sacrament of penance. And just as a man through asking to be baptized submits to the ministers of the Church, to whom the dispensation of that sacrament belongs, even so, by confessing his sin, a man submits to a minister of the Church, that, through the sacrament of penance dispensed by him, he may receive the pardon of his sins: nor can the minister apply a fitting remedy, unless he be acquainted with the sin, which knowledge he acquires through the penitent's confession. Therefore, confession is necessary for the salvation of a man who has fallen into actual mortal sin.

REPLY OBJ. 1: The infusion of grace suffices for the remission of sin; but after the sin has been forgiven, the sinner still owes a debt of temporal punishment. Moreover, the sacraments of grace are ordained in order that man may receive the infusion of grace, and before he receives them, either actually or in his intention, he does not receive grace. This is evident in the case of baptism, and applies to penance likewise. Again, the penitent expiates his temporal punishment by undergoing the shame of confession, by the power of the keys to which he submits, and by the enjoined satisfaction which the priest moderates according to the kind of sins made known to him in confession.

Nevertheless, the fact that confession is necessary for salvation is not due to its conducing to the satisfaction for sins, because this punishment to which one remains bound after the remission of sin is temporal, wherefore the way of salvation remains open without such punishment being expiated in this life: but it is due to its conducing to the remission of sin, as explained above.

REPLY OBJ. 2: Although we do not read that they confessed, it may be that they did; *for many things were done which were not recorded in writing* (cf. John 21:25). More-

statem excellentiae in sacramentis. Unde sine his quae ad sacramentum pertinent, potuit rem sacramenti conferre.

AD TERTIUM dicendum quod peccatum quod ex altero contractum est, scilicet originale, potest omnino ab extrinseco remedium habere, ut in parvulis patet: sed peccatum actuale, quod ex seipso quisque commisit, non potest expiari nisi aliquid cooperetur ille qui peccavit. Sed tamen non sufficit ad peccatum expiandum ex seipso, sicut sufficienter peccatum commisit: eo quod peccatum ex parte conversionis est finitum, ex qua parte peccator in ipsum inducitur, sed ex parte aversionis habet infinitatem; ex qua parte oportet quod peccati remissio incipiat, quia *quod est ultimum in generatione est primum in resolutione*, ut dicitur in III *Ethic.* Et ideo oportet quod etiam peccatum actuale ex alio medicinam habeat.

AD QUARTUM dicendum quod satisfactio non sufficeret ad expiandam poenam peccati ex quantitate poenae quae in satisfactione imponitur: sed sufficit inquantum est pars sacramenti virtutem sacramentalem habens. Et ideo oportet quod per dispensatores sacramentorum imponatur. Et ideo necessaria est confessio.

over, Christ has the power of excellence in the sacraments, so that he could bestow the reality of the sacrament without using the things which belong to the sacrament.

REPLY OBJ. 3: The sin that is contracted from another, namely, original sin, can be remedied by an entirely extrinsic cause, as in the case of infants: whereas actual sin, which a man commits of himself, cannot be expiated without some operation on the part of the sinner. Nevertheless, man is not sufficient to expiate his sin by himself, though he was sufficient to sin by himself, because sin is finite on the part of the thing to which it turns, in which respect the sinner returns to self; while, on the part of the aversion, sin derives infinity, in which respect the remission of sin must begin from someone else, because *that which is last in order of generation is first in the order of intention* (*Ethics* 3). Consequently, actual sin also must take its remedy from another.

REPLY OBJ. 4: Satisfaction would not suffice for the expiation of sin's punishment by reason of the severity of the punishment which is enjoined in satisfaction, but it does suffice as being a part of the sacrament having the sacramental power; thus, it ought to be imposed by the dispensers of the sacraments, and consequently confession is necessary.

Article 2

Whether Confession Is According to the Natural Law?

AD SECUNDUM SIC PROCEDITUR. Videtur quod confessio sit de iure naturali. Adam enim et Cain non tenebantur nisi ad praecepta legis naturae, sed reprehenduntur de hoc quod peccatum suum non sunt confessi. Ergo confessio peccati est de iure naturali.

PRAETEREA, praecepta illa quae manent in veteri lege et nova, sunt de iure naturali. Sed confessio fuit in veteri lege: ut dicitur Isaiae 43: *narra, si quid habes, ut iustificeris*. Ergo est de iure naturali.

PRAETEREA, Iob non erat subiectus nisi legi naturali. Sed ipse peccata confitebatur: quod patet per hoc quod ipse de se dicit, Iob 31: *si abscondi ut homo peccatum meum*. Ergo est de iure naturali.

SED CONTRA: Isidorus dicit quod *ius naturale est idem apud omnes*. Sed confessio non est eodem modo apud omnes. Ergo non est de iure naturali.

PRAETEREA, confessio fit ei qui habet claves. Sed claves Ecclesiae non sunt de iure naturali institutae. Ergo nec confessio.

RESPONDEO dicendum quod sacramenta sunt quaedam fidei protestationes: unde oportet ea fidei esse pro-

OBJECTION 1: It would seem that confession is according to the natural law. For Adam and Cain were bound to none but the precepts of the natural law, and yet they are reproached for not confessing their sin. Therefore, confession of sin is according to the natural law.

OBJ. 2: Further, those precepts which are common to the old and new law are according to the natural law. But confession was prescribed in the old law, as may be gathered from Isaiah 43:26: *tell, if you have anything to justify yourself*. Therefore, it is according to the natural law.

OBJ. 3: Further, Job was subject only to the natural law. But he confessed his sins, as appears from his words: *if, as a man, I have hid my sin* (Job 31:33). Therefore, confession is according to the natural law.

ON THE CONTRARY, Isidore says (*Etymologies* 5) that *the natural law is the same in all*. But confession is not in all in the same way. Therefore, it is not according to the natural law.

FURTHER, Confession is made to one who has the keys. But the keys of the Church are not an institution of the natural law; neither, therefore, is confession.

I ANSWER THAT, The sacraments are professions of faith, wherefore they ought to be proportionate to faith.

portionata. Fides autem est supra cognitionem rationis naturalis. Unde et sacramenta sunt supra rationis naturalis dictamen. Et quia ius naturale est *quod non opinio genuit, sed innata quaedam vis inseruit*, ut Tullius dicit; ideo sacramenta non sunt, de iure naturali, sed de iure divino, quod est supra naturale. Et quandoque etiam naturale dicitur, secundum quod cuilibet rei illud est naturale quod ei a suo Creatore imponitur: tamen proprie dicuntur naturalia quae ex principiis naturae causantur. Supra autem naturam sunt quae ipse Deus sibi reservat sine naturae ministerio operanda: sive in operationibus miraculorum, sive in revelationibus mysteriorum, sive in institutionibus sacramentorum. Et sic confessio quae necessitatem sacramentalem habet, non de iure naturali est, sed de divino.

Ad primum ergo dicendum quod Adam vituperatur ex hoc quod peccatum suum coram Deo non recognovit: confessio enim quae fit Deo per recognitionem peccati, est de iure naturali. Nunc autem loquimur de confessione quae fit homini.

Vel dicendum quod confiteri peccatum in casu est de iure naturali: scilicet cum quis in iudicio constitutus a iudice interrogatur; tunc enim non debet mentiri peccatum excusando vel negando, de quo Adam et Cain vituperantur. Sed confessio quae fit homini sponte ad remissionem peccatorum consequendam a Deo, non est de iure naturali.

Ad secundum dicendum quod praecepta legis naturae manent eodem modo in lege Moysi et in nova lege. Sed confessio, quamvis aliqualiter esset in lege Moysi, non tamen eodem modo sicut in lege nova, nec sicut in lege naturae. In lege autem naturae sufficiebat recognitio peccati interior apud Deum. Sed in lege Moysi oportebat aliquo signo exteriori peccatum protestari, sicut per oblationem hostiae pro peccato, ex quo et homini innotescere poterat eum peccasse. Non autem oportebat ut speciale peccatum a se commissum manifestaret, aut peccati circumstantias: sicut in nova lege oportet.

Ad tertium dicendum quod Iob loquitur de illa absconsione peccati quam facit deprehensus peccatum negando aut excusando: ut ex Glossa ibidem haberi potest.

Now faith surpasses the knowledge of natural reason, whose dictate is therefore surpassed by the sacraments. And since *the natural law is not begotten of opinion, but a product of a certain innate power*, as Cicero states (*On Rhetorical Invention* 2), consequently the sacraments are not part of the natural law, but of the divine law which is above nature. This latter, however, is sometimes called natural, insofar as whatever a thing derives from its Creator is natural to it, although, properly speaking, those things are said to be natural which are caused by the principles of nature. But such things are above nature as God reserves to himself; and these are wrought either through the agency of nature, in the working of miracles, in the revelation of mysteries, or in the institution of the sacraments. Hence confession, which is of sacramental necessity, is according to divine but not natural law.

Reply Obj. 1: Adam is reproached for not confessing his sin before God: because the confession which is made to God by the acknowledgment of one's sin is according to the natural law. Whereas here we are speaking of confession made to a man.

We may also reply that in such a case confession of one's sin is according to the natural law, namely, when one is called upon by the judge to confess in a court of law, for then the sinner should not lie by excusing or denying his sin, as Adam and Cain are blamed for doing. But confession made voluntarily to a man in order to receive from God the forgiveness of one's sins is not according to the natural law.

Reply Obj. 2: The precepts of the natural law avail in the same way in the law of Moses and in the new law. But although there was a kind of confession in the law of Moses, yet it was not after the same manner as in the new law, nor as in the law of nature; for in the law of nature it was sufficient to acknowledge one's sin inwardly before God; while in the law of Moses it was necessary for a man to declare his sin by some external sign, as by making a sin-offering, whereby the fact of his having sinned became known to another man; but it was not necessary for him to make known what particular sin he had committed, or what were its circumstances, as in the new law.

Reply Obj. 3: Job is speaking of the man who hides his sin by denying it or excusing himself when he is accused thereof, as we may gather from a Gloss (Gregory, *Morals on Job* 22.9) on the passage.

Article 3

Whether All Are Bound to Confession?

Ad tertium sic proceditur. Videtur quod non omnes ad confessionem teneantur. Quia, sicut dicit Hieronymus, *poenitentia est secunda tabula: post naufra-*

Objection 1: It would seem that not all are bound to confession, for on Isaiah 3:9, *they have proclaimed abroad their sin*, Jerome says, *penance is the second plank after ship-*

gium. Sed aliqui post baptismum naufragium non sunt passi. Ergo eis non competit poenitentia. Et sic nec confessio, quae est poenitentiae pars.

Praeterea, confessio facienda est iudici in quolibet foro. Sed aliqui sunt qui non habent hominem iudicem supra se. Ergo nec tenentur ad confessionem.

Praeterea, aliquis est qui non habet peccata nisi venialia. Sed de illis non tenetur homo confiteri. Ergo non quilibet tenetur ad confessionem.

Sed contra: Confessio contra satisfactionem et contritionem dividitur. Sed omnes tenentur ad contritionem et satisfactionem. Ergo et omnes tenentur ad confessionem.

Praeterea, hoc patet per *Decretalem de Poenitentia et Remissione*, ubi dicitur quod *omnes utriusque sexus, cum ad annos discretionis pervenerint, tenentur peccata confiteri*.

Respondeo dicendum quod ad confessionem dupliciter obligamur. Uno modo, ex iure divino: ex hoc ipso quod est medicina. Et secundum hoc non omnes tenentur ad confessionem, sed illi tantum qui peccatum mortale incurrunt post baptismum.

Alio modo, ex praecepto iuris positivi. Et sic tenentur omnes ex institutione Ecclesiae edita in Concilio Generali sub Innocentio III. Tum ut quilibet peccatorem se cognosceret: quia *omnes peccaverunt et egent gratia Dei*. Tum ut cum maiori reverentia ad Eucharistiam accedatur. Tum ut ecclesiarum rectoribus sui subditi innotescant: ne lupus inter gregem lateat.

Ad primum ergo dicendum quod, quamvis homo in hac mortali vita post baptismum naufragium evadere possit, quod est per peccatum mortale; non tamen evadere potest venialia, quibus ad naufragium disponitur, contra quae etiam poenitentia ordinatur. Et ideo manet poenitentiae locus etiam in illis qui non mortaliter peccant: et per consequens confessionis.

Ad secundum dicendum quod nullus est qui non habeat iudicem Christum, cui per suum vicarium confiteri debet. Qui quamvis eo inferior sit inquantum ipse praelatus est, tamen est eo superior inquantum peccator est ipse, et ille Christi minister.

Ad tertium dicendum quod ex vi sacramenti non tenetur aliquis venialia confiteri: sed ex institutione Ecclesiae, quando non habet alia quae confiteatur.

Vel potest dici, secundum quosdam, quod ex Decretali praedicta non obligantur nisi illi qui habent peccata mortalia: quod patet ex hoc quod dicit quod debet *omnia peccata* confiteri, quod de venialibus intelligi non potest, quia nullus omnia confiteri potest. Et secundum hoc, ille qui non habet mortalia, non tenetur ad confessionem venialium, sed sufficit ad praeceptum Ecclesiae implendum ut se sacerdoti repraesentet, et se ostendat absque

wreck. But some have not suffered shipwreck after baptism. Therefore, penance is not befitting them, and consequently neither is confession, which is a part of penance.

Obj. 2: Further, it is to the judge that confession should be made in any court. But some have no judge over them. Therefore, they are not bound to confession.

Obj. 3: Further, some have none but venial sins. Now a man is not bound to confess such sins. Therefore, not everyone is bound to confession.

On the contrary, Confession is condivided with satisfaction and contrition. Now all are bound to contrition and satisfaction. Therefore, all are bound to confession also.

Further, This appears from the *Decretals* (*On Repentance and Remission of Sins* 12), where it is stated that *all of either sex are bound to confess their sins as soon as they shall come to the age of discretion*.

I answer that, We are bound to confession on two counts: first, by the divine law, from the very fact that confession is a remedy, and in this way not all are bound to confession, but those only who fall into mortal sin after baptism.

Second, by a precept of positive law, and in this way all are bound by the precept of the Church laid down in the general council (*Lateran Council* 4, Can. 21) under Innocent III, both in order that everyone may acknowledge himself to be a sinner, because *all have sinned and need the grace of God* (Rom 3:23); and that the Eucharist may be approached with greater reverence; and lastly, that parish priests may know their flock, lest a wolf hide therein.

Reply Obj. 1: Although it is possible for a man, in this mortal life, to avoid shipwreck, i.e., mortal sin, after baptism, yet he cannot avoid venial sins, which dispose him to shipwreck, and against which also penance is ordained; therefore, there is still room for penance, and consequently for confession, even in those who do not commit mortal sins.

Reply Obj. 2: All must acknowledge Christ as their judge, to whom they must confess in the person of his vicar; and although the latter may be the inferior if the penitent be a prelate, yet he is the superior, insofar as the penitent is a sinner, while the confessor is the minister of Christ.

Reply Obj. 3: A man is bound to confess his venial sins not in virtue of the sacrament, but by the institution of the Church, when he has no other sins to confess.

We may also, with others, answer that the Decretal quoted above does not bind others than those who have mortal sins to confess. This is evident from the fact that it orders *all sins* to be confessed, which cannot apply to venial sins, because no one can confess all his venial sins. Accordingly, a man who has no mortal sins to confess is not bound to confess his venial sins, but it suffices for the fulfillment of the commandment of the Church that he present himself

conscientia mortalis esse: et hoc ei pro confessione reputatur.

before the priest, and declare himself to be unconscious of any mortal sin: and this will count for his confession.

Article 4

Whether It Is Lawful for a Man to Confess a Sin Which He Has Not Committed?

AD QUARTUM SIC PROCEDITUR. Videtur quod aliquis licite possit confiteri peccatum quod non habet. Quia, ut dicit Gregorius, *bonarum mentium est ibi culpam agnoscere ubi culpa non est*. Ergo ad bonam mentem pertinet ut de illis culpis se accuset quas non commisit.

PRAETEREA, aliquis per humilitatem reputat se deteriorem aliquo qui est manifestus peccator, et in hoc est commendandus. Sed quod corde quis aestimat, licet ore confiteri. Ergo licite potest confiteri se habere gravius peccatum quam habeat.

PRAETEREA, aliquis aliquando dubitat de peccato aliquo utrum sit mortale vel veniale. Et talis debet de illo, ut videtur, confiteri ut de mortali. Ergo aliquis debet confiteri aliquando peccatum quod non habet.

PRAETEREA, satisfactio ex confessione ordinatur. Sed aliquis potest satisfacere de peccato quod non commisit. Ergo etiam potest confiteri peccatum quod non fecit.

SED CONTRA: Quicumque dicit se fecisse quod non fecit, mentitur. Sed nullus in confessione mentiri debet: cum omne mendacium sit peccatum. Ergo nullus debet confiteri peccatum quod non fecit.

PRAETEREA, in iudicio exteriori non debet aliquod crimen alicui impingi quod non potest per testes idoneos probari. Sed testis in foro poenitentiae est conscientia. Ergo aliquis non debet se accusare de peccato quod conscientia non habet.

RESPONDEO dicendum quod per confessionem debet poenitens se confessori sub manifestare. Ille autem qui aliud sacerdoti de se loquitur quam sua conscientia habet, sive in bonum sive in malum, non se sacerdoti manifestat, sed magis occultat; Et ideo non est idonea confessio: sed ad hoc quod sit idonea, requiritur quod os cordi concordet, ut solum hoc os accuset quod conscientia tenet.

AD PRIMUM ergo dicendum, quod agnoscere culpam ubi non est, potest esse dupliciter.

Uno modo, ut intelligatur quantum ad substantiam actus. Et sic non est verum. Non enim ad bonam mentem pertinet, sed ad errantem, ut se actum aliquem commisisse agnoscat quem non commisit. Alio modo, quantum ad conditionem actus. Et sic verum est quod Gregorius dicit, quod iustus in actu qui de se bonus videtur, formidat ne aliquis defectus ex parte sua fuerit: et

OBJECTION 1: It would seem that it is lawful for a man to confess a sin which he has not committed. For, as Gregory says, *it is the mark of a good conscience to acknowledge a fault where there is none* (*Register* 12). Therefore, it is the mark of a good conscience to accuse oneself of those sins which one has not committed.

OBJ. 2: Further, by humility a man deems himself worse than another who is known to be a sinner, and in this he is to be praised. But it is lawful for a man to confess himself to be what he thinks he is. Therefore, it is lawful to confess having committed a more grievous sin than one has.

OBJ. 3: Further, sometimes one doubts about a sin, whether it be mortal or venial, in which case, seemingly, one ought to confess it as mortal. Therefore, a person must sometimes confess a sin which he has not committed.

OBJ. 4: Further, satisfaction originates from confession. But a man can do satisfaction for a sin which he has not committed. Therefore, he can also confess a sin which he has not done.

ON THE CONTRARY, Whosoever says he has done what he did not lies. But no one ought to lie in confession, since every lie is a sin. Therefore, no one should confess a sin which he has not committed.

FURTHER, In the public court of justice, no one should be accused of a crime which cannot be proved by means of proper witnesses. Now the witness, in the tribunal of penance, is the conscience. Therefore, a man ought not to accuse himself of a sin which is not on his conscience.

I ANSWER THAT, The penitent should, by his confession, make his state known to his confessor. Now he who tells the priest something other than what he has on his conscience, whether it be good or evil, does not make his state known to the priest, but hides it; wherefore his confession is unavailing: and in order for it to be effective his words must agree with his thoughts, so that his words accuse him only of what is on his conscience.

REPLY OBJ. 1: To acknowledge a fault where there is none may be understood in two ways:

First, as referring to the substance of the act, and then it is untrue; for it is a mark, not of a good, but of an erroneous conscience, to acknowledge having done what one has not done. Second, as referring to the circumstances of the act, and thus the saying of Gregory is true, because a just man fears lest, in any act which is good in itself, there should be any defect on his part. thus it is written: *I feared*

sic dicitur Iob 9: *verebar omnia opera mea*. Et ideo ad bonam mentem etiam pertinet ut hanc formidinem, quam corde tenet, lingua accuset.

Et per hoc etiam patet solutio ad secundum. Quia iustus, qui est vere humilis, non reputat se deteriorem quantum ad perpetrationem actus qui sit peior ex genere: sed timet ne in his quae bene agere videtur, per superbiam gravius delinquat.

Ad tertium dicendum quod, quando aliquis dubitat de aliquo peccato an sit mortale, tenetur illud confiteri, dubitatione manente. Quia qui aliquid committit vel omittit in quo dubitat esse peccatum mortale, peccat mortaliter, discrimini se committens. Et similiter periculo se committit qui de hoc quod dubitat esse mortale, negligit confiteri. Non tamen debet asserere illud mortale esse: sed cum dubitatione loqui, et iudicium sacerdotis expectare, cuius est discernere *inter lepram et lepram*.

Ad quartum dicendum quod ex hoc quod homo satisfacit pro peccato quod non commisit, non incurrit mendacium, sicut cum quis confitetur peccatum quod non credit se fecisse. Si autem dicat peccatum quod non fecit, dum credit se fecisse, non mentitur. Et ideo non peccat si eo modo dicat sicut est in corde suo.

all my works (Job 9:28). Therefore, it is also the mark of a good conscience that a man should accuse himself in words of this fear which he holds in his thoughts.

This suffices for the reply to the second objection, since a just man, who is truly humble, deems himself worse not as though he had committed an act generically worse, but because he fears lest in those things which he seems to do well, he may, by pride, sin more grievously.

Reply Obj. 3: When a man doubts whether a certain sin be mortal, he is bound to confess it so long as he remains in doubt, because he sins mortally by committing or omitting anything while doubting of its being a mortal sin, and thus leaving the matter to chance; and, moreover, he courts danger, if he neglect to confess that which he doubts may be a mortal sin. He should not, however, affirm that it was a mortal sin, but speak doubtfully, leaving the verdict to the priest, whose business it is to discern between *what is leprosy and what is not* (Deut 17:8).

Reply Obj. 4: A man does not commit a falsehood by making satisfaction for a sin which he did not commit, as when anyone confesses a sin which he thinks he has not committed. And if he mentions a sin that he has not committed, believing that he has, he does not lie; therefore, he does not sin, provided his confession tells what is in his heart.

Article 5

Whether One Is Bound to Confess at Once?

Ad quintum sic proceditur. Videtur quod statim teneatur confiteri. Dicit enim Hugo de Sancto Victore: *si necessitas non est quae praetendatur, contemptus non excusatur*. Sed quilibet tenetur vitare contemptum. Ergo quilibet tenetur statim confiteri cum potest.

Praeterea, quilibet tenetur plus facere ad evadendum morbum spiritualem quam ad evadendum morbum corporalem. Sed aliquis infirmus corporaliter non sine detrimento salutis medicum requirere tardat. Ergo videtur quod non possit esse sine detrimento salutis quod aliquis sacerdoti cuius copiam habet, non statim de peccato confiteatur.

Praeterea, illud quod sine termino debetur, statim debetur. Sed sine termino debet homo confessionem Deo. Ergo tenetur ad statim.

Sed contra: In *Decretali* simul datur tempus determinatum de confessione et de Eucharistiae perceptione. Sed aliquis non peccat si non percipiat Eucharistiam ante tempus a iure determinatum. Ergo non peccat si ante tempus illud non confiteatur.

Objection 1: It would seem that one is bound to confess at once. For Hugh of St. Victor says: *the contempt of confession is inexcusable, unless there be an urgent reason for delay* (*On the Sacraments* 2). But everyone is bound to avoid contempt. Therefore, everyone is bound to confess as soon as possible.

Obj. 2: Further, everyone is bound to do more to avoid spiritual disease than to avoid bodily disease. Now if a man who is sick in body were to delay sending for the physician, it would be detrimental to his health. Therefore, it seems that it must be detrimental to a man's health if he omits to confess immediately to a priest if there be one at hand.

Obj. 3: Further, that which is due always, is due at once. But man owes confession to God always. Therefore, he is bound to confess at once.

On the contrary, A fixed time both for confession and for receiving the Eucharist is determined by the *Decretals* (*On Repentance and Remission of Sins*). Now a man does not sin by failing to receive the Eucharist before the fixed time. Therefore, he does not sin if he does not confess before that time.

PRAETEREA, quicumque illud omittit ad quod ex praecepto tenetur, peccat mortaliter. Si ergo aliquis non statim confitetur quando habet copiam sacerdotis, si ad statim confitendum tenetur, peccaret mortaliter; et eadem ratione alio tempore; et sic deinceps. Et ita multa peccata mortalia homo incurreret pro una poenitentiae dilatione. Quod videtur inconveniens.

RESPONDEO dicendum quod, cum propositum confitendi sit annexum contritioni, tunc tenetur aliquis ad hoc propositum quando ad contritionem tenetur: scilicet quando peccata memoriae occurrunt, praecipue cum in periculo mortis existit, aut in aliquo articulo in quo sine peccati remissione oporteat eum peccatum incurrere; sicut, cum tenetur ad celebrandum, si desit copia sacerdotis, saltem conteri tenetur et habere propositum confitendi.

Sed ad confessionem actualiter faciendam obligatur aliquis dupliciter. Uno modo, per accidens: scilicet quando ad aliquid tenetur quod non potest sine peccato facere non confessus. Tunc enim confiteri tenetur: sicut si debeat Eucharistiam percipere, ad quam nullus post peccatum mortale nisi confessus accedere debet, copia, sacerdotis oblata et necessitate non urgente. Et inde venit obligatio qua Ecclesia omnes obligat ad semel in anno confitendum, quia instituit, ut semel in anno, scilicet in Paschate, omnes sacram communionem accipiant: et ideo ante tempus illud omnes confiteri tenentur.

Alio modo obligatur aliquis ad confessionem per se. Et sic videtur esse eadem ratio de confessione et de baptismo differendo; quia utrumque est sacramentum necessitatis. Ad baptismum autem percipiendum non tenetur aliquis statim postquam habet propositum baptismi, ita quod peccet mortaliter nisi statim baptizerut; nec est aliquod tempus determinatum ultra quod si baptismum differat, peccatum mortale incurrat; sed potest contingere quod in dilatione baptismi erit peccatum mortale vel non erit. Et hoc pensandum est ex causa dilationis: quia, sicut dicit Philosophus, VIII *Physic.*, voluntas non retardat facere opus volitum nisi propter aliquam causam rationabilem. Unde, si causa dilationis baptismi mortale peccatum annexum habeat, utpote si propter contemptum vel aliquod huiusmodi baptismum differat, dilatio erit peccatum mortale: alias non. Et ideo idem videtur esse de confessione, quae non est maioris necessitatis quam baptismus.

Et quia ea quae sunt de necessitate salutis tenetur homo in hac vita implere, ideo, si periculum mortis immineat, etiam per se loquendo, obligatur aliquis ad confessionem faciendam tunc vel baptismum suscipiendum. Et propter hoc etiam Iacobus simul praeceptum edidit de confessione facienda, et extrema unctione percipienda.

FURTHER, It is a mortal sin to omit doing what a commandment bids us to do. If, therefore, a man is bound to confess at once and omits to do so with a priest at hand, he would commit a mortal sin; and in like manner at any other time, and so on, so that he would fall into many mortal sins for the delay in confessing one, which seems unreasonable.

I ANSWER THAT, As the purpose of confessing is united to contrition, a man is bound to have this purpose when he is bound to have contrition, namely, when he calls his sins to mind, and chiefly when he is in danger of death, or when he is so circumstanced that unless his sin be forgiven, he must fall into another sin: for instance, if a priest be bound to say Mass, and a confessor is at hand, he is bound to confess or, if there be no confessor, he is bound at least to contrition and to have the purpose of confessing.

But to actual confession a man is bound in two ways. First, accidentally, viz. when he is bound to do something which he cannot do without committing a mortal sin unless he go to confession first, for then he is bound to confess; for instance, if he has to receive the Eucharist, to which no one can approach after committing a mortal sin without confessing first, if a priest be at hand, and there be no urgent necessity. Hence it is that the Church obliges all to confess once a year, because she commands all to receive Holy Communion once a year, namely, at Easter; therefore, all must go to confession before that time.

Second, a man is bound absolutely to go to confession; and here the same reason applies to delay of confession as to delay of baptism, because both are necessary sacraments. Now a man is not bound to receive baptism as soon as he makes up his mind to be baptized; and so he would not sin mortally, if he were not baptized at once: nor is there any fixed time beyond which, if he defer baptism, he would incur a mortal sin. Nevertheless, the delay of baptism may amount to a mortal sin, or it may not, and this depends on the cause of the delay, since, as the Philosopher says (*Physics* 8.15), the will does not defer doing what it wills to do, except for a reasonable cause. Therefore, if the cause of the delay of baptism has a mortal sin connected with it, e.g., if a man put off being baptized through contempt, or some like motive, the delay will be a mortal sin, but otherwise not: and the same seems to apply to confession, which is not more necessary than baptism.

Moreover, since man is bound to fulfill in this life those things that are necessary for salvation, therefore, if he be in danger of death, he is bound, even absolutely, then and there to make his confession or to receive baptism. For this reason too, James proclaimed at the same time the commandment about making confession and that about receiving extreme unction (Jas 5:14, 16).

Et ideo videtur probabilis illorum opinio qui dicunt quod non tenetur homo ad statim confitendum: quamvis periculosum, sit differre.

Alii autem dicunt quod tenetur contritus ad statim confitendum, debita opportunitate oblata, secundum rectam rationem. Nec obstat quod Decretalis terminum praefigat, ut *semel in anno* confiteatur: quia Ecclesia non indulget dilationi, sed prohibet negligentiam in maiori dilatione. Unde per decretalem illam non excusatur a culpa dilationis quantum ad forum conscientiae: sed excusatur a poena quantum ad forum Ecclesiae, ut non privetur debita sepultura si morte praeventus fuerit ante tempus illud. Sed hoc videtur nimis durum. Quia praecepta affirmativa non obligant ad statim, sed ad tempus determinatum; non quidem ex hoc quod tunc commode impleri possunt, quia tunc, si non daret aliquis eleemosynam de superfluo quandocumque pauper offerretur, peccaret mortaliter, quod falsum est; sed ex hoc quod tempus necessitatem urgentem adducit. Et ideo non oportet quod, si statim oblata opportunitate non confiteatur, etiam si maior opportunitas non expectetur, aliquis peccet mortaliter: sed quando ex articulo temporis necessitas confessionis inducitur. Nec hoc est ex indulgentia Ecclesiae quod non teneatur ad statim, sed ex natura praecepti affirmativi. Unde ante Ecclesiae statutum etiam minus debebatur.

Quidam vero dicunt quod saeculares non tenentur ante quadragesimale tempus confiteri, quod est eis poenitentiae tempus: sed religiosi tenentur ad statim quia totum tempus est eis poenitentiae tempus. Sed hoc nihil est: quia religiosi non tenentur ad alia quam alii homines, nisi ad quae ex voto se obligaverunt.

Ad primum ergo dicendum quod Hugo loquitur de illis qui sine sacramento decedunt.

Ad secundum dicendum quod non est de necessitate salutis corporalis quod statim medicum quaerat, nisi quando necessitas curationis incumbit. Et similiter est de morbo spirituali.

Ad tertium dicendum quod retentio rei alienae invito domino contrariatur praecepto negativo, quod obligat semper et ad semper. Et ideo tenetur semper ad statim reddendum secus autem est de impletione praecepti affirmativi, quod obligat semper sed non ad semper. Unde non tenetur aliquis ad statim implendum.

Therefore, the opinion seems probable of those who say that a man is not bound to confess at once, though it is dangerous to delay.

Others, however, say that a contrite man is bound to confess at once, as soon as he has a reasonable and proper opportunity. Nor does it matter that the Decretal fixes the time limit to an *annual confession*, because the Church does not favor delay, but forbids the neglect involved in a further delay. Therefore, by this Decretal the man who delays is excused, not from sin in the tribunal of conscience; but from punishment in the tribunal of the Church; so that such a person would not be deprived of proper burial if he were to die before that time. But this seems too severe, because affirmative precepts bind, not at once, but at a fixed time; and this, not because it is most convenient to fulfill them then (for in that case if a man were not to give alms of his superfluous goods, whenever he met with a man in need, he would commit a mortal sin, which is false), but because the time involves urgency. Consequently, if he does not confess at the very first opportunity, it does not follow that he commits a mortal sin, even though he does not await a better opportunity, unless it becomes urgent for him to confess through being in danger of death. Nor is it on account of the Church's indulgence that he is not bound to confess at once, but on account of the nature of an affirmative precept, so that before the commandment was made, there was still less obligation.

Others again say that secular persons are not bound to confess before Lent, which is the time of penance for them; but that religious are bound to confess at once, because, for them, all time is a time for penance. But this is not to the point; for religious have no obligations besides those of other men, with the exception of such as they are bound to by vow.

Reply Obj. 1: Hugh is speaking of those who die without this sacrament.

Reply Obj. 2: It is not necessary for bodily health that the physician be sent for at once, except when there is necessity for being healed: and the same applies to spiritual disease.

Reply Obj. 3: The retaining of another's property against the owner's will is contrary to a negative precept, which binds always and for always, and therefore one is always bound to make immediate restitution. It is not the same with the fulfillment of an affirmative precept, which binds always, but not at all times, wherefore one is not bound to fulfill it at once.

Article 6

Whether One Can Be Dispensed from Confession?

AD SEXTUM SIC PROCEDITUR. Videtur quod possit cum aliquo dispensari ne confiteatur homini. Praecepta enim quae sunt de iure positivo, subiacent dispensationi praelatorum Ecclesiae. Sed confessio est huiusmodi, ut ex dictis patet. Ergo potest dispensari cum aliquo ut non confiteatur.

PRAETEREA, illud quod ab homine institutum est, potest etiam ab homine dispensationem recipere. Sed confessio non legitur a Deo instituta, sed ab homine, Iac. 5: *confitemini alterutrum peccata vestra*. Habet autem Papa potestatem dispensandi in his quae per Apostolos instituta sunt: sicut patet de bigamis. Ergo etiam potest cum aliquo dispensari ne confiteatur.

SED CONTRA, poenitentia, cuius pars est confessio, est sacramentum necessitatis, sicut et baptismus. Cum ergo in baptismo nullus dispensare possit, nec in confessione aliquis dispensare poterit.

RESPONDEO dicendum quod ministri Ecclesiae instituuntur in Ecclesia divinitus fundata. Et ideo institutio Ecclesiae praesupponitur ad operationem ministrorum: sicut opus creationis praesupponitur ad opus naturae. Et quia Ecclesia fundatur in fide et sacramentis, ideo ad ministros novos articulos fidei edere aut editos removere, aut nova sacramenta instituere aut instituta removere, non pertinet: sed hoc est potestatis excellentiae, quae soli debetur Christo, qui est Ecclesiae *fundamentum*. Et ideo, sicut Papa non potest dispensare ut aliquis sine baptismo salvetur, ita nec quod salvetur sine confessione, secundum quod obligat ex ipsa vi sacramenti. Sed potest dispensare in confessione secundum quod obligat de praecepto Ecclesiae, ut possit ad diutius confessionem differre quam ab Ecclesia institutum sit.

AD PRIMUM ergo dicendum quod praecepta iuris divini non minus obligant quam praecepta iuris naturalis. Unde, sicut non potest dispensari in iure naturali, ita nec in iure positivo divino.

AD SECUNDUM dicendum quod praeceptum de confessione non est ab homine primo institutum, quamvis sit a Iacobo promulgatum: sed a Deo institutionem habuit, quamvis expressa ipsius institutio non legatur. Tamen quaedam praefiguratio ipsius invenitur: et in hoc quod Ioanni confitebantur peccata qui baptismo ipsius ad gratiam Christi praeparabantur; et in hoc quod Dominus sacerdotibus leprosos transmisit, qui, quamvis non essent novi Testamenti sacerdotes, tamen in eis novi Testamenti sacerdotium significabatur.

OBJECTION 1: It would seem that one can be dispensed from confessing his sins to a man. For precepts of positive law are subject to dispensation by the prelates of the Church. Now such is confession, as appears from what was said above (A. 3). Therefore, one may be dispensed from confession.

OBJ. 2: Further, a man can grant a dispensation in that which was instituted by a man. But we read of confession being instituted, not by God, but by a man: *confess your sins, one to another* (Jas 5:16). Now the Pope has the power of dispensation in things instituted by the apostles, as appears in the matter of bigamists. Therefore, he can also dispense a man from confessing.

ON THE CONTRARY, Penance, of which confession is a part, is a necessary sacrament, even as baptism is. Since, therefore, no one can be dispensed from baptism, neither can one be dispensed from confession.

I ANSWER THAT, The ministers of the Church are appointed in the Church which is founded by God. Thus they need to be appointed by the Church before exercising their ministry, just as the work of creation is presupposed to the work of nature. And since the Church is founded on faith and the sacraments, the ministers of the Church have no power to publish new articles of faith, or to do away with those which are already published, or to institute new sacraments, or to abolish those that are instituted, for this belongs to the power of excellence, which belongs to Christ alone, who is *the foundation* of the Church. Consequently, the Pope can neither dispense a man so that he may be saved without baptism, nor that he be saved without confession, insofar as it is obligatory in virtue of the sacrament. He can, however, dispense from confession, insofar as it is obligatory in virtue of the commandment of the Church; so that a man may delay confession longer than the limit prescribed by the Church.

REPLY OBJ. 1: The precepts of the divine law do not bind less than those of the natural law: wherefore, just as no dispensation is possible from the natural law, so neither can there be from positive divine law.

REPLY OBJ. 2: The precept about confession was not instituted by a man first of all, though it was promulgated by James: it was instituted by God, and although we do not read it explicitly, yet it was somewhat foreshadowed in the fact that those who were being prepared by John's baptism for the grace of Christ confessed their sins to him, and that the Lord sent the lepers to the priests, and though they were not priests of the New Testament, yet the priesthood of the New Testament was foreshadowed in them.

QUESTION 7

THE NATURE OF CONFESSION

Deinde considerandum est de quidditate confessionis.

Et circa hoc tria quaeruntur.

Primo: utrum Augustinus convenienter definiat confessionem.

Secundo: utrum confessio sit actus virtutis.

Tertio: utrum confessio sit actus poenitentiae virtutis.

We must now consider the nature of confession.

Under this head there are three points of inquiry:

(1) Whether Augustine fittingly defines confession?

(2) Whether confession is an act of virtue?

(3) Whether confession is an act of the virtue of penance?

Article 1

Whether Augustine Fittingly Defines Confession?

AD PRIMUM SIC PROCEDITUR. Videtur quod Augustinus inconvenienter confessionem definiat dicens: *confessio est per quam morbus latens spe veniae aperitur.* Morbus enim contra quem confessio ordinatur, peccatum est. Sed peccatum aliquando est apertum. Ergo non debuit dicere morbum latentem esse cuius confessio est medicina.

PRAETEREA, principium poenitentiae est timor. Sed confessio est pars poenitentiae. Ergo non debuit pro causa confessionis ponere spem, sed magis timorem.

PRAETEREA, illud quod sub sigillo ponitur, non aperitur, sed magis clauditur. Sed peccatum quod quis confitetur, sub sigillo confessionis ponitur. Ergo non aperitur in confessione peccatum, sed magis clauditur.

PRAETEREA, inveniuntur quaedam aliae definitiones ab ista differentes. Gregorius enim dicit quod confessio est *peccatorum detectio et ruptio vulneris.* Quidam vero dicunt quod confessio est *coram sacerdote legitima peccatorum declaratio.* Quidam autem dicunt sic: *confessio est sacramentalis delinquentis accusatio, ex erubescentia et per claves Ecclesiae satisfactoria, obligans ad peragendam poenitentiam iniunctam.* Ergo videtur quod praeassignata definitio, cum non omnia contineat quae in his continentur, insufficiens sit.

RESPONDEO dicendum quod in actu confessionis plura consideranda occurrunt: primo, ipsa substantia actus, sive genus eius, quod est manifestatio quaedam; secundo, de quo sit, scilicet peccatum; tertio, cui fiat, scilicet sacerdos; quarto, causa eius, scilicet spes veniae; quinto, effectus, scilicet absolutio, a parte poenae et obligatio ad aliam partem exsolvendam. In prima ergo definitione Augustini tangitur et substantia actus, in *apertio-*

OBJECTION 1: It would seem that Augustine defines confession unfittingly, when he says that *confession lays bare the hidden disease by the hope of pardon* (*Expositions of the Psalms* 21). For the disease against which confession is ordained is sin. Now sin is sometimes manifest. Therefore, it should not be said that confession is the remedy for a hidden disease.

OBJ. 2: Further, the beginning of penance is fear. But confession is a part of penance. Therefore, fear rather than hope should be set down as the cause of confession.

OBJ. 3: Further, that which is placed under a seal is not laid bare, but closed up. But the sin which is confessed is placed under the seal of confession. Therefore, sin is not laid bare in confession, but closed up.

OBJ. 4: Further, other definitions are to be found differing from the above. For Gregory says that *confession is the uncovering of sins, and the opening of the wound* (*Homilies on the Gospels* 40). Others say that confession is *a legal declaration of our sins in the presence of a priest.* Others define it thus: *confession is the sinner's sacramental self-accusation through shame for what he has done, through which the keys of the Church makes satisfaction for his sins, and binds him to perform the penance imposed on him.* Therefore, it seems that the definition in question is insufficient, since it does not include all that these include.

I ANSWER THAT, Several things offer themselves to our notice in the act of confession: first, the very substance or genus of the act, which is a kind of manifestation; second, the matter manifested, which is sin; third, the person to whom the manifestation is made, who is the priest; fourth, its cause, which is hope of pardon; fifth, its effect, which is release from part of the punishment and the obligation to pay the other part. Accordingly, the first definition, given

ne; et de quo fit confessio, cum dicitur *morbus latens*; et causa, in *spe veniae*. Et in aliis definitionibus tanguntur aliqua de illis quinque assignatis: ut cuilibet inspicienti patet.

AD PRIMUM ergo dicendum quod, quamvis sacerdos aliquando sciat eius peccatum ut homo, non tamen scit ut Christi vicarius: sicut etiam iudex aliquando scit aliquid ut homo quod nescit ut iudex. Et quantum ad hoc per confessionem aperitur.

Vel dicendum quod, quamvis actus exterior in aperto sit, actus interior, qui tamen principalior est, in occulto est. Et ideo oportet quod per confessionem aperiatur.

AD SECUNDUM dicendum quod confessio praesupponit caritatem, qua iam vivus aliquis efficitur: ut in littera dicitur. Contritio autem est in qua datur caritas. Timor autem servilis, qui est sine spe, est praevius ad caritatem. Sed habens caritatem magis movetur ex spe quam ex timore. Et ideo causa confessionis potius ponitur spes quam timor.

AD TERTIUM dicendum quod peccatum in qualibet confessione aperitur sacerdoti, et clauditur aliis confessionis sigillo.

AD QUARTUM dicendum quod non oportet in qualibet definitione omnia; tangere quae ad rem definitam concurrunt. Et ideo inveniuntur quaedam definitiones sive assignationes datae penes unam causam, quaedam penes aliam.

by Augustine, indicates the substance of the act, by saying that *it lays bare*; the matter of confession, by saying that it is a *hidden disease*; its cause, which is *the hope of pardon*; while the other definitions include one or other of the five things aforesaid, as may be seen by anyone who considers the matter.

REPLY OBJ. 1: Although the priest, as a man, may sometimes have knowledge of the penitent's sin, yet he does not know it as a vicar of Christ (even as a judge sometimes knows a thing, as a man, of which he is ignorant, as a judge), and in this respect it is made known to him by confession.

Or we may reply that although the external act may be in the open, yet the internal act, which is the cause of the external act, is hidden; and thus it needs to be revealed by confession.

REPLY OBJ. 2: Confession presupposes charity, which gives us life, as stated in the text (*Sentences* IV, D. 17). Now it is in contrition that charity is given; while servile fear, which is void of hope, is previous to charity: yet he that has charity is moved more by hope than by fear. Hence hope rather than fear is set down as the cause of confession.

REPLY OBJ. 3: In every confession sin is laid bare to the priest, and closed to others by the seal of confession.

REPLY OBJ. 4: It is not necessary that every definition should include everything connected with the thing defined: and for this reason we find some definitions or descriptions that indicate one cause, and some that indicate another.

Article 2

Whether Confession Is an Act of Virtue?

AD SECUNDUM SIC PROCEDITUR. Videtur quod confessio non sit actus virtutis. Omnis enim actus virtutis est de iure naturali: quia *ad virtutes apti sumus a natura*, ut Philosophus dicit, in II *Ethic*. Sed confessio non est de iure naturali. Ergo non est actus virtutis.

PRAETEREA, actus virtutis magis convenire potest innocenti quam ei qui peccavit. Sed confessio peccati de qua loquimur, non potest innocenti convenire. Ergo non est actus virtutis.

PRAETEREA, gratia quae est in sacramentis, aliquo modo differt a gratia quae est in virtutibus et donis. Sed confessio est pars sacramenti. Ergo non est actus virtutis.

SED CONTRA: Praecepta legis sunt de actibus virtutum. Sed confessio cadit sub praecepto. Ergo non est actus virtutis.

OBJECTION 1: It would seem that confession is not an act of virtue. For every act of virtue belongs to the natural law, since *we are naturally capable of virtue*, as the Philosopher says (*Ethics* 2.1). But confession does not belong to the natural law. Therefore, it is not an act of virtue.

OBJ. 2: Further, an act of virtue is more befitting to one who is innocent than to one who has sinned. But the confession of a sin, which is the confession of which we are speaking now, cannot be befitting an innocent man. Therefore, it is not an act of virtue.

OBJ. 3: Further, the grace which is in the sacraments differs somewhat from the grace which is in the virtues and gifts. But confession is part of a sacrament. Therefore, it is not an act of virtue.

ON THE CONTRARY, The precepts of the law are about acts of virtue. But confession comes under a precept. Therefore, it is an act of virtue.

PRAETEREA, non meremur nisi actibus virtutum. Sed confessio est meritoria: quia *caelum aperit*, ut in littera Magister dicit. Ergo videtur quod sit actus virtutis.

RESPONDEO dicendum quod ad hoc quod aliquid dicatur actus virtutis, ut prius dictum est, sufficit quod in sui ratione aliquam conditionem implicet quae ad virtutem pertineat. Quamvis autem non omnia quae ad virtutem requiruntur importet confessio, tamen importat ex suo nomine manifestationem alicuius quod in conscientia tenet aliquis: sic enim simul in unum os et cor conveniunt. Si enim quis aliquid proferat ore quod corde non teneat, non confessio, sed *fictio* dicitur. Haec autem conditio ad virtutem pertinet, ut aliquis ore confiteatur quod corde tenet. Et ideo confessio est bonum ex genere, et est actus virtutis. Sed tamen potest male fieri, nisi aliis debitis circumstantiis vestiatur.

AD PRIMUM ergo dicendum quod ad confessionem veri modo debito faciendam, ubi oportet et cui oportet, in generali inclinat ratio naturalis. Et secundum hoc confessio est de iure naturali. Sed determinatio circumstantiarum quando et quomodo et quid confiteri oporteat et cui, hoc est ex institutione iuris divini in confessione de qua loquimur. Et sic patet quod ius naturale inclinat ad confessionem mediante iure divino, quo circumstantiae determinantur: sicut etiam in omnibus est quae sunt de iure positivo.

AD SECUNDUM dicendum quod illius virtutis cuius obiectum est peccatum commissum, quamvis habitum possit innocens habere, tamen actum non habet, innocentia permanente. Et ideo etiam confessio peccatorum de qua nunc loquimur, non competit innocenti, quamvis sit actus virtutis.

AD TERTIUM dicendum quod, quamvis gratia sacramentorum et gratia virtutum sit alia et alia, non tamen sunt contrariae, sed disparatae. Et ideo non est inconveniens ut idem sit actus virtutis secundum quod ex libero arbitrio gratia informato procedit; et sit sacramentum, vel pars sacramenti, secundum quod est medicina in remedium peccati ordinata.

FURTHER, We do not merit except by acts of virtue. But confession is meritorious, for *it opens the gate of heaven*, as the Master says (*Sentences* IV, D. 17). Therefore, it seems that it is an act of virtue.

I ANSWER THAT, As stated above (I-II, Q. 18, A. 6–7; II-II, Q. 80; Q. 85, A. 3; Q. 109, A. 3), for an act to belong to a virtue it suffices that it be of such a nature as to imply some condition belonging to virtue. Now, although confession does not include everything that is required for virtue, yet its very name implies the manifestation of that which a man has on his conscience: for thus his lips and heart agree. For if a man professes with his lips what he does not hold in his heart, it is not a confession but a *fiction*. Now, to express in words what one has in one's thoughts is a condition of virtue; and, consequently, confession is a good thing generically, and is an act of virtue: yet it can be done badly, if it be devoid of other due circumstances.

REPLY OBJ. 1: Natural reason, in a general way, inclines a man to make confession in the proper way, to confess as he ought, what he ought, and when he ought, and in this way confession belongs to the natural law. But it belongs to the divine law to determine the circumstances, when, how, what, and to whom, with regard to the confession of which we are speaking now. Accordingly, it is evident that the natural law inclines a man to confession by means of the divine law, which determines the circumstances, as is the case with all matters belonging to the positive law.

REPLY OBJ. 2: Although an innocent man may have the habit of the virtue whose object is a sin already committed, he has not the act, so long as he remains innocent. Wherefore the confession of sins, of which confession we are speaking now, is not befitting an innocent man, though it is an act of virtue.

REPLY OBJ. 3: Though the grace of the sacraments differs from the grace of the virtues, they are not contrary but disparate. Hence there is nothing to prevent that which is an act of virtue, insofar as it proceeds from the free-will informed by grace, from being a sacrament, or part of a sacrament, insofar as it is ordained as a remedy for sin.

Article 3

Whether Confession Is an Act of the Virtue of Penance?

AD TERTIUM SIC PROCEDITUR. Videtur quod confessio non sit actus poenitentiae virtutis. Quia actus illius virtutis est quae est causa eius. Sed causa confessionis est *spes veniae*: ut ex definitione inducta apparet. Ergo videtur quod sit actus spei, et non poenitentiae.

OBJECTION 1: It would seem that confession is not an act of the virtue of penance. For an act belongs to the virtue which is its cause. Now the cause of confession is the *hope of pardon*, as appears from the definition given above (A. 1). Therefore, it seems that it is an act of hope and not of penance.

PRAETEREA, verecundia est pars temperantiae. Sed confessio *ex erubescentia* operatur: ut ex praeassignata definitione apparet. Ergo est actus temperantiae, et non poenitentiae.

PRAETEREA, actus poenitentiae innititur divinae misericordiae. Sed confessio magis innititur sapientiae: propter veritatem quae in ipsa esse debet. Ergo non est actus poenitentiae.

PRAETEREA, ad poenitentiam movet articulus de iudicio: propter timorem, qui poenitentiae origo est. Sed ad confessionem movet articulus de vita aeterna: quia est propter spem veniae. Ergo non est actus poenitentiae.

PRAETEREA, ad virtutem veritatis pertinet ut ostendat se quis talem qualis est. Sed hoc facit confitens. Ergo est actus virtutis quae dicitur veritas, et non poenitentiae.

SED CONTRA, poenitentia ordinatur ad destructionem peccati. Sed ad hoc idem ordinatur confessio. Ergo est actus poenitentiae.

RESPONDEO dicendum quod hoc in virtutibus considerandum est, quod, quando supra obiectum virtutis additur specialis ratio boni et difficilis, requiritur specialis virtus: sicut magni sumptus ad magnificentiam pertinent, quamvis communiter sumptus mediocres et donationes pertineant ad liberalitatem, ut patet II *Ethic.* et IV. Et similiter est in confessione veri: quae quamvis ad veritatis virtutem pertineat absolute, tamen, secundum quod aliqua ratio boni additur, ad aliam virtutem pertinere incipit. Et ideo dicit Philosophus, IV *Ethic.*, quod confessio quae fit in iudiciis, non pertinet ad veritatis virtutem, sed magis ad iustitiam. Et similiter confessio beneficiorum Dei in laudem divinam non pertinet ad virtutem veritatis, sed ad virtutem latriae. Et ita etiam confessio peccatorum ad remissionem eorum consequendam, non pertinet elicitive ad virtutem veritatis, ut quidam dicunt, sed ad virtutem poenitentiae. Imperative autem ad multas virtutes pertinere potest: secundum quod in finem multarum virtutum trahi potest confessionis actus.

AD PRIMUM ergo dicendum quod spes est confessionis causa non sicut eliciens, sed sicut imperans.

AD SECUNDUM dicendum quod erubescentia in illa definitione non ponitur quasi causa confessionis, cum magis nata sit impedire confessionis actum: sed quasi concausa ad liberandum a poena, inquantum ipsa erubescentia poena quaedam est; sicut etiam claves Ecclesiae concausae confessionis ad hoc sunt.

AD TERTIUM dicendum quod secundum quandam adaptationem partes poenitentiae tribus attributis Personarum adaptari possunt: ut contritio misericordiae vel bonitati respondeat, propter dolorem de malo; confessio sapientiae, propter veritatis manifestationem; satisfactio

OBJ. 2: Further, shame is a part of temperance. But confession arises *from shame*, as appears in the definition given above (A. 1, Obj. 4). Therefore, it is an act of temperance and not of penance.

OBJ. 3: Further, the act of penance leans on divine mercy. But confession leans rather on divine wisdom by reason of the truth which is required in it. Therefore, it is not an act of penance.

OBJ. 4: Further, we are moved to penance by the article of the Creed which is about the Judgment on account of fear, which is the origin of penance. But we are moved to confession by the article which is about life everlasting, because it arises from hope of pardon. Therefore, it is not an act of penance.

OBJ. 5: Further, it belongs to the virtue of truth that a man shows himself to be what he is. But this is what a man does in confession. Therefore, confession is an act of that virtue which is called truth, and not of penance.

ON THE CONTRARY, Penance is ordained for the destruction of sin. Now confession is ordained to this also. Therefore, it is an act of penance.

I ANSWER THAT, It must be observed with regard to virtues that when a special reason of goodness or difficulty is added over and above the object of a virtue, there is need of a special virtue: thus the expenditure of large sums is the object of magnificence, although the ordinary kind of average expenditure and gifts belongs to liberality, as appears from *Ethics* (2.7; 4.1). The same applies to the confession of truth, which, although it belongs to the virtue of truth absolutely, yet, on account of the additional reason of goodness, begins to belong to another kind of virtue. Hence the Philosopher says (*Ethics* 4.7) that a confession made in a court of justice belongs to the virtue of justice rather than to truth. In like manner, the confession of God's favors in praise of God belongs not to truth, but to religion: and so too the confession of sins, in order to receive pardon for them, is not the elicited act of the virtue of truth, as some say, but of the virtue of penance. It may, however, be the commanded act of many virtues, insofar as the act of confession can be directed to the end of many virtues.

REPLY OBJ. 1: Hope is the cause of confession not as eliciting, but as commanding.

REPLY OBJ. 2: In that definition shame is not mentioned as the cause of confession, since it is more of a nature to hinder the act of confession, but rather as the joint cause of delivery from punishment (because shame is in itself a punishment), since also the keys of the Church are the joint cause with confession, to the same effect.

REPLY OBJ. 3: By a certain adaptation the parts of penance can be ascribed to three attributes of the Persons, so that contrition may correspond to mercy or goodness, by reason of its being sorrow for evil; confession to wisdom, by reason of its being a manifestation of the truth; and sat-

potentiae, propter satisfaciendi laborem. Et quia contritio est prima pars poenitentiae, et efficaciam aliis partibus praebens, ideo eodem modo iudicatur de tota poenitentia sicut de contritione.

AD QUARTUM dicendum quod, quia confessio magis ex spe procedit quam ex timore, ideo magis innititur articulo de vita aeterna, quem respicit spes, quam articulo de iudicio, quem respicit timor: quamvis poenitentia ratione contritionis e converso se habeat.

AD QUINTUM patet solutio ex dictis.

isfaction to power, on account of the labor it entails. And since contrition is the first part of penance, and renders the other parts efficacious, for this reason the same is to be said of penance, as a whole, as of contrition.

REPLY OBJ. 4: Since confession results from hope rather than from fear, as stated above (A. 1), it is based on the article about eternal life which hope looks to, rather than on the article about the Judgment, which fear considers; although penance, in its aspect of contrition, is the opposite.

THE REPLY to the fifth objection is clear from what has been said.

45

QUESTION 8

THE MINISTER OF CONFESSION

Deinde considerandum est de ministro confessionis. Circa quod quaeruntur septem.

Primo: utrum necessarium sit confiteri sacerdoti.

Secundo: utrum in aliquo casu liceat aliis quam sacerdotibus confiteri.

Tertio: utrum extra casum necessitatis possit aliquis non sacerdos confessionem venialium audire.

Quarto: utrum sit necessarium quod homo confiteatur proprio sacerdoti.

Quinto: utrum possit aliquis alteri quam proprio sacerdoti confiteri ex privilegio vel mandato superioris.

Sexto: utrum poenitens in extremo vitae suae possit absolvi a quolibet sacerdote.

Septimo: utrum poena temporalis taxari debeat secundum quantitatem culpae.

We must now consider the minister of confession. Under this head there are seven points of inquiry:

(1) Whether it is necessary to confess to a priest?

(2) Whether it is ever lawful to confess to another than a priest?

(3) Whether outside a case of necessity one who is not a priest can hear the confession of venial sins?

(4) Whether it is necessary for a man to confess to his own priest?

(5) Whether it is lawful for anyone to confess to another than his own priest, in virtue of a privilege or of the command of a superior?

(6) Whether a penitent in danger of death can be absolved by any priest?

(7) Whether the temporal punishment should be enjoined in proportion to the sin?

Article 1

Whether It Is Necessary to Confess to a Priest?

AD PRIMUM SIC PROCEDITUR. Videtur quod non sit necessarium sacerdoti confiteri. Ad confessionem enim non obligamur nisi ex divina institutione. Sed divina iustitutio nobis proponitur Iac. 5, *confitemini alterutrum peccata vestra*, ubi noii fit mentio de sacerdote. Ergo non oportet confiteri sacerdoti.

PRAETEREA, poenitentia est necessitatis sacramentum, sicut et baptismus. Sed in baptismo, propter necessitatem sacramenti, est minister quilibet homo. Ergo et in poenitentia. Ergo sufficit cuilibet confiteri.

PRAETEREA, confessio est ad hoc necessaria ut taxetur poenitenti satisfactionis modus. Sed aliquando aliquis non sacerdos discretius posset poenitenti dare satisfactionis modum quam multi sacerdotes. Ergo non est necessarium quod confessio fiat sacerdoti.

PRAETEREA, confessio ad hoc est ordinata in Ecclesia ut rectores pecorum suorum vultum cognoscant. Sed quandoque rector vel praelatus non est sacerdos. Ergo confessio non semper facienda est sacerdoti.

SED CONTRA: Absolutio poenitentis, propter quam fit confessio, non pertinet nisi ad sacerdotes, quibus claves commissae sunt. Ergo confessio debet fieri sacerdoti.

OBJECTION 1: It would seem that it is not necessary to confess to a priest. For we are not bound to confession, except in virtue of its divine institution. Now its divine institution is made known to us in James 5:16: *confess your sins, one to another*, where there is no mention of a priest. Therefore, it is not necessary to confess to a priest.

OBJ. 2: Further, penance is a necessary sacrament, as is also baptism. But any man is the minister of baptism, on account of its necessity. Therefore, any man is the minister of penance. Now confession should be made to the minister of penance. Therefore, it suffices to confess to anyone.

OBJ. 3: Further, confession is necessary in order that the measure of satisfaction should be imposed on the penitent. Now, sometimes someone other than a priest might be more discreet than many priests are in imposing the measure of satisfaction on the penitent. Therefore, it is not necessary to confess to a priest.

OBJ. 4: Further, confession was instituted in the Church in order that the rectors might know their sheep by sight. But sometimes a rector or prelate is not a priest. Therefore, confession should not always be made to a priest.

ON THE CONTRARY, The absolution of the penitent, for the sake of which he makes his confession, is imparted by none but priests to whom the keys are entrusted. Therefore, confession should be made to a priest.

PRAETEREA, confessio praefiguratur in Lazari mortui vivificatione. Sed Dominus solum discipulis praecepit ut solverent Lazarum: ut patet Ioan. 11. Ergo sacerdotibus facienda est confessio.

RESPONDEO dicendum quod gratia, quae in sacramentis datur, a capite in membra descendit. Et ideo solus ille minister est sacramentorum, in quibus gratia datur, qui habet ministerium super corpus Christi verum. Quod solius sacerdotis est, qui consecrare Eucharistiam potest. Et ideo, cum in sacramento poenitentiae gratia conferatur, solus sacerdos minister est huius sacramenti. Et ideo ei soli facienda est sacramentalis confessio, quae ministro Ecclesiae fieri debet.

AD PRIMUM ergo dicendum quod Iacobus loquitur ex praesuppositione divinae institutionis. Et quia divinitus institutio praecesserat de confessione sacerdotibus facienda, per hoc quod eis potestatem remittendi peccata in Apostolis dedit, ut patet Ioan. 20; ideo intelligendum est quod Iacobus sacerdotibus confessionem esse faciendam monuit.

AD SECUNDUM dicendum quod baptismus est magis sacramentum necessitatis quam poenitentia quoad confessionem et absolutionem: quia quandoque baptismus praetermitti non potest sine periculo salutis aeternae, ut patet in pueris qui non habent usum rationis; sed non est ita de confessione et absolutione, quae tantum ad adultos pertinent, in quibus contritio cum proposito confitendi et desiderio absolutionis sufficit ad liberandum a morte aeterna. Et ideo non est simile de baptismo et confessione.

AD TERTIUM dicendum quod in satisfactione non solum attendenda est quantitas poenae, sed etiam virtus eius secundum quod est pars sacramenti. Et sic requirit sacramentorum dispensatorem: quamvis etiam ab alio quam a sacerdote quantitas poenae taxari possit.

AD QUARTUM dicendum quod cognoscere vultum pecoris ad duo potest necessarium esse. Primo, quod coordinetur gregi Christi. Et sic cognoscere vultum pecoris pertinet ad curam et sollicitudinem pastoralem, quae incumbit quandoque illis qui non sunt sacerdotes. Secundo, ad hoc quod provideatur ei conveniens medicamentum salutis. Et sic cognoscere vultum pecoris pertinet ad eum cuius est medicamentum salutis, scilicet sacramentum Eucharistiae et alia, praebere, scilicet ad sacerdotem. Et ad talem cognitionem pecoris confessio ordinatur.

FURTHER, Confession is foreshadowed in the raising of the dead Lazarus to life. Now our Lord commanded none but the disciples to loose Lazarus (John 11:44). Therefore, confession should be made to a priest.

I ANSWER THAT, The grace which is given in the sacraments descends from the Head to the members. Thus, he alone who exercises a ministry over Christ's true body is a minister of the sacraments, wherein grace is given; and this belongs to a priest alone, who can consecrate the Eucharist. Therefore, since grace is given in the sacrament of penance, none but a priest is the minister of the sacrament: and consequently sacramental confession, which should be made to a minister of the Church, should be made to none but a priest.

REPLY OBJ. 1: James speaks on the presupposition of the divine institutions: and since confession had already been prescribed by God to be made to a priest, in that he empowered them, in the person of the apostles, to forgive sins, as related in John 20:23, we must take the words of James as conveying an admonishment to confess to priests.

REPLY OBJ. 2: Baptism is a sacrament of greater necessity than penance, as regards confession and absolution, because sometimes baptism cannot be omitted without loss of eternal salvation, as in the case of children who have not come to the use of reason: whereas this cannot be said of confession and absolution, which regard none but adults, in whom contrition, together with the purpose of confessing and the desire of absolution, suffices to deliver them from everlasting death. Consequently, there is no parity between baptism and confession.

REPLY OBJ. 3: In satisfaction we must consider not only the quantity of the punishment but also its power, inasmuch as it is part of a sacrament. In this way it requires a dispenser of the sacraments, though the quantity of the punishment may be fixed by another than a priest.

REPLY OBJ. 4: It may be necessary for two reasons to know the sheep by sight. First, in order to register them as members of Christ's flock, and to know the sheep by sight thus belongs to the pastoral charge and care, which is sometimes the duty of those who are not priests. Second, that they may be provided with suitable remedies for their health; and to know the sheep by sight thus belongs to the man, i.e., the priest, whose business it is to provide remedies conducive to health, such as the sacrament of the Eucharist, and other like things. It is to this knowledge of the sheep that confession is ordained.

Article 2

Whether It Is Ever Lawful to Confess to Another than a Priest?

AD SECUNDUM SIC PROCEDITUR. Videtur quod in nullo casu liceat aliis quam sacerdotibus confiteri. Quia confessio *sacramentalis accusatio* est: ut ex supra posita definitione habetur. Sed dispensatio sacramenti ad illum tantum pertinet qui est sacramenti minister. Cum ergo minister sacramenti poenitentiae sit sacerdos, videtur quod nulli alii sit confessio facienda.

PRAETEREA, confessio in quolibet iudicio ad sententiam ordinatur. Sed sententia in foro contentioso non a suo iudice lata nulla est: et ideo non facienda est confessio nisi iudici. Sed iudex in foro conscientiae non est nisi sacerdos, qui habet potestatem ligandi et solvendi. Ergo non est alii confessio facienda.

PRAETEREA, in baptismo, quia quilibet potest baptizare, si baptizat laicus, etiam absque necessitate, non debet a sacerdote baptismus iterari. Sed si aliquis confiteatur laico in casu necessitatis, iterum tenetur sacerdoti confiteri, si articulum necessitatis evadat. Ergo confessio non potest fieri laico in casu necessitatis.

SED CONTRA est quod in littera determinatur.

RESPONDEO dicendum quod, sicut baptismus est sacramentum necessitatis, ita et poenitentia. Baptismus autem, quia est sacramentum necessitatis, duplicem habet ministrum: unum cui ex officio baptizare incumbit, scilicet sacerdotem; alium cui ratione necessitatis dispensatio baptismi committitur. Et ita etiam minister poenitentiae cui confessio est facienda ex officio, est sacerdos: sed in necessitate etiam laicus vicem sacerdotis supplet, ut ei confessio fieri possit.

AD PRIMUM ergo dicendum quod in sacramento poenitentiae non solum est aliquid ex parte ministri, scilicet absolutio et satisfactionis iniunctio; sed etiam aliquid ex parte ipsius qui suscipit sacramentum, quod est etiam de essentia sacramenti, sicut contritio et confessio. Satisfactio autem iam incipit esse a ministro, inquantum eam iniungit; et a poenitente, inquantum eam implet. Et ad plenitudinem sacramenti utrumque debet concurrere, quando possibile est. Sed quando necessitas imminet, debet facere poenitens quod ex parte sua est, scilicet conteri et confiteri cui potest: qui quamvis sacramentum perficere non possit, ut faciat id quod ex parte sacerdotis est, absolutionem scilicet, tamen defectum sacerdotis Summus Sacerdos supplet. Nihilominus confessio laico ex desiderio sacerdotis facta sacramentalis est quodammodo: quamvis non sit sacramentum perfectum, quia deest ei id quod est ex parte sacerdotis.

OBJECTION 1: It would seem that it is never lawful to confess to another than a priest. For confession is a *sacramental accusation*, as appears from the definition given above (Q. 7, A. 1). But the dispensing of a sacrament belongs to none but the minister of a sacrament. Since, then, the proper minister of penance is a priest, it seems that confession should be made to no one else.

OBJ. 2: Further, in every court of justice confession is ordained to the sentence. Now in a disputed case the sentence is void if pronounced by another than the proper judge, so that confession should be made to none but a judge. But, in the court of conscience, the judge is none but a priest, who has the power of binding and loosing. Therefore, confession should be made to no one else.

OBJ. 3: Further, in the case of baptism, since anyone can baptize, if a layman has baptized, even without necessity, the baptism should not be repeated by a priest. But if anyone confess to a layman in a case of necessity, he is bound to repeat his confession to a priest, when the cause for urgency has passed. Therefore, confession should not be made to a layman in a case of necessity.

ON THE CONTRARY, There stands the authority of the text (*Sentences* IV, D. 17).

I ANSWER THAT, Just as baptism is a necessary sacrament, so is penance. And baptism, through being a necessary sacrament, has a twofold minister: one whose duty it is to baptize in virtue of his office, who is the priest, and another, to whom the conferring of baptism is committed in a case of necessity. In like manner, the minister of penance, to whom in virtue of his office confession should be made, is a priest; but in a case of necessity even a layman may take the place of a priest, and hear a person's confession.

REPLY OBJ. 1: In the sacrament of penance there is not only something on the part of the minister, viz. the absolution and imposition of satisfaction, but also something on the part of the recipient, which is also essential to the sacrament, viz. contrition and confession. Now satisfaction originates from the minister insofar as he enjoins it, and from the penitent who fulfills it; and, for the fullness of the sacrament, both these things should concur when possible. But when there is reason for urgency, the penitent should fulfill his own part, by being contrite and confessing to whom he can; and although this person cannot perfect the sacrament so as to fulfill the part of the priest by giving absolution, yet this defect is supplied by the High Priest. Nevertheless, confession made to a layman through lack of a priest is quasi-sacramental, although it is not a perfect sacrament on account of the absence of the part which belongs to the priest.

AD SECUNDUM dicendum quod, quamvis laicus non sit iudex eius qui sibi confitetur absolute, tamen ratione necessitatis accipit iudicium super eum, secundum quod confitens ex desiderio sacerdotis se ei subdit.

AD TERTIUM dicendum quod per sacramenta homo non solum Deo, sed Ecclesiae oportet quod reconcilietur. Ecclesiae autem reconciliari non potest nisi sanctificatio Ecclesiae ad eum perveniat. In baptismo autem sanctificatio Ecclesiae ad hominem pervenit per ipsum elementum exterius adhibitum, quod *verbo vitae* sanctificatur, secundum formam Ecclesiae, a quocumque. Et ideo, ex quo semel baptizatus est a quocumque, non oportet quod iterum baptizetur. Sed in poenitentia Ecclesiae sanctificatio non pervenit ad hominem nisi per ministrum: quia non est ibi aliquod elementum corporale exterius adhibitum, quod ex sanctificatione invisibilem gratiam conferat. Et ideo, quamvis ille laico confessus in articulo necessitatis consecutus sit veniam a Deo, eo quod propositum confitendi, secundum mandatum Dei quod percepit, sicut potuit implevit; non tamen adhuc Ecclesiae reconciliatus est, ut ad sacramenta Ecclesiae admitti debeat, nisi prius a sacerdote absolvatur; sicut ille qui baptismo flaminis baptizatus est, ad Eucharistiam non admittitur. Et ideo oportet quod iterum confiteatur sacerdoti, cum copiam habere, potuerit. Et praecipue quia sacramentum poenitentiae perfectum non fuit. Unde oportet quod perficiatur: ut ex ipsa perceptione sacramenti pleniorem effectum consequatur; et ut mandatum de poenitentiae sacramento recipiendo impleat.

REPLY OBJ. 2: Although a layman is not the judge of the person who confesses to him, yet, on account of the urgency, he does take the place of a judge over him, absolutely speaking, insofar as the penitent submits to him through lack of a priest.

REPLY OBJ. 3: By means of the sacraments man must be reconciled not only to God, but also to the Church. Now he cannot be reconciled to the Church, unless the hallowing of the Church reach him. In baptism the hallowing of the Church reaches a man through the element itself applied externally, which is sanctified by *the word of life* (Eph 5:26), by whomsoever it is conferred: and so when once a man has been baptized, no matter by whom, he must not be baptized again. On the other hand, in penance the hallowing of the Church reaches man by the minister alone, because in that sacrament there is no bodily element applied externally through the hallowing of which grace may be conferred. Consequently, although the man who, in a case of necessity, has confessed to a layman, has received forgiveness from God, because he fulfilled so far as he could the purpose which he conceived in accordance with God's command, he is not yet reconciled to the Church so as to be admitted to the sacraments, unless he first be absolved by a priest, even as he who has received the baptism of desire is not admitted to the Eucharist. Therefore, he must confess again to a priest, as soon as there is one at hand, and the more so since, as stated above (ad 1), the sacrament of penance was not perfected, and so it needs yet to be perfected, in order that by receiving the sacrament, the penitent may receive a more plentiful effect, and that he may fulfill the commandment about receiving the sacrament of penance.

Article 3

Whether, Outside a Case of Necessity, Anyone Who is Not a Priest May Hear the Confession of Venial Sins?

AD TERTIUM SIC PROCEDITUR. Videtur quod, extra casum necessitatis, non possit aliquis non sacerdos confessionem venialium audire. Quia sacramentum aliquod committitur laico, dispensandum ratione necessitatis. Sed confessio venialium non est de necessitate. Ergo non committitur laico.

PRAETEREA, contra venialia ordinatur extrema unctio, sicut et poenitentia. Sed illa non potest dari a laico: ut patet Iac. 5. Ergo nec confessio venialium potest ei fieri.

SED CONTRA est quod dicit Beda in littera.

OBJECTION 1: It would seem that, outside a case of necessity, no one but a priest may hear the confession of venial sins. For the dispensation of a sacrament is committed to a layman by reason of necessity. But the confession of venial sins is not necessary. Therefore, it is not committed to a layman.

OBJ. 2: Further, extreme unction is ordained against venial sin, just as penance is. But the former may not be given by a layman, as appears from James 5:14. Therefore, neither can the confession of venial sins be made to a layman.

ON THE CONTRARY, There is the authority of Bede on James 5:16: *Confess . . . one to another*, quoted in the text (*Sentences* IV, D. 17).

RESPONDEO dicendum quod per peccatum veniale homo nec a Deo nec a sacramentis Ecclesiae separatur. Et ideo non indiget novae gratiae collatione ad eius dimissionem, neque indiget reconciliari Ecclesiae. Et propter hoc, non oportet quod venialia aliquis sacerdoti confiteatur: quia ipsa confessio laico facta sacramentale quoddam est (quamvis non sit sacramentum perfectum) et ex caritate procedens; et talibus natum est veniale remitti, sicut per tunsionem pectoris et aquam benedictam.

ET PER HOC patet solutio ad primum. Quia venialia non indigent sacramenti perceptione ad dimissionem sui, sed sufficit ibi aliquod sacramentale, ut aqua benedicta et aliquid huiusmodi.

AD SECUNDUM dicendum quod extrema unctio non datur directe contra veniale, nec aliquod sacramentum.

I ANSWER THAT, By venial sin man is separated neither from God nor from the sacraments of the Church: wherefore he does not need to receive any further grace for the forgiveness of such a sin, nor does he need to be reconciled to the Church. Consequently, a man does not need to confess his venial sins to a priest. And since confession made to a layman is a sacramental, although it is not a perfect sacrament, and since it proceeds from charity, it has a natural aptitude to remit sins, just as the beating of one's breast, or the sprinkling of holy water.

THIS SUFFICES for the reply to the first objection, because there is no need to receive a sacrament for the forgiveness of venial sins, and a sacramental, such as holy water or the like, suffices for the purpose.

REPLY OBJ. 2: Extreme unction is not given directly as a remedy for venial sin, nor is any other sacrament.

Article 4

Whether It Is Necessary for One to Confess to One's Own Priest?

AD QUARTUM SIC PROCEDITUR. Videtur quod non sit necessarium quod homo confiteatur proprio sacerdoti. Gregorius enim dicit: *Apostolico moderamine et pietatis officio a nobis constitutum est quod sacerdotibus monachis, Apostolorum figuram tenentibus, liceat praedicare, baptizare, communionem dare, pro peccatoribus orare, poenitentiam imponere, atque peccata solvere.* Sed monachi non sunt proprii sacerdotes aliquorum: cum non habeant curam animarum. Ergo, cum confessio fiat propter absolutionem sufficit quod fiat cuicumque sacerdoti.

PRAETEREA, sicut sacerdos est minister huius sacramenti, ita et Eucharistiae. Sed quilibet sacerdos potest conficere. Ergo quilibet sacerdos potest sacramentum poenitentiae ministrare. Ergo non oportet quod fiat proprio sacerdoti.

PRAETEREA, illud ad quod determinate tenemur, non est in nostra electione constitutum. Sed sacerdos cui confiteri debemus est in nostra potestate constitutus: ut patet per Augustinum in littera. Dicit enim: *qui vult confiteri peccata, ut inveniat gratiam, quaerat sacerdotem qui sciat solvere et ligare.* Ergo videtur quod non sit necessarium quod sacerdoti proprio aliquis confiteatur.

PRAETEREA, quidam sunt, sicut praelati, qui non videntur habere proprium sacerdotem: cum non habeant superiorem. Sed isti tenentur ad confessionem. Ergo non semper tenetur homo confiteri proprio sacerdoti.

PRAETEREA, *illud quod est institutum pro caritate, contra caritatem non militat*: ut Bernardus dicit. Sed confessio, quae pro caritate instituta est, contra caritatem

OBJECTION 1: It would seem that it is not necessary to confess to one's own priest. For Gregory (Cf. *Register* 16, Q. 1) says: *by our apostolic authority and in discharge of our solicitude we have decreed that priests, who as monks imitate the example of the apostles, may preach, baptize, give communion, pray for sinners, impose penances, and absolve from sins.* Now monks are not the proper priests of anyone, since they have not the care of souls. Since, therefore, confession is made for the sake of absolution it suffices for it to be made to any priest.

OBJ. 2: Further, the minister of this sacrament is a priest, as also of the Eucharist. But any priest can perform the Eucharist. Thus, any priest can administer the sacrament of penance, and therefore there is no need to confess to one's own priest.

OBJ. 3: Further, when we are bound to one thing in particular it is not left to our choice. But the choice of a discreet priest is left to us as appears from the authority of Augustine quoted in the text (*Sentences* 9, D. 17), for he says in *On True and False Penance*: *he who wishes to confess his sins, in order to find grace, must seek a priest who knows how to loose and to bind.* Therefore, it seems unnecessary to confess to one's own priest.

OBJ. 4: Further, there are some, such as prelates, who seem to have no priest of their own, since they have no superior: yet they are bound to confession. Therefore, a man is not always bound to confess to his own priest.

OBJ. 5: Further, *that which is instituted for the sake of charity does not militate against charity*, as Bernard observes (*De Praecept. et Dispens.* II). Now confession, which was in-

militaret si homo ad confitendum uni sacerdoti esset obligatus: ut puta si peccator sciat sacerdotem suum haereticum, aut sollicitatorem ad malum, aut fragilem, qui ad peccatum quod quis ei confitetur sit pronus; vel si revelator confessionis esse probabiliter aestimetur; vel si peccatum contra ipsum commissum sit de quo quis confiteri debet. Ergo videtur quod non semper oporteat confiteri proprio sacerdoti.

Praeterea, in eo quod est necessarium ad salutem, non sunt homines arctandi: ne impediantur a via salutis. Sed magna arctatio videtur si oporteat uni homini confiteri de necessitate: et per hoc multi possent a confessione retrahi, vel timore vel verecundia vel aliquo huiusmodi. Ergo, cum confessio sit de necessitate salutis, non debent homines ad hoc arctari, ut videtur, quod proprio sacerdoti confiteantur.

Sed contra: Est decretalis Innocentii, qui instituit quod *omnes utriusque sexus semel in anno proprio sacerdoti confiteantur.*

Praeterea, sicut episcopus se habet ad dioecesim suam, ita sacerdos ad suam parochiam. Sed non licet uni episcopo in dioecesi alterius episcopale officium exercere, secundum statuta canonum. Ergo nec licet uni sacerdoti parochianum alterius audire.

Respondeo dicendum quod alia sacramenta non consistunt in hoc quod ad sacramentum accedens aliquid agat, sed solum ut recipiat, sicut patet in baptismo et huiusmodi: sed actus recipientis requiritur ad percipiendum utilitatem sacramenti, in eo qui est suae voluntatis arbiter constitutus, quasi removens prohibens, scilicet fictionem. Sed in poenitentia actus accedentis ad sacramentum est de substantia sacramenti: eo quod contritio, confessio et satisfactio sunt poenitentiae partes, quae sunt actus poenitentis. Actus autem nostri, cum in nobis principium habeant, non possunt nobis ab alio dispensari nisi per imperium. Unde oportet quod ille qui dispensator huius sacramenti constituitur, sit talis qui possit imperare aliquid agendum. Imperium autem non competit alicui in alium nisi qui habet super eum iurisdictionem. Et ideo de necessitate huius sacramenti est, non solum ut minister habeat ordinem, sicut in aliis sacramentis, sed etiam quod habeat iurisdictionem. Et ideo, sicut ille qui non est sacerdos non potest hoc sacramentum conferre, ita nec ille qui non habet iurisdictionem. Et propter hoc oportet, sicut sacerdoti, ita proprio sacerdoti confessionem fieri. Cum enim sacerdos non absolvat nisi ligando ad aliquid faciendum, ille solus potest absolvere qui potest per imperium ad aliquid faciendum ligare.

Ad primum ergo dicendum quod Gregorius loquitur de illis monachis qui iurisdictionem habent, utpote quibus alicuius parochiae cura est commissa; de quibus

stituted for the sake of charity, would militate against charity if a man were bound to confess to any particular priest: e.g., if the sinner know that his own priest is a heretic, or a man of evil influence, or weak and prone to the very sin that he wishes to confess to him, or reasonably suspected of breaking the seal of confession, or if the penitent has to confess a sin committed against his confessor. Therefore, it seems that one need not always confess to one's own priest.

Obj. 6: Further, men should not be straitened in matters necessary for salvation, lest they be hindered in the way of salvation. But it seems a great inconvenience to be bound of necessity to confess to one particular man, and many might be hindered from going to confession through either fear, shame, or something else of the kind. Therefore, since confession is necessary for salvation, men should not be straitened, as apparently they would be, by having to confess to their own priest.

On the contrary, There stands a decree of Pope Innocent III in the Fourth Lateran Council appointing *all of either sex to confess once a year to their own priest.*

Further, As a bishop is to his diocese, so is a priest to his parish. Now it is unlawful, according to canon law (*Decretals*), for a bishop to exercise the episcopal office in another diocese. Therefore, it is not lawful for one priest to hear the confession of another's parishioner.

I answer that, The other sacraments do not consist in an action of the recipient, but only in his receiving something, as is evident with regard to baptism and so forth, though the action of the recipient is required as removing an obstacle, i.e., insincerity, in order that he may receive the benefit of the sacrament, if he has come to the use of his free-will. On the other hand, the action of the man who approaches the sacrament of penance is essential to the sacrament, since contrition, confession, and satisfaction, which are acts of the penitent, are parts of penance. Now our actions, since they have their origin in us, cannot be dispensed by others, except through their command. Hence whoever is appointed a dispenser of this sacrament must be such as to be able to command something to be done. Now a man is not competent to command another unless he have jurisdiction over him. Consequently, it is essential to this sacrament not only for the minister to be in orders, as in the case of the other sacraments, but also for him to have jurisdiction: wherefore he that has no jurisdiction cannot administer this sacrament any more than one who is not a priest. Therefore, confession should be made not only to a priest, but to one's own priest; for since a priest does not absolve a man except by binding him to do something, he alone can absolve, who, by his command, can bind the penitent to do something.

Reply Obj. 1: Gregory is speaking of those monks who have jurisdiction through having charge of a parish; about whom some had maintained that from the very fact

aliqui dicebant quod, hoc ipso quod monachi erant, non poterant absolvere et poenitentias iniungere. Quod falsum est.

AD SECUNDUM dicendum quod sacramentum Eucharistiae non requirit imperium in aliquem hominem. Secus autem est in hoc sacramento, ut dictum est. Et ideo ratio non sequitur. Et tamen non licet Eucharistiam ab alio quam a proprio sacerdote accipere: quamvis verum sit sacramentum quod ab eo percipitur.

AD TERTIUM dicendum quod electio discreti sacerdotis non est nobis commissa ut nostro arbitrio facienda, sed de licentia superioris, si forte proprius sacerdos esset minus idoneus ad apponendum peccato salutare remedium.

AD QUARTUM dicendum quod, quia praelatis incumbit sacramenta dispensare, quae non nisi mundi tractare debent, ideo concessum est eis a iure quod possunt sibi eligere proprios sacerdotes confessores, qui quantum ad hoc sunt eis superiores: sicut etiam unus medicus ab alio curatur, non inquantum medicus, sed inquantum infirmus.

AD QUINTUM dicendum quod in casibus illis in quibus probabiliter timet poenitens periculum sibi vel sacerdoti ex confessione ei facta, debet recurrere, ad superiorem, vel ab eodem petere licentiam alteri confitendi. Quod si licentiam habere non possit, idem est iudicium quod de illo qui non habet copiam sacerdotis. Unde magis debet eligere laico confiteri. Nec in hoc transgreditur aliquis praeceptum Ecclesiae: quia praecepta iuris positivi non se extendunt ultra intentionem. praecipientis, quae est finis praecepti; haec autem est caritas, secundum Apostolum. Nec iterum fit aliqua iniuria sacerdoti: quia *privilegium meretur amittere, qui concessa sibi abutitur potestate.*

AD SEXTUM dicendum quod in hoc quod oportet proprio sacerdoti confiteri, non arctatur via salutis, sed sufficiens ad salutem via statuitur. Peccaret autem sacerdos si non esset; facilis ad praebendum licentiam alteri confitendi: quia multi sunt adeo infirmi quod potius sine confessione morerentur quam tali sacerdoti confiterentur. Unde illi qui sunt nimis solliciti ut conscientias subditorum per confessionem sciant, multis damnationis laqueum iniiciunt si per consequens sibi ipsis.

that they were monks, they could not absolve or impose penance, which is false.

REPLY OBJ. 2: The sacrament of the Eucharist does not require the power of command over a man, whereas this sacrament does, as stated above: and so the argument proves nothing. Nevertheless, it is not lawful to receive the Eucharist from another than one's own priest, although it is a real sacrament that one receives from another.

REPLY OBJ. 3: The choice of a discreet priest is not left to us in such a way that we can do just as we like; but it is left to the permission of a higher authority, if perchance one's own priest happens to be less suitable for applying a salutary remedy to our sins.

REPLY OBJ. 4: Since it is the duty of prelates to dispense the sacraments, which the clean alone should handle, they are allowed by law (*On Repentance and Remission of Sins*) to choose a priest for their confessor, who in this respect is the prelate's superior, even as one physician is cured by another not as a physician, but as a patient.

REPLY OBJ. 5: In those cases wherein the penitent has reason to fear some harm to himself or to the priest by reason of his confessing to him, he should have recourse to the higher authority, or ask permission of the priest himself to confess to another; and if he fails to obtain permission, the case is to be decided as for a man who has no priest at hand; so that he should rather choose a layman and confess to him. Nor does he disobey the law of the Church by so doing, because the precepts of positive law do not extend beyond the intention of the lawgiver, which is the end of the precept, and in this case, is charity, according to the Apostle (1 Tim. 1:5). Nor is any injury done to the priest, for *he deserves to forfeit his privilege for abusing the power intrusted to him* (Gratian, *Decretals*).

REPLY OBJ. 6: The necessity of confessing to one's own priest does not straiten the way of salvation, but determines it sufficiently. A priest, however, would sin if he were not easy in giving permission to confess to another, because many are so weak that they would rather die without confession than confess to such a priest. Wherefore those priests who are too anxious to probe the consciences of their subjects by means of confession lay a snare of damnation for many, and consequently for themselves.

Article 5

Whether It Is Lawful for Anyone to Confess to Another than His Own Priest, in Virtue of a Privilege or a Command Given by a Superior?

AD QUINTUM SIC PROCEDITUR. Videtur quod non possit aliquis alteri quam proprio sacerdoti confiteri etiam ex privilegio vel mandato superioris. Quia non potest aliquod privilegium indulgeri in praeiudicium alterius. Sed hoc esset in praeiudicium alterius sacerdotis, si alius confessionem subditi sui audiat. Ergo non potest per privilegium, seu licentiam seu mandatum superioris, obtineri.

PRAETEREA, illud per quod impeditur divinum mandatum, non potest per mandatum vel privilegium alicuius hominis concedi. Sed mandatum divinum est ad rectores ecclesiarum ut diligenter *vultum pecoris sui agnoscant*, Proverb 27: quod impeditur si alius quam ipse confessionem eius audiat. Ergo hoc non potest per alicuius hominis privilegium vel mandatum ordinari.

PRAETEREA, ille qui audit confessionem alicuius, est proprius iudex eius: alias non posset eum ligare et solvere. Sed unius hominis non possunt esse plures proprii iudices vel proprii sacerdotes: quia tunc teneretur pluribus obedire, quod est impossibile, si contraria praeciperent vel incompossibilia. Ergo non potest aliquis confiteri nisi proprio sacerdoti, etiam ex superioris licentia.

PRAETEREA, iniuriam sacramento facit qui sacramentum iterat super eandem materiam: vel ad minus inutiliter facit. Sed qui confessus est alii sacerdoti, tenetur iterum confiteri proprio sacerdoti si petat: quia non est absolutus ab obedientia qua ei tenetur ad hoc. Ergo non potest licite fieri quod alii quam proprio sacerdoti confiteatur.

SED CONTRA: Ea quae sunt ordinis possunt habenti similem ordinem committi ab eo qui ea facere potest. Sed superior, ut episcopus, potest confessionem audire illius qui est de parochia alicuius presbyteri: quia etiam aliquando aliqua sibi reservat, cum sit principalior rector. Ergo etiam potest committere alicui sacerdoti alteri quod ipse audiat.

PRAETEREA, quidquid potest inferior, potest superior. Sed ipse sacerdos potest suo parochiano dare licentiam quod alteri confiteatur. Ergo multo fortius eius superior hoc potest.

PRAETEREA, potestatem quam habet sacerdos in populo, habet ab episcopo. Sed ex illa potestate potest confessionem audire. Ergo et eadem ratione alius cui episcopus potestatem concedit.

RESPONDEO dicendum quod sacerdos aliquis potest dupliciter impediri ne alicuius confessionem audiat: uno modo, propter defectum iurisdictionis; alio modo, propter impedimentum executionis ordinis, sicut excommu-

OBJECTION 1: It would seem that it is not lawful for anyone to confess to another than his own priest, even in virtue of a privilege or command given by a superior. For no privilege should be given that wrongs a third party. Now it would be prejudicial to the subject's own priest if he were to confess to another. Therefore, this cannot be allowed by a superior's privilege, permission, or command.

OBJ. 2: Further, that which hinders the observance of a divine command cannot be the subject of a command or privilege given by man. Now it is a divine command to the rectors of churches to *know the countenance of their own cattle* (Prov 27:23); and this is hindered if another than the rector hear the confession of his subjects. Therefore, this cannot be prescribed by any human privilege or command.

OBJ. 3: Further, he that hears another's confession is the latter's own judge, else he could not bind or loose him. Now one man cannot have several priests or judges of his own, for then he would be bound to obey several men, which would be impossible if their commands were contrary or incompatible. Therefore, one may not confess to another than one's own priest, even with the superior's permission.

OBJ. 4: Further, it is derogatory to a sacrament, or at least useless, to repeat a sacrament over the same matter. But he who has confessed to another priest is bound to confess again to his own priest, if the latter requires him to do so, because he is not absolved from his obedience, whereby he is bound to him in this respect. Therefore, it cannot be lawful for anyone to confess to another than his own priest.

ON THE CONTRARY, He that can perform the actions of an order can depute the exercise thereof to anyone who has the same order. Now a superior, such as a bishop, can hear the confession of anyone belonging to a priest's parish, for sometimes he reserves certain cases to himself, since he is the chief rector. Therefore, he can also depute another priest to hear that man.

FURTHER, A superior can do whatever his subject can do. But the priest himself can give his parishioner permission to confess to another. Much more, therefore, can his superior do this.

FURTHER, The power which a priest has among his people comes to him from the bishop. Now it is through that power that he can hear confessions. Therefore, in like manner, another can do so to whom the bishop gives the same power.

I ANSWER THAT, A priest may be hindered in two ways from hearing a man's confession: first, through lack of jurisdiction; second, through being prevented from exercising his order, as those who are excommunicate, degraded,

nicati et degradati et huiusmodi. Quicumque autem iurisdictionem habet, potest ea quae sunt iurisdictionis committere. Et ideo, si aliquis impediatur quod alterius confessionem audire non possit per iurisdictionis defectum, potest sibi per quemcumque iurisdictionem habentem immediatam in illos, committi quod confessionem audiat et absolvat, sive per ipsum sacerdotem, sive per episcopum, sive per Papam. Si autem propter executionis ordinis impedimentum audire non possit, potest sibi concedi quod confessionem audiat per eum qui impedimentum removere potest.

AD PRIMUM ergo dicendum quod praeiudicium non fit alicui nisi ei subtrahatur quod est in favorem eius indultum. Iurisdictionis autem potestas non est commissa alicui homini in favorem suum, sed in utilitatem plebis et honorem Dei. Et ideo, si superioribus praelatis expedire videatur ad salutem plebis et honorem Dei promovendum, quod aliis quae sunt iurisdictionis committant, in nullo fit praeiudicium inferioribus praelatis: nisi illis qui *quaerunt quae sua sunt, non quae Iesu Christi*, et qui gregi praesunt, non ut eos pascant, sed ut ab eis pascantur.

AD SECUNDUM dicendum quod rector ecclesiae debet *vultum pecoris sui cognoscere* dupliciter. Uno modo, per sollicitam exterioris conversationis considerationem, qua invigilare debet super gregem sibi commissum. Et in hac cognitione non oportet quod credat subito, sed certitudinem facti, inquantum potest, inquirat. Alio modo, per confessionis manifestationem. Et quantum ad hanc cognitionem, non potest maiorem certitudinem accipere quam ut subdito credat: quia hoc est ad subveniendum conscientiae ipsius. Unde in foro confessionis creditur homini et pro se et contra se: non autem in foro exterioris iudicii. Et ideo ad hanc cognitionem sufficit quod; credat subdito dicenti se alteri absolvere valenti fuisse confessum. Et sic patet quod talis cognitio pecoris per privilegium alicui indultum de confessione audienda non impeditur.

AD TERTIUM dicendum quod inconveniens esset si duo aequaliter super eandem plebem constituantur. Sed quod duo quorum unus alio principalior est, super eandem plebem constituantur, non est inconveniens. Et secundum hoc, super eandem plebem immediate sunt et sacerdos parochialis, et episcopus, et Papa: et, quilibet eorum potest ea quae sunt iurisdictionis ad ipsum pertinentia alteri committere. Sed si superior committat, qui et principalior est, dupliciter potest committere. Aut ita quod eum vice sui constituat: sicut Papa et episcopus suos poenitentiarios constituunt. Et tunc talis est principalior quam inferior praelatus, sicut poenitentiarius Papae quam episcopus, et poenitentiarius episcopi quam sacerdos parochialis: et magis tenetur ei confitens obedire. Alio modo, ut eum coadiutorem illius sacerdotis con-

and so forth. Now, whoever has jurisdiction can depute to another whatever comes under his jurisdiction; so that if a priest is hindered from hearing a man's confession through want of jurisdiction, anyone who has immediate jurisdiction over that man, priest, bishop, or Pope, can depute that priest to hear his confession and absolve him. If, on the other hand, the priest cannot hear the confession on account of an impediment to the exercise of his order, anyone who has the power to remove that impediment can permit him to hear confessions.

REPLY OBJ. 1: No wrong is done to a person unless what is taken away from him was granted for his own benefit. Now the power of jurisdiction is not granted a man for his own benefit, but for the good of the people and for the glory of God. Hence, if the higher prelates deem it expedient for the furthering of the people's salvation and God's glory to commit matters of jurisdiction to others, no wrong is done to the inferior prelates, except to those who *seek the things that are their own; not the things that are Jesus Christ's* (Phil 2:21), and who rule their flock not by feeding it, but by feeding on it.

REPLY OBJ. 2: The rector of a church should *know the countenance of his own cattle* in two ways. First, by an assiduous attention to their external conduct, so as to watch over the flock committed to his care: and in acquiring this knowledge he should not believe his subject, but, as far as possible, inquire into the truth of facts. Second, by the manifestation of confession; and with regard to this knowledge, he cannot arrive at any greater certainty than by believing his subject, because this is necessary that he may help his subject's conscience. Consequently, in the tribunal of confession the penitent is believed whether he speak for himself or against himself, but not in the court of external judgment: wherefore it suffices for this knowledge that he believe the penitent when he says that he has confessed to one who could absolve him. It is therefore clear that this knowledge of the flock is not hindered by a privilege granted to another to hear confessions.

REPLY OBJ. 3: It would be inconvenient, if two men were placed equally over the same people, but there is no inconvenience if over the same people two are placed one of whom is over the other. In this way the parish priest, the bishop, and the Pope are placed immediately over the same people, and each of them can commit matters of jurisdiction to some other. Now a higher superior delegates a man in two ways: first, so that the latter takes the superior's place, as when the Pope or a bishop appoints his penitentiaries; and then the man thus delegated is higher than the inferior prelate, as the Pope's penitentiary is higher than a bishop, and the bishop's penitentiary than a parish priest, and the penitent is bound to obey the former rather than the latter. Second, so that the delegate is appointed the coadjutor of this other priest; and since a co-adjutor is subordinate to

stituat. Et quia coadiutor ordinatur ad eum cui coadiutor datur, ideo coadiutor est minus principalis. Et ideo poenitens non tantum obedire tenetur ei quantum proprio sacerdoti.

AD QUARTUM dicendum quod nullus tenetur confiteri peccata quae non habet. Et ideo, si aliquis poenitentiario episcopi, vel alteri ab episcopo commissionem habenti, confessus fuerit, cum sint sibi dimissa peccata et quoad Deum et quoad Ecclesiam, non tenetur confiteri proprio sacerdoti, quantumcumque petat. Sed propter statutum Ecclesiae de confessione facienda proprio sacerdoti semel in anno, eodem modo se debet habere sicut ille qui habet solum venialia. Talis enim solum venialia confiteri debet, ut quidam dicunt: vel profiteri se a peccato mortali immunem. Et sacerdos ei in foro conscientiae credere debet et tenetur.

Si tamen iterum confiteri teneretur, non frustra primo confessus fuisset: quia quanto pluribus sacerdotibus confitetur quis, tanto plus de poena remittitur ei; tum ex erubescentia confessionis, quae in poenam satisfactoriam computatur; tum ex vi clavium. Unde toties posset confiteri quod ab omni poena liberaretur. Nec reiteratio facit iniuriam sacramento, nisi illi in quo sanctificatio adhibetur vel per characteris impressionem, vel per materiae consecrationem: quorum neutrum est in poenitentia. Unde bonum est quod ille qui auctoritate episcopi confessionem audit, inducat confitentem quod confiteatur proprio sacerdoti. Quod si noluerit, nihilominus eum absolvere debet.

the person he is appointed to help, he holds a lower rank, and the penitent is not so bound to obey him as his own priest.

REPLY OBJ. 4: No man is bound to confess sins that he has no longer. Consequently, if a man has confessed to the bishop's penitentiary, or to someone else having faculties from the bishop, his sins are forgiven both before the Church and before God, so that he is not bound to confess them to his own priest, however much the latter may insist: but on account of the ecclesiastical precept (*On Repentance and Remission of Sins*) which prescribes confession to be made once a year to one's own priest, he is under the same obligation as one who has committed none but venial sins. For such a one, according to some, is bound to confess none but venial sins, or he must declare that he is free from mortal sin, and the priest, in the tribunal of conscience, ought, and is bound, to believe him.

If, however, he were bound to confess again, his first confession would not be useless, because the more priests one confesses to, the more is the punishment remitted, both by reason of the shame in confessing, which is reckoned as a satisfactory punishment, and by reason of the power of the keys: so that one might confess so often as to be delivered from all punishment. Nor is repetition derogatory to a sacrament, except in those wherein there is some kind of sanctification, either by the impressing of a character, or by the consecration of the matter, neither of which applies to penance. Hence it would be well for him who hears confessions by the bishop's authority to advise the penitent to confess to his own priest, yet he must absolve him, even if he declines to do so.

Article 6

Whether a Penitent, at the Point of Death, Can Be Absolved by Any Priest?

AD SEXTUM SIC PROCEDITUR. Videtur quod in fine vitae poenitens non possit a quolibet sacerdote absolvi. Quia ad absolutionem requiritur aliqua iurisdictio, ut dictum est. Sed sacerdos non acquirit iurisdictionem super illum qui in fine poenitet. Ergo non potest eum in fine absolvere.

PRAETEREA, ille qui sacramentum baptismi in articulo mortis ab alio quam proprio sacerdote recipit, non debet a proprio sacerdote iterum baptizari. Si ergo quilibet sacerdos in articulo mortis posset absolvere a quolibet peccato, non deberet poenitens, si evadit, ad suum sacerdotem recurrere. Quod falsum est: quia alias sacerdos non haberet *cognitionem de vultu pecoris sui*.

PRAETEREA, in articulo mortis, sicut licet alieno sacerdoti baptizare, ita et non-sacerdoti. Sed non-sacerdos nunquam potest absolvere in foro poenitentiali. Ergo

OBJECTION 1: It would seem that a penitent, at the point of death, cannot be absolved by any priest. For absolution requires jurisdiction, as stated above (A. 5). Now a priest does not acquire jurisdiction over a man who repents at the point of death. Therefore, he cannot absolve him.

OBJ. 2: Further, he that, when in danger of death, receives the sacrament of baptism from another than his own priest does not need to be baptized again by the latter. If, therefore, any priest can absolve, from any sin, a man who is in danger of death, the penitent, if he survive the danger, need not go to his own priest; which is false, since otherwise the priest would not *know the countenance of his cattle*.

OBJ. 3: Further, when there is danger of death, baptism can be conferred not only by a strange priest, but also by one who is not a priest. But one who is not a priest can never

nec sacerdos in articulo mortis eum qui non est sibi subditus.

Sed contra: Necessitas spiritualis est maior quam corporalis. Sed aliquis in necessitate ultima potest aliorum rebus uti, etiam invitis dominis, ad subveniendum corporali necessitati. Ergo et in articulo mortis, ad subveniendum spirituali necessitati, potest a non suo sacerdote absolvi.

Praeterea, ad idem sunt auctoritates positae in littera.

Respondeo dicendum quod quilibet sacerdos, quantum est de virtute clavium, habet potestatem indifferenter in omnes, in quantum ad omnia peccata: sed quod non possit omnes ab omnibus peccatis absolvere, hoc est quia per ordinationem Ecclesiae habet iurisdictionem limitatam, vel omnino nullam habet. Sed quia *necessitas legem non habet*, ideo quando necessitatis articulus imminet, per Ecclesiae ordinationem; non impeditur quin absolvere possit, ex quo habet claves, etiam sacramentaliter: et tantum consequitur ex absolutione alterius sicut si a proprio sacerdote absolveretur. Nec solum a peccatis tunc potest a quolibet sacerdote absolvi, sed etiam ab excommunicatione, a quocumque sit lata. Et haec absolutio etiam ad iurisdictionem pertinet, quae per legem ordinationis Ecclesiae coarctatur.

Ad primum ergo dicendum quod aliquis potest uti iurisdictione alterius ex eius voluntate: quia ea quae iurisdictionis sunt committi possunt. Unde, quia Ecclesia acceptat ut quilibet sacerdos absolvere possit in articulo mortis, ideo ex hoc ipso quis usum iurisdictionis habet, quamvis iurisdictione careat.

Ad secundum dicendum quod non oportet eum recurrere ad proprium sacerdotem ut iterum a peccatis solvatur, a quibus in articulo mortis absolutus est: sed ut innotescat ei quod est absolutus. Nec similiter oportet quod absolutus ab excommunicatione ad iudicem vadat, qui alias absolvere potuisset, absolutionem petens, sed satisfactionem offerens.

Ad tertium dicendum quod baptismus habet ex ipsa sanctificatione materiae efficaciam: et ideo, a quocumque conferatur alicui, ille sacramentum recipit. Sed vis sacramentalis poenitentiae consistit in sanctificatione ministri. Et ideo ille qui laico confitetur, quamvis impleat quod ex parte sua est de sacramentali confessione, tamen sacramentalem absolutionem non consequitur. Et ideo aliquid valet ei quantum ad diminutionem poenae, quae fit per confessionis meritum et poenam: sed non consequitur diminutionem illam poenae quae est ex vi clavium. Et ideo oportet quod iterum sacerdoti confitea-

absolve in the tribunal of penance. Therefore, neither can a priest absolve a man who is not his subject when he is in danger of death.

On the contrary, Spiritual necessity is greater than bodily necessity. But it is lawful in a case of extreme necessity for a man to make use of another's property, even against the owner's will, in order to supply a bodily need. Therefore, in danger of death a man may be absolved by another than his own priest, in order to supply his spiritual need.

Further, The authorities quoted in the text prove the same (*Sentences* IV, D. 20, Cap. "Non Habet").

I answer that, If we consider the power of the keys, every priest has power over all men equally and over all sins: and it is due to the fact that, by the ordination of the Church, he has a limited jurisdiction or none at all that he cannot absolve all men from all sins. But since *necessity knows no law* (*Decretals*) in cases of necessity the ordination of the Church does not hinder him from being able to absolve, since he has the keys sacramentally: and the penitent will receive as much benefit from the absolution of this other priest as if he had been absolved by his own. Moreover, a man can then be absolved by any priest not only from his sins, but also from excommunication by whomsoever pronounced, because such absolution is also a matter of that jurisdiction which by the ordination of the Church is confined within certain limits.

Reply Obj. 1: One person may act on the jurisdiction of another according to the latter's will, since matters of jurisdiction can be deputed. Since, therefore, the Church recognizes absolution granted by any priest at the hour of death, from this very fact a priest has the use of jurisdiction, though he lack the power of jurisdiction.

Reply Obj. 2: He needs to go to his own priest not that he may be absolved again from the sins from which he was absolved when in danger of death, but that his own priest may know that he is absolved. In like manner, he who has been absolved from excommunication needs to go to the judge who in other circumstances could have absolved him, not in order to seek absolution, but in order to offer satisfaction.

Reply Obj. 3: Baptism derives its efficacy from the sanctification of the matter itself, so that a man receives the sacrament whosoever baptizes him: whereas the sacramental power of penance consists in a sanctification pronounced by the minister, so that if a man confess to a layman, although he fulfills his own part of the sacramental confession, he does not receive sacramental absolution. Wherefore his confession avails him somewhat as to the lessening of his punishment, owing to the merit derived from his confession and to his repentance, but he does not receive that diminution of his punishment which re-

tur. Et magis sic confessus decedens punitur post hanc vitam quam si sacerdoti fuisset confessus.

sults from the power of the keys; and consequently he must confess again to a priest; and one who has confessed thus is more punished hereafter than if he had confessed to a priest.

Article 7

Whether the Temporal Punishment Is Imposed According to the Degree of the Fault?

AD SEPTIMUM SIC PROCEDITUR. Videtur quod poena temporalis, cuius reatus post poenitentiam manet, non taxetur secundum quantitatem culpae. Taxatur enim secundum quantitatem delectationis quae fuit in peccato: ut patet Apoc. 18, *quantum glorificavit se et in deliciis fuit, tantum date illi tormentum et luctum.* Sed quandoque ubi est maior delectatio, ibi est minor culpa: quia *peccata carnalia, quae plus habent delectationis quam spiritualia, minus habent de culpa,* secundum Gregorium. Ergo poena non taxatur secundum quantitatem culpae.

PRAETEREA, eodem modo aliquis obligatur per praecepta moralia in nova lege et veteri. Sed in veteri lege debebatur pro peccatis poena septem dierum: ut scilicet septem diebus immundi essent. Cum ergo in novo Testamento imponatur poena septennis pro uno peccato mortali, videtur quod quantitas poenae non respiciat quantitatem culpae.

PRAETEREA, maius est peccatum homicidii in laico quam fornicationis in sacerdote: quia circumstantia quae sumitur ex specie peccati, magis aggravat quam quae sumitur ex conditione personae. Sed laico pro homicidio imponitur septennis poenitentia, sacerdoti pro fornicatione decem annorum, secundum Canones. Ergo poena non taxatur secundum quantitatem culpae.

PRAETEREA, maximum peccatum est quod in ipsum corpus Christi committitur; quia tanto gravius quis peccat quanto maior est in quem peccatur. Sed pro effusione sanguinis Christi in sacramento Altaris contenti iniungitur poenitentia quadraginta dierum, vel parum amplius; pro fornicatione autem simplici iniungitur poenitentia septennis, secundum Canones. Ergo quantitas poenae non respondet quantitati culpae.

SED CONTRA: Isaiae 27: *in mensuram contra mensuram, curri abiecta fuerit, iudicabo eam.* Ergo quantitas iudicii punitionis peccati est secundum quantitatem culpae.

PRAETEREA, homo reducitur ad aequalitatem iustitiae per poenam inflictam. Sed hoc non esset si quanti-

OBJECTION 1: It would seem that the temporal punishment, the debt of which remains after penance, is not imposed according to the degree of fault. For it is imposed according to the degree of pleasure derived from the sin, as appears from Revelation 18:7: *as much as she hath glorified herself and lived in delicacies, so much torment and sorrow give ye her.* Yet sometimes where there is greater pleasure, there is less fault, since *carnal sins, which afford more pleasure than spiritual sins, are less guilty,* according to Gregory (*Morals on Job,* 33.2). Therefore, the punishment is not imposed according to the degree of fault.

OBJ. 2: Further, in the new law one is bound to punishment for mortal sins in the same way as in the old law. Now in the old law the punishment for sin was due to last seven days: in other words, they had to remain unclean seven days for one mortal sin. Since therefore, in the New Testament, a punishment of seven years is imposed for one mortal sin, it seems that the quantity of the punishment does not answer to the degree of fault.

OBJ. 3: Further, the sin of murder in a layman is more grievous than that of fornication in a priest, because the circumstance which is taken from the species of a sin is more aggravating than that which is taken from the person of the sinner. Now a punishment of seven years' duration is appointed for a layman guilty of murder, while for fornication a priest is punished for ten years, according to the Canons (*Decretals*). Therefore, punishment is not imposed according to the degree of fault.

OBJ. 4: Further, a sin committed against the very body of Christ is most grievous, because the greater the person sinned against, the more grievous the sin. Now for spilling the blood of Christ in the Sacrament of the Altar, a punishment of forty days or a little more is enjoined, while a punishment of seven years is prescribed for fornication, according to the Canons (*Decretals*). Therefore, the quantity of the punishment does not answer to the degree of fault.

ON THE CONTRARY, It is written: *in measure against measure, when it shall be cast off, you will judge it* (Isa 27:8). Therefore, the quantity of punishment adjudicated for sin answers the degree of fault.

FURTHER, Man is reduced to the equality of justice by the punishment inflicted on him. But this would not be so

tas culpae et poenae non sibi responderent. Ergo unum alteri respondet.

RESPONDEO dicendum quod poena post dimissionem culpae exigitur ad duo: scilicet ad debitum solvendum, et ad remedium praestandum. Potest ergo taxatio poenae considerari quantum ad duo. Primo, quantum ad debitum. Et sic quantitas poenae radicaliter respondet quantitati culpae antequam de ea aliquid dimittatur. Sed tamen quantum per primum eorum quae poenam nata sunt remittere plus remittitur, secundum hoc per aliud minus remittendum vel solvendum restat: quia quanto per contritionem plus de poena dimissum est, tanto per confessionem minus dimittendum restat. Secundo, quantum ad remedium vel illius qui peccavit, vel aliorum. Et sic quandoque pro minori peccato iniungitur maior poena. Vel quia peccato unius difficilius potest resisti quam peccato alterius: sicut iuveni imponitur pro fornicatione maior poena quam seni, quamvis minus peccet. Vel quia in uno peccatum est periculosius, sicut in sacerdote, quam in alio. Vel quia multitudo magis prona est ad illud peccatum, et ideo per poenam unius alii sunt exterrendi.

Poena ergo in foro poenitentiae quantum ad utrumque taxanda est. Et ideo non semper pro maiori peccato maior poena imponitur. Sed poena purgatorii solum est ad solvendum debitum: quia iam ulterius non manet locus peccandi. Et ideo illa poena taxatur solum secundum quantitatem peccati: considerata tamen contritionis quantitate, et confessione et absolutione; quia per omnia haec de poena aliquid dimittitur. Unde etiam a sacerdote in iniungendo satisfactionem sunt consideranda.

AD PRIMUM ergo dicendum quod in verbis illis duo tanguntur ex parte culpae, scilicet glorificatio, et deliciae. Quorum primum pertinet ad elationem peccantis, qua Deo resistit; secundum ad delectationem peccati. Quamvis autem sit minor delectatio quandoque in maiori culpa, tamen est ibi semper maior elatio. Et ideo ratio non procedit.

AD SECUNDUM dicendum quod illa poena septem dierum non erat expiativa a poena debita peccato: unde etiam, si post illos dies moreretur, in purgatorio puniretur. Sed expiabat ab irregularitate, a qua omnia sacrificia legalia expiabant.

Nihilominus, ceteris paribus, plus peccat homo in nova lege quam in veteri: propter sanctificationem ampliorem, qua sanctificatur in baptismo; et propter beneficia Dei potiora humano generi exhibita. Et hoc patet ex hoc quod dicitur Heb. 10: *quanto putatis deteriora mereri supplicia*, etc.

if the quantity of the fault and of the punishment did not mutually correspond. Therefore, one answers to the other.

I ANSWER THAT, After the forgiveness of sin, a punishment is required for two reasons, viz. to pay the debt, and to afford a remedy. Hence the punishment may be imposed in consideration of two things. First, in consideration of the debt, and in this way the quantity of the punishment corresponds radically to the quantity of the fault before anything of the latter is forgiven: yet the more there is remitted by the first of those things which are of a nature to remit punishment, the less there remains to be remitted or paid by the other, because the more contrition remits of the punishment, the less there remains to be remitted by confession. Second, consideration of the remedy is either as regards the one who sinned, or as regards others: and thus sometimes a greater punishment is enjoined for a lesser sin; either because one man's sin is more difficult to resist than another's (thus a heavier punishment is imposed on a young man for fornication than on an old man, though the former's sin be less grievous), or because one man's sin, for instance, a priest's, is more dangerous to others than another's sin, or because the people are more prone to that particular sin, so that it is necessary by the punishment of the one man to deter others.

Consequently, in the tribunal of penance, the punishment has to be imposed with due regard to both these things: and so a greater punishment is not always imposed for a greater sin. On the other hand, the punishment of purgatory is only for the payment of the debt, because there is no longer any possibility of sinning, so that this punishment is meted only according to the measure of sin, with due consideration, however, for the degree of contrition, and for confession and absolution, since all these lessen the punishment somewhat: wherefore the priest in enjoining satisfaction should bear them in mind.

REPLY OBJ. 1: In the words quoted two things are mentioned with regard to the sin, namely, *glorification* and *delectation*, the first of which regards the uplifting of the sinner whereby he resists God, while the second regards the pleasure of sin. And although sometimes there is less pleasure in a greater sin, yet there is greater uplifting: therefore, the argument does not proceed.

REPLY OBJ. 2: This punishment of seven days did not expiate the punishment due for the sin, so that even if the sinner died after that time, he would be punished in purgatory: but it was in expiation of the irregularity incurred, from which all the legal sacrifices expiated.

Nevertheless, other things being equal, a man sins more grievously under the new law than under the old, on account of the more plentiful sanctification received in baptism, and on account of the more powerful blessings bestowed by God on the human race. This is evident from Hebrews 10:29: *how much more, do you think, he deserves worse punishments.*

Nec tamen hoc verum est universaliter, quod exigatur pro quolibet peccato mortali septennis poenitentia: sed hoc est quasi quaedam regula communis, ut in pluribus competens, quam tamen oportet dimittere consideratis diversis peccatorum circumstantiis.

AD TERTIUM dicendum quod episcopus vel sacerdos cum maiori periculo suo et aliorum peccat. Et ideo sollicitius retrahunt eum canones a peccato quam alios, maiorem poenam iniungendo, secundum quod est in remedium: quamvis quandoque non debeatur tanta ex debito. Unde in purgatorio non tanta ab eo exigitur.

AD QUARTUM dicendum quod poena illa est intelligenda quando nolente sacerdote hoc accidit. Si enim sponte funderetur, multo graviori poena dignus esset.

And yet it is not universally true that a seven years' penance is exacted for every mortal sin: but it is a kind of general rule applicable to the majority of cases, which must, nevertheless, be disregarded, with due consideration for the various circumstances of sins and penitents.

REPLY OBJ. 3: A bishop or priest sins with greater danger to others or to himself; thus, the canons are more anxious to withdraw him from sin by inflicting a greater punishment, inasmuch as it is intended as a remedy; although sometimes so great a punishment is not strictly due. Hence he is punished less in purgatory.

REPLY OBJ. 4: This punishment refers to the case when this happens against the priest's will: for if he spilled it willingly he would deserve a much heavier punishment.

QUESTION 9

THE QUALITY OF CONFESSION

Deinde considerandum est de qualitate confessionis. Circa quod quaeruntur quattuor.

Primo: utrum confessio possit esse informis.

Secundo: utrum oporteat confessionem esse integram.

Tertio: utrum possit aliquis per alium, vel per scriptum confiteri.

Quarto: utrum illae sexdecim conditiones quae a magistris assignantur, ad confessionem requirantur.

We must now consider the quality of confession. Under this head there are four points of inquiry:

(1) Whether confession can be lacking in form?

(2) Whether confession ought to be entire?

(3) Whether one can confess through another, or by writing?

(4) Whether the sixteen conditions, which are assigned by the masters, are necessary for confession?

Article 1

Whether Confession Can Be Lacking in Form?

AD PRIMUM SIC PROCEDITUR. Videtur quod confessio non possit esse informis. Eccli. 17 dicitur: *a mortuo, velut qui non est, perit confessio.* Sed ille qui non habet caritatem, est mortuus: quia ipsa est animae vita. Ergo absque caritate non potest esse confessio.

PRAETEREA, confessio dividitur contra contritionem et satisfactionem. Sed contritio et satisfactio nunquam possunt extra caritatem fieri. Ergo nec confessio.

PRAETEREA, in confessione oportet quod os cordi concordet: quia hoc ipsum nomen confessionis requirit. Sed ille qui adhuc manet in affectu peccati quod confitetur, non habet cor ori conforme: quia corde peccatum tenet quod ore damnat. Ergo talis non confitetur.

SED CONTRA, quilibet tenetur ad confessionem mortalium. Sed si aliquis semel confessus est etiam in mortali existens, non tenetur ulterius ad confitendum eadem peccata: quia, cum nullus sciat se caritatem habere, nullus sciret se confessum fuisse. Ergo non est de necessitate confessionis quod sit caritate formata.

RESPONDEO dicendum quod confessio est actus virtutis, et pars sacramenti. Secundum autem quod est actus virtutis, est actus meritorius proprie. Et sic confessio non valet sine caritate, quae est principium merendi. Sed secundum quod est pars sacramenti, sic ordinat confitentem ad sacerdotem, qui habet claves Ecclesiae, qui per confessionem conscientiam confitentis cognoscit. Et secundum hoc, confessio potest esse etiam in eo qui non est contritus: quia potest peccata sua confiteri sacerdoti,

OBJECTION 1: It would seem that confession cannot be lacking in form. For it is written: *confessing perishes from the dead as nothing* (Sir 17:26). But a man without charity is dead, because charity is the life of the soul. Therefore, there can be no confession without charity.

OBJ. 2: Further, confession is condivided with contrition and satisfaction. But contrition and satisfaction are impossible without charity. Therefore, confession is also impossible without charity.

OBJ. 3: Further, it is necessary in confession that the word should agree with the thought, for the very name of confession requires this. Now if a man confess while remaining attached to sin, his word is not in accord with his thought, since in his heart he holds to sin while he condemns it with his lips. Therefore, such a man does not confess.

ON THE CONTRARY, Every man is bound to confess his mortal sins. Now if a man in mortal sin has confessed once, he is not bound to confess the same sins again, because, as no man knows himself to have charity, no man would know himself to have confessed. Therefore, it is not necessary that confession should be informed by charity.

I ANSWER THAT, Confession is an act of virtue and a part of a sacrament. Insofar as it is an act of virtue, it has the property of being meritorious, and thus is of no avail without charity, which is the principle of merit. But insofar as it is part of a sacrament, it subordinates the penitent to the priest who has the keys of the Church, and who by means of the confession knows the conscience of the person confessing. In this way it is possible for confession to be in one who is not contrite, for he can make his sins known to the priest,

61

et clavibus Ecclesiae se subiicere. Et quamvis tunc non percipiat absolutionis fructum, tamen, recedente fictione, percipere incipiet. Et sic etiam est in aliis sacramentis. Unde non tenetur iterare confessionem qui fictus accedit: sed tenetur postmodum fictionem suam confiteri.

Ad primum ergo dicendum quod auctoritas illa intelligenda est quantum ad fructum confessionis percipiendum, quem nullus extra caritatem existens percipit.

Ad secundum dicendum quod contritio et satisfactio fiunt Deo, sed confessio fit homini. Et ideo de ratione contritionis et satisfactionis est quod homo sit Deo per caritatem unitus: non autem de ratione confessionis.

Ad tertium dicendum quod ille qui peccata quae habet narrat, vere loquitur. Et sic cor concordat verbis quantum ad substantiam confessionis, quamvis cor discordet a confessionis fine.

and subject himself to the keys of the Church: and though he does not receive the fruit of absolution then, yet he will begin to receive it when he is sincerely contrite, as happens in the other sacraments. Wherefore he is not bound to repeat his confession, but to confess his lack of sincerity.

Reply Obj. 1: These words must be understood as referring to the receiving of the fruit of confession, which none can receive who is not in the state of charity.

Reply Obj. 2: Contrition and satisfaction are offered to God, but confession is made to man: hence it is essential to contrition and satisfaction, but not to confession, that man should be united to God by charity.

Reply Obj. 3: He who declares the sins which he has, speaks the truth; and thus his thought agrees with his lips or words as to the substance of confession, though it is discordant with the purpose of confession.

Article 2

Whether Confession Should Be Entire?

Ad secundum sic proceditur. Videtur quod non oporteat confessionem esse integram, ut scilicet omnia peccata uni sacerdoti confiteatur aliquis. Quia erubescentia facit ad diminutionem poenae. Sed quanto pluribus sacerdotibus quis confitetur, tanto maiorem erubescentiam patitur. Ergo fructuosior est confessio si pluribus sacerdotibus dividatur.

Praeterea, confessio ad hoc necessaria est in poenitentia ut poena secundum arbitrium sacerdotis peccato taxetur. Sed sufficiens poena potest imponi a diversis sacerdotibus de diversis peccatis. Ergo non oportet uni sacerdoti omnia peccata confiteri.

Praeterea, potest contingere quod post confessionem factam et satisfactionem perfectam, recordetur quis alicuius peccati mortalis quod dum confitebatur iri memoria non habebat, et tunc copiam proprii sacerdotis, cui primo confessus fuerit, haberi non poterit. Ergo poterit illud solum peccatum alteri confiteri. Et sic diversa peccata diversis sacerdotibus confitebitur.

Praeterea, sacerdoti non debet fieri confessio de peccatis nisi propter absolutionem. Sed quandoque sacerdos qui confessionem audit, potest de quibusdam peccatis absolvere, non de omnibus. Ergo ad minus in tali casu non oportet quod confessio sit integra.

Sed contra: Hypocrisis est impedimentum poenitentiae. Sed dividere confessionem ad *hypocrisim pertinet*: ut Augustinus dicit. Ergo confessio debet esse integra.

Praeterea, confessio est poenitentiae pars. Sed poenitentia debet esse integra. Ergo et confessio.

Objection 1: It would seem that it is not necessary for confession to be entire, that is to say, for a man to confess all his sins to one priest. For shame conduces to the diminution of punishment. Now the greater the number of priests to whom a man confesses, the greater his shame. Therefore, confession is more fruitful if it be divided among several priests.

Obj. 2: Further, confession is necessary in penance in order that punishment may be enjoined for sin according to the judgment of the priest. Now a sufficient punishment for different sins can be imposed by different priests. Therefore, it is not necessary to confess all one's sins to one priest.

Obj. 3: Further, it may happen that a man, after going to confession and performing his penance, remembers a mortal sin which escaped his memory while confessing, and that his own priest to whom he confessed first is no longer available, so that he can only confess that sin to another priest, and thus he will confess different sins to different priests.

Obj. 4: Further, the sole reason for confessing one's sins to a priest is in order to receive absolution. Now sometimes, the priest who hears a confession can absolve from some of the sins, but not from all. Therefore, in such a case at least the confession need not be entire.

On the contrary, Hypocrisy is an obstacle to penance. But it *savors of hypocrisy* to divide one's confession, as Augustine says (*On True and False Penance*). Therefore, confession should be entire.

Further, Confession is a part of penance. But penance should be entire. Therefore, confession should also.

RESPONDEO dicendum quod in medicina corporali oportet quod medicus non unum solum morbum, contra quem medicinam dare debet, cognoscat, sed etiam universaliter totam habitudinem ipsius infirmi: eo quod unus morbus ex adiunctione alterius aggravatur, et medicina quae uni morbo competeret, alteri nocumentum praestaret. Et similiter est in peccatis: quia unum aggravatur ex adiunctione alterius; et illud quod uni peccato esset conveniens medicina, alteri incentivum praestaret, cum quandoque aliquis contrariis peccatis infectus sit, ut Gregorius, in *Pastorali*, docet. Et ideo de necessitate confessionis est quod homo omnia peccata confiteatur quae in memoria habet: quod si non faciat, non est confessio, sed confessionis simulatio.

AD PRIMUM ergo dicendum quod, etsi erubescentia sit multiplicior quando dividit diversa peccata diversis, tamen omnes simul non sunt ita magnae erubescentiae sicut illa una qua quis omnia peccata sua simul confitetur. Quia unum peccatum per se consideratum non ita demonstrat malam dispositionem peccantis sicut quando est cum pluribus aliis consideratum: quia in unum peccatum aliquis quandoque ex ignorantia vel infirmitate labitur; sed multitudo peccatorum demonstrat malitiam peccantis, vel magnam corruptionem eiusdem.

AD SECUNDUM dicendum quod poena a diversis sacerdotibus imposita non esset sufficiens: quia quilibet consideraret tantum unum peccatum per se, et non gravitatem ipsius quam habet ex adiunctione alterius; et quandoque poena quae contra unum peccatum daretur, esset promotiva alterius peccati.

Et praeterea sacerdos confessionem audiens vicem Dei gerit. Et ideo debet ei fieri hoc modo confessio sicut fit Deo in contritione. Unde, sicut non esset contritio nisi quis de omnibus peccatis contereretur, ita non esset confessio nisi quis de omnibus quae memoriae occurrerint confiteatur.

AD TERTIUM dicendum quod quidam dicunt quod, quando aliquis recordatur eorum quae prius oblitus erat, debet iterum etiam ea quae prius confessus fuit confiteri: et praecipue si non potest eundem habere cui ante confessus fuerat, qui omnia cognoscit, ut totius culpae quantitas uni sacerdoti innotescat. Sed hoc non videtur necessarium. Quia peccatum habet quantitatem et ex seipso, et ex adiunctione alterius. Peccatorum autem de quibus confessus est, manifestavit quantitatem quam ex seipsis habent. Ad hoc autem quod sacerdos utramque quantitatem huius peccati cuius fuerat oblitus cognoscat, sufficit quod hoc peccatum confitens dicat explicite, et alia in generali, dicendo quod, cum alia multa confiteretur, huius oblitus fuit.

AD QUARTUM dicendum quod, etiam si sacerdos non de omnibus possit absolvere, tamen tenetur sibi om-

I ANSWER THAT, In prescribing medicine for the body, the physician should know not only the disease for which he is prescribing, but also the general constitution of the sick person, since one disease is aggravated by the addition of another, and a medicine which would be adapted to one disease would be harmful to another. The same is to be said in regard to sins, for one is aggravated when another is added to it; and a remedy which would be suitable for one sin might prove an incentive to another, since sometimes a man is guilty of contrary sins, as Gregory says (*Book of Pastoral Rule* 3.3). Hence it is necessary for confession that man confess all the sins that he calls to mind, and if he fails to do this, it is not a confession, but a pretense of confession.

REPLY OBJ. 1: Although a man's shame is multiplied when he makes a divided confession to different confessors, yet all his different shames together are not so great as that with which he confesses all his sins together. For one sin considered by itself does not prove the evil disposition of the sinner as when it is considered in conjunction with several others, because a man may fall into one sin through ignorance or weakness, but a number of sins proves the malice of the sinner, or his great corruption.

REPLY OBJ. 2: The punishment imposed by different priests would not be sufficient, because each would only consider one sin by itself, and not the gravity which it derives from being in conjunction with another. Moreover, sometimes the punishment which would be given for one sin would foster another.

Furthermore, the priest in hearing a confession takes the place of God, so that confession should be made to him just as contrition is made to God: therefore, as there would be no contrition unless one were contrite for all the sins which one calls to mind, so is there no confession unless one confess all the sins that one remembers committing.

REPLY OBJ. 3: Some say that when a man remembers a sin which he had previously forgotten, he ought to confess again the sins which he had confessed before, especially if he cannot go to the same priest to whom his previous confession was made, in order that the total quantity of his sins may be made known to one priest. But this does not seem necessary, because sin takes its quantity both from itself and from the conjunction of another; and as to the sins which he confessed he had already manifested their quantity which they have of themselves, while as to the sin which he had forgotten, in order that the priest may know the quantity which it has under both the above heads, it is enough that the penitent declare it explicitly, and confess the others in general, saying that he had confessed many sins in his previous confession, but had forgotten this particular one.

REPLY OBJ. 4: Although the priest may be unable to absolve the penitent from all his sins, yet the latter is bound to

nia confiteri, ut quantitatem totius culpae cognoscat, et de illis de quibus non potest absolvere, ad superiorem remittat.

confess all to him that he may know the total quantity of his guilt, and refer him to the superior with regard to the sins from which he cannot absolve him.

Article 3

Whether One May Confess Through Another, or by Writing?

AD TERTIUM PROCEDITUR. Videtur quod possit per alium quis confiteri, vel per scriptum. Quia confessio necessaria est ad hoc ut conscientia poenitentis sacerdoti pandatur. Sed homo potest etiam per alium, vel per scriptum suam conscientiam sacerdoti manifestare. Ergo sufficit per alium, vel per scriptum confiteri.

PRAETEREA, quidam non intelliguntur a propriis sacerdotibus, propter linguae diversitatem: et tales non possunt nisi per alios confiteri. Ergo non est de necessitate sacramenti quod per seipsum quis confiteatur. Et ita videtur quod, si per alium quis confessus fuerit qualitercumque, sufficiat ei ad salutem.

PRAETEREA, de necessitate sacramenti est quod homo proprio sacerdoti confiteatur, ut ex dictis patet. Sed aliquando proprius sacerdos est absens, cui non potest poenitens propria voce loqui; posset autem per scriptum ei suam conscientiam manifestare. Ergo videtur quod per scriptum ei suam conscientiam transmittere debeat.

SED CONTRA: Homo ad confessionem peccatorum sicut ad confessionem fidei obligatur. Sed confessio fidei *ore* est facienda: ut patet Rom. 10. Ergo et confessio peccatorum.

PRAETEREA, qui per seipsum peccavit, per seipsum debet poenitere. Sed confessio est poenitentiae pars. Ergo poenitens debet confiteri propria voce.

RESPONDEO dicendum quod confessio non solum est actus virtutis, sed etiam pars sacramenti. Quamvis autem ad eam secundum quod est actus virtutis, sufficeret qualitercumque fieret, etsi non esset tanta difficultas in uno modo sicut in alio; tamen, secundum quod est pars sacramenti, habet determinatum actum, sicut et alia sacramenta habent determinatam materiam. Et sicut in baptismo ad significandam interiorem ablutionem assumitur illud elementum cuius est maximus usus in abluendo, ita in actu sacramentali ad manifestandum ordinate assumitur ille actus quo maxime consuevimus manifestare, scilicet per proprium verbum. Alii enim modi sunt inducti in supplementum istius.

AD PRIMUM ergo dicendum quod, sicut in baptismo non sufficit qualitercumque abluere, sed per elementum determinatum; ita nec in poenitentia sufficit qualitercumque peccata manifestare, sed oportet quod per actum determinatum manifestentur.

OBJECTION 1: It would seem that one may confess through another, or by writing. For confession is necessary in order that the penitent's conscience may be made known to the priest. But a man can make his conscience known to the priest through another or by writing. Therefore, it is enough to confess through another or by writing.

OBJ. 2: Further, some are not understood by their own priests on account of a difference of language, and consequently cannot confess save through others. Therefore, it is not essential to the sacrament that one should confess by oneself, so that if anyone confesses through another in any way whatever, it suffices for his salvation.

OBJ. 3: Further, it is essential to the sacrament that a man should confess to his own priest, as appears from what has been said (Q. 8). Now sometimes a man's own priest is absent so that the penitent cannot speak to him with his own voice. But he could make his conscience known to him by writing. Therefore, it seems that he ought to manifest his conscience to him by writing to him.

ON THE CONTRARY, Man is bound to confess his sins even as he is bound to confess his faith. But confession of faith should be made *with the mouth*, as appears from Romans 10:10. Therefore, the confession of sins should also.

FURTHER, Whoever sinned by himself should, by himself, do penance. But confession is part of penance. Therefore, the penitent should confess his own sins.

I ANSWER THAT, Confession is not only an act of virtue, but also part of a sacrament. Now, although insofar as it is an act of virtue it matters not how it is done, even if it be easier to do it in one way than in another, yet, insofar as it is part of a sacrament, it has a determinate act, just as the other sacraments have a determinate matter. And as in baptism, in order to signify the inward washing, we employ that element which is chiefly used in washing, so in the sacramental act which is intended for manifestation we generally make use of that act which is most commonly employed for the purpose of manifestation, that is, our own words; for other ways have been introduced as supplementary to this.

REPLY OBJ. 1: Just as in baptism it is not enough to wash with anything, but it is necessary to wash with a determinate element, so neither does it suffice, in penance, to manifest one's sins in any way, but they must be declared by a determinate act.

AD SECUNDUM dicendum quod in eo qui usum linguae non habet, sicut mutus vel qui est alterius linguae, sufficit quod per scriptum, aut per nutum, aut interpretem confiteatur, quia non exigitur ab homine plus quam possit: quamvis homo non debeat baptismum accipere nisi in aqua. Quia aqua est omnino ab exteriori, et nobis ab alio exhibetur. Sed actus confessionis est a nobis: et ideo, quando non possumus uno modo, debemus secundum quod possumus confiteri.

AD TERTIUM dicendum quod in absentia proprii sacerdotis potest etiam laico fieri confessio. Et ideo non oportet quod per scriptum fiat: quia plus pertinet ad necessitatem confessionis actus quam ille cui fit confessio.

REPLY OBJ. 2: It is enough for one who does not have the use of a language, such as a mute man or one of a different tongue, to confess by writing, or by signs, or by an interpreter, because a man is not bound to do more than he can, although a man is not able or obliged to receive baptism except with water, which is from an entirely external source and is applied to us by another: whereas the act of confession is from within and is performed by ourselves, so that when we cannot confess in one way, we must confess as we can.

REPLY OBJ. 3: In the absence of one's own priest, confession may be made even to a layman, so that there is no necessity to confess in writing, because the act of confession is more essential than the person to whom confession is made.

Article 4

Whether the Sixteen Conditions Usually Assigned are Necessary for Confession?

AD QUARTUM SIC PROCEDITUR. Videtur quod illae sexdecim conditiones quae a magistris assignantur, his versibus contentae, non requirantur ad confessionem: *Sit simplex, humilis confessio, pura, fidelis: Atque frequens, nuda, discreta, libens, verecunda: Integra, secreta, lacrimabilis, accelerata: Fortis et accusans, et sit parere parata. Fides* enim et *simplicitas* et *fortitudo* sunt per se virtutes. Ergo non debent poni conditiones confessionis.

PRAETEREA, *purum* est quod non habet permixtionem. Similiter *simplex* compositionem et mixtionem aufert. Ergo superflue utrumque ponitur.

PRAETEREA, peccatum semel commissum nullus tenetur confiteri nisi semel. Ergo, si homo peccatum non iterat, non oportet quod sit *frequens*.

PRAETEREA, confessio ad satisfactionem ordinatur. Sed satisfactio quandoque est publica. Ergo et confessio non semper debet esse *secreta*.

PRAETEREA, illud quod non est in potestate nostra, non requiritur a nobis. Sed *lacrimas emittere* non est in potestate nostra. Ergo non requiritur a confitentem

RESPONDEO dicendum quod dictarum conditionum quaedam sunt de necessitate confessionis, quaedam de bene esse ipsius. Ea autem quae sunt de necessitate confessionis, vel competunt ei secundum quod est actus virtutis; vel secundum quod est pars sacramenti.

Si primo modo, aut ratione virtutis in genere; aut ratione specialis virtutis cuius est actus; aut ex ipsa ratione actus. Virtutis autem in genere sunt quattuor conditiones: ut in II *Ethic* dicitur. Prima est ut aliquis sit *sciens*. Et quantum ad hoc, confessio dicitur esse *discreta*: secundum quod in actu omnis virtutis prudentia requiritur.

OBJECTION 1: It would seem that the conditions assigned by the masters, and contained in the following lines, are not requisite for confession: *let confession be simple, humble, pure, faithful and frequent, naked, discrete, willing, modest, complete, secret, tearful, speedy, courageous and accusing, and let it be ready to obey.* For *fidelity, simplicity,* and *courage* are virtues by themselves, and therefore should not be reckoned as conditions of confession.

OBJ. 2: Further, a thing is *pure* when it is not mixed with anything else: and *simplicity,* in like manner, removes composition and admixture. Therefore, one or the other is superfluous.

OBJ. 3: Further, no one is bound to confess more than once a sin which he has committed but once. Therefore, if a man does not commit a sin again, his penance need not be *frequent.*

OBJ. 4: Further, confession is directed to satisfaction. But satisfaction is sometimes public. Therefore, confession should not always be *secret.*

OBJ. 5: Further, that which is not in our power is not required of us. But it is not in our power *to shed tears.* Therefore, it is not required of those who confess.

I ANSWER THAT, Some of the above conditions are essential to confession, and some are requisite for its wellbeing. Now those things which are essential to confession belong to it either as to an act of virtue, or as part of a sacrament.

If in the first way, it is either by reason of virtue in general, or by reason of the special virtue of which it is the act, or by reason of the act itself. Now there are four conditions of virtue in general, as stated in *Ethics* (2.4). The first is *knowledge,* in respect of which confession is said to be *discreet,* inasmuch as prudence is required in every act of

Est autem haec discretio ut maiora cum maiori pondere confiteatur. Secunda conditio est ut sit *eligens*: quia actus virtutum debent esse voluntarii. Et quantum ad hoc dicit *libens*. Tertia conditio est ut *propter hoc*, scilicet debitum finem, operetur. Et quantum ad hoc, dicit quod debet esse *pura*: ut scilicet recta sit intentio. Quarta est ut *immobiliter operetur*. Et quantum ad hoc, dicit quod debet esse *fortis*: ut scilicet propter verecundiam non dimittat.

Est autem confessio actus virtutis poenitentiae. Quae quidem primo initium sumit in horrore turpitudinis peccati. Et quantum ad hoc, confessio debet esse *verecunda*: ut scilicet non se iactet de peccatis propter aliquam saeculi vanitatem admixtam. Secundo, progreditur ad dolorem de peccato commisso. Et quantum ad hoc, debet esse *lacrimabilis*. Tertio, in abiectione sui terminatur. Et quantum ad hoc, debet esse *humilis*: ut se miserum confiteatur et infirmum.

Sed ex propria ratione huius actus qui est confessio, habet quod sit manifestativa. Quae quidem manifestatio per quattuor impediri potest. Primo, per falsitatem. Et quantum ad hoc, dicit *fidelis*, idest vera. Secundo, per obscuritatem. Et contra hoc dicit *nuda*: ut non involvat obscuritatem verborum. Tertio, per verborum *multiplicationem*. Et contra hoc dicit *simplex*: ut non recitet in confessione nisi quod ad quantitatem peccati pertinet. Quarto, ut non subtrahatur aliquid de his quae manifestanda sunt. Et contra hoc dicit *integra*.

Secundum autem quod confessio est pars sacramenti, sic concernit iudicium sacerdotis, qui est minister sacramenti. Unde oportet quod sit *accusans* ex parte confitentis; *parere parata* per comparationem ad sacerdotem; *secreta* quantum ad conditionem fori, in quo de occultis conscientiae agitur.

Sed de bene esse confessionis est quod sit *frequens*; et quod sit *accelerata*, ut scilicet statim confiteatur.

AD PRIMUM ergo dicendum quod non est inconveniens quod conditio unius virtutis in actu alterius inveniatur qui ab ipsa imperatur; vel quia medium quod est unius virtutis principaliter, etiam aliae virtutes per participationem habent.

AD SECUNDUM dicendum quod haec conditio *pura* intentionis excludit perversitatem, a qua homo mundatur: sed *simplex* alieni admixtionem excludit.

AD TERTIUM dicendum quod hoc non est de necessitate confessionis, sed de bene esse.

AD QUARTUM dicendum quod, propter scandalum aliorum qui possunt ex peccatis auditis ad malum inclinari, non debet confessio fieri in publico, sed in occulto. Ex poena autem satisfactoria non scandalizatur ita ali-

virtue: and this discretion consists in giving greater weight to greater sins. The second condition is *choice*, because acts of virtue should be voluntary, and in this respect confession is said to be *willing*. The third condition is that the act be done for a *particular purpose*, viz. the due end, and in this respect confession is said to be *pure*, i.e., with a right intention. The fourth condition is that one should *act immovably*, and in this respect it is said that confession should be *courageous*, viz. that the truth should not be forsaken through shame.

Now confession is an act of the virtue of penance. First of all, it takes its origin in the horror which one conceives for the shamefulness of sin, and in this respect confession should be *full of shame*, so as not to be a boastful account of one's sins, by reason of some worldly vanity accompanying it. Then it goes on to deplore the sin committed, and in this respect it is said to be *tearful*. Third, it culminates in self-abjection, and in this respect it should be *humble*, so that one confesses one's misery and weakness.

By reason of its very nature, that is, confession, this act is one of manifestation, which manifestation can be hindered by four things: first, by falsehood, and in this respect confession is said to be *faithful*, i.e., true. Second, by the use of vague words, and against this confession is said to be *naked*, so as not to be wrapped up in vague words; third, by *multiplicity* of words, in which respect it is said to be *simple*, indicating that the penitent should relate only such matters as affect the gravity of the sin; fourth, none of those things should be suppressed which should be made known, and in this respect confession should be *entire*.

Insofar as confession is part of a sacrament it is subject to the judgment of the priest who is the minister of the sacrament. Wherefore it should be an *accusation* on the part of the penitent, should manifest his *readiness to obey* the priest, and should be *secret* as regards the nature of the court wherein the hidden affairs of conscience are tried.

The well-being of confession requires that it should be *frequent*; and *not delayed*, i.e., that the sinner should confess at once.

REPLY OBJ. 1: There is nothing unreasonable in one virtue being a condition of the act of another virtue, through this act being commanded by that virtue; or through the mean which belongs to one virtue principally belonging to other virtues by participation.

REPLY OBJ. 2: The condition *pure* excludes perversity of intention, from which man is cleansed: but the condition *simple* excludes the introduction of unnecessary matter.

REPLY OBJ. 3: This is not necessary for confession, but is a condition of its well-being.

REPLY OBJ. 4: Confession should be made not publicly but privately, lest others be scandalized, and led to do evil through hearing the sins confessed. On the other hand, the penance enjoined in satisfaction does not give rise to scan-

quis: quia quandoque pro parvo vel nullo peccato similia opera satisfactoria fiunt.

AD QUINTUM dicendum quod intelligendum est de lacrimis mentis.

dal, since similar works of satisfaction are done sometimes for slight sins, and sometimes for none at all.

REPLY OBJ. 5: We must understand this to refer to tears of the heart.

QUESTION 10

THE EFFECT OF CONFESSION

Deinde considerandum est de effectu confessionis. Circa quod quaeruntur quinque.

Primo: utrum confessio liberet a morte peccati.

Secundo: utrum confessio liberet aliquo modo a poena.

Tertio: utrum confessio aperiat paradisum.

Quarto: utrum confessio tribuat spem salutis.

Quinto: utrum confessio generalis deleat peccata mortalia oblita.

We must now consider the effect of confession. Under this head there are five points of inquiry:

(1) Whether confession delivers one from the death of sin?

(2) Whether confession delivers one in any way from punishment?

(3) Whether confession opens paradise to us?

(4) Whether confession gives hope of salvation?

(5) Whether a general confession blots out mortal sins that one has forgotten?

Article 1

Whether Confession Delivers One from the Death of Sin?

AD PRIMUM SIC PROCEDITUR. Videtur quod confessio non *liberet a morte* peccati. Confessio enim contritionem sequitur. Sed contritio sufficienter delet culpam. Ergo confessio non liberat a morte peccati.

PRAETEREA, sicut mortale est culpa, ita etiam veniale. Sed per confessionem *fit veniale quod prius fuit mortale*, ut in littera dicitur. Ergo per confessionem non remittitur culpa, sed culpa in culpam mutatur.

SED CONTRA: Confessio est pars poenitentiae sacramenti. Sed poenitentia a culpa liberat. Ergo et confessio.

RESPONDEO dicendum quod poenitentia, inquantum est sacramentum, praecipue in confessione perficitur: quia per eam homo ministris Ecclesiae se subdit, qui sunt sacramentorum dispensatores. Contritio enim votum confessionis annexum habet: et satisfactio pro iudicio sacerdotis cui fit confessio, taxatur. Et quia in sacramento poenitentiae gratia infunditur, per quam fit remissio peccatorum, sicut in baptismo; ideo eodem modo confessio ex vi absolutionis coniunctae remittit culpam sicut et baptismus. Liberat enim baptismus a morte peccati non solum secundum quod actu percipitur, sed etiam secundum quod in voto habetur: sicut patet in illis qui iam sanctificati ad baptismum accedunt. Et si aliquis impedimentum non praestaret, ex ipsa collatione baptismi gratiam consequeretur remittentem peccata, si prius ei remissa non fuissent. Et similiter dicendum est de confessione adiuncta absolutioni quod, secundum quod in voto poenitentis praecessit, a culpa liberavit; postmodum autem in actu confessionis et ab-

OBJECTION 1: It would seem that confession does not *deliver one from the death* of sin. For confession follows contrition. But contrition sufficiently blots out guilt. Therefore, confession does not deliver one from the death of sin.

OBJ. 2: Further, just as mortal sin is a fault, so is venial. Now confession *renders venial that which was mortal before*, as stated in the text (*Sentences* IV, D. 17). Therefore, confession does not blot out guilt, but one guilt is changed into another.

ON THE CONTRARY, Confession is part of the sacrament of penance. But penance delivers from guilt. Therefore, confession does also.

I ANSWER THAT, Penance, as a sacrament, is perfected chiefly in confession, because by the latter a man submits to the ministers of the Church, who are the dispensers of the sacraments: for contrition has the desire of confession united thereto, and satisfaction is enjoined according to the judgment of the priest who hears the confession. And since in the sacrament of penance, as in baptism, that grace is infused whereby sins are forgiven, therefore confession in virtue of the absolution granted remits guilt, even as baptism does. Now baptism delivers one from the death of sin not only by being received actually, but also by being received in desire, as is evident with regard to those who approach the sacrament of baptism after being already sanctified. And unless a man offers an obstacle, he receives, through the very fact of being baptized, grace whereby his sins are remitted, if they are not already remitted. The same is to be said of confession, to which absolution is added because it delivered the penitent from guilt through being previously in his desire. Afterwards at the time of actual

solutionis gratia augetur; et etiam remissio peccatorum daretur, si praecedens dolor de peccatis non sufficiens ad contritionem fuisset, et ipse tunc obicem gratiae non praeberet. Et ideo, sicut de baptismo dicitur quod liberat a morte, ita etiam de confessione dici potest.

AD PRIMUM ergo dicendum quod contritio habet votum confessionis annexum. Et ideo eo modo liberat a culpa poenitentes sicut desiderium baptismi baptizandos.

AD SECUNDUM dicendum quod veniale non sumitur pro culpa, sed pro poena de facili expiabili. Unde non sequitur quod culpa in culpam convertatur, sed penitus annihilatur. Dicitur enim veniale tripliciter: uno modo ex genere, sicut verbum otiosum; alio modo ex causa, idest veniae causam in se habens, sicut peccatum ex infirmitate; alio modo ex eventu, sicut accipitur hic, quia per confessionem hoc evenit quod de culpa praeterita homo veniam consequatur.

confession and absolution he receives an increase of grace, and forgiveness of sins would also be granted to him, if his previous sorrow for sin was not sufficient for contrition, and if at the time he offered no obstacle to grace. Consequently, just as it is said of baptism that it delivers from death, so can it be said of confession.

REPLY OBJ. 1: Contrition has the desire of confession attached to it, and therefore it delivers penitents from death in the same way as the desire of baptism delivers those who are going to be baptized.

REPLY OBJ. 2: In the text venial does not designate guilt, but punishment that is easily expiated, and so it does not follow that one guilt is changed into another but that it is wholly done away. For 'venial' is taken in three senses: first, for what is venial generically, such as an idle word; second, for what is venial in its cause, for example, having within itself a motive of pardon, such as sins due to weakness; third, for what is venial in the result, in which sense it is understood here, because the result of confession is that man's past guilt is pardoned.

Article 2

Whether Confession Delivers from Punishment in Some Way?

AD SECUNDUM SIC PROCEDITUR. Videtur quod confessio non liberet aliquo modo a poena. Quia peccato non debetur nisi poena aeterna, vel temporalis. Sed poena aeterna per contritionem dimittitur, poena autem temporalis per satisfactionem. Ergo per confessionem nihil dimittitur de poena.

PRAETEREA, *voluntas pro facto reputatur*: ut in littera dicitur. Sed ille qui contritus est, habuit propositum confitendi. Ergo tantum valuit sibi sicut si fuisset confessus. Et ita per confessionem quam postea facit, nihil de poena dimittitur.

SED CONTRA, confessio poenam habet. Sed per omnia opera poenalia expiatur poena peccato debita. Ergo et per confessionem.

RESPONDEO dicendum quod confessio, simul cum absolutione, habet vim liberandi a poena dupliciter. Uno modo, ex ipsa vi absolutionis. Et sic quidem liberat, in voto existens, a poena aeterna, sicut etiam a culpa: quae quidem poena est condemnans et ex toto exterminans. A qua homo liberatus, adhuc manet obligatus ad poenam temporalem, secundum quod poena est medicina purgans et promovens. Et haec poena restat in purgatorio patienda etiam his qui a poena inferni liberati sunt. Quae quidem poena est improportionata viribus poenitentis in hoc mundo viventis: sed per vim clavium in tantum minuitur quod proportionata viribus poeniten-

OBJECTION 1: It would seem that confession in no way delivers from punishment. For sin deserves no punishment but what is either eternal or temporal. Now eternal punishment is remitted by contrition, and temporal punishment by satisfaction. Therefore, nothing of the punishment is remitted by confession.

OBJ. 2: Further, *the will is taken for the deed* (Cf. *Decretals*), as stated in the text (*Sentences* IV, D. 17). Now he that is contrite has the intention to confess. Hence his intention avails him as though he had already confessed, and so the confession which he makes afterwards remits no part of the punishment.

ON THE CONTRARY, Confession is a penal work. But all penal works expiate the punishment due to sin. Therefore, confession does also.

I ANSWER THAT, Confession together with absolution has the power to deliver from punishment for two reasons. First, from the power of absolution itself: and thus the very desire of absolution delivers a man from eternal punishment, as also from the guilt. Now this punishment is one of condemnation and total banishment, and when a man is delivered from that he still remains bound to a temporal punishment, insofar as punishment is a cleansing and perfecting remedy; and so this punishment remains to be suffered in purgatory by those who also have been delivered from the punishment of hell. Which temporal punishment is beyond the powers of the penitent dwelling in this world,

tis remanet, ita quod satisfaciendo se in hac vita purgare potest.

Alio modo diminuit poenam ex ipsa natura actus confitentis, qui habet poenam erubescentiae annexam. Et ideo quanto aliquis pluries de eisdem peccatis confitetur, tanto magis poena minuitur.

ET PER HOC patet responsio ad primum.

AD SECUNDUM dicendum quod voluntas pro facto non reputatur in his quae sunt ab alio, sicut est de baptismo: non enim tantum valet voluntas suscipiendi baptismum sicut ipsius susceptio. Sed reputatur voluntas pro facto in his quae sunt omnino ab homine. Et iterum quantum ad praemium essentiale: non autem quantum ad poenae remotionem et huiusmodi, respectu quorum attenditur meritum accidentaliter et secundario. Et ideo confessus et absolutus minus in purgatorio punietur quam contritus tantum.

but is so far diminished by the power of the keys that it is within the ability of the penitent, and he is able, by making satisfaction, to cleanse himself in this life.

Second, confession diminishes the punishment in virtue of the very nature of the act of the one who confesses, for this act has the punishment of shame attached to it, so that the more often one confesses the same sins, the more is the punishment diminished.

THIS SUFFICES for the reply to the first objection.

REPLY OBJ. 2: The will is not taken for the deed, if this is done by another, as in the case of baptism: for the will to receive baptism is not worth as much as the reception of baptism. But a man's will is taken for the deed when the latter is something done by him entirely. Again, this is true of the essential reward, but not of the removal of punishment and the like, which come under the head of accidental and secondary reward. Consequently, one who has confessed and received absolution will be less punished in purgatory than one who has gone no further than contrition.

Article 3

Whether Confession Opens Paradise?

AD TERTIUM SIC PROCEDITUR. Videtur quod confessio non *aperiat paradisum*. Quia diversorum diversi sunt effectus. Sed apertio paradisi effectus est baptismi. Ergo non est effectus confessionis.

PRAETEREA, in id quod clausum est, ante apertionem intrari non potest. Sed ante confessionem moriens paradisum intrare potest. Ergo confessio non aperit paradisum.

SED CONTRA, confessio facit hominem subiici Clavibus Ecclesiae. Sed per eas aperitur paradisus. Ergo et per confessionem.

RESPONDEO dicendum quod a paradisi introitu prohibetur aliquis per culpam et reatum poenae. Et quia haec impedimenta confessio amovet, ut ex dictis patet, ideo dicitur paradisum aperire.

AD PRIMUM ergo dicendum quod, quamvis baptismus et poenitentia sint diversa sacramenta, tamen agunt in vi unius passionis Christi, per quam aditus paradisi est apertus.

AD SECUNDUM dicendum quod ante votum confessionis paradisus clausus erat peccanti mortaliter, quamvis postea per contritionem, votum confessionis importantem, apertus sit etiam ante confessionem actualiter factam. Non tamen obstaculum reatus est totaliter amotum ante confessionem et satisfactionem.

OBJECTION 1: It would seem that confession does not *open paradise*. For different sacraments have different effects. But it is the effect of baptism to open paradise. Therefore, it is not the effect of confession.

OBJ. 2: Further, it is impossible to enter by a closed door before it be opened. But a dying man can enter heaven before making his confession. Therefore, confession does not open paradise.

ON THE CONTRARY, Confession makes a man submit to the keys of the Church. But paradise is opened by those keys. Therefore, it is opened by confession.

I ANSWER THAT, Guilt and the debt of punishment prevent a man from entering into paradise: and since confession removes these obstacles, as shown above (A. 1–2), it is said to open paradise.

REPLY OBJ. 1: Although baptism and penance are different sacraments, they act in virtue of Christ's one Passion, whereby a way was opened unto paradise.

REPLY OBJ. 2: If the dying man was in mortal sin, paradise was closed to him before he conceived the desire to confess his sin, although afterwards it was opened by contrition implying a desire for confession, even before he actually confessed. Nevertheless, the obstacle of the debt of punishment was not entirely removed before confession and satisfaction.

Article 4

Whether Confession Gives Hope of Salvation?

AD QUARTUM SIC PROCEDITUR. Videtur quod effectus confessionis poni non debeat quod *tribuit spem salutis*. Quia spes ex omnibus meritoriis actibus provenit. Et sic non videtur esse proprius effectus confessionis.

PRAETEREA, per tribulationem ad spem pervenimus: ut patet Rom. 5. Sed tribulationem homo praecipue in satisfactione sustinet. Ergo tribuere spem salutis magis est satisfactionis quam confessionis.

SED CONTRA, per confessionem homo fit *humilior et mitior*: sicut in littera Magister dicit. Sed per hoc homo accipit spem salutis. Ergo confessionis effectus est tribuere spem salutis.

RESPONDEO dicendum quod spes remissionis peccatorum non est nobis nisi per Christum. Et quia homo per confessionem se subiicit clavibus Ecclesiae ex passione Christi virtutem habentibus, ideo dicitur quod confessio spem salutis tribuit.

AD PRIMUM ergo dicendum quod ex actibus non potest esse spes salutis principaliter, sed ex gratia Redemptoris. Et quia confessio gratiae Redemptoris innititur, ideo spem salutis tribuit, non solum ut actus meritorius, sed ut pars sacramenti.

AD SECUNDUM dicendum quod tribulatio spem salutis tribuit per experimentum propriae virtutis, et purgationem a poena: sed confessio etiam modo praedicto.

OBJECTION 1: It would seem that *hope of salvation* should not be reckoned an effect of confession. For hope arises from all meritorious acts. Therefore, seemingly, it is not the proper effect of confession.

OBJ. 2: Further, we arrive at hope through tribulation, as appears from Romans 5:3–4. Now man suffers tribulation chiefly in satisfaction. Therefore, satisfaction rather than confession gives hope of salvation.

ON THE CONTRARY, Confession makes a man *more humble and more wary*, as the Master states in the text (*Sentences* IV, D. 17). But the result of this is that man conceives a hope of salvation. Therefore, it is the effect of confession to give hope of salvation.

I ANSWER THAT, We can have no hope for the forgiveness of our sins except through Christ: and since by confession a man submits to the keys of the Church, which derive their power from Christ's Passion, therefore do we say that confession gives hope of salvation.

REPLY OBJ. 1: It is not our actions, but the grace of our Redeemer, that is the principal cause of the hope of salvation: and since confession relies upon the grace of our Redeemer, it gives hope of salvation not only as a meritorious act, but also as part of a sacrament.

REPLY OBJ. 2: Tribulation gives hope of salvation by making us exercise our own virtue, and by paying off the debt of punishment: while confession does so also in the way mentioned above.

Article 5

Whether a General Confession Suffices to Blot Out Forgotten Mortal Sins?

AD QUINTUM SIC PROCEDITUR. Videtur quod confessio generalis non sufficiat ad delendum peccata mortalia oblita. Peccatum enim per confessionem deletum non est necesse iterum confiteri; si ergo peccata oblita per confessionem generalem dimitterentur, non esset necessarium quod, cum ad notitiam redeunt, aliquis ea confiteretur.

PRAETEREA, quicumque non est conscius alicuius peccati, vel non habet peccatum, vel est oblitus sui peccati. Si ergo per generalem confessionem peccata mortalia oblita dimittuntur, quicumque non est sibi conscius de aliquo peccato mortali, per generalem confessionem potest esse certus quod sit immunis a peccato mortali. Quod est contra Apostolum, I Cor. 4: *nihil mihi conscius sum, sed non in hoc iustificatus sum.*

OBJECTION 1: It would seem that a general confession does not suffice to blot out forgotten mortal sins. For there is no necessity to confess again a sin which has been blotted out by confession. If, therefore, forgotten sins were forgiven by a general confession, there would be no need to confess them when they are called to mind.

OBJ. 2: Further, whoever is not conscious of sin either is not guilty of sin, or has forgotten his sin. If, therefore, mortal sins are forgiven by a general confession, whoever is not conscious of a mortal sin can be certain that he is free from mortal sin whenever he makes a general confession: which is contrary to what the Apostle says, *I am not conscious to myself of anything, yet am I not hereby justified* (1 Cor 4:4).

PRAETEREA, nullus ex negligentia reportat commodum. Sed non potest esse sine negligentia quod aliquis peccatum mortale obliviscatur antequam ei dimittatur. Ergo non reportat ex hoc tale commodum quod sine speciali confessione de peccato ei dimittatur.

PRAETEREA, magis est elongatum a cognitione confitentis illud quod est omnino ignoratum, quam illud cuius est oblitus. Sed peccata per ignorantiam commissa generalis confessio non delet: quia tunc haeretici, qui nesciunt aliqua peccata, in quibus sunt, esse peccata, aut etiam aliqui simplices per generalem confessionem absolverentur; quod falsum est. Ergo generalis confessio non tollit peccata oblita.

SED CONTRA: Psalmus: *accedite ad eum et illuminamini, et facies vestrae non confundentur.* Sed iste qui confitetur omnia quae scit, accedit ad Deum quantum potest. Plus autem ab eo requiri non potest. Ergo non confunditur, ut repulsam patiatur, sed veniam consequitur.

PRAETEREA, ille qui confitetur veniam consequitur nisi sit fictus. Sed ille qui confitetur omnia peccata quae in memoria habet, aliquorum oblitus, non ex hoc est fictus: quia ignorantiam facti patitur, quae a peccato excusat. Ergo veniam consequitur. Et sic peccata quae oblita sunt relaxantur: *cum impium sit dimidiam sperare veniam.*

RESPONDEO dicendum quod confessio operatur praesupposita contritione, quae culpam delet. Et sic confessio directe ordinatur ad dimissionem poenae: quod quidem facit et ex erubescentia quam habet; et ex vi clavium, quibus se confitens subiicit. Contingit autem quandoque quod per contritionem praecedentem peccatum aliquod deletum est quoad culpam, sive in generali, si eius memoria tunc non habebatur, sive in speciali, et tamen ante confessionem aliquis illius peccati oblitus est. Et tunc confessio generalis sacramentalis operatur ad dimissionem poenae ex vi clavium, quibus se confitens subiicit nullum obstaculum, quantum in ipso est, ponens. Sed ex illa parte qua erubescentia confessionis peccati poenam minuebat, poena ipsius de quo quis specialiter coram sacerdote non erubuit, non est diminuta.

AD PRIMUM ergo dicendum quod in confessione sacramentali non solum requiritur absolutio, sed iudicium sacerdotis satisfactionem imponentis. Et ideo, quamvis iste absolutione sit functus, tamen tenetur confiteri ut suppleatur quod defuit sacramentali confessioni.

AD SECUNDUM dicendum quod confessio non operatur, ut dictum est, nisi contritione praesupposita. De qua quando vera fuerit, non potest aliquis scire: sicut nec scire potest an gratiam habeat per certitudinem. Et ideo non potest scire utrum per confessionem genera-

OBJ. 3: Further, no man profits by neglect. Now a man cannot forget a mortal sin before it is forgiven him without neglect. Therefore, he does not profit by his forgetfulness so that the sin is forgiven him without special mention of it in confession.

OBJ. 4: Further, that which the penitent knows nothing about is further from his knowledge than that which he has forgotten. Now a general confession does not blot out sins committed through ignorance, else heretics, who are not aware that certain things they have done are sinful, and certain simple people would be absolved by a general confession, which is false. Therefore, a general confession does not take away forgotten sins.

ON THE CONTRARY, It is written: *come to him and be enlightened, and your faces shall not be confounded* (Ps 33:6). Now he who confesses all the sins of which he is conscious approaches to God as much as he can: nor can more be required of him. Therefore, he will not be confounded by being repelled, but will be forgiven.

FURTHER, He that confesses is pardoned unless he be insincere. But he who confesses all the sins that he calls to mind is not insincere through forgetting some, because he suffers from ignorance of fact, which excuses from sin. Therefore, he receives forgiveness, and then the sins which he has forgotten, are loosened, since *it is wicked to hope for half a pardon* (*Sentences* IV, Dist. 15).

I ANSWER THAT, Confession produces its effect on the presupposition that there is contrition which blots out guilt: so that confession is directly ordained to the remission of punishment, which it causes in virtue of the shame which it includes, and by the power of the keys, to which a man submits by confessing. Now it happens sometimes that by previous contrition a sin has been blotted out as to the guilt, either in a general way (if it was not remembered at the time) or in particular (and yet is forgotten before confession), and then general sacramental confession works for the remission of the punishment in virtue of the keys, to which man submits by confessing, provided he offers no obstacle so far as he is concerned. Yet so far as the shame of confessing a sin diminishes its punishment, the punishment is not diminished for that man who does not express his shame for a sin before the priest.

REPLY OBJ. 1: In sacramental confession, not only is absolution required, but also the judgment of the priest who imposes satisfaction is awaited. Therefore, although the latter has given absolution, nevertheless the penitent is bound to confess in order to supply what was wanting to the sacramental confession.

REPLY OBJ. 2: As stated above, confession does not produce its effect, unless contrition be presupposed; concerning which no man can know whether it be true contrition, even as neither can one know for certain if he has grace. Consequently, a man cannot know for certain

lem sit sibi peccatum oblitum dimissum per certitudinem: quamvis possit per coniecturas aliquas aestimare.

AD TERTIUM dicendum quod iste non reportat commodum ex negligentia. Quia non ita plenam remissionem consequitur sicut alias consecutus fuisset. Nec tantum meretur. Et tenetur iterum confiteri cum ad memoriam peccatum venerit.

AD QUARTUM dicendum quod ignorantia iuris non excusat, quia ipsa peccatum est: sed ignorantia facti excusat. Unde aliquis de hoc quod non confitetur peccata; quae nescit esse peccata propter ignorantiam iuris divini, non excusatur a fictione. Excusaretur autem si nesciret ea esse peccata propter ignorantiam particularis circumstantiae: sicut si cognovit alienam quam credidit esse suam. Sed oblivio de actu peccati habet ignorantiam facti. Et ideo excusat a peccato fictionis in confessione, quod fructum absolutionis et confessionis impedit.

whether a forgotten sin has been forgiven him in a general confession, although he may think so on account of certain conjectural signs.

REPLY OBJ. 3: He does not profit by his neglect, since he does not receive such full pardon as he would otherwise have received, nor is his merit so great. Moreover, he is bound to confess the sin when he calls it to mind.

REPLY OBJ. 4: Ignorance of the law does not excuse, because it is a sin by itself: but ignorance of fact does excuse. Therefore, if a man omits to confess a sin because he does not know it to be a sin through ignorance of the divine law, he is not excused from insincerity. On the other hand, he would be excused if he did not know it to be a sin through being unaware of some particular circumstance, for instance, if he knew another's wife, thinking her his own. Now forgetfulness of an act of sin comes under the head of ignorance of fact, wherefore it excuses from the sin of insincerity in confession, which is an obstacle to the fruit of absolution and confession.

QUESTION 11

THE SEAL OF CONFESSION

Deinde quaeritur de sigillo confessionis.

Et circa hoc quaeruntur quinque.

Primo: utrum in quolibet casu teneatur homo celare ea quae habet sub sigillo confessionis.

Secundo: utrum sigillum confessionis se extendat ad alia quam illa quae sunt de confessione.

Tertio: utrum solus sacerdos sigillum confessionis habeat.

Quarto: utrum sacerdos possit aliis revelarer de licentia confitentis.

Quinto: utrum teneatur ea celare etiam si aliter ea noverit.

We must now inquire about the seal of confession.

Under this head there are five points of inquiry:

(1) Whether in every case a man is bound to hide what he knows under the seal of confession?

(2) Whether the seal of confession extends to other matters than those which have reference to confession?

(3) Whether the priest alone is bound by the seal of confession?

(4) Whether, by permission of the penitent, the priest can make known to another a sin of his which he knew under the seal of confession?

(5) Whether he is bound to hide even what he knows through other sources besides?

Article 1

Whether in Every Case the Priest Is Bound to Hide the Sins
Which He Knows Under the Seal of Confession?

AD PRIMUM SIC PROCEDITUR. Videtur quod non in quolibet casu teneatur sacerdos celare peccata quae sub sigillo confessionis novit. Quia, sicut dicit Bernardus, *quod est institutum pro caritate, contra caritatem non militat*. Sed celatio confessionis in aliquo casu contra caritatem militaret: sicut si aliquis in confessione scit aliquem haereticum, quem non potest inducere ad hoc quod desistat a corruptione plebis; et similiter de illo qui scit per confessionem affinitatem esse inter aliquos qui contrahere volunt. Ergo talis debet confessionem revelare.

PRAETEREA, illud ad quod quis obligatur ex praecepto Ecclesiae tantum, non est necesse observari mandato Ecclesiae in contrarium facto. Sed celatio confessionis est introducta ex statuto Ecclesiae tantum. Si ergo per Ecclesiam praecipiatur quod quicumque scit aliquid de tali peccato dicat, ille qui scit per confessionem debet dicere.

PRAETEREA, magis debet homo conservare conscientiam suam quam famam alterius: quia caritas ordinata est. Sed aliquando aliquis peccatum celans incurrit propriae conscientiae damnum: sicut cum in testimonium adducitur pro peccato illo et iurare cogitur de veritate dicenda; vel cum aliquis abbas scit per confessio-

OBJECTION 1: It would seem that the priest is not bound in every case to hide the sins which he knows under the seal of confession. For, as Bernard says (*De Proecep. et Dispens.* II), *that which is instituted for the sake of charity does not militate against charity*. Now the secret of confession would militate against charity in certain cases: for instance, if a man knew through confession that a certain man was a heretic, whom he cannot persuade to desist from misleading the people; or, in like manner, if a man knew, through confession, that certain people who wish to marry are related to one another. Therefore, such ought to reveal what they know through confession.

OBJ. 2: Further, that which is obligatory solely on account of a precept of the Church need not be observed, if the commandment be changed to the contrary. Now the secret of confession was introduced solely by a precept of the Church. If, therefore, the Church were to prescribe that anyone who knows anything about such and such a sin must make it known, a man that had such knowledge through confession would be bound to speak.

OBJ. 3: Further, a man is bound to safeguard his conscience rather than the good name of another, because there is order in charity. Now it happens sometimes that a man by hiding a sin injures his own conscience—for instance, if he be called upon to give witness of a sin of which he has knowledge through confession, and is forced

75

nem alicuius prioris subiecti sibi peccatum cuius occasio inducit ipsum ad ruinam si ei prioratum dimittat, unde tenetur ei auferre propter debitum pastoralis curae, auferendo autem videtur confessionem publicare. Ergo videtur quod in aliquo casu liceat confessionem publicare.

PRAETEREA, aliquis sacerdos per confessionem alicuius quam audit, potest accipere conscientiam quod sit praelatione indignus. Sed quilibet tenetur contradicere promotioni indignorum, si sua intersit. Cum ergo contradicendo suspicionem inducere videatur de peccato, et sic quodammodo confessionem revelare, videtur quod quandoque oporteat confessionem revelare.

SED CONTRA: Est quod dicit *Decretalis de Poenitentia et Remissione: caveat sacerdos ne verbo vel signo vel alio quovis modo prodat aliquatenus peccatorem.*

PRAETEREA, sacerdos debet Deo, cuius minister est, conformari. Sed Deus peccata quae per confessionem panduntur non revelat, sed tegit. Ergo nec sacerdos revelare debet.

RESPONDEO dicendum quod in sacramentis ea quae exterius geruntur sunt signa rerum quae interius contingunt. Et ideo confessio qua quis sacerdoti se subiicit, signum est interioris, qua quis Deo subiicitur. Deus autem peccatum illius qui se sibi subiicit per poenitentiam, tegit. Unde et hoc oportet in sacramento poenitentiae significari. Et ideo de necessitate sacramenti est quod quis confessionem celet; et tanquam violator sacramenti peccat qui confessionem revelat. Et praeter hoc sunt: aliae utilitates huius celationis: quia per hoc homines magis ad confessionem attrahuntur; et simplicius etiam peccata confitentur.

AD PRIMUM ergo dicendum quod quidam dicunt quod sacerdos non tenetur servare sub sigillo confessionis nisi peccata de quibus poenitens emendationem promittit: aliter potest ea dicere ei qui potest prodesse et non obesse.

Sed haec opinio videtur erronea: cum sit contra veritatem sacramenti. Sicut enim baptismus est sacramentum quamvis quis fictus accedat, nec est immutatum aliquid propter hoc de essentialibus sacramenti; ita confessio non desinit esse sacramentalis quamvis ille qui confitetur emendationem non proponat. Et ideo nihilominus sub occulto tenendum est.

Nec tamen sigillum confessionis contra caritatem militat. Quia caritas non requirit quod opponatur remedium peccato quod homo nescit. Illud autem quod sub confessione scitur est quasi nescitum: cum illud nesciat ut homo, sed ut Deus.

to swear to tell the truth—or when an abbot knows through confession the sin of a prior who is subject to him, which sin would be an occasion of ruin to the latter, if he suffers him to retain his priorship, wherefore he is bound to deprive him of the dignity of his pastoral charge, and yet in depriving him he seem to divulge the secret of confession. Therefore, it seems that in certain cases it is lawful to reveal a confession.

OBJ. 4: Further, it is possible for a priest through hearing a man's confession to be conscious that the latter is unworthy of ecclesiastical preferment. Now everyone is bound to prevent the promotion of the unworthy, if it is his business. Since, then, by raising an objection he seems to raise a suspicion of sin, and so to reveal the confession somewhat, it seems that it is necessary sometimes to divulge a confession.

ON THE CONTRARY, The *Decretals* says (*On Repentance and Remission of Sins*): *let the priest beware lest he betray the sinner, by word, or sign, or in any other way whatever.*

FURTHER, The priest should conform himself to God, whose minister he is. But God does not reveal the sins which are made known to him in confession, but hides them. Neither, therefore, should the priest reveal them.

I ANSWER THAT, Those things which are done outwardly in the sacraments are the signs of what takes place inwardly: wherefore confession, whereby a man subjects himself to a priest, is a sign of the inward submission whereby one submits to God. Now God hides the sins of those who submit to him by penance; wherefore this also should be signified in the sacrament of penance, and consequently the sacrament demands that the confession should remain hidden, and he who divulges a confession sins by violating the sacrament. Besides this there are other advantages in this secrecy, because thereby men are more attracted to confession, and confess their sins with greater simplicity.

REPLY OBJ. 1: Some say that the priest is not bound by the seal of confession to hide other sins than those in respect of which the penitent promises amendment; otherwise he may reveal them to one who can be a help and not a hindrance.

But this opinion seems erroneous, since it is contrary to the truth of the sacrament; for just as though the person baptized be insincere, yet his baptism is a sacrament, and there is no change in the essentials of the sacrament on that account, so confession does not cease to be sacramental although he that confesses does not purpose amendment. Therefore, this notwithstanding, it must be held secret.

Neither does the seal of confession militate against charity on that account, because charity does not require a man to find a remedy for a sin which he knows not: and that which is known in confession, is, as it were, unknown, since a man knows it, not as man, but as God.

Tamen aliquod remedium adhibere debet in praedictis casibus, quantum potest sine revelatione confessionis: sicut monendo eos qui confitentur, et aliis diligentiam apponendo ne corrumpantur per haeresim. Potest etiam dicere praelato quod diligentius vigilet super gregem suum: ita tamen quod non dicat aliquid quod verbo vel nutu confitentem prodat.

AD SECUNDUM dicendum quod praeceptum de confessione servanda consequitur ipsum sacramentum. Et ideo, sicut praeceptum de confessione sacramentali facienda est de iure divino, et non potest aliqua dispensatione vel iussione humana homo absolvi ab eo, ita nullus ad revelationem confessionis potest ab homine cogi vel licentiari. Unde, si praecipiatur sub poena excommunicationis iam latae quod dicat si aliquid scit de tali peccato, non debet dicere: quia debet aestimare quod intentio praecipientis est, si sciat ut homo. Et si etiam exprimeret de confessione, interrogatus non deberet dicere. Nec excommunicationem incurreret: quia non est subiectus superiori suo nisi ut homo; hoc autem non scit ut homo, sed ut Deus.

AD TERTIUM dicendum quod homo non adducitur in testimonium nisi ut homo. Et ideo sine laesione conscientiae potest iurare se nescire quod scit tantum ut Deus.

Similiter etiam potest praelatus sine laesione conscientiae impunitum dimittere peccatum quod scit tantum ut Deus, vel sine aliquo remedio. Quia non tenetur adhibere remedium nisi eo modo quo ad ipsum refertur. Unde in his quae ad ipsum deferuntur in foro poenitentiae, debet in eodem foro, inquantum potest, adhibere remedium: ut abbas in casu praedicto admoneat eum ut prioratui resignet. Vel, si noluerit, potest ex aliqua alia occasione absolvere eum a cura prioratus: ita tamen quod omnis suspicio vitetur de confessionis revelatione.

AD QUARTUM dicendum quod ex multis aliis causis redditur aliquis indignus ad praelationis officium quam ex peccato: sicut ex defectu scientiae vel aetatis, vel alicuius huiusmodi. Et ideo, qui contradicit, nec suspicionem de crimine facit, nec confessionem revelat.

Nevertheless, in the cases quoted one should apply some kind of remedy, so far as this can be done without divulging the confession, e.g., by admonishing the penitent, and by watching over the others lest they be corrupted by heresy. He can also tell the prelate to watch over his flock with great care, yet so as by neither word nor sign to betray the penitent.

REPLY OBJ. 2: The precept concerning the secret of confession follows from the sacrament itself. Therefore, just as the obligation of making a sacramental confession is of divine law, so that no human dispensation or command can absolve one from it, even so no man can be forced or permitted by another man to divulge the secret of confession. Consequently, if he be commanded under pain of excommunication to be incurred *ipso facto*, to say whether he knows anything about such and such a sin, he ought not to say it, because he should assume that the intention of the person in commanding him thus, was that he should say what he knew as man. And even if he were expressly interrogated about a confession, he ought to say nothing, nor would he incur the excommunication, for he is not subject to his superior save as a man, and he knows this not as a man, but as God.

REPLY OBJ. 3: A man is not called upon to witness except as a man, wherefore without wronging his conscience he can swear that he does not know what he knows only as God.

In like manner, a superior can, without wronging his conscience, leave a sin unpunished which he knows only as God, or he may forbear to apply a remedy, since he is not bound to apply a remedy except according as it comes to his knowledge. Wherefore with regard to matters which come to his knowledge in the tribunal of penance, he should apply the remedy, as far as he can, in the same court: thus as to the case in point, the abbot should advise the prior to resign his office, and if the latter refuse, he can absolve him from the priorship on some other occasion, yet so as to avoid all suspicion of divulging the confession.

REPLY OBJ. 4: A man is rendered unworthy of ecclesiastical preferment by many other causes besides sin, for instance, by lack of knowledge, age, or the like: so that by raising an objection one does not raise a suspicion of crime or divulge the secret of confession.

Article 2

Whether the Seal of Confession Extends to Other Matters Than Those Which Have Reference to Confession?

AD SECUNDUM SIC PROCEDITUR. Videtur quod sigillum confessionis se extendat ad alia quam illa quae sunt de confessione. Quia de confessione non sunt nisi

OBJECTION 1: It would seem that the seal of confession extends to other matters besides those which have reference to confession. For sins alone have reference to

peccata. Sed aliquando cum peccatis alia multa quis narrat, quae ad confessionem non pertinent. Ergo, cum illa sacerdoti dicantur ut Deo, videtur quod etiam ad illa sigillum confessionis se extendat.

PRAETEREA, aliquando aliquis dicit alicui aliquod secretum, et ille recipit, *sub sigillo confessionis*. Ergo sigillum confessionis se extendit ad illa quae non sunt de confessione.

SED CONTRA, sigillum confessionis est aliquid annexum sacramentali confessioni. Sed ea quae annexa sunt alicui sacramento, non se extendunt ultra sacramentum illud. Ergo sigillum confessionis non se extendit nisi ad ea de quibus est confessio.

RESPONDEO dicendum quod sigillum confessionis directe non se extendit nisi ad illa de quibus est sacramentalis confessio. Sed indirecte id quod non cadit sub sacramentali confessione, etiam ad sigillum confessionis pertinet: sicut illa per quae posset peccator vel peccatum deprehendi. Nihilominus tamen alia summo studio sunt celanda: tum propter scandalum; tum propter pronitatem quae ex consuetudine accidere posset.

ET PER HOC patet responsio ad primum.

AD SECUNDUM dicendum quod aliquis non debet de facili aliquid recipere hoc modo. Si tamen recipiat, tenetur ex promissione hoc modo celare ac si in confessione haberet: quamvis sub sigillo confessionis non habeat.

confession. Now sometimes besides sins other matters are told which have no reference to confession. Therefore, since such things are told to the priest as to God, it seems that the seal of confession extends to them also.

OBJ. 2: Further, sometimes one person tells another a secret, which the latter receives *under the seal of confession*. Therefore, the seal of confession extends to matters having no relation to confession.

ON THE CONTRARY, The seal of confession is connected with sacramental confession. But those things which are connected with a sacrament do not extend outside the bounds of the sacrament. Therefore, the seal of confession does not extend to matters other than those which have reference to sacramental confession.

I ANSWER THAT, The seal of confession does not extend directly to other matters than those which have reference to sacramental confession, yet indirectly matters also which are not connected with sacramental confession are affected by the seal of confession, those, for instance, which might lead to the discovery of a sinner or of his sin. Nevertheless, these matters also must be most carefully hidden, both on account of scandal and to avoid leading others into sin through their becoming familiar with it.

THIS SUFFICES for the reply to the first objection.

REPLY OBJ. 2: A confidence ought not easily to be accepted in this way: but if it be done the secret must be kept in the way promised, as though one had the secret in confession, though not under the seal of confession.

Article 3

Whether the Priest Alone is Bound by the Seal of Confession?

AD TERTIUM SIC PROCEDITUR. Videtur quod non solum sacerdos sigillum confessionis habeat. Quia aliquando aliquis confitetur sacerdoti per interpretem, necessitate urgente. Sed interpres, ut videtur, tenetur confessionem celare. Ergo etiam non-sacerdos aliquid sub sigillo confessionis habet.

PRAETEREA, aliquando aliquis in casu necessitatis potest laico confiteri. Sed ille tenetur peccata celare: cum sibi dicantur sicut Deo. Ergo non solum sacerdos sigillum confessionis habet.

PRAETEREA, aliquando aliquis se sacerdotem fingit ut conscientiam alicuius exploret per hanc fraudem. Et ille etiam, ut videtur, peccat si confessionem revelet. Ergo non solum sacerdos sigillum confessionis habet.

SED CONTRA: Solus sacerdos minister est huius sacramenti. Sed sigillum confessionis est annexum huic

OBJECTION 1: It would seem that not only the priest is bound by the seal of confession. For sometimes a priest hears a confession through an interpreter, if there be an urgent reason for so doing. But it seems that the interpreter is bound to keep the confession secret. Therefore, one who is not a priest knows something under the seal of confession.

OBJ. 2: Further, it is possible sometimes in cases of urgency for a layman to hear a confession. But he is bound to secrecy with regard to those sins, since they are told to him as to God. Therefore, not only the priest is bound by the seal of confession.

OBJ. 3: Further, it may happen that a man pretends to be a priest, so that by this deceit he may know what is on another's conscience: and it would seem that he also sins if he divulges the confession. Therefore, not only the priest is bound by the seal of confession.

ON THE CONTRARY, A priest alone is the minister of this sacrament. But the seal of confession is connected with

sacramento. Ergo solus sacerdos habet sigillum confessionis.

PRAETEREA, homo tenetur ea quae in confessione audit celare, si non scit ea ut homo, sed ut Deus. Sed solus sacerdos est minister Dei. Ergo solus sacerdos tenetur occultare.

RESPONDEO dicendum quod sigillum confessionis competit sacerdoti inquantum est minister huius sacramenti: quod nihil est aliud quam debitum confessionem celandi, sicut clavis est potestas absolvendi. Tamen, sicut aliquis qui non est sacerdos, in, aliquo casu participat aliquid de actu clavis, dum confessionem audit propter necessitatem; ita etiam participat aliquid de actu sigilli confessionis, et tenetur celare; quamvis, proprie loquendo, sigillum confessionis non habeat.

ET PER HOC patet solutio ad obiecta.

this sacrament. Therefore, the priest alone is bound by the seal of confession.

FURTHER, The reason why a man is bound to keep secret what he hears in confession is because he knows them not as man, but as God. But the priest alone is God's minister. Therefore, he alone is bound to secrecy.

I ANSWER THAT, The seal of confession affects the priest as minister of this sacrament: which seal is nothing else than the obligation of keeping the confession secret, even as the key is the power of absolving. Yet as one who is not a priest in a particular case has a kind of share in the act of the keys (when he hears a confession in a case of urgency) so also does he have a certain share in the act of the seal of confession, and is bound to secrecy, though properly speaking he is not bound by the seal of confession.

THIS SUFFICES for the replies to the objections.

Article 4

Whether by the Penitent's Permission a Priest May Reveal to Another a Sin
Which He Knows Under the Seal of Confession?

AD QUARTUM SIC PROCEDITUR. Videtur quod de licentia confitentis non possit sacerdos peccatum quod habet sub sigillo confessionis, alteri prodere. Quod enim non potest superior, non potest inferior. Sed Papa non posset aliquem licentiare quod peccatum quod habet in confessione, alteri proderet. Ergo nec ille qui confitetur potest ipsum licentiare.

PRAETEREA, illud quod est institutum propter bonum commune, non potest ex arbitrio unius mutari. Sed celatio confessionis est instituta propter bonum totius Ecclesiae, ut homines confidentius ad confessionem accedant. Ergo ille qui confitetur non potest licentiare sacerdotem ad dicendum.

PRAETEREA, si possit licentiari sacerdos, videtur dari *pallium malitiae* malis sacerdotibus: quia possent praetendere sibi licentiam datam, et sic impune peccarent. Quod est inconveniens. Et sic videtur quod non possit a confitente licentiari.

PRAETEREA, ille cui iste revelabit, non habebit peccatum hoc sub sigillo confessionis. Et sic poterit peccatum publicari quod iam deletum est. Quod est inconveniens. Ergo non potest licentiare.

SED CONTRA: Superior potest mittere peccatorem cum litteris ad inferiorem sacerdotem de voluntate ipsius. Ergo de voluntate confitentis potest sacerdos peccatum revelare alteri.

PRAETEREA, *qui potest aliquid facere per se, potest etiam per alterum facere*. Sed confitens potest peccatum

OBJECTION 1: It would seem that a priest may not, by the penitent's permission, reveal to another a sin which he knows under the seal of confession. For an inferior may not do what his superior may not. Now the Pope cannot give permission for anyone to divulge a sin which he knows through confession. Neither, therefore, can the penitent give him such a permission.

OBJ. 2: Further, that which is instituted for the common good of the Church cannot be changed at the will of an individual. Now the secrecy of confession was instituted for the good of the whole Church, in order that men might have greater confidence in approaching the confessional. Therefore, the penitent cannot allow the priest to divulge his confession.

OBJ. 3: Further, if the priest could grant such a permission, this would seem to *palliate the wickedness* of bad priests, for they might pretend to have received the permission and so they might sin with impunity, which would be unbecoming. Therefore, it seems that the penitent cannot grant this permission.

OBJ. 4: Further, the one to whom this sin is divulged does not know that sin under the seal of confession. Thus he may publish a sin which is already blotted out, which is unbecoming. Therefore, this permission cannot be granted.

ON THE CONTRARY, If the sinner consent, a superior may refer him by letter to an inferior priest. Therefore, with the consent of the penitent the priest may reveal a sin of his to another.

FURTHER, *Whosoever can do a thing of his own authority, can do it through another*. But the penitent can by his

suum quod fecit, per se alteri revelare. Ergo potest per sacerdotem facere.

Respondeo dicendum quod duo sunt propter quae tenetur sacerdos peccatum occultare: primo, et principaliter, quia ipsa occultatio est de essentia sacramenti, inquantum scit illud ut Deus, cuius vicem gerit ad confessionem; alio modo, propter scandalum vitandum. Potest autem confitens facere quod sacerdos illud quod sciebat ut Deus, sciat etiam ut homo: quod facit dum licentiat eum ad dicendum. Et ideo, si dicat, non frangit sigillum confessionis. Tamen debet vitare scandalum dicendo: ne fractor sigilli praedicti reputetur.

Ad primum ergo dicendum quod Papa non potest licentiare sacerdotem ad dicendum, quia non potest facere quod illud sciat ut homo. Quod tamen facere potest ille qui confitetur.

Ad secundum dicendum quod non tollitur illud quod est institutum propter bonum commune: quia sigillum confessionis non frangitur, quia dicitur quod alio modo scitur.

Ad tertium dicendum quod ex hoc non datur aliqua impunitas malis sacerdotibus: quia imminet eis probatio, si accusantur, quod de licentia confitentis revelaverunt.

Ad quartum dicendum quod ille ad quem notitia peccati devenit mediante sacerdote de voluntate confitentis, participat in aliquo actu sacerdotis. Et ideo simile est de eo et de interprete: nisi forte peccator velit quod ille absolute sciat et libere.

own authority reveal his sin to another. Therefore, he can do it through the priest.

I answer that, There are two reasons for which the priest is bound to keep a sin secret: first and chiefly, because this very secrecy is essential to the sacrament, insofar as the priest knows that sin as it is known to God, whose place he holds in confession: second, in order to avoid scandal. Now the penitent can make the priest know, as a man, what he knew before only as God knows it, and he does this when he allows him to divulge it: so that if the priest does reveal it, he does not break the seal of confession. Nevertheless he should beware of giving scandal by revealing the sin, lest he be deemed to have broken the seal.

Reply Obj. 1: The Pope cannot permit a priest to divulge a sin, because he cannot make him to know it as a man, whereas he that has confessed it, can.

Reply Obj. 2: When that is told which was known through another source, that which is instituted for the common good is not taken away, because the seal of confession is not broken.

Reply Obj. 3: This does not bestow impunity on wicked priests, because they are in danger of having to prove that they had the penitent's permission to reveal the sin, if they should be accused of the contrary.

Reply Obj. 4: He that is informed of a sin through the priest with the penitent's consent shares in an act of the priest's, so that the same applies to him as to an interpreter, unless perchance the penitent wish him to know it unconditionally and freely.

Article 5

Whether a Man May Reveal That Which He Knows Through Confession and Through Some Other Source Besides?

Ad quintum sic proceditur. Videtur quod illud quod quis scit per confessionem et etiam alio modo, nullo modo possit alteri revelare. Non enim frangitur sigillum confessionis nisi dum peccatum quod scitur in confessione revelatur. Si ergo iste revelat peccatum quod in confessione audivit, qualitercumque alias sciat, sigillum confessionis frangere videtur.

Praeterea, quicumque confessionem alicuius audit, ei obligatur ad hoc quod peccata ipsius non revelet. Sed si aliquis promitteret alicui tenere privatum quod ei dicitur, quantumcumque post sciret, deberet privatum tenere. Ergo quod quis in confessione audivit, quantumcumque alias sciat, debet privatum haberi.

Praeterea, duorum quod est altero potentius trahit ad se reliquum. Sed scientia qua scit peccatum ut

Objection 1: It would seem that a man may not reveal what he knows through confession and through some other source besides. For the seal of confession is not broken unless one reveals a sin known through confession. If, therefore, a man divulges a sin which he knows through confession, no matter how he knows it otherwise, he seems to break the seal.

Obj. 2: Further, whoever hears someone's confession is under obligation to him not to divulge his sins. Now if one were to promise someone to keep something secret, he would be bound to do so, even if he knew it through some other source. Therefore, a man is bound to keep secret what he knows through the confession, no matter how he knows it otherwise.

Obj. 3: Further, the stronger of two things draws the other to itself. Now the knowledge whereby a man knows

Deus, est potentior et dignior scientia qua scit peccatum ut homo. Ergo trahit ad se eam. Et ita non poterit revelari: secundum quod scientia qua scit ut Deus, exigit.

PRAETEREA, secretum confessionis institutum est ad vitandum scandalum, et ne homines a confessionibus retrahantur. Sed si aliquis posset dicere illud quod in confessione audivit, etiam si aliter sciret, nihilominus scandalum sequeretur. Ergo nullo modo potest dicere.

SED CONTRA: Nullus potest alium obligare ad quod non erat obligatus, nisi sit suus praelatus, qui obliget eum praecepto. Sed ille qui sciebat alicuius peccatum per visum, non erat obligatus ad celandum. Ergo ille qui ei confitetur, cum non sit praelatus suus, non potest eum obligare ad celandum per hoc quod ei confitetur.

PRAETEREA, secundum hoc posset impediri iustitia Ecclesiae, si aliquis, ut evaderet sententiam excommunicationis quae in ipsum ferenda erat propter aliquod peccatum de quo convictus est, confitetur ei qui sententiam ferre debet. Sed iustitiae executio est in praecepto. Ergo non tenetur celare peccatum quod quis in confessione audivit, si alias ipsum scit.

RESPONDEO dicendum quod circa hoc est triplex opinio. Quidam enim dicunt quod illud quod in confessione aliquis audivit, non potest aliquo modo dicere si sciat alias, sive ante sive post. Quidam vero dicunt quod per confessionem praecluditur sibi via ne possit aliquid dicere quod prius scivit: non autem quin possit dicere si post alio modo sciat.

Utraque autem opinio, dum nimium sigillo confessionis attribuit, praeiudicium veritati et iustitiae servandae facit. Posset enim aliquis ad peccandum esse pronior si non timeret ab illo accusari cui confessus est, si coram illo peccatum iteraret. Similiter etiam multum iustitiae perire poterit si testimonium ferre aliquis non posset de eo quod vidit, post confessionem de hoc factam. Nec obstat quod quidam dicunt, quod debet protestari se non tenere privatum hoc. Quia hoc non posset protestari nisi postquam peccatum esset sibi dictum. Et tunc quilibet sacerdos posset revelare peccatum, protestationem faciendo, si hoc ipsum ad revelandum liberum redderet.

Et ideo alia opinio est, et verior, quod illud quod homo alias scit, sive ante confessionem sive post, non tenetur celare quantum ad id quod scit ut homo: potest enim dicere, *scio illud quia vidi*. Tenetur tamen celare illud inquantum scit ut Deus: non enim potest hoc dicere, *ego audivi hoc in confessione*. Tamen, propter scandalum vitandum, debet abstinere ne de hoc loquatur, nisi immineat necessitas.

AD PRIMUM ergo dicendum quod, quando aliquis dicit se vidisse quod in confessione audivit, non revelat

a sin as God is stronger and more excellent than the knowledge whereby he knows a sin as man. Therefore, it draws the latter to itself: and consequently a man cannot reveal that sin, because this is demanded by his knowing it as God.

OBJ. 4: Further, the secrecy of confession was instituted in order to avoid scandal, and to prevent men being shy of going to confession. But if a man might say what he had heard in confession, though he knew it otherwise, scandal would result all the same. Therefore, he can by no means say what he has heard.

ON THE CONTRARY, No one can put another under a new obligation unless he is his superior, who can bind him by a precept. But he who knew of a sin by witnessing it was not bound to keep it secret. Therefore, he that confesses to him, not being his superior, cannot put him under an obligation of secrecy by confessing to him.

FURTHER, The justice of the Church would be hindered if a man, in order to escape a sentence of excommunication incurred on account of some sin of which he has been convicted, were to confess to the person who has to sentence him. Now, the execution of justice falls under a precept. Therefore, a man is not bound to keep a sin secret which he has heard in confession but knows from some other source.

I ANSWER THAT, There are three opinions about this question. For some say that a man can by no means tell another what he has heard in confession, even if he knew it from some other source either before or after the confession: while others assert that the confession debars him from speaking of what he knew already, but not from saying what he knew afterwards and in another way.

Now both these opinions, by exaggerating the seal of confession, are prejudicial to the truth and to the safeguarding of justice. For a man might be more inclined to sin if he had no fear of being accused by his confessor supposing that he repeated the sin in his presence: and furthermore it would be most prejudicial to justice if a man could not bear witness to a deed which he has seen committed again after being confessed to him. Nor does it matter that, as some say, he ought to declare that he cannot keep it secret, for he cannot make such a declaration until the sin has already been confessed to him, and then every priest could, if he wished, divulge a sin, by making such a declaration, if this made him free to divulge it.

Consequently, there is a third and truer opinion, namely that what a man knows through another source either before or after confession, he is not bound to keep secret insofar as he knows it as a man, for he can say: *I know so and so since I saw it.* But he is bound to keep it secret insofar as he knows it as God knows it, for he cannot say: *I heard so and so in confession.* Nevertheless, on account of the scandal he should refrain from speaking of it unless there is an urgent reason.

REPLY OBJ. 1: If a man says that he has seen what he has heard in the confessional, he does not reveal what he

quod in confessione habet nisi per accidens. Sicut qui scit aliquid per auditum et visum, non revelat quod vidit, per se loquendo, si dicat se audivisse; sed per accidens, quia dicit auditum cui accidit visum esse. Et ideo talis sigillum confessionis non frangit.

AD SECUNDUM dicendum quod non obligatur audiens confessionem quod non revelet peccatum simpliciter: sed prout est in confessione auditum. Nullo enim casu dicere debet se audivisse in confessione.

AD TERTIUM quod hoc intelligendum est de duobus quae habent oppositionem. Sed scientia qua scit aliquis peccatum ut Deus, et illa qua scit ut homo, non sunt opposita. Ideo ratio non procedit.

AD QUARTUM dicendum quod non debet ita vitari peccatum ex una parte quod ex alia iustitia relinquatur: *veritas* enim *non est propter scandalum dimittenda*. Et ideo, quando imminet periculum iustitiae, non debet dimitti revelatio eius quod quis in confessione audivit, si aliter scit, propter scandalum: dum tamen scandalum, quantum in se est, evitare nitatur.

heard in confession, save indirectly: even as one who knows something through hearing and seeing it, does not, properly speaking, divulge what he saw, if he says he heard it, but only indirectly, because he says he has heard what he incidentally saw. Hence he does not break the seal of confession.

REPLY OBJ. 2: The confessor is not forbidden to reveal a sin simply, but to reveal it as heard in confession: for in no case is he allowed to say that he has heard it in the confessional.

REPLY OBJ. 3: This is true of things that are in opposition to one another: whereas to know a sin as God knows it, and to know it as man knows it, are not in opposition. Thus the argument proves nothing.

REPLY OBJ. 4: It would not be right to avoid scandal so as to desert justice: for *the truth should not be gainsaid for fear of scandal.* Therefore, when justice and truth are in the balance a man should not be deterred by the fear of giving scandal from divulging what he has heard in confession, provided he knows it from some other source: although he ought to avoid giving scandal, as far as he is able.

QUESTION 12

Deinde considerandum est de satisfactione. De qua quattuor consideranda sunt: primo, de eius quidditate; secundo, de ipsius possibilitate; tertio, de eiusdem qualitate; quarto, de his per quae homo Deo satisfacit.

Circa primum quaeruntur tria.

Primo: utrum satisfactio sit virtus, vel actus virtutis.

Secundo: utrum sit actus iustitiae.

Tertio: utrum definitio satisfactionis quae in littera ponitur, convenienter assignetur.

We must now consider satisfaction, about which there are four considerations: (1) Its nature; (2) Its possibility; (3) Its quality; (4) The means whereby man offers satisfaction to God.

Under the first head there are three points of inquiry:

(1) Whether satisfaction is a virtue or an act of virtue?

(2) Whether it is an act of justice?

(3) Whether the definition of satisfaction contained in the text is suitable?

Article 1

Whether Satisfaction Is a Virtue or an Act of Virtue?

AD PRIMUM SIC PROCEDITUR. Videtur quod satisfactio non sit neque virtus, neque actus virtutis. Omnis enim virtutis actus est meritorius. Sed satisfactio non est meritoria, ut videtur: quia meritum gratuitum est, sed satisfactio debitum attendit. Ergo satisfactio non est actus virtutis.

PRAETEREA, omnis actus virtutis est voluntarius. Sed aliquando fit alicui satisfactio de aliquo eo invito: ut quando aliquis pro offensa in alterum commissa a iudice punitur. Ergo satisfactio non est virtutis actus.

PRAETEREA, secundum Philosophum, VIII *Ethic., in virtute moris principale est electio*. Sed satisfactio non fit per electionem, sed respicit principaliter exteriora opera. Ergo non est virtutis actus.

SED CONTRA: Satisfactio ad poenitentiam pertinet. Sed poenitentia est virtus. Ergo satisfactio est actus virtutis.

PRAETEREA, nullus actus operatur ad deletionem peccati nisi sit actus virtutis: quia contrarium destruitur per suum contrarium. Sed per satisfactionem peccatum totaliter annihilatur. Ergo satisfactio est virtutis actus.

RESPONDEO dicendum quod aliquis actus dicitur esse actus virtutis dupliciter. Uno modo, materialiter. Et sic quilibet actus qui malitiam non habet implicitam, vel defectum debitae circumstantiae, actus virtutis dici potest, quia quolibet tali actu potest uti virtus in suum finem: sicut est ambulare, loqui, et huiusmodi.

Alio modo dicitur actus aliquis esse actus virtutis formaliter, quia in suo nomine formam et rationem virtutis implicitam habet: sicut fortiter sustinere dicitur actus fortitudinis. Formale autem cuiuslibet virtutis moralis

OBJECTION 1: It would seem that satisfaction is neither a virtue nor an act of virtue. For every act of virtue is meritorious; whereas, seemingly, satisfaction is not, since merit is gratuitous, while satisfaction answers to a debt. Therefore, satisfaction is not an act of virtue.

OBJ. 2: Further, every act of virtue is voluntary. But sometimes a man has to make satisfaction for something against his will, as when anyone is punished by the judge for an offense against another. Therefore, satisfaction is not an act of virtue.

OBJ. 3: Further, according to the Philosopher (*Ethics* 8.13): *choice holds the chief place in moral virtue*. But satisfaction is not an act of choice, but regards chiefly external works. Therefore, it is not an act of virtue.

ON THE CONTRARY, Satisfaction belongs to penance. But penance is a virtue. Therefore, satisfaction is also an act of virtue.

FURTHER, Nothing but an act of virtue has the effect of blotting out sin, for one contrary is destroyed by the other. Now satisfaction destroys sin altogether. Therefore, it is an act of virtue.

I ANSWER THAT, An act is said to be the act of a virtue in two ways. First, materially; and thus any act which implies no malice or defect of a due circumstance may be called an act of virtue, because virtue can make use of any such act for its end, e.g., to walk, to speak, and so forth.

Second, an act is said to belong to a virtue formally because its very name implies the form and nature of virtue; thus to suffer courageously is an act of courage. Now the formal element in every moral virtue is the observance of

est ratio medii. Unde omnis actus qui rationem medii importat, aptus virtutis formaliter est. Et quia aequalitas medium est, quod suo nomine satisfactio importat, non enim dicitur aliquid *satisfactum* nisi secundum proportionem aequalitatis ad aliquid; constat quod satisfactio etiam formaliter est actus virtutis.

AD PRIMUM ergo dicendum quod, quamvis satisfacere in se sit debitum, tamen, inquantum satisfaciens voluntate hoc opus exequitur, rationem gratuiti accipit ex parte operantis: et sic operans *facit de necessitate virtutem.* Ex hoc enim debitum diminuere habet meritum, quod necessitatem importat, quae voluntati contrariatur. Unde, si voluntas necessitati consentiat, non ratio meriti tolletur.

AD SECUNDUM dicendum quod actus virtutis non. requirit voluntarium in eo qui patitur, sed in eo qui facit: quia illius actus est. Et ideo, cum ille in quem iudex vindictam exercet, se habeat ut patiens ad satisfactionem, non ut agens; non oportet quod in eo voluntaria sit satisfactio, sed in iudice faciente.

AD TERTIUM dicendum quod principale in virtute potest accipi dupliciter. Uno modo, principale in ipsa inquantum est virtus. Et sic ea quae ad rationem pertinent, vel magis ei propinqua sunt, principaliora sunt in virtute. Et sic electio et interiores actus in virtute, inquantum virtus est, principaliores sunt.

Alio modo potest accipi principale in virtute inquantum est talis virtus. Et sic principalius in ipsa est ex quo determinationem recipit. Actus autem interiores in aliquibus virtutibus determinantur per exteriores: quia electio, quae est communis omnibus virtutibus, ex hoc quod est electio talis actus, efficitur propria huius virtutis. Et sic actus exteriores in aliquibus virtutibus sunt principaliores. Et ita etiam est in satisfactione.

a mean. Therefore, every act that implies the observance of a mean is formally an act of virtue. And since equality is the mean implied in the name of *satisfaction* (for a thing is said to be satisfied by reason of an equal proportion to something), it is evident that satisfaction also is formally an act of virtue.

REPLY OBJ. 1: Although to make satisfaction is due in itself, yet insofar as the deed is done voluntarily by the one who offers satisfaction, it becomes something gratuitous on the part of the agent, so that *he makes a virtue of necessity.* For debt diminishes merit through being necessary, and consequently against the will, so that if the will consent to the necessity, the element of merit is not forfeited.

REPLY OBJ. 2: An act of virtue demands voluntariness not in the patient but in the agent, for it is his act. Consequently, since he on whom the judge wreaks vengeance is the patient and not the agent as regards satisfaction, it follows that satisfaction should be voluntary not in him but in the judge as agent.

REPLY OBJ. 3: The chief element of virtue can be understood in two ways. First, as being the chief element of virtue as virtue, and thus the chief element of virtue denotes whatever belongs to the nature of virtue or is most akin to it; thus choice and other internal acts hold the chief place in virtue.

Second, the chief element of virtue may be taken as denoting that which holds the first place in such and such a virtue; and then the first place belongs to that which gives its determination. Now the interior act in certain virtues is determined by some external act, since choice, which is common to all virtues, becomes proper to such and such a virtue through being directed to such and such an act. Therefore, external acts hold the chief place in certain virtues; and this is the case with satisfaction.

Article 2

Whether Satisfaction Is an Act of Justice?

AD SECUNDUM SIC PROCEDITUR. Videtur quod satisfactio non sit actus iustitiae. Quia satisfactio fit ad hoc quod reconcilietur ei quem offendit. Sed reconciliatio, cum sit amoris, ad caritatem pertinet. Ergo satisfactio est actus caritatis, et non iustitiae.

PRAETEREA, causae peccatorum in nobis sunt passiones animae, quibus ad malum incitamur. Sed iustitia, secundum Philosophum, non est circa passiones, sed circa operationes. Cum ergo ad satisfactionem pertineat *peccatorum causas excidere*, ut in littera dicitur, videtur quod non sit actus iustitiae.

PRAETEREA, cavere in futurum non est actus iustitiae, sed magis prudentiae, cuius pars ponitur cautela.

OBJECTION 1: It would seem that satisfaction is not an act of justice, for the purpose of satisfaction is that one may be reconciled to the person offended. But reconciliation, being an act of love, belongs to charity. Therefore, satisfaction is an act of charity and not of justice.

OBJ. 2: Further, the causes of sin in us are the passions of the soul, which incline us to evil. But justice, according to the Philosopher (*Ethics* 5.2–3), is not about passions, but about operations. Since, therefore, satisfaction aims at *removing the causes of sin*, as stated in the text (*Sentences* IV, D. 15), it seems that it is not an act of justice.

OBJ. 3: Further, to be careful about the future is not an act of justice but of prudence, of which caution is a part. But

Sed hoc pertinet ad satisfactionem: quia ipsius est *suggestionibus peccatorum aditum non indulgere*. Ergo satisfactio non est actus iustitiae.

SED CONTRA: Nulla virtus attendit rationem debiti nisi iustitia. Sed satisfactio *honorem debitum Deo impendit*: ut Anselmus ait. Ergo satisfactio est actus iustitiae.

PRAETEREA, nulla virtus habet rerum exteriorum adaequationem perficere nisi iustitia. Sed hoc fit per satisfactionem, qua constituitur aequalitas emendae ad offensam praecedentem. Ergo satisfactio est iustitiae actus.

RESPONDEO dicendum quod, secundum Philosophum, in V *Ethic.*, medium iustitiae accipitur secundum adaequationem rei ad rem in proportionalitate aliqua. Unde, cum talem adaequationem ipsum nomen 'satisfactionis' importet, quia hoc adverbium 'satis' aequalitatem proportionis designat, constat quod satisfactio formaliter iustitiae actus est.

Sed iustitiae actus, secundum Philosophum, est vel *sui ad alterum*, ut quando aliquis reddit alteri quod ei debet; vel *alterius ad alterum*, sicut quando iudex facit iustitiam inter duos. Quando autem est actus iustitiae sui ad alterum, aequalitas in ipso faciente constituitur: quando autem alterius ad alterum, aequalitas constituitur in iustum passo. Et quia 'satisfactio' aequalitatem in ipso faciente exprimit, dicit actum iustitiae quae est sui ad alterum, proprie loquendo.

Sed sui ad alterum potest aliquis facere iustitiam vel in actionibus et passionibus, vel in rebus exterioribus: sicut et iniuria fit alteri vel subtrahendo res, vel per aliquam actionem laedendo. Et quia usus rerum exteriorum est dare, ideo actum iustitiae secundum quod aequalitatem in rebus exterioribus constituit, proprie dicit hoc quod est reddere: sed satisfacere manifeste aequalitatem in actionibus demonstrat, quamvis quandoque unum pro alio ponatur.

Et quia adaequatio non est nisi inaequalium, ideo satisfactio inaequalitatem actionum praesupponit, quae quidem offensam constituit: et ideo habet respectum ad offensam praecedentem. Nulla autem pars iustitiae respicit offensam praecedentem nisi iustitia vindicativa. Quae aequalitatem constituit iri eo qui iustum patitur, indifferenter, sive sit patiens idem quod agens, ut quando aliquis sibi ipsi poenam infert, sive non sit idem quod agens, ut quando iudex alium punit, ad utrumque vindicativa iustitia se habente. Similiter et poenitentia, quae aequalitatem tantum in faciente importat, quia ipsemet poenam tenet: ut sic quodammodo poenitentia vindicativae iustitiae species sit.

Et per hoc constat quod satisfactio, quae aequalitatem respectu offensae praecedentis in faciente importat, opus iustitiae est quantum ad illam partem quae poenitentia dicitur.

it belongs to satisfaction *to give no opening to the suggestions of sin*. Therefore, satisfaction is not an act of justice.

ON THE CONTRARY, No virtue but justice considers the notion of that which is due. But satisfaction *gives due honor to God*, as Anselm states (*Why God Became Man* 1). Therefore, satisfaction is an act of justice.

FURTHER, No virtue save justice establishes equality between external things. But this is done by satisfaction, which establishes equality between amendment and the previous offense. Therefore, satisfaction is an act of justice.

I ANSWER THAT, According to the Philosopher (*Ethics* 5.3–4), the mean of justice is considered with regard to an equation between thing and thing according to a certain proportion. Wherefore, since the very name of satisfaction implies an equation of the kind, because the adverb *satis*, 'enough,' denotes an equality of proportion, it is evident that satisfaction is formally an act of justice.

Now the act of justice, according to the Philosopher (*Ethics* 5.2, 4), is either an act done *by one man to another*, as when a man pays another what he owes him, or an act done *by one man between two others*, as when a judge does justice between two men. When it is an act of justice of one man to another, the equality is set up in the agent, while when it is something done between two others, the equality is set up in the subject that has suffered an injustice. And since 'satisfaction' expresses equality in the agent, it denotes, properly speaking, an act of justice of one man to another.

Now a man may do justice to another either in actions and passions, or in external things; even as one may do an injustice to another either by taking something away, or by a hurtful action. And since to give is to use an external thing, the act of justice, insofar as it establishes equality between external things, it signifies, properly speaking, a 'giving back': but to make satisfaction clearly points to equality between actions, although sometimes one is put for the other.

Now equalization concerns only such things as are unequal, wherefore satisfaction presupposes inequality among actions which inequality constitutes an offense; so that satisfaction regards a previous offense. But no part of justice regards a previous offense except vindictive justice, which establishes equality indifferently, whether the patient be the same subject as the agent, as when anyone punishes himself, or whether they be distinct, as when a judge punishes another man, since vindictive justice deals with both cases. The same applies to penance, which implies equality in the agent only, since it is the penitent who holds to the penance, so that penance is in a way a species of vindictive justice.

This proves that satisfaction, which implies equality in the agent with respect to a previous offense, is a work of justice, as to that part which is called penance.

AD PRIMUM ergo dicendum quod satisfactio, ut ex dictis patet, est quaedam iniuriae illatae recompensatio. Unde, sicut iniuria illata immediate ad inaequalitatem iustitiae pertingebat, et per consequens ad inaequalitatem amicitiae oppositam; ita et satisfactio directe ad aequalitatem iustitiae perducit, et ad aequalitatem amicitiae ex consequenti. Et quia actus aliquis elicitive ab illo habitu procedit ad cuius finem immediate ordinatur, imperative autem ab illo ad cuius finem ultimo tendit, ideo satisfactio elicitive est a iustitia, sed imperative a caritate.

AD SECUNDUM dicendum quod, quamvis iustitia sit principalior circa operationes, tamen etiam ex consequenti est circa passiones, inquantum sunt, operationum causae. Sed, sicut iustitia cohibet iram, ne alteri laesionem iniuste inferat; et concupiscentiam, ne ad alienum torum accedat; sic etiam satisfactio potest *peccatorum causas excidere*.

AD TERTIUM dicendum quod quaelibet virtus moralis participat actus prudentiae, eo quod formaliter ipsa complet in eis rationem virtutis: cum secundum eam medium accipiatur in singulis virtutibus moralibus, ut patet per definitionem virtutis in II *Ethic.*

REPLY OBJ. 1: Satisfaction, as appears from what has been said, is compensation for injury inflicted. Therefore, as the injury inflicted entailed of itself an inequality of justice, and consequently an inequality opposed to friendship, so satisfaction brings back directly equality of justice and consequently equality of friendship. And since an act is elicited by the habit to whose end it is immediately directed, but is commanded by that habit to whose end it is directed ultimately, hence satisfaction is elicited by justice but is commanded by charity.

REPLY OBJ. 2: Although justice is chiefly about operations, yet it is consequently about passions, insofar as they are the causes of operations. Wherefore as justice curbs anger, lest it inflict an unjust injury on another, and concupiscence, lest it invade another's marriage right, so satisfaction *removes the causes of other sins*.

REPLY OBJ. 3: Each moral virtue shares in the act of prudence because this virtue completes in it the conditions essential to virtue, since each moral virtue takes its mean according to the ruling of prudence, as is evident from the definition of virtue given in *Ethics* (2.6).

Article 3

Whether the Definition of Satisfaction Given in the Text is Suitable?

AD TERTIUM SIC PROCEDITUR. Videtur quod definitio satisfactionis in littera inconvenienter ponatur ab Augustino. Dicit enim quod satisfactio est *peccatorum causas excidere et eorum suggestionibus aditum non indulgere*. Causa enim actualis peccati fomes est. Sed in hac vita non possumus fomitem excidere. Ergo satisfactio non est *peccatorum causas excidere*.

PRAETEREA, causa peccati est fortior quam peccatum. Sed homo per se non potest peccatum excidere. Ergo multo minus causas peccati. Et sic idem quod prius.

PRAETEREA, satisfactio, cum sit pars poenitentiae, praeteritum respicit, non futurum. Sed *non indulgere aditum suggestionibus peccatorum* respicit futurum. Ergo non debet poni in definitione satisfactionis.

PRAETEREA, satisfactio dicitur respectu offensae praeteritae. Sed de offensa praecedenti nulla fit mentio. Ergo inconvenienter assignatur definitio satisfactionis.

PRAETEREA, Anselmus ponit aliam definitionem, in Libro *Cur Deus homo*, scilicet: *satisfactio est honorem debitum Deo impendere*. In qua nulla fit mentio horum quae Augustinus hic ponit. Ergo altera earum videtur esse incompetens.

OBJECTION 1: It would seem that the definition of satisfaction given in the text (*Sentences* IV, D. 15) and quoted from Augustine (Gennadius, *Book of Ecclesiastical Dogmas* 54) is unsuitable—namely, that *satisfaction is to uproot the causes of sins, and to give no opening to the suggestions thereof*. For the cause of actual sin·is the *fomes*. But we cannot remove the *fomes* in this life. Therefore, satisfaction does not consist in *removing the causes of sins*.

OBJ. 2: Further, the cause of sin is stronger than sin itself. But man by himself cannot remove sin. Much less, therefore, can he remove the cause of sin; and so the same conclusion follows.

OBJ. 3: Further, since satisfaction is a part of penance, it regards the past and not the future. Now *to give no opening to the suggestions of sin* regards the future. Therefore, it should not be put in the definition of satisfaction.

OBJ. 4: Further, satisfaction regards a past offense. Yet no mention is made of this. Therefore, the definition of satisfaction is unsuitable.

OBJ. 5: Further, Anselm gives another definition (*Why God Became Man* 1): *satisfaction consists in giving God due honor*, wherein no reference is made to the things mentioned by Augustine (Gennadius, cf. Obj. 1) in this definition. Therefore, one or the other is unsuitable.

PRAETEREA, honorem debitum Deo potest innocens impendere. Sed satisfacere non competit innocenti. Ergo definitio Anselmi est male assignata.

RESPONDEO dicendum quod iustitia non ad hoc tantum tendit ut inaequalitatem praecedentem auferat puniendo culpam praeteritam, sed ut in futurum aequalitatem custodiat: quia, secundum Philosophum, in II *Ethic.*, *poenae medicinae sunt.* Unde et satisfactio, quae est iustitiae actus poenam inferentis, est medicina curans peccata praeterita et praeservans a futuris. Et ideo, quando homo homini satisfacit, et praeterita recompensat et de futuris cavet.

Et secundum hoc, dupliciter potest satisfactio definiri. Uno modo, respectu culpae praeteritae, quam recompensando curat. Et sic dicitur quod satisfactio est *illatae iniuriae recompensatio secundum iustitiae aequalitatem.* Et in idem videtur redire definitio Anselmi, qui dicit quod satisfacere est *honorem debitum Deo impendere*, ut consideretur debitum ratione culpae commissae.

Alio modo potest definiri secundum quod praeservat a culpa futura. Et sic definit eam hic Augustinus. Praeservatio autem a morbo corporali fit per ablationem causarum quibus morbus consequi potest: eis enim ablatis, non potest morbus sequi. Sed in morbo spirituali non est ita: quia liberum arbitrium non cogitur; unde, causis praecedentibus, potest vitari quamvis difficulter; causis amotis, potest incurri. Et ideo in satisfactionis definitione duo ponit: scilicet abscisionem causarum, quantum ad primum; et renitentiam liberi arbitrii ad ipsum peccatum, quantum ad secundum.

AD PRIMUM ergo dicendum quod accipiendae sunt causae proximae peccati actualis: quae dicuntur duo, scilicet libido ex consuetudine vel actu peccati relicta, et aliquae reliquiae peccati praeteriti; et exteriores occasiones ad peccandum, ut locus, societas mala, et huiusmodi. Et tales causae in hac vita per satisfactionem tolluntur: quamvis fomes, qui est causa remota peccati actualis, non tollatur totaliter in hac vita per satisfactionem, etsi debilitetur.

AD SECUNDUM dicendum quod, quia causa mali vel privationis, eo modo quo causam habet, non est nisi bonum deficiens; bonum autem facilius tollitur quam constituatur: ideo facilius est causas privationis et mali abscindere quam ipsum malum removere, quod non removetur nisi per constructionem boni. Quod patet in caecitate et causis eius. Et tamen causae peccati praedictae non sunt sufficientes causae, cum ex eis non de necessitate sequatur peccatum: sed sunt occasiones quaedam. Nec iterum satisfactio sine Dei auxilio fit: quia sine caritate esse non potest, ut dicetur.

AD TERTIUM dicendum quod, quamvis poenitentia ex prima sui intentione respiciat praeteritum, tamen etiam ex consequenti futurum respicit, inquantum est medicina praeservans; et sic etiam satisfactio.

OBJ. 6: Further, an innocent man can give due honor to God: whereas satisfaction is not compatible with innocence. Therefore, Anselm's definition is faulty.

I ANSWER THAT, Justice aims not only at removing inequality already existing by punishing the past fault, but also at safeguarding equality for the future, because according to the Philosopher (*Ethics* 2.3) *punishments are medicinal.* Therefore, satisfaction, which is the act of justice inflicting punishment, is a medicine healing past sins and preserving from future sins: so that when one man makes satisfaction to another, he offers compensation for the past, and takes heed for the future.

Accordingly, satisfaction may be defined in two ways: first with regard to past sin, which it heals by making compensation, and thus it is defined as *compensation for an inflicted injury according to the equality of justice.* The definition of Anselm amounts to the same, for he says that *satisfaction consists in giving God due honor*; where duty is considered in respect of the sin committed.

Second, satisfaction may be defined considered as preserving us from future sins, and thus Augustine defines it. Now preservation from bodily sickness is assured by removing the causes from which the sickness may ensue, for if they be taken away the sickness cannot follow. But it is not thus in spiritual diseases, for the free-will cannot be forced, so that even in the presence of their causes, they can, though with difficulty, be avoided, while they can be incurred even when their causes are removed. Hence he puts two things in the definition of satisfaction, namely, removal of the causes, as to the first, and the free-will's refusal to sin.

REPLY OBJ. 1: By causes we must understand the proximate causes of actual sin, which are twofold: viz. the lust of sin through the habit or act of a sin that has been given up, and those things which are called the remnants of past sin; and external occasions of sin, such as place, bad company and so forth. Such causes are removed by satisfaction in this life, albeit the *fomes*, which is the remote cause of actual sin, is not entirely removed by satisfaction in this life though it is weakened.

REPLY OBJ. 2: Since the cause of evil or of privation (according as it has a cause) is nothing else than a defective good, and since it is easier to destroy good than to set it up, it follows that it is easier to uproot the causes of privation and of evil than to remove the evil itself, which can only be removed by setting up good, as may be seen in the case of blindness and its causes. Yet the aforesaid are not sufficient causes of sin, for sin does not, of necessity, ensue therefrom, but they are occasions of sin. Nor again can satisfaction be made without God's help, since it is not possible without charity, as we shall state further on (Q. 14, A. 2).

REPLY OBJ. 3: Although penance was primarily instituted and intended with a view to the past, yet as a consequence it regards the future insofar as it is a safeguarding remedy; and the same applies to satisfaction.

AD QUARTUM dicendum quod Augustinus definit satisfactionem secundum quod fit Deo: cui secundum rei veritatem nihil subtrahi potest, quamvis peccator, quantum in se est, aliquid subtrahat. Et ideo in satisfactione tali principalius requiritur emendatio in futurum quam recompensatio praeteritorum. Et propter hoc ex parte ista Augustinus definivit satisfactionem.

Nihilominus tamen ex cautela futurorum cognosci potest recompensatio praeteritorum, quae fit circa eadem converso modo. In praeterita enim respicientes causas peccatorum propter peccata detestamur, a peccatis incipientes detestationis motum: sed in cautela a causis incipimus, ut, causis subtractis, facilius peccata vitemus.

AD QUINTUM dicendum quod non est inconveniens quod de eodem dentur diversae assignationes secundum diversa quae in ipso inveniuntur. Et sic est in proposito, ut ex dictis patet.

AD SEXTUM dicendum quod intelligitur debitum quod debemus Deo ratione culpae commissae: quia debitum poenitentia respicit, ut prius dictum est.

REPLY OBJ. 4: Augustine (Gennadius, *Book of Ecclesiastical Dogmas* 54) defined satisfaction as made to God, from whom, in reality, nothing can be taken, though the sinner for his own part takes something away. Consequently, in such satisfaction amendment for future time is of greater weight than compensation for the past. And on account of this Augustine defines satisfaction from this point of view.

And yet it is possible to gauge the compensation for the past from the heed taken for the future, for the latter regards the same object as the former, but in the opposite way: since when looking at the past we detest the causes of sins on account of the sins themselves, which are the starting-point of the movement of detestation. Whereas when taking heed of the future, we begin from the causes, that by their removal we may avoid sins the more easily.

REPLY OBJ. 5: There is no reason why the same thing should not be described in different ways according to the various things found in it: and such is the case here, as explained above.

REPLY OBJ. 6: By debt is meant the debt we owe to God by reason of the sins we have committed, because penance regards a debt, as stated above (A. 2).

THE POSSIBILITY OF SATISFACTION

Deide considerandum est de possibilitate satisfactionis.

Circa quod duo quaeruntur.
Primo: utrum homo possit Deo satisfacere.
Secundo: utrum aliquis pro alio satisfacere possit.

We must now consider the possibility of satisfaction.

Under this head there are two points of inquiry:
(1) Whether man can make satisfaction to God?
(2) Whether one man can make satisfaction for another?

Article 1

Whether Man Can Make Satisfaction to God?

AD PRIMUM SIC PROCEDITUR. Videtur quod homo non possit Deo satisfacere. Satisfactio enim debet aequari offensae, ut ex dictis patet. Sed offensa in Deum commissa est infinita: quia quantitatem recipit ab eo in quem committitur; cum plus offendat qui principem percutit quam alium quemquam. Cum ergo actio hominis non possit esse infinita, videtur quod homo Deo satisfacere non possit.

PRAETEREA, servus, quia totum quod habet domini est, non potest aliquid domino recompensare. Sed nos servi Dei sumus, quidquid boni habemus ab ipso habentes. Cum ergo satisfactio sit recompensatio offensae praeteritae, videtur quod Deo satisfacere non possumus.

PRAETEREA, ille cuius totum quod habet non sufficit ad unum debitum exsolvendum, non potest pro alio debito satisfacere. Sed quidquid homo est et potest et habet, non sufficit ad solvendum debitum pro beneficio conditionis: unde Isaiae 40 dicitur quod *ligna Libani non sufficient ad holocaustum.* Ergo nullo modo potent satisfactio esse pro debito offensae commissae.

PRAETEREA, homo totum tempus suum debet in Dei servitium expendere. Sed tempus amissum non potest recuperari: propter quod est *gravis iactura temporis,* ut Seneca dicit. Ergo non potest homo recompensationem Deo facere. Et sic idem quod prius.

PRAETEREA, peccatum actuale mortale est gravius quam originale. Sed pro originali nemo potuit satisfacere nisi Deus et homo. Ergo neque pro actuali.

SED CONTRA: Sicut Hieronymus dicit: *qui dicit Deum aliquid impossibile homini praecepisse, anathema*

OBJECTION 1: It would seem that man cannot make satisfaction to God. For satisfaction should balance the offense, as shown above (Q. 12, A. 2–3). But an offense against God is infinite, since it is measured by the person against whom it is committed, for it is a greater offense to strike a prince than anyone else. Therefore, as no action of man can be infinite, it seems that he cannot make satisfaction to God.

OBJ. 2: Further, a slave cannot make compensation for a debt, since all that he has is his master's. But we are the slaves of God, and whatever good we have, we owe to him. Therefore, as satisfaction is compensation for a past offense, it seems that we cannot offer it to God.

OBJ. 3: Further, if all that a man has suffices not to pay one debt, he cannot pay another debt. Now all that man is, all that he can do, and all that he has, does not suffice to pay what he owes for the blessing of creation, wherefore it is written that *the wood of Libanus shall not be enough for a burnt offering* (Isa 40:16). Therefore, by no means can he make satisfaction for the debt resulting from the offense committed.

OBJ. 4: Further, man is bound to spend all his time in the service of God. Now time once lost cannot be recovered, wherefore, as Seneca observes (Liber i, Epistula. i, *ad Lucilium*) loss of time is a very grievous matter. Therefore, man cannot make compensation to God, and the same conclusion follows as before.

OBJ. 5: Further, mortal actual sin is more grievous than original sin. But none could satisfy for original sin unless he were both God and man. Neither, therefore, can he satisfy for actual sin.

ON THE CONTRARY, Jerome says: *whoever maintains that God has commanded anything impossible to man, let*

sit. Sed satisfactio est in praecepto, Luc. 3: *facite dignos fructus poenitentiae.* Ergo possibile est Deo satisfacere.

PRAETEREA, Deus est magis misericors quam aliquis homo. Sed homini est possibile satisfacere. Ergo et Deo.

PRAETEREA, debita satisfactio est cum poena culpae aequatur: quia *iustitia est idem quod contra-passum,* ut Pythagorici dixerunt. Sed contingit aequalem poenam assumere delectationi quae fuit in peccando. Ergo contingit Deo satisfacere.

RESPONDEO dicendum quod homo Deo debitor efficitur, uno modo, ratione beneficii accepti; alio modo, ratione peccati commissi. Et sicut gratiarum actio, vel latria, vel si quid est huiusmodi, respicit debitum accepti beneficii; ita satisfactio respicit debitum peccati commissi.

In his autem *honoribus qui sunt ad parentes et deos,* etiam secundum Philosophum, impossibile est aequivalens reddere secundum quantitatem, sed sufficit quod homo reddat quod potest: quia amicitia non exigit aequivalens nisi secundum quod possibile est. Et hoc etiam est aequale aliqualiter, scilicet *secundum proportionalitatem*: quia, sicut se habet hoc quod Deo est debitum ad ipsum Deum, ita hoc quod iste potest reddere ad eum. Et sic aliquo modo forma iustitiae conservatur.

Et similiter est ex parte satisfactionis. Unde non potest homo Deo satisfacere si ly *satis* aequalitatem quantitatis importet: contingit autem si importet aequalitatem proportionis, ut dictum est. Et hoc, sicut sufficit ad rationem iustitiae, ita sufficit ad rationem satisfactionis.

AD PRIMUM ergo dicendum quod, sicut offensa habuit quandam infinitatem ex infinitate divinae maiestatis, ita satisfactio accipit quandam infinitatem ex infinitate divinae misericordiae, prout est gratia informata, per quam acceptum redditur quod homo reddere potest.

Quidam tamen dicunt quod habet infinitamen ex parte aversionis, et sic gratis dimittitur: sed ex parte conversionis finita est, et sic pro ea satisfieri potest. Sed hoc nihil est. Quia satisfactio non respondet peccato nisi secundum quod est offensa Dei: quod non habet ex parte conversionis, sed solum ex parte aversionis.

Alii vero dicunt quod etiam quantum ad aversionem pro peccato satisfieri potest, virtute meriti Christi, quod quodammodo infinitum fuit. Et hoc in idem redit quod prius dictum est: quia per fidem Mediatoris gratia data est credentibus. Si tamen alio modo gratiam daret, sufficeret satisfactio per modum praedictum.

AD SECUNDUM dicendum quod homo, qui *ad imaginem Dei factus est,* aliquid libertatis participat, inquan-

him be anathema (Pelagius, *Exposition of the Faith*). But satisfaction is commanded: *bring forth fruits worthy of penance* (Luke 3:8). Therefore, it is possible to make satisfaction to God.

FURTHER, God is more merciful than any man. But it is possible to make satisfaction to a man. Therefore, it is possible to make satisfaction to God.

FURTHER, There is due satisfaction when the punishment balances the fault, since *justice is the same as counter-passion,* as the Pythagoreans said (Aristotle, *Ethics* 5.5; Cf. II-II, Q. 61, A. 4). Now punishment may equal the pleasure contained in a sin committed. Therefore, satisfaction can be made to God.

I ANSWER THAT, Man becomes God's debtor in two ways: first, by reason of favors received, second, by reason of sin committed: and just as thanksgiving or worship or the like regard the debt for favors received, so satisfaction regards the debt for sin committed.

Now *in giving honor to one's parents or to the gods,* as indeed the Philosopher says (*Ethics* 8.14), it is impossible to repay them measure for measure, but it suffices that man repay as much as he can, for friendship does not demand measure for measure, but what is possible. Yet even this is equal somewhat, viz. *according to proportion,* for as the debt due to God is in comparison with God, so is what man can do in comparison with himself. And thus in another way is the form of justice preserved.

It is the same as regards satisfaction. Consequently, man cannot make satisfaction to God if the *satis,* 'enough', denotes quantitative equality; but he can if it denotes proportionate equality, as explained above, and as this suffices for justice, so does it suffice for satisfaction.

REPLY OBJ. 1: Just as the offense derived a certain infinity from the infinity of the divine majesty, so does satisfaction derive a certain infinity from the infinity of divine mercy, insofar as it is informed by grace, whereby whatever man is able to repay becomes acceptable.

Others, however, say that the offense is infinite as regards the aversion, and in this respect it is pardoned gratuitously, but that it is finite as turning to a mutable good, in which respect it is possible to make satisfaction for it. But this is not to the point, since satisfaction does not answer to sin except as it is an offense against God, which is a matter not of turning to a creature but of turning away from God.

Others again say that even as regards the aversion it is possible to make satisfaction for sin in virtue of Christ's merit, which was, in a way, infinite. And this comes to the same as what we said before, since grace is given to believers through faith in the Mediator. If, however, he were to give grace otherwise, satisfaction would suffice in the way explained above.

REPLY OBJ. 2: Man, *who was made to God's image,* has a certain share of liberty insofar as he is master of his actions

tum est dominus suorum actuum per liberum arbitrium. Et ideo ex hoc quod per liberum arbitrium agit, Deo satisfacere potest: quia, quamvis Dei sit prout a Deo est sibi concessum, libere tamen traditum est, ut eius dominus sit. Quod servo non competit.

Ad tertium dicendum quod ratio illa concludit quod Deo aequivalens satisfactio fieri non possit: non autem quod non possit sibi sufficiens fieri. Quamvis enim posse suum totum homo debeat, non tamen ab eo exigitur de necessitate ut totum quod possit faciat: quia hoc est ei impossibile secundum statum praesentis vitae, ut totum posse suum in aliquid unum expendat; cum oporteat circa multa esse sollicitum. Sed est quaedam mensura homini adhibita quae ab eo requiritur, scilicet impletio mandatorum Dei: et super ea potest aliquid erogare ut satisfaciat.

Ad quartum dicendum quod, quamvis homo non possit tempus praeteritum recuperare, potest tamen in futuro recompensare illud quod in praeterito facere debuisset: quia non debuit, debito praecepti, totum quod potuit, ut dictum est.

Ad quintum dicendum quod originale peccatum, etsi minus habeat de ratione peccati quam actuale, tamen est gravius malum: quia est ipsius humanae naturae infectio. Et ideo per imius hominis puri satisfactionem expiari non potuit, sicut actuale.

through his free-will; so that, through acting by his free-will, he can make satisfaction to God, for though it belongs to God insofar as it was bestowed on him by God, yet it was freely bestowed on him that he might be his own master, which cannot be said of a slave.

Reply Obj. 3: This argument proves that it is impossible to make equivalent satisfaction to God, but not that it is impossible to make sufficient satisfaction to him. For though man owes God all that he is able to give him, yet it is not necessary for his salvation that he should actually do the whole of what he is able to do, for it is impossible for him, according to his present state of life, to put forth his whole power into any one single thing, since he has to be heedful about many things. And so his conduct is subject to a certain measure, viz. the fulfillment of God's commandments, over and above which he can offer something by way of satisfaction.

Reply Obj. 4: Though man cannot recover the time that is past, he can in the time that follows make compensation for what he should have done in the past, since the commandment did not exact from him the fulfillment of his whole power, as stated above (ad 3).

Reply Obj. 5: Though original sin has less of the nature of sin than actual sin has, yet it is a more grievous evil, because it is an infection of human nature itself, so that, unlike actual sin, it could not be expiated by the satisfaction of a mere man.

Article 2

Whether One Man Can Fulfill Satisfactory Punishment for Another?

Ad secundum sic proceditur. Videtur quod poenam satisfactoriam non possit unus pro alio explere. Quia ad satisfactionem meritum requiritur. Sed unus pro altero non potest mereri vel demereri: cum sit scriptum: *reddes tu unicuique secundum opera sua.* Ergo unus pro alio non potest satisfacere.

Praeterea, satisfactio contra contritionem et confessionem dividitur. Sed unus pro alio non potest conteri aut confiteri. Ergo nec satisfacere.

Praeterea, unus pro alio orando etiam sibi meretur. Si ergo aliquis pro alio satisfacere potest, satisfaciendo pro alio pro se satisfacit. Et ita ab eo qui pro altero satisfacit, non exigitur alia satisfactio pro peccatis propriis.

Praeterea, si unus pro alio satisfacere potest, ergo ex quo unus sibi suscipit debitum poenae, alius statim a debito liberatur. Ergo, si moriatur postquam tota poena debita ab alio suscepta est, statim evolabit. Vel, si adhuc puniatur, duplex poena reddetur pro eodem pec-

Objection 1: It would seem that one man cannot fulfill satisfactory punishment for another. For merit is requisite for satisfaction. Yet one man cannot merit or demerit for another, since it is written: *you will render to every man according to his works* (Ps 61:12). Therefore, one man cannot make satisfaction for another.

Obj. 2: Further, satisfaction is condivided with contrition and confession. But one man cannot be contrite or confess for another. Neither, therefore, can one make satisfaction for another.

Obj. 3: Further, by praying for another one merits also for oneself. If, therefore, a man can make satisfaction for another, he satisfies for himself by satisfying for another, so that if a man satisfy for another he need not make satisfaction for his own sins.

Obj. 4: Further, if one can satisfy for another, as soon as he takes the debt of punishment on himself, this other is freed from his debt. Therefore, the latter will go straight to heaven, if he die after the whole of his debt of punishment has been taken up by another; else, if he be punished all the

cato: scilicet illius qui satisfacere incipit, et illius qui punitur in purgatorio.

SED CONTRA: Galat. 6 dicitur: *alter alterius onera portate*. Ergo videtur quod unus possit onus poenitentiae impositae pro alio suscipere.

PRAETEREA, caritas magis potest apud Deum quam apud homines. Sed unus potest apud homines pro alterius amore debitum eius solvere. Ergo multo fortius hoc in divino iudicio fieri potest.

RESPONDEO dicendum quod poena satisfactoria est ad duo: scilicet ad solutionem debiti; et ad medicinam pro peccato vitando. Inquantum ergo est ad remedium sequentis peccati, sic satisfactio unius non prodest alteri, quia ex ieiunio unius caro alterius non domatur, nec ex actibus unius alius bene agere consuevit: nisi secundum accidens, inquantum aliquis per bona opera potest alteri mereri augmentum gratiae, quae efficacissimum remedium est ad vitandum peccatum. Sed hoc est per modum meriti magis quam per modum satisfactionis.

Sed quantum ad solutionem debiti, unus potest pro alio satisfacere: dummodo sit in caritate, ut opera eius satisfactoria esse possint.

Nec oportet quod maior poena imponatur ei qui pro altero satisfacit quam principali imponeretur: ut quidam dicunt, hac ratione moti, quia poena propria magis satisfacit quam aliena. Quia poena habet vim satisfaciendi maxime ratione caritatis, qua homo ipsam sustinet. Et quia maior caritas apparet, in hoc quod aliquis pro altero satisfacit quam si ipse satisfaceret, ideo minor poena requiritur in eo qui pro alio satisfacit quam in principali requireretur. Unde dicitur in *Vitis Patrum* quod propter caritatem unius qui, alterius fratris caritate ductus, poenitentiam fecit pro peccato quod non commiserat, alteri peccatum quod commiserat, dimissum est.

Nec exigitur etiam, quantum ad absolutionem debiti, quod ille pro quo fit satisfactio, sit impotens ad satisfaciendum. Quia, etiam si esset potens, alio satisfaciente pro ipso, ipse a debito immunis esset. Sed hoc requiritur inquantum poena satisfactoria est in remedium. Unde non est permittendum quod aliquis pro alio poenitentiam agat, nisi defectus aliquis appareat in poenitente: vel corporalis, per quem fit impotens ad sustinendum; vel spiritualis, per quem non sit promptus ad portandum poenam.

AD PRIMUM ergo dicendum quod praemium essentiale redditur secundum dispositionem hominis: quia secundum capacitatem videntium erit plenitudo visionis divinae. Et ideo, sicut unus non disponitur per actum alterius, ita unus alteri non meretur praemium essentiale: nisi meritum eius habeat efficaciam infinitam, sicut Christi, cuius merito solo pueri per baptismum ad vitam aeternam perveniunt. Sed poena temporalis pro

same, a double punishment will be paid for the same sin, viz. by him who has begun to make satisfaction, and by he who is punished in purgatory.

ON THE CONTRARY, It is written: *bear ye one another's burdens* (Gal 6:2). Therefore, it seems that one can bear the burden of punishment laid upon another.

FURTHER, Charity avails more before God than before man. Now before man, one can pay another's debt for love of him. Much more, therefore, can this be done before the judgment seat of God.

I ANSWER THAT, Satisfactory punishment has a twofold purpose, viz. to pay the debt, and to serve as a remedy for the avoidance of sin. Accordingly, as a remedy against future sin the satisfaction of one does not profit another, for the flesh of one man is not tamed by another's fast; nor does one man acquire the habit of well-doing through the actions of another, except accidentally insofar as a man, by his good actions, may merit an increase of grace for another, since grace is the most efficacious remedy for the avoidance of sin. But this is by way of merit rather than of satisfaction.

On the other hand, as regards the payment of the debt, one man can satisfy for another, provided he be in a state of charity, so that his works may avail for satisfaction.

Nor is it necessary that he who satisfies for another should undergo a greater punishment than the principal would have to undergo (as some maintain, who argue that a man profits more by his own punishment than by another's), because punishment derives its power of satisfaction chiefly from charity whereby man bears it. And since greater charity is evidenced by a man satisfying for another than for himself, less punishment is required of him who satisfies for another, than of the principal: wherefore we read in the *Lives of the Fathers* 5.5 of one who, for love of his brother, did penance for a sin which his brother had not committed, and that on account of his charity his brother was released from a sin which he had committed.

Nor is it necessary that the one for whom satisfaction is made should be unable to make satisfaction himself, for even if he were able, he would be released from his debt when the other satisfied in his stead. But this is necessary insofar as the satisfactory punishment is medicinal: so that a man is not to be allowed to do penance for another unless there be evidence of some defect in the penitent, either bodily, so that he is unable to bear it, or spiritual, so that he is not ready to undergo it.

REPLY OBJ. 1: The essential reward is bestowed on a man according to his disposition because the fullness of the sight of God will be according to the capacity of those who see him. Hence, just as one man is not disposed thereto by another's act, so one man does not merit the essential reward for another unless his merit has infinite efficacy, as the merit of Christ, whereby children come to eternal life through baptism. On the other hand, the temporal punish-

peccato debita post culpae remissionem non taxatur secundum dispositionem eius cui debetur: quia quandoque ille qui est melior, habet maioris poenae reatum. Et ideo quantum ad poenae remissionem, unus alteri potest mereri; et actus unius efficitur alterius, caritate mediante, per quam *omnes unum sumus in Christo*.

Ad secundum dicendum quod contritio ordinatur contra culpam, quae ad dispositionem bonitatis vel malitiae hominis pertinet. Et ideo per contritionem unius alius a culpa non liberatur. Similiter per confessionem homo se sacramentis Ecclesiae subiicit. Non autem potest unus sacramentum pro alio accipere: quia in sacramento gratia suscipienti datur, non alii. Et ideo non est similis ratio de satisfactione, contritione et confessione.

Ad tertium dicendum quod in solutione debiti attenditur quantitas poenae: sed in merito attenditur radix caritatis. Et ideo ille qui ex caritate pro alio meretur, saltem merito congrui, etiam sibi magis meretur. Non autem qui pro alio satisfacit, pro se satisfacit: quia illa quantitas poenae non sufficit ad utrumque peccatum. Tamen sibi meretur maius quam sit dimissio poenae, scilicet vitam aeternam.

Ad quartum dicendum quod, si ipsemet ad aliquam poenam se obligasset, non prius a debito esset immunis quam si eam solvisset. Et ideo poenam ipse patietur, quandiu ille satisfactionem pro eo fecerit. Quam si non fecerit, tunc uterque est debitor illius poenae, unus pro commisso, alius pro omisso. Et ita non sequitur quod peccatum unum bis puniatur.

ment due to sin after the guilt has been forgiven is not measured according to the disposition of the man to whom it is due, since sometimes the better man owes a greater debt of punishment. Consequently, one man can merit for another as regards release from punishment, and one man's act becomes another's, by means of charity whereby we are *all one in Christ* (Gal 3:28).

Reply Obj. 2: Contrition is ordained against the guilt which affects a man's disposition to goodness or malice, so that one man is not freed from guilt by another's contrition. In like manner, by confession a man submits to the sacraments of the Church: nor can one man receive a sacrament instead of another, since in a sacrament grace is given to the recipient, not to another. Consequently, there is no comparison between satisfaction, contrition, and confession.

Reply Obj. 3: In the payment of the debt we consider the measure of the punishment, whereas in merit we regard the root which is charity: thus he that through charity merits for another at least congruously merits more for himself; yet he that satisfies for another does not also satisfy for himself, because the measure of the punishment does not suffice for the sins of both, although by satisfying for another he merits something greater than the release from punishment, viz. eternal life.

Reply Obj. 4: If this man bound himself to undergo a certain punishment, he would not be released from the debt before paying it: thus he himself will suffer the punishment, as long as the other makes satisfaction for him: and if he do not this, then both are debtors in respect of fulfilling this punishment, one for the sin committed, the other for his omission, so that it does not follow that one sin is twice punished.

QUESTION 14

THE QUALITY OF SATISFACTION

Deinde considerandum est de qualitate satisfactionis.

Et circa hoc quaeruntur quinque.

Primo: utrum homo possit de uno peccato sine alio satisfacere.

Secundo: utrum ille qui de omnibus peccatis prius contritus fuit et postea in peccatum incidit, de aliis peccatis, quae sibi per contritionem fuerunt dimissa, satisfacere possit extra caritatem existens.

Tertio: utrum homo postquam caritatem habuit, valere sibi incipiat satisfactio praecederis.

Quarto: utrum opera extra caritatem facta sint alicuius boni meritoria.

Quinto: utrum opera praedicta valeant ad poenae infernalis mitigationem.

We must now consider the quality of satisfaction.

Under this head there are five points of inquiry:

(1) Whether a man can satisfy for one sin without satisfying for another?

(2) Whether, if a man fall into sin after being contrite for all his sins, he can, now that he has lost charity, satisfy for his other sins which were pardoned him through his contrition?

(3) Whether a man's previous satisfaction begins to avail when he recovers charity?

(4) Whether works done without charity merit any good?

(5) Whether such works avail for the mitigation of the pains of hell?

Article 1

Whether a Man Can Satisfy for One Sin Without Satisfying for Another?

AD PRIMUM SIC PROCEDITUR. Videtur quod homo possit de uno peccato sine alio satisfacere. Eorum enim quae non habent connexionem ad invicem, unum potest auferri sine alio. Sed peccata non habent ad invicem connexionem: alias qui haberet unum haberet omnia. Ergo unum potest expiari sine alio per satisfactionem.

PRAETEREA, Deus est magis misericors quam homo. Sed homo recipit unius debiti solutionem sine alio. Ergo et Deus satisfactionem unius peccati sine alio.

PRAETEREA, *satisfactio,* ut in littera dicitur, *est peccatorum causas excidere, nec suggestionibus aditum indulgere.* Sed contingit hoc de uno peccato sine alio: ut scilicet luxuriam refrenet et avaritiae insistat. Ergo de uno peccato potest fieri satisfactio sine alio.

SED CONTRA: Isaiae 58, ieiunium eorum qui *ad contentiones et lites ieiunabant,* Deo acceptum non erat, licet ieiunium sit satisfactionis opus. Sed non potest fieri satisfactio nisi per opus Deo acceptum. Ergo non potest qui habet aliquod peccatum, Deo satisfacere.

PRAETEREA, satisfactio est medicina curans peccata praeterita et praeservans a futuris, ut dictum est. Sed peccata non possunt sine gratia curari. Ergo, cum quod-

OBJECTION 1: It would seem that a man can satisfy for one sin without satisfying for another. For when several things are not connected together one can be taken away without another. Now sins are not connected together, else whoever had one would have them all. Therefore, one sin can be expiated by satisfaction without another.

OBJ. 2: Further, God is more merciful than man. But man accepts the payment of one debt without the payment of another. Therefore, God accepts satisfaction for one sin without the other.

OBJ. 3: Further, as stated in the text (*Sentences* I, D. 15), *satisfaction is to uproot the causes of sin, and give no opening to the suggestions thereof.* Now this can be done with regard to one sin and not another, as when a man curbs his lust and perseveres in covetousness. Therefore, we can make satisfaction for one sin without satisfying for another.

ON THE CONTRARY, The fast of those who fasted *for debates and strifes* (Isa 58:4–5) was not acceptable to God, though fasting be a work of satisfaction. Now satisfaction cannot be made save by works that are acceptable to God. Therefore, he that has a sin on his conscience cannot make satisfaction to God.

FURTHER, Satisfaction is a remedy for the healing of past sins, and for preserving from future sins, as stated above (Q. 12, A. 3). But without grace it is impossible to

libet peccatum gratiam auferat, non potest de uno peccato sine alio fieri satisfactio.

RESPONDEO dicendum quod quidam dixerunt quod potest de uno peccato satisfieri sine alio: ut Magister in littera dicit. Sed hoc non potest esse. Cum enim per satisfactionem tolli debeat offensa praecedens, oportet quod talis sit modus satisfactionis qui competat ad tollendum offensam. Offensae autem ablatio est amicitiae restitutio. Et ideo, si aliquid sit quod amicitiae restitutionem impediat, etiam apud homines satisfactio esse non potest. Cum ergo quodlibet peccatum amicitiam caritatis impediat, quae est hominis ad Deum, impossibile est quod homo de uno peccato satisfaciat alio retento: sicut nec homini satisfaceret qui pro alapa sibi data ei se prosterneret et aliam simul daret.

AD PRIMUM ergo dicendum quod, quia peccata non habent connexionem ad invicem in aliquo uno, unum potest quis incurrere sine alio. Sed unum et idem est secundum quod omnia peccata remittuntur. Et ideo remissiones diversorum peccatorum connexae sunt. Et ideo de uno sine alio satisfieri non potest.

AD SECUNDUM dicendum quod in obligatione debiti non est nisi inaequalitas iustitiae opposita, quia unus rem alterius habet. Et ideo ad restitutionem non exigitur nisi quod restituatur aequalitas iustitiae. Quod quidem potest fieri de uno debito et non de alio. Sed ubi est offensa, ibi est inaequalitas non tantum iustitiae opposita, sed etiam amicitiae. Et ideo ad hoc quod per satisfactionem offensa tollatur, non solum oportet quod aequalitas iustitiae restituatur per recompensationem aequalis poenae, sed etiam quod restituatur amicitiae aequalitas. Quod non potest fieri dum aliquid est quod amicitiam impediat.

AD TERTIUM dicendum quod *unum peccatum suo pondere ad aliud trahit*, ut Gregorius dicit. Ideo qui unum peccatum retinet, non sufficienter causas alterius peccati excidit.

avoid sins. Therefore, since each sin excludes grace, it is not possible to make satisfaction for one sin and not for another.

I ANSWER THAT, Some have held that it is possible to make satisfaction for one sin and not for another, as the Master states (*Sentences* IV, D. 15). But this cannot be. For since the previous offense has to be removed by satisfaction, the mode of satisfaction must be consistent with the removal of the offense. Now removal of offense is renewal of friendship: therefore, if there be anything to hinder the renewal of friendship, there can be no satisfaction. Since, therefore, every sin is a hindrance to the friendship of charity, which is the friendship of man for God, it is impossible for man to make satisfaction for one sin while holding to another: even as neither would a man make satisfaction who threw himself at another's feet for having slapped him, and then gave him another slap.

REPLY OBJ. 1: As sins are not connected together in some single one, a man can incur one without incurring another; whereas all sins are remitted by reason of one same thing, so that the remissions of various sins are connected together. Consequently, satisfaction cannot be made for one and not for another.

REPLY OBJ. 2: When a man is under obligation to another by reason of a debt, the only inequality between them is that which is opposed to justice, so that for restitution nothing further is required than that the equality of justice should be reinstated, and this can be done in respect of one debt without another. But when the obligation is based on an offense, there is inequality not only of justice but also of friendship, so that for the offense to be removed by satisfaction, not only must the equality of justice be restored by the payment of a punishment equal to the offense, but also the equality of friendship must be reinstated, which is impossible so long as an obstacle to friendship remains.

REPLY OBJ. 3: By its weight, *one sin drags us down to another*, as Gregory says (*Morals on Job* 25): so that when a man holds to one sin, he does not sufficiently cut himself off from the causes of further sin.

Article 2

Whether, When Deprived of Charity, a Man Can Make Satisfaction for Sins for Which He Was Previously Contrite?

AD SECUNDUM SIC PROCEDITUR. Videtur quod qui de omnibus peccatis contritus fuit prius, et postea in peccatum incidit, de aliis peccatis, quae sibi per contritionem dimissa fuerunt, satisfacere possit extra caritatem existens. Dixit enim Daniel Nabuchodonosor, Dan. 4: *peccata tua eleemosynis redime*. Sed ipse adhuc pecca-

OBJECTION 1: It would seem that if a man fall into sin after being contrite for all his sins, he can, now that he has lost charity, satisfy for his other sins which were already pardoned him through his contrition. For Daniel said to Nabuchadnezzar: *redeem your sins with alms* (Dan 4:24). Yet he was still a sinner, as is shown by his subsequent pun-

tor erat: quod sequens poena demonstrat. Ergo potest in peccato existens satisfacere.

PRAETEREA, *nemo scit utrum sit dignus odio vel amore*, Eccle. 9. Si ergo non possit fieri satisfactio nisi ab eo qui est in caritate, nullus sciret se satisfacere. Et hoc est inconveniens.

PRAETEREA, ex intentione quam homo habet in principio actus, totus actus informatur. Sed poenitens, quando poenitentiam inchoavit, in caritate erat. Ergo tota satisfactio sequens ex illa caritate intentionem informante efficaciam habebit.

PRAETEREA, satisfactio consistit in quadam adaequatione poenae ad culpam. Sed talis adaequatio poenae potest etiam fieri in eo qui caritatem non habet. Ergo, etc.

SED CONTRA: Proverb. 10: *universa delicta operit caritas*. Sed satisfactionis est delere delicta. Ergo sine caritate non habet suam virtutem.

PRAETEREA, praecipuum opus in satisfaciendo est eleemosyna. Sed eleemosyna extra caritatem facta non valet: ut patet I Cor. 13: *si distribuero in cibos pauperum*, etc. Ergo nec satisfactio aliqua est.

RESPONDEO dicendum quod quidam dixerunt quod, postquam omnia peccata per praecedentem: contritionem remissa sunt, si aliquis ante satisfactionem peractam in peccatum decidat, et iri peccato existens satisfaciat, quod satisfactio talis ei valeat, ita quod, si in peccato illo moreretur, in inferno de illis peccatis non puniretur.

Sed hoc non potest esse. Quia in satisfactione oportet quod, etiam amicitia restituta, iustitiae aequalitas restituatur, cuius contrarium amicitiam tollit, ut Philosophus, in IX *Ethic.*, dicit. Aequalitas autem in satisfactione ad Deum non est secundum aequivalentiam, sed magis secundum acceptationem ipsius. Et ideo oportet quod, etsi iam offensa sit dimissa per praecedentem contritionem, quod opera satisfactoria sint Deo accepta. Quod dat eis caritas. Et ideo sine caritate opera facta non sunt satisfactoria.

AD PRIMUM ergo dicendum quod consilium Daniel intelligitur quod a peccato cessaret, et poeniteret, et sic per eleemosynas satisfaceret.

AD SECUNDUM dicendum quod, sicut homo nescit pro certo utrum caritatem habuerit in satisfaciendo vel habeat, ita etiam nescit pro certo utrum plene satisfecerit. Et ideo dicitur Eccli. 5: *de propitiatu peccatorum noli esse sine metu*. Nec tamen exigitur quod propter hunc metum homo satisfactionem expletam iteret, si conscientiam peccati mortalis non habet. Quamvis enim poenam non expiet per huiusmodi satisfactionem, tamen non incurrit reatum omissionis ex satisfactione ne-

ishment. Therefore, a man can make satisfaction while in a state of sin.

OBJ. 2: Further, *man knows not whether he is worthy of love or hatred* (Sir 9:1). If, therefore, one cannot make satisfaction unless one be in a state of charity, it would be impossible to know whether one had made satisfaction, which would be unseemly.

OBJ. 3: Further, a man's entire action takes its form from the intention which he had at the beginning. But a penitent is in a state of charity when he begins to repent. Therefore, his whole subsequent satisfaction will derive its efficacy from the charity which informs his intention.

OBJ. 4: Further, satisfaction consists in a certain equalization of guilt to punishment. But these things can be equalized even in one who is devoid of charity. Therefore, etc.

ON THE CONTRARY, *Charity covers all sins* (Prov 10:12). But satisfaction has the power of blotting out sins. Therefore, it is powerless without charity.

FURTHER, The chief work of satisfaction is almsgiving. But alms given by one who is devoid of charity avail nothing, as is clearly stated, *if I should distribute all my goods to feed the poor . . . and have not charity, it profits me nothing* (1 Cor 13:3). Therefore, there can be no satisfaction with mortal sin.

I ANSWER THAT, Some have said that if, when all a man's sins have been pardoned through contrition, and before he has made satisfaction for them, he falls into sin and then makes satisfaction, such satisfaction will be valid, so that if he die in that sin, he will not be punished in hell for the other sins.

But this cannot be, because satisfaction requires the reinstatement of friendship and the restoration of the equality of justice, the contrary of which destroys friendship, as the Philosopher states (*Ethics* 9.1, 3). Now in satisfaction made to God, the equality is based not on equivalence but rather on God's acceptation: so that, although the offense be already removed by previous contrition, the works of satisfaction must be acceptable to God, and for this they are dependent on charity. Consequently, works done without charity are not satisfactory.

REPLY OBJ. 1: Daniel's advice meant that he should give up sin and repent, and so make satisfaction by giving alms.

REPLY OBJ. 2: Even as man knows not for certain whether he had charity when making satisfaction, or whether he has it now, so too he knows not for certain whether he made full satisfaction; therefore, Sirach 5:5 says: *be not without fear about sin forgiven*. And yet man need not, on account of that fear, repeat the satisfaction made if he is not conscious of a mortal sin. For although he may not have expiated his punishment by that satisfaction, he does not incur the guilt of omission through neglecting to make

glecta: sicut nec ille qui accedit ad Eucharistiam sine conscientia peccati mortalis cui subiacet, reatum indignae sumptionis incurrit.

AD TERTIUM dicendum quod intentio illa interrupta est per peccatum sequens. Et ideo non dat vim aliquam operibus post peccatum factis.

AD QUARTUM dicendum quod non potest fieri adaequatio sufficiens nec secundum divinam acceptationem, nec secundum aequivalentiam: et ideo ratio illa non sequitur.

satisfaction; even as he who receives the Eucharist without being conscious of a mortal sin of which he is guilty does not incur the guilt of receiving unworthily.

REPLY OBJ. 3: His intention was interrupted by his subsequent sin, so that it gives no virtue to the works done after that sin.

REPLY OBJ. 4: Sufficient equalization is impossible both as to the divine acceptation and as to equivalence: so that the argument proves nothing.

Article 3

Whether Previous Satisfaction Begins to Avail After Man is Restored to Charity?

AD TERTIUM SIC PROCEDITUR. Videtur quod, postquam homo caritatem habuerit, valere incipiat satisfactio praecedens. Super illud Levit. 25, *si attenuatus fuerit frater tuus* etc., dicit Glossa quod *fructus bonae conversionis debet computari ex eo tempore quo peccavit.* Sed non computarentur nisi aliquam efficaciam acciperent ex caritate sequenti. Ergo post caritatem recuperatam valere incipiunt.

PRAETEREA, sicut efficacia satisfactionis impeditur per peccatum, ita efficacia baptismi impeditur per fictionem. Sed baptismus incipit valere recedente fictione. Ergo satisfactio recedente peccato.

PRAETEREA, si alicui pro peccatis commissis iniuncta fuerint multa ieiunia, et in peccatum cadens ea perfecerit, non iniungitur, cum iterum confiteatur, ut ieiunia illa iteret. Iniungeretur autem ei si per ea satisfactio non impleretur. Ergo per poenitentiam sequentem opera praecedentia satisfaciendi efficaciam accipiunt.

SED CONTRA: Opera extra caritatem facta ideo non erant satisfactoria quia fuerunt mortua. Sed per poenitentiam non vivificantur. Ergo nec incipiunt esse satisfactoria.

PRAETEREA, caritas non informat actum nisi qui ab ipsa aliqualiter procedit. Sed opera non possunt esse Deo accepta, ac per hoc nec satisfactoria, nisi sint caritate informata. Ergo, cum opera facta extra caritatem nullo modo ex caritate processerint, vel de cetero procedere possint, nullo modo poterunt in satisfactionem computari.

RESPONDEO dicendum quod quidam dixerunt quod opera in caritate facta, quae viva dicuntur, sunt meritoria vitae aeternae, et satisfactoria respectu poenae, dimittendae; et quod per caritatem sequentem opera extra caritatem facta vivificantur quantum ad hoc quod sunt

OBJECTION 1: It would seem that when a man has recovered charity his previous satisfaction begins to avail, because on Leviticus 25:25: *if your brother, being impoverished*, the Gloss says that *the fruit of a man's good works should be counted from the time when he sinned.* But they would not be counted unless they derived some efficacy from his subsequent charity. Therefore, they begin to avail after he recovers charity.

OBJ. 2: Further, as the efficacy of satisfaction is hindered by sin, so the efficacy of baptism is hindered by insincerity. Now baptism begins to avail when insincerity ceases. Therefore, satisfaction begins to avail when sin is taken away.

OBJ. 3: Further, if a man is given as a penance for the sins he has committed to fast for several days, and then, after falling again into sin, he completes his penance, he is not told, when he goes to confession a second time, to fast once again. But he would be told to do so, if he did not fulfill his duty of satisfaction by them. Therefore, his previous works become valid for satisfaction through his subsequent repentance.

ON THE CONTRARY, Works done without charity were not satisfactory through being dead works. But they are not informed by penance. Therefore, they do not begin to be satisfactory.

FURTHER, Charity does not inform a work, unless in some way that work proceeds therefrom. But works cannot be acceptable to God, and therefore cannot be satisfactory, unless they be informed by charity. Since, then, the works done without charity in no way proceeded from charity, nor can ever proceed from it, they can by no means count towards satisfaction.

I ANSWER THAT, Some have said that works done while in a state of charity, which are called living works, are meritorious in respect of eternal life, and satisfactory in respect of paying off the debt of punishment; and that by subsequent charity, works done without charity are informed so

satisfactoria, sed non quantum ad hoc quod sunt meritoria vitae aeternae.

Sed hoc non potest esse. Quia utrumque habent ex eadem ratione opera ex caritate facta, scilicet ex hoc quod sunt Deo grata. Unde, sicut caritas adveniens non potest ea gratificare quantum ad unum, ita nec quantum ad aliud.

AD PRIMUM ergo dicendum quod non debet intelligi quod fructus computetur a tempore quo primo in peccato fuit: sed a tempore in quo peccare cessavit, quo scilicet ultimo in peccato fuit. Vel intelligitur quando statim post peccatum contritus fuit, et fecit multa bona antequam confiteretur.

Vel dicendum quod, quanto est maior contritio, tanto magis diminuit de poena; et quanto aliquis plura bona facit in peccato existens, magis se ad gratiam contritionis disponit; et ideo probabile est quod minoris poenae sit debitor. Et propter hoc deberet a sacerdote discrete computari, ut ei minorem poenam iniungat, inquantum invenit eum melius dispositum.

AD SECUNDUM dicendum quod baptismus imprimit characterem in anima, non autem satisfactio. Et ideo adveniens caritas, quae fictionem tollit et peccatum, facit quod baptismus effectum suum habeat; non autem facit hoc de satisfactione. Et praeterea baptismus ex ipso opere operato iustificat, quod non est hominis, sed Dei. Et ideo non eodem modo mortificatur sicut et satisfactio, quae est opus hominis.

AD TERTIUM dicendum quod aliquae satisfactiones sunt ex quibus manet aliquis effectus in satisfacientibus etiam postquam actus satisfactionis transit: sicut ex ieiunio manet corporis debilitatio, ex eleemosynarum largitione substantiae diminutio, et sic de similibus. Et tales satisfactiones in peccatis factae non oportet quod iterentur: quia quantum ad hoc quod de eis manet, per poenitentiam Deo acceptae sunt. Satisfactiones autem quae non relinquunt aliquem effectum in satisfaciente postquam actus transit, oportet quod iterentur: sicut est de oratione et similibus. Actus autem interior, quia totaliter transit, nullo modo vivificatur, sed oportet quod iteretur.

as to be satisfactory, but not so as to be meritorious of eternal life.

But this is impossible, because works done in charity produce both these effects for the same reason, namely, because they are pleasing to God: thus just as charity by its advent cannot make works done without charity to be pleasing in one respect, so neither can it make them pleasing in the other respect.

REPLY OBJ. 1: This means that the fruits are reckoned, not from the time when he was first in sin, but from the time when he ceased to sin, that is, when he was last in sin; unless he was contrite as soon as he had sinned, and did many good actions before he confessed.

Or we may say that the greater the contrition the more it alleviates the punishment, and the more good actions a man does while in sin, the more he disposes himself to the grace of contrition, so that it is probable that he owes a smaller debt of punishment. For this reason the priest should use discretion in taking them into account, so as to give him a lighter penance, according as he finds him better disposed.

REPLY OBJ. 2: Baptism imprints a character on the soul, whereas satisfaction does not. Hence the advent of charity, which removes both insincerity and sin, causes baptism to have its effect, whereas it does not do this for satisfaction. Moreover, baptism confers justification in virtue of the deed which is not man's deed but God's, wherefore it does not become a lifeless deed as satisfaction does, which is a deed of man.

REPLY OBJ. 3: Sometimes satisfaction is such as to leave an effect in the person who makes satisfaction even after the act of satisfaction has been done; thus fasting leaves the body weak, and almsgiving results in a diminution of a person's substance, and so on. In such cases there is no need to repeat the works of satisfaction if they have been done while in a state of sin, because through penance they are acceptable to God in the result they leave behind. But when a work of satisfaction leaves behind no effect in the person that does satisfaction, it needs to be repeated, as in the case of prayer and so forth. Interior works, since they pass away altogether, are in no way informed, and must be repeated.

Article 4

Whether Works Done Without Charity Merit Any, at Least Temporal, Good?

AD QUARTUM SIC PROCEDITUR. Videtur quod opera extra caritatem facta sint alicuius boni meritoria, saltem temporalis. Quia sicut se habet poena ad malum actum, ita se habet praemium ad bonum. Sed nullum

OBJECTION 1: It would seem that works done without charity merit some, at least a temporal, good. For as punishment is to the evil act, so is reward to a good act. Now no evil deed is unpunished by God, the *just judge*. There-

malum factum apud Deum, *iustum iudicem*, est impunitum. Ergo nec aliquod bonum irremuneratum. Et sic per illud bonum aliquid meretur.

PRAETEREA, merces non datur nisi merito. Sed operibus extra caritatem factis merces datur: ut dicitur, Matth., 6, de illis qui propter gloriam humanam opera bona faciunt, quod *receperunt mercedem suam*. Ergo illa fuerunt alicuius boni meritoria.

PRAETEREA, duo existentes in peccato quorum unus multa bona facit ex genere et circumstantia, alius autem nulla, non aequaliter propinque se habent ad accipiendum bona a Deo: alias non esset ei consulendum ut aliquid boni faceret. Sed qui magis appropinquat Deo, magis de bonis eius percipit. Ergo iste per opera bona quae facit, aliquid a Deo meretur.

SED CONTRA: Est quod Augustinus dicit, quod *peccator non est dignus pane quo vescitur*. Ergo non potest aliquid a Deo mereri.

PRAETEREA, qui nihil est, non potest aliquid mereri. Sed peccator, non habens caritatem, nihil est secundum esse spirituale: ut patet I Cor. 13. Ergo non potest aliquid mereri.

RESPONDEO dicendum quod meritum proprie dicitur actio qua efficitur ut ei qui agit sit iustum. aliquid dari. Sed iustitia dupliciter dicitur. Uno modo, proprie: quae scilicet respicit debitum ex parte recipientis. Alio modo, quasi similitudinarie, quae respicit debitum ex parte dantis: aliquid enim decet dantem dare quod tamen non habet recipiens debitum recipiendi. Et sic iustitia dicitur *decentia divinae bonitatis*: sicut Anselmus dicit quod *Deus iustus est cum peccatoribus parcit, quia eum decet*. Et secundum hoc, etiam meritum dupliciter dicitur. Uno modo, actus per quem efficitur ut ipse agens habeat debitum recipiendi. Et hoc vocatur *meritum condigni*. Alio modo, per quem efficitur ut sit debitum dandi in dante secundum decentiam ipsius. Et ideo hoc meritum dicitur *meritum congrui*.

Cum autem in omnibus illis quae gratis dantur, prima ratio dandi sit amor, impossibile est quod aliquid tale, sibi debitum faciat qui amicitia caret. Et ideo, cum omnia bona, et temporalia et aeterna, ex divina liberalitate donentur, nullus acquirere potest debitum recipiendi aliquod illorum nisi per caritatem ad Deum. Et ideo opera extra caritatem facta non sunt meritoria ex condigno neque aeterni neque temporalis alicuius boni apud Deum.

Sed quia divinam bonitatem decet ut, ubicumque dispositionem invenit, perfectionem adiiciat; ideo ex merito congrui dicitur aliquis mereri aliquod bonum per opera bona extra caritatem facta. Et secundum hoc, ope-

fore, no good deed is unrewarded, and so every good deed merits some good.

OBJ. 2: Further, reward is not given except for merit. Now some reward is given for works done without charity, wherefore it is written of those who do good actions for the sake of human glory that *they have received their reward* (Matt 6:5). Therefore, those works merit some good.

OBJ. 3: Further, if there be two men in sin, one of whom does many deeds that are good in themselves and in their circumstances, while the other does none, they are not equally near to the reception of good things from God; else the latter need not be advised to do any good deeds. Now, he that is nearer to God receives more of his good things. Therefore, the former, on account of his good works, merits some good from God.

ON THE CONTRARY, Augustine says that *the sinner is not worthy of the bread he eats*. Therefore, he cannot merit anything from God.

FURTHER, He that is nothing can merit nothing. But a sinner, through not having charity, is nothing in respect of spiritual being, according to 1 Corinthians 13:2. Therefore, he can merit nothing.

I ANSWER THAT, Properly speaking, a merit is an action on account of which it is just that the agent should be given something. Now justice is twofold: first, there is justice properly so called, which regards something due on the part of the recipient. Second, there is metaphorical justice, so to speak, which regards something due on the part of the giver, for it may be right for the giver to give something to which the receiver has no claim. In this sense the *fitness of the divine goodness* is justice; thus Anselm says (*Proslogion* 10) that *God is just when he spares the sinner, because this is befitting*. And in this way merit is also twofold. The first is an act in respect of which the agent himself has a claim to receive something, and this is called *merit of condignity*. The second is an act the result of which is that there is a duty of giving in the giver by reason of fittingness, wherefore it is called *merit of congruity*.

Now since in all gratuitous givings, the primary reason of the giving is love, it is impossible for anyone, properly speaking, to lay claim to a gift, if he lack friendship. Wherefore, as all things whether temporal or eternal are bestowed on us by the bounty of God, no one can acquire a claim to any of them, save through charity towards God: so that works done without charity are not condignly meritorious of any good from God either eternal or temporal.

But since it is befitting the goodness of God that wherever he finds a disposition he should grant the perfection, a man is said to merit congruously some good by means of good works done without charity. Accordingly, such works

ra ista ad triplex bonum valent: scilicet ad temporalium consecutionem; ad dispositionem ad gratiam; et ad assuetudinem bonorum operum.

Quia tamen hoc meritum non proprie dicitur meritum, ideo magis concedendum est quod huiusmodi opera non sint alicuius meritoria, quam quod sint.

AD PRIMUM ergo dicendum quod, sicut Philosophus dicit, VIII *Ethic.*, quia filius per omnia quae facere potest, nihil aequale reddere patri potest his quae a patre recipit; ideo nunquam pater debitor filii efficitur. Et multo minus homo potest propter aequivalentiam operis Dominum sibi constituere debitorem. Et ideo nullum opus nostrum ex quantitate suae bonitatis habet quod aliquid mereatur: sed ex vi caritatis, quae facit ea quae sunt amicorum esse communia. Unde, quantumcumque sit opus bonum extra caritatem factum, non facit, proprie loquendo, quod aliquid recipiendi a Deo faciens debitum habeat. Sed opus malum ex quantitate suae malitiae secundum aequivalentiam poenam meretur: quia ex parte Dei non sunt nobis aliqua mala facta, sicut bona. Et ideo, quamvis opus malum mereatur poenam ex condigno, non tamen opus bonum sine caritate meretur ex condigno praemium.

AD SECUNDUM et ad tertium dicendum quod procedunt de merito congrui. Aliae autem rationes procedunt de merito condigni.

avail for a threefold good: acquisition of temporal goods, disposition to grace, habituation to good works.

Since, however, this is not merit properly so called, we should grant that such works are not meritorious of any good, rather than that they are.

REPLY OBJ. 1: As the Philosopher states (*Ethics* 8.14), since no matter what a son may do, he can never give back to his father the equal of what he has received from him, a father can never become his son's debtor. Much less can man make God his debtor on account of equivalence of work. Consequently, no work of ours can merit a reward by reason of its measure of goodness, but it can by reason of charity, which makes friends hold their possessions in common. Therefore, no matter how good a work may be, if it be done without charity it does not give man a claim to receive anything from God. On the other hand, an evil deed deserves an equivalent punishment according to the measure of its malice, because no evil has been done to us on the part of God, like the good which he has done. Therefore, although an evil deed deserves condign punishment, nevertheless a good deed without charity does not merit condign reward.

REPLY OBJ. 2 AND 3: These arguments consider merit of congruity; while the other arguments consider merit of condignity.

Article 5

Whether the Aforesaid Works Avail for the Mitigation of the Pains of Hell?

AD QUINTUM SIC PROCEDITUR. Videtur quod opera praedicta non valent ad poenae infernalis mitigationem. Quia secundum quantitatem culpae erit quantitas poenae in inferno. Sed opera extra caritatem non minuunt quantitatem peccati. Ergo nec infernalis poenae.

PRAETEREA, poena infernalis, quamvis sit duratione infinita, tamen intensione finita est. Sed quodlibet finitum consumitur aliqua finita subtractione facta. Si ergo opera extra caritatem facta aliquid subtraherent de poena debita pro peccatis, contingeret tantum multiplicari illa opera quod totaliter tolleretur poena inferni. Quod falsum est.

PRAETEREA, suffragia Ecclesiae sunt magis efficacia quam opera extra caritatem facta: sed, sicut ait Augustinus, in *Enchiridion, damnatis in inferno non prosunt suffragia Ecclesiae.* Poenae ergo multo minus per opera extra caritatem facta mitigantur.

OBJECTION 1: It would seem that the aforesaid works do not avail for the mitigation of the pains of hell. For the measure of punishment in hell will answer to the measure of guilt. But works done without charity do not diminish the measure of guilt. Neither, therefore, do they lessen the pains of hell.

OBJ. 2: Further, the pain of hell, though infinite in duration, is nevertheless finite in intensity. Now anything finite is done away with by finite subtraction. If, therefore, works done without charity canceled any of the punishment due for sins, those works might be so numerous that the pain of hell would be done away with altogether: which is false.

OBJ. 3: Further, the suffrages of the Church are more efficacious than works done without charity. But, according to Augustine (*Handbook on Faith, Hope, and Charity* 110), *the suffrages of the Church do not profit the damned in hell.* Much less, therefore, are those pains mitigated by works done without charity.

Sed contra: Est quod Augustinus dicit, in *Enchiridion*, quia ad hoc prosunt ut sit plena remissio, vel ut tolerabilior fiat damnatio.

Praeterea, maius est facere bonum quam dimittere malum. Sed dimittere malum semper vitat poenam, etiam in eo qui caritate caret. Ergo multo fortius facere bonum.

Respondeo dicendum quod diminuere poenam infernalem potest intelligi dupliciter. Uno modo, quod quis liberetur a poena quam iam meruit. Et sic, cum nullus liberetur a poena nisi sit absolutus a culpa, quia effectus non diminuuntur neque tolluntur nisi diminuta vel ablata causa; per opera extra caritatem facta, quia neque culpam tollere neque diminuere possunt, poena inferni mitigari non potest.

Alio modo, quod meritum poenae impediatur. Et sic huiusmodi opera minuunt poenam inferni. Primo, quia homo reatum omissionis evadit qui huiusmodi opera perficit. Secundo, quia huiusmodi opera aliquo modo ad bonum disponunt: ut homo ex minori contemptu etiam peccata faciat: vel etiam a inultis peccatis per huiusmodi opera retrahatur.

Sed diminutionem vel dilationem temporalis poenae merentur huiusmodi opera, sicut dicitur de Achab, III Reg. 21, eodem modo sicut et bonorum temporalium consecutionem.

Quidam autem dicunt quod diminuunt poenam inferni, non subtrahendo aliquid de ipsa quantum ad substantiam, sed fortificando subiectum at melius sustinere possit. Sed hoc non potest esse. Quia fortificatio non est nisi ex ablatione passibilitatis. Passibilitas autem est secundum mensuram culpae. Et ideo, si culpa non minuitur, nec subiectum fortificari potest.

Quidam etiam dicunt quod diminuitur poena quantum ad vermem conscientiae, licet non quantum ad ignem. Sed hoc etiam nihil est. Quia sicut poena ignis aequatur culpae, ita et poena remorsionis conscientiae. Unde similis ratio est de utroque.

Et per hoc patet solutio ad obiecta.

On the contrary, Augustine also says (*Handbook on Faith, Hope, and Charity* 110): *whomsoever they profit either receive a full pardon, or at least find damnation itself more tolerable.*

Further, It is a greater thing to do a good deed than to omit an evil deed. But the omission of an evil deed always avoids a punishment, even in one who lacks charity. Much more, therefore, do good deeds void punishment.

I answer that, Mitigation of the pains of hell can be understood in two ways: first, as though one were delivered from the punishment which he already deserved, and thus, since no one is delivered from punishment unless he be absolved from guilt (for an effect is not diminished or taken away unless its cause be diminished or taken away), the pain of hell cannot be mitigated by works done without charity, since they are unable to remove or diminish guilt.

Second, so that the demerit of punishment is hindered; and thus the aforesaid works diminish the pain of hell: first, because he who does such works escapes being guilty of omitting them; second, because such works dispose one somewhat to good, so that a man sins less from contempt, and indeed is drawn away from many sins thereby.

These works do, however, merit a diminution or postponement of temporal punishment, as in the case of Achab (1 Kgs 21:27), as also the acquisition of temporal goods.

Some, however, say that they mitigate the pains of hell not by subtracting any of their substance, but by strengthening the subject, so that he is more able to bear them. But this is impossible, because there is no strengthening without a diminution of passibility. Now passibility is according to the measure of guilt, wherefore if guilt is not removed, neither can the subject be strengthened.

Some again say that the punishment is mitigated as to the remorse of conscience, though not as to the pain of fire. But neither will this stand, because as the pain of fire is equal to the guilt, so also is the pain of the remorse of conscience: so that what applies to one applies to the other.

This suffices for the replies to the objections.

QUESTION 15

THE MEANS OF MAKING SATISFACTION

Deinde considerandum est de his per quae satisfactio fit.

Circa quod quaeruntur tria.

Primo: utrum satisfactionem oporteat fieri per opera poenalia.

Secundo: utrum flagella, quibus a Deo in hac vita homo punitur, sint satisfactoria.

Tertio: utrum convenienter enumerentur opera satisfactoria, cum dicitur quod sunt tria, scilicet eleemosyna, ieiunium et oratio.

We must now consider the means of making satisfaction.

Under this head there are three points of inquiry:

(1) Whether satisfaction must be made by means of penal works?

(2) Whether the scourges by which God punishes man in this life are satisfactory?

(3) Whether the works of satisfaction are suitably reckoned by saying that there are three, namely, almsgiving, fasting, and prayer?

Article 1

Whether Satisfaction Must Be Made by Means of Penal Works?

AD PRIMUM SIC PROCEDITUR. Videtur quod satisfactionem non oporteat fieri per opera poenalia. Quia per satisfactionem oportet fieri recompensationem ad divinam offensam. Sed nulla recompensatio videtur fieri per opera poenalia: quia *Deus non delectatur in poenis nostris*. Ergo non oportet satisfactionem per opera poenalia fieri.

PRAETEREA, quanto aliquod opus ex maiori caritate procedit, tanto minus est poenale: quia, *caritas poenam non habet*, I Ioan. 4. Si ergo oportet opera satisfactoria esse poenalia, quanto magis sunt ex caritate facta, minus erunt satisfactoria. Quod falsum est.

PRAETEREA, satisfacere, ut dicit Anselmus, est *honorem debitum Deo impendere*. Sed hoc etiam aliis quam operibus poenalibus fieri potest. Ergo satisfactionem non oportet poenalibus operibus fieri.

SED CONTRA: Est quod Gregorius dicit: *iustum est ut peccator tanto maiora sibi inferat lamenta per poenitentiam, quanto maiora intulit damna per culpam.*

PRAETEREA, per satisfactionem oportet peccati vulnus sanari perfecte. Sed peccatorum medicinae sunt poenae: ut Philosophus dicit, II *Ethic.* 3. Ergo oportet quod per poenalia opera satisfactio fiat.

RESPONDEO dicendum quod satisfactio respectum habet et ad praeteritam offensam, pro qua recompensatio fit per satisfactionem; et etiam ad futuram culpam, a qua per eam praeservamur. Et quantum ad utrumque exigit quod satisfactio per opera poenalia fiat. Recompensatio enim offensae importat adaequationem quam oportet esse eius qui offendit ad eum in quem offensa

OBJECTION 1: It would seem that satisfaction need not be made by means of penal works. For satisfaction should make compensation for the offense committed against God. Now, seemingly, no compensation is given to God by penal works, for *God does not delight in our sufferings*, as is clear from Tobias 3:22. Therefore, satisfaction need not be made by means of penal works.

OBJ. 2: Further, the greater the charity from which a work proceeds, the less penal is that work, for *charity hath no pain*, according to 1 John 4:18. If, therefore, works of satisfaction need to be penal, the more they proceed from charity, the less satisfactory will they be: which is false.

OBJ. 3: Further, satisfaction, as Anselm states, *consists in giving due honor to God* (*Why God Became Man*). But this can be done by other means than penal works. Therefore, satisfaction does not need to be made by penal works.

ON THE CONTRARY, Gregory says: *it is just that the sinner, by his repentance, should inflict on himself so much the greater suffering as he has brought greater harm on himself by his sin* (*Homilies on the Gospels* 20).

FURTHER, The wound caused by sin should be perfectly healed by satisfaction. Now punishment is the remedy for sins, as the Philosopher says (*Ethics* 2.3). Therefore, satisfaction should be made by means of penal works.

I ANSWER THAT, As stated above, satisfaction regards both the past offense, for which compensation is made by its means, and also future sin, from which we are preserved thereby: and in both respects satisfaction needs to be made by means of penal works. For compensation for an offense implies equality, which must be between the offender and the person whom he offends. Now equalization in human

commissa est. Adaequatio autem in humana iustitia autenditur per subtractionem ab uno qui plus habuit iusto, et additionem ad alterum cui subtractum est aliquid. Deo autem quamvis, quantum ex parte sua est, nihil subtrahi possit, tamen peccator, quantum in ipso est, aliquid ei subtraxit peccando, ut dictum est. Unde oportet, ad hoc quod recompensatio fiat, quod aliquid subtrahatur de peccante per satisfactionem quod in honorem Dei cedat. Opus autem bonum, ex hoc quod est huiusmodi, non subtrahit aliquid ab operante, sed magis perficit ipsum. Unde subtractio non potest fieri per opus bonum nisi poenale sit. Et ideo, ad hoc quod aliquod opus sit satisfactorium, oportet quod, sit bonum, ut in honorem Dei sit; et poenale, ut aliquid peccatori subtrahatur.

Similiter etiam poena a culpa futura praeservat; quia non facile homo ad peccata redit ex quo poenam expertus est. Unde, secundum Philosophum, *poenae medicinae sunt.*

AD PRIMUM ergo dicendum quod, quamvis Deus non delectetur in poenis ut sunt poenae, delectatur tamen in eis ut sunt iustae. Et sic satisfactoriae esse possunt.

AD SECUNDUM dicendum quod, sicut in satisfactione consideratur poenalitas, ita in merito consideratur difficultas. Diminutio autem difficultatis ex parte ipsius actus diminuit, ceteris paribus, meritum: sed diminutio difficultatis ex promptitudine voluntatis non diminuit meritum, sed auget. Et similiter diminutio poenalitatis ex promptitudine voluntatis, quod facit caritas, non diminuit efficaciam satisfactionis, sed auget.

AD TERTIUM dicendum quod debitum pro peccato est recompensatio offensae, quae sine poena peccantis non fit. Et de tali debito Anselmus intelligit.

justice consists in taking away from one that which he has too much of, and giving it to the person from whom something has been taken. And, although nothing can be taken away from God so far as he is concerned, yet the sinner for his part deprives him of something by sinning as stated above. Consequently, in order that compensation be made, something by way of satisfaction that may conduce to the glory of God must be taken away from the sinner. Now a good work, as such, does not deprive the agent of anything, but perfects him: so that the deprivation cannot be effected by a good work unless it be penal. Therefore, in order that a work be satisfactory it needs to be good, that it may conduce to God's honor, and it must be penal, so that something may be taken away from the sinner thereby.

Again, punishment preserves from future sin, because a man does not easily fall back into sin when he has had experience of the punishment. Therefore, according to the Philosopher (*Ethics* 2.3), *punishments are medicinal.*

REPLY OBJ. 1: Though God does not delight in our punishments as such, yet he does insofar as they are just, and thus they can be satisfactory.

REPLY OBJ. 2: Just as in satisfaction we have to note the penality of the work, so, in merit, we must observe its difficulty. Now if the difficulty of the work itself be diminished, other things being equal, the merit is also diminished; but if the difficulty be diminished on the part of the promptitude of the will, this does not diminish the merit, but increases it; and, in like manner, diminution of the penality of a work, on account of the will being made more prompt by charity, does not lessen the efficacy of satisfaction, but increases it.

REPLY OBJ. 3: That which is due for sin is compensation for the offense, and this cannot be done without punishment of the sinner. It is of this debt that Anselm speaks.

Article 2

Whether the Scourges of the Present Life Are Satisfactory?

AD SECUNDUM SIC PROCEDITUR. Videtur quod flagella quibus a Deo in hac vita punimur, non possint satisfactoria esse. Nihil enim potest esse satisfactorium nisi quod est meritorium, ut ex dictis patet. Sed non meremur nisi per ea quae in nobis sunt. Cum ergo flagella quibus a Deo punimur, non sint in nobis, videtur quod satisfactoria esse non possunt.

PRAETEREA, satisfactio tantum bonorum est. Sed huiusmodi flagella in malis inducuntur, et praecipue eis debentur. Ergo non possunt esse satisfactoria.

PRAETEREA, satisfactio respicit peccata praeterita. Sed aliquando ista flagella infliguntur illis qui peccata

OBJECTION 1: It would seem that the scourges whereby we are punished by God in this life cannot be satisfactory. For nothing but what is meritorious can be satisfactory, as is clear from what has been said. But we do not merit except by what is in our own power. Since, therefore, the scourges with which God punishes us are not in our power, it seems that they cannot be satisfactory.

OBJ. 2: Further, only the good make satisfaction. But these scourges are inflicted on the wicked also, and are deserved by them most of all. Therefore, they cannot be satisfactory.

OBJ. 3: Further, satisfaction regards past sins. But these scourges are sometimes inflicted on those who have no sins,

non habent: sicut de Iob patet. Ergo videtur quod non sint satisfactoria.

SED CONTRA: Est quod dicitur Rom. 5: *tribulatio patientiam operatur, patientia autem probationem*: idest *a peccato purgationem*, ut Glossa ibidem dicit. Ergo flagella peccata purgant. Et sic sunt satisfactoria.

PRAETEREA, Ambrosius dicit: *etsi fides*, idest peccati conscientia, *desit, poena satisfacit*. Ergo huiusmodi flagella sunt satisfactoria.

RESPONDEO dicendum quod recompensatio offensae praeteritae potest fieri et ab eo qui offendit, et ab alio. Quando autem fit ab alio, talis recompensatio vindicationis magis quam satisfactionis rationem habet: quando autem fit ab ipso qui offendit, etiam rationem satisfactionis habet. Unde, si flagella quae pro peccatis a Deo infliguntur, fiant aliquo modo ipsius patientis, rationem satisfactionis accipiunt. Fiunt autem ipsius inquantum ea acceptat ad purgationem peccatorum, eis utens patienter. Si autem omnino eis per impatientiam dissentiat, tunc non efficiuntur aliquo modo ipsius. Et ideo non habent rationem satisfactionis, sed vindicationis tantum.

AD PRIMUM ergo dicendum quod, quamvis illa flagella non sint omnino in potestate nostra, tamen quantum ad aliquid sunt, ut scilicet eis patienter utamur. Et sic homo facit de necessitate virtutem. Unde et meritoria et satisfactoria esse possunt.

AD SECUNDUM dicendum quod, sicut *ex eodem igne*, ut Gregorius dicit, *aurum rutilat et palea fumat*, ita etiam eisdem flagellis et boni purgantur et mali magis infitiuntur per impatientiam. Et ideo, quamvis flagella sint communia, tamen satisfactio tantum est bonorum.

AD TERTIUM dicendum quod flagella respectum habent ad culpam praeteritam semper: sed non semper ad culpam personae, sed ad culpam naturae. Si enim in humana natura nulla culpa praecessisset, nulla poena fuisset. Sed quia culpa in natura praecessit, personae alicui divinitus poena infertur sine culpa personae, ad meritum virtutis et cautelam peccati sequentis. Et haec duo etiam necessaria sunt in satisfactione. Oportet enim esse opus meritorium, ut honor Deo exhibeatur; et oportet esse virtutum custodiam, ut a futuris peccatis praeservemur.

as in the case of Job. Therefore, it seems that they are not satisfactory.

ON THE CONTRARY, Romans 5:3–4 states: *tribulation works patience, and patience trial*, which the Gloss explains as *deliverance from sin*. Therefore, scourges purge sin, and are thus satisfactory.

FURTHER, Ambrose says: *although faith*, i.e., the consciousness of sin, *be lacking, the punishment satisfies* (*Expositions of the Psalms* 118). Therefore, the scourges of this life are satisfactory.

I ANSWER THAT, Compensation for a past offense can be enforced either by the offender or by another. When it is enforced by another, such compensation is of a vindictive rather than of a satisfactory nature, whereas when it is made by the offender it is also satisfactory. Consequently, if the scourges which are inflicted by God on account of sin become in some way the act of the sufferer, they acquire a satisfactory character. Now they become the act of the sufferer insofar as he accepts them for the cleansing of his sins by taking advantage of them patiently. If, however, he refuse to submit to them patiently, then they do not become his personal act in any way, and are not of a satisfactory, but merely of a vindictive, character.

REPLY OBJ. 1: Although these scourges are not altogether in our power, yet in some respect they are, insofar as we use them patiently. In this way man makes a virtue of necessity, so that such things can become both meritorious and satisfactory.

REPLY OBJ. 2: As Augustine observes, even as *the same fire makes gold glisten and straw smoke* (*The City of God* 1.8), so by the same scourges are the good cleansed and the wicked worsened on account of their impatience. Hence, though the scourges are common to both, satisfaction is only on the side of the good.

REPLY OBJ. 3: These scourges always regard past guilt: not always the guilt of the person, but sometimes the guilt of nature. For had there not been guilt in human nature, there would have been no punishment. But since guilt preceded in nature, punishment is inflicted by God on a person without the person's fault, that his virtue may be meritorious, and that he may avoid future sin. Moreover, these two things are necessary in satisfaction. For the work needs to be meritorious, that honor may be given to God, and it must be a safeguard of virtue, that we may be preserved from future sins.

Article 3

Whether the Works of Satisfaction Are Suitably Enumerated?

AD TERTIUM SIC PROCEDITUR. Videtur quod inconvenienter enumerentur opera satisfactoria, cum dicitur quod sunt tria: eleemosyna, ieiunium et oratio. Quia

OBJECTION 1: It would seem that the works of satisfaction are unsuitably enumerated by saying that there are three, namely, almsgiving, fasting, and prayer. For a work of

opus satisfactorium debet esse poenale. Sed oratio poenam non habet, cum sit contra poenae tristitiam medicina, sed delectationem: unde dicitur Iac. 5: *tristatur aliquis in vobis? Oret et psallat.* Ergo non debet computari inter opera satisfactoria.

Praeterea, omne peccatum; vel est carnale vel spirituale. Sed, sicut dicit Hieronymus, *ieiunio sanantur pestes corporis, oratione pestes mentis.* Ergo non debet esse aliquod aliud opiis satisfactorium.

Praeterea, satisfactio est necessaria ad emundationem peccatorum. Sed eleemosyna ab omnibus peccatis emundat, Luc. 11: *date eleemosynam, et omnia munda sunt vobis.* Ergo alia duo sunt superflua.

Sed contra: Videtur quod debeant esse plura. Quia *contraria contrariis curantur.* Sed multo plura sunt peccatorum genera quam tria. Ergo debent plura satisfactionis opera computari.

Praeterea, peregrinationes etiam iniunguntur pro satisfactione, et disciplinae sive flagelliones, quae non computantur sub aliquo horum. Ergo debent plura satisfactionis opera computari.

Respondeo dicendum quod satisfactio debet esse talis per quam aliquid nobis subtrahamus ad honorem Dei. Nos autem non habemus nisi tria bona: scilicet bona animae, et bona corporis, et bona fortunae, scilicet exteriora. Ex bonis quidem fortunae subtrahimus nobis aliquid per eleemosynam: sed ex bonis corporalibus per ieiunium. Ex bonis autem animae non oportet quod aliquid subtrahamus nobis quantum ad essentiam vel quantum ad diminutionem ipsorum, quia per ea efficimur Deo accepti: sed per hoc quod ea submittimus Deo totaliter. Et hoc fit per orationem.

Competit etiam iste numerus ex parte illa qua satisfactio peccatorum causas excidit. Quia radices peccatorum tres ponuntur, I Ioan. 2: scilicet *concupiscentia carnism et concupiscentia oculorum, et superbia vitae.* Et contra concupiscentiam carnis ordinatur ieiunium; contra concupiscentiam oculorum ordinatur eleemosyna; contra superbiam vitae ordinatur oratio; ut Augustinus dicit, super Matthaeum.

Competit etiam quantum ad hoc quod satisfactio peccatorum est suggestionibus aditum non indulgere; Quia omne peccatum vel in Deum committimus: et contra hoc ordinatur oratio. Vel in proximum: et contra hoc eleemosyna. Vel in nos ipsos: et contra hoc ordinatur ieiunium.

Ad primum ergo dicendum quod, secundum quosdam, duplex est oratio. Quaedam quae est contemplativorum, quorum *conversatio in caelis est.* Et talis, quia totaliter est delectabilis, non est satisfactoria. Alia est quae pro peccatis gemitus fundit. Et talis habet poenam; et est satisfactionis pars.

satisfaction should be penal. But prayer is not penal, since it is a remedy against penal sorrow and is a source of pleasure, wherefore it is written: *Is any of you sad? Let him pray. Is he cheerful in mind? Let him sing* (Jas 5:13). Therefore, prayer should not be reckoned among the works of satisfaction.

Obj. 2: Further, every sin is either carnal or spiritual. Now, on Mark 9:28: *this kind can go out by nothing but prayer and fasting,* Jerome says, *diseases of the body are healed by fasting; diseases of the mind, by prayer.* Therefore, no other work of satisfaction is necessary.

Obj. 3: Further, satisfaction is necessary in order for us to be cleansed from our sins. But almsgiving cleanses from all sins, according to Luke 11:41: *give alms, and behold all things are clean unto you.* Therefore, the other two are in excess.

Obj. 4: On the other hand, it seems that there should be more. For *contrary heals contrary.* But there are many more than three kinds of sin. Therefore, more works of satisfaction should be enumerated.

Obj. 5: Further, pilgrimages and scourgings are also enjoined as works of satisfaction, and are not included among the above. Therefore, they are not sufficiently enumerated.

I answer that, Satisfaction should be of such a nature as to involve something taken away from us for the honor of God. Now we have but three kinds of goods: bodily, spiritual, and goods of fortune, or external goods. By almsgiving we deprive ourselves of some goods of fortune, and by fasting we retrench goods of the body. As to goods of the soul, there is no need to deprive ourselves of any of them, either in whole or in part, since thereby we become acceptable to God, but we should submit them entirely to God, which is done by prayer.

This number is shown to be suitable insofar as satisfaction uproots the causes of sin, for these are reckoned to be three (1 John 2:16), namely, *concupiscence of the flesh, concupiscence of the eyes*, and *pride of life.* Fasting is directed against concupiscence of the flesh, almsgiving against concupiscence of the eyes, and prayer against pride of life, as Augustine says (*Expositions of the Psalms* 42).

This number is also shown to be suitable insofar as satisfaction does not open a way to the suggestions of sin, because every sin is committed either against God, and this is prevented by prayer, or against our neighbor, and this is remedied by almsgiving, or against ourselves, and this is forestalled by fasting.

Reply Obj. 1: According to some, prayer is twofold. There is the prayer of contemplatives whose *conversation is in heaven*: and this, since it is altogether delightful, is not a work of satisfaction. The other is a prayer which pours forth sighs for sin; this is penal and a part of satisfaction.

Vel dicendum melius quod quaelibet oratio habet rationem satisfactionis, quia, quamvis habeat suavitatem spiritus, habet tamen afflictionem carnis: quia, ut dicit Gregorius, super Ezech., *dum crescit in nobis fortitudo amoris intimi, infirmamur procul dubio fortitudine carnis.* Unde etiam *nervus femoris Iacob ex lucta angeli emarcuisse* legitur in Genesi.

Ad secundum dicendum quod peccatum carnale dicitur dupliciter. Uno modo, quod in ipsa delectatione carnis completur: ut gula et luxuria. Alio modo, quod completur in his quae ad carnem ordinantur, quamvis non in delectatione carnis, sed in delectatione animae magis: ut avaritia. Unde talia peccata sunt quasi media inter spiritualia et carnalia. Et ideo oportet quod eis etiam aliqua satisfactio respondeat propria, scilicet eleemosyna.

Ad tertium dicendum quod, quamvis singula istorum per quandam convenientiam singulis peccatis approprientur, quia congruum est ut in quo quis peccaverit, in hoc puniatur, et quod peccati commissi per satisfactionem radix abscindatur; tamen quodlibet horum pro quolibet peccato satisfacere potest. Unde ei qui non potest unum ex his perficere, iniungatur aliud. Et praecipue eleemosyna aliorum vices supplere potest: inquantum alia satisfactionis opera per eleemosynam quisque sibi mercatur quodammodo in illis quibus eleemosynam tribuit. Unde non oportet quod, si eleemosyna omnia mundat peccata, quod propter hoc aliae satisfactiones superfluant.

Ad quartum dicendum quod, quamvis sint multa peccata in specie, tamen omnia ad illas tres radices, vel ad illa tria peccatorum genera quibus diximus dictas satisfactiones respondere, reducuntur.

Ad quintum dicendum quod quidquid ad afflictionem corporis pertinet, totum ad ieiunium refertur; et quidquid in proximi utilitate expenditur, totum eleemosynae rationem habet; et similiter quaecumque latria exhibeatur Deo, orationis accipit rationem. Et ideo etiam unum opus potest habere plures rationes satisfaciendi.

It may also be replied, and better, that every prayer has the character of satisfaction, for though it be sweet to the soul it is painful to the body, since, as Gregory says (*Homilies on Ezekiel*, Hom. 14), *doubtless, when our soul's love is strengthened, our body's strength is weakened;* hence we read that the sinew of Jacob's thigh shrank through his wrestling with the angel (Gen 32:24–25).

Reply Obj. 2: Carnal sin is twofold: one which is completed in carnal delectation, as gluttony and lust, and another which is completed in things relating to the flesh though it be completed in the delectation of the soul rather than of the flesh, as covetousness. Hence such like sins are between spiritual and carnal sins, so that they need a satisfaction proper to them, viz. almsgiving.

Reply Obj. 3: Although each of these three, by a kind of likeness, is appropriated to some particular kind of sin because it is reasonable that whereby a man sins, in that he should be punished, and that satisfaction should cut out the very root of the sin committed, yet each of them can satisfy for any kind of sin. Hence if a man is unable to perform one of the above, another is imposed upon him, chiefly almsgiving which can take the place of the others, insofar as in those to whom a man gives alms he purchases other works of satisfaction thereby. Consequently, even if almsgiving washes all sins away, it does not follow that other works are in excess.

Reply Obj. 4: Though there are many kinds of sins, all are reduced to those three roots or to those three kinds of sin, to which, as we have said, the aforesaid works of satisfaction correspond.

Reply Obj. 5: Whatever relates to affliction of the body is all referred to fasting, and whatever is spent for the benefit of one's neighbor is a kind of alms, and whatever act of worship is given to God becomes a kind of prayer, so that even one work can be satisfactory in several ways.

QUESTION 16

THE RECIPIENTS OF PENANCE

Deinde considerandum est de suscipientibus hoc sacramentum.

Circa quod tria quaeruntur.

Primo: utrum poenitentia possit esse in innocentibus.

Secundo: utrum in sanctis qui sunt in gloria.

Tertio: utrum in angelis bonis seu malis.

We must now consider the recipients of the sacrament of penance.

Under this head there are three points of inquiry:

(1) Whether penance can be in the innocent?

(2) Whether it can be in the saints in glory?

(3) Whether in the good or bad angels?

Article 1

Whether Penance Can Be in the Innocent?

AD PRIMUM SIC PROCEDITUR. Videtur quod in innocentibus poenitentia esse non possit. Quia poenitentia est *commissa mala plangere*. Sed innocentes nullum malum commiserunt. Ergo in eis poenitentia non est.

PRAETEREA, poenitentia ex suo nomine importat poenam. Sed innocentibus non debetur poena. Ergo non est in eis poenitentia.

PRAETEREA, poenitentia in idem coincidit cum vindicativa iustitia. Sed, omnibus existentibus innocentibus, vindicativa iustitia locum non haberet. Ergo nec poenitentia. Et ita non est in innocentibus.

SED CONTRA: Omnes virtutes simul infunduntur. Sed poenitentia est virtus. Curn ergo iri baptismo innocentibus infundantur aliae virtutes, infunditur etiam poenitentia.

PRAETEREA, ille qui nunquam fuit infirmus corporaliter, dicitur sanabilis. Ergo et similiter qui nunquam fuit infirmus spiritualiter. Sed, sicut sanatio in actu a vulnere peccati non est nisi per actum poenitentiae, ita nec sanabilitas nisi per habitum. Ergo ille qui nunquam habuit infirmitatem peccati, habet habitum poenitentiae.

RESPONDEO dicendum quod habitus medius est inter potentiam et actum. Et quia, remoto priori removetur posterius, non autem e converso; ideo, remota potentia ad actum, removetur habitus, non autem remoto actu. Et quia subtractio materiae tollit actum, propter hoc quod actus non potest esse sine materia in quam transit; ideo habitus alicuius virtutis competit alicui cui non suppetit materia, propter hoc quod suppetere potest, et ita in actum exire: sicut pauper homo potest habere habitum magnificentiae, sed non actum, quia non habet magnitudinem divitiarum, quae sunt materia magnificentiae; sed potest habere habitum. Et ideo, cum innocentes in statu

OBJECTION 1: It would seem that penance cannot be in the innocent. For penance consists in *bewailing one's evil deeds*: whereas the innocent have done no evil. Therefore, penance cannot be in them.

OBJ. 2: Further, the very name of penance implies punishment. But the innocent do not deserve punishment. Therefore, penance is not in them.

OBJ. 3: Further, penance coincides with vindictive justice. But if all were innocent, there would be no room for vindictive justice. Therefore, there would be no penance. Thus there is none in the innocent.

ON THE CONTRARY, All the virtues are infused together. But penance is a virtue. Since, therefore, other virtues are infused into the innocent at baptism, penance is infused with them.

FURTHER, A man is said to be curable though he has never been sick in body: and it is therefore similar with one who has never been sick spiritually. Now, even as there can be no actual cure from the wound of sin without an act of penance, so is there no possibility of cure without the habit of penance. Therefore, one who has never had the disease of sin has the habit of penance.

I ANSWER THAT, Habit comes between power and act: and since the removal of what precedes entails the removal of what follows, but not conversely, the removal of the habit ensues from the removal of the power to act, but not from the removal of the act. And because removal of the matter entails the removal of the act, since there can be no act without the matter into which it passes, hence the habit of a virtue is possible in one for whom the matter is not available, for the reason that it can be available, so that the habit can proceed to its act—thus a poor man can have the habit of magnificence, but not the act, because he is not possessed of great wealth which is the matter of magnificence, but he

innocentiae non habeant peccata commissa, quae sunt materia poenitentiae, sed possunt habere, actus poenitentiae in eis esse non potest, sed habitus potest. Et hoc si gratiam habeant, cum qua omnes virtutes infunduntur.

AD PRIMUM ergo dicendum quod, quamvis non commiserint, possunt tamen committere. Et ideo eis habitum poenitentiae habere competit. Sed tamen habitus iste nunquam in actum exire potest, nisi forte respectu venialium peccatorum: quia peccata mortalia tollunt ipsum. Nec tamen est frustra: quia est perfectio potentiae naturalis.

AD SECUNDUM dicendum quod, quamvis non sit eis debita poena actu, tamen in eis est possibile esse aliquid pro quo eis poena debeatur.

AD TERTIUM dicendum quod, remanente potentia ad peccandum, adhuc haberet locum vindicativa iustitia secundum habitum: quamvis non secundum actum, si peccata actu non essent.

can be possessed thereof. And so, since the innocent in the state of innocence do not have sins that they have committed, which are the matter of repentance, but they could have had them, the act of repentance cannot exist in them, but the habit can. And it does if they have grace, with which all the virtues are infused.

REPLY OBJ. 1: Although the innocent have committed no sin, nevertheless they can, so that they are competent to have the habit of penance. Yet this habit can never proceed to its act, except perhaps with regard to their venial sins, because mortal sins destroy the habit. Nevertheless it is not without its purpose, because it is a perfection of the natural power.

REPLY OBJ. 2: Although they deserve no punishment actually, yet it is possible for something to be in them for which they would deserve to be punished.

REPLY OBJ. 3: So long as the power to sin remains, there would be room for vindictive justice as to the habit, though not as to the act, if there were no actual sins.

Article 2

Whether the Saints in Glory Have Penance?

AD SECUNDUM SIC PROCEDITUR. Videtur quod sancti homines qui sunt in gloria, non habeant poenitentiam. Quia, sicut dicit Gregorius, in *Moralia*: *beati peccatorum recordantur sicut nos sani sine dolore dolorum memoramur*. Sed poenitentia est dolor cordis. Ergo sancti in patria non habent poenitentiam.

PRAETEREA, sancti in patria sunt Christo conformes. Sed in Christo non fuit poenitentia: quia nec fides, quae est principium poenitentiae. Ergo nec sanctis in patria erit poenitentia.

PRAETEREA, frustra est habitus qui ad actum non reducitur. Sed sancti in patria non poenitebunt actu: quia sic eis esset aliquid contra votum. Ergo non est in eis habitus poenitentiae.

SED CONTRA: Poenitentia est pars iustitiae. Sed *iustitia est perpetua et immortalis*, et in patria remanebit. Ergo et poenitentia.

PRAETEREA, in *Vitis Patrum* legitur a quodam patre dictum quod etiam Abraham poenitebit de hoc quod non plura bona fecit. Sed magis debet homo poenitere de malo commisso quam de bono omisso ad quod non tenebatur (quia de bono tali loquitur). Ergo erit ibi poenitentia de malis commissis.

RESPONDEO dicendum quod virtutes cardinales remanebunt in patria, sed secundum actus quos habent in fine suo. Et ideo, cum poenitentia virtus sit pars iusti-

OBJECTION 1: It would seem that the saints in glory have not penance. For, as Gregory says (*Morals on Job*, 4), *the blessed remember their sins, even as we, without grief, remember our griefs after we have been healed.* But penance is grief of the heart. Therefore, the saints in heaven have not penance.

OBJ. 2: Further, the saints in heaven are conformed to Christ. But there was no penance in Christ, since there was no faith which is the principle of penance. Therefore, there will be no penance in the saints in heaven.

OBJ. 3: Further, a habit is useless if it is not reduced to its act. But the saints in heaven will not repent actually, because, if they did, there would be something in them against their wish. Therefore, the habit of penance will not be in them.

OBJ. 4: On the other hand, penance is a part of justice. But *justice is perpetual and immortal* (Wis 1:15), and will remain in heaven. Therefore, penance will also.

OBJ. 5: Further, we read in the *Lives of the Fathers* that one of them said that even Abraham will repent of not having done more good. But one ought to repent of evil done more than of good left undone, and which one was not bound to do, for such is the good in question. Therefore, repentance will be there of evil done.

I ANSWER THAT, The cardinal virtues will remain in heaven, but only as regards the acts which they exercise in respect of their end. Wherefore, since the virtue of penance

tiae, quae est habitus cardinalis, quicumque habet habitum poenitentiae in hac vita, habebit in futura. Sed non habebit eundem actum quem nunc habet, sed alium: scilicet gratias agere Deo pro misericordia relaxante peccata.

AD PRIMUM ergo dicendum quod illa auctoritas probat quod non habent eundem actum quem hic habet poenitentia. Et hoc concedimus.

AD SECUNDUM dicendum quod Christus non potuit peccare. Et ideo materia huius virtutis non competit sibi nec actu nec potentia. Et propter hoc non est simile de ipso et de aliis.

AD TERTIUM dicendum quod poenitere, proprie loquendo, prout dicit actum poenitentiae qui nunc est, non erit in patria. Nec tamen habitus frustra erit: quia alium actum habebit.

QUARTUM concedimus.

SED QUIA quinta ratio probat quod etiam idem actus poenitentiae erit in patria qui modo est: ideo dicendum ad quintum quod voluntas nostra in patria omnino erit conformis voluntati Dei. Unde, sicut Deus voluntate antecedente vult omnia esse bona et per consequens nihil esse mali, non autem voluntate consequente; ita etiam est de beatis. Et talis voluntas improprie dicitur ab illo sancto patre poenitentia.

is a part of justice which is a cardinal virtue, whoever has the habit of penance in this life will have it in the life to come. But he will not have the same act as now, but another, namely, thanksgiving to God for his mercy in pardoning his sins.

REPLY OBJ. 1: This argument proves that they do not have the same act as penance has now; and we grant this.

REPLY OBJ. 2: Christ could not sin, wherefore the matter of this virtue was lacking in his respect both actually and potentially: so that there is no comparison between him and others.

REPLY OBJ. 3: Repentance, properly speaking, considered as that act of penance which is in this life, will not be in heaven: and yet the habit will not be without its use, for it will have another act.

WE GRANT the fourth objection.

BUT SINCE the fifth objection proves that there will be the same act of penance in heaven as now, we answer the latter by saying that in heaven one will be altogether conformed to the will of God. Hence as God by his antecedent will, but not by his consequent will, wishes that all things should be good, and therefore that there should be no evil, so is it with the blessed. It is this will that this holy father improperly calls penance.

Article 3

Whether an Angel, Good or Bad, Can Be the Subject of Penance?

AD TERTIUM SIC PROCEDITUR. Videtur quod etiam angelus, bonus seu malus, sit susceptivus poenitentiae. Quia timor est initium poenitentiae. Sed in eis est timor: Iac. 2, *daemones credunt et contremiscunt*. Ergo in eis potest esse poenitentia.

PRAETEREA, Philosophus dicit, IX *Ethic.*, quod *poenitudine replentur mali*, et haec est maxima poena eis. Sed daemones maxime sunt pravi, nec aliqua poena eis deest. Ergo daemones possunt poenitere.

PRAETEREA, facilius movetur aliquid in id quod est secundum naturam, quam in id quod est contra naturam: sicut aqua quae per violentiam calefacta est, etiam per seipsam ad naturalem proprietatem redit. Sed angelus potest mutari in peccatum, quod est contra omnem naturam eorum. Ergo multo fortius potest revocari in id quod est secundum naturam. Sed hoc facit poenitentia. Ergo sunt susceptibiles poenitentiae.

PRAETEREA, idem iudicium est, secundum Damascenum, de angelis et de animabus separatis. Sed in animabus separatis potest esse poenitentia, ut quidam di-

OBJECTION 1: It would seem that even a good or bad angel can be a subject of penance. For fear is the beginning of penance. But fear is in the angels, according to James 2:19: *the devils . . . believe and tremble*. Therefore, there can be penance in them.

OBJ. 2: Further, the Philosopher says (*Ethics* 9.4) that *evil men are full of repentance*, and this is a great punishment for them. Now the devils are exceeding evil, nor is there any punishment that they lack. Therefore, they can repent.

OBJ. 3: Further, a thing is more easily moved to that which is according to its nature than to that which is against its nature: thus water which has by violence been heated returns to its natural property of itself. Now angels can be moved to sin, which is contrary to their common nature. Much more, therefore, can they return to that which is in accord with their nature. But this is done by penance. Therefore, they are susceptible to penance.

OBJ. 4: Further, what applies to angels applies equally to separated souls, as Damascene says (*On the Orthodox Faith* 2.4). But there can be penance in separated souls, as some

cunt: sicut in animabus beatis quae sunt in patria. Ergo et in angelis potest esse poenitentia.

SED CONTRA: Per poenitentiam homo reparatur ad vitam, peccato dimisso. Sed hoc est impossibile in angelis. Ergo non sunt susceptibiles poenitentiae.

PRAETEREA, Damascenus dicit quod *homo fungitur poenitentia propter corporis infirmitatem*. Sed angeli sunt incorporei. Ergo in eis non potest esse poenitentia.

RESPONDEO dicendum quod poenitentia in nobis dupliciter accipitur. Uno modo, secundum quod est passio: sic enim nihil aliud est quam dolor vel tristitia de malo commisso. Et quamvis, secundum quod est passio, non sit nisi in concupiscibili, tamen aliquis actus voluntatis similitudinarie poenitentia dicitur, quo quis detestatur quod facit: sicut amor et aliae passiones dicuntur in intellectivo appetitu.

Alio modo accipitur secundum quod est virtus. Et hoc modo detestari malum commissum cum emendationis proposito et intentione expiandi, vel Deum placandi de offensa commissa, est actus eius. Detestatio autem competit alicui secundum quod habet: ordinem naturalem ad bonum. Et quia in nulla creatura talis ordinatio totaliter tollitur, ideo etiam in damnatis talis detestatio manet: et per consequens poenitentiae passio, vel simile ei, ut dicitur Sap. 5: *intra se poenitentiam agentes*. Et haec quidem poenitentia, cum non sit habitus, sed passio vel actus, nullo modo in beatis angelis esse potest, in quibus peccata commissa non praecesserunt: sed in malis angelis est, cum sit eadem ratio de his et de animabus damnatis, quia, secundum Damascenum, *quod homini est mors, est angelis casus*. Sed peccatum angeli est irremissibile. Et quia peccatum ut remissibile est vel expiabile, est propria materia ipsius virtutis quae poenitentia dicitur; ideo, cum materia non possit eis competere, non adest eis potentia exeundi in actum. Et ideo nec habitus eis convenit. Et ideo angeli susceptivi virtutis poenitentiae esse non possunt.

AD PRIMUM ergo dicendum quod ex timore in eis generatur aliquis poenitentiae motus, sed non quae sit virtus.

ET SIMILITER dicendum ad secundum.

AD TERTIUM dicendum quod quidquid in eis est naturale, totum est bonum et ad bonum inclinans: sed liberum arbitrium est in eis in malitia obstinatum. Et quia motus virtutis et vitii non sequitur inclinationem naturae, sed magis motum liberi arbitrii; ideo non oportet quod, quamvis naturaliter inclinentur ad bonum, quod motus virtutis in eis sit vel esse possit.

AD QUARTUM dicendum quod non est eadem ratio de angelis sanctis et de animabus sanctis: quia in animabus sanctis praecessit, vel praecedere potuit peccatum remissibile; non autem in angelis. Et ita, quamvis sint si-

say, as in the souls of the blessed in heaven. Therefore, there can be penance in the angels.

ON THE CONTRARY, By penance man obtains pardon for the sin he has committed. But this is impossible in the angels. Therefore, they are not subjects of penance.

FURTHER, Damascene says (*On the Orthodox Faith* 2.4) that *man is subject to penance on account of the weakness of his body*. But the angels are not united to a body. Therefore, no penance can be in them.

I ANSWER THAT, In us, penance is taken in two senses: first, as a passion, and thus it is nothing but pain or sorrow on account of a sin committed; and though as a passion it is only in the concupiscible part, yet by way of comparison the name of penance is given to that act of the will, whereby a man detests what he has done, even as love and other passions are spoken of as though they were in the intellectual appetite.

Second, penance is taken as a virtue, and in this way its act consists in the detestation of evil done, together with the purpose of amendment and the intention of expiating the evil, or of placating God for the offense committed. Now detestation of evil befits a person according as he is naturally ordained to good. And since this order or inclination is not entirely destroyed in any creature, it remains even in the damned, and consequently the passion of repentance, or something like it, remains in them too, as stated in Wisdom 5:3: *repenting within themselves*, etc. This repentance, as it is not a habit, but a passion or act, can by no means be in the blessed angels, who have not committed any sins: but it is in the wicked angels, since the same applies to them as to the lost souls, for, according to Damascene (*On the Orthodox Faith* 2.4), *death is to men what the fall is to an angel*. But no forgiveness is possible for the sin of an angel. Now sin is the proper object of the virtue itself which we call penance, insofar as it can be pardoned or expiated. Therefore, since the wicked angels cannot have the matter, they have not the power to produce the act, so that neither can they have the habit. Hence the angels cannot be subjects of the virtue of penance.

REPLY OBJ. 1: A certain movement of penance is engendered in them from fear, but not such as is a virtue.

THIS SUFFICES for the reply to the second objection.

REPLY OBJ. 3: Whatever is natural in them is entirely good, and inclines to good: but their free-will is fixed on evil. And since the movement of virtue and vice follows the inclination, not of nature, but of the free-will, there is no need that there should be movements of virtue in them either actually or possibly, although they are inclined to good by nature.

REPLY OBJ. 4: There is no parity between the holy angels and the beatified souls, because in the latter there has been or could have been a sin that could be pardoned, but not in the former: so that though they are like as to their

miles quantum ad statum praesentem, non tamen quantum ad statum praeteritum, quem poenitentia respicit directe.

present state, they differ as to their previous states, which penance regards directly.

QUESTION 17

THE KEYS OF THE CHURCH

Consequenter considerandum est de potestate ministrorum huius sacramenti, quae ad claves pertinet. Circa quod, primo videndum est de clavibus; secundo, de excommunicatione; tertio, de indulgentia; haec enim duo sunt annexa potestati clavium.

Circa primum consideranda sunt quattuor: primo, de entitate et quidditate clavium; secundo, de effectu earum; tertio, de ministris clavium; quarto, de his in quibus potest exerceri usus clavium.

Circa primum quaeruntur tria.

Primo: utrum claves in Ecclesia esse debeant.

Secundo: utrum clavis sit potestas ligandi atque solvendi.

Tertio: utrum sint duae claves vel una.

We must now consider the power of the ministers of this sacrament, which power depends on the keys. About this there are three considerations: (1) The keys; (2) Excommunication; (3) Indulgences. These last two things are connected with the power of the keys.

The first of these considerations will be fourfold: (1) The nature and meaning of the keys; (2) The use of the keys; (3) The ministers of the keys; (4) Those on whom the use of the keys can be exercised.

Under the first head there are three points of inquiry:

(1) Whether there ought to be keys in the Church?

(2) Whether the key is the power of binding and loosing?

(3) Whether there are two keys or only one?

Article 1

Whether There Should Be Keys in the Church?

AD PRIMUM SIC PROCEDITUR. Videtur quod claves in Ecclesia esse non debeant. Non enim requiruntur claves ad intrandum domum cuius ostium est apertum. Sed Apoc. 4 dicitur: *vidi, et ecce in caelo ostium apertum*: quod Christus est, qui de seipso dicit: *ego sum ostium*. Ergo ad introitum caeli Ecclesia clavibus non indiget.

PRAETEREA, clavis est ad aperiendum et claudendum. Sed hoc solius Christi est, qui *aperit et nemo claudit, claudit et nemo aperit*, Apoc. 3. Ergo Ecclesia in ministris suis claves non habet.

PRAETEREA, cuicumque clauditur caelum, aperitur infernus, et e contrario. Ergo quicumque habet claves caeli, habet claves inferni. Sed Ecclesia non dicitur habere claves inferni. Ergo nec claves caeli habet.

SED CONTRA: Est quod dicitur Matth. 16: *tibi dabo claves, regni caelorum*.

PRAETEREA, omnis dispensator debet habere claves eorum quae dispensat. Sed ministri Ecclesiae sunt *dispensatores divinorum mysteriorum*, ut patet I Cor. 4. Ergo debent habere claves.

RESPONDEO dicendum quod in corporalibus dicitur clavis instrumentum quo ostium aperitur. Regni autem ostium nobis per peccatum clauditur, et quantum ad maculam, et quantum ad reatum poenae. Et ideo, potestas qua tale obstaculum Regni removetur, dicitur clavis.

OBJECTION 1: It seems that the power of the keys should not exist in the Church. For keys are not required for entering a home whose door is open. But Revelation 4:1 says, *I saw and behold in heaven a door was open*; which is Christ, who says of himself, *I am the door* (John 10:7). Therefore, the Church does not need keys for entering heaven.

OBJ. 2: Further, a key is needed for opening and shutting. But this belongs to Christ alone, *who opens and no man shuts, who shuts and no man opens* (Rev 3:7). Therefore, the Church has no keys in the hands of her ministers.

OBJ. 3: Further, hell is opened to whomever heaven is closed, and vice versa. Therefore, whoever has the keys of heaven has the keys of hell. But the Church is not said to have the keys of hell. Therefore, neither has she the keys of heaven.

ON THE CONTRARY, It is written: *To you will I give the keys of the kingdom of heaven* (Matt 16:19).

FURTHER, Every dispenser should have the keys of the things that he dispenses. But the ministers of the Church are the *dispensers of the divine mysteries*, as appears from 1 Corinthians 4:1. Therefore, they ought to have the keys.

I ANSWER THAT, In material things a key is an instrument for opening a door. Now the door of the kingdom is closed to us through sin both as to the stain and as to the debt of punishment. Wherefore the power of removing this obstacle is called a key.

Haec autem potestas est in divina Trinitate per auctoritatem. Et ideo dicitur a quibusdam quod habet *clavem auctoritatis*.

Sed in Christo homine fuit haec potestas ad removendum praedictum obstaculum per meritum passionis, quae etiam dicitur ianuam aperire. Et ideo dicitur habere, secundum quosdam, *claves excellentiae*.

Sed quia *ex latere dormientis in cruce sacramenta fluxerunt, quibus Ecclesia fabricatur*, ideo in sacramentis Ecclesiae efficacia passionis manet. Et propter hoc etiam ministris Ecclesiae, qui sunt dispensatores sacramentorum, potestas aliqua ad praedictum obstaculum removendum est collata, non propria, sed virtute divina et passionis Christi. Et haec potestas metaphorice clavis Ecclesiae dicitur, quae est *clavis ministerii*.

AD PRIMUM ergo dicendum quod ostium caeli, quantum est de se, semper est apertum: sed alicui clausum dicitur propter impedimentum intrandi in caelum quod in ipso est. Impedimentum autem totius humanae naturae, ex peccato primi hominis consecutum, per passionem Christi amotum est. Et ideo Ioannes post passionem *vidit in caelo ostium apertum*. Sed adhuc quotidie alicui manet clausum propter peccatum originale, quod contrahit vel actuale, quod committit. Et propter hoc indigemus sacramentis et clavibus Ecclesiae.

AD SECUNDUM dicendum quod hoc intelligitur de clausione qua limbum clausit, ne aliquis ultra in illum descendat; et de apertione qua paradisum aperuit, remoto impedimento naturae per suam passionem.

AD TERTIUM dicendum quod clavis inferni, qua aperitur et clauditur, est potestas gratiam conferendi, per quam homini aperitur infernus, ut de peccato educatur, quod est inferni porta; et clauditur, ne ultra homo in peccatum labatur, gratia sustentatus. Gratiam autem conferre solius Dei est. Et ideo clavem inferni sibi soli retinuit. Sed clavis regni est potestas etiam dimittendi reatum poenae, per quem homo a regno prohibetur. Et ideo magis potest dari homini clavis regni quam clavis inferni: non enim idem sunt, ut ex dictis patet. Aliquis enim de inferno educitur per remissionem aeternae poenae, qui non in instanti in regnum introducitur, propter reatum temporalis poenae, qui manet.

Vel dicendum est, ut quidam dicunt, quod eadem est clavis inferni et caeli, quia ex hoc ipso quod alicui aperitur unum, clauditur alterum: sed denominatur a digniori.

Now this power is in the divine Trinity by authority; hence some say that God has the *key of authority*.

But in Christ as man this power existed for removing the aforesaid obstacle by the merit of his Passion, which is also said to open the door; hence some say that he has the *keys of excellence*.

And since *the sacraments of which the Church is built flowed from the side of Christ while he lay asleep on the cross* (Augustine, *Expositions of the Psalms* 138) the efficacy of the Passion abides in the sacraments of the Church. Therefore, a certain power for the removal of the aforesaid obstacle is bestowed on the ministers of the Church, who are the dispensers of the sacraments, not by their own, but by a divine, power, and by the Passion of Christ. This power is called metaphorically the Church's key, and is the *key of ministry*.

REPLY OBJ. 1: The door of heaven, considered in itself, is ever open, but it is said to be closed to someone on account of some obstacle against entering therein, which is in himself. The obstacle which the entire human nature inherited from the sin of the first man was removed by Christ's Passion; hence, after the Passion, John saw *a door opened in heaven*. Yet that door still remains closed to this or that man on account of the original sin which he has contracted, or the actual sin which he has committed: hence we need the sacraments and the keys of the Church.

REPLY OBJ. 2: This refers to his closing limbo, so that thenceforth no one should go there, and to his opening of paradise, the obstacle of nature being removed by his Passion.

REPLY OBJ. 3: The key whereby hell is opened and closed is the power of bestowing grace, whereby hell is opened to man, so that he is taken out from sin which is the door of hell, and closed, so that by the help of grace man should no more fall into sin. Now the power of bestowing grace belongs to God alone, wherefore he kept this key to himself. But the key of the kingdom is also the power to remit the debt of temporal punishment, which debt prevents man from entering the kingdom. Consequently, the key of the kingdom can be given to man rather than the key of hell, for they are not the same, as is clear from what has been said. For a man may be set free from hell by the remission of the debt of eternal punishment, without being at once admitted to the kingdom on account of his yet owing a debt of temporal punishment.

It may also be replied, as some state, that the key of heaven is also the key of hell, since if one is opened to a man, the other, for that very reason, is closed to him, but it takes its name from the better of the two.

Article 2

Whether the Key Is the Power of Binding and Loosing?

AD SECUNDUM SIC PROCEDITUR. Videtur quod clavis non sit *potestas ligandi et solvendi, qua ecclesiasticus iudex dignos recipere, indignos excludere debet a regno*: ut ex littera habetur, et ex Glossa Hieronymi, Matth. 16. Potestas enim spiritualis in sacramento collata est idem quod character. Sed clavis et character non videntur idem esse: quia per characterem homo Deo comparatur, per claves autem ad subditos. Ergo clavis non est *potestas*.

PRAETEREA, iudex ecclesiasticus non dicitur nisi ille qui habet iurisdictionem: quae simul cum ordine non datur. Sed claves in ordinis susceptione conferuntur. Ergo non debuit de *ecclesiastico iudice* in definitione clavium mentio fieri.

PRAETEREA, ad id quod aliquis habet ex seipso, non indiget aliqua potestate activa per quam inducatur ad actum. Sed eo ipso quod aliquis est dignus, ad regnum admittitur. Ergo non pertinet ad potestatem clavium *dignos ad regnum admittere*.

PRAETEREA, peccatores indigni sunt regno. Sed Ecclesia pro peccatoribus orat ut ad regnum perveniant. Ergo non *excludit indignos*, sed magis admittit, quantum in se est.

PRAETEREA, in omnibus agentibus ordinatis ultimus finis pertinet ad principale agens, non ad agens instrumentale. Sed principale agens ad salutem hominis est Deus. Ergo ad eum pertinet ad regnum admittere, quod est ultimus finis; et non ad habentem claves, qui est sicut instrumentum vel minister.

RESPONDEO dicendum quod, secundum Philosophum, in II *de Anima*, potentiae per actus definiuntur. Unde, cum clavis sit potentia quaedam, oportet quod per actum vel per usum suum definiatur; et quod in actu obiectum exprimatur, a quo speciem recipit actus et modus agendi, ex quo apparet potentia ordinata. Actus autem potestatis spiritualis non est ut caelum aperiat absolute, quia iam apertum est, ut dictum est: sed ut quantum ad hunc aperiat. Quod quidem ordinate fieri non potest nisi idoneitate eius cui aperiendum est caelum pensata. Et ideo in praedicta definitione clavis ponitur genus, scilicet *potestas*; et subiectum potestatis, scilicet *iudex ecclesiasticus*; et actus, scilicet *excludere et recipere*, secundum duos actus materialis clavis, aperire et claudere; cuius obiectum tangit in hoc quod dicit *a regno*; modum autem in hoc quod *dignitas et indignitas* in illis in quos actus exercetur pensatur.

AD PRIMUM ergo dicendum quod ad duo quorum unum est causa alterius, una potestas ordinatur: sicut

OBJECTION 1: It would seem that the key is not *the power of binding and loosing, whereby the ecclesiastical judge has to admit the worthy to the kingdom and exclude the unworthy*, as stated in the text (*Sentences* IV, D. 16). For the spiritual power conferred in a sacrament is the same as the character. But the key and the character do not seem to be the same, since by the character man is referred to God, whereas by the key he is referred to his subjects. Therefore, the key is not a *power*.

OBJ. 2: Further, an ecclesiastical judge is only one who has jurisdiction, which is not given at the same time as holy orders. But the keys are given in the conferring of holy orders. Therefore, there should have been no mention of the *ecclesiastical judge* in the definition of the keys.

OBJ. 3: Further, when a man has something of himself, he needs not to be reduced to act by some active power. Now a man is admitted to the kingdom from the very fact that he is worthy. Therefore, it does not concern the power of the keys to *admit the worthy to the kingdom*.

OBJ. 4: Further, sinners are unworthy of the kingdom. But the Church prays for sinners that they may go to heaven. Therefore, she does not *exclude the unworthy*, but admits them, so far as she is concerned.

OBJ. 5: Further, in every ordered series of agents, the last end belongs to the principal and not to the instrumental agent. But the principal agent in view of man's salvation is God. Therefore, admission to the kingdom, which is the last end, belongs to him, and not to those who have the keys, who are as instrumental or ministerial agents.

I ANSWER THAT, According to the Philosopher (*On the Soul* 2), powers are defined from their acts. Wherefore, since the key is a kind of power, it should be defined from its act or use, and reference to the act should include its object from which it takes its species, and the mode of acting whereby the power is shown to be well-ordered. Now the act of the spiritual power is to open heaven not absolutely, since it is already open, as stated above, but for this or that man; and this cannot be done in an orderly manner without due consideration of the worthiness of the one to be admitted to heaven. Hence the aforesaid definition of the key gives the genus, namely, *power*; the subject of the power, namely, the *ecclesiastical judge*; and the act, *of excluding or admitting*, corresponding to the two acts of a material key which are to open and shut. The object of which act is referred to in the words *from the kingdom*, and the mode in the words *worthy and unworthy*, because account is taken of the worthiness or unworthiness of those on whom the act is exercised.

REPLY OBJ. 1: The same power is directed to two things, of which one is the cause of the other, as heat, in

in igne calor ad calefaciendum et dissolvendum. Et quia omnis gratia et remissio in corpore mystico ex capite suo provenit, ideo eadem potestas videtur esse per essentiam qua sacerdos conficere potest, et qua potest solvere et ligare si iurisdictio adsit: nec differt nisi ratione, secundum quod ad diversos effectus comparatur; sicut etiam ignis dicitur secundum aliam rationem calefactivus, et liquefactivus. Et quia nihil est aliud character ordinis sacerdotalis quam potestas exercendi illud ad quod principaliter ordo sacerdotii ordinatur (sustinendo quod sit idem quod spiritualis potestas), ideo character et potestas conficiendi et potestas clavium est unum et idem per essentiam, sed differt ratione.

AD SECUNDUM dicendum quod omnis potestas spiritualis datur cum aliqua consecratione. Et ideo clavis cum ordine datur. Sed executio clavis indiget materia debita, quae est plebs subdita per iurisdictionem. Et ideo, antequam iurisdictionem habeat, habet claves, sed non habet actum clavium. Et quia clavis per actum definitur, ideo in definitione clavis ponitur aliquid ad iurisdictionem pertinens.

AD TERTIUM dicendum quod aliquis potest esse dignus aliquo dupliciter. Aut ita quod ipsum habendi ius habeat. Et sic quilibet dignus iam habet caelum apertum. Aut ita quod insit ei congruitas ad hoc quod ei detur. Et sic dignos quibus nondum totaliter apertum est caelum, potestas clavium respicit.

AD QUARTUM dicendum quod, sicut Deus non obdurat impertiendo malitiam, sed non conferendo gratiam, ita sacerdos dicitur excludere, non quod impedimentum ad intrandum ponat, sed quia impedimentum positum non amovet, quia ipse amovere non potest nisi prius Deus amoverit. Et ideo rogatur Deus ut ipse absolvat, ut sic sacerdotis absolutio locum habeat.

AD QUINTUM dicendum quod actus sacerdotis non est immediate super regnum, sed super sacramenta, quibus homo ad regnum pervenit.

fire, is directed to make a thing hot and to melt it. And since every grace and remission in a mystical body comes to it from its head, it seems that it is essentially the same power whereby a priest can consecrate, and whereby he can loose and bind, if he has jurisdiction, and that there is only a logical difference, according as it is referred to different effects, even as fire in one respect is said to have the power of heating, and in another, the power of melting. And because the character of the priestly order is nothing else than the power of exercising that act to which the priestly order is chiefly ordained (if we maintain that it is the same as a spiritual power), therefore the character, the power of consecrating, and the power of the keys are one and the same essentially, but differ logically.

REPLY OBJ. 2: All spiritual power is conferred by some kind of consecration. Therefore, the key is given together with the order: yet the use of the key requires due matter, i.e., a people subject through jurisdiction, so that until he has jurisdiction, the priest has the keys but he cannot exercise the act of the keys. And since the key is defined from its act, its definition contains a reference to jurisdiction.

REPLY OBJ. 3: A person may be worthy to have something in two ways, either so as to have a right to possess it, and thus whoever is worthy has heaven already opened to him—or so that it is fitting that he should receive it, and thus the power of the keys admits those who are worthy, but to whom heaven is not yet fully opened.

REPLY OBJ. 4: Even as God hardens not by imparting malice but by withholding grace, so a priest is said to exclude not as though he placed an obstacle to entrance, but because he does not remove an obstacle which is there, since he cannot remove it unless God has already removed it. And so God is asked to absolve, so that the priest's absolution may take place.

REPLY OBJ. 5: The priest's act does not bear immediately on the kingdom, but on the sacraments, by means of which man wins to the kingdom.

Article 3

Whether There Are Two Keys or Only One?

AD TERTIUM SIC PROCEDITUR. Videtur quod non sint duae claves, sed tantum una. Ad unam enim seram non requiritur nisi una clavis. Sed sera ad quam amovendam ordinantur Ecclesiae claves est peccatum. Ergo contra unum peccatum non indiget Ecclesia duabus clavibus.

PRAETEREA, claves in collatione ordinis conferuntur. Sed scientia non est ex infusione semper, sed quandoque ex acquisitione: nec ab omnibus ordinatis habe-

OBJECTION 1: It would seem that there are not two keys but only one. For one lock requires but one key. Now the lock for the removal of which the keys of the Church are required is sin. Therefore, the Church does not require two keys for one sin.

OBJ. 2: Further, the keys are given when holy orders are conferred. But knowledge is not always due to infusion, but sometimes is acquired, nor is it possessed by all those who

tur, sed a quibusdam non ordinatis. Ergo scientia non est clavis. Et sic est una tantum clavis, scilicet *potestas iudicandi.*

PRAETEREA, potestas quam habet sacerdos super corpus mysticum, dependet ex potestate quam habet super corpus Christi verum. Sed potestas ad conficiendum corpus Christi verum est una tantum. Ergo clavis, quae est potestas respiciens corpus Christi mysticum, est una tantum.

SED CONTRA: Videtur quod sint plures quam duae. Quia sicut ad actum hominis requiritur scientia et potentia, ita et voluntas. Sed *scientia discernendi* ponitur clavis, et similiter *potentia iudicandi.* Ergo et *voluntas absolvendi* deberet dici clavis.

PRAETEREA, tota Trinitas peccatum remittit. Sed sacerdos per claves est minister remissionis peccatorum. Ergo debet habere tres claves, ut Trinitati configuretur.

RESPONDEO dicendum quod in omni actu qui requirit idoneitatem ex parte recipientis, duo sunt necessaria ei qui debet actum illum exercere: scilicet iudicium de idoneitate recipientis; et expletio actus. Et ideo etiam in actu iustitiae per quem redditur alicui hoc quo dignus est, oportet esse iudicium quo discernatur an iste sit dignus, et ipsa redditio. Et ad utrumque horum auctoritas, sive potestas quaedam exigitur: non enim dare possumus nisi quod in potestate nostra habemus; nec iudicium dici potest nisi vim coactivam habeat, eo quod iudicium ad unum iam terminatur; quae quidem determinatio in speculativis fit per virtutem priorum principiorum, quibus resisti non potest, et in rebus practicis per vim imperativam in iudicante existentem. Et quia actus clavis requirit idoneitatem in eo in quem exercetur, quia *recipit* per *clavem iudex ecclesiasticus dignos et excludit indignos,* ut ex dicta definitione patet; ideo indiget iudicio discretionis, quo idoneitatem indicat, et ipso receptionis actu, et ad utrumque potestas quaedam sive auctoritas requiritur. Et secundum hoc, sunt duae claves: quarum una pertinet ad iudicium de idoneitate eius qui absolvendus est; et alia ad ipsam absolutionem. Et hae duae claves non distinguuntur in essentia auctoritatis qua utrumque ex officio sibi competit: sed ex comparatione ad actus, quorum unus alium praesupponit.

AD PRIMUM ergo dicendum quod ad unam seram aperiendam una clavis immediate ordinatur: sed non est inconveniens quod una ad actum alterius ordinetur. Et sic est in proposito. Secunda enim clavis, quae dicitur *potestas ligandi et solvendi,* est quae immediate seram aperit peccati: sed clavis quae dicitur scientia, ostendit cui aperienda sit sera illa.

are ordained, and it is possessed by some who are not ordained. Therefore, knowledge is not a key, so that there is but one key, viz. *the power of judging.*

OBJ. 3: Further, the power which the priest has over the mystic body of Christ flows from the power which he has over Christ's true body. Now the power of consecrating Christ's true body is but one. Therefore, there is only one key that is the power regarding the mystical body of Christ.

OBJ. 4: On the other hand, it seems that there are more than two keys. For just as knowledge and power are requisite for man to act, so is will. But the *knowledge of discretion* is reckoned as a key, and so is the *power of judging.* Therefore, the *will to absolve* should be counted as a key.

OBJ. 5: Further, all three divine Persons remit sins. Now the priest, through the keys, is the minister for the remission of sins. Therefore, he should have three keys, so that he may be conformed to the Trinity.

I ANSWER THAT, Whenever an act requires fitness on the part of the recipient, two things are necessary in the one who has to perform the act, viz. judgment of the fitness of the recipient, and accomplishment of the act. Therefore, in the act of justice, whereby a man is given what he deserves, there needs to be a judgment in order to discern whether he deserves to receive. Again, an authority or power is necessary for both these things, for we cannot give save what we have in our power; nor can there be judgment without the right to enforce it, since judgment is determined to one particular thing, which determination it derives, in speculative matters, from the first principles which cannot be resisted, and in practical matters from the power of command vested in the one who judges. And since the act of the key requires fitness in the person on whom it is exercised—because the ecclesiastical judge, by means of the key, *admits the worthy and excludes the unworthy,* as may be seen from the definition given above—therefore the judge requires both judgment of discretion whereby he judges a man to be worthy, and also the very act of receiving; and for both these things a certain power or authority is necessary. Accordingly, we may distinguish two keys, the first of which regards the judgment about the worthiness of the person to be absolved, while the other regards the absolution. These two keys are distinct, not in the essence of authority, since both belong to the minister by virtue of his office, but in comparison with their respective acts, one of which presupposes the other.

REPLY OBJ. 1: One key is ordained immediately to the opening of one lock, but it is not unfitting that one key should be ordained to the act of another. Thus it is in the case in point. For it is the second key, which is the *power of binding and loosing,* that opens the lock of sin immediately, but the key of knowledge shows to whom that lock should be opened.

AD SECUNDUM dicendum quod circa clavem scientiae duplex est opinio. Quidam enim dixerunt quod scientia secundum quod est habitus acquisitus vel infusus, dicitur hic clavis; et quod non est principalis clavis, sed in ordine ad aliam clavem clavis dicitur; et ideo, quando est sine alia clavi, non dicitur clavis, sicut in viro litterato qui non est sacerdos. Et similiter etiam quandoque hac clavi aliqui sacerdotes carent, quia non habent scientiam acquisitam neque infusam, qua absolvere et ligare possint: sed quandoque industria naturali ad hoc utuntur, quae secundum eos *claviola* dicitur. Et sic clavis scientiae quamvis cum ordine non tradatur, traditur tamen cum ordine quod sit clavis quod prius non erat. Et haec videtur opinio Magistri fuisse.

Sed hoc non videtur verbis Evangelii concordare, quae *claves* Petro dandas promittunt: et ita non solum una, sed duae in ordine dantur.

Et propter hoc alia opinio est quod scientia quae est habitus, non est clavis: sed auctoritas actum scientiae exercendi. Quae quandoque sine scientia est: quandoque autem scientia sine ipsa. Sicut patet etiam in iudiciis saecularibus: aliquis enim est iudex habens auctoritatem iudicandi qui non habet iuris scientiam; et aliquis e converso habet iuris scientiam qui non habet auctoritatem iudicandi. Et quia actus iudicii, ad quos quis ex auctoritate suscepta ordinatur, non autem ex scientia habita, sine utroque bene fieri non potest; ideo auctoritas iudicandi, quae clavis est, sine scientia non potest sine peccato accipi; sed scientia sine auctoritate sine peccato haberi potest.

AD TERTIUM dicendum quod potestas conficiendi est ad unum tantum actum alterius generis. Et ideo non connumeratur clavibus: nec multiplicatur sicut potestas clavium, quae est ad diversos actus. Quamvis secundum auctoritatis essentiam sit una, ut dictum est.

AD QUARTUM dicendum quod velle unicuique est liberum. Et ideo ad volendum non exigitur auctoritas. Et propter hoc voluntas non ponitur clavis.

AD QUINTUM dicendum quod tota Trinitas eodem modo remittit peccata sicut una Persona. Et ideo non oportet quod sacerdos, qui minister est Trinitatis, tres claves habeat. Et praecipue cum voluntas, quae Spiritui Sancto appropriatur, clavem non requirat, ut dictum est.

REPLY OBJ. 2: There are two opinions about the key of knowledge. For some say that knowledge considered as a habit, acquired or infused, is the key in this case, and that it is not the principal key, but is called a key through being subordinate to another key: so that it is not called a key when the other key is wanting, for instance, in an educated man who is not a priest. And although priests lack this key at times through being without knowledge, acquired or infused, of loosing and binding, yet sometimes they make use of their natural endeavors, which they who hold this opinion call a *little key*, so that although knowledge be not bestowed together with holy orders, yet with the conferring of holy orders the knowledge becomes a key which it was not before. This seems to have been the opinion of the Master (*Sentences* IV, D. 19).

But this does not seem to agree with the words of the Gospel, whereby the *keys* are promised to Peter, so that not only one but two are given in holy orders.

For which reason the other opinion holds that the key is not knowledge considered as a habit, but the authority to exercise the act of knowledge, which authority is sometimes without knowledge, while the knowledge is sometimes present without the authority. This may be seen even in secular courts, for a secular judge may have the authority to judge without having the knowledge of the law, while another man, on the contrary, has knowledge of the law without having the authority to judge. And since the act of judging to which a man is bound through the authority which is vested in him, and not through his habit of knowledge, cannot be well performed without both of the above, the authority to judge, which is the key of knowledge, cannot be accepted without sin by one who lacks knowledge; whereas knowledge void of authority can be possessed without sin.

REPLY OBJ. 3: The power of consecrating is directed to only one act of another kind, wherefore it is not numbered among the keys, nor is it multiplied as the power of the keys, which is directed to different acts, although as to the essence of power and authority it is but one, as stated above.

REPLY OBJ. 4: Everyone is free to will, so that no one needs authority to will; wherefore will is not reckoned as a key.

REPLY OBJ. 5: All three Persons remit sins in the same way as one Person, wherefore there is no need for the priest, who is the minister of the Trinity, to have three keys: and all the more, since the will, which is appropriated to the Holy Spirit, requires no key, as stated above (ad 4).

QUESTION 18

THE EFFECT OF THE KEYS

Deinde considerandum est de effectu clavium.

Circa quod quaeruntur quattuor.

Primo: utrum potestas clavium se extendat ad remissionem culpae.

Secundo: utrum sacerdos possit remittere peccatum quoad poenam.

Tertio: utrum sacerdos per potestatem clavium ligare possit.

Quarto: utrum possit etiam ligare et solvere secundum proprium arbitrium.

We must now consider the effect of the keys.

Under this head there are four points of inquiry:

(1) Whether the power of the keys extends to the remission of guilt?

(2) Whether a priest can remit sin as to the punishment?

(3) Whether a priest can bind in virtue of the power of the keys?

(4) Whether he can loose and bind according to his own judgment?

Article 1

Whether the Power of the Keys Extends to the Remission of Guilt?

AD PRIMUM SIC PROCEDITUR. Videtur quod potestas clavium se extendat ad remissionem culpae. Ioan. 20 dicitur discipulis: *quorum remiseritis peccata, remittuntur eis*. Sed hoc non dicitur quantum ad manifestationem tantum, ut Magister in littera dicit: quia sic sacerdos novi Testamenti non haberet maiorem potestatem quam sacerdos veteris. Ergo exercet potestatem in culpae remissionem.

PRAETEREA, in poenitentia datur gratia ad remissionem peccati. Sed huius sacramenti dispensator est sacerdos ex vi clavium. Ergo, cum gratia non opponatur peccato ex parte poenae, sed ex parte culpae, videtur quod sacerdos ad remissionem culpae operetur ex vi clavium.

PRAETEREA, maiorem virtutem recipit sacerdos ex sua consecratione quam aqua baptismi ex sua sanctificatione. Sed aqua baptismi vim accipit *ut corpus tangat et cor abluat*, secundum Augustinum. Ergo multo fortius sacerdos in sui consecratione hanc potestatem accipit ut cor a culpae macula abluere possit.

SED CONTRA: Supra Magister dixit quod Deus hanc potestatem non contulit ministro quod ad interiorem mundationem cooperaretur ei. Sed, si peccata quoad culpam remittat, cooperaretur ei in mundatione interiori. Ergo potestas clavium non extendit se ad culpae dimissionem.

PRAETEREA, peccatum non remittitur nisi per Spiritum Sanctum. Sed dare Spiritum Sanctum non est alicuius hominis: ut in Libro Primo Magister dixit. Ergo nec peccata remittere quoad culpam.

OBJECTION 1: It would seem that the power of the keys extends to the remission of guilt. For it was said to the disciples: *whose sins you will forgive, they are forgiven them* (John 20:23). Now this was not said in reference to the declaration only, as the Master states (*Sentences* IV, D. 18), for in that case the priest of the New Testament would have no more power than the priest of the Old Testament. Therefore, he exercises a power over the remission of the guilt.

OBJ. 2: Further, in penance grace is given for the remission of sin. Now the priest is the dispenser of this sacrament by virtue of the keys. Therefore, since grace is opposed to sin not on the part of the punishment, but on the part of the guilt, it seems that the priest operates unto the remission of sin by virtue of the keys.

OBJ. 3: Further, the priest receives more power by his consecration than the baptismal water by its sanctification. Now the baptismal water receives the power *to touch the body and cleanse the heart*, as Augustine says (*Tractates on John* 80). Much more, therefore, does the priest, in his consecration, receive the power to cleanse the heart from the stain of sin.

ON THE CONTRARY, The Master stated above (*Sentences* IV, D. 18) that God has not bestowed on the minister the power to cooperate with him in the inward cleansing. Now if he remitted sins as to the guilt, he would cooperate with God in the inward cleansing. Therefore, the power of the keys does not extend to the remission of guilt.

FURTHER, Sin is not remitted save by the Holy Spirit. But no man has the power to give the Holy Spirit, as the Master said above (*Sentences* I, D. 14). Neither, therefore, can he remit sins as to their guilt.

RESPONDEO dicendum quod *sacramenta*, secundum Hugonem, *ex sanctificatione invisibilem gratiam continent*. Sed haec sanctificatio quandoque ad necessitatem sacramenti requiritur tam in materia quam in ministro, sicut patet in confirmatione: et tunc vis sacramentalis est in utroque coniunctim. Quandoque autem ex necessitate sacramenti non requiritur nisi sanctificatio materiae, sicut est in baptismo, quia non habet ministrum determinatum, quantum ad sui necessitatem: et tunc tota vis sacramentalis consistit in materia. Quandoque vero de necessitate sacramenti requiritur consecratio vel sanctificatio ministri sine aliqua sanctificatione materiae: et tunc tota vis sacramentalis consistit in ministro, sicut est in poenitentia. Unde eodem modo se habet potestas clavium quae est in sacerdote ad effectum sacramenti poenitentiae, sicut se habet virtus quae est in aqua baptismi ad effectum baptismi. Baptismus autem et sacramentum poenitentiae conveniunt quodammodo in effectu: quia utrumque contra culpam ordinatur directe, quod non est de aliis sacramentis.

Sed in hoc differunt, quia sacramentum poenitentiae, eo quod habet actus suscipientis quasi materiales, non potest dari nisi adultis, in quibus requiritur praeparatio ad suscipiendum effectum sacramentorum. Sed baptismus quandoque datur adultis, et quandoque pueris et aliis carentibus usu rationis: et ideo per baptismum datur gratia et remissio peccatorum pueris sine aliqua sui praeparatione praecedente; non autem adultis, in quibus praeexigitur praeparatio removens fictionem. Quae quidem praeparatio quandoque praecedit sufficieris ad gratiae susceptionem antequam baptismus actu percipiatur, sed non ante votum baptismi, post tempus propalatae veritatis. Quandoque autem talis praeparatio tempore non praecedit, sed est simul cum baptismi susceptione: et tunc per baptismi susceptionem gratia remissionis culpae confertur. Sed per poenitentiae sacramentum nunquam datur gratia nisi praeparatio adsit, vel prius fuerit. Unde virtus clavium operatur ad culpae remissionem, vel in voto existens vel in actu se exercens, sicut et aqua baptismi.

Sed, sicut baptismus non agit sicut principale agens, sed sicut instrumentum, non quidem pertingeris ad ipsam gratiae susceptionem creandam, etiam instrumentaliter, sed disponens ad gratiam, per quam fit remissio culpae, ita est de potestate clavium. Unde solus Deus remittit per se culpam; et in virtute eius agit instrumentaliter et baptismus ut instrumentum inanimatum, et sacerdos ut *instrumentum animatum*, quod dicitur servus, secundum Philosophum, in VIII *Ethic*. 6. Et ideo sacerdos agit ut minister.

Et sic patet quod potestas clavium ordinatur aliquo modo ad remissionem culpae, non sicut causans, sed si-

I ANSWER THAT, According to Hugh, *the sacraments, by virtue of their sanctification, contain an invisible grace* (*On the Sacraments* 2). Now this sanctification is sometimes essential to the sacrament both as regards the matter and as regards the minister, as may be seen in confirmation, and then the sacramental virtue is in both together. Sometimes, however, the essence of the sacrament requires only sanctification of the matter, as in baptism, which has no fixed minister on whom it depends necessarily, and then the whole virtue of the sacrament is in the matter. Again, sometimes the essence of the sacrament requires the consecration or sanctification of the minister without any sanctification of the matter, and then the entire sacramental virtue is in the minister, as in penance. Hence the power of the keys which is in the priest stands in the same relation to the effect of penance as the virtue in the baptismal water does to the effect of baptism. Now baptism and the sacrament of penance agree somewhat in their effect, since each is directly ordained against guilt, which is not the case in the other sacraments.

Yet they differ in this, that the sacrament of penance, since the acts of the recipient are as its matter, cannot be given save to adults, who need to be disposed for the reception of the sacramental effect; whereas baptism is given sometimes to adults, sometimes to children and others who lack the use of reason, so that by baptism children receive grace and remission of sin without any previous disposition, while adults do not, for they require to be disposed by the removal of insincerity. This disposition sometimes precedes their baptism by priority of time, being sufficient for the reception of grace before they are actually baptized, but not before they have come to the knowledge of the truth and have conceived the desire for baptism. At other times, this disposition does not precede the reception of baptism by a priority of time, but is simultaneous with it, and then the grace of the remission of guilt is bestowed through the reception of baptism. On the other hand, grace is never given through the sacrament of penance unless the recipient be disposed either simultaneously or before. Hence the power of the keys operates unto the remission of guilt either through being desired or through being actually exercised, even as the waters of baptism.

But just as baptism acts not as a principal agent but as an instrument, and does not go so far as to cause the reception itself of grace, even instrumentally, but merely disposes the recipient to the grace whereby his guilt is remitted, so is it with the power of the keys. Hence God alone directly remits guilt, and baptism acts through his power instrumentally, as an inanimate instrument, and the priest as an *animate instrument*, such as a servant is, according to the Philosopher (*Ethics* 8.11): and consequently the priest acts as a minister.

Hence it is clear that the power of the keys is ordained, in a manner, to the remission of guilt, not as causing that

cut disponens ad eam. Unde, si ante absolutionem aliquis non fuisset perfecte dispositus ad gratiam suscipiendam, in ipsa confessione et absolutione sacramentali gratiam consequeretur, si obicem non poneret. Si enim clavis nullo modo ad culpae remissionem ordinaretur, sed ad dimissionem poenae tantum ut quidam dicunt, non exigeretur votum recipiendi effectum clavium ad culpae remissionem: sicut non exigitur votum suscipiendi alia sacramenta, quae non ordinantur ad culpam sed contra poenam. Sed hoc facit videri quod non ordinantur ad culpae dimissionem: quia semper usus clavium, ad hoc quod effectum habeat, requirit praeparationem ex parte recipientis sacramentum. Et similiter videretur de baptismo, si nunquam daretur nisi adultis.

AD PRIMUM ergo dicendum quod, sicut Magister dicit in littera, sacerdotibus commissa est potestas remittendi peccata, non ut propria virtute remittant, quia hoc Dei est; sed ut operationem Dei remittentis ostendant tanquam ministri. Sed hoc contingit tribus modis. Uno modo, ut ostendant eam non praesentem, sed promittant eam futuram, sine hoc quod aliquid operentur ad ipsam. Et sic sacramenta veteris legis operationem Dei significabant. Unde et sacerdos veteris legis ostendebat tantum, et nihil operabatur.

Alio modo, ut significent praesentem, et nihil ad eam operentur. Et sic quidam dicunt quod sacramenta novae legis significant collationem gratiae, quam Deus in ipsa sacramentorum collatione dat, sine hoc quod in sacramentis sit aliqua virtus operans ad gratiam. Et secundum hanc opinionem etiam potestas clavium esset tantum ostendens divinam operationem in culpae remissione in ipsa sacramentali collatione facta.

Tertio modo, ut significent divinam operationem in remissionem culpae praesentem, et ad ipsam aliquid dispositive et instrumentaliter operentur. Et sic, secundum aliam opinionem, quae sustinetur communius, sacramenta novae legis emundationem ostendunt divinitus factam. Et hoc modo etiam sacerdos novi Testamenti ostendit absolutos a culpa: quia proportionaliter oportet loqui de sacramentis, et potestate ministrorum. Nec obstat quin claves Ecclesiae ad remissionem culpae disponant quia culpa iam est remissa: sicut nec quod baptismus disponat, quantum in se est, in eo qui iam sanctificatus est.

AD SECUNDUM dicendum quod neque sacramentum poenitentiae, neque sacramentum baptismi, operando pertingit directe ad gratiam nec ad culpae remissionem: sed dispositive.

UNDE ETIAM patet responsio ad tertium.

remission, but as disposing thereto. Consequently, if a man before receiving absolution were not perfectly disposed for the reception of grace, he would receive grace at the very time of sacramental confession and absolution, provided he offered no obstacle. For if the key were in no way ordained to the remission of guilt, but only to the remission of punishment, as some hold, it would not be necessary to have a desire of receiving the effect of the keys in order to have one's sins forgiven, just as it is not necessary to have a desire of receiving the other sacraments which are ordained not to the remission of guilt, but against punishment. But this enables us to see that it is not ordained unto the remission of guilt, because the use of the keys, in order to be effective, always requires a disposition on the part of the recipient of the sacrament. And the same would apply to baptism, were it never given save to adults.

REPLY OBJ. 1: As the Master says in the text (*Sentences* IV, D. 18), the power of forgiving sins was entrusted to priests, not that they may forgive them by their own power, for this belongs to God, but that as ministers they may declare the operation of God who forgives. Now this happens in three ways. First, by a declaration, not of present, but of future forgiveness, without cooperating therein in any way: and thus the sacraments of the old law signified the divine operation, so that the priest of the old law did but declare and did not operate the forgiveness of sins.

Second, by a declaration of present forgiveness without cooperating in it at all: and thus some say that the sacraments of the new law signify the bestowal of grace, which God gives when the sacraments are conferred without the sacraments containing any power productive of grace, according to which opinion even the power of the keys would merely declare the divine operation that has its effect in the remission of guilt when the sacrament is conferred.

Third, by signifying the divine operation causing then and there the remission of guilt, and by cooperating towards this effect dispositively and instrumentally: and then, according to another and more common opinion, the sacraments of the new law declare the cleansing effected by God. In this way also the priest of the New Testament declares the recipient to be absolved from guilt, because in speaking of the sacraments, what is ascribed to the power of the ministers must be consistent with the sacrament. Nor is it unreasonable that the keys of the Church should dispose the penitent to the remission of his guilt from the fact that the guilt is already remitted, even as neither is it unreasonable that baptism, considered in itself, causes a disposition in one who is already sanctified.

REPLY OBJ. 2: Neither the sacrament of penance nor the sacrament of baptism by its operation causes grace or the remission of guilt directly, but only dispositively.

HENCE the reply to the third objection is evident.

Aliae rationes ostendunt quod ad remissionem culpae directe clavium potestas non operetur. Quod concedendum est.

The other arguments show that the power of the keys does not effect the remission of guilt directly, and this is to be granted.

Article 2

Whether a Priest Can Remit Sin as to the Punishment?

AD SECUNDUM SIC PROCEDITUR. Videtur quod sacerdos non possit remittere peccatum quoad poenam. Peccato enim debetur poena aeterna et temporalis. Sed adhuc post absolutionem sacerdotis manet poenitens obligatus ad poenam temporalem, in purgatorio vel in hoc mundo faciendam. Ergo non dimittit aliquo modo poenam.

PRAETEREA, sacerdos non potest praeiudicare iustitiae divinae. Sed ex divina iustitia taxata est poenitentibus poena quam debent subire. Ergo sacerdos non potest de ea aliquid remittere.

PRAETEREA, ille qui parvum peccatum commisit, non est minus susceptivus effectus clavium quam ille qui commisit maius peccatum. Sed si aliquid de poena per officium sacerdotis de maiori peccato dimittitur, possibile est esse adeo parvum peccatum cui non debeatur plus de poena quam illud quod de maiori peccato dimissum est. Ergo poterit totam poenam illius peccati parvi dimittere. Quod falsum est.

PRAETEREA, tota poena temporalis peccato debita est unius rationis. Si ergo per primam absolutionem dimittatur aliquid de poena, et per secundam ab eodem peccato absolutionem poterit aliquid remitti. Et sic tantum poterit multiplicari absolutio quod vi clavium tota poena tolletur: cum secunda absolutio non sit minoris efficaciae quam prima. Et sic peccatum remanebit omnino impunitum. Quod est inconveniens.

SED CONTRA: Clavis est potestas ligandi et solvendi. Sed potest sacerdos iniungere poenam temporalem. Ergo et potest absolvere a poena.

PRAETEREA, sacerdos non potest dimittere peccatum quantum ad culpam, ut in littera dicitur: nec quantum ad poenam aeternam, pari ratione. Si ergo non potest remittere quantum ad poenam temporalem, nullo modo remittere poterit. Quod est omnino contrarium dictis Evangelii.

RESPONDEO dicendum quod idem iudicium est de effectu quem potestas clavium actualiter exercita complet in eo in quo contritio tempore praecessit, et effectu baptismi qui iam habenti gratiam datur. Aliquis enim per fidem et contritionem praecedentem baptismum gratiam remissionis peccatorum quantum ad culpam consecutus est: sed quando actualiter postea bapti-

OBJECTION 1: It would seem that a priest cannot remit sin as to the punishment. For sin deserves eternal and temporal punishment. But after the priest's absolution the penitent is still obliged to undergo temporal punishment either in purgatory or in this world. Therefore, the priest does not remit the punishment in any way.

OBJ. 2: Further, the priest cannot anticipate the judgment of God. But divine justice appoints the punishment which penitents have to undergo. Therefore, the priest cannot remit any part of it.

OBJ. 3: Further, a man who has committed a slight sin is not less susceptible to the power of the keys than one who has committed a graver sin. Now, if the punishment for the graver sin be lessened in any way through the priestly administrations, it would be possible for a sin to be so slight that the punishment which it deserves is no greater than that which has been remitted for the graver sin. Therefore, the priest would be able to remit the entire punishment due for the slight sin: which is false.

OBJ. 4: Further, the whole of the temporal punishment due for a sin is of one kind. If, therefore, by a first absolution something is taken away from the punishment, it will be possible for something more to be taken away by a second absolution, so that the absolution can be so often repeated that by virtue of the keys the whole punishment will be taken away, since the second absolution is not less efficacious than the first: and consequently that sin will be altogether unpunished, which is unfitting.

ON THE CONTRARY, The key is the power of binding and loosing. But the priest can enjoin a temporal punishment. Therefore, he can absolve from punishment.

FURTHER, The priest cannot remit sin either as to the guilt, as stated in the text (*Sentences* IV, D. 18), or as to the eternal punishment, for a like reason. If, therefore, he cannot remit sin as to the temporal punishment, he would be unable to remit sin in any way, which is altogether contrary to the words of the Gospel.

I ANSWER THAT, Whatever may be said of the effect of baptism conferred on one who has already received grace applies equally to the effect of the actual exercise of the power of the keys on one who has already been contrite. For a man may, through faith and contrition, obtain the grace of the remission of his sins as to their guilt previous to baptism; but when, afterwards, he actually receives baptism, his

smum suscipit, gratia augetur, et a reatu poenae totaliter absolvitur, eo quod fit particeps passionis Christi.

Et similiter illi qui per contritionem consecutus est remissionem peccatorum quantum ad culpam, et per consequens quantum ad reatum poenae aeternae, quae simul cum culpa dimittitur, ex vi clavium, ex passione Christi efficaciam habentium, augetur gratia et remittitur temporalis poena, cuius reatus adhuc remanserat post culpae remissionem. Non tamen totus, sicut in baptismo: sed pars eius. Quia in baptismo regeneratus homo configuratur passioni Christi totaliter efficaciam passionis Christi, quae sufficit ad omnem poenam delendam, in se suscipiens, ut nihil de prioris peccati actualis poena remaneat: quia non debet alicui imputari ad poenam nisi quod ipsemet fecit; in baptismo autem homo, novam vitam suscipieris, fit per gratiam baptismalem novus homo; et ideo nullus reatus poenae in eo remanet pro praecedenti peccato.

Sed in poenitentia non mutatur homo in aliam vitam: quia non est regeneratio, sed sanatio quaedam. Ideo ex vi clavium, quae operatur in sacramento poenitentiae, non tota poena remittitur, sed aliquid de poena temporali, cuius reatus post absolutionem a poena aeterna remanere potuit. Nec solum a poena illa quam habet vel suscipit ab ea poenitens in confitendo, ut quidam dicunt: quia sic confessio et sacramentalis absolutio non esset nisi in onus, quod non competit sacramentis novae legis. Sed etiam de illa poena quae in purgatorio debetur remittitur, ut minus in purgatorio puniatur absolutus ante satisfactionem decedens, quam si ante absolutionem decederet.

AD PRIMUM ergo dicendum quod sacerdos non remittit totam poenam temporalem, sed partem. Et ideo adhuc manet obligatus ad poenam satisfactoriam.

AD SECUNDUM dicendum quod passio Christi sufficienter satisfecit *pro peccatis totius mundi*. Et ideo sine praeiudicio divinae iustitiae aliquid de poena sibi debita remitti potest, secundum quod effectus passionis ad ipsum per sacramenta Ecclesiae pertingit.

AD TERTIUM dicendum quod pro quolibet peccato oportet aliquam poenam satisfactoriam remanere, et per quam medicina contra ipsum praestetur. Et ideo, quamvis virtute absolutionis dimittatur aliqua quantitas poenae debitae pro aliquo magno peccato, non oportet quod tanta quantitas poenae dimittatur respectu cuiuslibet peccati, quia secundum hoc aliquod peccatum remaneret omnino sine poena: sed virtute clavium de poenis singulorum peccatorum proportionaliter dimittitur.

grace is increased, and he is entirely absolved from the debt of punishment, since he is then made a partaker of the Passion of Christ.

In like manner, when a man through contrition has received the pardon of his sins as to their guilt, and consequently as to the debt of eternal punishment (which is remitted together with the guilt), by virtue of the keys which derive their efficacy from the Passion of Christ, his grace is increased and the temporal punishment is remitted, the debt of which remained after the guilt had been forgiven. However, this temporal punishment is not entirely remitted, as in baptism, but only partly, because the man who is regenerated in baptism is conformed to the Passion of Christ by receiving into himself entirely the efficacy of Christ's Passion, which suffices for the blotting out of all punishment, so that nothing remains of the punishment due to his preceding actual sins. For nothing should be imputed to a man unto punishment save what he has done himself, and in baptism man begins a new life, and becomes a new man by the baptismal water; and thus, no debt for previous sin remains in him.

On the other hand, in penance a man does not take on a new life, since in it he is not born again, but healed. Consequently, by virtue of the keys which produce their effect in the sacrament of penance, the punishment is not entirely remitted, but something is taken off the temporal punishment, the debt of which could remain after the eternal punishment had been remitted. Nor does this apply only to the temporal punishment which the penitent owes at the time of confession, as some hold, (for then confession and sacramental absolution would be mere burdens, which cannot be said of the sacraments of the new law), but also to the punishment due in purgatory, so that one who has been absolved and dies before making satisfaction is less punished in purgatory than if he had died before receiving absolution.

REPLY OBJ. 1: The priest does not remit the entire temporal punishment, but part of it; wherefore the penitent still remains obliged to undergo satisfactory punishment.

REPLY OBJ. 2: Christ's Passion was sufficiently satisfactory *for the sins of the whole world*, so that without prejudice to divine justice something can be remitted from the punishment which a sinner deserves, insofar as the effect of Christ's Passion reaches him through the sacraments of the Church.

REPLY OBJ. 3: Some satisfactory punishment must remain for each sin, so as to provide a remedy against it. And therefore, although by virtue of the absolution some measure of the punishment due to a grave sin is remitted, it does not follow that the same measure of punishment is remitted for each sin, because in that case some sin would remain without any punishment at all: but by virtue of the keys the punishments due to various sins are remitted in due proportion.

AD QUARTUM dicendum quod quidam dicunt quod in prima absolutione tantum dimittitur vi clavium quantum dimitti potest: sed tamen valet iterata confessio, tum propter instructionem; tum propter maiorem certitudinem; tum propter intercessionem confessoris; tum propter verecundiae meritum.

Sed hoc non videtur verum. Quia, si haec esset ratio confessionem iterandi, non tamen esset ratio iterandi absolutionem: praecipue in eo qui non habet aliquam causam dubitationis de praecedenti absolutione; ita enim poterit dubitare post secundam absolutionem sicut post primam. Sicut videmus quod sacramentum extremae unctionis non iteratur super eundem morbum, eo quod totum quod per sacramentum fieri potuit, semel factum est. Et praeterea in secunda confessione non requireretur quod haberet claves ille cui fit confessio, si nihil ibi vis clavium operatur.

Et ideo dicunt alii quod etiam in secunda absolutione vi clavium dimittitur de poena. Quia in secunda absolutione gratiae confertur augmentum: et quanto maior gratia recipitur, minus de impuritate praecedentis peccati manet; et ideo minor poena purgans debetur. Unde etiam in prima absolutione alicui plus et minus dimittitur de poena secundum quod plus se ad gratiam disponit. Et potest esse tanta dispositio quod etiam ex vi contritionis tota poena tollitur, ut praedictum est. Unde etiam non est inconveniens si per frequentem confessionem etiam tota poena tollatur, ut peccatum omnino remaneat impunitum, pro quo poena Christi satisfecit.

REPLY OBJ. 4: Some say that at the first absolution as much as possible is remitted by virtue of the keys, and that, nevertheless, the second confession is valid, on account of the instruction received, on account of the additional surety, on account of the prayers of the priest or confessor, and lastly on account of the merit of the shame.

But this does not seem to be true, for though there might be a reason for repeating the confession, there would be no reason for repeating the absolution, especially if the penitent has no cause to doubt about his previous absolution; for he might just as well doubt after the second as after the first absolution: even as we see that the sacrament of extreme unction is not repeated during the same sickness, for the reason that all that could be done through the sacrament has been done once. Moreover, in the second confession, there would be no need for the confessor to have the keys if the power of the keys had no effect therein.

For these reasons others say that even in the second absolution something of the punishment is remitted by virtue of the keys, because when absolution is given a second time, grace is increased, and the greater the grace received, the less there remains of the blemish of the previous sin, and the less punishment is required to remove that blemish. Hence even when a man is first absolved, his punishment is more or less remitted by virtue of the keys, according as he disposes himself more or less to receive grace; and this disposition may be so great that even by virtue of his contrition the whole punishment is remitted, as we have already stated (Q. 5, A. 2). Therefore, it is also not unfitting if by frequent confession even the whole punishment is taken away, so that sin remains entirely unpunished, for which the suffering of Christ made satisfaction.

Article 3

Whether the Priest Can Bind Through the Power of the Keys?

AD TERTIUM SIC PROCEDITUR. Videtur quod sacerdos per potestatem clavium ligare non possit. Virtutes enim sacramentales ordinantur contra peccatum ut medicina. Sed ligare non est medicina peccati, sed magis aggravatio morbi, ut videtur. Ergo sacerdos per vim clavium, quae est vis sacramentalis, non potest ligare.

PRAETEREA, sicut absolvere vel aperire est amovere obstaculum, ita ligare est obstaculum ponere. Sed obstaculum regni peccatum est, quod nobis ex alio imponi non potest: quia non nisi voluntate peccatur. Ergo sacerdos ligare non potest.

PRAETEREA, claves ex passione Christi efficaciam habent. Sed ligare non est effectus passionis. Ergo ex clavium potestate non potest sacerdos ligare.

OBJECTION 1: It would seem that the priest cannot bind by virtue of the power of the keys. For the sacramental power is ordained as a remedy against sin. Now binding is not a remedy for sin, but seemingly is rather conducive to an aggravation of the disease. Therefore, by the power of the keys, which is a sacramental power, the priest cannot bind.

OBJ. 2: Further, just as to loose or to open is to remove an obstacle, so to bind is to place an obstacle. Now an obstacle to heaven is sin, which cannot be placed on us by an extrinsic cause, since no sin is committed except by the will. Therefore, the priest cannot bind.

OBJ. 3: Further, the keys derive their efficacy from Christ's Passion. But binding is not an effect of the Passion. Therefore, the priest cannot bind by the power of the keys.

SED CONTRA: Est quod dicitur Matth. 16: *quodcumque ligaveris super terram, erit ligatum et in caelis.*

PRAETEREA, *potestates rationales sunt ad opposita.* Sed potestas clavium est potestas rationalis: cum habeat discretionem adiunctam. Ergo habet se ad opposita. Ergo, si potest solvere, potest et ligare.

RESPONDEO dicendum quod operatio sacerdotis in usu clavium est conformis Dei operationi, cuius minister est. Deus autem habet operationem et in culpam et in poenam. Sed in culpam ad absolvendum quidem directe, ad ligandum autem indirecte, inquantum *obdurare* dicitur dum gratiam non largitur. Sed in poenam habet operationem directe quantum ad utrumque: quia et poenam parcit, et poenam infligit. Similiter ergo et sacerdos, etsi in absolvendo ex vi clavium habeat aliquam operationem ordinatam ad culpae dimissionem modo iam dicto, non tamen ligando aliquam operationem habet in culpam: nisi ligare dicatur inquantum non absolvit sed ligatos ostendit. Sed in poenam habet potestatem et ligandi et solvendi. Solvit enim a poena quam dimittit, sed ligat ad poenam quae remanet. Sed ad hanc ligare dupliciter dicitur. Uno modo, considerando ipsam quantitatem poenae in communi: et sic non ligat, nisi inquantum non solvit sed ligatum ostendit. Alio modo, considerando poenam hanc vel illam determinate: et sic ligat ad poenam imponendo eam.

AD PRIMUM ergo dicendum quod illud residuum poenae ad quod obligat, est medicina purgans peccati impuritatem.

AD SECUNDUM dicendum quod obstaculum regni non solum est peccatum, sed etiam poena: quam qualiter sacerdos imponat, dictum est.

AD TERTIUM dicendum quod etiam passio Christi obligat nos ad poenam aliquam, per quam ei conformemur.

ON THE CONTRARY, Matthew 16:19 states: *whatsoever you will bind on earth will be bound also in heaven.*

FURTHER, *Rational powers are directed to opposites* (*Metaphysics* 9.2). But the power of the keys is a rational power, since it has discretion connected with it. Therefore, it is directed to opposites. Therefore, if it can loose, it can bind.

I ANSWER THAT, The operation of the priest in using the keys is conformed to God's operation, whose minister he is. Now God's operation extends both to guilt and to punishment: to the guilt indeed, so as to loose it directly, but to bind it indirectly, insofar as he is said *to harden* when he withholds his grace. But his operation extends to punishment directly in both respects, because he both spares and inflicts it. In like manner, therefore, although the priest in absolving exercises an operation ordained to the remission of guilt in the way mentioned above (A. 1), nevertheless, in binding, he exercises no operation on the guilt (unless he be said to bind by not absolving the penitent and by declaring him to be bound). But he has the power both of binding and of loosing with regard to the punishment. For he looses from the punishment which he remits, while he binds as to the punishment which remains. This he does in two ways—first, as regards the quantity of the punishment considered in general, and thus he does not bind save by not loosing, and declaring the penitent to be bound; second, as regards this or that particular punishment, and thus he binds to punishment by imposing it.

REPLY OBJ. 1: The remainder of the punishment to which the priest binds the penitent is the medicine which cleanses the latter from the blemish of sin.

REPLY OBJ. 2: Not only sin, but also punishment is an obstacle to heaven: and how the latter is enjoined by the priest has been said in the article.

REPLY OBJ. 3: Even the Passion of Christ binds us to some punishment through which we are conformed to him.

Article 4

Whether the Priest Can Bind and Loose According to His Own Judgment?

AD QUARTUM SIC PROCEDITUR. Videtur quod sacerdos possit ligare et solvere secundum proprium arbitrium. Hieronymus enim dicit: *mensuram temporis in agendo poenitentiam non satis aperte praefigunt canones pro unoquoque crimine, ut de singulis dicat qualiter unumquodque sit emendandum, sed magis arbitrio sacerdotis intelligentis relinquendum statuunt.* Ergo videtur quod ipse secundum suum arbitrium possit ligare et solvere.

PRAETEREA, *Dominus laudavit villicum iniquitatis, quod prudenter fecisset,* quia debitoribus domini sui re-

OBJECTION 1: It seems that the priest can bind and loose according to his own judgment. For Jerome says: *the canons do not fix the length of time for doing penance so precisely as to say how each sin is to be amended, but leave the decision of this matter to the judgment of a discreet priest.* Therefore, it seems that he can bind and loose according to his own judgment.

OBJ. 2: Further, *the Lord commended the unjust steward for as much as he had done wisely* (Luke 16:5), because

misisset largiter. Sed Deus magis pronus est ad miserendum quam aliquis dominus temporalis. Ergo videtur quod laudabilior sit quantum plus de poena dimiserit.

PRAETEREA, *omnis actio Christi nostra est instructio.* Sed ipse quibusdam peccantibus nullam poenam imposuit, sed solum emendationem vitae: ut patet de adultera, Ioan. 8. Ergo videtur quod ad arbitrium suum possit etiam sacerdos, qui est vicarius Christi, dimittere totam poenam vel partem.

SED CONTRA: Gregorius dicit: *falsam poenitentiam dicimus quae non secundum auctoritatem sanctorum Patrum pro qualitate criminis imponitur.* Ergo videtur quod non omnino sit in arbitrio sacerdotis.

PRAETEREA, ad actum clavium requiritur discretio. Sed, si esset omnino in voluntate sacerdotis dimittere et imponere de poena quantum vellet, non esset ibi necessaria discretio: quia nunquam ibi indiscretio posset accidere. Ergo non est omnino in arbitrio sacerdotis.

RESPONDEO dicendum quod sacerdos operatur in usu clavium sicut instrumentum et minister Dei. Nullum autem instrumentum habet efficacem actum nisi secundum quod movetur a principali agente. Et ideo dicit Dionysius, in fine *Eccles. Hier.*, quod *sacerdotibus utendum est virtutibus hierarchicis quando divinitas eos moverit.* In cuius signum, Matth. 16, ante potestatem clavium Petro traditam fit mentio de revelatione divinitatis ei facta; et Ioan. 20 praemittitur potestati remissionis Apostolis datae Spiritus Sancti donum, quo *filii Dei aguntur.* Unde, si praeter illum motum divinum uti sua potestate praesumpserit, non consequeretur effectum, ut Dionysius dicit. Et praeter hoc, a divino ordine averteretur, et sic culpam incurreret.

Et quia poenae satisfactoriae infligendae ut medicinae sunt, sicut medicinae in arte determinatae non omnibus competunt, sed variandae sunt secundum arbitrium medici non propriam voluntatem sequentis, sed scientiam medicinae; ita poenae satisfactoriae in canone determinatae non omnibus competunt, sed variandae sunt secundum arbitrium sacerdotis divino instinctu regulatum. Sicut ergo medicus aliquando prudenter non dat medicinam efficacem, quae ad morbi curationem sufficiat, ne propter debilitatem naturae maius periculum oriatur; ita sacerdos, divino instinctu motus, non semper totam poenam quae uni peccato debetur iniungit, ne infirmus aliquis ex magnitudine poenae desperet, et a poenitentia totaliter recedat.

AD PRIMUM ergo dicendum quod arbitrium istud debet esse divino instinctu regulatum.

he had allowed a liberal discount to his master's debtors. But God is more inclined to mercy than any temporal lord. Therefore, it seems that the more punishment the priest remits, the more he is to be commended.

OBJ. 3: Further, *Christ's every action is our instruction.* Now on some sinners he imposed no punishment, but only amendment of life, as in the case of the adulterous woman (John 8:11). Therefore, it seems that the priest also, who is the vicar of Christ, can, according to his own judgment, remit the punishment either wholly or in part.

ON THE CONTRARY, Gregory VII says: *we declare it a mock penance if it is not imposed according to the authority of the holy fathers in proportion to the sin* (Cf. Acts 5.5). Therefore, it seems that it does not altogether depend on the priest's judgment.

FURTHER, The act of the keys requires discretion. Now, if the priest could remit and impose as much as he liked of a penance, he would have no need of discretion, because there would be no room for indiscretion. Therefore, it does not altogether depend on the priest's judgment.

I ANSWER THAT, In using the keys, the priest acts as the instrument and minister of God. Now, no instrument can have an efficacious act except insofar as it is moved by the principal agent. Wherefore Dionysius says that *priests should use their hierarchical powers according as they are moved by God* (*On the Ecclesiastical Hierarchies*). A sign of this is that before the power of the keys was conferred on Peter mention is made of the revelation of divinity made to him (Matt 16:17); and before the power of forgiveness, the gift of the Holy Spirit is given to the apostles (John 20:22), for by it *they act as sons of God* (Rom 8:14). Consequently, if anyone were to presume to use his power against that divine motion, he would not realize the effect, as Dionysius states (*On the Ecclesiastical Hierarchies*). And besides, he would be turned away from the divine order, and consequently would be guilty of a sin.

Moreover, since satisfactory punishments are medicinal, just as the medicines prescribed by the medical art are not suitable to all but have to be changed according to the judgment of a medical man, who follows not his own will but his medical science, so the satisfactory punishments appointed by the canons are not suitable to all, but have to be varied according to the judgment of the priest guided by the divine instinct. Therefore, just as sometimes the physician prudently refrains from giving a medicine sufficiently efficacious to heal the disease, lest a greater danger should arise on account of the weakness of nature, so the priest, moved by divine instinct, sometimes refrains from enjoining the entire punishment due to one sin, lest by the severity of the punishment the sick man come to despair and turn away altogether from repentance.

REPLY OBJ. 1: This judgment should be guided entirely by the divine instinct.

Ad secundum dicendum quod etiam de hoc laudatur villicus quod prudenter fecit. Et ideo in remissione poenae debitae discretio adhibenda est.

Ad tertium dicendum quod Christus habuit potestatem excellentiae in sacramentis. Unde ipse ex auctoritate poenam totam vel partem poterat dimittere sicut volebat. Nec est simile de his qui operantur tantum ut ministri.

Reply Obj. 2: The steward is commended also for having done wisely. Therefore, in the remission of the due punishment, there is need for discretion.

Reply Obj. 3: Christ had the power of excellence in the sacraments, so that, by his own authority, he could remit the punishment wholly or in part, just as he chose. Therefore, there is no comparison between him and those who act merely as ministers.

QUESTION 19

THE MINISTERS AND THE USE OF THE KEYS

Deinde considerandum est de ministris clavium et usu earum.

Circa quod quaeruntur sex.

Primo: utrum sacerdos legalis claves habuerit.

Secundo: utrum Christus claves habuerit.

Tertio: utrum soli sacerdotes claves habeant.

Quarto: utrum sancti homines non sacerdotes usum clavium habeant.

Quinto: utrum mali sacerdotes usum clavium habeant efficacem.

Sexto: utrum schismatici et haeretici, excommunicati et suspensi et degradati, usum clavium habeant.

We must now consider the ministers and the use of the keys.

Under this head there are six points of inquiry:

(1) Whether the priest of the law had the keys?

(2) Whether Christ had the keys?

(3) Whether priests alone have the keys?

(4) Whether holy men who are not priests have the use of the keys?

(5) Whether wicked priests have the effective use of the keys?

(6) Whether those who are schismatics, heretics, excommunicate, suspended or degraded, have the use of the keys?

Article 1

Whether the Priest of the Law Had the Keys?

AD PRIMUM SIC PROCEDITUR. Videtur quod sacerdos legalis claves habuerit. Clavis enim est sequela ordinis. Sed ipsi habuerunt ordinem, ex quo sacerdotes dicebantur. Ergo etiam habuerunt clavem sacerdotes legales.

PRAETEREA, sicut supra Magister dicit, claves sunt duae, scilicet *scientia discernendi et potentia iudicandi.* Sed ad utramque sacerdotes legales habuerunt auctoritatem. Ergo habebant claves.

PRAETEREA, sacerdos legalis habebat aliquam potestatem super reliquum populum. Non temporalem: quia sic potestas regia non fuisset distincta a sacerdotali. Ergo spiritualem. Et haec est clavis. Ergo habebat clavem.

SED CONTRA: Claves ordinantur ad aperiendum regnum caelorum, quod aperiri non potest ante Christi passionem. Ergo sacerdos legalis clavem non habuit.

PRAETEREA, sacramenta veteris legis gratiam non conferebant. Sed aditus regni caelestis aperiri non potuit nisi per gratiam. Ergo per illa sacramenta non poterat aperiri. Et sic etiam sacerdos, qui minister eorum erat, claves regni caelestis non habebat.

RESPONDEO dicendum quod quidam dixerunt quod in veteri lege erant claves apud sacerdotes, quia eis erat commissum imponere poenam pro delicto, ut dicitur Levit. 5, quod ad claves pertinere videtur: sed fuerunt

OBJECTION 1: It would seem that the priests of the law had the keys. For the possession of the keys results from having holy orders. But they had orders, since they were called priests. Therefore, the priests of the law had the keys.

OBJ. 2: Further, as the Master states (*Sentences* IV, D. 18), there are two keys, *knowledge of discretion and power of judgment.* But the priests of the law had authority for both of these: therefore, they had the keys.

OBJ. 3: Further, the priests of the law had some power over the rest of the people. This power was not temporal, else the kingly power would not have differed from the priestly power. Therefore, it was a spiritual power: and this is the key. Therefore, they had the key.

ON THE CONTRARY, The keys are ordained to the opening of the heavenly kingdom, which could not be opened before Christ's Passion. Therefore, the priest of the law had not the keys.

FURTHER, The sacraments of the old law did not confer grace. Now the gate of the heavenly kingdom could not be opened except by means of grace. Therefore, it could not be opened by means of those sacraments, so that the priests who administered them did not have the keys of the heavenly kingdom.

I ANSWER THAT, Some have held that, under the old law, the keys of the kingdom were in the hands of the priests, because the right of imposing punishment for sin was conferred on them, as related in Leviticus 5, which

131

tunc incompletae, nunc autem per Christum in sacerdotibus novae legis perfectae sunt.

Sed hoc videtur esse contra intentionem Apostoli, in Epistola ad Heb. 9. Ibi enim sacerdotium Christi praefertur sacerdotio legali per hoc quod *Christus assistit Pontifex futurorum bonorum*, ad tabernaculum caeleste introducens *per proprium sanguinem*: non manufactum, in quod introducebat sacerdotium veteris legis *per sanguinem hircorum et taurorum*. Unde patet quod sacerdotii illius potestas non se extendebat ad caelestia, sed ad figuras caelestium. Et ideo, secundum alios, dicendum quod non habebant claves, sed in eis clavium figura praecessit.

AD PRIMUM ergo dicendum quod clavis regni caelestis consequitur ad sacerdotium quo homo in caelestia introducitur. Non autem talis erat ordo sacerdotii Levitici. Et ideo claves caeli non habuerunt, sed claves terreni tabernaculi.

AD SECUNDUM dicendum quod sacerdotes veteris legis habebant auctoritatem discernendi et iudicandi, sed non ut admitteretur homo ab eis iudicatus in caelestia, sed in figuras caelestium.

AD TERTIUM dicendum quod habebant spiritualem potestatem, quia per sacramenta legalia non a culpis, sed ab irregularitatibus purgabant homines, ut *ad manufactum tabernaculum* aditus purgatis per eos pateret.

right seems to belong to the keys; but these keys were incomplete then, whereas now they are complete as perfected by Christ on the priests of the new law.

But this seems to be contrary to the intent of the Apostle in the Epistle to the Hebrews (9:11–12). For there, the priesthood of Christ is given the preference over the priesthood of the law, inasmuch as Christ came *a high priest of the good things to come*, and brought us *by his own blood* into a tabernacle not made with hand, into which the priesthood of the old law brought men *by the blood of goats and of oxen*. Hence it is clear that the power of that priesthood did not reach to heavenly things but to the shadow of heavenly things: and so, we must say with others that they had not the keys, but that the keys were foreshadowed in them.

REPLY OBJ. 1: The keys of the kingdom go with the priesthood whereby man is brought into the heavenly kingdom, but such was not the priesthood of Levi; hence it had the keys, not of heaven, but of an earthly tabernacle.

REPLY OBJ. 2: The priests of the old law had authority to discern and judge, yet not to admit those they judged into heaven, but only into the shadow of heavenly things.

REPLY OBJ. 3: They had no spiritual power, since, by the sacraments of the law, they cleansed men not from their sins but from irregularities, so that those who were cleansed by them could enter into *a tabernacle which was made by hand*.

Article 2

Whether Christ Had the Key?

AD SECUNDUM SIC PROCEDITUR. Videtur quod Christus non habuerit clavem. Clavis enim characterem ordinis consequitur. Sed Christus non habuit characterem. Ergo non habuit clavem.

PRAETEREA, Christus habuit in sacramentis potestatem excellentiae, ut effectum sacramenti sine sacramentalibus posset conferre. Sed clavis est sacramentale quoddam. Ergo non indigebat clavi. Et sic frustra eam habuisset.

SED CONTRA est quod dicitur Apoc. 3: *haec dicit qui habet clavem David*, etc.

RESPONDEO dicendum quod virtus aliquid agendi est in instrumento et in per se agente non eodem modo, sed in per se agente perfectius. Potestas autem clavium quam nos habemus, et aliorum sacramentorum virtus est instrumentalis: sed in Christo est ut in per se agente ad salutem nostram, per auctoritatem quidem inquantum est Deus, sed per meritum inquantum est homo. Clavis autem de ratione sua exprimit potestatem aperiendi et claudendi, sive aliquis aperiat quasi principale

OBJECTION 1: It would seem that Christ did not have the key. For the key goes with the character of holy orders. But Christ did not have a character. Therefore, he had not the key.

OBJ. 2: Further, Christ had power of excellence in the sacraments, so that he could produce the sacramental effect without the sacramental rite. Now the key is something sacramental. Therefore, he needed no key, and it would have been useless to him to have it.

ON THE CONTRARY, Revelation 3:7 says: *these things say . . . he that has the key of David*, etc.

I ANSWER THAT, The power to do a thing is both in the instrument and in the principal agent, but not in the same way, since it is more perfectly in the latter. Now, like other sacramental powers, the power of the keys which we have is instrumental, whereas it is in Christ as principal agent in the matter of our salvation: by authority, if we consider him as God, by merit, if we consider him as man. But the very notion of a key expresses a power to open and shut, whether this be done by the principal agent or by an instru-

agens, sive quasi minister. Et ideo in Christo oportet ponere clavem, sed altero modo quam sit in eius ministris. Et ideo dicitur quod habet clavem excellentiae.

AD PRIMUM ergo dicendum quod character de sua ratione dicit aliquid ab aliquo derivatum. Et ideo potestas clavium quae est in nobis a Christo derivata, sequitur characterem quo Christo conformamur. Sed in Christo non consequitur characterem, sed principalem formam.

AD SECUNDUM dicendum quod clavis illa quam Christus habuit, non erat sacramentalis, sed sacramentalis clavis principium.

ment. Consequently, we must admit that Christ had the key, but in a higher way than his ministers; hence he is said to have the key of excellence.

REPLY OBJ. 1: A character implies the notion of something derived from another; hence the power of the keys which we receive from Christ results from the character whereby we are conformed to Christ, whereas in Christ it results not from a character, but from the principal form.

REPLY OBJ. 2: The key which Christ had was not sacramental, but the origin of the sacramental key.

Article 3

Whether Priests Alone Have the Keys?

AD TERTIUM SIC PROCEDITUR. Videtur quod non soli sacerdotes claves habeant. Dicit enim Isidorus quod *ostiarii inter bonos et malos habent iudicium: dignos recipiunt, indignos reiiciunt.* Sed haec est definitio clavium, ut ex dictis patet. Ergo non solum sacerdotes, sed etiam ostiarii clavem habent.

PRAETEREA, claves sacerdotibus dantur dum per unctionem potestatem divinitus accipiunt. Sed reges etiam potestatem in populum fidelem divinitus habent, et unctione sanctificantur. Ergo non soli sacerdotes habent claves.

PRAETEREA, sacerdotium est ordo uni singulari personae conveniens. Sed clavem aliquando videtur habere tota una congregatio: quia quaedam capitula excommunicationem inferre possunt, quod ad potestatem clavium pertinet. Ergo non soli sacerdotes clavem habent.

PRAETEREA, mulier non est sacerdotalis, ordinis susceptiva: quia ei docere non competit, secundum Apostolum, I Cor. 14. Sed aliquae mulieres videntur habere claves: sicut abbatissae, quae habent spiritualem potestatem in subditas. Ergo non soli sacerdotes habent clavem.

SED CONTRA: Est quod Ambrosius dicit: *hoc ius,* scilicet ligandi et solvendi, *solum sacerdotibus est concessum.*

PRAETEREA, per potestatem clavium efficitur aliquis medius inter populum et Deum. Sed hoc tantum sacerdotibus competit, qui *constituuntur in his quae sunt ad Deum, ut offerant dona et sacrificia pro peccatis,* ut dicitur Heb. 5. Ergo soli sacerdotes claves habent.

RESPONDEO dicendum quod clavis est duplex. Una quae se extendit ad ipsum caelum immediate, removendo impedimenta introitus in caelum per remissionem peccati. Et haec vocatur *clavis ordinis.* Et hanc soli sacer-

OBJECTION 1: It would seem that not only priests have the keys. For Isidore says (*Etymologies* 7.12) that the *porters have to tell the good from the bad, so as to admit the good and keep out the bad.* Now this is the definition of the keys, as appears from what has been said (Q. 17, A. 2). Therefore, not only priests but even porters have the keys.

OBJ. 2: Further, the keys are conferred on priests when by being anointed they receive power from God. But kings of Christian peoples also receive power from God and are consecrated by being anointed. Therefore, not only priests have the keys.

OBJ. 3: Further, the priesthood is an order belonging to an individual person. But sometimes a number of people together seem to have the key, because certain chapters can pass a sentence of excommunication, which pertains to the power of the keys. Therefore, not only priests have the key.

OBJ. 4: Further, a woman is not capable of receiving the priesthood, since she is not competent to teach, according to the Apostle (1 Cor 14:34). But some women (abbesses, for instance, who exercise a spiritual power over their subjects) seem to have the keys. Therefore, not only priests have the keys.

ON THE CONTRARY, Ambrose says: *this right,* viz. of binding and loosing, *is granted to priests alone* (*On Penance* 1).

FURTHER, By receiving the power of the keys, a man is set up between the people and God. But this belongs to the priest alone, who is *ordained . . . in the things that appertain to God, that he may offer up gifts and sacrifices for sins* (Heb 5:1). Therefore, only priests have the keys.

I ANSWER THAT, There are two kinds of key. One reaches to heaven itself directly by remitting sin and thus removing the obstacles to the entrance into heaven; and this is called the *key of order.* Priests alone have this key,

dotes habent: quia ipsi soli ordinantur populo in his quae directe *sunt ad Deum*.

Alia clavis est quae non directe se extendit ad ipsum caelum, sed mediante, militante Ecclesia, per quam aliquis ad caelum vadit: dum per eam aliquis excluditur vel admittitur ad consortium Ecclesiae militantis per excommunicationem et absolutionem. Et haec vocatur *clavis iurisdictionis in foro causarum*. Et ideo nonsacerdotes etiam hanc habere possunt: sicut archidiaconi, et electi, et alii qui excommunicare possunt. Sed non proprie dicitur clavis caeli, sed quaedam dispositio ad ipsam.

AD PRIMUM ergo dicendum quod ostiarii habent Clavem custodiendi ea quae in templo materiali continentur; et habent iudicium a tali templo excludendi et admittendi, non quidem sua auctoritate iudicantes qui sint digni vel indigni, sed iudicium sacerdotum exequentes; ut sic quodammodo executores potestatis sacerdotis videantur.

AD SECUNDUM dicendum quod reges non habent aliquam potestatem in spiritualibus, et ideo clavem regni caelestis non accipiunt: sed solum in temporalibus, quae etiam non nisi a Deo esse potest, ut patet Rom. 13. Nec per unctionem in aliquo ordine consecrantur: sed excellentia potestatis ipsorum a Christo descendere significatur, et ut ipsi sub Christo in populo Christiano regnent.

AD TERTIUM dicendum quod, sicut in politicis quandoque iudex habet totam potestatem, sicut est in regno; quandoque autem multi in diversis officiis constituti, vel etiam ex aequo, ut dicitur VIII *Ethic.*: ita etiam spiritualis iurisdictio potest haberi ab uno solo, sicut ab episcopo; et pluribus simul, sicut a capitulo. Et sic habent clavem iurisdictionis, non tamen clavem ordinis, simul omnes.

AD QUARTUM dicendum quod mulier, secundum Apostolum, est in statu subiectionis, et ideo non potest habere aliquam spiritualem iurisdictionem: quia etiam secundum Philosophum, in VIII *Ethic.* corruptio urbanitatis est quando ad mulierem dominium pervenit. Unde mulier non habet neque clavem ordinis neque clavem iurisdictionis. Sed committitur mulieri aliquis usus clavium: sicut habere correctionem in subditas mulieres, propter periculum quod imminere posset si viri mulieribus cohabitarent.

because they alone are ordained for the people in the things which *appertain to God* directly.

The other key reaches to heaven not directly but through the medium of the Church Militant. By this key a man goes to heaven, since by it a man is shut out from or admitted to the fellowship of the Church Militant through excommunication or absolution. This is called the *key of jurisdiction in the external court*, wherefore even those who are not priests can have this key, e.g., archdeacons, bishops elect, and others who can excommunicate. But it is not properly called a key of heaven, but a disposition thereto.

REPLY OBJ. 1: The porters have the key for taking care of those things which are contained in a material temple, and they have to judge whether a person should be excluded from or admitted to that temple; which judgment they pronounce, not by their own authority, but in pursuance to the priest's judgment, so that they appear to be the administrators of the priestly power.

REPLY OBJ. 2: Kings have no power in spiritual matters, so that they do not receive the key of the heavenly kingdom. Their power is confined to temporal matters, and this too can only come to them from God, as appears from Romans 13:1. Nor are they consecrated by the unction of a sacred order: their anointing is merely a sign that the excellence of their power comes down to them from Christ, and that, under Christ, they reign over the Christian people.

REPLY OBJ. 3: Just as in civil matters the whole power is sometimes vested in a judge, as in a kingdom, whereas sometimes it is vested in many exercising various offices but acting together with equal rights (*Ethics* 8.10–11), so too, spiritual jurisdiction may be exercised both by one alone, e.g., a bishop, and by many together, e.g., by a chapter, and thus they have the key of jurisdiction, but they have not all together the key of order.

REPLY OBJ. 4: According to the Apostle (1 Tim 2:11; Titus 2:5), woman is in a state of subjection: wherefore she can have no spiritual jurisdiction, since the Philosopher also says (*Ethics* 8) that it is a corruption of public life when the government comes into the hands of a woman. Consequently, a woman has neither the key of order nor the key of jurisdiction. Nevertheless, a certain use of the keys is allowed to women, such as the right to correct other women who are under them, on account of the danger that might threaten if men were to dwell under the same roof.

Article 4

Whether Holy Men Who Are Not Priests Have the Keys?

AD QUARTUM SIC PROCEDITUR. Videtur quod etiam sancti homines non sacerdotes usum clavium habeant. Absolutio enim et ligatio, quae fit per claves, effi-beant.

OBJECTION 1: It would seem that holy men, even those who are not priests, have the use of the keys. For loosing and binding, which are the effects of the keys, derive

caciam habet ex merito passionis Christi. Sed illi maxime passioni Christi conformantur qui per patientiam et alias virtutes Christum passum sequuntur. Ergo videtur quod, etiam si non habeant sacerdotalem ordinem, quod possint ligare et solvere.

PRAETEREA, Heb. 7 dicitur: *sine ulla contradictione, quod minus est a maiori benedicitur.* Sed in spiritualibus, secundum Augustinum, *hoc est maius esse quod melius.* Ergo meliores, qui scilicet plus de caritate habent, possunt alios benedicere absolvendo. Et sic idem quod prius.

SED CONTRA, *cuius est potentia, eius est actio,* secundum Philosophum. Sed clavis, quae est potestas spiritualis, est tantum sacerdotum. Ergo et usus eius non nisi sacerdotibus convenire potest.

RESPONDEO dicendum quod agens per se et agens instrumentale in hoc differunt quod agens instrumentale non inducit in effectu similitudinem suam, sed similitudinem principalis agentis; principale autem agens inducit similitudinem suam. Et ideo ex hoc aliquid constituitur principale agens quod habet aliquam formam quam in alterum transfundere potest: non autem ex hoc constituitur agens instrumentale, sed ex hoc quod est applicatum a principali agente ad effectum aliquem inducendum. Cum ergo in actu clavium principale ageris sit Christus, ut Deus per auctoritatem et ut homo per meritum, ex ipsa plenitudine divinae bonitatis in eo et ex perfectione gratiae consequitur quod possit in actum clavium. Sed homo alius non potest in actum clavium sicut per se agens: quia nec ipse alteri gratiam, qua remittuntur peccata, dare potest, nec sufficienter mereri. Et ideo non est nisi sicut agens instrumentale. Unde ille qui effectum clavium consequitur, non assimilatur utenti clavibus, sed Christo. Et propter hoc, quantumcumque aliquis habeat de gratia, non potest pertingere ad effectum clavium nisi applicetur ad hoc quasi minister per ordinis susceptionem.

AD PRIMUM ergo dicendum quod, sicut inter instrumentum et effectum non exigitur similitudo secundum convenientiam in forma, sed secundum proportionem instrumenti ad effectum; ita etiam nec inter instrumentum et principale agens. Et talis similitudo est in sanctis hominibus ad Christum passum. Et talis similitudo eis usum clavium non confert.

AD SECUNDUM dicendum quod, quamvis purus homo non possit alteri ex condigno mereri gratiam, tamen unius meritum potest cooperari ad salutem alterius. Ideo duplex est benedictio. Una quae est ab ipso homine puro sicut merente per proprium actum. Et talis potest fieri a quolibet sancto, in quo Christus habitat per gratiam. Et hoc requirit maioritatem bonitatis ad minus inquantum huiusmodi. Alia est benedictio qua homo benedicit ut

their efficacy from the merit of Christ's Passion. Now those are most conformed to Christ's Passion who follow Christ through suffering by patience and other virtues. Therefore, it seems that even if they have not the priestly order, they can bind and loose.

OBJ. 2: Further, it is written: *without all contradiction, that which is less is blessed by the greater* (Heb 7:7). Now in spiritual matters, according to Augustine, *to be better is to be greater* (On the Trinity 6.8). Therefore, those who are better, i.e., who have more charity, can bless others by absolving them. Hence the same conclusion follows.

ON THE CONTRARY, *Action belongs to that which has the power,* as the Philosopher says (On Sleep and Sleeplessness 1). But the key, which is a spiritual power, belongs to priests alone. Therefore, priests alone are competent to have the use of the keys.

I ANSWER THAT, There is this difference between a principal and an instrumental agent, that the latter does not produce its own likeness in the effect, but the likeness of the principal agent, whereas the principal agent produces its own likeness. Consequently, a thing becomes a principal agent through having a form which it can reproduce in another, whereas an instrumental agent is not constituted thus, but through being applied by the principal agent in order to produce a certain effect. Since, therefore, in the act of the keys the principal agent by authority is Christ as God, and by merit is Christ as man, it follows that on account of the very fullness of divine goodness in him, and of the perfection of his grace, he is competent to exercise the act of the keys. But another man is not competent to exercise this act as principal agent, since neither can he give another man grace whereby sins are remitted, nor can he merit sufficiently; hence he is nothing more than an instrumental agent. Consequently, the recipient of the effect of the keys is likened not to the one who uses the keys, but to Christ. Therefore, no matter how much grace a man may have, he cannot produce the effect of the keys, unless he be appointed to that purpose by receiving orders.

REPLY OBJ. 1: Just as between instrument and effect there is need or likeness, not of a similar form, but of aptitude in the instrument for the effect, so is it as regards the instrument and the principal agent. The former is the likeness between holy men and the suffering Christ, nor does it bestow on them the use of the keys.

REPLY OBJ. 2: Although a mere man cannot merit grace for another man condignly, yet the merit of one man can cooperate in the salvation of another. Hence there is a twofold blessing. One proceeds from a mere man, as meriting by his own act: this blessing can be conferred by any holy person in whom Christ dwells by his grace, insofar as he excels in goodness the person whom he blesses. The other blessing is when a man blesses as applying a bless-

benedictionem quae est ex merito Christi instrumentaliter alicui applicans. Et quantum ad hanc requiritur maioritas ordinis, et non virtutis.

ing instrumentally through the merit of Christ, and this requires excellence of order and not of virtue.

Article 5

Whether Wicked Priests Have the Use of the Keys?

AD QUINTUM SIC PROCEDITUR. Videtur quod mali sacerdotes usum clavium non habeant. Ioan. 20, ubi usus clavium Apostolis traditur, Spiritus Sancti donum promittitur. Sed mali non habent Spiritum Sanctum. Ergo non habent usum clavium.

PRAETEREA, nullus sapiens rex dispensationem sui thesauri suo inimico committit. Sed usus clavium in dispensatione consistit thesauri caelestis Regis, qui est ipsa Sapientia. Ergo mali, qui per peccata sunt eius hostes, non habent usum clavium.

PRAETEREA, Augustinus dicit quod *sacramentum gratiae, dat Deus etiam per malos, ipsam vero gratiam non nisi per seipsum vel per sanctos suos.* Et ideo remissionem peccatorum per seipsum facit, vel per ipsius Columbae membra. Sed remissio peccatorum est usus clavium. Ergo peccatores, qui non sunt Columbae membra, usum clavium non habent.

PRAETEREA, intercessio mali sacerdotis non habet aliquam efficaciam ad reconciliandum: quia, secundum Gregorium, *cum is qui displicet ad interpellandum mittitur, irati animis ad deteriora provocatur.* Sed usus clavium fit per quandam intercessionem: ut patet in forma absolutionis. Ergo non habent efficacem clavium usum.

SED CONTRA: Nullus potest scire de alio an sit in statu salutis. Si ergo nullus posset uti clavibus in absolvendo nisi existens in statu salutis, nullus sciret se esse absolutum. Quod est valde inconveniens.

PRAETEREA, iniquitas ministri non potest auferre liberalitatem domini. Sed sacerdos est solum minister. Ergo non potest sua malitia donum a Deo transmissum per eum nobis auferre.

RESPONDEO dicendum quod, sicut participatio formae quae est inducenda in effectum, non facit instrumentum; ita nec subtractio talis formae tollit usum instrumenti. Et ideo, cum homo sit tantum instrumentaliter agens in usu clavium, quantumcumque sit per peccatum gratia privatus, per quam fit remissio peccatorum, nullo modo privatur usu clavium.

AD PRIMUM ergo dicendum quod donum Spiritus Sancti exigitur ad usum clavium non ut sine quo fieri non possit, sed quia sine eo incongrue fit ex parte uten-

OBJECTION 1: It would seem that wicked priests have not the use of the keys. For in the passage where the use of the keys is bestowed on the apostles (John 20:22–23), the gift of the Holy Spirit is promised. But wicked men have not the Holy Spirit. Therefore, they have not the use of the keys.

OBJ. 2: Further, no wise king entrusts his enemy with the dispensation of his treasure. Now the use of the keys consists in dispensing the treasure of the King of heaven, who is Wisdom itself. Therefore, the wicked, who are his enemies on account of sin, have not the use of the keys.

OBJ. 3: Further, Augustine says that God *gives the sacrament of grace even through wicked men, but grace itself only by himself or through his saints* (*On Baptism* 21). Hence he forgives sin by himself, or by those who are members of the Dove. But the remission of sins is the use of the keys. Therefore, sinners, who are not members of the Dove, have not the use of the keys.

OBJ. 4: Further, the prayer of a wicked priest cannot effect reconciliation, for, as Gregory says, *if an unacceptable person is sent to intercede, anger is provoked to yet greater severity* (*Book of Pastoral Rule* 1.11). But the use of the keys implies a kind of intercession, as appears in the form of absolution. Therefore, wicked priests cannot use the keys effectively.

ON THE CONTRARY, No man can know whether another man is in the state of grace. If, therefore, no one could use the keys in giving absolution unless he were in a state of grace, no one would know that he had been absolved, which would be very unfitting.

FURTHER, The wickedness of the minister cannot void the liberality of his lord. But the priest is no more than a minister. Therefore, he cannot by his wickedness take away from us the gift which God has given through him.

I ANSWER THAT, Just as participation of a form to be induced into an effect does not make a thing to be an instrument, so neither does the loss of that form prevent that thing being used as an instrument. Consequently, since man is merely an instrument in the use of the keys, however much he may through sin be deprived of grace whereby sins are forgiven, yet he is by no means deprived of the use of the keys.

REPLY OBJ. 1: The gift of the Holy Spirit is requisite for the use of the keys not as being indispensable for the purpose, but because it is unbecoming for the user to use them

tis: quamvis subiiciens se clavibus effectum clavium consequatur.

Ad secundum dicendum quod rex terrenus in thesauro suo defraudari et decipi potest: et ideo hosti eius dispensationem non committit. Sed Rex caelestis defraudari non potest: quia totum ad ipsius honorem cedit, etiam quod aliqui clavibus male utuntur; quia novit ex malis elicere bona, et per malos etiam multa bona facere. Et ideo non est simile.

Ad tertium dicendum quod Augustinus loquitur de remissione peccatorum secundum quod sancti homines cooperantur ad ipsam, non ex vi clavium, sed ex merito congrui. Et ideo dicit quod etiam per malos sacramenta ministrat. Et inter alia sacramenta etiam absolutio, quae est usus clavium, computari debet. Sed per *membra Columbae*, idest per sanctos homines, facit remissionem peccatorum inquantum eorum intercessionibus peccata remittit.

Vel potest dici quod *membra Columbae* nominat omnes ab Ecclesia non praecisos. Qui enim ab eis sacramenta recipiunt, gratiam consequuntur: non autem qui recipiunt ab illis qui sunt ab Ecclesia praecisi, quia hoc ipso peccant; excepto baptismo, quem in casu necessitatis licet ab excommunicato recipere.

Ad quartum dicendum quod intercessio quam sacerdos malus ex propria persona facit, non habet efficaciam: sed illa quam facit ut minister Ecclesiae, habet efficaciam ex merito Christi. Utroque tamen modo debet intercessio sacerdotis populo subiecto prodesse.

without it, though he that submits to them receives their effect.

Reply Obj. 2: An earthly king can be cheated and deceived in the matter of his treasure, and so he does not entrust his enemy with the dispensation thereof. But the King of heaven cannot be cheated, because all tends to his own glory, even the abuse of the keys by some, for he can make good come out of evil and produce many good effects through evil men. Hence the comparison fails.

Reply Obj. 3: Augustine speaks of the remission of sins insofar as holy men cooperate in it not by virtue of the keys, but by merit of congruity. Hence he says that God confers the sacraments even through evil men. And among the other sacraments, absolution, which is the use of the keys, should be reckoned. But through *members of the Dove*, i.e., holy men, he grants forgiveness of sins, insofar as he remits sins on account of their intercession.

We might also reply that by *members of the Dove* he means all who are not cut off from the Church, for those who receive the sacraments from them receive grace, whereas those who receive the sacraments from those who are cut off from the Church do not receive grace, because they sin in so doing, except in the case of baptism, which, in cases of necessity, may be received even from one who is excommunicate.

Reply Obj. 4: The prayer which the wicked priest proffers on his own account is not efficacious: but that which he makes as a minister of the Church is efficacious through the merit of Christ. Yet in both ways the priest's prayer should profit those who are subject to him.

Article 6

Whether Those Who Are Schismatics, Heretics, Excommunicate,
Suspended or Degraded Have the Use of the Keys?

Ad sextum sic proceditur. Videtur quod schismatici et haeretici, excommunicati et suspensi et degradati, usum clavium habeant. Sicut enim potestas clavium dependet ab ordine, ita et potestas conficiendi. Sed non possunt amittere usum potestatis conficiendi: quia, si conficiunt, confectum est, quamvis peccent conficientes. Ergo etiam non possunt amittere usum clavium.

Praeterea, omnis potestas spiritualis activa, in eo qui habet usum liberi arbitrii, exit in actum quando vult. Sed potestas clavium adhuc manet in praedictis: quia, cum non detur nisi in ordine, oporteret reordinari eos quando ad Ecclesiam redeunt. Ergo, cum sit potentia activa, possunt in actum eius exire cum voluerint.

Objection 1: It would seem that those who are schismatics, heretics, excommunicate, suspended or degraded have the use of the keys. For just as the power of the keys results from holy orders, so does the power of consecration. But the above cannot lose the use of the power of consecration, since if they do consecrate it is valid, though they sin in doing so. Therefore, neither can they lose the use of the keys.

Obj. 2: Further, any active spiritual power in one who has the use of his free-will can be exercised by him when he wills. Now the power of the keys remains in the aforesaid, for, since it is only conferred with holy orders, they would have to be reordained when they return to the Church. Therefore, since it is an active power, they can exercise it when they will.

PRAETEREA, spiritualis gratia magis impeditur per culpam quam per poenam. Sed excommunicatio et suspensio et degradatio sunt poenae quaedam. Cum ergo propter culpam non amittat aliquis usum clavium, videtur quod nec propter ista.

SED CONTRA: Augustinus dicit quod *Ecclesiae caritas peccata dimittit*. Caritas autem est quae facit Ecclesiae unionem. Cum ergo praedicti sint ab Ecclesiae unione divisi, videtur quod usum clavium non habent in remittendis peccatis.

PRAETEREA, nullus absolvitur a peccato secundum hoc quod peccat. Sed aliquis a praedictis absolutionem petens peccat, contra praeceptum Ecclesiae faciens. Ergo per eos a peccato absolvi non potest. Et sic idem quod prius.

RESPONDEO dicendum quod in omnibus praedictis manet clavium potestas quantum ad essentiam, sed usus impeditur ex defectu materiae. Cum enim usus clavium in utente praelationem requirat respectu eius in quem utitur, ut dictum est, propria materia in quam exercetur usus clavium, est homo subditus. Et quia per ordinationem Ecclesiae subditur unus alteri, ideo etiam per Ecclesiae praelatos potest subtrahi alicui ille qui erat ei subiectus. Unde, cum Ecclesia haereticos et schismaticos, et alios huiusmodi, privet subtrahendo subditos, vel simpliciter vel quantum ad aliquid, quantum ad hoc quo privati sunt, non possunt usum clavium habere.

AD PRIMUM ergo dicendum quod materia sacramenti Eucharistiae, in quam suam potestatem exercet sacerdos, non est homo, sed panis triticeus; et in baptismo homo simpliciter. Unde, sicut si subtraheretur haeretico panis triticeus, conficere non posset; ita, si subtrahatur praelato praelatio, nec absolvere poterit. Potest tamen baptizare et conficere: quamvis ad sui damnationem.

AD SECUNDUM dicendum quod propositio habet veritatem quando non deest materia, sicut est in proposito.

AD TERTIUM dicendum quod ex ipsa culpa non subtrahitur materia, sicut per aliquam poenam. Unde poena non impedit per contrarietatem ad effectum inducendum, sed ratione praedicta.

OBJ. 3: Further, spiritual grace is hindered by guilt more than by punishment. Now excommunication, suspension and degradation are punishments. Therefore, since a man does not lose the use of the keys on account of guilt, it seems that he does not lose it on account of the aforesaid.

ON THE CONTRARY, Augustine says that the *charity of the Church forgives sins* (*Tractates on John* 121). Now it is the charity of the Church which unites its members. Since, therefore, the above are disunited from the Church, it seems that they have not the use of the keys in remitting sins.

FURTHER, No man is absolved from sin by sinning. Now it is a sin for anyone to seek absolution of his sins from the above, for he disobeys the Church in so doing. Therefore, he cannot be absolved by them: and so the same conclusion follows.

I ANSWER THAT, In all the above the power of the keys remains as to its essence, but its use is hindered on account of the lack of matter. For since the use of the keys requires in the user authority over the person on whom they are used, as stated above (Q. 17, A. 2), the proper matter on whom one can exercise the use of the keys is a man under one's authority. And since it is by appointment of the Church that one man has authority over another, so a man may be deprived of his authority over another by his ecclesiastical superiors. Consequently, since the Church deprives heretics, schismatics, and the like by withdrawing their subjects from them either altogether or in some respect, insofar as they are thus deprived they cannot have the use of the keys.

REPLY OBJ. 1: The matter of the sacrament of the Eucharist, on which the priest exercises his power, is not a man but wheaten bread, and in baptism, the matter is simply a man. Wherefore, just as if a heretic were to be without wheaten bread, he could not consecrate, so neither can a prelate absolve if he be deprived of his authority, yet he can baptize and consecrate, although to his own damnation.

REPLY OBJ. 2: The assertion is true, provided matter be not lacking as it is in the case in point.

REPLY OBJ. 3: Sin, of itself, does not remove matter, as certain punishments do: so that punishment is a hindrance not because it is contrary to the effect, but for the reason stated.

QUESTION 20

THOSE ON WHOM THE POWER OF THE KEYS CAN BE EXERCISED

Deinde considerandum est de his in quos usus clavium exerceri potest.

Circa quod tria quaeruntur.

Primo: utrum sacerdos possit in quemlibet hominem uti clave quam habet.

Secundo: utrum sacerdos possit semper suum subditum absolvere.

Tertio: utrum aliquis possit uti clavibus in suum superiorem.

We must now consider those on whom the power of the keys can be exercised.

Under this head there are three points of inquiry:

(1) Whether a priest can use the key which he has on any man?

(2) Whether a priest can always absolve his subject?

(3) Whether anyone can use the keys on his superior?

Article 1

Whether a Priest Can Use the Key Which He Has on Any Man?

AD PRIMUM SIC PROCEDITUR. Videtur quod sacerdos possit uti clave quam habet in quemlibet hominem. Potestas enim clavium in sacerdote descendit ex illa Domini auctoritate quae dicit: *accipite Spiritum Sanctum: quorum remiseritis peccata, remittuntur eis.* Sed illud indeterminate dixit de omnibus. Ergo habens clavem indeterminate potest ea uti in quoslibet.

PRAETEREA, clavis corporalis quae aperit unam seram, aperit omnes alias eiusdem modi. Sed omne peccatum cuiuslibet hominis est eiusdem rationis obstaculum respectu introitus caeli. Ergo, si potest unum hominem sacerdos per clavem quam habet absolvere, poterit et quoscumque alios.

PRAETEREA, sacerdotium novi Testamenti est perfectius quam veteris. Sed sacerdos veteris Testamenti poterat uti sua potestate quam habebat discernendi inter lepram et lepram, indifferenter in omnes. Ergo multo fortius sacerdos Evangelicus potest uti potestate sua in omnes.

SED CONTRA: Est quod dicitur XVI, qu. i: *nulli, sacerdotum liceat parochianum alterius absolvere aut ligare.* Ergo non quilibet potest quemlibet absolvere.

PRAETEREA, iudicium spirituale debet esse ordinatius quam temporale. Sed in iudicio temporali non potest quilibet iudex quemlibet iudicare. Ergo, cum usus clavium sit iudicium quoddam, non potest sacerdos sua clavi uti in quemlibet.

RESPONDEO dicendum quod ea quae circa singularia operari oportet, non eodem modo omnibus competunt. Unde sicut, post generalia medicinae praecepta, oportet adhiberi medicos, quibus praecepta universalia

OBJECTION 1: It would seem that a priest can use the key which he has on any man. For the power of the keys was bestowed on priests by divine authority in the words: *receive ye the Holy Spirit; whose sins you shall forgive, they are forgiven them* (John 20:22–23). But this was said without any restriction. Therefore, he that has the key can use it on any without restriction.

OBJ. 2: Further, a material key that opens one lock, opens all locks of the same pattern. Now every sin of every man is the same kind of obstacle against entering into heaven. Therefore, if a priest can, by means of the key which he has, absolve one man, he can do the same for all others.

OBJ. 3: Further, the priesthood of the New Testament is more perfect than that of the Old Testament. But the priest of the Old Testament could use the power which he had of discerning between different kinds of leprosy with regard to all indiscriminately. Much more, therefore, can the priest of the Gospel use his power with regard to all.

ON THE CONTRARY, It is written in the *Decretals*: *it is not lawful for every priest to loose or bind another priest's parishioner.* Therefore, a priest cannot absolve everybody.

FURTHER, Judgment in spiritual matters should be better regulated than in temporal matters. But in temporal matters a judge cannot judge everybody. Therefore, since the use of the keys is a kind of judgment, it is not within the competency of a priest to use his key with regard to everyone.

I ANSWER THAT, That which has to do with singular matters is not equally in the power of all. Thus, even as besides the general principles of medicine, it is necessary to have physicians who adapt those general principles to

medicinae singulis infirmis secundum quod debent aptentur; ita in quolibet principatu, praeter illum qui universaliter praecepta legis tradit, oportet esse aliquos qui ea singulis secundum quod debent adaptent. Et propter hoc in caelesti hierarchia sub Potestatibus, qui indistincte praesunt, ponuntur Principatus, qui singulis provinciis distribuuntur, et sub his Angeli, qui singulis hominibus in custodiam deputantur: ut patet ex his quae dicta sunt in Secundo Libro. Unde et ita esse debet in praelatione Ecclesiae militantis: ut apud aliquem esset praelatio indistincte in omnes; et sub hoc essent alii qui super diversos distinctam potestatem acciperent. Et quia usus clavium requirit aliquam praelationis potestatem per quam ille in quem usus clavium communicatur, efficitur materia propria illius actus: ideo ille qui habet indistinctam potestatem super omnes, potest uti clavibus in omnes; illi autem qui sub eo distinctas potestates acceperunt, non in quoslibet uti possunt clavibus, sed in eos tantum qui eis in sortem venerunt; nisi in necessitatis articulo, ubi nemini sacramenta sunt deneganda.

AD PRIMUM ergo dicendum quod ad absolutionem a peccato requiritur duplex potestas: scilicet potestas ordinis, et potestas iurisdictionis. Prima quidem potestas aequaliter est in omnibus sacerdotibus, non autem secunda. Et ideo ubi Dominus, Ioan. 20, dedit omnibus Apostolis communiter potestatem remittendi peccata, intelligitur de potestate quae consequitur ordinem. Unde et sacerdotibus, quando ordinantur, illa verba dicuntur. Sed Petro singulariter dedit potestatem dimittendi peccata, Matth. 16: ut intelligatur quod ipse prae aliis habet potestatem iurisdictionis. Potestas autem ordinis, quantum est de se, se extendit ad omnes absolvendos: et ideo indeterminate Dominus dixit, *quorum remiseritis peccata*; intelligens tamen quod usus illius potestatis esse deberet praesupposita potestate Petro collata secundum ipsius ordinationem.

AD SECUNDUM dicendum quod etiam clavis materialis non potest aperire nisi seram propriam: nec aliqua virtus activa potest agere nisi in propriam materiam. Materia autem propria potestatis ordinis efficitur aliquis per iurisdictionem. Et ideo non potest aliquis clave uti in eum in quem iurisdictio non datur.

AD TERTIUM dicendum quod populus Israel unus populus erat, et unum tantummodo templum habebat. Unde non oportebat sacerdotum iurisdictiones distingui sicut in Ecclesia, in qua congregantur diversi populi et nationes.

individual patients or diseases, according to their various requirements, so in every kingdom, besides that one who proclaims the universal precepts of law, there is need for others to adapt those precepts to individual cases, according as each case demands. For this reason, in the heavenly hierarchy also, under the Powers who rule indiscriminately, a place is given to the Principalities, who are appointed to individual kingdoms, and to the Angels, who are given charge over individual men, as we have explained above (I, Q. 113, A. 1–2). Consequently, there should be a like order of authority in the Church Militant, so that an indiscriminate authority over all should be vested in one individual, and that there should be others under him, having distinct authority over various people. Now the use of the keys implies a certain power to exercise authority, whereby the one on whom the keys are used becomes the proper matter of that act. Therefore, he that has power over all indiscriminately can use the keys on all, whereas those who have received authority over distinct persons cannot use the keys on everyone, but only on those over whom they are appointed, except in cases of necessity, when the sacraments should be refused to no one.

REPLY OBJ. 1: A twofold power is required in order to absolve from sins, namely, power of order and power of jurisdiction. The former power is equally in all priests, but not the latter. And therefore, when our Lord (John 20:23) gave all the apostles in general the power of forgiving sins, this is to be understood of the power which results from receiving holy orders, wherefore these words are addressed to priests when they are ordained. But to Peter he gave, in a singular manner, the power of forgiving sins (Matt 16:19), so that it may be understood that he had the power of jurisdiction over all the others. But the power of order, considered in itself, extends to all who can be absolved: wherefore our Lord said indeterminately, *whose sins you shall forgive, they are forgiven them*, on the understanding that this power should be used in dependence on the power given to Peter, according to his appointment.

REPLY OBJ. 2: A material key can open only its own lock, nor can any active force act save on its own matter. Now a man becomes the matter of the power of order by jurisdiction: and consequently no one can use the key in respect of another over whom he has not jurisdiction.

REPLY OBJ. 3: The people of Israel were one people, and had but one temple, so that there was no need for a distinction in priestly jurisdiction, as there is now in the Church which comprises various peoples and nations.

Article 2

Whether a Priest Can Always Absolve His Subject?

AD SECUNDUM SIC PROCEDITUR. Videtur quod sacerdos non possit semper suum subditum absolvere. Sicut enim Augustinus in littera dicit, *nullus officio sacerdotis uti debet nisi immunis ab illis sit quae in aliis iudicat*. Sed quandoque contingit quod sacerdos est particeps criminis quod subditus suus commisit: sicut cum mulierem subditam cognovit. Ergo videtur quod non semper possit in suos subditos potestate clavium uti.

PRAETEREA, per potestatem clavium homo ab omnibus defectibus curatur. Sed quandoque alicui peccato annexus est irregularitatis defectus, vel excommunicationis sententia, a qua simplex sacerdos liberare non potest. Ergo videtur quod non possit uti clavium potestate in illos qui talibus irretiti sunt.

PRAETEREA, sacerdotii nostri iudicium et potestas per iudicium veteris sacerdotii figuratur. Sed minoribus iudicibus secundum legem non omnia competebat discutere, sed ad superiores recurrebant: ut dicitur Exod. 24: *si quid natum fueri quaestionis inter vos*, etc. Ergo videtur quod nec sacerdos de gravibus peccatis possit subditum suum absolvere, sed debeat ad superiorem remittere.

SED CONTRA: *Cuicumque committitur principale, committitur et accessorium*. Sed sacerdotibus committitur quod subditis suis Eucharistiam dispensent, ad quam ordinatur absolutio a peccatis quibuscumque. Ergo sacerdos ab omnibus peccatis potest absolvere quantum est de clavium potestate.

PRAETEREA, gratia omne peccatum tollit, quantumcumque sit parva. Sed sacerdos sacramenta dispensat, quibus gratia datur. Ergo, quantum est de potestate clavium, de omnibus peccatis absolvere potest.

RESPONDEO dicendum quod potestas ordinis, quantum est de se, extendit se ad omnia peccata remittenda: sed quia ad usum huius potestis requiritur iurisdictio, quae a maioribus in inferiores descendit, ideo potest superior aliqua sibi reservare, in quibus iudicium inferiori non committat. Alias de quolibet potest simplex sacerdos iurisdictionem habens absolvere.

Sunt autem quinque casus in quibus oportet quod simplex sacerdos poenitentem as superiorem remittat. Primus est quando est solemnis poenitentia imponenda: quia eius minister proprius est episcopus. Secundus est de excommunicatis, quando inferior sacerdos non potest absolvere. Tertius, quando invenit irregularitatem contractum, pro cuius dispensatione debet ad superiorem remittere. Quartus de incendiariis. Quintus, quando est consuetudo in aliquo episcopatu quod enormia cri-

OBJECTION 1: It would seem that a priest cannot always absolve his subject. For, as Augustine says, *no man should exercise the priestly office, unless he be free from those things which he condemns in others* (*On True and False Penance*). But a priest might happen to share in a sin committed by his subject; for instance, by knowledge of a woman who is his subject. Therefore, it seems that he cannot always use the power of the keys on his subjects.

OBJ. 2: Further, by the power of the keys a man is healed of all his shortcomings. Now it happens sometimes that a sin has attached to it a defect of irregularity or a sentence of excommunication from which a simple priest cannot absolve. Therefore, it seems that he cannot use the power of the keys on such as are shackled by these things in the above manner.

OBJ. 3: Further, the judgment and power of our priesthood was foreshadowed by the judgment of the ancient priesthood. Now according to the law, the lesser judges were not competent to decide all cases, and had recourse to the higher judges, according to Exodus 24:14: *if any question shall arise among you, you shall refer it to them*. It seems, therefore, that a priest cannot absolve his subject from graver sins, but should refer him to his superior.

ON THE CONTRARY, *Whoever has charge of the principal has charge of the accessory* (*Decretals*). Now priests are charged with the dispensation of the Eucharist to their subjects, to which sacrament the absolution of sins is subordinate (Q. 17, A. 2) Therefore, as far as the power of the keys is concerned, a priest can absolve his subject from any sins whatever.

FURTHER, Grace, however small, removes all sin. But a priest dispenses sacraments whereby grace is given. Therefore, as far as the power of the keys is concerned, he can absolve from all sins.

I ANSWER THAT, The power of order, considered in itself, extends to the remission of all sins. But since, as stated above, the use of this power requires jurisdiction which inferiors derive from their superiors, it follows that the superior can reserve certain matters to himself, the judgment of which he does not commit to his inferior; otherwise, any simple priest who has jurisdiction can absolve from any sin.

Now there are five cases in which a simple priest must refer his penitent to his superior. The first is when a public penance has to be imposed, because in that case the bishop is the proper minister of the sacrament. The second is the case of those who are excommunicated, when the inferior priest cannot absolve a penitent through the latter being excommunicated by his superior. The third case is when he finds that an irregularity has been contracted, for the dispensation of which he has to have recourse to his superior.

mina, ad terrorem, reservantur episcopo. Quia consuetudo dat vel aufert in talibus potestatem.

AD PRIMUM ergo dicendum quod in tali casu nec sacerdos deberet audire confessionem mulieris cum qua peccavit de illo peccato, sed deberet ad alium mittere. Nec illa deberet ei confiteri, sed deberet petere licentiam ad alium eundi; vel ad superiorem recurrere, si ille licentiam denegaret. Tum propter periculum. Tum quia est minor verecundia. Si tamen absolveret, absoluta esset. Quod enim Augustinus dicit, quod non debet esse in eodem crimine, intelligendum est secundum congruitatem, non secundum necessitatem sacramenti.

AD SECUNDUM dicendum quod poenitentia ab omnibus defectibus culpae liberat, non autem ab omnibus defectibus poenae: quia adhuc post peractam poenitentiam de homicidio aliquis remanet irregularis. Unde sacerdos potest de crimine absolvere, et pro poena amovenda debet ad superiorem remittere: nisi in excommunicatione, quia absolutio ab ipsa debet praecedere absolutionem a peccato, quia, quandiu aliquis est excommunicatus, non potest recipere aliquod Ecclesiae sacramentum.

AD TERTIUM dicendum quod ratio illa procedit quantum ad haec in quibus sibi superiores potestates iurisdictionem reservant.

The fourth is the case of arson. The fifth is when it is the custom in a diocese for the more heinous crimes to be reserved to the bishop in order to inspire fear, because custom in these cases either gives the power or takes it away.

REPLY OBJ. 1: In this case the priest should not hear the confession of his accomplice with regard to that particular sin, but must refer her to another. Nor should she confess to him, but should ask permission to go to another, or should have recourse to his superior if he refused, both on account of the danger, and for the sake of less shame. If, however, he were to absolve her it would be valid: because when Augustine says that they should not be guilty of the same sin, he is speaking of what is congruous, not of what is essential to the sacrament.

REPLY OBJ. 2: Penance delivers man from all defects of guilt, but not from all defects of punishment, since even after doing penance for murder, a man remains irregular. Hence a priest can absolve from a crime, but for the remission of the punishment he must refer the penitent to the superior, except in the case of excommunication, absolution from which should precede absolution from sin, for as long as a man is excommunicated, he cannot receive any sacrament of the Church.

REPLY OBJ. 3: This objection considers those cases in which superiors reserve the power of jurisdiction to themselves.

Article 3

Whether a Man Can Use the Keys with Regard to His Superior?

AD TERTIUM SIC PROCEDITUR. Videtur quod aliquis non possit uti clavibus in suum superiorem. Actus enim sacramentalis quilibet requirit propriam materiam. Sed propria materia usus clavium est persona subiecta, ut dictum est. Ergo in eo qui non est subditus, non potest clavibus sacerdos uti.

PRAETEREA, Ecclesia militans imitatur triumphantem. Sed in caelesti Ecclesia inferior angelus nunquam *purgat* aut *illuminat* aut *perficit* superiorem. Ergo nec aliquis inferior sacerdos potest uti actione hierarchica, quae est per absolutionem, in superiorem.

PRAETEREA, iudicium conscientiae debet esse ordinatius quam iudicium exterioris fori. Sed in exteriori foro inferior non potest excommunicare aut absolvere superiorem. Ergo videtur quod nec in foro poenitentiali.

SED CONTRA: Superior praelatus etiam *circumdatus est infirmitate*, et contingit ipsum peccare. Sed remedium contra peccatum est potestas clavium. Ergo, cum ipse non possit in seipsum clave uti, quia non potest esse

OBJECTION 1: It would seem that a man cannot use the keys in respect of a superior. For every sacramental act requires its proper matter. Now the proper matter for the use of the keys is a person who is subject, as stated above (Q. 19, A. 6). Therefore, a priest cannot use the keys in respect of one who is not his subject.

OBJ. 2: Further, the Church Militant is an image of the Church Triumphant. Now in the heavenly Church an inferior angel never *cleanses, enlightens*, or *perfects* a higher angel. Therefore, neither can an inferior priest exercise on a superior a hierarchical action such as absolution.

OBJ. 3: Further, the judgment of penance should be better regulated than the judgment of an external court. Now in the external court an inferior cannot excommunicate or absolve his superior. Therefore, seemingly, neither can he do so in the penitential court.

ON THE CONTRARY, The higher prelate is also *compassed with infirmity*, and may happen to sin. Now the power of the keys is the remedy for sin. Therefore, since he cannot use the key on himself, for he cannot be both judge

simul iudex et reus, videtur quod possit inferior in ipsum clavis potestate uti.

PRAETEREA, absolutio, quae fit per virtutem clavium, ordinatur ad perceptionem Eucharistiae. Sed inferior potest superiori Eucharistiam dispensare, si petat. Ergo et clavium potestate in ipsum uti, si se ei subiecerit.

RESPONDEO dicendum quod potestas clavium quantum est de se, extendit se ad omnes, ut dictum est: sed quod in aliquem sacerdos non possit potestate clavium uti, contingit ex hoc quod eius potestas est ad aliquos speciaiter limitata. Unde ille qui limitavit, potest extendere in quem voluerit. Et propter hoc etiam potestatem sibi dare potest in seipsum quamvis ipse in seipsum uti clavium potestate non possit, quia potestas clavium requirit pro materia aliquem subiectum, et ita alium; sibi ipsi enim aliquis subiectus esse non potest.

AD PRIMUM ergo dicendum quod, quamvis episcopus quem simplex sacerdos absolvit, sil superior eo simpliciter, est tamen inferior eo inquantum ei se ut peccatorem subiicit.

AD SECUNDUM dicendum quod in angelis non potest accidere aliquis defectus ratione cuius inferioribus suis superiores subdantur, sicut accidit in hominibus. Et ideo non est simile.

AD TERTIUM dicendum quod iudicium exterius est secundum homines: sed iudicium confessionis est quoad Deum, apud quem aliquis redditur minor ex hoc quod peccat, non autem apud hominum praelationes. Et ideo in exteriori iudicio, sicut nullus in seipsum sententiam dare potest excommunicationis, ita nec alteri committere, nec se excommunicare. Sed in foro conscientiae potest alteri committere suam absolutionem: qua ipse uti non possit.

Vel dicendum quod absolutio in foro confessionis est principaliter potestatis clavium, et ex consequenti respicit iurisdictionem. Sed excommunicatio respicit totaliter iurisdictionem. Quantum autem ad potestatem ordinis omnes sunt aequales, non autem quantum ad iurisdictionem. Et ideo non est simile.

and accused at the same time, it seems that an inferior can use the power of the keys on him.

FURTHER, Absolution, which is given through the power of the keys, is ordained to the reception of the Eucharist. But an inferior can give the Eucharist to his superior, if the latter asks him to. Therefore, he can use the power of the keys on him if he submit to him.

I ANSWER THAT, The power of the keys, considered in itself, is applicable to all, as stated above (A. 2): and that a priest is unable to use the keys on some particular person is due to his power being limited to certain individuals. Therefore, he who limited his power can extend it to whom he wills, so that he can give him power over himself, although he cannot use the power of the keys on himself, because this power requires to be exercised on a subject and therefore on someone else, for no man can be subject to himself.

REPLY OBJ. 1: Although the bishop whom a simple priest absolves is his superior absolutely speaking, yet he is beneath him insofar as he submits himself as a sinner to him.

REPLY OBJ. 2: In the angels there can be no defect by reason of which the higher angel can submit to the lower, such as there can happen to be among men; and so there is no comparison.

REPLY OBJ. 3: External judgment is according to men, whereas the judgment of confession is according to God, in whose sight a man is lessened by sinning, which is not the case in human prelacy. Therefore, just as in external judgment no man can pass sentence of excommunication on himself, so neither can he empower another to excommunicate him. On the other hand, in the tribunal of conscience he can give another the power to absolve him, though he cannot use that power himself.

It may also be replied that absolution in the tribunal of the confessional belongs principally to the power of the keys and consequently to the power of jurisdiction, whereas excommunication regards jurisdiction exclusively. And, as to the power of orders, all are equal, but not as to jurisdiction. Therefore, there is no comparison.

QUESTION 21

EXCOMMUNICATION

Consequenter videndum est de excommunicatione. De qua primo considerandum est de definitione excommunicationis, et congruitate, et causa; secundo, de eo qui potest excommunicare et excommunicari; tertio, de participatione cum excommunicatis; quarto, de absolutione ab excommunicatione.

Circa primum quaeruntur quattuor.

Primo: utrum convenienter excommunicatio definiatur.

Secundo: utrum Ecclesia debeat aliquem excommunicare.

Tertio: utrum aliquis pro aliquo temporali damno sit excommunicandus.

Quarto: utrum excommunicatio iniuste lata aliquem effectum habeat.

We must now treat of excommunication, about which we shall consider: (1) The definition, congruity and cause of excommunication; (2) Who has the power to excommunicate; (3) Communication with excommunicated persons; (4) Absolution from excommunication.

Under the first head there are four points of inquiry:

(1) Whether excommunication is suitably defined?

(2) Whether the Church should excommunicate anyone?

(3) Whether anyone should be excommunicated for inflicting temporal harm?

(4) Whether an excommunication unjustly pronounced has any effect?

Article 1

Whether Excommunication Is Suitably Defined as Separation From the Communion of the Church, Etc?

AD PRIMUM SIC PROCEDITUR. Videtur quod incompetens sit haec definitio excommunicationis a quibusdam posita: *excommunicatio est separatio a communione Ecclesiae quoad fructum et suffragia generalia.* Suffragia enim Ecclesiae valent eis pro quibus fiunt. Sed Ecclesia orat pro eis qui extra Ecclesiam sunt: sicut pro haereticis et paganis. Ergo etiam pro excommunicatis, qui extra Ecclesiam sunt. Et sic eis suffragia Ecclesiae valent.

PRAETEREA, nullus amittit suffragia Ecclesiae nisi per culpam. Sed excommunicatio non est culpa, sed poena. Ergo per excommunicationem non separatur aliquis a suffragiis Ecclesiae communibus.

PRAETEREA, fructus Ecclesiae non videtur esse aliud quam suffragia: non enim potest intelligi de fructu bonorum temporalium, quia haec excommunicatis non auferuntur. Ergo inconvenienter utrumque ponitur.

PRAETEREA, excommunicatio minor quaedam excommunicatio est. Sed per eam homo non perdit suffragia Ecclesiae. Ergo definitio non est conveniens.

RESPONDEO dicendum quod ille qui per baptismum in Ecclesia ponitur, ad duo adscribitur: scilicet ad coetum fidelium; et ad participationem sacramentorum. Et hoc secundum praesupponit primum: quia in sacra-

OBJECTION 1: It would seem that excommunication is unsuitably defined by some thus: *excommunication is separation from the communion of the Church as to fruit and general suffrages.* For the suffrages of the Church avail for those for whom they are offered. But the Church prays for those who are outside the Church, such as for heretics and pagans. Therefore, she prays also for the excommunicated, since they are outside the Church, and so the suffrages of the Church avail for them.

OBJ. 2: Further, no one loses the suffrages of the Church except by his own fault. Now excommunication is not a fault, but a punishment. Therefore, excommunication does not deprive a man of the general suffrages of the Church.

OBJ. 3: Further, the fruit of the Church seems to be the same as the Church's suffrages, for it cannot mean the fruit of temporal goods, since excommunication does not deprive a man of these. Therefore, there is no reason for mentioning both.

OBJ. 4: Further, there is a kind of excommunication called minor, by which man is not deprived of the suffrages of the Church. Therefore, this definition is unsuitable.

I ANSWER THAT, When a man enters the Church by baptism, he is admitted to two things, viz. the body of the faithful and the participation of the sacraments: and this latter presupposes the former, since the faithful are united

mentis participandis etiam fideles communicant. Et ideo aliquis potest extra Ecclesiam fieri per excommunicationem dupliciter. Uno modo, ita quod separaretur tantum a participatione sacramentorum. Et haec erit excommunicatio minor. Alio modo, ita quod excludatur ab utroque. Et sic erit excommunicatio maior, quae hic definitur. Non autem potest esse tertium, scilicet quod excludatur a communione fidelium et non a participatione sacramentorum, ratione iam dicta: quia scilicet fideles in sacramentis communicant. Sed communicatio fidelium est duplex: quaedam in spiritualibus, sicut mutuae orationes, et conventus ad sacra percipienda; quaedam in corporalibus actibus legitimis. Qui quidem legitimi actus et licita communio his versibus continentur: *Si pro delictis anathema quis efficiatur: Os, orare, vale, communio, mensa negatur. Os* scilicet, ne osculum detur; *orare*, ne cum excommunicatis oremus; *vale*, ne salutentur; *communio*, ne scilicet in sacramentis cum ipsis aliquis communicet; *mensa negatur*, ne aliquis cum eis comedat.

Praemissa ergo definitio importat separationem a sacramentis, in hoc quod dicit, quantum ad fructum; et a communione fidelium quantum ad spiritualia, in hoc quod dicit, et suffragia Ecclesiae communia.

Alia autem definitio invenitur quae datur secundum separationem ab utrisque actibus, quae talis est: *excommunicatio est a qualibet licita communione vel legitimo actu separatio.*

AD PRIMUM ergo dicendum quod pro infidelibus oratur, sed ipsi orationis fructum non percipiunt nisi ad fidem convertantur. Similiter et pro excommunicatis orari potest: quamvis non inter orationes quae pro membris Ecclesiae fiunt. Et tamen fructum non percipiunt quandiu in excommunicatione manent: sed oratur ut detur eis spiritus poenitentiae, ut ab excommunicatione solvantur.

AD SECUNDUM dicendum quod suffragia alicuius valent alicui secundum quod ei continuantur. Potest tamen actio unius alteri continuari dupliciter. Uno modo, ex vi caritatis, quae omnes fideles connectit ut sint unum in Deo: sicut dicitur in Psalmo 118: *particeps ego sum*, etc. Et hanc continuationem excommunicatio non intercipit. Quia iuste quis excommunicari non potest nisi pro culpa mortali, per quam a caritate iam divisus est, etiam si non excommunicetur. Iniusta autem excommunicatio caritatem alicui auferte non potest: cum sit de *maximis bonis*, quae non possunt alicui invito auferri.

Alio modo, per intentionem suffragia facientis, quae in aliquem fertur pro quo fiunt. Et hanc continuationem excommunicatio intercipit: quia Ecclesia per excommunicationis sententiam separat excommunicatos ab universitate fidelium, pro quibus suffragia facit; unde suf-

together in the participation of the sacraments. Consequently, a person may be expelled from the Church in two ways. First, by being deprived merely of the participation of the sacraments, and this is the minor excommunication. Second, by being deprived of both, and this is the major excommunication, of which the above is the definition. Nor can there be a third consisting in the privation of communion with the faithful but not of the participation of the sacraments, for the reason already given, namely because the faithful communicate together in the sacraments. Now, there are two things the faithful share in. They share in spiritual things, like mutual prayers and the agreement for receiving sacred things, which legal acts and licit communion are contained in these verses: *if for his crimes anyone is made anathema, he is denied mouth, prayer, farewell, communion, table. He is denied mouth*, namely, he may not be given a kiss of peace; *prayer*, lest we pray with those excommunicated; *farewell*, lest they be greeted; *communion*, namely, so that no one shares with them in the sacraments; *table*, lest anyone eat with them.

Accordingly, the above definition includes privation of the sacraments in the words *as to the fruit*, and from partaking together with the faithful in spiritual things, in the words, *and the general prayers of the Church*.

Another definition is given which expresses the privation of both kinds of acts, and is as follows: *excommunication is the privation of all lawful communion with the faithful.*

REPLY OBJ. 1: Prayers are said for unbelievers, but they do not receive the fruit of those prayers unless they be converted to the faith. In like manner, prayers may be offered up for those who are excommunicated, but not among the prayers that are said for the members of the Church. Yet they do not receive the fruit so long as they remain under the excommunication, but prayers are said for them that they may receive the spirit of repentance, so that they may be loosed from excommunication.

REPLY OBJ. 2: One man's prayers profit another insofar as they can reach to him. Now the action of one man may reach to another in two ways. First, by virtue of charity, which unites all the faithful, making them one in God, according to Psalm 118:63: *I am a partaker with all them that fear you*. Now excommunication does not interrupt this union, since no man can be justly excommunicated except for a mortal sin, whereby a man is already separated from charity, even without being excommunicated. An unjust excommunication cannot deprive a man of charity, since this is one of the *greatest of all goods*, of which a man cannot be deprived against his will.

Second, through the intention of the one who prays, which intention is directed to the person he prays for, and this union is interrupted by excommunication, because by passing sentence of excommunication the Church severs a man from the whole body of the faithful, for whom she

fragia Ecclesiae ei non prosunt, quae pro tota Ecclesia fiunt. Nec ex persona Ecclesiae, oratio pro eis inter membra Ecclesiae fieri potest: quamvis aliqua persona privata possit ad eius conversionem aliquod suffragium per intentionem dirigere.

Ad tertium dicendum quod fructus spiritualis Ecclesiae non solum est ex suffragiis, sed etiam ex perceptione sacramentorum et ex convictu fidelium.

Ad quartum dicendum quod minor excommunicatio non habet perfectam rationem excommunicationis, sed aliquid ipsius participat. Et ideo non oportet quod, totaliter ei excommunicationis definitio conveniat, sed solum quoad aliquid.

prays. Hence those prayers of the Church which are offered up for the whole Church do not profit those who are excommunicated. Nor can prayers be said for them among the members of the Church as speaking in the Church's name, although a private individual may say a prayer with the intention of offering it for their conversion.

Reply Obj. 3: The spiritual fruit of the Church is derived not only from her prayers, but also from the sacraments received and from the faithful dwelling together.

Reply Obj. 4: The minor excommunication does not fulfill all the conditions of excommunication but only a part of them. Hence the definition of excommunication need not apply to it in every respect, but only in some.

Article 2

Whether the Church Should Excommunicate Anyone?

Ad secundum sic proceditur. Videtur quod Ecclesia nullum debeat excommunicare. Quia excommunicatio maledictio quaedam est. Sed Rom. 12 prohibemur maledicere. Ergo Ecclesia excommunicare non debet.

Praeterea, Ecclesia, militans debet imitari triumphantem. Sed, ut in Epistola Iudae legitur, *Michael, cum altercaretur cum diabolo de Moysi corpore, non est ausus iudicium inferre blasphemiae, sed ait: Imperet tibi Deus.* Ergo nec Ecclesia militans debet alicui iudicium maledictionis et excommunicationis inferre.

Praeterea, nullus est in manum hostis tradendus nisi omnino desperatus. Sed per excommunicationem traditur aliquis in manum Satanae: ut patet I Cor. 5. Cum ergo de nemine sit desperandum in vita ista, Ecclesia nullum debet excommunicare.

Sed contra: Est quod Apostolus, I Cor. 5, mandat quendam excommunicari.

Praeterea, Matth. 18 dicitur, de illo qui Ecclesiam audire contemnit: *sit tibi sicut ethnicus et publicanus.* Sed ethnici sunt extra Ecclesiam. Ergo illi qui Ecclesiam audire contemnunt per excommunicationem extra Ecclesiam sunt ponendi.

Respondeo dicendum quod iudicium Ecclesiae conforme debet esse iudicio Dei. Deus autem peccatores multipliciter punit, ut ad bonum eos trahat: uno modo, flagellis castigando; alio modo, hominem sibi relinquendo, ut, auxiliis subtractis quibus a malo praepediebatur, suam infirmitatem cognoscat, et humilis ad Deum redeat, a quo superbus discesserat. Et quantum ad utrumque Ecclesia in excommunicationis sententia imi-

Objection 1: It would seem that the Church ought not to excommunicate anyone, because excommunication is a kind of curse, and we are forbidden to curse (Rom 12:14). Therefore, the Church should not excommunicate.

Obj. 2: Further, the Church Militant should imitate the Church Triumphant. Now we read in the epistle of Jude 1:9 that when *Michael the Archangel disputing with the devil contended about the body of Moses, he did not dare to bring against him the judgment of blasphemy, but said, "May the Lord rebuke you."* Therefore, the Church Militant ought not to judge any man by cursing or excommunicating him.

Obj. 3: Further, no man should be given into the hands of his enemies, unless there be no hope for him. Now by excommunication a man is given into the hands of Satan, as is clear from 1 Corinthians 5:5. Since, then, we should never give up hope about anyone in this life, the Church should not excommunicate anyone.

On the contrary, The Apostle ordered a man to be excommunicated (1 Cor 5:5).

Further, It is written about the man who refuses to hear the Church: *let him be to you as the heathen or publican* (Matt 18:17). But heathens are outside the Church. Therefore, they also who refuse to hear the Church should be banished from the Church by excommunication.

I answer that, The judgment of the Church should be conformed to the judgment of God. Now God punishes the sinner in many ways in order to draw him to good, either by chastising him with stripes, or by leaving him to himself so that, being deprived of those helps whereby he was kept out of evil, he may acknowledge his weakness, and humbly return to God whom he had abandoned in his pride. In both these respects the Church by passing sen-

tatur divinum iudicium. Inquantum enim eum a communione fidelium separat *ut erubescat*, imitatur divinum iudicium quo per flagella castigat. Inquantum autem a suffragiis et aliis spiritualibus separat, imitatur divinum iudicium quo hominem sibi relinquit, ut per humilitatem seipsum cognoscens ad Deum redeat.

AD PRIMUM ergo dicendum quod maledictio potest esse dupliciter. Uno modo, ita quod in malo quod irrogat vel dicit, per intentionem sistat. Et sic maledictio omnibus modis est prohibita. Alio modo, ita quod malum, quod quidem maledicendo imprecatur, ad bonum illius ordinet qui maledicitur. Et sic maledictio quandoque est licita et salutifera: sicut etiam medicus quandoque nocumentum infert infirmo, ut sectionem, per quam ab infirmitate liberetur.

AD SECUNDUM dicendum quod diabolus incorrigibilis est: et ideo non susceptibilis alicuius boni per excommunicationis poenam.

AD TERTIUM dicendum quod ex hoc ipso quod aliquis suffragiis Ecclesiae privatur, triplex incommodum incurrit, per tria quae quis ex suffragiis Ecclesiae consequitur. Valent enim ad augmentum gratiae eis qui habent, vel ad merendum eis qui non habent. Et quantum ad hoc Magister Sententiarum dicit quod *gratia Dei per excommunicationem subtrahitur*.

Valent etiam ad custodiam virtutis. Et quantum ad hoc dicit quod *protectio subtrahitur*: non quod omnino a Dei providentia excludantur, sed ab illa protectione qua filios Ecclesiae speciliori modo custodit. Valent etiam ad defendendum ab hoste. Et quantum ad hoc dicit quod *diabolo maior potestas faciendi in ipsum datur*, et spiritualiter et corporaliter.

Unde in primitiva Ecclesia, quando oportebat per signa homines ad fidem invitare, sicut Spiritus Sancti donum visibili signo manifestabatur, ita et excommunicatio corporali vexatione a diabolo innotescebat. Nec est inconveniens si ille qui non est desperatus hosti datur: quia non datur ei quasi damnandus, sed quasi corrigendus; cum in potestate Ecclesiae sit ex eius manu ipsum cum voluerit eripere.

tence of excommunication imitates the judgment of God. For by severing a man from the communion of the faithful *that he may blush*, she imitates the judgment whereby God chastises man with stripes; and by depriving him of prayers and other spiritual things, she imitates the judgment of God in leaving man to himself, in order that by humility he may learn to know himself and return to God.

REPLY OBJ. 1: A curse may be pronounced in two ways: first, so that the intention of the one who curses is fixed on the evil which he invokes or pronounces, and cursing in this sense is altogether forbidden. Second, so that the evil which a man invokes in cursing is intended for the good of the one who is cursed, and thus cursing is sometimes lawful and salutary: thus a physician makes a sick man undergo pain, for instance, by cutting him in order to deliver him from his sickness.

REPLY OBJ. 2: The devil cannot be brought to repentance, wherefore the pain of excommunication cannot do him any good.

REPLY OBJ. 3: From the very fact that a man is deprived of the prayers of the Church, he incurs a triple loss, corresponding to the three things which a man acquires through the Church's prayers. For they bring an increase of grace to those who have it, or merit grace for those who have it not; and in this respect the Master of the Sentences says: *the grace of God is taken away by excommunication* (*Sentences* IV, D. 18).

They also prove a safeguard of virtue; and in this respect he says that *protection is taken away*, not that the excommunicated person is withdrawn altogether from God's providence, but that he is excluded from that protection with which he watches over the children of the Church in a more special way. Moreover, they are useful as a defense against the enemy, and in this respect he says that *the devil receives greater power of assaulting the excommunicated person, both spiritually and corporally*.

Hence in the early Church, when men had to be enticed to the faith by outward signs (thus the gift of the Holy Spirit was shown openly by a visible sign), so too excommunication was evidenced by a person being troubled in his body by the devil. Nor is it unreasonable that one for whom there is still hope be given over to the enemy, for he is given not to damnation, but to correction, since the Church has the power to rescue him from the hands of the enemy, whenever he is willing.

Article 3

Whether Anyone Should Be Excommunicated for Inflicting Temporal Harm?

Ad tertium sic proceditur. Videtur quod nullus pro temporali damno debeat excommunicari. Quia poena non debet excedere culpam. Sed poena excommunicationis est privatio alicuius boni spiritualis, quod omnibus bonis temporalibus praeeminet. Ergo pro temporalibus nullus est excommunicandus.

Praeterea, *nulli malum pro malo reddere debemus,* secundum Apostoli praeceptum. Sed hoc esset malum pro malo reddere, si pro tali damno quis excommunicatur. Ergo nullo modo hoc debet fieri.

Sed contra est quod Petrus Ananiam et Saphiram pro defraudatione pretii agri sententia mortis damnavit. Ergo et Ecclesiae licet pro temporalibus damnis excommunicare.

Respondeo dicendum quod per excommunicationem iudex ecclesiasticus excommunicatos excludit a regno quodammodo. Unde, cum non debeat a regno excludere nisi indignos, ut ex definitione clavis patuit; nec aliquis reddatur indignus nisi per peccatum mortale caritatem amiserit, quae est via ducens ad regnum: ideo nullus excommunicari debet nisi pro peccato mortali. Et quia in damnificando aliquem corporaliter vel in rebus temporalibus aliquis mortaliter peccat; et contra caritatem facit, ideo pro damno temporali illato Ecclesiae aliquem excommunicare potest.

Sed quia excommunicatio est gravissima poenarum; *poenae* autem *medicinae sunt,* secundum Philosophum, in II *Ethic.;* sapientis autem medici est a levioribus incipere medicinis et minus periculosis: ideo excommunicatio infligi non debet, etiam pro peccato mortali, nisi contumax fuerit, vel non veniendo ad iudicium, vel ante terminationem iudicii sine licentia recedendo, vel determinationi non parendo. Tunc enim, post quam monitus fuerit, si obedire contempserit, contumax reputatur; et excommunicari debet a iudice, iam non habente quod contra ipsum faciat amplius.

Ad primum ergo dicendum quod culpae quantitas non mensuratur ex nocumento quod quis facit, sed ex voluntate qua quis facit, contra caritatem agens. Et ideo, quamvis poena excommunicationis excedat nocumentum, non tamen excedit quantitatem culpae.

Ad secundum dicendum quod, cum aliquis per poenam aliquam corrigitur, non redditur ei malum, sed bonum: quia *poenae medicinae sunt,* ut dictum est.

Objection 1: It would seem that no man should be excommunicated for inflicting a temporal harm. For the punishment should not exceed the fault. But the punishment of excommunication is the privation of a spiritual good, which surpasses all temporal goods. Therefore, no man should be excommunicated for temporal injuries.

Obj. 2: Further, *we should render to no man evil for evil,* according to the precept of the Apostle (Rom 12:17). But this would be rendering evil for evil, if a man were to be excommunicated for doing such an injury. Therefore, this ought by no means to be done.

On the contrary, Peter sentenced Ananias and Sapphira to death for keeping back the price of their piece of land (Acts 5:1–10). Therefore, it is lawful for the Church to excommunicate for temporal injuries.

I answer that, By excommunication the ecclesiastical judge excludes a man, in a sense, from the kingdom. Wherefore, since he ought not to exclude from the kingdom others than the unworthy, as was made clear from the definition of the keys (Q. 17, A. 2), and since no one becomes unworthy unless he loses charity (which is the way leading to the kingdom) by committing a mortal sin, it follows that no man should be excommunicated except for a mortal sin. And since by injuring a man in his body or in his temporalities, one may sin mortally and act against charity, the Church can excommunicate a man for having inflicted temporal injury on anyone.

Yet, as excommunication is the most severe punishment, and since *punishments are remedies,* according to the Philosopher (*Ethics* 2), and again since a prudent physician begins with lighter and less risky remedies, therefore excommunication should not be inflicted even for a mortal sin, unless the sinner be obstinate, either by not coming up for judgment, or by going away before judgment is pronounced, or by failing to obey the decision of the court. For then, if, after due warning, he refuse to obey, he is reckoned to be obstinate, and the judge, not being able to proceed otherwise against him, must excommunicate him.

Reply Obj. 1: A fault is not measured by the extent of the damage a man does, but by the will with which he does it, acting against charity. Wherefore, though the punishment of excommunication exceeds the harm done, it does not exceed the measure of the sin.

Reply Obj. 2: When a man is corrected by being punished, evil is not rendered to him, but good: since *punishments are remedies,* as stated above.

Article 4

Whether an Excommunication Unjustly Pronounced Has Any Effect?

AD QUARTUM SIC PROCEDITUR. Videtur quod excommunicatio iniuste lata nullo modo effectum habeat. Quia per excommunicationem *protectio et gratia Dei subtrahitur*, quae non iniuste subtrahi potest. Ergo excommunicatio iniuste lata non habet effectum.

PRAETEREA, Hieronymus dicit quod *est de supercilio Pharisaeorum aestimare esse ligatum vel solutum qui ligatur vel solvitur iniuste.* Sed eorum supercilium erat superbum et erroneum. Ergo excommunicatio iniusta nullum habet effectum.

SED CONTRA: Secundum Gregorium, *praecepta pastoris, sive iusta sive iniusta, timenda sunt.* Non autem essent timenda nisi aliquid nocerent etiam iniusta. Ergo, etc.

RESPONDEO dicendum quod excommunicatio potest dici iniusta dupliciter. Uno modo, ex parte excommunicantis: sicut cum ex odio vel ex ira aliquis excommunicat. Et tunc excommunicatio nihilominus habet effectum suum, quaevis ille qui excommunicat peccet: quia iste iuste patitur, quamvis ille iniuste faciat.

Alio modo, ex parte excommunicationis ipsius: vel quia causa excommunicationis est indebita; vel quia infertur sententia iuris ordine praetermisso. Et tunc, si sit talis error ex parte sententiae qui sententiam nullam esse faciat, non habet effectum: quia non est excommunicatio. Si autem non annullet sententiam, habet effectum suum. Et debet excommunicatus humiliter obedire, et erit ei ad meritum; vel absolutionem petere debet ab excommunicante; vel ad superiorem iudicem recurrere. Si autem contemneret, eo ipso mortaliter peccaret.

Contingit autem quandoque quod est debita causa ex parte excommunicantis quae non est debita ex parte excommunicati: sicut cum quis pro falso crimine in iudicio probato excommunicatur. Et tunc, si humiliter sustinet, humilitatis mentum recompensat excommunicationis damnum.

AD PRIMUM ergo dicendum quod, quamvis homo gratiam Dei iniuste amittere non possit, potest tamen iniuste amittere illa quae ex parte nostra sunt quae ad gratiam Dei disponunt: sicut patet si subtrahatur alicui doctrinae verbum quod ei debetur. Et hoc modo excommunicatio gratiam Dei subtrahere dicitur, ut in praedictis patet.

OBJECTION 1: It would seem that an excommunication which is pronounced unjustly has no effect at all. For excommunication deprives a man of the *protection and grace of God*, which cannot be forfeited unjustly. Therefore, excommunication has no effect if it be unjustly pronounced.

OBJ. 2: Further, on Matthew 16:19: *I will give to you the keys*, Jerome says, *it is a pharisaical severity to reckon as really bound or loosed that which is bound or loosed unjustly.* But that severity was proud and erroneous. Therefore, an unjust excommunication has no effect.

ON THE CONTRARY, According to Gregory, *the sentence of the pastor is to be feared whether it be just or unjust* (*Homilies on the Gospels* 26). Now there would be no reason to fear an unjust excommunication if it did not hurt. Therefore, etc.

I ANSWER THAT, An excommunication may be unjust for two reasons. First, on the part of its author, as when anyone excommunicates through hatred or anger, and then nevertheless the excommunication takes effect, though its author sins, because the one who is excommunicated suffers justly, even if the author act wrongly in excommunicating him.

Second, on the part of the excommunication, through there being no proper cause, or through the sentence being passed without the forms of law being observed. In this case, if the error on the part of the sentence be such as to render the sentence void, this has no effect, for there is no excommunication; but if the error does not annul the sentence, this takes effect, and the person excommunicated should humbly submit (which will be credited to him as a merit), and either seek absolution from the person who has excommunicated him, or appeal to a higher judge. If, however, he were to contemn the sentence, he would *ipso facto* sin mortally.

But sometimes it happens that there is sufficient cause on the part of the excommunicator, but not on the part of the excommunicated, as when a man is excommunicated for a crime which he has not committed, but which has been proved against him: in this case, if he submit humbly, the merit of his humility will compensate him for the harm of excommunication.

REPLY OBJ. 1: Although a man cannot lose God's grace unjustly, yet he can unjustly lose those things which on our part dispose us to receive grace: for instance, a man may be deprived of the instruction which he ought to have. It is in this sense that excommunication is said to deprive a man of God's grace, as was explained above (A. 2).

AD SECUNDUM dicendum quod Hieronymus loquitur quantum ad culpas, et non quantum ad poenas: quae possunt etiam iniuste infligi a rectoribus ecclesiarum.

REPLY OBJ. 2: Jerome is speaking of sin, not of its punishments, which can be inflicted unjustly by ecclesiastical superiors.

QUESTION 22

WHO CAN EXCOMMUNICATE AND BE EXCOMMUNICATED

Deinde considerandum est de his qui possunt excommunicare et excommunicari.

Circa quod quaeruntur sex.

Primo: utrum quilibet sacerdos possit excommunicare.

Secundo: utrum non-sacerdos excommunicare possit.

Tertio: utrum excommunicatus vel suspensus possit excommunicare.

Quarto: utrum aliquis seipsum, vel aequalem vel superiorem possit excommunicare.

Quinto: utrum aliqua universitas excommunicari poscit.

Sexto: utrum semel excommunicatus excommunicari possit ulterius.

We must now consider those who can excommunicate or be excommunicated.

Under this head there are six points of inquiry:

(1) Whether every priest can excommunicate?

(2) Whether one who is not a priest can excommunicate?

(3) Whether one who is excommunicated or suspended can excommunicate?

(4) Whether anyone can excommunicate himself, or an equal, or a superior?

(5) Whether a university can be excommunicated?

(6) Whether one who is already excommunicated can be excommunicated again?

Article 1

Whether Every Priest Can Excommunicate?

AD PRIMUM SIC PROCEDITUR. Videtur quod quilibet sacerdos possit excommunicare. Excommunicatio enim est actus clavium. Sed quilibet sacerdos habet claves. Ergo quilibet potest excommunicare.

PRAETEREA, maius est solvere et ligare in foro poenitentiae: quam in foro iudicii. Sed quilibet sacerdos potest sibi subditos in foro poenitentiali absolvere et ligare. Ergo etiam potest sibi subditos quilibet sacerdos excommunicare.

SED CONTRA, ea in quibus imminet periculum, sunt maioribus reservanda. Sed poena excommunicationis est valde periculosa, nisi cum moderamine fiat. Ergo non debet cuilibet sacerdoti committi.

RESPONDEO dicendum quod in foro conscientiae causa agitur inter hominem et Deum: in foro autem exterioris iudicii causa agitur hominis ad hominem. Et ideo absolutio vel ligatio quae unum hominem obligat quoad Deum tantum, pertinet ad forum poenitentiae; sed illa quae hominem obligat in comparatione ad alios homines, ad forum publicum exterioris iudicii pertinet. Et quia homo per excommunicationem a communione fidelium separatur, ideo excommunicatio ad forum exterius pertinet. Et ideo illi soli possunt excommunicare qui habent iurisdictionem in foro iudiciali. Et propter hoc soli episcopi propria auctoritate at maiores praelati,

OBJECTION 1: It would seem that every priest can excommunicate. For excommunication is an act of the keys. But every priest has the keys. Therefore, every priest can excommunicate.

OBJ. 2: Further, it is a greater thing to loose and bind in the tribunal of penance than in the tribunal of judgment. But every priest can loose and bind his subjects in the tribunal of penance. Therefore, every priest can excommunicate his subjects.

ON THE CONTRARY, Matters fraught with danger should be left to the decision of superiors. Now the punishment of excommunication is fraught with many dangers, unless it be inflicted with moderation. Therefore, it should not be entrusted to every priest.

I ANSWER THAT, In the tribunal of conscience the plea is between man and God, whereas in the outward tribunal it is between man and man. Thus, the loosing or binding of one man in relation to God alone belongs to the tribunal of penance, whereas the binding or loosing of a man in relation to other men belongs to the public tribunal of external judgment. And since excommunication severs a man from the communion of the faithful, it belongs to the external tribunal. Consequently, those alone can excommunicate who have jurisdiction in the judicial tribunal. Hence of their own authority only bishops and higher prelates, according to the more common opinion, can excommuni-

secundum communiorem opinionem, possunt excommunicare: sed presbyteri parochiales non nisi ex commissione eis facta, vel in certis casibus, sicut in furto et rapina et huiusmodi, in quibus est eis a iure concessum quod excommunicare possint.

Alii autem dixerunt quod etiam sacerdotes parochiales possunt excommunicare. Sed praedicta opinio est rationabilior.

AD PRIMUM ergo dicendum quod excommunicatio non est actus clavis directe, sed magis respectu exterioris iudicii. Sed sententia excommunicationis, quamvis in exteriori iudicio promulgetur, quia tamen aliquo modo pertinet ad aditum regni, secundum quod Ecclesia militans est via ad triumphantem; ideo etiam talis iurisdictio per quam homo excommunicare potest, clavis potest dici. Et secundum hoc a quibusdam distinguitur quod est *clavis ordinis*, quam omnes sacerdotes habent; et *clavis iurisdictionis in foro iudiciali*, quam habent soli iudices exterioris fori. Utramque tamen Deus Petro contulit, Matth. 16: et ab ipso in alios descendit qui utramque habent.

AD SECUNDUM dicendum quod sacerdotes parochiales habent quidem iurisdictionem in subditos suos quantum ad forum conscientiae, sed non quantum ad forum iudiciale: quia non possunt conveniri coram eis in causis contentiosis. Et ideo excommunicare non possunt: sed absolvere possunt in foro poenitentiali. Et quamvis forum poenitentiale sit dignius, tamen in foro iudiciali maior solemnitas requiritur; quia iri eo oportet quod non solum Deo, sed etiam homini satisfiat.

cate, whereas parish priests can do so only by commission or in certain cases, as those of theft, rape, and the like, in which the law allows them to excommunicate.

Others, however, have maintained that even parish priests can excommunicate: but the former opinion is more reasonable.

REPLY OBJ. 1: Excommunication is an act of the keys not directly, but with respect to the external judgment. The sentence of excommunication, however, though it is promulgated by an external verdict, still, as it belongs somewhat to the entrance to the kingdom insofar as the Church Militant is the way to the Church Triumphant, this jurisdiction whereby a man is competent to excommunicate can be called a key. It is in this sense that some distinguish between the *key of orders*, which all priests have, and the *key of jurisdiction in the tribunal of judgment*, which none have but the judges of the external tribunal. Nevertheless, God bestowed both on Peter (Matt 16:19), from whom they are derived by others, whichever of them they have.

REPLY OBJ. 2: Parish priests have jurisdiction indeed over their subjects in the tribunal of conscience, but not in the judicial tribunal, for they cannot summon them in contentious cases. Hence they cannot excommunicate, but they can absolve them in the tribunal of penance. And though the tribunal of penance is higher, yet more solemnity is requisite in the judicial tribunal, because therein it is necessary to make satisfaction not only to God but also to man.

Article 2

Whether Those Who Are Not Priests Can Excommunicate?

AD SECUNDUM SIC PROCEDITUR. Videtur quod non-sacerdotes excommunicare non possint. Quia excommunicatio est actus clavium, ut in IV *Sententiarum* dicitur. Sed non-sacerdotes non habent claves. Ergo excommunicare non possunt.

PRAETEREA, plus requiritur ad excommunicationem quam ad absolutionem in foro poenitentiae. Sed non-sacerdos in foro poenitentiae absolvere non potest. Ergo nec excommunicationem inferre.

SED CONTRA est quod archidiaconi legati et electi excommunicant, qui quandoque non sunt sacerdotes. Ergo non solum sacerdotes excommunicare possunt.

RESPONDEO dicendum quod sacramenta, in quibus gratia confertur, dispensare ad solos sacerdotes pertinet. Et ideo ipsi soli possunt absolvere et ligare in foro poenitentiali. Sed excommunicatio non directe respicit gratiam, sed ex consequenti, inquantum homo suffragiis Ecclesiae privatur, quae ad gratiam disponunt vel in gra-

OBJECTION 1: It would seem that those who are not priests cannot excommunicate. For excommunication is an act of the keys, as stated in the *Sentences* IV, Dist. 18. But those who are not priests have not the keys. Therefore, they cannot excommunicate.

OBJ. 2: Further, more is required for excommunication than for absolution in the tribunal of penance. But one who is not a priest cannot absolve in the tribunal of penance. Neither, therefore, can he excommunicate.

ON THE CONTRARY, Archdeacons, legates and bishops elect excommunicate, and yet sometimes they are not priests. Therefore, not only priests can excommunicate.

I ANSWER THAT, Priests alone are competent to dispense the sacraments wherein grace is given: therefore, they alone can loose and bind in the tribunal of penance. On the other hand, excommunication regards grace not directly but consequently, insofar as it deprives a man of the Church's prayers, by which he is disposed for grace or

tia conservant. Et ideo etiam non-sacerdotes, dummodo iurisdictionem habeant in foro contentioso, possunt excommunicare.

AD PRIMUM ergo dicendum quod, quamvis non habeant clavem ordinis, habent tamen clavem iurisdictionis.

AD SECUNDUM dicendum quod ista duo se habent sicut excedentia et excessa. Et ideo alicui competit unum cui non competit aliud.

preserved therein. Consequently, even those who are not priests, provided they have jurisdiction in a contentious court, can excommunicate.

REPLY OBJ. 1: Though they have not the key of orders, they have the key of jurisdiction.

REPLY OBJ. 2: These two are related to one another as something exceeding and something exceeded (A. 1; Q. 24, A. 1) and consequently one of them may be within the competency of someone while the other is not.

Article 3

Whether a Man Who Is Excommunicated or Suspended Can Excommunicate Another?

AD TERTIUM SIC PROCEDITUR. Videtur quod excommunicatus vel suspensus excommunicare possit. Ille enim qui est excommunicatus vel suspensus, neque ordinem neque iurisdictionem amittit: quia neque reordinatur cum absolvitur, neque cura iterum ei committitur. Sed excommunicatio non requirit nisi ordinem vel iurisdictionem. Ergo etiam excommunicatus vel suspensus excommunicare possunt.

PRAETEREA, maius est conficere corpus Christi quam excommunicare. Sed excommunicati conficere possunt. Ergo et excommunicare possunt.

SED CONTRA, ligatus corporaliter non potest alium ligare. Sed vinculum spirituale est fortius quam corporale. Ergo excommunicatus non potest alium excommunicare: cum excommunicatio sit vinculum spirituale.

RESPONDEO dicendum quod usus iurisdictionis est in comparatione ad alium hominem. Et ideo, cum omnis excommunicatus a communione fidelium separetur, quilibet excommunicatus usu iurisdictionis privatur. Et quia excommunicatio est iurisdictionis, ideo excommunicatus excommunicare non potest.

Et eadem ratio est de suspenso a iurisdictione. Si enim sit suspensus ab ordine tantum, tunc non potest ea quae sunt ordinis, sed potest ea quae sunt iurisdictionis. Et e converso si sit suspensus a iurisdictione et non ab ordine. Si autem ab utroque, tunc neutrum potest.

AD PRIMUM ergo dicendum quod, quamvis non amittat iurisdictionem, amittit tamen iurisdictionis usum.

AD SECUNDUM dicendum quod conficere consequitur potestatem characteris, qui indelebilis est. Et ideo homo, ex quo characterem ordinis habet, semper potest conficere licet non semper ei liceat. Secus autem est de

OBJECTION 1: It would seem that one who is excommunicated or suspended can excommunicate another. For such a one has lost neither holy orders nor jurisdiction, since he is neither ordained anew when he is absolved nor is his jurisdiction renewed. But excommunication requires nothing more than holy orders or jurisdiction. Therefore, even one who is excommunicated or suspended can excommunicate.

OBJ. 2: Further, it is a greater thing to consecrate the body of Christ than to excommunicate. But such persons can consecrate. Therefore, they can excommunicate.

ON THE CONTRARY, One whose body is bound cannot bind another. But a spiritual bond is stronger than a physical one. Therefore, one who is excommunicated cannot excommunicate another, since excommunication is a spiritual bond.

I ANSWER THAT, Jurisdiction can only be used in relation to another man. Consequently, since every excommunicated person is severed from the communion of the faithful, he is deprived of the use of jurisdiction. And as excommunication requires jurisdiction, an excommunicated person cannot excommunicate.

The same reason applies to one who is suspended from jurisdiction. For if he be suspended from holy orders only, then he cannot exercise his order, but he can use his jurisdiction, while, on the other hand, if he be suspended from jurisdiction and not from holy orders, he cannot use his jurisdiction, though he can exercise his order: and if he be suspended from both, he can exercise neither.

REPLY OBJ. 1: Although an excommunicated or suspended person does not lose his jurisdiction, yet he does lose its use.

REPLY OBJ. 2: The power of consecration results from the power of the character which is indelible, wherefore, from the very fact that a man has the character of holy orders, he can always consecrate, though not always licitly.

excommunicatione, quae iurisdictionem sequitur, quae auferri potest et ligari.

It is different with the power of excommunication which results from jurisdiction, for this can be taken away and bound.

Article 4

Whether a Man Can Excommunicate Himself, His Equal, or His Superior?

AD QUARTUM SIC PROCEDITUR. Videtur quod aliquis possit seipsum, vel aequalem vel superiorem excommunicare. Quia angelus Dei maior erat Paulo: Math. 11. *Qui minor est in regno caelorum, maior est eo quo nemo inter natos mulierum maior*. Sed Paulus excommunicavit *angelum de caelo*: ut patet Galat. i. Ergo homo potest superiorem excommunicare.

PRAETEREA, sacerdos aliquando excommunicat in generali pro furto, vel pro aliquo huiusmodi. Sed potest contingere quod ipsemet fecit, vel superior aut aequalis. Ergo aliquis potest se, vel aequalem vel superiorem excommunicare.

PRAETEREA, aliquis potest superiorem absolvere in foro poenitentiali, vel aequalem: sicut cum episcopi suis subditis confitentur, et cum unus sacerdos alteri venialia confitetur. Ergo videtur quod etiam excommunicare aliquis superiorem vel aequalem possit.

SED CONTRA, excommunicatio est actus iurisdictionis. Sed aliquis non habet in se iurisdictionem quia in eadem causa non potest quis esse reus et iudex. Nec iterum in superiorem vel aequalem. Ergo non potest aliquis superiorem vel aequalem, aut se excommunicare.

RESPONDEO dicendum quod, cum per iurisdictionem aliquis constituatur in gradu superioritatis respectu eius in quem habet iurisdictionem, quia iudex est eius; ideo nullus habet in seipsum, vel in superiorem vel aequalem iurisdictionem. Et per consequens nullus potest seipsum excommunicare, vel superiorem aut aequalem.

AD PRIMUM ergo dicendum quod Apostolus loquitur sub hypothesi, idest, si poneretur angelus peccare: sic enim non esset Apostolo superior, sed inferior. Nec est inconveniens quod in conditionalibus quarum antecedentia impossibilia sunt, et consequentia impossibilia sint.

AD SECUNDUM dicendum quod in tali casu nullus excommunicatur: quia *par in parem non habet imperium*.

AD TERTIUM dicendum quoad absolutio et ligatio in foro confessionis est quoad Deum tantum, apud quem aliquis alio superior redditur inferior per peccatum. Sed excommunicatio est in iudicio exteriori, in quo aliquis non amittit superioritatem ex hoc ipso quod peccat. Unde non est similis ratio de utroque.

OBJECTION 1: It would seem that a man can excommunicate himself, his equal, or his superior. For an angel of God was greater than Paul, according to Matthew 11:11: *he that is lesser in the kingdom of heaven is greater then he, a greater than whom hath not risen among men that are born of women*. Now Paul excommunicated an *angel from heaven* (Gal 1:8). Therefore, a man can excommunicate his superior.

OBJ. 2: Further, sometimes a priest pronounces a general excommunication for theft or the like. But it might happen that he, or his equal, or a superior has done such things. Therefore, a man can excommunicate himself, his equal, or a superior.

OBJ. 3: Further, a man can absolve his superior or his equal in the tribunal of penance, as when a bishop confesses to his subject, or one priest confesses venial sins to another. Therefore, it seems that a man may also excommunicate his superior or his equal.

ON THE CONTRARY, Excommunication is an act of jurisdiction. But no man has jurisdiction over himself (since one cannot be both judge and defendant in the same trial), or over his superior, or over an equal. Therefore, a man cannot excommunicate his superior, or his equal, or himself.

I ANSWER THAT, Since by jurisdiction a man is placed above those over whom he has jurisdiction through being their judge, it follows that no man has jurisdiction over himself, his superior, or his equal, and that, consequently, no one can excommunicate either himself, or his superior, or his equal.

REPLY OBJ. 1: The Apostle is speaking hypothetically, i.e., supposing an angel were to sin, for in that case he would not be higher than the Apostle, but lower. Nor is it absurd that, if the antecedent of a conditional sentence be impossible, the consequence be impossible also.

REPLY OBJ. 2: In that case no one would be excommunicated, since *no man has power over his peer*.

REPLY OBJ. 3: Loosing and binding in the tribunal of confession affects our relation to God only, in whose sight a man from being above another sinks below him through sin; while on the other hand excommunication is the affair of an external tribunal in which a man does not forfeit his superiority on account of sin.

Et tamen etiam in foro confessionis aliquis non potest seipsum absolvere; nec superiorem aut aequalem, nisi ex commissione sibi facta. De venialibus autem potest: quia venialia ex quibuslibet sacramentis gratiam conferentibus remittuntur; unde remissio venialium sequitur potestatem ordinis.

Hence there is no comparison between the two tribunals. Nevertheless, even in the tribunal of confession, a man cannot absolve himself, or his superior, or his equal, unless the power to do so be committed to him. This does not apply to venial sins, because they can be remitted through any sacraments which confer grace; hence remission of venial sins follows the power of orders.

Article 5

Whether a Sentence of Excommunication Can Be Passed on a University?

Ad quintum sic proceditur. Videtur quod in aliquam universitatem sententia excommunicationis ferri possit. Contingit enim quod aliqua universitas sibi in malitia colligatur. Sed pro malitia in qua quis contumax exstitit, debet excommunicatio ferri. Ergo potest in aliquam universitatem ferri excommunicatio.

Praeterea, illud quod est gravissimum in excommunicatione, est separatio a sacramentis Ecclesiae. Sed aliquando tota civitas interdicitur a divinis. Ergo et excommunicari universitas aliqua potest.

Sed contra est Glossa Augustini, Matth. 13, quae dicit quod princeps et multitudo non est excommunicanda.

Respondeo dicendum quod excommunicari non debet aliquis nisi pro peccato mortali. Peccatum autem in actu consistit. Actus autem non est communitatis, sed singularium personarum, ut frequenter. Et ideo singuli de communitate excommunicari possunt, non autem ipsa communitas.

Et si sit quandoque etiam actus alicuius totius multitudinis, ut quando multi navem trahunt quam nullus trahere posset, tamen non est probabile quod aliqua communitas ita tota ad malum consentiat quin aliqui sint dissentientes. Et quia non est Dei, qui iudicat omnem terram, ut condemnet iustum cum impio, ut dicitur Gen. 18; ideo Ecclesia, quae Dei iudicium imitari debet, satis provide statuit ut communitas non excommunicetur, *ne, collectis zizaniis, simul eradicetur et triticum.*

Ad primum ergo patet solutio ex dictis.

Ad secundum dicendum quod suspensio non tanta poena est quanta excommunicatio: quia suspensi non fraudantur Ecclesiae suffragiis, sicut excommunicati. Unde etiam aliquis sine peccato proprio suspenditur: sicut et totum regnum ponitur sub interdicto pro peccato regis. Et ideo non est simile de excommunicatione et suspensione.

Objection 1: It would seem that sentence of excommunication can be passed on a university. For it is possible for a number of people to be united together in wickedness. Now, when a man is obstinate in his wickedness he should be excommunicated. Therefore, a university can be excommunicated.

Obj. 2: Further, the most grievous effect of an excommunication is privation of the sacraments of the Church. But sometimes a whole country is laid under an interdict. Therefore, a university can be excommunicated.

On the contrary, A Gloss of Augustine (*Epistle* 250) on Matthew 12 asserts that the sovereign and a body of people cannot be excommunicated.

I answer that, No man should be excommunicated except for a mortal sin. Now sin consists in an act: and acts do not belong to communities, but, generally speaking, to individuals. Wherefore individual members of a community can be excommunicated, but not the community itself.

And although sometimes an act belongs to a whole multitude, as when many draw a boat which none of them could draw by himself, yet it is not probable that a community would so wholly consent to evil that there would be no dissentients. Now God, who judges all the earth, does not condemn the just with the wicked (Gen 18:25). Therefore the Church, who should imitate the judgments of God, prudently decided that a community should not be excommunicated, *lest the wheat be uprooted together with the tares and cockle.*

The reply to the first objection is evident from what has been said.

Reply Obj. 2: Suspension is not so great a punishment as excommunication, since those who are suspended are not deprived of the prayers of the Church, as the excommunicated are. Wherefore a man can be suspended without having committed a sin himself, just as a whole kingdom is laid under an interdict on account of the king's crime. Hence there is no comparison between excommunication and suspension.

Article 6

Whether a Man Can Be Excommunicated Who Is Already Under Sentence of Excommunication?

AD SEXTUM SIC PROCEDITUR. Videtur quod ille qui semel est excommunicatus, ulterius excommunicari non possit. I Cor. 5 dicit Apostolus: *quid mihi est de his qui foris sunt iudicare?* Sed excommunicati iam sunt extra Ecclesiam. Ergo super eos Ecclesia iudicium non habet, ut possit eos iterum excommunicare.

PRAETEREA, excommunicatio est separatio quaedam a divinis et a communione fidelium. Sed postquam est aliquis privatus aliquo, non potest iterum illo privari. Ergo unus excommunicatus non debet iterum excommunicari.

SED CONTRA, excommunicatio quaedam poena est et medicinale remedium. Sed poenae omnes et medicinae iterantur cum causa exigit. Ergo excommunicatio iterari potest.

RESPONDEO dicendum quod ille qui excommunicatus est una excommunicatione, potest iterum excommunicari: vel per eiusdem excommunicationis iterationem, ad maiorem sui confusionem, ut vel sic a peccato resiliat; vel propter alias causas. Et tunc tot sunt principales excommunicationes quot causae pro quibus quis excommunicatur.

AD PRIMUM ergo dicendum quod Apostolus loquitur de paganis et aliis infidelibus, qui non habent characterem, per quem annumerati sint populo Dei. Sed quia character baptismalis, quo quis populo Dei annumeratur, est indelebilis, ideo semper remanet aliquo modo de Ecclesia baptizatus. Et sic semper Ecclesia de illo iudicare potest.

AD SECUNDUM dicendum quod privatio, quamvis non recipiat maius et minus secundum se, recipit tamen secundum causam suam. Et secundum hoc, excommunicatio potest iterari. Et magis est elongatus a suffragiis Ecclesiae qui pluries est excommunicatus, quam qui semel tantum.

OBJECTION 1: It would seem that a man who is already under sentence of excommunication cannot be excommunicated any further. For the Apostle says: *what have I to do to judge them that are without?* (1 Cor 5:12). Now those who are excommunicated are already outside the Church. Therefore, the Church cannot exercise any further judgment on them, so as to excommunicate them again.

OBJ. 2: Further, excommunication is privation of divine things and of the communion of the faithful. But when a man has been deprived of a thing, he cannot be deprived of it again. Therefore, one who is excommunicated cannot be excommunicated again.

ON THE CONTRARY, Excommunication is a punishment and a healing medicine. Now punishments and medicines are repeated when necessary. Therefore, excommunication can be repeated.

I ANSWER THAT, A man who is under sentence of one excommunication can be excommunicated again, either by a repetition of the same excommunication, for his greater shame so that he may renounce sin, or for some other cause. And then there are as many principal excommunications as there are causes for his being excommunicated.

REPLY OBJ. 1: The Apostle is speaking of heathens and of other unbelievers who have no sacramental character, whereby they are numbered among the people of God. But since the baptismal character whereby a man is numbered among God's people is indelible, one who is baptized always belongs to the Church in some way, so that the Church is always competent to sit in judgment on him.

REPLY OBJ. 2: Although privation does not receive more or less in itself, yet it can as regards its cause. In this way an excommunication can be repeated, and a man who has been excommunicated several times is further from the Church's prayers than one who has been excommunicated only once.

QUESTION 23

COMMUNICATION WITH EXCOMMUNICATED PERSONS

Deinde considerandum est de participatione cum excommunicatis.

Circa quod quaeruntur tria.

Primo: utrum liceat excommunicato participare in puris corporalibus.

Secundo: utrum participans excommunicato sit excommunicatus.

Tertio: utrum participare excommunicato in casibus non concessis semper sit peccatum mortale.

We must now consider communication with those who are excommunicated.

Under this head there are three points of inquiry:

(1) Whether it is lawful to communicate in matters purely corporal with one who is excommunicated?

(2) Whether one who communicates with an excommunicated person is excommunicated?

(3) Whether it is always a mortal sin to communicate with an excommunicated person in matters not permitted by law?

Article 1

Whether It Is Lawful, in Matters Purely Corporal, to Communicate With an Excommunicated Person?

AD PRIMUM SIC PROCEDITUR. Videtur quod liceat excommunicato communicare in pure corporalibus. Excommunicatio enim est actus clavium. Sed potestas clavium se extendit ad spiritualia tantum. Ergo per excommunicationem non prohibetur quin unus alii in corporalibus communicare possit.

PRAETEREA, *quod est institutum pro caritate, contra caritatem non militat.* Sed ex praecepto caritatis tenemur inimicis subvenire, quod sine aliqua communicatione fieri non potest. Ergo licet alicui excommunicato in corporalibus communicare.

SED CONTRA est quod dicitur I Cor. 5: *cum eiusmodi nec cibum sumere.*

RESPONDEO dicendum quod duplex est excommunicatio. Una est minor, quae separat tantum a participatione sacramentorum, sed non a communione fidelium. Et ideo tali excommunicato licet communicare, sed non licet ei sacramenta conferre.

Alia est maior excommunicatio: et haec separat hominem a sacramentis Ecclesiae et a communione fidelium. Et ideo tali excommunicato communicare non licet. Sed quia Ecclesia excommunicationem ad medelam, et non ad interitum inducit, excipiuntur ab hac generalitate quaedam in quibus communicare licet, scilicet in his quae pertinent ad salutem. Quia in talibus homo licite cum excommunicato loqui potest: et etiam alia verba

OBJECTION 1: It would seem that it is lawful, in matters purely corporal, to communicate with an excommunicated person. For excommunication is an act of the keys. But the power of the keys extends only to spiritual matters. Therefore, excommunication does not prevent one from communicating with another in matters corporal.

OBJ. 2: Further, *what is instituted for the sake of charity does not militate against charity* (Cf. Q. 11, A. 1, Ob. 1). But we are bound by the precept of charity to succor our enemies, which is impossible without some sort of communication. Therefore, it is lawful to communicate with an excommunicated person in corporal matters.

ON THE CONTRARY, 1 Corinthians 5:11 states: *with such an one not so much as to eat.*

I ANSWER THAT, Excommunication is twofold: there is minor excommunication, which deprives a man merely of a share in the sacraments, but not of the communion of the faithful. Hence it is lawful to communicate with a person lying under an excommunication of this kind, but not to give him the sacraments.

The other is major excommunication, which deprives a man of the sacraments of the Church and of the communion of the faithful. Hence it is not lawful to communicate with one who lies under such an excommunication. But, since the Church resorts to excommunication to repair and not to destroy, exception is made from this general law in certain matters wherein communication is lawful, viz. in those which concern salvation, for one is allowed to speak

interserere, ut facilius salutis verba ex familiaritate recipiantur.

Excipiuntur etiam quaedam personae, ad quas specialiter pertinet provisio excommunicati: ut uxor, filius, servus rusticus et serviens. Sed hoc intelligendum est de filiis non emancipatis: alias tenentur vitare patrem. De aliis autem intelligitur quod licet excommunicato communicare si ante excommunicationem se ei subdiderunt: non autem si post. Quidam autem intelligunt e converso, scilicet quod superiores possunt licite communicare inferioribus. Alii vero contradicunt. Sed ad minus in his communicare eis debent in quibus sunt eis obligati: quia, sicut inferiores obligantur ad absequium superiorum, ita superiores ad providentiam inferiorum.

Sunt etiam quidam casiis excepti: sicut *quando ignoratur excommunicatio*; et quando aliqui sunt *peregrini et viatores in terra excommunicatorum*, qui licite possunt ab eis *emere*, vel etiam *accipere* eleemosynam. Et similiter etiam si aliquis videat excommunicatum in necessitate: quia tunc ex praecepto caritatis tenetur ei providere.

Et ista hoc versu continentur: *utile, lex, humile, res ignorata, necesse*: ut *utile* referatur ad verba salutis, *lex* ad matrimonium, *humile* ad subiectionem. Cetera patent.

AD PRIMUM ergo dicendum quod corporalia ad spiritualia, ordinantur. Et ideo potestas quae se extendit ad spiritualia, etiam ad corporalia, se extendere potest: sicut ars quae est de fine, imperat de his quae sunt ad finem.

AD SECUNDUM dicendum quod in illo casu in quo aliquis ex praecepto caritatis communicare tenetur, non prohibetur communio, ut ex dictis patet.

of such matters with an excommunicated person; and one may even speak of other matters so as to put him at his ease and to make the words of salvation more acceptable.

Moreover, exception is made in favor of certain people whose business it is to be in attendance on the excommunicated person, namely, his wife, child, slave, vassal or subordinate. This, however, is to be understood of children who have not attained their majority, else they are forbidden to communicate with their father: and as to the others, the exception applies to them if they have entered his service before his excommunication, but not if they did so afterwards. Some understand this exception to apply in the opposite way, viz. that the master can communicate with his subjects: while others hold the contrary. At any rate, it is lawful for them to communicate with others in matters wherein they are under an obligation to them, for just as subjects are bound to serve their master, so is the master bound to look after his subjects.

Again certain cases are excepted; as *when the fact of the excommunication is unknown*, or in the case of *strangers or travelers in the country of those who are excommunicated*, for they are allowed *to buy* from them, or *to receive* alms from them. Likewise, if anyone were to see an excommunicated person in distress he then would be bound by the precept of charity to assist him.

These are all contained in the following line: *utility, law, lowliness, ignorance of fact, necessity*, where *utility* refers to salutary words, *law* to marriage, and *lowliness* to subjection. The others need no explanation.

REPLY OBJ. 1: Corporal matters are subordinate to spiritual matters. Wherefore the power which extends to spiritual things can also extend to matters touching the body: even as the art which considers the end commands in matters ordained to the end.

REPLY OBJ. 2: In a case where one is bound by the precept of charity to hold communication, the prohibition ceases, as is clear from what has been said.

Article 2

Whether a Person Incurs Excommunication for Communicating With One Who Is Excommunicated?

AD SECUNDUM SIC PROCEDITUR. Videtur quod participans excommunicato non sit excommunicatus. Plus enim separatus est ab Ecclesia gentilis quam excommunicatus. Sed ille qui participat gentili aut Iudaeo, non est excommunicatus. Ergo nec ille qui participat Christiano excommunicato.

PRAETEREA, si ille qui participat excommunicato est excommunicatus, eadem ratione qui participat participanti erit excommunicatus: et sic in infinitum procedet.

OBJECTION 1: It would seem that a person does not incur excommunication for communicating with one who is excommunicated. For a heathen or a Jew is more separated from the Church than a person who is excommunicated. But one does not incur excommunication for communicating with a heathen or a Jew. Neither, therefore, does one for communicating with an excommunicated Christian.

OBJ. 2: Further, if a man incurs excommunication for communicating with an excommunicated person, for the same reason a third would incur excommunication for

Quod videtur absurdum. Ergo non est excommunicatus qui excommunicato participat.

SED CONTRA est quod excommunicatus est positus extra communionem. Ergo qui ei communicat, a communione Ecclesiae recedit. Et sic videtur quod sit excommunicatus.

RESPONDEO dicendum quod excommunicatio potest in aliquem ferri dupliciter. Aut ita quod ipse sit excommunicatus cum omnibus ei participantibus. Et tunc non est dubium quod quicumque participat ei, est excommunicatus maiori excommunicatione. Aut est excommunicatus simpliciter. Et tunc aut participat aliquis in crimine, ei praebendo consilium, auxilium aut favorem: et sic iterum est excommunicatus maiori excommunicatione. Aut in aliis, sicut in verbo vel in osculo vel in mensa: et sic est excommunicatus minori excommunicatione.

AD PRIMUM ergo dicendum quod Ecclesia non ita intendit corrigere infideles sicut fideles, quorum cura sibi incumbit. Et ideo non arcet a communione infidelium, sicut a communione fidelium illorum quos excommunicat, super quos habet aliquam potestatem.

AD SECUNDUM dicendum quod excommunicato minori excommunicatione licet communicare. Et sic excommunicatio non transit in tertiam personam.

communicating with him, and thus on to infinity, which would seem absurd. Therefore, one does not incur excommunication for communicating with one who is excommunicated.

ON THE CONTRARY, An excommunicated person is banished from communion. Therefore, whoever communicates with him leaves the communion of the Church: and hence he seems to be excommunicated.

I ANSWER THAT, A person may incur excommunication in two ways. First, so that the excommunication includes both himself and whosoever communicates with him: and then, without any doubt, whoever communicates with him incurs a major excommunication. Second, so that the excommunication is simply pronounced on him; and then a man may communicate with him either in his crime, by counsel, help or favor, in which case again he incurs the major excommunication, or he may communicate with him in other things by speaking to him, greeting him, or eating with him, in which case he incurs the minor excommunication.

REPLY OBJ. 1: The Church has no intention of correcting unbelievers as well as the faithful who are under her care: hence she does not sever those whom she excommunicates from the fellowship of unbelievers, as she does from the communion of the faithful over whom she exercises a certain power.

REPLY OBJ. 2: It is lawful to hold communion with one who has incurred a minor excommunication, so that excommunication does not pass on to a third person.

Article 3

Whether it is Always a Mortal Sin to Communicate with an Excommunicated Person in Other Cases Than Those in Which It Is Allowed?

AD TERTIUM SIC PROCEDITUR. Videtur quod participare cum excommunicato in casibus non concessis semper sit peccatum mortale. Quia Decretalis quaedam respondet quod propter metum mortis non debet aliquis excommunicato communicare, quia aliquis debet prius subire mortem quam mortaliter peccet. Sed haec ratio nulla esset nisi participare excommunicato esset peccatum mortale. Ergo, etc.

PRAETEREA, facere contra praeceptum Ecclesiae est peccatum mortale. Sed Ecclesia praecipit quod excommunicato nullus communicet. Ergo participare excommunicato est peccatum mortale.

PRAETEREA, nullus arcetur a perceptione Eucharistiae pro peccato veniali. Sed ille qui participat excommunicato in casibus non concessis arcetur a perceptione Eucharistiae: quia incurrit minorem excommunicatio-

OBJECTION 1: It would seem that it is always a mortal sin to hold communion with an excommunicated person in other cases than those in which it is allowed. Because a certain Decretal (*Decretals*) declares that not even through fear of death should anyone hold communion with an excommunicated person, since one ought to die rather than commit a mortal sin. But this would not be reasonable unless it were always a mortal sin to hold communion with an excommunicated person. Therefore, etc.

OBJ. 2: Further, it is a mortal sin to act against a commandment of the Church. But the Church forbids anyone to hold communion with an excommunicated person. Therefore, it is a mortal sin to hold communion with one who is excommunicated.

OBJ. 3: Further, no man is debarred from receiving the Eucharist on account of a venial sin. But a man who holds communion with an excommunicated person, outside those cases in which it is allowed, is debarred from re-

nem. Ergo participans excommunicato in casibus non concessis peccat mortaliter.

PRAETEREA, nullus debet excommunicari maiori excommunicatione nisi pro peccato mortali. Sed aliquis, secundum iura, potest excommunicari maiori excommunicatione propter hoc quod excommunicato participat. Ergo excommunicato participare est peccatum mortale.

SED CONTRA: A peccato mortali nullus potest absolvere nisi super eum habeat iurisdictionem. Sed potest absolvere a participatione cum excommunicatis quilibet sacerdos. Ergo non est peccatum mortale.

PRAETEREA, *pro mensura peccati debet esse poenitentiae modus*. Sed pro participatione excommunicationis secundum communem consuetudinem non imponitur poena debita mortali peccato, sed magis debita veniali. Ergo non est peccatum mortale.

RESPONDEO dicendum quod quidam dicunt quod, quandocumque aliquis participat excommunicato vel verbo vel quocumque dictorum modorum secundum quos ei communicare non licet, peccat mortaliter, nisi in casibus exceptis a iure. Sed quia hoc videtur valde grave, quod homo pro uno verbo levi, quo excommunicatum alloquitur, mortaliter peccet; et multis excommunicantes laqueum damnationis inficerent, quod in eos retorqueretur: ideo aliis probabilius videtur quod non semper peccat mortaliter, sed solum quando in crimine sibi participat, vel in divinis, vel in contemptum Ecclesiae.

AD PRIMUM ergo dicendum quod Decretalis illa loquitur de participatione in divinis.

Vel dicendum quod similis ratio est de peccato mortali et de veniali quantum ad hoc quod, sicut peccatum mortale non potest bene fieri, ita nec veniale. Et ideo, sicut homo debet prius sustinere mortem quam peccet mortaliter, ita etiam quam peccet venialiter: illo modo debiti quo debet venialia vitare.

AD SECUNDUM dicendum quod praeceptum Ecclesiae directe respicit spiritualia, et ex consequenti legitimos actus. Et ideo qui communicat eis in divinis, facit contra praeceptum, et mortaliter peccat: qui autem participat eis in aliis, facit praeter praeceptum, et venialiter peccat.

AD TERTIUM dicendum quod aliquis etiam sine aliqua culpa quandoque ab Eucharistia arctatur, sicut patet in suspensis vel interdictis: quia tales poenae quandoque alicui pro culpa alterius, quae in eis punitur, inferuntur.

ceiving the Eucharist, since he incurs a minor excommunication. Therefore, it is a mortal sin to hold communion with an excommunicated person, save in those cases in which it is allowed.

OBJ. 4: Further, no one should incur a major excommunication save for a mortal sin. Now, according to the law (*Decretals*) a man may incur a major excommunication for holding communion with an excommunicated person. Therefore, it is a mortal sin to hold communion with one who is excommunicated.

ON THE CONTRARY, None can absolve a man from mortal sin unless he have jurisdiction over him. But any priest can absolve a man for holding communion with those who are excommunicated. Therefore, it is not a mortal sin.

FURTHER, *The measure of the penalty should be according to the measure of the sin* (Deut 25:3). Now the punishment appointed by common custom for holding communion with an excommunicated person is not that which is inflicted for mortal sin, but rather that which is due for venial sin. Therefore, it is not a mortal sin.

I ANSWER THAT, Some hold that it is always a mortal sin to hold communion with an excommunicated person, by word or in any of the forbidden ways mentioned above (A. 2), except in those cases allowed by law (*Decretals*). But since it seems very hard that a man should be guilty of a mortal sin by uttering just a slight word to an excommunicated person, and that by excommunicating a person one would endanger the salvation of many, and lay a snare which might turn to one's own hurt, it seems to others more probable that he is not always guilty of a mortal sin, but only when he holds communion with him in a criminal deed, or in an act of divine worship, or through contempt of the Church.

REPLY OBJ. 1: This Decretal is speaking of holding communion in divine worship.

It may also be replied that the same reason applies both to mortal and venial sin, since just as one cannot do well by committing a mortal sin, so neither can one by committing a venial sin: so that just as it is a man's duty to suffer death rather than commit a mortal sin, so is it his duty to do so sooner than commit a venial sin, inasmuch as it is his duty to avoid venial sin.

REPLY OBJ. 2: The commandment of the Church regards spiritual matters directly, and legitimate actions as a consequence: hence by holding communion in divine worship one acts against the commandment and commits a mortal sin; but by holding communion in other matters, one acts beside the commandment and sins venially.

REPLY OBJ. 3: Sometimes a man is debarred from the Eucharist even without his own fault, as in the case of those who are suspended or under an interdict, because these penalties are sometimes inflicted on one person for the sin of another who is thus punished.

AD QUARTUM dicendum quod, quamvis, participare excommunicato sit peccatum veniale, tamen participare pertinaciter est peccatum mortale. Et propter hoc potest aliquis excommunicari secundum iura.

REPLY OBJ. 4: Although it is a venial sin to hold communion with one who is excommunicated, yet to do so obstinately is a mortal sin: and for this reason one may be excommunicated according to the law.

QUESTION 24

ABSOLUTION FROM EXCOMMUNICATION

Deinde considerandum est de absolutione ab excommunicatione.

Circa quod tria quaeruntur.

Primo: utrum quilibet sacerdos possit subditum suum ab excommunicatione absolvere.

Secundo: utrum aliquis possit invitus ab excommunicatione absolvi.

Tertio: utrum aliquis possit absolvi ab una excommunicatione et non ab alia.

We must now consider absolution from excommunication.

Under this head there are three points of inquiry:

(1) Whether any priest can absolve his subject from excommunication?

(2) Whether a man can be absolved from excommunication against his will?

(3) Whether a man can be absolved from one excommunication without being absolved from another?

Article 1

Whether Any Priest Can Absolve His Subject from Excommunication?

AD PRIMUM SIC PROCEDITUR. Videtur quod quilibet sacerdos subditum suum possit ab excommunicatione absolvere. Maius enim est vinculum peccati quam excommunicationis. Sed quilibet sacerdos potest suum subditum a peccato absolvere. Ergo multo fortius ab excommunicatione.

PRAETEREA, remota causa removetur effectus. Sed excommunicationis causa est peccatum mortale. Ergo, cum possit quilibet sacerdos a peccato illo mortali absolvere, poterit ab excommunicatione similiter.

SED CONTRA, eiusdem potestatis est excommunicare et excommunicatum absolvere. Sed sacerdotes inferiores non possunt suos subditos excommunicare. Ergo nec absolvere.

RESPONDEO dicendum quod a minori excommunicatione quilibet potest absolvere qui potest a peccato participationis absolvere. Si autem est maior aut est lata a iudice: et sic ille qui tulit, vel eius superior, potest absolvere. Vel est lata a iure: et tunc episcopus, vel etiam sacerdos potest absolvere, exceptis sex casibus quos sibi iuris conditor, scilicet Papa, reservavit.

Primus est quando aliquis iniicit manus in clericum vel religiosum; secundus est de illo qui incendit ecclesiam, et est denuntiatus; tertius est de illo qui frangit ecclesiam, et denuntiatus est; quartus est de illo qui in divinis communicat scienter excommunicatis nominaliter a Papa; quintus, de illo qui falsificat litteras Sedis Apostolicae; sextus de illo qui excommunicatis in crimine communicat.

OBJECTION 1: It would seem that any priest can absolve his subject from excommunication. For the chains of sin are stronger than those of excommunication. But any priest can absolve his subject from sin. Therefore, much more can he absolve him from excommunication.

OBJ. 2: Further, when the cause is removed, the effect is removed. But the cause of excommunication is mortal sin. Therefore, since any priest can give absolution from that mortal sin, he could likewise from excommunication.

ON THE CONTRARY, It belongs to the same power to excommunicate as to absolve from excommunication. But priests of inferior degree cannot excommunicate their subjects. Neither, therefore, can they absolve them.

I ANSWER THAT, Anyone can absolve from minor excommunication who can absolve from the sin of participation in the sin of another. But in the case of a major excommunication, this is pronounced either by a judge, and then he who pronounced sentence or his superior can absolve, or it is pronounced by law, and then the bishop or even a priest can absolve except in the six cases which the Pope, who is the maker of laws, reserves to himself.

The first is the case of a man who lays hands on a cleric or a religious; the second is of one who breaks into a church and is denounced for so doing; the third is of the man who sets fire to a church and is denounced for the deed; the fourth is of one who knowingly communicates in the divine worship with those whom the Pope has excommunicated by name; the fifth is the case of one who tampers with the letters of the Holy See; the sixth is the case of one who communicates in a crime of one who is excommunicated.

Non enim debet absolvi nisi ab eo qui excommunicavit, etiam si non sit eius subditus: nisi, propter difficultatem accedendi ad ipsum, absolveretur ab episcopo, vel a sacerdote proprio, praestita iuratoria cautione quod parebit mandato illius iudicis qui sententiam tulit.

A primo autem casu octo excipiuntur. Primus est in articulo mortis, in quo a qualibet excommunicatione potest quis a quolibet sacerdote absolvi; secundus, si sit ostiarius alicuius potentis et non ex odio vel proposito percussit; tertius, si percutiens sit mulier; quartus, si sit servus, et dominus laederetur de eius absentia, qui non est in culpa; quintus, si regularis regularem, et non sit enormis excessus; sextus, si sit pauper; septimus, si sit impubes, vel senex, vel valetudinarius; octavus, si habeat inimicitias capitales.

Sunt etiam alii casus in quibus percutiens clericum excommunicationem non incurrit. Primo, si causa disciplinae, ut magister vel praelatus, percusserit; secundo, si iocosa levitate; tertio, si invenerit eum turpiter agentem cum uxore vel matre vel sorore vel filia; quarto, si statim vim vi repellat; quinto, si ignoret eum esse clericum; sexto, si inveniat eum in apostasia post tertiam admonitionem; septimo, si transfert se clericus ad actum penitus contrarium, ut si fiat miles, vel ad bigamiam transeat.

Ad primum ergo dicendum quod, quamvis vinculum peccati sit maius simpliciter quam, excommunicatio, tamen quoad aliquid vinculum excommunicationis est maius, inquantum non solum obligat quoad Deum, sed etiam in facie Ecclesiae. Et ideo in absolvendo ab excommunicatione requiritur iurisdictio in exteriori foro: non autem in absolutione a peccato; nec exigitur cautio iuramenti, sicut exigitur in absolutione ab excommunicatione; per iuramentum enim controversiae quae sunt inter homines terminantur, secundum Apostolum.

Ad secundum dicendum quod, cum excommunicatus non sit particeps sacramentorum Ecclesiae, sacerdos non potest absolvere excommunicatum a culpa nisi sit prius absolutus ab excommunicatione.

For he should not be absolved except by the person who excommunicated him, even though he be not subject to him, unless, by reason of the difficulty of appearing before him, he be absolved by the bishop or by his own priest, after binding himself by oath to submit to the command of the judge who pronounced the excommunication on him.

There are, however, eight exceptions to the first case: (1) in the hour of death, when a person can be absolved by any priest from any excommunication; (2) if the striker be the porter of a man in authority, and the blow be given neither through hatred nor of set purpose; (3) if the striker be a woman; (4) if the striker be a servant, whose master is not at fault and would suffer from his absence; (5) if a religious strike a religious, unless he strike him very grievously; (6) if the striker be a poor man; (7) if he be a minor, an old man, or an invalid; (8) if there be a deadly feud between them.

There are, besides, seven cases in which the person who strikes a cleric does not incur excommunication: (1) if he do it for the sake of discipline, as a teacher or a superior; (2) if it be done for fun; (3) if the striker find the cleric behaving with impropriety towards his wife, his mother, his sister or his daughter; (4) if he return blow for blow at once; (5) if the striker be not aware that he is striking a cleric; (6) if the latter be guilty of apostasy after the triple admonition; (7) if the cleric exercise an act which is altogether contrary to the clerical life, e.g., if he become a soldier, or if he be guilty of bigamy.

Reply Obj. 1: Although the chains of sin are in themselves greater than those of excommunication, yet in a certain respect the chains of excommunication are greater, inasmuch as they bind a man not only in the sight of God, but also in the eye of the Church. Hence absolution from excommunication requires jurisdiction in the external forum, whereas absolution from sin does not. Nor is there need of giving one's word by oath, as in the case of absolution from excommunication, because, as the Apostle declares (Heb 6:16), controversies between men are decided by oath.

Reply Obj. 2: As an excommunicated person has no share in the sacraments of the Church, a priest cannot absolve him from his guilt, unless he be first absolved from excommunication.

Article 2

Whether Anyone Can Be Absolved Against His Will?

Ad secundum sic proceditur. Videtur quod nullus possit absolvi invitus. Spiritualia enim non conferuntur invito alicui. Sed absolutio ab excommunicatione est beneficium spirituale. Ergo non potest praestari invito.

Objection 1: It would seem that no man can be absolved against his will. For spiritual things are not conferred on anyone against his will. Now absolution from excommunication is a spiritual favor. Therefore, it cannot be granted to a man against his will.

PRAETEREA, excommunicationis causa est contumacia. Sed quando aliquis non vult absolvi, excommunicationem contemnens, tunc est maxime contumax. Ergo non potest absolvi.

SED CONTRA, excommunicatio contra voluntatem alicui potest inferri. Sed quae contra voluntatem eveniunt, etiam contra voluntatem amoveri possunt: sicut patet de bonis fortunae. Ergo excommunicatio potest tolli ab aliquo invito.

RESPONDEO dicendum quod malum culpae et poenae in hoc differunt quod culpae principium est in nobis, quia omne peccatum voluntarium est; poenae autem principium quandoque extra nos est. Non enim requiritur ad poenam quod sit voluntaria: immo est magis de ratione poenae quod sit contra voluntatem. Et ideo, sicut peccata non committuntur nisi voluntate, ita non remittuntur alicui invito: sed excommunicatio sicut in aliquem invitum ferri potest, ita et invitus ab ea absolvi poterit.

AD PRIMUM ergo dicendum quod propositio habet veritatem de illis bonis spiritualibus quae in voluntate nostra consistunt: sicut sunt virtutes, quae non possunt a nolentibus perdi. Scientia enim, quamvis sit spirituale bonum, tamen potest a nolente per infirmitatem amitti. Et ideo ratio non est ad propositum.

AD SECUNDUM dicendum quod, etiam manente contumacia, potest aliquis discrete excommunicationem iuste latam remittere, si videat saluti illius expedire in cuius medicinam excommunicatio lata est.

OBJ. 2: Further, the cause of excommunication is contumacy. But when, through contempt of the excommunication, a man is unwilling to be absolved, he shows a high degree of contumacy. Therefore, he cannot be absolved.

ON THE CONTRARY, Excommunication can be pronounced on a man against his will. Now things that happen to a man against his will can be removed from him against his will, as is clear from the goods of fortune. Therefore, excommunication can be removed from a man against his will.

I ANSWER THAT, Evil of fault and evil of punishment differ in this, that the origin of fault is within us, since all sin is voluntary, whereas the origin of punishment is sometimes without, since punishment does not need to be voluntary. In fact, the nature of punishment is rather to be against the will. Wherefore, just as a man commits no sin except willingly, so no sin is forgiven him against his will. On the other hand, just as a person can be excommunicated against his will, so can he be absolved therefrom.

REPLY OBJ. 1: The assertion is true of those spiritual goods which depend on our will, such as the virtues, which we cannot lose unwillingly; for knowledge, although a spiritual good, can be lost by a man against his will through sickness. Hence the argument is not to the point.

REPLY OBJ. 2: It is possible for excommunication to be removed from a man even though he be contumacious, if it seem to be for the good of the man for whom the excommunication was intended as a medicine.

Article 3

Whether a Man Can Be Absolved From One Excommunication Without Being Absolved from All?

AD TERTIUM SIC PROCEDITUR. Videtur quod aliquis non possit absolvi ab una excommunicatione nisi absolvatur ab omnibus. Effectus enim debet proportionari suae causae. Sed causa excommunicationis est peccatum. Cum ergo aliquis non possit absolvi ab uno peccato nisi absolvatur ab omnibus, nec in excommunicatione hoc esse poterit.

PRAETEREA, excommunicationis absolutio in Ecclesia fit. Sed ille qui una excommunicatione est irretitus, extra Ecclesiam est. Ergo, quandiu una manet, ab alia absolvi non potest.

SED CONTRA, excommunicatio quaedam poena est. Sed ab una poena aliquis liberatur alia remanente. Ergo ab una excommunicatione, alia remanente, quis absolvi potest.

OBJECTION 1: It would seem that a man cannot be absolved from one excommunication without being absolved from all. For an effect should be proportionate to its cause. Now the cause of excommunication is a sin. Since, then, a man cannot be absolved from one sin without being absolved from all, neither can this happen as regards excommunication.

OBJ. 2: Further, absolution from excommunication is pronounced in the Church. But a man who is under the ban of one excommunication is outside the Church. Therefore, so long as one remains, a man cannot be loosed from another.

ON THE CONTRARY, Excommunication is a punishment. Now a man can be loosed from one punishment while another remains. Therefore, a man can be loosed from one excommunication and yet remain under another.

RESPONDEO dicendum quod excommunicationes non habent connexionem in aliquo. Et ideo possibile est quod aliquis ab una absolvatur, et in altera remaneat.

Sed circa hoc sciendum est quod aliquis quandoque est excommunicatus pluribus excommunicationibus ab uno iudice. Et tunc, quando absolvitur ab una, intelligitur ab omnibus absolvi: nisi contrarium exprimatur; vel nisi in causa qua quis absolutionem impetrat de uno tantum casu excommunicationis, cum pluribus excommunicatus sit. Quandoque est excommunicatus a diversis iudicibus. Et tunc absolutus ab una excommunicatione, non propter hoc est absolutus ab altera: nisi omnes alii, ad petitionem eius, absolutionem eius confirmaverint; vel nisi omnes demandent uni absolutionem.

AD PRIMUM ergo dicendum quod omnia peccata habent connexionem in aversione voluntatis a Deo, cum quo non potest esse peccatorum remissio: et ideo unum peccatum sine altero remitti non potest. Sed excommunicationes non habent aliquam talem connexionem. Nec iterum absolutio ab excommunicatione impeditur propter voluntatis contrarietatem. Et ideo ratio non sequitur.

AD SECUNDUM dicendum quod, sicut pluribus de causis erat aliquis extra Ecclesiam, ita possibile est quod ista separatio removeatur quantum ad unam causam, et maneat quantum ad alteram.

I ANSWER THAT, Excommunications are not connected together in any way, and so it is possible for a man to be absolved from one, and yet remain under another.

It must be observed, however, that sometimes a man lies under several excommunications pronounced by one judge; and then, when he is absolved from one, he is understood to be absolved from all, unless the contrary be expressed, or unless he ask to be absolved from excommunication on one count only, whereas he was excommunicated under several. On the other hand, sometimes a man lies under several sentences of excommunication pronounced by several judges; and then, when absolved from one excommunication, he is not therefore absolved from the others, unless at his prayer they all confirm his absolution, or unless they all depute one to absolve him.

REPLY OBJ. 1: All sins are connected together in aversion from God, which is incompatible with the forgiveness of sin: wherefore one sin cannot be forgiven without another. But excommunications have no such connection. Nor again is absolution from excommunication hindered by contrariety of the will, as stated above (A. 2). Hence the argument does not follow.

REPLY OBJ. 2: Just as such a man was for several reasons outside the Church, so is it possible for his separation to be removed on one count and to remain on another.

QUESTION 25

INDULGENCES

Consequenter considerandum est de indulgentia. Et primo, de ea secundum se; secundo, de facientibus indulgentiam; tertio, de recipientibus eam.

Circa primum quaeruntur tria.

Primo: utrum per indulgentiam possit aliquid remitti de poena satisfactoria.

Secundo: utrum indulgentiae tantum valeant quantum pronuntiantur.

Tertio: utrum pro temporali subsidio sit indulgentia facienda.

We must now consider indulgence: (1) In itself; (2) Those who grant indulgence; (3) Those who receive it.

Under the first head there are three points of inquiry:

(1) Whether an indulgence remits any part of the punishment due for the satisfaction of sins?

(2) Whether indulgences are as effective as they claim to be?

(3) Whether an indulgence should be granted for temporal assistance?

Article 1

Whether an Indulgence Can Remit Any Part of the Punishment Due for the Satisfaction of Sins?

AD PRIMUM SIC PROCEDITUR. Videtur quod per indulgentiam non possit aliquid remitti de poena satisfactoria. Quia super illud II Tim. 2, *negare seipsum non potest*, dicit Glossa: *quod faceret si dicta sua non impleret.* Sed ipse dicit, Deut. 25: *secundum mensuram delicti erit et plagarum modus.* Ergo non potest aliquid remitti de poena satisfactionis taxata secundum quantitatem culpae.

PRAETEREA, inferior non potest, absolvere ab eo ad quod superior obligavit. Sed Deus, absolvendo a culpa, obligat ad poenam temporalem: ut dicit Hugo de Sancto Victore. Ergo nullus homo potest absolvere a poena illa aliquid dimittendo.

PRAETEREA, hoc ad potestatem excellentiae pertinet ut sine sacramentis effectus sacramentorum tradatur. Sed nullus habet potestatem excellentiae in sacramentis nisi Christus. Cum ergo satisfactio sit pars sacramenti, operans ad dimissionem poenae debitae, videtur quod nullus homo purus possit dimittere debitum poenae sine satisfactione.

PRAETEREA, potestas ministris Ecclesiae non est tradita *in destructionem, sed in aedificationem.* Sed hoc ad destructionem pertinet, si satisfactio, quae est ad utilitatem nostram, inquantum remedium praebet, tolleretur. Ergo potestas ministrorum Ecclesiae ad hoc se non extendit.

SED CONTRA: II Cor. 2: *nam et ego quod donavi, si quid, propter vos donavi in persona Christi*: Glossa, *idest, ac si Christus donasset.* Sed Christus poterat relaxare abs-

OBJECTION 1: It would seem that an indulgence cannot remit any part of the punishment due for the satisfaction of sins. Because a Gloss on 2 Timothy 2:13: *he cannot deny himself*, says, *he would do this if he did not keep his word.* Now God himself said: *according to the measure of the sin shall the measure also of the stripes be* (Deut 25:2). Therefore, nothing can be remitted from the satisfactory punishment which is appointed according to the measure of sin.

OBJ. 2: Further, an inferior cannot absolve from an obligation imposed by his superior. But when God absolves us from sin, he binds us to temporal punishment, as Hugh of St. Victor declares (*Tract. vi Sum. Sent.*). Therefore, no man can absolve from that punishment by remitting any part of it.

OBJ. 3: Further, the granting of the sacramental effect without the sacraments belongs to the power of excellence. Now none but Christ has the power of excellence in the sacraments. Since, then, satisfaction is a part of the sacrament of penance, conducing to the remission of the punishment due, it seems that no mere man can remit the debt of punishment without satisfaction.

OBJ. 4: Further, the power of the ministers of the Church was given them, not *unto destruction*, but *unto edification* (2 Cor 10:8). But it would be conducive to destruction if satisfaction, which was intended for our good inasmuch as it serves for a remedy, were done away with. Therefore, the power of the ministers of the Church does not extend to this.

ON THE CONTRARY, It is written: *for what I have pardoned, if I have pardoned anything, for your sakes have I done it in the person of Christ* (2 Cor 2:10), and a Gloss

169

que omni satisfactione poenam peccati: ut patet Ioan. 8 de muliere adultera. Ergo et Paulus potuit. Ergo et Papa, qui non est minoris potestatis in Ecclesia quam Paulus fuerit.

PRAETEREA, Ecclesia generalis non potest errare: quia ille qui *in omnibus exauditus est pro sua reverentia*, dixit Petro, super cuius confessione Ecclesia fundata est: *ego pro te rogavi, Petre, ut non deficiat fides tua*, Luc. 22. Sed Ecclesia generalis indulgentias approbat et facit. Ergo indulgentiae aliquid valent.

RESPONDEO dicendum quod ab omnibus conceditur indulgentias aliquid valere: quia impium esset dicere quod Ecclesia aliquid vanum faceret. Sed quidam dicunt quod non valent ad absolvendum a reatu poenae quam quis in purgatorio secundum iudicium Dei meretur, sed valent ad absolvendum ab obligatione qua sacerdos obligavit poenitentem ad poenam aliquam, vel ad quam etiam ordinatur ex canonum statutis.

Sed haec opinio non videtur vera. Primo, quia est expresse contra privilegium Petro datum, ut quod in terra remitteret, in caelo remitteretur. Unde remissio quae fit quantum ad forum Ecclesiae, valet etiam quantum ad forum Dei. Et praeterea, Ecclesia, huiusmodi indulgentias faciens, magis damnificaret quam adiuvaret: quia remitteret ad graviores poenas, scilicet purgatorii, absolvendo a poenitentiis iniunctis.

Et ideo aliter dicendum est, quod valent, et quantum ad forum Ecclesiae et quantum ad iudicium Dei, ad remissionem poenae residuae post contritionem et absolutionem et confessionem, sive sit iniuncta sive non. Ratio autem quare valere possunt, est unitas corporis mystici: in qua multi in operibus poenitentiae supererogaverunt ad mensuram debitorum suorum; et multas etiam tribulationes iniustas sustinuerunt patienter, per quas multitudo poenarum poterat expiari, si eis deberetur; quorum meritorum tanta est copia quod omnem poenam debitam nunc viventibus excedunt. Et praecipue propter meritum Christi: quod etsi in sacramentis operatur, non tamen efficacia eius in sacramentis includitur, sed sua infinitate excedit efficaciam sacramentorum.

Dictum est autem supra quod unus pro alio satisfacere potest. Sancti autem, in quibus superabundantia operum satisfactionis invenitur, non determinate pro isto qui remissione indiget, huiusmodi opera fecerunt, alias absque omni indulgentia consequerentur remissionem: sed communiter pro tota Ecclesia, sicut Apostolus ait se

adds: *that is, as though Christ himself had pardoned*. But Christ could remit the punishment of a sin without any satisfaction, as evidenced in the case of the adulterous woman (John 8). Therefore, Paul could do so likewise. Therefore, the Pope can too, since his power in the Church is not less than Paul's.

FURTHER, The universal Church cannot err, since he who *was heard for his reverence* (Heb 5:7) said to Peter, on whose profession of faith the Church was founded: *I have prayed for you that your faith fail not* (Luke 22:32). Now, the universal Church approves and grants indulgences. Therefore, indulgences have some value.

I ANSWER THAT, All admit that indulgences have some value, for it would be blasphemy to say that the Church does anything in vain. But some say that they do not avail to free a man from the debt of punishment which he has deserved in purgatory according to God's judgment, and that they merely serve to free him from the obligation imposed on him by the priest as a punishment for his sins, or from the canonical penalties he has incurred.

But this opinion does not seem to be true. First, because it is expressly opposed to the privilege granted to Peter, to whom it was said (Matt 16:19) that whatsoever he should loose on earth should be loosed also in heaven. Therefore, whatever remission is granted in the court of the Church holds good in the court of God. Moreover, the Church by granting such indulgences would do more harm than good, since by remitting the punishment she had enjoined on a man, she would deliver him to be punished more severely in purgatory.

Hence we must say on the contrary that indulgences hold good both in the Church's court and in the judgment of God, for the remission of the punishment which remains after contrition, absolution, and confession, whether this punishment be enjoined or not. The reason why they so avail is the oneness of the mystical body in which many have performed works of satisfaction exceeding the requirements of their debts; in which, too, many have patiently borne unjust tribulations whereby a multitude of punishments would have been paid, had they been incurred. So great is the quantity of such merits that it exceeds the entire debt of punishment due to those who are living at this moment: and this is especially due to the merits of Christ: for though he acts through the sacraments, yet his efficacy is in no way restricted to them, but infinitely surpasses their efficacy.

Now one man can satisfy for another, as we have explained above (Q. 13, A. 2). And the saints in whom this superabundance of satisfactions is found did not perform their good works for this or that particular person who needs the remission of his punishment (else he would have received this remission without any indulgence at all), but

implere ea quae desunt passionum Christi in corpore suo pro Ecclesia, ad quam scribit, Coloss. I.

Et sic praedicta merita sunt communia toti Ecclesiae. Ea autem quae sunt communia multitudinis alicuius, distribuuntur singulis de multitudine secundum arbitrium eius qui multitudini praeest. Unde, sicut aliquis consequeretur remissionem poenae si alius pro eo satisfecisset, ita si satisfactio alterius sibi per eum qui potest distribuatur.

AD PRIMUM ergo dicendum quod remissio, quae per indulgentias fit, non tollit quantitatem poenae ad culpam: quia pro culpa unius alius sponte poenam sustinuit.

AD SECUNDUM dicendum quod iste qui indulgentias suscipit, non absolvitur, simpliciter loquendo, a debito poenae: sed datur sibi unde debitum solvat.

AD TERTIUM dicendum quod effectus sacramentalis absolutionis est diminutio reatus. Et hic effectus non inducitur per indulgentias: sed pro eo faciens indulgentias solvit poenam quam debuit, de bonis Ecclesiae communibus, ut ex dictis patet.

AD QUARTUM dicendum quod maius remedium praebetur contra peccata vitanda ex gratia quam ex assuetudine nostrorum operum. Et quia ex affectu quem accipiens indulgentias concipit ad causam pro qua indulgentia datur, ad gratiam disponitur; ideo etiam per indulgentias remedium ad peccata vitanda datur. Et ideo non est in destructionem indulgentias dare, nisi inordinate dentur.

Tamen consulendum est eis qui indulgentias consequuntur, ne propter hoc ab operibus poenitentiae iniunctis abstineant: ut etiam ex his remedium consequantur, quamvis a debito poenae essent immunes; et praecipue quia quandoque sunt plurium debitores quam credant.

they performed them for the whole Church in general, even as the Apostle declares that he fills up *those things that are wanting of the sufferings of Christ . . . for his body, which is the Church*, to whom he wrote (Col 1:24).

These merits, then, are the common property of the whole Church. Now those things which are the common property of a multitude are distributed to the various individuals according to the judgment of him who rules them all. Hence, just as one man would obtain the remission of his punishment if another were to satisfy for him, so would he too if another's satisfactions be applied to him by one who has the power to do so.

REPLY OBJ. 1: The remission which is granted by means of indulgences does not destroy the proportion between punishment and sin, since someone has spontaneously taken upon himself the punishment due for another's guilt, as explained above.

REPLY OBJ. 2: He who gains an indulgence is not, strictly speaking, absolved from the debt of punishment, but is given the means whereby he may pay it.

REPLY OBJ. 3: The effect of sacramental absolution is the removal of a man's guilt, an effect which is not produced by indulgences. But he who grants indulgences pays the debt of punishment which a man owes out of the common stock of the Church's goods, as explained above.

REPLY OBJ. 4: Grace affords a better remedy for the avoidance of sin than do our repeated works. And since he who gains an indulgence is disposed to grace through the love which he conceives for the cause for which the indulgence is granted, it follows that indulgences provide a remedy against sin. Consequently, it is not harmful to grant indulgences unless this be done without discretion.

Nevertheless, those who gain indulgences should be advised not on this account to omit the penitential works imposed on them, so that they may derive a remedy from these also, even though they may be quit of the debt of punishment; and all the more, seeing that they are often more in debt than they think.

Article 2

Whether Indulgences Are as Effective as They Claim to Be?

AD SECUNDUM SIC PROCEDITUR. Videtur quod indulgentiae non valeant tantum quantum pronuntiantur. Indulgentiae enim non habent effectum nisi ex vi clavium. Sed ex vi clavium non potest habens clavem dimittere de poena peccati nisi aliquid determinatum, considerata quantitate peccati et contritionis poenitentis.

OBJECTION 1: It would seem that indulgences are not as effective as they claim to be. For indulgences have no effect save from the power of the keys. Now by the power of the keys, he who has that power can only remit some fixed part of the punishment due for sin after taking into account the measure of the sin and of the penitent's sorrow. Since,

Ergo, cum indulgentiae fiant pro libito instituentis indulgentiam, videtur quod non valeant tantum quantum pronuntiantur.

PRAETEREA, per debitum poenae homo a gloriae adeptione retardatur, quam summe appetere debet. Sed si indulgentiae tantum valent quantum pronuntiantur, in brevi homo, per indulgentias discurrens, posset ab omni reatu temporalis poenae immunis reddi. Ergo videtur quod deberet his acquirendis, omnibus aliis operibus dimissis, homo vacare.

PRAETEREA, aliquando datur indulgentia quod qui dat auxilium ad aliquam fabricam erigendam, tertiam partem remissionis peccatorum consequatur. Si ergo indulgentiae tantum valent quantum praedicantur, tunc qui dat unum denarium, et secundo unum, et iterum tertium, plenam absolutionem ab omni peccatorum poena consequentur. Quod videtur absurdum.

PRAETEREA, quandoque datur hoc modo indulgentia quod qui vadit ad aliquam ecclesiam septem annos remissionis consequatur. Si ergo tantum valet indulgentia quantum praedicatur, ille qui habet domum iuxta ecclesiam illam, vel clerici ecclesiae, qui quotidie vadunt, consequuntur tantum quantum ille qui a remotis partibus venit: quod videtur iniustum. Et iterum, ut videtur, pluries indulgentiam consequetur in die, cum pluries vadat.

PRAETEREA, idem videtur remittere alicui poenam ultra iustam aestimationem, quam remittere absque causa: quia quantum ad hoc quod excedit, non recompensatur. Sed ille qui facit indulgentiam, non posset remittere absque causa poenam in toto vel in parte alicui: ut sidiceret Papa alicui: *ego remitto tibi omnem poenam debitam pro peccato.* Ergo videtur quod nec possit aliquid dimittere ultra iustam aestimationem. Sed indulgentiae plerumque praedicantur ultra iustam aestimationem. Ergo non tantum valent quantum praedicantur.

SED CONTRA: Iob 13: *numquid Deus indiget mendacio nostro, ut pro eo loquamur dolos?* Ergo Ecclesia, praedicando indulgentias, non mentitur. Et ita tantum valent quantum praedicantur.

PRAETEREA, I Cor. 15 dicit Apostolus: *si inanis est praedicatio nostra, inanis est et fides nostra.* Ergo quicumque in praedicatione falsum dicit, fidem, quantum est in se, evacuat, et ita mortaliter peccat. Si ergo non tantum valent indulgentiae quantum praedicantur, omnes mortaliter peccant indulgentiam praedicantes. Quod est absurdum.

RESPONDEO dicendum quod circa hoc est multiplex opinio. Quidam enim dicunt quod huiusmodi indulgentiae non tantum valent quantum praedicantur, sed unicuique tantum valent quantum fides et devotio sua ex-

then, indulgences depend on the mere will of the grantor, it seems that they are not as effective as they claim to be.

OBJ. 2: Further, the debt of punishment keeps man back from the attainment of glory, which he ought to desire above all things. Now, if indulgences are as effective as they claim to be, a man setting himself to gain indulgences might become immune from all debt of temporal punishment. Therefore, it would seem that a man ought to put aside all other kinds of works, and devote himself to gain indulgences.

OBJ. 3: Further, sometimes an indulgence whereby a man is remitted a third part of the punishment due for his sins is granted if he contribute towards the erection of a certain building. If, therefore, indulgences produce the effect which is claimed for them, he who gives a penny, and then another, and then again a third, would obtain a plenary absolution from all punishment due for his sins, which seems absurd.

OBJ. 4: Further, sometimes an indulgence is granted so that for visiting a church a man obtains a seven years' remission. If, then, an indulgence avails as much as is claimed for it, a man who lives near that church, or the clergy attached thereto who go there every day, obtain as much indulgence as one who comes from a distance (which would appear unjust). Moreover, seemingly they would gain the indulgence several times a day, since they go there repeatedly.

OBJ. 5: Further, to remit a man's punishment beyond a just estimate seems to amount to the same as to remit it without reason, because insofar as he exceeds that estimate, he limits the compensation. Now he who grants an indulgence cannot without cause remit a man's punishment either wholly or partly, even though the Pope were to say to anyone: *I remit to all the punishment you owe for your sins.* Therefore, it seems that he cannot remit anything beyond the just estimate. Now indulgences are often published which exceed that just estimate. Therefore, they do not avail as much as is claimed for them.

ON THE CONTRARY, It is written: *has God any need of your lie that you should speak deceitfully for him?* (Job 13:7). Therefore, the Church in publishing indulgences does not lie; and so they avail as much as is claimed for them.

FURTHER, The Apostle says: *If . . . our preaching is vain, your faith is also vain* (1 Cor 15:11–19). Therefore, whoever utters a falsehood in preaching, so far as he is concerned, makes faith void and so sins mortally. If, therefore, indulgences are not as effective as they claim to be, all who publish indulgences would commit a mortal sin: which is absurd.

I ANSWER THAT, On this point there are many opinions. For some maintain that indulgences have not the efficacy claimed for them, but that they simply avail each individual in proportion to his faith and devotion. And

igit. Sed dicunt quod Ecclesia ad hoc ita pronuntiat ut quadam pia fraude homines ad bene faciendum alliciat: sicut mater quae, promittens filio pomum, ipsum ad ambulandum provocat.

Sed hoc videtur valde periculosum dicere. Sicut enim dicit Augustinus, in *Epistola ad Hieronymum, si in sacra Scriptura deprehenditur aliquid falsitatis, iam robur auctoritatis sacrae Scripturae perit.* Et similiter, si in praedicatione Ecclesiae aliqua falsitas deprehenderetur, non essent documenta Ecclesiae alicuius auctoritatis ad roborandam fidem.

Et ideo alii dixerunt quod valent tantum quantum pronuntiantur, secundum iustam aestimationem: non tamen dantis indulgentiam, qui minus forte aestimat quod dat; aut secundum aestimationem recipientis, qui nimis parum aestimare posset quod datur; sed secundum aestimationem quae iusta est secundum iudicium bonorum, pensata conditione personae et utilitate et necessitate Ecclesiae; quia uno tempore Ecclesia plus indiget quam alio.

Sed haec etiam opinio stare non potest, ut videtur. Primo, quia secundum hoc indulgentiae non valerent ad remissionem, sed magis ad commutationem quandam. Et praeterea, praedicatio Ecclesiae a mendacio non excusaretur: cum quandoque indulgentia praedicetur longe maior quam iusta aestimatio possit requirere, omnibus praedictis conditionibus pensatis; sicut quando dat Papa indulgentiam quod pergens ad unam ecclesiam habeat septem annos indulgentiae; cuiusmodi etiam indulgentiae a beato Gregorio in stationibus Romae institutae sunt.

Et ideo alii dicunt quod quantitas remissionis in indulgentiis non est mensuranda secundum devotionem tantum suscipientis, ut prima opinio dicebat; neque secundum quantitatem eius quod datur, sicut dicebat secunda; sed secundum causam pro qua indulgentia datur, ex qua reputatur dignus ut talem indulgentiam consequatur. Unde secundum quod accedit ad illam causam, secundum hoc consequitur remissionem indulgentiae vel in toto vel in parte.

Sed hoc iterum non potest salvare consuetudinem Ecclesiae, quae interdum pro eadem causa maiorem indulgentiam ponit: sicut, rebus eodem modo se habentibus, quandoque datur unus annus visitantibus ecclesiam unam, quandoque quadraginta dies, prout gratiam Papa facere voluerit indulgentiam constituens. Unde quantitas remissionis non est mensuranda ex causa quae facit indulgentia dignum.

Et ideo aliter dicendum est quod quantitas effectus sequitur quantitatem suae causae. Causa autem remissionis poenae in indulgentiis non est nisi abundantia meritorum Ecclesiae, quae se habet sufficienter ad totam poenam expiandam: non autem causa remissionis effec-

consequently those who maintain this say that the Church publishes her indulgences in such a way as to induce men to do well by a kind of pious fraud, just as a mother entices her child to walk by holding out an apple.

But this seems a very dangerous assertion to make. For as Augustine states (*Epistle to Jerome* 78), *if any error were discovered in Sacred Scripture, the authority of Sacred Scripture would perish.* In like manner, if any error were to be found in the Church's preaching, her doctrine would have no authority in settling questions of faith.

Hence others have maintained that indulgences avail as much as is claimed for them, according to a just estimate, not of him who grants it—who perhaps puts too high a value on it—nor of the recipient—for he may prize too highly the gift he receives—but a just estimate according to the estimate of good men who consider the condition of the person affected, and the utility and needs of the Church, for the Church's needs are greater at one time than at another.

Yet, neither, seemingly, can this opinion stand. First, because in that case indulgences would no longer be a remission, but rather a mere commutation. Moreover, the preaching of the Church would not be excused from untruth, since, at times, indulgences are granted far in excess of the requirements of this just estimate, taking into consideration all the aforesaid conditions, as, for example, when the Pope granted to anyone who visited a certain church an indulgence of seven years, which indulgence was granted by Blessed Gregory for the Roman Stations.

Hence others say that the quantity of remission accorded in an indulgence is not to be measured by the devotion of the recipient, as the first opinion suggested, nor according to the quantity of what is given, as the second opinion held; but according to the cause for which the indulgence is granted, and according to which a person is held deserving of obtaining such an indulgence. Thus according as a man approached near to that cause, so would he obtain remission in whole or in part.

But neither will this explain the custom of the Church, who assigns now a greater, now a lesser, indulgence for the same cause: thus, under the same circumstances, now a year's indulgence, now one of only forty days, according as the graciousness of the Pope, who grants the indulgence, is granted to those who visit a church. Wherefore the amount of the remission granted by the indulgence is not to be measured by the cause for which a person is worthy of an indulgence.

We must therefore say otherwise that the quantity of an effect is proportionate to the quantity of the cause. Now the cause of the remission of punishment effected by indulgences is no other than the abundance of the Church's merits, and this abundance suffices for the remission of all

tiva est vel devotio aut labor aut datum recipientis indulgentiam, aut causa pro qua fit indulgentia. Unde non oportet ad aliquid horum proportionare quantitatem remissionis, sed ad merita Ecclesiae, quae semper superabundant: et ideo, secundum quod applicantur ad istum, secundum hoc remissionem consequitur. Ad hoc autem quod applicentur isti requiritur auctoritas dispensandi huiusmodi thesaurum; et unio eius cui dispensatur ad eum qui merebatur, quod est per caritatem; et ratio dispensationis secundum quam salvetur intentio illorum qui opera meritoria fecerunt; fecerunt enim ad honorem Dei et utilitatem Ecclesiae in generali. Unde quaecumque causa adsit quae in utilitatem Ecclesiae et honorem Dei vergat, sufficiens est ratio indulgentias faciendi.

Et ideo, secundum alios, dicendum quod indulgentiae simpliciter tantum valent quantum praedicantur: dummodo ex parte dantis sit auctoritas, et ex parte recipientis *caritas*, et ex parte causae pietas, quae comprehendit honorem Dei et proximi utilitatem. Nec in hoc fit *nimio magnum forum de misericordia Dei*, ut quidam dicunt, nec divinae iustitiae derogatur: quia nihil de poena dimittitur, sed unius poena alteri computatur.

AD PRIMUM ergo dicendum quod clavis est duplex: scilicet ordinis, et iurisdictionis. Clavis ordinis sacramentale quoddam est. Et quia sacramentorum effectus non sunt determinati ab homine sed a Deo, non potest taxare sacerdos quantum per clavem ordinis in foro confessionis de poena debita dimittat, sed tantum dimittitur quantum Deus ordinavit. Sed clavis iurisdictionis non est quid sacramentale, et effectus eius arbitrio hominis subiacet. Et huius clavis effectus est remissio quae est per indulgentias: cum non pertineat ad dispensationem sacramentorum talis dimissio, sed ad dispensationem bonorum communium Ecclesiae. Et ideo etiam legati non sacerdotes indulgentias facere possunt. Unde in arbitrio dantis indulgentiam est taxare quantum per indulgentiam de poena dimittatur. Si tamen inordinate remittat, ita quod homines quasi pro nihilo ab operibus poenitentiae revocentur, peccat faciens tales indulgentias, nihilominus quis plenam indulgentiam consequitur.

AD SECUNDUM dicendum quod, quamvis huiusmodi indulgentiae multum valeant ad remissionem poenae, tamen alia opera satisfactionis sunt magis meritoria respectu praemii essentialis: quod in infinitum melius est quam dimissio poenae temporalis.

punishment. The effective cause of the remission is not the devotion, or toil, or gift of the recipient; nor, again, is it the cause for which the indulgence was granted. We cannot, then, estimate the quantity of the remission by any of the foregoing, but solely by the merits of the Church—and these are always superabundant. Consequently, according as these merits are applied to a person so does he obtain remission. That they should be so applied demands, first, authority to dispense this treasure; second, union between the recipient and him who merited it (and this is brought about by charity); third, a reason for so dispensing this treasury, so that the intention, namely, of those who wrought these meritorious works is safeguarded, since they did them for the honor of God and for the good of the Church in general. Hence whenever the cause assigned tends to the good of the Church and the honor of God, there is sufficient reason for granting an indulgence.

Hence, according to others, indulgences have precisely the efficacy aimed for them, provided that he who grants them have the authority, that the recipient have *charity*, and that, as regards the cause, there be piety which includes the honor of God and the profit of our neighbor. Nor in this view have we *too great a market of the divine mercy* (St. Bonaventure, *Commentary on the Sentences* IV, D. 20) as some maintain, nor again does it derogate from divine justice, for no punishment is remitted, but the punishment of one is imputed to another.

REPLY OBJ. 1: As stated above (Q. 19, A. 3) there are two keys, the key of orders and the key of jurisdiction. The key of orders is a sacramental: and as the effects of the sacraments are fixed, not by men but by God, the priest cannot decide in the tribunal of confession how much shall be remitted by means of the key of orders from the punishment due; it is God who appoints the amount to be remitted. On the other hand, the key of jurisdiction is not something sacramental, and its effect depends on a man's decision. The remission granted through indulgences is the effect of this key, since it does not belong to the dispensation of the sacraments, but to the distribution of the common property of the Church: hence it is that legates, even though they be not priests, can grant indulgences. Consequently, the decision of how much punishment is to be remitted by an indulgence depends on the will of the one who grants that indulgence. If, however, he remits punishment without sufficient reason, so that men are enticed to substitute mere nothings, as it were, for works of penance, he sins by granting such indulgences, although the indulgence is gained fully.

REPLY OBJ. 2: Although indulgences avail much for the remission of punishment, yet works of satisfaction are more meritorious in respect of the essential reward, which infinitely transcends the remission of temporal punishment.

AD TERTIUM dicendum quod, quando datur indulgentia indeterminate, qui dant auxilium ad fabricam ecclesiae, intelligitur tale auxilium quod sit conveniens ei qui auxilium dat: et secundum quod accedit ad hoc, secundum hoc plus vel minus de indulgentia consequitur. Unde etiam aliquis pauper dans unum denarium consequitur totam indulgentiam: non autem dives, quem non decet ad opus tam pium ita parum dare; sicut non diceretur rex alicui homini auxilium facere si ei obolum daret.

AD QUARTUM dicendum quod ille qui est vicinus ecclesiae, et ecclesiae sacerdotes et clerici consequuntur tantam indulgentiam sicut illi qui venirent a mille diaetis: quia remissio non proportionatur labori, ut dictum est, sed meritis quae dispensantur. Sed ille qui plus laboraret, acquireret plus de merito.

Sed hoc intelligendum quando indistincte indulgentia datur. Quandoque enim distinguitur. Sicut Papa, in generalibus absolutionibus, illis qui transeunt mare, dat quinque annos; aliis, qui transeunt montes, tres; aliis unum.

Nec tamen quotiescumque vadit infra tempus indulgentiae, toties eam consequitur. Quandoque autem ad determinatum tempus datur, ut cum dicitur, *quicumque vadit ad ecclesiam talem usque ad tale tempus, habeat tantum de indulgentia*: intelligitur *semel tantum*. Sed si in aliqua Ecclesia sit indulgentia perennis, sicut in ecclesia beati Petri quadraginta dierum, tunc, quoties aliquis vadit, toties indulgentiam consequitur.

AD QUINTUM dicendum quod causa non requiritur ad hoc quod secundum eam mensurari debeat remissio poenae: sed ad hoc quod intentio illorum quorum merita communicantur, ad ipsum pervenire possint. Bonum autem unius continuatur alteri dupliciter. Uno modo, per caritatem: et sic etiam sine indulgentiis aliquis est omnium bonorum particeps quae fiunt, si in caritate sit. Alio modo, per intentionem facientis. Et sic per indulgentias, si causa legitima adsit, potest intentio illius qui pro utilitate Ecclesia operatus est, ad istum continuari.

REPLY OBJ. 3: When an indulgence is granted in a general way to anyone that helps towards the building of a church, we must understand this to mean a help proportionate to the giver: and insofar as he approaches to this, he will gain the indulgence more or less fully. Consequently, a poor man by giving one penny would gain the full indulgence, but not so a rich man, whom it would not become to give so little to so holy and profitable a work; just as a king would not be said to help a man if he gave him an small coin.

REPLY OBJ. 4: A person who lives near the church, and the priest and clergy of the church, gain the indulgence as much as those who come perhaps a distance of a thousand days' journey: because the remission, as stated above, is proportionate, not to the toil, but to the merits which are applied.

Yet he who toils most gains most merit. This, however, is to be understood of those cases in which an indulgence is given in an undeterminate manner. For sometimes a distinction is expressed: thus the Pope at the time of general absolution grants an indulgence of five years to those who come from across the seas; three years to those who come from across the mountains; to others, an indulgence of one year.

Nor does a person gain the indulgence each time he visits the church during the term of indulgence, because sometimes it is granted for a fixed time; thus when it is said, *whoever visits such and such a church until such and such a day, shall gain so much indulgence*, we must understand that it can be gained only once. On the other hand, if there be a continual indulgence in a certain church, as the indulgence of forty days to be gained in St. Peter's Basilica, then a person gains the indulgence as often as he visits the church.

REPLY OBJ. 5: An indulgence requires a cause not as a measure of the remission of punishment, but in order that the intention of those whose merits are applied may reach to this particular individual. Now one person's good is applied to another in two ways: first, by charity; and in this way, even without indulgences, a person shares in all the good deeds done, provided he has charity; second, by the intention of the person who does the good action; and in this way, provided there be a lawful cause, the intention of a person who has done something for the profit of the Church may reach to some individual through indulgences.

Article 3

Whether an Indulgence Ought to Be Granted for Temporal Help?

AD TERTIUM SIC PROCEDITUR. Videtur quod pro temporali subsidio non debeat fieri indulgentia. Quia remissio peccatorum est quoddam spirituale; sed dare spi-

OBJECTION 1: It would seem that an indulgence ought not to be granted for temporal help. For the remission of sins is something spiritual. Now to exchange a spiritual for

rituale pro temporali est simonia. Ergo hoc fieri non debet.

PRAETEREA, spiritualia subsidia sunt magis necessaria quam temporalia. Sed pro spiritualibus subsidiis non videntur fieri indulgentiae. Ergo multo minus pro temporalibus fieri debent.

SED CONTRA est communis Ecclesiae consuetudo, quae pro peregrinationibus et eleemosynis faciendis indulgentias facit.

RESPONDEO dicendum quod temporalia ad spiritualia ordinantur: quia propter spiritualia debemus uti temporalibus. Et ideo pro temporalibus simpliciter non potest fieri indulgentia: sed pro temporalibus ordinatis ad spiritualia; sicut repressio inimicorum Ecclesiae, qui pacem Ecclesiae perturbant, sicut constructio ecclesiarum et pontium, et aliarum eleemosynarum. Et per hoc patet quod non fit ibi simonia: quia non datur spirituale pro temporali.

UNDE PATET solutio ad primum.

AD SECUNDUM dicendum quod etiam pro pure spiritualibus potest fieri indulgentia, et fit quandoque: sicut quicumque orat pro rege Franciae, habet decem dies pro indulgentia a Papa Innocentio IV. Et similiter crucem praedicantibus datur quandoque eadem indulgentia quae crucem accipientibus.

a temporal thing is simony. Therefore, this ought not to be done.

OBJ. 2: Further, spiritual assistance is more necessary than temporal. But indulgences do not appear to be granted for spiritual assistance. Much less, therefore, ought they to be granted for temporal help.

ON THE CONTRARY, It is the common custom of the Church to grant indulgences for pilgrimages and almsgiving.

I ANSWER THAT, Temporal things are subordinate to spiritual matters, since we must make use of temporal things on account of spiritual things. Consequently, an indulgence must not be granted for the sake of temporal matters as such, but insofar as they are subordinate to spiritual things: such as the quelling of the Church's enemies, who disturb her peace; or such as the building of a church, of a bridge, and other forms of almsgiving. It is therefore evident that there is no simony in these transactions, since a spiritual thing is exchanged, not for a temporal but for a spiritual commodity.

HENCE the reply to the first objection is clear.

REPLY OBJ. 2: Indulgences can be, and sometimes are, granted even for purely spiritual matters. Thus Pope Innocent IV granted an indulgence of ten days to all who prayed for the king of France; and in like manner sometimes the same indulgence is granted to those who preach a crusade as to those who take part in it.

QUESTION 26

THOSE WHO CAN GRANT INDULGENCES

Deinde considerandum est de his qui possunt indulgentias facere.

Circa quod quattuor quaeruntur:

Primo: utrum quilibet sacerdos parochialis possit indulgentias facere.

Secundo: utrum diaconus vel non-sacerdos possit eas facere.

Tertio: utrum episcopus possit eas facere.

Quarto: utrum existens in peccato mortali possit eas facere.

We must now consider those who can grant indulgences.

Under this head there are four points of inquiry:

(1) Whether every parish priest can grant indulgences?

(2) Whether a deacon or another who is not a priest can grant indulgences?

(3) Whether a bishop can grant them?

(4) Whether they can be granted by one who is in mortal sin?

Article 1

Whether Every Parish Priest Can Grant Indulgences?

AD PRIMUM SIC PROCEDITUR. Videtur quod quilibet sacerdos parochialis possit indulgentias facere. Indulgentia enim habet efficaciam ex abundantia meritorum Ecclesiae. Sed non est aliqua congregatio in qua non sit aliqua meritorum abundantia. Ergo quilibet sacerdos potest facere indulgentiam si habet plebem subiectam: et similiter quilibet praelatus.

PRAETEREA, praelatus quilibet gerit personam totius multitudinis sicut unus homo gerit personam suam. Sed quilibet potest alteri communicare bona sua pro altero satisfaciendo. Ergo et praelatus potest communicare bona multitudinis sibi commissae. Et sic videtur quod possit indulgentias facere.

SED CONTRA, minus est excommunicare quam indulgentias facere. Sed hoc non potest sacerdos parochialis. Ergo nec illud.

RESPONDEO dicendum quod indulgentiae effectum habent secundum quod opera satisfactoria unius alteri computantur, non solum ex vi caritatis, sed ex intentione operantis aliquo modo directa ad ipsum. Sed intentio alicuius potest ad alterum dirigi tripliciter: aut in speciali, aut in generali, aut in singulari. In singulari quidem, sicut cum quis pro alio satisfacit determinate. Et sic quilibet potest alteri sua opera communicare. In speciali autem, sicut cum quis orat pro congregatione sua et familiaribus et benefactoribus, et ad hoc etiam ordinat sua opera satisfactoria. Et sic ille qui congregationi praeest, potest opera illa alii communicare, applicando intentionem illorum qui sunt de congregatione sua ad hunc determinate. Sed in generali, sicut cum quis opera sua ordinat ad bonum commune in generali. Et sic ille

OBJECTION 1: It would seem that every parish priest can grant indulgences. For an indulgence derives its efficacy from the superabundance of the Church's merits. Now there is no congregation without some superabundance of merits. Therefore, every priest who has charge of a congregation can grant indulgences, and, in like manner, so can every prelate.

OBJ. 2: Further, every prelate stands for a multitude, just as an individual stands for himself. But any individual can assign his own goods to another, and thus offer satisfaction for a third person. Therefore, a prelate can assign the property of the multitude subject to him, and so it seems that he can grant indulgences.

ON THE CONTRARY, To excommunicate is less than to grant indulgences. But a parish priest cannot do the former. Therefore, he cannot do the latter.

I ANSWER THAT, Indulgences are effective inasmuch as the works of satisfaction done by one person are applied to another not only by virtue of charity, but also by the intention of the person who did them being directed in some way to the person to whom they are applied. Now a person's intention may be directed to another in three ways: specifically, generically and individually. Individually, as when one person offers satisfaction for another particular person; and thus anyone can apply his works to another. Specifically, as when a person prays for the congregation to which he belongs, for the members of his household, or for his benefactors, and directs his works of satisfaction to the same intention: in this way the superior of a congregation can apply those works to some other person by applying the intention of those who belong to his congregation

qui praeest Ecclesiae generaliter, potest opera illa communicare, applicando incentionem suam ad hunc vel ad illum.

Et quia homo est pars congregationis, et congregatio est pars Ecclesiae, ideo in intentione privati boni intentio boni congregationis includitur, et boni totius Ecclesiae. Et ideo ille qui praeest Ecclesiae potest communicare ea quae sunt congregationis, et huius hominis; et ille qui praeest congregationi, ea quae sunt huius hominis; sed non convertitur.

Sed neque prima communicatio neque secunda indulgentia dicitur, sed solum tertia: propter duo. Primo, quia per illas communicationes, quamvis homo solvatur a reatu poenae quantum ad Deum, tamen non solvitur a debito faciendi satisfactionem iniunctam ad quam obligatus est ex praecepto Ecclesiae. Sed per tertiam communicationem homo etiam ab hoc debito solvitur. Secundo, quia in una persona, vel in una congregatione, non est indeficientia meritorum, ut sibi et omnibus aliis valere possint. Unde iste non absolvitur a poena debita pro toto, nisi tantum determinate pro eo fiat quantum debebatur. Sed in Ecclesia tota est indeficientia meritorum: praecipue propter meritum Christi. Et ideo solus ille qui praeficitur Ecclesiae, potest indulgentias facere.

Sed, cum Ecclesia sit *congregatio fidelium*; congregatio autem hominum sit duplex, scilicet oeconomica, ut illi qui sunt de una familia, et politica, sicut illi qui sunt de uno populo: Ecclesia assimilatur congregationi politicae, quia ipse populus Ecclesia dicitur; sed conventus diversi vel parochia in una dioecesi, assimilantur congregationi in diversis familiis vel in diversis officiis. Et ideo solus episcopus proprie praelatus Ecclesiae dicitur: et ideo ipse solus, quasi sponsus, anulum Ecclesiae recipit. Et ideo ipse solus habet potestatem plenam in dispensatione sacramentorum, et iurisdictionem in foro causarum, quasi persona publica: alii autem secundum quod ab eis committitur. Sed sacerdotes qui plebibus praeficiuntur, non sunt simpliciter praelati, sed quasi coadiutores: unde in consecratione sacerdotum episcopus dicit, *quanto fragiliores sumus, tanto magis auxiliis his indigemus*. Et propter hoc etiam non omnia sacramenta dispensant. Unde sacerdotes parochiales, vel abbates, aut alii huiusmodi praelati, non possunt indulgentias facere.

Et per hoc patet responsio ad obiecta.

to some fixed individual. Generically, as when a person directs his works for the good of the Church in general; and thus he who presides over the whole Church can communicate those works by applying his intention to this or that individual.

And since a man is a member of a congregation, and a congregation is a part of the Church, hence the intention of private good includes the intention of the good of the congregation, and of the good of the whole Church. Therefore, he who presides over the Church can communicate what belongs to an individual congregation or to an individual man: and he who presides over a congregation can communicate what belongs to an individual man, but not conversely.

Yet neither the first nor the second communication is called an indulgence, but only the third; and this for two reasons. First, because, although those communications loose man from the debt of punishment in the sight of God, yet he is not freed from the obligation of fulfilling the satisfaction enjoined, to which he is bound by a commandment of the Church; whereas the third communication frees man even from this obligation. Second, because in one person or even in one congregation there is not such an unfailing supply of merits as to be sufficient both for the one person or congregation and for all others; and consequently the individual is not freed from the entire debt of punishment unless satisfaction is offered for him individually, to the very amount that he owes. On the other hand, in the whole Church there is an unfailing supply of merits, chiefly on account of the merit of Christ. Consequently, he alone who is at the head of the Church can grant indulgences.

Since, however, the Church is the *congregation of the faithful*, and since a congregation of men is of two kinds, the domestic, composed of members of the same family, and the civil, composed of members of the same nationality, the Church is like a civil congregation, for the people themselves are called the Church; while the various assemblies or parishes of one diocese are likened to a congregation in the various families and services. Hence a bishop alone is properly called a prelate of the Church, wherefore he alone, like a bridegroom, receives the ring of the Church. Consequently, full power in the dispensation of the sacraments, and jurisdiction in the public tribunal, belong to him alone as the public person, but to others by delegation from him. Those priests who have charge of the people are not prelates strictly speaking, but assistants; hence, in consecrating priests the bishop says: *the more fragile we are, the more we need these assistants*: and for this reason they do not dispense all the sacraments. Hence parish priests, abbots, or other like prelates cannot grant indulgences.

This suffices for the replies to the objections.

Article 2

Whether a Deacon or Another Who Is Not a Priest Can Grant an Indulgence?

AD SECUNDUM SIC PROCEDITUR. Videtur quod diaconus non possit indulgentias facere, vel alius nonsacerdos. Quia remissio peccatorum est effectus clavium. Sed non habet claves nisi solus sacerdos. Ergo ipse solus potest indulgentias facere.

PRAETEREA, plenior remissio poenae est in indulgentiis quam in foro poenitentiali. Sed hoc non potest nisi sacerdos. Ergo nec illud.

SED CONTRA, eidem confertur dispensatio thesauri Ecclesiae cui committitur regimen Ecclesiae. Sed hoc committitur quandoque non-sacerdoti. Ergo potest indulgentias facere: nam ex dispensatione thesauri Ecclesiae efficaciam habent.

RESPONDEO dicendum quod potestas faciendi indulgentias sequitur iurisdictionem, ut supra dictum est. Et quia diaconi et alii non-sacerdotes possunt habere iurisdictionem, vel commissam, sicut legati, vel ordinariam, sicut electi; ideo possunt indulgentias facere etiam non-sacerdotes; quamvis non possunt absolvere in foro poenitentiali, quod est ordinis.

ET PER HOC patet solutio ad obiecta. Indulgentias enim facere pertinet ad clavem iurisdictionis, et non ad clavem ordinis.

OBJECTION 1: It would seem that a deacon or one that is not a priest cannot grant an indulgence. For remission of sins is an effect of the keys. Now none but a priest has the keys. Therefore, a priest alone can grant indulgences.

OBJ. 2: Further, a fuller remission of punishment is granted by indulgences than by the tribunal of penance. But a priest alone has power in the latter, and, therefore, he alone has power in the former.

ON THE CONTRARY, The distribution of the Church's treasury is entrusted to the same person as the government of the Church. Now this is entrusted sometimes to one who is not a priest. Therefore, he can grant indulgences, since they derive their efficacy from the distribution of the Church's treasury.

I ANSWER THAT, The power of granting indulgences follows jurisdiction, as stated above (Q. 25, A. 2). And since deacons and others, who are not priests, can have jurisdiction either delegated, as legates, or ordinary, as bishops elect, it follows that even those who are not priests can grant indulgences, although they cannot absolve in the tribunal of penance, since this follows the reception of holy orders.

THIS SUFFICES for the replies to the objections, because the granting of indulgences belongs to the key of jurisdiction and not to the key of orders.

Article 3

Whether a Bishop Can Grant Indulgences?

AD TERTIUM SIC PROCEDITUR. Videtur quod etiam episcopus non possit indulgentias facere. Quia thesaurus Ecclesiae est communis toti Ecclesiae. Sed id quod est commune toti Ecclesiae, non potest dispensari nisi per illum qui toti Ecclesiae praeest. Ergo solus Papa potest indulgentias facere.

PRAETEREA, nullus potest remittere poenas a iure determinatas nisi ille qui habet potestatem ius condendi. Sed poenae satisfactoriae sunt pro peccatis determinatae in iure. Ergo remittere huiusmodi poenas potest solus Papa, qui est conditor iuris.

SED CONTRA est consuetudo Ecclesiae, secundum quam episcopi dant indulgentias.

RESPONDEO dicendum quod Papa habet plenitudinem pontificialis potestatis, quasi rex in regno. Sed episcopi assumuntur *in partem sollicitudinis*, quasi iudices singulis civitatibus praepositi: propter quod eos solos in suis litteris Papa *fratres* vocat, reliquos autem omnes vo-

OBJECTION 1: It would seem that even a bishop cannot grant indulgences. For the treasury of the Church is the common property of the whole Church. Now the common property of the whole Church cannot be distributed save by him who presides over the whole Church. Therefore, the Pope alone can grant indulgences.

OBJ. 2: Further, none can remit punishments fixed by law save the one who has the power to make the law. Now punishments in satisfaction for sins are fixed by law. Therefore, the Pope alone can remit these punishments, since he is the maker of the law.

ON THE CONTRARY, There is the custom of the Church in accordance with which bishops grant indulgences.

I ANSWER THAT, The Pope has the plenitude of pontifical power, being like a king in his kingdom: whereas the bishops are appointed *to a share in his solicitude*, like judges over each city. Hence them alone the Pope, in his letters, addresses as *brethren*, whereas he calls all others his *sons*.

cat *filios*. Et ideo potestas faciendi indulgentias plene residet in Papa: quia potest facere prout vult, causa tamen existente legitima. Sed in episcopis est taxata secundum ordinationem Papae. Et ideo possunt facere secundum quod eis est taxatum, et non amplius.

Et per hoc patet solutio ad obiecta.

Therefore, the plenitude of the power of granting indulgences resides in the Pope, because he can grant them as he chooses, provided the cause be a lawful one: while, in bishops, this power resides subject to the Pope's ordination, so that they can grant them within fixed limits and not beyond.

This suffices for the replies to the objections.

Article 4

Whether Indulgences Can Be Granted by One Who Is in Mortal Sin?

Ad quartum sic proceditur. Videtur quod ille qui est in peccato mortali, non possit facere indulgentias. Quia rivus cui fons non influit, nihil profluere potest. Sed praelato in peccato mortali existenti non influit fons gratiae, scilicet Spiritus Sanctus. Ergo non potest in alios profluere faciendo indulgentias.

Praeterea, maius est facere indulgentiam quam recipere. Sed ille qui est in peccato mortali non recipit, ut dicetur. Ergo nec facere potest.

Sed contra, indulgentiae fiunt per potestatem praelatis Ecclesiae traditam. Sed peccatum mortale non tollit potestatem, sed bonitatem. Ergo potest aliquis in peccato mortali existens indulgentias facere.

Respondeo dicendum quod facere indulgentias pertinet ad iurisdictionem. Sed per peccatum homo non amittit iurisdictionem. Et ideo indulgentiae aeque valent si fiant ab eo qui est in peccato mortali, sicut si fierent ab eo qui est sanctissimus: cum non remittat poenam ex vi meritorum suorum, sed ex vi meritorum reconditorum in thesauris Ecclesiae.

Ad primum ergo dicendum quod iste praelatus in peccato mortali indulgentias faciens non profluit de suo aliquid. Et ideo non requiritur quod influxum recipiat a fonte ad hoc quod eius indulgentiae valeant.

Ad secundum dicendum quod maius est facere indulgentias quam recipere quantum, ad potestatem: sed est minus quantum ad propriam utilitatem.

Objection 1: It would seem that indulgences cannot be granted by one who is in mortal sin. For a stream can no longer flow if it is cut off from its source. Now the source of grace which is the Holy Spirit is cut off from one who is in mortal sin. Therefore, such a one can convey nothing to others by granting indulgences.

Obj. 2: Further, it is a greater thing to grant an indulgence than to receive one. But one who is in mortal sin cannot receive an indulgence, as we shall show presently (Q. 27, A. 1). Neither, therefore, can he grant one.

On the contrary, Indulgences are granted in virtue of the power conferred on the prelates of the Church. Now mortal sin takes away not power but goodness. Therefore, one who is in mortal sin can grant indulgences.

I answer that, The granting of indulgences belongs to jurisdiction. But a man does not, through sin, lose jurisdiction. Consequently, indulgences are equally valid whether they be granted by one who is in mortal sin, or by a most holy person; since he remits punishment, not by virtue of his own merits, but by virtue of the merits laid up in the Church's treasury.

Reply Obj. 1: The prelate who, while in a state of mortal sin, grants an indulgence, does not pour forth anything of his own, and so it is not necessary that he should receive an influx from the source, in order that he may grant a valid indulgence.

Reply Obj. 2: To grant an indulgence is more than to receive one, if we consider the power, but it is less, if we consider the personal profit.

QUESTION 27

THOSE WHOM INDULGENCES AVAIL

Deinde considerandum est de his quibus valet indulgentia.

Circa quod quaeruntur quattuor.

Primo: utrum indulgentia valeat existentibus in mortali peccato.

Secundo: utrum valeat religiosis.

Tertio: utrum valeat non facienti illud pro quo indulgentia datur.

Quarto: utrum valeat ei qui indulgentiam facit.

We must now consider those whom indulgences avail.

Under this head there are four points of inquiry:

(1) Whether indulgences avail those who are in mortal sin?

(2) Whether they avail religious?

(3) Whether they avail a person who does not fulfill the conditions for which the indulgence is given?

(4) Whether they avail him who grants them?

Article 1

Whether an Indulgence Avails Those Who Are in Mortal Sin?

AD PRIMUM SIC PROCEDITUR. Videtur quod indulgentia valeat existentibus in peccato mortali. Quia aliquis potest alteri mereri, etiam in peccato mortali existenti, gratiam et multa alia bona. Sed indulgentiae habent efficaciam ex hoc quod merita sanctorum applicantur ad istum. Ergo habent effectum in illis qui sunt in peccato mortali.

PRAETEREA, ubi est maior indigentia, magis habet locum misericordia. Sed ille qui est in peccato mortali maxime indiget. Erigo ei maxime debet fieri misericordia per indulgentias.

SED CONTRA, membrum mortuum non suscipit influentiam ab aliis vivis. Sed ille qui est in peccato mortali est quasi membrum mortuum. Ergo per indulgentias non suscipit influentiam ex meritis vivorum membrorum.

RESPONDEO dicendum quod quidam dicunt indulgentias valere etiam existentibus in mortali peccato. Non quidem ad dimissionem poenae, quia nulli potest dimitti poena nisi cui dimissa est culpa; qui enim non est consecutus operationem Dei in remissionem culpae, non potest consequi remissionem poenae a ministro Ecclesiae, neque in indulgentiis neque in foro poenitentiali: valent tamen eis ad acquirendum gratiam.

Sed hoc non videtur verum. Quia, quamvis merita illa quae per indulgentiam communicantur, possunt valere ad merendum gratiam, non tamen propter hoc dispensantur, sed determinate ad remissionem poenae. Et ideo non valent existentibus in mortali. Et ideo in omnibus indulgentiis fit mentio de *vere contritis et confessis.*

OBJECTION 1: It would seem that an indulgence avails those who are in mortal sin. For one person can merit grace and many other good things for another, even though he be in mortal sin. Now indulgences derive their efficacy from the application of the saints' merits to an individual. Therefore, they are effective in one who is in mortal sin.

OBJ. 2: Further, the greater the need, the more room there is for pity. Now a man who is in mortal sin is in very great need. Therefore, all the more should pity be extended to him by indulgence.

ON THE CONTRARY, A dead member receives no influx from the other members that are living. But one who is in mortal sin is like a dead member. Therefore, he receives no influx through indulgences from the merits of living members.

I ANSWER THAT, Some hold that indulgences avail those even who are in mortal sin for the acquiring of grace, but not for the remission of their punishment, since none can be freed from punishment who is not yet freed from guilt. For he who has not yet been reached by God's operation unto the remission of guilt cannot receive the remission of his punishment from the minister of the Church, neither by indulgences nor in the tribunal of penance.

But this opinion seems to be untrue. Because, although those merits which are applied by means of an indulgence might possibly avail a person so that he could merit grace (by way of congruity and impetration), yet it is not for this reason that they are applied, but for the remission of punishment. Hence they do not avail those who are in mortal sin, and consequently *true contrition and confession* are demanded as conditions for gaining all indulgences.

181

Si autem fieret communicatio per hunc modum, *facio te participem meritorum totius Ecclesiae*, vel *unius congregationis*, vel *unius specialis personae*, sic posset valere ad merendum aliquid illi qui est in peccato mortali, ut praedicta opinio dicit.

ET PER HOC patet solutio ad primum.

AD SECUNDUM dicendum quod, quamvis sit magis indigens qui est in peccato mortali, tamen est minus capax.

If, however, the merits were applied by such a form as this: *I grant you a share in the merits of the whole Church—or of one congregation, or of one specified person*, then they might avail a person in mortal sin so that he could merit something, as the foregoing opinion holds.

THIS SUFFICES for the reply to the first objection.

REPLY OBJ. 2: Although he who is in mortal sin is in greater need of help, yet he is less capable of receiving it.

Article 2

Whether Indulgences Avail Religious?

AD SECUNDUM SIC PROCEDITUR. Videtur quod indulgentiae non valeant religiosis. Non enim competit eis suppleri ex quorum abundantia aliis suppletur. Sed ex superabundantia operum satisfactionis quae sunt in religiosis, aliis suppletur per indulgentias. Ergo eis non competit per indulgentiam suppleri.

PRAETEREA, in Ecclesia non debet aliquid fieri quod inducat religionis dissolutionem. Sed si religiosis indulgentiae prodessent, esset occasio dissolutionis disciplinae regularis: quia religiosi nimis vagarentur per huiusmodi indulgentias, et poenas impositas in capitulo sibi negligerent. Ergo religiosis non prosunt.

SED CONTRA, nullus ex bono reportat damnum. Sed religio bonum est. Ergo religiosi non consequuntur hoc damnum, ut eis indulgentiae non valeant.

RESPONDEO dicendum quod tam saecularibus quam religiosis valent indulgentiae, dummodo sint in caritate, et servent ea quae pro indulgentiis indicuntur: non enim religiosi sunt minus adiuvabiles meritis aliorum quam saeculares.

AD PRIMUM ergo dicendum quod, quamvis religiosus sit in statu perfectionis, tamen ipse sine peccato vivere non potest. Et ideo, si aliquando propter peccatum aliquod commissum fit reus poenae, potest per indulgentiam ab hoc expiari. Non enim est inconveniens si ille qui est simpliciter superabundans, aliquo tempore indigeat et quantum ad aliquid, et sic indiget supplemento quo sublevetur. Unde dicitur Galat. 6: *alter alterius onera portate*.

AD SECUNDUM dicendum quod propter indulgentias non debet dissolvi regularis observantia: quia religiosi magis merentur religionem suam servando, quantum ad praemium vitae aeternae, quam indulgentias exquirendo; quamvis minus quantum ad dimissionem poenae, quod est minus bonum. Nec iterum par indulgentias dimittuntur poenae iniunctae in capitulo: quia in capitulo agitur quasi forum iudiciale magis quam poenitentiale;

OBJECTION 1: It would seem that indulgences do not avail religious. For there is no reason to bring supplies to those who supply others out of their own abundance. Now indulgences are derived from the abundance of works of satisfaction to be found in religious. Therefore, it is unreasonable for them to profit by indulgences.

OBJ. 2: Further, nothing detrimental to religious life should be done in the Church. But if indulgences were to avail religious, this would be detrimental to regular discipline, because religious would become lax on account of indulgences, and would neglect the penances imposed in chapter. Therefore, indulgences do not avail religious.

ON THE CONTRARY, Good brings harm to no man. But the religious life is a good thing. Therefore, it does not take away from religious the profit to be derived from indulgences.

I ANSWER THAT, Indulgences avail both seculars and religious, provided they have charity and satisfy the conditions for gaining the indulgences: for religious can be helped by indulgences no less than persons living in the world.

REPLY OBJ. 1: Although religious are in the state of perfection, yet they cannot live without sin: and so if at times they are liable to punishment on account of some sin, they can expiate this debt by means of indulgences. For it is not unreasonable that one who is well off absolutely speaking should be in want at times and in some respect, and thus need to be supplied with what he lacks. Hence it is written: *bear ye one another's burdens* (Gal 6:2).

REPLY OBJ. 2: There is no reason why indulgences should be detrimental to religious observance, because, as to the reward of eternal life, religious merit more by observing their rule than by gaining indulgences; although, as to the remission of punishment, which is a lesser good, they merit less. Nor again do indulgences remit the punishment enjoined in chapter, because the chapter is a judicial rather than a penitential tribunal; hence even those who are not

unde etiam non-sacerdotes capitulum tenent. Sed absolvitur a poena iniuncta vel debita pro peccato in foro poenitentiali.

priests hold chapter. Absolution from punishment enjoined or due for sin is given in the tribunal of penance.

Article 3

Whether an Indulgence Can Ever Be Granted to One Who Does Not Fulfill the Conditions Required?

AD TERTIUM SIC PROCEDITUR. Videtur quod ei qui non facit hoc pro quo indulgentia datur, possit quandoque indulgentia dari. Quia ei qui non potest operari, voluntas pro facto reputatur. Sed aliquando fit indulgentia pro aliqua eleemosyna facienda, quam aliquis pauper facere non potest, et tamen libenter faceret. Ergo indulgentia ei valet.

PRAETEREA, unus potest pro alio satisfacere. Sed indulgentia ad remissionem poenae operatur sicut et satisfactio. Ergo unus pro alio potest indulgentiam accipere. Et sic ille consequetur indulgentiam qui non facit hoc pro quo indulgentia datur.

SED CONTRA, remota causa removetur effectus. Si ergo aliquis non facit hoc pro quo indulgentia datur, quod est indulgentiae causa, indulgentiam non consequitur.

RESPONDEO dicendum quod, non existente conditione non consequitur illud quod sub conditione datur. Unde, cum indulgentia detur sub hac conditione quod aliquis aliquid faciat vel det, si illud non exerceat, indulgentiam non consequitur.

AD PRIMUM ergo dicendum quod hoc intelligitur quantum ad praemium essentiale: sed non quantum ad accidentalia aliqua praemia, sicut est dimissio poenae, vel aliquid huiusmodi.

AD SECUNDUM dicendum quod opus proprium potest quis applicare per intentionem cuicumque voluerit: et ideo potest pro quocumque vult satisfacere. Sed; indulgentia non potest applicari ad alterum nisi ex intentione eius qui dat indulgentiam. Et ideo, cum ipse applicet ad facientem vel dantem hoc aut illud, non potest ille qui hoc facit ad alterum hanc intentionem transferre. Si tamen sic fieret indulgentia, *ille qui facit, vel pro quo hoc fit, habeat tantam indulgentiam,* valeret ei pro quo fit. Nec tamen iste qui facit hoc opus, daret alteri indulgentiam: sed ille qui indulgentiam sub tali forma facit.

OBJECTION 1: It would seem that an indulgence can sometimes be granted to one who does not fulfill the required conditions, because when a person is unable to perform a certain action his will is taken for the deed. Now, sometimes an indulgence is to be gained by giving alms, which a poor man is unable to do, though he would do so willingly. Therefore, he can gain the indulgence.

OBJ. 2: Further, one man can make satisfaction for another. Now an indulgence is directed to the remission of punishment, just as satisfaction is. Therefore, one man can gain an indulgence for another; and so a man can gain an indulgence without doing that for which the indulgence is given.

ON THE CONTRARY, If the cause is removed, the effect is removed. If, therefore, a person fails to do that for which an indulgence is granted, and which is the cause of the indulgence, he does not gain the indulgence.

I ANSWER THAT, Failing the condition of a grant, no grant ensues. Hence, as an indulgence is granted on the condition that a person does or gives a certain thing, if he fails in this, he does not gain the indulgence.

REPLY OBJ. 1: This is true of the essential reward, but not of certain accidental rewards, such as the remission of punishment and the like.

REPLY OBJ. 2: A person can by his intention apply his own action to whomever he desires, and so he can make satisfaction for whomever he chooses. On the other hand, an indulgence cannot be applied to someone except in accordance with the intention of the grantor. Hence, since he applies it to the doer or giver of a particular action or thing, the doer cannot transfer this intention to another. If, however, the indulgence were expressed thus: *whosoever does this, or for whomsoever this is done, shall gain so much indulgence*, it would avail the person for whom it is done. Nor would the person who does this action give the indulgence to another, but he who grants the indulgence in this form.

Article 4

Whether an Indulgence Avails the Person Who Grants It?

AD QUARTUM SIC PROCEDITUR. Videtur quod indulgentia non valeat ei qui facit. Quia facere indulgentias est iurisdictionis. Sed nullus in seipsum potest exercere eu quae sunt iurisdictionis. Ergo nullus potest indulgentiae a se factae particeps esse.

PRAETEREA, secundum hoc, ille qui facit indulgentiam posset pro aliquo modico facto sibi poenam remittere omnium peccatorum, et ita impune peccare. Quod videtur absonum.

PRAETEREA, eiusdem potestatis est facere indulgentias et excommunicare. Sed aliquis non potest excommunicare seipsum. Ergo nec indulgentiae quam facit particeps esse potest.

SED CONTRA est quia tunc esset ipse peioris conditionis quam alii, si ipse non posset uti thesauro Ecclesiae, quem aliis dispensat.

RESPONDEO dicendum quod, indulgentia debet ex aliqua causa dari, ad hoc quod aliquis per indulgentiam ad actum aliquem provocetur qui in utilitatem Ecclesiae et in honorem Dei vergat. Praelatus autem, cui cura Ecclesiae utilitatis et honoris divini propagandi est commissa, non habet causam, ut seipsum ad hoc provocet. Et ideo non potest facere sibi indulgentiam. Sed potest uti indulgentia quam pro aliis facit, quia aliis subesi causa faciendi.

AD PRIMUM ergo dicendum quod actus iurisdictionis non potest aliquis in seipsum exercere. Sed eis quae auctoritate iurisdictionis dantur aliis, potest etiam praelatus uti, tam in temporalibus quam in spiritualibus; sicut etiam sacerdos sibi Eucharistiam accipit, quam aliis dat. Et ita etiam episcopus potest accipere sibi suffragia Ecclesiae, quae aliis dispensat, quorum effectus immediatus est remissio poenae per indulgentias, et non iurisdictionis.

AD SECUNDUM patet solutio ex dictis.

AD TERTIUM dicendum quod excommunicatio profertur per modum sententiae, quam nullus in seipsum ferre potest: eo quod in iudicio non potest idem esse iudex et reus. Indulgentia autem datur non per modum sententiae, sed per modum dispensationis cuiusdam: quam homo potest facere ad seipsum.

OBJECTION 1: It would seem that an indulgence does not avail him who grants it. For the granting of an indulgence belongs to jurisdiction. Now no one can exercise jurisdiction on himself. Thus no one can excommunicate himself. Therefore, no one can participate in an indulgence granted by himself.

OBJ. 2: Further, if this were possible, he who grants an indulgence might gain the remission of the punishment of all his sins for some small deed, so that he would sin with impunity, which seems senseless.

OBJ. 3: Further, to grant indulgences and to excommunicate belong to the same power. Now a man cannot excommunicate himself. Therefore, he cannot share in the indulgence of which he is the grantor.

ON THE CONTRARY, He would be worse off than others if he could not make use of the Church's treasury which he dispenses to others.

I ANSWER THAT, An indulgence should be given for some reason, in order for anyone to be enticed by the indulgence to perform some action that conduces to the good of the Church and to the honor of God. Now the prelate to whom is committed the care of the Church's good and of the furthering of God's honor does not need to entice himself thereto. Therefore, he cannot grant an indulgence to himself alone; but he can avail himself of an indulgence that he grants for others, since it is based on a cause for granting it to them.

REPLY OBJ. 1: A man cannot exercise an act of jurisdiction on himself, but a prelate can avail himself of those things which are granted to others by the authority of his jurisdiction, both in temporal and in spiritual matters: thus also a priest gives himself the Eucharist which he gives to others. And so a bishop too can apply to himself the suffrages of the Church which he dispenses to others, the immediate effect of which suffrages, and not of his jurisdiction, is the remission of punishment by means of indulgences.

THE REPLY to the second objection is clear from what has been said.

REPLY OBJ. 3: Excommunication is pronounced by way of sentence, which no man can pronounce on himself, for the reason that in the tribunal of justice the same man cannot be both judge and accused. On the other hand, an indulgence is not given under the form of a sentence, but by way of dispensation, which a man can apply to himself.

QUESTION 28

THE SOLEMN RITE OF PENANCE

Consequenter considerandum est de solemnitate poenitentiae.

Circa quod tria quaeruntur.

Primo: utrum aliqua poenitentia possit publicari vel solemnizari.

Secundo: utrum solemnis poenitentia possit iterari.

Tertio: de ritu solemnis poenitentiae.

We must now consider the solemn rite of penance.

Under this head there are three points of inquiry:

(1) Whether a penance can be published or solemnized?

(2) Whether a solemn penance can be repeated?

(3) Whether public penance should be imposed on women?

Article 1

Whether a Penance Should Be Published or Solemnized?

AD PRIMUM SIC PROCEDITUR. Videtur quod non debeat aliqua poenitentia publicari vel solemnizari. Quia non licet sacerdoti, etiam metu, peccatum alicuius confiteri, quantumcumque publicum. Sed per poenitentiam solemnem publicatur peccatum. Ergo non debet solemnizari.

PRAETEREA, iudicium debet esse secundum conditionem fori. Sed poenitentia est quoddam iudicium quod in foro occulto agitur. Ergo non debet publicari vel solemnizari.

PRAETEREA, *poenitentia omnes defectus revocat ad perfectum*: ut Ambrosius dicit. Sed solemnizatio facit contrarium, quia poenitentem multis defectibus innectit: non enim laicus potest post solemnem poenitentiam ad clericatum promoveri, nec clericus ad superiores ordines. Ergo poenitentia non est solemnizanda.

SED CONTRA: Poenitentia est quoddam sacramentum. Sed in quolibet sacramento solemnitas quaedam adhibetur. Ergo et in poenitentia adhiberi debet.

PRAETEREA, medicina debet respondere morbo. Sed peccatum quandoque est publicum, quod multos ad exemplum peccandi trahit. Ergo et poenitentia, quae est medicina eius, debet esse publica et solemnis, qua multi aedificentur.

RESPONDEO dicendum quod aliqua poenitentia debet esse publica et solemnis, propter quattuor. Primo, ut peccatum publicum publicam habeat medicinam. Secundo, quia maxima confusione in hoc mundo etiam est dignus qui gravissimum scelus commisit. Tertio, ut aliis sit ad terrorem. Quarto, ut sit ad exemplum poenitendi: ne desperent qui in gravibus peccatis detinentur.

OBJECTION 1: It would seem that a penance should not be published or solemnized. Because it is not lawful for a priest, even through fear, to divulge anyone's sin, however notorious it may be. Now a sin is published by a solemn penance. Therefore, a penance should not be solemnized.

OBJ. 2: Further, the judgment should follow the nature of the tribunal. Now penance is a judgment pronounced in a secret tribunal. Therefore, it should not be published or solemnized.

OBJ. 3: Further, *every deficiency is made good by penance*, as Ambrose states. Now solemnization has a contrary effect, since it involves the penitent in many deficiencies: for a layman cannot be promoted to the ranks of the clergy, nor can a cleric be promoted to higher orders after doing solemn penance. Therefore, penance should not be solemnized.

ON THE CONTRARY, Penance is a sacrament. Now some kind of solemnity is observed in every sacrament. Therefore, there should be some solemnity in penance.

FURTHER, The medicine should suit the disease. Now a sin is sometimes public, and by its example draws many to sin. Therefore, the penance which is its medicine should also be public and solemn so as to give edification to many.

I ANSWER THAT, Some penances should be public and solemn for four reasons. First, so that a public sin may have a public remedy; second, because he who has committed a very grave crime deserves the greatest shame even in this life; third, in order to deter others; fourth, that he may be an example of repentance, lest those should despair, who have committed grievous sins.

AD PRIMUM ergo dicendum quod sacerdos non revelat confessionem talem poenitentiam iniungendo, quamvis suspicio oriatur illum aliquod enorme peccatum commisisse. Non enim culpa pro certo scitur ex poena, quia quandoque aliquis poenitentiam pro alio facit: sicut legitur in *Vitis Patrum* de quodam qui, ut socium suum ad poenitentiam provocaret, ipse cum eo poenitentiam egit. Si autem sit peccatum publicum, ipse poenitens, exequendo poenitentiam, confessionem a se factam manifestat.

AD SECUNDUM dicendum quod poenitentia solemnis, quantum ad iniunctionem, non exit forum occultum: quia, sicut occulte quis confitetur, ita occulte ei poenitentia iniungitur. Sed executio exit forum occultum. Et hoc non est inconveniens.

AD TERTIUM dicendum quod poenitentia, quamvis revocet omnes defectus restituendo in pristinam gratiam, non tamen restituit in pristinam dignitatem. Et ideo etiam mulieres post peractam poenitentiam de fornicatione non velantur, quia dignitatem virginitatis non recuperant. Et similiter post publicam poenitentiam peccator non redit ad hanc dignitatem ut possit ad clericatum assumi, et episcopus talem ordinans potestate ordinandi privari debet: nisi forte necessitas ecclesiae id exposcat, aut consuetudo; tunc enim dispensative recipitur ad minores ordines, non autem ad sacros ordines. Primo, propter dignitatem ordinum istorum. Secundo, propter timorem recidivi. Tertio, propter scandalum vitandum, quod posset in populo oriri ex memoria praecedentium peccatorum. Quarto, quia non haberet frontem alios corrigendi, cum peccatum eius fuerit publicum.

REPLY OBJ. 1: The priest does not divulge the confession by imposing such a penance, though people may suspect the penitent of having committed some great sin. For a man is not certainly taken to be guilty because he is punished, since sometimes one does penance for another: thus we read in the *Lives of the Fathers* of a certain man who, in order to incite his companion to do penance, did penance together with him. And if the sin be public, the penitent, by fulfilling his penance, shows that he has been to confession.

REPLY OBJ. 2: A solemn penance, as to its imposition, does not go beyond the limits of a secret tribunal, since, just as the confession is made secretly, so the penance is imposed secretly. It is the execution of the penance that goes beyond the limits of the secret tribunal: and there is nothing objectionable in this.

REPLY OBJ. 3: Although penance cancels all deficiencies by restoring man to his former state of grace, yet it does not always restore him to his former dignity. Hence women after doing penance for fornication are not given the veil, because they do not recover the honor of virginity. In like manner, after doing public penance a sinner does not recover his former dignity so as to be eligible for the clerical state, and a bishop who would ordain such a one ought to be deprived of the power of ordaining, unless perhaps the needs of the Church or custom require it. In that case such a one would be admitted to minor orders by way of exception, but not to the sacred orders. First, on account of the dignity of the latter; second, for fear of relapse; third, in order to avoid the scandal which the people might take through recollection of his former sins; fourth, because he would not have the face to correct others, by reason of the publicity of his own sin.

Article 2

Whether a Solemn Penance Can Be Repeated?

AD SECUNDUM SIC PROCEDITUR. Videtur quod solemnis poenitentia iterari possit. Sacramenta enim quae characterem non imprimunt, cum sua solemnitate iterantur: sicut Eucharistia et extrema unctio et huiusmodi. Sed poenitentia non imprimit characterem. Ergo cum sua solemnitate iterari debet.

PRAETEREA, poenitentia solemnizatur propter gravitatem et manifestationem peccati. Sed post peractam poenitentiam contingit similia peccata committere, vel etiam graviora. Ergo solemnis poenitentia iterum debet adhiberi.

SED CONTRA, solemnis poenitentia significat electionem primi hominis de paradiso. Sed haec tantum se-

OBJECTION 1: It would seem that a solemn penance can be repeated. For those sacraments which do not imprint a character can be solemnized a second time, such as the Eucharist, extreme unction, and the like. But penance does not imprint a character; therefore, it can be solemnized over again.

OBJ. 2: Further, penance is solemnized on account of the gravity and publicity of the sin. Now, after doing penance, a person may commit the same sins over again, or even more grievous sins. Therefore, the solemn penance should be imposed again.

ON THE CONTRARY, Solemn penance signifies the expulsion of the first man from paradise. Now this was done

mel est facta. Ergo et poenitentia solemnis tantum semel debet fieri.

Respondeo dicendum quod solemnis poenitentia iterari non debet, propter tria: primo, ne ex iteratione vilescat. Secundo, propter significationem. Tertio, quia solemnizatio est quasi quaedam professio perpetuo poenitentiam conservandi: et ideo iteratio solemnitati resistit.

Si tamen postmodum peccaverit, non clauditur ei locus poenitentiae: sed poenitentia solemnis iterum ei iniungenda non est.

Ad primum ergo dicendum quod in illis sacramentis in quibus, solemnitas iteratur, iteratio solemnitati non repugnat, ut est in proposito. Et ideo non est simile.

Ad secundum dicendum quod, quamvis ratione criminis deberetur sibi eadem poenitentia, tamen solemnitatis iteratio non competit, propter praedictas causas.

but once. Therefore, solemn penance should be imposed once only.

I answer that, Solemn penance ought not to be repeated for three reasons. First, lest frequency bring it into contempt. Second, on account of its signification; for it signifies the expulsion of the first man from paradise, which happened only once. Third, because the solemnization indicates, in a way, that one makes profession of continual repentance. Therefore, repetition is inconsistent with solemnization.

And if the sinner fall again, he is not precluded from doing penance, but a solemn penance should not be imposed on him again.

Reply Obj. 1: In those sacraments which are solemnized again and again, repetition is not inconsistent with solemnity, as it is in the present case. Hence the comparison fails.

Reply Obj. 2: Although, if we consider his crime, he ought to do the same penance again, yet the repeated solemnization is not becoming for the reasons stated above.

Article 3

Whether Solemn Penance Should Be Imposed on Women and
Clerics, and Whether Any Priest Can Impose It?

Ad tertium sic proceditur. Videtur quod mulieribus non sit imponenda. Quia vir cui imponitur solemnis poenitentia, debet comam abiicere. Sed hoc non competit mulieri: ut patet I Cor. 11. Ergo non debet agere solemnem poenitentiam.

Item, videtur quod clericis sit imponenda. Quia imponitur propter gravitatem delicti. Sed idem peccatum gravius est in clerico quam in laico. Ergo magis debet imponi clerico quam laico.

Item, videtur quod a quolibet sacerdote possit imponi. Quia absolvere in foro poenitentiali est eius qui habet claves. Sed simplex sacerdos habet claves. Ergo potest esse minister huius poenitentiae.

Respondeo dicendum quod omnis solemnis poenitentia est publica, sed non convertitur. Poenitentia enim solemnis hoc modo fit. In capite quadragesimae tales poenitentes praesentant se cum presbyteris suis episcopis civitatum ante fores ecclesiae sacco induti, nudis pedibus, vultibus demissis, coma deposita; et eis in ecclesia deductis, episcopus cum omni clero septem psalmos poenitentiales dicit, et postmodum eis manum imponit aqua benedicta aspersa, et cinerem capitibus imponit, cilicio: colla eorum operit, et denuntiat eis lacrimabiliter quod, sicut Adam eiectus est; de paradiso, ita ipsi de ecclesia eiiciuntur; et iubet ministris ut eos ab ecclesia

Objection 1: It would seem that solemn penance should not be imposed on women. For when this penance is imposed on a man, he has to cut his hair off. But this does not become a woman, according to 1 Corinthians 11:15. Therefore, she should not do solemn penance.

Obj. 2: It also seems that it ought to be imposed on clerics. For it is enjoined on account of a grievous crime. Now the same sin is more grievous in a cleric than in a layman. Therefore, it ought to be imposed on a cleric more than on a layman.

Obj. 3: It also seems that it can be imposed by any priest, for to absolve in the tribunal of penance belongs to one who has the keys. Now an ordinary priest has the keys. Therefore, he can administer this penance.

I answer that, Every solemn penance is public, but not vice versa. For solemn penance is done as follows: on the first day of Lent, these penitents clothed in sackcloth, with bare feet, their faces to the ground, and their hair shorn away, accompanied by their priests, present themselves to the bishop of the city at the door of the church. Having brought them into the church, the bishop with all his clergy recites the seven penitential psalms, and then imposes his hand on them, sprinkles them with holy water, puts ashes on their heads, covers their shoulders with a hairshirt, and sorrowfully announces to them that as Adam was expelled from paradise, so are they expelled from the

pellant, clero eos prosequente cum hoc responsorio, *in sudore vultus tui*, etc. In Cena autem Domini quolibet anno a suis presbyteris m ecclesia reducuntur, et erunt ibi usque ad octavas Paschae: ita tamen quod non communicabunt nec pacem accipient. Et sic fiet quolibet anno quousque aditus ecclesiae est eis interdictus. Ultima autem reconciliatio reservatur episcopo, ad quem solum spectat solemnis poenitentiae impositio.

Potest autem imponi viris et mulieribus: sed non clericis, propter scandalum. Non autem talis poenitentia debet imponi nisi pro peccato *quod totam commoverit urbem.*

Publica autem et non solemnis, quae in facie Ecclesiae fit sed non cum solemnitate praedicta, sicut peregrinatio per mundum cum baculo cubitali, haec potest iterari; et a simplici sacerdote iniungi; et potest etiam clerico imponi.

Quandoque tamen solemnis ponitur publica. Et secundum hoc, auctoritates quaedam varie loquuntur de solemni.

AD PRIMUM ergo dicendum quod mulier habet comam in signum subiectionis, non autem vir. Et ideo non competit ut in poenitentia mulieri coma deponatur, sicut viro.

AD SECUNDUM dicendum quod, quamvis in eodem genere peccati clericus plus peccet quam laicus, tamen non iniungitur ei poenitentia solemnis, ne ordo veniat in contemptum. Unde defertur non personae, sed ordini.

AD TERTIUM dicendum quod magna peccata indigent maiori cautela ad sui curationem. Et ideo iniunctio poenitentiae solemnis, quae non nisi pro gravissimis peccatis fit, soli episcopo reservatur.

church. He then orders the ministers to put them out of the church, and the clergy follow reciting the responsory: *in the sweat of your brow*, etc. Every year on the day of our Lord's Supper they are brought back into the church by their priests, and there shall they be until the octave day of Easter, without, however, being admitted to Communion or to the kiss of peace. This shall be done every year as long as entrance into the church is forbidden to them. The final reconciliation is reserved to the bishop, who alone can impose solemn penance (Cap. lxiv, dist. 50).

This penance can be imposed on men and women; but not on clerics, for fear of scandal. Nor ought such a penance to be imposed except for a crime *which has disturbed the whole of the city.*

On the other hand, public but not solemn penance is that which is done in the presence of the Church, but without the foregoing solemnity, such as a pilgrimage throughout the world with a staff. A penance of this kind can be repeated, and can be imposed by a mere priest, even on a cleric.

Sometimes, however, a solemn penance is taken to signify a public one: so that authorities speak of solemn penance in different senses.

REPLY OBJ. 1: The woman's hair is a sign of her subjection while a man's is not. Hence it is not proper for a woman to put aside her hair when doing penance, as it is for a man.

REPLY OBJ. 2: Although in the same kind of sin, a cleric offends more grievously than a layman, yet a solemn penance is not imposed on him, lest his orders should be an object of contempt. Thus deference is given not to the person but to his orders.

REPLY OBJ. 3: Grave sins need great care in their cure. Hence the imposition of a solemn penance, which is only applied for the most grievous sins, is reserved to the bishop.

Question 29

The Sacrament of Extreme Unction

Post hoc considerandum est de sacramento extremae unctionis. De quo quinque videnda sunt: primo, de essentialibus ipsius, et de eius institutione; secundo, de effectu ipsius; tertio, de ministro ipsius; quarto, de eo cui conferri debet, et in qua parte; quinto, de eius iteratione.

Circa primum quaeruntur novem.

Primo: utrum extrema unctio sit aeramentum.

Secundo: utrum sit unum sacramentum.

Tertio: utrum hoc sacramentum fuerit a Christo institutum.

Quarto: utrum oleum olivae sit conveniens materia huius sacramenti.

Quinto: utrum oporteat oleum esse consecratum.

Sexto: utrum huius sacramenti materia debeat per episcopum consecrari.

Septimo: utrum hoc sacramentum habeat aliquam formam.

Octavo: utrum forma huius sacramenti debeat proferri per orationem deprecativam.

Nono: utrum praedicta oratio sit competens forma huius sacramenti.

We must now consider the sacrament of extreme unction, in respect of which five points have to be considered: (1) Its essentials and institution; (2) Its effect; (3) Its minister; (4) On whom should it be conferred and in what parts; (5) Its repetition.

Under the first head there are nine points of inquiry:

(1) Whether extreme unction is a sacrament?

(2) Whether it is one sacrament?

(3) Whether this sacrament was instituted by Christ?

(4) Whether olive oil is a suitable matter for this sacrament?

(5) Whether the oil ought to be consecrated?

(6) Whether the matter of this sacrament should be consecrated by a bishop?

(7) Whether this sacrament has any form?

(8) Whether the form of this sacrament should take the shape of a deprecatory phrase?

(9) Whether this is a suitable form for this sacrament?

Article 1

Whether Extreme Unction is a Sacrament?

Ad primum sic proceditur. Videtur quod extrema unctio non sit sacramentum. Quia sicut oleum assumitur ad infirmos, ita ad catechumenos. Sed unctio quae fit oleo ad catechumenos non est sacramentum. Ergo nec extrema unctio, quae fit oleo ad infirmos.

Praeterea, sacramenta veteris legis fuerunt signa sacramentorum novae legis. Sed extrema unctio non habuit aliquam figuram in veteri lege. Ergo non est sacramentum novae legis.

Praeterea, secundum Dionysium, omne sacramentum vel ad *purgandum* est, vel ad *illuminandum*, vel ad *perficiendum*. Sed extrema unctio non ponitur nec ad purgandum nec ad illuminandum, quia hoc soli baptismo attribuitur: nec ad perficiendum, quia hoc, secundum ipsum Dionysium, pertinet ad chrisma et ad Eucharistiam. Ergo extrema unctio non est sacramentum.

Sed contra: Sacramenta Ecclesiae sufficienter subveniunt defectibus hominum secundum quemlibet sta-

Objection 1: It would seem that extreme unction is not a sacrament. For just as oil is used on sick people, so is it on catechumens. But anointing of catechumens with oil is not a sacrament. Therefore, neither is extreme unction, which is done with oil for the sick.

Obj. 2: Further, the sacraments of the old law were figures of the sacraments of the new law. But there was no figure of extreme unction in the old law. Therefore, it is not a sacrament of the new law.

Obj. 3: Further, according to Dionysius (*On the Ecclesiastical Hierarchies* 3.5) every sacrament aims at either *cleansing*, or *enlightening*, or *perfecting*. Now extreme unction does not aim at cleansing or enlightening, for this is ascribed to baptism alone, or perfecting, for according to Dionysius (*On the Ecclesiastical Hierarchies* 2), this belongs to confirmation and the Eucharist. Therefore, extreme unction is not a sacrament.

On the contrary, The sacraments of the Church supply man's defects sufficiently with respect to every state

tum. Sed exeuntibus non subvenit aliud quam extrema unctio. Ergo ipsa est sacramentum.

PRAETEREA, sacramenta nihil aliud sunt quam quaedam spirituales medicinae. Sed extrema unctio est quaedam spiritualis medicina: quia valet ad remissionem peccatorum, ut habetur Iac. 5. Ergo est sacramentum.

RESPONDEO dicendum quod in his quae Ecclesia visibiliter, operatur, quaedam sunt sacramenta, ut baptismus; quaedam sacramentalia, ut exorcismus. Quorum est haec differentia, quia sacramentum dicitur illa actio Ecclesiae quae attingit ad effectum principaliter intentum in administratione sacramentorum: sed sacramentale dicitur illa actio quae, quamvis non pertingat ad illum effectum, tamen ordinatur aliquo modo ad illam actionem principalem. Effectus autem intentus in administratione sacramentorum est curatio morbi peccati: Isaiae 27, *hic est omnis fructus, ut tollatur peccatum.* Et ideo, cum ad hunc effectum pertingat extrema unctio, ut ex verbis Iacobi patet; nec ordinetur ad aliud sacramentum quasi ei annexum: constat quod extrema unctio non est sacramentale, sed sacramentum.

AD PRIMUM ergo dicendum quod oleum, quo catechumeni inunguntur, sua unctione non perducit ad peccati remissionem, quia hoc ad baptismum pertinet: sed aliquo modo ad baptismum disponit. Et ideo non est sacramentum illa unctio, sicut unctio extrema.

AD SECUNDUM dicendum quod hoc sacramentum immediate hominem ad gloriam disponit, cum exeuntibus a corpore detur. Et quia in veteri lege non erat adhuc tempus perveniendi ad gloriam, quia *neminem ad perfectum adduxit lex*; ideo illud sacramentum ibi praefigurari non debuit per aliquod sacramentum sibi respondens, sicut per figuram eiusdem generis. Quamvis per figuras remotas aliquo modo figuratum sit in omnibus curationibus quae leguntur in veteri lege.

AD TERTIUM dicendum quod Dionysius non facit aliquam mentionem de extrema unctione, sicut nec de poenitentia nec de matrimonio, quia ipse non intendit determinare de sacramentis nisi quatenus per ea innotescere potest ecclesiasticae hierarchiae ordinata dispositio quantum ad ministros et actiones ministrorum et recipientes. Tamen, cum per extremam unctionem aliquis consequatur gratiam et remissionem peccatorum, non est dubium quod habet vim illuminativam et purgativam, sicut baptismus: quamvis non ita plenam.

of life. Now nothing other than extreme unction does this for those who are departing from this life. Therefore, it is a sacrament.

FURTHER, The sacraments are neither more nor less than spiritual remedies. Now extreme unction is a spiritual remedy, since it avails for the remission of sins, according to James 5:15. Therefore, it is a sacrament.

I ANSWER THAT, Among the visible operations of the Church, some are sacraments, as baptism, and some are sacramentals, as exorcism. The difference between these is that a sacrament is an action of the Church that reaches to the principal effect intended in the administration of the sacraments, whereas a sacramental is an action which, though it does not reach to that effect, is nevertheless directed towards that principal action. Now the effect intended in the administration of the sacraments is the healing of the disease of sin: wherefore it is written: *this is all the fruit, that the sin . . . should be taken away* (Isa 27:9). Since, then, extreme unction reaches to this effect, as is clear from the words of James, and is not ordained to any other sacrament as an accessory to it, it is evident that extreme unction is not a sacramental but a sacrament.

REPLY OBJ. 1: The oil with which catechumens are anointed does not convey the remission of sins to them by its unction, for that belongs to baptism. It does, however, dispose them to receive baptism, as stated above (III, Q. 71, A. 31). Hence that unction is not a sacrament as extreme unction is.

REPLY OBJ. 2: This sacrament prepares man for glory immediately, since it is given to those who are departing from this life. And as, under the old law, it was not yet time to enter into glory, because *the law brought nobody to perfection* (Heb 7:19), so this sacrament had not to be foreshadowed therein by some corresponding sacrament, as by a figure of the same kind. Nevertheless, it was somewhat foreshadowed remotely by all the healings related in the Old Testament.

REPLY OBJ. 3: Dionysius makes no mention of extreme unction, as neither of penance, nor of matrimony, because he had no intention to decide any question about the sacraments save insofar as they serve to illustrate the orderly disposition of the ecclesiastical hierarchy, as regards the ministers, their actions, and the recipients. Nevertheless, since extreme unction confers grace and remission of sins, there is no doubt that it possesses an enlightening and cleansing power, even as baptism, though not so plentifully.

Article 2

Whether Extreme Unction is One Sacrament?

AD SECUNDUM SIC PROCEDITUR. Videtur quod extrema unctio non sit unum sacramentum. Quia unitas rei est ex sua materia et ex sua forma: cum ex eodem habeat res esse et unitatem. Sed forma huius sacramenti frequenter iteratur, etiam eadem vice; et materia pluries inuncto adhibetur, secundum diversas partes. Ergo non est unum sacramentum.

PRAETEREA, ipsa unctio est sacramentum, ridiculum enim est dicere quod oleum sit sacramentum. Sed sunt plures unctiones. Ergo sunt plura sacramenta.

PRAETEREA, unum sacramentum ab uno ministro perfici debet. Sed in aliquo casu extrema unctio non potest perfici ab uno ministro: sicut si post primam unctionem factam sacerdos moriatur; tunc enim alius sacerdos debet ulterius procedere. Ergo extrema unctio non est sacramentum unum.

SED CONTRA: Sicut se habet immersio ad baptismum ita se habet unctio ad hoc sacramentum. Sed plures immersiones sunt unum sacramentum baptismi. Ergo et plures unctiones sunt unum sacramentum.

PRAETEREA, si non esset unum sacramentum, tunc, facta prima unctione, non oporteret ad perfectionem sacramenti quod fieret secunda: quia quodlibet sacramentum per se habet esse perfectum. Sed hoc falsum est. Ergo est unum sacramentum.

RESPONDEO dicendum quod unum numero, per se loquendo, dicitur tripliciter. Uno modo, sicut indivisibile, quod nec actu nec potentia est plura: ut punctus et unitas. Alio modo, sicut continuum, quod quidem actu est unum, sed plura potentia: ut linea. Tertio modo, sicut perfectum aliquod quod ex pluribus partibus constituitur: ut domus, quae est multa quodammodo in actu, sed illa multa conveniunt in aliquo uno. Et hoc modo quodlibet sacramentum dicitur unum: inquantum multa quae sunt in uno sacramento, adunantur ad unum significandum vel causandum. Quia sacramentum significando causat. Et ideo, quando una actio sufficit ad perfectam significationem, unitas sacramenti consistit in illa actione tantum: sicut patet in confirmatione. Quando autem significatio sacramenti potest esse et in una et in multis actionibus, tunc sacramentum perfici potest et una actione et pluribus: sicut baptismus una immersione et tribus, quia ablutio, quae significatur in baptismo, potest esse per unam immersionem et per multas. Quando autem perfecta significatio non potest esse nisi per plures actiones, tunc plures actiones sunt de perfectione sacramenti: sicut patet in Eucharistia, quia refectio corporalis, quae significat spiritualem, non potest esse nisi per cibum et potum. Et similiter est in hoc sacramento: quia

OBJECTION 1: It would seem that extreme unction is not one sacrament, because the oneness of a thing depends on its matter and form, since being and oneness are derived from the same source. Now the form of this sacrament is said several times during the one administration, and the matter is applied to the person anointed in respect of various parts of his body. Therefore, it is not one sacrament.

OBJ. 2: Further, the unction itself is a sacrament, for it would be absurd to say that the oil is a sacrament. But there are several unctions. Therefore, there are several sacraments.

OBJ. 3: Further, one sacrament should be performed by one minister. But the case might occur that extreme unction could not be conferred by one minister: thus if the priest die after the first unction, another priest would have to proceed with the others. Therefore, extreme unction is not one sacrament.

ON THE CONTRARY, As immersion is to baptism, so is unction to this sacrament. But several immersions are but one sacrament of baptism. Therefore, the several unctions in extreme unction are also one sacrament.

FURTHER, If it were not one sacrament, then after the first unction, it would not be essential for the perfection of the sacrament that the second unction should be performed, since each sacrament has perfect being of itself. But that is not true. Therefore, it is one sacrament.

I ANSWER THAT, Strictly speaking, a thing is one numerically in three ways. First, as something indivisible, which is neither actually nor potentially several, such a point and unity. Second, as something continuous, which is actually one, but potentially several, such as a line. Third, as something complete that is composed of several parts, such as a house, which is, in a way, several things even actually, although those several things go together towards making one. In this way, each sacrament is said to be one thing inasmuch as the many things which are contained in one sacrament are united together for the purpose of signifying or causing one thing, because a sacrament is a sign of the effect it produces. Hence when one action suffices for a perfect signification, the unity of the sacrament consists in that action only, as may be seen in confirmation. When, however, the signification of the sacrament can be both in one and in several actions, then the sacrament can be complete both in one and in several actions, even as baptism in one immersion and in three, since the washing which is signified in baptism can be completed by one immersion and by several. But when the perfect signification cannot be expressed except by means of several actions, then these several actions are essential for the perfection of the sacrament, as is exemplified in the Eucharist, for the refreshment of the

curatio interiorum vulnerum non potest perfecte significari nisi per appositionem medicinae ad diversas vulnerum radices. Et ideo plures actiones sunt de perfectione huius sacramenti.

Ad primum ergo dicendum quod unitas totius perfecta non tollitur per diversitatem materiae aut formae quae est iri partibus totius. Sicut constat quod non est eadem materia carnis et ossis, ex quibus constituitur unus homo, nec eadem forma. Et similiter in sacramento Eucharistiae, et in hoc sacramento, pluralitas materiae et formae unitatem sacramenti non tollit.

Ad secundum dicendum quod, quamvis illae actiones sint plures simpliciter, tamen uniuntur in una perfecta actione, quae est unctio omnium exteriorum sensuum, quibus hauritur morbus interior.

Ad tertium dicendum quod, quamvis in Eucharistia, si post consecrationem panis moriatur sacerdos, alius sacerdos possit procedere ad consecrationem vini, incipiens ubi ille dimisit, vel etiam incipere a capite supra aliam materiam; tamen in extrema unctione non potest a capite incipere, sed debet semper procedere: quia unctio in eadem parte facta tantum valet ac si consecraretur bis eadem hostia, quod nullo modo faciendum est. Nec tamen ministrorum pluralitas tollit unitatem huius sacramenti: quia instrumentaliter tantum operantur; mutatio autem martellorum non tollit unitatem operationis fabri.

body which signifies that of the soul can only be attained by means of meat and drink. It is the same in this sacrament, because the healing of the internal wounds cannot be perfectly signified save by the application of the remedy to the various sources of the wounds. Hence several actions are essential to the perfection of this sacrament.

Reply Obj. 1: The unity of a complete whole is not destroyed by reason of a diversity of matter or form in the parts of that whole. Thus it is evident that there is neither the same matter nor the same form in the flesh and in the bones of which one man is composed. In like manner, both in the sacrament of the Eucharist and in this sacrament, the diversity of matter and form does not destroy the unity of the sacrament.

Reply Obj. 2: Although those actions are several simply, yet they are united together in one complete action, namely, the anointing of all the external senses, whence arises the internal malady.

Reply Obj. 3: Although, in the Eucharist, if the priest should die after the consecration of the bread, another priest can go on with the consecration of the wine beginning where the other left off, or can begin over again with fresh matter, in extreme unction he cannot begin over again, but should always go on, because to anoint the same part a second time would produce as much effect as if one were to consecrate a host a second time, which ought by no means to be done. Nor does the plurality of ministers destroy the unity of this sacrament, because they only act as instruments, and the unity of a smith's work is not destroyed by his using several hammers.

Article 3

Whether This Sacrament Was Instituted by Christ?

Ad tertium sic proceditur. Videtur quod hoc sacramentum non fuerit institutum a Christo. Quia de institutione: sacramentorum quae Christus instituit, fit mentio in Evangelio: sicut de Eucharistia et baptismo. Sed nulla fit mentio de extrema unctione. Ergo non est a Christo instituta.

Praeterea, Magister expresse dicit, in Quarto, 23 dist., quod est institutum ab Apostolis. Ergo ipse Christus per se non instituit.

Praeterea, sacramentum Eucharistiae, quod Christus instituit, etiam ipse per se exhibuit. Sed hoc sacramentum ipse nulli exhibuit. Ergo per se non instituit.

Sed contra: Sacramenta novae legis sunt digniora quam sacramenta veteris legis. Sed omnia sacramenta veteris legis sunt ab ipso Deo instituta. Ergo, multo for-

Objection 1: It would seem that this sacrament was not instituted by Christ. For mention is made in the Gospel of the institution of those sacraments which Christ instituted, for instance, the Eucharist and baptism. But no mention is made of extreme unction. Therefore, it was not instituted by Christ.

Obj. 2: Further, the Master says explicitly (*Sentences* IV, D. 23) that it was instituted by the apostles. Therefore, Christ did not institute it himself.

Obj. 3: Further, Christ showed forth the sacraments which he instituted, as in the case of the Eucharist and baptism. But he did not bestow this sacrament on anyone. Therefore, he did not institute it himself.

On the contrary, The sacraments of the new law are more excellent than those of the old law. But all the sacraments of the old law were instituted by God. Therefore,

tius, omnia sacramenta novae legis habent institutionem ab ipso Christo.

PRAETEREA, eiusdem est instituere, et statutum removere. Sed Ecclesia, quae iri successoribus Apostolorum habet eandem auctoritatem quam Apostoli habuerunt, non posset auferre sacramentum extremae unctionis. Ergo Apostoli non instituerunt, sed ipse Christus.

RESPONDEO dicendum quod circa hoc est duplex opinio. Quidam dicunt quod sacramentum illud, et confirmationis, Christus non instituit per se, sed Apostolis instituendum dimisit: quia haec duo, propter plenitudinem gratiae quae in eis confertur, non potuerunt ante Spiritus Sancti missionem plenissimam institui. Unde sunt ita sacramenta novae legis quod in veteri figuram non habuerunt. Sed haec ratio non multum cogit: quia, sicut Christus ante passionem promisit plenam Spiritus Sancti missionem, ita potuit instituere huiusmodi sacramentum.

Et ideo alii dicunt quod omnia sacramenta Christus instituit per seipsum: sed quaedam per seipsum promulgavit, quae sunt maioris difficultatis ad credendum; quaedam autem Apostolis promulganda reservavit, sicut extremam unctionem et confirmationem. Et haec opinio pro tanto videtur probabilior, quia sacramenta ad fundamentum legis pertinent; et ideo ad legislatorem pertinet eorum institutio. Et iterum, quia ex institutione efficaciam habent: quae eis non nisi divinitus inest.

AD PRIMUM ergo dicendum quod multa Dominus fecit et dixit quae in Evangeliis non continentur. Illa enim praecipue curaverunt Evangelistae tradere quae ad necessitatem salutis et Ecclesiae dispositionem pertinent. Et ideo potius institutionem baptismi et poenitentiae et Eucharistiae et ordinis factam a Christo narraverunt quam sacramentum extremae unctionis, quae neque est de necessitate salutis, neque ad dispositionem sive distinctionem Ecclesiae pertinet. Tamen etiam de olei unctione fit mentio in Evangelio, Marc. 6, ubi dicitur quod Apostoli *oleo ungebant infirmos*.

AD SECUNDUM dicendum quod Magister dicit ab Apostolis institutum, quia per doctrinam Apostolorum nobis promulgata est eius institutio.

AD TERTIUM dicendum quod Christus non exhibuit aliquod sacramentum nisi quod ipse accepit in exemplum. Accipere autem poenitentiam et extremam unctionem sibi non competebat: quia sine peccato erat. Et ideo ipse non exhibuit.

much more do all the sacraments of the new law owe their institution to Christ himself.

FURTHER, To make an institution and to remove it belongs to the same authority. Now the Church, who enjoys the same authority in the successors of the apostles as the apostles themselves possessed, cannot do away with the sacrament of extreme unction. Therefore, the apostles did not institute it, but Christ himself.

I ANSWER THAT, There are two opinions on this point. For some hold that this sacrament and confirmation were not instituted by Christ himself, but were left by him to be instituted by the apostles; for the reason that these two sacraments, on account of the plenitude of grace conferred in them, could not be instituted before the mission of the Holy Spirit in perfect plenitude. Hence they are sacraments of the new law in such a way as not to be foreshadowed in the old law. But this argument is not very cogent, since, just as Christ, before his Passion, promised the mission of the Holy Spirit in his plenitude, so could he institute these sacraments.

Wherefore others hold that Christ himself instituted all the sacraments, but that he himself promulgated some which present greater difficulty to our belief, while he reserved some to be promulgated by the apostles, such as extreme unction and confirmation. This opinion seems much the more probable, as the sacraments belong to the foundation of the law, wherefore their institution pertains to the lawgiver; besides, they derive their efficacy from their institution, which efficacy is given them by God alone.

REPLY OBJ. 1: Our Lord did and said many things which are not related in the Gospel. For the Evangelists particularly took care to hand down those things that pertain to the necessity of salvation and the order of ecclesiastical disposition. Hence they related the institution by Christ of baptism, penance, the Eucharist and orders, rather than of extreme unction and confirmation, which are not necessary for salvation, nor do they concern the building or division of the Church. As a matter of fact, however, an anointing done by the apostles is mentioned in the Gospel where it is said that they *anointed the sick with oil* (Mark 6:13).

REPLY OBJ. 2: The Master says it was instituted by the apostles because its institution was made known to us by the teaching of the apostles.

REPLY OBJ. 3: Christ did not show forth any sacrament except such as he received by way of example: but he could not be a recipient of penance and extreme unction, since there was no sin in him; hence he did not show them forth.

Article 4

Whether Olive Oil Is a Suitable Matter for This Sacrament?

AD QUARTUM SIC PROCEDITUR. Videtur quod oleum olivae non sit conveniens materia huius sacramenti. Quia hoc sacramentum immediate ad incorruptionem ordinat. Sed incorruptio significatur per balsamum, quod in chrismate ponitur. Ergo chrisma esset convenientior materia huius sacramenti.

PRAETEREA, hoc sacramentum est spiritualis medicatio. Sed spiritualis medicatio per vini appositionem significatur: sicut patet Luc. 10, in parabola de sauciato. Ergo vinum esset convenientior materia huius sacramenti.

PRAETEREA, ubi est maius periculum, ibi debet esse commune remedium. Sed oleum non est commune remedium: quia non invenitur in qualibet terra. Ergo, cum hoc sacramentum detur exeuntibus, qui sunt in maximo periculo, videtur quod oleum olivae non sit materia conveniens,

SED CONTRA: Est quod Iac. 5 oleum materia huius sacramenti determinatur. Sed oleum proprie non dicitur nisi oleum olivae. Ergo hoc est materia huius sacramenti.

PRAETEREA, spiritualis sanatio per olei inunctionem significatur: ut patet Isaiae 1, ubi dicitur: *plaga tumens non est curata medicamine neque fota oleo*. Ergo conveniens materia huius sacramenti est oleum.

RESPONDEO dicendum quod spiritualis curatio quae in fine adhibetur, debet esse perfecta, quia post eam alia non relinquitur; et lenis, ut spes, quae exeuntibus est maxime necessaria, non frangatur, sed foveatur. Oleum autem lenitivum est, et penetrativum usque ad intima, et etiam diffusivum. Et ideo quantum ad utrumque praedictorum est conveniens materia huius sacramenti. Et quia oleum principaliter nominatur olivae liquor, cum alii liquores ex similitudine ad ipsum olei nomen accipiant; ideo oleum olivae etiam debet esse quod assumitur in materia huius sacramenti.

AD PRIMUM ego dicendum quod incorruptio gloriae est res non contenta in hoc sacramento: nec oportet quod tali rei significatio materiae respondeat. Unde non oportet quod balsamum ponatur materia huius sacramenti: quia balsamum, propter odorem, pertinet ad *bonitatem famae*, qua de cetero non indigent, propter se, exeuntes; sed indigent tantum *nitore conscientiae*, qui in oleo significatur.

AD SECUNDUM dicendum quod vinum sanat mordicando: sed oleum leniendo. Et ideo curatio per vinum magis pertinet ad poenitentiam quam ad hoc sacramentum.

AD TERTIUM dicendum quod oleum olivae, quamvis non ubique crescat, tamen de facili potest ad quemli-

OBJECTION 1: It would seem that olive oil is not a suitable matter for this sacrament. For this sacrament is ordained immediately to the state of incorruption. Now incorruption is signified by balsam, which is contained in chrism. Therefore, chrism would be a more suitable matter for this sacrament.

OBJ. 2: Further, this sacrament is a spiritual healing. Now spiritual healing is signified by the use of wine, as may be gathered from the parable of the wounded man (Luke 10:34). Therefore, wine would be a more suitable matter for this sacrament.

OBJ. 3: Further, where there is the greater danger, the remedy should be a common one. But olive oil is not a common remedy, since the olive is not found in every country. Therefore, since this sacrament is given to the dying, who are in the greatest danger, it seems that olive oil is not a suitable matter.

ON THE CONTRARY, Oil is appointed (Jas 5:14) as the matter of this sacrament. Now, oil is properly said only of olive oil. Therefore, this is the matter of this sacrament.

FURTHER, Spiritual healing is signified by anointing with oil, as is evident from where we read: *swelling sores are not . . . dressed nor fomented with oil* (Isa 1:6). Therefore, the suitable matter for this sacrament is oil.

I ANSWER THAT, The spiritual healing which is given at the end of life ought to be complete, since there is no other to follow; it ought also to be gentle, lest hope, of which the dying stand in utmost need, be shattered rather than fostered. Now oil has a softening effect, both penetrating to the very heart of a thing and easily spreading over it. Hence in both the foregoing respects it is a suitable matter for this sacrament. And since oil is, above all, the name of the liquid extract of olives, for other liquids are only called oil from their likeness to it, it follows that olive oil is the matter which should be employed in this sacrament.

REPLY OBJ. 1: The incorruption of glory is something not contained in this sacrament: and there is no need for the matter to signify such a thing. Hence it is not necessary for balsam to be included in the matter of this sacrament, because on account of its fragrance it is indicative *of a good name*, which is no longer necessary, for its own sake, to those who are dying; they need only a *clear conscience*, which is signified by oil.

REPLY OBJ. 2: Wine heals by its roughness, oil by its softness; therefore, healing with wine pertains to penance rather than to this sacrament.

REPLY OBJ. 3: Though olive oil is not produced everywhere, yet it can easily be transported from one place to an-

bet locum transferri. Et praeterea hoc sacramentum non est tantae necessitatis quod exeuntes sine hoc sacramento non possint salutem consequi.

other. Moreover, this sacrament is not so necessary that the dying cannot obtain salvation without it.

Article 5

Whether the Oil Ought To Be Consecrated?

AD QUINTUM SIC PROCEDITUR. Videtur quod non oporteat esse oleum consecratum. Quia hoc sacramentum habet unam sanctificationem in usu per formam verborum. Ergo superfluit alia sanctificatio, si ad materiam ipsius fiat.

PRAETEREA, sacramenta habent efficaciam et significationem in ipsa materia. Sed significatio effectus huius sacramenti competit oleo ex naturali proprietate, efficacia autem ex institutione divina. Ergo non est necessaria aliqua sanctificatio materiae.

PRAETEREA, baptismus est perfectius sacramentum quam extrema unctio. Sed in baptismo non praeexigitur materiae sanctificatio, quantum est de necessitate sacramenti. Ergo nec in extrema unctione.

SED CONTRA est, quia in omnibus aliis unctionibus est materia consecrata prius. Ergo, cum hoc sacramentum sit quaedam unctio, requirit materiam consecratam.

RESPONDEO dicendum quod quidam dicunt quod oleum simplex est materia huius sacramenti; et in ipsa sanctificatione olei, quae est per episcopum, perficitur sacramentum. Sed hoc patet esse falsum ex his quae de Eucharistia dicta sunt, ubi ostensum est quod solum illud sacramentum consistit in consecratione materiae.

Et ideo dicendum quod hoc sacramentum consistit in ipsa unctione, sicut baptismus in ablutione: et materia huius sacramenti est oleum sanctificatum. Potest autem triplex ratio assignari quare exigitur materiae sanctificatio in hoc sacramento et in quibusdam aliis. Prima est, quia omnis efficacia sacramentorum a Christo descendit. Et ideo sacramenta illa quibus ipse est usus, habent efficaciam ex ipso usu suo: sicut *tactu suae carnis vim regenerativam contulit aquis*. Sed hoc sacramento non est usus, nec aliqua corporali unctione. Et ideo in omnibus unctionibus requiritur sanctificatio materiae.

Secunda causa est propter plenitudinem gratiae, quae confertur non solum ut tollat culpam, sed etiam reliquias et infirmitatem corporis.

Tertia est ex hoc quod effectus eius corporalis, scilicet sanatio, non causatur ex materiae naturali proprietate. Et ideo oportet quod haec efficacia sibi per sanctificationem detur.

OBJECTION 1: It would seem that the oil need not be consecrated, because there is a sanctification in the use of this sacrament through the form of words. Therefore, another sanctification is superfluous if it be applied to the matter.

OBJ. 2: Further, the efficacy and signification of the sacraments are in their very matter. But the signification of the effect of this sacrament is suitable to oil on account of its natural properties, and the efficacy of it is due to the divine institution. Therefore, its matter does not need to be sanctified.

OBJ. 3: Further, baptism is a more perfect sacrament than extreme unction. But so far as the essentials of the sacrament are concerned, the baptismal matter needs no sanctification. Neither, therefore, does the matter of extreme unction need to be sanctified.

ON THE CONTRARY, In all other anointings the matter is previously consecrated. Therefore, since this sacrament is an anointing, it requires consecrated matter.

I ANSWER THAT, Some hold that mere oil is the matter of this sacrament, and that the sacrament itself is perfected in the consecration of the oil by the bishop. But this is clearly false, since we proved when treating of the Eucharist that that sacrament alone consists in the consecration of the matter (Q. 2, A. 1).

We must therefore say that this sacrament consists in the anointing itself, just as baptism consists in the washing, and that the matter of this sacrament is consecrated oil. Three reasons may be assigned why consecrated matter is needed in this sacrament and in certain others. The first is that all sacramental efficacy is derived from Christ: therefore, those sacraments which he himself used derived their efficacy from his use of them, even as *by the contact of his flesh, he bestowed the force of regeneration on the waters*. But he did not use this sacrament, nor any bodily anointing; therefore, in all anointings a consecrated matter is required.

The second reason is that this sacrament confers a plenitude of grace, so as to take away not only sin, but also the remnants of sin and bodily sickness.

The third reason is that its effect on the body, namely, bodily health, is not caused by a natural property of the matter. Therefore, it has to derive this efficacy from being consecrated.

AD PRIMUM ergo dicendum quod prima sanctificatio est materiae secundum se: sed secunda magis pertinet ad usum ipsius, secundum quod est actu conferens effectum suum. Et ideo neuter superfluit: quia etiam instrumenta efficaciam accipiunt ab artifice et dum fiunt, et dum ad actum applicantur.

AD SECUNDUM dicendum quod illa efficacia quae est ex institutione sacramenti, applicatur huic materiae per sanctificationem.

AD TERTIUM patet solutio ex dictis.

REPLY OBJ. 1: The first consecration sanctifies the matter in itself, but the second regards rather the use of the matter considered as actually producing its effect. Hence neither is superfluous, because instruments also receive their efficacy from the craftsman both when they are made and when they are used for action.

REPLY OBJ. 2: The efficacy which the sacrament derives from its institution is applied to this particular matter when it is consecrated.

THE REPLY to the third objection is gathered from what has been said.

Article 6

Whether the Matter of This Sacrament Ought To Be Consecrated by a Bishop?

AD SEXTUM PROCEDITUR. Videtur quod non oporteat materiam huius sacramenti esse consecratam per episcopum. Quia dignior est consecratio materiae in sacramento Eucharistiae quam in hoc sacramento. Sed in Eucharistia materiam sacerdos potest consecrare. Ergo et in hoc sacramento.

PRAETEREA, in operibus corporalibus ars dignior nunquam praeparat materiam inferiori: quia dignior est quae utitur quam quae materiam praeparat, ut dicitur II *Physic.* Sed episcopus est supra sacerdotem. Ergo non praeparat materiam in illo sacramento quo sacerdos utitur. Sed sacerdos dispensat hoc sacramentum, ut dicetur. Ergo consecratio materiae ad episcopum non pertinet.

SED CONTRA est quia in aliis unctionibus etiam materia per episcopum consecratur. Ergo ita debet esse in ista.

RESPONDEO dicendum quod minister sacramenti non propria virtute effectum sacramenti inducit ut principale agens, sed per efficaciam sacramenti quod dispensat. Quae quidem efficacia primo est a Christo, et ab ipso in alios descendit ordinate: scilicet in populum mediantibus ministris, qui sacramenta dispensant; et in ministros inferiores mediantibus superioribus qui materiam sanctificant. Et ideo in omnibus sacramentis quae indigent materia sanctificata, prima sanctificatio materiae fit per episcopum, et usus quandoque per sacerdotem, ut ostendatur sacerdotalis potestas ab episcopali derivata: secundum illud Psalmi: *sicut unguentum in capite, quod prius descendit in barbam*, deinde usque ad *oram vestimenti.*

AD PRIMUM ergo dicendum quod sacramentum Eucharistiae consistit in ipsa materiae sanctificatione, non autem in usu. Et ideo, proprie loquendo, illud quod est materia sacramenti, non est quid consecratum. Unde

OBJECTION 1: It would seem that the matter of this sacrament need not be consecrated by a bishop. For the consecration of the Eucharistic elements surpasses that of the matter in this sacrament. But a priest can consecrate the matter in the Eucharist. Therefore, he can do so in this sacrament also.

OBJ. 2: Further, in material works the higher art never prepares the matter for the lower, because the art which applies the matter is more excellent than that which prepares it, as stated in *Physics* 2.25. Now a bishop is above a priest. Therefore, he does not prepare the matter of a sacrament which is applied by a priest. But a priest dispenses this sacrament, as we shall state further on (Q. 31). Therefore, the consecration of the matter does not belong to a bishop.

ON THE CONTRARY, In other anointings also the matter is consecrated by a bishop. Therefore, the same applies to this.

I ANSWER THAT, The minister of a sacrament produces the effect, not by his own power, as though he were the principal agent, but by the efficacy of the sacrament which he dispenses. This efficacy comes, in the first place, from Christ, and from him flows down to others in due order, namely, to the people through the medium of the ministers who dispense the sacraments, and to the lower ministers through the medium of the higher ministers who sanctify the matter. Therefore, in all the sacraments which require a sanctified matter, the first consecration of the matter is performed by a bishop, and the application thereof sometimes by a priest, in order to show that the priest's power is derived from the bishop's, according to Psalm 132:2: *like the precious ointment on the head*, that is, Christ, *that ran down upon the beard of Aaron first*, and then *to the skirt of his garment.*

REPLY OBJ. 1: The sacrament of the Eucharist consists in the consecration of the matter and not in its use. Consequently, strictly speaking, that which is the matter of the sacrament is not a consecrated thing. Hence no consecra-

non praeexigitur aliqua sanctificatio circa materiam per episcopum facta. Sed exigitur sanctificatio altaris et huiusmodi, et etiam ipsius sacerdotis, quae non nisi per episcopum fieri potest. Unde in illo etiam sacramento ostenditur potestas sacerdotalis ab episcopo derivata: ut Dionysius dicit. Ideo autem illam consecrationem materiae potest facere sacerdos quae est in se sacramentum, et non illam quae ut sacramentale quoddam ordinatur ad sacramentum, quod consistit in usu fidelium, quia quantum ad corpus Christi verum nullus ordo est supra sacerdotium, sed quantum ad corpus Christi mysticum episcopalis: ordo est supra sacerdotalem, ut infra dicetur.

Ad secundum dicendum quod materia sacramenti non est talis materia ut in qua fiat aliquid per eum qui ea utitur, sicut est in artibus mechanicis: sed ut cuius virtute aliquid fiat, et sic percipiat aliquid de ratione causae agentis, inquantum est instrumentum quoddam divinae operationis. Et ideo oportet quod a superiori arte vel potestate talis virtus materiae acquiratur. Quia in causis agentibus, quanto aliquod agens est prius, tanto est perfectius: in causis autem pure materialibus, quanto materia est prior, tanto imperfectior.

tion of the matter by a bishop is required beforehand. But the altar and suchlike things, even the priest himself, need to be consecrated, all of which can be done by none but a bishop: so that in this sacrament also, the priest's power is shown to be derived from the bishop's, as Dionysius observes (*On the Ecclesiastical Hierarchies* 3). The reason why a priest can perform that consecration of matter which is a sacrament by itself, and not that which, as a sacramental, is directed to a sacrament consisting in something used by the faithful, is that in respect of Christ's true body no order is above the priesthood, whereas, in respect of Christ's mystic body, the episcopate is above the priesthood, as we shall state further on (Q. 40, A. 4).

Reply Obj. 2: The sacramental matter is not one that is made into something else by him that uses it, as occurs in the mechanical arts: it is one in virtue of which something is done, so that it partakes somewhat of the nature of an efficient cause insofar as it is the instrument of a divine operation. Hence the matter needs to acquire this virtue from a higher art or power, since among efficient causes, the more prior the cause, the more perfect it is, whereas in material causes, the more prior the matter, the more imperfect it is.

Article 7

Whether This Sacrament Has a Form?

Ad septimum sic proceditur. Videtur quo hoc sacramentum non habeat aliquam formam cum enim efficacia sacramentorum sit a institutione et item a forma, oportet quo forma tradatur ab ipso qui sacramentum instituit. Sed forma huius sacramenti non inveniti tradita neque a Christo neque ab Apostoli. Ergo hoc sacramentum non habet aliqua formam.

Praeterea, ea quae sunt de necessita sacramenti, observantur eodem modo apud omnes. Sed nihil magis est de necessitate sacramenti habentis formam quam ipsa forma. Ergo cum non sit aliqua, forma communiter observata ab omnibus in hoc sacramento, quia diversi diversis verbis utuntur, videtur quod hoc sacramentum, non habeat aliquam formam.

Praeterea, in baptismo non requiritur forma nisi ad sanctificationem materiae, qua est *aqua verbo vitae diluendis criminibus sanctificata*. Sed hoc sacramentum habet materiam prius sanctificatam. Non ergo indiget aliqua forma verborum.

Sed contra: Est quod Magister dicit quod omne sacramentum novae legis consistit in rebus et in verbis. Verba autem sunt formi sacramenti. Cum ergo hoc sit sacramentum novae legis, videtur quod habeat formam.

Objection 1: It would seem that this sacrament has no form. For since the efficacy of the sacraments is derived from their institution, as also from their form, the latter must be appointed by the institutor of the sacrament. But there is no account of the form of this sacrament being instituted either by Christ or by the apostles. Therefore, this sacrament has no form.

Obj. 2: Further, whatever is essential to a sacrament is observed everywhere in the same way. Now nothing is so essential to a sacrament that has a form, as that very form. Therefore, as in this sacrament there is no form commonly used by all, since various words are in use, it seems that this sacrament has no form.

Obj. 3: Further, in baptism no form is needed except for the sanctification of the matter, because the water is *sanctified by the word of life so as to wash sin away*, as Hugh states (*On the Sacraments* 2). Now the matter of this sacrament is already consecrated. Therefore, it needs no form of words.

On the contrary, The Master says (*Sentences* IV, D. 1) that every sacrament of the new law consists in things and words. Now the words are the sacramental form. Therefore, since this is a sacrament of the new law, it seems that it has a form.

PRAETEREA, ad hoc est ritus universali Ecclesiae, quae quibusdam verbis utitur in collatione huius sacramenti.

RESPONDEO dicendum quod quidam dixerunt quod nulla forma est de necessitate huius sacramenti. Sed hoc videtur derogare effectu huius sacramenti. Quia omne sacramentum efficit significando. Significatio autem materiae non determinatur ad effectum determinatum cum ad multa se possit habere, nisi per formam verborum. Et ideo in omnibus sacramentis novae legis, quae *efficiunt quod figurant*, oportet esse et res et verba. Et praeterea Iacobus totam vim sacramenti huius videtur constituere in *oratione*, quae est forma huius sacramenti, ut dicetur. Et ideo praedicta opinio praesumptuosa videtur, et erronea. Et propter hoc dicendum, sicut communiter dicitur, quod habet formam determinatam, sicut et alia sacramenta.

AD PRIMUM ergo dicendum quod sacra Scriptura omnibus communiter proponitur. Et ideo forma baptismi, qui ab omnibus dari potest, debet in sacra Scriptura exprimi. Et similiter forma Eucharistiae, quae exprimit sacramenti illius fidem, quae est de necessitate salutis. Sed formae aliorum sacramentorum non inveniuntur in Scriptura traditae, sed Ecclesia ex traditione Apostolorum habet, qui a Domino acceperunt: ut dicit Apostolus, I Cor. ii: *ego accepi a Domino quod, et tradidi vobis.*

AD SECUNDUM dicendum quod illa verba quae sunt de essentia formae, scilicet oratio deprecativa, ab omnibus dicuntur; sed alia, quae sunt de bene esse, non observantur ab omnibus.

AD TERTIUM dicendum quod materia baptismi habet quandam sanctificationem per se ex ipso tactu carnis Salvatoris: sed ex forma verborum accipit sanctificationem actu sanctificantem. Et similiter, post sanctificationem materiae huius sacramenti secundum se, requiritur sanctificatio in usu, per quam actu sanctificet.

FURTHER, This is confirmed by the rite of the universal Church, who uses certain words in the bestowal of this sacrament.

I ANSWER THAT, Some have held that no form is essential to this sacrament. This, however, seems derogatory to the effect of this sacrament, since every sacrament signifies its effect. Now the matter is indifferent as regards its effect, and consequently cannot be determined to any particular effect save by the form of words. Hence in all the sacraments of the new law, since *they effect what they signify*, there must be things and words. Moreover, James 5:14–15 seems to ascribe the whole force of this sacrament to *prayer*, which is the form thereof, as we shall state further on (ad 2; A. 8–9). Wherefore the foregoing opinion seems presumptuous and erroneous; and for that reason we should hold with the common opinion that this, like all the other sacraments, has a fixed form.

REPLY OBJ. 1: Sacred Scripture is proposed to all alike: and so, the form of baptism, which can be conferred by all, should be expressed in Sacred Scripture, as also the form of the Eucharist, which in regard to that sacrament, expresses faith which is necessary for salvation. Now the forms of the other sacraments are not contained in Sacred Scripture, but were handed down to the Church by the apostles, who received them from our Lord, as the Apostle declares: *for I have received of the Lord that which also I delivered to you* (1 Cor 11:23).

REPLY OBJ. 2: The words which are essential to the form, that is, the prayer of deprecation, are said by all; but other words which pertain to the well-being of it are not said by all.

REPLY OBJ. 3: The matter of baptism has a certain sanctification of its own from the very contact of our Savior's flesh; but the form of words sanctifies it so that it has a sanctifying force. In like manner, when the matter of this sacrament has been sanctified in itself, it requires sanctification in its use, so that it may sanctify actually.

Article 8

Whether the Form of This Sacrament Should Be Expressed by Way of Assertion or of Petition?

AD OCTAVUM SIC PROCEDITUR. Videtur quod forma huius sacramenti debeat proferri per orationem indicativam, et non deprecativam. Quia sacramenta novae legis habent certum effectum. Sed certitudo effectus non exprimitur in formis sacramentorum nisi per orationem indicativam, cum dicitur, *hoc est corpus meum*, vel, *ego te baptizo*. Ergo debet esse forma huius sacramenti oratio indicativa.

PRAETEREA, in formis sacramentorum debet exprimi intentio ministri, quae requiritur ad sacramentum.

OBJECTION 1: It would seem that the form of this sacrament should be expressed by way of assertion rather than of petition. For all the sacraments of the new law have a sure effect. But sureness of effect is not expressed in the sacramental forms except by way of assertion, as when we say: *this is my body* or *I baptize you*. Therefore, the form of this sacrament should be expressed as an assertion.

OBJ. 2: Further, the intention of the minister should be expressed in the sacramental forms because it is essential to

Sed intentio conferendi sacramentum non exprimitur nisi per orationem indicativam. Ergo, etc.

PRAETEREA, in quibusdam ecclesiis dicuntur huiusmodi verba in collatione huius sacramenti: *ungo hos oculos oleo sanctificato in nomine Patris*, etc.: et hoc est conforme aliis formis sacramentorum. Ergo videtur quod in hoc consistat forma huius sacramenti.

SED CONTRA: Illud quod est forma sacramenti, ab omnibus oportet quod servetur. Sed verba praedicta non dicuntur secundum consuetudinem omnium ecclesiarum, sed tantum verba deprecativa, scilicet: *per istam sanctam unctionem, et suam piis simam misericordiam, indulgeat tibi Dominus quidquid deliquisti per visum*, etc. Ergo forma huius sacramenti est oratio deprecativa.

PRAETEREA, hoc videtur ex verbis Iacobi, qui attribuit efficaciam huius sacramenti orationi: *oratio fidei*, inquit, *sanabit infirmum*. Ergo, cum efficacia sacramenti sit ex forma, videtur quod forma huius sacramenti sit praedicta oratio.

RESPONDEO dicendum quod oratio deprecativa est forma huius sacramenti: ut patet per verba Iacobi; et ex usu Romanae Ecclesiae quae solum verbis deprecativis utitur in collatione huius sacramenti. Cuius ratio multiplex assignatur.

Primo, quia suscipiens sacramentum hoc est viribus propriis destitutus. Unde indiget orationibus sublevari.

Secundo, quia datur exeuntibus, qui iam desinunt esse de foro Ecclesiae, et in solius Dei manu requiescunt. Unde ei per orationem committuntur.

Tertio, quia hoc sacramentum non habet aliquem effectum qui semper ex operatione ministri consequatur, omnibus quae sunt de essentia sacramenti rite peractis: sicut character in baptismo et confirmatione; et transubstantiatio in Eucharistia; et remissio peccati in poenitentia, existente contritione, quae est de essentia sacramenti poenitentiae, non autem de essentia huius sacramenti. Et ideo in hoc sacramento non potest esse forma indicativi modi, sicut in praedictis sacramentis.

AD PRIMUM ergo dicendum quod hoc sacramentum, sicut et praedicta, quantum est de se habet certitudinem, sed potest impediri ex fictione recipientis, etiam si sacramento se subiiciat per intentionem, quod nullum effectum consequatur. Et propter hoc non est simile de hoc et de aliis sacramentis, in quibus semper aliquis effectus consequitur.

AD SECUNDUM dicendum quod per ipsum actum, qui ponitur in forma, scilicet, *per istam sanctam unctionem*, satis exprimitur intentio.

AD TERTIUM dicendum quod verba illa indicativi modi quae secundum morem quorundam praemittun-

the sacrament. But the intention of conferring a sacrament is not expressed except by an assertion. Therefore, etc.

OBJ. 3: Further, in some churches the following words are said in the conferring of this sacrament: *I anoint these eyes with consecrated oil in the name of the Father*, etc., which is in keeping with the forms of the other sacraments. Therefore, it seems that such is the form of this sacrament.

ON THE CONTRARY, The form of a sacrament must be one that is observed everywhere. Now the words employed according to the custom of all the churches are not those quoted above, but take the form of a petition, namely: *through this holy unction, and his most tender mercy, may the Lord pardon you whatever sins you have committed by sight*, etc. Therefore, the form of this sacrament is expressed as a petition.

FURTHER, This seems to follow from the words of James, who ascribes the effect of this sacrament to prayer: *the prayer of faith*, he says, *shall save the sick man* (5:15). Since, then, a sacrament takes its efficacy from its form, it seems that the form of this sacrament is expressed as a petition.

I ANSWER THAT, The form of this sacrament is expressed by way of a petition, as appears from the words of James, and from the custom of the Roman Church, who uses nothing other than words of supplication in conferring this sacrament. Several reasons are assigned for this:

first, because the recipient of this sacrament is deprived of his strength, so that he needs to be helped by prayers;

second, because it is given to the dying, who are on the point of quitting the courts of the Church, and rest in the hands of God alone, for which reason they are committed to him by prayer;

third, because the effect of this sacrament is not such that it always results from the minister's prayer, even when all essentials have been duly observed, as is the case with the character in baptism and confirmation, transubstantiation in the Eucharist, and remission of sin in penance (given contrition), which remission is essential to the sacrament of penance but not to this sacrament. Consequently, the form of this sacrament cannot be expressed in the indicative mood, as in the sacraments just mentioned.

REPLY OBJ. 1: This sacrament, like the others mentioned, considered in itself, is sure of its effect; yet this effect can be hindered through the insincerity of the recipient (though by his intention he submits to the sacrament), so that he receives no effect at all. Hence there is no parity between this sacrament and the others in which some effect always ensues.

REPLY OBJ. 2: The intention is sufficiently expressed by the act which is mentioned in the form, namely, *by this holy unction.*

REPLY OBJ. 3: These words in the indicative mood which some are wont to say before the prayer are not the

tur orationi, non sunt forma huius sacramenti: sed sunt quaedam dispositio ad formam, inquantum intentio ministri determinatur ad actum illum per illa verba.

sacramental form, but are a preparation for the form, insofar as they determine the intention of the minister.

Article 9

Whether the Foregoing Prayer Is a Suitable Form for This Sacrament?

Ad nonum sic proceditur. Videtur quod praedicta oratio non sit competens forma huius sacramenti. Quia in formis aliorum sacramentorum fit mentio de materia: sicut patet in confirmatione. Quae non fit in verbis praedictis. Ergo non est conveniens forma.

Praeterea, sicut effectus huius sacramenti provenit in nos per misericordiam divinam, ita et aliorum sacramentorum. Sed in formis aliorum sacramentorum non fit mentio de misericordia divina, sed magis de Trinitate et de passione. Ergo similiter debet esse hic.

Praeterea, duplex effectus huius sacramenti in littera ponitur. Sed in verbis praedictis non fit mentio nisi de uno, scilicet de remissione peccatorum: non autem de corporali sanatione, ad quam Iacobus ordinat orationem fidei, dicens: *oratio fidei sanabit infirmum*. Ergo forma praedicta est incompetens.

Respondeo dicendum quod praedicta oratio est competens forma huius sacramenti. Quia tangit sacramentum, in hoc quod dicitur, *per istam sanctam unctionem*; et illud quod operatur in sacramento, scilicet *divinam misericordiam*; et effectum, scilicet *remissionem peccatorum*.

Ad primum ergo dicendum quod materia huius sacramenti potest intelligi per actum unctionis: non autem materia confirmationis per actum in forma expressum. Et ideo non est simile.

Ad secundum dicendum quod misericordia respicit miseriam. Et quia hoc sacramentum datur in statu miseriae, scilicet infirmitatis, ideo potius hic quam in aliis fit mentio de misericordia.

Ad tertium dicendum quod in forma debet exprimi effectus principalis, et qui semper inducitur ex sacramento nisi sit defectus ex parte recipientis. Non autem talis effectus est corporalis sanitas, ut ex dictis patet, quamvis quandoque sequatur. Ratione cuius Iacobus hunc effectum attribuit orationi, quae est forma huius sacramenti.

Objection 1: It would seem that the foregoing prayer is not a suitable form for this sacrament. For in the forms of the other sacraments mention is made of the matter, for instance in confirmation, whereas this is not done in the aforesaid words. Therefore, it is not a suitable form.

Obj. 2: Further, just as the effect of this sacrament is bestowed on us by the mercy of God, so are the effects of the other sacraments. But mention is made in the forms of the other sacraments, not of the divine mercy, but rather of the Trinity and of the Passion. Therefore, the same should be done here.

Obj. 3: Further, this sacrament is stated in the text (*Sentences* IV, D. 23) to have a twofold effect. But in the foregoing words mention is made of only one effect, viz. the remission of sins, and not of the healing of the body to which end James directs the prayer of faith to be made: *the prayer of faith shall save the sick man* (Jas 5:15). Therefore, the above form is unsuitable.

I answer that, The prayer given above (A. 8) is a suitable form for this sacrament, for it includes the sacrament by the words: *by this holy unction*, and that which works in the sacrament, namely, *the mercy of God*, and the effect, namely, *remission of sins*.

Reply Obj. 1: The matter of this sacrament may be understood in the act of anointing, whereas the matter of confirmation cannot be implied by the act expressed in the form. And therefore it is not similiar.

Reply Obj. 2: The object of mercy is misery: and because this sacrament is given when we are in a state of misery, i.e., of sickness, mention of mercy is made in this rather than in other sacraments.

Reply Obj. 3: The form should contain mention of the principal effect, and of that which always ensues in virtue of the sacrament, unless there be something lacking on the part of the recipient. Now bodily health is not an effect of this kind, as we shall state further on (Q. 30, A. 1–2), though it does ensue at times, for which reason James ascribes this effect to the prayer which is the form of this sacrament.

Question 30

The Effect of Extreme Unction

Deinde considerandum est de effectu huius sacramenti.

Circa quod quaeruntur tria.

Primo: utrum extrema unctio valeat ad remissionem peccatorum.

Secundo: utrum sanitas corporalis sit effectus huius sacramenti.

Tertio: utrum hoc sacramentum characterem imprimat.

We must now consider the effect of this sacrament.

Under this head there are three points of inquiry:

(1) Whether extreme unction avails for the remission of sins?

(2) Whether bodily health is an effect of this sacrament?

(3) Whether this sacrament imprints a character?

Article 1

Whether Extreme Unction Avails for the Remission of Sins?

Ad primum sic proceditur. Videtur quod extrema unctio non valeat ad remissionem peccatorum. Ad hoc enim quod per unum potest effici, aliud non exigitur. Sed in eo qui extremam unctionem accipit, requiritur poenitentia ad peccatorum remissionem. Ergo per extremam unctionem non dimittuntur peccata.

Praeterea, in peccato non sunt nisi tria: macula, reatus poenae, et reliquiae peccati. Sed per extremam unctionem non remittitur peccatum quoad maculam sine contritione: quae etiam sine unctione remittit. Nec iterum quoad poenarii: quia adhuc, si convalescat, tenetur perficere satisfactionem iniunctam. Nec quoad reliquias culpae: quia adhuc remanent dispositiones ex actibus praecedentibus relictae, ut patet post convalescentiam. Ergo nullo modo per extremam unctionem fit peccatorum remissio.

Praeterea, remissio peccatorum non fit successive, sed in instanti. Sed extrema unctio non fit tota simul: quia plures unctiones requiruntur. Ergo eius effectus non est remissio peccatorum.

Sed contra: Est quod dicitur Iac. 5: *si in peccatis est, dimittentur ei.*

Praeterea, omne sacramentum novae legis gratiam confert. Sed per gratiam fit remissio peccatorum. Ergo extrema unctio, cum sit sacramentum novae legis, operatur ad remissionem peccati.

Respondeo dicendum quod quodlibet sacramentum est institutum principaliter ad unum effectum, quamvis etiam alios ex consequenti inducere possit. Et quia sacramentum efficit quod figurat, ideo ex ipsa significatione sacramenti debet accipi eius principalis effectus. Adhibetur autem hoc sacramentum secundum

Objection 1: It would seem that extreme unction does not avail for the remission of sins. For when a thing can be attained by one means, no other is needed. Now repentance is required in the recipient of extreme unction for the remission of his sins. Therefore, sins are not remitted by extreme unction.

Obj. 2: Further, there are no more than three things in sin: the stain, the debt of punishment, and the remnants of sin. Now extreme unction does not remit the stain without contrition, and this remits sin even without unction; nor does it remit the punishment, for if the recipient recover, he is still bound to fulfill the satisfaction enjoined; nor does it take away the remnants of sin, since the dispositions remaining from preceding acts still remain, as may easily be seen after recovery. Therefore, remission of sins is by no means the effect of extreme unction.

Obj. 3: Further, remission of sins takes place, not successively, but instantaneously. On the other hand, extreme unction is not done all at once, since several anointings are required. Therefore, the remission of sins is not its effect.

On the contrary, James 5:15 says: *if he is in sins, they shall be forgiven him.*

Further, Every sacrament of the new law confers grace. Now grace effects the forgiveness of sins. Therefore, since extreme unction is a sacrament of the new law, its effect is the remission of sins.

I answer that, Each sacrament was instituted for the purpose of one principal effect, though it may, in consequence, produce other effects besides. And since a sacrament causes what it signifies, the principal effect of a sacrament must be gathered from its signification. Now this sacrament is conferred by way of a kind of medicament,

modum cuiusdam medicationis: sicut baptismus per modum ablutionis. Medicina autem est ad pellendum infirmitatem. Unde principaliter hoc sacramentum est institutum ad sanandum infirmitatem peccati: ut sicut baptismus est quaedam spiritualis regeneratio, et poenitentia quaedam spiritualis suscitatio, ita et extrema unctio est quaedam spiritualis sanatio vel medicatio. Sicut autem corporalis medicatio praesupponit corporalem vitam in medicato, ita spiritualis spiritualem. Et ideo hoc sacramentum non datur contra defectus quibus spiritualis vita tollitur, scilicet contra peccatum originale et mortale: sed contra illos defectus quibus homo spiritualiter infirmatur, ut non habeat perfectum vigorem ad actus vitae gratiae vel gloriae. Et hic defectus nihil est aliud quam quaedam debilitas et ineptitudo quae in nobis relinquitur ex peccato actuali vel originali. Et contra hanc debilitatem homo roboratur per hoc sacramentum.

Sed quia hoc robur gratia facit, quae secum non compatitur peccatum, ideo ex consequenti, si invenit peccatum aliquod, vel mortale vel veniale, quoad culpam, tollit ipsum, dummodo non ponatur obex ex parte recipientis: sicut etiam de Eucharistia et confirmatione supra dictum est. Et ideo etiam Iacobus de remissione peccati conditionaliter loquitur, dicens: *si in peccatis sit, dimittentur ei* quoad culpam. Non enim semper delet peccatum, quia non semper invenit; sed semper remittit quoad debilitatem praedictam, quam quidam *reliquias peccati* dicunt.

Quidam vero dicunt quod principaliter est institutum contra veniale: quod quidem non potest, dum haec vita agitur, perfecte curari; et ideo sacramentum exeuntium, specialiter contra veniale ordinatur. Sed hoc non videtur verum. Quia poenitentia sufficienter, etiam in vita, delet venialia quoad culpam. Quod autem non potest evitari post peractam poenitentiam, non aufert praecedenti poenitentiae suum effectum. Et iterum hoc pertinet ad debilitatem praedictam.

Unde dicendum quod principalis effectus huius sacramenti est remissio peccatorum quoad reliquias peccati; et ex consequenti etiam quoad culpam, si eam inveniat.

AD PRIMUM ergo dicendum quod, quamvis effectus principalis alicuius sacramenti possit haberi sine actuali perceptione illius sacramenti, vel sine sacramento, vel per aliud sacramentum ex consequenti; nunquam tamen haberi potest sine proposito illius sacramenti. Et ideo, quia poenitentia est principaliter instituta contra actualem culpam, quodcumque aliud sacramentum actualem culpam deleat ex consequenti, non excludit necessitatem poenitentiae.

AD SECUNDUM dicendum quod extrema unctio aliquo modo quantum ad illa tria remittit peccatum. Quamvis enim culpa quoad maculam sine contritio-

even as baptism is conferred by way of washing, and the purpose of a medicament is to expel sickness. Hence the chief object of the institution of this sacrament is to cure the sickness of sin. Therefore, just as baptism is a spiritual regeneration, and penance a spiritual resurrection, so extreme unction is a spiritual healing or cure. Now just as a bodily cure presupposes bodily life in the one who is cured, so does a spiritual cure presuppose spiritual life. Hence this sacrament is not an antidote to those defects which deprive man of spiritual life, namely, original and mortal sin, but is a remedy for such defects as weaken man spiritually, so as to deprive him of perfect vigor for acts of the life of grace or of glory; which defects consist in nothing else but a certain weakness and unfitness, the result in us of actual or original sin, against which weakness man is strengthened by this sacrament.

Since, however, this strength is given by grace, which is incompatible with sin, it follows that in consequence, if it finds any sin, either mortal or venial, it removes it as far as the guilt is concerned, provided there be no obstacle on the part of the recipient; just as we have stated to be the case with regard to the Eucharist and confirmation (III, Q. 73, A. 7; III, Q. 79, A. 3). Hence, too, James speaks of the remission of sin as being conditional, for he says: *if he be in sins, they shall be forgiven him*, viz. as to the guilt. Now, it does not always blot out sin, since it does not always find any: but it always remits in respect of the aforesaid weakness which some call the *remnants of sin*.

Some, however, maintain that it is instituted chiefly as a remedy for venial sin which cannot be cured perfectly in this lifetime: for which reason the sacrament of the dying is ordained specially against venial sin. But this does not seem to be true, since penance also blots out venial sins sufficiently during this life as to their guilt, and that we cannot avoid them after doing penance does not cancel the effect of the previous penance; moreover, this is part of the weakness mentioned above.

Consequently, we must say that the principal effect of this sacrament is the remission of sin as to its remnants, and, consequently, even as to its guilt, if it find it.

REPLY OBJ. 1: Although the principal effect of a sacrament can be obtained without actually receiving that sacrament (either without any sacrament at all, or indirectly by means of some other sacrament), yet it never can be obtained without the purpose of receiving that sacrament. And so, since penance was instituted chiefly against actual sin, whichever other sacrament may blot out sin indirectly, it does not exclude the necessity of penance.

REPLY OBJ. 2: Extreme unction remits sin in some way as to those three things. For, although the stain of sin is not washed out without contrition, yet this sacrament, by the

ne non dimittatur, tamen hoc sacramentum per gratiam quam infundit, facit quod ille motus liberi arbitrii in peccatum sit contritio: sicut etiam in Eucharistia et confirmatione potest accidere. Similiter etiam et reatum poenae temporalis diminuit: sed ex consequenti, inquantum debilitatem tollit, quia eandem poenam levius portat fortis quam debilis. Unde non oportet quod propter hoc minuatur satisfactionis mensura. Reliquiae autem peccati non dicuntur hic dispositiones ex actibus relictae, quae sunt quidam habitus inchoati: sed quaedam spiritualis debilitas in ipsa mente existens, qua sublata, et eisdem habitibus vel dispositionibus manentibus, non ita potest inclinari mens ad peccatum.

AD TERTIUM dicendum quod, quando sunt multae actiones ordinatae ad unum effectum, ultima est formalis respectu omnium praecedentium, et agit in virtute earum. Et ideo in ultima unctione gratia infunditur, quae effectum sacramento praebet.

grace which it bestows, makes the movement of the free will towards sin to be one of contrition, just as may occur in the Eucharist and confirmation. Again it diminishes the debt of temporal punishment; and this indirectly, inasmuch as it takes away weakness, for a strong man bears the same punishment more easily than a weak man. Hence it does not follow that the measure of satisfaction is diminished. As to the remnants of sin, they do not mean here those dispositions which result from acts, and are inchoate habits so to speak, but a certain spiritual debility in the mind, which debility being removed, though such like habits or dispositions remain, the mind is not so easily prone to sin.

REPLY OBJ. 3: When many actions are ordained to one effect, the last is formal with respect to all the others that precede, and acts by virtue of them: wherefore by the last anointing is infused grace which gives the sacrament its effect.

Article 2

Whether Bodily Health is an Effect of This Sacrament?

AD SECUNDUM SIC PROCEDITUR. Videtur quod sanitas corporalis non sit effectus huius sacramenti. Omne enim sacramentum est medicina spiritualis. Sed spiritualis medicina ad spiritualem sanitatem ordinatur, sicut corporalis ad corporalem. Ergo sanitas corporalis non est effectus huius sacramenti.

PRAETEREA, sacramentum semper habet effectum suum in eo qui non fictus accedit. Sed quandoque non sanatur corporaliter suscipiens hoc sacramentum, quantumcumque devotus accipiat. Ergo sanitas corporalis non est effectus eius.

PRAETEREA, efficacia huius sacramenti nobis ostenditur Iac. 5. Sed ibi non attribuitur sanatio effectus unctioni, sed orationi: dicit enim: *oratio fidei, sanabit infirmum*. Ergo corporalis sanatio non est effectus huius sacramenti.

SED CONTRA: Operatio Ecclesiae habet maiorem efficaciam post Christi passionem quam ante. Sed ante oleo inuncti per Apostolos sanabantur: ut patet Marc. 6. Ergo et nunc habet effectum in corporali sanatione.

PRAETEREA, sacramenta significando efficiunt. Sed baptismus per ablutionem corporalem, quam exterius facit, significat et efficit spiritualem. Ergo et extrema unctio per sanationem corporalem, quam exterius efficit, significat et causat spiritualem.

RESPONDEO dicendum quod, sicut baptismus per ablutionem corporalem facit spiritualem emundationem

OBJECTION 1: It would seem that bodily health is not an effect of this sacrament. For every sacrament is a spiritual remedy. Now a spiritual remedy is ordained to spiritual health, just as a bodily remedy is ordained to health of the body. Therefore, bodily health is not an effect of this sacrament.

OBJ. 2: Further, the sacraments always produce their effect in those who approach them in the proper dispositions. Now sometimes the recipient of this sacrament does not receive bodily health, no matter how devoutly he receives it. Therefore, bodily health is not its effect.

OBJ. 3: Further, the efficacy of this sacrament is shown to us in the fifth chapter of James. Now healing is ascribed there as the effect, not of the anointing, but of the prayer, for he says: *the prayer of faith shall save the sick man* (Jas 5:15). Therefore, bodily healing is not an effect of this sacrament.

ON THE CONTRARY, The operation of the Church is more efficacious since Christ's Passion than before. Now, before the Passion, those whom the apostles anointed with oil were healed (Mark 6:13). Therefore, unction has its effect now in healing bodies.

FURTHER, The sacraments produce their effect by signifying it. Now baptism signifies and effects a spiritual washing, through the bodily washing in which it consists outwardly. Therefore, extreme unction signifies and causes a spiritual healing through the bodily healing which it effects externally.

I ANSWER THAT, Just as baptism causes a spiritual cleansing from spiritual stains by means of a bodily wash-

a maculis spiritualibus, ita hoc sacramentum per medicationem sacramentalem exteriorem facit sanationem interiorem: et sicut ablutio baptismi habet effectum corporalis ablutionis, quia etiam corporalem mundationem habet; ita extrema unctio habet effectum corporalis medicationis, scilicet corporalem sanationem. Sed haec est differentia, quia corporalis ablutio ex ipsa naturali proprietate elementi facit corporalem mundationem: et ideo semper eam facit. Sed extrema unctio non facit corporalem sanationem ex proprietate naturali materiae, sed virtute divina, quae rationabiliter operatur. Et quia ratio operans nunquam inducit secundarium effectum nisi secundum quod expedit ad principalem, ideo ex hoc sacramento non sequitur corporalis sanatio semper, sed quando expedit ad spiritualem sanationem. Et tunc semper eam inducit: dummodo non sit impedimentum ex parte recipientis.

Ad primum ergo dicendum quod obiectio illa probat quod corporalis sanitas non sit effectus principalis huius sacramenti; et hoc verum est.

Ad secundum patet solutio ex dictis.

Ad tertium dicendum quod oratio illa est forma huius sacramenti, ut dicetur. Et ideo hoc sacramentum, et sua forma, habet efficaciam, quantum est de se, ad sanationem corporalem.

ing, so this sacrament causes an inward healing by means of an outward sacramental healing: and even as the baptismal washing has the effect of a bodily washing, since it effects even a bodily cleansing, so too, extreme unction has the effect of a bodily remedy, namely, a healing of the body. But there is a difference, for the bodily washing causes a bodily cleansing by a natural property of the bodily element, and consequently always causes it, whereas extreme unction causes a bodily healing not by a natural property of the matter, but by the divine power, which works reasonably. And since reasonable working never produces a secondary effect except insofar as it is required for the principal effect, it follows that a bodily healing does not always ensue from this sacrament, but only when it is requisite for the spiritual healing: and then it produces it always, provided there be no obstacle on the part of the recipient.

Reply Obj. 1: This objection proves that bodily health is not the principal effect of this sacrament: and this is true.

The reply to the second objection is clear from what has been said above (cf. Q. 29, A. 8).

Reply Obj. 3: This prayer is the form of this sacrament, as stated above (Q. 29, A. 8–9). Hence, so far as its form is concerned, this sacrament derives from it its efficacy in healing the body.

Article 3

Whether This Sacrament Imprints a Character?

Ad tertium sic proceditur. Videtur quod hoc sacramentum imprimat characterem. Character enim signum distinctivum est. Sed, sicut baptizatus distinguitur a non baptizato, ita unctus a non uncto. Ergo, sicut baptismus imprimit characterem, ita et extrema unctio.

Praeterea, in ordinis et confirmationis sacramentis est unctio, sicut in hoc sacramento. Sed in illis imprimitur character. Ergo et in isto.

Praeterea, in omni sacramento est aliquid quod est res tantum, et aliquid quod est sacramentum tantum, et aliquid quod est res et sacramentum. Sed non potest aliquid assignari in hoc sacramento quod sit res et sacramentum nisi character. Ergo in hoc sacramento imprimitur character.

Sed contra: Nullum sacramentum imprimens characterem iteratur. Hoc autem iteratur, ut dicetur. Ergo non imprimit characterem.

Objection 1: It would seem that this sacrament imprints a character. For a character is a distinctive sign. Now just as one who is baptized is distinguished from one who is not, so is one who is anointed from one who is not. Therefore, just as baptism imprints a character, so does extreme unction.

Obj. 2: Further, there is an anointing in the sacraments of holy orders and confirmation, as there is in this sacrament. But a character is imprinted in those sacraments. Therefore, a character is imprinted in this one also.

Obj. 3: Further, every sacrament contains something that is a reality only, something that is a sacrament only, and something that is both reality and sacrament. Now nothing in this sacrament can be assigned as both reality and sacrament except a character. Therefore, in this sacrament a character is imprinted.

On the contrary, No sacrament that imprints a character is repeated. But this sacrament is repeated, as we shall state further on (Q. 33). Therefore, it does not imprint a character.

Praeterea, distinctio quae fit secundum characterem sacramentalem, est distinctio eorum qui sunt in praesenti Ecclesia. Sed extrema unctio confertur ei qui exit de praesenti Ecclesia. Ergo non decet quod in eo character conferatur.

Respondeo dicendum quod character non imprimitur nisi in illis sacramentis in quibus homo ad aliquod sacrum deputatur. Sed hoc sacramentum est solum in remedium, et non deputatur per ipsum homo ad aliquod sacrum agendum vel suscipiendum. Et ideo non imprimitur in eo character.

Ad primum ergo dicendum quod character facit distinctionem statuum quantum ad ea quae in Ecclesia sunt agenda; et talem distinctionem homo non habet ab aliis per hoc quod ipse est inunctus.

Ad secundum dicendum quod unctio quae fit in ordine et confirmatione, est unctio consecrationis, qua homo deputatur ad aliquod sacrum. Sed haec unctio est unctio medicationis. Et ideo non est simile.

Ad tertium dicendum quod in hoc sacramento res et sacramentum non est character, sed quaedam interior devotio, quae est spiritualis unctio.

Further, A sacramental character causes a distinction among those who are in the present Church. But extreme unction is given to one who is departing from the present Church. Therefore, it would not be fitting for it to imprint a character.

I answer that, A character is not imprinted except in those sacraments whereby man is deputed to some sacred duty. Now this sacrament is for no other purpose than a remedy, and man is not deputed thereby to do or receive anything holy. Therefore, it does not imprint a character.

Reply Obj. 1: A character marks a distinction of states with regard to duties which have to be performed in the Church, a distinction which a man does not receive by being anointed.

Reply Obj. 2: The unction of orders and confirmation is the unction of consecration whereby a man is deputed to some sacred duty, whereas this unction is remedial. Hence the comparison fails.

Reply Obj. 3: In this sacrament, that which is both reality and sacrament is not a character, but a certain inward devotion which is a kind of spiritual anointing.

QUESTION 31

THE MINISTER OF EXTREME UNCTION

Deinde considerandum est de administratione huius sacramenti.

Circa quod tria quaeruntur.

Primo: utrum laicus possit hoc sacramentum conferre.

Secundo: utrum diaconus.

Tertio: utrum solus episcopus.

We must now consider the minister of this sacrament.

Under this head there are three points of inquiry:

(1) Whether a layman can confer this sacrament?

(2) Whether a deacon can?

(3) Whether none but a bishop can confer it?

Article 1

Whether a Layman Can Confer This Sacrament?

AD PRIMUM SIC PROCEDITUR. Videtur quod etiam laicus possit hoc sacramentum conferre. Quia hoc sacramentum habet efficaciam ex oratione, ut Iacobus dicit. Sed oratio laici quandoque est a Deo accepta sicut sacerdotis. Ergo potest hoc sacramentum conferre.

PRAETEREA, de quibusdam Patribus in Aegypto legitur quod oleum ad infirmos transmittebant et sanabantur. Et similiter de beata Genovefa quod oleo infirmos ungebat. Ergo hoc sacramentum potest conferri etiam a laicis.

SED CONTRA est quia in hoc sacramento fit remissio peccatorum. Sed laici non habent potestatem dimittendi peccata. Ergo, etc.

RESPONDEO dicendum quod, secundum Dionysium, in *Eccles. Hier.*, sunt quidam exercentes actiones hierarchicas, et quidam recipientes tantum, qui sunt laici. Et ideo nullius sacramenti dispensatio laico ex officio competit: sed quod baptizare possunt in causa necessitatis est divina dispensatione factum, ut nulli regenerationis spiritualis facultas desit.

AD PRIMUM ergo dicendum quod oratio illa non fit a sacerdote in persona sua, quia, cum sit quandoque peccator, non esset exaudibilis: sed fit in persona totius Ecclesiae, in cuius persona orare potest quasi persona publica; non autem laicus, qui persona privata est.

AD SECUNDUM dicendum quod illae unctiones non erant sacramentales: sed ex quadam devotione recipientium talem unctionem, et meritis unguentium vel oleum mittentium, consequebatur effectus sanitatis corporalis per *gratiam sanitatum*, non per gratiam sacramentalem.

OBJECTION 1: It would seem that even a layman can confer this sacrament. For this sacrament derives its efficacy from prayer, as James declares (Jas 5:15). But a layman's prayer is sometimes as acceptable to God as a priest's. Therefore, he can confer this sacrament.

OBJ. 2: Further, we read of certain fathers in Egypt that they sent the oil to the sick, and that these were healed. It is also related of the Blessed Genevieve that she anointed the sick with oil. Therefore, this sacrament can be conferred even by lay people.

ON THE CONTRARY, Remission of sins is given in this sacrament. But laymen have not the power to forgive sins. Therefore, etc.

I ANSWER THAT, According to Dionysius (*On the Ecclesiastical Hierarchies* 5) there are some who exercise hierarchical actions, and some who are recipients only. Hence laymen are officially incompetent to dispense any sacrament: and that they can baptize in cases of necessity is due to the divine dispensation, in order that no one may be deprived of spiritual regeneration.

REPLY OBJ. 1: This prayer is not said by the priest in his own person, for since sometimes he is in sin, he would not in that case be heard. But it is said in the person of the whole Church, in whose person he can pray as a public official, whereas a layman cannot, for he is a private individual.

REPLY OBJ. 2: These unctions were not sacramental. It was due to the devotion of the recipients of the unction, and to the merits of those who anointed them, that they procured the effects of bodily health through the *grace of healing* (1 Cor 12:9), but not through sacramental grace.

Article 2

Whether Deacons Can Confer This Sacrament?

AD SECUNDUM SIC PROCEDITUR. Videtur quod diaconi possint hoc sacramentum conferre. Quia secundum Dionysium, diaconi habent virtutem *purgativam*. Sed hoc sacramentum est institutum ad purgandum tantum ab infirmitate mentis et corporis. Ergo diaconi possunt conferre.

PRAETEREA, dignius sacramentum est baptismus quam hoc de quo hic agimus. Sed diaconi possunt baptizare: ut patet de beato Laurentio. Ergo possunt hoc sacramentum conferre.

SED CONTRA est quod dicitur Iac. 5: *inducat presbyteros Ecclesiae.*

RESPONDEO dicendum quod diaconus habet vim purgativam tantum, non illuminativam. Unde, cum illuminatio fiat per gratiam, nullum sacramentum in quo gratia confertur, diaconus potest dare ex officio. Et ideo nec hoc: cum in eo gratia conferatur.

AD PRIMUM ergo dicendum quod hoc sacramentum illuminando per gratiae collationem purgat. Et ideo diacono eius collatio non competit.

AD SECUNDUM dicendum quod hoc sacramentum non est necessitatis, sicut baptismus. Unde non ita committitur dispensatio eius omnibus in articulo necessitatis, sed solum illis quibus ex officio competit. Diaconis autem etiam baptizare non competit ex officio.

OBJECTION 1: It would seem that deacons can confer this sacrament. For, according to Dionysius (*On the Ecclesiastical Hierarchies* 5), deacons have the power *to cleanse*. Now this sacrament was instituted precisely to cleanse from sickness of the mind and body. Therefore, deacons also can confer it.

OBJ. 2: Further, baptism is a more excellent sacrament than the one of which we are speaking. But deacons can baptize, as is clear from Blessed Laurence. Therefore, they can confer this sacrament also.

ON THE CONTRARY, It is written: *let him bring in the priests of the Church* (Jas 5:14).

I ANSWER THAT, A deacon has the power to cleanse but not to enlighten. Hence, since enlightenment is an effect of grace, no sacrament whereby grace is conferred can be given by a deacon in virtue of his office: and so he cannot confer this sacrament, since grace is bestowed therein.

REPLY OBJ. 1: This sacrament cleanses by enlightening through the bestowal of grace: wherefore a deacon is not competent to confer it.

REPLY OBJ. 2: This is not a necessary sacrament, as baptism is. Hence its bestowal is not committed to all in cases of necessity, but only to those who are competent to do so in virtue of their office. Nor are deacons competent to baptize in virtue of their office.

Article 3

Whether None but a Bishop Can Confer This Sacrament?

AD TERTIUM SIC PROCEDITUR. Videtur quod solus episcopus possit hoc sacramentum conferre. Quia hoc sacramentum unctione perficitur, sicut et confirmatio. Sed solus Episcopus potest confirmare. Ergo solus potest hoc sacramentum conferre.

PRAETEREA, qui non potest quod minus est, non potest quod est maius. Sed maior est usus materiae sanctificatae quam sanctificatio eius: quia est finis ipsius. Ergo, cum sacerdos non possit sanctificare materiam, non potest materia sanctificata uti.

SED CONTRA, huius sacramenti minister *inducendus est* ad eum qui suscipit sacramentum; ut patet Iac. 5. Sed episcopus non posset accedere ad omnes infirmos suae dioecesis. Ergo non solus episcopus potest hoc sacramentum conferre.

RESPONDEO dicendum quod, secundum Dionysium, episcopus proprie habet *perficiendi* officium, sicut

OBJECTION 1: It would seem that none but a bishop can confer this sacrament. For this sacrament consists in an anointing, just as confirmation does. Now none but a bishop can confirm. Therefore, only a bishop can confer this sacrament.

OBJ. 2: Further, he who cannot do what is less cannot do what is greater. Now the use of consecrated matter surpasses the act of consecrating the matter, since the former is the end of the latter. Therefore, since a priest cannot consecrate the matter, neither can he use the matter after it has been consecrated.

ON THE CONTRARY, The minister of this sacrament *has to be brought in* to the recipient, as is clear from James 5:14. Now a bishop cannot go to all the sick people of his diocese. Therefore, the bishop is not the only one who can confer this sacrament.

I ANSWER THAT, According to Dionysius (*On the Ecclesiastical Hierarchies* 5), the office *of perfecting* belongs to

sacerdos *illuminandi*. Unde illa sacramenta dispensanda solis episcopis reservantur quae suscipientem in aliquo statu perfectionis super alios ponunt. Hoc autem non est in hoc sacramento, cum omnibus detur. Et ideo per simplices sacerdotes potest administrari.

AD PRIMUM ergo dicendum quod confirmatio imprimit characterem, quo collocatur homo in statu perfectionis, ut supra dictum est. Non autem hoc est in hoc sacramento. Et ideo non est simile.

AD SECUNDUM dicendum quod, quamvis in genere causae finalis usus materiae sanctificatae sit potior quam sanctificatio materiae, tamen in genere causae efficientis sanctificatio materiae est potior: quia ab eodem pendet usus sicut ab activa causa. Et ideo sanctificatio requirit altiorem virtutem activam quam usus.

a bishop, just as it belongs to a priest to *enlighten*. Therefore, those sacraments are reserved to a bishop's dispensation which place the recipient in a state of perfection above others. But this is not the case with this sacrament, for it is given to all. Consequently, it can be given by ordinary priests.

REPLY OBJ. 1: Confirmation imprints a character, whereby man is placed in a state of perfection, as stated above (III, Q. 63, A. 1–2, 6). But this does not take place in this sacrament; hence there is no comparison.

REPLY OBJ. 2: Although the use of consecrated matter is of more importance than the consecration of the matter from the point of view of the final cause, nevertheless, from the point of view of efficient cause, the consecration of the matter is the more important, since the use of the matter is dependent thereon as on its active cause: hence the consecration of the matter demands a higher power than the use of the matter does.

QUESTION 32

HOW EXTREME UNCTION SHOULD BE CONFERRED

Deinde considerandum est de his quibus hoc sacramentum conferri debet, et in qua parte corporis.

Circaquod septem quaeruntur.

Primo: utrum sanis debeat hoc sacramentum conferri.

Secundo: utrum debeat conferri in qualibet infirmitate.

Tertio: utrum debeat conferri furiosis et amentibus.

Quarto: utrum pueris.

Quinto: utrum totum corpus hoc sacramento inungi debeat.

Sexto: utrum convenienter determinentur partes in quibus inungitur.

Septimo: utrum mutilati in praedictis partibus inungi debeant.

We must now consider on whom this sacrament should be conferred and on what part of the body.

Under this head there are seven points of inquiry:

(1) Whether this sacrament should be conferred on those who are in good health?

(2) Whether it should be conferred in any kind of sickness?

(3) Whether it should be conferred on madmen and imbeciles?

(4) Whether it should be given to children?

(5) Whether, in this sacrament, the whole body should be anointed?

(6) Whether certain parts are suitably assigned to be anointed?

(7) Whether those who are deformed in the above parts ought to be anointed on them?

Article 1

Whether This Sacrament Ought to Be Conferred on Those Who Are in Good Health?

AD PRIMUM SIC PROCEDITUR. Videtur quod etiam sanis conferri debeat hoc sacramentum. Quia principalior effectus huius sacramenti est sanatio mentis quam sanatio corporis, ut dictum est. Sed etiam sani corpore indigent sanatione mentis. Ergo eis etiam debet hoc sacramentum conferri.

PRAETEREA, hoc sacramentum est exeuntium, sicut baptismus intrantium. Sed omnibus intrantibus baptismus datur. Ergo omnibus exeuntibus debet dari hoc sacramentum. Sed quandoque illi qui sunt in propinquo exitu, sani sunt: sicut illi qui decapitandi sunt. Ergo talibus debet hoc sacramentum dari.

SED CONTRA est quod dicitur Iac. 5: *infirmatur quis in vobis*, etc. Ergo solum infirmis competit.

RESPONDEO dicendum quod hoc sacramentum est quaedam spiritualis curatio, ut dictum est, quae quidem per quendam corporalis curationis modum significatur. Et ideo illis quibus corporalis curatio non competit, scilicet sanis, non debet hoc sacramentum conferri.

AD PRIMUM ergo dicendum quod, quamvis spiritualis sanitas sit principalis effectus huius sacramenti, ta-

OBJECTION 1: It would seem that this sacrament should be conferred even on those who are in good health. For the healing of the mind is a more important effect of this sacrament than the healing of the body, as stated above (Q. 30, A. 2). Now even those who are healthy in body need to be healed in mind. Therefore, this sacrament should be conferred on them also.

OBJ. 2: Further, this is the sacrament of those who are departing this life, just as baptism is the sacrament of those who are entering this life. Now baptism is given to all who enter. Therefore, this sacrament should be given to all who are departing. But sometimes those who are near departure are in good health, for instance, those who are to be beheaded. Therefore, this sacrament should be conferred on them.

ON THE CONTRARY, It is written: *is any man sick among you* (Jas 5:14), etc. Therefore, none but the sick are competent to receive this sacrament.

I ANSWER THAT, This sacrament is a spiritual healing, as stated above (Q. 30, A. 1–2), and is signified by way of a healing of the body. Hence this sacrament should not be conferred on those who are not subjects for bodily healing, namely, those who are in good health.

REPLY OBJ. 1: Although spiritual health is the principal effect of this sacrament, yet this same spiritual healing

men oportet quod per curationem corporalem significetur curatio spiritualis, etiam si corporalis sanatio non sequatur. Et ideo solum illis hoc sacramento sanitas spirirualis dari potest quibus corporalis curatio competit, scilicet infirmis: sicut ille solus potest baptismum suscipere qui potest corporalis ablutionis esse particeps, non autem puer in ventre matris existens.

AD SECUNDUM dicendum quod baptismus etiam non est nisi illorum intrantium qui corporali ablutioni subiici possunt. Et ideo hoc sacramentum illorum tantum exeuntium est quibus corporalis curatio competit.

needs to be signified by a healing of the body, although bodily health may not actually ensue. Consequently, spiritual health can be conferred by this sacrament on those alone who are competent to receive bodily healing, viz. the sick; even as he alone can receive baptism who is capable of a bodily washing, and not a child still in the mother's womb.

REPLY OBJ. 2: Even those who are entering into life cannot receive baptism unless they are capable of a bodily washing. And so those who are departing this life cannot receive this sacrament, unless they be subjects for a bodily healing.

Article 2

Whether This Sacrament Ought to Be Given in Any Kind of Sickness?

AD SECUNDUM SIC PROCEDITUR. Videtur quod hoc sacramentum dari debeat in qualibet infirmitate. Quia Iac. 5, ubi hoc sacramentum traditur, nulla infirmitas determinatur. Ergo omnibus infirmantibus debet hoc sacramentum conferri.

PRAETEREA, quanto remedium est dignius, tanto debet esse generalius. Sed hoc sacramentum est dignius quam medicina corporalis. Cum ergo medicina corporalis omnibus infirmis detur, videtur quod etiam hoc sacramentum.

SED CONTRA, hoc sacramentum dicitur ab omnibus *extremae unctionis*. Sed non omnis infirmitas ad extremum vitae perducit: cum quaedam aegritudines sint causa longioris vitae, ut dicit Philosophus. Ergo non omnibus infirmantibus debet hoc sacramentum dari.

RESPONDEO dicendum quod hoc sacramentum est ultimum remedium quod Ecclesia potest conferre, immediate quasi disponens ad gloriam. Et ideo illis tantum infirmantibus debet exhiberi qui sunt in statu exeuntium, propter hoc quod aegritudo nata est inducere mortem, et de periculo timetur.

AD PRIMUM ergo dicendum quod quaelibet infirmitas augmentata potest mortem inducere. Et ideo, si genera infirmitatum pensentur, in qualibet aegritudine potest dari hoc sacramentum: quia Apostolus non determinat infirmitatem aliquam. Sed si pensetur infirmitatis modus et status, non semper debet infirmantibus hoc sacramentum dari.

AD SECUNDUM dicendum quod medicina corporalis habet pro principali effectu sanitatem corporalem, qua omnes infirmi in quolibet statu indigent. Sed hoc sacramentum habet pro principali effectu illam sospitatem quae exeuntibus et iter ad gloriam agentibus est necessaria. Et ideo non est simile.

OBJECTION 1: It would seem that this sacrament should be given in any kind of sickness. For no kind of sickness is determined in the fifth chapter of James where this sacrament is delivered to us. Therefore, this sacrament should be given in all kinds of sickness.

OBJ. 2: Further, the more excellent a remedy is, the more generally should it be available. Now this sacrament is more excellent than bodily medicine. Since, then, bodily medicine is given to all manner of sick persons, it seems that this sacrament should be given in like manner to all.

ON THE CONTRARY, This sacrament is called by all 'extreme unction.' Now it is not every sickness that brings man to the extremity of his life, since some ailments prolong life, according to the Philosopher (*On Length and Brevity of Life* 1). Therefore, this sacrament should not be given in every case of sickness.

I ANSWER THAT, This sacrament is the last remedy that the Church can give, since it is an immediate preparation for glory. Therefore, it ought to be given to only those who are so sick as to be in a state of departure from this life, through their sickness being of such a nature as to cause death, the danger of which is feared.

REPLY OBJ. 1: Any sickness can cause death if it be aggravated. Hence if we consider the different kinds of disease, there is none in which this sacrament cannot be given; and for this reason the apostle does not determine any particular one. But if we consider the degree and the stage of the complaint, this sacrament should not be given to every sick person.

REPLY OBJ. 2: The principal effect of bodily medicine is bodily health, which all sick people lack, whatever be the stage of their sickness. But the principal effect of this sacrament is that immunity from disorder which is needed by those who are taking their departure from this life and setting out for the life of glory. Hence the comparison fails.

Article 3

Whether This Sacrament Ought to Be Given to Madmen and Imbeciles?

Ad tertium sic proceditur. Videtur quod furiosis et amentibus hoc sacramentum dari debeat. Quia tales aegritudines sunt periculosissimae, et cito ad mortem disponunt. Sed periculo debet adhiberi remedium. Ergo hoc sacramentum, quod est in remedium infirmitatis humanae, debet talibus conferri.

Praeterea, dignius sacramentum est baptismus quam istud. Sed baptismus datur furiosis, ut supra dictum est. Ergo et hoc sacramentum eis debet dari.

Sed contra, hoc sacramentum non est dandum nisi recognoscentibus ipsum. Sed tales non sunt furiosi et amentes. Ergo eis dari non debet.

Respondeo dicendum quod ad effectum huius sacramenti percipiendum plurimum valet devotio suscipientis, et personale meritum conferentium, et generale totius ecclesiae: quod patet ex hoc quod per modum deprecationis forma huius sacramenti confertur. Et ideo illis qui non possunt recognoscere et cum devotione suscipere hoc sacramentum, dari non debet: et praecipue furiosis et amentibus, qui possent irreverentiam sacramento per aliquam immunditiam facere; nisi haberent lucida intervalla, quibus sacramenta recognoscerent, et sic eis conferri in statu illo possent.

Ad primum ergo dicendum quod, quamvis in periculo mortis tales quandoque sint, tamen remedium per devotionem propriam non potest eis applicari. Et ideo non debet eis conferri.

Ad secundum dicendum quod baptismus non requirit motum liberi arbitrii, quia datur contra originale principaliter, quod non curatur in nobis ex nostro libero arbitrio. Sed in hoc sacramento requiritur motus liberi arbitrii. Et ideo non est simile. Et praeterea baptismus est sacramentum necessitatis: non extrema unctio.

Objection 1: It would seem that this sacrament should be given to madmen and imbeciles. For these diseases are full of danger and cause death quickly. Now, when there is danger it is the time to apply the remedy. Therefore, this sacrament, which was intended as a remedy to human weakness, should be given to such people.

Obj. 2: Further, baptism is a greater sacrament than this. Now baptism is conferred on mad people, as stated above (III, Q. 68, A. 12). Therefore, this sacrament also should be given to them.

On the contrary, This sacrament should be given to none but such as acknowledge it. Now this does not apply to madmen and imbeciles. Therefore, it should not be given to them.

I answer that, The devotion of the recipient, the personal merit of the minister, and the general merits of the whole Church are of great account towards the reception of the effect of this sacrament. This is evident from the fact that the form of this sacrament is pronounced by way of a prayer. Hence it should not be given those who cannot acknowledge it, and especially to madmen and imbeciles, who might dishonor the sacrament by their offensive conduct, unless they have lucid intervals when they would be capable of acknowledging the sacrament, for then the sacrament should be given as to children the same in that state.

Reply Obj. 1: Although such people are sometimes in danger of death, yet the remedy cannot be applied to them on account of their lack of devotion. Hence it should not be given to them.

Reply Obj. 2: Baptism does not require a movement of the free-will, because it is given chiefly as a remedy for original sin, which, in us, is not taken away by a movement of the free-will. On the other hand, this sacrament requires a movement of the free-will; wherefore the comparison fails. Moreover, baptism is a necessary sacrament, while extreme unction is not.

Article 4

Whether This Sacrament Should Be Given to Children?

Ad quartum sic proceditur. Videtur quod debeat dari pueris. Quia eisdem infirmitatibus quandoque laborant pueri et adulti. Sed eidem morbo debet adhiberi idem remedium. Ergo, sicut adultis, ita et pueris debet hoc sacramentum dari.

Praeterea, hoc sacramentum datur ad purgandum reliquias peccati, ut supra dictum est, tam origina-

Objection 1: It would seem that this sacrament ought to be given to children. For children sometimes suffer from the same ailments as adults. Now the same disease requires the same remedy. Therefore, this sacrament should be given to children the same as to adults.

Obj. 2: Further, this sacrament is given in order to remove the remnants of sin, whether original or actual, as

lis quam actualis. Sed in pueris sunt reliquiae originalis peccati. Ergo eis debet hoc sacramentum dari.

Sed contra est quod nulli debet dari hoc sacramentum cui non competit forma sacramenti. Sed forma huius sacramenti non competit pueris: quia non peccaverunt per visum et auditum, ut in forma exprimitur. Ergo eis dari non debet hoc sacramentum.

Respondeo dicendum quod hoc sacramentum exigit actualem devotionem in suscipiente, sicut et Eucharistia. Unde, sicut Eucharistia non debet dari pueris, ita nec hoc sacramentum.

Ad primum ergo dicendum quod infirmitates in pueris non sunt ex peccato actuali causatae, sicut in adultis. Et contra illas praecipue infirmitates hoc sacramentum datur quae sunt ex peccato causatae quasi peccati reliquiae.

Ad secundum dicendum quod non datur contra reliquias originalis peccati nisi secundum quod sunt per actualia peccata quodammodo confortatae. Unde principaliter contra actualia peccata datur, ut ex ipsa forma patet: quae non sunt in pueris.

stated above (Q. 30, A. 1). Now the remnants of original sin are in children. Therefore, this sacrament should be given to them.

On the contrary, This sacrament should be given to none but those to whom the form applies. But the form of this sacrament does not apply to children, since they have not sinned by sight and hearing, as expressed in the form. Therefore, this sacrament should not be given to them.

I answer that, This sacrament, like the Eucharist, requires actual devotion in the recipient. Therefore, just as the Eucharist ought not to be given to children, so neither ought this sacrament to be given to them.

Reply Obj. 1: Children's infirmities are not caused by actual sin, as in adults, and this sacrament is given chiefly as a remedy for infirmities that result from sins, being the remnants of sin, as it were.

Reply Obj. 2: This sacrament is not given as a remedy for the remnants of original sin, except insofar as they gather strength, so to speak, from actual sins. Hence from the very form it appears that it is given chiefly as a remedy for actual sins, which are not in children.

Article 5

Whether the Whole Body Should Be Anointed in This Sacrament?

Ad quintum sic proceditur. Videtur quod hoc sacramento totum corpus inungi debeat. Quia secundum Augustinum, *tota anima est in toto corpore.* Sed praecipue datur hoc sacramentum ad sanandum animam. Ergo in corpore toto debet inunctio fieri.

Praeterea, ubi est morbus, ibi debet apponi medicina. Sed quandoque morbus est universalis et in toto corpore, sicut febris. Ergo totum corpus debet inungi.

Praeterea, in baptismo totum corpus immergitur. Ergo et hic totum deberet inungi.

Sed contra est universalis Ecclesiae ritus, secundum quem non inungitur infirmus nisi in determinatis partibus corporis.

Respondeo dicendum quod hoc sacramentum per modum curationis exhibetur. Curatio autem corporalis non oportet quod fiat per medicinam toti corpori appositam, sed illis partibus ubi est radix morbi. Et ideo etiam unctio sacramentalis debet fieri in illis partibus tantum in quibus est radix spiritualis infirmitatis.

Ad primum ergo dicendum quod anima, quamvis sit tota in qualibet parte corporis quantum ad essentiam, non tamen quantum ad potentias, quae sunt radices ac-

Objection 1: It would seem that the whole body should be anointed in this sacrament. For, according to Augustine, *the whole soul is in every part of the body* (*On the Trinity* 6.6). Now this sacrament is given chiefly in order to heal the soul. Therefore, the whole body ought to be anointed.

Obj. 2: Further, the remedy should be applied to the part affected by the disease. But sometimes the disease is general, and affects the whole body, as a fever does. Therefore, the whole body should be anointed.

Obj. 3: Further, in baptism the whole body is dipped under the water. Therefore, in this sacrament the whole body should be anointed.

On the contrary, According to the rite observed throughout the Church, in this sacrament the sick man is anointed only in certain fixed parts of the body.

I answer that, This sacrament is shown to us under the form of a healing. Now bodily healing has to be effected by applying the remedy not to the whole body, but to those parts where the root of the disease is seated. Consequently, the sacramental unction also ought to be applied to those parts only in which the spiritual sickness is rooted.

Reply Obj. 1: Although the whole soul is, as to its essence, in each part of the body, it is not as to its powers which are the roots of sinful acts. Hence certain fixed parts

tuum peccati. Et ideo oportet quod in determinatis partibus fiant, in quibus illae potentiae habent esse.

Ad secundum dicendum quod non semper apponitur medicina ubi est morbus: sed congruentius ubi est radix morbi.

Ad tertium dicendum quod baptismus fit per modum ablutionis. Ablutio autem corporalis non purgat maculam ab aliqua parte nisi cui apponitur. Et ideo baptismus toti corpori adhibetur. Secus autem est de extrema unctione, ratione iam dicta.

have to be anointed, those, namely, in which powers have their being.

Reply Obj. 2: The remedy is not always applied to the part affected by the disease, but, with greater reason, to the part where the root of the disease is seated.

Reply Obj. 3: Baptism is given under the form of washing: and a bodily washing cleanses only the part to which it is applied; for this reason baptism is applied to the whole body. It is different with extreme unction for the reason given above.

Article 6

Whether the Parts To Be Anointed Are Suitably Assigned?

Ad sextum sic proceditur. Videtur quod inconvenienter determinentur istae partes: ut scilicet infirmans inungatur in oculis, in naribus, in auribus, in labiis, in manibus et pedibus. Quia sapiens medicus curat morbum in radice. Sed *de corde exeunt cogitationes, quae coinquinant hominem,* ut dicitur Matth. 15. Ergo in pectore debet fieri inunctio.

Praeterea, puritas mentis non minus est necessaria exeuntibus quam intrantibus. Sed intrantes unguntur chrismate in vertice a sacerdote ad significandum mentis puritatem. Ergo et exeuntes hoc sacramento ungi debent in vertice.

Praeterea, ibi debet adhiberi remedium ubi est maior vis morbi. Sed spiritualis morbus praecipue viget in renibus viris, et mulieribus in umbilico: ut dicitur Iob 40, *potestas eius in lumbis eius,* secundum expositionem Gregorii. Ergo ibi debet fieri inunctio.

Praeterea, sicut per pedes peccatur, ita et per alia membra corporis. Ergo, sicut inunguntur pedes, ita et alia corporis membra inungi debent.

Respondeo dicendum quod principia peccandi iri nobis sunt eadem quae et principia agendi, quia peccatum consistit iri actu. Principia autem agendi in nobis sunt tria: primum est dirigens, scilicet vis cognoscitiva; secundum est imperans, scilicet vis appetitiva; tertium est exequens, scilicet vis motiva. Omnis autem nostra cognitio a sensu ortum habet. Et quia ubi est in nobis prima origo peccati, ibi debet unctio adhiberi, ideo inunguntur loca quinque sensuum: scilicet oculi, propter visum; aures, propter auditum; nares, propter odoratum; os, propter gustum; manus, propter tactum, qui in pulpis digitorum praecipue viget. Sed propter appetitivam unguntur a quibusdam renes. Propter motivam

Objection 1: It would seem that these parts are unsuitably assigned, namely, that the eyes, nose, ears, lips, hands, and feet should be anointed. For a wise physician heals the disease in its root. Now *from the heart come forth thoughts . . . that defile a man* (Matt 15:19–20). Therefore, the breast ought to be anointed.

Obj. 2: Further, purity of mind is not less necessary to those who are departing this life than to those who are entering it. Now those who are entering are anointed with chrism on the head by the priest, to signify purity of mind. Therefore, in this sacrament those who are departing should be anointed on the head.

Obj. 3: Further, the remedy should be applied where the disease is most virulent. Now spiritual sickness is most virulent in the loins in men, and in the navel in women, according to how Gregory expounds upon Job 40:11: *his strength is in his loins, and his force in the navel of his belly* (*Morals on Job* 32.11). Therefore, these parts should be anointed.

Obj. 4: Further, sins are committed with other parts of the body no less than with the feet. Therefore, as the feet are anointed, so ought other members of the body to be anointed.

I answer that, The principles of sinning are the same in us as the principles of action, for a sin is an act. Now there are in us three principles of action: the first is the directing principle, namely, the cognitive power; the second is the commanding principle, namely, the appetitive power; the third is the executive principle, namely, the motive power. Now all our knowledge has its origin in the senses. And, since the remedy for sin should be applied where sin originates in us first, for that reason the places of the five senses are anointed: namely, the eyes on account of the sight; the ears on account of the hearing; the nostrils on account of the smell; the mouth on account of the taste; the hands on account of the touch, which is keenest in the finger tips. In

unguntur pedes, qui surit principalius eius instrumentum. Et quia primum principium est cognoscitiva, ideo illa unctio ab omnibus observatur quae fit ad quinque sensus, quasi de necessitate sacramenti. Sed quidam non servant alias, quidam vero servant illam quae ad pedes et non quae ad renes: quia appetitiva et motiva sunt secundaria principia.

AD PRIMUM ergo dicendum quod cognitio a corde non exit nisi per aliquam imaginationem, quae est *motus a sensu factus*, ut dicitur in II *de Anima*. Et ideo cor non est prima radix cogitationis, sed organa sensuum: nisi quatenus cor est principium totius corporis. Sed hoc principium est radix remota.

AD SECUNDUM dicendum quod intrantes debent acquirere puritatem: sed exeuntes debent eam purgare. Et ideo exeuntes debent inungi in illis partibus quibus contingit puritatem mentis inquinari.

AD TERTIUM dicendum quod secundum quorumdam consuetudinem fit in renibus, propter hoc quod ibi maxime viget appetitus concupiscibilis. Sed appetitiva non est prima radix, ut dictum est.

AD QUARTUM dicendum quod organa corporis quibus actus peccati exercentur, sunt pedes, manus et lingua, quibus etiam exhibetur unctio; et membra genitalia, quibus, propter immunditiam illarum partium et honestatem sacramenti, non debet unctio adhiberi.

some places too the loins are anointed on account of the appetite. And the feet are anointed on account of the motive power, of which they are the chief instrument. And since the cognitive power is the first principle of human activity, the anointing of the five senses is observed by all as being essential to the sacrament. But some do not observe the other unctions—some anoint the feet but not the loins—because the appetitive and motive powers are secondary principles.

REPLY OBJ. 1: No thought arises in the heart without an act of the imagination which is a *movement proceeding from sensation* (*On the Soul* 2). Hence the primary root of thought is not the heart, but the sensory organs, except insofar as the heart is a principle of the whole body, albeit a remote principle.

REPLY OBJ. 2: Those who enter have to receive purity of the mind, whereas those who are departing have to cleanse the mind. Hence the latter need to be anointed in those parts in respect of which the mind's purity may be sullied.

REPLY OBJ. 3: According to a certain custom it is done on the loins because it is there that the concupiscible appetite most flourishes. But the appetitive power is not the first root, as was said.

REPLY OBJ. 4: The bodily organs which are the instruments of sin are the feet, hands, and tongue, all of which are anointed, and the organs of generation, which it would be unbecoming to anoint on account of their uncleanliness and out of respect for the sacrament.

Article 7

Whether Those Who Are Deformed in Those Parts Should Be Anointed?

AD SEPTIMUM SIC PROCEDITUR. Videtur quod mutilati non sunt ungendi illis unctionibus quae partibus illis competunt. Quia sicut hoc sacramentum exigit determinatam dispositionem in suscipiente, ut scilicet sit infirmus, ita et determinatam partem. Sed ille qui non habet infirmitatem, non potest inungi. Ergo nec ille qui non habet partem illam in qua debet fieri unctio.

PRAETEREA, ille qui est caecus a nativitate, non delinquit per visum. Sed in unctione quae fit ad oculos, fit mentio de *delicto per visum*. Ergo talis unctio caeco nato non deberet fieri. Et sic de aliis.

SED CONTRA est quod defectus corporis non impedit aliquod aliud sacramentum. Ergo nec istud impedire debet. Sed de necessitate istius sacramenti est quaelibet unctionum. Ergo omnes debent fieri mutilatis.

RESPONDEO dicendum quod mutilati inungi debent quam propinquius esse potest ad partes illas: in quibus

OBJECTION 1: It would seem that those who are deformed should not be anointed in those parts. For just as this sacrament demands a certain disposition on the part of the recipient, namely, that he should be sick, so it demands that he should be anointed in a certain part of the body. Now he that is not sick cannot be anointed. Therefore, neither can he be anointed who lacks the part to be anointed.

OBJ. 2: Further, a man born blind does not sin by his sight. Yet in the anointing of the eyes mention is made of *sins by sight*. Therefore, this anointing ought not to be applied to one born blind, and in like manner as regards the other senses.

ON THE CONTRARY, Bodily deformity is not an impediment to any other sacrament. Therefore, it should not be an impediment to this one. Now each of the anointings is essential to the sacrament. Therefore, all should be applied to those who are deformed.

I ANSWER THAT, Even those who are deformed should be anointed, and that as near as possible to the part which

unctio fieri debuerat. Quia, quamvis non habeant membra, habent tamen potentias animae quae illis membris debentur, saltem in radice: et interius peccare possunt per ea quae ad partes illas pertinent, quamvis non exterius.

Et per hoc patet solutio ad obiecta.

ought to have been anointed. For though they have not the members, nevertheless, they have, at least in the root, the powers of the soul corresponding to those members, and they may commit inwardly the sins that pertain to those members, though they cannot outwardly.

This suffices for the replies to the objections.

QUESTION 33

THE REPETITION OF EXTREME UNCTION

Deinde considerandum est de iteratione huius sacramenti.

Circa quod duo quaeruntur.

Primo: utrum hoc sacramentum debeat iterari.

Secundo: utrum in eadem infirmitate debeat iterari.

We must now consider the repetition of this sacrament.

Under this head there are two points of inquiry:
(1) Whether this sacrament ought to be repeated?
(2) Whether it ought to be repeated during the same sickness?

Article 1

Whether This Sacrament Ought to Be Repeated?

AD PRIMUM SIC PROCEDITUR. Videtur quod hoc sacramentum non debeat iterari. Quia dignior est unctio quae fit homini, quam quae fit lapidi. Sed unctio altaris non iteratur, nisi altare illud fractum fuerit. Ergo nec unctio extrema, quae adhibetur homini, debet iterari.

PRAETEREA, post ultimum nihil est. Sed haec unctio dicitur *extrema*. Ergo non debet iterari.

SED CONTRA, hoc sacramentum est quaedam spiritualis curatio per modum curationis corporalis exhibita. Sed curatio corporis iteratur. Ergo et hoc sacramentum iterari debet.

RESPONDEO dicendum quod nullum sacramentum quod habet effectum perpetuum, debet iterari: quia ostenderetur sacramentum non fuisse efficax ad faciendum illum effectum, et sic fieret iniuria illi sacramento. Sacramentum autem quod habet effectum non perpetuum, potest iterari sine iniuria, ut effectus deperditus iterato recuperetur. Et quia sanitas corporis et mentis, quae sunt effectus huius sacramenti, possunt amitti postquam fuerint per sacramentum effecta, ideo hoc sacramentum sine sui iniuria potest iterari.

AD PRIMUM ergo dicendum quod unctio lapidis fit ad ipsius altaris consecrationem, quae est perpetuo in lapide quandiu altare manet: et ideo non potest iterari. Sed haec unctio non fit ad consecrationem hominis: cum non imprimatur character. Et ideo non est simile.

AD SECUNDUM dicendum quod illud quod secundum aestimationem hominum est extremum, quandoque secundum rei veritatem non est extremum. Et sic dicitur hoc sacramentum extrema unctio, quia non debet dari nisi illis quorum mors est propinqua secundum aestimationem hominum.

OBJECTION 1: It would seem that this sacrament ought not to be repeated. For the anointing of a man is of greater import than the anointing of a stone. But the anointing of an altar is not repeated, unless the altar be shattered. Neither, therefore, should extreme unction, whereby a man is anointed, be repeated.

OBJ. 2: Further, nothing comes after what is extreme. But this unction is called *extreme*. Therefore, it should not be repeated.

ON THE CONTRARY, This sacrament is a spiritual healing applied under the form of a bodily cure. But a bodily cure is repeated. Therefore, this sacrament also can be repeated.

I ANSWER THAT, No sacramental or sacrament having a perpetual effect can be repeated, because this would imply that the sacrament had failed to produce that effect; and this would be derogatory to the sacrament. On the other hand, a sacrament whose effect does not last forever can be repeated without disparaging that sacrament, in order that the lost effect may be recovered. And since health of body and soul, which is the effect of this sacrament, can be lost after it has been effected, it follows that this sacrament can, without disparagement thereto, be repeated.

REPLY OBJ. 1: The stone is anointed in order that the altar may be consecrated, and the stone remains consecrated as long as the altar remains; hence it cannot be anointed again. But a man is not consecrated by being anointed, since it does not imprint a character on him. Hence there is no comparison.

REPLY OBJ. 2: What men think to be extreme is not always extreme in reality. It is thus that this sacrament is called extreme unction, because it ought not to be given save to those whose death men think to be nigh.

Article 2

Whether This Sacrament Ought to Be Repeated During the Same Sickness?

Ad secundum sic proceditur. Videtur quod in eadem infirmitate non debeat iterari. Quia uni morbo non debetur nisi una medicina. Sed hoc sacramentum est quaedam spiritualis medicina. Ergo contra unum morbum non debet iterari.

Praeterea, secundum hoc posset aliquis infirmus tota die inungi, si in eodem morbo posset iterari unctio. Quod est absurdum.

Sed contra est quod aliquando morbus diu durat post sacramenti perceptionem: et sic reliquiae peccatorum contrahuntur, contra quas principaliter hoc sacramentum datur. Ergo iterato debet inungi.

Respondeo dicendum quod hoc sacramentum non respicit tantum infirmitatem, sed etiam infirmitatis statum: quia non debet dari nisi infirmis qui, secundum humanam aestimationem, videntur morti appropinquare. Quaedam autem infirmitates non sunt diuturnae. Unde, si in eis datur hoc sacramentum tunc eum homo ad statum illum perveniat quod sit in periculo mortis, non recedit a statu illo nisi infirmitate curata, et ita iterum non debet inungi: sed, si recidivum patiatur, erit alia infirmitas, et poterit alia fieri inunctio. Quaedam vero sunt aegritudines diuturnae: ut ethica et hydropisis, et huiusmodi. Et in talibus non debet fieri unctio, nisi quando videntur perducere ad periculum mortis. Et si homo illum articulum evadat, eadem infirmitate durante, et iterum ad similem statum per illam aegritudinem reducatur, iterum potest inungi: quia iam quasi est alius status infirmitatis, quamvis non sit alia infirmitas simpliciter.

Et per hoc patet solutio ad obiecta.

Objection 1: It would seem that this sacrament ought not to be repeated during the same sickness. For one disease demands one remedy. Now this sacrament is a spiritual remedy. Therefore, it ought not to be repeated for one sickness.

Obj. 2: Further, if a sick man could be anointed more than once during one disease, this might be done for a whole day: which is absurd.

On the contrary, Sometimes a disease lasts long after the sacrament has been received, so that the remnants of sin, against which chiefly this sacrament is given, would be contracted. Therefore, it ought to be given again.

I answer that, This sacrament regards not only the sickness, but also the state of the sick man, because it ought not to be given except to those sick people who seem, in man's estimation, to be nigh to death. Now some diseases do not last long; so that if this sacrament is given at the time that the sick man is in a state of danger of death, he does not leave that state except the disease be cured, and thus he needs not to be anointed again. But if he has a relapse, it will be a second sickness, and he can be anointed again. On the other hand some diseases are of long duration, as hectic fever, dropsy and the like, and those who lie sick of them should not be anointed until they seem to be in danger of death. And if the sick man escape that danger while the disease continues, and be brought again thereby to the same state of danger, he can be anointed again, because it is, as it were, another state of sickness, although strictly speaking, it is not another sickness.

This suffices for the replies to the objections.

QUESTION 34

THE SACRAMENT OF HOLY ORDERS

Post hoc considerandum est de sacramento ordinis. Et primo, de ordine in communi; secundo, de distinctione ordinum; tertio, de conferentibus ordinem; quarto, de impedimentis ordinandorum; quinto, de his quae sunt ordinibus annexa.

De ipso autem ordine in communi tria videnda sunt: primo, de eius entitate et quidditate, et partibus eius; secundo, de eius effectu; tertio, de suscipientibus ipsum.

Circa primum quaeruntur quinque.

Primo: utrum in Ecclesia esse debeat.

Secundo: utrum convenienter definiatur.

Tertio: utrum sit sacramentum.

Quarto: utrum eius forma exprimatur convenienter.

Quinto: utrum hoc sacramentum materiam habeat.

In the next place we must consider the sacrament of holy orders: (1) Holy orders in general; (2) The difference of holy orders; (3) Those who confer holy orders; (4) The impediments to receiving holy orders; (5) Things connected with holy orders.

Concerning holy orders in general three points have to be considered: (1) Its essence, quiddity, and parts; (2) Its effect; (3) The recipients of holy orders.

Under the first head there are five points of inquiry:

(1) Whether there should be holy orders in the Church?

(2) Whether it is fittingly defined?

(3) Whether it is a sacrament?

(4) Whether its form is expressed properly?

(5) Whether this sacrament has any matter?

Article 1

Whether There Should Be Orders in the Church?

AD PRIMUM SIC PROCEDITUR. Videtur quod ordo in Ecclesia esse non debeat. Ordo enim requirit subiectionem et praelationem. Sed subiectio videtur repugnare *libertati in quam vocati sumus per Christum.* Ergo ordo in Ecclesia esse non debet.

PRAETEREA, ille qui in ordine constituitur, alio superior fit. Sed in Ecclesia quilibet debet se altero inferiorem reputare: Philipp. 2, *superiores invicem arbitrantes.* Ergo non debet in Ecclesia esse ordo.

PRAETEREA, ordo invenitur in angelis propter distinctionem eorum in naturalibus et gratuitis. Sed omnes homines sunt in natura unum: gratiarum etiam dona quis eminentius habeat, ignotum est. Ergo ordo in Ecclesia esse non potest.

SED CONTRA: Rom. 13: *quae a Deo sunt, ordinata sunt.* Sed Ecclesia a Deo est: quia ipse eam aedificavit sanguine suo. Ergo ordo in Ecclesia esse debet.

PRAETEREA, status Ecclesiae est medius inter statum naturae et gloriae. Sed in natura invenitur ordo, quo quaedam aliis superiora sunt: et similiter in gloria, ut patet in angelis. Ergo in Ecclesia debet esse ordo.

RESPONDEO dicendum quod Deus sua opera in sui similitudinem producere voluit quantum possibile fuit,

OBJECTION 1: It would seem that there should not be an order in the Church. For order requires subjection and preeminence. But subjection seemingly is incompatible *with the liberty whereunto we are called by Christ.* Therefore, there should not be an order in the Church.

OBJ. 2: Further, he who has received an order becomes another's superior. But in the Church everyone should deem himself lower than another: *let each esteem others better than themselves* (Phil 2:3). Therefore, an order should not be in the Church.

OBJ. 3: Further, we find order among the angels on account of their differing in natural and gratuitous gifts. But all men are one in nature, and it is not known who has the higher gifts of grace. Therefore, an order should not be in the Church.

ON THE CONTRARY, *Those things that are of God are in order.* (Rom 13:1). Now the Church is of God, for he himself built it with his blood. Therefore, there ought to be holy orders in the Church.

FURTHER, The state of the Church is between the state of nature and the state of glory. Now we find order in nature in that some things are above others, and likewise in glory, as in the angels. Therefore, there should be holy orders in the Church.

I ANSWER THAT, God wished to produce his works in likeness to himself, as far as possible, in order that they

ut perfecta essent, et per ea cognosci posset. Et ideo, ut in suis operibus repraesentaretur non solum secundum quod in se est, sed etiam secundum quod aliis influit, hanc legem naturalem imposuit omnibus, ut ultima per media perficerentur et media per prima, ut Dionysius dicit. Et ideo, ut ista pulchritudo Ecclesiae non deesset, posuit ordinem in ea, ut quidam aliis sacramenta traderet, suo modo Deo in hoc assimilati, quasi Deo cooperantes: sicut et in corpore naturali quaedam membra aliis influunt.

AD PRIMUM ergo dicendum quod subiectio servitutis repugnat libertati: quae servitus est cum aliquis dominatur ad sui utilitatem subiectis utens. Talis autem subiectio non requiritur in ordine, per quem qui praesunt salutem subditorum quaerere debent, non propriam utilitatem.

AD SECUNDUM dicendum quod quilibet debet se reputare inferiorem merito, sed non officio. Ordines autem officia quaedam sunt.

AD TERTIUM dicendum quod ordo in angelis non attenditur secundum distinctionem naturae nisi per accidens, inquantum ad distinctionem naturae sequitur in eis distinctio gratiae. Attenditur autem per se secundum distinctionem in gratia: quia eorum ordines respiciunt participationem divinorum, et communicationem in statu gloriae, quae est secundum mensuram gratiae, quasi gratiae finis et effectus quodammodo. Sed ordines Ecclesiae militantis respiciunt participationem sacramentorum et communicationem, quae sunt causa gratiae, et quodammodo gratiam praecedunt. Et sic non est de necessitate nostrorum ordinum gratia gratum faciens, sed solum potestas dispensandi sacramenta. Et propter hoc ordo non attenditur per distinctionem gratiae gratum facientis, sed per distinctionem potestatis.

might be perfect and that he might be known through them. Hence, that he might be portrayed in his works not only according to what he is in himself, but also according as he acts on others, he laid this natural law on all things, that last things should be reduced and perfected by middle things, and middle things by the first, as Dionysius says (*On the Ecclesiastical Hierarchies* 5). Wherefore that this beauty might not be lacking to the Church, he established holy orders in her so that some should deliver the sacraments to others, being thus made like to God in their own way, as cooperating with God; even as in the natural body, some members act on others.

REPLY OBJ. 1: The subjection of slavery is incompatible with liberty; for slavery consists in lording over others and employing them for one's own profit. Such subjection is not required in holy orders, whereby those who preside have to seek the salvation of their subjects and not their own profit.

REPLY OBJ. 2: Each one should esteem himself lower in merit, not in office; and holy orders are a kind of office.

REPLY OBJ. 3: Order among the angels does not arise from difference of nature, unless accidentally, insofar as difference of grace results in them from difference of nature. But in them it results directly from their difference in grace; because their orders regard their participation of divine things, and their communicating them in the state of glory, which is according to the measure of grace, as being the end and effect, so to speak, of grace. On the other hand, the orders of the Church Militant regard the participation in the sacraments and the communication thereof, which are the cause of grace and, in a way, precede grace; and consequently our holy orders do not require sanctifying grace, but only the power to dispense the sacraments; for which reason holy orders does not correspond to the difference of sanctifying grace, but to the difference of power.

Article 2

Whether Holy Orders Is Properly Defined?

AD SECUNDUM SIC PROCEDITUR. Videtur quod inconvenienter ordo a Magistro *Sententiarum*, 24 distinctione, definiatur, ubi dicitur: *ordo est signaculum quoddam Ecclesiae, per quod spiritualis potestas traditur ordinato.* Pars enim non debet poni genus totius. Sed *character*, qui per *signaculum* exponitur in consequenti definitione, est pars ordinis: quia dividitur contra id quod est res tantum, vel sacramentum tantum, cum sit res et sacramentum. Ergo signaculum non debet poni quasi genus ordinis.

OBJECTION 1: It would seem that holy orders is improperly defined by the Master (*Sentences* IV, D. 53), where it is said, *order is a seal of the Church, whereby spiritual power is conferred on the person ordained.* For a part should not be described as the genus of the whole. Now the *character* which is denoted by the *seal* in a subsequent definition is a part of holy orders, since it is placed in contradistinction with that which is either reality only, or sacrament only, since it is both reality and sacrament. Therefore, seal should not be mentioned as the genus of holy orders.

PRAETEREA, sicut in sacramento ordinis imprimitur character, ita in sacramento baptismi. Sed in definitione baptismi non ponebatur character. Ergo nec in definitione ordinis debet poni.

PRAETEREA, in baptismo etiam quaedam spiritualis datur potestas accedendi ad sacramenta: et iterum est quoddam signaculum, cum sit sacramentum. Ergo haec definitio convenit baptismo. Et sic inconvenienter assignatur de ordine.

PRAETEREA, ordo relatio quaedam est quae in utroque extremorum salvatur. Extrema autem huius relationis sunt superior et inferior. Ergo inferiores habent ordinem sicut et superiores. Sed in eis non est aliqua potestas praeeminentiae, qualis ponitur hic in definitione ordinis, ut patet per expositionem sequentem, ubi ponitur *promotio potestatis*. Ergo inconvenienter definitur hic ordo.

RESPONDEO dicendum quod definitio quam Magister de ordine ponit, convenit ordini secundum quod est Ecclesiae sacramentum. Et ideo duo ponit: signum exterius, ibi, *signaculum quoddam* etc., idest, signum quoddam; et effectum interiorem, ibi, *quo spiritualis potestas* etc.

AD PRIMUM ergo dicendum quod *signaculum* non ponitur hic pro charactere interiori: sed pro eo quod exterius geritur, quod est signum interioris potestatis et causa. Et sic etiam sumitur *character* in alia definitione.

Si tamen pro interiori charactere sumeretur, non esset inconveniens. Quia divisio sacramenti in illa tria non est in partes integrales, proprie loquendo. Quia illud quod est res tantum, non est de essentia sacramenti. Quod est etiam sacramentum tantum, transit: et sacramentum manere dicitur. Unde relinquitur quod ipse character interior sit essentialiter et principaliter ipsum sacramentum ordinis.

AD SECUNDUM dicendum quod baptismus, quamvis in eo conferatur aliqua spiritualis potestas recipiendi alia sacramenta, ratione cuius characterem imprimit, non tamen hic est principalis effectus eius: sed ablutio interior, propter quam baptismus fieret etiam priori causa non existente. Sed ordo potestatem principaliter importat. Et ideo character, qui est spiritualis potestas, in definitione ordinis ponitur, non autem in definitione baptismi.

AD TERTIUM dicendum quod in baptismo datur quaedam potentia spiritualis ad recipiendum, et ita quodammodo passiva. *Potestas* autem proprie nominat *potentiam activam cum aliqua praeeminentia*. Et ideo haec definitio baptismo non competit.

AD QUARTUM dicendum quod nomen *ordinis* dupliciter accipitur. Quandoque enim significat ipsam relationem. Et sic est tam in inferiori quam in superiori, ut ob-

OBJ. 2: Further, just as a character is imprinted in the sacrament of holy orders, so is it in the sacrament of baptism. Now character was not mentioned in the definition of baptism. Therefore, neither should it be mentioned in the definition of holy orders.

OBJ. 3: Further, in baptism there is also given a certain spiritual power to approach the sacraments; and again it is a seal, since it is a sacrament. Therefore, this definition is applicable to baptism; and consequently it is improperly applied to holy orders.

OBJ. 4: Further, order is a kind of relation, and relation is realized in both its terms. Now the terms of the relation of order are the superior and the inferior. Therefore, inferiors have order as well as superiors. Yet there is no power of preeminence in them, such as is mentioned here in the definition of holy orders, as appears from the subsequent explanation (*Sentences* IV, D. 53), where *promotion to power* is mentioned. Therefore, holy orders is improperly defined there.

I ANSWER THAT, The Master's definition of order applies to holy orders as a sacrament of the Church. Hence he mentions two things, namely the outward sign, a *kind of seal*, i.e., a kind of sign, and the inward effect, *whereby spiritual power*, etc.

REPLY OBJ. 1: *Seal* stands here, not for the inward character, but for the outward action, which is the sign and cause of inward power; and this is also the sense of *character* in the other definition.

If, however, it be taken for the inward character, the definition would not be unsuitable; because the division of a sacrament into those three things is not a division into integral parts, properly speaking, since what is reality only is not essential to the sacrament, and that which is the sacrament is transitory, while that which is sacrament and reality is said to remain. Therefore, it follows that inward character itself is essentially and principally the sacrament of order.

REPLY OBJ. 2: Although in baptism there is conferred a spiritual power to receive the other sacraments, for which reason it imprints a character, nevertheless this is not its principal effect, but the inward cleansing; wherefore baptism would be given even though the former motive did not exist. On the other hand, 'order' denotes power principally. Wherefore the character which is a spiritual power is included in the definition of holy orders, but not in that of baptism.

REPLY OBJ. 3: In baptism there is given a certain spiritual potentiality to receive, and consequently a somewhat passive potentiality. But *power* properly denotes *active potentiality, together with some kind of preeminence*. Hence this definition is not applicable to baptism.

REPLY OBJ. 4: The word 'order' is used in two ways. For sometimes it denotes the relation itself, and thus it is both in the inferior and in the superior, as the objection states;

iectio tangit. Et sic non accipitur hic. Aliquando autem accipitur pro ipso gradu qui ordinem primo modo acceptum facit. Et quia ratio ordinis prout est relatio, invenitur ubi primo aliquid superius alteri occurrit, ideo hic gradus eminens per potestatem spiritualem ordo nominatur.

but it is not thus that we use the word here. On the other hand, it denotes the degree which results in the order taken in the first sense. And since the notion of order as relation is observed where we first meet with something higher than another, it follows that this degree of preeminence by spiritual power is called order.

Article 3

Whether Holy Orders Is a Sacrament?

AD TERTIUM SIC PROCEDITUR. Videtur quod ordo non sit sacramentum. *Sacramentum* enim, ut dicit Hugo de Sancto Victore, *est materiale elementum*. Sed ordo non nominat aliquid huiusmodi, sed magis relationem vel potestatem: quia ordo est pars potestatis, secundum Isidorum. Ergo non est sacramentum.

PRAETEREA, sacramenta non sunt de Ecclesia triumphante. Sed ordo est ibi: ut patet de angelis. Ergo ordo non est sacramentum.

PRAETEREA, sicut praelatio spiritualis, quae est ordo, datur cum quadam consecratione, ita et praelatio saecularis: quia et reges inunguntur, ut dictum est. Sed regia dignitas non est sacramentum. Ergo nec ordo de quo loquimur.

SED CONTRA est quia ab omnibus enumeratur inter septem Ecclesiae sacramenta.

PRAETEREA, *propter quod unumquodque, et illud magis*. Sed propter ordinem fit homo dispensator aliorum sacramentorum. Ergo ordo habet magis rationem quod sit sacramentum quam etiam alia.

RESPONDEO dicendum quod sacramentum, ut ex dictis patet, nihil est aliud quam quaedam sanctificatio homini exhibita cum aliquo signo visibili. Unde, cum in susceptione ordinis quaedam consecratio homini exhibeatur per visibilia signa, constat ordinem esse sacramentum.

AD PRIMUM ergo dicendum quod, quamvis ordo in suo nomine non exprimat aliquod materiale elementum, tamen ordo non confertur sine aliquo elemento materiali.

AD SECUNDUM dicendum quod potestates proportionari debent illis ad quae sunt. Communicatio autem divinorum, ad quam datur spiritualis potestas, non fit angelis per aliqua sensibilia signa, sicut in hominibus contingit. Et ideo potestas spiritualis, quae est ordo, non adhibetur angelis cum aliquibus signis visibilibus sicut hominibus. Et ideo in hominibus est ordo sacramentum, sed non in angelis.

AD TERTIUM dicendum quod non omnis benedictio quae hominibus adhibetur, vel consecratio, est sacramentum. Quia et monachi et abbates benedicuntur:

OBJECTION 1: It would seem that holy orders is not a sacrament. For a *sacrament*, according to Hugh of St. Victor (*On the Sacraments* 1) *is a material element*. Now 'order' denotes nothing of the kind, but rather relation or power; since 'order' is a part of power according to Isidore. Therefore, it is not a sacrament.

OBJ. 2: Further, the sacraments do not concern the Church Triumphant. Yet order is there, as in the angels. Therefore, it is not a sacrament.

OBJ. 3: Further, just as spiritual authority, which is holy orders, is given by means of consecration, so is secular authority, since kings also are anointed, as stated above (Q. 19, A. 1). But the kingly power is not a sacrament. Therefore, neither is holy orders of which we speak now.

ON THE CONTRARY, It is numbered among the seven sacraments of the Church by everyone.

FURTHER, *The cause of a thing being such, is still more so.* Now holy orders is the cause of man being the dispenser of the other sacraments. Therefore, holy orders has more reason for being a sacrament than the others.

I ANSWER THAT, As stated above (Q. 29, A. 1; III, Q. 60), a sacrament is nothing else than a sanctification conferred on man with some outward sign. Wherefore, since by receiving holy orders a consecration is conferred on man by visible signs, it is clear that holy orders is a sacrament.

REPLY OBJ. 1: Although holy orders does not by its name express a material element, it is not conferred without some material element.

REPLY OBJ. 2: Power must be proportionate to the purpose for which it is intended. Now the communication of divine things, which is the purpose for which spiritual power is given, is not effected among the angels by means of sensible signs, as is the case among men. Hence the spiritual power that is holy orders is not bestowed on the angels by visible signs, as on men. Therefore, holy orders is a sacrament among men, but not among angels.

REPLY OBJ. 3: Not every blessing or consecration given to men is a sacrament, for both monks and abbots are blessed, and yet such blessings are not sacraments, and in

tamen illae benedictiones non sunt sacramenta. Et similiter nec regalis unctio. Quia per huiusmodi benedictiones non ordinantur aliqui ad dispensationem divinorum sacramentorum, sicut per benedictiones ordinis.

like manner neither is the anointing of a king; because by such blessings men are not ordained to the dispensing of the divine sacraments as by the blessing of holy orders. Hence the comparison fails.

Article 4

Whether the Form of This Sacrament Is Suitably Expressed?

AD QUARTUM SIC PROCEDITUR. Videtur quod forma huius sacramenti inconvenienter in littera exprimatur. Quia sacramenta efficaciam habent ex forma. Sed efficacia sacramentorum est ex *virtute divina*, quae in eis *secretius operatur salutem*. Ergo in forma huius sacramenti deberet fieri mentio de virtute divina per invocationem Trinitatis: sicut in aliis sacramentis.

PRAETEREA, imperare est eius qui habet auctoritatem. Sed auctoritas non residet apud eum qui sacramenta dispensat, sed ministerium tantum. Ergo non deberet uti imperativo modo, ut diceret sic: *agite* vel *accipite* hoc vel illud, vel aliquid huiusmodi.

PRAETEREA, in forma sacramenti non debet fieri mentio nisi de illis quae sunt de essentia sacramenti. Sed usus potestatis acceptae non est de essentia huius sacramenti, sed consequitur ad ipsum. Ergo non debet de eo fieri mentio in forma huius sacramenti.

PRAETEREA, omnia sacramenta ordinant ad aeternam remunerationem. Sed in formis aliorum sacramentorum non fit mentio de remuneratione. Ergo nec in forma huius sacramenti deberet de ea fieri mentio, sicut fit cum dicitur: *habiturus partem si fideliter*, etc.

RESPONDEO dicendum quod hoc sacramentum principaliter consistit in potestate tradita. Potestas autem a potestate traducitur sicut simile ex simili. Et iterum potestas per usum innotescit: quia potentiae notificantur per actus. Et ideo in forma ordinis exprimitur usus ordinis per actum qui imperatur; et exprimitur traductio potestatis per imperativum modum.

AD PRIMUM ergo dicendum quod alia sacramenta non ordinantur principaliter ad effectus similes potestati per quam sacramenta dispensantur, sicut hoc sacramentum. Et ideo in hoc sacramento est quasi quaedam communicatio univoca unde in aliis sacramentis exprimitur aliquid ex parte divinae virtutis, cui effectus sacramenti assimilatur: non autem in hoc sacramento.

AD SECUNDUM dicendum quod, quamvis in episcopo, qui est minister huius sacramenti, non sit auctoritas respectu collationis huius sacramenti, tamen habet aliquam potestatem respectu potestatis ordinis quae confertur per ipsum, inquantum a sua potestate derivatur.

OBJECTION 1: It would seem that the form of this sacrament is unsuitably set forth in the text (*Sentences* IV, D. 24). Because the sacraments take their efficacy from their form. Now the efficacy of the sacraments is from the *divine power*, which *works our salvation* in them *in a most hidden manner*. Therefore, the form of this sacrament should include a mention of the divine power by the invocation of the Trinity, as in the other sacraments.

OBJ. 2: Further, to command pertains to one who has authority. Now, the dispenser of the sacrament exercises no authority, but only ministry. Therefore, he should not use the imperative mood by saying *do* or *receive* this or that, or some similar expression.

OBJ. 3: Further, mention should not be made in the sacramental form except of such things as are essential to the sacrament. But the use of the power received is not essential to this sacrament, but is consequent upon it. Therefore, it should not be mentioned in the form of this sacrament.

OBJ. 4: Further, all the sacraments direct us to an eternal reward. But the forms of the other sacraments make no mention of a reward. Therefore, neither should any mention be made thereof in the form of this sacrament, as in the words: *since you will have a share, if faithfully*, etc.

I ANSWER THAT, This sacrament consists chiefly in the power conferred. Now power is conferred by power, as like proceeds from like; and again power is made known by its use, since powers are manifested by their acts. Hence in the form of holy orders the use of the order is expressed by the act which is commanded; and the conferring of power is expressed by employing the imperative mood.

REPLY OBJ. 1: The other sacraments are not ordained chiefly to effects similar to the power whereby the sacraments are dispensed, as this sacrament is. Thus in this sacrament there is a kind of universal communication. Hence in the other sacraments something is expressed on the part of the divine power to which the effect of the sacrament is likened, but not in this sacrament.

REPLY OBJ. 2: Although the bishop who is the minister of this sacrament has no authority in respect of the conferring of this sacrament, nevertheless he has some power with regard to the power of holy orders, which power he confers insofar as it is derived from his.

AD TERTIUM dicendum quod usus potestatis est effectus potestatis in genere causae efficientis: et sic non habet quod in definitione ordinis ponatur. Sed est quodammodo causa in genere causae finalis. Et ideo secundum hanc rationem poni potest in definitione ordinis.

AD QUARTUM dicendum, quod aliter se habet in hoc, et in aliis sacramentis; nam per hoc sacramentum confertur officium aliquod, vel potestas aliquid faciendi, et ideo convenienter fit mentio remunerationis acquirendae, si fideliter administretur: sed in aliis non confertur simile officium, vel similis potestas ad agendum, et ideo in illis nulla remunerationis mentio fit. Ad alia igitur sacramenta velut passive quodammodo se habet suscipiens, quia recipit ea propter proprium statum perficiendum tantum: sed ad hoc sacramentum se habet quodammodo active, quia illud suscipit propter hierarchicas functiones in Ecclesia exercendas: unde quamvis alia eo ipso quod gratiam conferunt, ordinent ad salutem, proprie tamen ad remunerationem non ordinant, sicut hoc sacramentum.

REPLY OBJ. 3: The use of power is the effect of power in the genus of efficient cause, and from this point of view it has no reason to be mentioned in the definition of holy orders. But it is somewhat a cause in the genus of final cause, and from this point of view it can be placed in the definition of holy orders.

REPLY OBJ. 4: Here there is a difference between this and the other sacraments. For by this sacrament an office or the power to do something is conferred; and so it is fitting that mention be made of the reward to be obtained if it be administered faithfully. But in the other sacraments no such office or power to act is conferred, and so no mention of reward is made in them. Accordingly, the recipient is somewhat passive in relation to the other sacraments, because he receives them for the perfecting of his own state only, whereas in relation to this sacrament he holds himself somewhat actively, since he receives it for the sake of exercising hierarchical duties in the Church. Therefore, although the other sacraments from the very fact that they give grace direct the recipient to salvation, properly speaking they do not direct him to a reward in the same way as this sacrament does.

Article 5

Whether This Sacrament Has Any Matter?

AD QUINTUM SIC PROCEDITUR. Videtur quod hoc sacramentum non habeat materiam. Quia in omni sacramento quod habet materiam, virtus operans in sacramento est in materia. Sed in rebus materialibus quae hic adhibentur, sicut sunt claves et candelabra et huiusmodi, non videtur esse aliqua virtus sanctificandi. Ergo non habet materiam.

PRAETEREA, in isto sacramento confertur plenitudo *gratiae septiformis*, ut in littera dicitur sicut in confirmatione. Sed materia confirmationis praeexigit sanctificationem. Cum ergo ea quae in hoc sacramento videntur esse materialia, non sint praesanctificata, videtur quod non sint materia huius sacramenti.

PRAETEREA, in quolibet sacramento habente materiam requiritur contactus materiae ad eum qui suscipit sacramentum. Sed, ut a quibusdam dicitur, contactus dictorum materialium ab eo qui suscipit sacramentum, non est de necessitate sacramenti, sed solum porrectio. Ergo praedictae res materiales non sunt materia huius sacramenti.

SED CONTRA est quia omne sacramentum consistit in rebus et verbis. Sed res in quolibet sacramento sunt materia ipsius. Ergo et res quae in hoc sacramento adhibentur, sunt materia huius sacramenti.

OBJECTION 1: It would seem that this sacrament has no matter. For in every sacrament that has matter, the power that works in the sacrament is in the matter. But in the material objects which are used here, such as keys, candlesticks, and so forth, there is not apparently any power of sanctification. Therefore, it has no matter.

OBJ. 2: Further, in this sacrament the fullness of *sevenfold grace* is conferred, as stated in the text (*Sentences* IV, D. 24), just as in confirmation. But the matter of confirmation requires to be consecrated beforehand. Since, then, the things which appear to be material in this sacrament are not consecrated beforehand, it would seem that they are not the matter of the sacrament.

OBJ. 3: Further, in any sacrament that has matter there needs to be contact of matter with the recipient of the sacrament. Now, as some say, it is not essential to this sacrament that there be contact between the aforesaid material objects and the recipient of the sacrament, but only that they be presented to him. Therefore, the aforesaid material objects are not the matter of this sacrament.

ON THE CONTRARY, Every sacrament consists of things and words. Now in any sacrament the thing is the matter. Therefore, the things employed in this sacrament are its matter.

PRAETEREA, plus requiritur ad dispensandum sacramenta quam ad suscipiendum sacramenta. Sed baptismus, in quo datur potestas ad suscipiendum sacramenta, indiget materia. Ergo et ordo, in quo datur potestas ad ea dispensanda.

RESPONDEO dicendum quod materia in sacramentis exterius adhibita significat virtutem in sacramentis agentem ex extrinseco omnino advenire. Unde, cum effectus proprius huius sacramenti, scilicet character, non percipiatur ex aliqua operatione ipsius qui ad sacramentum accedit, sicut erat in poenitentia, sed omnino ex extrinseco adveniat, competit ei materiam habere. Tamen diversimode ab aliis sacramentis quae materiam habent. Quia hoc quod in sacramento confertur, in aliis sacramentis derivatur tantum a Deo, non a ministro, qui sacramentum dispensat: sed illud quod in hoc sacramento traditur, scilicet spiritualis potestas, derivatur etiam ab eo qui sacramentum dat, sicut potestas imperfecta a perfecta. Et ideo efficacia aliorum sacramentorum principaliter consistit in materia, quae virtutem divinam significat et continet ex sanctificatione per ministerium adhibita: sed efficacia huius sacramenti principaliter residet penes eum qui sacramentum dispensat: materia autem adhibetur magis ad determinandum potestatem, quae traditur particulariter ab habente eam complete, quam ad potestatem causandam. Quod patet ex hoc quod materia competit usui potestatis.

ET PER HOC patet solutio ad primum.

AD SECUNDUM dicendum quod materiam in aliis sacramentis oportet sanctificari propter virtutem quam continet. Sed non est ita in proposito.

AD TERTIUM dicendum quod, sustinendo illud dictum, ex dictis apparet causa eius. Quia enim potestas ordinis non accipitur a materia sed a ministro, ideo porrectio materiae magis est de essentia sacramenti quam tactus. Tamen ipsa verba formae videntur ostendere quod tactus materiae sit de essentia sacramenti: quia dicitur, *accipe* hoc vel illud.

FURTHER, More is requisite to dispense the sacraments than to receive them. Yet baptism, wherein the power is given to receive the sacraments, needs a matter. Therefore, holy orders does also, wherein the power is given to dispense them.

I ANSWER THAT, The matter employed outwardly in the sacraments signifies that the power which works in the sacraments comes entirely from without. Wherefore, since the effect proper to this sacrament, namely, the character, is not received through any operation of the one who approaches the sacrament, as was the case in penance, but comes wholly from without, it is fitting that it should have a matter, yet otherwise than the other sacraments that have matter; because that which is bestowed in the other sacraments comes from God alone, and not from the minister who dispenses the sacrament; whereas that which is conferred in this sacrament, namely, the spiritual power, comes also from him who gives the sacrament, as imperfect from perfect power. Hence the efficacy of the other sacraments resides chiefly in the matter which both signifies and contains the divine power through the sanctification applied by the minister; whereas the efficacy of this sacrament resides chiefly with him who dispenses the sacrament. And the matter is employed to show the powers conferred in particular by one who has it completely, rather than to cause power; and this is clear from the fact that the matter is in keeping with the use of power.

THIS SUFFICES for the reply to the first objection.

REPLY OBJ. 2: It is necessary for the matter to be consecrated in the other sacraments, on account of the power it contains; but it is not so in the case in point.

REPLY OBJ. 3: If we admit this assertion, the reason for it is clear from what we have said; for, since the power of order is received from the minister and not from the matter, the presenting of the matter is more essential to the sacrament than contact therewith. However, the words themselves of the form would seem to indicate that contact with the matter is essential to the sacrament, for it is said: *Receive this or that.*

QUESTION 35

THE EFFECT OF HOLY ORDERS

Deinde considerandum est de effectu Huius sacramenti.

Circa quod quaeruntur quinque.

Primo: utrum in sacramento ordinis gratia conferatur.

Secundo: utrum imprimatur character.

Tertio: utrum character ordinis praesupponat characterem baptismalem.

Quarto: utrum praesupponat characterem confirmationis.

Quinto: utrum character unius ordinis praesupponat characterem alterius.

We must next consider the effect of this sacrament.

Under this head there are five points of inquiry:

(1) Whether sanctifying grace is conferred in the sacrament of holy orders?

(2) Whether a character is imprinted in connection with all the orders?

(3) Whether the character of holy orders presupposes of necessity the character of baptism?

(4) Whether it presupposes of necessity the character of confirmation?

(5) Whether the character of one order presupposes of necessity the character of another order?

Article 1

Whether Sanctifying Grace Is Conferred in the Sacrament of Holy Orders?

AD PRIMUM SIC PROCEDITUR. Videtur quod in sacramento ordinis non conferatur gratia gratum faciens. Quia communiter dicitur quod sacramentum ordinis ordinatur contra defectum ignorantiae. Sed contra ignorantiam non datur gratia gratum faciens, sed gratia gratis data: quia gratia gratum faciens magis respicit affectum. Ergo in hoc sacramento ordinis non datur gratia gratum faciens.

PRAETEREA, ordo distinctionem importat. Sed membra Ecclesiae non distinguuntur per gratiam gratum facientem, sed secundum gratiam gratis datam, de qua dicitur, I Cor. 12: *divisiones gratiarum sunt*. Ergo in ordine non datur gratia gratum faciens.

PRAETEREA, nulla causa praesupponit effectum suum. Sed in eo qui accedit ad ordines praesupponitur gratia, per quam fit idoneus ad exacutionem ordinis. Ergo talis gratia non confertur in ordinis collatione.

SED CONTRA: Sacramenta novae legis *efficiunt quod figurant*. Sed ordo per numerum septenarium significat septem dona Spiritus Sancti, ut in littera dicitur. Ergo dona Spiritus Sancti, quae non sunt sine gratia gratum faciente, in ordine dantur.

PRAETEREA, ordo est sacramentum novae legis. Sed in definitione talis sacramenti ponitur ut *causa gratiae existat*. Ergo causat gratiam in suscipiente.

OBJECTION 1: It would seem that sanctifying grace is not conferred in the sacrament of holy orders. For it is commonly agreed that the sacrament of holy orders is directed to counteract the defect of ignorance. Now, not sanctifying grace but gratuitous grace is given to counteract ignorance, for sanctifying grace has more to do with the will. Therefore, sanctifying grace is not given in the sacrament of holy orders.

OBJ. 2: Further, 'order' implies distinction. Now the members of the Church are distinguished not by sanctifying but by gratuitous grace, of which it is said: *there are diversities of graces* (1 Cor 12:4). Therefore, sanctifying grace is not given in holy orders.

OBJ. 3: Further, no cause presupposes its effect. But grace is presupposed in one who receives holy orders, so that he may be worthy to receive them. Therefore, this same grace is not given in the conferring of holy orders.

ON THE CONTRARY, The sacraments of the new law *cause what they signify*. Now holy orders by its sevenfold number signifies the seven gifts of the Holy Spirit, as stated in the text (*Sentences* IV, D. 24). Therefore, the gifts of the Holy Spirit, which are not apart from sanctifying grace, are given in holy orders.

FURTHER, Holy orders is a sacrament of the new law. Now the definition of a sacrament of that kind includes the words, *that it may be a cause of grace*. Therefore, it causes grace in the recipient.

Respondeo dicendum quod *Dei perfecta sunt opera*, ut dicitur Deut. 32. Et ideo cuicumque datur potentia aliqua divinitus, dantur ea per quae executio illius potentiae potest congrue fieri. Et hoc etiam in naturalibus patet: quia animalibus dantur membra quibus potentiae animae possunt exire in actus suos, nisi sit defectus ex parte materiae. Sicut autem gratia gratum faciens est necessaria ad hoc quod homo digne sacramenta recipiat, ita etiam ad hoc quod homo digne sacramenta dispenset. Et ideo, sicut in baptismo, per quem fit homo susceptivus aliorum sacramentorum, datur gratia gratum faciens; ita in sacramento ordinis, per quod homo ordinatur ad aliorum sacramentorum dispensationem.

Ad primum ergo dicendum quod ordo datur non in remedium unius personae, sed totius Ecclesiae. Unde quod dicitur *contra ignorantiam dari*, non est intelligendum ita quod per susceptionem ordinis pellatur ignorantia in suscipiente: sed quia suscipiens ordinem praeficitur ad pellendam ignorantiam in plebe.

Ad secundum dicendum quod, quamvis dona gratiae gratum facientis communia sint omnibus membris Ecclesiae, tamen illorum actus donorum secundum quae attenditur distinctio in membris Ecclesiae idoneus susceptor aliquis esse non potest nisi caritas adsit: quae quidem sine gratia gratum faciente esse non potest.

Ad tertium dicendum quod ad idoneam executionem ordinum non sufficit bonitas qualiscumque, sed requiritur bonitas excellens: ut sicut illi qui ordinem suscipiunt super plebem constituuntur gradu ordinis, ita et superiores sint merito sanctitatis. Et ideo praeexigitur gratia quae sufficiebat ad hoc quod digne connumerentur in plebe Christi: sed confertur in ipsa susceptione ordinis amplius gratiae munus, per quod ad maiora reddantur idonei.

I answer that *The works of God are perfect* (Deut 32:4); and consequently whoever receives power from above receives also those things that render him competent to exercise that power. This is also the case in natural things, since animals are provided with members by which their soul's powers are enabled to proceed to their respective actions unless there be some defect on the part of matter. Now just as sanctifying grace is necessary in order that man receive the sacraments worthily, so is it that he may dispense them worthily. Therefore, as in baptism sanctifying grace is given whereby a man is adapted to receive the other sacraments, so is it in the sacrament of holy orders whereby man is ordained to the dispensation of the other sacraments.

Reply Obj. 1: Holy orders is given as a remedy not to one person but to the whole Church. Hence, although it is said *to be given in order to counteract ignorance*, it does not mean that by receiving holy orders a man has his ignorance driven out of him, but that the recipient of holy orders is set in authority to expel ignorance from among the people.

Reply Obj. 2: Although the gifts of sanctifying grace are common to all the members of the Church, nevertheless a man cannot be the worthy recipient of those gifts in respect of which the members of the Church are distinguished from one another unless he have charity, and this cannot be apart from sanctifying grace.

Reply Obj. 3: The worthy exercise of holy orders requires not any kind of goodness but excellent goodness, in order that as they who receive orders are set above the people in the degree of holy orders, so they may be above them by the merit of holiness. Hence they are required to have the grace that suffices to make them worthy members of Christ's people, but when they receive holy orders they are given a yet greater gift of grace, whereby they are rendered apt for greater things.

Article 2

Whether in the Sacrament of Holy Orders a Character Is Imprinted in Connection with All the Orders?

Ad secundum sic proceditur. Videtur quod in sacramento ordinis non imprimatur character quantum ad omnes ordines. Quia ordinis character est quaedam spiritualis potestas. Sed quidam ordines non ordinantur nisi ad quosdam actus corporales, scilicet ostiarii vel acolythi. Ergo in eis non imprimitur character.

Praeterea, omnis character est indelebilis. Ergo per characterem homo ponitur in tali statu a quo non possit recedere. Sed illi qui habent aliquos ordines, possunt licite redire ad laicatum. Ergo non imprimitur character in omnibus ordinibus.

Objection 1: It would seem that in the sacrament of holy orders a character is not imprinted in connection with all the orders. For the character of holy orders is a spiritual power. Now some orders are directed only to certain bodily acts, for instance, those of the porter or of the acolyte. Therefore, a character is not imprinted in these orders.

Obj. 2: Further, every character is indelible. Therefore, a character places a man in a state whence he cannot withdraw. Now those who have certain orders can lawfully return to the laity. Therefore, a character is not imprinted in all the orders.

PRAETEREA, per characterem homo adscribitur ad aliquid sacrum dandum vel accipiendum. Sed ad susceptionem sacramentorum homo sufficienter ordinatur per characterem baptismalem. Dispensator autem sacramentorum non constituitur aliquis nisi in ordine sacerdotali. Ergo in aliis ordinibus non imprimitur character.

SED CONTRA: Omne sacramentum in quo non imprimitur character, est iterabile. Sed nullus ordo est iterabilis. Ergo in quolibet ordine imprimitur character.

PRAETEREA, character est signum distinctivum. Sed in quolibet ordine est aliqua distinctio. Ergo quilibet ordo imprimit characterem.

RESPONDEO dicendum quod circa hoc fuit triplex opinio. Quidam enim dixerunt quod in solo ordine sacerdotali character imprimitur. Sed hoc non est verum. Quia actum diaconi nullus potest exercere licite nisi diaconus. Et ita patet quod habet aliquam specialem potestatem in dispensatione sacramentorum, quam alii non habent.

Et propter hoc alii dixerunt quod in sacris ordinibus imprimitur character, non autem in minoribus. Sed hoc iterum nihil est. Quia per quemlibet ordinem aliquis constituitur supra plebem in aliquo gradu potestatis ordinatae ad sacramentorum dispensationem.

Unde, cum character sit signum distinctivum ab aliis, oportet quod in omnibus character imprimatur. Cuius etiam signum est quod perpetuo manent, et nunquam iterantur. Et haec est tertia opinio: quae communior est.

AD PRIMUM ergo dicendum quod quilibet ordo vel habet actum circa ipsum sacramentum, vel ordinatum ad sacramentorum dispensationem: sicut ostiarii habent actum admittendi homines ad divinorum sacramentorum inspectionem, et sic de aliis. Et ideo in omnibus requiritur spiritualis potestas.

AD SECUNDUM dicendum quod, quantumcumque homo ad laicatum se transferat, semper tamen manet in eo character. Quod patet ex hoc quod, si ad clericatum revertatur, non iterum ordinem quem habuerat, suscipit.

AD TERTIUM dicendum sicut ad primum.

OBJ. 3: Further, by means of a character a man is appointed to give or to receive some sacred thing. Now a man is sufficiently adapted to the reception of the sacraments by the character of baptism, and a man is not appointed to dispense the sacraments except in the order of priesthood. Therefore, a character is not imprinted in the other orders.

ON THE CONTRARY, Every sacrament in which a character is not imprinted can be repeated. But no order can be repeated. Therefore, a character is imprinted in each order.

FURTHER, A character is a distinctive sign. Now there is something distinct in every order. Therefore, every order imprints a character.

I ANSWER THAT, There have been three opinions on this point. For some have said that a character is imprinted only in the order of priesthood; but this is not true, since none but a deacon can exercise the act of the diaconate, and so it is clear that in the dispensation of the sacraments, he has a spiritual power which others have not.

For this reason others have said that a character is impressed in the sacred, but not in the minor, orders. But this again comes to nothing, since each order sets a man above the people in some degree of authority directed to the dispensation of the sacraments.

Wherefore since a character is a sign whereby one thing is distinguished from another, it follows that a character is imprinted in each order. And this is confirmed by the fact that they remain forever and are never repeated. This is the third and more common opinion.

REPLY OBJ. 1: Each order either has an act connected with the sacrament itself, or adapts a man to the dispensation of the sacraments; thus porters exercise the act of admitting men to witness the divine sacraments, and so forth. Consequently, a spiritual power is required in each.

REPLY OBJ. 2: For all that a man may return to the laity, the character always remains in him. This is evident from the fact that if he return to the clerical state, he does not receive again the order which he had already.

THE REPLY to the third objection is the same as to the first.

Article 3

Whether the Character of Holy Orders Presupposes the Baptismal Character?

AD TERTIUM SIC PROCEDITUR. Videtur quod character ordinis non praesupponat characterem baptismalem. Quia per characterem ordinis homo efficitur dispensator sacramentorum: per characterem baptismalem susceptivus eorundem. Sed potestas activa non praesupponit de necessitate passivam: quia potest esse

OBJECTION 1: It would seem that the character of holy orders does not presuppose the character of baptism. For the character of holy orders makes a man a dispenser of the sacraments; while the character of baptism makes him a recipient of them. Now active power does not necessarily presuppose passive power, for it can be without it, as in God.

sine ea, sicut patet in Deo. Ergo character ordinis non praesupponit de necessitate characterem baptismalem.

PRAETEREA, potest contingere quod aliquis non sit baptizatus qui se baptizatum existimat probabiliter. Si ergo talis ad ordines accedat, non consequetur characterem ordinis, si character ordinis praesupponit characterem baptismalem. Et sic ea quae faciet vel in consecratione vel in absolutione, nihil erunt, et in hoc Ecclesia decipietur. Quod est inconveniens.

SED CONTRA, baptismus est *ianua sacramentorum*. Ergo, cum ordo sit quoddam sacramentum, praesupponit baptismum.

RESPONDEO dicendum quod nihil potest aliquis accipere cuius receptivam potentiam non habet. Per characterem autem baptismalem efficitur homo receptivus aliorum sacramentorum. Unde qui characterem baptismalem non habet, nullum alterum sacramentum recipere potest. Et character ordinis baptismalem characterem praesupponit.

AD PRIMUM ergo dicendum quod in eo qui habet potentiam activam a se, potentia activa non praesupponit passivam. Sed in eo qui habet potentiam activam ab altero, praeexigitur ad potentiam activam potentia passiva, quae recipere possit potentiam activam.

AD SECUNDUM dicendum quod talis, si ad sacerdotium promoveatur, non est sacerdos, nec conficere potest, nec absolvere in foro poenitentiali. Unde secundum canones debet iterato baptizari et ordinari. Et si etiam in episcopum promoveatur, illi quos ordinat non habent ordinem. Sed tamen pie credi potest quod, quantum ad ultimos effectus sacramentorum, Summus Sacerdos suppleret defectum; et quod non permitteret hoc ita latere quod Ecclesiae posset periculum imminere.

Therefore, the character of holy orders does not necessarily presuppose the character of baptism.

OBJ. 2: Further, it may happen that a man is not baptized, and yet think with probability that he has been baptized. If, therefore, such a person present himself for holy orders, he will not receive the character of holy orders, supposing the character of holy orders to presuppose the character of baptism; and consequently whatever he does by way of consecration or absolution will be invalid, and the Church will be deceived therein, which is inadmissible.

ON THE CONTRARY, Baptism is the *door of the sacraments*. Therefore, since holy orders is a sacrament, it presupposes baptism.

I ANSWER THAT, No one can receive what he has not the power to receive. Now the character of baptism gives a man the power to receive the other sacraments. Therefore, he that has not the baptismal character can receive no other sacrament; and consequently the character of holy orders presupposes the character of baptism.

REPLY OBJ. 1: In one who has active power of himself, the active does not presuppose the passive power; but in one who has active power from another, passive power, whereby he is enabled to receive the active power, is prerequisite to active power.

REPLY OBJ. 2: Such a man, if he be ordained to the priesthood, is not a priest, and he can neither consecrate nor absolve in the tribunal of penance. Therefore, according to the canons he must be baptized and reordained (*Decretals*). And even though he be raised to the episcopate, those whom he ordains receive not the holy orders. Yet it may piously be believed that as regards the ultimate effects of the sacraments, the High Priest will supply the defect, and that he would not allow this to be so hidden as to endanger the Church.

Article 4

Whether the Character of Holy Orders Necessarily Presupposes the Character of Confirmation?

AD QUARTUM SIC PROCEDITUR. Videtur quod praesupponat de necessitate characterem confirmationis. Quia in his quae sunt ordinata ad invicem, sicut medium praesupponit primum, ita ultimum praesupponit medium. Sed character confirmationis praesupponit baptismalem quasi primum. Ergo character ordinis praesupponit characterem confirmationis quasi medium.

PRAETEREA, qui ad alios confirmandos ponuntur, maxime debent esse firmi. Sed illi qui sacramentum ordinis suscipiunt sunt aliorum confirmatores. Ergo ipsi maxime debent habere sacramentum confirmationis.

OBJECTION 1: It would seem that the character of holy orders necessarily presupposes the character of confirmation. For in things subordinate to one another, as the middle presupposes the first, so does the last presuppose the middle. Now the character of confirmation presupposes that of baptism as being the first. Therefore, the character of holy orders presupposes that of confirmation as being in the middle.

OBJ. 2: Further, those who are appointed to confirm should themselves be most firm. Now those who receive the sacrament of holy orders are appointed to confirm others. Therefore, they especially should have received the sacrament of confirmation.

SED CONTRA, Apostoli receperunt potestatem ordinis ante Ascensionem, Ioan. 20, ubi dictum est: *accipite Spiritum Sanctum*. Sed confirmati sunt post Ascensionem per adventum Spiritus Sancti. Ergo ordo non praesupponit confirmationem.

RESPONDEO dicendum quod ad susceptionem ordinis praeexigitur aliquid quasi de necessitate sacramenti, et aliquid de congruitate. De necessitate enim sacramenti exigitur quod ille qui accedit ad ordines sit susceptivus, quod competit ei per baptismum. Et ideo character baptismalis praesupponitur de necessitate sacramenti, ita quod sine eo sacramentum ordinis conferri non potest. Sed de congruitate requiritur omnis perfectio per quam aliquis reddatur idoneus ad executionem ordinis: et unum de istis est ut sit confirmatus. Et ideo de congruitate character ordinis characterem confirmationis praesupponit, et non de necessitate.

AD PRIMUM ergo dicendum quod non est similis habitudo huius medii ad ultimum, et primi ad medium: quia per characterem baptismalem fit homo susceptivus sacramenti confirmationis, non autem per sacramentum confirmationis fit susceptivus sacramenti ordinis. Et ideo non est similis ratio.

AD SECUNDUM dicendum quod illa ratio procedit de idoneitate quantum ad congruitatem.

ON THE CONTRARY, The apostles received the power of holy orders before the Ascension, where it is said: *receive the Holy Spirit* (John 20:22). But they were confirmed after the Ascension by the coming of the Holy Spirit. Therefore, holy orders does not presuppose confirmation.

I ANSWER THAT, For the reception of holy orders something is prerequisite for the validity of the sacrament, and something as congruous to the sacrament. For the validity of the sacrament it is required that one who presents himself for holy orders should be capable of receiving them, and this is competent to him through baptism; wherefore the baptismal character is prerequisite for the validity of the sacrament, so that the sacrament of holy orders cannot be conferred without it. On the other hand, as congruous to the sacrament a man is required to have every perfection whereby he becomes adapted to the exercise of holy orders, and one of these is that he be confirmed. Wherefore the character of holy orders presupposes the character of confirmation as congruous but not as necessary.

REPLY OBJ. 1: In this case the middle does not stand in the same relation to the last as the first to the middle, because the character of baptism enables a man to receive the sacrament of confirmation, whereas the character of confirmation does not enable a man to receive the sacrament of holy orders. Hence the comparison fails.

REPLY OBJ. 2: This argument considers aptness by way of congruity.

Article 5

Whether the Character of One Order Necessarily Presupposes the Character of Another Order?

AD QUINTUM SIC PROCEDITUR. Videtur quod character unius ordinis praesupponat de necessitate characterem alterius ordinis. Quia maior est convenientia ordinis ad ordinem quam ordinis ad aliud sacramentum. Sed character ordinis praesupponit characterem alterius sacramenti, scilicet baptismi. Ergo multo fortius character unius ordinis praesupponit characterem alterius.

PRAETEREA, ordines sunt quidam gradus. Sed nullus potest pervenire ad posteriorem gradum nisi priorem ascenderit. Ergo nullus potest accipere characterem ordinis sequentis nisi prius accipiat ordinem praecedentem.

SED CONTRA, si omittatur aliquid in sacramento quod sit de necessitate sacramenti, oportet quod sacramentum iteretur. Sed si aliquis accipiat sequentem ordinem praetermisso primo, non reordinabitur, sed conferetur sibi quod deerat, secundum statuta canonum. Ergo praecederis ordo non est de necessitate sequentis.

OBJECTION 1: It would seem that the character of one order necessarily presupposes the character of another order. For there is more in common between one order and another than between order and another sacrament. But the character of order presupposes the character of another sacrament, namely, baptism. Much more, therefore, does the character of one order presuppose the character of another.

OBJ. 2: Further, the orders are degrees of a kind. Now no one can reach a further degree unless he first mount the previous degree. Therefore, no one can receive the character of a subsequent order unless he has first received the preceding order.

ON THE CONTRARY, If anything necessary for a sacrament be omitted in that sacrament, the sacrament must be repeated. But if one receive a subsequent order without receiving a preceding order he is not reordained, but he receives what was lacking, according to the canonical statutes (*Decretals*). Therefore, the preceding order is not necessary for the following.

RESPONDEO dicendum quod non est de necessitate superiorum ordinum quod aliquis minores ordines prius habeat: quia potestates sunt distinctae; et una, quantum est de sui ratione, non requirit aliam in eodem subiecto. Et ideo etiam in primitiva Ecclesia aliqui ordinabantur in presbyteros qui prius inferiores ordines non susceperant: et tamen poterant omnia quae inferiores ordines possunt; quia inferior potestas comprehenditur in superiori virtute, sicut sensus in intellectu et ducatus in regno. Sed postea per constitutionem Ecclesiae determinatum est quod ad maiores ordines se non ingerat qui prius in minoribus officiis se non humiliavit. Et inde est quod qui ordinantur per saltum, secundum canones, non reordinantur, sed id quod omissum fuerat de praecedentibus ordinibus eis confertur.

AD PRIMUM ergo dicendum quod magis conveniunt ordines ad invicem secundum similitudinem speciei quam ordo cum baptismo: sed secundum proportionem potentiae ad actum magis convenit baptismus cum ordine quam ordo cum ordine. Quia per baptismum acquirit homo potentiam passivam recipiendi ordines: non autem per ordinem inferiorem datur potentia passiva recipiendi maiores ordines.

AD SECUNDUM dicendum quod ordines non sunt gradus qui occurrant in actione una vel in uno motu, ut oporteat ad ultimum per primum devenire: sed sunt sicut gradus in diversis rebus constituti. Sicut est gradus inter hominem et angelum: nec oportet quod ille qui sit angelus, prius fuerit homo. Similiter etiam est gradus inter caput et omnia membra corporis: nec oportet quod illud quod est caput, prius fuerit pes. Et similiter est in proposito.

I ANSWER THAT, It is not necessary for the higher orders that one should have received the minor orders, because their respective powers are distinct, and one, considered in its essentials, does not require another in the same subject. Hence even in the early Church some were ordained priests without having previously received the lower orders and yet they could do all that the lower orders could, because the lower power is comprised in the higher, even as sense in understanding, and dukedom in kingdom. Afterwards, however, it was decided by the legislation of the Church that no one should present himself to the higher orders who had not previously humbled himself in the lower offices. And hence it is that according to the Canons (*Decretals*) those who are ordained without receiving a preceding order are not reordained, but receive what was lacking to them of the preceding order.

REPLY OBJ. 1: Orders have more in common with one another as regards specific likeness than holy orders has with baptism. But as regards proportion of power to action, baptism has more in common with holy orders than one order with another, because baptism confers on man the passive power to receive holy orders, whereas a lower order does not give him the passive power to receive higher orders.

REPLY OBJ. 2: Orders are not degrees combining in one action or in one movement, so that it be necessary to reach the last through the first; but they are like degrees consisting in things of different kinds, such as the degrees between man and angel, and it is not necessary that one who is an angel be first of all a man. Such also are the degrees between the head and all members of the body; nor is it necessary that that which is the head should be previously a foot. Thus it is in the case in point.

QUESTION 36

THE QUALITIES OF THOSE RECEIVING HOLY ORDERS

Deinde considerandum est de qualitate suscipientium hoc sacramentum.

Circa quod quaeruntur quinque.

Primo: utrum in suscipientibus hoc sacramentum requiratur bonitas vitae.

Secundo: utrum requiratur scientia totius sacrae Scripturae.

Tertio: utrum ex ipso merito vitae aliquis ordinis gradus consequatur.

Quarto: utrum promovens indignos ad ordines peccet.

Quinto: utrum aliquis in peccato existens possit sine peccato ordine suscepto uti.

We must next consider the qualities required of those who receive the sacrament of holy orders.

Under this head there are five points of inquiry:

(1) Whether goodness of life is required of those who receive this sacrament?

(2) Whether the knowledge of the whole of Sacred Scripture is required?

(3) Whether the degree of holy orders is obtained by mere merit of life?

(4) Whether he who raises the unworthy to holy orders sins?

(5) Whether one who is in sin can, without committing a sin, exercise the holy orders he has received?

Article 1

Whether Goodness of Life Is Required of Those Who Receive Holy Orders?

AD PRIMUM SIC PROCEDITUR. Videtur quod in suscipientibus ordines non requiratur bonitas vitae. Quia per ordinem aliquis ordinatur ad dispensationem sacramentorum. Sed sacramenta possunt dispensari a bonis et malis. Ergo non requiritur bona vita.

PRAETEREA, non est maius ministerium quod Deo in sacramentis exhibetur, quam quod ipsi corporaliter exhibetur. Sed a ministerio ipsius corporali non repulit Dominus mulierem peccatricem et infamem: ut patet Luc. 7. Ergo nec a ministerio eius in sacramentis tales sunt amovendi.

PRAETEREA, per omnem gratiam datur aliquod remedium contra peccatum. Sed illis qui habent peccatum, non debet aliquod remedium denegari quod eis valere possit. Cum ergo in sacramento ordinis gratia conferatur, videtur quod debeat etiam peccatoribus hoc sacramentum dari.

SED CONTRA: Levit. 21: *homo de semine Aaron qui habuerit maculam, non offerat panes coram Domino, nec accedat ad ministerium eius.* Sed per *maculam*, ut dicit Glossa, omne *vitium* intelligitur. Ergo ille qui est aliquo vitio irretitus, non debet ad ministerium ordinis adhiberi.

PRAETEREA, Hieronymus dicit quod *non solum episcopi, presbyteri et diaconi debent magnopere providere ut cunctum populum cui praesident sermone et conversatione praecedant, verum etiam inferiores gradus, et omnes qui Domini oraculo deserviunt: quia vehementer Eccle-*

OBJECTION 1: It would seem that goodness of life is not required of those who receive holy orders. For by holy orders a man is ordained to the dispensation of the sacraments. But the sacraments can be administered by good and wicked. Therefore, goodness of life is not requisite.

OBJ. 2: Further, the service of God in the sacraments is no greater than service offered to him in the body. Now our Lord did not cast aside the sinful and notorious woman from rendering him a bodily service (Luke 7). Therefore, neither should the like be debarred from his service in the sacraments.

OBJ. 3: Further, by every grace a remedy is given against sin. Now those who are in sin should not be refused a remedy that may avail them. Since, then, grace is given in the sacrament of holy orders, it would seem that this sacrament ought also to be conferred on sinners.

ON THE CONTRARY, *Whosoever of the seed of Aaron throughout their families has a blemish, he shall not offer bread to his God, neither shall he approach to minister to him* (Lev. 21:17–18). Now *blemish* signifies all kinds *of vice* according to a Gloss. Therefore, he who is shackled by any vice should not be admitted to the ministry of orders.

FURTHER, Commenting on the words of Titus 2:15, *let no man despise you,* Jerome says that *not only should bishops, priests, and deacons take very great care to be examples of speech and conduct to those over whom they are placed, but also the lower grades, and without exception all who*

siam Dei destruit meliores: esse laicos quam clericos. Ergo in omnibus ordinibus requiritur sanctitas vitae.

RESPONDEO dicendum quod, sicut Dionysius dicit, 3 cap. *Eccles. Hier.*: *ut subtiliores et clariores essentiae, repletae influxu solarium splendorum, lumen in eis supereminens, ad similitudinem solis, ad alia corpora invehunt; sic in omni divino non est audendum aliis dux esse, nisi secundum omnem habitum suum factus deiformissimus et Deo simillimus.* Unde, cum in quolibet ordine aliquis constituatur dux aliis in rebus divinis, quasi praesumptuosus mortaliter peccat qui cum conscientia peccati mortalis ad ordines accedit. Et ideo sanctitas vitae requiritur ad ordinem de necessitate praecepti. Sed non de necessitate sacramenti. Unde, si malus ordinatur, nihilominus ordinem habet: tamen cum peccato.

AD PRIMUM ergo dicendum quod, sicut vera sacramenta sunt quae peccator dispensat, ita verum sacramentum ordinis recipit: et sicut indigne dispensat, ita indigne recipit.

AD SECUNDUM dicendum quod illud ministerium erat tantum in executione corporalis obsequii: quod etiam licite peccatores facere possunt. Secus autem est de ministerio spirituali, ad quod applicantur ordinati: quia per ipsum efficiuntur medii inter Deum et plebem; et ideo debent de bona conscientia nitere quoad Deum, et bona fama quoad homines.

AD TERTIUM dicendum quod aliquae medicinae sunt quae exigunt robur naturae, alias cum periculo mortis assumuntur: et aliae sunt quae debilibus dari possunt. Ita etiam in spiritualibus quaedam sacramenta sunt ordinata ad remedium peccati: et talia peccatoribus sunt exhibenda, sicut baptismus et poenitentia. Illa vero quae perfectionem gratiae conferunt, requirunt hominem per gratiam confortatum.

serve the household of God, since it is most disastrous to the Church if the laity be better than the clergy. Therefore, holiness of life is requisite in all the orders.

I ANSWER THAT, As Dionysius says (*On the Ecclesiastical Hierarchies* 3), *even as the more subtle and clear essences, being filled by the outpouring of the solar radiance, like the sun enlighten other bodies with their brilliant light, so in all things pertaining to God a man must not dare to become a leader of others unless in all his habits he be most deiform and godlike.* Wherefore, since in every order a man is appointed to lead others in divine things, he who being conscious of mortal sin presents himself for holy orders is guilty of presumption and sins mortally. Consequently, holiness of life is requisite for holy orders as a matter of precept, but not as essential to the sacrament; and if a wicked man be ordained, he receives the order nonetheless, and yet with sin.

REPLY OBJ. 1: Just as the sinner dispenses sacraments validly, so does he receive validly the sacrament of holy orders, and as he dispenses unworthily, even so he receives unworthily.

REPLY OBJ. 2: The service in point consisted only in the exercise of bodily homage, which even sinners can offer lawfully. It is different with the spiritual service to which the ordained are appointed, because thereby they are made to stand between God and the people. Wherefore they should shine with a good conscience before God, and with a good name before men.

REPLY OBJ. 3: Certain medicines require a robust constitution, else it is mortally dangerous to take them; others can be given to the weak. So too in spiritual things certain sacraments are ordained as remedies for sin, and the like are to be given to sinners, as baptism and penance, while others, which confer the perfection of grace, require a man made strong by grace.

Article 2

Whether Knowledge of All Sacred Scripture Is Required?

AD SECUNDUM SIC PROCEDITUR. Videtur quod requiratur scientia totius Sacrae Scripturae. Quia ille debet habere legis scientiam a cuius ore lex requiritur. Sed *legem requirunt de ore sacerdotis*, ut patet Malach. 2. Ergo ipse debet legis totius habere scientiam.

PRAETEREA, I Petr. 3: *parati semper ad satisfactionem omni poscenti vos rationem de ea quae in vobis est fide et spe.* Sed reddere rationem de his quae sunt fidei et spei, est illorum qui perfectam scientiam sacrarum Scripturarum habent. Ergo talem scientiam debent habere illi qui ponuntur in ordinibus, quibus verba praedicta dicuntur.

OBJECTION 1: It would seem that knowledge of all Sacred Scripture is required. For one from whose lips we seek the law should have knowledge of the law. Now *the laity seek the law at the mouth of the priest* (Mal 2:7). Therefore, he should have knowledge of the whole law.

OBJ. 2: Further, 1 Peter 3:15 says, *always be ready to give an account of the hope and faith that is in you to the satisfaction of everyone who asks.* Now to give a reason for things pertaining to faith and hope belongs to those who have perfect knowledge of Sacred Scripture. Therefore, like knowledge should be possessed by those who are placed in orders, and to whom the aforesaid words are addressed.

PRAETEREA, nullus congrue legit qui non intelligit quod legit: quia *legere et non intelligere negligere est*, ut dicit Cato. Sed ad lectores, qui est quasi infimus ordo, pertinet legere Vetus Testamentum, ut in littera dicitur. Ergo ad eos pertinet habere totius veteris Testamenti intellectum. Et multo fortius ad alios superiores ordines.

SED CONTRA est quod multi promoventur ad sacerdotium qui penitus de talibus nihil sciunt, etiam in religionibus multis. Ergo videtur quod talis scientia non requiratur.

PRAETEREA, in *Vitis Patrum* legitur aliquos simplices monachos ad sacerdotium promotos, qui erant sanctissimae vitae. Ergo non requiritur praedicta scientia in ordinandis.

RESPONDEO dicendum quod in quolibet actu hominis, si debeat esse ordinatus, oportet quod adsit directio rationis. Unde ad hoc quod ordinis officium exequatur, oportet quod habeat tantam de scientia quae sufficiat ad hoc quod dirigatur in actum ordinis illius. Et ideo etiam talis scientia requiritur in eo qui debet ad ordines promoveri: et non quod universaliter in tota Scriptura sit instructus, sed plus vel minus secundum quod ad plura vel pauciora se eius officium extendit; ut scilicet illi qui aliis praeponuntur curam animarum suscipientes, sciant ea quae ad doctrinam fidei et morum pertinent, et alii sciant ea quae ad executionem sui ordinis spectant.

AD PRIMUM ergo dicendum quod sacerdos habet duos actus: unum principalem, supra corpus Christi verum; et alium secundarium, supra corpus Christi mysticum. Secundus autem actus dependet a primo, sed non convertitur. Et ideo aliqui ad sacerdotium promoventur quibus committitur primus actus tantum: sicut religiosi quibus cura animarum non committitur. Et a talium ore lex non requiritur, sed solum quod sacramenta conficiant. Et ideo talibus sufficit si tantum de scientia habeant quod ea quae ad sacramentum perficiendum spectant, rite servare possint.

Alii autem promoventur ad alium actum, qui est supra corpus Christi mysticum. Et a talium ore populus legem requirit. Unde scientia legis in eis debet esse: non quidem ut sciant omnes difficiles quaestiones legis, quia in his debet ad superiores recursus haberi; sed sciant ea quae populus debet credere et observare de lege. Sed ad superiores sacerdotes, scilicet episcopos, pertinet ut etiam ea quae difficultatem in lege facere possunt, sciant: et tanto magis quanto in maiori gradu collocantur.

AD SECUNDUM dicendum quod ratio reddenda de fide et spe non est intelligenda talis quae sufficiat ad probandum quae fidei vel spei sunt, cum utrumque de invisibilibus sit: sed ut sciant in communi probabilitatem

OBJ. 3: Further, no one is competent to read what he understands not, since *to read without intelligence is negligence*, as Cato declares (*Rudiment.*). Now it belongs to the lector (which is the lower order) to read the Old Testament, as stated in the text (*Sentences* IV, D. 24). Therefore, he should understand the whole of the Old Testament; and much more those in the higher orders.

ON THE CONTRARY, Many are raised to the priesthood who know nothing at all of these things, even in many religious orders. Therefore, it appears that this knowledge is not required.

FURTHER, We read in the *Lives of the Fathers* that certain simple monks were promoted to the priesthood who had the holiest lives. Therefore, the aforesaid knowledge is not required in those to be ordained.

I ANSWER THAT, For any human act to be rightly ordered there must be the direction of reason. Wherefore in order that a man exercise the office of an order, it is necessary for him to have as much knowledge as suffices for his direction in the act of that order. And consequently one who is to be raised to orders is required to have that knowledge, and to be instructed in Sacred Scripture, not the whole, but more or less, according as his office is of a greater or lesser extent—that is, those who are placed over others, and receive the care of souls, know things pertaining to the doctrine of faith and morals, and that others know whatever concerns the exercise of their order.

REPLY OBJ. 1: A priest exercises a twofold action: the one, which is principal, over the true body of Christ; the other, which is secondary, over the mystical body of Christ. The second act depends on the first, but not conversely. Wherefore some are raised to the priesthood to whom the first act alone is deputed, for instance, those religious who are not empowered with the care of souls. The law is not sought at the mouth of these, but they are only required for the celebration of the sacraments; and consequently it is enough for them to have such knowledge as enables them to observe rightly those things that regard the celebration of the sacrament.

Others are raised to exercise the other act which is over the mystical body of Christ, and it is at the mouth of these that the people seek the law; wherefore they ought to possess knowledge of the law, not indeed to know all the difficult points of the law (for in these they should have recourse to their superiors), but to know what the people have to believe and fulfill in the law. To the higher priests, namely, the bishops, it belongs to know even those points of the law which may offer some difficulty, and to know them the more perfectly according as they are in a higher position.

REPLY OBJ. 2: The reason that we have to give for our faith and hope does not denote one that suffices to prove matters of faith and hope, since they are both of things invisible; it means that we should be able to give general

utriusque ostendere. Ad quod non requiritur multum magna scientia.

AD TERTIUM dicendum quod ad lectorem non pertinet tradere intellectum sacrae Scripturae populo, quia hoc est superiorum ordinum: sed solum pronuntiare. Et ideo ab eo non exigitur quod habeat tantum de scientia quod sacram Scripturam intelligat: sed solum quod recte pronuntiare sciat. Et quia talis scientia de facili addiscitur et a multis, ideo probabiliter aestimari potest quod ordinatus talem scientiam acquiret, si etiam tunc eam non habeat: maxime si in via ad hoc esse videatur.

proofs of the probability of both, and for this there is not much need of great knowledge.

REPLY OBJ. 3: The lector has not to explain Sacred Scripture to the people (for this belongs to the higher orders), but merely to voice the words. Therefore, he is not required to have so much knowledge as to understand Sacred Scripture, but only to know how to pronounce it correctly. And since such knowledge is obtained easily and from many persons, it may be supposed with probability that the ordained will acquire that knowledge even if he have it not already, especially if it appears that he is on the road to acquire it.

Article 3

Whether One Obtains the Degrees of Holy Orders by the Merit of One's Life?

AD TERTIUM SIC PROCEDITUR. Videtur quod ex ipso merito vitae aliquis ordinis gradus consequatur. Quia, sicut dicit Chrysostomus, *non omnis sacerdos sanctus est, sed omnis sanctus sacerdos est.* Sed ex merito vitae aliquis efficitur sanctus. Ergo et sacerdos. Et multo fortius alios ordines habens.

PRAETEREA, in rebus naturalibus ex hoc ipso aliqua in gradu superiori collocantur quod Deo appropinquant, et magis de eius bonitatibus participant: ut Dionysius dicit, 4 cap. *Eccles. Hier.* Sed ex merito sanctitatis et scientiae aliquis efficitur Deo propinquior, et plus de eius bonitatibus recipiens: ergo ex hoc ipso in gradu ordinis collocatur.

SED CONTRA, sanctitas semel habita potest amitti. Sed ordo semel habitus nunquam amittitur. Ergo ordo non consistit in ipso merito sanctitatis.

RESPONDEO dicendum quod causa debet esse proportionata suo effectui. Et ideo, sicut in Christo, a quo descendit gratia in omnes homines, oportet quod sit gratiae plenitudo; ita in ministris Ecclesiae, quorum non est dare gratiam, sed gratiae sacramenta, non constituitur gradus ordinis ex hoc quod habeat gratiam, sed ex hoc quod percipit aliquod gratiae sacramentum.

AD PRIMUM ergo dicendum quod Chrysostomus accipit sacerdotis nomen quantum ad rationem interpretationis, secundum quod *sacerdos* idem est quod *sacra dans:* sic enim quilibet iustus, inquantum sacra merita alicui in auxilium dat, sacerdotis interpretationem habet. Non autem loquitur secundum nominis significationem. Est enim hoc nomen *sacerdos* institutum ad significandum eum *qui sacra dat in sacramentorum dispensatione.*

OBJECTION 1: It would seem that a man obtains the degrees of orders by the mere merit of his life. For, according to Chrysostom (*Opus Imperfectum*, Hom. 43), *not every priest is a saint, but every saint is a priest.* Now a man becomes a saint by the merit of his life. Consequently, he thereby also becomes a priest, and *a fortiori* has he the other orders.

OBJ. 2: Further, in natural things, men obtain a higher degree from the very fact that they are near God, and have a greater share of his favors, as Dionysius says (*On the Ecclesiastical Hierarchies* 4). Now it is by merit of holiness and knowledge that a man approaches nearer to God and receives more of his favors. Therefore, by this alone he is raised to the degree of holy orders.

ON THE CONTRARY, Holiness once possessed can be lost. But when once a man is ordained he never loses his orders. Therefore, holy orders does not consist in the mere merit of holiness.

I ANSWER THAT, A cause should be proportionate to its effect. And consequently as in Christ, from whom grace comes down on all men, there must be fullness of grace, so in the ministers of the Church, to whom it belongs, not to give grace, but to give the sacraments of grace, the degree of holy orders does not result from their having grace, but from their participating in a sacrament of grace.

REPLY OBJ. 1: Chrysostom is speaking of the priest in reference to the reason for which he is so called, the word 'sacerdos' signifying *dispenser of holy things:* for in this sense every righteous man, insofar as he assists others by the sacraments, may be called a priest. But he is not speaking according to the actual meaning of the words; for this word 'priest' is employed to signify one *who gives sacred things by dispensing the sacraments.*

AD SECUNDUM dicendum quod res naturales efficiuntur in gradu super alia secundum quod in ea agere possunt ex forma sua: et ideo ex hoc ipso quod formam nobiliorem habent, in altiori gradu constituuntur. Sed ministri Ecclesiae non proponuntur aliis ut eis ex propriae sanctitatis virtute aliquid attribuant, quia hoc solius Dei est: sed sicut ministri et quodammodo instrumenta illius effluxus qui fit a capite in membra. Et ideo non est simile quantum ad dignitatem ordinis; quamvis sit simile quantum ad congruitatem.

REPLY OBJ. 2: Natural things acquire a degree of superiority over others from the fact that they are able to act on them by virtue of their form; wherefore from the very fact that they have a higher form they obtain a higher degree. But the ministers of the Church are placed over others not to confer anything on them by virtue of their own holiness (for this belongs to God alone), but as ministers, and as instruments, so to say, of the outpouring from the Head to the members. Hence the comparison fails as regards the dignity of holy orders, although it applies as to congruity.

Article 4

Whether He Who Raises the Unworthy to Holy Orders Commits a Sin?

AD QUARTUM SIC PROCEDITUR. Videtur quod promovens indignos ad ordines non peccet. Quia episcopus indiget coadiutoribus in minoribus officiis constitutis. Sed non posset eos invenire in sufficienti numero si talem idoneitatem requireret in eis qualis a sanctis describitur. Ergo, si aliquos non idoneos promovet, videtur quod sit excusabilis.

PRAETEREA, Ecclesia non solum indiget ministris ad dispensationem spiritualium, sed ad gubernationem temporalium. Sed quandoque illi qui non habent scientiam vel sanctitatem vitae, possunt esse utiles ad gubernationem temporalium: vel propter potentiam saecularem, vel propter industriam naturalem. Ergo videtur quod tales sine peccato possent promoveri.

PRAETEREA, quilibet tenetur vitare peccatum quantum potest. Si ergo episcopus peccat indignos promovens debet adhibere maximam, diligentiam ad sciendum an illi qui accedunt ad ordines sint digni, ut fieret diligens inquisitio de moribus et scientia eorum. Quod non videtur alicubi observari.

SED CONTRA: Peius est promovere malos ad sacra mysteria quam iam promotos non corrigere. Sed Heli mortaliter peccavit non corrigens filios suos de malitia sua: unde, *retrorsum cadens mortuus est*, ut dicitur I Regum 4. Ergo non sine peccato evadit si indignos promovet.

PRAETEREA, spiritualia temporalibus sunt praeponenda in Ecclesia. Sed mortaliter peccaret qui res Ecclesiae temporales scienter sub periculo poneret. Ergo multo fortius qui poneret res spirituales sub periculo. Sed sub periculo ponit res spirituales quicumque indignos promovet: quia *cuius vita despicitur*, ut dicit Gregorius, *restat ut eius praedicatio contemnatur*, et eadem ratione omnia spiritualia ab eis exhibita. Ergo indignos promovens mortaliter peccat.

OBJECTION 1: It would seem that he who raises the unworthy to holy orders commits no sin. For a bishop needs assistants appointed to the lesser offices. But he would be unable to find them in sufficient number if he were to require of them such qualifications as the saints enumerate. Therefore, if he should raise some who are not qualified, it seems to be excusable.

OBJ. 2: Further, the Church needs not only ministers for the dispensation of things spiritual, but also for the supervision of temporalities. But sometimes men without knowledge or holiness of life may be useful for the conduct of temporal affairs either because of their worldly power or on account of their natural industry. Therefore, seemingly the like can be promoted without sin.

OBJ. 3: Further, everyone is bound to avoid sin as far as he can. If, therefore, a bishop sins in promoting the unworthy, he is bound to take the utmost pains to know whether those who present themselves for holy orders be worthy by making a careful inquiry about their morals and knowledge, and yet seemingly this is not done anywhere.

ON THE CONTRARY, It is worse to raise the wicked to the sacred ministry than not to correct those who are raised already. But Eli sinned mortally by not correcting his sons for their wickedness; wherefore *he fell backwards . . . and died* (2 Sam 1:30). Therefore, he who promotes the unworthy does not escape sin.

FURTHER, Spiritual things must be set before temporal things in the Church. Now a man would commit a mortal sin were he knowingly to endanger the temporalities of the Church. Much more, therefore, is it a mortal sin to endanger spiritual things. But whoever promotes the unworthy endangers spiritual things, since according to Gregory (*Homilies on the Gospels* 12) *if a man's life is contemptible, his preaching is liable to be despised*; and for the same reason all the spiritual things that he dispenses. Therefore, he who promotes the unworthy sins mortally.

RESPONDEO dicendum quod a Domino describitur *fidelis servus, qui est constitutus supra familiam, ut det illis tritici mensuram.* Et ideo infidelitatis reus est qui alicui supra mensuram eius divina tradit. Hoc autem facit quicumque indignos promovet. Et ideo crimen mortale committit, quasi summo Domino infidelis: et praecipue cum hoc in detrimentum Ecclesiae vergat et honoris divini, qui per bonos ministros promovetur. Esset enim infidelis terreno domino qui in eius officio aliquos inutiles poneret.

AD PRIMUM ergo dicendum quod Deus nunquam ita deserit Ecclesiam suam quin inveniantur idonei ministri sufficientes ad necessitatem plebis si digni promoverentur et indigni repellerentur. Et, si non possunt tot ministri inveniri quot modo sunt, *melius esset habere paucos ministros bonos quam multos malos*, ut dicit beatus Clemens.

AD SECUNDUM dicendum quod temporalia non sunt quaerenda nisi propter spiritualia. Unde omne incommodum temporale deberet eligi, et omne lucrum sperni, propter spirituale bonum promovendum.

AD TERTIUM dicendum quod ad minus hoc requiritur quod nesciat ordinans aliquid contrarium sanctitati in ordinando esse. Sed etiam exigitur amplius ut, secundum mensuram ordinis vel officii iniungendi, diligentior cura apponatur ut habeatur certitudo de qualitate promovendorum, saltem ex testimonio aliorum. Et hoc est quod Apostolus dicit, I Tim. 5: *nemini cito manum imposueris.*

I ANSWER THAT, Our Lord describes *the faithful servant whom he has set over his household to give them their measure of wheat.* Hence he is guilty of unfaithfulness who gives any man divine things above his measure: and whoever promotes the unworthy does this. Therefore, he commits a mortal crime as being unfaithful to his sovereign Lord, especially since this is detrimental to the Church and to the divine honor which is promoted by good ministers. For a man would be unfaithful to his earthly lord were he to place unworthy subjects in his offices.

REPLY OBJ. 1: God never so abandons his Church that apt ministers are not to be found sufficient for the needs of the people, if the worthy be promoted and the unworthy set aside. And though it were impossible to find as many ministers as there are now, *it were better to have few good ministers than many bad ones*, as the blessed Clement declares.

REPLY OBJ. 2: Temporal things are not to be sought except for the sake of spiritual things. Thus all temporal advantage should count for nothing and all gain be despised for the advancement of spiritual good.

REPLY OBJ. 3: It is at least required that the ordainer know that nothing contrary to holiness is in the candidate for ordination. But besides this he is required to take the greatest care, in proportion to the order or office to be enjoined, so as to be certain of the qualifications of those to be promoted, at least from the testification of others. This is the meaning of the Apostle when he says: *impose not hands lightly on any man* (1 Tim 5:22).

Article 5

Whether a Man Who Is in Sin Can Without Sin Exercise the Holy Orders He Has Received?

AD QUINTUM SIC PROCEDITUR. Videtur quod aliquis in peccato existens possit sine peccato ordine suscepto uti. Quia peccat si non utatur, cum ex officio tenetur. Si ergo utendo peccat, non potest peccatum vitare. Quod est inconveniens.

PRAETEREA, *dispensatio est iuris relaxatio.* Ergo, quamvis de iure esset ei illicitum uti ordine suscepto, tamen ex dispensatione ei liceret.

PRAETEREA, quicumque communicat alicui in peccato mortali, peccat mortaliter. Si ergo peccator in usu ordinis peccat mortaliter, tunc etiam peccat mortaliter qui ab eo aliquid divinorum accipit, vel ab eo exigit. Quod videtur absurdum.

PRAETEREA, si utendo ordine sub peccat, ergo quilibet actus ordinis quem facit, est peccatum mortale. Et ita, cum in una executione ordinis multi actus concur-

OBJECTION 1: It would seem that one who is in sin can without sin exercise the order he has received. For since by virtue of his office he is bound to exercise his order, he sins if he fails to do so. If, therefore, he sins by exercising it, he cannot avoid sin: which is inadmissible.

OBJ. 2: Further, *a dispensation is a relaxation of the law.* Therefore, although by rights it would be unlawful for him to exercise the order he has received, it would be lawful for him to do so by dispensation.

OBJ. 3: Further, whoever cooperates with another in a mortal sin, sins mortally. If, therefore, a sinner sins mortally by exercising his order, he who receives or demands any divine thing from him also sins mortally: and this seems absurd.

OBJ. 4: Further, if he sins by exercising his order, it follows that every act of his order that he performs is a mortal sin; and consequently since many acts concur in the one

rant, videtur quod multa peccata mortalia committat. Quod valde durum videtur.

SED CONTRA: Est quod dicit Dionysius, in *Epistola ad Demophilum. Talis*, scilicet qui non est illuminatus, *audax videtur sacerdotalibus manum apponens; et non timet neque verecundatur divina praeter dignitatem exequens, et putans Deum ignorare quae ipse in seipso cognovit; et decipere existimat falso nomine Patrem ab ipso appellatum: et audet ipsius immundas infamias, non enim dicam orationes, super divina signa Christiformiter enuntiare.* Ergo sacerdos est quasi blasphemus et deceptor qui indigne suum ordinem exequitur. Et sic mortaliter peccat. Et eadem ratione quilibet alius ordinatus.

PRAETEREA, sanctitas requiritur in susceptione ordinis ut sit idoneus ad exequendum. Sed peccat mortaliter qui cum peccato mortali ad ordines accedit. Ergo multo fortius peccat mortaliter in qualibet executione sui ordinis.

RESPONDEO dicendum quod lex praecipit ut *homo iuste, ea quae sunt iusta* exequatur. Et ideo quicumque hoc quod sibi competit ex ordine facit indigne, quod iustum est iniuste exequitur, et contra praeceptum legis facit, ac per hoc mortaliter peccat. Quicumque autem cum peccato mortali aliquod sacrum officium pertractat, non est dubium quin indigne illud facit. Unde patet quod mortaliter peccat.

AD PRIMUM ergo dicendum quod non est perplexus, ut necessitatem peccandi habeat: quia potest peccatum dimittere, vel officio resignare ex quo obligabatur ad ordinis executionem.

AD SECUNDUM dicendum quod ius naturale est indispensabile. Hoc autem est de iure naturali, ut homo sancta sancte pertractet. Unde contra hoc nullus potest dispensare.

AD TERTIUM dicendum quod, quandiu minister Ecclesiae qui est in peccato mortali ab Ecclesia sustinetur, ab eo sacramenta eius subditus recipere debet: quia ad hoc est ei obligatus. Sed tamen, praeter necessitatis articulum, non esset tutum quod eum induceret ad aliquid sui ordinis exequendum durante tali conscientia quod ille in peccato mortali esset. Quam tamen deponere posset: quia iri instanti homo a divina gratia emundatur.

AD QUARTUM dicendum quod, quandocumque exhibet se in aliquo actu ut minister Ecclesiae, mortaliter peccat, et toties quoties huiusmodi actum facit: quia, ut Dionysius dicit, 1 cap. *Eccles. Hier.*, *immundis nec symbola*, idest sacramentalia signa, *tangere fas est.* Unde, quando tangunt res sacras quasi suo officio utentes, peccant mortaliter.

Secus autem esset si in aliqua necessitate aliquod sacrum contingerent vel exequerentur in illo casu in quo

exercise of his order, it would seem that he commits many mortal sins: which seems very hard.

ON THE CONTRARY, Dionysius says (*Epistle to Demophilus*): *it seems presumptuous for such a man*, namely, one who is not enlightened, *to lay hands on priestly things; he is not afraid nor ashamed, all unworthy that he is to take part in divine things, with the thought that God does not see what he sees in himself; he thinks, by false pretense, to cheat him whom he falsely calls his Father; he dares to utter in the person of Christ words polluted by his infamy, I will not call them prayers, over the divine symbols.* Therefore, a priest is a blasphemer and a cheat if he exercises his order unworthily, and thus he sins mortally: and in like manner any other person in orders.

FURTHER, Holiness of life is required in one who receives an order, that he may be qualified to exercise it. Now a man sins mortally if he present himself for orders in mortal sin. Much more, therefore, does he sin mortally whenever he exercises his order.

I ANSWER THAT, The law prescribes that *man should follow justly after that which is just* (Deut 16:20). Wherefore whoever fulfills unworthily the duties of his order follows unjustly after that which is just, and acts contrary to a precept of the law, and thereby sins mortally. Now anyone who exercises a sacred office in mortal sin without doubt does so unworthily. Hence it is clear that he sins mortally.

REPLY OBJ. 1: He is not perplexed as though he were in the necessity of sinning; for he can renounce his sin, or resign his office whereby he was bound to the exercise of his order.

REPLY OBJ. 2: The natural law allows of no dispensation; and it is of natural law that man must handle holy things holily. Therefore, no one can dispense from this.

REPLY OBJ. 3: So long as a minister of the Church who is in mortal sin is recognized by the Church, his subject must receive the sacraments from him, since this is the purpose for which he is bound to him. Nevertheless, outside the case of necessity, it would not be safe to induce him to an execution of his order as long as he is conscious of being in mortal sin, which conscience, however, he can lay aside, since a man is repaired in an instant by divine grace.

REPLY OBJ. 4: When any man performs an action as a minister of the Church while in a state of mortal sin, he sins mortally and as often as he performs that action, since, as Dionysius says (*On the Ecclesiastical Hierarchies* 1), *it is wrong for the unclean even to touch the symbols*, i.e., the sacramental signs. Hence when they touch sacred things in the exercise of their office they sin mortally.

It would be otherwise if they were to touch some sacred thing or perform some sacred duty in a case of necessity,

et laicis liceret: sicut si baptizaret in articulo necessitatis, vel si corpus Christi in terram proiectum colligeret.

when it would be allowable even to a layman, for instance, if they were to baptize in a case of urgency or gather up Christ's body should it be cast to the ground.

QUESTION 37

THE DISTINCTION OF ORDERS AND OF THEIR ACTS

Consequenter agendum est de distinctione ordinum, et eorum actibus, et characteris impressione.

Circa quod quaeruntur quinque.

Primo: utrum ordo debeat in plures distingui.

Secundo: quot sint.

Tertio: utrum debeant distingui per sacros et non sacros.

Quarto: utrum actus ordinum convenienter assignentur.

Quinto: quando ordinum characteres imprimuntur.

In the next place we must consider the distinction of the orders and their acts, and the imprinting of the character.

Under this head there are five points of inquiry:

(1) Whether holy orders should be divided into several kinds?

(2) How many are there?

(3) Whether they ought to be divided into those that are sacred and those that are not?

(4) Whether the acts of the orders are rightly assigned in the text?

(5) When are the characters of the orders imprinted?

Article 1

Whether We Ought to Distinguish Several Orders?

AD PRIMUM SIC PROCEDITUR. Videtur quod non debeant plures ordines distingui. Quanto enim aliqua virtus est maior, tanto minus est multiplicata. Sed hoc sacramentum est dignius aliis sacramentis: in quantum constituit suscipientes in aliquo gradu super alios. Cum ergo alia sacramenta non distinguantur in plura quae recipiant praedicationem totius, nec hoc sacramentum debet in plures ordines distingui.

PRAETEREA, si dividitur, aut est divisio totius in partes integrales, aut in partes subiectivas. Non autem in partes integrales: quia sic non reciperent praedicationem totius. Ergo est divisio in partes subiectivas. Sed partes subiectivae recipiunt in plurali praedicationem generis remoti sicut generis proximi: sicut homo et asinus sunt plura *animalia*, et plura *corpora animata*. Ergo et sacerdotium et diaconatus, sicut sunt plures ordines, ita sunt plura sacramenta: cum *sacramentum* sit quasi genus ad ordines.

PRAETEREA, secundum Philosophum, VIII *Ethic.*, regimen in quo unus tantum principatur, est nobilius regimen communitatis quam aristocratia, qua diversi in diversis officiis constituuntur. Sed regimen Ecclesiae debet esse nobilissimum. Ergo non deberet esse in Ecclesia distinctio ordinum ad diversos actus, sed tota potestas deberet apud unum residere. Et sic deberet esse tantum unus ordo.

SED CONTRA: Ecclesia est corpus Christi mysticum, simile corpori naturali, secundum Apostolum. Sed in

OBJECTION 1: It would seem that we ought not to distinguish several orders. For the greater a power is, the less is it multiplied. Now this sacrament ranks above the others insofar as it places its recipients in a degree above other persons. Since, then, the other sacraments are not divided into several of which the whole is predicated, neither ought this sacrament to be divided into several orders.

OBJ. 2: Furthermore, if it is divided, either it is a division of the whole into integral parts or into subjective parts. It is not in integral parts, for then they would not receive the predication of the whole. Therefore, it is a division into subjective parts. But subjective parts receive in the plural the predication of the remote genus as well as proximate genus, as man and ass are several *animals*, and several *animate bodies*. Therefore also, the priesthood and diaconate are like several orders; so also, several sacraments, since *sacrament* is as the genus for holy orders.

OBJ. 3: Further, according to the Philosopher (*Ethics* 8.10) the form of authority in which one alone governs is a better government of the common good than aristocracy, where different persons occupy different offices. But the government of the Church should be the best of all. Therefore, in the Church there should be no distinction of orders for different acts, but the whole power should reside in one person; and consequently there ought to be only one order.

ON THE CONTRARY, The Church is Christ's mystical body, like to our natural body, according to the Apostle.

corpore naturali sunt diversa membrorum officia. Ergo et in Ecclesia debent esse diversi ordines.

PRAETEREA, ministerium novi Testamenti est dignius quam veteris: ut patet II Cor. 3. Sed in veteri Testamento non solum sacerdotes, sed etiam ministri eorum, levitae, sanctificabantur. Ergo et in novo Testamento debent consecrari per ordinis sacramentum non solum sacerdotes, sed ministri eorum. Et ita oportet quod sint plures ordines.

RESPONDEO dicendum quod ordinum multitudo est inducta in Ecclesia propter tria. Primo quidem, propter Dei sapientiam commendandam, quae in distinctione ordinata rerum maxime relucet, tam in naturalibus quam in spiritualibus. Quod significatur in hoc quod *regina Saba, videns ordinem ministrorum Salomonis, non habebat ultra spiritum*, deficiens in admiratione sapientiae illius.

Secundo, ad subveniendum humanae infirmitati: quia per unum non poterant omnia quae ad divina mysteria pertinebant expleri sine magno gravamine. Et ideo distinguuntur ordines diversi ad diversa officia: et hoc patet per hoc quod Dominus, Num. 11, dedit Moysi *septuaginta senes populi* in adiutorium.

Tertio, ut via proficiendi hominibus amplior detur, dum plures in diversis officiis distribuuntur, ut omnes sint Dei cooperatores: quo *nihil est divinius*, ut Dionysius dicit.

AD PRIMUM ergo dicendum quod illa sacramenta dantur ad effectus aliquos percipiendos: sed hoc sacramentum datur principaliter ad actus aliquos agendos. Et ideo secundum diversitatem actuum oportet quod ordinis sacramentum distinguatur: sicut potentiae distinguuntur per actus.

AD SECUNDUM dicendum quod distinctio ordinis non est totius integralis in partes, neque totius universalis, sed totius potestativi. Cuius haec est natura, quod totum secundum completam rationem est in uno, in aliis autem est aliqua participatio ipsius. Et ita est hic. Tota enim plenitudo huius sacramenti est in uno ordine, scilicet sacerdotio: sed in aliis est quaedam participatio ordinis. Et hoc significatum est in hoc quod Dominus dixit, Num. 11, Moysi: *auferam de spiritu tuo et tradam eis, ut sustentent tecum onus populi*. Et ideo omnes ordines sunt unum sacramentum.

AD TERTIUM dicendum quod in regno, quamvis tota potestatis plenitudo resideat penes regem, non tamen excluduntur ministrorum potestates, quae sunt participationes quaedam regiae potestatis. Et similiter est in ordine. In aristocratia autem apud nullum residet plenitudo potestatis, sed apud omnes.

Now in the natural body there are various offices of the members. Therefore, in the Church also there should be various orders.

FURTHER, The ministry of the New Testament is superior to that of the Old Testament (2 Cor 3). Now in the Old Testament not only the priests, but also their ministers, the Levites, were consecrated. Therefore, likewise in the New Testament not only the priests but also their ministers should be consecrated by the sacrament of order; and consequently there ought to be several orders.

I ANSWER THAT, Multiplicity of orders was introduced into the Church for three reasons. First, to show forth the wisdom of God, which is reflected in the orderly distinction of things both natural and spiritual. This is signified in the statement that *when the queen of Sheba saw the order of Solomon's servants she had no longer any spirit in her* (1 Kgs 10:4–5), for she was breathless from admiration of his wisdom.

Second, in order to succor human weakness, because it would be impossible for one man, without his being heavily burdened, to fulfill all things pertaining to the divine mysteries; and so various orders are severally appointed to the various offices; and this is shown by the Lord giving Moses *seventy ancients* to assist him (Num 11:16).

Third, so that a path for advancing further might be given to men when they distribute more people among different offices so that all may be God's cooperators, than which *nothing is more divine*, as Dionysius says (*On the Ecclesiastical Hierarchies* 3).

REPLY OBJ. 1: The other sacraments are given that certain effects may be received; but this sacrament is given chiefly that certain acts may be performed. Hence the sacrament of holy orders ought to be differentiated according to the diversity of acts, even as powers are differentiated by their acts.

REPLY OBJ. 2: The division of holy orders is not that of an integral whole into its parts, nor of a universal whole, but of a potential whole, the nature of which is that the notion of the whole is found to be complete in one part, but in the others by some participation thereof. Thus it is here: for the entire fullness of the sacrament is in one order, namely, the priesthood, while in the other sacraments there is a participation of holy orders. And this is signified by the Lord saying: *I will take of your spirit and give to them, that they may bear with you the burden of the people* (Num 11:17). Therefore, all the orders are one sacrament.

REPLY OBJ. 3: In a kingdom, although the entire fullness of power resides in the king, this does not exclude the ministers having a power which is a participation of the kingly power. It is the same in holy orders. In the aristocratic form of government, on the contrary, the fullness of power resides in no one, but in all.

Article 2

Whether There Are Seven Orders?

AD SECUNDUM SIC PROCEDITUR. Videtur quod non sint septem ordines. Ordines enim Ecclesiae ordinantur ad actus hierarchicos. Sed tres sunt tantum actus hierarchici, scilicet *purgare, illuminare* et *perficere*. Secundum quos Dionysius distinguit tres ordines, in 5 cap. *Eccles. Hier.* Ergo non sunt septem.

PRAETEREA, omnia sacramenta habent efficaciam et auctoritatem ex institutione Christi, vel saltem Apostolorum eius. Sed in doctrina Christi et Apostolorum non fit mentio nisi de presbyteris et diaconibus. Ergo videtur quod non sint alii ordines.

PRAETEREA, per sacramentum ordinis constituitur aliquis dispensator aliorum sacramentorum. Sed alia sacramenta sunt sex. Ergo debent esse tantum sex ordines.

SED CONTRA: Videtur quod debeant esse plures. Quia, quanto aliqua virtus est altior, tanto est minus multiplicabilis. Sed potestas hierarchica est altiori modo in angelis quam in nobis: ut Dionysius dicit. Cum ergo in hierarchia angelica sint novem ordines, totidem deberent esse in Ecclesia, vel plures.

PRAETEREA, prophetia psalmorum est nobilior inter omnes alias prophetias. Sed ad pronuntiandum in Ecclesia alias prophetias est unus ordo, scilicet lectorum. Ergo et ad pronuntiandum psalmos deberet esse alius ordo: et praecipue cum in Decretis, dist. 21, *psalmista* secundus ab ostiario inter ordines ponatur.

RESPONDEO dicendum quod quidam sufficientiam ordinum assumunt per quandam adaptationem ad gratias gratis datas, de quibus habetur I Cor. 12. Dicunt enim quod *sermo sapientiae* competit episcopo, quia ipse aliorum ordinator est, quod ad sapientiam pertinet; *sermo scientiae* sacerdoti, quia debet habere clavem scientiae; *fides* diacono, qui praedicat Evangelium; *opera virtutum* subdiacono, qui se ad opera perfectionis extendit per votum continentiae; *interpretatio sermonum* acolytho, quod significatur in lumine quod defert; *gratia sanitatum* exorcistae; *gratia linguarum* psalmistae; *prophetia* lectori; *discretio spirituum* ostiario, qui quosdam repellit et quosdam admittit.

Sed hoc nihil est. Quia gratiae gratis datae non dantur eidem, sicut omnes ordines dantur eidem: dicitur enim I Cor. 12: *Divisiones gratiarum sunt*. Et iterum ponuntur quaedam quae ordines non dicuntur: scilicet episcopatus et *psalmistatus*.

Et ideo alii assignant secundum quandam assimilationem ad caelestem hierarchiam, in quibus ordines distinguuntur secundum purgationem, illuminationem et

OBJECTION 1: It would seem that there are not seven orders. For the orders of the Church are directed to the hierarchical acts. But there are only three hierarchical acts, namely, *to cleanse, to enlighten* and *to perfect*, for which reason Dionysius distinguishes three orders (*On the Ecclesiastical Hierarchies* 5). Therefore, there are not seven.

OBJ. 2: Further, all the sacraments derive their efficacy and authenticity from their institution by Christ, or at least by his apostles. But no mention except of priests and deacons is made in the teaching of Christ and his apostles. Therefore, seemingly there are no other orders.

OBJ. 3: Further, by the sacrament of holy orders a man is appointed to dispense the other sacraments. But there are only six other sacraments. Therefore, there should be only six orders.

OBJ. 4: On the other hand, it would seem that there ought to be more. For the higher a power is, the less is it subject to multiplication. Now the hierarchical power is in the angels in a higher way than in us, as Dionysius says (*On the Ecclesiastical Hierarchies* 1). Since, then, there are nine orders in the angelic hierarchy, there should be as many, or more, in the Church.

OBJ. 5: Further, the prophecy of the Psalms is the most noble of all the prophecies. Now there is one order, namely of lectors, for reading the other prophecies in the Church. Therefore, there ought to be another order for reading the Psalms, especially since the *psalmist* is reckoned as the second order after the porter (*Decretals*).

I ANSWER THAT, Some show the sufficiency of the orders from their correspondence with the gratuitous graces which are indicated in 1 Corinthians 12. For they say that the *word of wisdom* belongs to the bishop, because he is the ordainer of others, which pertains to wisdom; the *word of knowledge* to the priest, for he ought to have the key of knowledge; *faith* to the deacon, for he preaches the Gospel; the *working of miracles* to the subdeacon, who sets himself to do deeds of perfection by the vow of continency; *interpretation of speeches* to the acolyte, this being signified by the light which he bears; the *grace of healing* to the exorcist; *diverse kinds of tongues* to the psalmist; *prophecy* to the lector; and the *discerning of spirits* to the porter, for he excludes some and admits others.

But this is of no account, for the gratuitous graces are not given, as the orders are, to one same man. For it is written: *there are distributions of graces* (1 Cor 12:4). Moreover, the episcopate (Cf. Q. 40, A. 5) and *the office of psalmist* are included, which are not orders.

Wherefore others account for the orders by likening them to the heavenly hierarchy, where the orders are distinguished in reference to cleansing, enlightening, and per-

perfectionem. Dicunt enim quod ostiarius *purgat* exterius, segregando bonos a malis etiam corporaliter; interius vero acolythus, quia per lumen quod portat significat se interiores tenebras pellere; sed utroque modo exorcista, quia diabolum, quem expellit, utroque modo perturbat. Sed *illuminatio*, quae fit per doctrinam, quantum ad doctrinam propheticam fit per lectores; quantum ad Apostolicam fit per subdiaconos; quantum ad Evangelicam fit per diaconos. Sed *perfectio* communis, utpote quae est poenitentiae et baptismi et huiusmodi, fit per sacerdotem; excellens vero per episcopum, ut consecratio sacerdotum et virginum; sed excellentissima per Summum Pontificem, in quo est plenitudo auctoritatis.

Sed hoc nihil est. Tum quia ordines caelestis hierarchiae non distinguuntur per praedictas actiones hierarchicas: cum quaelibet cuilibet ordinum conveniat. Tum quia, secundum Dionysium, solis episcopis convenit perficere, illuminare autem sacerdotibus, purgare autem ministris omnibus.

Et ideo alii appropriant ordines septem donis: ut sacerdotio respondeat donum sapientiae, quae nos *pane vitae et intellectus cibat*, sicut sacerdos nos pane caelesti reficit; sed timor ostiario, quia nos separat a malis; et sic intermedii ordines respondent mediis donis.

Sed hoc iterum nihil est. Quia in quolibet ordine septiformis gratia datur.

Et ideo aliter dicendum quod ordinis sacramentum ad sacramentum Eucharistiae ordinatur, quod est *sacramentum sacramentorum*, ut Dionysius dicit. Sicut enim templum et altare, et vasa et vestes, ita et ministeria quae ad Eucharistiam ordinantur, consecratione indigent: et haec consecratio est ordinis sacramentum. Et ideo distinctio ordinis est accipienda secundum relationem ad Eucharistiam.

Quia potestas ordinis aut est ad consecrationem Eucharistiae ipsius, aut ad aliquod ministerium ordinandum ad hoc. Si primo inodo, sic est ordo *sacerdotum*. Et ideo, cum ordinantur, accipiunt calicem cum vino et patenam cum pane, potestatem accipientes consecrandi corpus et sanguinem Christi.

Cooperatio autem ministrorum est vel in ordine ad ipsum sacramentum, vel in ordine ad suscipientes. Si primo modo, sic tripliciter. Primo enim est ministerium quo minister cooperatur sacerdoti in ipso sacramento, quantum ad dispensationem, sed non quantum ad consecrationem, quam solus sacerdos facit. Et hoc pertinet ad diaconum. Unde in littera dicitur quod *ad diaconum pertinet ministrare sacerdotibus in omnibus quae aguntur*

fecting. Thus they say that the porter *cleanses* outwardly, by separating even in the body the good from the wicked; that the acolyte cleanses inwardly, because by the light which he bears he signifies that he dispels inward darkness; and that the exorcist cleanses both ways, for he casts out the devil who disturbs a man both ways. But *enlightening*, which is effected by teaching, is done by lectors as regards prophetic doctrine; by subdeacons as to apostolic doctrine; and by deacons as to the gospel doctrine; while ordinary *perfection*, such as the perfection of penance, baptism, and so forth is the work of the priest; excellent perfection, such as the consecration of priests and virgins, is the work of the bishop; while the most excellent perfection is the work of the Sovereign Pontiff in whom resides the fullness of authority.

But this again is of no account; both because the orders of the heavenly hierarchy are not distinguished by the aforesaid hierarchical actions, since each of them is applicable to every order; and because, according to Dionysius (*On the Ecclesiastical Hierarchies* 5), perfecting belongs to the bishops alone, enlightening to the priests, and cleansing to all the ministers.

Wherefore others suit the orders to the seven gifts, so that the priesthood corresponds to the gift of wisdom, which *feeds us with the bread of life and understanding*, even as the priest refreshes us with the heavenly bread; fear to the porter, for he separates us from the wicked; and thus the intermediate orders to the intermediate gifts.

But this again is of no account, since the sevenfold grace is given in each one of the orders.

Consequently, we must answer differently by saying that the sacrament of order is directed to the sacrament of the Eucharist, which is the sacrament of sacraments, as Dionysius says (*On the Ecclesiastical Hierarchies* 3). For just as temple, altar, vessels, and vestments need to be consecrated, so do the ministers who are ordained for the Eucharist; and this consecration is the sacrament of order. Hence the distinction of orders is derived from their relation to the Eucharist.

For the power of order is directed either to the consecration of the Eucharist itself, or to some ministry in connection with this sacrament of the Eucharist. If in the former way, then it is the order *of priests*; hence when they are ordained, they receive the chalice with wine, and the paten with the bread, because they are receiving the power to consecrate the body and blood of Christ.

The cooperation of the ministers is directed either to the sacrament itself, or to the recipients. If the former, this happens in three ways. For in the first place, there is the ministry whereby the minister cooperates with the priest in the sacrament itself, by dispensing, but not by consecrating, for this is done by the priest alone; and this belongs to the deacon. Hence in the text (*Sentences* IV, D. 24) it is said that *it belongs to the deacon to minister to the priests in whatever is*

in sacramentis Christi. Unde et ipsi sanguinem dispensant. Secundo est ministerium ordinatum ad materiam sacramenti ordinandam in sacris vasis ipsius sacramenti. Et hoc pertinet ad subdiaconum. Unde dicitur in littera quod corporis et sanguinis Domini vasa portant, et oblationes in altari ponunt. Et ideo accipiunt calicem de manu episcopi, sed vacuum, cum ordinantur. Tertio est ministerium ordinatum ad praesentandum materiam sacramenti. Et hoc competit acolytho. Ipse enim, ut in littera dicitur, urceolum cum vino et aqua praeparat. Unde accipiunt urceolum vacuum.

Sed ministerium ad praeparationem recipientium ordinatum non potest esse nisi super immundos: quia qui mundi sunt, iam sunt ad sacramenta percipienda idonei. Triplex autem est genus immundorum, secundum Dionysium. Quidam enim sunt omnino infideles, credere nolentes. Et hi totaliter etiam a visione divinorum et a coetu fidelium arcendi sunt. Et hoc pertinet ad ostiarios. Quidam autem sunt volentes credere, sed non instructi, scilicet catechumeni. Et ad horum instructionem ordinatur ordo lectorum. Et ideo prima rudimenta doctrinae fidei, scilicet vetus Testamentum, eis legendum committitur. Quidam vero sunt fideles et instructi, sed impedimentum habentes ex daemonis potestate, scilicet energumeni. Et ad hoc habet ministerium ordo exorcistarum.

Et sic patet ratio numeri et gradus ordinum.

Ad primum ergo dicendum quod Dionysius loquitur de ordinibus non secundum quod sunt sacramenta, sed secundum quod ad hierarchicas actiones ordinantur. Et ideo secundum actiones illas tres ordines distinguit. Quorum primus habet omnes tres, scilicet episcopus; secundus habet duas, scilicet sacerdos; sed tertius habet unam, scilicet purgare, scilicet diaconus, qui *minister* dicitur; et sub hoc omnes inferiores ordines comprehenduntur. Sed ordines habent quod sint sacramenta ex relatione ad maximum sacramentorum. Et ideo secundum hoc debet numerus ordinum accipi.

Ad secundum dicendum quod in primitiva Ecclesia, propter paucitatem ministrorum, omnia inferiora ministeria diaconibus committebantur: ut patet per Dionysium, 3 cap. *Eccles. Hier.*, ubi dicit: *ministrorum alii stant ad portas templi clausas, alii aliud quid proprii ordinis operantur, alii autem sacerdotibus proponunt super altare sacrum panem et benedictionis calicem.* Nihilominus erant omnes praedictae potestates, sed implicite, in una diaconi potestate. Sed postea ampliatus est cultus divinus, et Ecclesia quod implicite habebat in uno ordine,

done in Christ's sacraments, wherefore he dispenses Christ's blood. Second, there is the ministry directed to the disposal of the sacramental matter in the sacred vessels of the sacrament, and this belongs to subdeacons. Wherefore it is stated in the text (*Sentences* IV, D. 24) that they carry the vessels of our Lord's body and blood, and place the oblation on the altar; hence, when they are ordained, they receive the chalice from the bishop's hand, but it is empty. Third, there is the ministry directed to the proffering of the sacramental matter, and this belongs to the acolyte. For he, as stated in the text (*Sentences* IV, D. 24), prepares the cruet with wine and water; wherefore he receives an empty cruet.

The ministry directed to the preparation of the recipients can be exercised only over the unclean, since those who are clean are already apt for receiving the sacraments. Now the unclean are of three kinds, according to Dionysius (*On the Ecclesiastical Hierarchies* 3). For some are absolute unbelievers and unwilling to believe; and these must be altogether debarred from beholding divine things and from the assembly of the faithful; this belongs to the porters. Some, however, are willing to believe, but are not as yet instructed, namely, catechumens, and to the instruction of such persons the order of lectors is directed, who are therefore entrusted with the reading of the first rudiments of the doctrine of faith, namely, the Old Testament. But some are believers and instructed, yet lie under an impediment through the power of the devil, namely, those who are possessed: and to this ministry the order of exorcists is directed.

Thus the reason and number of the degrees of orders is made clear.

Reply Obj. 1: Dionysius is speaking of the orders not as sacraments, but as directed to hierarchical actions. Wherefore he distinguishes three orders corresponding to those actions. The first of these orders, namely, the bishop, has all three actions; the second, namely, the priest, has two; while the third has one, namely, to cleanse; this is the deacon who is called a *minister*: and under this last all the lower orders are comprised. But the orders derive their sacramental nature from their relation to the greatest of the sacraments, and consequently the number of orders depends on this.

Reply Obj. 2: In the early Church, on account of the fewness of ministers, all the lower ministries were entrusted to the deacons, as Dionysius says (*On the Ecclesiastical Hierarchies* 3), where he says: *some of the ministers stand at the closed door of the Church; others are otherwise occupied in the exercise of their own order; others place the sacred bread and the chalice of benediction on the altar and offer them to the priests.* Nevertheless, all the power to do all these things was included in the one power of the deacon, though implicitly. But afterwards the divine worship devel-

explicite tradidit in diversis. Et secundum hoc dicit Magister in littera quod *Ecclesia* alios ordines *sibi instituit.*

Ad tertium dicendum quod ordines ordinantur principaliter ad sacramentum Eucharistiae, ad alia autem per consequens: quia etiam alia sacramenta ab eo quod in sacramento continetur, derivantur. Unde non oportet quod distinguantur ordines secundum sacramenta.

Ad quartum dicendum quod angeli differunt specie: et propter hoc in eis potest esse modus diversus recipiendi divina. Et ideo etiam diversae hierarchiae in eis distinguuntur. Sed in ordinibus tantum est una hierarchia, propter imum modum accipiendi divina, qui consequitur humanam speciem, scilicet per similitudinem rerum sensibilium. Et ideo distinctio ordinum in angelis non potest esse per comparationem ad aliquod sacramentum, sicut est apud nos: sed solum per comparationem ad hierarchicas actiones quas in inferiores exercet quilibet ordo in eis. Et secundum hoc nostri ordines eis respondent: quia in nostra hierarchia sunt tres ordines secundum hierarchicas actiones distincti, sicut in qualibet hierarchia una angelorum.

Ad quintum dicendum quod psalmistatus non est ordo, sed officium ordini annexum: quia enim psalmi cum cantu pronuntiantur, ideo dicitur psalmista cantor. *Cantor* autem non est nomen ordinis specialis. Tum quia cantare pertinet ad totum chorum. Tum quia non habet aliquam specialem relationem ad Eucharistiae sacramentum. Tum quia officium quoddam est: quod inter ordines largo modo acceptos computatur quandoque.

oped, and the Church committed expressly to several persons that which had hitherto been committed implicitly in one order. This is what the Master means, when he says in the text (*Sentences* IV, D. 24) that the *Church herself instituted* other orders.

Reply Obj. 3: The orders are directed to the sacrament of the Eucharist chiefly, and to the other sacraments consequently, for even the other sacraments flow from that which is contained in that sacrament. Hence it does not follow that the orders ought to be distinguished according to the sacraments.

Reply Obj. 4: The angels differ specifically (I, Q. 50, A. 4): for this reason it is possible for them to have various modes of receiving divine things, and hence also they are divided into various hierarchies. But in men there is only one hierarchy, because they have only one mode of receiving divine things, which results from the human species, namely, through the images of sensible objects. Consequently, the distinction of orders in the angels cannot bear any relation to a sacrament as it is with us, but only a relation to the hierarchical actions which among them each order exercises on the orders below. In this respect our orders correspond to theirs, since in our hierarchy there are three orders distinguished according to the three hierarchical actions, even as in each angelic hierarchy.

Reply Obj. 5: The office of psalmist is not an order, but an office annexed to an order. For the psalmist is also named 'cantor' because the psalms are recited with chant. Now 'cantor' is not the name of a special order, both because it belongs to the whole choir to sing, and because he has no special relation to the sacrament of the Eucharist. Since, however, it is a particular office, it is sometimes reckoned among the orders, taking these in a broad sense.

Article 3

Whether Holy Orders Should Be Divided into Those That Are Sacred and Those That Are Not?

Ad tertium sic proceditur. Videtur quod ordines non debeant distingui per sacros et non sacros. Omnes enim ordines sacramenta quaedam sunt. Sed omnia sacramenta sunt sacra. Ergo omnes ordines sunt sacri.

Praeterea, secundum ordines Ecclesiae non deputatur aliquis, nisi ad divina officia. Sed omnia talia sunt sacra. Ergo omnes ordines sunt sacri.

Sed contra est quod ordines sacri impediunt matrimonium contrahendum et dirimunt iam contractum. Sed quattuor inferiores ordines non impediunt contrahendum nec dirimunt contractum. Ergo non sunt sacri ordines.

Respondeo dicendum quod ordo sacer dicitur dupliciter. Uno modo, secundum se. Et sic quilibet ordo est

Objection 1: It would seem that the orders ought not to be divided into those that are sacred and those that are not. For all the orders are sacraments, and all the sacraments are sacred. Therefore, all the orders are sacred.

Obj. 2: Further, by the orders of the Church a man is not appointed to any other than divine offices. Now all these are sacred. Therefore, all the orders also are sacred.

On the contrary, The sacred orders are an impediment to the contracting of marriage and annul the marriage that is already contracted. But the four lower orders neither impede the contracting nor annul the contract. Therefore, these are not sacred orders.

I answer that, An order is said to be sacred in two ways. First, in itself, and thus every order is sacred, since it

sacer: cum sit sacramentum quoddam. Alio modo, ratione materiae circa quam habet aliquem actum. Et sic ordo sacer dicitur qui habet aliquem actum circa rem aliquam consecratam. Et sic sunt tantum tres ordines sacri: scilicet sacerdos; et diaconus, qui habet actum circa corpus Christi et sanguinem consecratum; et subdiaconus, qui habet actum circa vasa consecrata. Et ideo etiam eis continentia indicitur, ut mundi sint qui sancta tractant.

ET PER HOC patet solutio ad obiecta.

is a sacrament. Second, by reason of the matter about which it exercises an act, and thus an order is called sacred if it exercises an act about some consecrated thing. In this sense there are only three sacred orders: namely, the priesthood and diaconate, which exercise an act about the consecrated body and blood of Christ, and the subdiaconate, which exercises an act about the consecrated vessels. Hence continency is enjoined them, that they who handle holy things may themselves be holy and clean.

THIS SUFFICES for the replies to the objections.

Article 4

Whether the Acts of the Orders Are Rightly Assigned in the Text?

AD QUARTUM SIC PROCEDITUR. Videtur quod actus ordinum inconvenienter in littera assignentur. Quia per absolutionem praeparatur aliquis ad corpus Christi sumendum. Sed praeparatio suscipientium sacramentum pertinet ad inferiores ordines. Ergo inconvenienter absolutio a peccatis inter actus ponitur sacerdotis.

PRAETEREA, homo per baptismum est immediate Deo configuratus, characterem configurantem suscipiens. Sed orare et offerre oblationes sunt actus immediate ad Deum ordinati. Ergo quilibet baptizatus potest hos actus facere, et non soli sacerdotes.

PRAETEREA, diversorum ordinum diversi sunt actus. Sed oblationes in altari ponere et epistolam legere ad subdiaconum pertinet. Crucem etiam ferunt subdiaconi coram Papa. Ergo hi non debent poni actus diaconi.

PRAETEREA, eadem veritas continetur in novo et in veteri Testamento. Sed legere vetus Testamentum est lectorum. Ergo, eadem ratione, et legere novum: et non diaconorum.

PRAETEREA, Apostoli nihil aliud praedicaverunt quam Evangelium Christi, ut patet Rom. 1. Sed doctrina Apostolorum committitur subdiaconibus enuntianda. Ergo et doctrina Evangelii.

PRAETEREA, secundum Dionysium, quod est superioris ordinis, non debet inferiori convenire. Sed ministrare cum urceolo est actus subdiaconorum. Ergo non debet acolythis attribui.

PRAETEREA, actus spirituales debent corporalibus praeeminere. Sed acolythus non habet nisi actum corporalem. Ergo exorcista non habet actum spiritualem pellendi daemones: cum sit inferior.

PRAETEREA, quae magis conveniunt, iuxta se ponenda sunt. Sed legere vetus Testamentum maxime debet convenire cum lectore novi Testamenti, quod competit superioribus ministris. Ergo legere vetus Te-

OBJECTION 1: It would seem that the acts of the orders are not rightly assigned in the text (*Sentences* IV, D. 24). For a person is prepared by absolution to receive Christ's body. Now the preparation of the recipients of a sacrament belongs to the lower orders. Therefore, absolution from sins is unfittingly reckoned among the acts of a priest.

OBJ. 2: Further, man is made like to God immediately in baptism by receiving the character which causes this likeness. But prayer and the offering of oblations are acts directed immediately to God. Therefore, every baptized person can perform these acts, and not priests alone.

OBJ. 3: Further, different orders have different acts. But it belongs to the subdeacon to place the oblations on the altar, and to read the epistle; and subdeacons carry the cross before the Pope. Therefore, these acts should not be assigned to the deacon.

OBJ. 4: Further, the same truth is contained in the Old and in the New Testament. But it belongs to the lectors to read the Old Testament. Therefore, it should belong to them likewise, and not to deacons, to read the New Testament.

OBJ. 5: Further, the apostles preached naught else but the Gospel of Christ (Rom 1:15). But the teaching of the apostles is entrusted to subdeacons to be read by them. Therefore, the Gospel teaching should be also.

OBJ. 6: Further, according to Dionysius (*On the Ecclesiastical Hierarchies* 5) that which belongs to a higher order should not be applicable to a lower order. But it is an act of subdeacons to minister with the cruets. Therefore, it should not be assigned to acolytes.

OBJ. 7: Further, spiritual actions should rank above bodily actions. But the acolyte's act is merely corporeal. Therefore, the exorcist has not the spiritual act of casting out devils, since he is of inferior rank.

OBJ. 8: Further, things that have most in common should be placed beside one another. Now the reading of the Old Testament must have most in common with the reading of the New Testament, which latter belongs to the

stamentum non debet poni actus lectoris, sed magis acolythi: et praecipue cum lumen corporale quod acolythi deferunt, significet lumen spirituale doctrinae.

PRAETEREA, in quolibet actu ordinis spiritualis debet esse aliqua vis spiritualis quam habeant ordinati prae aliis. Sed in apertione et clausione ostiorum non habent aliam potestatem ostiarii quam alii homines. Ergo non debet poni actus ipsorum.

RESPONDEO dicendum quod, cum consecratio quae fit in ordinis sacramento, ordinetur ad sacramentum Eucharistiae, ut dictum est; ille est principalis actus uniuscuiusque ordinis secundum quem magis proxime ordinatur ad Eucharistiae sacramentum. Et secundum hoc etiam unus ordo est alio eminentior, secundum quod unus actus magis de proximo ad praedictum sacramentum ordinatur. Sed quia ad Eucharistiae sacramentum, quasi dignissimum, multa ordinantur; ideo non est inconveniens ut, praeter principalem actum, etiam multos actus unus ordo habeat; et tanto plures quanto est eminentior, quia virtus, quanto est superior, tanto ad plura se extendit.

AD PRIMUM ergo dicendum quod duplex est praeparatio suscipientium sacramentum. Quaedam remota: et haec per ministros efficitur. Quaedam proxima, qua statim efficiuntur idonei ad sacramentorum susceptionem. Et haec pertinet ad sacerdotes. Quia etiam in naturalibus ab eodem agente fit materia in ultima dispositione ad formam, et recipit formam. Et quia in proxima dispositione ad Eucharistiam fit aliquis per hoc quod a peccatis purgatur, ideo omnium sacramentorum quae sunt instituta principaliter ad purgationem peccatorum, est minister proprius sacerdos: scilicet baptismi, poenitentiae et extremae unctionis.

AD SECUNDUM dicendum quod actus aliqui immediate ad Deum ordinantur dupliciter. Uno modo, ex parte unius personae tantum, sicut facere orationes singulares, et vovere, et huiusmodi. Et talis actus competit cuilibet baptizato. Alio modo, ex parte totius Ecclesiae. Et sic solus sacerdos habet actus immediate ad Deum ordinatos: quia ipse solus potest gerere personam totius Ecclesiae qui consecrat Eucharistiam, quae est sacramentum universalis Ecclesiae.

AD TERTIUM dicendum quod oblationes a populo oblatae per sacerdotem offeruntur. Et ideo duplex ministerium circa oblationes est necessarium. Unum ex parte populi: et hoc est subdiaconi, qui accipit oblationes a populo et altari imponit, vel offert diacono. Aliud ex parte sacerdotis: et hoc diaconi est, qui oblationes ministrat ipsi sacerdoti. Et in hoc est actus principalis utriusque ordinis. Et propter hoc ordo diaconi est superior. Legere autem epistolam non est actus diaconi: nisi secundum quod actus inferiorum ordinum superioribus attribuun-

higher ministers. Therefore, the reading of the Old Testament should be reckoned the act, not of the lector, but rather of the acolyte; especially since the bodily light which the acolytes carry signifies the light of spiritual doctrine.

OBJ. 9: Further, in every act of a special order, there should be some special power which the person ordained has to the exclusion of other persons. But in opening and shutting doors the porter has no special power that other men have not. Therefore, this should not be reckoned their act.

I ANSWER THAT, Since the consecration conferred in the sacrament of holy orders is directed to the sacrament of the Eucharist, as stated above (A. 2), the principal act of each order is that whereby it is most nearly directed to the sacrament of the Eucharist. In this respect, too, one order ranks above another, insofar as one act is more nearly directed to that same sacrament. But because many things are directed to the Eucharist, as being the most exalted of the sacraments, it follows not unfittingly that one order has many acts besides its principal act, and all the more as it ranks higher, since a power extends to the more things the higher it is.

REPLY OBJ. 1: The preparation of the recipients of a sacrament is twofold. One is remote and is effected by the ministers: another is proximate, whereby they are rendered apt at once for receiving the sacraments. This latter belongs to priests, since even in natural things matter receives from one and the same agent both the ultimate disposition to the form, and the form itself. And since a person acquires the proximate disposition to the Eucharist by being cleansed from sin, it follows that the priest is the proper minister of all those sacraments which are chiefly instituted for the cleansing of sins: namely, baptism, penance, and extreme unction.

REPLY OBJ. 2: Acts are directed immediately to God in two ways: in one way, on the part of one person only, for instance, the prayers of individuals, vows, and so forth; such acts befit any baptized person. In another way, on the part of the whole Church, and thus the priest alone exercises acts immediately directed to God: for to impersonate the whole Church belongs to him alone who consecrates the Eucharist, which is the sacrament of the universal Church.

REPLY OBJ. 3: The offerings made by the people are offered through the priest. Hence a twofold ministry is necessary with regard to offerings. One on the part of the people: and this belongs to the subdeacon who receives the offerings from the people and places them on the altar or offers them to the deacon. The other is on the part of the priest, and belongs to the deacon, who hands the offerings to the priest. This is the principal act of both orders, and for this reason the deacon's order is the higher. But to read the epistle does not belong to a deacon, except as the acts of lower

tur. Similiter etiam crucem ferre. Et hoc secundum consuetudinem aliquarum ecclesiarum. Quia in actibus secundariis non est inconveniens diversas consuetudines esse.

AD QUARTUM dicendum quod doctrina est remota praeparatio ad sacramentum suscipiendum: et ideo pronuntiatio doctrinae ministris committitur. Sed doctrina veteris Testamenti adhuc est magis remota quam doctrina novi: quia non instruit de hoc sacramento nisi in figuris. Et ideo novum Testamentum superioribus ministris pronuntiandum committitur, vetus autem inferioribus. Doctrina etiam novi Testamenti perfectior est quam Dominus per seipsum tradidit, quam ipsius manifestatio per Apostolos. Et ideo Evangelium diaconis, epistola subdiaconis committuntur.

ET SECUNDUM HOC patet solutio ad quintum.

AD SEXTUM dicendum quod acolythi habent actum super urceolum tantum, non super ea quae in urceolo continentur. Sed subdiaconus habet actum super contentis in urceolo: quia utitur aqua et vino ad ponendum in calice, et aquam iterum manibus sacerdotis praebet. Et diaconus, sicut et subdiaconus, solum actum habet super calicem, non super contenta: sed sacerdos super contenta. Et ideo, sicut subdiaconus in sui ordinatione accipit calicem vacuum, sacerdos plenum; ita acolythus urceolum vacuum, sed subdiaconus plenum. Et sic est quaedam connexio in ordinibus.

AD SEPTIMUM dicendum quod corporales actus acolythi magis de proximo ordinantur ad actum sacrorum ordinum quam actus exorcistarum, quamvis sit aliquo modo spiritualis: quia acolythi habent ministerium super vasa in quibus materia sacramenti continetur, quantum ad vinum, quod vase continente indiget propter sui humiditatem. Et ideo inter minores ordines ordo acolythorum superior est.

AD OCTAVUM dicendum quod actus acolythorum se habet propinquius ad actus principales superiorum ministrorum quam actus aliorum minorum ordinum, ut per se patet. Et similiter etiam quantum ad actus secundarios, quibus populum per doctrinam disponunt: quia acolythus doctrinam novi Testamenti visibiliter figurat lumen portans, sed lector recitando figuras alias. Ideo acolythus est superior. Similiter etiam exorcista. Quia, sicut se habet actus lectorum ad actum secundarium diaconi et subdiaconi, ita se habet actus exorcistae ad secundarium actum sacerdotis, scilicet ligare et solvere, per quem totaliter homo a servitute diaboli liberatur.

Et in hoc patet ordinatissimus ordinis progressus. Quia sacerdoti, quantum ad actum eius principalem, scilicet consecrare corpus Christi, cooperantur tantum tres

orders are ascribed to the higher; and in like manner to carry the cross. Moreover, this depends on the customs of Churches, because in secondary acts it is not unfitting for customs to vary.

REPLY OBJ. 4: Doctrine is a remote preparation for the reception of a sacrament; wherefore the announcement of doctrine is entrusted to the ministers. But the doctrine of the Old Testament is more remote than that of the New Testament, since it contains no instruction about this sacrament except in figures. Thus, announcing of the New Testament is entrusted to the higher ministers, and that of the Old Testament to the lower ministers. Moreover, the doctrine of the New Testament is more perfect as delivered by our Lord himself than as made known by his apostles. Therefore, the Gospel is committed to deacons and the Epistle to subdeacons.

THIS SUFFICES for the reply to the fifth objection.

REPLY OBJ. 6: Acolytes exercise an act over the cruet alone, and not over the contents of the cruet; whereas the subdeacon exercises an act over the contents of the cruet, because he handles the water and wine to the end that they be put into the chalice, and again he pours the water over the hands of the priest; and the deacon, like the subdeacon, exercises an act over the chalice only, not over its contents, whereas the priest exercises an act over the contents. Therefore, as the subdeacon at his ordination receives an empty chalice, while the priest receives a full chalice, so the acolyte receives an empty cruet, but the subdeacon a full one. Thus there is a certain connection among the orders.

REPLY OBJ. 7: The bodily acts of the acolyte are more intimately connected with the act of holy orders than the act of the exorcist, although the latter is, in a fashion, spiritual. For the acolytes exercise a ministry over the vessels in which the sacramental matter is contained as regards the wine, which needs a vessel to hold it on account of its wetness. Hence of all the minor orders, the order of acolytes is the highest.

REPLY OBJ. 8: The act of the acolyte is more closely connected with the principal acts of the higher ministers than the acts of the other minor orders, as is self-evident; and again as regards the secondary acts whereby they prepare the people by doctrine. For the acolyte, by bearing a light, represents the doctrine of the New Testament in a visible manner, while the lector by his recital represents it differently: wherefore the acolyte is of higher rank. It is the same with the exorcist, for as the act of the lector is compared with the secondary act of the deacon and subdeacon, so is the act of the exorcist compared with the secondary act of the priest, namely, to bind and to loose, by which man is wholly freed from the slavery of the devil.

This, too, shows the degrees of order to be most orderly, since only the three higher orders cooperate with the priest in his principal act, which is to consecrate the body

superiores ordines. Sed quantum ad actum eius secundarium, qui est absolvere et ligare, cooperantur superiores et inferiores.

AD NONUM dicendum quod quidam dicunt quod in susceptione ordinis ostiario datur quaedam vis divina ut arcere possit aliquos ab introitu templi, sicut in Christo: fuit quando eiecit vendentes de Templo. Sed hoc magis pertinet ad gratiam gratis datam quam ad gratiam sacramenti.

Et ideo dicendum quod suscipit potestatem ut ex officio hoc agere possit: quamvis etiam et hoc ab aliis fieri possit, sed non ex officio. Et ita est in omnibus actibus minorum ordinum, quod possunt per alios licite fieri, quamvis illi ad hoc non habeant officium. Sicut etiam in domo non consecrata potest dici missa, quamvis consecratio ecclesiae ad hoc ordinetur ut in ea missa dicatur.

of Christ, while both the higher and lower orders cooperate with him in his secondary act, which is to loose and bind.

REPLY OBJ. 9: Some say that in receiving the order the porter is given a divine power to debar others from entering the Church, even as Christ had, when he cast out the sellers from the Temple. But this belongs to a gratuitous grace rather than to a sacramental grace.

Wherefore we should reply that he receives the power to do this by virtue of his office, although others may do so, yet not from the office. It is the case in all the acts of the minor orders that they can be lawfully exercised by others, even though these have no office to that effect: just as Mass may be said in an unconsecrated building, although the consecration of a church is directed to the purpose that Mass be said there.

Article 5

Whether the Character Is Imprinted on a Priest When the Chalice Is Handed to Him?

AD QUINTUM SIC PROCEDITUR. Videtur quod sacerdoti character non imprimatur in ipsa calicis porrectione. Quia consecratio sacerdotis fit cum quadam unctione, sicut et confirmatio. Sed in confirmatione in ipsa unctione imprimitur character. Ergo et in sacerdotio: et non in calicis porrectione.

PRAETEREA, Dominus dedit discipulis sacerdotalem potestatem quando dixit: *accipite Spiritum sanctum: quorum remiseritis peccata*, etc., Ioan. 20. Sed Spiritus datur per manus impositionem. Ergo in ipsa manus impositione imprimitur character ordinis.

PRAETEREA, sicut consecrantur ministri, ita et vestes ministrorum: sed vestes sola benedictio consecrat. Ergo in ipsa benedictione episcopi consecratio sacerdotis efficitur.

PRAETEREA, sicut sacerdoti datur calix, ita et vestis sacerdotalis. Ergo, si in datione calicis imprimitur character, eadem ratione et in datione casulae. Et sic haberet duos characteres: quod falsum est.

PRAETEREA, ordo diaconi conformior est ordini sacerdotis quam ordo subdiaconi. Sed, si character imprimeretur sacerdoti in ipsa calicis porrectione, subdiaconus conformior esset sacerdoti quam diaconus: quia subdiaconus characterem, recipit in ipsa calicis porrectione, non autem diaconus. Ergo character sacer dotalis non imprimitur iri ipsa calicis porrectione.

OBJECTION 1: It would seem that the character is not imprinted on the priest at the moment when the chalice is handed to him. For the consecration of a priest is done by anointing as in confirmation. Now in confirmation the character is imprinted at the moment of anointing and therefore also in the priesthood: not at the handing of the chalice.

OBJ. 2: Further, our Lord gave his disciples the priestly power when he said: *receive ye the Holy Spirit: whose sins you shall forgive* (John 20:22–23), etc. Now the Holy Spirit is given by the imposition of hands. Therefore, the character of holy orders is given at the moment of the imposition of hands.

OBJ. 3: Further, as the ministers are consecrated, even so are the ministers' vestments. Now the blessing alone consecrates the vestments. Therefore, the consecration of the priest also is effected by the mere blessing of the bishop.

OBJ. 4: Further, as a chalice is handed to the priest, even so is the priestly vestment. Therefore, if a character is imprinted at the giving of the chalice, so likewise is there at the giving of the chasuble, and thus a priest would have two characters: but this is false.

OBJ. 5: Further, the deacon's order is more closely allied to the priest's order than is the subdeacon's. But if a character is imprinted on the priest at the moment of the handing of the chalice, the subdeacon would be more closely allied to the priest than the deacon; because the subdeacon, not the deacon, receives the character at the handing of the chalice. Therefore, the priestly character is not imprinted at the handing of the chalice.

PRAETEREA, acolythorum ordo magis appropinquat ad actum sacerdotis per hoc quod habet actum super urceolum, quam per hoc quod habet actum super candelabrum. Sed magis imprimitur character in acolythatu quando accipiunt candelabrum, quam quando accipiunt urceum: quia nomen acolythi cerei portationem significat. Ergo et in sacerdotio non imprimitur character quando calicem accipit.

SED CONTRA, principalis actus ordinis sacerdotis est consecrare corpus Christi. Sed ad hoc datur sibi potestas in acceptione calicis. Ergo tunc imprimitur character.

RESPONDEO dicendum quod, sicut dictum est, eiusdem est formam aliquam inducere, et materiam de proximo praeparare ad formam. Unde episcopus in collatione ordinum duo facit: praeparat enim ordinandos ad ordinis susceptionem; et ordinis potestatem tradit.

Praeparat quidem et instruendo eos de proprio officio; et aliquid circa eos operando ut idonei sint potestatem accipiendi. Quae quidem operatio in tribus consistit: scilicet benedictione, manus impositione, et unctione. Per benedictionem divinis obsequiis mancipantur. Et ideo benedictio omnibus datur. Sed per manus impositionem datur plenitudo gratiae, per quam ad magna officia sunt idonei. Et ideo solis diaconibus et sacerdotibus fit manus impositio, quia eis competit dispensatio sacramentorum: quamvis uni sicut principali, alteri sicut ministro. Sed unctione ad aliquod sacramentum tractandum consecrantur. Et ideo unctio solis sacerdotibus fit, qui propriis manibus corpus Christi tangunt: sicut etiam calix inungitur, qui tenet sanguinem, et patena, quae continet corpus.

Sed potestatis collatio fit per hoc quod datur eis aliquid quod ad proprium actum pertinet. Et quia principalis actus sacerdotis est consecrare corpus et sanguinem Christi, ideo in ipsa datione calicis, sub forma verborum determinata, character sacerdotalis imprimitur.

AD PRIMUM ergo dicendum quod in confirmatione non datur officium operandi super aliquam materiam exteriorem. Et ideo character ibi non imprimitur in aliqua exhibitione alicuius rei, sed in sola manus impositione et unctione. Sed in ordine sacerdotali aliter est. Et ideo non est simile.

AD SECUNDUM dicendum quod Dominus discipulis dedit potestatem sacerdotalem quantum ad principalem actum, ante passionem in Cena, quando dixit: *accipite et manducate*. Unde subiunxit: *hoc facite in meam commemorationem*. Sed post resurrectionem dedit eis potestatem sacerdotalem quantum ad actum secundarium, qui est ligare et solvere.

OBJ. 6: Further, the order of acolytes approaches nearer to the priestly act by exercising an act over the cruet than by exercising an act over the torch. Yet the character is imprinted on the acolytes when they receive the torch rather than when they receive the cruet, because the name of acolyte signifies candle-bearer. Therefore, the character is not imprinted on the priest when he receives the chalice.

ON THE CONTRARY, The principal act of the priest's order is to consecrate Christ's body. Now he receives the power to this effect at the handing of the chalice. Therefore, the character is imprinted on him then.

I ANSWER THAT, As stated above (A. 4), to cause the form and to give the matter its proximate preparation for the form belong to the same agent. Therefore, the bishop in conferring holy orders does two things, for he prepares the candidates for the reception of holy orders and delivers to them the power of order.

He prepares them both by instructing them in their respective offices and by doing something to them, so that they may be adapted to receive the power. This preparation consists of three things: namely, blessing, imposition of hands, and anointing. By the blessing they are enlisted in the divine service; thus the blessing is given to all. By the imposition of hands the fullness of grace is given, whereby they are qualified for exalted duties; thus only deacons and priests receive the imposition of hands, because they are competent to dispense the sacraments, although the latter as principal dispensers, the former as ministers. But by the anointing they are consecrated for the purpose of handling the sacrament; thus the anointing is done to the priests alone who touch the body of Christ with their own hands, even as a chalice is anointed because it holds the blood, and the paten because it holds the body.

The conferring of power is effected by giving them something pertaining to their proper act. And since the principal act of a priest is to consecrate the body and blood of Christ, the priestly character is imprinted at the very giving of the chalice under the prescribed form of words.

REPLY OBJ. 1: In confirmation there is not given the office of exercising an act on an exterior matter, wherefore the character is not imprinted in that sacrament at the handing of some particular thing, but at the mere imposition of hands and anointing. But it is otherwise in the priestly order, and consequently the comparison fails.

REPLY OBJ. 2: Our Lord gave his disciples the priestly power as regards the principal act before his Passion, at the Supper when he said: *take ye and eat* (Matt 26:26), wherefore he added: *do this for a commemoration of me* (Luke 22:19). After the resurrection, however, he gave them the priestly power as to its secondary act, which is to bind and loose.

Ad tertium dicendum quod in vestibus non requiritur alia consecratio nisi quod divino cultui mancipentur. Et ideo sufficit eis pro consecratione benedictio. Sed aliter est de ordinatis, ut ex dictis patet.

Ad quartum dicendum quod vestis sacerdotalis non significat potestatem sacerdoti datam, sed idoneitatem quae in eo requiritur ad actum potestatis exequendum. Et ideo nec sacerdoti nec alicui alii imprimitur character in alicuius vestis datione.

Ad quintum dicendum quod potestas diaconi est media inter potestatem subdiaconi et sacerdotis: sacerdos enim directe habet potestatem super corpus Christi, subdiaconus autem super vasa tantum, sed diaconus super corpus in vase contentum. Unde eius non est tangere corpus Christi, sed portare corpus in patena, et dispensare sanguinem cum calice. Et ideo eius potestas ad actum principalem non potuit exprimi nec per dationem vasis tantum, nec per dationem materiae. Sed exprimitur potestas eius ad actum secundarium, in hoc quod datur ei liber Evangeliorum: et in hac potestate intelligitur alia. Et ideo in ipsa libri datione imprimitur character.

Ad sextum dicendum quod principalior actus acolythi est quo ministrat in urceolo quam quo ministrat in candelabro: quamvis denominetur ab actu secundario, propter hoc quod est magis notus et magis proprius ei. Et ideo in datione urceoli imprimitur acolytho character, virtute verborum ab episcopo prolatorum.

Reply Obj. 3: Vestments require no other consecration except to be set aside for the divine worship, wherefore the blessing suffices for their consecration. But it is different with those who are ordained, as explained above.

Reply Obj. 4: The priestly vestment signifies not the power given to the priest, but the aptitude required of him for exercising the act of that power. Therefore, a character is imprinted neither on the priest nor on anyone else at the giving of a vestment.

Reply Obj. 5: The deacon's power is midway between the subdeacon's and the priest's. For the priest exercises a power directly on Christ's body, the subdeacon on the vessels only, and the deacon on Christ's body contained in a vessel. Hence it is not for him to touch Christ's body, but to carry the body on the paten, and to dispense the blood with the chalice. Consequently, his power, as to the principal act, could not be expressed either by the giving of the vessel only, or by the giving of the matter; and thus his power is expressed as to the secondary act alone, by his receiving the book of the Gospels, and this power is understood to contain the other; wherefore the character is impressed at the handing of the book.

Reply Obj. 6: The act of the acolyte whereby he serves with the cruet ranks before his act of carrying the torch; although he takes his name from the secondary act, because it is better known and more proper to him. Hence the acolyte receives the character when he is given the cruet by virtue of the words uttered by the bishop.

QUESTION 38

THOSE WHO CONFER ORDERS

Deinde considerandum est de conferentibus hoc sacramentum.

Circa quod quaeruntur duo.

Primo: utrum solus episcopus possit; hoc sacramentum conferre.

Secundo: utrum haereticus, vel quicumque ab Ecclesia praecisus, possit hoc sacramentum conferre.

We must now consider those who confer this sacrament.

Under this head there are two points of inquiry:

(1) Whether a bishop alone can confer this sacrament?

(2) Whether a heretic or any other person cut off from the Church can confer this sacrament?

Article 1

Whether a Bishop Alone Confers the Sacrament of Holy Orders?

AD PRIMUM SIC PROCEDITUR. Videtur quod non tantum episcopus ordinis sacramentum conferat. Quia manus impositio ad consecrationem aliquid facit. Sed sacerdotibus qui ordinantur non solum episcopus manus imponit, sed etiam sacerdotes adstantes. Ergo non solus episcopus confert ordinis sacramentum.

PRAETEREA, tunc unicuique datur potestas ordinis quando ei exhibetur quod ad actum sui ordinis pertinet. Sed subdiacono datur urceolus cum aqua, bacili et manutergio, ab archidiacono: similiter acolythis candelabrum cum cereo et urceolus vacuus. Ergo non solus episcopus confert ordinis sacramentum.

PRAETEREA, illa quae ordinis sunt, non possunt alicui committi qui non habet ordinem. Sed conferre ordines minores committitur aliquibus qui non sunt episcopi, sicut presbyteris cardinalibus. Ergo conferre ordines non est episcopalis ordinis.

PRAETEREA, *cuicumque committitur principale, et accessorium*. Sed ordinis sacramentum ordinatur ad Eucharistiam sicut accessorium ad principale. Cum ergo sacerdos consecret Eucharistiam, ipse etiam poterit ordines conferre.

PRAETEREA, plus distat sacerdos a diacono quam episcopus ab episcopo. Sed episcopus potest consecrare episcopum. Ergo et sacerdos potest promovere diaconum.

SED CONTRA: Nobiliori modo applicantur ad divinum cultum ministri per ordines quam vasa sacra. Sed consecratio vasorum pertinet ad solum episcopum. Ergo multo fortius consecratio ministrorum.

OBJECTION 1: It would seem that not only a bishop confers the sacrament of order. For the imposition of hands has something to do with the consecration. Now not only the bishop but also the assisting priests lay hands on the priests who are being ordained. Therefore, not only a bishop confers the sacrament of order.

OBJ. 2: Further, a man receives the power of order when that which pertains to the act of his order is handed to him. Now the cruet with water, bowl, and towel, is given to the subdeacon by the archdeacon; as also the candlestick with candle, and the empty cruet, to the acolyte. Therefore, not only the bishop confers the sacrament of order.

OBJ. 3: Further, that which belongs to an order cannot be entrusted to one who has not the order. Now the conferring of minor orders is entrusted to certain persons who are not bishops; for instance, to cardinal presbyters. Therefore, the conferring of orders does not belong to the episcopal order.

OBJ. 4: Further, *whoever is entrusted with the principal is entrusted with the accessory also*. Now the sacrament of order is directed to the Eucharist, as accessory to principal. Since, then, a priest consecrates the Eucharist, he can also confer orders.

OBJ. 5: Further, there is a greater distinction between a priest and a deacon than between bishop and bishop. But a bishop can consecrate a bishop. Therefore, a priest can ordain a deacon.

ON THE CONTRARY, Ministers are applied by their orders to the divine worship in a more noble way than the sacred vessels. But the consecration of the vessels belongs to a bishop only. Much more, therefore, does the consecration of ministers.

PRAETEREA, sacramentum ordinis est excellentius quam confirmationis. Sed solus episcopus confirmat. Ergo multo magis solus confert ordinis sacramentum.

PRAETEREA, virgines per benedictionem non constituuntur in aliquo gradu spiritualis potestatis, sicut ordinati constituuntur. Sed virgines benedicere est solius episcopi. Ergo multo magis solus ipse potest aliquos ordinare.

RESPONDEO dicendum quod potestas episcopalis habet se ad potestatem ordinum inferiorum sicut politica, quae coniectat bonum commune, ad inferiores artes et virtutes, quae coniectant aliquod bonum speciale, ut ex dictis patet. Politica autem, ut dicitur in I *Ethic.*, ponit legem inferioribus artibus: scilicet, quis quam debeat exercere, et quantum et qualiter. Et ideo ad episcopum pertinet in omnibus divinis ministeriis alios collocare. Unde ipse solus confirmat: quia confirmati in quodam officio confitendi fidem constituuntur. Ideo etiam solus ipse virgines benedicit, quae figuram gerunt Ecclesiae Christo desponsatae, cuius cura ipsi principaliter committitur. Ipse etiam in ministeriis ordinum ordinandos consecrat, et vasa quibus debent uti eis determinat sua consecratione: sicut et officia saecularia in civitatibus distribuuntur ab eo qui habet excellentiorem potestatem, sicut a rege.

AD PRIMUM ergo dicendum quod in impositione manuum non datur character sacerdotalis ordinis, ut ex dictis patet, sed gratia secundum quam, ad exequendum ordinem sint idonei. Et quia indigent amplissima gratia, ideo sacerdotes manus cum episcopo imponunt eis qui in sacerdotes promoventur: sed diaconis solus episcopus.

AD SECUNDUM dicendum quod, quia archidiaconus est quasi *princeps ministerii*, ideo omnia quae ad ministerium pertinent ipse tradit: sicut cereum, quo acolythus diacono servit ante Evangelium ipsum portando, et urceum, quo servit subdiacono; et similiter dat subdiacono ea quibus superioribus ordinibus servit. Sed tamen in illis non consistit principalis actus subdiaconi, sed in hoc quod cooperatur circa materiam sacramenti. Et ideo characterem accipit in eo quod datur ei calix ab episcopo. Sed acolythus accipit characterem ex verbis episcopi in hoc quod accipit praedicta ab archidiacono: et magis in acceptione urcei quam candelabri. Unde non sequitur quod archidiaconus ordinem conferat.

AD TERTIUM dicendum quod Papa, qui habet plenitudinem potestatis pontificalis, potest committere nonepiscopo ea quae ad episcopalem dignitatem pertinent, dummodo illa non habeant immediatam relationem ad verum corpus Christi. Et ideo ex eius commissione ali-

FURTHER, The sacrament of order ranks higher than the sacrament of confirmation. Now a bishop alone confirms. Much more, therefore, does a bishop alone confer the sacrament of order.

FURTHER, Virgins are not placed in a degree of spiritual power by their consecration, as the ordained are. Yet a bishop alone can consecrate a virgin. Therefore, much more can he alone ordain.

I ANSWER THAT, The episcopal power stands in the same relation to the power of the lower orders as does political science, which seeks the common good, to the lower acts and virtues, which seek some special good, as appears from what was said above (Q. 37, A. 1). Now political science, as stated in *Ethics* 1.2, lays down the law to lower sciences, namely, what science each one ought to cultivate, and both how far and in what way it should be pursued. Wherefore it belongs to a bishop to assign others to places in all the divine services. Hence he alone confirms, because those who are confirmed receive the office, as it were, of confessing the faith; again he alone blesses virgins who are images of the Church, Christ's spouse, the care of which is entrusted chiefly to him; and he it is who consecrates the candidates for ordination to the ministry of holy orders, and, by his consecration, appoints the vessels that they are to use; even as secular offices in various cities are allotted by him who holds the highest power, for instance, by the king.

REPLY OBJ. 1: As stated above (Q. 37, A. 5), at the imposition of hands there is given not the character of the priestly order, but grace which makes a man fit to exercise his order. And since those who are raised to the priesthood need most copious grace, the priests together with the bishop lay hands on them, but the bishop alone lays hands on deacons.

REPLY OBJ. 2: Since the archdeacon is, as it were, *minister-in-chief*, all things pertaining to the ministry are handed by him, for instance, the candle with which the acolyte serves the deacon by carrying it before him at the Gospel, and the cruet with which he serves the subdeacon; and in like manner he gives the subdeacon the things with which the latter serves the higher orders. And yet, the principal act of the subdeacon does not consist in these things, but in his cooperation as regards the matter of the sacrament; wherefore he receives the character through the chalice being handed to him by the bishop. On the other hand, the acolyte receives the character by virtue of the words of the bishop when the aforesaid things—the cruet rather than the candlestick—are handed to him by the archdeacon. Hence it does not follow that the archdeacon ordains.

REPLY OBJ. 3: The Pope, who has the fullness of episcopal power, can entrust one who is not a bishop with things pertaining to the episcopal dignity, provided they bear no immediate relation to the true body of Christ. Hence by virtue of his commission a simple priest can confer the mi-

quis sacerdos simplex potest conferre minores ordines et confirmare: non autem aliquis non sacerdos. Nec iterum sacerdos maiores ordines, qui habent immediatam relationem ad corpus Christi, supra quod consecrandum Papa non habet maiorem potestatem quam simplex sacerdos.

AD QUARTUM dicendum quod, quamvis sacramentum Eucharistiae sit maximum sacramentum in se, tamen non collocat in aliquo officio, sicut ordinis sacramentum. Et ideo non est similis ratio.

AD QUINTUM dicendum quod ad communicandum alteri quod quis habet, non exigitur solum propinquitas, sed completio potestatis. Et quia sacerdos non habet completam potestatem in hierarchicis officiis, sicut episcopus, ideo non sequitur quod possit diaconos facere, quamvis ille ordo sit sibi propinquus.

nor orders and confirm; but not one who is not a priest. Nor can a priest confer the higher orders which bear an immediate relation to Christ's body, over the consecration of which the Pope's power is no greater than that of a simple priest.

REPLY OBJ. 4: Although the Eucharist is in itself the greatest of the sacraments, it does not place a man in an office as does the sacrament of order. Hence the comparison fails.

REPLY OBJ. 5: In order to bestow what one has on another, it is necessary not only to be near him but also to have fullness of power. And since a priest has not fullness of power in the hierarchical offices, as a bishop has, it does not follow that he can raise others to the diaconate, although the latter order is near to his.

Article 2

Whether Heretics and Those Who Are Cut Off From the Church Can Confer Holy Orders?

AD SECUNDUM SIC PROCEDITUR. Videtur quod haeretici et ab Ecclesia praecisi non possint ordines conferre. Maius est enim conferre ordines quam aliquem absolvere vel ligare. Sed haereticus non potest absolvere aut ligare. Ergo nec ordines conferre.

PRAETEREA, sacerdos ab Ecclesia separatus conficere potest quia in eo character indelebiliter manet, per quem hoc potest. Sed episcopus non accipit aliquem characterem in sui promotione. Ergo non est necesse quod episcopalis potestas remaneat in eo post separationem eius ab Ecclesia.

PRAETEREA, in nulla communitate ille qui a communitate expellitur potest officia communitatis disponere. Sed ordines sunt quaedam officia Ecclesiae. Ergo ille qui extra Ecclesiam ponitur non potest ordines conferre.

PRAETEREA, sacramenta habent efficaciam ex passione Christi. Sed haereticus non continuatur, passioni Christi: neque per propriam fidem, cum sit infidelis; neque per fidem Ecclesiae, cum sit ab Ecclesia separatus. Ergo non potest sacramentum ordinis conferre.

PRAETEREA, in ordinis collatione exigitur benedictio. Sed haereticus non potest benedicere: quinimmo benedictio sua in maledictionem convertitur, ut patet per auctoritates in littera inductas. Ergo non potest ordines conferre.

SED CONTRA: Est quod aliquis episcopus in haeresim lapsus, quando reconciliatur, non iterum consecratur. Ergo non amisit potestatem quam habebat ordines conferendi.

OBJECTION 1: It would seem that heretics and those who are cut off from the Church cannot confer orders. For to confer orders is a greater thing than to loose or bind anyone. But a heretic cannot loose or bind. Neither, therefore, can he ordain.

OBJ. 2: Further, a priest that is separated from the Church can consecrate, because the character whence he derives this power remains in him indelibly. But a bishop receives no character when he is raised to the episcopate. Therefore, he does not necessarily retain the episcopal power after his separation from the Church.

OBJ. 3: Further, in no community can one who is expelled therefrom dispose of the offices of the community. Now orders are offices of the Church. Therefore, one who is outside the Church cannot confer orders.

OBJ. 4: Further, the sacraments derive their efficacy from Christ's Passion. Now a heretic is not united to Christ's Passion: neither by his own faith, since he is an unbeliever, nor by the faith of the Church, since he is severed from the Church. Therefore, he cannot confer the sacrament of orders.

OBJ. 5: Further, a blessing is necessary in the conferring of orders. But a heretic cannot bless; in fact, his blessing is turned into a curse, as appears from the authorities quoted in the text (*Sentences* IV, D. 25). Therefore, he cannot ordain.

ON THE CONTRARY, When a bishop who has fallen into heresy is reconciled, he is not reconsecrated. Therefore, he did not lose the power which he had of conferring orders.

PRAETEREA, maior est potestas conferendi ordines quam potestas ordinum. Sed potestas ordinum non amittitur propter haeresim vel aliquod huiusmodi. Ergo nec potestas conferendi ordines.

PRAETEREA, sicut baptizans exhibet tantum ministerium exterius, ita et conferens ordines, Deo interius operante. Sed nulla ratione aliquis ab Ecclesia praecisus amittit baptizandi potestatem. Ergo nec ordines conferendi.

RESPONDEO dicendum quod circa hoc ponuntur in littera quattuor opiniones. Quidam enim dixerunt quod haeretici, quandiu ab Ecclesia tolerantur, habent potestatem ordines conferendi, non autem postquam fuerunt praecisi: similiter nec degradati et alii huiusmodi. Et haec est prima opinio.

Sed hoc non potest esse. Quia omnis potestas quae datur cum aliqua consecratione, nullo casu contingente tolli potest, sicut nec ipsa consecratio annullari: quia etiam altare vel chrisma semel consecrata perpetuo consecrata manent. Unde, cum episcopalis potestas cum quadam consecratione detur, oportet quod perpetuo maneat, quantumcumque aliquis peccet, vel ab Ecclesia praecidatur.

Et ideo alii dixerunt quod praecisi ab Ecclesia qui in Ecclesia episcopalem potestatem habuerunt, retinent potestatem alios ordinandi et promovendi, sed promoti ab eis hoc non habent. Et haec est quarta opinio.

Sed hoc non potest esse. Quia si illi qui fuerunt in Ecclesia promoti, retinent potestatem quam acceperunt, patet quod, exequendo suam potestatem veram consecrationem faciunt. Et ideo vere tribuunt omnem potestatem quae cum consecratione datur. Et sic ordinati ab eis, vel promoti, habent eandem potestatem quam et ipsi.

Et ideo alii dixerunt quod etiam praecisi ab Ecclesia possunt ordines conferre et alia sacramenta, dummodo formam debitam et intentionem servent, et quantum ad primum effectum, qui est collatio sacramenti, et quantum ad ultimum, qui est collatio gratiae. Et haec est secunda opinio.

Sed hoc etiam non potest stare. Quia ex hoc ipso quod aliquis haeretico praeciso ab Ecclesia, in sacramentis communicat, peccat. Et ita fictus accedit, et gratiam consequi non potest: nisi forte in baptismo in articulo necessitatis.

Et ideo alii dicunt quod vera sacramenta conferunt, sed cum eis gratiam non dant: non propter inefficaciam sacramentorum, sed propter peccata recipientium ab eis sacramenta contra prohibitionem Ecclesiae. Et haec est tertia opinio, quae vera est.

AD PRIMUM ergo dicendum quod effectus absolutionis non est aliud quam remissio peccatorum, quae per gratiam fit. Et ideo haereticus non potest absolvere: sicut

FURTHER, The power to ordain is greater than the power of orders. But the power of orders is not forfeited on account of heresy and the like. Neither, therefore, is the power to ordain.

FURTHER, As the one who baptizes exercises a merely outward ministry, so does one who ordains, while God works inwardly. But one who is cut off from the Church by no means loses the power to baptize. Neither, therefore, does he lose the power to ordain.

I ANSWER THAT, On this question four opinions are mentioned in the text (*Sentences* IV, D. 25). For some said that heretics, so long as they are tolerated by the Church, retain the power to ordain, but not after they have been cut off from the Church; as neither do those who have been degraded and the like. This is the first opinion.

Yet this is impossible, because, happen what may, no power that is given with a consecration can be taken away so long as the thing itself remains, any more than the consecration itself can be annulled, for even an altar or chrism once consecrated remains consecrated forever. Wherefore, since the episcopal power is conferred by consecration, it must endure forever, however much a man may sin or be cut off from the Church.

For this reason others said that those who are cut off from the Church after having episcopal power in the Church retain the power to ordain and raise others, but that those who are raised by them have not this power. This is the fourth opinion.

But this again is impossible, for if those who were ordained in the Church retain the power they received, it is clear that by exercising their power they consecrate validly, and therefore they validly confer whatever power is given with that consecration, and thus those who receive ordination or promotion from them have the same power as they.

Therefore, others said that even those who are cut off from the Church can confer orders and the other sacraments, provided they observe the due form and intention, both as to the first effect, which is the conferring of the sacrament, and as to the ultimate effect, which is the conferring of grace. This is the second opinion.

But this again is inadmissible, since by the very fact that a person communicates in the sacraments with a heretic who is cut off from the Church, he sins, and thus approaches the sacrament insincerely and cannot obtain grace, except perhaps in baptism in a case of necessity.

Hence others say that they confer the sacraments validly, but do not confer grace with them, not that the sacraments are lacking in efficacy, but on account of the sins of those who receive the sacraments from such persons despite the prohibition of the Church. This is the third and the true opinion.

REPLY OBJ. 1: The effect of absolution is nothing else but the forgiveness of sins which results from grace, and consequently a heretic cannot absolve, as neither can he

nec gratiam in sacramentis conferre. Et iterum ad absolutionem requiritur iurisdictio, quam non habet ab Ecclesia praecisus.

AD SECUNDUM dicendum quod in promotione episcopi datur sibi potestas quae perpetuo manet in eo: quamvis dici non possit character, quia per eam non ordinatur homo directe ad Deum, sed ad corpus Christi mysticum. Et tamen indelebilitem manet sicut character, et per consecrationem datur.

AD TERTIUM dicendum quod illi qui promoventur ab haereticis, quamvis accipiant ordinem, non tamen recipiunt executionem, ut licite possint in suis ordinibus ministrare, ratione illa quam obiectio tangit.

AD QUARTUM dicendum quod per fidem Ecclesiae continuatur passioni Christi. Quia, quamvis in ea non sint secundum se, sunt tamen in ea secundum formam Ecclesiae, quam servant.

AD QUINTUM dicendum quod hoc est referendum ad ultimum effectum sacramentorum, ut tertia opinio dicit.

confer grace in the sacraments. Moreover, in order to give absolution it is necessary to have jurisdiction, which one who is cut off from the Church has not.

REPLY OBJ. 2: When a man is raised to the episcopate he receives a power which he retains forever. This, however, cannot be called a character, because a man is not thereby placed in direct relation to God, but to Christ's mystical body. Nevertheless it remains indelibly, even as would the character, because it is given by consecration.

REPLY OBJ. 3: Those who are ordained by heretics, although they receive an order, do not receive the exercise thereof so as to minister lawfully in their orders, for the very reason indicated in the objection.

REPLY OBJ. 4: They are united to the passion of Christ by the faith of the Church, for although in themselves they are severed from it, they are united to it as regards the form of the Church which they observe.

REPLY OBJ. 5: This refers to the ultimate effect of the sacraments, as the third opinion maintains.

QUESTION 39

THE IMPEDIMENTS TO HOLY ORDERS

Deinde considerandum est de impedimentis huius sacramenti.

Circa quod quaeruntur sex.

Primo: utrum sexus femineus impediat huius sacramenti susceptionem.

Secundo: utrum carentia usus rationis.

Tertio: utrum servitus.

Quarto: utrum homicidium.

Quinto: utrum illegitima nativitas.

Sexto: utrum defectus membrorum.

We must next consider the impediments to this sacrament.

Under this head there are six points of inquiry:

(1) Whether the female sex is an impediment to receiving this sacrament?

(2) Whether lack of the use of reason is?

(3) Whether the state of slavery is?

(4) Whether homicide is?

(5) Whether illegitimate birth is?

(6) Whether lack of members is?

Article 1

Whether the Female Sex Is an Impediment to Receiving Holy Orders?

AD PRIMUM SIC PROCEDITUR. Videtur quod sexus femineus non impediat ordinis susceptionem. Quia officium prophetiae est maius quam officium sacerdotis: quia propheta est medium inter Deum et sacerdotes, sicut sacerdos est inter Deum et populum. Sed prophetiae officium aliquando mulieribus est concessum: ut patet IV *Reg*. Ergo et sacerdotii officium eis competere potest.

PRAETEREA, sicut ordo ad quandam perfectionem pertinet, ita et praelationis officium, et martyrium, et religionis status. Sed praelatio committitur mulieribus in novo Testamento, ut patet de abbatissis: et in veteri, ut patet de Debbora, quae iudicavit Israel, Iudic. 4. Competit etiam eis martyrium, et religionis status. Ergo et ordo Ecclesiae.

PRAETEREA, ordinum potestas in anima fundatur. Sed sexus non est in anima. Ergo diversitas sexus non facit distinctionem in receptione ordinum.

SED CONTRA: Est quod dicitur I Tim. 2: *mulierem in Ecclesia docere non permitto, nec dominari in virum*.

PRAETEREA, in ordinandis praeexigitur corona: quamvis non de necessitate sacramenti. Sed corona et tonsura non competunt mulieribus: ut patet I Cor. ii. Ergo nec ordinum susceptio.

RESPONDEO dicendum quod quaedam requiruntur in recipiente sacramentum quasi de necessitate sacramenti: quae si desunt, non potest aliquis suscipere neque sacramentum neque rem sacramenti, quaedam vero re-

OBJECTION 1: It would seem that the female sex is no impediment to receiving orders. For the office of prophet is greater than the office of priest, since a prophet stands midway between God and priests, just as the priest does between God and people. Now the office of prophet was sometimes granted to women, as may be gathered from 2 Kgs 22:14. Therefore, the office of priest also may be competent to them.

OBJ. 2: Further, just as order pertains to a kind of preeminence, so does a position of authority, as well as martyrdom and the religious state. Now authority is entrusted to women in the New Testament, as in the case of abbesses, and in the Old Testament, as in the case of Deborah, who judged Israel (Judg 2). Moreover, martyrdom and the religious life are also befitting to them. Therefore, the orders of the Church are also competent to them.

OBJ. 3: Further, the power of orders is founded in the soul. But sex is not in the soul. Therefore, difference in sex makes no difference to the reception of orders.

ON THE CONTRARY, It is said: *I suffer not a woman to teach in the Church, nor to use authority over the man* (1 Tim 2:12).

FURTHER, The crown is required previous to receiving orders, although not for the validity of the sacrament. But the crown or tonsure is not befitting to women according to 1 Corinthians 11:6. Neither, therefore, is the receiving of orders.

I ANSWER THAT, Certain things are required in the recipient of a sacrament as being requisite for the validity of the sacrament, and if such things be lacking, one can receive neither the sacrament nor the reality of the sacrament.

quiruntur non de necessitate sacramenti, sed de necessitate praecepti, propter congruitatem ad sacramentum. Et sine talibus aliquis suscipit sacramentum, sed non rem sacramenti. Dicendum ergo quod sexus virilis requiritur ad susceptionem ordinum non solum secundo modo, sed etiam primo. Unde, etsi mulieri exhibeantur omnia quae in ordinibus fiunt, ordinem non suscipit. Quia, cum sacramentum sit signum, in his quae in sacramento aguntur requiritur non solum res, sed signum rei: sicut dictum est quod in extrema unctione exigitur quod sit infirmus ut significetur curatione indigens. Cum igitur in sexu femineo non possit significari aliqua eminentia gradus, quia mulier statum subiectionis, habet; ideo non potest ordinis sacramentum suscipere.

Quidam autem dixerunt quod sexus virilis est de necessitate praecepti, sed non de necessitate sacramenti, quia etiam in Decretis fit mentio de diaconissa et presbytera. Sed diaconissa dicitur quae in aliquo actu diaconi participat, sicut quae legit homiliam in ecclesia. Presbytera autem dicitur vidua, quia *presbyter* idem est quod *senior*.

AD PRIMUM ergo dicendum quod prophetia non est sacramentum, sed Dei donum. Unde ibi non exigitur significatio, sed solum res. Et quia secundum rem in his quae sunt animae mulier non differt a viro, cum quandoque mulier inveniatur melior quantum ad animam viris multis; ideo donum prophetiae et alia huiusmodi potest recipere, sed non ordinis sacramentum.

ET PER HOC patet solutio ad secundum et tertium.

De abbatissis tamen dicitur quod non habent praelationem ordinariam, sed quasi ex commissione, propter periculum cohabitationis virorum ad mulieres. Debbora autem in temporalibus praefuit, non in sacerdotalibus: sicut et nunc possunt mulieres temporaliter dominari.

Other things, however, are required not for the validity of the sacrament, but for its lawfulness, as being congruous to the sacrament; and without these one receives the sacrament, but not the reality of the sacrament. Accordingly, we must say that the male sex is required for receiving orders not only in the second, but also in the first way. Therefore, even though a woman were made the object of all that is done in conferring orders, she would not receive orders, for since a sacrament is a sign, not only the thing, but the signification of the thing, is required in all sacramental actions; thus it was stated above (Q. 32, A. 2) that in extreme unction it is necessary to have a sick man, in order to signify the need of healing. Accordingly, since it is not possible in the female sex to signify eminence of degree, for a woman is in the state of subjection, it follows that she cannot receive the sacrament of order.

Some, however, have asserted that the male sex is necessary for the lawfulness and not for the validity of the sacrament, because even in the *Decretals* mention is made of deaconesses and priestesses. But deaconess there denotes a woman who shares in some act of a deacon, namely who reads the homilies in the Church; and priestess means a widow, for the word 'presbyter' means 'elder'.

REPLY OBJ. 1: Prophecy is not a sacrament but a gift of God. Wherefore there it is not the signification, but only the thing which is necessary. And since in matters pertaining to the soul, woman does not differ from man as to the thing (for sometimes a woman is found to be better than many men as regards the soul), it follows that she can receive the gift of prophecy and the like, but not the sacrament of holy orders.

THIS SUFFICES for the reply to the second and third objections.

However, as to abbesses, it is said that they have not ordinary authority, but delegated as it were, on account of the danger of men and women living together. But Deborah exercised authority in temporal, not in priestly matters, even as now woman may have temporal power.

Article 2

Whether Boys and Those Who Lack the Use of Reason Can Receive Holy Orders?

AD SECUNDUM SIC PROCEDITUR. Videtur quod pueri, et qui carent usu rationis, non possint ordines suscipere. Quia, ut in littera dicitur, sacri canones in suscipientibus ordines certum et determinatum tempus statuerunt aetatis. Sed hoc non esset si pueri recipere possent ordinis sacramentum. Ergo, etc.

PRAETEREA, ordinis sacramentum est dignius quam matrimonium. Sed pueri, et alii carentes usu rationis,

OBJECTION 1: It would seem that boys and those who lack the use of reason cannot receive orders. For, as stated in the text (*Sentences* IV, D. 25), the sacred canons have appointed a certain fixed age in those who receive orders. But this would not be if boys could receive the sacrament of orders. Therefore, etc.

OBJ. 2: Further, the sacrament of orders ranks above the sacrament of matrimony. Now children and those who

non possunt contrahere matrimonium. Ergo nec ordines suscipere.

PRAETEREA, *cuius est potentia, eius est actus*: secundum Philosophum, in libro *de Somno et Vigilia*. Sed actus ordinis requirit usum rationis. Ergo et ordinum potestas.

SED CONTRA: Ille qui est ante annos discretionis promotus ad ordines, sine iteratione ipsorum quandoque in eis conceditur ministrare: ut patet, *Extra de Clerico per saltum promoto*. Hoc autem non esset si ordinem non suscepisset. Ergo puer potest ordines suscipere.

PRAETEREA, alia sacramenta in quibus character imprimitur, possunt pueri suscipere, ut baptismum et confirmationem. Ergo pari ratione et ordines.

RESPONDEO dicendum quod per pueritiam et alios defectus quibus tollitur usus rationis, praestatur impedimentum actui. Et ideo omnia illa sacramenta quae actum requirunt suscipientis sacramentum, talibus non competunt: sicut poenitentia, matrimonium et huiusmodi. Sed quia potestates infusae sunt priores actibus, sicut et naturales, quamvis acquisitae sunt posteriores; remoto autem posteriori non tollitur prius: ideo omnia sacramenta in quibus non requiritur actus suscipientis de necessitate sacramenti, sed potestas aliqua spiritualis divinitus datur, possunt pueri suscipere, et alii qui usu rationis carent; hac tamen distinctione habita, quod in minoribus ordinibus requiritur discretionis tempus de honestate, propter dignitatem sacramenti, sed non de necessitate praecepti neque de necessitate sacramenti. Unde aliqui, si necessitas adsit et spes profectus, ad minores ordines possunt ante annos discretionis promoveri sine peccato, et suscipient ordinem: quia, quamvis tunc non sint idonei ad officia quae eis committuntur, tamen per assuefactionem idonei reddentur. Sed ad maiores ordines requiritur usus rationis et de honestate et necessitate praecepti: propter votum continentiae, quod habent annexum et quia etiam eis sacramenta tractanda committuntur. Sed ad episcopatum, ubi in corpus mysticum accipitur potestas, requiritur actus suscipientis curam pastoralem. Et ideo est etiam de necessitate consecrationis episcopalis quod usum rationis habeat.

Quidam autem dicunt quod ad omnes ordines requiritur usus rationis de necessitate sacramenti. Sed eorum dictum ratione vel auctoritate non confirmatur.

AD PRIMUM ergo dicendum quod non omne quod est de necessitate praecepti, est de necessitate sacramenti, ut dictum est.

AD SECUNDUM dicendum quod matrimonium causat consensus, qui sine usu rationis esse non potest. Sed in receptione ordinis non requiritur aliquis actus ex par-

lack the use of reason cannot contract matrimony. Neither, therefore, can they receive orders.

OBJ. 3: Further, *act and power are in the same subject*, according to the Philosopher (*On Sleep and Sleeplessness* 1). Now the act of orders requires the use of reason. Therefore, the power of orders does also.

ON THE CONTRARY, One who is raised to orders before the age of discretion is sometimes allowed to exercise them without being reordained (*Extra De Clerico Per Saltum Promoto*). But this would not be the case if he had not received orders. Therefore, a boy can receive holy orders.

FURTHER, Boys can receive other sacraments in which a character is imprinted, namely, baptism and confirmation. Therefore, in like manner they can receive holy orders.

I ANSWER THAT, Boyhood and other defects which remove the use of reason occasion an impediment to act. Wherefore the like are unfit to receive all those sacraments which require an act on the part of the recipient of the sacrament, such as penance, matrimony, and so forth. But since infused powers, like natural powers, precede acts—although acquired powers follow acts—and the removal of that which comes after does not entail the removal of what comes first, it follows that children and those who lack the use of reason can receive all the sacraments in which an act on the part of the recipient is not required for the validity of the sacrament, but some spiritual power is conferred from above; with this difference, however, that in the minor orders the age of discretion is required out of respect for the dignity of the sacrament, but not for its lawfulness, nor for its validity. Hence some can without sin be raised to the minor orders before the years of discretion, if there be an urgent reason for it and hope of their proficiency, and they are validly ordained; for although at the time they are not qualified for the offices entrusted to them, they will become qualified by being habituated thereto. For the higher orders, however, the use of reason is required both out of respect for, and for the lawfulness of the sacrament, not only on account of the vow of continency annexed thereto, but also because the handling of the sacraments is entrusted to them. But for the episcopate whereby a man receives power also over the mystical body, the act of accepting the pastoral care of souls is required; wherefore the use of reason is necessary for the validity of episcopal consecration.

Some, however, maintain that the use of reason is necessary for the validity of the sacrament in all the orders. But this statement is not confirmed either by authority or by reason.

REPLY OBJ. 1: As stated in the Article, not all that is necessary for the lawfulness of a sacrament is required for its validity.

REPLY OBJ. 2: The cause of matrimony is consent, which cannot be without the use of reason. Whereas in the reception of orders no act is required on the part of the re-

te recipientis. Quod patet ex hoc quod nullus actus ex parte eorum exprimitur in eorum consecratione. Et ideo non est simile.

AD TERTIUM dicendum quod eiusdem est actus et potentia: sed tamen aliquando potentia praecedit, sicut liberum arbitrium usum suum. Et sic est in proposito.

cipients, since no act on their part is expressed in their consecration. Hence there is no comparison.

REPLY OBJ. 3: Act and power are in the same subject; yet sometimes a power, such as the free-will, precedes its act; and thus it is in the case in point.

Article 3

Whether the State of Slavery Is an Impediment to Receiving Holy Orders?

AD TERTIUM SIC PROCEDITUR. Videtur quod servitus non impediat aliquem a susceptione ordinum. Subiectio enim corporalis non repugnat praelationi spirituali. Sed in servo est subiectio corporalis. Ergo non impeditur quin debeat suscipere praelationem spiritualem, quae in ordine datur.

PRAETEREA, illud quod est occasio humilitatis, non debet impedire susceptionem alicuius sacramenti. Sed servitus est huiusmodi: unde Apostolus consuluit quod, *si aliquis possit, magis utatur servitute*, I Cor. 7. Ergo non debet impedire a promotione ordinis.

PRAETEREA, magis est turpe clericum in servum vendi, quam servum in clericum promoveri. Sed licite clericus in servum vendi potest: quia episcopus Nolanus, scilicet beatus Paulinus, seipsum in servum vendidit, ut in Dialogis legitur. Ergo multo fortius potest servus in clericum promoveri.

SED CONTRA: Videtur quod impediat quantum ad necessitatem sacramenti. Quia mulier non potest suscipere sacramentum ratione subiectionis. Sed maior subiectio est in servo: quia mulier non datur viro in ancillam; propter quod, non est de pedibus sumpta. Ergo et servus sacramentum non suscipit.

PRAETEREA, aliquis ex quo suscipit ordinem, tenetur in ordine ministrare. Sed non potest simul ministrare domino suo carnali, et in spirituali ministerio. Ergo videtur quod non possit ordinem suscipere: quia dominus debet conservari indemnis.

RESPONDEO dicendum quod in susceptione ordinis mancipatur homo divinis officiis. Et quia nullus potest dare quod suum non est, ideo servus, qui non habet potestatem sui, non potest ad ordines promoveri. Si tamen promovetur, ordinem suscipit: quia libertas non est de necessitate sacramenti, sed de necessitate praecepti; cum non impediat potestatem, sed actum tantum. Et similis ratio est de omnibus qui sunt aliis obligati: ut ratiociniis detenti, et huiusmodi personae.

OBJECTION 1: It would seem that the state of slavery is not an impediment to receiving holy orders. For corporal subjection is not incompatible with spiritual authority. But in a slave there is corporal subjection. Therefore, he is not hindered from receiving the spiritual authority which is given in holy orders.

OBJ. 2: Further, that which is an occasion for humility should not be an impediment to the reception of a sacrament. Now such is slavery, for the Apostle counsels a man, *if possible, rather to remain in slavery* (1 Cor 7:21). Therefore, it should not hinder him from being raised to orders.

OBJ. 3: Further, it is more disgraceful for a cleric to become a slave than for a slave to be made a cleric. Yet a cleric may lawfully be sold as a slave; for a bishop of Nola, Blessed Paulinus, sold himself as a slave, as related by Gregory (*Dialogues* 3). Much more, therefore, can a slave be made a cleric.

OBJ. 4: On the contrary, it would seem that it is an impediment to the validity of the sacrament. For a woman, on account of her subjection, cannot receive the sacrament of holy orders. But greater still is the subjection in a slave; since woman was not given to man as his handmaid (for which reason she was not made from his feet). Therefore, neither can a slave receive this sacrament.

OBJ. 5: Further, a man, from the fact that he receives an order, is bound to minister in that order. But he cannot at the same time serve his carnal master and exercise his spiritual ministry. Therefore, it would seem that he cannot receive holy orders, since the master must be indemnified.

I ANSWER THAT, By receiving orders a man pledges himself to the divine offices. And since no man can give what is not his, a slave who has not the disposal of himself cannot be raised to orders. If, however, he be raised, he receives the order, because freedom is not required for the validity of the sacrament, although it is requisite for its lawfulness, since it hinders not the power, but the act only. The same reason applies to all who are under an obligation to others, such as those who are in debt and like persons.

AD PRIMUM ergo dicendum quod in susceptione spiritualis potestatis est aliqua obligatio ad aliqua etiam corporaliter agenda. Et ideo per corporalem subiectionem impeditur.

AD SECUNDUM dicendum quod ex multis aliis, quae non praestant impedimentum executioni ordinum, potest aliquis occasionem humilitatis accipere. Et ideo ratio non sequitur.

AD TERTIUM dicendum quod beatus Paulinus ex abundantia caritatis, Spiritu Dei ductus, hoc fecit. Quod rei eventus probat: quia per eius servitutem multi de grege suo sunt de servitute liberati. Et ideo non est ad consequentiam trahendum: quia, *ubi Spiritus Domini, ibi libertas*, II Cor. 3.

AD QUARTUM dicendum quod signa sacramentalia ex naturali similitudine repraesentant. Mulier autem habet subiectionem a natura, sed non servus. Et ideo non est simile.

AD QUINTUM dicendum quod, si est promotus sciente domino et non reclamante, ex hoc ipso efficitur ingenuus. Si autem eo nesciente, tunc episcopus et ille qui praesentavit tenentur domino in duplum quam sit pretium servi, si sciverunt ipsum esse servum. Alias, si servus habeat peculium, debet seipsum redimere: alioquin redigetur in servitutem domini sui, non obstante quod ordinem suum exequi non potest.

REPLY OBJ. 1: The reception of spiritual power involves also an obligation to certain bodily actions, and consequently it is hindered by bodily subjection.

REPLY OBJ. 2: A man may take an occasion for humility from many other things which do not prove a hindrance to the exercise of holy orders. And thus the argument does not proceed.

REPLY OBJ. 3: The blessed Paulinus did this out of the abundance of his charity, being led by the spirit of God; as was proved by the result of his action, since by his becoming a slave many of his flock were freed from slavery. Hence we must not draw a conclusion from this particular instance, since *where the spirit of the Lord is, there is liberty* (2 Cor 3:17).

REPLY OBJ. 4: The sacramental signs signify by reason of their natural likeness. Now a woman is a subject by her nature, whereas a slave is not. Hence the comparison fails.

REPLY OBJ. 5: If he be ordained, his master knowing and not dissenting, by this very fact he becomes a freedman. But if his master be in ignorance, the bishop and he who presented him are bound to pay the master double the slave's value, if they knew him to be a slave. Otherwise, if the slave has possessions of his own, he is bound to buy his freedom, else he would have to return to the bondage of his master, notwithstanding the impossibility of his exercising his order.

Article 4

Whether a Man Should Be Debarred From Receiving Holy Orders on Account of Homicide?

AD QUARTUM SIC PROCEDITUR. Videtur quod propter homicidium aliquis non debeat prohiberi a sacris ordinibus. Quia ordines nostri sumpserunt initium a levitarum officio: ut in praecedenti distinctione dictum est. Sed levitae *consecraverunt manus suas* in sanguinis effusione fratrum suorum, ut patet Exod. 32. Ergo et in novo Testamento non debent aliqui ab assumptione ordinum prohiberi propter sanguinis effusionem.

PRAETEREA, propter actum virtutis nullus debet impediri ab aliquo sacramento. Sed aliquando sanguis effunditur per iustitiam, sicut a iudice: et peccaret habens officium si non effunderet. Ergo non impeditur propter hoc a sacramenti susceptione.

PRAETEREA, poena non debetur nisi culpae. Sed aliquis sine culpa quandoque homicidium committit: sicut se defendendo, vel etiam casualiter. Ergo non debet incurrere irregularitatis poenam.

OBJECTION 1: It would seem that a man ought not to be debarred from receiving holy orders on account of homicide. For our orders originated with the office of the Levites, as stated in the previous Distinction (*Sentences* IV, D. 24). But the Levites *consecrated their hands* by shedding the blood of their brethren (Exod 32:29). Therefore, neither should anyone in the New Testament be debarred from receiving holy orders on account of the shedding of blood.

OBJ. 2: Further, no one should be debarred from a sacrament on account of an act of virtue. Now blood is sometimes shed for justice's sake, for instance, by a judge; and he who has the office would sin if he did not shed it. Therefore, he is not hindered on that account from receiving holy orders.

OBJ. 3: Further, punishment is not due save for a fault. Now, sometimes a person commits homicide without fault, for instance, by defending himself, or again by mishap. Therefore, he ought not to incur the punishment of irregularity.

Sed contra hoc sunt plura canonum statuta, et Ecclesiae consuetudo.

Respondeo dicendum quod omnes ordines referuntur ad Eucharistiae sacramentum, quod est sacramentum pacis nobis factae per effusionem sanguinis Christi. Et quia homicidium maxime contrariatur paci; et homicidae magis conformantur occidentibus Christum quam ipsi Christo occiso, cui omnes ministri praedicti sacramenti debent conformari: ideo de necessitate praecepti est quod non sit homicida qui ad ordines promovetur; quamvis non sit de necessitate sacramenti.

Ad primum ergo dicendum quod vetus lex inferebat poenam sanguinis, non autem nova lex. Et ideo non est simile de ministris veteris et novae legis, quae est *iugum suave et onus leve*.

Ad secundum dicendum quod irregularitas non incurritur propter peccatum tantum, sed principaliter propter ineptitudinem personae ad sacramentum Eucharistiae ministrandum. Et ideo iudex, et omnes qui in causa sanguinis ei participant, sunt irregulares, propter hoc quod effusio sanguinis non decet ministros dicti sacramenti.

Ad tertium dicendum quod nullus facit nisi illud cuius est causa, quod est voluntarium in homine. Et ideo ille qui ignorans hominem occidit homicidio casuali, non dicitur homicida, nec irregularitatem incurrit: nisi operam dederit illicitae rei, vel nisi omiserit debitam diligentiam, quia iam quodammodo efficitur voluntarium. Nec hoc est propter hoc quod culpa careat: quia etiam sine culpa incurritur irregularitas. Et ideo etiam ille qui se defendendo in aliquo casu non peccat; homicidium committendo, nihilominus irregularis est.

On the contrary, Against this there are many canonical statutes (*Decretals*), as also the custom of the Church.

I answer that, All the orders bear a relation to the sacrament of the Eucharist, which is the sacrament of the peace vouchsafed to us by the shedding of Christ's blood. And since homicide is most opposed to peace, and those who slay are conformed to Christ's slayers rather than to Christ slain, to whom all the ministers of the aforesaid sacrament ought to be conformed, it follows that it is illicit, although not invalid, for homicides to be raised to holy orders.

Reply Obj. 1: The old law inflicted the punishment of blood, whereas the new law does not. Hence the comparison fails between the ministers of the Old Testament and those of the New, which is a *sweet yoke and a light burden* (Matt 11:30).

Reply Obj. 2: Irregularity is incurred not only on account of sin, but chiefly on account of a person being unfit to administer the sacrament of the Eucharist. Hence the judge and all who take part with him in a cause of blood are irregular, because the shedding of blood is unbecoming to the ministers of that sacrament.

Reply Obj. 3: No one does a thing without being the cause thereof, and in man this is something voluntary. Hence he who by mishap slays a man without knowing that it is a man is not called a homicide, nor does he incur irregularity (unless he was occupying himself in some unlawful manner, or failed to take sufficient care, since in this case the slaying becomes somewhat voluntary). But this is not because he is not in fault, since irregularity is incurred even without fault. Wherefore even he who in a particular case slays a man in self-defense without committing a sin is nonetheless irregular.

Article 5

Whether Those of Illegitimate Birth Should Be Debarred from Receiving Holy Orders?

Ad quintum sic proceditur. Videtur quod illegitime nati non debeant impediri a susceptione ordinum. Quia *filius non debet portare iniquitatem patris*. Portaret autem si propter hoc impediretur ab ordinibus suscipiendis. Ergo, etc.

Praeterea, magis impeditur aliquis propter defectum proprium quam alienum. Sed a susceptione ordinum propter illicitum concubitum suum non semper aliquis impeditur. Ergo nec propter illicitum concubitum patris sui.

Sed contra est quod dicitur Deut. 23; *non ingredietur mamzer, hoc est de scorto natus, ecclesiam Dei, usque*

Objection 1: It would seem that those who are of illegitimate birth should not be debarred from receiving holy orders. For the *son should not bear the iniquity of the father* (Ezek 18:20); and yet he would if this were an impediment to his receiving holy orders. Therefore, etc.

Obj. 2: Further, one's own fault is a greater impediment than the fault of another. Now unlawful intercourse does not always debar a man from receiving holy orders. Therefore, neither should he be debarred by the unlawful intercourse of his father.

On the contrary, It is written: *a bastard, that is to say, one born of a prostitute, shall not enter into the Church*

in decimam generationem. Ergo multo minus debet promoveri ad ordines.

Respondeo dicendum quod ordinati in quadam dignitate prae aliis constituuntur. Ideo ex quadam honestate requiritur in eis claritas quaedam, non de necessitate sacramenti, sed de necessitate praecepti: ut scilicet sint bonae famae, bonis moribus ornati, non publice poenitentes. Et quia obscuratur hominis claritas ex vitiosa origine, ideo etiam ex illegitimo toro nati a susceptione ordinum repelluntur, nisi cum eis dispensetur: et tanto est difficilior eorum dispensatio quanto eorum origo est turpior.

Ad primum ergo dicendum quod irregularitas non est poena iniquitati debita. Et ideo patet quod illegitime nati non portant iniquitatem patris ex hoc quod irregulares sunt.

Ad secundum dicendum quod ea quae per actum committuntur, possunt per poenitentiam et actum contrarium aboleri: non autem ea quae ex natura sunt. Et ideo non est simile de vitioso actu et de vitiosa origine.

of the Lord until the tenth generation (Deut 23:2). Much less, therefore, should he be ordained.

I answer that, Those who are ordained are placed in a position of dignity over others. Hence by a kind of propriety, it is requisite that they should be without reproach, not for the validity but for the lawfulness of the sacrament, namely, that they should be of good repute, bedecked with a virtuous life, and not publicly penitent. And since a man's good name is bedimmed by a sinful origin, therefore those also who are born of an illegitimate union are debarred from receiving orders unless they receive a dispensation; and this is the more difficult to obtain according as their origin is more discreditable.

Reply Obj. 1: Irregularity is not a punishment due for sin. Hence it is clear that those who are of illegitimate birth do not bear the iniquity of their father through being irregular.

Reply Obj. 2: What a man does by his own act can be removed by repentance and by a contrary act; not so the things which are from nature. Hence the comparison fails between sinful act and sinful origin.

Article 6

Whether Lack of Members Should Be an Impediment?

Ad sextum sic proceditur. Videtur quod propter defectum membrorum non debeat aliquis impediri. Quia *afflictio, non debet addi afflicto.* Ergo non debet privari ordinis gradu propter poenam corporalis defectus.

Praeterea, plus exigitur ad actum ordinis integritas discretionis quam integritas corporis. Sed aliqui possunt promoveri ante annos discretionis. Ergo et cum corporis defectu.

Sed contra, tales prohibebantur a ministerio veteris legis. Ergo multo fortius debent in nova prohiberi.

De bigamia vero dicetur in tractatu de matrimonio.

Respondeo dicendum quod, sicut ex dictis patet, aliquis efficitur ineptus ad susceptionem ordinum vel propter impedimentum actus, vel propter impedimentum claritatis personae. Et ideo patientes defectum iri membris impediuntur a susceptione ordinis si sit talis defectus qui maculam notabilem inferat, per quem obscuretur personae claritas, ut abscissio nasi; vel periculum in executione facere possit. Alias non impeditur. Haec autem integritas exigitur de necessitate praecepti, sed non de necessitate sacramenti.

Et per haec patet solutio ad obiecta.

Objection 1: It would seem that a man ought not to be debarred from receiving holy orders on account of a lack of members. For *one who is afflicted should not receive additional affliction.* Therefore, a man ought not to be deprived of the degree of orders on account of a bodily defect.

Obj. 2: Further, integrity of discretion is more necessary for the act of orders than integrity of body. But some can be ordained before the years of discretion. Therefore, they can also be ordained though deficient in body.

On the contrary, The like were debarred from the ministry of the old law (Lev 21:18). Much more, therefore, should they be debarred in the new law.

We shall speak of bigamy in the treatise on matrimony (Q. 66).

I answer that, As appears from what we have said above (A. 3–5), a man is disqualified from receiving holy orders either on account of an impediment to the act, or on account of an impediment affecting his personal comeliness. Hence he who suffers from a lack of members is debarred from receiving holy orders if the defect be such as to cause a notable blemish, whereby a man's comeliness is obscured (for instance, if his nose be cut off) or the exercise of his order endangered; otherwise, he is not debarred. This integrity, however, is necessary for the lawfulness and not for the validity of the sacrament.

This suffices for the replies to the objections.

QUESTION 40

THE THINGS ANNEXED TO HOLY ORDERS

Deinde considerandum est de his quae sunt annexa sacramento ordinis.

Et circa hoc quaeruntur septem.

Primo: utrum ordinati debeant habere coronae rasuram et tonsuram.

Secundo: utrum corona sit ordo.

Tertio: utrum per acceptionem coronae aliquis abrenuntiet corporalibus bonis.

Quarto: utrum supra sacerdotalem debet esse potestas episcopalis.

Quinto: utrum episcopatus sit ordo.

Sexto: utrum supra episcopos possit esse aliqua potestas superior.

Septimo: utrum vestes ministrorum convenienter sint institutae.

We must now consider the things that are annexed to the sacrament of holy orders.

Under this head there are seven points of inquiry:

(1) Whether those who are ordained ought to be shaven and tonsured in the form of a crown?

(2) Whether the tonsure is an order?

(3) Whether by receiving the tonsure one renounces temporal goods?

(4) Whether above the priestly order there should be an episcopal power?

(5) Whether the episcopate is an order?

(6) Whether in the Church there can be any power above the episcopate?

(7) Whether the vestments of the ministers are fittingly instituted by the Church?

Article 1

Whether Those Who Are Ordained Ought to Wear the Tonsure?

AD PRIMUM SIC PROCEDITUR. Videtur quod ordinati non debeant coronae rasuram habere. Quia Dominus comminatur captivitatem et dispersionem his qui sic attonduntur: ut patet Deut. 32, *de captivitate inimicorum denudati capitis*; et Ierem. 49, *dispergam in omnem ventum eos qui attonsi sunt in comam.* Sed ministris Christi non debetur captivitas, sed libertas. Ergo coronae rasura et tonsura eis non competit.

PRAETEREA, veritas debet respondere figurae. Sed figura coronae praecessit in veteri lege in tonsura Nazaraeorum, sicut in littera dicitur. Ergo, cum Nazaraei non essent ordinati ad ministerium divinum, videtur quod ministris Ecclesiae non debeatur tonsura vel rasura coronae. Et hoc etiam videtur per hoc quod conversi, qui non sunt ministri Ecclesiae, tonduntur in religionibus.

PRAETEREA, per capillos superflua significantur: quia capilli ex superfluis generantur. Sed ministri altaris omnem superfluitatem a se debent expellere. Ergo totaliter debent caput radere, et non in modum coronae.

SED CONTRA: Quia, secundum Gregorium, *servire Deo regnare est.* Sed corona est signum regni. Ergo illis

OBJECTION 1: It would seem that those who are ordained ought not to wear the tonsure in the shape of a crown. For the Lord threatened captivity and dispersion to those who were shaven in this way in Deuteronomy 32:42: *and of the captivity of the bare head of the enemies,* and Jeremiah 49:32: *I will scatter into every wind them that have their hair cut round.* Now the ministers of Christ should not be captives, but free. Therefore, shaving and tonsure in the shape of a crown does not become them.

OBJ. 2: Further, the truth should correspond to the figure. Now the crown-shaped tonsure was prefigured in the old law by the tonsure of the Nazarenes, as stated in the text (*Sentences* IV, D. 24). Therefore, since the Nazarenes were not ordained to the divine ministry, it would seem that the ministers of the Church should not receive the tonsure or shave the head in the form of a crown. The same would seem to follow from the fact that lay brothers, who are not ministers of the Church, receive a tonsure in the religious orders.

OBJ. 3: Further, the hair signifies superfluity, because it grows from that which is superfluous. But the ministers of the Church should cast off all superfluity. Therefore, they should shave the head completely and not in the shape of a crown.

ON THE CONTRARY, According to Gregory, *to serve God is to reign* (*Expositions of the Psalms* 101.23). Now a

269

qui ad divinum ministerium applicantur, corona competit.

Praeterea, *capilli in velamen dati sunt*: ut patet I Cor, 11. Sed ministri altaris debent habere mentem revelatam. Ergo competit eis rasura coronae.

Respondeo dicendum quod eis qui ad divina ministeria applicantur competit rasura et tonsura in modum coronae, ratione figurae. Quia corona est signum regni et perfectionis: cum sit circularis. Illi autem qui divinis ministeriis applicantur, adipiscuntur regiam dignitatem, et perfecti in virtute esse debent.

Competit etiam eis ratione subtractionis capillorum: et ex parte superiori per rasuram, ne mens eorum temporalibus occupationibus a contemplatione divinorum retardetur; et ex parte inferiori per tonsuram, ne eorum sensus temporalibus obvolvantur.

Ad primum ergo dicendum quod Dominus comminatur illis qui hoc ad cultum daemonum faciebant.

Ad secundum dicendum quod ea quae fiebant in veteri Testamento imperfecte repraesentant ea quae sunt in novo. Et ideo ea quae pertinent ad ministros novi Testamenti non solum significabantur per officia levitarum, sed per omnes illos qui aliquam perfectionem profitebantur. Nazaraei autem profitebantur perfectionem quandam in depositione comae, significantes temporalium contemptum. Quamvis non in modum coronae deponerent, sed omnino totum: quia nondum erat tempus regalis et perfecti sacerdotii.

Et similiter etiam conversi tonduntur propter renuntiationem temporalium. Sed non raduntur: quia non occupantur divinis ministeriis, in quibus divina oporteat eos mente contemplari.

Ad tertium dicendum quod non solum debet significari temporalium abiectio, sed etiam regalis dignitas in forma coronae. Et ideo non debet totaliter coma tolli. Et etiam ne indecens videatur.

crown is the sign of royalty. Therefore, a crown-shaped tonsure is becoming to those who are devoted to the divine ministry.

Further, According to 1 Corinthians 11:15, *hair is given us for a covering*. But the ministers of the altar should have the mind uncovered. Therefore, the tonsure is becoming to them.

I answer that, It is becoming for those who apply themselves to the divine ministry to be shaven or tonsured in the form of a crown by reason of the figure. For a crown is the sign of royalty and of perfection, since it is circular; and those who are appointed to the divine service acquire a royal dignity and ought to be perfect in virtue.

It is also becoming to them as it involves the hair being taken both from the higher part of the head by shaving, lest their mind be hindered by temporal occupations from contemplating divine things, and from the lower part by clipping, lest their senses be entangled in temporal things.

Reply Obj. 1: The Lord threatens those who did this for the worship of demons.

Reply Obj. 2: The things that were done in the Old Testament represent imperfectly the things of the New Testament. Hence things pertaining to the ministers of the New Testament were signified not only by the offices of the Levites, but also by all those persons who professed some degree of perfection. Now the Nazarenes professed a certain perfection by having their hair cut off, thus signifying their contempt of temporal things, although they did not have it cut in the shape of a crown, but cut it off completely, for as yet it was not the time of the royal and perfect priesthood.

In like manner, lay brothers have their hair cut because they renounce temporalities. but they do not shave the head because they are not occupied in the divine ministry, so as to have to contemplate divine things with the mind.

Reply Obj. 3: Not only the renunciation of temporalities, but also the royal dignity has to be signified by the form of a crown; wherefore the hair should not be cut off entirely. Also, this would be unbecoming.

Article 2

Whether the Tonsure Is an Order?

Ad secundum sic proceditur. Videtur quod corona sit ordo. Quia in actibus Ecclesiae spiritualia corporalibus respondent. Sed corona est quoddam corporale signum quod Ecclesia adhibet. Ergo videtur quod significatum interius ei respondeat. Et ita in coronatione imprimetur character, et erit ordo.

Praeterea, sicut ab episcopo solum datur confirmatio et alii ordines, ita et corona. Sed in confirmatione

Objection 1: It would seem that the tonsure is an order. For in the acts of the Church the spiritual corresponds to the corporal. Now the tonsure is a corporal sign employed by the Church. Therefore, seemingly there is some interior signification corresponding thereto, so that a person receives a character when he receives the tonsure, and consequently the latter is an order.

Obj. 2: Further, just as confirmation and the other orders are given by a bishop alone, so is the tonsure. Now a

et aliis ordinibus imprimitur character. Ergo et in corona. Et sic idem quod prius.

PRAETEREA, ordo importat quendam dignitatis gradum. Sed clericus, hoc ipso quod clericus est, in gradu supra populum constituitur. Ergo corona, per quam efficitur clericus, est aliquis ordo.

SED CONTRA: Nullus ordo datur nisi in missae celebratione. Sed corona datur etiam absque officio missae. Ergo non est ordo.

PRAETEREA, in collatione cuiuslibet ordinis fit mentio de aliqua potestate data. Non autem in collatione coronae. Ergo non est ordo.

RESPONDEO dicendum quod ministri Ecclesiae a populo separantur ad vacandum divino cultui. In cultu autem divino quaedam sunt quae per potentias determinatas sunt exercenda: et ad hoc datur spiritualis potestas ordinis. Quaedam autem sunt quae communiter a toto ministrorum collegio fiunt: sicut dicere divinas laudes. Et ad hoc non praeexigitur aliqua potestas ordinis, sed solum quaedam deputatio ad tale officium. Et hoc fit per coronam. Et ideo non est ordo, sed praeambulum ad ordinem.

AD PRIMUM ergo dicendum quod corona habet interius aliquod spirituale quod ei respondet sicut signum significato. Sed haec non est aliqua spiritualis potestas. Et ideo in corona non imprimitur character, nec est ordo.

AD SECUNDUM dicendum quod, quamvis per coronam non imprimatur character, tamen deputatur homo ad divinum cultum. Et ideo talis deputatio debet fieri per summum ministrorum, scilicet per episcopum: qui etiam vestes benedicit et vasa et omnia quae ad divinum cultum applicantur.

AD TERTIUM dicendum quod ex hoc quod aliquid est clericus, est in altiori statu quam laicus: non tamen habet ampliorem potestatis gradum, quod ad ordinem requiritur.

character is imprinted in confirmation, and the other orders. Therefore, one is imprinted likewise in receiving the tonsure. And thus as before.

OBJ. 3: Further, 'order' denotes a degree of dignity. Now a cleric, by the very fact of being a cleric, is placed on a degree above the people. Therefore, the tonsure by which he is made a cleric is an order.

ON THE CONTRARY, No order is given except during the celebration of Mass. But the tonsure is given even outside the office of the Mass. Therefore, it is not an order.

FURTHER, In the conferring of every order mention is made of some power granted, but not in the conferring of the tonsure. Therefore, it is not an order.

I ANSWER THAT, The ministers of the Church are severed from the people in order that they may give themselves entirely to the divine worship. Now in the divine worship are certain actions that have to be exercised by virtue of certain definite powers, and for this purpose the spiritual power of order is given; while other actions are performed by the whole body of ministers in common, for instance, the recital of the divine praises. For such things it is not necessary to have the power of order, but only to be deputed to such an office; and this is done by the tonsure. Consequently, it is not an order but a preamble to orders.

REPLY OBJ. 1: The tonsure has some spiritual thing inwardly corresponding to it, like a sign signified, but this is not a spiritual power. Therefore, a character is not imprinted in the tonsure as in an order.

REPLY OBJ. 2: Although a man does not receive a character in the tonsure, nevertheless he is appointed to the divine worship. Hence this appointment should be made by the supreme minister, namely the bishop, who moreover blesses the vestments and vessels and whatsoever else is employed in the divine worship.

REPLY OBJ. 3: A man through being a cleric is in a higher state than a layman; but as regards power he has not the higher degree that is required for holy orders.

Article 3

Whether by Receiving the Tonsure a Man Renounces Temporal Goods?

AD TERTIUM SIC PROCEDITUR. Videtur quod per acceptionem coronae aliquis renuntiet temporalibus bonis. Ipsi enim dicunt, cum coronantur: *Dominus pars hereditatis meae*. Sed, sicut dicit Hieronymus, *Dominus cum his temporalibus fieri dedignatur pars*: ergo abrenuntiant temporalibus.

PRAETEREA, iustitia ministrorum novi Testamenti debet abundare super ministros veteris testamenti: ut

OBJECTION 1: It would seem that men renounce temporal goods by receiving the tonsure, for when they are tonsured they say, *the Lord is the portion of my inheritance*. But as Jerome says (*Epistle to Nepotian*), *the Lord disdains to be made a portion together with these temporal things*. Therefore, he renounces temporalities.

OBJ. 2: Further, the justice of the ministers of the New Testament ought to abound more than that of the ministers

patet Matth. 5. Sed ministri veteris Testamenti, scilicet levitae, *non acceperunt partem hereditatis cum fratribus suis*. Ergo nec ministri novi Testamenti habere debent.

PRAETEREA, Hugo dicit quod *postquam aliquis est factus clericus, deinceps debet stipendiis ecclesiae sustentari*. Sed hoc non esset si patrimonium suum retineret. Ergo videtur quod abrenuntiet in hoc quod clericus fit.

SED CONTRA: Est quod Ieremias fuit de ordine sacerdotali: ut patet Ierem. 1. Sed ipse habuit possessionem ex hereditatis iure: ut patet Ierem. 32. Ergo clerici possunt habere patrimonialia bona.

PRAETEREA, si hoc non possent, non videretur tunc differentia inter religiosos et clericos saeculares.

RESPONDEO dicendum quod clerici, in hoc quod coronam accipiunt, non renuntiant patrimonio, nec aliis rebus temporalibus. Quia terrenorum possessio non contrariatur divino cultui, ad quem clerici deputantur, sed nimia eorum sollicitudo: quia, ut dicit Gregorius, *affectus in crimine est*.

AD PRIMUM ergo dicendum quod Dominus dedignatur pars fieri ut ex aequo cum aliis diligatur: ita scilicet quod aliquis ponat finem suum in Deo et in rebus mundi. Non tamen dedignatur fieri pars eorum qui res mundi ita possident quod per eas a cultu divino non retrahuntur.

AD SECUNDUM dicendum quod levitae in veteri Testamento habebant ius in hereditate paterna. Sed ideo non acceperunt partem cum aliis tribubus, quia erant per omnes tribus dispergendi: quod fieri non potuisset si unam determinatam partem cepissent, sicut aliae tribus.

AD TERTIUM dicendum quod, si sint indigentes clerici ad sacros ordines promoti, episcopus qui eos promovit tenetur eis providere: alias non tenetur. Ipsi autem ex ordine suscepto tenentur ecclesiae ministrare. Verbum autem Hugonis intelligitur de illis qui non habent unde sustententur.

of the Old Testament (Matt 5:20). But the ministers of the Old Testament, namely the Levites, *did not receive a portion of inheritance with their brethren* (Deut 10; 18). Therefore, neither should the ministers of the New Testament.

OBJ. 3: Further, Hugh says (*On the Sacraments* 2) that *after a man is made a cleric, he must from thenceforward live on the pay of the Church*. But this would not be so were he to retain his patrimony. Therefore, he would seem to renounce it by becoming a cleric.

ON THE CONTRARY, Jeremiah was of the priestly order (Jer 1:1). Yet he retained possession of his inheritance (Jer 32:8). Therefore, clerics can retain their patrimony.

FURTHER, If this were not so there would seem to be no difference between religious and the secular clergy.

I ANSWER THAT, Clerics by receiving the tonsure do not renounce their patrimony or other temporalities, since the possession of earthly things is not contrary to the divine worship to which clerics are appointed, although excessive care for such things is. For, as Gregory says, *it is not wealth but the love of wealth that is sinful* (*Morals on Job* 10.30).

REPLY OBJ. 1: The Lord disdains to be a portion as being loved equally with other things, so that a man place his end in God and the things of the world. He does not, however, disdain to be the portion of those who so possess the things of the world as not to be withdrawn thereby from the divine worship.

REPLY OBJ. 2: In the Old Testament the Levites had a right to their paternal inheritance; and the reason why they did not receive a portion with the other tribes was because they were scattered throughout all the tribes, which would have been impossible if, like the other tribes, they had received one fixed portion of the soil.

REPLY OBJ. 3: Clerics promoted to holy orders, if they are poor, must be provided for by the bishop who ordained them; otherwise, he is not so bound. And they are bound to minister to the Church in the order they have received. The words of Hugh refer to those who have no means of livelihood.

Article 4

Whether Above the Priestly Order There Ought to Be an Episcopal Power?

AD QUARTUM SIC PROCEDITUR. Videtur quod supra sacerdotalem ordinem non debet esse aliqua potestas episcopalis. Sicut enim in littera dicitur, *ordo sacerdotalis ab Aaron sumpsit exordium*. Sed in veteri lege nullus erat supra Aaron. Ergo nec in nova lege debet aliqua potestas esse supra sacerdotalem.

PRAETEREA, potestas ordinatur secundum actus. Sed nullus actus sacer potest esse maior quam consecra-

OBJECTION 1: It would seem that there ought not to be an episcopal power above the priestly order. For as stated in the text (*Sentences* IV, D. 24) *the priestly order originated from Aaron*. Now, in the old law there was no one above Aaron. Therefore, neither in the new law ought there to be any power above that of the priests.

OBJ. 2: Further, powers rank according to acts. Now no sacred act can be greater than to consecrate the body of

re corpus Christi, ad quod est potestas sacerdotalis. Ergo supra sacerdotalem potestatem non debet esse episcopalis.

PRAETEREA, sacerdos in offerendo gerit figuram Christi in Ecclesia, qui se Patri pro nobis obtulit. Sed in Ecclesia nullus est maior Christo: quia *ipse est caput Ecclesiae*. Ergo nulla potestas debet esse supra sacerdotalem potestatem.

SED CONTRA: Potestas tanto est altior quanto ad plura se extendit. Sed potestas sacerdotalis, ut Dionysius dicit, extendit se ad *purgandum* et *illuminandum* tantum; episcopalis autem ad hoc et ad *perficiendum*. Ergo supra sacerdotalem potestatem debet esse episcopalis.

PRAETEREA, divina ministeria debent esse magis ordinata quam humana. Sed humanorum officiorum ordo exigit ut in quolibet officio praeponatur unus qui sit princeps illius officii: sicut praeponitur, militibus dux. Ergo et sacerdotibus debet aliquis praeponi qui sit sacerdotum princeps. Et hic est episcopus. Ergo episcopalis potestas debet esse supra sacerdotalem.

RESPONDEO dicendum quod sacerdos habet duos actus: principalem, scilicet consecrare verum corpus Christi; et secundarium, scilicet praeparare populum ad susceptionem huius sacramenti, ut prius dictum est. Quantum autem ad primum actum, actus sacerdotis non dependet ab aliqua superiori potestate nisi divina. Sed quantum ad secundum, dependet ab aliqua superiori potestate et humana. Omnis enim potestas quae non potest exire in actum nisi praesuppositis quibusdam ordinationibus, dependet ab illa potestate quae illas ordinationes facit. Sacerdos autem non potest absolvere, et ligare nisi praesupposita praelationis iurisdictione, qua sibi subdantur illi quos absolvit. Potest autem consecrare quamlibet materiam a Christo determinatam, nec aliud requiritur, quantum est de necessitate sacramenti: quamvis ex quadam congruitate praesupponatur actus episcopalis in consecratione altaris vel vestium et huiusmodi. Et ita patet quod oportet esse supra sacerdotalem potestatem episcopalem quantum ad actum secundarium sacerdotis, non quantum ad primum.

AD PRIMUM ergo dicendum quod Aaron sacerdos fuit et pontifex, idest *sacerdotum princeps*. Sumpsit ergo sacerdotalis potestas ab ipso exordium inquantum fuit sacerdos sacrificia offerens: quod etiam minoribus sacerdotibus licebat. Sed non ab eo inquantum fuit pontifex: per quam potestatem poterat aliqua facere, ut *ingredi semel in anno sancta sanctorum*, quod aliis non licebat.

AD SECUNDUM dicendum quod quantum ad illum actum non est aliqua potestas superior, sed quantum ad alium, ut dictum est.

AD TERTIUM dicendum quod, sicut omnium rerum naturalium perfectiones praeexistunt exemplariter

Christ, to which the priestly power is directed. Therefore, there should not be an episcopal above the priestly power.

OBJ. 3: Further, the priest, in offering, represents Christ in the Church, who offered himself for us to the Father. Now no one is above Christ in the Church, since *he is the head of the Church*. Therefore, there should not be an episcopal above the priestly power.

ON THE CONTRARY, A power is so much the higher according as it extends to more things. Now the priestly power, according to Dionysius (*On the Ecclesiastical Hierarchies* 5), extends only to *cleansing* and *enlightening*, whereas the episcopal power extends both to this and to *perfecting*. Therefore, the episcopal should be above the priestly power.

FURTHER, The divine ministries should be more orderly than human ministries. Now the order of human ministries requires that in each office there should be one person to preside, just as a general is placed over soldiers. Therefore, there should also be appointed over priests one who is the chief priest, and this is the bishop. Therefore, the episcopal should be above the priestly power.

I ANSWER THAT, A priest has two acts: one is the principal, namely, to consecrate the body of Christ; the other is secondary, namely, to prepare God's people for the reception of this sacrament, as stated above (Q. 37, A. 2, 4). As regards the first act, the priest's power does not depend on a higher power save God's; but as to the second, it depends on a higher and that a human power. For every power that cannot exercise its act without certain ordinances depends on the power that makes those ordinances. Now a priest cannot loose and bind, except we presuppose him to have the jurisdiction of authority, whereby those whom he absolves are subject to him. But he can consecrate any matter determined by Christ, nor is anything else required for the validity of the sacrament; although, on account of a certain congruousness, the act of the bishop is pre-required in the consecration of the altar, vestments, and so forth. Hence it is clear that the episcopal ought to be above the priestly power as regards the priest's secondary act, but not as regards his primary act.

REPLY OBJ. 1: Aaron was both priest and pontiff, that is, *chief priest*. Accordingly, the priestly power originated from him insofar as he was a priest offering sacrifices, which was lawful even to the lesser priests; but it does not originate from him as pontiff, by which power he was able to do certain things: for instance, to *enter once a year the Holy of Holies*, which it was unlawful for the other priests to do.

REPLY OBJ. 2: There is no higher power with regard to this act, but with regard to another, as stated above.

REPLY OBJ. 3: Just as the perfections of all natural things preexist in God as their exemplar, so was Christ the

in Deo, ita Christus fuit exemplar omnium officiorum ecclesiasticorum. Unde unusquisque minister Ecclesiae quantum ad aliquid gerit typum Christi, ut ex littera patet: et tamen ille est superior qui secundum maiorem perfectionem Christum repraesentat. Sacerdos autem repraesentat Christum, in hoc quod per seipsum aliquod ministerium implevit: sed episcopus in hoc quod alios ministros instituit et Ecclesiam fundavit. Unde ad episcopum pertinet mancipare aliquid divinis officiis, quasi cultum divinum ad similitudinem Christi statuens. Et propter hoc etiam episcopus specialiter sponsus dicitur ecclesiae, sicut et Christus.

exemplar of all ecclesiastical offices. Wherefore each minister of the Church is, in some respect, a copy of Christ, as stated in the text (*Sentences* IV, D. 24). Yet he is the higher who represents Christ according to a greater perfection. Now a priest represents Christ in that he fulfilled a certain ministry by himself, whereas a bishop represents him in that he instituted other ministers and founded the Church. Hence it belongs to a bishop to dedicate a thing to the divine offices, as establishing the divine worship after the manner of Christ. For this reason also a bishop is especially called the bridegroom of the Church, even as Christ is.

Article 5

Whether the Episcopate Is an Order?

AD QUINTUM SIC PROCEDITUR. Videtur quod episcopatus sit ordo. Primo, per hoc quod Dionysius assignat hos tres ordines ecclesiasticae hierarchiae, episcopum, sacerdotem et ministrum. In littera etiam dicitur quod *est ordo episcoporum quadripartitus*.

PRAETEREA, ordo nihil aliud est quam quidam potestatis gradus in spiritualibus dispensandis. Sed episcopi possunt dispensare aliqua sacramenta quae non possunt dispensare sacerdotes: sicut confirmationem et ordinem. Ergo episcopatus est ordo.

PRAETEREA, in Ecclesia non est aliqua spiritualis potestas nisi ordinis vel iurisdictionis. Sed ea quae pertinent ad episcopalem potestatem non sunt iurisdictionis: alias possent committi non-episcopo, quod falsum est. Ergo sunt potestatis ordinis. Ergo episcopus habet aliquem ordinem quem non habet sacerdos simplex. Et sic episcopatus est ordo.

SED CONTRA: Est quod unus ordo non dependet a praecedenti, quantum ad necessitatem sacramenti. Sed episcopalis potestas dependet a sacerdotali: quia nullus potest recipere episcopalem potestatem nisi prius habeat sacerdotalem. Ergo episcopatus non est ordo.

PRAETEREA, maiores ordines non conferuntur nisi in sabbatis. Sed episcopalis potestas traditur in Dominicis. Ergo non est ordo.

RESPONDEO dicendum quod ordo potest accipi dupliciter. Uno modo, secundum quod est sacramentum. Et sic, ut prius dictum est, ordinatur omnis ordo ad Eucharistiae sacramentum. Unde, cum episcopus non habeat potestatem superiorem sacerdote quantum ad hoc, episcopatus non erit ordo.

Alio modo potest considerari ordo secundum quod est officium quoddam respectu quarundam actionum

OBJECTION 1: It would seem that the episcopate is an order. First of all, because Dionysius (*On the Ecclesiastical Hierarchies* 5) assigns these three orders to the ecclesiastical hierarchy: the bishop, the priest, and the minister. In the text also (*Sentences* IV, D. 24) it is stated that *the episcopal order is fourfold*.

OBJ. 2: Further, order is nothing else but a degree of power in the dispensing of spiritual things. Now bishops can dispense certain sacraments which priests cannot dispense, namely, confirmation and holy orders. Therefore, the episcopate is an order.

OBJ. 3: Further, in the Church there is no spiritual power other than of order or jurisdiction. But things pertaining to the episcopal power are not matters of jurisdiction, else they might be committed to one who is not a bishop, which is false. Therefore, they belong to the power of order. Therefore, the bishop has an order which a simple priest has not; and thus the episcopate is an order.

ON THE CONTRARY, One order does not depend on a preceding order as regards the validity of the sacrament. But the episcopal power depends on the priestly power, since no one can receive the episcopal power unless he have previously the priestly power. Therefore, the episcopate is not an order.

FURTHER, The greater orders are not conferred except on Saturdays. But the episcopal power is bestowed on Sundays (Dist. lxxv, can. *Ordinationes*). Therefore, it is not an order.

I ANSWER THAT, Order may be understood in two ways. In one way as a sacrament, and thus, as already stated (Q. 37, A. 2, 4), every order is directed to the sacrament of the Eucharist. Wherefore, since the bishop has not a higher power than the priest, in this respect the episcopate is not an order.

In another way, order may be considered as an office in relation to certain sacred actions: and thus, since in hierar-

sacrarum. Et sic, cum episcopus habeat potestatem in actionibus hierarchicis respectu corporis mystici supra sacerdotem, episcopatus erit ordo. Et secundum hoc loquuntur auctoritates inductae.

UNDE PATET solutio ad primum.

AD SECUNDUM dicendum quod ordo, prout est sacramentum imprimens characterem, ordinatur specialiter ad sacramentum Eucharistiae, in quo ipse Christus continetur: quia per characterem ipsi Christo configuramur. Et ideo, licet detur aliqua potestas spiritualis episcopo in sui promotione respectu aliquorum sacramentorum, non tamen illa potestas habet rationem characteris. Et propter hoc episcopatus non est ordo, secundum quod ordo est sacramentum quoddam.

AD TERTIUM dicendum quod potestas episcopalis non est tantum iurisdictionis, sed etiam ordinis, ut ex dictis patet, secundum quod ordo communiter accipitur.

chical actions a bishop has in relation to the mystical body a higher power than the priest, the episcopate is an order. It is in this sense that the authorities quoted speak.

HENCE the reply to the first objection is clear.

REPLY OBJ. 2: Order, considered as a sacrament which imprints a character, is specially directed to the sacrament of the Eucharist, in which Christ himself is contained, because by a character we are made like to Christ himself (III, Q. 63, A. 3). Hence, although at his promotion a bishop receives a spiritual power in respect of certain sacraments, this power nevertheless has not the nature of a character. For this reason the episcopate is not an order, in the sense in which an order is a sacrament.

REPLY OBJ. 3: The episcopal power is one not only of jurisdiction but also of order, as stated above, taking order in the sense in which it is generally understood.

Article 6

Whether in the Church There Can Be Anyone Above the Bishops?

AD SEXTUM SIC PROCEDITUR. Videtur quod supra episcopos non possit esse aliquis superior in Ecclesia. Quia omnes episcopi sunt Apostolorum successores. Sed potestas quae est data uni Apostolorum, scilicet Petro, Matth. 16, est data omnibus Apostolis Ioan. 20. Ergo episcopi sunt pares, et unus non est supra alium.

PRAETEREA, ritus Ecclesiae magis debet esse conformis ritui Iudaeorum quam ritui gentilium. Sed distinctio episcopalis dignitatis, et ordinatio unius super alium, ut in littera dicitur, *est a gentilibus introducta*: in veteri autem lege non erat. Ergo nec in Ecclesia episcopus unus super alium esse debet.

PRAETEREA, superior potestas non potest conferri per inferiorem, neque aequalis per aequalem: quia, *sine ulla contradictione, quod minus est a maiori benedicitur*, Heb. 7. Unde etiam sacerdos non promovet episcopum neque sacerdotem: sed episcopus sacerdotem. Sed episcopus potest quemlibet episcopum promovere: quia etiam Ostiensis episcopus consecrat Papam. Ergo episcopalis dignitas in omnibus est aequalis. Et sic unus episcopus non debet aliis subesse, ut in littera dicitur.

SED CONTRA: Est quod legitur in Concilio Constantinopolitano: *veneramur, secundum Scripturas et secundum canonum definitiones, sanctissimum antiquae Romae Episcopum primum esse et maximum episcoporum, et post ipsum Constantinopolitanum episcopum.* Ergo unus episcopus est super alium.

PRAETEREA, beatus Cyrillus, episcopus Alexandrinus, dicit: *ut membra maneamus in capite nostro Apo-*

OBJECTION 1: It would seem that there cannot be anyone in the Church higher than the bishops. For all the bishops are the successors of the apostles. Now the power so given to one of the apostles, namely Peter (Matt 16:19), was given to all the apostles (John 20:23). Therefore, all bishops are equal, and one is not above another.

OBJ. 2: Further, the rite of the Church ought to be more conformed to the Jewish rite than to that of the gentiles. Now the distinction of the episcopal dignity and the appointment of one over another, *were introduced by the gentiles*, as stated in the text (*Sentences* IV, D. 24); and there was no such thing in the old law. Therefore, neither in the Church should one bishop be above another.

OBJ. 3: Further, a higher power cannot be conferred by a lower, nor equal by equal, because *without all contradiction that which is less is blessed by the greater*; hence a priest does not consecrate a bishop or a priest, but a bishop consecrates a priest. But a bishop can consecrate any bishop, since the bishop of Ostia consecrates even the Pope. Therefore, the episcopal dignity is equal in all matters, and consequently one bishop should not be subject to another, as stated in the text (*Sentences* IV, D. 24).

ON THE CONTRARY, We read in the council of Constantinople: *in accordance with the Scriptures and the statutes and definitions of the canons, we venerate the most holy bishop of ancient Rome, the first and greatest of bishops, and after him the bishop of Constantinople.* Therefore, one bishop is above another.

FURTHER, The blessed Cyril, bishop of Alexandria, says: *that we may remain members of our apostolic head, the*

stolico throno Romanorum Pontificum, a quo nostrum est quaerere quid credere et quid tenere debeamus, ipsum venerantes, ipsum rogantes prae omnibus. Quoniam ipsius solius est reprehendere, corripere, statuere, disponere; solvere et ligare, loco illius qui ipsum aedificavit, et nulli alii quod suum est plenum, sed ipsi soli dedit; cui omnes iure divino caput inclinant, et primates mundi tanquam ipsi Domino Iesu Christo obediunt. Ergo episcopi alicui subsunt etiam de iure divino.

RESPONDEO dicendum quod, ubicumque sunt multa regimina ordinata in unum, oportet esse aliquod universale regimen super particularia regimina. Quia in omnibus virtutibus et actibus, ut dicitur in I *Ethic.*, est ordo secundum ordinem finium. *Bonum* autem *commune est divinius quam bonum speciale.* Et ideo supra potestatem regitivam quae coniectat bonum speciale, oportet esse potestatem universalem respectu boni communis: alias non posset esse colligatio ad unum. Et ideo, cum tota Ecclesia sit unum corpus, oportet, si ista unitas debet conservari, quod sit aliqua potestas regitiva respectu totius Ecclesiae, supra potestatem episcopalem, qua unaquaeque specialis ecclesia regitur. Et haec est potestas Papae. Et ideo illi qui hanc potestatem negant, *schismatici* dicuntur, quasi *divisores* ecclesiasticae unitatis. Et inter episcopum simplicem et Papam sunt alii gradus dignitatum, correspondentes gradibus unionis, secundum quos una congregatio vel communitas includit aliam: sicut communitas provinciae includit communitatem civitatis, et communitas regni communitatem unius provinciae, et communitas totius mundi communitatem unius regni.

AD PRIMUM ergo dicendum quod, quamvis omnibus Apostolis data sit communiter potestas ligandi et solvendi, tamen, ut in hac potestate ordo aliquis significaretur, primo soli Petro data est, ut ostendatur quod ab eo in alios ista potestas debeat descendere. Propter quod etiam ei dixit singulariter, *confirma fratres tuos*, et, *pasce oves meas*, idest: *loco mei*, ut dicit Chrysostomus, *praepositus et caput esto fratrum: ut ipsi te in loco meo assumentes, ubique terrarum te in throno tuo sedentem praedicent et confirment.*

AD SECUNDUM dicendum quod ritus Iudaeorum non erat diffusus in diversis regnis et provinciis, sed tantum in una gente. Et ideo non oportebat quod sub eo qui habebat potestatem principalem alii pontifices distinguerentur. Sed Ecclesiae ritus, sicut et gentilium ritus, per diversas nationes diffunditur. Et ideo oportet quod, quantum ad hoc, magis gentilium ritui quam Iudaeorum status Ecclesiae conformetur.

AD TERTIUM dicendum quod potestas sacerdotis exceditur a potestate episcopi quasi a potestate alterius generis. Sed potestas episcopi exceditur a potestate Papae quasi a potestate eiusdem generis. Et ideo omnem actum

throne of the Roman Pontiffs, of whom it is our duty to seek what we are to believe and what we are to hold, venerating him, beseeching him above others; for his it is to reprove, to correct, to appoint, to loose, and to bind in place of him who set up that very throne, and who gave the fullness of his own to no other, but to him alone, to whom by divine right all bow the head, and the primates of the world are obedient as to our Lord Jesus Christ himself. Therefore, bishops are subject to someone even by divine right.

I ANSWER THAT, Wherever there are several authorities directed to one purpose, there must be one universal authority over the particular authorities, because in all virtues and acts the order is according to the order of their ends (*Ethics* 1.1–2). Now *the common good is more divine than the particular good.* Therefore, above the governing power which aims at a particular good there must be a universal governing power in respect of the common good, otherwise there would be no cohesion towards the one object. Hence, since the whole Church is one body, it is necessary, if this unity is to be preserved, that there be a governing power in respect of the whole Church above the episcopal power whereby each particular Church is governed, and this is the power of the Pope. Consequently, those who deny this power are called *schismatics* as causing a *division* in the unity of the Church. Again, between a simple bishop and the Pope, there are other degrees of rank corresponding to the degrees of union, in respect of which one congregation or community includes another; thus the community of a province includes the community of a city, and the community of a kingdom includes the community of one province, and the community of the whole world includes the community of one kingdom.

REPLY OBJ. 1: Although the power of binding and loosing was given to all the apostles in common, nevertheless in order to indicate some order in this power it was given first of all to Peter alone, to show that this power must come down from him to the others. For this reason Christ said to him in the singular: *confirm your brethren* (Luke 22:32), and, *feed my sheep* (John 21:17), as though to say, according to Chrysostom: *be the head and leader of brothers, so that they, accepting you in my place, may preach and confirm your seat on your throne, everywhere in the world.*

REPLY OBJ. 2: The Jewish rite was not spread abroad in various kingdoms and provinces, but was confined to one nation; hence there was no need to distinguish various pontiffs under the one who had the chief power. But the rite of the Church, like that of the gentiles, is spread abroad through various nations; and consequently in this respect it is necessary for the constitution of the Church to be like the rite of the gentiles rather than that of the Jews.

REPLY OBJ. 3: The priestly power is surpassed by the episcopal power, as by a power of a different kind; but the episcopal is surpassed by the papal power as by a power of the same kind. Hence a bishop can perform every hi-

hierarchicum quem potest facere Papa in ministratione sacramentorum, potest facere episcopus: non autem omnem actum quem potest facere episcopus, potest facere sacerdos in sacramentorum collatione. Et ideo, quantum ad ea quae sunt episcopalis ordinis, omnes episcopi sunt aequales. Et propter hoc quilibet alium potest consecrare.

erarchical act that the Pope can; whereas a priest cannot perform every act that a bishop can in conferring the sacraments. Wherefore, as regards matters pertaining to the episcopal order, all bishops are equal, and for this reason any bishop can consecrate another bishop.

Article 7

Whether the Vestments of the Ministers Are Fittingly Instituted in the Church?

AD SEPTIMUM SIC PROCEDITUR. Videtur quod vestes ministrorum non convenienter sint in Ecclesia institutae. Ministri enim novi Testamenti magis tenentur ad castitatem quam ministri veteris. Sed inter alias vestes ministrorum veteris Testamenti erant *feminalia*, in signum castitatis. Ergo multo fortius nunc esse debent inter vestes ministrorum Ecclesiae.

PRAETEREA, sacerdotium novi Testamenti est dignius quam sacerdotium veteris. Sed veteres sacerdotes habebant *mitras*, quod est signum dignitatis. Ergo sacerdotes novae legis eas debent habere.

PRAETEREA, sacerdos est propinquior ordinibus ministrorum quam ordo episcopalis. Sed episcopi utuntur vestibus ministrorum: scilicet *dalmatica*, quae est vestis diaconi; et *tunica*, quae est vestis subdiaconi. Ergo multo fortius debent uti eis simplices sacerdotes.

PRAETEREA, in veteri lege pontifex deferebat *superhumerale*: quod significabat *onus Evangelii*, ut dicit Beda. Hoc autem maxime pontificibus nostris incumbit. Ergo debent habere superhumerale.

PRAETEREA, in *rationali*, quo utebantur pontifices veteris legis, scribebatur *doctrina et veritas*. Sed veritas maxime in nova lege declarata est. Ergo pontificibus novae legis competit.

PRAETEREA, *lamina aurea*, in qua scriptum erat dignissimum nomen Dei, erat dignissimum ornamentum legis veteris. Ergo illud maxime debuit transferri in novam legem.

PRAETEREA, ea quae exterius geruntur in ministris Ecclesiae, sunt signa interioris potestatis. Sed archiepiscopus non habet alterius generis potestatem quam episcopus, ut dictum est. Ergo non debet habere *pallium*, quod non habent episcopi.

PRAETEREA, potestatis plenitudo residet penes Romanum Pontificem. Sed ipse non habet *baculum*. Ergo nec alii episcopi debent habere.

OBJECTION 1: It would seem that the vestments of the ministers are not fittingly instituted in the Church. For the ministers of the New Testament are more bound to chastity than were the ministers of the Old Testament. Now among the vestments of the Old Testament there were the *thigh coverings* as a sign of chastity. Much more, therefore, should they have a place among the vestments of the Church's ministers.

OBJ. 2: Further, the priesthood of the New Testament is more worthy than the priesthood of the Old. But the priests of the Old Testament had *mitres*, which are a sign of dignity. Therefore, the priests of the New Testament should also have them.

OBJ. 3: Further, the priest is nearer than the episcopal order to the orders of ministers. Now the bishop uses the vestments of the ministers, namely, the *dalmatic*, which is the deacon's vestment, and the *tunic*, which is the subdeacon's. Much more, therefore, should simple priests use them.

OBJ. 4: Further, in the old law the pontiff wore the *ephod*, which signified the *burden of the Gospel*, as Bede observes (*On the Tabernacle* 3). Now this is especially incumbent on our pontiffs. Therefore, they ought to wear the ephod.

OBJ. 5: Further, *doctrine and truth* were inscribed on the *breastpiece* which the pontiffs of the Old Testament wore. Now truth was made known especially in the new law. Therefore, it is becoming to the pontiffs of the new law.

OBJ. 6: Further, the *golden plate* on which was written the most admirable name of God was the most admirable of the adornments of the old law. Therefore, it should especially have been transferred to the new law.

OBJ. 7: Further, the things which the ministers of the Church wear outwardly are signs of inward power. Now the archbishop has no other kind of power than a bishop, as stated above (A. 6). Therefore, he should not have the *pallium* which other bishops have not.

OBJ. 8: Further, the fullness of power resides in the Roman Pontiff. But he has not a *crozier*. Therefore, other bishops should not have one.

RESPONDEO dicendum quod vestes ministrorum designant idoneitatem quae in eis requiritur ad tractandum divina. Et quia quaedam sunt quae in omnibus requiruntur, et quaedam requiruntur in superioribus quae non ita exiguntur in inferioribus; ideo quaedam vestes sunt omnibus ministris communes, quaedam autem superiorum tantum.

Et ideo omnibus ministris competit *amictus* humeros tegens, quo significatur fortitudo ad divina officia exequenda, quibus mancipatur; et similiter *alba*, quae significat puritatem vitae; et *cingulum*, quod significat repressionem carnis.

Sed subdiaconus ulterius habet *manipulum*, quo significatur extersio minimarum macularum, quia manipulus est quasi sudarium ad extergendum vultum: ipsi enim primo ad sacra tractanda admittuntur. Habent etiam *tunicam strictam*, per quam doctrina Christi significatur: unde et in veteri lege in ipsa *tintinnabula* pendebant. Subdiaconi enim primo admittuntur ad doctrinam novae legis annuntiandam.

Sed diaconus habet amplius *stolam* in sinistro humero: in signum quod applicatur ad ministerium in ipsis sacramentis. Et *dalmaticam*, quae est vestis larga, sic dicta quia in Dalmatiae partibus primo usus eius fuit: ad designandum quod ipse primo dispensator sacramentorum ponitur, ipse enim sanguinem dispensat; in dispensatione autem largitas requiritur.

Sed sacerdoti in utroque humero ponitur *stola*: ut ostendatur quod ei plena potestas dispensandi sacramenta datur, non ut ministro alterius; et ideo stola descendit usque ad inferiora. Habet etiam *casulam*, quae significat caritatem: quia sacramentum consecrat caritatis, scilicet Eucharistiam.

Sed episcopis adduntur novem ornamenta super sacerdotes, quae sunt caligae, sandalia, succinctorium, tunica, dalmatica, mitra, chirothecae, anulus et baculus: quia novem sunt quae supra sacerdotes possunt, scilicet clericos ordinare, virgines benedicere, basilicas dedicare, clericos deponere, synodos celebrare, chrisma conficere, vestes et vasa consecrare. Vel per *caligas* significatur rectitudo gressuum. Per *sandalia*, quae pedes tegunt, contemptus terrenorum. Per *succinctorium*, quo stola ligatur cum alba, amor honestatis. Per *tunicam*, perseverantia: quia Ioseph *tunicam talarem* dicitur habuisse, quasi descendentem usque ad talos, per quos significatur extremitas vitae. Per *dalmaticam*, largitas in operibus misericordiae. Per *chirothecas*, cautela in opere. Per *mitram*, scientia utriusque Testamenti: unde et duo cornua habet. Per *baculum* cura pastoralis, qua debet *colligere vagos*, quod significat curvitas in capite baculi; *sustentare infirmos*, quod ipse stipes significat baculi; sed *pungere lentos*, quod significat stimulus in pede baculi; unde versus: *colligite, sustenta, stimula, vaga, morbida, lenta*. Per *anulum*,

I ANSWER THAT, The vestments of the ministers denote the qualifications required of them for handling divine things. And since certain things are required of all, and some are required of the higher that are not so exacted of the lower ministers, therefore certain vestments are common to all the ministers, while some pertain to the higher ministers only.

Accordingly, it is becoming to all the ministers to wear the *amice* which covers the shoulders, thereby signifying courage in the exercise of the divine offices to which they are deputed, and the *alb*, which signifies a pure life, and the *cincture*, which signifies restraint of the flesh.

But the subdeacon wears in addition the *maniple* on the left arm: this signifies the wiping away of the least stains (since a maniple is a kind of handkerchief for wiping the face) for they are the first to be admitted to the handling of sacred things. They also have the *narrow tunic*, signifying the doctrine of Christ; wherefore in the old law *little bells* hung therefrom, and subdeacons are the first admitted to announce the doctrine of the new law.

The deacon has in addition the *stole* over the left shoulder, as a sign that he is deputed to a ministry in the sacraments themselves, and the *dalmatic* (which is a full vestment, so called because it first came into use in Dalmatia), to signify that he is the first to be appointed to dispense the sacraments: for he dispenses the blood, and in dispensing one should be generous.

But in the case of the priest the *stole* hangs from both shoulders, to show that he has received full power to dispense the sacraments, and not as the minister of another man, for which reason the stole reaches right down. He also wears the *chasuble*, which signifies charity, because it is he who consecrates the sacrament of charity, namely, the Eucharist.

Bishops have nine ornaments besides those which the priest has: these are the stockings, sandals, subcingulum, tunic, dalmatic, mitre, gloves, ring, and crozier. For there are nine things which they can do, but priests cannot: namely, ordain clerics, bless virgins, consecrate bishops, impose hands, dedicate churches, depose clerics, celebrate synods, consecrate chrism, bless vestments and vessels. We may also say that the *stockings* signify his upright walk; the *sandals* which cover the feet, his contempt of earthly things; the *subcingulum* which girds the stole with the alb, his love of probity; the *tunic*, perseverance, for Joseph is said (Gen 37:23) to have had a long tunic called a 'talaric' because it reached down to the ankles, which denote the end of life; the *dalmatic*, generosity in works of mercy; the *gloves*, prudence in action; the *mitre*, knowledge of both Testaments, for which reason it has two crests; the *crozier*, his pastoral care, whereby he has *to gather together the wayward* (this is denoted by the curve at the head of the crozier), *to uphold the weak* (this is denoted by the stem of the crozier), and *to spur on the laggards* (this is denoted by

sacramenta fidei, qua Ecclesia desponsatur Christo: ipsi enim sunt Ecclesiae sponsi loco Christi.

Sed ulterius archiepiscopi pallium habent, in signum privilegiatae potestatis: significat enim torquem auream quam solebant legitime certantes accipere.

AD PRIMUM ergo dicendum quod sacerdotibus veteris legis indicebatur continentia illo tantum tempore quo ad suum ministerium accedebant. Et ideo, in signum castitatis tunc servandae, in sacrificiorum oblatione feminalibus utebantur. Sed ministris novi testamenti indicitur perpetua continentia. Et ideo non est simile.

AD SECUNDUM dicendum quod mitra illa non erat signum alicuius dignitatis: fuit enim sicut quoddam galerum, ut Hieronymus dicit. Sed cidaris, quae erat signum dignitatis, solum pontificibus dabatur: sicut et nunc mitra.

AD TERTIUM dicendum quod potestas ministrorum est in episcopo sicut in origine: non autem in sacerdote, quia ipse non confert illos ordines. Et ideo magis episcopus quam sacerdos vestibus ministrorum utitur.

AD QUARTUM dicendum quod loco superhumeralis utitur stola: quae ad idem significandum est ad quod erat superhumerale.

AD QUINTUM dicendum quod pallium succedit loco rationalis.

AD SEXTUM dicendum quod pro illa lamina habet pontifex noster crucem, ut Innocentius dicit: sicut pro feminalibus habet sandalia, pro linea albam, pro balteo cingulum, pro podere tunicam, et pro ephod amictum, pro rationali pallium, pro cidari mitram.

AD SEPTIMUM dicendum quod, quamvis non habeat alterius generis potestatem, tamen eandem habet ampliorem. Et ideo, ad hanc perfectionem designandam, sibi pallium datur, quo undique circumdatur.

AD OCTAVUM dicendum quod Romanus Pontifex non utitur baculo, quia Petrus misit ipsum ad suscitandum quendam discipulum suum, qui postea factus est episcopus Treverensis. Et ideo in dioecesi Treverensi Papa baculum portat, et non in aliis locis. Vel etiam in signum quod non habet coarctatam potestatem, quod curvatio baculi significat.

the point at the foot of the crozier). Hence the line: *gather, uphold, spur on, the wayward, the weak, and the laggard.* The *ring* signifies the sacraments of that faith whereby the Church is espoused to Christ. For bishops are espoused to the Church in the place of Christ.

Furthermore, archbishops have the *pallium* in sign of their privileged power, for it signifies the golden chain which those who fought rightfully were wont to receive.

REPLY OBJ. 1: The priests of the old law were enjoined continency only for the time of their attendance for the purpose of their ministry. Therefore, as a sign of the chastity which they had then to observe, they wore the thigh coverings while offering sacrifices. But the ministers of the New Testament are enjoined perpetual continency; and so the comparison fails.

REPLY OBJ. 2: The mitre was not a sign of dignity, for it was a kind of hat, as Jerome says (*Epistle to Fabiola*). But the diadem, which was a sign of dignity, was given to the pontiffs alone, as the mitre is now.

REPLY OBJ. 3: The power of the ministers resides in the bishop as their source, but not in the priest, for he does not confer those orders. Wherefore the bishop, rather than the priest, wears those vestments.

REPLY OBJ. 4: Instead of the ephod, they wear the stole, which is intended for the same signification as the ephod.

REPLY OBJ. 5: The pallium takes the place of the breast-piece.

REPLY OBJ. 6: Instead of that plate, our pontiff wears the cross, as Innocent III says (*On the Mystery of the Sacred Altar* 1), just as the thigh coverings are replaced by the sandals, the linen garment by the alb, the belt by the girdle, the long or talaric garment by the tunic, the ephod by the amice, the breastpiece by the pallium, the diadem by the mitre.

REPLY OBJ. 7: Although he has not another kind of power, he has the same power more fully, and so in order to designate this perfection, he receives the pallium which surrounds him on all sides.

REPLY OBJ. 8: The Roman Pontiff does not use a pastoral staff because Peter sent his to restore to life a certain disciple who afterwards became bishop of Trier. Hence in the diocese of Trier the Pope carries a crozier, but not elsewhere; or else it is a sign of his not having a restricted power (denoted by the curve of the staff.)

QUESTION 41

MATRIMONY AS DIRECTED TO AN OFFICE OF NATURE

Post haec considerandum est de matrimonio. Et primo agendum est de eo inquantum est in officium naturae; secundo, inquantum est sacramentum; tertio, inquantum absolute et secundum se consideratur.

Circa primum quaeruntur quattuor.

Primo: utrum sit de iure naturali.

Secundo: utrum nunc sit in praecepto.

Tertio: utrum eius actus sit licitus.

Quarto: utrum possit esse meritorius.

In the next place we must consider matrimony. We must treat of it: (1) As directed to an office of nature; (2) As a sacrament; (3) As considered absolutely and in itself.

Under the first head there are four points of inquiry:

(1) Whether it is of natural law?

(2) Whether it is a matter of precept?

(3) Whether its act is lawful?

(4) Whether its act can be meritorious?

Article 1

Whether Matrimony Is of Natural Law?

AD PRIMUM SIC PROCEDITUR. Videtur quod matrimonium non sit naturale. Quia *ius naturale est quod natura omnia animalia docuit.* Sed in aliis animalibus est coniunctio sexuum absque matrimonio. Ergo matrimonium non est de iure naturali.

PRAETEREA, id quod est de iure naturali, invenitur in hominibus secundum quemlibet statum eorum. Sed matrimonium non fuit in quolibet statu hominum: quia, sicut dicit Tullius, in I *Rhetoric., homines a principio sylvestres erant, et tunc nemo scivit proprios liberos nec certas nuptias*, in quibus matrimonium consistit. Ergo non est naturale.

PRAETEREA, naturalia sunt eadem apud omnes. Sed non eodem modo est matrimonium apud omnes: cum pro diversis legibus diversimode matrimonium celebretur. Ergo non est naturale.

PRAETEREA, illa sine quibus potest salvari naturae intentio, non videntur esse naturalia. Sed natura intendit conservationem speciei per generationem, quae potest esse sine matrimonio, ut patet in fornicariis. Ergo matrimonium non est naturale.

SED CONTRA: Est quod in principio *Digestorum* dicitur: *ius naturale est maris et feminae coniunctio, quam nos matrimonium appellamus.*

PRAETEREA, Philosophus, VIII *Ethic.*, dicit quod *homo est magis naturaliter coniugale animal quam politicum.* Sed *homo est naturaliter animal politicum et gregale,* ut ipse dicit. Ergo est naturaliter coniugale. Et sic coniugium, sive matrimonium, est naturale.

RESPONDEO dicendum quod aliquid dicitur esse naturale dupliciter. Uno modo, sicut ex principiis naturae

OBJECTION 1: It would seem that matrimony is not natural. Because *the natural law is what nature has taught all animals* (*Digests*). But in other animals the sexes are united without matrimony. Therefore, matrimony is not of natural law.

OBJECTION 1: Further, that which is of natural law is found in all men with regard to their every state. But matrimony was not in every state of man, for as Cicero says (*On Rhetorical Invention*), *at the beginning men were savages and then no man knew his own children, nor was he bound by any marriage tie*, in which matrimony consists. Therefore, it is not natural.

OBJ. 3: Further, natural things are the same among all. But matrimony is not in the same way among all, since its practice varies according to the various laws. Therefore, it is not natural.

OBJ. 4: Further, those things without which the intention of nature can be maintained would seem not to be natural. But nature intends the preservation of the species by generation, which is possible without matrimony, as in the case of fornicators. Therefore, matrimony is not natural.

ON THE CONTRARY, At the commencement of the *Digests* it is stated: *the union of male and female, which we call matrimony, is of natural law.*

FURTHER, The Philosopher (*Ethics* 8.12) says that *man is an animal more inclined by nature to conjugal than political society.* But *man is naturally a political and gregarious animal*, as the same author asserts (*Politics* 1.2). Therefore, he is naturally inclined to conjugal union, and thus the conjugal union or matrimony is natural.

I ANSWER THAT, A thing is said to be natural in two ways. First, as resulting of necessity from the principles of

ex necessitate causatum: ut moveri sursum est naturale igni, etc. Et sic matrimonium non est naturale: nec aliquid eorum quae mediante libero arbitrio complentur.

Alio modo dicitur naturale ad quod natura inclinat, sed mediante libero arbitrio completur: sicut actus virtutum dicuntur naturales. Et hoc modo matrimonium est naturale: quia ratio naturalis ad ipsum inclinat dupliciter. Primo, quantum ad principalem eius finem, qui est bonum prolis. Non enim intendit natura solum generationem prolis, sed traductionem et promotionem usque ad perfectum statum hominis inquantum homo est, qui est status virtutis. Unde, secundum Philosophum, tria a parentibus habemus: scilicet *esse, nutrimentum* et *disciplinam.* Filius autem a parente educari et instrui non posset nisi determinatos et certos parentes haberet. Quod non esset nisi esset aliqua obligatio viri ad mulierem determinatam, quae matrimonium facit.

Secundo, quantum ad secundarium finem matrimonii, qui est mutuum obsequium sibi a coniugibus in rebus domesticis impensum. Sicut enim naturalis ratio dictat ut homines simul cohabitent, quia unus non sufficit sibi in omnibus quae ad vitam pertinent, ratione cuius dicitur homo *naturaliter politicus*; ita etiam eorum quibus indigetur ad humanam vitam, quaedam opera sunt competentia viris, quaedam mulieribus. Unde natura monet ut sit quaedam associatio viri ad mulierem, in qua est matrimonium. Et has duas causas ponit Philosophus in VIII *Ethicorum.*

AD PRIMUM ergo dicendum quod natura hominis ad aliquid inclinat dupliciter. Uno modo, quia est conveniens naturae generis: et hoc est commune omnibus animalibus. Alio modo, quod est conveniens naturae differentiae, qua species humana *abundat a genere*, inquantum est rationalis: sicut est prudentiae actus vel temperantiae. Et sicut natura generis, quamvis sit una in omnibus animalibus, non tamen est eodem modo in omnibus, ita etiam non inclinat eodem modo in omnibus, sed secundum quod unicuique competit.

Ad matrimonium, ergo inclinat natura hominis ex parte differentiae, quantum ad rationem secundam assignatam. Unde Philosophus hanc rationem assignant hominibus supra alia animalia. Sed quantum ad rationem primam inclinat ex parte generis. Unde dicit quod *filiorum procreatio communis est omnibus animalibus.* Tamen ad hoc non inclinat eodem modo in omnibus. Quia quaedam animalia sunt quorum filii, statim nati, possunt sufficienter sibi victum quaerere, vel ad quorum sustentationem mater sufficit: et in his non est aliqua maris ad feminam determinatio. In illis autem quorum filii indigent utriusque sustentatione, sed ad parvum tempus, invenitur aliqua determinatio quantum ad tempus illud: sicut in avibus quibusdam patet. Sed in homine, quia in-

nature; thus upward movement is natural to fire. In this way matrimony is not natural, nor are any of those things that come to pass at the intervention or motion of the free-will.

Second, that is said to be natural to which nature inclines, although it comes to pass through the intervention of the free-will; thus acts of virtue and the virtues themselves are called natural. And in this way matrimony is natural, because natural reason inclines to it in two ways. First, in relation to the principal end of matrimony, namely, the good of the offspring. For nature intends not only the begetting of offspring, but also its education and development until it reach the perfect state of man as man, and that is the state of virtue. Hence, according to the Philosopher (*Ethics* 8.11–12), we derive three things from our parents, namely, *existence, nourishment,* and *education.* Now a child cannot be brought up and instructed unless it have certain and definite parents, and this would not be the case unless there were a tie between the man and a definite woman, and it is in this that matrimony consists.

Second, in relation to the secondary end of matrimony, which is the mutual services which married persons render one another in household matters. For just as natural reason dictates that men should live together, since one is not self-sufficient in all things concerning life, for which reason man is described as being *naturally inclined to political society*, so too among those works that are necessary for human life some are becoming to men, others to women. Wherefore nature inculcates that society of man and woman which consists in matrimony. These two reasons are given by the Philosopher (*Ethics* 8.11–12).

REPLY OBJ. 1: Man's nature inclines to a thing in two ways. In one way, because that thing is becoming to the nature of the genus, and this is common to all animals; in another way because it is becoming to the nature of the difference, whereby the human species insofar as it is rational *overflows the genus*; such is an act of prudence or temperance. And just as the nature of the genus, though one in all animals, yet is not in all in the same way, so neither does it incline in the same way in all, but in a way befitting each one.

Accordingly, man's nature inclines to matrimony on the part of the difference, as regards the second reason given above; wherefore the Philosopher (*Ethics* 8.11–12; *Politics* 1) gives this reason in men over other animals; but as regards the first reason it inclines on the part of the genus; wherefore he says that *the begetting of offspring is common to all animals.* Yet nature does not incline thereto in the same way in all animals; since there are animals whose offspring are able to seek food immediately after birth, or are sufficiently fed by their mother; and in these there is no tie between male and female; whereas in those whose offspring needs the support of both parents, although for a short time, there is a certain tie, as may be seen in certain birds. In man, however, since the child needs the parents'

diget filius cura parentum usque ad magnum tempus, est maxima determinatio masculi ad feminam, ad quam etiam natura generis inclinat.

AD SECUNDUM dicendum quod verbum Tullii potest esse verum quantum ad aliquam gentem (si tamen accipiatur principium proximum illius gentis, per quod ab aliis gentibus est distincta): quia in omnibus producitur ad effectum hoc ad quod naturalis ratio inclinat. Non autem est verum universaliter: quia a principio humani generis sacra Scriptura recitat fuisse coniugia.

AD TERTIUM dicendum quod, secundum Philosophum, in VII *Ethic.*, natura humana non est immobilis, sicut divina. Et ideo diversificantur ea quae sunt de iure naturali secundum diversos status et conditiones hominum: quamvis ea quae sunt in rebus divinis naturaliter nullo modo varientur.

AD QUARTUM dicendum quod natura non tantum intendit esse in prole, sed esse perfectum. Ad quod exigitur matrimonium, ut ex dictis patet.

care for a long time, there is a very great tie between male and female, to which tie even the generic nature inclines.

REPLY OBJ. 2: The assertion of Cicero may be true of some particular nation, provided we understand it as referring to the proximate beginning of that nation when it became a nation distinct from others; for that to which natural reason inclines is not realized in all things. But this statement is not universally true, since Sacred Scripture states that there has been matrimony from the beginning of the human race.

REPLY OBJ. 3: According to the Philosopher (*Ethics* 7), human nature is not unchangeable as the divine nature is. Hence things that are of natural law vary according to the various states and conditions of men; although those which naturally pertain to things divine in no way vary.

REPLY OBJ. 4: Nature intends not only being in the offspring, but also perfect being, for which matrimony is necessary, as shown above.

Article 2

Whether Matrimony Still Comes Under a Precept?

AD SECUNDUM SIC PROCEDITUR. Videtur quod matrimonium adhuc maneat sub praecepto. Quia praeceptum obligat quandiu non revocatur. Sed prima institutio matrimonii fuit sub praecepto, ut in littera dicitur: nec unquam hoc praeceptum legitur revocatum; immo confirmatum, Matth. 19: *quod Deus coniunxit homo non separet*. Ergo adhuc est matrimonium sub praecepto.

PRAETEREA, praecepta iuris naturalis secum dum omne tempus obligant. Sed matrimonium est de iure naturali, ut dictum est. Ergo, etc.

PRAETEREA, bonum speciei est melius quam bonum individui: quia *bonum gentis est divinius quam bonum unius hominis*, ut dicitur I *Ethic.* Sed praeceptum primo homini datum ad conservationem individui per actum nutritivae, adhuc obligat. Ergo multo magis praeceptum de matrimonio, quod pertinet ad conservationem speciei.

PRAETEREA, ubi manet eadem ratio obligans, eadem obligatio manere debet. Sed propter hoc obligabantur homines ad matrimonium antiquo tempore, ne multiplicatio humani generis cessaret. Cum ergo hoc idem sequatur si quilibet libere potest a matrimonio abstinere, videtur quod matrimonium sit in praecepto.

OBJECTION 1: It would seem that matrimony still comes under a precept. For a precept is binding so long as it is not recalled. But the primary institution of matrimony came under a precept, as stated in the text (*Sentences* IV, D. 26); nor do we read anywhere that this precept was recalled, but rather that it was confirmed: *what God has joined together let no man put asunder* (Matt 19:6). Therefore, matrimony still comes under a precept.

OBJ. 2: Further, the precepts of natural law are binding in respect of all time. Now matrimony is of natural law, as stated above (A. 1). Therefore, etc.

OBJ. 3: Further, the good of the species is better than the good of the individual, *for the good of the State is more divine than the good of one man* (*Ethics* 1.2). Now the precept given to the first man concerning the preservation of the good of the individual by the act of the nutritive power is still in force. Much more, therefore, does the precept concerning matrimony still hold, since it refers to the preservation of the species.

OBJ. 4: Further, where the reason of an obligation remains the same, the obligation must remain the same. Now the reason why men were bound to marry in olden times was lest the human race should cease to multiply. Since, then, the result would be the same if each one were free to abstain from marriage, it would seem that matrimony comes under a precept.

Sed contra: Est quod dicitur I Cor. 7: *qui non iungit matrimonio virginem suam, melius facit*, scilicet quam qui iungit. Ergo contractus matrimonii nunc non est sub praecepto.

Praeterea, nulli debetur praemium pro transgressione praecepti. Sed virginibus debetur speciale praemium, scilicet aureola. Ergo matrimonium non est sub praecepto.

Respondeo dicendum quod natura inclinat ad aliquid dupliciter. Uno modo, sicut ad id quod est necessarium ad perfectionem unius. Et talis inclinatio quemlibet obligat: quia naturales perfectiones omnibus sunt communes. Alio modo: inclinat ad aliquid quod est necessarium multitudini. Et cum multa sint huiusmodi, quorum unum impedit aliud, ex tali obligatione non obligatur quilibet homo per modum praecepti, alias quilibet homo obligaretur ad agriculturam et ad aedificatoriam et ad huiusmodi officia, quae sunt necessaria communitati humanae: sed inclinationi naturae satisfit cum per diversos diversa complentur de praedictis.

Cum ergo ad perfectionem humanae multitudinis sit necessarium aliquos contemplativae vitae inservire, quae maxime per matrimonium impeditur; inclinatio naturae ad matrimonium non obligat per modum praecepti, etiam secundum philosophos. Unde Theophrastus probat quod sapienti non expedit nubere.

Ad primum ergo dicendum quod praeceptum illud non est revocatum. Nec tamen obligat unumquemque, ratione iam dicta: nisi illo tempore quo paucitas hominum exigebat ut quilibet generationi vacaret.

Ad secundum et tertium patet responsio ex dictis.

Ad quartum dicendum quod natura humana communiter ad diversa officia et actus inclinat, ut dictum est: sed quia est diversimode in diversis, secundum quod individuatur in hoc vel in illo, unum magis inclinat ad unum illorum officiorum, alium ad aliud. Et ex hac diversitate, simul cum divina providentia, quae omnia moderatur, contingit quod unus eligat unum officium, ut agriculturam, alius aliud. Et sic etiam contingit quod quidam eligunt matrimonialem vitam, et quidam contemplativam. Unde nullum periculum imminet.

On the contrary, It is written: *he that does not give his virgin in marriage does better* (1 Cor 7:38), namely, than he that gives her in marriage. Therefore, the contract of marriage is not now a matter of precept.

Further, No one deserves a reward for breaking a precept. Now a special reward, namely, the aureole, is due to virgins (Q. 96, A. 5). Therefore, matrimony does not come under a precept.

I answer that, Nature inclines to a thing in two ways. In one way as to that which is necessary for the perfection of the individual, and such an obligation is binding on each one, since natural perfections are common to all. In another way, it inclines to that which is necessary for the perfection of the community; and since there are many things of this kind, one of which hinders another, such an inclination does not bind each man by way of precept; else each man would be bound to agriculture and building and other such offices as are necessary to the human community; but the inclination of nature is satisfied by the accomplishment of those various offices by various individuals.

Accordingly, since the perfection of the human community requires that some should devote themselves to the contemplative life, to which marriage is a very great obstacle, the natural inclination to marriage is not binding by way of precept, even according to the philosophers. Hence Theophrastus proves that it is not advisable for a wise man to marry, as Jerome relates (*Against Jovinian* 1).

Reply Obj. 1: This precept has not been recalled, and yet it is not binding on each individual, for the reason given above, except at that time when the paucity of men required each one to betake himself to the begetting of children.

The replies to objections 2 and 3 are clear from what has been said.

Reply Obj. 4: Human nature has a general inclination to various offices and acts, as already stated. But since it is variously in various subjects, as individualized in this or that one, it inclines one subject more to one of those offices, and another subject more to another, according to the difference of temperament of various individuals. And it is owing to this difference, as well as to divine providence which governs all, that one person chooses one office such as husbandry, and another person another. And so it is too that some choose the married life and some the contemplative. Therefore, no danger threatens.

Article 3

Whether the Marriage Act Is Always Sinful?

Ad tertium sic proceditur. Videtur quod actus matrimonialis, semper sit peccatum. I Cor. 7: *qui nubunt, sint tanquam non nubentes*. Sed non nubentes

Objection 1: It would seem that the marriage act is always sinful. For it is written: *let they who have wives be as if they had none* (1 Cor 7:29). But those who are not married

non habent actum matrimonialem. Ergo etiam nubentes peccant in actu illo.

PRAETEREA, Isaiae 59: *iniquitates nostrae diviserunt inter nos et Deum nostrum*. Sed actus matrimonialis dividit hominem a Deo: unde Exodi 19 praecipitur populo qui debebat Deum videre, quod non accederent ad uxores suas; et Hieronymus dicit quod *in actu matrimoniali Spiritus Sanctus prophetarum corda non tangit*. Ergo est iniquitas.

PRAETEREA, illud quod secundum se est turpe, nullo modo potest bene fieri. Sed actus matrimonialis habet concupiscentiam adiunctam, quae semper est turpis. Ergo semper est peccatum.

PRAETEREA, nihil *excusatur* nisi peccatum. Sed actus matrimonialis indiget excusari per bona matrimonii, ut Magister dicit. Ergo est peccatum.

PRAETEREA, de similibus specie idem est iudicium. Sed concubitus matrimonialis est eiusdem speciei cum actu adulterii: quia ad idem terminantur, scilicet speciem humanam. Ergo, cum actus adulterii sit peccatum, et actus matrimonii.

PRAETEREA, superfluitas in passionibus corrumpit virtutem. Sed semper in actu matrimoniali est superfluitas delectationis: adeo quod absorbet rationem, quae est principale hominis bonum; unde Philosophus dicit, in VII *Ethic.*, quod *impossibile est hominem aliquid in ipsa intelligere*. Ergo actus matrimonialis semper est peccatum.

SED CONTRA: I Cor. 7 dicitur: *virgo, si nubat, non peccat*; et I Tim. 5: *volo iuvenculas nubere, procreare filios*. Sed procreatio filiorum non potest esse sine carnali coniunctione. Ergo actus matrimonialis non est peccatum: alias Apostolus non voluisset illud.

PRAETEREA, nullum peccatum est in praecepto. Sed actus matrimonialis est in praecepto: I Cor. 7, *uxori vir debitum reddat*. Ergo non est peccatum.

RESPONDEO dicendum quod, supposito quod natura corporalis sit a Deo bona instituta, impossibile est dicere quod ea quae pertinent ad conservationem naturae corporalis, et ad quae natura inclinat, sint universaliter mala. Et ideo, cum inclinatio sit naturae ad prolis procreationem, per quam natura speciei conservatur, impossibile est dicere quod actus quo procreatur proles sit universaliter illicitus, ut in eo medium virtutis invenire non possit: nisi ponatur, secundum quorundam insaniam, quod res corruptibiles creatae sunt a malo deo. Ex quo forte ista opinio derivatur quae in littera tangitur. Et ideo est pessima haeresis.

AD PRIMUM ergo dicendum quod Apostolus in verbis illis non prohibuit matrimonii actum, sicut nec rerum possessionem cum dixit, *qui utuntur hoc mundo,*

do not perform the marriage act. Therefore, even those who are married sin in that act.

OBJ. 2: Further, *your iniquities have divided between you and your God* (Isa 59:2). Now the marriage act divides man from God; wherefore the people who were to see God were commanded not to go near their wives (Exod 19:11, 20). And Jerome says that *in the marriage act the Holy Spirit touches not the hearts of the prophets* (*Epistle to Ageruchia*; *Against Jovinian* 18). Therefore, it is sinful.

OBJ. 3: Further, that which is shameful in itself can by no means be well done. Now the marriage act is always connected with concupiscence, which is always shameful. Therefore, it is always sinful.

OBJ. 4: Further, nothing *is the object of excuse* save sin. Now the marriage act needs to be excused by the marriage blessings, as the Master says (*Sentences* IV, D. 26). Therefore, it is a sin.

OBJ. 5: Further, things alike in species are judged alike. But marriage intercourse is of the same species as the act of adultery, since its end is the same, namely, the human species. Therefore, since the act of adultery is a sin, the marriage act is likewise.

OBJ. 6: Further, excess in the passions corrupts virtue. Now there is always excess of pleasure in the marriage act, so much so that it absorbs the reason, which is man's principal good; thus the Philosopher says that *in that act it is impossible to understand anything* (*Ethics* 7.11). Therefore, the marriage act is always a sin.

ON THE CONTRARY, 1 Corinthians 7:28 says that *if a virgin marry she has not sinned*, and 1 Timothy 5:14 that *I will that the young should marry and bear children* (1 Tim 5:14). But there can be no bearing of children without carnal union. Therefore, the marriage act is not a sin; else the Apostle would not have approved of it.

FURTHER, No sin is a matter of precept. But the marriage act is a matter of precept: *let the husband render the debt to his wife* (1 Cor 7:3). Therefore, it is not a sin.

I ANSWER THAT, If we suppose the corporeal nature to be created by the good God, we cannot hold that those things which pertain to the preservation of the corporeal nature and to which nature inclines are altogether evil; therefore, since the inclination to beget offspring, whereby the specific nature is preserved, is from nature, it is impossible to maintain that the act of begetting children is altogether unlawful, so that it be impossible to find the mean of virtue therein; unless we suppose, as some are mad enough to assert, that corruptible things were created by an evil god. From this, perhaps, the opinion mentioned in the text is derived (*Sentences* IV, D. 26); thus this is a most wicked heresy.

REPLY OBJ. 1: By these words the Apostle did not forbid the marriage act, as neither did he forbid the possession of things when he said: *those who make use of this world,*

sint quasi non utentes: sed in utroque fruitionem prohibuit. Quod patet ex ipso modo loquendi. Non enim dixit, *sint non utentes*, vel *non habentes*: sed, *quasi non utentes vel non habentes*.

Ad secundum dicendum quod Deo coniungimur et secundum habitum gratiae, et secundum actum contemplationis et amoris. Quod ergo primam coniunctionem separat, semper est peccatum. Non autem quod separat secundam: quia aliqua occupatio licita circa res inferiores animum distrahit, ut actu Deo coniungi non sit idoneus. Et hoc praecipue accidit in carnali coniunctione, in qua detinetur mens propter delectationem intensam. Et propter hoc illis quibus competit divina contemplari aut sacra tractare, indicitur pro tempore; isto abstinentia ab uxoribus. Et secundum hoc etiam dicitur quod Spiritus Sanctus, quantum ad actum revelationis secretorum, non tangebat mentes prophetarum in usu matrimonii.

Ad tertium dicendum quod turpitudo illa concupiscentiae quae actum matrimonialem semper comitatur, non est turpitudo culpae, sed poenae, ex peccato primo proveniens: ut scilicet inferiores vires et membra corporis rationi non obediant. Et propter hoc ratio non sequitur.

Ad quartum dicendum quod illud proprie *excusari* dicitur quod aliquam similitudinem mali habet et tamen non est malum, vel non tantum quantum apparet. Quorum quaedam excusantur a toto, quaedam a tanto. Et quia actus matrimonialis propter corruptionem concupiscentiae habet similitudinem actus inordinati, ideo pro bono matrimonii excusatur a toto, ut non sit peccatum.

Ad quintum dicendum quod, quamvis sint idem specie naturae, tamen differunt in specie moris, quam una circumstantia variat, scilicet accedere ad suam vel non suam. Sicut etiam occidere hominem per violentiam, vel per iustitiam, facit diversam speciem moris, quamvis sit una species naturae: et tamen unum est licitum, aliud illicitum.

Ad sextum dicendum quod superfluum passionis quod virtutem corrumpit, non solum impedit rationis actum, sed tollit rationis ordinem. Quod non facit delectationis intensio in actu matrimoniali: quia, etsi tunc non ordinetur homo, tamen a ratione est praeordinatus.

as though not using it (1 Cor 7:31). In each case he forbade resting in the enjoyment, which is clear from the way in which he expresses himself: for he did not say *let them not use it*, or *let them not have them*, but let them be *as if they used it not* and *as if they had none*.

Reply Obj. 2: We are united to God by the habit of grace and by the act of contemplation and love. Therefore, whatever severs the former of these unions is always a sin, but not always that which severs the latter, since a lawful occupation about lower things distracts the mind so that it is not fit for actual union with God; and this is especially the case in carnal intercourse, in which the mind is withheld by the intensity of pleasure. For this reason those who have to contemplate divine things or handle sacred things are enjoined not to have to do with their wives for that particular time; and it is in this sense that the Holy Spirit, as regards the actual revelation of hidden things, did not touch the hearts of the prophets at the time of the marriage act.

Reply Obj. 3: The shamefulness of concupiscence that always accompanies the marriage act is a shamefulness not of guilt, but of punishment inflicted for the first sin, inasmuch as the lower powers and the members do not obey reason. Hence the argument does not follow.

Reply Obj. 4: Properly speaking, a thing is said *to be excused* when it has some appearance of evil, and yet is not evil, or not as evil as it seems, because some things excuse wholly, others in part. And since the marriage act, by reason of the corruption of concupiscence, has the appearance of an inordinate act, it is wholly excused by the marriage blessing, so as not to be a sin.

Reply Obj. 5: Although they are the same as to their natural species, they differ as to their moral species, which varies in respect of one circumstance, namely, intercourse with one's wife and with another than one's wife; just as to kill a man by assault or by justice differentiates the moral species, although the natural species is the same; and yet the one is lawful and the other unlawful.

Reply Obj. 6: The excess of passions that corrupts virtue not only hinders the act of reason, but also destroys the order of reason. The intensity of pleasure in the marriage act does not do this, since, although for the moment man is not being directed, he was previously directed by his reason.

Article 4

Whether the Marriage Act Is Meritorious?

Ad quartum sic proceditur. Videtur quod actus matrimonialis non sit meritorius. Chrysostomus enim dicit, super Matth.1: *matrimonium, etsi utentibus se poe-*

Objection 1: It would seem that the marriage act is not meritorious. For Chrysostom says in his commentary on Matthew: *although marriage brings no punishment to*

nam non inferat, mercedem tamen non praestat. Sed meritum respectu mercedis dicitur. Ergo actus matrimonialis non est meritorius.

Praeterea, illud quod est meritorium dimittere non est laudabile. Sed laudabilis est virginitas, per quam matrimonium dimittitur. Ergo matrimonialis actus non est meritorius.

Praeterea, qui utitur indulgentia sibi facta, beneficio recepto utitur. Sed ex hoc quod alicui praestatur beneficium, non meretur. Ergo actus matrimonialis non est meritorius.

Praeterea, meritum in difficultate consistit: sicut et virtus. Sed actus matrimonialis non habet difficultatem, sed delectationem. Ergo non est meritorius.

Praeterea, illud quod non potest fieri sine peccato veniali, non est meritorium: quia non potest homo simul mereri et demereri. Sed in actu matrimoniali semper est peccatum veniale: quia etiam primus motus in huiusmodi delectatione est peccatum veniale. Ergo actus praedictus non potest esse meritorius.

Sed contra: Omnis actus in quo impletur praeceptum, est meritorius si ex caritate fiat. Sed actus matrimonialis est huiusmodi: quia dicitur I Cor. 7: *uxori vir debitum reddat.* Ergo, etc.

Praeterea, omnis actus virtutis est meritorius. Sed actus praedictus est actus iustitiae: quia dicitur *redditio debiti.* Ergo meritorius est.

Respondeo dicendum quod, cum nullus actus ex deliberata voluntate procedens sit indifferens, ut in II libro dictum est; actus matrimonialis semper est peccatum vel meritorius, in eo qui gratiam habet. Si enim ad actum matrimonialem virtus inducat vel iustitiae, ut debitum reddat, vel religionis, ut proles ad cultum Dei procreetur, est meritorius. Si autem moveat libido sistens infra bona matrimonii, ut scilicet nullo modo ad aliam accedere vellet, est peccatum veniale. Si autem extra bona matrimonii efferatur, ut scilicet cum quacumque muliere id facere proponeret, est peccatum mortale. Natura autem movere non potest quin vel ordinetur ratione, et sic erit motus virtutis; vel non ordinetur, et sic erit motus libidinis.

Ad primum ergo dicendum quod radix merendi quantum ad praemium substantiale est ipsa caritas. Sed quantum ad aliquod accidentale praemium ratio meriti existit in difficultate actus. Et sic actus matrimonii non est meritorius, sed primo modo.

Ad secundum dicendum quod homo potest mereri et in minoribus bonis et in maioribus. Unde, quando aliquis minora bona dimittit ut maiora faciat, laudandus est, a minus meritorio actu discedens.

Ad tertium dicendum quod indulgentia quandoque est de minoribus malis. Et sic indulgetur actus matrimonii prout ad ipsum movet libido infra terminos

those who use it, it affords them no reward (Hom. 1 in the *Opus Imperfectum*). Now merit bears a relation to reward. Therefore, the marriage act is not meritorious.

Obj. 2: Further, to refrain from what is meritorious deserves not praise. Yet virginity, whereby one refrains from marriage, is praiseworthy. Therefore, the marriage act is not meritorious.

Obj. 3: Further, he who avails himself of an indulgence granted him avails himself of a favor received. But a man does not merit by receiving a favor. Therefore, the marriage act is not meritorious.

Obj. 4: Further, merit, like virtue, consists in difficulty. But the marriage act affords not difficulty, but pleasure. Therefore, it is not meritorious.

Obj. 5: Further, that which cannot be done without venial sin is never meritorious, for a man cannot both merit and demerit at the same time. Now there is always a venial sin in the marriage act, since even the first movement in such like pleasures is a venial sin. Therefore, the aforesaid act cannot be meritorious.

On the contrary, Every act whereby a precept is fulfilled is meritorious if it be done from charity. Now such is the marriage act, for it is said: *let the husband render the debt to his wife* (1 Cor 7:3). Therefore, etc.

Further, Every act of virtue is meritorious. Now the aforesaid act is an act of justice, for it is called the *rendering of a debt.* Therefore, it is meritorious.

I answer that, Since no act proceeding from a deliberate will is indifferent, as stated in the Book II of the *Sentences,* the marriage act is always either sinful or meritorious in one who is in a state of grace. For if the motive for the marriage act be a virtue, whether of justice, that they may render the debt, or of religion, that they may beget children for the worship of God, it is meritorious. But if the motive be lust, yet not excluding the marriage blessings, namely, that he would by no means be willing to go to another woman, it is a venial sin; while if he exclude the marriage blessings, so as to be disposed to act in like manner with any woman, it is a mortal sin. And nature cannot move without being either directed by reason, and thus it will be an act of virtue, or not so directed, and then it will be an act of lust.

Reply Obj. 1: The root of merit, as regards the essential reward, is charity itself; but as regards an accidental reward, the reason for merit consists in the difficulty of an act; and thus the marriage act is not meritorious except in the first way.

Reply Obj. 2: Man can merit in lesser things and in greater things: and so when someone foregoes a lesser good so that he might do the greater, his abandoning a less meritorious act is to be praised.

Reply Obj. 3: An indulgence sometimes has to do with lesser evils; and thus the marital act is indulged according as sexual desire moves one to it while remaining within the

matrimonii consistens: sic enim est veniale peccatum. Sed prout ad ipsum movet virtus, ut est meritorius, non habet indulgentiam, nisi secundum quod est indulgentia de mirioribus bonis, quae idem est quod concessio. Nec est inconveniens quod ille qui tali concessione utitur, mereatur: quia bonus usus beneficiorum Dei meritorius est.

AD QUARTUM dicendum quod difficultas, laboris requiritur ad meritum praemii accidentalis: sed ad meritum praemii essentialis requiritur difficultas consistens in ordinatione medii. Et hoc est etiam in actu matrimoniali.

AD QUINTUM dicendum quod primus motus, secundum quod dicitur peccatum veniale, est motus appetitus in aliquod inordinatum delectabile. Quod non est in actu matrimoniali. Et ideo ratio non sequitur.

bounds of marriage, for thus it is a venial sin. But according as virtue moves one to it, so that it is meritorious, it does not require an indulgence unless as to the indulgence of lesser goods, which is the same as a concession. Nor is it unfitting that that man who takes advantage of this concession merits: for the good use of the benefits of God is meritorious.

REPLY OBJ. 4: Difficulty of a work is required for the merit of the accidental prize, but for meriting the essential prize, the difficulty required consists in ordering to the mean, and this is also in the marital act.

REPLY OBJ. 5: The first movement, according to which it is called venial sin, is the motion of the appetite toward something inordinately delectable, which is not in the marital act; and thus the argument does not follow.

QUESTION 42

MATRIMONY AS A SACRAMENT

Deinde considerandum est de matrimonio inquantum est sacramentum.

Circa quod quaeruntur quattuor.

Primo: utrum sit sacramentum.

Secundo: utrum debuerit institui ante peccatum.

Tertio: utrum conferat gratiam.

Quarto: utrum carnalis commixtio sit de integritate matrimonii.

We must next consider matrimony as a sacrament.

Under this head there are four points of inquiry:

(1) Whether matrimony is a sacrament?

(2) Whether it ought to have been instituted before sin was committed?

(3) Whether it confers grace?

(4) Whether carnal intercourse belongs to the integrity of matrimony?

Article 1

Whether Matrimony Is a Sacrament?

AD PRIMUM SIC PROCEDITUR. Videtur quod matrimonium non sit sacramentum. Omne enim sacramentum novae legis habet aliquam formam, quae est de essentia sacramenti. Sed benedictio quae fit per sacerdotes in nuptiis, non est de essentia matrimonii. Ergo non est sacramentum.

PRAETEREA, sacramentum, secundum Hugonem, est *materiale elementum*. Sed matrimonium non habet pro materia aliquod materiale elementum. Ergo non est sacramentum.

PRAETEREA, sacramenta habent efficaciam ex passione Christi. Sed per matrimonium non conformatur homo passioni Christi, quae fuit poenalis: cum habeat delectationem adiunctam. Ergo non est sacramentum.

PRAETEREA, omne sacramentum novae legis *efficit quod figurat*. Sed matrimonium non efficit coniunctionem Christi et Ecclesiae, quam significat. Ergo matrimonium non est sacramentum.

PRAETEREA, in aliis sacramentis est aliquid quod est *res et sacramentum*. Sed hoc non potest inveniri in matrimonio: cum non imprimat characterem; alias non iteraretur. Ergo non est sacramentum.

SED CONTRA: Est quod dicitur Ephes. 5: *sacramentum hoc magnum est*. Ergo, etc.

PRAETEREA, sacramentum est *sacrae rei signum*. Sed matrimonium est huiusmodi. Ergo, etc.

RESPONDEO dicendum quod sacramentum importat aliquod remedium sanctitatis homini contra peccatum exhibitum per sensibilia signa. Unde, cum hoc inveniatur in matrimonio, inter sacramenta computatur.

OBJECTION 1: It would seem that matrimony is not a sacrament. For every sacrament of the new law has a form that is essential to the sacrament. But the blessing given by the priest at a wedding is not essential to matrimony. Therefore, it is not a sacrament.

OBJ. 2: Further, a sacrament, according to Hugh (*On the Sacraments* 1), is *a material element*. But matrimony has not a material element for its matter. Therefore, it is not a sacrament.

OBJ. 3: Further, the sacraments derive their efficacy from Christ's Passion. But matrimony, since it has pleasure adjoined to it, does not conform man to Christ's Passion, which was painful. Therefore, it is not a sacrament.

OBJ. 4: Further, every sacrament of the new law *causes that which it signifies*. Yet matrimony does not cause the union of Christ with the Church, which union it signifies. Therefore, matrimony is not a sacrament.

OBJ. 5: Further, in the other sacraments there is something which is *reality and sacrament*. But this is not to be found in matrimony, since it does not imprint a character, else it would not be repeated. Therefore, it is not a sacrament.

ON THE CONTRARY, It is written: *this is a great sacrament* (Eph 5:32). Therefore, etc.

FURTHER, A sacrament is the *sign of a sacred thing*. But such is matrimony. Therefore, etc.

I ANSWER THAT, A sacrament denotes a sanctifying remedy against sin offered to man under sensible signs. Therefore, since this is the case in matrimony, it is reckoned among the sacraments.

AD PRIMUM ergo dicendum quod verba quibus consensus matrimonialis exprimitur, sunt forma huius sacramenti: non autem benedictio sacerdotis, quae est quoddam sacramentale.

AD SECUNDUM dicendum quod sacramentum matrimonii perficitur per actum eius qui sacramento illo utitur, sicut poenitentia. Et ideo, sicut poenitentia non habet aliam materiam nisi ipsos actus sensui subiectos, qui sunt loco materialis elementi, ita est de matrimonio.

AD TERTIUM dicendum quod, quamvis matrimonium non conformet passioni Christi quantum ad poenam, conformat tamen ei quantum ad caritatem, per quam pro Ecclesia sibi in sponsam coniungenda passus est.

AD QUARTUM dicendum quod unio Christi ad Ecclesiam non est res contenta in hoc sacramento, sed res significata non contenta: et talem rem nullum sacramentum efficit. Sed habet aliam rem contentam et significatam, quam efficit, ut dicetur Magister autem ponit rem non contentam, quia erat huius opinionis quod non haberet rem aliquam contentam.

AD QUINTUM dicendum quod etiam in hoc sacramento sunt illa tria. Quia *sacramenta tantum* sunt actus exterius apparentes; sed *res et sacramentum* est obligatio quae innascitur viri ad mulierem ex talibus actibus; sed *res ultima contenta* est effectus huius sacramenti; *non contenta* autem est res quam Magister determinat.

REPLY OBJ. 1: The words whereby the marriage consent is expressed are the form of this sacrament, and not the priest's blessing, which is a sacramental.

REPLY OBJ. 2: The sacrament of matrimony, like that of penance, is perfected by the act of the recipient. Wherefore just as penance has no other matter than the sensible acts themselves, which take the place of the material element, so it is in matrimony.

REPLY OBJ. 3: Although matrimony is not conformed to Christ's Passion as regards pain, it is as regards charity, whereby he suffered for the Church who was to be united to him as his spouse.

REPLY OBJ. 4: The union of Christ with the Church is not the reality contained in this sacrament, but is the reality signified and not contained—and no sacrament causes a reality of that kind—but it has another both contained and signified which it causes, as we shall state further on (ad 5). The Master, however, asserts that it is a non-contained reality (*Sentences* IV, D. 26), because he was of the opinion that matrimony has no reality contained therein.

REPLY OBJ. 5: In this sacrament also those three things (III, Q. 66, A. 1) are to be found, for the acts externally apparent are the *sacrament only*; the bond between husband and wife resulting from those acts is *reality and sacrament*; and the *ultimate reality contained* is the effect of this sacrament, while the *non-contained* reality is that which the Master assigns (*Sentences* IV, D. 26).

Article 2

Whether Matrimony Ought to Have Been Instituted Before Sin?

AD SECUNDUM SIC PROCEDITUR. Videtur quod matrimonium non debuit institui ante peccatum. Quia illud quod est de iure naturali, non indiget institutione. Sed matrimonium est huiusmodi, ut ex dictis patet. Ergo non debuit institui.

PRAETEREA, sacramenta sunt quaedam medicinae contra morbum peccati. Sed medicina non praeparatur nisi morbo. Ergo ante peccatum non debuit institui.

PRAETEREA, ad idem sufficit una institutio. Sed matrimonium fuit institutum etiam post peccatum, ut in littera dicitur. Ergo ante peccatum non fuit institutum.

PRAETEREA, institutio sacramenti debet esse a Deo. Sed ante peccatum verba quae ad matrimonium pertinent determinate, non sunt dicta a Deo, sed ab Adam: illa autem verba quae Deus dixit *crescite et multiplicamini*,

OBJECTION 1: It would seem that matrimony ought not to have been instituted before sin. For that which is of natural law needs not to be instituted. Now such is matrimony, as stated above (Q. 41, A. 1). Therefore, it ought not to have been instituted.

OBJ. 2: Further, sacraments are medicines against the disease of sin. But a medicine is not prepared except for an actual disease. Therefore, it should not have been instituted before sin.

OBJ. 3: Further, one institution suffices for one thing. Now matrimony was instituted also after sin, as stated in the text (*Sentences* IV, D. 26). Therefore, it was not instituted before sin.

OBJ. 4: Further, the institution of a sacrament must come from God. Now before sin, the words relating to matrimony were not definitely said by God, but by Adam; the words which God uttered, *increase and multiply* (Gen 1:22),

dicta sunt etiam brutis, in quibus non est matrimonium. Ergo matrimonium non fuit institutum ante peccatum.

PRAETEREA, matrimonium est sacramentum novae legis. Sed sacramenta novae legis a Christo initium sumpserunt. Ergo non debuit ante peccatum institui.

SED CONTRA: Est quod dicitur Matth. 19: *non legistis quod ab initio qui fecit homines, masculum et feminam fecit eos?*

PRAETEREA, matrimonium est institutum ad procreationem prolis. Sed ante peccatum erat necessaria homini procreatio prolis. Ergo ante peccatum debuit matrimonium institui.

RESPONDEO dicendum quod natura inclinat ad matrimonium intendens aliquod bonum, quod quidem variatur secundum diversos hominum status. Et ideo oportet quod illud bonum diversimode in diversis statibus hominum instituatur. Et ideo matrimonium, secundum quod ordinatur ad procreationem prolis, quae erat necessaria etiam peccato non existente, institutum fuit ante peccatum. Secundum autem quod remedium praebet contra vulnus peccati, institutum fuit post peccatum tempore legis naturae. Secundum autem determinationem personarum, institutionem habuit in lege Moysi. Sed secundum quod repraesentat mysterium coniunctionis Christi et Ecclesiae, institutionem habuit in nova lege: et secundum hoc est sacramentum novae legis. Quantum autem ad alias utilitates quae ex matrimonio consequuntur, sicut est amicitia et mutuum obsequium sibi a coniugibus impensum, habet institutionem in lege civili.

Sed quia de ratione sacramenti est quod sit signum et remedium, ideo quantum ad medias institutiones competit ei ratio sacramenti; sed quantum ad primam institutionem, competit ei quod sit in officium naturae; quantum vero ad ultimam, quod sit in officium civilitatis.

AD PRIMUM ergo dicendum quod illa quae in communi sunt de iure naturali, indigent institutione quantum ad eorum determinationem, quae diversimode competit secundum diversos status: sicut de iure naturali est quod maleficia puniantur, sed quod talis poena tali culpae apponatur, per determinationem iuris positivi fit.

AD SECUNDUM dicendum quod matrimonium non est tantum in remedium contra peccatum, sed principaliter est in officium naturae. Et sic institutum fuit ante peccatum, non autem prout est in remedium.

AD TERTIUM dicendum quod, secundum diversa quae oportet in matrimonio determinari, non est inconveniens quod habuerit diversas institutiones. Et sic illa diversa institutio non est eiusdem secundum idem.

were addressed also to the brute creation where there is no marriage. Therefore, matrimony was not instituted before sin.

OBJ. 5: Further, matrimony is a sacrament of the new law. But the sacraments of the new law took their origin from Christ. Therefore, it ought not to have been instituted before sin.

ON THE CONTRARY, Matthew 19:4 says: *have you not read that he who made man from the beginning made them male and female?*

FURTHER, Matrimony was instituted for the begetting of children. But the begetting of children was necessary to man before sin. Therefore, matrimony ought to have been instituted before sin.

I ANSWER THAT, Nature inclines to marriage with a certain good in view, which good varies according to the different states of man; therefore, it was necessary for matrimony to be variously instituted in the various states of man in reference to that good. Consequently, matrimony as directed to the begetting of children, which was necessary even when there was no sin, was instituted before sin. According as it affords a remedy for the wound of sin, it was instituted after sin at the time of the natural law. Its institution belongs to the Mosaic law as regards personal disqualifications. It was instituted in the new law insofar as it represents the mystery of Christ's union with the Church, and in this respect it is a sacrament of the new law. As regards other advantages resulting from matrimony, such as the friendship and mutual services which husband and wife render one another, its institution belongs to the civil law.

Since, however, a sacrament is essentially a sign and a remedy, it follows that the nature of sacrament applies to matrimony as regards the intermediate institution; that it is fittingly intended to fulfill an office of nature as regards the first institution; and, as regards the last-mentioned institution, that it is directed to fulfill an office of society.

REPLY OBJ. 1: Things which are of natural law in a general way need to be instituted as regards their determination, which is subject to variation according to various states; just as it is of natural law that evil-doers be punished, but that such and such a punishment be appointed for such and such a crime is determined by positive law.

REPLY OBJ. 2: Matrimony is not only for a remedy against sin, but is chiefly for an office of nature. And thus it was instituted before sin, but not as intended for a remedy.

REPLY OBJ. 3: There is no reason why matrimony should not have had several institutions corresponding to the various things that had to be determined in connection with marriage. Hence these various institutions are not of the same thing in the same respect.

AD QUARTUM dicendum quod matrimonium ante peccatum institutum fuit a Deo in hoc quod homini mulierem in adiutorium de costa formavit, et dixit eis, *crescite et multiplicamini.* Quod quamvis aliis animalibus dixerit, non tamen per ea eodem modo implendum sicut per homines. Adam vero verba illa protulit a Deo inspiratus ut intelligeret matrimoni institutionem a Deo factam.

AD QUINTUM dicendum quod, quantum ad hoc quod matrimonium est sacramentum novae legis, non fuit ante Christum institutum, ut ex dictis patet.

REPLY OBJ. 4: Before sin, matrimony was instituted by God when he fashioned a helpmate for man out of his rib, and said to them: *increase and multiply.* And although this was said also to the other animals, it was not to be fulfilled by them in the same way as by men. But Adam brought forth those words, inspired by God, as he understood the institution of marriage to have been done by God.

REPLY OBJ. 5: As was clearly stated, matrimony was not instituted before Christ as a sacrament of the new law.

Article 3

Whether Matrimony Confers Grace?

AD TERTIUM SIC PROCEDITUR. Videtur quod matrimonium non conferat gratiam. Quia secundum Hugonem, *sacramenta ex sanctificatione invisibilem gratiam conferunt.* Sed matrimonium non habet aliquam sanctificationem quae sit de essentia eius. Ergo non confertur gratia in ipso.

PRAETEREA, omne sacramentum conferens gratiam confert ipsam ex materia et forma sua. Sed actus, qui sunt materia in hoc sacramento, non sunt causa gratiae: quia hoc esset Pelagiana haeresis, scilicet quod actus nostri sint causa gratiae. Verba etiam exprimentia consensum non sunt causa gratiae: nam ex eis non fit aliqua sanctificatio. Ergo in matrimonio nullo modo gratia datur.

PRAETEREA, gratia ordinata contra vulnus peccati es necessaria omnibus habentibus vulnus illud. Sed in omnibus invenitur concupiscentiae vulnus. Si ergo in matrimonio detur gratia contra vulnus concupiscentiae, debent omnes homines matrimonium contrahere. Et sic esset valde stultum a matrimonio abstinere.

PRAETEREA, infirmitas non accipit medicamentum ab eo a quo accipit intensionem. Sed per matrimonium concupiscentia accipit intensionem: quia, sicut dicit Philosophus, in III *Ethic., insatiabilis est concupiscentiae appetitus, et per operationem congruam augetur.* Ergo videtur quod in matrimonio non conferatur remedium gratiae contra concupiscentiam.

SED CONTRA: Definitio et definitum debent converti. Sed in definitione sacramenti ponitur causalitas gratiae. Ergo, cum matrimonium sit sacramentum, erit gratiae causa.

PRAETEREA, Augustinus dicit quod *matrimonium est aegrotis in remedium.* Sed non est in remedium nisi inquantum aliquam efficaciam habet. Ergo habet aliquid efficaciae ad reprimendum concupiscentiam. Sed con-

OBJECTION 1: It would seem that matrimony does not confer grace. For, according to Hugh, *the sacraments, by virtue of their sanctification, confer an invisible grace (On the Sacraments 1).* But matrimony has no sanctification essential to it. Therefore, grace is not conferred therein.

OBJ. 2: Further, every sacrament that confers grace confers it by virtue of its matter and form. Now the acts which are the matter in this sacrament are not the cause of grace (for it would be the heresy of Pelagius to assert that our acts cause grace); and the words expressive of consent are not the cause of grace, since no sanctification results from them. Therefore, grace is by no means given in matrimony.

OBJ. 3: Further, the grace that is directed against the wound of sin is necessary to all who have that wound. Now the wound of concupiscence is to be found in all. Therefore, if grace were given in matrimony against the wound of concupiscence, all men ought to contract marriage, and it would be very stupid to refrain from matrimony.

OBJ. 4: Further, sickness does not seek a remedy where it finds aggravation. Now, concupiscence is aggravated by matrimony, because, according to the Philosopher (*Ethics* 3.12), *the desire of concupiscence is insatiable, and is increased by congenial actions.* Therefore, it would seem that grace is not conferred in matrimony as a remedy for concupiscence.

ON THE CONTRARY, Definition and thing defined should be convertible. Now causality of grace is included in the definition of a sacrament. Since, then, matrimony is a sacrament, it is a cause of grace.

FURTHER, Augustine says that *matrimony affords a remedy to the sick (On the Good of Widowhood 8; On the Literal Meaning of Genesis 9.7).* But it is not a remedy except insofar as it has some efficacy. Therefore, it has some

cupiscentia non reprimitor nisi per gratiam. Ergo in ipso confertur gratia.

Respondeo dicendum quod circa hoc fuit triplex opinio. Quidam enim dixerunt quod matrimonium nullo modo est causa gratiae, sed est tantum signum. Sed hoc non potest stare. Quia secundum hoc in nullo abundaret a sacramentis veteris legis: unde non esset aliqua ratio quare sacramentis novae legis annumeraretur. Quod enim remedium praebat satisfaciendo concupiscentiae, ne in praeceps ruat dum nimis arctatur, habuit etiam in veteri lege ex ipsa natura actus.

Et ideo alii dixerunt quod confertur ibi gratia in ordine ad recessum a malo, quia excusatur actus a peccato; qui sine matrimonio peccatum esset. Sed hoc esset nimis parum: quia hoc etiam in veteri lege habuit.

Et ideo dicunt quod facit recedere a malo inquantum constringit concupiscentiam ne extra bona matrimonii feratur: non autem per gratiam illam fit aliquod auxilium ad bene operandum. Sed hoc non potest stare. Quia eadem gratia est quae impedit peccatum, et quae ad bonum inclinat: sicut idem calor qui aufert frigus, et qui calefacit.

Unde alii dicunt quod matrimonium, inquantum in fide Christi contrahitur, habet ut conferat gratiam adiuvantem ad illa operanda quae in matrimonio requiruntur. Et hoc probabilius est. Quia ubicumque datur divinitus aliqua facultas, dantur etiam auxilia quibus homo convenienter uti possit facultate illa: sicut patet quod omnibus potentiis animae respondent aliqua membra corporis, quibus in actum exire possint. Unde, cum in matrimonio detur homini ex divina institutione facultas utendi uxore sua ad procreationem prolis, datur etiam gratia sine qua id convenienter facere non posset: sicut etiam de potestate ordinis supra dictum est. Et sic ista gratia data est ultima res contenta in hoc sacramento.

Ad primum ergo dicendum quod, sicut habet aqua baptismi quod *corpus tangat et cor abluat* ex tactu carnis Christi; ita matrimonium hoc habet ex hoc quod Christus sua passione illud repraesentavit; et non principaliter ex aliqua sanctificatione sacerdotis.

Ad secundum dicendum quod, sicut aqua baptismi cum forma verborum non operatur immediate ad gratiam, sed ad characterem; ita actus exteriores et verba exprimentia consensum directe faciunt nexum quendam, qui est sacramentum matrimonii; et huiusmodi nexus ex virtute divinae institutionis dispositive operatur ad gratiam.

efficacy for the repression of concupiscence. Now concupiscence is not repressed except by grace. Therefore, grace is conferred therein.

I answer that, There have been three opinions on this point. For some (Peter Lombard, *Sentences* IV, D. 2) said that matrimony is in no way the cause of grace, but only a sign thereof. But this cannot be maintained, for in that case it would in no respect surpass the sacraments of the old law. Wherefore there would be no reason for reckoning it among the sacraments of the new law; since even in the old law by the very nature of the act it was able to afford a remedy to concupiscence, lest the latter run riot when held in too strict restraint.

Hence others (St. Albert Magnus, *Commentary on the Sentences* IV, D. 26) said that grace is conferred therein as regards the withdrawal from evil, because the act is excused from sin, for it would be a sin apart from matrimony. But this would be too little, since it had this also in the old law.

And so they say that it makes man withdraw from evil, by restraining the concupiscence lest it tend to something outside the marriage blessings, but that this grace does not enable a man to do good works. But this cannot be maintained, since the same grace hinders sin and inclines to good, just as the same heat expels cold and gives heat.

Hence others (St. Bonaventure, *Commentary on the Sentences* IV, D. 26) say that matrimony, inasmuch as it is contracted in the faith of Christ, is able to confer the grace helping those things to be done which are required in marriage. And this is more probable, since wherever a certain divine faculty is given, help is also given by which man can fittingly make use of that faculty; thus it is clear that to all the soul's powers there correspond bodily members by which they can proceed to act. Therefore, since in matrimony man receives by divine institution the faculty to use his wife for the begetting of children, he also receives the grace without which he cannot fittingly do so, just as with the power of holy orders spoken of above (Q. 35, A. 1). So also what grace is now given in this sacrament is like the reality contained.

Reply Obj. 1: Just as the baptismal water by virtue of its contact with Christ's body (III, Q. 66, A. 3) is able to *touch the body and cleanse the heart* (St. Augustine, *Tractates on John* 80) so is matrimony able to do so through Christ having represented it by his Passion, and not principally through any blessing of the priest.

Reply Obj. 2: Just as the water of baptism together with the form of words does not result immediately in the infusion of grace, but in the imprinting of the character, so the outward acts and the words expressive of consent directly effect a certain tie which is the sacrament of matrimony; and this tie by virtue of its divine institution works dispositively to the infusion of grace.

AD TERTIUM dicendum quod ratio illa procederet nisi contra concupiscentiae morbum posset aliquod efficacius remedium adhiberi. Adhibetur autem maius remedium per opera spiritualia et carnis mortificationem ab illis qui matrimonio non utuntur.

AD QUARTUM dicendum quod contra concupiscentiam potest praestari remedium dupliciter. Uno modo, ex parte ipsius concupiscentiae, ut reprimatur in sua radice. Et sic remedium praestat matrimonium per gratiam quae in eo datur.

Alio modo, ex parte actus eius. Et hoc dupliciter. Uno modo, ut actus ad quem concupiscentia inclinat exterius, turpitudine careat. Et hoc fit per bona matrimonii, quae honestant carnalem concupiscentiam. Alio modo, ut actus turpitudinem habens impediatur. Quod fit ex ipsa natura actus: quia, dum concupiscentiae satisfit in actu coniugali, ad alias corruptelas non ita incitat. Propter quod dicit Apostolus: *melius est nubere quam uri*. Quamvis enim opera concupiscentiae congrua secundum se nata sint concupiscentiam augere, tamen secundum quod ratione ordinantur, ipsam reprimunt: quia ex similibus actibus similes relinquuntur dispositiones et habitus.

REPLY OBJ. 3: This argument would hold if no more efficacious remedy could be employed against the disease of concupiscence; but a yet more powerful remedy is found in spiritual works and mortification of the flesh by those who make no use of matrimony.

REPLY OBJ. 4: A remedy can be employed against concupiscence in two ways. First, on the part of concupiscence by repressing it in its root, and thus matrimony affords a remedy by the grace given therein.

Second, on the part of its act, and this in two ways: first, by depriving the act to which concupiscence inclines of its outward shamefulness, and this is done by the marriage blessings which justify carnal concupiscence; second, by hindering the shameful act, which is done by the very nature of the act. For concupiscence, being satisfied by the conjugal act, does not incline so much to other wickedness. For this reason the Apostle says: *it is better to marry than to burn* (1 Cor 7:9). For, though the works congenial to concupiscence are in themselves of a nature to increase concupiscence, yet insofar as they are directed according to reason they repress concupiscence, because similar acts result in similar dispositions and habits.

Article 4

Whether Carnal Intercourse Is an Integral Part of This Sacrament?

AD QUARTUM SIC PROCEDITUR. Videtur quod carnalis commixtio sit de integritate matrimonii. In ipsa enim institutione matrimonii dictum est: *erunt duo in carne una*. Sed hoc non fit nisi per carnalem commixtionem. Ergo est de integritate matrimonii.

PRAETEREA, illud quod pertinet ad sacramenti significationem, est de necessitate sacramenti, ut praedictum est. Sed carnalis commixtio pertinet ad significationem sacramenti, ut in littera dicitur. Ergo est de integritate sacramenti.

PRAETEREA, huiusmodi sacramentum ordinatur ad conservationem speciei. Sed conservatio speciei non potest fieri sine carnali commixtione. Ergo est de integritate sacramenti.

PRAETEREA, matrimonium est sacramentum secundum quod remedium contra concupiscentiam praestat, de quo dicit Apostolus, I Cor. 7, *quod melius est nubere quam uri*. Sed hoc remedium non praestat his qui carnaliter non commiscentur. Ergo idem quod prius.

SED CONTRA: In paradiso fuit matrimonium. Sed ibi non fuit carnalis copula. Ergo commixtio carnalis non est de integritate matrimonii.

OBJECTION 1: It would seem that carnal intercourse is an integral part of marriage. For at the very institution of marriage it was declared: *they shall be two in one flesh* (Gen 2:24). Now this is not brought about save by carnal intercourse. Therefore, it is an integral part of marriage.

OBJ. 2: Further, that which belongs to the signification of a sacrament is necessary for the sacrament, as we have stated above (A. 2; Q. 9, A. 1). Now carnal intercourse belongs to the signification of matrimony, as stated in the text (*Sentences* IV, D. 26). Therefore, it is an integral part of the sacrament.

OBJ. 3: Further, this sacrament is directed to the preservation of the species. But the species cannot be preserved without carnal intercourse. Therefore, it is an integral part of the sacrament.

OBJ. 4: Further, matrimony is a sacrament inasmuch as it affords a remedy against concupiscence; according to the Apostle's saying: *it is better to marry than to burn* (1 Cor 7:9). But it does not afford this remedy to those who have no carnal intercourse. Therefore, the same conclusion follows as before.

ON THE CONTRARY, There was matrimony in paradise, and yet there was no carnal intercourse. Therefore, carnal intercourse is not an integral part of matrimony.

PRAETEREA, sacramentum ex suo nomine sanctificationem importat. Sed sine carnali commixtione est matrimonium sanctius, ut in littera dicitur. Ergo carnalis commixtio non est de necessitate sacramenti.

RESPONDEO dicendum quod duplex est integritas: una quae attenditur secundum perfectionem primam, quae consistit in ipso esse rei; alia quae attenditur secundum perfectionem secundam, quae consistit in operatione. Quia ergo carnalis commixtio est quaedam operatio sive usus matrimonii, per quod facultas ad hoc datur; ideo erit carnalis commixtio de secunda perfectione matrimonii, et non de prima.

AD PRIMUM ergo dicendum quod Adam exposuit integritatem matrimonii quantum ad utramque perfectionem: quia res ex suo actu innotescit.

AD SECUNDUM dicendum quod significatio rei contentae est de necessitate sacramenti. Et ad hanc significationem non pertinet carnalis commixtio, sed ad rem non contentam: ut ex dictis patet.

AD TERTIUM dicendum quod res non pervenit ad finem suum nisi per actum proprium. Unde ex hoc quod finis matrimonii non habetur sine carnali commixtione, ostenditur quod sit de integritate secunda, et non de prima.

AD QUARTUM dicendum quod ante commixtionem carnalem est matrimonium in remedium ex gratia, quae in eo datur, quamvis non ex actu. Quod pertinet ad integritatem secundam.

FURTHER, A sacrament by its very name denotes a sanctification. But matrimony is holier without carnal intercourse, according to the text (*Sentences* D. 26). Therefore, carnal intercourse is not necessary for the sacrament.

I ANSWER THAT, Integrity is twofold. One regards the primal perfection consisting in the very essence of a thing; the other regards the secondary perfection consisting in operation. Since, then, carnal intercourse is an operation or use of marriage which gives the faculty for that intercourse, it follows that carnal intercourse belongs to the latter, and not to the former, integrity of marriage (III, Q. 29, A. 2).

REPLY OBJ. 1: Adam expressed the integrity of marriage in regard to both perfections, because a thing is known by its operation.

REPLY OBJ. 2: Signification of the thing contained is necessary for the sacrament. Carnal intercourse belongs not to this signification, but to the thing not contained, as appears from what was said above (A. 1).

REPLY OBJ. 3: A thing does not reach its end except by its own act. Wherefore, from the fact that the end of matrimony is not attained without carnal intercourse, it follows that it belongs to the second and not to the first integrity.

REPLY OBJ. 4: Before carnal intercourse marriage is a remedy by virtue of the grace given in it, although not by virtue of the act, which belongs to the second integrity.

QUESTION 43

THE BETROTHAL

Consequenter considerandum est de matrimonio absolute considerato. Ubi primo agendum est de sponsalibus; secundo, de matrimonii ratione; tertio, de eius causa efficiente, scilicet de consensu; quarto, de eius bonis; quinto, de impedimentis ipsius; sexto, de secundis nuptiis; septimo, de quibusdam matrimonio annexis.

Circa primum quaeruntur tria.

Primo: quid sint sponsalia.

Secundo: qui possunt contrahere sponsalia.

Tertio: utrum sponsalia dirimi possint.

In the next place we must consider matrimony absolutely; and here we must treat: (1) Of the betrothal; (2) Of the nature of matrimony; (3) Of its efficient cause, namely the consent; (4) Of its blessings; (5) Of the impediments thereto; (6) Of second marriages; (7) Of certain things annexed to marriage.

Under the first head there are three points of inquiry:

(1) What is the betrothal?

(2) Who can contract a betrothal?

(3) Whether a betrothal can be canceled?

Article 1

Whether a Betrothal Is a Promise of Future Marriage?

AD PRIMUM SIC PROCEDITUR. Videtur quod sponsalia non convenienter dicantur *futurarum nuptiarum promissio*, ut habetur ex verbis Nicolai Papae. Quia, sicut dicit Isidorus, *est aliquis sponsus, non quia promittit, sed quia spondet et sponsores dat*. Sed a sponsalibus dicitur aliquis sponsus. Ergo male dicitur *promissio*.

PRAETEREA, quicumque promittit aliquid, debet compelli ad solvendum. Sed illi qui sponsalia contraxerunt, non compelluntur per Ecclesiam ad matrimonium contrahendum. Ergo sponsalia non sunt *promissio*.

PRAETEREA, in sponsalibus non est quandoque sola promissio, sed adiicitur iuramentum, et aliquae arrhae. Ergo videtur quod non debuerint solum per promissionem definiri.

PRAETEREA, matrimonia debent esse libera et absoluta. Sed sponsalia quandoque fiunt sub aliqua conditione, etiam accipiendae pecuniae. Ergo non convenienter dicuntur promissio *nuptiarum*.

PRAETEREA, promissio, quae est de rebus futuris, vituperatur Iac. 4: Sed circa sacramenta non debet aliquid esse vituperabile. Non ergo debet fieri *futurarum nuptiarum* promissio.

PRAETEREA, nullus dicitur sponsus nisi a sponsalibus. Sed aliquis dicitur sponsus ex praesentibus nuptiis, ut in littera dicitur. Ergo sponsalia non semper sunt *futurarum nuptiarum* promissio.

RESPONDEO dicendum quod consensus in coniugalem copulam per verba de futuro non facit matrimo-

OBJECTION 1: It would seem that a betrothal is not rightly defined *a promise of future marriage*, as expressed in the words of Pope Nicholas I (*Response to Consultation of the Bulgarians* 3). For as Isidore says (*Etymologies* 4), *a man is betrothed not by a mere promise, but by giving his troth and providing sureties*. Now a person is called a bridegroom by reason of his betrothal. Therefore, it is wrongly described as a *promise*.

OBJ. 2: Further, whoever promises a thing must be compelled to fulfill his promise. But those who have contracted a betrothal are not compelled by the Church to fulfill the marriage. Therefore, a betrothal is not a *promise*.

OBJ. 3: Further, sometimes a betrothal does not consist of a mere promise, but an oath is added, as also certain pledges. Therefore, seemingly it should not be defined as a mere promise.

OBJ. 4: Further, marriage should be free and absolute. But a betrothal is sometimes expressed under a condition even of money to be received. Therefore, it is not fittingly described as a promise of *marriage*.

OBJ. 5: Further, promising about the future is blamed in James 4:13. But there should be nothing blameworthy about the sacraments. Therefore, one ought not to make a promise of *future marriage*.

OBJ. 6: Further, no man is called a spouse except on account of his betrothal. But a man is said to be a spouse on account of actual marriage, according to the text (*Sentences* IV, D. 27). Therefore, betrothals are not always a promise of *future marriage*.

I ANSWER THAT, Consent to conjugal union if expressed in words of the future does not make a marriage,

297

nium, sed matrimonii promissionem. Et haec promissio dicitur *sponsalia a spondendo*, ut dicit Isidorus: *nam, ante usum tabularum matrimonii, cautiones dabant, quibus spondebant se invicem consentire in iure matrimonii, et fideiussores dabant.*

Fit autem ista promissio dupliciter: scilicet absolute, et sub conditione. Absolute quattuor modis. Primo, nuda promissione: ut cum dicitur, *accipiam te in meam*, et e converso. Secundo, datis arrhis sponsalitiis: ut pecunia, vel aliquid huiusmodi. Tertio, anuli subarrhatione. Quarto, interveniente iuramento.

Si autem fiat dicta promissio sub conditione, distinguendum est. Quia aut est conditio honesta, ut cum dicitur, *accipiam te si parentibus placeat*: et tunc, stante conditione stat promissio, et non stante non stat. Aut est inhonesta. Et hoc dupliciter. Quia aut est contraria bonis matrimonii, ut si dicam, *accipiam te si venena sterilitatis procures*: et tunc non contrahuntur sponsalia. Aut non est contraria bonis matrimonii, ut si dicam, *accipiam te si furtis meis consentias*: et tunc stat promissio, sed tollenda est conditio.

AD PRIMUM ergo dicendum quod ipsa sponsalia et sponsorum datio est promissionis confirmatio. Et ideo ab hoc denominatur, quasi a perfectiori.

AD SECUNDUM dicendum quod ex tali promissione obligatur unus alteri ad matrimonium contrahendum: et peccat mortaliter non solvens promissum, nisi legitimum impedimentum interveniat. Et secundum hoc Ecclesia cogit, iniungendo poenitentiam pro peccato. Tamen in foro contentioso non compellitur: quia *matrimonia coacta consueverunt malos exitus habere*. Nisi forte iuramentum intervenerit. Quia tunc cogendus est, ut quidam dicunt. Quamvis aliis non videatur, propter causam praedictam: praecipue si de uxoricidio timeretur.

AD TERTIUM dicendum quod illa addita non sunt nisi ad confirmandam promissionem. Unde non sunt aliud quam promissio.

AD QUARTUM dicendum quod conditio illa quae apponitur, non tollit matrimonii libertatem. Quia, si est inhonesta, debet abiici. Si autem honesta, aut de bonis simpliciter, ut si dicatur, *accipiam te si placet parentibus*: et haec conditio non tollit libertatem sponsalium, sed auget ei honestatem. Aut est de utilibus, ut si dicat, *contraham tecum si dabis mihi centum*: et tunc hoc non ponitur quasi ad vendendum consensum matrimonii, sed intelligitur ut promissio dotis; unde matrimonium libertatem non perdit.

Quandoque autem apponitur conditio pecuniae per modum poenae. Et tunc, quia matrimonia debent esse

but a promise of marriage; and this promise is called *a betrothal from plighting one's troth*, as Isidore says. *For before the use of writing-tablets, they used to give pledges of marriage, by which they plighted their mutual consent under the marriage code, and they provided guarantors (Etymologies 4).*

This promise is made in two ways, namely, absolutely or conditionally. Absolutely, in four ways: first, a mere promise, by saying: *I will take you for my wife*, and conversely; second, by giving betrothal pledges, such as money and the like; third, by giving an engagement ring; fourth, by the addition of an oath.

If, however, this promise be made conditionally, we must draw a distinction; for it is either an honorable condition, for instance, if it were said: *I will take you, if your parents consent*, and then the promise holds if the condition is fulfilled, and does not hold if the condition is not fulfilled; or else the condition is dishonorable, and this in two ways: for either it is contrary to the marriage blessings, as if I were to say: *I will take you if you promise means of sterility*, and then no betrothal is contracted; or else it is not contrary to the marriage blessings, as were one to say: *I will take you if you consent to my thefts*, and then the promise holds, but the condition should be removed.

REPLY OBJ. 1: The betrothal itself and giving of sureties are a ratification of the promise, wherefore it is denominated from these as from that which is more perfect.

REPLY OBJ. 2: By this promise one party is bound to the other in respect of contracting marriage; and he who does not fulfill his promise sins mortally, unless a lawful impediment arise; and the Church uses compulsion in the sense that she enjoins a penance for the sin. But he is not compelled by sentence of the court, because *compulsory marriages are wont to have evil results*; unless the parties be bound by oath, for then he ought to be compelled, in the opinion of some, although others think differently on account of the reason given above, especially if there be fear of one taking the other's life.

REPLY OBJ. 3: Such things are added only in confirmation of the promise, and consequently they are not distinct from it.

REPLY OBJ. 4: The condition that is appended does not destroy the liberty of marriage; for if it be unlawful, it should be renounced; and if it be lawful, it is either about things that are good simply, as were one to say, *I will take you, if your parents consent*, and such a condition does not destroy the liberty of the betrothal, but gives it an increase of rectitude; or else it is about things that are useful, as were one to say: *I will marry you if you pay me a hundred pounds*, and then this condition is appended, not as asking a price for the consent of marriage, but as referring to the promise of a dowry; so that the marriage does not lose its liberty.

Sometimes, however, the condition appended is the payment of a sum of money by way of penalty, and then,

libera, talis conditio non stat; nec potest exigi poena illa ab eo qui non vult matrimonium complere.

Ad quintum dicendum quod Iacobus non intendit prohibere quod omnino aliquis nullam promissionem faciat de futuris: sed quod non promittat quasi fiduciam habens de vita sua. Unde docet quod debet apponi conditio, *si Deus voluerit*. Quae etiam si verbis non exprimatur, corde tamen debet intelligi.

Ad sextum dicendum quod in matrimonio potest considerari ipsa coniunctio matrimonialis, et actus eius. Et a sponsione primi in futurum dicitur sponsus a sponsalibus contractis per verba de futuro. Et a sponsione secundi dicitur aliquis sponsus etiam quando contractum est matrimonium per verba de praesenti: quia ex hoc ipso matrimonii spondet actum. Tamen a prima sponsione dicuntur sponsalia proprie, quae sunt quaedam sacramentalia matrimonii, sicut exorcismus baptismi.

since marriage should be free, such a condition does not hold, nor can such a penalty be exacted from a person who is unwilling to fulfill the promise of marriage.

Reply Obj. 5: James does not intend to forbid altogether the making of promises about the future, but the making of promises as though one were certain of one's life; hence he teaches that we ought to add the condition: *if the Lord will*, which, though it be not expressed in words, ought nevertheless to be impressed on the heart.

Reply Obj. 6: In marriage we may consider both the marriage union and the marriage act; and on account of his promise of the first as future a man is called a 'spouse' from his having contracted his betrothals by words expressive of the future; but from the promise of the second a man is called a 'spouse' even when the marriage has been contracted by words expressive of the present, because by this very fact he promises the marriage act. However, properly speaking, betrothals are so called from the promise in the first sense, because betrothals are a kind of sacramental annexed to matrimony, as exorcism to baptism.

Article 2

Whether Seven Years Is Fittingly Assigned as the Age for Betrothal?

Ad secundum sic proceditur. Videtur quod tempus septennii non sit competenter assignatum sponsalibus contrahendis. Contractus enim qui per alios fieri potest, non requirit discretionem in illis ad quos pertinet. Sed sponsalia fieri possunt per parentes, utroque illorum ignorante quorum sunt sponsalia. Ergo ita possunt fieri ante septennium sicut post.

Praeterea, sicut ad contractum sponsalium requiritur aliquis rationis usus, ita ad consentiendum in; peccatum mortale. Sed, sicut Gregorius narrat, in IV *Dialog.*, quidam puer propter blasphemiae peccatum extinctus est. Ergo ante septennium possunt sponsalia contrahi.

Praeterea, sponsalia ad matrimonium ordinantur. Sed in matrimonio non assignatur unum tempus puellae et puero. Ergo nec in sponsalibus septennium utrique assignari debet.

Praeterea, ex tunc aliqui possunt sponsalia contrahere ex quo eis possunt futurae nuptiae placere. Sed signa talis placentiae frequenter apparent in pueris ante septennium. Ergo ante illud tempus possunt contrahi sponsalia.

Praeterea, si aliqui ante septimum annum contrahunt sponsalia, et postea, post septennium ante tempus pubertatis, contrahunt per verba de praesenti, reputantur inter eos esse sponsalia. Sed hoc non est ex secundo contractu: quia tunc non intendunt sponsalia, sed matri-

Objection 1: It would seem that seven years is not fittingly assigned as the age for betrothal. For a contract that can be formed by others does not require discretion in those whom it concerns. Now a betrothal can be arranged by the parents without the knowledge of either of the persons betrothed. Therefore, a betrothal can be arranged before the age of seven years as well as after.

Obj. 2: Further, just as some use of reason is necessary for the contract of betrothal, so is there for the consent to mortal sin. Now, as Gregory says (*Dialogues* 4), a boy of five years of age was carried off by the devil on account of the sin of blasphemy. Therefore, a betrothal can take place before the age of seven years.

Obj. 3: Further, a betrothal is directed to marriage. But for marriage the same age is not assigned to boy and girl. Therefore, neither in betrothal ought seven years be assigned to both.

Obj. 4: Further, one can become betrothed as soon as future marriage can please one. Now signs of this agreeableness are often apparent in boys before the age of seven. Therefore, they can become betrothed before that age.

Obj. 5: Further, if persons become betrothed before they are seven years old, and subsequently after the age of seven and before the age of maturity renew their promise in words expressive of the present, they are reckoned to be betrothed. Now this is not by virtue of the second contract,

monium contrahere. Ergo ex primo. Et sic ante septennium possunt sponsalia contrahi.

PRAETEREA, in his quae communiter fiunt a pluribus, quod deest uni suppletur ab altero: sicut patet in trahentibus navem. Sed contractus sponsalium est quaedam actio communis inter contrahentes. Ergo, si unus sit pubes, potest contrahere cum puella quae non habet septem annos sponsalia: quia quod uni deficit de tempore, alteri superabundat.

PRAETEREA, si aliqui iuxta aetatem pubertatis, quamvis ante eam, contrahunt per verba de praesenti, reputatur inter eos matrimonium esse. Ergo, pari ratione, si ante septennium, dummodo sint propinqui, contrahunt per verba de futuro, reputabuntur inter eos esse sponsalia.

RESPONDEO dicendum quod septennium est tempus determinatum a iure sponsalibus contrahendis satis rationabiliter. Quia, cum sponsalia sint quaedam promissio futurorum, ut dictum est, oportet quod illorum sint qui aliquo modo promittere possunt. Quod non est nisi illorum qui habent aliquam prudentiam de futuris: quae usum rationis requirit. Respectu cuius triplex gradus notatur, secundum Philosophum, in I *Ethic.*: primus est cum quis neque intelligit per se, neque ab alio capere potest; secundus status est quo homo ab aliis capere potest, sed ipse per se non sufficit ad intelligendum; tertius est cum homo et ab alio iam capere potest, et per seipsum considerare. Et quia ratio paulatim in homine convalescit, secundum quod quietantur motus et fluxibilitates humorum, ideo primum statum rationis obtinet homo ante primum septennium: et propter hoc illo tempore nulli contractui aptus est, et ita nec sponsalibus. Sed ad secundum statum incipit pervenire in fine primi septennii: unde etiam tunc temporis pueri ad scholas ponuntur. Sed ad tertium statum incipit homo pervenire in fine secundi septennii, quantum ad ea quae ad personam ipsius pertinent, in qua ratio naturalis citius convalescit: sed quantum ad ea quae extra ipsum sunt, in fine tertii septennii.

Et ideo ante primum septennium nulli contractui homo aptus est. Sed in fine primi septennii incipit esse aptus ad aliqua promittendum in futurum, praecipue de his ad quae ratio naturalis inclinat magis: non autem ad obligandum se perpetuo vinculo, quia adhuc non firmam voluntatem habet. Et ideo tali tempore possunt contrahere sponsalia. Sed in fine secundi septennii, iam potest obligare se de his quae ad personam ipsius pertinent, vel ad religionem vel ad coniugium. Sed post tertium septennium etiam potest de aliis se obligare. Et secundum leges constituitur ei potestas de rebus suis disponendi post viginti quinque annos.

AD PRIMUM ergo dicendum quod, si ante annos pubertatis fiat contractus sponsalium per alium, ambo vel

since they intend to contract not betrothal but marriage. Therefore, it is by the virtue of the first; and thus espousals can be contracted before the age of seven.

OBJ. 6: Further, when a thing is done by many persons in common, if one fails he is supplied by another, as in the case of those who row a boat. Now the contract of betrothal is an action common to the contracting parties. Therefore, if one be of mature age, he can contract a betrothal with a girl who is not seven years old, since the lack of age in one is more than counterbalanced in the other.

OBJ. 7: Further, those who at about the age of puberty, but before it, enter into the marriage contract by words expressive of the present are reputed to be married. Therefore, in like manner if they contract marriage by words expressive of the future, before yet close on the age of puberty, they are to be reputed as betrothed.

I ANSWER THAT, The age of seven years is fixed reasonably enough by law for the contracting of betrothals, for since a betrothal is a promise of the future, as already stated (A. 1), it follows that they are within the competency of those who can make a promise in some way, and this is only for those who can have some foresight of the future, and this requires the use of reason, of which three degrees are to be observed, according to the Philosopher (*Ethics* 1.4). The first is when a person neither understands by himself nor is able to learn from another; the second stage is when a man can learn from another but is incapable by himself of consideration and understanding; the third degree is when a man is both able to learn from another and to consider by himself. And since reason develops in man little by little, in proportion as the movement and fluctuation of the humors is calmed, man reaches the first stage of reason before his seventh year; and consequently during that period he is unfit for any contract, and therefore for betrothal. But he begins to reach the second stage at the end of his first seven years, wherefore children at that age are sent to school. But man begins to reach the third stage at the end of his second seven years, as regards things concerning his person, when his natural reason develops; but as regards things outside his person, at the end of his third seven years.

Hence before his first seven years a man is not fit to make any contract, but at the end of that period he begins to be fit to make certain promises for the future, especially about those things to which natural reason inclines us more, though he is not fit to bind himself by a perpetual obligation, because as yet he has not a firm will. Hence at that age betrothals can be contracted. But at the end of the second seven years he can already bind himself in matters concerning his person, either to religion or to wedlock. And after the third seven years he can bind himself in other matters also; and according to the laws he is given the power of disposing of his property after his twenty-fifth year.

REPLY OBJ. 1: If the parties are betrothed by another person before they reach the age of puberty, either of them

alter reclamare possunt. Unde nihil tunc actum est: adeo quod nec aliqua affinitas contrahatur ex hoc. Et ideo sponsalia quae inter aliquos per personas alias contrahuntur, robur habent inquantum illi inter quos contrahuntur, ad aetatem debitam venientes, non reclamant, ex quo intelliguntur consentire de his quae per alios facta sunt.

Ad secundum dicendum quod quidam dicunt quod ille puer de quo Gregorius narrat non fuit damnatus, nec mortaliter peccavit, sed visio illa ostensa fuit ad patrem contristandum, qui in puero illo peccaverat non corrigens eum. Sed hoc est expresse contra intentionem Gregorii dicentis quod *pater pueri, animam parvuli filii negligens, non parvulum peccatorem gehennae ignibus nutrivit*.

Et ideo dicendum quod ad peccatum mortale sufficit etiam consensus in praesens. Sed in sponsalibus est consensus in futurum. Maior autem discretio rationis requiritur ad providendum in futurum quam ad consentiendum in actum unum praesentem. Et ideo ante potest homo peccare mortaliter quam possit se obligare ad aliquid futurum.

Ad tertium dicendum quod in tempore contractus matrimonii non solum requiritur dispositio ex parte usus rationis, sed etiam ex parte corporis, ut sit tempus generationi aptum. Et quia puella in duodecimo anno ad hoc venit ut possit esse actui generationis apta, puer autem in finem secundi septennii, ut Philosophus ait, in IX *Animalium*; simul autem usum discretionis accipiunt, qui tantum iri sponsalibus requiritur: ideo in sponsalibus determinatur unum tempus utrique, non autem in matrimonio.

Ad quartum dicendum quod illa placentia quae est in pueris ante septennium, non procedit ex perfecto usu rationis, cum nondum sint plene susceptibiles disciplinae: sed magis contingit ex motu naturae quam ex aliqua ratione. Et ideo non sufficit talis placentia ad sponsalia contrahendum.

Ad quintum dicendum quod, quamvis per secundum contractum in casu illo non faciunt matrimonium, tamen ostendunt se ratam habere priorem promissionem. Et ideo prior contractus accipit firmitatem.

Ad sextum dicendum quod trahentes navem agunt per modum unius causae: et ideo quod deest urii potest suppleri ex altero. Sed sponsalia contrahentes agunt ut distinctae personae: quia sponsalia non nisi inter duos esse possunt. Unde in utroque requiritur quod sit sufficiens ad contrahendum. Et ideo defectus unius sponsalia impedit, nec ex altero potest suppleri.

Ad septimum dicendum quod iri sponsalibus etiam similiter, si appropinquant contrahentes ad tempus septennii, contractus sponsalium habet robur: quia, secun-

or both can demur; wherefore in that case the betrothal does not take effect, so that neither does any affinity result therefrom. Hence a betrothal made between certain persons by some other takes effect insofar as those between whom the betrothal is arranged do not demur when they reach the proper age, whence they are understood to consent to what others have done.

Reply Obj. 2: Some say that the boy of whom Gregory tells this story was not damned, and that he did not sin mortally; and that this vision was for the purpose of making the father sorrowful, for he had sinned in the boy through failing to correct him. But this is contrary to the express intention of Gregory, who says (*Dialogues* 4) that *the boy's father, having neglected the soul of his little son, fostered no little sinner for the flames of hell.*

Consequently, it must be said that for a mortal sin it is sufficient to give consent to something present, whereas in a betrothal the consent is to something future; and greater discretion of reason is required for looking to the future than for consenting to one present act. Therefore, a man can sin mortally before he can bind himself to a future obligation.

Reply Obj. 3: Regarding the age for the marriage contract, a disposition is required not only on the part of the use of reason, but also on the part of the body, in that it is necessary to be of an age adapted to procreation. And since a girl becomes apt for the act of procreation in her twelfth year, and a boy at the end of his second seven years, as the Philosopher says (*History of Animals* 7), whereas the age is the same in both for attaining the use of reason (which is the sole condition for betrothal), hence it is that the one age is assigned for both as regards betrothal, but not as regards marriage.

Reply Obj. 4: This agreeableness in regard to boys under the age of seven does not result from the perfect use of reason, since they are not as yet possessed of complete self-control; it results rather from the movement of nature than from any process of reason. Consequently, this agreeableness does not suffice for contracting a betrothal.

Reply Obj. 5: In this case, although the second contract does not amount to marriage, nevertheless the parties show that they ratify their former promise; wherefore the first contract is confirmed by the second.

Reply Obj. 6: Those who row a boat act by way of one cause, and consequently what is lacking in one can be supplied by another. But those who make a contract of betrothal act as distinct persons, since a betrothal can only be between two parties; therefore, it is necessary for each to be qualified to contract, and thus the defect of one is an obstacle to their betrothal, nor can it be supplied by the other.

Reply Obj. 7: It is true that in the matter of betrothal if the contracting parties are close upon the age of seven, the contract of betrothal is valid, since, according to the

dum Philosophum, in II *Physic., quod parum deest, quasi nihil deesse videtur.*

Haec autem propinquitas a quibusdam determinatur tempus sex mensium. Sed melius est quod determinetur secundum conditionem contrahentium: quia in quibusdam magis acceleratur usus rationis quam in aliis.

Philosopher (*Physics* 2.56), *when little is lacking it seems as though nothing were lacking.*

Some fix the margin at six months. But it is better to determine it according to the condition of the contracting parties, since the use of reason comes sooner to some than to others.

Article 3

Whether a Betrothal Can Be Dissolved?

AD TERTIUM SIC PROCEDITUR. Videtur quod sponsalia dirimi non possunt altero religionem intrante. Quia de pecunia quam alteri promisi, non possum alteri licite oblationem facere. Sed ille qui sponsalia contrahit, corpus suum promittit mulieri. Ergo non potest se offerre Deo ulterius in religionem.

ITEM, videtur quod non debeant dirimi quando alter coniugum ad longinquam regionem se transfert. Quia *in dubiis semper tutior pars est eligenda.* Se tutius esset quod eum expectaret. Ergo tenetur eum expectare.

ITEM, videtur quod nec dirimantur per aegritudinem quam aliquis incurrit post contracta sponsalia. Quia pro poena nullus debet puniri. Sed vir qui infirmitatem incurrit, punitur in eo quod ei ius suum aufertur, quod in illa habebat quae sibi fuerat desponsata. Ergo propter corporalem infirmitatem non debent sponsalia dirimi.

ITEM, videtur quod nec propter affinitatem intervenientem: utpote si sponsus consanguineam sponsae fornicario concubitu cognoscat. Quia secundum hoc sponsa puniretur pro peccato sponsi. Quod non est conveniens.

ITEM, videtur quod non possint se invicem absolvere. Quia hoc est maximae levitatis, ut primo contrahant et postmodum se absolvant. Sed talia non debent ab Ecclesia sustineri. Ergo etc.

ITEM, videtur quod nec propter alterius fornicationem. Quia adhuc per sponsalia unus non accipit potestatem in corpus alterius. Et ita videtur quod in nullo contra invicem peccent si interim fornicantur. Et sic sponsalia dirimi non debent per hoc.

ITEM, videtur quod nec per contractum cum alia per verba de praesenti. Quia venditio secunda non derogat venditioni primae. Ergo nec secundus contractus potest derogare primo.

ITEM, videtur quod nec per defectum aetatis possint dirimi. Quia quod non est, non potest dissolvi. Sed ante

OBJECTION 1: It would seem that a betrothal cannot be dissolved if one of the parties enter religion. For if I have promised a thing to someone, I cannot lawfully pledge it to someone else. Now he who betroths himself promises his body to the woman. Therefore, he cannot make a further offering of himself to God in religion.

OBJ. 2: Again, seemingly it should not be dissolved when one of the parties leaves for a distant country, because *in doubtful matters one should always choose the safer course.* Now the safer course would be to wait for him. Therefore, she is bound to wait for him.

OBJ. 3: Again, seemingly neither is it dissolved by sickness contracted after betrothal, for no man should be punished for being under a penalty. Now the man who contracts an infirmity would be punished if he were to lose his right to the woman betrothed to him. Therefore, a betrothal should not be dissolved on account of a bodily infirmity.

OBJ. 4: Again, neither seemingly should a betrothal be dissolved on account of a supervening affinity, for instance, if the spouse were to commit fornication with a kinswoman of his betrothed; for in that case the affianced bride would be penalized for the sin of her affianced spouse, which is unreasonable.

OBJ. 5: Again, seemingly they cannot set one another free; for it would be a proof of greatest fickleness if they contracted together and then set one another free; and such conduct ought not to be tolerated by the Church. Therefore, etc.

OBJ. 6: Again, neither seemingly ought a betrothal to be dissolved on account of the fornication of one of the parties. For a betrothal does not yet give the one power over the body of the other; wherefore it would seem that they in no way sin against one another if meanwhile they commit fornication. Consequently, a betrothal should not be dissolved on that account.

OBJ. 7: Again, neither seemingly on account of his contracting with another woman by words expressive of the present. For a subsequent sale does not void a previous sale. Therefore, neither should a second contract void a previous one.

OBJ. 8: Again, neither seemingly should it be dissolved on account of deficient age; since what is not cannot be

aetatem determinatam nulla fuerunt sponsalia. Ergo dirimi non possunt.

RESPONDEO dicendum quod in omnibus praedictis casibus sponsalia contracta dirimuntur, sed diversimode. Quia in duobus, scilicet cum quis ad religionem confugit, et cum alter coniugum cum altero per verba de praesenti contrahit, ipso iure sponsalia dirimuntur. Sed iri aliis casibus dirimi debent secundum iudicium Ecclesiae.

AD PRIMUM ergo dicendum quod talis promissio solvitur per mortem spiritualem: cum sit spiritualis tantum, ut dictum est.

AD SECUNDUM dicendum quod dubium illud determinatur ex hoc quod alter non comparet tempore statuto ad rnatrimonium perficiendum. Unde, si ex parte eius non defuit quin matrimonium compleret, potest licite alteri nubere sine peccato aliquo. Si autem per eum stetit quod matrimonium non est completum, debet agere poenitentiam de peccato fractae promissionis, aut iuramenti, si iuramentum intervenit: et contrahere cum alia, si vult, iudicio Ecclesiae.

AD TERTIUM dicendum quod si, ante contractum matrimonium, aliquam gravem infirmitatem incurrat alter eorum inter quos sunt contracta sponsalia, quae ipsum debilitet nimis, ut epilepsia aut paralysis; aut eum deformet, ut abscissio nasi vel orbitas oculorum aut aliquid huiusmodi; aut quae sunt contra bonum prolis, utpote lepra, quae solet prolem inficere: possunt sponsalia dirimere, ne sibi invicem displiceant, et matrimonium sic contractum malum exitum sortiatur. Nec pro poena punitur aliquis: sed ex poena damnum reportat. Quod non est inconveniens.

AD QUARTUM dicendum quod, si sponsus cognovit consanguineam sponsae vel e converso, tunc dirimi debent sponsalia. Et ad hoc probandum sola fama sufficit, propter scandalum vitandum. Causae enim quae in futurum expectant effectus suos, impediuntur a suis effectibus non solum ex eo quod est, sed ex eo quod futurum est. Unde, sicut affinitas, si esset tempore contractus sponsalium, impedivisset contractum illum; ita, si interveniat ante matrimonium, quod est effectus quidam sponsalium, prior contractus ab effectu suo impeditur. Nec in hoc aliquid detrahitur alteri; immo ei confertur, quia absolvitur ab eo qui per fornicationem se Deo odiosum reddidit.

AD QUINTUM dicendum, quod quidam non recipiunt istum casum. Sed contra eos est *Decretalis*, quae expresse dicit: *ad instar*, inquit, *eorum qui societatem interpositione fidei contrahunt, et postea eandem remittunt, potest in patientia tolerari, si mutuo se absolvunt qui sponsalia contraxerunt.*

dissolved. Now a betrothal is null before the requisite age. Therefore, it cannot be dissolved.

I ANSWER THAT, In all the cases mentioned above the betrothal that has been contracted is dissolved, but in different ways. For in two of them—namely, when a party enters religion, and when either of the affianced spouses contracts with another party by words expressive of the present—the betrothal is dissolved by law, whereas in the other cases it has to be dissolved according to the judgment of the Church.

REPLY OBJ. 1: Such a promise is dissolved by spiritual death, for that promise is purely spiritual, as we shall state further on (Q. 61, A. 2).

REPLY OBJ. 2: This doubt is solved by either party not putting in an appearance at the time fixed for completing the marriage. Wherefore if it was no fault of that party that the marriage was not completed, he or she can lawfully marry without any sin. But if he or she was responsible for the non-completion of the marriage, this responsibility involves the obligation of doing penance for the broken promise—or oath if the promise was confirmed by oath—and he or she can contract with another if they wish it, subject to the judgment of the Church.

REPLY OBJ. 3: If either of the betrothed parties incur an infirmity which notably weakens the subject (as epilepsy or paralysis), or causes a deformity (as loss of the nose or eyes, and the like), or is contrary to the good of the offspring (as leprosy, which tends to be transmitted to the children), the betrothal can be dissolved, lest the betrothed be displeasing to one another, and the marriage thus contracted have an evil result. Nor is one punished for being under a penalty, although one incurs a loss from one's penalty, and this is not unreasonable.

REPLY OBJ. 4: If the affianced bridegroom has carnal knowledge of a kinswoman of his spouse, or vice versa, the betrothal must be dissolved; and for proof it is sufficient that the fact be the common talk, in order to avoid scandal; for causes whose effects mature in the future are voided of their effects not only by what actually is, but also by what happens subsequently. Hence just as affinity, had it existed at the time of the betrothal, would have prevented that contract, so, if it supervene before marriage, which is an effect of the betrothal, the previous contract is voided of its effect. Nor does the other party suffer in consequence: rather, he or she gains, being set free from one who has become hateful to God by committing fornication.

REPLY OBJ. 5: Some do not admit this case. Yet they have against them the *Decretals*, which says expressly: *just as those who enter into a contract of fellowship by pledging their faith to one another and afterwards give it back, so it may be patiently tolerated that those who are betrothed to one another should set one another free.*

Sed ad hoc dicunt quod Ecclesia magis hoc sustinet ne peius eveniat, quam hoc sit de iure. Sed hoc non videtur exemplo convenire quod decretalis adducit.

Et ideo dicendum quod non semper est levitatis retractare quae prius firmata sunt: quia *incertae sunt providentiae nostrae*, ut dicitur in libro Sapientiae.

Ad sextum dicendum quod, quamvis non dederint sibi mutuo potestatem corporis sponsalia contrahentes, tamen ex hoc efficiuntur sibi invicem suspecti de non servanda fide in futurum. Et ideo potest sibi praecavere unus contra alium, sponsalia dirimendo.

Ad septimum dicendum quod ratio illa teneret si esset unius rationis uterque contractus. Sed secundus contractus matrimonii est fortior primo. Et ideo solvit ipsum.

Ad octavum dicendum quod, quamvis non fuerint vera sponsalia, tamen fuit ibi quidam modus sponsalium. Et ideo, ne videatur approbare ad annos legitimos veniens, debet petere solutionem sponsalium iudicio Ecclesiae faciendam, propter bonum exemplum.

Yet to this they say that the Church allows this lest worse happen, rather than because it is according to strict law. But this does not seem to agree with the example quoted by the Decretal.

Accordingly, we must reply that it is not always a proof of fickleness to retract an agreement, since *our counsels are uncertain* (Wis 9:14).

Reply Obj. 6: Although when they become betrothed they have not yet given one another power over one another's body, yet if this were to happen it would make them suspicious of one another's fidelity; and so one can ensure himself against the other by breaking off the engagement.

Reply Obj. 7: This argument would hold if each contract were of the same kind; whereas the second contract of marriage has greater force than the first, and consequently dissolves it.

Reply Obj. 8: Although it was not a true betrothal, there was a betrothal of a kind; and consequently, lest approval should seem to be given when they come to the lawful age, they should seek a dissolution of the betrothal by the judgment of the Church, for the sake of a good example.

QUESTION 44

THE DEFINITION OF MATRIMONY

Deinde considerandum est de ratione matrimonii. Circa quod quaeruntur tria.

Primo: utrum matrimonium sit in genere coniunctionis.

Secundo: utrum convenienter nominetur.

Tertio: utrum convenienter definiatur.

We must now consider the nature of matrimony. Under this head there are three points of inquiry:

(1) Whether matrimony is a kind of joining?

(2) Whether it is fittingly named?

(3) Whether it is fittingly defined?

Article 1

Whether Matrimony Is a Kind of Joining?

AD PRIMUM SIC PROCEDITUR. Videtur quod matrimonium non sit in genere coniunctionis. Quia vinculum quo aliqua ligantur, differt a coniunctione ipsa, sicut causa ab effectu. Sed matrimonium est vinculum quoddam quo iuncti matrimonio ligantur. Ergo non est in genere coniunctionis.

PRAETEREA, omne sacramentum est sensibile signum. Sed nulla relatio est accidens sensibile. Ergo matrimonium, cum sit sacramentum, non erit in genere relationis. Et ita nec in genere coniunctionis.

PRAETEREA, coniunctio est relatio aequiparentiae, sicut aequalitas. Sed non est una numero aequalitatis relatio in utroque extremorum: ut Avicenna dicit. Ergo nec una coniunctio. Et sic, si matrimonium est in genere coniunctionis, non est unum tantum matrimonium inter duos coniuges.

SED CONTRA: Relatio est secundum quam aliqua ad invicem referuntur. Sed secundum matrimonium aliqua ad invicem referuntur: dicitur enim maritus vir uxoris, et uxor mariti uxor. Ergo matrimonium est in genere relationis. Nec est aliud quam coniunctio.

PRAETEREA, unio duorum ad aliquid unum non fit nisi secundum coniunctionem. Hoc autem fit per matrimonium: ut patet Genes. 2, *erunt duo in carne una.* Ergo matrimonium est in genere coniunctionis.

RESPONDEO dicendum quod coniunctio adunationem quandam importat. Unde ubicumque est adunatio aliquorum, ibi est aliqua coniunctio. Ea autem quae ordinantur ad aliquid unum, dicuntur in ordine ad illud adunari: sicut multi homines adunantur ad unam militiam vel negotiationem exequendam, ex qua dicuntur commilitones ad invicem, vel socii negotiationis. Et ideo, cum per matrimonium ordinentur aliqui ad unam generationem et educationem prolis; et iterum ad unam vitam domesticam; constat quod in matrimonio est ali-

OBJECTION 1: It would seem that matrimony is not a kind of joining. For the bond whereby things are tied together differs from their joining as cause from effect. Now matrimony is the bond whereby those who are joined in matrimony are tied together. Therefore, it is not a kind of joining.

OBJ. 2: Further, every sacrament is a sensible sign. But no relation is a sensible accident. Therefore, since matrimony is a sacrament, it is not a kind of relation, and consequently neither is it a kind of joining.

OBJ. 3: Further, a joining is a relation of equiparance as well as of equality. Now, according to Avicenna, the relation of equality is not identically the same in each extreme. Neither, therefore, is there an identically same joining; and consequently if matrimony is a kind of joining, there is not only one matrimony between man and wife.

ON THE CONTRARY, It is by relation that things are related to one another. Now by matrimony certain things are related to one another; for the husband is the wife's husband, and the wife is the husband's wife. Therefore, matrimony is a kind of relation, nor is it other than a joining.

FURTHER, The union of two things into one can result only from their being joined. Now such is the effect of matrimony: *they shall be two in one flesh* (Gen 2:23). Therefore, matrimony is a kind of joining.

I ANSWER THAT, A joining denotes a kind of uniting, and so wherever things are united there must be a joining. Now things directed to one purpose are said to be united in their direction to it; thus many men are united in following one military calling or in pursuing one business, in relation to which they are called fellow-soldiers or business partners. Hence, since by marriage certain persons are directed to one begetting and upbringing of children, and again to one family life, it is clear that in matrimony there is a joining in respect of which we speak of husband and wife; and

qua coniunctio secundum quam dicitur maritus et uxor. Et talis coniunctio, ex hoc quod ordinatur ad aliquod unum, est matrimonium. Coniunctio autem corporum vel animorum ad matrimonium consequitur.

AD PRIMUM ergo dicendum quod matrimonium est vinculum quo ligantur formaliter, non effective. Ideo non oportet quod sit aliud a coniunctione.

AD SECUNDUM dicendum quod, quamvis ipsa relatio non sit sensibile accidens, tamen causae eius possunt esse sensibiles. Nec in sacramento requiritur quod sit sensibile illud quod est res et sacramentum: hoc enim modo se habet in hoc sacramento praedicta coniunctio. Sed verba exprimentia consensum, quae sunt sacramentum tantum, et causa praedictae coniunctionis, sunt sensibilia.

AD TERTIUM dicendum quod relatio fundatur in aliquo sicut in causa, ut similitudo in qualitate; et in aliquo sicut in subiecto, ut in ipsis similibus. Et ex utraque parte potest attendi unitas et diversitas ipsius. Quia ergo in similitudine non est eadem qualitas numero, sed specie, in utroque simili; et iterum subiecta similitudinis sunt duo numero; et similiter est de aequalitate: ideo et aequalitas et similitudo omnibus modis est alia numero in utroque similium et aequalium. Sed relatio quae est matrimonium, ex una parte habet unitatem in utroque extremorum, scilicet ex parte; causae, quia ad eandem numero generationem ordinatur: sed ex parte subiecti habet diversitatem secundum numerum. Et ideo haec relatio est una et multiplex. Et secundum quod est multiplex ex parte subiecti, significatur his nominibus, *uxor et maritus*: secundum autem quod est una, significatur hoc nomine, *matrimonium*.

this joining, through being directed to some one thing, is matrimony; while the joining together of bodies and minds is a result of matrimony.

REPLY OBJ. 1: Matrimony is the bond by which they are tied formally, not effectively, and so it need not be distinct from the joining.

REPLY OBJ. 2: Although relation is not itself a sensible accident, its causes may be sensible. Nor is it necessary in a sacrament for that which is both reality and sacrament (III, Q. 66, A. 1) to be sensible (for such is the relation of the aforesaid joining to this sacrament), whereas the words expressive of consent, which are sacrament only and are the cause of that same joining, are sensible.

REPLY OBJ. 3: A relation is founded on something as its cause—for instance, likeness is founded on quality—and on something as its subject—for instance, in the things themselves that are like. On either hand we may find unity and diversity of relation. Since, then, it is not the same identical quality that conduces to likeness, but the same specific quality in each of the like subjects, and since, moreover, the subjects of likeness are two in number, and the same applies to equality, it follows that both equality and likeness are in every way numerically distinct in either of the like or equal subjects. But the relations of matrimony, on the one hand, have unity in both extremes, namely, on the part of the cause, since it is directed to the one identical begetting; whereas on the part of the subject there is numerical diversity. The fact of this relation having a diversity of subjects is signified by the terms *husband and wife*, while its unity is denoted by its being called *matrimony*.

Article 2

Whether Matrimony Is Fittingly Named?

AD SECUNDUM SIC PROCEDITUR. Videtur quod *matrimonium* incongrue nominetur. Quia denominatio debet fieri a digniori. Sed pater dignior est matre. Ergo magis debet denominari a patre quam a matre coniunctio utriusque.

PRAETEREA, res debet denominari ab eo quod est de essentia sua: quia *ratio quam significat nomen, est definitio*, ut dicitur in IV *Metaphys*. Sed nuptiae non sunt de essentia matrimonii. Ergo non debet matrimonium *nuptiae* appellari.

PRAETEREA, species non potest proprio nomine nominari ab eo quod est generis. Sed coniunctio est genus ad matrimonium. Ergo non potest proprie coniugium nominari.

OBJECTION 1: It would seem that *matrimony* is unfittingly named. For a thing should be named after that which ranks higher. But the father ranks above the mother. Therefore, the union of father and mother should rather be named after the father.

OBJ. 2: Further, a thing should be named from that which is essential to it, since a *definition expresses the nature signified by a name* (*Metaphysics* 4.28). Now nuptials are not essential to matrimony. Therefore, matrimony should not be called *nuptials*.

OBJ. 3: Further, a species cannot take its proper name from that which belongs to the genus. Now joining is the genus of matrimony. Therefore, it should not be called a conjugal union.

SED IN CONTRARIUM est communis usus loquentium.

RESPONDEO dicendum quod in matrimonio est tria considerare. Primo, essentiam ipsius, quae est coniunctio. Et secundum hoc vocatur *coniugium*.

Secundo, causam eius, quae est desponsatio. Et secundum hoc vocantur *nuptiae* a *nubere*: quia in ipsa solemnitate desponsationis, qua matrimonium perficitur, capita nubentium velantur.

Tertio, effectum, qui est proles. Et sic dicitur *matrimonium*: ut Augustinus dicit, contra Faustum, *ob hoc quod mulier non debet ad aliud nubere nisi ut sit mater*. Potest etiam dici matrimonium quasi *matris munium*, idest officium: quia feminis incumbit maxime educandae prolis officium. Vel dicitur matrimonium quasi *matrem muniens*: quia iam habet quo defendatur et muniatur, scilicet virum. Vel dicitur matrimonium quasi *matrem monens*, ne virum relinquat alteri adhaerens. Vel dicitur matrimonium quasi *materia unius*, quia in eo fit coniunctio ad unam prolem materialiter inducendam: ut dicatur matrimonium a *monos* et *materia*. Vel dicitur matrimonium, ut Isidorus dicit, a *matre* et *nato*: quia per matrimonium efficitur aliqua mater nati.

AD PRIMUM ergo dicendum quod, quamvis pater sit dignior quam mater, tamen circa prolem mater magis est officiosa quam pater. Vel ideo quia mulier ad hoc principaliter facta est ut sit homini in adiutorium prolis. Non autem vir propter hoc factus est. Unde magis pertinet ad rationem matrimonii mater quam pater.

AD SECUNDUM dicendum quod aliquando essentialia cognoscuntur per accidentalia. Et ideo etiam per accidentalia aliqua nominari possunt: cum nomen detur causa rei innotescendae.

AD TERTIUM dicendum quod aliquando species nominatur ab eo quod est generis propter imperfectionem speciei: quando scilicet complete habet generis rationem, nec tamen aliquid addit quod ad dignitatem pertineat; sicut proprium accidentale retinet nomen proprii communis. Aliquando autem propter perfectionem: quando in una specie complete invenitur ratio generis, et non in alia; sicut animal denominatur ab *anima*, quae competit animato corpori, quod est genus animalis, sed animatio non invenitur perfecte in animatis quae non sunt animalia. Et similiter est in proposito: quia coniunctio viri ad mulierem per matrimonium est maxima, cum sit et animarum et corporum. Et ideo coniugium nominatur.

I ANSWER THAT, Three things may be considered in matrimony. First, its essence, which is a joining together, and in reference to this it is called the *conjugal union*.

Second, its cause, which is the wedding, and in reference to this it is called the *nuptial union* from *nubere*, 'to veil', because at the wedding ceremony, whereby the marriage is completed, the heads of those who are wedded are covered with a veil.

Third, the effect, which is the offspring, and in reference to this it is called *matrimony*, as Augustine says (*Against Faustus* 19.26), because *a woman's sole purpose in marrying should be motherhood*. Matrimony may also be resolved into *matris munium*, i.e., a mother's duty, since the duty of bringing up the children chiefly devolves on the women; or into *matrem muniens*, because it provides the mother with a protector and support in the person of her husband; or into *matrem monens*, as admonishing her not to leave her husband and take up with another man; or into *materia unius*, because it is a joining together for the purpose of providing the matter of one offspring (as though it were derived from *monos* and *materia*); or into *matre* and *nato*, as Isidore says (*Etymologies* 9), because it makes a woman the mother of a child.

REPLY OBJ. 1: Although the father ranks above the mother, the mother has more to do with the offspring than the father has. Or we may say that woman was made chiefly in order to be man's helpmate in relation to the offspring, whereas the man was not made for this purpose. Therefore, the mother has a closer relation to the nature of marriage than the father has.

REPLY OBJ. 2: Sometimes essentials are known by accidentals, wherefore some things can be named even after their accidentals, since a name is given to a thing for the purpose that it may become known.

REPLY OBJ. 3: Sometimes a species is named after something pertaining to the genus on account of an imperfection in the species, namely, when it has the generic nature completely, yet adds nothing pertaining to dignity; thus the accidental property retains the name of 'property' which is common to it and to the definition. Sometimes, however, it is on account of a perfection, when we find the generic nature completely in one species and not in another; thus animal is named from *anima*, 'soul', and this belongs to an animate body, which is the genus of animal; yet animation is not found perfectly in those animate beings that are not animals. It is thus with the case in point, for the joining of husband and wife by matrimony is the greatest of all joinings, since it is a joining of soul and body, wherefore it is called a conjugal union.

Article 3

Whether Matrimony Is Fittingly Defined in the Text?

AD TERTIUM SIC PROCEDITUR. Videtur quod inconvenienter definiatur in littera. Quia in *mariti* definitione oportet quod matrimonium ponatur: quia maritus est qui est mulieri matrimonio iunctus. Sed ipse ponit *maritalem coniunctionem* in definitione matrimonii. Ergo videtur quod sit circulatio in definitionibus istis.

PRAETEREA, per matrimonium, sicut vir efficitur maritus mulieris, ita mulier uxor viri. Ergo non debet magis dici coniunctio *maritalis* quam *uxoria*.

PRAETEREA, consuetudo ad genus moris pertinet. Sed frequenter matrimonio iuncti sunt valde moribus diversi. Ergo non debet poni in definitione matrimonii, *individuam vitae consuetudinem retinens*.

PRAETEREA, inveniuntur aliae definitiones de matrimonio datae. Quia secundum Hugonem, matrimonium est *duarum idonearum personarum legitimus de coniunctione consensus*. Secundum quosdam autem *matrimonium est consortium communis vitae et communicatio divini et humani iuris*. Et quaeritur qualiter hae definitiones differant.

RESPONDEO dicendum quod, sicut dictum est, in matrimonio tria considerantur: scilicet causa ipsius, et essentia eius, et effectus. Et secundum hoc tres definitiones inveniuntur de matrimonio datae. Nam definitio Hugonis tangit causam, scilicet consensum: et per se nota est.

Definitio autem in littera posita tangit essentiam matrimonii, scilicet *coniunctionem*: Et addit determinatum subiectum, in hoc quod dicit *inter legitimas personas*. Ponit etiam differentiam contrahentem ad speciem, in hoc quod dicit maritalis: quia, cum matrimonium sit coniunctio in ordine ad aliquid unum, talis coniunctio in speciem trahitur per illud ad quod ordinatur; et hoc est id quod ad maritum pertinet. Ponit etiam virtutem huius coniunctionis, quia indissolubilis est, in hoc quod dicit, *individuam*, etc.

Sed alia definitio tangit effectum ad quem ordinatur matrimonium, scilicet *vita communis* in rebus domesticis. Et quia omnis communicatio aliqua lege ordinatur, ideo ponitur ordinativum istius communionis, scilicet *ius divinum et humanum*. Aliae autem communicationes, ut negotiatorum et militantium, solo iure humano institutae sunt.

AD PRIMUM ergo dicendum quod aliquando priora, ex quibus debet dari definitio, non sunt nominata; et ideo in definitione aliquorum poliuntur aliqua posteriora simpliciter quae sunt priora quoad nos; sicut in de-

OBJECTION 1: It would seem that matrimony is unfittingly defined in the text (*Sentences* IV, D. 27). For it is necessary to mention matrimony in defining *maritus*, husband, since it is the husband who is joined to the woman in matrimony. Now *marital union* is put in the definition of matrimony. Therefore, it seems that these definitions are circular.

OBJ. 2: Further, matrimony makes the woman the man's wife no less than it makes the man the woman's husband. Therefore, it should not be described as a *marital* union rather than an *uxorial* union.

OBJ. 3: Further, habit pertains to morals. Yet it often happens that married persons differ very much in habit. Therefore, the words *involving their living together in undivided partnership* should have no place in the definition of matrimony.

OBJ. 4: Further, we find other definitions given of matrimony, for according to Hugh (*Summa Sent.* vii, 6), *matrimony is the lawful consent of two apt persons to be joined together*. Also, according to some, *matrimony is the fellowship of a common life and a community regulated by divine and human law*; and we ask how these definitions differ.

I ANSWER THAT, As stated above (A. 2), three things are to be considered in matrimony: namely, its cause, its essence, and its effect. Accordingly, we find three definitions given of matrimony. For the definition of Hugh indicates the cause, namely, the consent, and this definition is self-evident.

The definition given in the text indicates the essence of matrimony, namely, the *union*, and adds determinate subjects by the words *between lawful persons*. It also points to the difference of the contracting parties in reference to the species, by the word *marital*, for, since matrimony is a joining together for the purpose of some one thing, this joining together is specified by the purpose to which it is directed, and this is what pertains to the husband. It also indicates the force of this joining—for it is indissoluble—by the words *involving*, etc.

The remaining definition indicates the effect to which matrimony is directed, namely, the *common life* in family matters. And since every community is regulated by some law, the code according to which this community is directed, namely, *divine and human law*, finds a place in this definition, while other communities, such as those of traders or soldiers, are established by human law alone.

REPLY OBJ. 1: Sometimes the prior things from which a definition ought to be given are not known to us, and consequently certain things are defined from things that are posterior simply, but prior to us; thus in the definition

finitione qualitatis ponitur *quale* a Philosopho, cum dicit: *qualitas est secundum quam quales dicimur*. Et ita etiam hic in definitione matrimonii ponitur *maritalis*: ut sit sensus quod matrimonium est *coniunctio ad ea quae mariti officium requirit*, quae non poterant uno nominari nomine.

AD SECUNDUM dicendum quod per hanc differentiam tangitur finis coniunctionis, ut dictum est. Et quia, ut dicit Apostolus, *vir non est propter mulierem, sed mulier propter virum*, ideo haec differentia potius debet sumi a viro quam a muliere.

AD TERTIUM dicendum quod, sicut vita civilis non importat actum singularem huius vel illius, sed ea quae ad communicationem civilem pertinent; ita vita coniugalis nihil aliud est quam conversatio ad communicationem talem pertinens. Et ideo quantum ad hanc vitam semper consuetudo est individua: quamvis sit diversa quantum ad actus singulares utriusque.

AD QUARTUM patet solutio ex dictis.

of quality the Philosopher employs the word *such* when he says (*Categories*) that *quality is that whereby we are said to be such*. Thus, too, in defining matrimony we say that it is a *marital union*, by which we mean that matrimony is a *union for the purpose of those things required by the marital office*, all of which could not be expressed in one word.

REPLY OBJ. 2: As stated (A. 2), this difference indicates the end of the union. And since, according to the Apostle, the *man is not for the woman, but the woman for the man* (1 Cor 11:9), it follows that this difference should be indicated in reference to the man rather than the woman.

REPLY OBJ. 3: Just as the civic life denotes not the individual act of this or that one, but the things that concern the common action of the citizens, so the conjugal life is nothing else than a particular kind of companionship pertaining to that common action. Therefore, as regards this same life, the partnership of married persons is always indivisible, although it is divisible as regards the act belonging to each party.

THE REPLY to the fourth objection is clear from what has been said above.

QUESTION 45

THE CONSENT OF MATRIMONY IN ITSELF

Consequenter considerandum est de consensu. Ubi primo agendum est de consensu secundum se considerato; secundo, de consensu iuramento vel carnali copula firmato; tertio, de consensu coacto et conditionato; quarto, de obiecto consensus.

Circa primum quaeruntur quinque.

Primo: utrum consensus sit causa efficiens matrimonii.

Secundo: utrum consensum oporteat per verba exprimi.

Tertio: utrum consensus expressus per verba de futuro faciat matrimonium.

Quarto: utrum consensus expressio per verba, si desit interior consensus, faciat matrimonium.

Quinto: utrum consensus in occulto factus per verba de praesenti faciat matrimonium.

In the next place we have to consider the consent: (1) The consent considered in itself; (2) The consent confirmed by oath or by carnal intercourse; (3) Compulsory consent and conditional consent; (4) The object of the consent.

Under the first head there are five points of inquiry:

(1) Whether the consent is the efficient cause of matrimony?

(2) Whether the consent needs to be expressed in words?

(3) Whether consent given in words expressive of the future makes a marriage?

(4) Whether consent given in words expressive of the present, without inward consent, makes a marriage?

(5) Whether consent given secretly in words expressive of the present makes a marriage?

Article 1

Whether Consent Is the Efficient Cause of Matrimony?

AD PRIMUM SIC PROCEDITUR: Videtur quod consensus non sit causa efficiens matrimonii. Sacramenta enim non sunt a voluntate humana, sed ab institutione divina. Sed consensus ad voluntatem pertinet. Ergo non est causa matrimonii, sicut nec aliorum sacramentorum.

PRAETEREA, idem non est causa sui ipsius. Sed matrimonium nihil aliud videtur esse quam consensus: quia consensus ipse significat coniunctionem Christi ad Ecclesiam. Ergo consensus non est causa matrimonii.

PRAETEREA, unius debet esse una causa. Sed matrimonium inter duos est unum, ut dictum est. Consensus autem duorum sunt diversi, quia diversorum sunt, et in diversa: ab una enim parte est consensus in virum, ex alia in uxorem. Ergo mutuus consensus non est causa matrimonii.

SED CONTRA: Est quod Chrysostomus dicit: *matrimonium non facit coitus, sed voluntas.*

PRAETEREA, unus non accipit potestatem in eo quod est libere alterius, nisi per eius consensum. Sed per matrimonium accipit uter que coniugum potestatem in corpus alterius, ut patet I Cor. 7, cum prius uterque liberam

OBJECTION 1: It would seem that consent is not the efficient cause of matrimony. For the sacraments depend not on the human will but on the divine institution, as shown above (*Sentences* IV, D. 2; III, Q. 64, A. 2). But consent belongs to the human will. Therefore, it is no more the cause of matrimony than of the other sacraments.

OBJ. 2: Further, nothing is its own cause. But seemingly matrimony is nothing else than the consent, since it is the consent which signifies the union of Christ with the Church. Therefore, consent is not the cause of matrimony.

OBJ. 3: Further, of one thing there should be one cause. Now there is one marriage between two persons, as stated above (Q. 44, A. 1); whereas the consents of the two parties are distinct, for they are given by different persons and to different things, since on the one hand there is consent to take a husband, and on the other hand consent to take a wife. Therefore, mutual consent is not the cause of matrimony.

ON THE CONTRARY, Chrysostom says: *it is not coition but consent that makes a marriage* (Hom. 32 in the *Opus Imperfectum*).

FURTHER, One person does not receive power over that which is at the free disposal of another without the latter's consent. Now by marriage each of the married parties receives power over the other's body (1 Cor 7:4), whereas be-

potestatem sui corporis haberet. Ergo consensus facit matrimonium.

RESPONDEO dicendum quod in omnibus sacramentis est aliqua spiritualis operatio, mediante materiali operatione quae eam significat: sicut per ablutionem corporalem in baptismo fit ablutio interior spiritualis. Unde, cum in matrimonio sit quaedam spiritualis coniunctio, inquantum matrimonium est sacramentum; et aliqua materialis, secundum quod est in officium naturae et civilis vitae: oportet quod mediante materiali fiat spiritualis virtute divina. Unde, cum coniunctiones materialium contractuum fiant per mutuum consensum, oportet quod hoc modo etiam fiat matrimonialis coniunctio.

AD PRIMUM ergo dicendum quod sacramentorum prima causa est *divina virtus, quae in eis operatur salutem*: sed causae secundae instrumentales sunt materiales operationes ex divina institutione habentes efficaciam. Et sic consensus in matrimonio est causa.

AD SECUNDUM dicendum quod matrimonium non est ipse consensus, sed quaedam unio ordinatorum ad unum, ut dictum est, quam consensus facit. Nec consensus, proprie loquendo, coniunctionem Christi ad Ecclesiam significat: sed voluntatem eius, qua factum est ut Ecclesiae coniungeretur.

AD TERTIUM dicendum quod, sicut matrimonium est unum ex parte eius in quod fit coniunctio, quamvis sit multiplex ex parte coniunctorum; ita etiam consensus est unus ex parte eius in quod consentitur, scilicet praedictae coniunctionis, quamvis multiplex ex parte consentientium. Nec est directe consensus in virum, sed in coniunctionem ad virum, ex parte uxoris; et similiter, ex parte viri, consensus in coniunctionem ad uxorem.

fore this each had free power over his own body. Therefore, consent makes a marriage.

I ANSWER THAT, In every sacrament there is a spiritual operation by means of a material operation which signifies it; thus in baptism the inward spiritual cleansing is effected by a bodily cleansing. Wherefore, since in matrimony there is a kind of spiritual joining together, insofar as matrimony is a sacrament, and a certain material joining together, insofar as it is directed to an office of nature and of civil life, it follows that the spiritual joining is the effect of the divine power by means of the material joining. Therefore, seeing that the joinings of material contracts are effected by mutual consent, it follows that the joining together of marriage is effected in the same way.

REPLY OBJ. 1: The first cause of the sacraments is the *divine power which works in them the welfare of the soul*; but the second or instrumental causes are material operations deriving their efficacy from the divine institution, and thus consent is the cause in matrimony.

REPLY OBJ. 2: Matrimony is not the consent itself, but the union of persons directed to one purpose, as stated above (Q. 44, A. 1), and this union is the effect of the consent. Moreover, the consent, properly speaking, signifies not the union of Christ with the Church, but his will whereby his union with the Church was brought about.

REPLY OBJ. 3: Just as marriage is one on the part of the object to which the union is directed, whereas it is more than one on the part of the persons united, so too the consent is one on the part of the thing consented to, namely, the aforesaid union, whereas it is more than one on the part of the persons consenting. Nor is the direct object of consent a husband, but union with a husband, on the part of the wife, even as it is union with a wife on the part of the husband.

Article 2

Whether the Consent Needs to Be Expressed in Words?

AD SECUNDUM SIC PROCEDITUR. Videtur quod non oportet consensum per verba exprimi. Quia sicut per matrimonium redigitur homo in potestatem alterius, ita per votum. Sed votum obligat quoad Deum etiam si non exprimatur verbis. Ergo et consensus facit matrimonii obligationem etiam sine expressione verborum.

PRAETEREA, matrimonium potest esse inter aliquos qui suum consensum sibi mutuo verbis exprimere non possunt, quia vel sunt muti, vel diversarum linguarum. Ergo expressio consensus per verba non requiritur ad matrimonium.

PRAETEREA, si omittatur illud quod est de necessitate sacramenti quacumque ex causa, non est sacramentum. Sed in aliquo casu est matrimonium sine expressio-

OBJECTION 1: It would seem that there is no need for the consent to be expressed in words. For a man is brought under another's power by a vow just as he is by matrimony. Now a vow is binding in God's sight, even though it be not expressed in words. Therefore, consent also makes a marriage binding, even without being expressed in words.

OBJ. 2: Further, there can be marriage between persons who are unable to express their mutual consent in words, through being dumb or of different languages. Therefore, expression of the consent by words is not required for matrimony.

OBJ. 3: Further, if that which is essential to a sacrament be omitted for any reason whatever, there is no sacrament. Now there is a case of marriage without the expression of

ne verborum: sicut quando puella tacet prae verecundia, parentibus eam viro tradentibus. Ergo expressio verborum non est de necessitate matrimonii.

SED CONTRA: Matrimonium est sacramentum quoddam. Sed in omni sacramento requiritur aliquod sensibile signum. Ergo et in matrimonio. Et ita oportet ibi saltem esse verba exprimentia consensum sensibiliter.

PRAETEREA, in matrimonio fit contractus inter virum et mulierem. Sed in quolibet contractu oportet esse expressionem verborum, quibus se mutuo homines obligent. Ergo et in matrimonio oportet esse consensum per verba expressum.

RESPONDEO dicendum quod, sicut ex dictis patet, coniunctio matrimonialis fit ad modum obligationis in contractibus materialibus. Et quia materiales contractus non possunt fieri nisi sibi, invicem voluntatem suam verbis promant qui contrahunt, ideo etiam oportet, quod consensus matrimonium faciens verbis exprimatur: ut expressio verborum se habeat ad matrimonium sicut ablutio exterior ad baptismum.

AD PRIMUM ergo dicendum quod in voto non est aliqua sacramentalis obligatio, sed spiritualis tantum. Et ideo non oportet quod fiat ad modum materialium contractuum ad hoc quod obliget, sicut est de matrimonio.

AD SECUNDUM dicendum quod, quamvis non possint vota, sua mutuo verbis tales exprimere, possunt tamen exprimere nutibus. Et tales nutus pro verbis computantur.

AD TERTIUM dicendum quod, sicut dicit Hugo de Sancto Victore, *eos qui coniunguntur sic oportet consentire ut invicem se spontanee recipiant: quod iudicatur fieri si in desponsatione non contradicant.* Unde verba parentum computantur in casu, illo ac si essent puellae: sunt enim sufficiens signum quod sunt eius, ex quo non contradicit.

words, as when the maid is silent through bashfulness when her parents give her away to the bridegroom. Therefore, the expression of words is not essential to matrimony.

ON THE CONTRARY, Matrimony is a sacrament. Now a sensible sign is required in every sacrament. Therefore, it is also required in matrimony, and consequently there must be at least words by which the consent is made perceptible to the senses.

FURTHER, In matrimony there is a contract between husband and wife. Now in every contract there must be expression of the words by which men bind themselves mutually to one another. Therefore, in matrimony also the consent must be expressed in words.

I ANSWER THAT, As stated above (A. 1), the marriage union is effected in the same way as the bond in material contracts. And since material contracts are not feasible unless the contracting parties express their will to one another in words, it follows that the consent which makes a marriage must also be expressed in words, so that the expression of words is to marriage what the outward washing is to baptism.

REPLY OBJ. 1: In a vow there is not a sacramental but only a spiritual bond, wherefore there is no need for it to be done in the same way as material contracts in order that it be binding, as in the case of matrimony.

REPLY OBJ. 2: Although the like cannot plight themselves to one another in words, they can do so by signs, and such signs count for words.

REPLY OBJ. 3: According to Hugh of St. Victor (Tract. vii, *Sum. Sent.*), *persons who are being married should give their consent by accepting one another freely, and this is judged to be the case if they show no dissent when they are being wedded.* Hence in such a case the words of the parents are taken as being the maid's, for the fact that she does not contradict them is a sign that they are her words.

Article 3

Whether Consent Given in Words Expressive of the Future Makes a Marriage?

AD TERTIUM SIC PROCEDITUR. Videtur quod consensus expressus per verba de futuro matrimonium faciat. Quia sicut se habet praesens ad praesens, ita futurum ad futurum. Sed consensus per verba de praesenti expressus facit matrimonium in praesenti. Ergo consensus expressus per verba de futuro facit matrimonium in futuro.

PRAETEREA, sicut in matrimonio fit quaedam obligatio, per verba exprimentia consensum, ita et in aliis civilibus contractibus. Sed in aliis contractibus non differt

OBJECTION 1: It would seem that consent given in words expressive of the future makes a marriage. For as present is to present, so is future to future. But consent given in words expressive of the present makes a marriage in the present. Therefore, consent given in words expressive of the future makes a marriage in the future.

OBJ. 2: Further, in other civil contracts, just as in matrimony, a certain obligation results from the words expressing consent. Now in other contracts, it matters not whether

utrum per verba de praesenti vel de futuro obligatio fiat. Ergo nec in matrimonio differt.

PRAETEREA, per votum religionis homo contrahit matrimonium spirituale cum Deo. Sed votum religionis fit per verba de futuro, et obligat. Ergo et similiter potest fieri matrimonium per verba de futuro.

SED CONTRA: Est quia ille qui consentit in aliquam per verba de futuro, et postea cum alia per verba de praesenti, secundum iura debet habere secundam uxorem. Sed hoc non esset si consensus per verba de futuro faceret matrimonium: quia ex quo verum est; matrimonium cum una, ea vivente non potest contrahi cum alia. Ergo consensus per verba de futuro non facit matrimonium.

PRAETEREA, qui promittit aliquid se facturum, nondum facit illud. Sed qui consentit per verba de futuro, promittit se cum aliqua contracturum matrimonium. Ergo non contrahit adhuc cum illa.

RESPONDEO dicendum quod causae sacramentales significando efficiunt: unde *hoc efficiunt quod significant*. Et quia, cum aliquis consensum suum per verba de futuro exprimit, non significat se facere matrimonium, sed promittit se facturum, ideo talis expressio consensus non facit matrimonium, sed sponsionem eius, quae sponsalia nominantur.

AD PRIMUM ergo dicendum quod, cum consensus exprimitur per verba de praesenti, et verba sunt praesentia, et in praesens consentitur pro eodem tempore. Sed quando consensus fit per verba de futuro, verba sunt praesentia, sed consentitur in futurum. Et ideo non pro eodem tempore. Et propter hoc non est simile.

AD SECUNDUM dicendum quod etiam in aliis contractibus qui verbis futuris utitur non transfert potestatem rei suae in alterum, ut si dicat, *dabo tibi*: sed solum quando verbis praesentibus utitur.

AD TERTIUM dicendum quod in voto professionis actus spiritualis matrimonii per verba de fututo exprimitur, scilicet obedientia vel observantia regulae: et non ipsum matrimonium spirituale. Si autem spirituale matrimonium in futurum voveatur, non est matrimonium spirituale: quia nondum ex hoc aliquis est monachus, sed se futurum monachum pollicetur.

the obligation is effected by words of the present or of the future tense. Therefore, neither does it make any difference in matrimony.

OBJ. 3: Further, by the religious vow man contracts a spiritual marriage with God. Now the religious vow is expressed in words of the future tense, and is binding. Therefore, carnal marriage also can be effected by words of the future tense.

ON THE CONTRARY, A man who consents in words of the future tense to take a particular woman as his wife, and after, by words of the present tense, consents to take another, according to law must take the second for his wife (*Decretals*). But this would not be the case if consent given in words of the future tense made a marriage, since from the very fact that his marriage with the one is valid, he cannot, as long as she lives, marry another. Therefore, consent given in words of the future tense does not make a marriage.

FURTHER, He who promises to do a certain thing does it not yet. Now he who consents in words of the future tense promises to marry a certain woman. Therefore, he does not marry her yet.

I ANSWER THAT, The sacramental causes produce their effect by signifying it; hence *they effect what they signify*. Since, therefore, when a man expresses his consent by words of the future tense he does not signify that he is marrying, but promises that he will marry, it follows that a consent expressed in this manner does not make a marriage, but a promise of marriage, and this promise is known as a betrothal.

REPLY OBJ. 1: When consent is expressed in words of the present tense, not only are the words actually present, but consent is directed to the present, so that they coincide in point of time; but when consent is given in words of the future tense, although the words are actually present, the consent is directed to a future time, and hence they do not coincide in point of time. For this reason the comparison fails.

REPLY OBJ. 2: Even in other contracts, a man who uses words referring to the future does not transfer the power over his property to another person—for instance, if he were to say *I will give you*—but only when he uses words indicative of the present.

REPLY OBJ. 3: In the vow of religious profession it is not the spiritual marriage itself that is expressed in words which refer to the future, but an act of the spiritual marriage, namely, obedience or observance of the rule. If, however, a man vows spiritual marriage in the future, it is not a spiritual marriage, for a man does not become a monk by taking such a vow, but promises to become one.

Article 4

Whether, in the Absence of Inward Consent, a Marriage Is
Made by Consent Given in Words of the Present?

AD QUARTUM SIC PROCEDITUR. Videtur quod consensus expressio, etiam per verba, si desit interior consensus, faciat matrimonium. Quia *fraus et dolus nemini patrocinari debet*, secundum iura. Sed ille qui verbis exprimit Consensum quem in corde non habet, dolum committit. Ergo non debet sibi patrocinari, ut ab obligatione matrimonii liber reddatur.

PRAETEREA, consensus mentalis alterius non potest esse alicui notus nisi quatenus per verba exprimitur. Si ergo expressio verborum non sufficit, sed consensus interior requiritur in utroque coniugum, tunc neuter poterit scire de altero an sit ei verus coniux. Et ita erit fornicator quandocumque matrimonio utetur.

PRAETEREA, si aliquis probatur per verba de praesenti in aliquam consensisse, cogitur per excommunicationis sententiam ut eam habeat iri uxorem, quamvis dicat consensum mentalem defuisse, etiam si postea cum alia contraxerit consensu mentali verbis expresso. Sed hoc non esset si requireretur consensus mentalis ad matrimonium. Ergo non requiritur.

SED CONTRA: Est quod Innocentius III dicit, in decretali quadam, in casu isto loqueris: *sine consensu nequeunt cetera foedus perficere coniugale.*

PRAETEREA, intentio requiritur in omnibus sacramentis: Sed ille qui corde non consentit, non habet intentionem matrimonii contrahendi. Ergo non fit matrimonium.

RESPONDEO dicendum quod, sicut se habet ablutio exterior ad baptismum, ita se habet expressio verborum ad hoc sacramentum, ut dictum est. Unde sicut, si aliquis ablutionem exteriorem reciperet non intendens recipere sacramentum sed ludum et dolum facere, non esset baptizatus; ita expressio verborum sine interiori consensu matrimonium non facit.

AD PRIMUM ergo dicendum quod ibi sunt duo: scilicet defectus consensus, qui sibi patrocinatur in foro conscientiae, ut non adstringatur vinculo matrimonii, quamvis non in foro Ecclesiae, in quo iudicatur secundum allegata; et dolus verborum, et hic non patrocinatur nec in foro poenitentiae nec in foro Ecclesiae, quia in utroque pro hoc punitur.

AD SECUNDUM dicendum quod, si desit consensus mentalis ex parte unius, ex neutra parte est matrimonium: quia matrimonium consistit in mutua coniunctione, ut dictum est. Tamen probabiliter potest credi do-

OBJECTION 1: It would seem that even in the absence of inward consent a marriage is made by consent expressed in words of the present. For *fraud and deceit should benefit no man*, according to the law (*Decretals*). Now he who gives consent in words without consenting in heart commits a fraud. Therefore, he should not benefit by it through being released of the bond of marriage.

OBJ. 2: Further, the mental consent of one person cannot be known to another except insofar as it is expressed in words. If, then, the expression of the words is not enough, and inward consent is required in both parties, neither of them will be able to know that he is truly married to the other; and consequently whenever he uses marriage he will commit fornication.

OBJ. 3: Further, if a man is proved to have consented to take a certain woman to wife in words of the present tense, he is compelled under pain of excommunication to take her as his wife, even though he should say that he was wanting in mental consent, notwithstanding that afterwards he may have contracted marriage with another woman by words expressive of consent in the present. But this would not be the case if mental consent were requisite for marriage. Therefore, it is not required.

ON THE CONTRARY, Innocent III says in a Decretal (*Register*) in reference to this case: *other things cannot complete the marriage bond in the absence of consent.*

FURTHER, Intention is necessary in all the sacraments. Now he who consents not in his heart has no intention of contracting marriage; therefore, he does not contract a marriage.

I ANSWER THAT, The outward cleansing stands in the same relation to baptism as the expression of words to this sacrament, as stated above (A. 2). Wherefore, just as were a person to receive the outward cleansing with the intention not of receiving the sacrament, but of acting in jest or deceit, he would not be baptized; so, too, expression of words without inward consent makes no marriage.

REPLY OBJ. 1: There are two things here: namely, the lack of consent—which benefits him in the tribunal of his conscience so that he is not bound by the marriage tie, although not in the tribunal of the Church where judgment is pronounced according to the evidence—and the deceit in the words, which does not benefit him, neither in the tribunal of his conscience nor in the tribunal of the Church, since in both he is punished for this.

REPLY OBJ. 2: If mental consent is lacking in one of the parties, on neither side is there marriage, since marriage consists in a mutual joining together, as stated above (Q. 44, A. 1). However, one may believe that in all probabil-

lus non esse, nisi signa evidentia doli appareant: quia de quolibet praesumendum est bonum nisi probetur contrarium. Unde ille ex cuius parte dolus non est, a peccato excusatur per ignorantiam.

AD TERTIUM dicendum quod in tali casu Ecclesia compellit eum ad standum cum prima uxore, quia secundum ea iudicat *quae foris apparent*: nec decipitur in iustitia, quamvis decipiatur in facto: Sed ille debet potius excommunicationem sustinere quam ad primam uxorem accedat; vel in alias regiones remotas fugere.

ity there is no fraud unless there be evident signs thereof; because we must presume good of everyone unless there be proof of the contrary. Consequently, the party in whom there is no fraud is excused from sin on account of ignorance.

REPLY OBJ. 3: In such a case the Church compels him to hold to his first wife, because the Church judges according *to outward appearances*; nor is she deceived in justice, although she is deceived in the facts of the case. Yet such a man ought to bear the excommunication rather than return to his first wife; or else he should go far away into another country.

Article 5

Whether Consent Given Secretly in Words of the Present Makes a Marriage?

AD QUINTUM SIC PROCEDITUR. Videtur quod consensus in occulto factus per verba de praesenti non faciat matrimonium. Res enim in potestate alterius existens non transfertur in potestatem alterius nisi consentiente illo in cuius potestate erat. Sed puella erat in potestate patris. Ergo non potest per matrimonium transire in potestatem viri nisi patre consentiente. Et ita, si fiat in occulto consensus, etiam per verba de praesenti expressus, non erit matrimonium.

PRAETEREA, sicut in matrimonio est actus noster quasi de essentia sacramenti, ita in poenitentia. Sed sacramentum poenitentiae non perficitur nisi mediantibus Ecclesiae ministris, qui sunt sacramentorum dispensatores. Ergo nec matrimonium perfici potest in occulto, absque sacerdotali benedictione.

PRAETEREA, baptismus, quia potest in occulto et in aperto fieri, non prohibetur ab Ecclesia fieri in occulto. Sed Ecclesia prohibet clandestina matrimonia. Ergo non possunt fieri in occulto.

PRAETEREA, inter eos qui in secundo gradu sibi attinent, matrimonium contrahi non potest quia Ecclesia prohibuit. Sed similiter Ecclesia prohibuit clandestina matrimonia. Ergo non possunt esse vera matrimonia.

SED CONTRA: Posita causa ponitur effectus. Sed causa efficiens matrimonii est consensus per verba de praesenti expressus. Ergo, sive fiat in publico sive in occulto, matrimonium sequetur.

PRAETEREA, ubi est debita materia et debita forma, ibi est sacramentum. Sed in occulto, matrimonio servatur debita forma, quia sunt ibi verba de praesenti consensum exprimentia; et debita materia, quia sunt legitimae personae ad contrahendum. Ergo, est ibi verum matrimonium.

OBJECTION 1: It would seem that consent given secretly in words of the present does not make a marriage. For a thing that is in one person's power is not transferred to the power of another without the consent of the person in whose power it was. Now the maid is in her father's power. Therefore, she cannot by marriage be transferred to a husband's power without her father's consent. Wherefore if consent be given secretly, even though it should be expressed in words of the present, there will be no marriage.

OBJ. 2: Further, in penance, just as in matrimony, our act is, as it were, essential to the sacrament. But the sacrament of penance is not made complete except by means of the ministers of the Church, who are the dispensers of the sacraments. Therefore, neither can marriage be perfected without the priest's blessing.

OBJ. 3: Further, the Church does not forbid baptism to be given secretly, since one may baptize either privately or publicly. But the Church does forbid the celebration of clandestine marriages (*Decretals*). Therefore, they cannot be done secretly.

OBJ. 4: Further, marriage cannot be contracted by those who are related in the second degree, because the Church has forbidden it. But the Church has also forbidden clandestine marriages. Therefore, they cannot be valid marriages.

ON THE CONTRARY, Given the cause, the effect follows. Now the efficient cause of matrimony is consent expressed in words of the present. Therefore, whether this be done in public or in private, the result is a marriage.

FURTHER, Wherever there is the due matter and the due form of a sacrament, there is the sacrament. Now in a secret marriage there is the due matter, since there are persons who are able lawfully to contract, and the due form, since there are the words of the present expressive of consent. Therefore, there is a true marriage.

Respondeo dicendum quod, sicut in aliis sacramentis quaedam sunt de essentia sacramenti, quibus omissis non est sacramentum; quaedam autem ad solemnitatem sacramenti pertinent, quibus omissis verum perficitur sacramentum, quamvis peccet qui omittit: ita etiam consensus expressus per verba de praesenti, inter personas legitimas ad contrahendum, matrimonium facit. Quia haec duo sunt de essentia sacramenti: alia autem omnia sunt de solemnitate sacramenti, quia ad hoc adhibentur ut matrimonium convenientius fiat. Unde, si omittantur, verum est matrimonium: quamvis peccent sic contrahentes, nisi per aliquam legitimam causam excusentur.

Ad primum ergo dicendum quod puella non est in potestate patris quasi ancilla, ut sui corporis potestatem non habeat, sed quasi filia ad educandum. Et ideo, secundum hoc quod libera est, potest se in potestate alterius absque consensu patris dare; sicut etiam potest aliquis vel aliqua intrare religionem absque consensu parentum, cum sit persona libera.

Ad secundum dicendum quod actus noster in poenitentia, quamvis sit de essentia sacramenti, non est sufficiens ad inducendum proximum effectum, scilicet absolutionem a peccatis: et ideo oportet quod ad perfectionem sacramenti interveniat actus sacerdotis. Sed in matrimonio actus nostri sunt causa sufficiens ad inducendum proximum effectum, qui est obligatio: quia quicumque est sui iuris, potest se alteri obligare. Et ideo sacerdotis benedictio non requiritur in matrimonio quasi de essentia sacramenti.

Ad tertium dicendum quod etiam prohibitum est quod baptismum nullus accipiat nisi a sacerdote, nisi in articulo necessitatis. Matrimonium autem non est sacramentum necessitatis. Et ideo non est similis ratio.

Prohibentur autem clandestina matrimonia propter pericula quae inde evenire solent. Quia frequenter in talibus est aliqua fraus ex altera parte; frequenter etiam ad alia coniugia transeunt, dum poenitent de his quae subito facta surit; et multa alia mala inde accidunt. Et speciem turpitudinis praeter hoc habent.

Ad quartum dicendum quod non sunt prohibita clandestina matrimonia quasi contra essentialia matrimonii existentia, sicut sunt prohibita matrimonia illegitimarum personarum, quae sunt materia indebita huic sacramento. Et ideo non est simile.

I answer that, Just as in the other sacraments certain things are essential to the sacrament, and if they are omitted there is no sacrament, while certain things belong to the solemnization of the sacrament, and if these be omitted the sacrament is nevertheless validly performed, although it is a sin to omit them; so, too, consent expressed in words of the present between persons lawfully qualified to contract makes a marriage. For these two conditions are essential to the sacrament, while all else belongs to the solemnization of the sacrament, as being done in order that the marriage may be more fittingly performed. Hence if these be omitted it is a true marriage, although the contracting parties sin unless they have a lawful motive for being excused.

Reply Obj. 1: The maid is in her father's power not as a female slave without power over her own body, but as a daughter for the purpose of education. Hence, insofar as she is free, she can give herself into another's power without her father's consent, even as a son or daughter, since they are free, may enter religion without their parent's consent.

Reply Obj. 2: In penance our act, although essential to the sacrament, does not suffice for producing the proximate effect of the sacrament, namely, forgiveness of sins, and consequently it is necessary that the act of the priest intervene in order that the sacrament be perfected. But in matrimony our acts are the sufficient cause for the production of the proximate effect, which is the marriage bond, because whoever has the right to dispose of himself can bind himself to another. Consequently, the priest's blessing is not required for matrimony as being essential to the sacrament.

Reply Obj. 3: It is also forbidden to receive baptism otherwise than from a priest, except in a case of necessity. But matrimony is not a necessary sacrament: and consequently the comparison fails.

However, clandestine marriages are forbidden on account of the evil results to which they are liable, since it often happens that one of the parties is guilty of fraud in such marriages; frequently, too, they have recourse to other nuptials when they repent of having married in haste; and many other evils result therefrom. Besides, there is something disgraceful about them.

Reply Obj. 4: Clandestine marriages are not forbidden as though they were contrary to the essentials of marriage in the same way as the marriages of unlawful persons, who are undue matter for this sacrament; and hence there is no comparison.

QUESTION 46

THE CONSENT TO WHICH AN OATH OR CARNAL INTERCOURSE IS ADDED

Deinde considerandum est de consensu cui advenit iuramentum vel copula carnalis.

Circa quod quaeruntur duo.

Primo: utrum iuramentum adiunctum consensui per verba de fututor expresso, faciat matrimonium.

Secundo: utrum copula carnalis eidem consensui adveniens faciat matrimonium.

We must now consider the consent to which an oath or carnal intercourse is appended.

Under this head there are two points of inquiry:

(1) Whether an oath added to the consent that is expressed in words of the future tense makes a marriage?

(2) Whether carnal intercourse supervening to such a consent makes a marriage?

Article 1

Whether an Oath Added to the Consent That Is Expressed in
Words of the Future Tense Makes a Marriage?

AD PRIMUM SIC PROCEDITUR. Videtur quod iuramentum adiunctum consensui per verba de futuro expresso, faciat matrimonium. Nullus enim potest se obligare ut faciat contra ius divinum. Sed implere iuramentum est de iure divino: ut patet Matth. 5: *reddes autem Domino iuramenta tua*. Ergo per nullam obligationem sequentem potest evenire quod homo non debeat tenere iuramentum prius factum. Si ergo post consensum in aliquam per verba de futuro iuramento firmatum, aliquis alteri se obligat per verba de praesenti; videtur quod nihilominus debeat iuramentum primum servare. Sed hoc non esset nisi iuramento illo esset matrimonium illud perfectum. Ergo iuramentum adiunctum consensui per verba de futuro, facit matrimonium.

PRAETEREA, veritas divina fortior est quam veritas humana. Sed per iuramentum veritate divina firmatur aliquid. Cum ergo verba exprimentia consensum de praesenti, in quibus est sola veritas humana, matrimonium perficiant; videtur quod multo amplius id efficere possint verba de futuro iuramento firmata.

PRAETEREA, secundum Apostolum, ad Heb., *omnis controversiae finis est iuramentum*. Ergo, in iudicio saltem, plus standum est iuramento quam simplici verbo. Si ergo aliquis simplici verbo consentiat in aliquam per verba de praesenti postquam consenserit in aliam per verba de futuro iuramento firmata, videtur quod iudicio Ecclesiae debeat compelli stare cum prima, et non cum secunda.

PRAETEREA, verba de futuro simpliciter prolata faciunt sponsalia. Sed iuramentum ibi aliquid operatur.

OBJECTION 1: It would seem that if an oath be added to a consent that is expressed in words of the future tense, it makes a marriage. For no one can bind himself to act against the divine law. But the fulfilling of an oath is of divine law, according to Matthew 5:33: *you shall render your oaths to the Lord*. Consequently, no subsequent obligation can relieve a man of the obligation to keep an oath previously taken. If, therefore, after consenting to marry a woman by words expressive of the future and confirming that consent with an oath, a man binds himself to another woman by words expressive of the present, it would seem that nonetheless he is bound to keep his former oath. But this would not be the case unless that oath made the marriage complete. Therefore, an oath affixed to a consent expressed in words of the future tense makes a marriage.

OBJ. 2: Further, divine truth is stronger than human truth. Now an oath confirms a thing with the divine truth. Since, then, words expressive of consent in the present, in which there is mere human truth, complete a marriage, it would seem that much more is this the case with words of the future confirmed by an oath.

OBJ. 3: Further, according to the Apostle, *an oath for confirmation is the end of all controversy* (Heb 6:16); wherefore in a court of justice, at any rate, one must stand by an oath rather than by a mere affirmation. Therefore, if a man consent to marry a woman by a simple affirmation expressed in words of the present, after having consented to marry another in words of the future confirmed by oath, it would seem that in the judgment of the Church he should be compelled to take the first and not the second as his wife.

OBJ. 4: Further, the simple uttering of words relating to the future makes a betrothal. But the addition of an oath

319

Ergo facit plus quam sponsalia. Sed ultra sponsalia non est nisi matrimonium. Ergo faciunt matrimonium.

SED CONTRA: Quod futurum est, non est. Sed iuramentum additum non facit quin verba futuro significent consensum de futuro. Ergo adhuc matrimonium non est.

PRAETEREA, postquam perfectum est matrimonium, non oportet quod alius consensus interveniat ad matrimonium. Sed post iuramentum advehit alius consensus, qui matrimonium facit: alias frustra iuraretur illud esse futurum. Ergo non facit matrimonium.

RESPONDEO dicendum quod iuramentum adhibetur ad confirmationem dictorum. Unde illud tantum confirmat quod in dictis significatur, nec significatum mutat. Et ideo, cum verba de futuro ex ipsa significatione sua habeant quod matrimonium non faciant, quia quod futurum promittitur nondum fit; etiam si iuramentum adveniat, nondum est matrimonium factum, sicut Magister in littera dicit.

AD PRIMUM ergo dicendum quod implere iuramentum licitum est de iure divino, non autem implere iuramentum illicitum. Unde, si aliqua obligatio sequens iuramentum faciat illud illicitum, cum prius fuisset licitum, non derogat iuri divino qui iuramentum prius factum non servat. Et ita est in proposito. Illicite enim iuratur quod illicite promittitur. Promissio autem de alieno est illicita. Unde consensus sequens per verba de praesenti, quo quis transfert dominium sui corporis in aliam, facit praecedens iuramentum esse illicitum, quod prius licitum erat.

AD SECUNDUM dicendum quod veritas divina efficacissima est ad firmandum illud cui adhibetur.

UNDE PATET solutio ad tertium.

AD QUARTUM dicendum quod iuramentum aliquid operatur, non novam obligationem faciens, sed factam confirmans. Et sic gravius peccat qui eam violat.

must have some effect. Therefore, it makes something more than a betrothal. Now, beyond a betrothal there is nothing but marriage. Therefore, it makes a marriage.

ON THE CONTRARY, What is future is not yet. Now, the addition of an oath does not make words of the future tense signify anything else than consent to something future. Therefore, it is not a marriage yet.

FURTHER, After a marriage is complete, no further consent is required for the marriage. But after the oath there is yet another consent which makes the marriage, else it would be useless to swear to a future marriage. Therefore, it does not make a marriage.

I ANSWER THAT, An oath is employed in confirmation of one's words; wherefore it confirms that only which is signified by the words, nor does it change their signification. Consequently, since it belongs to words of the future tense, by their very signification, not to make a marriage, since what is promised in the future is not done yet, even though an oath be added to the promise, the marriage is not made yet, as the Master says in the text (*Sentences* IV, D. 28).

REPLY OBJ. 1: The fulfilling of a lawful oath is of divine law, but not the fulfilling of an unlawful oath. Wherefore if a subsequent obligation makes that oath unlawful, whereas it was lawful before, he who does not keep the oath he took previously does not disobey the divine law. And so it is in the case in point, since he swears unlawfully who promises unlawfully, and a promise about another's property is unlawful. Consequently, the subsequent consent by words of the present, whereby a man transfers the power over his body to another woman, makes the previous oath unlawful which was lawful before.

REPLY OBJ. 2: The divine truth is most efficacious in confirming that to which it is applied.

HENCE the reply to the third objection is clear.

REPLY OBJ. 4: The oath has some effect, not by causing a new obligation, but confirming that which is already made, and thus he who violates it sins more grievously.

Article 2

Whether Carnal Intercourse After Consent Expressed in Words of the Future Makes a Marriage?

AD SECUNDUM SIC PROCEDITUR. Videtur quod carnalis copula, post verba de futuro consensum exprimentia, faciat matrimonium. Quia maius est consentire facto quam verbo. Sed ille qui carnaliter commiscetur, facto consentit promissioni quam prius fecit. Ergo videtur quod multo magis per hoc fiat matrimonium quam si solis verbis de praesenti consensus fieret.

PRAETEREA, consensus non solum expressus, sed etiam interpretativus, facit matrimonium. Sed nulla po-

OBJECTION 1: It would seem that carnal intercourse after consent expressed in words of the future makes a marriage. For consent by deed is greater than consent by word. But he who has carnal intercourse consents by deed to the promise he has previously made. Therefore, it would seem that much more does this make a marriage than if he were to consent to mere words referring to the present.

OBJ. 2: Further, not only explicit but also interpretive consent makes a marriage. Now there can be no better in-

test esse maior interpretatio consensus quam carnalis copula. Ergo perficitur matrimonium per hoc.

PRAETEREA, omnis coniunctio carnalis praeter matrimonium facta est peccatum. Sed mulier non videtur peccare admittens sponsum ad carnalem copulam. Ergo per hoc fit matrimonium.

PRAETEREA, *non remittitur peccatum nisi restituatur ablatum*. Sed aliquis non potest mulieri quam defloravit sub specie matrimonii, restituere ablatum, nisi eam coniugio ducat. Ergo videtur quod si etiam, post carnalem copulam, cum alia contraxerit per verba de praesenti, quod teneatur ad primam redire. Quod non esset nisi inter eos esset matrimonium. Ergo carnalis copula, post consensum de futuro, facit matrimonium.

SED CONTRA: Est quod dicit Nicolaus Papa 1: *si consensus in nuptiis defuerit, cetera, etiam cum ipso coitu celebrata, frustrantur.*

PRAETEREA, quod consequitur ad aliquid, non facit ipsum. Sed carnalis copula sequitur ipsum matrimonium, sicut effectus causam. Ergo non potest facere matrimonium.

RESPONDEO dicendum quod de matrimonio possumus loqui dupliciter. Uno modo, quantum ad forum conscientiae. Et sic in rei veritate carnalis copula non habet quod perficiat matrimonium cuius sponsalia praecesserunt per verba de futuro, si consensus interior desit: quia verba de praesenti etiam consensum exprimentia, si consensus mentalis deesset, non facerent matrimonium.

Alio modo, quantum ad iudicium Ecclesiae. Et quia in exteriori iudicio secundum ea *quae foris patent* iudicatur, cum nihil possit expressius significare consensum quam carnalis copula, secundum iudicium Ecclesiae carnalis copula consequens sponsalia matrimonium facere iudicatur, nisi aliqua signa expressa doli vel fraudis appareant.

AD PRIMUM ergo dicendum quod ille qui carnaliter commiscetur, facto consentit in carnalem copulam secundum rei veritatem: sed in matrimonium non consentit ex hoc ipso nisi secundum interpretationem iuris.

AD SECUNDUM, dicendum quod interpretatio illa non mutat rei veritatem, sed iudicium quod de rebus exterius fit.

AD TERTIUM dicendum quod, si sponsa sponsum admittat credens eum velle matrimonium consummare, excusatur a peccato: nisi aliqua signa expressa fraudis appareant, sicut si sunt multum distantis conditionis vel quantum ad nobilitatem vel quantum ad fortunam, vel aliud signum evidens appareat. Sed tamen sponsus peccat et fornicando; et, quod plus est, fraude quam facit.

AD QUARTUM dicendum quod in tali casu sponsus, antequam aliam duxerit, tenetur eam ducere in uxorem

terpretation of consent than carnal intercourse. Therefore, marriage is completed thereby.

OBJ. 3: Further, all carnal union outside marriage is a sin. But the woman, seemingly, does not sin by admitting her betrothed to carnal intercourse. Therefore, it makes a marriage.

OBJ. 4: Further, *sin is not forgiven unless restitution be made*, as Augustine says (Ep. cliii *ad Macedon.*). Now a man cannot reinstate a woman whom he has violated under the pretense of marriage unless he marry her. Therefore, it would seem that even if after his carnal intercourse he happen to contract with another by words of the present tense, he is bound to return to the first; and this would not be the case unless he were married to her. Therefore, carnal intercourse after consent referring to the future makes a marriage.

ON THE CONTRARY, Pope Nicholas I says (*Response to the Consultation of the Bulgarians* 3), *without the consent to marriage, other things, including coition, are of no effect.*

FURTHER, That which follows a thing does not make it. But carnal intercourse follows the actual marriage, as effect follows cause. Therefore, it cannot make a marriage.

I ANSWER THAT, We may speak of marriage in two ways. First, in reference to the tribunal of conscience, and thus in very truth carnal intercourse cannot complete a marriage the promise of which has previously been made in words expressive of the future, if inward consent is lacking, since words, even though expressive of the present, would not make a marriage in the absence of mental consent, as stated above (Q. 45, A. 4).

Second, in reference to the judgment of the Church; and since in the external tribunal judgment is given *in accordance with external evidence*, and since nothing is more expressly significant of consent than carnal intercourse, it follows that in the judgment of the Church carnal intercourse following on betrothal is declared to make a marriage, unless there appear clear signs of deceit or fraud (*Decretals*).

REPLY OBJ. 1: In reality, he who has carnal intercourse consents by deed to the act of sexual union, and does not merely for this reason consent to marriage except according to the interpretation of the law.

REPLY OBJ. 2: This interpretation does not alter the truth of the matter, but changes the judgment which is about external things.

REPLY OBJ. 3: If the woman admit her betrothed, thinking that he wishes to consummate the marriage, she is excused from the sin unless there be clear signs of fraud: for instance, if they differ considerably in birth or fortune, or some other evident sign appear. Nevertheless, the affianced husband is guilty of fornication, and should be punished for this fraud he has committed.

REPLY OBJ. 4: In a case of this kind the affianced husband, before his marriage with the other woman, is bound

si sint aequalis conditionis, vel si sponsa sit melioris conditionis. Sed si aliam duxerit, factus est iam impotens ad solvendum illud ad quod tenebatur. Et ideo sufficit si ei de nuptiis provideat. Et ad hoc etiam non tenetur, ut quidam dicunt, si sponsus sit multo melioris conditionis, aut aliquod signum evidens fraudis fuerit: quia praesumi probabiliter potest quod sponsa non fuerit decepta, sed decipi se finxerit.

to marry the one to whom he was betrothed, if she be his equal or superior in rank. But if he has married another woman, he is no longer able to fulfill his obligation, wherefore it suffices if he provide for her marriage. Nor is he bound even to do this, according to some, if her affianced husband is of much higher rank than she, or if there be some evident sign of fraud, because it may be presumed that in all probability she was not deceived but contrived herself to be.

QUESTION 47

COMPULSORY AND CONDITIONAL CONSENT

Deinde considerandum est de consensu coacto et conditionato.

Circa quod quaeruntur sex.

Primo: utrum aliquis consensus possit esse coactus.

Secundo: utrum aliqua coactio cadat in constantem virum.

Tertio: utrum consensus coactus faciat matrimonium.

Quarto: utrum consensus coactus faciat matrimonium ex parte cogentis.

Quinto: utrum consensus conditionatus matrimonium faciat.

Sexto: utrum aliquis possit cogi a patre ad matrimonium contrahendum.

We must now consider compulsory and conditional consent.

Under this head there are six points of inquiry:

(1) Whether compulsory consent is possible?

(2) Whether a constant man can be compelled by fear?

(3) Whether compulsory consent invalidates marriage?

(4) Whether compulsory consent makes a marriage as regards the party using compulsion?

(5) Whether conditional consent makes a marriage?

(6) Whether one can be compelled by one's father to marry?

Article 1

Whether a Compulsory Consent Is Possible?

AD PRIMUM SIC PROCEDITUR. Videtur quod nullus consensus possit esse coactus. Coactio enim in libero arbitrio cadere non potest secundum aliquem, statum eius: ut in II libro, dist. 25 dictum est. Sed consensus est actus liberi arbitrii. Ergo non potest esse coactus.

PRAETEREA, violentum, quod est idem quod coactum, secundum Philosophum, *est cuius principium est extra, nihil conferente vim passo.* Sed omnis consensus principium est intra. Ergo nullus consensus potest esse coactus.

PRAETEREA, omne peccatum consensu perficitur. Sed illud quo perficitur peccatum, cogi non potest: quia, secundum Augustinum, *nullus peccat in eo quod vitare non potest.* Cum ergo vis a iuristis definiatur esse *maioris rei impetus qui repelli non potest,* videtur quod consensus non possit esse coactus vel violentus.

PRAETEREA, dominium libertati opponitur. Sed coactio ad dominium pertinet, ut patet in quadam Tullii definitione: dicit enim quod *vis est impetus dominantis retinens rem intra terminos alienos.* Ergo vis in liberum arbitrium non cadit. Et ita nec in consensum, qui est actus eius.

OBJECTION 1: It would seem that no consent can be compulsory. For, as stated above (*Sentences* II, D. 25, I-II, Q. 6, A. 4) the free-will cannot be compelled. Now consent is an act of the free-will. Therefore, it cannot be compelled.

OBJ. 2: Further, 'violent' is the same as 'compulsory.' Now, according to the Philosopher (*Ethics* 3.1), *a violent action is one the principle of which is without, the patient concurring not at all.* But the principle of consent is always within. Therefore, no consent can be compulsory.

OBJ. 3: Further, every sin is perfected by consent. But that which perfects a sin cannot be compulsory, for, according to Augustine (*On Free Choice of the Will* 3.18), *no one sins in what he cannot avoid.* Since, then, violence is defined by jurists (*Digesta Iustiniani*) as the *force of a stronger being that cannot be repulsed,* it would seem that consent cannot be compulsory or violent.

OBJ. 4: Furthermore, domination is opposed to freedom. But compulsion belongs to domination, as is clear in a certain definition from Cicero: for he says that *force is the impetus of the dominant thing retaining a thing within foreign boundaries.* Therefore, force does not happen to a free will; and thus neither does it happen in consent, which is its act.

Sed contra: Illud quod esse non potest, non potest aliquid impedire. Sed coactio consensus impedit matrimonium, ut in littera dicitur. Ergo consensus cogi potest.

Praeterea, in matrimonio est quidam contractus. Sed in contractibus potest esse voluntas coacta: unde legislator in integrum restitutionem adiudicat, ratum non habens *quod vi metusve causa factum est*. Ergo et in matrimonio potest esse consensus coactus.

Respondeo dicendum quod duplex est coactio vel violentia. Una quae facit necessitatem absolutam. Et tale violentum dicitur a Philosopho violentum simpliciter: ut cum quis aliquem corporaliter impellit ad motum. Alia quae facit necessitatem conditionatam. Et hanc vocat Philosophus violentum mixtum: sicut cum quis proiicit merces in mare ne periclitetur. Et in isto violento, quamvis hoc quod fit non sit per se voluntarium, tamen, consideratis circumstantiis, hic et nunc voluntarium est. Et quia *actus in particularibus sunt*, ideo simpliciter voluntarium est, sed secundum quid involuntarium. Unde haec violentia vel coactio potest esse de consensu, qui est actus voluntatis: non autem prima. Et quia haec coactio fit ex hoc quod timetur aliquod periculum imminens, ideo ista vis idem est quod *metus*, qui voluntatem cogit quodammodo. Sed prima vis cadit et in corporalibus actibus.

Et quia Legislator considerat non solum interiores actus, sed magis exteriores, ideo per vim intelligit coactionem simpliciter: propter quod *vim* contra *metum* dividit. Sed nunc agitur de consensu interiori, in quem non cadit coactio seu vis quae a metu distinguitur. Et ideo, quantum ad propositum pertinet, idem est coactio quod metus. Est autem metus, secundum iuris-peritos, *instantis vel futuri periculi causa mentis trepidatio*.

Et per hoc patet solutio ad obiecta. Nam primae rationes procedunt de coactione prima; secundae de secunda.

On the contrary, That which cannot be, cannot be an impediment. But compulsory consent is an impediment to matrimony, as stated in the text (*Sentences* IV, D. 29). Therefore, consent can be compelled.

Further, In marriage there is a contract. Now the will can be compelled in the matter of contracts; for which reason the law adjudges that restitution should be made of the whole, for it does not ratify *that which was done under compulsion or fear* (*Sentences* IV, D. 29). Therefore, in marriage also it is possible for the consent to be compulsory.

I answer that, Compulsion or violence is twofold. One is the cause of absolute necessity, and violence of this kind the Philosopher calls violent simply (*Ethics* 3.1), as when by bodily strength one forces a person to move. The other causes conditional necessity, and the Philosopher calls this a mixed violence, as when a person throws his merchandise overboard in order to save himself. In the latter kind of violence, although the thing done is not voluntary in itself, yet taking into consideration the circumstances of place and time it is voluntary. And since *actions are about particulars*, it follows that it is voluntary simply, and involuntary in a certain respect (Cf. I-II, Q. 6, A. 6). Wherefore this latter violence or compulsion is consistent with consent, but not the former. And since this compulsion results from one's *fear* of a threatening danger, it follows that this violence coincides with fear which, in a manner, compels the will, whereas the former violence has to do with bodily actions.

Moreover, since the law considers not merely internal actions, but rather external actions, consequently it takes violence to mean absolute compulsion, for which reason it draws a distinction between *violence* and *fear*. Here, however, it is a question of internal consent, which cannot be influenced by compulsion or violence as distinct from fear. Therefore, as to the question at issue, compulsion and fear are the same, for, according to lawyers, fear is *the agitation of the mind occasioned by danger imminent or future* (*Ethics* 3.1).

This suffices for the replies to the objections: for the first set of arguments consider the first kind of compulsion, and the second set of arguments consider the second.

Article 2

Whether a Constant Man Can Be Compelled by Fear?

Ad secundum sic proceditur. Videtur quod coactio metus non cadat in constantem virum. Quia de ratione constantis est quod non trepidet in periculis. Cum ergo metus sit trepidatio mentis ratione periculi imminentis, videtur quod non cogatur metu.

Objection 1: It would seem that a constant man cannot be compelled by fear. For the nature of a constant man is not to be agitated in the midst of dangers. Since, then, fear is agitation of the mind occasioned by imminent danger, it would seem that he is not compelled by fear.

Praeterea, *omnium terribilissimum est mors*, secundum Philosophum, in III *Ethic.*, quasi perfectissimum inter terribilia. Sed constantes non coguntur morte: quia fortis etiam pericula mortis sustinet. Ergo nullus metus cadit in constantem virum.

Praeterea, inter alia pericula praecipue timetur a bonis periculum famae. Sed timor infamiae non reputatur timor cadens in constantem virum: quia, ut dicit lex, *timor infamiae non continetur illo edicto, Quod metus causa factum est.* Ergo nec aliquis alius metus cadit in constantem virum.

Praeterea, metus in eo qui metu cogitur peccatum relinquit: quia facit eum promittere quod non vult solvere, et sic facit eum mentiri. Sed non est constantis aliquod peccatum, etiam minimum, pro aliquo timore facere. Ergo nullus metus cadit in constantem virum.

Sed contra: Abraham et Isaac constantes fuerunt. Sed in eis cecidit metus: quia ratione metus dixerunt uxores suas sibi esse sorores. Ergo metus potest cadere in constantem virum.

Praeterea, ubicumque est violentum mixtum, est aliquis metus cogens. Sed aliquis quantumcumque constans potest pati tale violentum: quia, si sit in mari, merces proiiciet tempore naufragii. Ergo metus potest cadere in constantem virum.

Respondeo dicendum quod cadere metum in aliquem est aliquem metu cogi. Cogitur autem aliquis metu quando aliquid facit quod alias non vellet, ad evitandum aliquid quod timet. In hoc autem constans ab inconstanti distinguitur quantum ad duo. Primo, quantum ad qualitatem periculi quod timetur. Quia constans sequitur rationem rectam, per quam scit quid pro quo dimittendum sit vel faciendum. Semper autem minus malum vel maius bonum eligendum est. Et ideo constans ad minus malum sustinendum cogitur metu maioris mali: non autem cogitur ad maius malum ut vitet minus malum. Sed inconstans cogitur ad maius malum propter metum minoris mali: sicut ad peccatum propter metum corporalis poenae. Sed pertinax e contra non potest cogi etiam ad minus malum sustinendum vel faciendum ut evitet maius malum. Unde constans est medius inter inconstantem et pertinacem.

Secundo differunt quantum ad aestimationem periculi imminentis. Quia fortis non nisi ex forti aestimatione et probabili cogitur: sed inconstans ex levi, Proverb. 28: *fugit impius nemine per sequente.*

Ad primum ergo dicendum quod constans, sicut et de forti dicit Philosophus, est intrepidus, non quod om-

Obj. 2: Further, *of all fearsome things death is the limit*, according to the Philosopher (*Ethics* 3.6), as though it were the most perfect of all things that inspire fear. But the constant man is not compelled by death, since the brave face even mortal dangers. Therefore, no fear influences a constant man.

Obj. 3: Further, of all dangers a good man fears most that which affects his good name. But the fear of disgrace is not reckoned to influence a constant man, because, according to the law, *fear of disgrace is not included under the ordinance, "That which is done through fear"* (*Digesti veteris*, Bk. 4, tit. 2, sec. 7). Therefore, neither does any other kind of fear influence a constant man.

Obj. 4: Further, in him who is compelled by fear, fear leaves a sin, for it makes him promise what he is unwilling to fulfill, and thus it makes him lie. But a constant man does not commit a sin, not even a very slight one, for fear. Therefore, no fear influences a constant man.

On the contrary, Abraham and Isaac were constant. Yet they were influenced by fear, since on account of fear each said that his wife was his sister (Gen 12:12; 26:7). Therefore, fear can influence a constant man.

Further, Wherever there is mixed violence, it is fear that compels. But however constant a man may be, he may suffer violence of that kind, for if he be on the sea, he will throw his merchandise overboard if menaced with shipwreck. Therefore, fear can influence a constant man.

I answer that, By fear influencing a man we mean his being compelled by fear. A man is compelled by fear when he does that which otherwise he would not wish to do, in order to avoid that which he fears. Now the constant differs from the inconstant man in two respects. First, in respect of the quality of the danger feared, because the constant man follows right reason, whereby he knows whether to omit this rather than that, and whether to do this rather than that. Now the lesser evil or the greater good is always to be preferred; and therefore the constant man is compelled to bear with the lesser evil through fear of the greater evil, but he is not compelled to bear with the greater evil in order to avoid the lesser. But the inconstant man is compelled to bear with the greater evil through fear of a lesser evil, namely, to commit sin through fear of bodily suffering. On the contrary, the obstinate man cannot be compelled even to permit or to do a lesser evil in order to avoid a greater. Hence the constant man is a mean between the inconstant and the obstinate.

Second, they differ as to their estimate of the threatening evil, for a constant man is not compelled unless for grave and probable reasons, while the inconstant man is compelled by trifling motives: *the wicked man flees when no man pursues* (Prov 28:1).

Reply Obj. 1: The constant man, like the brave man, is fearless, as the Philosopher states (*Ethics* 3.4), not that he

nino non timeat, sed quia non timet quae non oportet, vel nisi quando oportet.

AD SECUNDUM dicendum quod peccata sunt maxima malorum. Et ideo ad haec nullo modo potest homo constans cogi: immo magis debet homo mori quam talia sustinere, ut etiam Philosophus, III *Ethic.*, dicit.

Sed quaedam damna corporalia sunt minora quibusdam aliis. Inter quae sunt praecipua quae ad personam pertinent, sicut mors, verbera, dehonestatio per stuprum, et servitus. Et ideo ex istis constans cogitur ad alia damna corporalia. Et haec continentur hoc versu: *stupri sive status, verberis atque necis.* Nec differt utrum haec pertineant ad personam propriam, vel uxoris, vel filiorum, vel aliorum huiusmodi.

AD TERTIUM dicendum quod infamia quamvis sit magnum damnum, tamen ei de facili occurri potest. Et ideo non reputatur cadere in constantem virum metus infamiae, secundum iura.

AD QUARTUM dicendum quod constans non cogitur ad mentiendum, quia tunc vult dare: sed tamen postea vult petere restitutionem; vel saltem iudici denuntiare, si se promisit non petiturum restitutionem. Non potest autem promittere se non denuntiaturum: cum hoc sit contra bonum iustitiae, ad quod cogi non potest, ut scilicet contra iustitiam faciat.

is altogether without fear, but because he fears not what he ought not to fear, or where, or when he ought not to fear.

REPLY OBJ. 2: Sin is the greatest of evils, and consequently a constant man can in no way be compelled to sin. Indeed, a man should die rather than suffer the like, as again the Philosopher says (*Ethics* 3.6, 9).

Yet certain bodily injuries are less grievous than certain others; and chief among them are those which relate to the person, such as death, blows, the stain resulting from rape, and slavery. Therefore, the like compel a constant man to suffer other bodily injuries. They are contained in the verse: *rape, status, blows, and death.* Nor does it matter whether they refer to his own person, or to the person of his wife or children, or the like.

REPLY OBJ. 3: Although disgrace is a greater injury, it is easy to remedy it. Hence fear of disgrace is not reckoned to influence a constant man according to law.

REPLY OBJ. 4: The constant man is not compelled to lie, because at the time he wishes to give; yet afterwards he wishes to ask for restitution, or at least to appeal to the judge if he promised not to ask for restitution. But he cannot promise not to appeal, for since this is contrary to the good of justice, he cannot be compelled thereto, namely, to act against justice.

Article 3

Whether Compulsory Consent Invalidates a Marriage?

AD TERTIUM SIC PROCEDITUR. Videtur quod consensus coactus non tollat matrimonium. Quia sicut ad matrimonium requiritur consensus, ita ad baptismum requiritur intentio. Sed coactus timore ad recipiendum baptismum, recipit sacramentum. Ergo coactus ad consentiendum aliquo timore matrimonio obligatur.

PRAETEREA, violentum mixtum, secundum Philosophum, plus habet de voluntario quam de involuntario. Sed non potest aliter consensus esse coactus nisi per violentum mixtum. Ergo non omnino excluditur voluntarium. Et ita adhuc est matrimonium.

PRAETEREA, ei qui consentit in matrimonium coactus, consulendum videtur quod in matrimonio illo stet: quia *speciem mali* habet promittere et non solvere, a quo Apostolus vult nos abstinere. Hoc autem non esset si consensus coactus omnino matrimonium tolleret. Ergo, etc.

SED CONTRA: Est quod *Decretalis* dicit: *cum consensus locum non habeat ubi metus vel Coactio intercidit, necesse est ut, ubi communis consensus requiritur, coactionis*

OBJECTION 1: It would seem that compulsory consent does not invalidate a marriage. For just as consent is necessary for matrimony, so is intention necessary for baptism. Now one who is compelled by fear to receive baptism receives the sacrament. Therefore, one who is compelled by fear to consent is bound by his marriage.

OBJ. 2: Further, according to the Philosopher (*Ethics* 3.1), that which is done on account of mixed violence is more voluntary than involuntary. Now consent cannot be compelled except by mixed violence. Therefore, it is not entirely involuntary, and consequently the marriage is valid.

OBJ. 3: Further, seemingly he who has consented to marriage under compulsion ought to be counseled to stand to that marriage; because to promise and not to fulfill has an *appearance of evil*, and the Apostle wishes us to refrain from all such things (1 Thess 5:22). But that would not be the case if compulsory consent invalidated a marriage altogether. Therefore, etc.

ON THE CONTRARY, The *Decretals* says: *since there is no room for consent where fear or compulsion enters in, it follows that where a person's consent is required, every pre-*

materia repellatur. Sed in matrimonio requiritur communis consensus. Ergo, etc.

PRAETEREA, matrimonium significat coniunctionem Christi ad Ecclesiam, quae fit secundum libertatem amoris. Ergo non potest fieri per consensum coactum.

RESPONDEO dicendum quod vinculum matrimonii est perpetuum. Unde illud quod perpetuitati repugnat, matrimonium tollit. Metus autem *qui cadit in constantem virum*, perpetuitatem contractus tollit: quia potest peti restitutio in integrum. Et ideo haec coactio tollit matrimonium, et non alia. Constans autem vir iudicatur *virtuosus*, qui est *mensura* in omnibus operibus humanis, ut Philosophus dicit, in III *Ethic.*

Quidam autem dicunt quod, si adsit consensus, quamvis coactus, interius est matrimonium quantum ad Deum; sed non quantum ad statum Ecclesiae, quae praesumit ibi non fuisse consensum interiorem propter metum. Sed hoc nihil est. Quia Ecclesia non debet praesumere de aliquo peccatum quousque non probetur. Peccavit autem si dixit se consentire, et non consensit. Unde Ecclesia praesumit eum consensisse, sed iudicat consensum illum extortum non esse sufficientem ad faciendum matrimonium.

AD PRIMUM ergo dicendum quod intentio non est causa efficiens sacramenti in baptismo, sed solum eliciens actionem agentis. Sed consensus est causa efficiens in matrimonio. Et ideo non est simile.

AD SECUNDUM dicendum quod ad matrimonium non sufficit quodcumque voluntarium, sed Voluntarium complete: quia debet esse perpetuum. Et ideo per violentum mixtum impeditur.

AD TERTIUM quod in matrimonio illo stet, sed solum quando timetur periculum de dissolutione. Alias autem non peccat: quia non solvere promissa quae nolens facit, non est species mali.

text for compulsion must be set aside. Now mutual contract is necessary in marriage. Therefore, etc.

FURTHER, Matrimony signifies the union of Christ with the Church, which union is according to the liberty of love. Therefore, it cannot be the result of compulsory consent.

I ANSWER THAT, The marriage bond is everlasting. Hence whatever is inconsistent with its perpetuity invalidates marriage. Now the fear *which compels a constant man* deprives the contract of its perpetuity, since its complete rescission can be demanded. Therefore, this compulsion by fear, which influences a constant man, invalidates marriage, but not the other compulsion. Now a constant man is reckoned a *virtuous man* who, according to the Philosopher (*Ethics* 3.4), is a *measure* in all human actions.

However, some say that if there be consent, although compulsory, the marriage is valid in conscience and in God's sight, but not in the eyes of the Church, who presumes that there was no inward consent on account of the fear. But this is of no account, because the Church should not presume a person to sin until it be proved; and he sinned if he said that he consented whereas he did not consent. Wherefore the Church presumes that he did consent, but judges this compulsory consent to be insufficient for a valid marriage.

REPLY OBJ. 1: The intention is not the efficient cause of the sacrament in baptism; it is merely the cause that elicits the action of the agent. Yet the consent is the efficient cause in matrimony. Hence the comparison fails.

REPLY OBJ. 2: Not any kind of voluntariness suffices for marriage: it must be completely voluntary, because it has to be perpetual; and consequently it is invalidated by violence of a mixed nature.

REPLY OBJ. 3: He ought not always to be advised to stand to that marriage, but only when evil results are feared from its dissolution. Nor does he sin if he does otherwise, because there is no appearance of evil in not fulfilling a promise that one has made unwillingly.

Article 4

Whether Compulsory Consent Makes a Marriage as Regards the Party Who Uses Compulsion?

AD QUARTUM SIC PROCEDITUR. Videtur quod consensus coactus saltem ex parte cogentis faciat matrimonium. Quia matrimonium est signum spiritualis coniunctionis. Sed spiritualis coniunctio, quae est per caritatem, potest esse ad eum qui non habet caritatem. Ergo et matrimonium est ad eum qui non vult.

PRAETEREA, si illa quae fuit coacta, postmodum consentiat, erit matrimonium verum. Sed iste qui coegit primo, ex consensu illius non ligatur. Ergo ex primo consensu ligabatur matrimonio.

OBJECTION 1: It would seem that compulsory consent makes a marriage, at least as regards the party who uses compulsion. For matrimony is a sign of a spiritual union. But spiritual union, which is by charity, may be with one who has not charity. Therefore, marriage is possible with one who does not will it.

OBJ. 2: Further, if she who was compelled consents afterwards, it will be a true marriage. But he who compelled her before is not bound by her consent. Therefore, he was married to her by virtue of the consent he gave before.

SED CONTRA, matrimonium est relatio aequiparantiae. Sed talis relatio aequaliter est in utroque. Ergo, si sit impedimentum ex parte unius, non erit matrimonium ex parte alterius.

RESPONDEO dicendum quod, cum matrimonium sit quaedam relatio; et non possit innasci relatio in uno extremorum sine hoc quod fiat in alio: ideo quidquid impedit matrimonium in uno, impedit ipsum in altero; quia non potest esse quod aliquis sit vir non uxoris, vel aliqua sit uxor non habens virum, sicut mater non habens filium. Et ideo dicitur communiter quod *matrimonium non claudicat.*

AD PRIMUM ergo dicendum quod, quamvis actus amantis possit transire in non amantem, tamen unio inter eos non potest esse nisi sit mutua amatio. Et ideo dicit Philosophus, in VIII *Ethic.*, quod ad amicitiam, quae in quadam unione consistit, requiritur redamatio.

AD SECUNDUM dicendum quod ex consensu libero illius qui prius coactus est, non fit matrimonium nisi inquantum consensus praecedens in altero adhuc manet in suo vigore. Unde, si dissentiret, non fieret matrimonium.

ON THE CONTRARY, Matrimony is an equiparant relation. Now a relation of that kind is equally in both terms. Therefore, if there is an impediment on the part of one, there will be no marriage on the part of the other.

I ANSWER THAT, Since marriage is a kind of relation, and a relation cannot arise in one of the terms without arising in the other, it follows that whatever is an impediment to matrimony in the one is an impediment to matrimony in the other; since it is impossible for a man to be the husband of one who is not his wife, or for a woman to be a wife without a husband, just as it is impossible to be a mother without having a child. Hence it is a common saying that *marriage is not lame.*

REPLY OBJ. 1: Although the act of the lover can be directed to one who loves not, there can be no union between them unless love be mutual. Wherefore the Philosopher says (*Ethics* 8.2) that friendship, which consists in a kind of union, requires a return of love.

REPLY OBJ. 2: Marriage does not result from the consent of her who was compelled before, except insofar as the other party's previous consent remains in force; wherefore if he were to withdraw his consent, there would be no marriage.

Article 5

Whether Conditional Consent Makes a Marriage?

AD QUINTUM SIC PROCEDITUR. Videtur quod nec per consensum conditionatum fiat matrimonium. Quia quod sub conditione ponitur, non simpliciter enuntiatur. Sed in matrimonio oportet esse verba simpliciter exprimentia consensum. Ergo conditio alicuius consensus non facit matrimonium.

PRAETEREA, matrimonium debet esse certum. Sed ubi dicitur aliquid sub conditione, ponitur illud sub dubio. Ergo talis consensus non facit matrimonium.

SED CONTRA, in aliis contractibus fit obligatio sub conditione, et stat stante conditione. Ergo, cum matrimonium sit contractus quidam, videtur quod possit fieri per conditionatum consensum.

RESPONDEO dicendum quod conditio apposita aut est de praesenti, aut est de futuro. Si de praesenti, et non est contraria matrimonio, sive sit honesta sive inhonesta, stat matrimonium stante conditione, et ea non stante, non stat. Sed, si sit contraria bonis matrimonii, non efficitur matrimonium.

Si autem sit conditio de futuro, aut est necessaria, sicut solem oriri cras. Et tunc est matrimonium: quia talia futura iam sunt praesentia in causis suis. Aut est contingens, ut datio pecuniae vel acceptatio parentum. Et tunc

OBJECTION 1: It would seem that not even a conditional consent makes a marriage, because a statement is not made simply if it is made subject to a condition. But in marriage the words expressive of consent must be uttered simply. Therefore, a conditional consent makes no marriage.

OBJ. 2: Further, marriage should be certain. But where a statement is made under a condition it is rendered doubtful. Therefore, a like consent makes no marriage.

ON THE CONTRARY, In other contracts an obligation is undertaken conditionally and holds so long as the condition holds. Therefore, since marriage is a contract, it would seem that it can be made by a conditional consent.

I ANSWER THAT, The condition made is either of the present or of the future. If it is of the present and is not contrary to marriage, whether it be moral or immoral, the marriage holds if the condition is verified, and is invalid if the condition is not verified. If, however, it be contrary to the marriage blessings, the marriage is invalid.

But if the condition refer to the future, it is either necessary, as that the sun will rise tomorrow—and then the marriage is valid, because such future things are present in their causes—or else it is contingent, as the payment of a sum of

idem est iudicium de tali consensu sicut de consensu qui fit per verba de futuro. Unde non facit matrimonium.

ET PER HOC patet solutio ad obiecta.

money, or the consent of the parents, and then the judgment about a consent of this kind is the same as about a consent expressed in words of the future tense; wherefore it makes no marriage.

THIS SUFFICES for the replies to the objections.

Article 6

Whether One Can Be Compelled by a Father's Command to Marry?

AD SEXTUM SIC PROCEDITUR. Videtur quod aliquis praecepto patris possit compelli ad matrimonium contrahendum. Dicitur enim ad Coloss. 3: *filii, obedite parentibus vestris per omnia.* Ergo etiam in hoc eis obedire tenentur.

PRAETEREA, Gen. 28, Isaac *praecepit* Iacob quod *non acciperet uxorem de filiabus Chanaan.* Nec praecepisset nisi de iure praecipere potuisset. Ergo filius in hoc tenetur obedire patri.

PRAETEREA, nullus debet promittere, praecipue per iuramentum, pro illo quem non potest cogere ad servandum. Sed parentes promittunt futura matrimonia pro filiis, et etiam iuramento firmant. Ergo possunt praecepto cogere filios adimplendum.

PRAETEREA, pater spiritualis, scilicet Papa, potest compellere praecepto ad matrimonium spirituale, scilicet ad episcopatum accipiendum. Ergo potest et pater carnalis ad matrimonium carnale.

SED CONTRA: Patre imperante matrimonium, filius potest sine peccato religionem intrare. Ergo non tenetur ei in hoc obedire.

PRAETEREA, si teneretur obedire, sponsalia per parentes contracta absque consensu filiorum essent stabilia. Sed hoc est contra iura. Ergo, etc.

RESPONDEO dicendum quod, cum in matrimonio sit quasi quaedam servitus perpetua, pater non potest cogere filium ad matrimonium per praeceptum, cum sit liberae conditionis. Sed potest eum inducere ex rationabili causa. Et tunc, sicut se habet filius ad causam illam, ita se habet ad praeceptum patris: ut, si causa illa cogat de necessitate vel de honestate, et praeceptum similiter cogat; alias non.

AD PRIMUM ergo dicendum quod verbum Apostoli non intelligitur in illis in quibus est liber sui sicut pater. Et huiusmodi est matrimonium, per quod etiam filius fit pater.

AD SECUNDUM dicendum quod Iacob alias tenebatur ad faciendum hoc quod mandabat Isaac: tum propter malitiam illarum mulierum; tum quia semen Chanaan

OBJECTION 1: It would seem that one can be compelled by one's father's command to marry. For Colossians 3:20 says: *children, obey your parents in all things.* Therefore, they are bound to obey them in this also.

OBJ. 2: Further, Isaac *charged* Jacob *not to take a wife from the daughters of Canaan* (Gen 28:1). But he would not have charged him thus unless he had the right to command it. Therefore, a son is bound to obey his father in this.

OBJ. 3: Further, no one should promise for one whom he cannot compel to keep the promise, especially with an oath. Now parents promise future marriages for their children, and even confirm their promise by oath. Therefore, they can compel their children to keep that promise.

OBJ. 4: Further, our spiritual father, namely, the Pope, can by his command compel a man to a spiritual marriage, namely, to accept a bishopric. Therefore, a carnal father can compel his son to marriage.

ON THE CONTRARY, A son may lawfully enter religion though his father command him to marry. Therefore, he is not bound to obey him in this.

FURTHER, If he were bound to obey, a betrothal contracted by the parents would hold good without their children's consent. But this is against the law (*Decretals*). Therefore, etc.

I ANSWER THAT, Since in marriage there is a kind of perpetual service, as it were, a father cannot by his command compel his son to marry, since the latter is of free condition: but he may induce him for a reasonable cause; and thus the son will be affected by his father's command in the same way as he is affected by that cause, so that if the cause be compelling as indicating either obligation or fitness, his father's command will compel him in the same measure: otherwise, he may not compel him.

REPLY OBJ. 1: The words of the Apostle do not refer to those matters in which a man is his own master as the father is. Such is marriage, by which the son also becomes a father.

REPLY OBJ. 2: There were other motives why Jacob was bound to do what Isaac commanded him, both on account of the wickedness of those women, and because the seed

de terra quae semini Patriarcharum promittebatur, erat disperdendum. Et ideo Isaac praecipere poterat.

Ad tertium dicendum quod non iurant nisi illa conditione subintellecta, *si illis placuerit.* Et ipsi obligantur ad eos bona fide inducendum.

Ad quartum dicendum quod quidam dicunt quod Papa non potest praecipere alicui quod accipiat episcopatum, quia consensus debet liber esse. Sed, hoc posito, periret ecclesiasticus ordo. Nisi enim aliquis posset cogi ad suscipiendum regimen Ecclesiae, Ecclesia conservari non posset: cum quandoque illi qui sunt idonei ad hoc, nolint suscipere nisi coacti.

Et ideo dicendum quod non est simile hinc inde. Quia non est aliqua corporalis servitus in matrimonio spirituali, sicut iri corporali. Est enim spirituale matrimonium sicut quoddam officium dispensandae reipublicae: I Cor. 4, *sic nos existimet homo,* etc.

of Canaan was to be cast forth from the land which was promised to the seed of the patriarchs. Hence Isaac could command this.

Reply Obj. 3: They do not swear except with the implied condition *if it please them*; and they are bound to induce them in good faith.

Reply Obj. 4: Some say that the Pope cannot command a man to accept a bishopric, because consent should be free. But if this be granted there would be an end of ecclesiastical order, for unless a man can be compelled to accept the government of a church, the Church could not be preserved, since sometimes those who are qualified for the purpose are unwilling to accept unless they be compelled.

Therefore, we must reply that the two cases are not parallel; for there is no bodily service in a spiritual marriage as there is in the bodily marriage; because the spiritual marriage is a kind of office for dispensing the public good: *let a man so account of us as of the ministers of Christ, and the dispensers of the mysteries of God* (1 Cor 4:1).

QUESTION 48

THE OBJECT OF CONSENT

Deinde considerandum est de obiecto consensus.
Circa quod quaeruntur duo.
Primo: utrum consensus qui facit matrimonium, sit consensus in carnalem copulam.
Secundo: utrum consensus in aliquam propter causam inhonestam faciat matrimonium.

We must now consider the object of the consent.
Under this head there are two points of inquiry:
(1) Whether the consent that makes a marriage is a consent to carnal intercourse?
(2) Whether consent to marry a person for an immoral motive makes a marriage?

Article 1

Whether the Consent That Makes a Marriage Is a Consent to Carnal Intercourse?

AD PRIMUM SIC PROCEDITUR. Videtur quod Consensus qui facit matrimonium, sit consensus in carnalem copulam: Dicit enim Hieronymus quod *voventibus virginitatem non solum nubere, sed velle nubere damnabile est.* Sed non esset damnabile nisi esset virginitati contrarium: cui nuptiae non contrariantur nisi ratione carnalis copulae. Ergo consensus voluntatis qui est in nuptiis, est in carnalem copulam.

PRAETEREA, omnia quae sunt in matrimonio inter virum et uxorem, possunt esse licita inter fratrem et sororem, excepta carnali copula. Sed non potest fieri licite inter eos consensus matrimonialis. Ergo consensus matrimonialis est consensus in carnalem copulam.

PRAETEREA, si mulier dicat viro, *consentio in te, ut non cognoscas me,* non est consensus matrimonialis: quia est ibi aliquid contra substantiam praedicti consensus. Sed non esset nisi dictus consensus esset in carnalem copulam. Ergo, etc.

PRAETEREA, in qualibet re initium consummationi respondet. Sed matrimonium consummatur per carnalem copulam. Ergo, cum initietur per consensum, videtur quod consensus sit in carnalem copulam.

SED CONTRA: Nullus consentiens in carnalem copulam est virgo mente et carne. Sed beatus Ioannes Evangelista post consensum nuptialem fuit virgo mente et carne. Ergo non consensit in carnalem copulam.

PRAETEREA, effectus respondet causae. Sed consensus: est causa matrimonii. Cum ergo de essentia matrimonii non sit carnalis copula, videtur quod nec consensus qui matrimonium causat, sit in carnalem copulam.

RESPONDEO dicendum quod consensus qui matrimonium facit, est consensus in matrimonium: quia ef-

OBJECTION 1: It would seem that the consent which makes a marriage is a consent to carnal intercourse. For Jerome says that *for those who have vowed virginity it is wicked, not only to marry, but even to wish to marry.* But it would not be wicked unless it were contrary to virginity, and marriage is not contrary to virginity except by reason of carnal intercourse. Therefore, the will's consent in marriage is a consent to carnal intercourse.

OBJ. 2: Further, whatever there is in marriage between husband and wife is lawful between brother and sister, except carnal intercourse. But there cannot lawfully be a consent to marriage between them. Therefore, the marriage consent is a consent to carnal intercourse.

OBJ. 3: Further, if the woman say to the man: *I consent to take you provided, however, that you know me not*, it is not a marriage consent, because it contains something against the essence of that consent. Yet this would not be the case unless the marriage consent were a consent to carnal intercourse. Therefore, etc.

OBJ. 4: Further, in everything the beginning corresponds to the consummation. Now marriage is consummated by carnal intercourse. Therefore, since it begins by the consent, it would seem that the consent is to carnal intercourse.

ON THE CONTRARY, No one that consents to carnal intercourse is a virgin in mind and body. Yet Blessed John the evangelist, after consenting to marriage, was a virgin both in mind and body. Therefore, he did not consent to carnal intercourse.

FURTHER, The effect corresponds to its cause. Now consent is the cause of marriage. Since, then, carnal intercourse is not essential to marriage, seemingly neither is the consent which causes marriage a consent to carnal intercourse.

I ANSWER THAT, The consent that makes a marriage is a consent to marriage, because the proper effect of the

fectus proprius voluntatis est ipsum volitum. Unde, sicut carnalis copula se habet ad matrimonium, ita consensus qui matrimonium causat, est in carnalem copulam. Matrimonium autem, ut supra dictum est, non est essentialiter ipsa coniunctio carnalis: sed quaedam associatio viri et uxoris in ordine ad carnalem copulam et, alia quae ex consequenti ad virum et uxorem pertinent, secundum quod eis datur potestas in invicem respectu carnalis, copulae. Et haec associatio coniugalis *copula* dicitur. Unde patet quod bene dixerunt illi qui dixerunt quod consentire in matrimonium est consentire in carnalem copulam implicite, non explicite. Non enim debet intelligi nisi sicut implicite continetur effectus in causa: quia potestas carnalis copulae in quam consentitur, est causa carnalis copulae sicut potestas utendi re sua est causa usus.

AD PRIMUM ergo dicendum quod consensus iri rnatrimonium ideo est damnabilis post votum virginitatis, quia per talem consensum datur potestas ad id quod non licet: sicut peccaret qui daret potestatem alteri accipiendi illud quod ipse in deposito habet, non solum in hoc quod ei actualiter traderet. De consensu autem Beatae Virginis infra dicetur.

AD SECUNDUM dicendum quod inter fratrem et sororem non potest esse potestas in invicem ad carnalem copulam, sicut nec licite carnalis copula. Et ideo ratio non sequitur.

AD TERTIUM dicendum quod illa conditio explicita non solum actui, sed potestati contrariatur copulae carnalis. Et ideo est contraria matrimonio.

AD QUARTUM dicendum quod initiatum matrimonium respondet consummato sicut habitus vel potestas actui qui est operatio.

Rationes autem in contrarium ostendunt quod non sit consensus in carnalem copulam explicite. Et hoc est verum.

will is the thing willed. Wherefore, according as carnal intercourse stands in relation to marriage, so far is the consent that causes marriage a consent to carnal intercourse. Now, as stated above (Q. 44, A. 1; Q. 45, A. 1–2), marriage is not essentially the carnal union itself, but a certain joining together of husband and wife ordained to carnal intercourse, and a further consequent union between husband and wife, insofar as they each receive power over the other in reference to carnal intercourse. And this joining together is called the *nuptial bond*. Hence it is evident that they said well who asserted that to consent to marriage is to consent to carnal intercourse implicitly and not explicitly. For it should not be understood except as an effect is implicitly contained in its cause: for the power of carnal union, to which one consents, is the cause of carnal union, as the power of using what is one's own is the cause of its use.

REPLY OBJ. 1: The reason why consent to marriage after taking the vow of virginity is sinful is because that consent gives a power to do what is unlawful: even so would a man sin if he gave another man the power to receive that which he has in deposit, and not only by actually delivering it to him. We have spoken about the consent of the Blessed Virgin above (*Sentences* 4, D. 3; III, Q. 29, A. 2).

REPLY OBJ. 2: Between brother and sister there can be no power of one over the other in relation to carnal intercourse, even as neither can there be lawfully carnal intercourse itself. Consequently, the argument does not follow.

REPLY OBJ. 3: Such an explicit condition is contrary not only to the act but also to the power of carnal intercourse, and therefore it is contrary to marriage.

REPLY OBJ. 4: Marriage begun corresponds to marriage consummated as habit or power corresponds to the act which is operation.

The arguments on the contrary side show that consent is not given explicitly to carnal intercourse; and this is true.

Article 2

Whether Marriage Can Result from One Person's Consent to Take Another for a Base Motive?

AD SECUNDUM SIC PROCEDITUR. Videtur quod matrimonium non possit esse ex consensu alicuius in aliquam propter causam inhonestam. Unius enim una est ratio. Sed matrimonium est unum sacramentum. Ergo non potest fieri ex alterius finis intentione quam illius ad quem a Deo institutum est, scilicet ad procreationem prolis.

PRAETEREA, coniunctio matrimonii est a Deo: ut patet Matth. 19, *quod Deus coniunxit, homo non separet.* Sed coniunctio quae fit propter turpes causas, non est a Deo. Ergo non est matrimonium.

OBJECTION 1: It would seem that marriage cannot result from one person's consent to take another for a base motive. For there is but one reason for one thing. Now marriage is one sacrament. Therefore, it cannot result from the intention of any other end than that for which it was instituted by God; namely, the begetting of children.

OBJ. 2: Further, the marriage union is from God, according to Matthew 19:6: *what God hath joined together, let no man put asunder* (Matt 19:6). But a union that is made for immoral motives is not from God. Therefore, it is not a marriage.

PRAETEREA, in aliis sacramentis, si non servetur intentio Ecclesiae, non est verum sacramentum. Sed intentio Ecclesiae in sacramento matrimonii non est ad aliquam turpem causam. Ergo, si ex aliqua turpi causa matrimonium contrahatur, non erit verum matrimonium.

PRAETEREA, secundum Boetium, *cuius finis est bonus, ipsum quoque bonum est*. Sed matrimonium semper est bonum. Ergo non est matrimonium si propter malum finem fiat.

PRAETEREA, matrimonium significat coniunctionem Christi et Ecclesiae. Sed ibi non cadit aliqua turpitudo. Ergo non potest matrimonium contrahi propter aliquam turpem causam.

SED CONTRA: Est quod qui baptizat alium intentione lucrandi, vere baptizat. Ergo et qui contrahit cum aliqua intentione lucri, verum est matrimonium.

PRAETEREA, hoc idem probant exempla et auctoritates quae ponuntur in littera.

RESPONDEO dicendum quod causa finalis matrimonii potest accipi dupliciter: scilicet per se, et per accidens. Per se quidem causa matrimonii est ad quam matrimonium est de se ordinatum: et haec semper bona est, scilicet procreatio prolis et vitatio fornicationis. Sed per accidens causa finalis ipsius est hoc quod contrahentes intendunt ex matrimonio. Et quia hoc quod ex matrimonio intenditur consequitur ad matrimonium; et priora non variantur ex posterioribus, sed e converso: ideo ex illa causa non recipit matrimonium bonitatem vel malitiam, sed ipsi contrahentes, quorum est finis per se. Et quia *causae per accidens sunt infinitae*, ideo infinitae tales causae possunt esse in matrimonio, quarum sunt quaedam honestae et quaedam inhonestae.

AD PRIMUM ergo dicendum quod verum est de causa per se et principali. Sed quod habet unum finem per se et principalem, potest habere plures secundarios per se, et infinitos per accidens.

AD SECUNDUM dicendum quod coniunctio potest accipi pro ipsa relatione quae est matrimonium. Et talis semper est a Deo: et bona est, quacumque fiat causa. Vel pro actu eorum qui coniunguntur. Et sic est quandoque mala: et non est a Deo, simpliciter loquendo. Nec est inconveniens quod aliquis effectus sit a Deo cuius causa est mala: sicut proles quae ex adulterio suscipitur. Non enim est ex illa causa inquantum est mala, sed inquantum habet aliquid de bono, secundum quod est a Deo, quamvis non simpliciter sit a Deo.

AD TERTIUM dicendum quod intentio Ecclesiae qua intendit sacramentum tradere, est de necessitate cuiuslibet sacramenti, ita quod, ea non observata, nihil in sacramentis agitur. Sed intentio Ecclesiae qua intendit utilitatem ex sacramento provenientem, est de bene esse sacramenti, et non de necessitate eius. Unde, si non ob-

OBJ. 3: Further, in the other sacraments, if the intention of the Church be not observed, the sacrament is invalid. Now the intention of the Church in the sacrament of matrimony is not directed to a base purpose. Therefore, if a marriage be contracted for a base purpose, it will not be a valid marriage.

OBJ. 4: Further, according to Boethius, *a thing is good if its end be good* (*Concerning Different Topics* 2). But matrimony is always good. Therefore, it is not matrimony if it is done for an evil end.

OBJ. 5: Further, matrimony signifies the union of Christ with the Church; and in this there can be nothing base. Neither, therefore, can marriage be contracted for a base motive.

ON THE CONTRARY, He who baptizes another for the sake of gain baptizes validly. Therefore, if a man marries a woman for the purpose of gain it is a valid marriage.

FURTHER, The same conclusion is proved by the examples and authorities quoted in the text (*Sentences* IV, D. 30).

I ANSWER THAT, The final cause of marriage may be taken as twofold: namely, essential and accidental. The essential cause of marriage is the end to which it is by its very nature ordained, and this is always good, namely, the begetting of children and the avoiding of fornication. But the accidental final cause of it is that which the contracting parties intend as the result of marriage. And since that which is intended as the result of marriage is consequent upon marriage, and since that which comes first is not altered by what comes after, but conversely, marriage does not become good or evil by reason of that cause, but the contracting parties to whom this cause is the essential end. And since *accidental causes are infinite in number*, it follows that there can be an infinite number of such causes in matrimony, some of which are good and some bad.

REPLY OBJ. 1: This is true of the essential and principal cause; but that which has one essential and principal end may have several secondary essential ends, and an infinite number of accidental ends.

REPLY OBJ. 2: The joining together can be taken for the relation itself which is marriage, and that is always from God, and is good, whatever be its cause; or for the act of those who are being joined together, and thus it is sometimes evil and is not from God simply. Nor is it unreasonable that an effect be from God, the cause of which is evil, such as a child born of adultery; for it is not from that cause as evil, but as having some good insofar as it is from God, although it is not from God simply.

REPLY OBJ. 3: The intention of the Church whereby she intends to confer a sacrament is essential to each sacrament, so that if it be not observed, all sacraments are null. But the intention of the Church whereby she intends an advantage resulting from the sacrament belongs to the well-being and not to the essence of a sacrament; wherefore, if

servetur, nihilominus est verum sacramentum. Sed tamen praetermittens hanc intentionem peccat: sicut si in baptismo non intendatur sanitas mentis, quam Ecclesia intendit. Et similiter ille qui intendit matrimonium contrahere, quamvis matrimonium non ordinet ad illum finem quem Ecclesia intendit, nihilominus verum matrimonium contrahit.

AD QUARTUM dicendum quod illud malum intentum non est finis matrimonii, sed contrahentium.

AD QUINTUM dicendum quod ipsa unio est signum coniunctionis Christi et Ecclesiae, et non operatio unitorum. Et ideo ratio non sequitur.

it be not observed, the sacrament is nonetheless valid. Yet he who omits this intention sins; for instance, if in baptism one intend not the healing of the mind which the Church intends. In like manner, he who intends to marry, although he fail to direct it to the end which the Church intends, nevertheless contracts a valid marriage.

REPLY OBJ. 4: This evil which is intended is the end not of marriage, but of the contracting parties.

REPLY OBJ. 5: The union itself, and not the action of those who are united, is the sign of the union of Christ with the Church: wherefore the conclusion does not follow.

QUESTION 49

THE GOODS OF MATRIMONY

Consequenter considerandum est de bonis matrimonii.

Circa quod quaeruntur sex.

Primo: utrum debeant haberi aliqua bona ad excusandum matrimonium.

Secundo: utrum sufficienter assignentur.

Tertio: utrum bonum sacramenti sit principalius inter alia bona.

Quarto: utrum actus matrimonii per praedicta bona a peccato excusetur.

Quinto: utrum sine eis aliquando a peccatis excusari possit.

Sexto: utrum quando est sine eis, sit semper peccatum mortale.

In the next place we must consider the marriage goods.

Under this head there are six points of inquiry:

(1) Whether certain goods are necessary in order to excuse marriage?

(2) Whether those assigned are sufficient?

(3) Whether the sacrament is the principal among the goods?

(4) Whether the marriage act is excused from sin by the aforesaid goods?

(5) Whether it can ever be excused from sin without them?

(6) Whether in their absence it is always a mortal sin?

Article 1

Whether Certain Blessings are Necessary in Order to Excuse Marriage?

AD PRIMUM SIC PROCEDITUR. Videtur quod matrimonium non debeat habere aliqua bona quibus excusetur. Sicut enim conservatio individui, quae fit per ea quae ad nutritivam pertinent, est de intentione naturae, ita conservatio speciei, quae fit per matrimonium: et multo magis, quanto melius et dignius est bonum speciei quam bonum unius individui. Sed ad actum nutritivae excusandum non indigetur aliquibus. Ergo nec etiam ad excusandum matrimonium.

PRAETEREA, secundum Philosophum, in VIII *Ethic.*, amicitia quae est inter virum et uxorem est naturalis, et claudit in se *honestum, utile* et *delectabile*. Sed illud quod de se est honestum, non indiget aliqua excusatione. Ergo nec matrimonio debent attribui aliqua bona excusantia.

PRAETEREA, matrimonium est institutum in remedium et in officium. Sed secundum quod est in officium, non indiget excusatione: quia sic etiam in paradiso excusatione indiguisset, quod falsum est; ibi enim fuissent *honorabiles nuptiae et torus immaculatus*, ut Augustinus dicit. Similiter nec secundum quod est in remedium: sicut nec alia sacramenta, quae in remedium peccati sunt instituta. Ergo matrimonium huiusmodi excusantia habere non debet.

OBJECTION 1: It would seem that certain blessings are not necessary in order to excuse marriage. For just as the preservation of the individual (which is effected by the nutritive power) is intended by nature, so too is the preservation of the species, which is effected by marriage; and indeed so much the more as the good of the species is better and more exalted than the good of the individual. But no goods are necessary to excuse the act of the nutritive power. Neither, therefore, are they necessary to excuse marriage.

OBJ. 2: Further, according to the Philosopher (*Ethics* 8.12) the friendship between husband and wife is natural, and includes the *virtuous*, the *useful*, and the *pleasant*. But that which is virtuous in itself needs no excuse. Therefore, neither should any goods be assigned for the excuse of matrimony.

OBJ. 3: Further, matrimony was instituted as a remedy and as an office, as stated above (Q. 42, A. 2). Now it needs no excuse insofar as it is instituted as an office, since then it would also have needed an excuse in paradise, which is false, for there, as Augustine says, *marriage would have been without reproach and the marriage-bed without stain* (*On the Literal Meaning of Genesis* 9). In like manner, neither does it need an excuse insofar as it is intended as a remedy any more than do the other sacraments, which were instituted as remedies for sin. Therefore, matrimony does not need these excuses.

335

PRAETEREA, ad omnia quae honeste fieri possunt, virtutes dirigunt. Si ergo matrimonium aliquibus bonis potest honestari, non indiget aliis honestatibus quam animi virtutibus. Et sic non debent matrimonio aliqua bona assignari quibus honestetur: sicut nec aliis in quibus virtutes dirigunt.

SED CONTRA: Ubicumque est indulgentia, ibi est necessaria aliqua excusationis ratio. Sed matrimonium conceditur in statu infirmitatis *secundum indulgentiam*: ut patet I Cor. 7. Ergo indiget per aliqua bona excusari.

PRAETEREA, concubitus matrimonialis et fornicarius sunt eiusdem speciei quantum ad speciem naturae. Sed concubitus fornicarius de se est turpis. Ergo ad hoc quod matrimonialis non sit turpis, oportet ei aliquid addi quod ad honestatem eius pertineat, et in aliam speciem moris trahat.

RESPONDEO dicendum quod nullus sapiens debet iacturam aliquam sustinere nisi pro aliqua recompensatione alicuius aequalis vel melioris boni. Unde electio alicuius quod aliquam iacturam habet annexam, indiget alicuius boni adiunctione, per cuius recompensationem ordinetur et honestetur. In coniunctione autem viri et mulieris rationis iactura accidit: tum quia propter vehementiam delectationis absorbetur ratio, ut *non possit aliquid intelligere in ipso*, ut Philosophus dicit; tum etiam propter *tribulationem carnis*, quam oportet tales sustinere ex sollicitudine temporalium, ut patet I Cor. 7. Et ideo talis coniunctionis electio non potest esse ordinata nisi per recompensationem aliquorum ex quibus dicta coniunctio honestetur. Et haec sunt bona quae matrimonium excusant et honestum reddunt.

AD PRIMUM ergo dicendum quod in actu comestionis non est tam vehemens delectatio rationem absorbens sicut est in praedicta delectatione. Tum quia vis generativa, per quam originale traducitur, est infecta et corrupta: nutritiva autem, per quam non traducitur, est corrupta et non infecta. Tum etiam quia defectum individui quilibet magis sentit iri seipso quam defectum speciei. Unde ad excitandum ad comestionem, secundum quam defectui individui subvenitur, sufficit sensus ipsius defectus. Sed ad excitandum ad actum quo defectui speciei subvenitur, divina providentia delectationem apposuit in illo actu, quae etiam animalia bruta movet, in quibus non est infectio originalis peccati, Et ideo non est simile.

AD SECUNDUM dicendum quod ista bona quae matrimonium honestant, sunt de ratione matrimonii. Et ideo non indiget eis quasi exterioribus quibusdam ad honestandum, sed quasi causantibus in ipso honestatem quae ei secundum se competit.

AD TERTIUM dicendum quod matrimonium, ex hoc ipso quod est in officium vel in remedium, habet rationem utilis et honesti; sed utrumque horum ei competit

OBJ. 4: Further, the virtues are directed to whatever can be done aright. If, then, marriage can be righted by certain goods, it needs nothing else to right it besides the virtues of the soul; and consequently there is no need to assign to matrimony any goods whereby it is righted any more than to other things in which the virtues direct us.

ON THE CONTRARY, Wherever there is indulgence, there must be some reason for excuse. Now marriage is allowed in the state of infirmity *by indulgence* (1 Cor 7:6). Therefore, it needs to be excused by certain goods.

FURTHER, The intercourse of fornication and that of marriage are of the same species as regards the species of nature. But the intercourse of fornication is wrong in itself. Therefore, in order that the marriage intercourse be not wrong, something must be added to it to make it right, and draw it to another moral species.

I ANSWER THAT, No wise man should allow himself to lose a thing except for some compensation in the shape of an equal or better good. Therefore, for a thing that has a loss attached to it to be eligible, it needs to have some good connected with it, which by compensating for that loss makes that thing ordinate and right. Now there is a loss of reason incidental to the union of man and woman, both because the reason is carried away entirely on account of the vehemence of the pleasure, so that *it is unable to understand anything at the same time*, as the Philosopher says (*Ethics* 7.11); and again because of the *tribulation of the flesh* which such persons have to suffer from solicitude for temporal things (1 Cor 7:28). Consequently, the choice of this union cannot be made ordinate except by certain compensations whereby that same union is righted; and these are the goods which excuse marriage and make it right.

REPLY OBJ. 1: In the act of eating there is not such an intense pleasure overpowering the reason as in the aforesaid action, both because the generative power, whereby original sin is transmitted, is infected and corrupt, whereas the nutritive power, by which original sin is not transmitted, is neither corrupt nor infected; and again because each one feels in himself a defect of the individual more than a defect of the species. Hence, in order to entice a man to take food, which supplies a defect of the individual, it is enough that he feel this defect; but in order to entice him to the act whereby a defect of the species is remedied, divine providence attached pleasure to that act, which moves even irrational animals in which there is not the stain of original sin. Hence the comparison fails.

REPLY OBJ. 2: These goods which justify marriage belong to the nature of marriage, which consequently needs them not as extrinsic causes of its rectitude, but as causing in it that rectitude which belongs to it by nature.

REPLY OBJ. 3: From the very fact that marriage is intended as an office or as a remedy it has the aspect of something useful and right; nevertheless, both aspects belong to

ex hoc quod huiusmodi bona habet, quibus fit et officiosum et remedium concupiscentiae adhibens.

AD QUARTUM dicendum quod aliquis actus virtutis honestatur et virtute, quasi principio elicitivo; et circumstantiis, quasi formalibus principiis ipsius. Hoc autem modo se habent bona ad matrimonium sicut circumstantiae ad actus virtutis, ex quibus habet quod virtutis actus esse possit.

it from the fact that it has these goods by which it fulfills the office and affords a remedy to concupiscence.

REPLY OBJ. 4: An act of virtue may derive its rectitude both from the virtue as its inducing principle, and from its circumstances as its formal principles; and the goods of marriage are related to marriage as circumstances to an act of virtue which owes it to those circumstances that it can be an act of virtue.

Article 2

Whether the Goods of Marriage Are Sufficiently Enumerated?

AD SECUNDUM SIC PROCEDITUR. Videtur quod insufficienter bona matrimonii assignentur a Magistro Sententiarum: scilicet *fides, proles ei sacramentum*. Quia matrimonium non solum fit in hominibus ad prolem procreandam et nutriendam, sed, ad consortium communis vitae, propter operum communicationem, ut dicitur in VIII *Ethic*. Ergo, sicut ponitur proles bonum matrimonii, ita debet poni *communicatio operum*.

PRAETEREA, coniunctio Christi ad Ecclesiam, quam matrimonium significat, perficitur per caritatem. Ergo inter bona matrimonii magis debet poni caritas quam *fides*.

PRAETEREA, in matrimonio, sicut exigitur quod neuter coniugum ad alterius torum accedat, ita exigitur quod unus alteri debitum reddat. Sed primum pertinet ad fidem, ut Magister dicit. Ergo deberet etiam *iustitia*, propter redditionem debiti, inter bona matrimonii computari.

PRAETEREA, sicut in matrimonio, inquantum significat coniunctionem Christi et Ecclesiae, requiritur indivisibilitas, ita et *unitas*, ut sit *una unius*. Sed *sacramentum*, quod inter tria bona matrimonii computatur, pertinet ad indivisionem. Ergo deberet esse aliquid aliud quod pertineret ad unitatem.

SED CONTRA: Videtur quod superfluant. Quia unica virtus sufficit ad unum actum honestandum. Sed *fides* est una virtus. Ergo non oportuit alia duo addere ad honestandum matrimonium.

PRAETEREA, non ex eodem aliquid accipit rationem utilis et honesti: cum utile et honestum ex opposito bonum dividant. Sed ex prole matrimonium accipit rationem utilis. Ergo proles non debet computari inter bona quibus matrimonium honestatur.

PRAETEREA, nihil debet poni ut proprietas vel conditio sui ipsius. Sed haec bona ponuntur ut quaedam conditiones matrimonii. Ergo, cum matrimonium sit sa-

OBJECTION 1: It would seem that the goods of marriage are insufficiently enumerated by the Master (*Sentences* IV, D. 31) as *faith, offspring, and sacrament*. For the object of marriage among men is not only the begetting and feeding of children, but also the partnership of a common life, whereby each one contributes his share of work to the common stock, as stated in *Ethics* 8.12. Therefore, as the offspring is reckoned a good of matrimony, so also should the *communication of works*.

OBJ. 2: Further, the union of Christ with the Church, signified by matrimony, is the effect of charity. Therefore, charity rather than *faith* should be reckoned among the goods of matrimony.

OBJ. 3: Further, in matrimony, just as it is required that neither party have intercourse with another, so is it required that the one pay the marriage debt to the other. Now the former pertains to faith, according to the Master (*Sentences* IV, D. 31). Therefore, *justice* should also be reckoned among the goods of marriage on account of the payment of the debt.

OBJ. 4: Further, in matrimony, insofar as it signifies the union of Christ with the Church, just as indivisibility is required so also is *unity*, whereby *one man has one wife*. But the *sacrament*, which is reckoned among the three marriage goods, pertains to indivisibility. Therefore, there should be something else pertaining to unity.

OBJ. 5: On the other hand, it would seem that they are too many. For one virtue suffices to make one act right. Now *faith* is one virtue. Therefore, it was not necessary to add two other goods to make marriage right.

OBJ. 6: Further, the same cause does not make a thing both useful and virtuous, since the useful and the virtuous are opposite divisions of the good. Now marriage derives its character of useful from the offspring. Therefore, the offspring should not be reckoned among the goods that make marriage virtuous.

OBJ. 7: Further, nothing should be reckoned as a property or condition of itself. Now these goods are reckoned to be conditions of marriage. Therefore, since matrimony is a

cramentum, non debet poni *sacramentum* inter bona matrimonii.

Respondeo dicendum quod matrimonium est in officium naturae, et est sacramentum Ecclesiae. Inquantum ergo est in officium naturae, duobus ordinatur, sicut et quilibet alius virtutis actus. Quorum unum exigitur ex parte ipsius agentis: et haec est intentio finis debiti. Et sic ponitur bonum matrimonii *proles*. Aliud exigitur ex parte ipsius actus, qui est bonus in genere ex hoc quod cadit supra debitam materiam. Et sic est *fides*, per quam homo ad suam accedit et non ad aliam. Sed ulterius habet aliquam bonitatem inquantum est sacramentum. Et hoc significatur ipso nomine *sacramenti*.

Ad primum ergo dicendum quod in *prole* non solum intelligitur procreatio prolis, sed etiam educatio ipsius, ad quam sicut ad finem ordinatur tota communicatio operum quae est inter virum et uxorem inquantum sunt matrimonio coniunctim quia patres naturaliter *thesaurizant filiis*, ut patet II Cor. 12. Et sic in *prole*, quasi in principali fine, alius quasi secundarius includitur.

Ad secundum dicendum quod *fides* non accipitur hic prout est virtus theologica, sed prout est pars iustitiae: secundum quod fides dicitur ex hoc quod *fiunt dicta* in conservatione promissorum. Quia in matrimonio, cum sit quidam contractus, est quaedam promissio per quam talis vir tali mulieri determinatur.

Ad tertium dicendum quod, sicut in promissione matrimonii continetur ut neuter ad alium torum accedat, ita etiam quod sibi invicem debitum reddant. Et hoc etiam est principalius: cum sequatur ex ipsa mutua potestate in invicem data. Et ideo utrumque ad *fidem* pertinet. Sed in libro *Sententiarum* ponitur quod est minus manifestum.

Ad quartum dicendum quod in *sacramento* non solum intelligenda est indivisio, sed omnia illa quae consequuntur matrimonium ex hoc quod est signum coniunctionis Christi et Ecclesiae.

Vel dicendum quod unitas quam obiectio tangit, pertinet ad *fidem*, sicut et indivisio ad sacramentum.

Ad quintum dicendum quod *fides* non accipitur hic pro aliqua virtute: sed pro quadam conditione virtutis ex qua fides nominatur quae ponitur pars iustitiae.

Ad sextum dicendum quod, sicut debitus usus boni utilis accipit rationem honesti, non quidem ex. utili, sed ex ratione, quae rectum usum facit; ita etiam ordinatio ad aliquod bonum utile potest facere bonitatem honestatis ex vi rationis debitam ordinationem facientis. Et hoc modo matrimonium, ex hoc quod ordinatur ad prolem, et utile est, et nihilominus honestum, inquantum debite ordinatur.

Ad septimum dicendum quod, sicut Magister dicit, 31 dist. IV *Sent.*, *sacramentum* non dicitur hic ipsum ma-

sacrament, the *sacrament* should not be reckoned a good of matrimony.

I answer that, Matrimony is instituted both as an office of nature and as a sacrament of the Church. As an office of nature it is directed by two things, like every other virtuous act. One of these is required on the part of the agent and is the intention of the due end, and thus the *offspring* is accounted a good of matrimony. The other is required on the part of the act, which is good generically through being about a due matter: and thus we have *faith*, whereby a man has intercourse with his wife and with no other woman. Besides this it has a certain goodness as a sacrament, and this is signified by the very word *sacrament*.

Reply Obj. 1: 'Offspring' signifies not only the begetting of children, but also their education, to which as its end is directed the entire communion of works that exists between man and wife as united in marriage, since parents naturally *lay up* for their *children* (2 Cor 12:14); so that the *offspring* like a principal end includes another secondary end, as it were.

Reply Obj. 2: *Faith* is not taken here as a theological virtue, but as part of justice, insofar as faith signifies the *suiting of deed to word* by keeping one's promises; for since marriage is a contract, it contains a promise whereby this man is assigned to this woman.

Reply Obj. 3: Just as the marriage promise means that neither party is to have intercourse with a third party, so does it require that they should mutually pay the marriage debt. The latter is indeed the chief of the two, since it follows from the power which each receives over the other. Consequently, both these things pertain to *faith*, although the *Sentences* mentions that which is the less manifest.

Reply Obj. 4: By *sacrament* we are to understand not only indivisibility, but all those things that result from marriage being a sign of Christ's union with the Church.

We may also reply that the unity to which the objection refers pertains to *faith*, just as indivisibility belongs to the sacrament.

Reply Obj. 5: *Faith* here does not denote a virtue, but that condition of virtue which is a part of justice and is called by the name of faith.

Reply Obj. 6: Just as the right use of a useful good derives its rectitude not from the useful but from the reason which causes the right use, so too direction to a useful good may cause the goodness of rectitude by virtue of the reason causing the right direction; and in this way marriage, through being directed to the offspring, is useful, and nevertheless righteous, inasmuch as it is directed aright.

Reply Obj. 7: As the Master says (*Sentences* IV, D. 31), *sacrament* here does not mean matrimony itself, but its in-

trimonium, sed inseparabilitas eius, quae est eiusdem rei signum cuius est matrimonium.

Vel dicendum quod, quamvis matrimonium sit sacramentum, tamen aliud est matrimonio esse matrimonium, et aliud est ei esse sacramentum: quia non solum ad hoc est institutum ut sit in signum rei sacrae, sed etiam ut sit in officium naturae. Et ideo ratio sacramenti est quaedam conditio adveniens matrimonio secundum se considerato, ex quo etiam honestatem habet. Et ideo sacramentalitas eius, ut ita dicam, ponitur inter bona honestantia matrimonium. Et secundum hoc in tertio bono matrimonii, scilicet *sacramento*, non solum intelligitur inseparabilitas, sed etiam omnia quae ad significationem ipsius pertinent.

dissolubility, which is a sign of the same thing as matrimony is.

We may also reply that although marriage is a sacrament, marriage as marriage is not the same as marriage as a sacrament, since it was instituted not only as a sign of a sacred thing but also as an office of nature. Hence the sacramental aspect is a condition added to marriage considered in itself, from it is also derives its rectitude. Hence its sacramentality, if I may use the term, is reckoned among the goods which justify marriage; and accordingly this third good of marriage, that is, the *sacrament*, denotes not only its indissolubility, but also whatever pertains to its signification.

Article 3

Whether the Sacrament Is the Chief of the Marriage Goods?

AD TERTIUM SIC PROCEDITUR. Videtur quod *sacramentum* non sit principalius inter bona matrimonii. Quia *finis est potissimum in unoquoque*. Sed *proles* est matrimonii finis. Ergo proles est principalius matrimonii bonum.

PRAETEREA, principalius in ratione speciei est differentia, quae complet speciem, quam genus: sicut forma quam materia in constitutione rei naturalis. Sed *sacramentum* competiit matrimonio ex ratione sui generis; *proles* autem et *fides* ex ratione differentiae, inquantum est tale sacramentum. Ergo alia duo sunt magis principalia in matrimonio quam sacramentum.

PRAETEREA, sicut invenitur matrimonium sine prole et fide, ita invenitur sine inseparabilitate: sicut patet quando alter coniugum ante matrimonium consummatum ad religionem transit. Ergo nec ex hac ratione sacramentum est in matrimonio principalius:

PRAETEREA, effectus non potest esse principalior sua causa. Sed consensus, qui est causa matrimonii, frequenter immutatur. Ergo et matrimonium solvi potest. Et sic inseparabilitas non semper comitatur matrimonium.

PRAETEREA, sacramenta quae habent effectum perpetuum, imprimunt characterem. Sed in matrimonio non imprimitur character. Ergo non adest ei inseparabilitas perpetua. Et ideo, sicut est matrimonium sine *prole*, ita potest esse sine *sacramento*: Et sic idem quod prius.

SED CONTRA: Illud quod ponitur in definitione rei est sibi maxime essentiale. Sed indivisio, quae pertinet ad *sacramentum*, ponitur in definitione supra de matri-

OBJECTION 1: It would seem that the *sacrament* is not the chief of the marriage goods. For *the end is principal in everything*. Now the end of marriage is the *offspring*. Therefore, the offspring is the chief marriage good.

OBJ. 2: Further, in the specific nature the difference is more important than the genus, even as the form is more important than matter in the composition of a natural thing. Now *sacrament* refers to marriage on the part of its genus, while *offspring* and *faith* refer thereto on the part of the difference whereby it is a special kind of sacrament. Therefore, these other two are more important than sacrament in reference to marriage.

OBJ. 3: Further, just as we find marriage without offspring and without faith, so do we find it without indissolubility, as in the case where one of the parties enters religion before the marriage is consummated. Therefore, neither from this point of view is sacrament the most important marriage good.

OBJ. 4: Further, an effect cannot be more important than its cause. Now consent, which is the cause of matrimony, is often changed. Therefore, the marriage also can be dissolved; consequently, inseparability is not always a condition of marriage.

OBJ. 5: Further, the sacraments which produce an everlasting effect imprint a character. But no character is imprinted in matrimony. Therefore, it is not conditioned by a lasting inseparability. Consequently, just as there is marriage without *offspring* so is there marriage without *sacrament*, and thus the same conclusion follows as above.

ON THE CONTRARY, That which has a place in the definition of a thing is most essential thereto. Now inseparability, which pertains to *sacrament*, is placed in the definition

monio data, non autem *proles* vel *fides*. Ergo *sacramentum* inter alia est matrimonio essentialius.

PRAETEREA, virtus divina, quae in sacramentis operatur, est efficacior quam virtus humana. Sed *proles* et *fides* pertinent ad matrimonium secundum quod est in officium naturae humanae; *sacramentum* autem secundum quod est ex institutione divina. Ergo *sacramentum* est principalius in matrimonio quam alia duo.

RESPONDEO dicendum quod aliquid dicitur in re aliqua principalius, altero duorum modorum: aut quia altero essentialius; aut quia dignius. Si quia dignius, sic omnibus modis *sacramentum* est principalius inter tria bona coniugii. Quia pertinet ad matrimonium inquantum est sacramentum gratiae. Alia vero duo pertinent ad ipsum inquantum est quoddam naturae officium. Perfectio autem gratiae est dignior perfectione naturae.

Si autem dicatur principalius quod est essentialius, sic distinguendum est. Quia *fides* et *proles* possunt dupliciter considerari. Uno modo, in seipsis. Et sic pertinent ad usum matrimonii, per quem et proles producitur, et pactio coniugalis servatur. Sed indivisibilitas, quam *sacramentum* importat, pertinet ad ipsum matrimonium secundum se: quia ex hoc ipso quod per pactionem coniugalem sui potestatem sibi invicem in perpetuum coniuges tradunt, sequitur quod separari non possint. Et inde est quod matrimonium nunquam invenitur sine inseparabilitate: invenitur autem sine fide et prole, quia esse rei non dependet ab usu suo. Et secundum hoc sacramentum est essentialius matrimonio quam *fides* et *proles*.

Alio modo possunt considerari fides et proles secundum quod sunt in suis principiis: ut pro prole accipiatur intentio *prolis*, et pro *fide* debitum servandi fidem. Sine quibus etiam matrimonium esse non potest: quia haec in hoc matrimonio ex ipsa pactione coniugali causantur; ita quod, si aliquid contrarium huius exprimeretur in consensu qui matrimonium facit, non esset verum matrimonium. Et sic accipiendo fidem et prolem, proles est essentialissimum in matrimonio, et secundo fides, et tertio sacramentum: sicut etiam homini est essentialius esse naturae quam esse gratiae, quamvis esse gratiae sit dignius.

AD PRIMUM ergo dicendum quod finis secundum intentionem est primum in re, sed secundum consecutionem est ultimum. Et similiter *proles* se habet inter matrimonii bona. Et ideo quodammodo est principalius, et quodammodo non.

AD SECUNDUM dicendum quod sacramentum, prout ponitur tertium matrimonii bonum, pertinet ad matrimonium ratione suae differentiae: dicitur enim *sacramentum* ex significatione huius rei sacrae determinatae quam matrimonium significat.

of marriage (Q. 44, A. 3), while *offspring* and *faith* are not. Therefore, among the other goods *sacrament* is the most essential to matrimony.

FURTHER, The divine power which works in the sacraments is more efficacious than human power. But *offspring* and *faith* pertain to matrimony as it is an office of human nature, whereas *sacrament* pertains to it as instituted by God. Therefore, *sacrament* takes a more important part in marriage than the other two.

I ANSWER THAT, This or that may be more important to a thing in two ways: either because it is more essential or because it is more excellent. If the reason is because it is more excellent, then *sacrament* is in every way the most important of the three marriage goods, since it belongs to marriage considered as a sacrament of grace, while the other two belong to it as an office of nature; and a perfection of grace is more excellent than a perfection of nature.

If, however, it is said to be more important because it is more essential, we must draw a distinction; for *faith* and *offspring* can be considered in two ways. First, in themselves, and thus they regard the use of matrimony in begetting children and observing the marriage compact; while inseparability, which is denoted by *sacrament*, regards the very sacrament considered in itself, since from the very fact that by the marriage compact man and wife give to one another power over each other in perpetuity, it follows that they cannot be put asunder. Hence there is no matrimony without inseparability, whereas there is matrimony without faith and offspring, because the existence of a thing does not depend on its use; and in this sense sacrament is more essential to matrimony than faith and offspring.

Second, faith and offspring may be considered as in their principles, so that *offspring* denote the intention of having children, and *faith* the duty of remaining faithful, and there can be no matrimony without these also, since they are caused in matrimony by the marriage compact itself, so that if anything contrary to these were expressed in the consent which makes a marriage, the marriage would be invalid. Taking faith and offspring in this sense, it is clear that offspring is the most essential thing in marriage, second, faith, and third, sacrament; even as to man it is more essential to be in nature than to be in grace, although it is more excellent to be in grace.

REPLY OBJ. 1: The end as regards the intention stands first in a thing, but as regards the attainment it stands last. It is the same with *offspring* among the marriage goods; thus in a way it is the most important, and in another way it is not.

REPLY OBJ. 2: Sacrament, even as holding the third place among the marriage goods, belongs to matrimony by reason of its difference; for it is called *sacrament* from its signification of that particular sacred thing which matrimony signifies.

AD TERTIUM dicendum quod nuptiae, secundum Augustinum, sunt bona mortalium: unde *in resurrectione neque nubent neque nubentur*, ut dicitur Matth. 22. Et ideo vinculum matrimonii non se extendit ultra vitam in qua contrahitur: et ideo dicitur inseparabile, quia non potest in hac vita separari. Sed per mortem separari potest: sive corporalem, post carnalem coniunctionem; sive spiritualem, post spiritualem tantum.

AD QUARTUM dicendum quod, quamvis consensus qui facit matrimonium, non sit perpetuus materialiter, idest quantum ad substantiam actus, quia ille actus cessat et potest contrarius succedere; tamen, formaliter loquendo, est perpetuus, quia est de perpetuitate vinculi: alias non faceret matrimonium; non enim consensus ad tempus in aliquam matrimonium facit. Et dico *formaliter*, secundum quod actus accipit speciem ab obiecto. Et secundum hoc matrimonium ex consensu inseparabilitatem accipit.

AD QUINTUM dicendum quod in sacramentis in quibus imprimitur character, traditur potestas ad actus spirituales: sed in matrimonio ad actus corporales. Unde matrimonium, ratione potestatis quam in se invicem coniuges accipiunt convenit cum sacramentis in quibus character imprimitur, et ex hoc habet inseparabilitatem, ut Magister dicit: sed differt ab eis inquantum potestas illa est ad actus corporales. Et propter hoc non imprimit characterem spiritualem.

REPLY OBJ. 3: According to Augustine (*On the Good of Marriage* 19), marriage is a good of mortals, wherefore *in the resurrection they shall neither marry nor be married* (Matt 22:30). Hence the marriage bond does not last after the life in which it is contracted, and consequently it is said to be inseparable, because it cannot be sundered in this life. But it can be separated either by bodily death after carnal union, or by spiritual death after a merely spiritual union.

REPLY OBJ. 4: Although the consent which makes a marriage is not everlasting materially, i.e., in regard to the substance of the act, since that act ceases and a contrary act may succeed it, nevertheless formally speaking it is everlasting because it is a consent to an everlasting bond, else it would not make a marriage; for a consent to take a woman for a time makes no marriage. Hence it is everlasting *formally*, inasmuch as an act takes its species from its object; and thus it is that matrimony derives its inseparability from the consent.

REPLY OBJ. 5: In those sacraments wherein a character is imprinted, power is given to perform spiritual actions; but in matrimony, to perform bodily actions. Therefore, matrimony, by reason of the power which man and wife receive over one another, agrees with the sacraments in which a character is imprinted, and from this it derives its inseparability, as the Master says (*Sentences* IV, D. 31); yet it differs from them insofar as that power regards bodily acts; hence it does not confer a spiritual character.

Article 4

Whether the Marriage Act Is Excused by the Aforesaid Goods?

AD QUARTUM SIC PROCEDITUR. Videtur quod actus matrimonii non possit excusari per bona praedicta ut non sit omnino peccatum. Quia quicumque sustinet damnum maioris boni propter minus bonum, peccat: quia inordinate sustinet. Sed bonum rationis, quod laeditur in ipso actu coniugali, est maius quam haec tria coniugii bona. Ergo praedicta bona non sufficiunt ad excusandum coniugalem concubitum.

PRAETEREA, si bonum malo additur, in genere moris totum efficitur malum, non autem totum bonum: quia una circumstantia mala facit actum malum, non autem una bona facit ipsum bonum. Sed actus coniugalis secundum se est malus: alias excusatione non indigeret. Ergo bona matrimonii adiuncta non possunt ipsum bonum facere.

PRAETEREA, ubicumque est immoderatio passionis, ibi est vitium in moribus. Sed bona matrimonii non possunt efficere quin delectatio illius actus sit immoderata. Ergo non possunt excusare quin sit peccatum.

OBJECTION 1: It would seem that the marriage act cannot be altogether excused from sin by the aforesaid goods. For whoever allows himself to lose a greater good for the sake of a lesser good sins because he allows it inordinately. Now the good of reason, which is prejudiced in the marriage act, is greater than these three marriage goods. Therefore, the aforesaid goods do not suffice to excuse marital intercourse.

OBJ. 2: Further, if a moral good be added to a moral evil the sum total is evil and not good, since one evil circumstance makes an action evil, whereas one good circumstance does not make it good. Now the marriage act is evil in itself, else it would need no excuse. Therefore, the addition of the marriage goods cannot make the act good.

OBJ. 3: Further, wherever there is immoderate passion there is moral vice. Now the marriage goods cannot prevent the pleasure in that act from being immoderate. Therefore, they cannot excuse it from being a sin.

Praeterea, verecundia non est nisi de *turpi actu*, secundum Damascenum. Sed bona matrimonii non tollunt erubescentiam ab illo actu. Ergo non possunt excusare quin sit peccatum.

Sed contra: Concubitus coniugalis non differt a fornicario nisi per bona matrimonii. Si ergo haec non sufficerent excusare ipsum, tunc matrimonium semper illicitum remaneret.

Praeterea, bona matrimonii se habent ad actum eius sicut circumstantiae debitae, ut dictum est. Sed circumstantiae tales sufficienter faciunt quod actus aliquis non sit malus. Ergo et haec bona possunt excusare matrimonium ut nullo modo sit peccatum.

Respondeo dicendum quod actus dicitur excusari dupliciter. Uno modo, ex parte facientis: ita quod non imputetur facienti in culpam, quamvis sit malus, vel saltem non in tantam culpam; sicut ignorantia dicitur excusare peccatum in toto vel in parte. Alio modo dicitur excusari actus ex parte sui: ita scilicet quod non sit malus. Et hoc modo praedicta bona dicuntur excusare actum matrimonii.

Ex eodem autem habet actus aliquis quod non sit malus in genere moris, et quod sit bonus: quia non est aliquis actus indifferens, ut in II libro dictum est. Dicitur autem aliquis humanus actus bonus dupliciter. Uno modo, bonitate virtutis. Et sic habet actus quod sit bonus ex his quae ipsum in medio ponunt. Et hoc faciunt in actu matrimonii fides et proles, ut ex dictis patet. Alio modo, bonitate *sacramenti*, secundum quod actus non solum bonus, sed etiam sanctus dicitur. Et hanc bonitatem habet actus matrimonii ex indivisibilitate coniunctionis, secundum quam significat coniunctionem Christi ad Ecclesiam. Et sic patet quod praedicta bona sufficienter actum matrimonii excusant.

Ad primum ergo dicendum quod per matrimonii actum non incurrit homo in damnum rationis quantum ad habitum, sed solum quantum ad actum. Nec est inconveniens quod quandoque aliquis actus melior secundum genus suum interrumpatur pro aliquo minus bono actu: hoc enim sine peccato fieri potest, sicut patet in eo qui ab actu contemplationis cessat ut interdum actioni vacet.

Ad secundum dicendum quod ratio illa procederet si malum quod inseparabiliter comitatur concubitum, esset malum culpae. Nunc autem non est malum culpae, sed poena tantum, quae est inobedientia concupiscentiae ad rationem. Et ideo ratio non sequitur.

Ad tertium dicendum quod superabundantia passionis quae facit vitium, non attenditur secundum quantitativam ipsius intensionem, sed secundum proportionem ad rationem. Unde tunc solum passio reputatur immoderata quando limites rationis excedit. Delectatio

Obj. 4: Further, according to Damascene (*On the Orthodox Faith* 2.15), shame is only caused by a *disgraceful deed*. Now the marriage goods do not deprive that deed of its shame. Therefore, they cannot excuse it from sin.

On the contrary, The marriage act does not differ from fornication except by the marriage goods. If, therefore, these were not sufficient to excuse it, marriage would be always unlawful; and this is contrary to what was stated above (Q. 41, A. 3).

Further, The marriage goods are related to its act as its due circumstances, as stated above (A. 1). Now the like circumstances are sufficient to prevent an action from being evil. Therefore, these goods can excuse marriage so that it is in no way a sin.

I answer that, An act is said to be excused in two ways. First, on the part of the agent, so that although it be evil it is not imputed as sin to the agent, or at least not as so grave a sin. Thus ignorance is said to excuse a sin wholly or partly. Second, an act is said to be excused on its part, so that, namely, it is not evil; and it is thus that the aforesaid goods are said to excuse the marriage act.

Now it is from the same cause that an act is not morally evil and that it is good, since there is no such thing as an indifferent act, as was stated in the Second Book (*Sentences* II, D. 40; I-II, Q. 18, A. 9). Now a human act is said to be good in two ways. In one way by goodness of virtue, and thus an act derives its goodness from those things which place it in the mean. This is what faith and offspring do in the marriage act, as stated above (A. 2). In another way, by goodness of the *sacrament*, in which way an act is said to be not only good, but also holy, and the marriage act derives this goodness from the indissolubility of the union, in respect of which it signifies the union of Christ with the Church. Thus it is clear that the aforesaid goods sufficiently excuse the marriage act.

Reply Obj. 1: By the marriage act man does not incur harm to his reason as to habit, but only as to act. Nor is it unfitting that a certain act which is generically better be sometimes interrupted for some less good act; for it is possible to do this without sin, as in the case of one who ceases from the act of contemplation in order to devote himself to action in the meanwhile.

Reply Obj. 2: This argument would avail if the evil that is inseparable from carnal intercourse were an evil of sin. But in this case it is an evil not of sin, but of punishment alone, consisting in the rebellion of concupiscence against reason; and consequently the conclusion does not follow.

Reply Obj. 3: The excess of passion that amounts to a sin does not refer to the passion's quantitative intensity, but to its proportion to reason; wherefore it is only when a passion goes beyond the bounds of reason that it is reckoned to be immoderate. Now the pleasure attaching to the marriage

autem quae fit in actu matrimoniali, quamvis sit intensissima secundum quantitatem, non tamen excedit limites sibi a ratione praefixos ante principium suum: quamvis in ipsa delectatione ratio eos ordinare non possit.

Ad quartum dicendum quod turpitudo quae semper est in actu matrimoniali et erubescentiam facit, est turpitudo poenae, et non culpae: quia de quolibet defectu homo naturaliter erubescit.

act, while it is most intense in point of quantity, does not go beyond the bounds previously appointed by reason before the commencement of the act, although reason is unable to regulate them during the pleasure itself.

Reply Obj. 4: The turpitude that always accompanies the marriage act and always causes shame is the turpitude of punishment, not of sin, for man is naturally ashamed of any defect.

Article 5

Whether the Marriage Act Can Be Excused Without the Marriage Goods?

Ad quintum sic proceditur. Videtur quod actus matrimonialis excusari possit etiam sine bonis matrimonii. Qui enim a natura tantum movetur ad actum matrimonii, non videtur aliquod bonum matrimonii intendere: quia bona matrimonii pertinent ad gratiam vel virtutem. Sed quando aliquis solo appetitu naturali movetur ad actum praedictum, non videtur esse peccatum: quia nullum naturale est malum, cum *malum sit praeter naturam et praeter ordinem*, ut Dionysius dicit. Ergo actus matrimonii excusari potest etiam sine bonis matrimonii.

Praeterea, ille qui utitur coniuge ad fornicationem vitandam, non videtur aliquod bonum matrimonii intendere. Sed talis non peccat, ut videtur: quia ad hoc est matrimonium concessum humanae infirmitati, ut fornicatio vitetur, ut patet I Cor. 7. Ergo etiam sine bonis matrimonii potest actus eius excusari.

Praeterea, ille qui utitur re sua ad libitum, non facit contra iustitiam, et sic non peccat, ut videtur. Sed per matrimonium uxor efficitur res viri, et e converso. Ergo, si se invicem ad libitum utuntur libidine movente, non videtur esse peccatum. Et sic idem quod prius.

Praeterea, illud quod est bonum ex genere, non efficitur malum nisi ex mala intentione fiat. Sed actus matrimonii, quo quis suam cognoscit, est ex genere bonus. Ergo non potest malus esse nisi mala intentione fiat. Sed potest bona intentione fieri etiam si non intendat aliquod bonum matrimonii: puta cum quis salutem corporalem per hoc intendit servare aut consequi. Ergo videtur quod etiam sine matrimonii bonis actus ille possit excusari.

Sed contra: *Remota causa removetur effectus.* Sed causa honestatis actus matrimonialis sunt matrimonii bona. Ergo sine eis non potest actus matrimonialis excusari.

Praeterea, non differt actus praedictus ab actu fornicario nisi in praedictis bonis. Sed concubitus fornica-

Objection 1: It would seem that the marriage act can be excused even without the marriage goods. For he who is moved by nature alone to the marriage act apparently does not intend any of the marriage goods, since the marriage goods pertain to grace or virtue. Yet when a person is moved to the aforesaid act by the natural appetite alone, seemingly he commits no sin, for nothing natural is an evil, since *evil is contrary to nature and order*, as Dionysius says (*On the Divine Names* 4). Therefore, the marriage act can be excused even without the marriage goods.

Obj. 2: Further, he who has intercourse with his wife in order to avoid fornication does not seemingly intend any of the marriage goods. Yet he does not sin apparently, because marriage was granted to human weakness for the very purpose of avoiding fornication (1 Cor 7:2, 6). Therefore, the marriage act can be excused even without the marriage goods.

Obj. 3: Further, he who uses as he will that which is his own does not act against justice, and thus seemingly does not sin. Now marriage makes the wife the husband's own, and vice versa. Therefore, if they use one another at will through the instigation of lust, it would seem that it is no sin; and thus the same conclusion follows.

Obj. 4: Further, that which is good generically does not become evil unless it be done with an evil intention. Now the marriage act, whereby a husband knows his wife, is generically good. Therefore, it cannot be evil unless it be done with an evil intention. Now it can be done with a good intention even without intending any marriage good, for instance, by intending to keep or acquire bodily health. Therefore, it seems that this act can be excused even without the marriage goods.

On the contrary, *If the cause be removed, the effect is removed.* Now the marriage goods are the cause of rectitude in the marriage act. Therefore, the marriage act cannot be excused without them.

Further, The aforesaid act does not differ from the act of fornication except in the aforesaid goods. But the act of

rius semper est malus. Ergo, si non excusatur praedictis bonis, etiam matrimonialis actus semper erit malus.

RESPONDEO dicendum quod, sicut bona matrimonii, secundum quod sunt in habitu, faciunt matrimonium honestum et sanctum; ita etiam, secundum quod sunt in actuali intentione, faciunt actum matrimonii honestum, quantum ad illa duo bona matrimonii quae ipsius actum respiciunt. Unde quando coniuges conveniunt causa prolis procreandae, vel ut sibi invicem debitum reddant, quod ad *fidem* pertinet, totaliter excusantur a peccato. Sed tertium bonum non pertinet ad usum matrimonii, sed ad essentiam ipsius, ut dictum est. Unde facit ipsum matrimonium honestum: non autem actum eius, ut per hoc actus eius absque peccato reddatur, quia causa alicuius significationis conveniunt. Et ideo duobus solis modis coniuges absque omni peccato conveniunt: scilicet causa procreandae prolis, et debiti reddendi. Alias autem semper est ibi peccatum, ad minus veniale.

AD PRIMUM ergo dicendum quod proles prout est bonum sacramenti, addit supra prolem prout est bonum intentum a natura. Natura enim intendit prolem prout in ipsa salvatur bonum speciei: sed in prole secundum quod est bonum sacramenti matrimonii, ultra hoc intelligitur ut proles suscepta ulterius ordinetur in Deum. Et ideo oportet quod intentio naturae, qua prolem intendit, referatur, actu vel habitu, ad intentionem, prolis prout est bonum sacramenti: alias staretur in creatura, quod sine peccato esse non potest. Et ideo, quando natura tantum movet ad actum matrimonii, non excusatur a peccato omnino, nisi inquantum motus naturae ordinatur, actu vel habitu, ulterius ad prolem secundum quod est bonum sacramenti. Nec tamen sequitur quod motus naturae sit malus. Sed quod sit imperfectus, nisi ad aliquod bonum matrimonii ulterius ordinetur.

AD SECUNDUM dicendum quod, si aliquis per actum matrimonii intendat vitare fornicationem in coniuge, non est aliquod peccatum: quia hoc est quaedam redditio debiti, quae ad bonum *fidei* pertinet. Sed si intendat vitare fornicationem in se, sic est ibi aliqua superfluitas. Et secundum hoc est peccatum veniale. Nec ad hoc est matrimonium institutum nisi *secundum indulgentiam* quae est de peccatis venialibus.

AD TERTIUM dicendum quod una debita circumstantia non sufficit ad hoc quod actus sit bonus. Et ideo non oportet quod, qualitercumque quis re sua utatur, usus sit bonus: sed quando utitur re sua ut debet secundum omnes circumstantias.

AD QUARTUM dicendum quod, quamvis intendere sanitatis conservationem non sit per se malum, tamen haec intentio efficitur mala si ex aliquo sanitas intendatur quod non est ad hoc de se ordinatum: sicut qui ex

fornication is always evil. Therefore, the marriage act also will always be evil unless it be excused by the aforesaid goods.

I ANSWER THAT, Just as the marriage goods, insofar as they consist in a habit, make a marriage honest and holy, so too, insofar as they are in the actual intention, they make the marriage act honest, as regards those two marriage goods which relate to the marriage act. Hence when married persons come together for the purpose of begetting children, or of paying the debt to one another (which pertains to *faith*) they are wholly excused from sin. But the third good does not relate to the use of marriage, but to its excuse, as stated above (A. 3); wherefore it makes marriage itself honest, but not its act, as though its act were wholly excused from sin through being done on account of some signification. Consequently, there are only two ways in which married persons can come together without any sin at all, namely, in order to have offspring, and in order to pay the debt. Otherwise it is always at least a venial sin.

REPLY OBJ. 1: The offspring considered as a marriage good includes something besides the offspring as a good intended by nature. For nature intends offspring as safeguarding the good of the species, whereas the offspring as a good of the sacrament of marriage includes besides this the directing of the child to God. Therefore, the intention of nature which intends the offspring must be referred either actually or habitually to the intention of having an offspring as a good of the sacrament: otherwise the intention would go no further than a creature, and this is always a sin. Consequently, whenever nature alone moves a person to the marriage act, he is not wholly excused from sin, except insofar as the movement of nature is further directed actually or habitually to the offspring as a good of the sacrament. Nor does it follow that the instigation of nature is evil, but that it is imperfect unless it be further directed to some marriage good.

REPLY OBJ. 2: If a man intends by the marriage act to prevent fornication in his wife, it is no sin, because this is a kind of payment of the debt that comes under the good of *faith*. But if he intends to avoid fornication in himself, then there is a certain superfluity, and accordingly there is a venial sin, nor was the sacrament instituted for that purpose, except *by indulgence* which regards venial sins.

REPLY OBJ. 3: One due circumstance does not suffice to make a good act, and consequently it does not follow that, no matter how one should use one's own property, the use is good, but when one uses it as one ought according to all the circumstances.

REPLY OBJ. 4: Although it is not evil in itself to intend to keep oneself in good health, this intention becomes evil if one intend health by means of something that is not naturally ordained for that purpose; for instance, if one sought

sacramento baptismi tantum salutem corporalem quaereret. Et similiter etiam est in proposito in actu matrimonii.

only bodily health by the sacrament of baptism. The same applies to the marriage act in the question at issue.

Article 6

Whether It Is a Mortal Sin for a Man to Have Knowledge of His Wife with the Intention Not of a Marriage Good but Merely of Pleasure?

AD SEXTUM SIC PROCEDITUR. Videtur quod, quandocumque aliquis uxorem cognoscit non intendens aliquod bonum matrimonii sed solam delectationem, mortaliter peccet. Quia Hieronymus dicit, et habetur in littera: *voluptates quae de meretricum amplexibus capiuntur, in uxore damnandae sunt.* Sed non dicitur esse damnabile nisi peccatum mortale; ergo cognoscere uxorem propter voluptatem solam est semper peccatum mortale.

PRAETEREA, consensus in delectationem est peccatum mortale, ut in II libro dictum est. Sed quicumque cognoscit uxorem suam causa delectationis, consentit in delectationem. Ergo mortaliter peccat.

PRAETEREA, quicumque usum creaturae non refert in Deum, creatura fruitur: quod est peccatum mortale. Sed quicumque uxore propter solam delectationem utitur, hunc usum non refert in Deum. Ergo mortaliter peccat.

PRAETEREA, nullus debet excommunicari nisi pro peccato mortali. Sed aliquis uxorem sola libidine cognoscens ab introitu ecclesiae arcetur, ut in littera dicitur, quasi sit excommunicatus. Ergo omnis talis peccat mortaliter.

SED CONTRA: Est quia, secundum Augustinum, talis concubitus ponitur inter peccata quotidiana, pro quibus dicitur, *Pater noster* etc., ut habetur in littera. Sed talia non sunt peccata mortalia. Ergo, etc.

PRAETEREA, qui cibo utitur ad delectationem tantum, non peccat mortaliter. Ergo, pari ratione, qui utitur uxore tantum causa libidinis satiandae.

RESPONDEO dicendum quod quidam dicunt quod, quandocumque ad actum coniugalem libido principaliter movet, est peccatum mortale; sed quando movet ex latere, tunc est peccatum veniale; quando autem omnino delectationem respuit et displicet ei, tunc est omnino sine veniali peccato: ut sic delectationem in illo actu quaerere sit peccatum mortale; delectationem oblatam acceptare sit peccatum veniale; sed eam odire sit perfectionis.

Sed hoc non potest esse. Quia secundum Philosophum, in X *Ethic.*, idem iudicium est de delectatione et operatione: quia operationis bonae est delectatio bona, et malae mala. Unde, eum actus matrimonialis non sit

OBJECTION 1: It would seem that whenever a man has knowledge of his wife with the intention not of a marriage good but merely of pleasure he commits a mortal sin. For, according to Jerome as quoted in the text (*Sentences* IV, D. 31), *the pleasure taken in the embraces of a harlot is damnable in a husband* (*Commentary on Ephesians*). Now nothing but mortal sin is said to be damnable. Therefore, it is always a mortal sin to have knowledge of one's wife for mere pleasure.

OBJ. 2: Further, consent to pleasure is a mortal sin, as stated in the Second Book (*Sentences* II, D. 24). Now whoever knows his wife for the sake of pleasure consents to the pleasure. Therefore, he sins mortally.

OBJ. 3: Further, whoever fails to refer the use of a creature to God enjoys a creature, and this is a mortal sin. But whoever uses his wife for mere pleasure does not refer that use to God. Therefore, he sins mortally.

OBJ. 4: Further, no one should be excommunicated except for a mortal sin. Now according to the text (*Sentences* II, D. 24) a man who knows his wife for mere pleasure is debarred from entering the Church, as though he were excommunicate. Therefore, every such man sins mortally.

ON THE CONTRARY, As stated in the text (*Sentences* II, D. 24), according to Augustine (*Against Julian; On the Ten Strings; Sermon 41 on the Saints*), carnal intercourse of this kind is one of the daily sins, for which we say the *Our Father*. Now these are not mortal sins. Therefore, etc.

FURTHER, It is no mortal sin to take food for mere pleasure. Therefore, in like manner it is not a mortal sin for a man to use his wife merely to satisfy his desire.

I ANSWER THAT, Some say that whenever pleasure is the chief motive for the marriage act it is a mortal sin; that when it is an indirect motive it is a venial sin; and that when it spurns the pleasure altogether and is displeasing, it is wholly void of venial sin; so that it would be a mortal sin to seek pleasure in this act, a venial sin to take the pleasure when offered, but that perfection requires one to detest it.

But this is impossible, since according to the Philosopher (*Ethics* 10.3–4) the same judgment applies to pleasure as to action, because pleasure in a good action is good, and in an evil action, evil; wherefore, as the marriage act is not

per se malus, nec quaerere delectationem erit peccatum mortale semper.

Et ideo dicendum quod, si delectatio quaeratur ultra honestatem matrimonii, ut scilicet aliquis in coniuge non attendat quod coniux est, sed solum quod mulier, paratus idem facere cum ea si non esset coniux, est peccatum mortale. Et talis dicitur *ardentior amator uxoris*: quia ardor ille extra bona matrimonii effertur. Si autem quaeratur delectatio infra limites matrimonii, ut scilicet talis delectatio in alia non quaereretur quam in coniuge, sic est veniale peccatum.

AD PRIMUM ergo dicendum quod tunc voluptates meretricias vir in uxore quaerit quando nihil aliud in ea attendit quam quod in meretrice attenderet.

AD SECUNDUM dicendum quod consensus in delectationem concubitus qui est peccatum mortale, est peccatum mortale. Non autem talis est delectatio matrimonialis actus.

AD TERTIUM dicendum quod, quamvis delectationem non referat actu in Deum, non tamen ponit in ea ultimum voluntatis finem: alias eam ubicumque indifferenter quaereret. Et ideo non oportet quod creatura fruatur: sed utitur creatura propter se, se autem habitualiter propter Deum, quamvis non actu.

AD QUARTUM dicendum quod hoc non dicitur propter hoc quod ex hoc peccato homo excommunicationem mereatur: sed quia spiritualibus se reddit inhabilem, propter hoc quod in actu illo homo efficitur *totus caro*.

evil in itself, neither will it be always a mortal sin to seek pleasure therein.

Consequently, the right answer to this question is that if pleasure be sought in such a way as to exclude the honesty of marriage, so that, for example, someone should not turn to his wife because she is his wife, but only because she is a woman, prepared to do the same with her as if she were not his wife, that is a mortal sin. Wherefore such a man is said to be *too ardent a lover of his wife*, because his ardor carries him away from the goods of marriage. If, however, he seek pleasure within the bounds of marriage, so that it would not be sought in another than his wife, it is a venial sin.

REPLY OBJ. 1: A man seeks a harlot's pleasures in his own wife whenever he sees nothing else in her than what he might look for in a prostitute.

REPLY OBJ. 2: Consent to the pleasure of the intercourse that is a mortal sin is itself a mortal sin; but such is not the consent to the marriage act.

REPLY OBJ. 3: Although he does not actually refer the pleasure to God, he does not place his will's last end in it; otherwise, he would seek it anywhere indifferently. Hence it does not follow that he enjoys a creature; but he uses a creature actually for his own sake and himself habitually, though not actually, for God's sake.

REPLY OBJ. 4: The reason for this statement is not that man deserves to be excommunicated for this sin, but because he renders himself unfit for spiritual things, since in that act he becomes *flesh and nothing more*.

QUESTION 50

THE IMPEDIMENTS TO MATRIMONY IN GENERAL

Deinde considerandum est de impedimentis matrimonii. Et primo, in generali; secundo, in speciali.

In the next place we must consider the impediments of marriage: (1) In general; (2) In particular.

Article 1

Whether Impediments Are Fittingly Assigned to Marriage?

AD PRIMUM SIC PROCEDITUR. Videtur quod matrimonio inconvenienter impedimenta assignentur. Matrimonium enim quoddam sacramentum est contra alia divisum. Sed aliis non assignantur impedimenta. Ergo nec matrimonio assignari debent.

PRAETEREA, quanto aliquid est minus perfectum, tanto paucioribus modis impediri potest. Sed matrimonium inter alia sacramenta est minus perfectum. Ergo vel nulla, vel paucissima impedimenta ei assignari debent.

PRAETEREA, ubicumque est morbus, est necessarium remedium morbi. Sed concupiscentia, in cuius remedium matrimonium est indultum, est in omnibus. Ergo non debet esse aliquod impedimentum quod aliquam personam penitus illegitimam faciat ad contrahendum.

PRAETEREA, illegitimum dicitur quod est contra legem. Sed huiusmodi impedimenta quae in matrimonio assignantur, non sunt contra legem naturae: quia non similiter inveniuntur in quolibet statu humani generis; plures enim gradus consanguinitatis inveniuntur esse prohibiti uno tempore quam alio. Lex autem humana non potest, ut videtur, matrimonio impedimenta praestare: quia matrimonium non est ex institutione humana, sed divina, sicut et alia sacramenta. Ergo matrimonio non debent alia impedimenta assignari, quae faciant personas illegitimas ad contrahendum.

PRAETEREA, illegitimum et legitimum differunt per hoc quod est contra legem, vel non contra legem. Inter quae non cadit medium: cum sint opposita secundum affirmationem et negationem. Ergo non possunt esse aliqua matrimonii impedimenta quibus personae mediae inter legitimas et illegitimas constituantur.

PRAETEREA, coniunctio viri et mulieris non est licita nisi in matrimonio. Sed omnis coniunctio illicita dirimi debet. Ergo, si aliquid matrimonium contrahendum impediat, hoc dirimet contractum de facto. Et sic non

OBJECTION 1: It would seem unfitting for impediments to be assigned to marriage. For marriage is one sacrament divided from others. But no impediments are assigned to the others. Neither, therefore, should they be assigned to marriage.

OBJ. 2: Further, the less perfect a thing is, the fewer its obstacles. Now matrimony is the least perfect of the sacraments. Therefore, it should have either no impediments or very few.

OBJ. 3: Further, wherever there is disease, it is necessary to have a remedy for the disease. Now concupiscence, for whose remedy matrimony was granted (1 Cor 7:6), is in all. Therefore, there should not be any impediment making it altogether unlawful for a particular person to marry.

OBJ. 4: Further, 'unlawful' means against the law. Now these impediments that are assigned to matrimony are not against the natural law, because they are not found to be the same in each state of the human race, since more degrees of kindred come under prohibition at one time than at another. Nor, seemingly, can human law set impediments against marriage, since marriage, like the other sacraments, is not of human but of divine institution. Therefore, impediments should not be assigned to marriage, making it unlawful for a person to marry.

OBJ. 5: Further, unlawful and lawful differ as that which is against the law from that which is not, and between these there is no middle term, since they are opposed according to affirmation and negation. Therefore, there cannot be impediments to marriage, placing a person in a middle position between those who are lawful and those who are unlawful subjects of marriage.

OBJ. 6: Further, the union of man and woman is unlawful save in marriage. Now every unlawful union should be dissolved. Therefore, if anything prevent a marriage being contracted, it will *de facto* dissolve it after it has been

347

debent aliqua impedimenta matrimonio assignari quae impediant contrahendum et non dirimant contractum.

Praeterea, nullo impedimento potest a re aliqua removeri quod in definitione ipsius cadit. Sed indivisibilitas cadit in definitione matrimonii. Ergo non possunt esse aliqua impedimenta quae matrimonium contractum dirimant.

Sed contra: Videtur quod debeant esse infinita matrimonii impedimenta. Quia matrimonium quoddam bonum est. Sed infinitis modis est defectus boni: ut dicit Dionysium, 4 cap. de Div. Nom. Ergo infinita sunt matrimonii impedimenta.

Praeterea, impedimenta matrimonii accipiuntur secundum conditiones particularium personarum. Sed conditiones huiusmodi sunt infinitae. Ergo et matrimonii impedimenta.

Respondeo dicendum quod in matrimonio sunt quaedam quae sunt de essentia ipsius, et quaedam quae sunt de solemnitate eius, sicut et in aliis sacramentis. Et quia, remotis his quae non sunt de necessitate sacramenti, adhuc manet verum sacramentum; ideo impedimenta quae contrariantur his quae sunt de solemnitate sacramenti, non officiunt quin sit verum matrimonium. Et talia dicuntur impedire contrahendum, sed non dirimunt contractum: sicut prohibitio Ecclesiae, et tempus feriatum. Unde versus: *Ecclesiae vetitum, nec non tempus feriatum / Impediunt fieri, permittunt iuncta teneri.*

Impedimenta autem quae contrariantur his quae sunt de essentia matrimonii, faciunt ut non sit verum matrimonium. Et ideo dicuntur non solum impedire contrahendum, sed dirimere iam contractum. Quae his versibus continentur: *Error, conditio, votum, cognatio, crimen: / Cultus disparitas, vis, ordo, ligamen, honestas; / Si sit affinis, si forte coire nequibis: / Haec socianda vetant connubia, facta retractant.*

Horum autem numerus hoc modo accipi potest. Potest enim matrimonium impediri aut ex parte contractus matrimonii; aut ex parte contrahentium. Si primo modo, cum contractus matrimonii fiat per voluntarium consensum, qui tollitur per ignorantiam et per violentiam, erunt duo impedimenta matrimonii: scilicet *vis*, idest coactio; et *error* ex parte ignorantiae. Et ideo de istis duobus impedimentis supra Magister determinavit, ubi agebatur de causa matrimonii.

Nunc autem agit de impedimentis quae accipiuntur ex parte personarum contrahentium. Quae sic distinguuntur. Potest enim aliquis impediri a matrimonio contrahendo vel simpliciter; vel respectu alicuius personae. Si simpliciter, ut cum nulla possit matrimonium contrahere, hoc non potest esse nisi quia impeditur a

contracted; and thus impediments should not be assigned to marriage which hinder it from being contracted and dissolve it after it has been contracted.

Obj. 7: Further, no impediment can remove from a thing that which is part of its definition. Now indissolubility is part of the definition of marriage. Therefore, there cannot be any impediments which annul a marriage already contracted.

Obj. 8: On the other hand, it would seem that there should be an infinite number of impediments to marriage. For marriage is a good. Now good may be lacking in an infinite number of ways, as Dionysius says (*On the Divine Names* 3). Therefore, there is an infinite number of impediments to marriage.

Obj. 9: Further, the impediments to marriage arise from the conditions of individuals. But such conditions are infinite in number. Therefore, the impediments to marriage are also infinite.

I answer that, In marriage, as in other sacraments, there are certain things essential to marriage, and others that belong to its solemnization. And since even without the things that pertain to its solemnization it is still a true sacrament, as also in the case of the other sacraments, it follows that the impediments to those things that pertain to the solemnization of this sacrament do not derogate from the validity of the marriage. These impediments are said to hinder the contracting of marriage, but they do not dissolve the marriage once contracted: such are the veto of the Church, or the holy seasons. Hence the verse: *The veto of the Church and holy tide / Forbid the knot, but loose it not if tied.*

On the other hand, those impediments which regard the essentials of marriage make a marriage invalid, wherefore they are said not only to hinder the contracting of marriage, but to dissolve it if contracted; and they are contained in the following verse: *Error, station, vow, kinship, crime, / Disparity of cult, force, holy orders, / Marriage bond, honesty, affinity, impotence: / All these forbid marriage, and annul it though contracted.*

The reason for this number may be explained as follows. Marriage may be hindered either on the part of the contract or in regard to the contracting parties. If in the first way, since the marriage contract is made by voluntary consent and this is incompatible with either ignorance or violence, there will be two impediments to marriage, namely, *force*, i.e., compulsion, and *error*, in reference to ignorance. Wherefore the Master pronounced on these two impediments when treating of the cause of matrimony (*Sentences* IV, D. 29–30).

Here, however, he is treating of the impediments as arising from the contracting parties, and these may be differentiated as follows. A person may be hindered from contracting marriage either simply, or with some particular person. If simply, so that he be unable to contract marriage with any woman, this can only be because he is hindered from per-

matrimoniali actu. Quod quidem contingit dupliciter. Primo, quia non potest de facto: sive quia omnino non possit, et sic ponitur impedimentum *impotentia coeundi*; sive quia non libere possit, et sic ponitur impedimentum *servitutis conditio*. Secundo, quia non licite potest. Et hoc secundum quod ad continentiam obligatur. Quod contingit dupliciter. Vel quia obligatur ex officio suscepto: et sic est impedimentum *ordinis*. Vel ex voto emisso: et sic impedit *votum*.

Si autem aliquis impeditur a matrimonio non simpliciter, sed respectu alicuius personae: vel propter obligationem ad alteram personam: sicut qui uni matrimonio iunctus est, non potest alteri coniugi; et sic est *ligamen*, scilicet matrimonii. Vel quia deficit proportio ad alteram personam. Et hoc propter tria. Primo quidem, propter nimiam distantiam ad ipsam: et sic est *disparitas cultus*. Secundo, propter nimiam propinquitatem, et sic ponitur triplex impedimentum: scilicet *cognatio*, quae importat propinquitatem duarum, personarum secundum se; et *affinitas*, quae importat propinquitatem duarum personarum ratione tertiae matrimonio coniunctae; et *publicae honestatis iustitia*, in qua est propinquitas duarum personarum respectu tertiae per sponsalia iunctae. Tertio, propter indebitam coniunctionem ad ipsam primo factam. Et sic impedit *crimen* adulterii prius cum ipsa commissi.

Ad primum ergo dicendum quod etiam alia sacramenta impediri possunt, si aliquid quod sit de essentia vel solemnitate sacramenti subtrahatur, ut dictum est. Sed tamen magis matrimonio quam aliis sacramentis impedimenta assignantur, propter tres rationes. Primo, quia matrimonium consistit in duobus. Et ideo pluribus modis potest impediri quam alia sacramenta, quae uni personae competunt singulariter. Secundo, quia matrimonium habet in nobis causam, sed alia quaedam sacramenta solum in Deo. Unde et poenitentiae, quae habet causam in nobis aliquo modo, Magister supra quaedam impedimenta assignavit, ut hypocrisim, ludos et huiusmodi. Tertio, quia de aliis sacramentis est praeceptum vel consilium, sicut de bonis perfectioribus: sed de matrimonio est indulgentia, sicut de bono minus perfecto. Et ideo, ut detur occasio proficiendi in melius, plura impedimenta assignantur matrimonio quam aliis sacramentis.

Ad secundum dicendum quod perfectiora pluribus modis impediri possunt inquantum ad ea plura requiruntur. Si autem sit aliquod imperfectum ad quod plura requiruntur, illud etiam habebit plura impedimenta. Et sic est de matrimonio.

forming the marriage act. This happens in two ways. First, because he cannot *de facto*, either through being altogether unable—and thus we have the impediment of *impotence*—or through being unable to do so freely, and thus we have the impediment of the *condition of slavery*. Second, because he cannot do it lawfully because he is bound to continence, which happens in two ways, either through his being bound on account of the office he has undertaken to fulfill—and thus we have the impediment of *holy orders*—or on account of his having taken a vow—and thus *vow* is an impediment.

If, however, a person is hindered from marrying not simply but in reference to a particular person, this is either because he is bound to another person, and thus he who is married to one cannot marry another, which constitutes the impediment of the *bond* of marriage—or through lack of proportion to the other party, and this for three reasons. First, on account of too great a distance separating them, and thus we have *disparity of cult*; second, on account of their being too closely related, and thus we have three impediments, namely, *kinship*; then *affinity*, which denotes the close relationship between two persons in reference to a third united to one of them by marriage; and the *justice of public honesty*, where we have a close relationship between two persons arising out of the betrothal of one of them to a third person; third, on account of a previous undue union between him and the woman, and thus the *crime* of adultery previously committed with her is an impediment.

Reply Obj. 1: There may be impediments to the other sacraments also, in the omission either of that which is essential or of that which pertains to the solemnization of the sacrament, as stated above. However, impediments are assigned to matrimony rather than to the other sacraments for three reasons. First, because matrimony consists of two persons, and consequently can be impeded in more ways than the other sacraments which refer to one person taken individually; second, because matrimony has its cause in us and in God, while some of the other sacraments have their cause in God alone. Wherefore penance, which in a manner has a cause in us, is assigned certain impediments by the Master (*Sentences* IV, D. 16), such as hypocrisy, the public games, and so forth. Third, because other sacraments are objects of command or counsel, as being more perfect goods, whereas marriage is a matter of indulgence, as being a less perfect good (1 Cor 7:6). Wherefore, in order to afford an opportunity of proficiency towards a greater good, more impediments are assigned to matrimony than to the other sacraments.

Reply Obj. 2: The more perfect things can be hindered in more ways insofar as more conditions are required for them. And if an imperfect thing requires more conditions, there will be more impediments to it; and thus it is in matrimony.

Ad tertium dicendum quod ratio illa procederet si non essent alia remedia, quibus etiam posset efficacius morbo concupiscentiae subveniri. Quod falsum est.

Ad quartum dicendum quod personae illegitimae ad matrimonium contrahendum dicuntur ex eo quod sunt contra legem qua matrimonium statuitur. Matrimonium autem, inquantum est in officium naturae, statuitur lege naturae; inquantum est sacramentum, statuitur iure divino; inquantum est in officium communitatis, statuitur lege civili. Et ideo ex qualibet dictarum legum potest aliqua persona effici ad matrimonium illegitima. Nec est simile de aliis sacramentis, quae sunt sacramenta tantum. Et quia lex naturalis secundum diversos status respicit determinationes diversas; et ius positivum variatur etiam secundum diversas hominum conditiones in diversis temporibus: ideo Magister ponit in diversis temporibus diversas personas illegitimas fuisse.

Ad quintum dicendum quod lex potest aliquid prohibere vel universaliter, vel in parte quantum ad aliquos casus. Et ideo inter esse totaliter secundum legem, et esse totaliter contra legem, quae sunt contrarie opposita, et non secundum affirmationem et negationem, cadit medium esse aliqualiter secundum legem et aliqualiter contra legem. Et propter hoc ponuntur quaedam personae mediae inter simpliciter legitimas et simpliciter illegitimas.

Ad sextum dicendum quod illa impedimenta quae non dirimunt matrimonium contractum, impediunt quandoque contrahendum, non ut non fiat, sed ut non licite fiat. Et tamen, si fiat, matrimonium verum contractum est: quamvis contrahens peccet. Sicut, si aliquis consecraret post comestionem, peccaret contra statutum Ecclesiae faciens; nihilominus verum sacramentum perficeret, quia ieiunium consecrantis non est de necessitate sacramenti.

Ad septimum dicendum quod impedimenta praedicta non dicuntur dirimere matrimonium contractum quasi solventia verum matrimonium, quod rite contractum est: sed quia solvunt matrimonium quod contractum est de facto et non de iure. Unde, si impedimentorum aliquod matrimonio rite facto superveniat, matrimonium solvere non valet.

Ad octavum dicendum quod impedimenta quibus aliquod bonum per accidens impeditur, sunt infinita: sicut et omnes causae per accidens. Sed causae corrumpentes aliquod bonum per se, sunt determinatae, sicut etiam causae constituentes: quia causae destructionis et constructionis alicuius rei sunt oppositae, vel eaedem contrario modo sumptae.

Ad nonum dicendum quod conditiones particularium personarum in singulari sunt infinitae, sed in generali possunt reduci ad certum numerum: sicut in

Reply Obj. 3: This argument would hold if there were not other and more efficacious remedies for the disease of concupiscence; which is false.

Reply Obj. 4: Persons are said to be unlawful subjects for marriage through being contrary to the law whereby marriage is established. Now marriage as an office of nature is established by the natural law; as a sacrament, by the divine law; as an office of society, by the civil law. Consequently, a person may be rendered an unlawful subject of marriage by any of the aforesaid laws. Nor does the comparison with the other sacraments hold, for they are sacraments only. And since the natural law is particularized in various ways according to the various states of mankind, and since positive law, too, varies according to the various conditions of men, the Master asserts that at various times various persons have been unlawful subjects of marriage (*Sentences* IV, D. 34).

Reply Obj. 5: The law may forbid a thing either altogether, or in part and in certain cases. Hence between that which is altogether according to the law and that which is altogether against the law (which are opposed by contrariety and not according to affirmation and negation), that which is somewhat according to the law and somewhat against the law is a middle term. For this reason certain persons hold a middle place between those who are simply lawful subjects and those who are simply unlawful.

Reply Obj. 6: Those impediments which do not annul a marriage already contracted sometimes hinder a marriage from being contracted by rendering it not invalid but unlawful. And if it be contracted, it is a true marriage, although the contracting parties sin; just as by consecrating after breaking one's fast one would sin by disobeying the Church's ordinance, and yet it would be a valid sacrament because it is not essential to the sacrament that the consecrator be fasting.

Reply Obj. 7: When we say that the aforesaid impediments annul marriage already contracted, we do not mean that they dissolve a marriage contracted in due form, but that they dissolve a marriage contracted *de facto* and not *de jure*. Therefore, if an impediment supervene after a marriage has been contracted in due form, it cannot dissolve the marriage.

Reply Obj. 8: The impediments that hinder a good accidentally are infinite in number, like all accidental causes. But the causes which of their own nature corrupt a certain good are directed to that effect, and are determinate even as are the causes which produce that good; for the causes by which a thing is destroyed and those by which it is made are either contrary to one another, or the same but taken in a contrary way.

Reply Obj. 9: The conditions of particular persons taken individually are infinite in number, but taken in general, they may be reduced to a certain number, as is clear in

medicina patet et in omnibus artibus operativis, quae particularium, in quibus est actus, conditiones considerant.

medicine and all operative arts, which consider the conditions of the particular persons in whom the acts are.

QUESTION 51

THE IMPEDIMENT OF ERROR

Deinde considerandum est de impedimentis matrimonii in speciali. Et primo, de impedimento erroris. Circa quod quaeruntur duo.

Primo: utrum error de sui natura matrimonium impediat.

Secundo: quis error.

We must now consider the impediments to matrimony in particular, and in the first place the impediment of error. Under this head there are two points of inquiry:

(1) Whether error of its very nature is an impediment to matrimony?

(2) What kind of error?

Article 1

Whether Error Should Be Reckoned in Itself an Impediment to Marriage?

AD PRIMUM SIC PROCEDITUR. Videtur quod error non debeat poni matrimonii impedimentum per se. Consensus enim, qui est causa matrimonii, impeditur sicut et voluntarium. Sed voluntarium, secundum Philosophum, in III *Ethic.*, potest impediri per ignorantiam. Quae non est idem quod error: quia ignorantia nullam cognitionem ponit; sed error ponit, eo quod *approbare falsa pro veris sit error*, secundum Augustinum. Ergo non debuit hic poni impedimentum matrimonii error, sed magis ignorantia.

PRAETEREA, illud potest impedire matrimonium de sui natura quod habet contrarietatem ad bona matrimonii. Sed error non est huiusmodi. Ergo error de sui natura non impedit matrimonium.

PRAETEREA, sicut consensus requiritur ad matrimonium, ita intentio requiritur ad baptismum. Sed si aliquis baptizat Ioannem et credit baptizare Petrum, nihilominus vere baptizatus est. Ergo error non excludit matrimonium.

PRAETEREA, inter Liam et Iacob fuit verum matrimonium. Sed ibi fuit error. Ergo error non excludit matrimonium.

SED CONTRA: Est quod in *Digestis* dicitur: *quid tam contrarium est consensui quam error?* Sed consensus requiritur ad matrimonium. Ergo error matrimonium impedit.

PRAETEREA, consensus aliquid voluntarium nominat. Sed error impedit voluntarium: quia *voluntarium*, secundum Philosophum et Gregorium Nyssenum et Damascenum, *est cuius principium est in aliquo sciente singularia in quibus est actus*, quod erranti non competit. Ergo error matrimonium impedit.

OBJECTION 1: It would seem that error should not be reckoned in itself an impediment to marriage. For consent, which is the efficient cause of marriage, is hindered in the same way as the voluntary. Now the voluntary, according to the Philosopher (*Ethics* 3.1), may be hindered by ignorance. But ignorance is not the same as error, because ignorance excludes knowledge altogether, whereas error does not, since *error is to approve the false as though it were true*, according to Augustine (*On the Trinity* 9.11). Therefore, ignorance rather than error should have been reckoned here as an impediment to marriage.

OBJ. 2: Further, that which of its very nature can be an impediment to marriage is in opposition to the good of marriage. But error is not a thing of this kind. Therefore, error is not by its very nature an impediment to marriage.

OBJ. 3: Further, just as consent is required for marriage, so is intention required for baptism. Now if one were to baptize John, thinking to baptize Peter, John would be baptized nonetheless. Therefore, error does not annul matrimony.

OBJ. 4: Further, there was true marriage between Leah and Jacob, and yet, in this case, there was error. Therefore, error does not annul a marriage.

ON THE CONTRARY, It is said in the *Digests*: *what is more opposed to consent than error?* Now consent is required for marriage. Therefore, error is an impediment to matrimony.

FURTHER, Consent denotes something voluntary. Now error is an obstacle to the voluntary, since *the voluntary*, according to the Philosopher (*Ethics* 3.1), Damascene (*On the Orthodox Faith* 2.24), and Gregory of Nyssa (*The Nature of Man* 32), *is that which has its principle in one who has knowledge of singulars which are the matter of actions*. But this does not apply to one who is in error. Therefore, error is an impediment to matrimony.

RESPONDEO dicendum quod quidquid impedit causam de sui natura, impedit et effectum similiter. Consensus autem est causa matrimonii, ut dictum est. Et ideo quod evacuat consensum, evacuat matrimonium. Consensus autem voluntatis est actus, qui praesupponit actum intellectus. Deficiente autem primo, necesse est defectum contingere in secundo; et ideo, quando error cognitionem impedit, sequitur etiam in ipso consensu defectus. Et per consequens in matrimonio. Et sic error de iure naturali habet quod evacuet matrimonium.

AD PRIMUM ergo dicendum quod ignorantia differt, simpliciter loquendo, ab errore: quia ignorantia de sui ratione non importat aliquem cognitionis actum; sed error ponit, iudicium rationis perversum de aliquo. Tamen quantum ad hoc quod est impedire voluntarium, non differt utrum dicatur ignorantia vel error. Quia nulla ignorantia potest impedire voluntarium nisi quae habet errorem adiunctum: eo quod actus voluntatis praesupponit aestimationem sive iudicium de aliquo in quod fertur; unde, si est ibi ignorantia, oportet ibi esse errorem. Et ideo etiam ponitur error, quasi causa proxima.

AD SECUNDUM dicendum quod, quamvis non contrariatur secundum se matrimonio, contrariatur ei tamen quantum ad causam suam.

AD TERTIUM dicendum quod character baptismalis non causatur ex intentione baptizantis directe, sed ex elemento materiali exterius adhibito: intentio autem operatur solum ut dirigens elementum materiale ad effectum proprium. Sed vinculum coniugale ex ipso consensu causatur directe. Et ideo non est simile.

AD QUARTUM dicendum quod, sicut Magister, 30 dist. IV Sent., dicit, matrimonium quod fuit inter Liam et Iacob non fuit perfectum ex ipso concubitu, qui ex errore contigit; sed ex consensu qui postmodum accessit. Tamen uterque a peccato excusatur: ut in eadem distinctione.

I ANSWER THAT, Whatever hinders a cause of its very nature hinders the effect likewise. Now consent is the cause of matrimony, as stated above (Q. 45, A. 1). Hence whatever voids the consent voids marriage. Now consent is an act of the will, presupposing an act of the intellect; and if the first be lacking, the second must be lacking also. Hence, when error hinders knowledge, there follows a defect in the consent also, and consequently in the marriage. Therefore, it is possible according to the natural law for error to void marriage.

REPLY OBJ. 1: Simply speaking, ignorance differs from error, because ignorance does not of its very nature imply an act of knowledge, while error supposes a wrong judgment of reason about something. However, as regards being an impediment to the voluntary, it differs not whether we call it ignorance or error, since no ignorance can be an impediment to the voluntary unless it have error in conjunction with it, because the will's act presupposes an estimate or judgment about something which is the object of the will. Therefore, if there be ignorance there must also be error; and for this reason error is set down as being the proximate cause.

REPLY OBJ. 2: Although error is not of itself contrary to matrimony, it is contrary to it as regards the cause of matrimony.

REPLY OBJ. 3: The character of baptism is not caused directly by the intention of the baptizer, but by the material element applied outwardly; and the intention is effective only as directing the material element to its effect; whereas the marriage tie is caused by the consent directly. Hence the comparison fails.

REPLY OBJ. 4: According to the Master (*Sentences* IV, D.30) the marriage between Leah and Jacob was effected not by their coming together, which happened through an error, but by their consent which followed afterwards. Yet both are clearly to be excused from sin (*Sentences* IV, D. 30).

Article 2

Whether Every Error Is an Impediment to Matrimony?

AD SECUNDUM SIC PROCEDITUR. Videtur quod omnis error matrimonium impediat, et non solum error conditionis aut personae, ut in littera dicitur. Quia quod convenit alicui secundum se, convenit ei secundum totum suum ambitum. Sed error de sui natura habet quod matrimonium impediat, ut dictum est. Ergo omnis error matrimonium impedit.

PRAETEREA, si error inquantum huiusmodi matrimonium impedit, maior error magis debet impedire. Sed maior est error fidei; qui est in haereticis non credenti-

OBJECTION 1: It would seem that every error is an impediment to matrimony, and not, as stated in the text (*Sentences* IV, D. 30), only error about the condition or the person. For that which applies to a thing as such applies to it in all its bearings. Now error is of its very nature an impediment to matrimony, as stated above (A. 1). Therefore, every error is an impediment to matrimony.

OBJ. 2: Further, if error as such is an impediment to matrimony, the greater the error, the greater the impediment. Now the error concerning faith in a heretic who

bus hoc sacramentum, quam error personae. Ergo magis debet impedire quam error personae.

PRAETEREA, error non evacuat matrimonium nisi inquantum tollit voluntarium. Sed ignorantia cuiuslibet circumstantiae voluntarium tollit, ut patet in III *Ethic.* Ergo non solum error conditionis et personae matrimonium impediunt.

PRAETEREA, sicut conditio servitutis aliquid est annexum accidens personae, ita qualitas corporis aut animi. Sed error conditionis impedit matrimonium. Ergo, eadem ratione error qualitatis aut fortunae.

PRAETEREA, sicut ad conditionem personae pertinet servitus et libertas, ita nobilitas vel ignobilitas, aut status dignitatis et privatio eius. Sed error conditionis libertatis vel servitutis impedit matrimonium. Ergo et error aliorum dictorum.

PRAETEREA, sicut conditio servitutis impedit, ita etiam disparitas Cultus et impotentia coeundi, ut infra dicetur. Ergo, sicut error conditionis ponitur matrimonii impedimentum, ita error circa alia huiusmodi deberet impedimentum matrimonii poni.

SED CONTRA: Videtur quod nec error personae matrimonium impediat. Quia sicut emptio est quidam contractus, ita etiam matrimonium. Sed in emptione et venditione, si detur aurum aequivalens pro alio auro, non impeditur venditio. Ergo nec matrimonium impeditur si pro una muliere alia accipiatur,

PRAETEREA, potest contingere quod per multos annos isto errore detineantur, et filios et filias generent simul. Sed grave esset dicere quod tunc essent dividendi. Ergo error primus non frustravit matrimonium.

PRAETEREA, potest contingere quod frater viri in quem consentire credit mulier, offeratur ei, et cum eo commisceatur carnaliter. Et tunc videtur quod non possit redire ad illum in quem consentire se credidit, sed debeat stare cum fratre eius. Et sic error personae non impedit matrimonium.

RESPONDEO dicendum quod, sicut error ex hoc quod involuntarium causat, habet excusare peccatum, ita habet quod matrimonium impediat ex eodem. Error autem non excusat a peccato nisi sit illius circumstantiae cuius appositio vel remotio facit differentiam liciti et illiciti in actu. Si enim aliquis percutiat patrem baculo ferreo, quem credit ligneum esse, non excusatur a toto, quamvis forte a tanto: sed si credat quis percutere filium causa disciplinae, et percutiat patrem, excusatur a toto, adhibita debita diligentia. Unde oportet quod error qui matrimonium impedit, sit alicuius eorum quae

disbelieves in this sacrament is greater than an error concerning the person. Therefore, it should be a greater impediment than error about the person.

OBJ. 3: Further, error does not void marriage except as removing voluntariness. Now ignorance about any circumstance takes away voluntariness (*Ethics* 3.1). Therefore, it is not only error about condition or person that is an impediment to matrimony.

OBJ. 4: Further, just as the condition of slavery is an accident affecting the person, so are bodily or mental qualities. But error regarding the condition is an impediment to matrimony. Therefore, error concerning quality or fortune is equally an impediment.

OBJ. 5: Further, just as slavery or freedom pertains to the condition of person, so do high and low rank, or dignity of position and the lack thereof. Now error regarding the condition of slavery is an impediment to matrimony. Therefore, error about the other matters mentioned is also an impediment.

OBJ. 6: Further, just as the condition of slavery is an impediment, so are difference of worship and impotence, as we shall say further on (Q. 52, A. 2; Q. 58, A. 1; Q. 59, A. 1). Therefore, just as error regarding the condition is an impediment, so also should error about those other matters be reckoned an impediment.

OBJ. 7: On the other hand, it would seem that not even error about the person is an impediment to marriage. For marriage is a contract even as a sale is. Now in buying and selling the sale is not voided if one coin be given instead of another of equal value. Therefore, a marriage is not voided if one woman be taken instead of another.

OBJ. 8: Further, it is possible for them to remain in this error for many years and to beget between them sons and daughters. But it would be a grave assertion to maintain that they ought to be separated then. Therefore, their previous error did not void their marriage.

OBJ. 9: Further, it might happen that the woman is betrothed to the brother of the man whom she thinks that she is consenting to marry, and that she has had carnal intercourse with him; in which case, seemingly, she cannot go back to the man to whom she thought to give her consent, but should remain with his brother. Thus error regarding the person is not an impediment to marriage.

I ANSWER THAT, Just as error, through causing involuntariness, is an excuse from sin, so on the same count is it an impediment to marriage. Now error does not excuse from sin unless it refer to a circumstance the presence or absence of which makes an action lawful or unlawful. For if a man were to strike his father with an iron rod, thinking it to be of wood, he is not excused from sin wholly, although perhaps in part; but if a man were to strike his father, thinking to strike his son to correct him, he is wholly excused provided he took due care. Therefore error, in order to void marriage, must be about the essentials of mar-

sunt de essentia matrimonii. Duo autem includit ipsum matrimonium, scilicet personas duas quae coniunguntur, et mutuam potestatem in invicem, in qua matrimonium consistit. Primum autem tollitur per errorem personae; secundum per errorem conditionis, quia servus non potest potestatem sui corporis libere alteri tradere sine consensu domini sui. Et propter hoc hi duo errores matrimonium impediunt, et non alii.

Ad primum ergo dicendum quod error non habet ex natura generis quod impediat matrimonium, sed ex natura differentiae adiunctae: prout scilicet est error alicuius eorum quae sunt de essentia matrimonii.

Ad secundum dicendum quod error infidelis de matrimonio est circa ea quae sunt matrimonium consequentia, sicut an sit sacramentum, vel an sit licitum. Et ideo error talis matrimonium non impedit: sicut nec error circa baptismum impedit acceptionem characteris, dummodo intendat facere vel recipere quod Ecclesia dat, quamvis credat nihil esse.

Ad tertium dicendum quod non quaelibet circumstantiae ignorantia causat involuntarium quod excusat peccatum, ut dictum est. Et propter hoc ratio non sequitur.

Ad quartum dicendum quod diversitas fortunae non variat aliquid eorum quae sunt de essentia matrimonii, nec diversitas qualitatis, sicut facit conditio servitutis. Et ideo ratio non sequitur.

Ad quintum dicendum quod error nobilitatis, inquantum huiusmodi, non evacuat matrimonium: eadem ratione qua nec error qualitatis. Sed si error nobilitatis vel dignitatis redundat in errorem personae, tunc impedit matrimonium. Unde si consensus mulieris feratur in istam personam directe, error nobilitatis ipsius non impedit matrimonium. Si autem directe intendit consentire in filium regis, quicumque sit ille, tunc, si alius praesentetur ei quam filius regis, est error personae, et impedietur matrimonium.

Ad sextum dicendum quod error etiam aliorum impedimentorum matrimonii, quantum ad ea quae faciunt personas illegitimas, impedit matrimonium. Sed ideo de errore illorum non facit mentionem, quia illa impediunt matrimonium sive cum errore sint sive sine errore: ut, si aliqua contrahat cum subdiacono, sive sciat sive nesciat, non est matrimonium. Sed conditio servitutis non impedit si servitus sciatur. Et ideo non est simile.

Ad septimum dicendum quod pecunia in contractibus accipitur quasi mensura aliarum rerum, ut patet in V *Ethic.*, et non: quasi propter se quaesita. Et ideo, si non detur illa pecunia quae creditur sed alia aequivalens, nihil obest contractui. Sed si in re quaesita propter se esset

riage. Now marriage includes two things, namely, the two persons who are joined together and the mutual power over one another wherein marriage consists. The first of these is removed by error concerning the person, the second by error regarding the condition, since a slave cannot freely give power over his body to another, without his master's consent. For this reason these two errors, and no others, are an impediment to matrimony.

Reply Obj. 1: It is not from its generic nature that error is an impediment to marriage, but from the nature of the difference added to it; namely, from its being error about one of the essentials to marriage.

Reply Obj. 2: An error of faith about matrimony is about things consequent upon matrimony, for instance, on the question of its being a sacrament, or of its being lawful. Wherefore such an error as these is no impediment to marriage, as neither does an error about baptism hinder a man from receiving the character, provided he intend to receive what the Church gives, although he believe it to be nothing.

Reply Obj. 3: It is not any ignorance of a circumstance that causes the involuntariness which is an excuse from sin, as stated above; wherefore the argument does not follow.

Reply Obj. 4: Difference of fortune or of quality does not make a difference in the essentials to matrimony, as the condition of slavery does. Hence the argument does not follow.

Reply Obj. 5: Error about a person's rank, as such, does not void a marriage, for the same reason as neither does error about a personal quality. If, however, the error about a person's rank or position amounts to an error about the person, it is an impediment to matrimony. Hence, if the woman consent directly to this particular person, her error about his rank does not void the marriage; but if she intend directly to consent to marry the king's son, whoever he may be, then, if another man than the king's son be brought to her, there is error about the person, and the marriage will be void.

Reply Obj. 6: Error is an impediment to matrimony, although it be about other impediments to marriage, if it concern those things which render a person an unlawful subject of marriage. But the Master does not mention error about such things, because they are an impediment to marriage whether there be error about them or not; so that if a woman contract with a subdeacon, whether she know this or not, there is no marriage. But the condition of slavery is no impediment if the slavery be known. Hence the comparison fails.

Reply Obj. 7: In contracts money is regarded as the measure of other things (*Ethics* 5.5), and not as being sought for its own sake. Hence if the coin paid is not what it is thought to be but another of equal value, this does not void the contract. But if there be error about a thing sought

error, impediretur contractus: sicut si alicui venderetur asinus pro equo. Et similiter est in proposito.

AD OCTAVUM dicendum quod, quantumcumque fuerit cum ea, nisi de novo consentire velit, non est matrimonium.

AD NONUM dicendum quod, si ante non consenserat in fratrem eius, potest eum quem per errorem accepit retinere: nec potest ad fratrem eius redire, praecipue si sit cognita carnaliter ab eo quem accepit. Si autem consenserat in primum per verba de praesenti, non potest secundum habere primo vivente: sed potest vel secundum relinquere, vel ad primum redire. Et ignorantia facti excusat: sicut excusaretur si post consummatum matrimonium a consanguineo viri sui fraudulenter cognosceretur; quia fraus alterius non debet sibi praeiudicare.

for its own sake, the contract is voided—for instance, if one were to sell a donkey for a horse—and thus it is in the case in point.

REPLY OBJ. 8: No matter how long they have cohabited, unless she be willing to consent again, there is no marriage.

REPLY OBJ. 9: If she did not consent previously to marry his brother, she may hold to the one whom she took in error. Nor can she return to his brother, especially if there has been carnal intercourse between her and the man she took to husband. If, however, she had previously consented to take the first one in words of the present, she cannot have the second while the first lives. But she may either leave the second or return to the first; and ignorance of the fact excuses her from sin, just as she would be excused if after the consummation of the marriage a kinsman of her husband were to know her by fraud, since she is not to be blamed for the other's deceit.

QUESTION 52

THE IMPEDIMENT OF THE CONDITION OF SLAVERY

Deinde considerandum est de impedimento conditionis.

Circa quod quaeruntur quattuor.

Primo: utrum conditio, servitutis matrimonium impediat.

Secundo: utrum servus sine consensu domini possit matrimonium contrahere.

Tertio: utrum aliquis, postquam uxoratus est, possit se servum facere sine consensu uxoris.

Quarto: utrum filii debeant sequi conditionem patris vel matris.

We must now consider the impediment of the condition of slavery.

Under this head there are four points of inquiry:

(1) Whether the condition of slavery is an impediment to matrimony?

(2) Whether a slave can marry without his master's consent?

(3) Whether a man who is already married can make himself a slave without his wife's consent?

(4) Whether the children should follow the condition of their father or of their mother?

Article 1

Whether the Condition of Slavery Is an Impediment to Matrimony?

Ad primum sic proceditur. Videtur quod conditio servitutis non impediat matrimonium. Nihil enim impedit matrimonium nisi quod habet aliquam contrarietatem ad ipsum. Sed servitus non habet aliquam contrarietatem ad matrimonium: alias inter servos non possent esse coniugia. Ergo servitus non impedit matrimonium.

Praeterea, illud quod est contra naturam, non potest impedire illud quod est secundum naturam. Sed servitus est contra naturam: quia, sicut dicit Gregorius, *contra naturam est hominem homini velle dominari.* Quod etiam patet ex hoc quod homini dictum est *ut praesit piscibus maris,* etc.: non autem *ut praesit homini.* Ergo non potest impedire matrimonium, quod est naturale.

Praeterea, si impediat, aut hoc est de iure naturali, aut de iure positivo. Non de iure naturali: quia secundum ius naturale *omnes homines sunt aequales,* ut Gregorius dicit; et in principio *Digestorum* dicitur quod servitus non est de iure naturali. Positivum etiam ius descendit a naturali: ut Tullius dicit. Ergo secundum nullum ius servitus matrimonium impedire potest.

Praeterea, illud quod impedit matrimonium, aequaliter impedit sive sciatur sive ignoretur: ut patet de consanguinitate. Sed servitus unius cognita ab altero non impedit matrimonium. Ergo servitus, quantum in se est, non habet quod impediat matrimonium. Et ita

Objection 1: It would seem that the condition of slavery is no impediment to matrimony. For nothing is an impediment to marriage except what is in some way opposed to it. But slavery is in no way opposed to marriage, else there could be no marriage among slaves. Therefore, slavery is no impediment to marriage.

Obj. 2: Further, that which is contrary to nature cannot be an impediment to that which is according to nature. Now slavery is contrary to nature, for as Gregory says (*Book of Pastoral Rule* 2.6), *it is contrary to nature for man to wish to lord it over another man*; and this is also evident from the fact that it was said of man that he *should have dominion over the fishes of the sea* (Gen 1:26), but not that he *should have dominion over man.* Therefore, it cannot be an impediment to marriage, which is a natural thing.

Obj. 3: Further, if it is an impediment, this is either of natural law or of positive law. But it is not of natural law, since according to natural law *all men are equal,* as Gregory says (*Book of Pastoral Rule* 2.6), while it is stated at the beginning of the *Digests* that slavery is not of natural law; and positive law springs from the natural law, as Cicero says (*De Inventione* ii). Therefore, according to law, slavery is not an impediment to any marriage.

Obj. 4: Further, that which is an impediment to marriage is equally an impediment whether it be known or not, as in the case of consanguinity. Now the slavery of one party, if it be known to the other, is no impediment to their marriage. Therefore, slavery considered in itself is unable

non deberet poni per se matrimonii impedimentum ab aliis distinctum.

PRAETEREA, sicut contingit esse errorem circa servitutem ut putetur liber qui est servus, ita potest esse error de libertate ut putetur servus qui est liber. Sed libertas non ponitur matrimonii impedimentum. Ergo nec servitus deberet poni.

PRAETEREA, magis facit gravem societatem matrimonii, et plus impedit prolis bonum morius leprae quam servitus. Sed lepra non ponitur impedimentum matrimonii. Ergo nec servitus debet poni.

SED CONTRA: Est quod Decretalis dicit, *de Coniugio servorum*, quod error conditionis impedit contrahendum matrimonium et dirimit contractum.

PRAETEREA, matrimonium est de bonis per se expetendis, inquantum habet honestatem. Sed servitus est de per se fugiendis. Ergo matrimonium et servitus sunt contraria. Et sic servitus matrimonium impedit.

RESPONDEO dicendum quod matrimonii contractu obligatur unus coniugum alteri ad debitum reddendum. Et ideo, si ille qui se obligat, est impotens ad solvendum, ignorantia huius impotentiae in eo cui fit obligatio, tollit contractum. Sicut autem per impotentiam coeundi efficitur aliquis impotens ad solvendum debitum ut omnino non possit solvere, ita per servitutem ut libere debitum reddere non possit. Et ideo, impotentia coeundi ignorata impedit matrimonium, non autem si sciatur, ita conditio servitutis ignorata impedit matrimonium, non autem servitus scita.

AD PRIMUM ergo dicendum quod servitus contrariatur matrimonio quantum ad actum ad quem quis per matrimonium alteri obligatur, quem non potest libere exequi; et quantum ad bonum prolis, quae peioris conditionis efficitur et servitute parentis. Sed quia quilibet potest in eo quod sibi debetur sponte detrimentum aliquod subire, ideo, si alter coniugum scit alterius servitutem, nihilominus tenet matrimonium.

Similiter etiam, quia in matrimonio est aequalis obligatio ex utraque parte ad debitum reddendum, non potest aliquis requirere maiorem obligationem ex parte alterius quam ipse possit facere. Et propter hoc servus etiam si contrahit cum ancilla quam credit liberam, non propter hoc impeditur matrimonium.

Et sic patet quod servitus non impedit matrimonium nisi quando est ignorata ab alio coniuge, et si ille sit liberae conditionis. Et ideo nihil prohibet inter servos esse coniugia, vel inter liberum et ancillam.

to void a marriage; and consequently it should not be reckoned by itself as a distinct impediment to marriage.

OBJ. 5: Further, just as one may be in error about slavery, so as to think a person free who is a slave, so may one be in error about freedom, so as to think a person a slave whereas he is free. But freedom is not accounted an impediment to matrimony. Therefore, neither should slavery be so accounted.

OBJ. 7: Further, leprosy is a greater burden to the fellowship of marriage and is a greater obstacle to the good of the offspring than slavery is. Yet leprosy is not reckoned an impediment to marriage. Therefore, neither should slavery be so reckoned.

ON THE CONTRARY, A Decretal says that error regarding the condition hinders a marriage from being contracted and voids that which is already contracted.

FURTHER, Marriage is one of the goods that are sought for their own sake, because it is qualified by honesty; whereas slavery is one of the things to be avoided for their own sake. Therefore, marriage and slavery are contrary to one another; consequently, slavery is an impediment to matrimony.

I ANSWER THAT, In the marriage contract one party is bound to the other in the matter of paying the debt; wherefore if one who thus binds himself is unable to pay the debt, ignorance of this inability on the side of the party to whom he binds himself voids the contract. Now just as impotence in respect of coition makes a person unable to pay the debt, so that he is altogether disabled, so slavery makes him unable to pay it freely. Therefore, just as ignorance or impotence in respect of coition is an impediment if unknown, but not if known, as we shall state further on (Q. 58), so the condition of slavery is an impediment if unknown, but not if it be known.

REPLY OBJ. 1: Slavery is contrary to marriage as regards the act to which marriage binds one party in relation to the other, because it prevents the free execution of that act; and again as regards the good of the offspring, who become subject to the same condition by reason of the parent's slavery. Since, however, it is free to everyone to suffer detriment in that which is his due, if one of the parties knows the other to be a slave, the marriage is nonetheless valid.

Likewise, since in marriage there is an equal obligation on either side to pay the debt, neither party can exact of the other a greater obligation than that under which he lies; so that if a slave marry a bondswoman, thinking her to be free, the marriage is not thereby rendered invalid.

It is therefore evident that slavery is no impediment to marriage except when it is unknown to the other party, even though the latter be in a condition of freedom; and so nothing prevents marriage between slaves, or even between a freeman and a bondswoman.

Ad secundum dicendum quod nihil prohibet aliquid; esse contra naturam quantum ad primam intentionem ipsius, quod non est contra naturam quantum ad secundam intentionem eius. Sicut omnis corruptio et defectus et senium est contra naturam, ut dicitur in II *de Coelo*, quia natura intendit esse et perfectionem: non tamen est contra secundam intentionem naturae; quia ex quo natura non potest conservare esse in uno, conservat in altero, quod generatur corruptione alterius. Et quando natura non potest perducere ad maiorem perfectionem, inducit ad minorem: sicut, quando non potest facere masculum, facit feminam, quae est *mas occasionatus*, ut dicitur in XVI *de Animalibus*.

Similiter: etiam dico quod servitus est contra primam intentionem naturae, sed non est contra secundam. Quia naturalis ratio ad hoc inclinat, et hoc appetit natura, ut quilibet sit bonus: sed ex quo aliquis peccat, natura etiam inclinat ut ex peccato poenam reportet. Et sic servitus in poenam peccati introducta est. Nec est inconveniens aliquod naturale per hoc quod est contra naturam hoc modo impediri; sic enim matrimonium impeditur per impotentiam coeundi, quae est contra naturam modo praedicto.

Ad tertium dicendum quod ius naturale dictat quod poena sit pro culpa infligenda, et quod nullus sine culpa puniri debet: sed determinare poenam secundum conditionem personae et culpae est iuris positivi. Et ideo servitus, quae est poena, determinata est a iure positivo, et a naturali proficiscitur sicut determinatum ab indeterminato. Et eodem iure positivo determinate est factum quod servitus ignorata matrimonium impediat, ne aliquis sine culpa puniatur: est enim quaedam poena uxoris quod habeat virum servum, et e converso.

Ad quartum dicendum quod aliqua impedimenta sunt quale faciunt matrimonium illicitum. Et quia voluntas nostra non facit aliquid esse illicitum vel licitum, sed lex, cui voluntas subdi debet; ideo ignorantia talis impedimenti, quae voluntarium tollit, vel scientia, nihil facit ad hoc quod matrimonium teneat. Et tale impedimentum est affinitas vel votum, et cetera huiusmodi.

Quaedam autem impedimenta sunt quae faciunt matrimonium inefficax ad solutionem debiti. Et quia in voluntate nostra consistit debitum nobis relaxare, ideo talia impedimenta, si sint cognita, matrimonium non tollunt sed solum quando ignorantia voluntarium excludit. Et tale impedimentum est servitus et impotentia coeundi. Et quia etiam de se habent aliquam rationem impedimenti, ideo ponuntur specialia impedimenta praeter errorem. Non autem personae variatio ponitur speciale impedimentum praeter errorem: quia persona alia su-

Reply Obj. 2: Nothing prevents a thing being against nature as to the first intention of nature, and yet not against nature as to its second intention. Thus, as stated in *On the Heavens* II, all corruption, defect, and old age are contrary to nature because nature intends being and perfection, and yet they are not contrary to the second intention of nature, because nature, through being unable to preserve being in one thing, preserves it in another which is engendered of the other's corruption. And when nature is unable to bring a thing to a greater perfection it brings it to a lesser; thus when it cannot produce a male it produces a female, which is *a misbegotten male* (*On the Generation and Corruption* 2.3).

I say, then, in like manner that slavery is contrary to the first intention of nature. Yet it is not contrary to the second, because natural reason has this inclination, and nature has this desire, that everyone should be good; but from the fact that a person sins, nature has an inclination that he should be punished for his sin, and thus slavery was brought in as a punishment of sin. Nor is it unreasonable for a natural thing to be hindered by that which is unnatural in this way; for thus is marriage hindered by impotence of coition, which impotence is contrary to nature in the way mentioned.

Reply Obj. 3: The natural law requires punishment to be inflicted for guilt, and that no one should be punished who is not guilty; but the appointing of the punishment according to the circumstances of person and guilt belongs to positive law. Hence slavery, which is a definite punishment, is of positive law, and arises out of natural law as the determinate from that which is indeterminate. And it arises from the determination of the same positive law that slavery, if unknown, is an impediment to matrimony, lest one who is not guilty be punished; for it is a punishment to the wife to have a slave for a husband, and vice versa.

Reply Obj. 4: Certain impediments render a marriage unlawful; and since it is not our will that makes a thing lawful or unlawful, but the law to which our will ought to be subject, it follows that the validity or invalidity of a marriage is not affected either by ignorance (such as destroys voluntariness) of the impediment or by knowledge thereof; and such an impediment is affinity or a vow, and others of the same kind.

Other impediments, however, render a marriage ineffectual as to the payment of the debt; and since it is within the competency of our will to remit a debt that is due to us, it follows that such impediments, if known, do not invalidate a marriage, but only when ignorance of them destroys voluntariness. Such impediments are slavery and impotence of coition. And, because they have of themselves the nature of an impediment, they are reckoned as special impediments besides error; whereas a change of person is not reckoned a special impediment besides error, because

bintroducta non habet rationem impedimenti nisi ex intentione contrahentis.

AD QUINTUM dicendum quod libertas non impedit matrimonii actum. Unde libertas ignorata non impedit matrimonium.

AD SEXTUM dicendum quod lepra non impedit matrimonium quantum ad primum actum suum, quia leprosi debitum reddere possunt libere: quamvis aliqua gravamina matrimonio inferant quantum ad secundos effectus. Et ideo non impedit matrimonium sicut servitus.

the substitution of another person has not the nature of an impediment except by reason of the intention of one of the contracting parties.

REPLY OBJ. 5: Freedom does not hinder the marriage act, wherefore ignorance of freedom is no impediment to matrimony.

REPLY OBJ. 6: Leprosy does not hinder marriage as to its first act, since lepers can pay the debt freely, although they lay a burden upon marriage as to its secondary effects; wherefore it is not an impediment to marriage as slavery is.

Article 2

Whether a Slave Can Marry Without His Master's Consent?

AD SECUNDUM SIC PROCEDITUR. Videtur quod servus matrimonium contrahere non possit sine consensu domini. Nullus enim potest alicui dare quod est alterius sine consensu ipsius. Sed *servus est res domini.* Ergo non potest, contrahendo matrimonium, dare potestatem corporis sui uxori, sine consensu domini.

PRAETEREA, servus tenetur domino suo obedire. Sed dominus potest ei praecipere quod in matrimonium non consentiat. Ergo sine consensu eius matrimonium non potest contrahere.

PRAETEREA, post contractum matrimonium servus tenetur reddere debitum uxori etiam praecepto iuris divini. Sed eo tempore quo uxor debitum petit, potest dominus aliquod servitium servo imponere, quod facere non poterit si carnali copulae vacare velit. Ergo, si sine consensu domini posset servus contrahere matrimonium, privaretur dominus servitio sibi debito sine culpa. Quod esse non debet.

PRAETEREA, dominus potest vendere servum suum in extraneas regiones, quo uxor sua non potest eum sequi, vel propter infirmitatem corporis; vel propter periculum fidei imminens, puta si vendatur infidelibus; vel etiam domino uxoris non permittente, si sit ancilla. Et sic matrimonium dissolvetur. Quod est inconveniens. Ergo non potest servus sine consensu domini matrimonium contrahere.

PRAETEREA, favorabilior est obligatio qua homo divinis obsequiis se mancipat, quam illa qua homo se uxori subiicit. Sed servus, sine consensu domini non potest religionem intrare vel ad clericatum promoveri. Ergo multo minus potest sine eius consensu matrimonio iungi.

SED CONTRA: Galat. 3: *in Christo Iesu non est servus neque liber.* Ergo ad matrimonium contrahendum in fide Christi Iesu eadem est libertas liberis et servis.

OBJECTION 1: It would seem that a slave cannot marry without his master's consent. For no one can give a person that which is another's without the latter's consent. Now a *slave is his master's possession.* Therefore, he cannot give his wife power over his body by marrying without his master's consent.

OBJ. 2: Further, a slave is bound to obey his master. But his master may command him not to consent to marry. Therefore, he cannot marry without his consent.

OBJ. 3: Further, after marriage, a slave is bound even by a precept of the divine law to pay the debt to his wife. But at the time that his wife asks for the debt his master may demand of him a service which he will be unable to perform if he wish to occupy himself in carnal intercourse. Therefore, if a slave can marry without his master's consent, the latter would be deprived of a service due to him without any fault of his; and this ought not to be.

OBJ. 4: Further, a master may sell his slave into a foreign country where the latter's wife is unable to follow him through either bodily weakness, or imminent danger to her faith (for instance, if he be sold to unbelievers, or if her master be unwilling, supposing her to be a slavewoman): and thus the marriage will be dissolved, which is unfitting. Therefore, a slave cannot marry without his master's consent.

OBJ. 5: Further, the burden under which a man binds himself to the divine service is more advantageous than that whereby a man subjects himself to his wife. But a slave cannot enter religion or receive orders without his master's consent. Much less, therefore, can he be married without his consent.

ON THE CONTRARY, *In Christ Jesus there is neither slave nor free* (Gal 3:23). Therefore, both freeman and slaves enjoy the same liberty to marry in the faith of Christ Jesus.

PRAETEREA, servitus est de iure positivo: sed matrimonium de iure naturali et divino. Cum ergo ius positivum non praeiudicet iuri naturali aut divino, videtur quod servus absque domini consensu matrimonium contrahere possit.

RESPONDEO dicendum quod ius positivum, ut dictum est, progreditur a iure naturali. Et ideo servitus, quae est de iure positivo, non potest praeiudicare his quae sunt de iure naturali Sicut autem appetitus naturae est ad conservationem individui, ita est ad conservationem speciei per generationem. Unde, sicut servus non subditur domino quin libere possit comedere et dormire, et alia huiusmodi facere quae ad necessitatem corporis pertinent, sine quibus natura conservari non potest; ita non subditur ei quantum ad hoc quod non possit libere matrimonium contrahere, etiam domino nesciente aut contradicente.

AD PRIMUM ergo dicendum quod servus est res domini quantum ad ea quae naturalibus superadduntur: sed quantum ad naturalia omnes sunt pares. Unde in his quae ad actus naturales pertinent, servus potest alteri, invito domino, sui corporis potestatem per matrimonium praebere.

AD SECUNDUM dicendum quod servus domino suo tenetur obedire in his quae dominus licite potest praecipere. Sicut autem licite non potest dominus praecipere servo quod non comedat vel dormiat, ita etiam nec quod a matrimonio contrahendo abstineat: interest enim ad legislatorem qualiter quilibet re sua utatur. Et ideo, si dominus praecipiat servo quod non contrahat matrimonium, servus non tenetur domino obedire.

AD TERTIUM dicendum quod si servus, volente domino, matrimonium contraxerit, tunc debet praetermittere servitium domini imperantis et reddere debitum uxori: quia per hoc quod dominus concessit ut matrimonium servus contraheret, intelligitur ei concessisse omnia quae matrimonium requirit. Si autem matrimonium ignorante vel contradicente domino est contractum, non tenetur reddere debitum, sed potius domino obedire, si utrumque esse non possit.

Sed tamen in his multa particularia considerari debent, sicut et in omnibus humanis actibus: scilicet periculum castitatis imminens uxori, et impedimentum quod ex redditione debiti servitio imperato generatur, et aliis huiusmodi. Quibus omnibus rite pensatis, iudicari poterit cui magis servus obedire teneatur, domino vel uxori.

AD QUARTUM dicendum quod in tali casu dicitur quod dominus cogendus est ne servum vendat taliter quod faciat onera matrimonii graviora: praecipue cum non desit facultas ubicumque servum suum vendendi iusto pretio.

FURTHER, Slavery is of positive law; whereas marriage is of natural and divine law. Since, then, positive law is not prejudicial to the natural or the divine law, it would seem that a slave can marry without his master's consent.

I ANSWER THAT, As stated above (A. 1), the positive law arises out of the natural law, and consequently slavery, which is of positive law, cannot be prejudicial to those things that are of natural law. Now just as nature seeks the preservation of the individual, so does it seek the preservation of the species by means of procreation; wherefore even as a slave is not so subject to his master as not to be at liberty to eat, sleep, and do such things as pertain to the needs of his body and without which nature cannot be preserved, so he is not subject to him to the extent of being unable to marry freely, even without his master's knowledge or consent.

REPLY OBJ. 1: A slave is his master's possession in matters superadded to nature, but in natural things all are equal. Wherefore, in things pertaining to natural acts, a slave can by marrying give another person power over his body without his master's consent.

REPLY OBJ. 2: A slave is bound to obey his master in those things which his master can command lawfully; and just as his master cannot lawfully command him not to eat or sleep, so neither can he lawfully command him to refrain from marrying. For it is the concern of the lawgiver how each one uses his own, and consequently if the master command his slave not to marry, the slave is not bound to obey his master.

REPLY OBJ. 3: If a slave has married with his master's consent, he should omit the service commanded by his master and pay the debt to his wife; because the master, by consenting to his slave's marriage, implicitly consented to all that marriage requires. If, however, the marriage was contracted without the master's knowledge or consent, he is not bound to pay the debt, but in preference to obey his master, if the two things are incompatible.

Nevertheless, in such matters there are many particulars to be considered, as in all human acts, namely, the danger to which his wife's chastity is exposed, and the obstacle which the payment of the debt places in the way of the service commanded, and other like considerations, all of which, being duly weighed, it will be possible to judge which of the two in preference the slave is bound to obey, his master or his wife.

REPLY OBJ. 4: In such a case it is said that the master should be compelled not to sell the slave in such a way as to increase the weight of the marriage burden, especially since he is able to obtain anywhere a just price for his slave.

Ad quintum dicendum quod propter religionem et ordinis susceptionem aliquis obligatur divinis obsequiis quantum ad totum tempus. Sed vir tenetur debitum reddere uxori non semper, sed congruis temporibus. Et ideo non est simile.

Et praeterea ille, qui, intrat religionem et suscipit ordinem, obligat se ad aliqua opera quae sunt naturalibus superaddita, in quibus dominus potestatem eius habet, et non in naturalibus, ad quae obligat se. per matrimonium. Unde posset continentiam vovere sine consensu domini.

Reply Obj. 5: By entering religion or receiving orders a man is bound to the divine service for all time; whereas a husband is bound to pay the debt to his wife not always, but at a fitting time; hence the comparison fails.

Moreover, he who enters religion or receives orders binds himself to works that are superadded to natural works, and in which his master has power over him, but not in natural works to which a man binds himself by marriage. Hence he cannot vow continence without his master's consent.

Article 3

Whether Slavery Can Supervene to Marriage by a Man Selling Himself to Another as a Slave?

Ad tertium sic proceditur. Videtur quod servitus matrimonio non possit supervenire, ut vir se alteri in servum vendat. Quia quod in fraudem et praeiudicium alterius factum est, ratum esse non debet. Sed vir qui se in servum vendit, facit hoc quandoque in fraudem matrimonii, et ad minus in detrimentum uxoris. Ergo non debet valere talis venditio ad servitutem inducendam.

Praeterea, duo favorabilia praeiudicant uni non favorabili. Sed matrimonium et libertas sunt favorabilia, et repugnant servituti, quae non est favorabilis in iure. Ergo talis servitus debet penitus annullari.

Praeterea, in matrimonio vir et uxor ad paria iudicantur. Sed uxor non potest se in ancillam dare nolente marito. Ergo nec vir nolente uxore.

Praeterea; illud quod impedit rei generationem in naturalibus, destruit etiam rem generatam. Sed servitus viri, nesciente uxore, impedit matrimonium contractum antequam fiat. Ergo, si posset matrimonio supervenire, destrueret matrimonium. Quod est inconveniens.

Sed contra: Quilibet potest dare alteri quod suum est. Sed vir est sui iuris, cum sit liber. Ergo potest dare ius suum alteri.

Praeterea, servus potest, nolente domino, uxorem ducere, ut dictum est. Ergo, eadem ratione, vir potest domino se subiicere nolente uxore.

Respondeo dicendum quod vir subditur uxori solum in his quae ad actum naturae pertinent, in quibus sunt aequales: ad quae servitutis subiectio se non extendit. Et ideo vir, nolente uxore potest se alteri in servum dare. Non tamen ex hoc matrimonium dissolvetur: quia nullum impedimentum matrimonio superveniens potest dissolvere ipsum, ut dictum est.

Objection 1: It would seem that slavery cannot supervene to marriage by the husband selling himself to another as slave. For what is done by fraud and to another's detriment should not hold. But a husband who sells himself for a slave does so sometimes to cheat marriage, and at least to the detriment of his wife. Therefore, such a sale should not hold as to the effect of slavery.

Obj. 2: Further, two favorable things outweigh one that is not favorable. Now marriage and freedom are favorable things and are contrary to slavery, which in law is not a favorable thing. Therefore, such a slavery ought to be entirely annulled in marriage.

Obj. 3: Further, in marriage husband and wife are on a par with one another. Now the wife cannot surrender herself to be a slave without her husband's consent. Therefore, neither can the husband without his wife's consent.

Obj. 4: Further, in natural things that which hinders a thing being generated destroys it after it has been generated. Now bondage of the husband, if unknown to the wife, is an impediment to the act of marriage before it is performed. Therefore, if it could supervene to marriage, it would dissolve it; which is unreasonable.

On the contrary, Everyone can give another that which is his own. Now the husband is his own master, since he is free. Therefore, he can surrender his right to another.

Further, A slave can marry without his master's consent, as stated above (A. 2). Therefore, a husband can, in like manner, subject himself to a master without his wife's consent.

I answer that, A husband is subject to his wife in those things which pertain to the act of nature; in these things they are equal, and the subjection of slavery does not extend thereto. Wherefore the husband, without his wife's knowledge, can surrender himself to be another's slave. Nor does this result in a dissolution of the marriage, since no impediment supervening to marriage can dissolve it, as stated above (Q. 50, A. 1).

AD PRIMUM ergo dicendum quod fraus bene potest nocere ei qui fraudem fecit, sed non potest alteri praeiudicium generare. Et ideo, si vir in fraudem uxoris alteri det se in servum, ipse reportat damnum, inaestimabile bonum libertatis amittens: sed uxori nullum potest ex hoc praeiudicium generari, quin teneatur reddere debitum petenti, et ad omnia quae matrimonium requirit; non enim potest ab his retrahi domini sui praecepto.

AD SECUNDUM dicendum quod, quantum ad hoc quod servitus matrimonio repugnat, matrimonium servituti praeiudicat: quia tunc servus tenetur uxori debitum reddere etiam nolente domino.

AD TERTIUM dicendum quod, quamvis in actu matrimoniali, et in his quae ad naturam spectant, ad paria vir et uxor iudicentur, ad quae conditio servitutis se non extendit; tamen quantum ad dispensationem domus et alia huiusmodi superaddita, vir est caput uxoris et debet corrigere eam, non autem e converso. Et ideo uxor non potest se dare in ancillam nolente viro.

AD QUARTUM dicendum quod ratio illa procedit de rebus corruptibilibus: in quibus etiam multa impediunt generationem quae non sufficiunt ad destruendum rem generatam. Sed in rebus perpetuis potest impedimentum praestari ne res talis esse incipiat, non autem ut esse desistat: sicut patet de anima rationali. Et similiter etiam est de matrimonio, quod est perpetuum vinculum, praesenti vita manente.

REPLY OBJ. 1: The fraud can indeed hurt the person who has acted fraudulently, but it cannot be prejudicial to another person: wherefore if the husband, to cheat his wife, surrender himself to be another's slave, it will be to his own prejudice, through his losing the inestimable good of freedom; whereas this can in no way be prejudicial to the wife, and he is bound to pay her the debt when she asks, and to do all that marriage requires of him, for he cannot be taken away from these obligations by his master's command.

REPLY OBJ. 2: Insofar as slavery is opposed to marriage, marriage is prejudicial to slavery, since the slave is bound then to pay the debt to his wife, though his master be unwilling.

REPLY OBJ. 3: Although husband and wife are considered to be on a par in the marriage act and in things relating to nature, to which the condition of slavery does not extend, nevertheless, as regards the management of the household and other such additional matters, the husband is the head of the wife and should correct her, and not vice versa. Hence the wife cannot surrender herself to be a slave without her husband's consent.

REPLY OBJ. 4: This argument considers corruptible things; and yet even in these there are many obstacles to generation that are not capable of destroying what is already generated. But in things which have stability it is possible to have an impediment which prevents a certain thing from beginning to be, yet does not cause it to cease to be; as is clear of the rational soul. It is the same with marriage, which is a lasting tie so long as this life lasts.

Article 4

Whether Children Should Follow the Condition of Their Father?

AD QUARTUM SIC PROCEDITUR. Videtur quod filii debeant sequi conditionem patris. Quia denominatio fit a digniori. Sed pater in generatione est dignior quam mater. Ergo, etc.

PRAETEREA, esse rei magis dependet a forma quam a materia. Sed in generatione *pater dat formam, mater materiam*, ut dicitur XVI *de Animalibus*. Ergo magis debet sequi proles patrem quam matrem.

PRAETEREA, illud praecipue debet aliquid sequi cui magis similatur. Sed filius plus similatur patri quam matri: sicut et filia plus matri. Ergo ad minus filius plus debet sequi patrem, et filia matrem.

PRAETEREA, in sacra Scriptura non computatur genealogia per mulieres, sed per viros. Ergo proles magis sequitur patrem quam matrem.

OBJECTION 1: It would seem that children should follow the condition of their father. For dominion belongs to those of higher rank. Now in generating the father ranks above the mother. Therefore, etc.

OBJ. 2: Further, the being of a thing depends on the form more than on the matter. Now in generation *the father gives the form, and the mother the matter* (*On the Generation of Animals* 2.4). Therefore, the child should follow the condition of the father rather than of the mother.

OBJ. 3: Further, a thing should follow that chiefly to which it is most like. Now the son is more like the father than the mother, even as the daughter is more like the mother. Therefore, at least the son should follow the father in preference, and the daughter the mother.

OBJ. 4: Further, in Sacred Scripture genealogies are not traced through the women but through the men. Therefore, the children follow the father rather than the mother.

SED CONTRA: Si quis seminat in terra aliena, fructus sunt eius cuius est terra. Sed venter mulieris respectu seminis viri est sicut terra respectu sementis. Ergo, etc.

PRAETEREA, in aliis animalibus hoc videmus, quae ex diversis speciebus nascuntur, quod partus magis sequitur matrem quam patrem: unde muli qui nascuntur ex equa et asino, magis assimilantur equabus quam illi qui nascuntur ex asina et equo. Ergo similiter debet esse in hominibus.

RESPONDEO dicendum quod, secundum leges civiles, *partus sequitur ventrem*. Et hoc rationabiliter. Quia proles habet a patre complementum formale, sed a matre substantiam corporis. Servitus autem corporalis conditio est: cum servus sit quasi instrumentum domini in operando. Et ideo proles in libertate et servitute sequitur matrem. Sed in his quae pertinent ad dignitatem, quae est ex forma rei, sequitur patrem: sicut in honoribus et municipiis et haereditate, et aliis huiusmodi. Et huic etiam concordant canones; et lex Moysi, ut patet Exod. 21.

In quibusdam tamen terris, quae iure civili non reguntur, partus sequitur deteriorem conditionem: ut, si pater sit servus, quamvis mater sit libera, erunt filii servi (non tamen si post peractum matrimonium pater se in servum dedit nolente uxore); et similiter si sit e converso. Si autem uterque sit servilis conditionis, et pertineant ad diversos dominos, tunc dividunt filios si plures sint; vel, si unus tantum, unus alteri recompensabit de pretio et accipiet prolem natam in sui servitium. Tamen non est credibile quod talis consuetudo possit esse ita rationabilis sicut illud quod multorum sapientum diuturno consilio determinatum est.

Hoc etiam in naturalibus invenitur, quod receptum est in recipiente per modum recipientis, non per modum dantis. Et ideo rationabile est quod semen receptum in muliere ad conditionem ipsius trahatur.

AD PRIMUM ergo dicendum quod, quamvis pater sit dignius principium, tamen mater dat substantiam corporalem, ex parte cuius attenditur conditio servitutis.

AD SECUNDUM dicendum quod in his quae ad rationem speciei pertinent, magis similatur filius patri quam matri. Sed in materialibus conditionibus magis debet similari matri quam patri: quia res habet a forma esse specificum, sed conditiones materiales a materia.

AD TERTIUM dicendum: quod filius similatur patri ratione formae, quam habet in sui complemento, sicut et pater. Et ideo ratio non est ad propositum.

AD QUARTUM dicendum quod, quia honor filii magis est ex patre quam ex matre, ideo in genealogiis in Scripturis, et secundum communem consuetudinem, magis nominantur filii a patre quam a matre. Tamen in

ON THE CONTRARY, If a man sows on another's land, the produce belongs to the owner of the land. Now the woman's womb in relation to the seed of man is like the land in relation to the sower. Therefore, etc.

FURTHER, We observe that in animals born from different species the offspring follows the mother rather than the father, wherefore mules born of a mare and an ass are more like mares than those born of a she-ass and a horse. Therefore, it should be the same with men.

I ANSWER THAT, According to civil law (*Decretals*) the *offspring follows the womb*; and this is reasonable since the offspring derives its formal complement from the father, but the substance of the body from the mother. Now slavery is a condition of the body, since a slave is to the master a kind of instrument in working; wherefore children follow the mother in freedom and bondage. But in matters pertaining to dignity as proceeding from a thing's form, they follow the father, for instance, in honors, franchise, inheritance, and so forth. The canons are in agreement with this (*Decretals*) as also the law of Moses (Exod 21:4).

In some countries, however, where the civil law does not hold, the offspring follows the inferior condition, so that if the father be a slave, the children will be slaves although the mother be free; but not if the father gave himself up as a slave after his marriage and without his wife's consent; and the same applies if the case be reversed. And if both be of servile condition and belong to different masters, the children, if several, are divided among the latter, or if one only, the one master will compensate the other in value and will take the child thus born for his slave. However, it is incredible that this custom have as much reason in its favor as the decision of the time-honored deliberations of many wise men.

Moreover, in natural things it is the rule that what is received is in the recipient according to the mode of the recipient and not according to the mode of the giver; wherefore it is reasonable that the seed received by the mother should be drawn to her condition.

REPLY OBJ. 1: Although the father is a more noble principle, nevertheless the mother provides the substance of the body, and it is to this that the condition of slavery attaches.

REPLY OBJ. 2: As regards things pertaining to the specific nature the son is like the father rather than the mother, but in material conditions should be like the mother rather than the father, since a thing has its specific being from its form, but material conditions from matter.

REPLY OBJ. 3: The son is like the father in respect of the form which is his, and also the father's, complement. Hence the argument is not to the point.

REPLY OBJ. 4: It is because the son derives honor from his father rather than from his mother that in the genealogies of Scripture, and according to common custom, children are named after their father rather than after their

his quae ad servitutem spectant, magis matrem sequuntur.

mother. But in matters relating to slavery they follow the mother by preference.

QUESTION 53

THE IMPEDIMENT OF VOWS AND HOLY ORDERS

Deinde considerandum est de impedimento voti et ordinis.

Circa quod quaeruntur quattuor.

Primo: utrum votum simplex matrimonium dirimat.

Secundo: utrum votum solemne.

Tertio: utrum ordo matrimonium impediat.

Quarto: utrum aliquis post matrimonium sacrum ordinem suscipere possit.

We must now consider the impediment of vows and orders.

Under this head there are four points of inquiry:

(1) Whether a simple vow is a diriment impediment to matrimony?

(2) Whether a solemn vow is a diriment impediment?

(3) Whether order is an impediment to matrimony?

(4) Whether a man can receive a sacred order after being married?

Article 1

Whether a Marriage Already Contracted Should Be Annulled by the Obligation of a Simple Vow?

AD PRIMUM SIC PROCEDITUR. Videtur quod per obligationem voti simplicis matrimonium contractum dirimi debeat. Fortius enim vinculum debiliori praeiudicat. Sed vinculum voti est fortius quam vinculum matrimonii: quia hoc fit homini, illud autem Deo. Ergo vinculum voti praeiudicat vinculo matrimonii.

PRAETEREA, praeceptum Dei non est minus quam praeceptum Ecclesiae. Sed praeceptum Ecclesiae adeo obligat quod, si contra ipsum matrimonium contrahatur, dirimitur: sicut patet de illis qui contrahunt in aliquo gradu consanguinitatis ab Ecclesia prohibito. Ergo, cum servare votum sit praeceptum divinum, videtur quod qui contra votum divinum matrimonium contrahit, quod ex hoc matrimonium sit dirimendum.

PRAETEREA, in matrimonio potest homo uti carnali copula sine peccato. Sed ille qui facit votum simplex, nunquam potest carnaliter uxori commisceri sine peccato. Ergo Votum simplex matrimonium dirimit.

Probatio mediae. Constat quod ille qui post votum simplex continentiae matrimonium contrahit, peccat mortaliter: quia, secundum Hieronymum, *virginitatem voventibus non solum nubere, sed velle nubere damnabile.* Sed contractus matrimonii non est contra votum continentiae nisi ratione carnalis copulae. Ergo, quando primo carnaliter commiscetur uxori, mortaliter peccat. Et eadem ratione omnibus aliis vicibus: quia peccatum primo commissum non potest excusare a peccato sequenti,

PRAETEREA, vir et mulier in matrimonio debent esse pares praecipue quantum ad carnalem copulam. Sed ille qui votum simplex continentiae facit, nunquam po-

OBJECTION 1: It would seem that a marriage already contracted ought to be annulled by the obligation of a simple vow. For the stronger tie takes precedence over the weaker. Now a vow is a stronger tie than marriage, since the latter binds man to man, but the former binds man to God. Therefore, the obligation of a vow takes precedence of the marriage tie.

OBJ. 2: Further, God's commandment is no less binding than the commandment of the Church. Now the commandment of the Church is so binding that a marriage is void if contracted in despite thereof, as in the case of those who marry within the degrees of kindred forbidden by the Church. Therefore, since it is a divine commandment to keep a vow, it would seem that if a person marry in despite of a vow his marriage should be annulled for that reason.

OBJ. 3: Further, in marriage a man may have carnal intercourse without sin. Yet he who has taken a simple vow of chastity can never have carnal intercourse with his wife without sin. Therefore, a simple vow annuls marriage.

Proof of the middle: It is clear that it is a mortal sin to marry after taking a simple vow of continence, since according to Jerome, *for those who vow virginity it is damnable not only to marry, but even to wish to marry* (St. Augustine, *On the Good of Widowhood*). Now the marriage contract is not contrary to the vow of continence except by reason of carnal intercourse. Therefore, he sins mortally the first time he has intercourse with his wife, and for the same reason every other time, because a sin committed in the first instance cannot be an excuse for a subsequent sin.

OBJ. 4: Further, husband and wife should be equal in marriage, especially as regards carnal intercourse. But he who has taken a simple vow of continence can never ask for

test petere debitum sine peccato: quia hoc est expresse contra votum continentiae, ad quam ex voto tenetur. Ergo nec reddere potest sine peccato.

SED CONTRA est quod Papa Clemens dicit, quod votum simplex impedit matrimonium contrahendum, sed non dirimit contractum.

RESPONDEO dicendum quod per hoc res aliqua desinit esse in potestate alicuius per quod transit in dominium alterius. Promissio autem alicuius rei non transfert eam in dominium eius cui promittitur. Et ideo non ex hoc ipso quod aliquis rem promittit aliquam, desinit res illa esse in potestate sua. Cum ergo in voto simplici non sit nisi simplex promissio proprii corporis ad continentiam Deo servandam facta, post votum simplex adhuc remanet homo dominus sui corporis. Et ideo potest ipsum alteri dare, scilicet uxori: in qua datione sacramentum matrimonii consistit, quod indissolubile est. Et propter hoc votum simplex, quamvis impediat contrahendum, quia peccat contrahens matrimonium post votum simplex continentiae; tamen, quia verus contractus est, non potest matrimonium propter hoc dirimi.

AD PRIMUM ergo dicendum quod votum est fortius vinculum quam matrimonium quantum ad id cui fit, et ad quod ligat: quia per matrimonium homo ligatur uxori ad redditionem debiti, sed per votum Deo ad continentiam. Tamen quantum ad modum ligandi, matrimonium est fortius vinculum quam votum simplex: quia per matrimonium traditur actualiter vir in potestatem uxoris, non autem per votum simplex, ut dictum est; potior autem est semper conditio possidentis. Sed quantum ad hoc simili modo obligat votum simplex sicut sponsalia. Unde propter votum simplex sunt sponsalia dirimenda.

AD SECUNDUM dicendum quod praeceptum prohibens matrimonium inter consanguineos non habet inquantum est praeceptum Dei vel Ecclesiae, quod dirimat matrimonium contrahendum: sed inquantum facit quod consanguinei corpus non possit transire in potestatem consanguinei. Hoc autem non facit praeceptum prohibens matrimonium post votum simplex, ut ex dictis patet. Et ideo ratio non sequitur: ponitur enim pro causa quod non est causa.

AD TERTIUM dicendum quod ille qui contrahit matrimonium per verba de praesenti post votum simplex, non potest cognoscere uxorem suam sine peccato mortali: quia adhuc restat sibi facultas implendi votum continentiae ante matrimonium consummatum, Sed postquam iam matrimonium consummatum est, est sibi factum illicitum non reddere debitum uxori exigenti, tamen ex culpa sua. Et ideo ad hoc obligatio voti non se extendit, ut ex praedictis patet: tamen debet lamentum poenitentiae recompensare pro continentia non servata.

the debt without a sin, for this is clearly against his vow of continence, since he is bound to continence by vow. Therefore, neither can he pay the debt without sin.

ON THE CONTRARY, Pope Clement says (cap. Consuluit, *De His qui cler. vel vovent.*) that a simple vow is an impediment to the contract of marriage, but does not annul it after it is contracted.

I ANSWER THAT, A thing ceases to be in one man's power from the fact that it passes into the power of another. Now the promise of a thing does not transfer it into the power of the person to whom it is promised, wherefore a thing does not cease to be in a person's power for the reason that he has promised it. Since, then, a simple vow contains merely a simple promise of one's body to the effect of keeping continence for God's sake, a man still retains power over his own body after a simple vow, and consequently can surrender it to another, namely, his wife; and in this surrender consists the sacrament of matrimony, which is indissoluble. Therefore, although a simple vow is an impediment to the contracting of a marriage, since it is a sin to marry after taking a simple vow of continence, yet since the contract is valid, the marriage cannot be annulled on that account.

REPLY OBJ. 1: A vow is a stronger tie than matrimony as regards that to which man is tied, and the obligation under which he lies, because by marriage a man is tied to his wife with the obligation of paying the debt, whereas by a vow a man is tied to God with the obligation of remaining continent. But as to the manner in which he is tied, marriage is a stronger tie than a simple vow, since by marriage a man surrenders himself actually to the power of his wife, but not by a simple vow as explained above; and the possessor is always in the stronger position. In this respect a simple vow binds in the same way as a betrothal; wherefore a betrothal must be annulled on account of a simple vow.

REPLY OBJ. 2: The contracting of a marriage between blood relations is annulled by the commandment forbidding such marriages, not precisely because it is a commandment of God or of the Church, but because it makes it impossible for the body of a kinswoman to be transferred into the power of her kinsman, whereas the commandment forbidding marriage after a simple vow has not this effect, as already stated. Hence the argument is void, for it assigns as a cause that which is not a cause.

REPLY OBJ. 3: If after taking a simple vow a man contract marriage by words of the present, he cannot know his wife without mortal sin, because until the marriage is consummated he is still in a position to fulfill the vow of continence. But after the marriage has been consummated, through his fault it is unlawful for him not to pay the debt when his wife asks; therefore, this is not covered by his obligation to his vow, as explained above (ad 1). Nevertheless, he should atone for not keeping continence by his tears of repentance.

Ad quartum dicendum quod, quantum ad ea in quibus non est factus impotens votum continentiae servare, adhuc post contractum matrimonium obligatur ad servandum. Propter quod, mortua uxore, tenetur totaliter continere. Et quia ex matrimonii vinculo non obligatur ad debitum petendum, ideo non potest petere debitum sine peccato: quamvis possit sine peccato reddere debitum exigenti, postquam obligatus est ad hoc per carnalem copulam praecedentem. Hoc autem intelligendum est sive mulier expresse petat, sive interpretative, ut quando mulier verecunda est, et vir sentit eius voluntatem de redditione debiti: tunc enim sine peccato reddere potest, et praecipue si ei timet de periculo castitatis. Nec obstat quod non sunt pares in matrimonii actu: quia quilibet potest hoc quod suum est abrenuntiare.

Quidam tamen dicunt quod potest et petere et reddere: ne nimis onerosum reddatur matrimonium uxori semper exigenti. Sed, si recte inspiciatur, hoc est exigere interpretative.

Reply Obj. 4: After contracting marriage he is still bound to keep his vow of continence in those matters wherein he is not rendered unable to do so. Hence if his wife should die, he is bound to continence altogether. And since the marriage tie does not bind him to ask for the debt, he cannot ask for it without sin, although he can pay the debt without sin on being asked, when once he has incurred this obligation through the carnal intercourse that has already occurred. And this holds whether the wife ask expressly or interpretively, as when she is ashamed and her husband feels that she desires him to pay the debt, for then he may pay it without sin. This is especially the case if he fears to endanger her chastity: nor does it matter that they are equals in the marriage act, since everyone may renounce what is his own.

Some say, however, that he may both ask and pay lest the marriage become too burdensome to the wife who has always to ask; but if this be looked into rightly, it is the same as asking interpretively.

Article 2

Whether a Solemn Vow Dissolves a Marriage Already Contracted?

Ad secundum sic proceditur. Videtur quod nec etiam votum solemne matrimonium dirimat contractum. Quia, sicut Decretalis dicit, *apud Deum non minus obligat votum simplex quam solemne.* Sed matrimonium acceptatione divina stat vel dirimitur. Ergo, cum votum simplex non dirimat matrimonium, nec votum solemne dirimere poterit.

Praeterea, votum solemne non addit ita validum robur super votum simplex sicut iuramentum. Sed votum simplex, etiam iuramento superveniente, non dirimit matrimonium contractum. Ergo nec votum solemne.

Praeterea, votum solemne nihil habet quod non possit votum simplex habere. Quia votum simplex posset habere scandalum: cum possit esse in publico, sicut et solemne. Similiter et Ecclesia posset et deberet statuere quod votum simplex dirimat matrimonium iam contractum, ut multa peccata vitarentur. Ergo, qua ratione votum simplex non dirimit matrimonium, nec votum solemne dirimere debet.

Sed contra: Est quod ille qui facit votum solemne, contrahit matrimonium spirituale cum Deo, quod est multo dignius quam materiale matrimonium. Sed materiale matrimonium prius contractum dirimit matrimonium post contractum. Ergo votum solemne.

Praeterea, hoc etiam probari potest per multas auctoritates quae ponuntur in littera.

Objection 1: It would seem that not even a solemn vow dissolves a marriage already contracted. For, according to the *Decretals, in God's sight a simple vow is no less binding than a solemn one.* Now marriage stands or falls by virtue of the divine acceptance. Therefore, since a simple vow does not dissolve marriage, neither will a solemn vow dissolve it.

Obj. 2: Further, a solemn vow does not add the same force to a simple vow as an oath does. Now a simple vow, even though an oath be added thereto, does not dissolve a marriage already contracted. Neither, therefore, does a solemn vow.

Obj. 3: Further, a solemn vow has nothing that a simple vow cannot have. For a simple vow may give rise to scandal, since it may be public, like a solemn vow. Again, the Church could and should ordain that a simple vow dissolves a marriage already contracted, so that many sins may be avoided. Therefore, for the same reason that a simple vow does not dissolve a marriage already contracted, neither should a solemn vow dissolve it.

On the contrary, He who takes a solemn vow contracts a spiritual marriage with God, which is much more excellent than a material marriage. Now a material marriage already contracted annuls a marriage contracted afterwards. Therefore, a solemn vow does also.

Further, The same conclusion may be proved by many authorities quoted in the text (*Sentences* IV, D. 28).

RESPONDEO dicendum quod omnes dicunt quod, sicut votum solemne impedit contrahendum, ita dirimit iam contractum. Quidam autem assignant pro causa scandalum. Sed hoc nihil est. Quia et simplex votum quandoque habet scandalum: cum sit quandoque quodammodo publicum. Et praeterea insolubilitas matrimonii est *de veritate vitae*: quae *non est propter scandalum dimittenda*.

Et ideo alii dicunt quod hoc est propter statutum Ecclesiae. Sed hoc etiam non sufficit. Quia secundum hoc Ecclesia posset etiam contrarium statuere. Quod non videtur verum.

Et ideo dicendum est, cum aliis, quod votum solemne ex sui natura habet quod dirimat matrimonium contractum: inquantum scilicet per ipsum homo sui corporis amisit potestatem, Deo illud ad perpetuarii continentiam tradens, ut ex dictis patet; et ideo non potest seipsum tradere in potestatem uxoris matrimonium contrahendo. Et quia matrimonium quod sequitur tale votum, nullum est, ideo votum praedictum dirimere dicitur matrimonium contractum.

AD PRIMUM ergo dicendum quod votum simplex quoad Deum dicitur non minus obligare quam solemne in his quae ad Deum spectant, sicut est separatio a Deo per peccatum mortale: quia mortaliter peccat frangens votum simplex sicut solemne, quamvis gravius sit peccatum frangere votum solemne; ut sic comparatio in genere accipiatur, non in determinata quantitate reatus. Sed quantum ad matrimonium, per quod homo homini obligatur, non oportet quod sit aequalis obligationis etiam in genere: quia ad quaedam obligat votum solemne, et non simplex.

AD SECUNDUM dicendum quod iuramentum plus obligat ex parte eius ex quo fit obligatio, quam votum. Sed votum solemne plus obligat quantum ad modum obligandi: inquantum actualiter tradit hoc quod promittitur, quod non fit per iuramentum. Et ideo non sequitur ratio.

AD TERTIUM dicendum quod votum solemne habet actualem exhibitionem proprii corporis, quam non habet votum simplex, ut ex dictis patet. Et ideo ratio ex insufficienti procedit.

I ANSWER THAT, All agree that as a solemn vow is an impediment to the contracting of marriage, so it invalidates the contract. Some assign scandal as the reason. But this is futile, because even a simple vow sometimes leads to scandal since it is at times somewhat public. Moreover, the indissolubility of marriage belongs *to the truth of life*, which *is not to be set aside on account of scandal*.

Wherefore others say that it is on account of the ordinance of the Church. But this again is insufficient, since in that case the Church might decide the contrary, which is seemingly untrue.

Wherefore we must say with others that a solemn vow of its very nature dissolves the marriage contract, namely, inasmuch by it a man has lost the power over his own body, through surrendering it to God for the purpose of perpetual continence. Therefore, he is unable to surrender it to the power of a wife by contracting marriage. And since the marriage that follows such a vow is void, a vow of this kind is said to annul the marriage contracted.

REPLY OBJ. 1: With respect to God a simple vow is said to obligate one not less than a solemn vow in those matters which regard God, as separation from God is mortal sin; for he sins mortally who breaks a simple vow, just as he who breaks a solemn one, although it may be a more serious sin to break a solemn one, so that in this way the comparison is taken generically, not determined by the quantity of the guilt. But as regards marriage, whereby one man is under an obligation to another, there is no need for it to be of equal obligation even in general, since a solemn vow binds to certain things to which a simple vow does not bind.

REPLY OBJ. 2: An oath is more binding than a vow on the part of the cause of the obligation, but a solemn vow is more binding as to the manner in which it binds, insofar as it is an actual surrender of that which is promised; while an oath does not do this actually. Hence the conclusion does not follow.

REPLY OBJ. 3: A solemn vow implies the actual surrender of one's body, whereas a simple vow does not, as stated above (A. 1). Hence the argument does not suffice to prove the conclusion.

Article 3

Whether Holy Orders Is an Impediment to Matrimony?

AD TERTIUM SIC PROCEDITUR. Videtur quod ordo non impediat matrimonium. Quia nihil impeditur nisi a suo contrario. Sed ordo non est contrarius matrimonio: cum utrumque sit sacramentum. Ergo non impedit ipsum.

OBJECTION 1: It would seem that holy orders is not an impediment to matrimony. For nothing is an impediment to a thing except its contrary. But holy orders is not contrary to matrimony. Therefore, it is not an impediment thereto.

Praeterea, idem ordo est apud nos et apud Ecclesiam Orientalem. Sed apud Ecclesiam Orientalem non impedit matrimonium. Ergo nec apud Occidentalem.

Praeterea, matrimonium significat coniunctionem Christi et Ecclesiae. Sed hoc praecipue congruit significari in his qui sunt ministri Christi, scilicet ordinatis. Ergo ordo matrimonium non impedit.

Praeterea, omnes ordines ad aliquid spirituale ordinantur. Sed ordo non potest impedire matrimonium nisi ratione spiritualitatis. Ergo, si ordo impedit matrimonium, quilibet ordo impediet. Quod falsum est.

Praeterea, omnes ordinati possunt ecclesiastica beneficia habere, et privilegio clericali gaudere aequaliter. Si ergo propter hoc ordo matrimonium impediat quia uxorati non possunt habere beneficium ecclesiasticum nec gaudere privilegio clericali, ut iuristae dicunt; tunc quilibet ordo impedire deberet. Quod falsum est: ut patet per decretalem Alexandri, *de Clericis coniugatis*. Et sic nullus ordo, ut videtur, matrimonium impediet.

Sed contra: Est quod Decretalis dicit: *si in subdiaconatu et aliis superioribus ordinibus uxores accepisse noscuntur, eos uxores dimittere compellatis.* Quod non esset si esset verum matrimonium.

Praeterea, nullus vovens continentiam potest matrimonium contrahere. Sed quidam ordines sunt qui habent votum continentiae annexum, ut ex littera patet. Ergo talis ordo matrimonium impedit.

Respondeo dicendum quod ordo sacer de sui ratione habet, ex quadam congruentia, quod matrimonium impedire debeat: quia in sacris ordinibus constituti sacra vasa et sacramenta tractant, et ideo decens est ut munditiam corporalem per continentiam servent. Sed quod impediat matrimonium, ex constitutione Ecclesiae habet. Tamen aliter apud Latinos quam apud Graecos. Quia apud Graecos impedit matrimonium contrahendum solum ex vi ordinis. Sed apud: Latinos impedit ex vi ordinis, et ulterius ex voto continentiae, quod est ordinibus sacris annexum: quod etiam si quis verbo tenus non emittat, ex hoc ipso quod ordinem suscipit secundum ritum Occidentalis Ecclesiae, intelligitur emisisse. Et ideo apud Graecos et alios Orientales sacer ordo impedit matrimonium contrahendum, non tamen matrimonii prius contracti usum: possunt enim matrimonio prius contracto uti, quamvis non possint matrimonium de novo contrahere. Sed apud Occidentalem Ecclesiam impedit matrimonium et matrimonii usum: nisi forte, ignorante aut contradicente uxore, vir ordinem sacrum susceperit; quia ex hoc non potest ei aliquod praeiudicium gene-

Obj. 2: Further, holy orders is the same with us as with the Eastern Church. But they are not an impediment to matrimony in the Eastern Church. Therefore, neither are they in the Western.

Obj. 3: Further, matrimony signifies the union of Christ with the Church. Now this is most fittingly signified in those who are Christ's ministers, namely, those who are ordained. Therefore, holy orders is not an impediment to matrimony.

Obj. 4: Further, all the orders are directed to spiritual things. Now holy orders cannot be an impediment to matrimony except by reason of its spirituality. Therefore, if holy orders is an impediment to matrimony, every order will be an impediment, and this is untrue.

Obj. 5: Further, every ordained person can have ecclesiastical benefices, and can enjoy equally the privilege of clergy. If, therefore, orders are an impediment to marriage, because married persons cannot have an ecclesiastical benefice nor enjoy the privilege of clergy, as jurists assert (*Decretals*), then every order ought to be an impediment. Yet this is false, as shown by the *Decretals*: and consequently it would seem that no order is an impediment to marriage.

On the contrary, The Decretal says: *any person whom you shall find to have taken a wife after receiving the subdiaconate or the higher orders, you shall compel to put his wife away.* But this would not be so if the marriage were valid.

Further, No person who has vowed continence can contract marriage. Now some orders have a vow of continence connected with them, as appears from the text (*Sentences* IV, D. 37). Therefore, in that case order is an impediment to matrimony.

I answer that, By a certain fittingness the very nature of holy orders requires that it should be an impediment to marriage, because those who are in holy orders handle the sacred vessels and the sacraments: wherefore it is becoming that they keep their bodies clean by continence (Isa 52:11). But it is owing to the Church's ordinance that it is actually an impediment to marriage. However, it is not the same with the Latins as with the Greeks, since with the Greeks it is an impediment to the contracting of marriage solely by virtue of holy orders; whereas with the Latins it is an impediment by virtue of holy orders and also by virtue of the vow of continence which is annexed to the sacred orders; for, although this vow is not expressed in words, nevertheless a person is understood to have taken it by the very fact of his being ordained. Hence among the Greeks and other Eastern peoples a sacred order is an impediment to the contracting of matrimony but it does not forbid the use of marriage already contracted: for they can use marriage contracted previously, although they cannot be married again. But in the Western Church it is an impediment both to marriage and to the use of marriage, unless perhaps the hus-

rari. Quomodo autem ordines sacri distinguuntur a non sacris, nunc et in primitiva Ecclesia, dictum est.

Ad primum ergo dicendum quod, quamvis ordo sacer non habeat contrarietatem ad matrimonium inquantum sacramentum, habet tamen repugnantiam quandam ad ipsum ratione actus sui, qui spirituales actus impedit.

Ad secundum dicendum quod iam patet quod obiectio procedit ex falsis. Ordo enim ubique impedit matrimonium contrahendum, quamvis non ubique habeat votum annexum.

Ad tertium dicendum quod illi qui sunt in sacris ordinibus, significant Christum nobilioribus actibus, prout ex dictis in tractatu de ordine patet, quam illi qui sunt matrimonio coniuncti. Et ideo ratio non sequitur.

Ad quartum dicendum quod illi qui sunt in minoribus ordinibus constituti, ex vi ordinis non prohibentur matrimonium contrahere: quia, quamvis ordines illi deputentur ad aliqua spiritualia, non tamen immediate habent: accessum ad tractandum sacra, sicut illi qui sunt in sacris ordinibus. Sed secundum statutum Occidentalis Ecclesiae, matrimonii usus executionem ordinis non sacri impedit: propter servandam maiorem honestatem in officiis Ecclesiae. Et quia aliquis ex beneficio ecclesiastico tenetur ad executionem ordinis, et ex hoc ipso privilegio clericali gaudet, ideo haec apud Latinos clericis uxoratis auferuntur.

Et per hoc patet solutio ad ultimum.

band should receive a sacred order without the knowledge or consent of his wife, because this cannot be prejudicial to her. Of the distinction between sacred and non-sacred orders now and in the early Church we have spoken above (Q. 37, A. 3).

Reply Obj. 1: Although a sacred order is not contrary to matrimony as a sacrament, it has a certain incompatibility with marriage in respect of the latter's act, which is an obstacle to spiritual acts.

Reply Obj. 2: The objection is based on a false statement, since holy orders is everywhere an impediment to the contracting of marriage, although it has not everywhere a vow annexed to it.

Reply Obj. 3: Those who are in sacred orders signify Christ by more sublime actions, as appears from what has been said in the treatise on orders (Q. 37, A. 2, 4), than those who are married. Consequently, the conclusion does not follow.

Reply Obj. 4: Those who are in minor orders are not forbidden to marry by virtue of their order; for, although those orders are entrusted with certain spiritualities, they are not admitted to the immediate handling of sacred things, as those are who are in sacred orders. But according to the laws of the Western Church, the use of marriage is an impediment to the exercise of a non-sacred order, for the sake of maintaining a greater honesty in the offices of the Church. And since the holding of an ecclesiastical benefice binds a man to the exercise of his order, and since for this very reason he enjoys the privilege of clergy, it follows that in the Latin Church this privilege is forfeit to a married cleric.

This suffices for the reply to the last objection.

Article 4

Whether a Sacred Order Can Supervene to Matrimony?

Ad quartum sic proceditur. Videtur quod matrimonio ordo sacer supervenire non possit. Quia fortius praeiudicat minus forti. Sed fortius est vinculum spirituale quam corporale. Ergo, si matrimonio iunctus ordinem suscipiat, praeiudicium generabitur uxori, ut non possit debitum exigere: cum ordo sit vinculum spirituale, et matrimonium corporale. Et sic videtur quod non possit aliquis ordinem sacrum suscipere post matrimonium consummatum.

Praeterea, post matrimonium consummatum unus coniugum sine consensu alterius non potest continentiam vovere. Sed ordo sacer habet continentiae votum annexum. Ergo, si vir ordinem sacrum invita uxo-

Objection 1: It would seem that a sacred order cannot supervene to matrimony. For the stronger prejudices the weaker. Now a spiritual obligation is stronger than a bodily tie. Therefore, if a married man be ordained, this will prejudice the wife, so that she will be unable to demand the debt, since holy orders is a spiritual, and marriage a bodily bond. Hence it would seem that a man cannot receive a sacred order after consummating marriage.

Obj. 2: Further, after consummating the marriage, one of the parties cannot vow continence without the other's consent (Q. 61, A. 1). Now a sacred order has a vow of continence annexed to it. Therefore, if the husband be ordained

re acciperet, cogeretur uxor invita continentiam, servare: quia non posset alteri nubere, vivente viro.

PRAETEREA, etiam ad tempus non potest vir vacare orationi sine consensu uxoris, ut habetur I Cor. 7. Sed apud Orientales illi qui sunt in sacris constituti, tenentur ad continentiam tempore quo exequuntur officium. Ergo nec ipsi possunt ordinari sine consensu uxoris. Et multo minus Latini.

PRAETEREA, vir et uxor ad paria indicantur. Sed sacerdos graecus, defuncta uxore sua, non potest aliam ducere. Ergo nec uxor, defuncto viro. Sed non potest sibi auferri facultas nubendi post mortem viri per viri actum. Ergo vir non potest suscipere ordines post matrimonium.

PRAETEREA, matrimonium quantum opponitur ordini, tantum e converso. Sed ordo praecedens impedit matrimonium sequens. Ergo e converso.

SED CONTRA: Religiosi tenentur ad continentiam sicut illi qui sunt in sacris ordinibus. Sed post matrimonium potest aliquis religionem intrare, defuncta vel consentiente uxore. Ergo et ordinem suscipere.

PRAETEREA, aliquis potest fieri servus hominum post matrimonium. Ergo et servus Dei per susceptionem ordinis.

RESPONDEO dicendum quod matrimonium non impedit ordinis sacri susceptionem. Quia si matrimonio iunctus ad sacros ordines accedat etiam reclamante uxore, nihilominus characterem ordinis suscipit: sed executione ordinis caret. Si autem volente uxore, vel ipsa defuncta, sacrum ordinem accipiat, recipit ordinem et executionem.

AD PRIMUM ergo dicendum quod vinculum Ordinis solvit vinculum matrimonii ratione redditionis debiti, ex qua parte habet repugnantiam ad matrimonium, ex parte eius qui suscipit ordinem: quia non potest petere debitum, nec uxor ei tenetur reddere. Non tamen solvit ex parte alterius: quia ipse tenetur uxori debitum reddere, si non possit eam inducere ad continentiam.

AD SECUNDUM dicendum quod, si uxor sciat et de eius consensu vir ordinem sacrum susceperit, tenetur perpetuam continentiam Vovere: non tamen tenetur religionem intrare, si sibi non timeat de periculo castitatis, propter hoc quod vir eius solemne votum emisit. Secus autem esset si emisisset votum simplex. Si autem sine eius consensu suscepit, non tenetur: quia ex hoc sibi nullum praeiudicium generatur.

AD TERTIUM dicendum quod, sicut probabilius videtur, quamvis quidam contrarium dixerunt, quod etiam Graeci non debent accedere ad sacros ordines sine consensu uxorum. Quia ad minus tempore ministerii sui fraudarentur debiti redditione: quo fraudari non

without his wife's consent, she will be bound to remain continent against her will, since she cannot marry another man during her husband's lifetime.

OBJ. 3: Further, a husband may not even for a time devote himself to prayer without his wife's consent (1 Cor 7:5). But in the Eastern Church those who are in sacred orders are bound to continence for the time when they exercise their office. Therefore, neither may they be ordained without their wife's consent, and much less may the Latins.

OBJ. 4: Further, husband and wife are on a par with one another. Now a Greek priest cannot marry again after his wife's death. Therefore, neither can his wife after her husband's death. But she cannot be deprived by her husband's act of the right to marry after his death. Therefore, her husband cannot receive holy orders after marriage.

OBJ. 5: Further, holy orders is as much opposed to marriage as marriage to holy orders. Now a previous order is an impediment to a subsequent marriage. Therefore, etc.

ON THE CONTRARY, Religious are bound to continence like those who are in sacred orders. But a man may enter religion after marriage if his wife die, or if she consent. Therefore, he can also receive holy orders.

FURTHER, A man may become a man's slave after marriage. Therefore, he can become a slave of God by receiving orders.

I ANSWER THAT, Marriage is not an impediment to the reception of sacred orders, since if a married man receive sacred orders, even though his wife be unwilling, he receives the character of holy orders: but he lacks the exercise of his order. If, however, his wife consent, or if she be dead, he receives both the order and the exercise.

REPLY OBJ. 1: The bond of orders dissolves the bond of marriage as regards the payment of the debt, in respect of which it is incompatible with marriage on the part of the person ordained, since he cannot demand the debt, nor is the wife bound to pay it. But it does not dissolve the bond in respect of the other party, since the husband is bound to pay the debt to the wife if he cannot persuade her to observe continence.

REPLY OBJ. 2: If the husband receive sacred orders with the knowledge and consent of his wife, she is bound to vow perpetual continence, but she is not bound to enter religion, if she has no fear of her chastity being endangered through her husband having taken a solemn vow; it would have been different, however, if he had taken a simple vow. On the other hand, if he be ordained without her consent, she is not bound in this way, because the result is not prejudicial to her in any way.

REPLY OBJ. 3: It would seem more probable, although some say the contrary, that even a Greek ought not to receive sacred orders without his wife's consent, since at least at the time of his ministry she would be deprived of the payment of the debt, of which she cannot be deprived accord-

possunt, secundum ordinem iuris, si, eis contradicentibus aut ignorantibus, viri ordines susceperint.

AD QUARTUM dicendum quod, sicut dicitur, eo ipso quod mulier consentit, apud Graecos, quod vir suus ordinem suscipiat, obligat se ad hoc quod ipsa in perpetuum alteri non nubat: quia significatio matrimonii non servaretur, quae in matrimonio sacerdotis praecipue exigitur. Si autem sine consensu eius ordinatur, non videtur ad hoc teneri.

AD QUINTUM dicendum quod matrimonium habet pro causa nostrum consensum: non autem ordo, sed habet causam sacramentalem determinatam a Deo. Et ideo matrimonium potest impediri ex ordine praecedenti quod non sit verum matrimonium, non autem ordo ex matrimonio quod non sit verus ordo: quia sacramentorum virtus est immutabilis, sed actus humani possunt impediri.

ing to law if the husband should have been ordained without her consent or knowledge.

REPLY OBJ. 4: As stated, among the Greeks the wife, by the very fact of consenting to her husband's receiving a sacred order, binds herself never to marry another man, because the signification of marriage would not be safeguarded, and this is especially required in the marriage of a priest. If, however, he be ordained without her consent, it seems that she would not be under that obligation.

REPLY OBJ. 5: Marriage has for its cause our consent; not so holy orders, which has a sacramental cause appointed by God. Hence matrimony may be impeded by a previous order so as not to be true marriage; whereas holy orders cannot be impeded by marriage so as not to be truly holy orders, because the power of the sacraments is unchangeable, whereas human acts can be impeded.

QUESTION 54

THE IMPEDIMENT OF CONSANGUINITY

Deinde considerandum est de impedimento consanguinitatis.

Circa quod quaeruntur quattuor.

Primo: utrum consanguinitas convenienter a quibusdam definiatur.

Secundo: utrum convenienter distinguatur per gradus et lineas.

Tertio: utrum de iure naturali matrimonium impediat secundum aliquos gradus.

Quarto: utrum gradus impedientes matrimonium possint per statutum Ecclesiae determinari.

We must next consider the impediment of consanguinity.

Under this head there are four points of inquiry:

(1) Whether consanguinity is rightly defined by some?

(2) Whether it is fittingly distinguished by degrees and lines?

(3) Whether certain degrees are by natural law an impediment to marriage?

(4) Whether the impediment degrees can be fixed by the ordinance of the Church?

Article 1

Whether Consanguinity Is Rightly Defined?

AD PRIMUM SIC PROCEDITUR. Videtur quod definitio consanguinitatis, quam quidam ponunt, sit incompetens, scilicet: *consanguinitas est vinculum ab eodem stipite descendentium carnali propagatione contractum.* Omnes enim homines ab eodem stipite carnali propagatione descendunt, scilicet ab Adam. Si ergo recta esset praedicta definitio consanguinitatis, omnes homines essent ad invicem consanguinei. Quod falsum est.

PRAETEREA, vinculum non potest esse nisi aliquorum ad invicem convenientium: quia vinculum unit. Sed eorum qui descendunt ab uno stipite non est maior convenientia ad invicem quam aliorum hominum: cum conveniant specie et differant numero, sicut et alii homines. Ergo consanguinitas non est aliquod vinculum.

PRAETEREA, carnalis propagatio, secundum Philosophum, fit de *superfluo alimenti.* Sed tale superfluum magis habet convenientiam cum rebus comestis, cum quibus in substantia convenit, quam cum eo qui comedit. Cum ergo non nascatur aliquod vinculum consanguinitatis eius qui ex semine nascitur ad res comestas, nec ad generantem ex carnali propagatione nascetur aliquod propinquitatis vinculum.

PRAETEREA, Gen. 29, Laban dixit ad Iacob, *os meum et caro mea es,* ratione cognationis quae erat inter eos. Ergo talis propinquitas magis debet dici 'carnalitas' quam 'consanguinitas'.

PRAETEREA, carnalis propagatio est communis hominibus et animalibus. Sed in animalibus non contrahi-

OBJECTION 1: It would seem that consanguinity is unsuitably defined by some as follows: *consanguinity is the tie contracted between persons descending from the same common ancestor by carnal procreation.* For all men descend from the same common ancestor, namely Adam, by carnal procreation. Therefore, if the above definition of consanguinity is right, all men would be related by consanguinity, which is false.

OBJ. 2: Further, a tie is only between things in accord with one another, since a tie unites. Now there is not greater accordance between persons descended from a common ancestor than there is between other men, since they accord in species but differ in number, just as other men do. Therefore, consanguinity is not a tie.

OBJ. 3: Further, carnal procreation, according to the Philosopher (*On the Generation of Animals* 2.19), is effected from the *surplus food* (I, Q. 119, A. 2). Now this surplus has more in common with that which is eaten, since it agrees with it in substance, than with him who eats. Since, then, no tie of consanguinity arises between the person born of semen and that which he eats, neither will there be any tie of kindred between him and the person of whom he is born by carnal procreation.

OBJ. 4: Further, Laban said to Jacob: *you are my bone and my flesh* (Gen 29:14), on account of the relationship between them. Therefore, such a kinship should be called 'flesh relationship' rather than 'blood relationship'.

OBJ. 5: Further, carnal procreation is common to men and animals. But no tie of consanguinity is contracted

tur ex carnali propagatione consanguinitatis vinculum. Ergo nec in hominibus.

RESPONDEO dicendum quod, secundum Philosophum, in VIII Ethic., *omnis amicitia in aliqua communicatione consistit.* Et quia amicitia ligatio sive unio quaedam est, ideo communicatio quae est amicitiae causa, *vinculum* dicitur. Et ideo secundum; quamlibet communicationem denominantur aliqui quasi colligati ad invicem: sicut dicuntur concives qui habent politicam communicationem ad invicem, et commilitones qui conveniunt in militari negotio. Et eodem modo qui conveniunt in naturali communicatione dicuntur consanguinei. Et ideo in praedicta definitione ponitur quasi consanguinitatis genus, *vinculum*; quasi subiectum, *personae descendentes ab uno stipite*, quorum est huiusmodi vinculum; quasi principium, *carnalis propagatio.*

AD PRIMUM ergo dicendum quod virtus activa non recipitur secundum eandem perfectionem in instrumento secundum quam est in principali agente. Et quia omne movens motum est instrumentum, inde est quod virtus primi motoris in aliquo genere, per multa media deducta, tandem deficit, et pervenit ad aliquid quod est motum tantum et non movens. Virtus autem generantis movet non solum quantum ad id quod est speciei, sed etiam quantum ad id quod est individui, ratione cuius filius assimilatur patri etiam in accidentalibus, non solum in natura speciei. Nec tamen individualis virtus patris ita perfecte in filio est sicut erat in patre; et adhuc in nepote minus; et sic deinceps debilitatur. Et inde est quod virtus illa quandoque deficit, ut ultra; procedere non possit. Et quia consanguinitas est inquantum multi communicant in tali virtute ex uno in multos per propagationem inducta, *paulatim se consanguinitas dirimit*, ut Isidorus dicit. Et ideo non oportet accipere stipitem remotum in definitione consanguinitatis, sed propinquum, cuius virtus adhuc maneat in illis qui ex eo propagantur.

AD SECUNDUM dicendum quod iam patet ex dictis quod non solum conveniunt consanguinei in natura speciei, sed etiam in virtute propria ipsius individui ex uno in multos traducta: ex qua contingit quandoque quod filius assimilatur non solum patri, sed avo vel remotis parentibus, ut dicitur in XVIII *de Animalibus.*

AD TERTIUM dicendum quod convenientia magis attenditur secundum formam, secundum quam aliquid est actu, quam secundum materiam, secundum quam est in potentia: quod patet in hoc, quod carbo magis convenit cum igne quam cum arbore unde abscisum est lignum. Et similiter alimentum iam conversum in speciem nutriti per virtutem nutritivam, magis convenit cum ipso nutrito quam cum illa re unde sumptum est nutrimentum.

among animals from carnal procreation. Therefore, neither is there among men.

I ANSWER THAT, According to the Philosopher (*Ethics* 3.11–12) *all friendship is based on some kind of fellowship.* And since friendship is a knot or union, it follows that the fellowship which is the cause of friendship is called *a tie.* Wherefore in respect of any kind of a fellowship certain persons are denominated as though they were tied together: thus we speak of fellow-citizens who are connected by a common political life, of fellow-soldiers who are connected by the common business of soldiering, and in the same way those who are connected by the fellowship of nature are said to be tied by blood. Hence in the above definition *tie* is included as being the genus of consanguinity; the *persons descending from the same common ancestor*, who are thus tied together, are the subject of this tie; while *carnal procreation* is mentioned as being its origin.

REPLY OBJ. 1: An active force is not received into an instrument in the same degree of perfection as it has in the principal agent. And since every moved mover is an instrument, it follows that the power of the first mover in a particular genus when drawn out through many mediate movers fails at length, and reaches something that is moved and not a mover. But the power of a begetter moves not only as to that which belongs to the species, but also as to that which belongs to the individual, by reason of which the child is like the parent even in accidentals and not only in the specific nature. And yet this individual power of the father is not so perfect in the son as it was in the father, and still less so in the grandson, and thus it goes on failing; so that at length it ceases and can go no further. Since, then, consanguinity results from this power being communicated to many through being conveyed to them from one person by procreation, *it destroys itself little by little*, as Isidore says (*Etymologies* 9). Consequently, in defining consanguinity we must not take a remote common ancestor, but a near one, whose power still remains in those who are descended from him.

REPLY OBJ. 2: It is clear from what has been said that blood relations agree not only in the specific nature but also in that power peculiar to the individual which is conveyed from one to many, the result being that sometimes the child is not only like his father, but also his grandfather or his remote ancestors (*On the Generation of Animals*, 4.3).

REPLY OBJ. 3: Likeness depends more on form, whereby a thing is actually, than on matter, whereby a thing is potentially; for instance, charcoal has more in common with fire than with the tree from which the wood was cut. In like manner, food already transformed by the nutritive power into the substance of the person fed has more in common with the subject nourished than with that from which the nourishment was taken.

Ratio autem procederet secundum opinionem illorum qui dicebant quod tota natura rei est materia, et quod formae omnes sunt accidentia. Quod falsum est.

AD QUARTUM dicendum quod illud quod proxime convertitur in semen, est sanguis: ut probatur XV *de Animalibus*. Et propter hoc vinculum quod propagatione carnali contrahitur, convenientius dicitur 'consanguinitas' quam 'carnalitas'. Et quod aliquando unus consanguineus dicitur esse *caro alterius*, hoc est inquantum sanguis, qui in semen viri aut in menstruum convertitur, est potentia caro et os.

AD QUINTUM dicendum quod quidam dicunt quod ideo consanguinitatis vinculum contrahitur inter homines ex carnali propagatione, et tamen non inter alia animalia, quia quidquid est de veritate humanae naturae in omnibus hominibus, fuit in primo parente: quod non est de aliis animalibus. Sed secundum hoc, consanguinitas nunquam dirimi posset. Praedicta autem positio in II libro, dist. 30, improbata est.

Unde dicendum quod hoc ideo contingit quia animalia non coniunguntur ad amicitiae unitatem propter propagationem multorum ex uno parente proximo: sicut est de hominibus, ut dictum est.

The argument, however, would hold according to the opinion of those who asserted that the whole nature of a thing is from its matter and that all forms are accidents, which is false.

REPLY OBJ. 4: It is the blood that is proximately changed into the semen, as proved in *On the Generation of Animals* 1.18. Hence the tie contracted by carnal procreation is more fittingly called 'blood relationship' than 'flesh-relationship'. That sometimes one relation is called the *flesh of another* is because the blood which is transformed into the man's seed or into the menstrual fluid is potentially flesh and bone.

REPLY OBJ. 5: Some say that the reason why the tie of consanguinity is contracted among men through carnal procreation, and not among other animals, is because whatever belongs to the truth of human nature in all men was in our first parent, which does not apply to other animals. But according to this, matrimonial consanguinity would never come to an end. However, the above theory was disproved in the Second Book (*Sentences* II, D. 30: I, Q. 119, A. 1).

Wherefore we must reply that the reason for this is that animals are not united together in the union of friendship through the begetting of many from one proximate parent, as is the case with men, as stated above.

Article 2

Whether Consanguinity Is Fittingly Distinguished by Lines and Degrees?

AD SECUNDUM SIC PROCEDITUR. Videtur quod consanguinitas inconvenienter distinguatur per lineas et gradus. Dicitur enim linea consanguinitatis esse *ordinata collectio personarum consanguinitate coniunctarum ab eodem stipite descendentium, diversos continens gradus*. Sed nihil est aliud consanguinitas quam collectio talium personarum. Ergo linea consanguinitatis est idem quod consanguinitas. Nihil autem debet distingui per seipsum. Ergo consanguinitas non convenienter per lineas distinguitur.

PRAETEREA, illud secundum quod dividitur aliquid commune, non potest poni in definitione communis. Sed 'descensus' ponitur in definitione praedicta consanguinitatis. Consanguinitas ergo non potest dividi per lineam ascendentium, descendentium et transversalium.

PRAETEREA, definitio lineae est quod sit *inter duo puncta*. Sed duo puncta non faciunt nisi unum gradum. Ergo una linea habet tantum unum gradum. Et ita eadem videtur divisio consanguinitatis per lineas et per gradus.

PRAETEREA, gradus definitur esse *habitudo distantium personarum qua cognoscitur quanta distantia personae inter se differant*. Sed, cum consanguinitas sit

OBJECTION 1: It would seem that consanguinity is unfittingly distinguished by lines and degrees. For a line of consanguinity is described as *the ordered series of persons related by blood, and descending from a common ancestor in various degrees*. Now consanguinity is nothing else but a series of such persons. Therefore, a line of consanguinity is the same as consanguinity. Now a thing ought not to be distinguished by itself. Therefore, consanguinity is not fittingly distinguished into lines.

OBJ. 2: Further, that by which a common thing is divided should not be placed in the definition of that common thing. Now 'descent' is placed in the above definition of consanguinity. Therefore, consanguinity cannot be divided into ascending, descending, and collateral lines.

OBJ. 3: Further, a line is defined as being *between two points*. But two points make but one degree. Therefore, one line has but one degree, and for this reason it would seem that consanguinity should not be divided into lines and degrees.

OBJ. 4: Further, a degree is defined as *the relation between distant persons by which is known the distance between them*. Now since consanguinity is a kind of near-

propinquitas quaedam, distantia personarum consanguinitati opponitur magis quam sit eius pars. Ergo per gradus consanguinitas distingui non potest.

PRAETEREA, si consanguinitas per gradus distinguitur et cognoscitur, oportet quod illi qui sunt in eodem gradu, sint aequaliter consanguinei. Sed hoc falsum est: quia propatruus et eiusdem pronepos sunt in eodem gradu, non tamen sunt aequaliter consanguinei, ut Decretalis dicit. Ergo consanguinitas non recte distinguitur per gradus.

PRAETEREA, in rebus ordinatis quodlibet additum alteri facit alium gradum: sicut quaelibet unitas addita facit aliam speciem numeri. Sed persona addita personae non semper facit gradum alium consanguinitatis: quia in eodem gradu consanguinitatis est pater et patruus, qui adiungitur. Ergo non recte per gradus consanguinitas distinguitur.

PRAETEREA, inter duos propinquos semper est eadem consanguinitatis propinquitas: quia aequaliter distat unum extremorum ab alio et e converso. Sed gradus consanguinitatis non invenitur semper idem ex utraque parte: cum quandoque unus propinquus sit in tertio et, alius in quarto gradu. Ergo consanguinitatis propinquitas non potest sufficienter per gradus cognosci.

RESPONDEO dicendum quod consanguinitas est quaedam propinquitas in naturali communicatione fundata secundum actum generationis, qua natura propagatur. Unde, secundum Philosophum, in VIII *Ethic.*, ista communicatio est triplex. Una secundum habitudinem principii ad principiatum. Et haec est consanguinitas patris ad filium. Unde dicit quod *parentes diligunt filios ut sui ipsorum aliquid existentes*. Alia est secundum habitudinem principiati ad principium. Et haec est filii ad patrem. Unde dicit quod *filii diligunt parentes, ut ab illis existentes*. Tertia est secundum habitudinem eorum quae sunt ab uno principio ad invicem: sicut *fratres dicuntur ex eisdem nasci*, ut ipse ibidem dicit. Et quia punctus motus lineam facit, et propagatione quodammodo pater descendit in filium, ideo secundum tres dictas habitudines tres lineae consanguinitatis sumuntur: scilicet linea descendentium secundum primam habitudinem, linea ascendentium secundum secundam, linea transversalis secundum tertiam.

Sed quia propagationis motus non quiescit in uno termino, sed ultra progreditur, ideo contingit quod patris est accipere patrem, et filii filium, et sic deinceps. Et secundum hos diversos progressus diversi gradus in linea inveniuntur. Et quia gradus cuiuslibet rei est pars aliqua illius rei, gradus propinquitatis non potest esse ubi non est propinquitas. Et ideo identitas et nimia distantia gradum consanguinitatis tollunt: quia nullus est sibi ip-

ness, distance between persons is opposed to consanguinity rather than a part thereof.

OBJ. 5: Further, if consanguinity is distinguished and known by its degrees, those who are in the same degree ought to be equally related. But this is false, since a man's great-uncle and great-nephew are in the same degree, and yet they are not equally related, according to the *Decretals*. Therefore, consanguinity is not rightly divided into degrees.

OBJ. 6: Further, in ordinary things a different degree results from the addition of one thing to another, even as every additional unity makes a different species of number. Yet the addition of one person to another does not always make a different degree of consanguinity, since father and uncle are in the same degree of consanguinity, for they are side by side. Therefore, consanguinity is not rightly divided into degrees.

OBJ. 7: Further, if two persons be akin to one another there is always the same measure of kinship between them, since the distance from one extreme to the other is the same either way. Yet the degrees of consanguinity are not always the same on either side, since sometimes one relative is in the third and the other in the fourth degree. Therefore, the measure of consanguinity cannot be sufficiently known by its degrees.

I ANSWER THAT, Consanguinity is a certain nearness based on the natural communication by the act of procreation, whereby nature is propagated. Hence according to the Philosopher (*Ethics* 8.12) this communication is threefold. One corresponds to the relationship between cause and effect, and this is the consanguinity of father to son, wherefore he says that *parents love their children as being a part of themselves*. Another corresponds to the relation of effect to cause, and this is the consanguinity of son to father, wherefore he says that *children love their parents because they exist from them*. The third corresponds to the mutual relation between things that come from the same cause, as brothers *who are born of the same parents*, as he again says (*Ethics* 8.12). And since the movement of a point makes a line, and since a father by procreation may be said to descend to his son, hence it is that corresponding to these three relationships there are three lines of consanguinity: namely, the descending line corresponding to the first relationship, the ascending line corresponding to the second, and the collateral line corresponding to the third.

Since, however, the movement of propagation does not rest in one term but continues beyond, the result is that one can point to the father's father and to the son's son, and so on, and according to the various steps we take we find various degrees in one line. And seeing that the degrees of a thing are parts of that thing, there cannot be degrees of nearness where there is no nearness. Consequently, identity and extreme distance do away with degrees of consanguin-

si propinquus, sicut nec sibi similis. Et propter hoc nulla persona per seipsam facit aliquem gradum: sed, comparata alteri personae, gradum facit ad ipsam.

Sed tamen diversa est ratio computandi gradus in diversis lineis. Gradus enim consanguinitatis in linea ascendentium et descendentium contrahitur ex hoc quod una persona ex alia propagatur eorum inter quos gradus consideratur. Et ideo, secundum computationem canonicam et legalem, persona quae primo in progressu propagationis occurrit, vel ascendendo vel descendendo, distat ab aliquo, puta a Petro, in primo gradu, ut pater et filius; quae autem secundo utrinque occurrit, distat in secundo gradu, ut avus et nepos; et sic deinceps.

Sed consanguinitas quae est eorum qui sunt in linea transversali, contrahitur, non ex hoc quod unus eorum ex alio propagatur, sed quia uter que propagatur ex uno. Et ideo debet gradus consanguinitatis in hac linea consanguinitatis computari per comparationem ad unum principium ex quo propagantur. Et secundum hoc est diversa computatio canonica et legalis: quia legalis computatio attendit descensum a communi radice ex utraque parte; sed canonica tantum ex altera, ex illa scilicet ex qua maior numerus graduum invenitur. Unde secundum legalem computationem, frater et soror, vel duo fratres, attinent sibi in secundo gradu: quia uterque a radice communi distat per unum gradum. Et similiter filii duorum fratrum distant a se invicem in quarto.

Sed secundum computationem canonicam, duo fratres attinent sibi in primo gradu: quia neuter eorum distat a radice communi nisi per unum gradum. Sed filius unius fratrum distat ab altero fratre in secundo gradu: quia tantum distant a communi radice. Et ideo, secundum computationem canonicam, quoto gradu distat quis ab aliquo gradu superiori, toto distat a quolibet descendentium ab ipso, et nunquam minus: quia *propter quod unumquodque, illud magis.*

Unde, etsi alii descendentes a communi principio conveniunt cum aliquo ratione principii communis, non possunt propinquiores esse descendenti ex alia parte quam sit primum principium ei propinquum. Aliquando tamen plus distat aliquis ab aliquo descendente a communi principio quam distet ipse a principio: quia ille forte plus distat a communi principio quam ipse, et secundum remotiorem distantiam oportet consanguinitatem computari.

AD PRIMUM ergo dicendum quod obiectio illa procedit ex falsis. Consanguinitas enim non est collectio,

ity; since no man is kin to himself any more than he is like himself, for which reason there is no degree of consanguinity where there is but one person, but only when one person is compared to another.

Nevertheless there are different ways of counting the degrees in various lines. For the degree of consanguinity in the ascending and descending line is contracted from the fact that the one of the parties whose consanguinity is in question is descended from the other. Wherefore according to the canonical as well as the legal reckoning, the person who occupies the first place, whether in the ascending or in the descending line, is distant from a certain one, say Peter, in the first degree—for instance, father and son; while the one who occupies the second place in either direction is distant in the second degree, for instance, grandfather, grandson and so on.

But the consanguinity that exists between persons who are in collateral lines is contracted not through one being descended from the other, but through both being descended from one; wherefore the degrees of consanguinity in this line must be reckoned in relation to the one principle whence it arises. Here, however, the canonical and legal reckonings differ, for the legal reckoning takes into account the descent from the common stock on both sides, whereas the canonical reckoning takes into account only one, namely, that on which the greater number of degrees are found. Hence according to the legal reckoning brother and sister, or two brothers, are related in the second degree, because each is separated from the common stock by one degree; and in like manner the children of two brothers are distant from one another in the fourth degree.

But according to the canonical reckoning, two brothers are related in the first degree, since neither is distant more than one degree from the common stock; but the children of one brother are distant in the second degree from the other brother, because they are at that distance from the common stock. Hence, according to the canonical reckoning, by whatever degree a person is distant from some higher degree, by so much and never by less is he distant from each person descending from that degree, because *the cause of a thing being so is yet more so.*

Wherefore, although the other descendants from the common stock be related to some person on account of his being descended from the common stock, these descendants of the other branch cannot be more nearly related to him than he is to the common stock. Sometimes, however, a person is more distantly related to a descendant from the common stock, than he himself is to the common stock, because this other person may be more distantly related to the common stock than he is, and consanguinity must be reckoned according to the more distant degree.

REPLY OBJ. 1: This objection is based on a false premise: for consanguinity is not the series but a mutual

sed relatio quaedam aliquarum personarum ad invicem, quarum collectio lineam consanguinitatis facit.

AD SECUNDUM dicendum quod descensus Communiter sumptus attenditur secundum quamlibet consanguinitatis lineam: quia carnalis propagatio, ex qua vinculum consanguinitatis contrahitur, descensus quidam est. Sed descensus talis, scilicet a persona cuius consanguinitas quaeritur, lineam descendentium facit.

AD TERTIUM dicendum quod linea dupliciter accipi potest. Aliquando proprie, pro ipsa dimensione quae est prima species quantitatis continuae. Et sic linea recta continet tantum duo puncta in actu, quae terminant ipsam; sed infinita in potentia, quorum quolibet signato in actu, linea dividitur, et fiunt duae lineae. Aliquando vero linea sumitur pro his quae linealiter disponuntur. Et secundum hoc assignatur in numeris linea et figura, prout unitas post unitatem ponitur in aliquo numero. Et sic quaelibet unitas adiecta gradum facit in tali linea. Et similiter est de linea consanguinitatis. Unde una linea continet plures gradus.

AD QUARTUM dicendum quod, sicut similitudo non potest esse ubi non est aliqua diversitas, ita propinquitas non est ubi non est aliqua distantia. Et ideo distantia quaelibet non opponitur consanguinitati: sed talis distantia quae consanguinitatis propinquitatem excludit.

AD QUINTUM dicendum quod, sicut albedo dicitur maior dupliciter, uno modo ex intensione ipsius qualitatis, alio modo ex quantitate superficiei; ita consanguinitas dicitur maior vel minor uno modo intensive ex ipsa natura consanguinitatis, alio modo quasi dimensive; et sic quantitas consanguinitatis mensuratur ex personis inter quas consanguinitatis propagatio procedit. Et hoc secundo modo gradus consanguinitatis distinguuntur. Et ideo contingit quod aliquorum duorum qui sunt in eodem gradu consanguinitatis respectu alicuius personae, unus est sibi magis consanguineus quam alius, considerando primam quantitatem consanguinitatis: sicut pater et frater attinent alicui in primo gradu consanguinitatis, quia ex neutra parte incidit aliqua persona media; sed tamen, intensive loquendo, magis attinet alicui personae pater suus quam frater, quia frater non attinet ei nisi quantum est ex eodem patre. Et ideo, quanto est aliquis propinquior communi principio a quo consanguinitas descendit, tanto est magis consanguineus, quamvis non sit in propinquiori gradu. Et secundum hoc propatruus est magis consanguineus alicui quam pronepos eius, quamvis sit in eodem gradu.

AD SEXTUM dicendum quod, quamvis pater et patruus sint in eodem gradu respectu radicis consanguinitatis, quia uterque distat uno gradu ab avo; tamen respectu eius cuius consanguinitas quaeritur, non sunt in eodem gradu: quia pater est in primo gradu, patruus au-

relationship existing between certain persons, the series of whom forms a line of consanguinity.

REPLY OBJ. 2: Descent taken in a general sense attaches to every line of consanguinity, because carnal procreation, whence the tie of consanguinity arises, is a kind of descent; but it is a particular kind of descent, namely, from the person whose consanguinity is in question, that makes the descending line.

REPLY OBJ. 3: A line may be taken in two ways. Sometimes it is taken properly for the dimension itself that is the first species of continuous quantity: and thus a straight line contains actually but two points which terminate it, but infinite points potentially, any one of which being actually designated, the line is divided, and becomes two lines. But sometimes a line designates things which are arranged in a line, and thus we have line and figure in numbers, insofar as unity added to unity involves number. Thus every unity added makes a degree in a particular line, and it is the same with the line of consanguinity; wherefore one line contains several degrees.

REPLY OBJ. 4: Even as there cannot be likeness without a difference, so there is no nearness without distance. Hence not every distance is opposed to consanguinity, but such as excludes the nearness of blood relationship.

REPLY OBJ. 5: Even as whiteness is said to be greater in two ways, in one way through intensity of the quality itself, in another way through the quantity of the surface, so consanguinity is said to be greater or lesser in two ways. First, intensively by reason of the very nature of consanguinity; second, extensively as it were, and thus the degree of consanguinity is measured by the persons between whom there is the propagation of a common blood, and in this way the degrees of consanguinity are distinguished. Therefore, it happens that of two persons related to one person in the same degree of consanguinity, one is more akin to him than the other if we consider the quantity of consanguinity in the first way. Thus a man's father and brother are related to him in the first degree of consanguinity, because in neither case does any person come in between; and yet from the point of view of intensity a man's father is more closely related to him than his brother, since his brother is related to him only because he is of the same father. Hence the nearer a person is to the common ancestor from whom the consanguinity descends, the greater is his consanguinity, although he be not in a nearer degree. In this way a man's great-uncle is more closely related to him than his great-nephew, although they are in the same degree.

REPLY OBJ. 6: Although a man's father and uncle are in the same degree in respect of the root of consanguinity, since both are separated by one degree from the grandfather, nevertheless in respect of the person whose consanguinity is in question, they are not in the same degree, since

tem non potest esse propinquior quam in secundo, in quo est avus.

Ad septimum dicendum quod semper duae personae in aequali numero graduum distant a se invicem: quamvis quandoque non aequali numero graduum distent a communi principio, ut ex dictis patet.

the father is in the first degree whereas the uncle cannot be nearer than the second degree, in which the grandfather stands.

Reply Obj. 7: Two persons are always related in the same degree to one another, although they are not always distant in the same number of degrees from the common ancestor, as explained above.

Article 3

Whether Consanguinity Is, by Natural Law, an Impediment to Matrimony?

Ad tertium sic proceditur. Videtur quod consanguinitas de iure naturali non impediat matrimonium. Nulla enim mulier potest esse propinquior viro quam Eva fuit Adae, de qua dixit, Gen. 2: *hoc nunc os ex ossibus meis, et caro ex carne mea*. Sed Eva fuit matrimonio coniuncta Adae. Ergo consanguinitas nulla, quantum est de lege naturae, matrimonium impedit.

Praeterea, lex naturalis eadem est apud omnes. Sed apud barbaras nationes nulla persona coniuncta consanguinitate a matrimonio excluditur. Ergo consanguinitas, quantum est de lege naturae, matrimonium non impedit.

Praeterea, *ius naturale est quod natura omnia animalia docuit*, ut dicitur in principio *Digestorum*. Sed animalia bruta etiam cum matre coeunt. Ergo non est de lege naturae quod aliqua persona a matrimonio propter consanguinitatem repellatur.

Praeterea, nihil impedit matrimonium quod non contrariatur alicui bono matrimonii. Sed consanguinitas non contrariatur alicui bono matrimonii. Ergo non impedit ipsum.

Praeterea, eorum quae sunt magis propinqua et similia, melior et firmior est coniunctio. Sed matrimonium quaedam coniunctio est. Cum ergo consanguinitas sit propinquitas quaedam, matrimonium non impedit, sed magis iuvat.

Sed contra: Illud quod impedit bonum prolis, etiam matrimonium impedit secundum legem naturae. Sed consanguinitas impedit bonum prolis: quia, ut ex verbis Gregorii habetur, *experimento didicimus ex tali coniugio: sobolem non posse succrescere*. Ergo consanguinitas secundum legem naturae matrimonium impedit.

Praeterea, illud quod habet natura humana in prima sui conditione, est de lege naturae. Sed a prima sui conditione hoc habuit humana natura, quod pater et mater a matrimonio excluderentur: quod patet per hoc quod dicitur Gen. 2: *propter hoc relinquet homo patrem et matrem*; quod non potest intelligi quantum ad coha-

Objection 1: It would seem that consanguinity is not by natural law an impediment to marriage. For no woman can be more akin to a man than Eve was to Adam, since of her did he say: *this now is bone of my bones and flesh of my flesh* (Gen 2:23). Yet Eve was joined in marriage to Adam. Therefore, as regards the natural law no consanguinity is an impediment to marriage.

Obj. 2: Further, the natural law is the same for all. Now among the uncivilized nations no person is debarred from marriage by reason of consanguinity. Therefore, as regards the law of nature, consanguinity is no impediment to marriage.

Obj. 3: Further, *the natural law is what nature has taught all animals*, as stated at the beginning of the *Digests*. Now brute animals copulate even with their mother. Therefore, it is not of natural law that certain persons are debarred from marriage on account of consanguinity.

Obj. 4: Further, nothing that is not contrary to one of the goods of matrimony is an impediment to marriage. But consanguinity is not contrary to any of the goods of marriage. Therefore, it is not an impediment thereto.

Obj. 5: Further, things which are more akin and more similar to one another are better and more firmly united together. Now matrimony is a kind of union. Since, then, consanguinity is a kind of kinship, it does not hinder marriage but rather strengthens the union.

On the contrary, According to the natural law, whatever is an obstacle to the good of the offspring is an impediment to marriage. Now consanguinity hinders the good of the offspring, because in the words of Gregory (*Register* 31) quoted in the text (*Sentences* IV, D. 40): *we have learned by experience that the children of such a union cannot thrive*. Therefore, according to the law of nature consanguinity is an impediment to matrimony.

Further, That which belongs to human nature in its first condition is of natural law. Now it belonged to human nature from when it was first created that one should be debarred from marrying one's father or mother: in proof of which it was said, *wherefore a man shall leave father and mother* (Gen 2:24), which cannot be understood of cohab-

bitationem, et sic oportet quod intelligatur quantum ad matrimonii coniunctionem. Ergo consanguinitas impedit matrimonium secundum legem naturae.

Respondeo dicendum quod in matrimonio illud contra legem naturae esse dicitur per quod matrimonium redditur incompetens respectu finis ad quem est ordinatum. Finis autem matrimonii per se et primo est bonum prolis. Quod quidem per aliquam consanguinitatem, scilicet inter patrem et filiam vel filium et matrem, impeditur, non quidem ut totaliter tollatur, quia filia ex semine patris potest prolem suscipere et simul cum patre nutrire et instruere, in quibus bonum prolis consistit; sed ut non convenienti modo fiat. Inordinatum enim est quod filia patri per matrimonium iungatur in sociam, causa generandae prolis et educandae, quam oportet per omnia patri esse subiectam, velut ex eo procedentem. Et ideo de lege naturali est ut pater et mater a matrimonio repellantur. Et magis etiam mater quam pater: quia magis reverentiae quae debetur parentibus derogatur si filius matrem, quam si pater filiam ducit in uxorem, cum uxor viro aliqualiter debeat esse subiecta.

Sed finis matrimonii secundarius per se est concupiscentiae repressio. Cui deperiret si quaelibet consanguinea posset in matrimonium duci: quia magnus concupiscentiae aditus praeberetur nisi inter illas personas quas oportet in eadem domo conversari, esset carnalis copula interdicta. Et ideo lex divina non solum patrem et matrem exclusit a matrimonio, sed etiam alias coniunctas personas, quas oportet simul conversari, et quae debent invicem altera alterius pudicitiam custodire. Et hanc causam assignat divina lex dicens: *ne reveles turpitudinem* (talis vel talis), *quia turpitudo tua est.*

Sed per accidens finis matrimonii est confoederatio hominum et amicitiae multiplicatio, dum homo ad consanguineos uxoris sicut ad suos se habet. Et ideo huic multiplicationi amicitiae praeiudicium fieret si aliquis sanguine coniunctam uxorem duceret: quia ex hoc nova amicitia per matrimonium nulla accresceret. Et ideo, secundum leges humanas et statuta Ecclesiae, plures consanguinitatis gradus sunt a matrimonio separati.

Sic ergo ex dictis patet quod consanguinitas quantum ad aliquas personas impedit matrimonium de iure naturali; quantum ad aliquas, de iure divino; et quantum ad aliquas, de iure per homines instituto.

Ad primum ergo dicendum quod Eva, quamvis ex Adam prodiit, non tamen fuit filia Adae: quia non prodit ex eo per modum illum quo vir natus est generare sibi simile in specie, sed operatione divina, qua ita potuisset ex costa Adae fieri unus equus sicut facta est Eva. Et ideo non est tanta naturalis convenientia Evae ad Adam

itation, and consequently must refer to the union of marriage. Therefore, consanguinity is an impediment to marriage according to the natural law.

I answer that, In relation to marriage, a thing is said to be contrary to the natural law if it prevents marriage from reaching the end for which it was instituted. Now the essential and primary end of marriage is the good of the offspring, and this is hindered by a certain consanguinity, namely, that which is between father and daughter, or son and mother. It is not that the good of the offspring is utterly destroyed, since a daughter can have a child of her father's semen and with the father rear and teach that child in those things in which the good of the offspring consists, but that it is not effected in a becoming way. For it is out of order that a daughter be mated to her father in marriage for the purpose of begetting and rearing children, since in all things she ought to be subject to her father as proceeding from him. Hence by natural law a father and mother are debarred from marrying their children, and the mother still more than the father, since it is more derogatory to the reverence due to parents if the son marry his mother than if the father marry his daughter, since the wife should be to a certain extent subject to her husband.

The secondary essential end of marriage is the curbing of concupiscence; and this end would be forfeit if a man could marry any blood relation, since a wide scope would be afforded to concupiscence if those who have to live together in the same house were not forbidden to be mated in the flesh. Therefore, the divine law debars from marriage not only father and mother, but also other kinsfolk who have to live in close intimacy with one another and ought to safeguard one another's modesty. The divine law assigns this reason: *you shall not uncover the nakedness* of such and such a one, *because it is your own nakedness* (Lev 18:10).

Now, the accidental end of marriage is the binding together of mankind and the extension of friendship, for a husband regards his wife's kindred as his own. Hence it would be prejudicial to this extension of friendship if a man could take a woman of his kindred to wife, since no new friendship would accrue to anyone from such a marriage. Wherefore, according to human law and the ordinances of the Church, several degrees of consanguinity are debarred from marriage.

Accordingly, it is clear from what has been said that consanguinity is by natural law an impediment to marriage in regard to certain persons, by divine law in respect of some, and by human law in respect of others.

Reply Obj. 1: Although Eve was formed from Adam, she was not Adam's daughter because she was not formed from him after the manner in which it is natural for a man to beget his like in species, but by the divine operation, since from Adam's rib a horse might have been formed in the same way as Eve was. Hence the natural connection be-

sicut filiae ad patrem. Nec Adam est naturale principium Evae, sicut pater, filiae.

AD SECUNDUM dicendum quod non procedit ex lege naturali quod aliqui barbari parentibus carnaliter commisceantur: sed ex concupiscentiae ardore, qui legem naturae in eis obfuscavit.

AD TERTIUM dicendum quod coniunctio maris et feminae dicitur esse de iure naturali, quia natura hoc omnia animalia docuit. Sed hanc coniunctionem diversa animalia diversimode docuit, secundum diversas eorum conditiones. Commixtio autem carnalis ad parentes derogat reverentiae quae eis debetur: sicut enim parentibus indidit natura sollicitudinem filiis providendi, ita indidit reverentiam filiis ad parentes. Nulli autem generi animalium indidit sollicitudinem filiorum aut reverentiam parentum in omne tempus, nisi homini: aliis autem animalibus plus et minus necessarii sunt vel filii parentibus, vel parentes filiis. Unde etiam in quibusdam animalibus abhorret filius cognoscere matrem carnaliter, quandiu manet apud ipsum cognitio matris et reverentia quaedam ad ipsam: ut recitat Philosophus, IX *de Animalibus*, de camelo et equo. Et quia omnes honesti mores animalium in hominibus congregati sunt naturaliter, et perfectius quam in aliis, propter hoc homo naturaliter abhorret cognoscere non solum matrem, sed etiam filiam, quod est adhuc minus contra naturam, ut dictum est. Et iterum in aliis animalibus ex propagatione carnis non contrahitur consanguinitas, sicut in hominibus. Et ideo non est similis ratio.

AD QUARTUM dicendum quod ex iam dictis patet quomodo consanguinitas coniugum bono matrimonii contrarietur. Unde ratio procedit ex falsis.

AD QUINTUM dicendum quod non est inconveniens duarum unionum unam ab altera impediri: sicut, ubi est identitas, non est similitudo. Et similiter consanguinitatis vinculum potest impedire matrimonii coniunctionem.

tween Eve and Adam was not so great as between daughter and father, nor was Adam the natural principle of Eve as a father is of his daughter.

REPLY OBJ. 2: That certain barbarians are united carnally to their parents does not come from the natural law, but from the passion of concupiscence which has clouded the natural law in them.

REPLY OBJ. 3: Union of male and female is said to be of natural law, because nature has taught this to animals; yet she has taught this union to various animals in various ways, according to their various conditions. But carnal copulation with parents is derogatory to the reverence due to them. For just as nature has instilled into parents solicitude in providing for their offspring, so has it instilled into the offspring reverence towards their parents. Yet to no kind of animal save man has she instilled a lasting solicitude for his children or reverence for parents, but to other animals more or less, according as the offspring is more or less necessary to its parents, or the parents to their offspring. Hence, as the Philosopher attests concerning the camel and the horse, among certain animals the son abhors copulation with its mother as long as he retains knowledge of her and a certain reverence for her (*On the Generation of Animals* IX, 47). And since all honest customs of animals are united together in man naturally, and more perfectly than in other animals, it follows that man naturally abhors carnal knowledge not only of his mother, but also of his daughter, which is, however, less against nature, as stated above. And again, in other animals consanguinity is not contracted from propagation of the flesh, as it is in man. Hence the case is not similiar.

REPLY OBJ. 4: It has been shown how consanguinity between married persons is contrary to the goods of marriage. Hence the objection proceeds from false premises.

REPLY OBJ. 5: It is not unreasonable for one of two unions to be hindered by the other, even as where there is identity there is not likeness. In like manner, the tie of consanguinity may hinder the union of marriage.

Article 4

Whether the Degrees of Consanguinity That Are an Impediment to Matrimony Could Be Fixed by the Church as far as the Fourth Degree?

AD QUARTUM SIC PROCEDITUR. Videtur quod consanguinitatis gradus matrimonium impedientes non potuerunt taxari ab Ecclesia usque ad quartum gradum. Matth. 19 dicitur: *quos Deus coniunxit, homo non separet.* Sed illos qui coniunguntur infra quartum consanguinitatis gradum, Deus coniunxit: non enim divina lege eorum coniunctio prohibetur. Ergo nec debent humano statuto separari.

OBJECTION 1: It would seem that the degrees of consanguinity that are an impediment to marriage could not be fixed by the Church so as to reach to the fourth degree. For it is written: *what God has joined together, let no man put asunder* (Matt 19:6). But God joined those together who are married within the fourth degree of consanguinity, since their union is not forbidden by the divine law. Therefore, they should not be put asunder by a human law.

PRAETEREA, matrimonium est sacramentum sicut et baptismus. Sed non posset ex statuto Ecclesiae fieri quod ille qui ad baptismum accedit, non acciperet characterem baptismalem, si ex iure divino eius capax sit. Ergo nec Ecclesiae statutum facere potest quod matrimonium non sit inter illos qui per ius divinum matrimonialiter coniungi non prohibentur.

PRAETEREA, ius positivum non potest ea quae sunt naturalia removere vel ampliare. Sed consanguinitas est naturale vinculum, quod, quantum est de se, natum est matrimonium impedire. Ergo Ecclesia non potest aliquo statuto facere quod aliqui possint matrimonialiter coniungi vel non coniungi: sicut non potest facere quod sint consanguinei vel non consanguinei.

PRAETEREA, statutum iuris positivi debet aliquam rationabilem causam habere: quia secundum causam rationabilem quam habet, a iure naturali procedit. Sed causae quae assignantur de numero graduum, omnino videntur irrationabiles, cum nullam habeant habitudinem ad causata: sicut quod consanguinitas prohibeatur usque ad quartum gradum propter quattuor elementa; usque ad sextum, propter sex aetates mundi; usque ad septimum, propter septem dies quibus omne tempus agitur. Ergo videtur quod talis prohibitio nullum vigorem habeat.

PRAETEREA, ubi est eadem causa, debet esse idem effectus. Sed causa quare consanguinitas impedit matrimonium, est bonum prolis, repressio concupiscentiae, et multiplicatio amicitiae, ut ex dictis patet, quae omni tempore necessaria aequaliter sunt. Ergo debuissent aequaliter omni tempore gradus consanguinitatis matrimonium impedire. Quod non est verum: cum modo usque ad quartum, antiquitus usque ad septimum gradum matrimonium consanguinitas impedierit.

PRAETEREA, una et eadem coniunctio non potest esse in genere sacramenti et in genere stupri. Sed hoc contingeret si Ecclesia haberet potestatem statuendi diversum numerum in gradibus impedientibus matrimonium: sicut, si aliqui in quinto gradu, quando prohibitus fuit, coniuncti fuissent, talis coniunctio stuprum esset; sed postmodum eadem coniunctio, Ecclesia prohibitionem revocante, matrimonium esset. Et e converso posset accidere si aliqui gradus concessi possent postmodum ab Ecclesia interdici. Ergo videtur quod potestas Ecclesiae non se extendat ad hoc.

PRAETEREA, ius humanum debet imitari ius divinum. Sed secundum ius divinum, quod in lege veteri continetur, non aequaliter currit prohibitio graduum in sursum et deorsum: quia in veteri lege aliquis prohibebatur accipere in uxorem sororem patris sui, non tamen filiam fratris. Ergo nec modo debet aliqua prohibitio de nepotibus et patruis manere.

OBJ. 2: Further, matrimony is a sacrament, as also is baptism. Now, no ordinance of the Church could prevent one who is baptized from receiving the baptismal character if he be capable of receiving it according to the divine law. Therefore, neither can an ordinance of the Church forbid marriage between those who are not forbidden to marry by the divine law.

OBJ. 3: Further, positive law can neither void nor extend those things which are natural. Now consanguinity is a natural tie which is in itself of a nature to impede marriage. Therefore, the Church cannot by its ordinance permit or forbid certain people to marry, any more than she can make them to be consanguineous or not consanguineous.

OBJ. 4: Further, an ordinance of positive law should have some reasonable cause, since it is for this reasonable cause that it proceeds from the natural law. But the causes that are assigned for the number of degrees seem altogether unreasonable, since they bear no relation to their effect; for instance, that consanguinity be an impediment as far as the fourth degree on account of the four elements, as far as the sixth degree on account of the six ages of the world, or as far as the seventh degree on account of the seven days of which all time is comprised. Therefore, seemingly this prohibition is of no force.

OBJ. 5: Further, where the cause is the same, there should be the same effect. Now the causes for which consanguinity is an impediment to marriage are the good of the offspring, the curbing of concupiscence, and the extension of friendship, as stated above (A. 3), which are equally necessary for all time. Therefore, the degrees of consanguinity should have equally impeded marriage at all times; yet this is not true since consanguinity is now an impediment to marriage as far as the fourth degree, whereas formerly it was an impediment as far as the seventh.

OBJ. 6: Further, one and the same union cannot be a kind of sacrament and a kind of incest. But this would be the case if the Church had the power of fixing a different number in the degrees which are an impediment to marriage. Thus if certain parties related in the fifth degree were married when that degree was an impediment, their union would be incestuous, and yet this same union would be a marriage afterwards when the Church withdrew her prohibition. And the reverse might happen if certain degrees which were not an impediment were subsequently to be forbidden by the Church. Therefore, seemingly the power of the Church does not extend to this.

OBJ. 7: Further, human law should copy the divine law. Now, according to the divine law which is contained in the old law, the prohibition of degrees does not apply equally in the ascending and descending lines, since in the old law a man was forbidden to marry his father's sister but not his brother's daughter. Therefore, neither should there remain now a prohibition in respect of nephews and uncles.

SED CONTRA: Est quod Dominus dicit discipulis: *qui vos audit, me audit*. Ergo praeceptum Ecclesiae habet firmitatem sicut praeceptum Dei. Sed Ecclesia quandoque prohibuit, et quandoque concessit, aliquos gradus quos lex vetus non prohibuit. Ergo illi gradus matrimonium impediunt.

PRAETEREA, sicut olim matrimonia gentilium dispensabantur per leges civiles, ita nunc per statuta Ecclesiae. Sed olim lex civilis determinabat gradus consanguinitatis qui matrimonium impediunt: et qui non. Ergo et modo potest hoc fieri per Ecclesiae statutum.

RESPONDEO dicendum quod secundum diversa tempora invenitur consanguinitas secundum gradus diversos, matrimonium impedisse. In principio enim humani generis solus pater et mater a matrimonio repellebantur: eo quod tunc temporis erat paucitas hominum, et oportebat propagationi humani generis maximam curam impendere; unde non erant removendae nisi illae personae quae matrimonio incompetentes erant etiam quantum ad finem matrimonii principalem, qui est bonum prolis, ut dictum est.

Postmodum autem, multiplicato genere humano, per legem Moysi plures personae sunt exceptae, quae iam concupiscentiam reprimere incipiebat. Unde, ut dicit Rabbi Moyses, omnes illae personae exceptae sunt a matrimonio quae in una familia cohabitare solent: quia, si inter eos licite carnalis copula esse posset, magnum incentivum libidini praestaretur. Sed alios consanguinitatis gradus lex vetus permisit: immo quodammodo praecepit, ut scilicet de cognatione sua unusquisque uxorem acciperet, ne successionum confusio esset; quia tunc temporis cultus divinus per successionem generis propagabatur.

Sed postmodum in lege nova, quae est lex Spiritus et amoris, plures gradus consanguinitatis sunt prohibiti: quia iam per spiritualem gratiam, non per carnis originem cultus Dei derivatur et multiplicatur; unde oportet ut homines etiam magis a carnalibus retrahantur, spiritualibus vacantes; et ut amor amplius diffundatur.

Et ideo antiquitus usque ad remotiores gradus consanguinitatis matrimonium impediebatur: ut ad plures per consanguinitatem et affinitatem naturalis amicitia promanaret. Et rationabiliter usque ad septimum gradum. Tum quia ultra hoc non de facili remanebat communis radicis memoria. Tum quia septiformi Spiritus sancti gratiae congruebat.

Sed postmodum, circa haec ultima tempora, restrictum est Ecclesiae interdictum usque ad quartum gradum: quia ultra inutile et periculosum erat gra-

ON THE CONTRARY, Our Lord said to his disciples: *he that hears you hears me* (Luke 10:16). Therefore, a commandment of the Church has the same force as a commandment of God. Now the Church sometimes has forbidden and sometimes allowed certain degrees which the old law did not forbid. Therefore, those degrees are an impediment to marriage.

FURTHER, Even as of old the marriages of pagans were controlled by the civil law, so now is marriage controlled by the laws of the Church. Now formerly the civil law decided which degrees of consanguinity impede marriage, and which do not. Therefore, this can be done now by a commandment of the Church.

I ANSWER THAT, The degrees within which consanguinity has been an impediment to marriage have varied according to various times. For at the beginning of the human race father and mother alone were debarred from marrying their children, because then mankind was few in number, and it was necessary that the propagation of the human race should be ensured with very great care; consequently, only such persons were to be debarred as were unfitted for marriage even in respect of its principal end, which is the good of the offspring, as stated above (A. 3).

Afterwards, however, the human race having multiplied, more persons were excluded by the law of Moses, for they already began to curb concupiscence. Wherefore as Rabbi Moses says (*Guide for the Perplexed* 3.49) all those persons were debarred from marrying one another who are wont to live together in one household, because if a lawful carnal intercourse were possible between them, this would prove a very great incentive to lust. Yet the old law permitted other degrees of consanguinity—in fact, to a certain extent it commanded them: namely, that each man should take a wife from his kindred in order to avoid confusion of inheritances, because at that time the divine worship was handed down as the inheritance of the race.

But afterwards more degrees were forbidden by the new law, which is the law of the spirit and of love, because the worship of God is no longer handed down and spread abroad by a carnal birth but by a spiritual grace; wherefore it was necessary that men should be yet more withdrawn from carnal things by devoting themselves to things spiritual, and that love should be diffused more widely.

Hence in ancient times marriage was forbidden even within the more remote degrees of consanguinity, in order that consanguinity and affinity might be the sources of a wider natural friendship; and this was reasonably extended to the seventh degree, both because beyond this it was difficult to have any recollection of the common stock, and because this was in keeping with the sevenfold grace of the Holy Spirit.

Afterwards, however, towards these latter times the prohibition of the Church has been restricted to the fourth degree, because it became useless and dangerous to ex-

dus consanguinitatis prohibere. Inutile quidem, quia ad remotiores consanguineos quasi nullum foedus maioris amicitiae quam ad extraneos habebatur, *caritate in multorum cordibus frigescente*. Periculosum autem erat, quia, concupiscentia et negligentia praevalente, numerosam consanguineorum multitudinem homines non satis observabant: et sic laqueus damnationis multis iniiciebatur ex remotorum graduum prohibitione.

Satis etiam convenienter usque ad quartum gradum dicta prohibitio est restricta. Tum quia usque ad quartam generationem homines vivere consueverunt: ut sic non possit consanguinitatis memoria aboleri. Unde Dominus *in tertiam et quartam generationem* peccata parentum se visitaturum in filiis comminatur. Tum quia in qualibet generatione nova mixtio sanguinis, cuius identitas consanguinitatem facit, fit cum sanguine alieno; et quantum miscetur alteri, tantum receditur a primo. Et quia elementa sunt quattuor, quorum quodlibet tanto facilius est miscibile quanto est magis subtile; ideo in prima commixtione evanescit sanguinis identitas quantum ad primum elementum, quod est subtilissimum; in secunda, quantum ad secundum; in tertia, quantum ad tertium; in quarta, quantum ad quartum. Et sic convenienter post quartam generationem potest reiterari carnalis coniunctio.

AD PRIMUM ergo dicendum quod, sicut Deus non coniungit illos qui coniunguntur contra divinum praeceptum, ita nec coniungit illos qui coniunguntur contra Ecclesiae praeceptum, quod habet eandem obligationis efficaciam quam et divinum praeceptum.

AD SECUNDUM dicendum quod matrimonium non tantum est sacramentum, sed etiam est in officium. Et ideo magis subiacet ordinationi ministrorum Ecclesiae quam baptismus, qui est sacramentum tantum: quia, sicut contractus et officia humana determinantur legibus humanis, ita contractus et officia spiritualia lege Ecclesiae.

AD TERTIUM dicendum quod, quamvis consanguinitatis vinculum sit naturale, tamen non est naturale quod consanguinitas carnalem copulam impediat, nisi secundum aliquem gradum, ut dictum est. Et ideo Ecclesia suo statuto non facit quod aliqui sint vel non sint consanguinei, quia secundum omne tempus aequaliter, consanguinei remanent: sed facit quod carnalis copula sit licita vel illicita secundum diversa tempora in diversis gradibus consanguinitatis.

AD QUARTUM dicendum quod tales rationes assignatae magis dantur per modum adaptationis et congruentiae, quam per modum causae et necessitatis.

AD QUINTUM dicendum quod iam ex dictis patet quod non est eadem causa secundum diversa tempora gradus consanguinitatis prohibendi. Unde quod alio tempore utiliter conceditur, alio salubriter prohibetur.

tend the prohibition to more remote degrees of consanguinity. Useless, because *charity waxed cold in many hearts* (Matt 24:12), so that they had scarcely a greater bond of friendship with their more remote kindred than with strangers; and it was dangerous because through the prevalence of concupiscence and neglect men took no account of so numerous a kindred, and thus the prohibition of the more remote degrees became for many a snare leading to damnation.

Moreover, there is a certain fittingness in the restriction of the above prohibition to the fourth degree. First, because men tend to live until the fourth generation, so that consanguinity cannot lapse into oblivion, wherefore God threatened to visit the parent's sins on their children *to the third and fourth generation* (Exod 20:5). Second, because in each generation the blood, the identity of which causes consanguinity, receives a further addition of new blood, and the more another blood is added the less there is of the old. And because there are four elements, each of which is the more easily mixed with another according as it is more rarefied, it follows that at the first admixture the identity of blood disappears as regards the first element (which is most subtle); at the second admixture, as regards the second element; at the third, as to the third element; at the fourth, as to the fourth element. Thus after the fourth generation it is fitting for the carnal union to be repeated.

REPLY OBJ. 1: Even as God does not join together those who are joined together against the divine command, so does he not join together those who are joined together against the commandment of the Church, which has the same binding force as a commandment of God.

REPLY OBJ. 2: Matrimony is not only a sacrament but also fulfills an office; wherefore it is more subject to the control of the Church's ministers than baptism, which is a sacrament only, because just as human contracts and offices are controlled by human laws, so are spiritual contracts and offices controlled by the law of the Church.

REPLY OBJ. 3: Although the tie of consanguinity is natural, it is not natural that consanguinity forbid carnal intercourse, except as regards certain degrees, as stated above (A. 3). Therefore, the Church's commandment does not cause certain people to be consanguineous or not consanguineous, because they remain equally consanguineous at all times, but it makes carnal intercourse to be lawful or unlawful at different times for different degrees of consanguinity.

REPLY OBJ. 4: The reasons assigned are given as indicating aptness and congruousness rather than causality and necessity.

REPLY OBJ. 5: The reason for the impediment of consanguinity is not the same at different times; thus that which it was useful to allow at one time, it was beneficial to forbid at another.

AD SEXTUM dicendum quod statutum non imponit modum praeteritis, sed futuris. Unde, si modo prohiberetur quintus gradus, qui nunc est concessus, illi qui sunt in quinto gradu coniuncti, non essent separandi: nullum enim impedimentum matrimonio superveniens ipsum potest dirimere. Et sic coniunctio quae prius fuit matrimonium, non efficeretur per statutum Ecclesiae stuprum. Et similiter, si aliquis gradus concederetur qui nunc est prohibitus, illa coniunctio non efficeretur matrimonialis ex statuto Ecclesiae ratione primi contractus: quia possent separari si vellent. Sed tamen possent de novo contrahere, et alia coniunctio esset.

AD SEPTIMUM dicendum quod in gradibus consanguinitatis prohibendis Ecclesia praecipue observat rationem amoris. Et quia non est minor ratio amoris ad nepotem quam ad patruum, sed etiam maior, quanto propinquior est patri filius quam filio pater, ut dicitur in VIII *Ethic.*; propter hoc aequaliter prohibuit gradus consanguinitatis in patruis et nepotibus.

Sed lex vetus in personis prohibendis attendit praecipue cohabitationem, contra concupiscentiam prohibens illas personas ad quas facilior pateret accessus propter mutuam cohabitationem. Magis autem consuevit cohabitare neptis patruo quam amita nepoti: quia filia est idem quasi cum patris, cum sit aliquid eius; sed soror non est hoc modo idem cum fratre, cum non sit aliquid eius, sed magis ex eodem nascitur. Et ideo non erat eadem ratio prohibendi neptem et amitam.

REPLY OBJ. 6: A commandment does not affect the past but the future. Therefore, if the fifth degree which is now allowed were to be forbidden at any time, those in the fifth degree who are married would not have to separate, because no impediment supervening to marriage can annul it; and consequently a union which was a marriage from the first would not be made incestuous by a commandment of the Church. In like manner, if a degree which is now forbidden were to be allowed, such a union would not become a marriage on account of the Church's commandment by reason of the former contract, because they could separate if they wished. Nevertheless, they could contract anew, and this would be a new union.

REPLY OBJ. 7: In prohibiting the degrees of consanguinity the Church considers chiefly the point of view of affection. And since the reason for affection towards one's brother's son is not less but even greater than the reasons for affection towards one's father's brother, inasmuch as the son is more akin to the father than the father to the son (*Ethics* 8.12), therefore did the Church equally prohibit the degrees of consanguinity in uncles and nephews.

On the other hand, the old law in debarring certain persons looked chiefly to the danger of concupiscence arising from cohabitation; and debarred those persons who were in closer intimacy with one another on account of their living together. Now it is more usual for a niece to live with her uncle than an aunt with her nephew: because a daughter is more identified with her father, being part of him, whereas a sister is not in this way identified with her brother, for she is not part of him but is born of the same parent. Hence there was not the same reason for debarring a niece and an aunt.

QUESTION 55

THE IMPEDIMENT OF AFFINITY

Deinde considerandum est de impedimento affinitatis.

Circa quod quaeruntur undecim.

Primo: utrum affinitas ex matrimonio causetur.

Secundo: utrum maneat post mortem viri aut uxoris.

Tertio: utrum causetur ex illicito concubitu.

Quarto: utrum ex sponsalibus.

Quinto: utrum affinitas sit causa affinitatis.

Sexto: utrum affinitas matrimonium impediat.

Septimo: utrum affinitas habeat per seipsam gradus.

Octavo: utrum gradus eius extendantur sicut gradus consanguinitatis.

Nono: utrum matrimonium quod est inter consanguineos et affines, semper sit dirimendum per divortium.

Decimo: utrum ad dirimendum tale matrimonium sit procedendum per viam accusationis.

Undecimo: utrum in tali causa sit procedendum per testes.

We must consider next the impediment of affinity.

Under this head there are eleven points of inquiry:

(1) Whether affinity results from matrimony?

(2) Whether it remains after the death of husband or wife?

(3) Whether it is caused through unlawful intercourse?

(4) Whether it arises from a betrothal?

(5) Whether affinity is caused through affinity?

(6) Whether affinity is an impediment to marriage?

(7) Whether affinity in itself admits of degrees?

(8) Whether its degrees extend as far as the degrees of consanguinity?

(9) Whether marriages of persons related to one another by consanguinity or affinity should always be dissolved by divorce?

(10) Whether the process for the dissolution of like marriages should always be by way of accusation?

(11) Whether witnesses should be called in such a case?

Article 1

Whether Affinity is Contracted Through the Marriage of a Blood Relation?

AD PRIMUM SIC PROCEDITUR. Videtur quod ex matrimonio consanguinei affinitas non causetur. Quia *propter quod unumquodque, illud magis.* Sed mulier ducta in matrimonium non coniungitur alicui de consanguinitate viri nisi ratione viri. Cum ergo non fiat viro affinis, nec alicui consanguineorum viri affinis erit.

PRAETEREA, eorum quae sunt ab invicem separata, si urii aliquid coniungitur, non oportet propter hoc quod sit alteri coniunctum. Sed consanguinei iam sunt ab invicem separati. Ergo non oportet quod, si aliqua mulier coniungatur alicui viro, quod propter hoc coniungatur omnibus consanguineis eius per affinitatem.

PRAETEREA, relationes ex aliquibus unitionibus innascuntur. Sed nulla unitio fit in consanguineis viri per hoc quod ille duxit uxorem. Ergo non accrescit eis affinitatis relatio.

SED CONTRA: Vir et uxor efficiuntur *una caro.* Si ergo vir secundum carnem omnibus suis consanguineis attinet, et mulier eadem ratione attinebit eisdem.

OBJECTION 1: It would seem that a person does not contract affinity through the marriage of a blood relation. For *the cause of a thing being so is yet more so.* Now the wife is not connected with her husband's kindred except by reason of the husband. Since, then, she does not contract affinity with her husband, neither does she contract it with her husband's kindred.

OBJ. 2: Further, if certain things be separate from one another and something be connected with one of them, it does not follow that it is connected with the other. Now a person's blood relations are separate from one another. Therefore, it does not follow that if a certain woman be married to a certain man, that she is therefore connected with all his kindred.

OBJ. 3: Further, relations result from certain things being united together. Now the kindred of the husband do not become united together by the fact of his taking a wife. Therefore, they do not acquire any relationship of affinity.

ON THE CONTRARY, Husband and wife are made *one flesh.* Therefore, since the husband is related in the flesh to all his kindred, his wife will also be related to them all.

391

PRAETEREA, hoc patet per auctoritates in littera inductas.

RESPONDEO dicendum quod amicitia quaedam naturalis in communicatione naturali fundatur. Naturalis autem communicatio est duobus modis, secundum Philosophum, VIII *Ethic.*: uno modo, per carnis propagationem; alio modo, per coniunctionem ad carnis propagationem ordinatam. Unde ipse ibidem dicit quod *amicitia viri ad uxorem est naturalis.* Unde, sicut persona coniuncta alteri per carnis propagationem quoddam vinculum naturalis amicitiae facit, ita si coniungatur per carnalem copulam. Sed in hoc differt, quod persona coniuncta alicui per carnis propagationem, sicut filius patri, fit particeps eiusdem radicis et sanguinis: unde eodem genere vinculi colligatur filius consanguineis patris quo pater coniungebatur, scilicet consanguinitate; quamvis secundum alium gradum, propter maiorem distantiam a radice. Sed persona coniuncta per carnalem copulam non fit particeps eiusdem radicis, sed quasi extrinsecus adiuncta. Et ideo ex hoc efficitur aliud genus vinculi, quod 'affinitas' dicitur. Et hoc est quod in hoc versu dicitur: *mutat nupta genus, sed generata gradum*: quia scilicet persona generata fit in eodem genere attinentiae, sed alio gradu; per carnalem vero copulam fit in alio genere.

AD PRIMUM ergo dicendum quod, quamvis causa sit potior effectu, non tamen oportet semper quod nomen idem effectui et causae conveniat: quia quandoque illud quod est in effectu, invenitur in causa non eodem modo, sed altiori, et ideo non convenit causae et effectui per idem nomen, neque per eandem rationem; sicut patet in omnibus causis aequivoce agentibus. Et hoc modo coniunctio viri et uxoris est potior quam coniunctio uxoris ad consanguineos viri: non tamen debet dici affinitas, sed 'matrimonium', quod est unitas quaedam; sicut homo est sibi ipsi idem, non consanguineus.

AD SECUNDUM dicendum quod consanguinei sunt quodammodo separati et quodammodo coniuncti. Et ratione coniunctionis accidit quod persona quae uni coniungitur, aliquo modo omnibus coniungatur. Sed propter separationem et distantiam accidit quod persona quae uni coniungitur uno modo, alii coniungatur alio modo, vel secundum aliud genus vel secundum alium gradum.

AD TERTIUM dicendum quod relatio quandoque innascitur ex motu utriusque extremi, sicut paternitas et filiatio. Et talis relatio est realiter in utroque.

Quandoque vero innascitur ex motu alterius tantum. Et hoc contingit dupliciter. Uno modo, quando relatio innascitur ex motu unius sine motu alterius vel praece-

FURTHER, This is proved by the authorities quoted in the text (*Sentences* IV, D. 41).

I ANSWER THAT, A certain natural friendship is founded on natural fellowship. Now natural fellowship, according to the Philosopher, arises in two ways; first, from carnal procreation; second, from connection with orderly carnal procreation, wherefore he says that the *friendship of a husband towards his wife is natural* (*Ethics* 8.12). Consequently, even as a person through being connected with another by carnal procreation is bound to him by a tie of natural friendship, so does one person become connected with another through carnal intercourse. But there is a difference in this, that one who is connected with another through carnal procreation, as a son with his father, shares in the same common stock and blood, so that a son is connected with his father's kindred by the same kind of tie as the father was, namely, the tie of consanguinity, although in a different degree on account of his being more distant from the stock; whereas one who is connected with another through carnal intercourse does not share in the same stock, but is as it were an extraneous addition thereto; whence arises another kind of tie known by the name of 'affinity'. This is expressed in the verse: *marriage makes a new kind of connection, while birth makes a new degree*, because, to wit, the person begotten is in the same kind of relationship, but in a different degree, whereas through carnal intercourse he enters into a new kind of relationship.

REPLY OBJ. 1: Although a cause is more potent than its effect, it does not always follow that the same name is applicable to the cause as to the effect, because sometimes that which is in the effect is found in the cause not in the same but in a higher way; wherefore it is not applicable to both cause and effect under the same name or under the same aspect, as is the case with all equivocal agent causes. Thus, then, the union of husband and wife is stronger than the union of the wife with her husband's kindred, and yet it ought not to be named affinity, but 'matrimony', which is a kind of unity; even as a man is identical with himself, but not with his kinsman.

REPLY OBJ. 2: Blood relations are in a way separate, and in a way connected; and it happens in respect of their connection that a person who is connected with one of them is in some way connected with all of them. But on account of their separation and distance from one another it happens that a person who is connected with one of them in one way is connected with another in another way, either as to the kind of connection or as to the degree.

REPLY OBJ. 3: Sometimes a relation results from a movement in each extreme, for instance, fatherhood and sonship, and a relation of this kind is really in both extremes.

Sometimes it results from the movement of one only, and this happens in two ways. In one way, when a relation results from the movement of one extreme without

dente vel concomitante: sicut in Creatore et creatura pateti et sensibili et sensu, et scientia et scibili. Et tunc relatio est in uno secundum rem, et in altero secundum rationem tantum. Alio modo, quando innascitur ex motu unius sine motu alterius tunc existente, non tamen sine motu praecedente: sicut aequalitas fit inter duos homines per augmentum unius, sine hoc quod alius tunc augeatur vel minuatur; sed tamen prius ad hanc quantitatem quam habet per aliquem motum vel mutationem pervenit. Et ideo in utroque extremorum talis relatio realiter fundatur.

Et similiter est de consanguinitate et affinitate. Quia relatio fraternitatis quae innascitur aliquo puero nato alicui iam provecto, causatur quidem sine motu ipsius tunc existente, sed ex motu ipsius praecedente, scilicet generationis eius: hoc enim ei accidit quod ex motu alterius sibi nunc talis relatio innascitur. Similiter ex hoc quod iste descendit per generationem propriam ab eadem radice cum viro, provenit affinitas in ipso ad uxorem sine aliqua nova mutatione ipsius.

any movement previous to or concomitant of the other extreme, as in the Creator and the creature, the sensible and the sense, knowledge and the knowable object; and then the relation is in one extreme really and in the other logically only. In another way, when the relation results from the movement of one extreme without any concomitant movement, but not without a previous movement of the other; thus there results equality between two men by the increase of one, without the other either increasing or decreasing then, although previously he reached his actual quantity by some movement or change, so that this relation is founded really in both extremes.

It is the same with consanguinity and affinity, because the relation of brotherhood which comes to be in a grown child on the birth of a boy is caused without any movement of the former's at the time, but by virtue of that previous movement of his wherein he was begotten; wherefore at the time it happens that there results in him the aforesaid relation through the movement of another. Likewise, because this man descends through his own birth from the same stock as the husband, there results in him affinity with the latter's wife, without any new change in him.

Article 2

Whether After the Death of a Man, Affinity Remains Between His Blood Relations and His Wife?

AD SECUNDUM SIC PROCEDITUR. Videtur quod affinitas non manet post mortem viri inter consanguineos viri et uxorem. Quia, *cessante causa, cessat effectus*. Sed causa affinitatis fuit matrimonium, quod cessat in morte viri: quia tunc *solvitur mulier a lege viri*, ut dicitur Rom. 7. Ergo nec affinitas praedicta manet.

PRAETEREA, consanguinitas causat affinitatem. Sed consanguinitas viri cessat per mortem ad consanguineos suos. Ergo et affinitas uxoris ad eos.

SED CONTRA, affinitas ex consanguinitate causatur. Sed consanguinitas est perpetuum vinculum, quandiu personae vivunt inter quas est affinitas. Ergo et affinitas. Et ita non solvitur affinitas soluto matrimonio per mortem tertiae personae.

RESPONDEO dicendum quod relatio aliqua esse desinit dupliciter: uno modo ex corruptione subiecti, alio modo ex subtractione causae; sicut similitudo esse desinit quando alter similium moritur, vel quando qualitas quae erat causa similitudinis, subtrahitur. Sunt autem quaedam relationes quae habent pro causa actionem vel passionem aut motum, ut in V *Metaphys.* dicitur. Quarum quaedam causantur ex motu inquantum aliquid movetur actu: sicut ipsa relatio quae est moventis et

OBJECTION 1: It would seem that after the death of a man affinity does not remain between his blood relations and his wife. For *if the cause cease the effect ceases*. Now the cause of affinity was the marriage, which ceases after the husband's death, since then *the woman is loosed from the law of the husband* (Rom 7:2). Therefore, the aforesaid affinity ceases also.

OBJ. 2: Further, consanguinity is the cause of affinity. Now the consanguinity of the husband with his blood relations ceases at his death. Therefore, the wife's affinity with them ceases also.

ON THE CONTRARY, Affinity is caused by consanguinity. Now consanguinity binds persons together for all time as long as they live. Therefore, affinity does so also; and consequently affinity is not dissolved through the dissolution of the marriage by the death of a third person.

I ANSWER THAT, A relation ceases in two ways: in one way through the corruption of its subject; in another way by the removal of its cause. Thus likeness ceases when one of the like subjects dies, or when the quality that caused the likeness is removed. Now there are certain relations which have for their cause an action, a passion, or a movement (*Metaphysics* 5.20); and some of these are caused by movement through something being moved actually, such as is the relation between mover and moved; some of them are

moti. Quaedam autem inquantum habent aptitudinem ad motum; sicut motivum et mobile, dominus et servus. Quaedam autem ex hoc quod aliquid prius motum est: sicut pater et filius non ex hoc quod est generari nunc, ad invicem dicuntur; sed ex hoc quod est generatum esse.

Aptitudo autem ad motum, etiam ipsum moveri transit: sed motum esse perpetuum est, quia quod factum est, nunquam desinit esse factum. Et ideo paternitas et filiatio nunquam destruuntur per destructionem causae, sed solum per corruptionem subiecti, scilicet alterutrius extremorum. Et similiter dicendum est de affinitate, quae causatur ex hoc quod aliqui coniuncti sunt, non ex hoc quod coniunguntur. Unde non dirimitur, manentibus illis personis inter quas affinitas est contracta, quamvis moriatur persona ratione cuius contracta fuit.

AD PRIMUM ergo dicendum quod coniunctio matrimonii causat affinitatem non solum secundum hoc quod est actu coniungi, sed secundum hoc quod est prius coniunctum esse.

AD SECUNDUM dicendum quod consanguinitas non est proxima causa affinitatis: sed coniunctio ad consanguineum, non solum quae est, sed quae fuit. Et propter hoc ratio non sequitur.

caused through something being adapted to movement, for instance, the relations between the motive power and the movable, or between master and servant; and some of them result from something having been moved previously, such as the relation between father and son, for the relation between them is caused not by the son being begotten now, but by his having been begotten.

Now aptitude for movement and for being moved is transitory, whereas the fact of having been moved is everlasting, since what has been never ceases having been. Consequently, fatherhood and sonship are never dissolved through the removal of the cause, but only through the corruption of the subject, that is, of one of the subjects. The same applies to affinity, for this is caused by certain persons having been joined together, not by their being actually joined. Wherefore it is not done away with as long as the persons between whom affinity has been contracted survive, although the person through whom it was contracted should die.

REPLY OBJ. 1: The marriage tie causes affinity not only by reason of actual union, but also by reason of the union having been effected in the past.

REPLY OBJ. 2: Consanguinity is not the chief cause of affinity, but union with a blood relation, not only because that union is now, but because it has been. Hence the argument does not follow.

Article 3

Whether Unlawful Intercourse Causes Affinity?

AD TERTIUM SIC PROCEDITUR. Videtur quod illicitus concubitus affinitatem non causet. Quia affinitas est quaedam res honesta. Sed res honestae non causantur ex inhonestis. Ergo ex inhonesto concubitu non potest affinitas causari.

PRAETEREA, ubi est consanguinitas, non potest esse affinitas: quia affinitas, est *proximitas personarum ex carnali copula proveniens omni carens parentela*. Sed aliquando contingeret ad consanguineos et ad seipsum esse affinitatem, si illicitus concubitus affinitatem causaret: sicut quando homo carnaliter consanguineam suam incestuose cognoscit. Ergo affinitas non causatur, ex illicito concubitu.

PRAETEREA, illicitus concubitus est secundum naturam, et contra naturam. Sed ex illicito concubitu contra naturam non causatur affinitas, ut iura determinant. Ergo nec ex illicito concubitu secundum naturam tantum.

OBJECTION 1: It would seem that unlawful intercourse does not cause affinity. For affinity is an honorable thing. Now honorable things do not result from that which is dishonorable. Therefore, affinity cannot be caused by a dishonorable intercourse.

OBJ. 2: Further, where there is consanguinity there cannot be affinity; since affinity is a *relationship between persons that results from carnal intercourse and is altogether void of blood relationship*. Now if unlawful intercourse were a cause of affinity, it would sometimes happen that a man would contract affinity with his blood relations and with himself: for instance, when a man is guilty of incest with a blood relation. Therefore, affinity is not caused by unlawful intercourse.

OBJ. 3: Further, unlawful intercourse is according to nature or against nature. Now affinity is not caused by unnatural and unlawful intercourse, as decided by law (*Decretals*). Therefore, it is not caused only by unlawful intercourse according to nature.

SED CONTRA: Est quod *adhaerens meretrici unum corpus efficitur*, ut patet I Cor. 6. Sed ex hac causa matrimonium affinitatem causabat. Ergo, pari ratione, illicitus concubitus.

PRAETEREA, carnalis copula est causa affinitatis: ut patet per definitionem affinitatis, quae est talis: *affinitas est propinquitas personarum ex carnali copula proveniens omni carens parentela.* Sed carnalis copula est etiam in illicito concubitu. Ergo illicitus concubitus affinitatem causat.

RESPONDEO dicendum quod, secundum Philosophum, in VIII *Ethic.*, coniunctio viri et uxoris dicitur naturalis principaliter propter prolis productionem, et secundario propter operum communicationem: quorum primum pertinet ad matrimonium ratione carnalis copulae, sed secundum inquantum est quaedam societas in communem vitam. Primum autem horum est invenire in qualibet carnali copula ubi est commixtio seminum, quia ex tali copula potest proles produci: quamvis secunda desit. Et ideo, quia matrimonium affinitatem causabat secundum quod erat quaedam carnalis commixtio, etiam fornicarius concubitus affinitatem causat, inquantum habet aliquid de carnali coniunctione.

AD PRIMUM ergo dicendum quod in fornicario concubitu est aliquid naturale, quod est commune fornicationi et matrimonio: et ex hac parte affinitatem causat. Aliud est ibi inordinatum, per quod a matrimonio dividitur: et ex hac parte affinitas non causatur. Unde affinitas semper honesta remanet, quamvis causa aliquo modo sit inhonesta.

AD SECUNDUM dicendum quod non est inconveniens relationes ex opposito divisas eidem inesse ratione diversorum. Et ideo potest inter aliquas duas personas esse affinitas et consanguinitas, non solum per illicitum concubitum, sed etiam per licitum: sicut cum consanguineus meus ex parte patris, duxit in uxorem consanguineam meam ex parte matris. Unde, cum dicitur in definitione affinitatis inducta, *omni carens parentela*, intelligendum est, inquantum huiusmodi. Nec tamen sequitur quod aliquis consanguineam suam cognoscens sibi ipsi sit affinis: quia affinitas, sicut et consanguinitas, diversitatem requirit; sicut et similitudo.

AD TERTIUM dicendum quod concubitus contra naturam non habet commixtionem seminum quae possit esse causa generationis. Et ideo ex tali concubitu non causatur aliqua affinitas.

ON THE CONTRARY, He who is *joined to a harlot is made one body* (1 Cor 6:16). Now this is the reason why marriage caused affinity. Therefore, unlawful intercourse does so for the same reason.

FURTHER, Carnal intercourse is the cause of affinity, as shown by the definition of affinity, which definition is as follows: *affinity is the relationship of persons which results from carnal intercourse and is altogether void of blood relationship.* But there is carnal copulation even in unlawful intercourse. Therefore, unlawful intercourse causes affinity.

I ANSWER THAT, According to the Philosopher (*Ethics* 8.12) the union of husband and wife is said to be natural chiefly on account of the procreation of offspring, and second on account of the community of works, the former of which belongs to marriage by reason of carnal copulation, and the latter, insofar as marriage is a partnership directed to a common life. Now the former is to be found in every carnal union where there is a mingling of seeds, since such a union may be productive of offspring, but the latter may be wanting. Consequently, since marriage caused affinity insofar as it was a carnal mingling, it follows that also an unlawful intercourse causes affinity insofar as it has something of natural copulation.

REPLY OBJ. 1: In an unlawful intercourse there is something natural which is common to fornication and marriage, and in this respect it causes affinity. There is also something which is inordinate whereby it differs from marriage, and in this respect it does not cause affinity. Hence affinity remains honorable, although its cause is in a way dishonorable.

REPLY OBJ. 2: There is no reason why diverse relations should not be in the same subject by reason of different things. Consequently, there can be affinity and consanguinity between two persons not only on account of unlawful but also on account of lawful intercourse: for instance, if a blood relation of mine on my father's side marries a blood relation of mine on my mother's side. Hence in the above definition the words *which is altogether void of blood relationship* apply to affinity as such. Nor does it follow that a man by having intercourse with his blood relation contracts affinity with himself, since affinity, like consanguinity, requires diversity of subjects, as likeness does.

REPLY OBJ. 3: In unnatural copulation there is no mingling of seeds that makes generation possible; wherefore a like intercourse does not cause affinity.

Article 4

Whether Affinity Can Be Caused by Betrothal?

AD QUARTUM SIC PROCEDITUR. Videtur quod ex sponsalibus nulla affinitas causari possit. Quia affinitas est perpetuum vinculum. Sed sponsalia quandoque separantur. Ergo non possunt esse causa affinitatis.

PRAETEREA, si aliquis claustrum pudoris alicuius mulieris invasit et aperuit, sed non pervenit ad operis consummationem, non contrahitur ex hoc affinitas. Sed talis est magis propinquus carnali copulae quam ille qui sponsalia contrahit. Ergo ex sponsalibus affinitas non causatur.

PRAETEREA, in sponsalibus non fit nisi quaedam sponsio futurarum nuptiarum. Sed aliquando fit sponsio futurarum nuptiarum et ex hoc non contrahitur aliqua affinitas: sicut si fiat ante septennium, vel si aliquis habens perpetuum impedimentum tollens potentiam coeundi alicui mulieri spondeat futuras nuptias, aut si talis sponsio fiat inter personas quibus nuptiae per votum reddantur illicitae, vel alio quocumque modo. Ergo sponsalia non possunt esse causa affinitatis.

SED CONTRA est quod Alexander Papa prohibuit mulierem quandam cuidam viro matrimonio coniungi quia fratri suo fuerat desponsata. Quod non esset nisi per sponsalia affinitas contraheretur. Ergo, etc.

RESPONDEO dicendum quod, sicut sponsalia non habent perfectam rationem matrimonii sed sunt quaedam praeparatio ad matrimonium, ita ex sponsalibus non causatur affinitas sicut ex matrimonio, sed aliquid affinitati simile, quod dicitur publicae honestatis iustitia: quae impedit matrimonium sicut et affinitas et consanguinitas, secundum eosdem gradus. Et definitur sic: *Publicae honestatis iustitia est propinquitas ex sponsalibus proveniens, robur trahens ex Ecclesiae institutione propter eius honestatem.* Ex quo patet ratio nominis et causa: quia scilicet talis propinquitas ab Ecclesia instituta est propter honestatem.

AD PRIMUM ergo dicendum quod sponsalia non ratione sui, sed ratione eius ad quod ordinantur, causant hoc genus affinitatis quod dicitur *publicae honestatis iustitia.* Et ideo, sicut matrimonium est perpetuum vinculum, ita et praedictus affinitatis modus.

AD SECUNDUM dicendum quod vir et mulier efficiuntur in carnali copula *una caro* per commixtionem seminum. Unde, quantumcumque aliquis claustrum pudoris invadat vel frangat, nisi commixtio seminum sequatur, non contrahitur ex hoc affinitas. Sed matrimonium affinitatem causat non solum ratione carnalis copulae, sed etiam ratione societatis coniugalis, secundum quam etiam matrimonium naturale est. Unde et affinitas contrahitur ex ipso contractu matrimonii per

OBJECTION 1: It would seem that affinity cannot be caused by betrothal. For affinity is a lasting tie, whereas a betrothal is sometimes broken off. Therefore, it cannot cause affinity.

OBJ. 2: Furthermore, if someone violated some woman and penetrated her, but did not succeed in bringing the act to consummation, affinity is not contracted by this. Yet this is much more akin to carnal intercourse than a betrothal. Therefore, betrothal does not cause affinity.

OBJ. 3: Further, betrothal is nothing but a promise of future marriage. Now sometimes there is a promise of future marriage without affinity being contracted, for instance, if it take place before the age of seven years, or if a man having a perpetual impediment of impotence promise a woman future marriage, or if a like promise be made between persons for whom marriage is rendered unlawful by a vow, or in any other way whatever. Therefore, betrothal cannot cause affinity.

ON THE CONTRARY, Pope Alexander (*Decretals*) forbade a certain woman to marry a certain man, because she had been betrothed to his brother. Now this would not be the case unless affinity were contracted by betrothal. Therefore, etc.

I ANSWER THAT, Just as a betrothal has not the conditions of a perfect marriage, but is a preparation for marriage, so betrothal causes not affinity as marriage does, but something like affinity. This is called the justice of public honesty, which is an impediment to marriage even as affinity and consanguinity are, and according to the same degrees, and is defined thus: *the justice of public honesty is a relationship arising out of betrothal, and derives its force from ecclesiastical institution by reason of its honesty.* This indicates the reason of its name as well as its cause, namely, that this relationship was instituted by the Church on account of its honesty.

REPLY OBJ. 1: Betrothal, by reason not of itself but of the end to which it is directed, causes this kind of affinity known as *the justice of public honesty*; wherefore just as marriage is a lasting tie, so is the aforesaid kind of affinity.

REPLY OBJ. 2: In carnal intercourse man and woman become *one flesh* by the mingling of seeds. Wherefore it is not every invasion or penetration of the hymen that causes affinity to be contracted, but only such as is followed by a mingling of seeds. But marriage causes affinity not only on account of carnal intercourse, but also by reason of the conjugal fellowship, in respect of which also marriage is according to nature. Consequently, affinity results from the marriage contract itself expressed in words of the present

verba de praesenti ante carnalem copulam. Et similiter etiam ex sponsalibus, in quibus fit quaedam, pactio coniugalis societatis, contrahitur aliquid affinitati simile, scilicet publicae honestatis iustitia.

AD TERTIUM dicendum quod omnia impedimenta quae faciunt sponsalia non esse sponsalia, non permittunt ex pactione nuptiarum affinitatem fieri. Unde sive habens defectum aetatis, sive habens votum solemne continentiae, aut aliquod huiusmodi impedimentum, sponsalia de facto contrahat, ex hoc non sequitur aliqua affinitas, quia sponsalia nulla sunt, nec aliquis affinitatis modus.

Si tamen aliquis minor frigidus vel maleficiatus habens impedimentum perpetuum, ante annos pubertatis post septennium contrahat sponsalia cum adulta, ex tali contractu contrahitur publicae honestatis iustitia: quia adhuc non erat in actu impediendi, cum in tali aetate puer frigidus et non frigidus, quantum ad actum illum, sint aequaliter impotentes.

and before its consummation, and in like manner there results from betrothal, which is a promise of conjugal fellowship, something akin to affinity, namely, the justice of public honesty.

REPLY OBJ. 3: All those impediments which void a betrothal prevent affinity being contracted through a promise of marriage. Hence whether he who actually promises marriage be lacking in age, or be under a solemn vow of continence or any like impediment, no affinity nor anything akin to it results, because the betrothal is void.

If, however, a minor, laboring under insensibility or a curse, having a perpetual impediment, is betrothed before the age of puberty and after the age of seven years with a woman who is of age, from such a contract there results the impediment called justice of public honesty, because at the time the impediment was not actual, since at that age both a potent and an impotent boy are equally impotent in respect of the act in question.

Article 5

Whether Affinity Is a Cause of Affinity?

AD QUINTUM SIC PROCEDITUR. Videtur etiam quod affinitas sit causa affinitatis. Quia Iulius Papa dicit: *relictam consanguineorum uxoris suae nullus ducat uxorem,* ut habetur XXXV, qu. 3, cap. *Contradicimus.* Et in sequenti capitulo dicitur quod *duae consanguineorum uxores uni viro altera post alteram nubere prohibentur.* Sed hoc non est nisi ratione affinitatis quae contrahitur ex coniunctione ad affinem. Ergo affinitas est causa affinitatis.

PRAETEREA, carnalis commixtio coniungit sicut et carnalis propagatio: quia aequaliter computantur gradus affinitatis et consanguinitatis. Sed consanguinitas est causa affinitatis. Ergo et affinitas.

PRAETEREA, *quaecumque uni et eidem sunt eadem, sibi invicem sunt eadem.* Sed uxor viri alicuius efficitur eiusdem attinentiae cum omnibus consanguineis viri. Ergo et omnes consanguinei viri sui efficiuntur unum cum omnibus qui attinent mulieri per affinitatem. Et sic affinitas est, causa affinitatis.

SED CONTRA: Si affinitas ex affinitate causatur, aliquis qui cognovisset duas mulieres, neutram earum posset ducere in uxorem: quia secundum hoc altera efficeretur alteri affinis. Sed hoc est falsum. Ergo affinitas non causat affinitatem.

PRAETEREA, si affinitas ex affinitate nasceretur, aliquis contrahens cum uxore defuncti fieret affinis omnibus consanguineis prioris viri, ad quos mulier habet af-

OBJECTION 1: It would seem that affinity also is a cause of affinity. For Pope Julius I says (cap. *Contradicimus* 35, qu. iii): *no man may marry his wife's surviving blood relation;* and it is said in the next chapter (cap. *Porro duorum*) that *the wives of two cousins are forbidden to marry, one after the other, the same husband.* But this is only on account of affinity being contracted through union with a person related by affinity. Therefore, affinity is a cause of affinity.

OBJ. 2: Further, carnal intercourse makes persons akin even as carnal procreation, since the degrees of affinity and consanguinity are reckoned equally. But consanguinity causes affinity. Therefore, affinity does also.

OBJ. 3: Further, *things that are the same with one and the same are the same with one another.* But the wife contracts the same relations with all her husband's kindred. Therefore, all her husband's kindred are made one with all who are related by affinity to the wife, and thus affinity is the cause of affinity.

OBJ. 4: On the contrary, if affinity is caused by affinity, a man who knew two women can marry neither of them, because then the one would be related to the other by affinity. But this is false. Therefore, affinity does not cause affinity.

OBJ. 5: Further, if affinity arose out of affinity, a man by marrying another man's widow would contract affinity with all her first husband's kindred, since she is related to them

finitatem. Sed hoc non potest esse: quia maxime fieret affinis viro defuncto. Ergo, etc.

PRAETEREA, consanguinitas est fortius vinculum quam affinitas. Sed consanguinei uxoris non efficiuntur affines consanguineis viri. Ergo multo minus affines uxoris efficientur eis affines. Et sic idem quod prius.

RESPONDEO dicendum quod duplex est modus quo aliquid ex alio procedit: unus secundum quem aliquid procedit in similitudinem speciei, sicut ex homine generatur homo; alius secundum quem procedit dissimile in specie; et hic processus semper est in inferiorem speciem, ut patet in omnibus agentibus aequivoce. Primus autem modus processionis quotiescumque iteretur, semper manet eadem species: sicut, si ex homine generatur homo per actum generativae virtutis, ex hoc quoque generabitur homo, et sic deinceps. Secundus autem modus, sicut in principio facit aliam speciem, ita, quotiescumque iteretur, aliam speciem facit: ut, si ex puncto per motum procedit linea, non punctus quia punctus motus facit lineam, ex linea linealiter mota non procedit linea, sed superficies; et ex superficie corpus; et ulterius per talem modum processus aliquis non potest esse.

Invenimus autem in processu attinentiae duos modos quibus vinculum huiusmodi causatur. Unus per carnis propagationem: et hic semper facit eandem speciem attinentiae. Alius per matrimonialem coniunctionem: et hic facit aliam speciem in principio, sicut patet quod coniuncta matrimonialiter consanguineo, non fit consanguinea, sed affinis. Unde, si et ille modus procedendi iteratur, non erit affinitas, sed aliud attinentiae genus. Unde persona quae matrimonialiter affini coniungitur, non est affinis: sed est aliud genus affinitatis, quod dicatur secundum genus. Et rursus, si affini in secundo genere aliquis per matrimonium coniungatur, non erit affinis in secundo genere, sed in tertio. Ut hoc versu supra posito ostenditur: *mutat nupta genus, sed generata gradus.*

Et haec duo genera olim erant prohibita, propter publicae honestatis iustitiam magis quam propter affinitatem: quia deficiunt a vera affinitate, sicut illa attinentia quae ex sponsalibus contrahitur. Sed modo illa prohibitio cessavit. Et remanet sub prohibitione solum primum genus affinitatis, in quo est vera affinitas.

AD PRIMUM ergo dicendum quod alicui viro consanguineus uxoris suae efficitur affinis in primo genere, et uxor eius in secundo. Unde, mortuo viro qui erat affinis, non poterat eam ducere in uxorem propter secundum affinitatis genus. Similiter autem, si aliquis viduam in uxorem ducat, consanguineus prioris viri, qui est af-

by affinity. But this cannot be the case because he would become especially related by affinity to her deceased husband. Therefore, etc.

OBJ. 6: Further, consanguinity is a stronger tie than affinity. But the blood relations of the wife do not become blood relations of the husband. Much less, therefore, does affinity to the wife cause affinity to her blood relations, and thus the same conclusion follows.

I ANSWER THAT, There are two ways in which one thing proceeds from another: in one way, a thing proceeds from another in likeness of species, as a man is begotten of a man; in another way, one thing proceeds from another not in likeness of species, and this process is always towards a lower species, as instanced in all equivocal agents. In the first kind of procession, however often it be repeated, the same species always remains; thus if one man be begotten of another by an act of the generative power, of this man also another man will be begotten, and so on. But the second kind of procession, just as in the first instance it produces another species, so it makes another species as often as it is repeated. Thus by movement from a point there proceeds a line and not a point, because a point by being moved makes a line; and from a line moved lineally, there proceeds not a line but a surface, and from a surface a body, and in this way the procession can go no further.

Now in the procession of kinship we find two kinds whereby this tie is caused: one is by carnal procreation, and this always produces the same species of relationship; the other is by the marriage union, and this produces a different kind of relationship from the beginning; thus it is clear that a married woman is related to her husband's blood relations not by blood but by affinity. Wherefore if this kind of process be repeated, the result will be not affinity but another kind of relationship; and consequently a married party contracts with the affines of the other party a relation not of affinity, but of some other kind, which is called affinity of the second kind. And again if a person through marriage contracts relationship with an affine of the second kind, it will not be affinity of the second kind, but of a third kind, as indicated in the verse quoted above (A. 1): *marriage makes a new kind of connection, while birth makes a new degree.*

Formerly these two kinds were included in the prohibition under the head of the justice of public honesty rather than under the head of affinity, because they fall short of true affinity, in the same way as the relationship arising out of betrothal. Now, however, they have ceased to be included in the prohibition, which now refers only to the first kind of affinity in which true affinity consists.

REPLY OBJ. 1: A husband contracts affinity of the first kind with his wife's male blood relation, and affinity of the second kind with the latter's wife: hence if the latter man dies, the former cannot marry his widow on account of the second kind of affinity. Again, if a man marry a widow, a blood relation of her former husband, being connected

finis uxori in primo genere, efficitur affinis secundo viro in secundo genere: et uxor illius consanguinei, quae est affinis uxori viri huius in secundo genere, efficitur affinis viro secundo in tertio genere. Et quia tertium genus erat prohibitum, propter honestatem quandam magis quam propter affinitatem, ideo canon dicit: *duas consanguineorum uxores uni viro alteram post alteram nubere publicae honestatis iustitiae contradicit.* Sed talis prohibitio nunc cessavit.

AD SECUNDUM dicendum quod, quamvis carnalis coniunctio coniungat, non tamen eodem genere coniunctionis.

AD TERTIUM dicendum quod uxor viri efficitur eiusdem attinentiae cum consanguineis viri quantum ad eundem gradum, sed non quantum ad idem attinentiae genus.

Sed quia ex rationibus quae in oppositum inducuntur videtur ostendi quod nullum vinculum ex affinitate causetur, ad alias rationes respondendum est: ne antiqua Ecclesiae prohibitio irrationabilis videatur.

AD QUARTUM dicendum, quod mulier non efficitur affinis in primo genere viro cui coniungitur carnaliter, ut ex praedictis patet. Unde consequenter alii mulieri a viro eodem cognitae non efficitur affinis in secundo genere. Unde nec ducenti in uxorem unam earum efficitur alia affinis in tertio genere affinitatis. Et ita duas mulieres cognitas ab eodem viro nec antiqua iura eidem successive copulari prohibebant:

AD QUINTUM dicendum quod, sicut vir non est affinis uxori suae in primo genere, ita nec efficitur affinis secundo viro eiusdem uxoris in secundo genere. Et sic ratio non procedit.

AD SEXTUM dicendum quod mediante una persona non coniungitur mihi alia nisi ex hoc quod ei adiungitur. Unde, mediante muliere quae mihi est affinis, nulla persona fit mihi attinens nisi quae illi mulieri adiungitur. Quod non potest esse nisi per carnis propagationem ex ipsa, vel propter coniunctionem matrimonialem ad eam. Et utroque modo aliqua attinentia mediante praedicta muliere, secundum antiqua iura, mihi proveniebat: quia filius eius etiam ex alio viro efficitur mihi affinis in eodem genere, sed in alio gradu, ut ex regula prius data patet; et iterum secundus vir eius efficitur mihi affinis in secundo genere. Sed alii consanguinei illius mulieris non adiunguntur ei: sed ipsa vel adiungitur eis, sicut patri et matri, inquantum procedit ab eis; vel principio eorundem, sicut fratribus. Unde frater affinis meae, vel pater, non efficitur mihi affinis in aliquo genere.

with the widow by the first kind of affinity, contracts affinity of the second kind with her second husband; and the wife of this blood relation, being connected by affinity of the second kind with the widow, contracts affinity of the third kind with her second husband. And since the third kind of affinity was included in the prohibition on account of a certain honesty more than by reason of affinity, the canon says: *the justice of public honesty forbids the wives of two cousins to be married to the same man, the one after the other* (cap. *Porro duorum* 35, qu. iii). But this prohibition has now ceased.

REPLY OBJ. 2: Although carnal intercourse is a cause of people being connected with one another, it is not the same kind of connection.

REPLY OBJ. 3: The wife contracts the same connection with her husband's relatives as to the degree, but not as to the kind of connection.

Since, however, the arguments in the contrary sense would seem to show that no tie is caused by affinity, we must reply to them lest the time-honored prohibition of the Church seem unreasonable.

REPLY OBJ. 4: As stated above, a woman does not contract affinity of the first kind with the man to whom she is united in the flesh, wherefore she does not contract affinity of the second kind with a woman known by the same man; and consequently if a man marry one of these women, the other does not contract affinity of the third kind with him. And so the laws of bygone times did not forbid the same man to marry successively two women known by one man.

REPLY OBJ. 5: As a man is not connected with his wife by affinity of the first kind, so he does not contract affinity of the second kind with the second husband of the same wife. Thus the argument does not proceed.

REPLY OBJ. 6: One person is not connected with me through another, except they be connected together. Hence through a woman who is affine to me, no person becomes connected with me except such as is connected with her. Now, this cannot be except through carnal procreation from her, or through connection with her by marriage; and according to the old legislation, I contracted some kind of connection through her in both ways: because her son even by another husband becomes affine to me in the same kind and in a different degree of affinity, as appears from the rule given above; and again her second husband becomes affine to me in the second kind of affinity. But her other blood relations are not connected with him, but she is connected with them, either as with father or mother, inasmuch as she descends from them, or, as with her brothers, as proceeding from the same principle; wherefore the brother or father of my affine does not become affine to me in any kind of affinity.

Article 6

Whether Affinity Is an Impediment to Matrimony?

AD SEXTUM SIC PROCEDITUR. Videtur quod affinitas matrimonium non impediat. Nihil enim impedit matrimonium nisi quod est illi contrarium. Sed affinitas non contrariatur matrimonio: cum sit effectus eius. Ergo non impedit matrimonium.

PRAETEREA, uxor per matrimonium efficitur res quaedam viri. Sed consanguinei defuncti viri succedunt in rebus eius. Ergo possunt succedere in uxore. Ad quam tamen manet affinitas, ut ostensum est. Ergo affinitas non impedit matrimonium.

SED CONTRA est quod dicitur Levit. 18: *turpitudinem uxoris patris tui non revelabis.* Sed illa est tantum affinis. Ergo affinitas impedit matrimonium.

RESPONDEO dicendum quod affinitas praecedens matrimonium impedit contrahendum et dirimit contractum: eadem ratione qua et consanguinitas. Sicut enim inest necessitas quaedam cohabitandi consanguineis ad invicem, ita et affinibus. Et sicut est quoddam amicitiae vinculum inter consanguineos, ita inter affines. Sed si affinitas matrimonio superveniat, non potest ipsum dirimere, ut supra dictum est.

AD PRIMUM ergo dicendum quod affinitas non contrariatur matrimonio ex quo causatur: Sed contrariatur matrimonio quod cum affine contrahendum esset, inquantum impediret multiplicationem amicitiae et concupiscentiae repressionem, quae per matrimonium quaeruntur.

AD SECUNDUM dicendum quod res possessae a viro non efficiuntur aliquid unum cum ipso viro, sicut uxor efficitur una caro cum ipso. Unde, sicut consanguinitas impedit coniunctionem ad virum, ita et ad uxorem viri.

OBJECTION 1: It would seem that affinity is not an impediment to marriage. For nothing is an impediment to marriage except what is contrary to it. But affinity is not contrary to marriage, since it is caused by it. Therefore, it is not an impediment to marriage.

OBJ. 2: Further, by marriage the wife becomes a possession of the husband. Now the husband's kindred inherit his possessions after his death. Therefore, they can succeed to his wife, although she is affine to them, as shown above (A. 5). Therefore, affinity is not an impediment to marriage.

ON THE CONTRARY, It is written: *you shall not uncover the nakedness of your father's wife* (Lev 18:8). Now, she is only affine. Therefore, affinity is an impediment to marriage.

I ANSWER THAT, Affinity that precedes marriage hinders marriage being contracted and voids the contract, for the same reason as consanguinity. For just as there is a certain need for blood relations to live together, so is there for those who are connected by affinity; and just as there is a tie of friendship between blood relations, so is there between those who are affine to one another. If, however, affinity supervene to matrimony, it cannot void the marriage, as stated above (Q. 50, A. 7).

REPLY OBJ. 1: Affinity is not contrary to the marriage which causes it, but to a marriage being contracted with an affine, insofar as the latter would hinder the extension of friendship and the curbing of concupiscence, which are sought in marriage.

REPLY OBJ. 2: The husband's possessions do not become one with him as the wife is made one flesh with him. Wherefore just as consanguinity is an impediment to marriage or union with the husband according to the flesh, so is one forbidden to marry the husband's wife.

Article 7

Whether Affinity in Itself Admits of Degrees?

AD SEPTIMUM SIC PROCEDITUR. Videtur quod affinitas habeat etiam per seipsam gradus. Cuiuslibet enim propinquitatis est accipere aliquos per se gradus. Sed affinitas propinquitas quaedam est. Ergo habet gradus per se, sine gradibus consanguinitatis, ex quibus causatur.

PRAETEREA, in littera dicitur quod *soboles secundae coniunctionis non potest transire ad consortium affinitatis prioris viri.* Sed hoc non esset nisi filius affinis etiam es-

OBJECTION 1: It would seem that affinity in itself admits of degrees. For any kind of nearness can itself be the subject of degrees. Now affinity is a kind of nearness. Therefore, it has degrees in itself apart from the degrees of consanguinity by which it is caused.

OBJ. 2: Further, it is stated in the text (*Sentences* IV, D. 41) that *the child of a second marriage could not take a consort from within the degrees of affinity of the first husband.*

set affinis. Ergo affinitas habet per se gradus, sicut consanguinitas.

Sed contra, affinitas ex consanguinitate causatur. Ergo et omnes gradus affinitatis causantur ex gradibus consanguinitatis. Et sic non habet per se aliquos gradus.

Respondeo dicendum quod res non dividitur divisione per se nisi ratione illius quod competit sibi secundum genus suum: sicut animal per rationale et irrationale, non autem per album et nigrum. Carnis autem propagatio per se comparatur ad consanguinitatem, quia ex ea immediate consanguinitatis vinculum contrahitur: sed ad affinitatem non comparatur nisi mediante consanguinitate, quae est causa eius. Unde, cum gradus attinentiae per propagationem carnis distinguantur, distinctio graduum per se et immediate competit consanguinitati, sed affinitati mediante consanguinitate. Et ideo ad inveniendum gradus affinitatis est regula generalis quod, quoto gradu consanguinitatis attinet mihi vir, toto gradu affinitatis attinet mihi uxor.

Ad primum ergo dicendum quod gradus in propinquitate attinentiae non possunt accipi nisi secundum ascensum et descensum propagationis. Ad quam non comparatur affinitas nisi mediante consanguinitate. Et ideo non habet affinitas gradus per se, sed sumptos iuxta gradus consanguinitatis.

Ad secundum dicendum quod filius affinis meae ex alio matrimonio, non per se loquendo, sed quasi per accidens dicebatur antiquitus affinis. Unde prohibebatur a matrimonio magis propter publicae honestatis iustitiam quam propter affinitatem. Et propter hoc etiam illa prohibitio nunc est revocata.

But this would not be the case unless the son of an affine were also affine. Therefore, affinity, like consanguinity, admits itself of degrees.

On the contrary, Affinity is caused by consanguinity. Therefore, all the degrees of affinity are caused by the degrees of consanguinity, and so it has no degrees of itself.

I answer that, A thing does not of itself admit of being divided except in reference to something belonging to it by reason of its genus: thus animal is divided into rational and irrational, and not into white and black. Now carnal procreation has a direct relation to consanguinity, because the tie of consanguinity is immediately contracted through it; whereas it has no relation to affinity except through consanguinity, which is the latter's cause. Therefore, since the degrees of relationship are distinguished in reference to carnal procreation, the distinction of degrees is directly and immediately referable to consanguinity, and to affinity through consanguinity. Hence the general rule in seeking the degrees of affinity is that in whatever degree of consanguinity I am related to the husband, in that same degree of affinity I am related to the wife.

Reply Obj. 1: The degrees in nearness of relationship can only be taken in reference to ascent and descent of propagation, to which affinity is compared only through consanguinity. Wherefore affinity has no direct degrees, but derives them according to the degrees of consanguinity.

Reply Obj. 2: Formerly it used to be said that the son of my affine by a second marriage was affine to me not directly, but accidentally, as it were; wherefore he was forbidden to marry on account of the justice of public honesty, rather than affinity. And for this reason this prohibition is now revoked.

Article 8

Whether the Degrees of Affinity Extend in the Same Way as the Degrees of Consanguinity?

Ad octavum sic proceditur. Videtur quod gradus affinitatis non extendantur sicut gradus consanguinitatis. Quia vinculum affinitatis est minus forte quam consanguinitatis: cum affinitas ex consanguinitate causetur in diversitate speciei, sicut a causa aequivoca. Sed quanto fortius est vinculum, tanto diutius durat. Ergo vinculum affinitatis non durat usque ad tot gradus ad quot durat consanguinitas.

Praeterea, ius humanum debet imitari ius divinum. Sed secundum ius divinum aliqui gradus consanguinitatis erant prohibiti in quibus gradibus affinitas matrimonium non impediebat: sicut patet de uxore fratris, quam aliquis poterat ducere in uxorem ipso defuncto, non tamen propriam sororem. Ergo et nunc non debet esse prohibitio aequalis de affinitate et consanguinitate.

Objection 1: It would seem that the degrees of affinity do not extend in the same way as the degrees of consanguinity. For the tie of affinity is less strong than the tie of consanguinity, since affinity arises from consanguinity in diversity of species, as from an equivocal cause. Now the stronger the tie, the longer it lasts. Therefore, the tie of affinity does not last to the same number of degrees as consanguinity.

Obj. 2: Further, human law should imitate divine law. Now, according to the divine law certain degrees of consanguinity were forbidden, in which degrees affinity was not an impediment to marriage; for example, a man could marry a brother's wife, though he could not marry her sister. Therefore, now too the prohibition of affinity and consanguinity should not extend to the same degrees.

SED CONTRA, ex hoc ipso est mihi aliqua affinis quod meo consanguineo est coniuncta. Ergo in quocumque gradu sit vir mihi consanguineus, in illo gradu erit uxor mihi affinis. Et sic gradus affinitatis computari debent in eodem numero sicut gradus consanguinitatis.

RESPONDEO dicendum quod ex quo gradus affinitatis sumuntur iuxta gradus consanguinitatis, oportet quod tot sint gradus affinitatis quot sunt gradus consanguinitatis. Sed tamen, quia affinitas est minus vinculum quam consanguinitas, facilius, et olim et nunc, dispensatio fit in remotis gradibus affinitatis quam in remotis gradibus consanguinitatis.

AD PRIMUM ergo dicendum quod illa minoritas vinculi affinitatis respectu consanguinitatis, facit varietatem in genere attinentiae, non in gradibus. Et ideo illa ratio non est ad propositum.

AD SECUNDUM dicendum quod frater non poterat accipere uxorem fratris sui defuncti nisi in casu, scilicet quando moriebatur sine prole, *ut suscitaret semen fratri suo*. Quod tunc requirebatur, quando per propagationem carnis cultus religionis multiplicabatur: quod nunc locum non habet. Et sic patet quod non ducebat eam uxorem quasi gerens propriam personam, sed quasi supplens defectum fratris sui.

ON THE CONTRARY, A woman is connected with me by affinity from the very fact that she is married to a blood relation of mine. Therefore, in whatever degree her husband is related to me by blood, she is related to me in that same degree by affinity; and so the degrees of affinity should be reckoned in the same number as the degrees of consanguinity.

I ANSWER THAT, Since the degrees of affinity are reckoned according to the degrees of consanguinity, the degrees of affinity must be the same in number as those of consanguinity. Nevertheless, affinity being a lesser tie than consanguinity, both formerly and now, a dispensation is more easily granted in the more remote degrees of affinity than in the remote degrees of consanguinity.

REPLY OBJ. 1: The fact that the tie of affinity is less than the tie of consanguinity causes a difference in the kind of relationship, but not in the degrees. Hence this argument is not to the point.

REPLY OBJ. 2: A man could not take his deceased brother's wife except *in order to raise up seed to his brother*, in the case when the latter died without issue. This was requisite at a time when religious worship was propagated by means of the propagation of the flesh, which is not the case now. Hence it is clear that he did not marry her in his own person, as it were, but as supplying the place of his brother.

Article 9

*Whether a Marriage Contracted by Affines or Blood
Relations Should Always Be Annulled by Divorce?*

AD NONUM SIC PROCEDITUR. Videtur quod coniugium quod inter affines vel consanguineos est contractum, non semper sit per divortium dirimendum. Quia *quos Deus coniunxit, homo separare non debet*. Cum ergo Deus facere intelligatur quod facit Ecclesia, quae quandoque tales ignoranter coniungit, videtur quod, si postmodum in notitiam veniant, non sunt separandi.

PRAETEREA, favorabilius est vinculum matrimonii quam dominii. Sed homo per longi temporis praescriptionem acquirit dominium in re cuius non erat dominus. Ergo per diuturnitatem temporis matrimonium ratificatur, etiam si prius ratum non fuit.

PRAETEREA, de similibus simile est iudicium. Sed si matrimonium esset dirimendum propter consanguinitatem, tunc, in casu illo quando duo fratres habent duas sorores in uxores, si unus separatur propter consanguinitatem, et alius pari ratione separari deberet. Quod non

OBJECTION 1: It would seem that a marriage contracted by persons within the degrees of affinity or consanguinity ought not always to be annulled by divorce. For *what God has joined together let no man put asunder* (Matt 19:6). Since, then, it is understood that what the Church does God does, and since the Church sometimes through ignorance joins such persons together, it would seem that if subsequently this came to knowledge they ought not to be separated.

OBJ. 2: Further, the tie of marriage is more favored than the tie of ownership. Now, after a long time a man may acquire by prescription the ownership of a thing of which he was not the owner. Therefore, by length of time a marriage becomes good in law, although it was not so before.

OBJ. 3: Further, of like things we judge alike. Now if a marriage ought to be annulled on account of consanguinity, in the case when two brothers marry two sisters, if one be separated on account of consanguinity, the other ought to be separated for the same reason. But this does not seem

videtur. Ergo matrimonium non est separandum propter consanguinitatem vel affinitatem.

SED CONTRA, consanguinitas et affinitas impediunt contrahendum et dirimunt contractum. Ergo, si probatur affinitas vel consanguinitas, separandi sunt, etiam si de facto contraxerunt.

RESPONDEO dicendum quod, cum omnis concubitus praeter legitimum matrimonium sit peccatum mortale, quod Ecclesia omnibus modis impedire conatur, ad ipsam pertinet eos inter quos non potest esse verum matrimonium, separare: et praecipue consanguineos et affines, qui sine incestu contrahere non possunt carnaliter.

AD PRIMUM ergo dicendum quod, quamvis Ecclesia dono et auctoritate divina fulciatur, tamen, inquantum est hominum congregatio, aliquid de defectu humano in actibus eius pervenit, quod non est divinum. Et ideo illa coniunctio quae fit in facie Ecclesiae impedimentis ignoratis, non habet inseparabilitatem ex auctoritate divina, sed est contra auctoritatem divinam errore hominum inducta: qui excusat a peccato, cum sit error facti, quandiu manet. Et propter hoc, quando impedimentum ad notitiam pervenit Ecclesiae, debet praedictam coniunctionem separare.

AD SECUNDUM dicendum quod illa quae sine peccato esse non possunt, nulla praescriptione firmantur: quia, ut Innocentius dicit, *diuturnitas temporis non minuit peccatum, sed auget*. Nec ad hoc facit aliquod favor matrimonii, quod inter illegitimas personas esse non poterat.

AD TERTIUM dicendum quod res inter alios acta, aliis non praeiudicat in foro contentioso. Unde, quamvis unus frater repellatur a matrimonio unius sororum ex causa consanguinitatis, non propter hoc separat Ecclesia aliud matrimonium, quod non accusatur. Sed in foro conscientiae non oportet quod semper obligetur ob hoc alius frater ad dimittendum uxorem suam: quia frequenter tales accusationes ex malevolentia procedunt, et per falsos testes probantur; unde non oportet quod conscientiam suam informet ex his quae circa aliud matrimonium sunt facta. Sed distinguendum videtur in hoc. Quia aut habet certam scientiam de impedimento matrimonii, aut opinionem, aut neutrum. Si primo modo, nec exigere nec reddere debitum debet; si secundo, debet reddere, sed non exigere; si tertio, potest reddere et exigere.

to happen. Therefore, a marriage ought not to be annulled on account of affinity or consanguinity.

ON THE CONTRARY, Consanguinity and affinity forbid the contracting of a marriage and void the contract. Therefore, if affinity or consanguinity be proved, the parties should be separated even though they have actually contracted marriage.

I ANSWER THAT, Since all copulation apart from lawful marriage is a mortal sin, which the Church uses all her endeavors to prevent, it belongs to her to separate those between whom there cannot be valid marriage, especially those related by blood or by affinity, who cannot without incest be united in the flesh.

REPLY OBJ. 1: Although the Church is upheld by God's gift and authority, yet insofar as she is an assembly of men there results in her acts something of human frailty which is not divine. Therefore, a union effected in the presence of the Church who is ignorant of an impediment is not indissoluble by divine authority, but is brought about contrary to divine authority through man's error, which, being an error of fact, excuses from sin as long as it remains. Hence when the impediment comes to the knowledge of the Church, she ought to sever the aforesaid union.

REPLY OBJ. 2: That which cannot be done without sin is not ratified by any prescription, for as Innocent III says (*Fourth Lateran Council*), *length of time does not diminish sin but increases it*; nor can it in any way legitimize a marriage which could not take place between unlawful persons.

REPLY OBJ. 3: In contentious suits between two persons the verdict does not prejudice a third party, wherefore although the one brother's marriage with the one sister is annulled on account of consanguinity, the Church does not therefore annul the other marriage against which no action is taken. Yet in the tribunal of the conscience the other brother ought not on this account always to be bound to put away his wife, because such accusations frequently proceed from ill-will, and are proved by false witnesses. Hence he is not bound to form his conscience on what has been done about the other marriage, but seemingly one ought to draw a distinction, because either he has certain knowledge of the impediment of his marriage, or he has an opinion about it, or he has neither. In the first case, he can neither seek nor pay the debt; in the second, he must pay, but not ask; in the third he can both pay and ask.

Article 10

*Whether One Should Proceed by Way of Accusation for the Annulment of a Marriage
Contracted Between Affines and Blood Relations?*

AD DECIMUM SIC PROCEDITUR. Videtur quod ad separationem matrimonii quod est inter affines et consanguineos contractum, non sit procedendum per viam accusationis. Quia accusationem praecedit inscriptio, qua aliquis se ad talionem obligat si in probatione defecerit. Sed haec non requiruntur quando de matrimonii separatione agitur. Ergo ibi locum non habet accusatio.

PRAETEREA, in causa matrimonii audiuntur solum propinqui, ut in littera dicitur. Sed in accusationibus audiuntur etiam extranei. Ergo in causa separationis matrimonii non agitur per viam accusationis.

PRAETEREA, si matrimonium accusari deberet, tunc praecipue hoc esset faciendum quando minus difficile est quod separetur. Sed hoc est quando sunt sponsalia tantum contracta. Non autem tunc accusatur matrimonium. Ergo nunquam de cetero debet fieri accusatio.

PRAETEREA, ad accusandum non praecluditur via alicui per hoc quod non statim accusat. Sed hoc fit in matrimonio: quia, si primo tacuit quando matrimonium contrahebatur, non potest postea matrimonium accusare, quasi suspectus. Ergo, etc.

SED CONTRA, omne illicitum potest accusari. Sed matrimonium affinium vel consanguineorum est illicitum. Ergo de eo potest esse accusatio.

RESPONDEO dicendum quod accusatio ad hoc est instituta ne aliquis sustineatur quasi innocens qui culpam habet. Sicut autem ex ignorantia facti contingit quod aliquis homo reputatur innocens qui in culpa est, ita ex ignorantia alicuius circumstantiae contingit quod aliquod factum reputatur licitum quod est illicitum. Et ideo, sicut homo accusatur quandoque, ita et factum ipsum accusari potest. Et sic matrimonium accusatur quando, propter ignorantiam impedimenti, aestimatur legitimum quod est illegitimum.

AD PRIMUM ergo dicendum quod obligatio ad poenam talionis habet locum quando accusatur persona, de crimine, quia tunc agitur ad punitionem eius. Sed quando accusatur factum, tunc non agitur ad poenam facientis, sed ad impediendum quod est illicitum. Et ideo in matrimonio accusator non se obligat ad aliquam poenam: sed talis accusatio potest et verbis et scripto fieri, ita quod exprimatur et persona accusans matrimonium quod accusatur, et impedimentum propter quod accusatur.

OBJECTION 1: It would seem that one ought not to proceed by way of accusation in order to sever a marriage contracted between persons related by affinity or consanguinity. For accusation is preceded by inscription, whereby a man binds himself to suffer the punishment of retaliation, if he fail to prove his accusation. But this is not required when a matrimonial separation is at issue. Therefore, accusation has no place there.

OBJ. 2: Further, in a matrimonial lawsuit only the relatives are heard, as stated in the text (*Sentences* IV, D. 41). But in accusations even strangers are heard. Therefore, in a suit for matrimonial separation the process is not by way of accusation.

OBJ. 3: Further, if a marriage ought to be denounced, this should be done especially where it is least difficult to sever the tie. Now this is when only the betrothal has been contracted, and then it is not the marriage that is denounced. Therefore, accusation should never take place at any other time.

OBJ. 4: Further, a man is not prevented from accusing by the fact that he does not accuse at once. But this happens in marriage, for if he was silent at first when the marriage was being contracted, he cannot denounce the marriage afterwards without laying himself open to suspicion. Therefore, etc.

ON THE CONTRARY, Everything unlawful may be accused. But a marriage of people related by affinity or consanguinity is unlawful. Therefore, an accusation can be made concerning it.

I ANSWER THAT, Accusation is instituted lest the guilty be tolerated as though they were innocent. Now just as it happens through ignorance of fact that a guilty man is reputed innocent, so it happens through ignorance of a circumstance that a certain fact is deemed lawful whereas it is unlawful. Wherefore just as a man is sometimes accused, so is a fact sometimes an object of accusation. It is in this way that a marriage is denounced, when through ignorance of an impediment it is deemed lawful whereas it is unlawful.

REPLY OBJ. 1: The punishment of retaliation takes place when a person is accused of a crime, because then action is taken that he may be punished. But when it is a deed that is accused, action is taken not for the punishment of the doer, but in order to prevent what is unlawful. Hence in a matrimonial suit the accuser does not bind himself to a punishment; but such an accusation can be made either in words or in writing, so that it expresses both the person accusing the marriage, and the impediment for which it is accused.

AD SECUNDUM dicendum quod extranei non possunt scire consanguinitatem nisi per consanguineos, de quibus probabilius est quod sciant. Unde, quando ipsi tacent, suspicio habetur, contra extraneum quod ex malevolentia procedat, nisi per consanguineos probare voluerit. Unde repellitur ab accusatione quando sunt consanguinei qui tacent, et per quod probare non potest. Sed consanguinei, quantumcumque sint propinqui, non repelluntur ab accusatione quando accusatur matrimonium propter aliquod impedimentum perpetuum, quod impedit contrahendum et dirimit contractum. Sed quando accusatur ex hoc quod dicitur non fuisse contractum, tunc parentes tanquam suspecti sunt repellendi: nisi ex parte illius qui est inferior dignitate et divitiis, de quibus probabiliter aestimari potest quod: libenter vellent quod matrimonium staret.

AD TERTIUM dicendum quod, quando matrimonium nondum est contractum, sed sponsalia tantum, non potest accusari, quia non accusatur quod non est. Sed potest denuntiari impedimentum, ne matrimonium contrahatur.

AD QUARTUM dicendum quod ille qui tacuit primo, quandoque auditur postea, si velit matrimonium accusare, quandoque repellitur. Quod patet ex Decretali, quae sic dicit: *si post contractum matrimonium: aliquis appareat accusator, cum non prodierit in publicum quando, secundum consuetudinem, in ecclesiis edebatur: utrum vox suae accusationis debeat admitti; merito quaeri potest. Super quo respondemus quod, si tempore denuntiationis praemissae is qui iam coniunctos impetit, extra dioecesim existebat, vel alias denunciatio non potuit ad eius devenire notitiam, ut puta si nimiae infirmitatis fervore laborans sanae mentis patiebatur exilium, vel in annis erat tam teneris constitutus quod ad comprehensionem talium eius aetas sufficere non valebat, seu alia causa legitima fuerit impeditus, eius accusatio debet audiri. Alioquin, tanquam suspectus est procul dubio repellendus: nisi firmaverit iuramento quod post didicerit ea quae obiecerit, et ad hoc ex malitia non procedat.*

REPLY OBJ. 2: Strangers cannot know of the consanguinity except from the relatives, since these know with greater probability. Hence when these are silent, a stranger is liable to be suspected of acting from ill-will unless he wish the relatives to prove his assertion. Wherefore a stranger is debarred from accusing when there are relatives who are silent, and by whom he cannot prove his accusation. On the other hand, the relatives, however nearly related they be, are not debarred from accusing when the marriage is denounced on account of a perpetual impediment, which prevents the contracting of the marriage and voids the contract. When, however, the accusation is based on a denial of the contract having taken place, the parents should be debarred from witnessing as being liable to suspicion, except those of the party that is inferior in rank and wealth, for they, one is inclined to think, would be willing for the marriage to stand.

REPLY OBJ. 3: If the marriage is not yet contracted and there is only a betrothal, there can be no accusation, for what is not, cannot be accused. But the impediment can be denounced lest the marriage be contracted.

REPLY OBJ. 4: He who is silent at first is sometimes heard afterwards if he wish to denounce the marriage, and sometimes he is repulsed. This is made clear by the Decretal which runs as follows: *if an accuser present himself after the marriage has been contracted, since he did not declare himself when according to custom the banns were published in church, we may rightly ask whether he should be allowed to voice his accusation. In this matter we deem that a distinction should be made, so that if he who lodges information against persons already married was absent from the diocese at the time of the aforesaid publication, or if for some other reason this could not come to his knowledge—for instance, if through exceeding stress of weakness and fever he was not in possession of his faculties, or was of so tender years as to be too young to understand such matters, or if he were hindered by some other lawful cause—his accusation should be heard. Otherwise without doubt he should be repulsed as open to suspicion, unless he swear that the information lodged by him came to his knowledge subsequently and that he is not moved by ill-will to make his accusation.*

Article 11

Whether in a Suit of This Kind One Should Proceed by Hearing Witnesses, as in Other Suits?

AD UNDECIMUM SIC PROCEDITUR. Videtur quod in tali causa non sit procedendum per testes, sicut in aliis causis. Quia in aliis causis adducuntur ad testificandum quicumque sunt omni exceptione maiores. Sed hic non

OBJECTION 1: It would seem that in such a suit one ought not to proceed by hearing witnesses, in the same way as in other suits. For in other suits, any witnesses whatever may be called, provided they be unexceptionable. But here

admittuntur extranei, quamvis sint omni exceptione maiores. Ergo, etc.

PRAETEREA, testes suspecti de privato odio vel amore a testimonio repelluntur. Sed maxime possunt propinqui esse suspecti de amore respectu unius partis et odio ad partem alteram. Ergo non est audiendum eorum testimonium.

PRAETEREA, matrimonium est favorabilius quam aliae causae, in quibus de rebus pure corporalibus agitur. Sed in illis non potest idem esse testis et accusator. Ergo nec in matrimonio. Et ita videtur quod non convenienter in causa ista per testes procedatur.

SED CONTRA, testes inducuntur in causis ut super his de quibus dubitatur fiat iudici fides. Sed ita facienda est iudici fides in causa ista sicut in aliis causis: quia non debet praecipitare sententiam de eo quod non constat. Ergo procedendum est hic ex testibus, sicut in aliis causis.

RESPONDEO dicendum quod in hac causa oportet quod per testes veritas patefiat, sicut et in aliis. Tamen, ut iuristae dicunt, in hac causa multa specialia inveniuntur: scilicet, quod idem potest esse accusator et testis; et quod non iuratur de calumnia, cum sit causa quasi spiritualis; et quod consanguinei admittuntur ad testificandum, et quod non observatur omnino ordo iudiciarius quia, tali denuntiatione facta, contumax potest excommunicari lite non contestata; et valet hic testimonium de auditu; et post publicationem testium testes possunt induci. Et hoc totum est ut peccatum impediatur, quod in tali coniunctione esse potest.

ET PER HOC patet solutio ad obiecta.

strangers are not admitted, although they be unexceptionable. Therefore, etc.

OBJ. 2: Further, witnesses who are suspected of private hatred or love are debarred from giving evidence. Now relatives are especially open to suspicion of love for one party, and hatred for the other. Therefore, their evidence should not be taken.

OBJ. 3: Further, marriage is a more favorable suit than those others in which purely corporeal questions are at stake. Now in these the same person cannot be both accuser and witness. Neither, therefore, can this be in a matrimonial suit; and so it would appear that it is not right to proceed by hearing witnesses in a suit of this kind.

ON THE CONTRARY, Witnesses are called in a suit in order to give the judge evidence concerning matters of doubt. Now evidence should be afforded the judge in this suit as in other suits, since he must not pronounce a hasty judgment on what is not proven. Therefore, here as in other lawsuits witnesses should be called.

I ANSWER THAT, In this kind of lawsuit as in others, truth must be unveiled by witnesses. Yet, as the lawyers say, there are many things peculiar to this suit: namely, that the same person can be accuser and witness; that evidence is not taken on oath of calumny, since it is a quasi-spiritual lawsuit; that relatives are allowed as witnesses; that the juridical order is not perfectly observed, since if the denunciation has been made, and the suit is uncontested, the defendant may be excommunicated if contumacious; that hearsay evidence is admitted; and that witnesses may be called after the publication of the names of the witnesses. All this is in order to prevent the sin that may occur in such a union (*Decretals*).

THIS SUFFICES for the replies to the objections.

QUESTION 56

THE IMPEDIMENT OF SPIRITUAL RELATIONSHIP

Deinde considerandum est de impedimento cognationis spiritualis.

Circa quod quaeruntur quinque.

Primo: utrum spiritualis cognatio matrimonium impediat.

Secundo: ex qua causa contrahatur.

Tertio: inter quos.

Quarto: utrum transeat a viro in uxorem.

Quinto: utrum transeat ad filios carnales patris spiritualis.

We must now consider the impediment of spiritual relationship.

Under this head there are five points of inquiry:

(1) Whether spiritual relationship is an impediment to marriage?

(2) From what cause is it contracted?

(3) Between whom?

(4) Whether it passes from husband to wife?

(5) Whether it passes to the father's carnal children?

Article 1

Whether Spiritual Relationship Is an Impediment to Marriage?

AD PRIMUM SIC PROCEDITUR. Videtur quod spiritualis cognatio matrimonium non impediat. Nihil enim impedit matrimonium, nisi quod contrariatur alicui bono matrimonii. Sed spiritualis cognatio non contrariatur alicui bono matrimonii. Ergo non impedit matrimonium.

PRAETEREA, impedimentum perpetuum matrimonii non potest stare simul cum matrimonio. Sed cognatio spiritualis stat simul aliquando cum matrimonio, ut in littera dicitur: sicut cum aliquis in casu necessitatis filium suum baptizat; quia tunc fit uxori suae spirituali cognatione coniunctus, nec tamen matrimonium separatur. Ergo spiritualis cognatio matrimonium non impedit.

PRAETEREA, unio spiritus non transit in carnem. Sed matrimonium est carnalis coniunctio. Ergo, cum cognatio spiritualis sit unio spiritus, non potest transire ad matrimonium impediendum.

PRAETEREA, contrariorum non sunt iidem effectus. Sed spiritualis cognatio videtur esse contraria disparitati cultus: cum spiritualis cognatio sit *propinquitas proveniens ex datione sacramenti, vel tensione ad idem*; disparitas autem cultus consistit in sacramenti carentia, ut prius dictum est. Cum ergo disparitas cultus matrimonium impediat, videtur quod spiritualis cognatio non habeat hunc effectum.

SED CONTRA: Quanto aliquod vinculum sanctius est, tanto magis est custodiendum. Sed vinculum spirituale est sanctius quam corporale. Cum ergo vinculum propinquitatis corporalis matrimonium impediat, videtur etiam quod cognatio, spiritualis idem faciat.

OBJECTION 1: It would seem that spiritual relationship is not an impediment to marriage. For nothing is an impediment to marriage save what is contrary to a marriage good. Now spiritual relationship is not contrary to a marriage good. Therefore, it is not an impediment to marriage.

OBJ. 2: Further, a perpetual impediment to marriage cannot stand together with marriage. But spiritual relationship sometimes stands together with marriage, as stated in the text (*Sentences* IV, D. 42), as when a man in a case of necessity baptizes his own child, for then he contracts a spiritual relationship with his wife, and yet the marriage is not dissolved. Therefore, spiritual relationship is not an impediment to marriage.

OBJ. 3: Further, union of the spirit does not pass to the flesh. But marriage is a union of the flesh. Therefore, since spiritual relationship is a union of the spirit, it cannot become an impediment to marriage.

OBJ. 4: Further, contraries have not the same effects. Now spiritual relationship is apparently contrary to disparity of worship, since spiritual relationship is a *kinship resulting from the giving of a sacrament or the intention of so doing*, whereas disparity of worship consists in the lack of a sacrament, as stated above (Q. 50, A. 1). Since, then, disparity of worship is an impediment to matrimony, it would seem that spiritual relationship has not this effect.

ON THE CONTRARY, The holier the bond, the more is it to be safeguarded. Now a spiritual bond is holier than a bodily tie, and since the tie of bodily kinship is an impediment to marriage, it follows that spiritual relationship should also be an impediment.

PRAETEREA, in matrimonio coniunctio animarum est principalior quam coniunctio corporum: quia praecedit ipsam. Ergo multo fortius spiritualis cognatio matrimonium impedire potest quam carnalis.

RESPONDEO dicendum quod, sicut per carnalem propagationem homo accipit esse naturae, ita per sacramenta accipit esse spiritualis gratiae. Unde, sicut vinculum quod ex carnis propagatione contrahitur, est homini naturale inquantum est res quaedam naturae; ita vinculum quod contrahitur ex, sacramentorum susceptione, est aliquo modo naturale alicui inquantum est membrum Ecclesiae. Et ideo, sicut carnalis cognatio impedit matrimonium, ita spiritualis, ex Ecclesiae statuto.

Tamen distinguendum est de spirituali cognatione. Quia aut praecessit matrimonium; aut sequitur. Si praecessit, impedit contrahendum et dirimit contractum. Si sequitur, tunc non dirimit vinculum matrimonii: sed quantum, ad actum matrimonii est distinguendum. Quia aut spiritualis cognatio inducitur causa necessitatis, sicut cum pater baptizat filium in articulo mortis. Et tunc non impedit actum matrimonii ex neutra parte. Aut inducitur extra casum necessitatis, ex ignorantia tamen. Et tunc, si ille ex cuius actu inducitur, diligentiam adhibuit, est eadem ratio sicut et de primo. Aut ex industria, extra casum necessitatis. Et tunc ille ex cuius actu inducitur, amittit ius petendi debitum: sed tamen debet reddere, quia ex culpa eius non debet aliquod incommodum alius reportare.

AD PRIMUM ergo dicendum quod, quamvis spiritualis cognatio non impediat aliquod de principalibus bonis matrimonii, tamen impedit aliquod de secundariis bonis, quod est amicitiae multiplicatio. Quia spiritualis cognatio est sufficiens ratio amicitiae per se. Unde oportet quod ad alios per matrimonium familiaritas et amicitia quaeratur.

AD SECUNDUM dicendum quod matrimonium est vinculum perpetuum. Et ideo nullum impedimentum superveniens potest ipsum dirimere. Et sic quandoque contingit quod matrimonium et matrimonii impedimentum stant simul: non autem si impedimentum praecedat.

AD TERTIUM dicendum quod in matrimonio non est tantum coniunctio corporalis, sed etiam spiritualis. Et ideo propinquitas spiritus ei impedimentum praestat, sine hoc quod propinquitas spiritualis transire debeat in carnalem.

AD QUARTUM dicendum quod non est inconveniens quod duo contraria ad invicem contrarientur eidem: sicut magnum et parvum aequali. Et sic disparitas cultus et spiritualis cognatio matrimonio repugnant: quia in uno est maior distantia, in altero maior propinquitas

FURTHER, In marriage the union of souls ranks higher than union of bodies, for it precedes it. Therefore, with much more reason can a spiritual relationship hinder marriage than bodily relationship does.

I ANSWER THAT, Just as by carnal procreation man receives natural being, so by the sacraments he receives the spiritual being of grace. Wherefore just as the tie that is contracted by carnal procreation is natural to man, inasmuch as he is a natural being, so the tie that is contracted from the reception of the sacraments is after a fashion natural to man, inasmuch as he is a member of the Church. Therefore, as carnal relationship hinders marriage, even so does spiritual relationship by command of the Church.

We must, however, draw a distinction in reference to spiritual relationship, since either it precedes or follows marriage. If it precedes, it hinders the contracting of marriage and voids the contract. If it follows, it does not dissolve the marriage bond, but we must draw a further distinction in reference to the marriage act. For either the spiritual relationship is contracted in a case of necessity, as when a father baptizes his child who is at the point of death, and then it is not an obstacle to the marriage act on either side; or it is contracted without any necessity and through ignorance, in which case if the person whose action has occasioned the relationship acted with due caution, it is the same with him as in the former case; or it is contracted purposely and without any necessity, and then the person whose action has occasioned the relationship loses the right to ask for the debt, but is bound to pay if asked, because the fault of the one party should not be prejudicial to the other.

REPLY OBJ. 1: Although spiritual relationship does not hinder any of the chief marriage goods, it hinders one of the secondary goods, namely, the extension of friendship, because spiritual relationship is by itself a sufficient reason for friendship; wherefore intimacy and friendship with other persons need to be sought by means of marriage.

REPLY OBJ. 2: Marriage is a perpetual bond, wherefore no supervening impediment can sever it. Hence it happens sometimes that marriage and an impediment to marriage stand together, but not if the impediment precedes.

REPLY OBJ. 3: In marriage there is not only a bodily but also a spiritual union, and consequently kinship of spirit proves an impediment thereto, without spiritual kinship having to pass into a bodily relationship.

REPLY OBJ. 4: There is nothing unreasonable in two things that are contrary to one another being contrary to the same thing, as great and small are contrary to equal. Thus disparity of worship and spiritual relationship are opposed to marriage, because in one the distance is greater,

quam matrimonium requirat. Et ideo ex utraque parte matrimonium impeditur.

and in the other less, than required by marriage. Hence there is an impediment to marriage in either case.

Article 2

Whether Spiritual Relationship Is Contracted by Baptism Only?

AD SECUNDUM SIC PROCEDITUR. Videtur quod per solum baptismum spiritualis propinquitas contrahatur. Sicut enim se habet corporalis cognatio ad corporalem generationem, ita spiritualis ad spiritualem. Sed solus baptismus dicitur spiritualis generatio. Ergo per solum baptismum contrahitur spiritualis cognatio: sicut et per solam generationem carnalem carnalis cognatio.

PRAETEREA, sicut in confirmatione imprimitur character, ita in ordine. Sed ex susceptione ordinis non sequitur spiritualis cognatio. Ergo nec ex confirmatione. Et sic solum ex baptismo.

PRAETEREA, sacramenta sunt digniora sacramentalibus. Sed ex quibusdam sacramentis spiritualibus cognatio non sequitur: sicut patet in extrema unctione. Ergo multo minus ex catechismo, ut quidam dicunt.

PRAETEREA, inter sacramentalia baptismi multa alia praeter catechismum numerantur . Ergo ex catechismo non magis contrahitur spiritualis cognatio quam ex aliis.

PRAETEREA, oratio non est minus efficax ad promovendum in bonum quam instructio vel catechizatio. Sed ex oratione non contrahitur spiritualis cognatio. Ergo nec ex catechismo.

PRAETEREA, instructio quae fit baptizatis per praedicationem, non minus valet quam illa quae fit nondum baptizatis. Sed ex praedicatione non contrahitur aliqua cognatio spiritualis. Ergo nec ex catechismo.

SED CONTRA: I Cor. 4: *in Christo Iesu per Evangelium ego vos genui*: et sic spiritualis generatio causat spiritualem cognationem. Ergo ex praedicatione Evangelii et instructione fit spiritualis cognatio: et non solum ex baptismo.

PRAETEREA, sicut per baptismum tollitur peccatum originale, ita per poenitentiam actuale. Ergo, sicut baptismus causat spiritualem cognationem, ita et poenitentia.

PRAETEREA, 'pater' nomen cognationis est. Sed per poenitentiam et doctrinam et curam pastoralem, et multa huiusmodi, aliquis dicitur alteri spiritualis pater. Ergo ex multis aliis praeter baptismum et confirmationem spiritualis cognatio contrahitur.

RESPONDEO dicendum quod circa hoc est triplex opinio. Quidam enim dicunt quod spiritualis regeneratio, sicut per septiformem Spiritus Sancti gratiam datur,

OBJECTION 1: It would seem that spiritual relationship is contracted by baptism only. For as bodily kinship is to bodily birth, so is spiritual kinship to spiritual birth. Now baptism alone is called spiritual birth. Therefore, spiritual kinship is contracted by baptism only, even as only by carnal birth is carnal kinship contracted.

OBJ. 2: Further, a character is imprinted in holy orders as in confirmation. But spiritual relationship does not result from receiving holy orders. Therefore, it does not result from confirmation but only from baptism.

OBJ. 3: Further, sacraments are more excellent than sacramentals. Now spiritual relationship does not result from certain sacraments, for instance, from extreme unction. Much less, therefore, does it result from catechizing, as some maintain.

OBJ. 4: Further, many other sacramentals are attached to baptism besides catechizing. Therefore, spiritual relationship is not contracted from catechism any more than from the others.

OBJ. 5: Further, prayer is no less efficacious than instruction of catechism for advancement in good. But spiritual relationship does not result from prayer. Therefore, it does not result from catechism.

OBJ. 6: Further, the instruction given to the baptized by preaching to them avails no less than preaching to those who are not yet baptized. But no spiritual relationship results from preaching. Neither, therefore, does it result from catechism.

OBJ. 7: On the other hand, it is written: *in Christ Jesus by the gospel I have begotten you* (1 Cor 4:15). Now spiritual birth causes spiritual relationship. Therefore, spiritual relationship results from the preaching of the gospel and instruction, and not only from baptism.

OBJ. 8: Further, as original sin is taken away by baptism, so is actual sin taken away by penance. Therefore, just as baptism causes spiritual relationship, so also does penance.

OBJ. 9: Further, 'father' denotes relationship. Now, a man is called another's spiritual father in respect of penance, teaching, pastoral care, and many other like things. Therefore, spiritual relationship is contracted from many other sources besides baptism and confirmation.

I ANSWER THAT, There are three opinions on this question. Some say that as spiritual regeneration is bestowed by the sevenfold grace of the Holy Spirit, it is caused by means

ita per septem efficitur, incipiendo a primo pabulo salis sacri usque ad confirmationem per episcopum factam: et per quodlibet horum septem spiritualis cognatio contrahitur. Sed illud non videtur rationabile. Quia cognatio carnalis non contrahitur nisi per actum generationis completum: unde etiam affinitas non contrahitur nisi facta commixtione seminum ex qua potest sequi generatio carnalis. Spiritualis autem generatio non perficitur nisi per aliquod sacramentum. Et ideo inconveniens est quod spiritualis cognatio contrahatur nisi per aliquod sacramentum.

Et ideo alii dicunt quod per tria tantum sacramenta spiritualis cognatio contrahitur, scilicet per catechismum, baptismum et confirmationem. Sed isti propriam vocem videntur ignorare: quia catechismus non est sacramentum, sed sacramentale.

Et ideo alii dicunt quod tantum per duo sacramenta contrahitur, scilicet per confirmationem et baptismum. Et haec opinio est communior. Tamen de catechismo quidam horum dicunt quod est debile impedimentum: quia impedit contrahendum, sed non dirimit matrimonium contractum.

Ad primum ergo dicendum quod duplex est carnalis nativitas. Prima in utero: in qua adhuc quod natum est, est adeo debile quod non possit extra exponi sine periculo. Et huic nativitati similatur regeneratio per baptismum, in quo regeneratur aliquis adhuc quasi fovendus intra uterum Ecclesiae. Secunda est nativitas ex utero: quando iam id quod natum erat in utero, tantum roboratum est quod potest sine periculo exponi exterioribus, quae nata sunt corrumpere. Et huic assimilatur confirmatio, per quam homo roboratus exponitur in publicum ad confessionem nominis Christi. Et ideo congrue per utrumque istorum sacramentorum contrahitur spiritualis cognatio.

Ad secundum dicendum quod per ordinis sacramentum non fit aliqua regeneratio, sed quaedam promotio potestatis. Et propterea mulier non suscipit ordinem. Et sic non potest ex hoc aliquod impedimentum praestari matrimonio. Et ideo talis cognatio non computatur.

Ad tertium dicendum quod in catechismo fit quaedam professio futuri baptismi: sicut in sponsalibus quaedam sponsio futurarum nuptiarum. Unde, sicut in sponsalibus contrahitur quidam modus propinquitatis, ita et in catechismo, ad minus impediens contrahendum, ut quidam dicunt. Non tamen in aliis sacramentis.

Ad quartum dicendum quod talis professio fidei non fit in aliis sacramentalibus baptismi sicut in catechismo. Et ideo non est similis ratio.

Et similiter dicendum ad quintum, de oratione; et ad sextum, de praedicatione.

of seven things, beginning with the first taste of blessed salt and ending with confirmation given by the bishop; and they say that spiritual relationship is contracted by each of these seven things. But this does not seem reasonable, for carnal relationship is not contracted except by a perfect act of generation. Hence affinity is not contracted except there be mingling of seeds, from which it is possible for carnal generation to follow. Now spiritual generation is not perfected except by a sacrament; wherefore it does not seem fitting for spiritual relationship to be contracted otherwise than through a sacrament.

Hence others say that spiritual relationship is only contracted through three sacraments, namely, catechism, baptism, and confirmation, but these do not apparently know the meaning of what they say, since catechism is not a sacrament but a sacramental.

Wherefore others say that it is contracted through two sacraments only, namely, confirmation and baptism, and this is the more common opinion. Some, however, of these say that catechism is a weak impediment, since it hinders the contracting of marriage but does not void the contract.

Reply Obj. 1: Carnal birth is twofold. The first is in the womb, wherein that which is born is a weakling and cannot come forth without danger; and to this birth regeneration by baptism is likened, wherein a man is regenerated as though yet needing to be fostered in the womb of the Church. The second is birth from the womb, when that which was born in the womb is so far strengthened that it can without danger face the outer world, which has a natural corruptive tendency. To this is likened confirmation, whereby man being strengthened goes forth abroad to confess the name of Christ. Hence spiritual relationship is fittingly contracted through both these sacraments.

Reply Obj. 2: The effect of the sacrament of holy orders is not regeneration but the bestowal of power, for which reason it is not conferred on women, and consequently no impediment to marriage can arise therefrom. Hence this kind of relationship does not count.

Reply Obj. 3: In catechism one makes a profession of future baptism, just as in betrothal one enters an engagement of future marriage. Wherefore just as in betrothal a certain kind of propinquity is contracted, so is there in catechism, whereby marriage is rendered at least unlawful, as some say; but not in the other sacraments.

Reply Obj. 4: There is not made a profession of faith in the other sacramentals of baptism, as in catechism; wherefore the comparison fails.

The same answer applies to the fifth and sixth objections.

AD SEPTIMUM dicendum quod Apostolus eos ad fidem instruxerat per modum catechismi. Et sic aliquo modo talis instructio habebat ordinem ad spiritualem generationem.

AD OCTAVUM dicendum quod per sacramentum poenitentiae non contrahitur, proprie loquendo, spiritualis cognatio. Unde filius sacerdotis potest contrahere cum illa quam sacerdos in confessione audit: alias filius sacerdotis non inveniret in tota una parochia mulierem cum qua; contraheret. Nec obstat quod per poenitentiam tollitur peccatum actuale. Quia hoc non est per modum regenerationis, sed magis per modum sanationis.

Sed tamen per poenitentiam contrahitur quoddam foedus inter mulierem et sacerdotem confitentem, spirituali cognationi simile: ut tantum peccet eam carnaliter cognoscens ac si esset sua spiritualis filia. Et hoc ideo quia maxima familiaritas est inter sacerdotem et confitentem: et ob hoc ista prohibitio est inducta, ut tollatur peccandi occasio.

AD NONUM dicendum quod pater spiritualis dicitur ad similitudinem patris carnalis. Pater autem carnalis, ut Philosophus dicit, in VIII *Ethic.*, tria dat filio: *esse, nutrimentum et instructionem.* Et ideo spiritualis pater aliquis alicuius dicitur ratione alicuius horum trium. Tamen ex hoc quod est spiritualis pater non habet spiritualem cognationem, nisi conveniat cum patre quantum ad generationem, per quam est esse.

ET SIC etiam potest solvi octavum, quod praecessit.

REPLY OBJ. 7: The Apostle had instructed them in the faith by a kind of catechism; and consequently his instruction was directed to their spiritual birth.

REPLY OBJ. 8: Properly speaking, a spiritual relationship is not contracted through the sacrament of penance. Therefore, a priest's son can marry a woman whose confession the priest has heard, else in the whole parish he could not find a woman whom he could marry. Nor does it matter that by penance actual sin is taken away, for this is not a kind of birth, but a kind of healing.

Nevertheless, penance occasions a kind of bond between the woman penitent and the priest that has a resemblance to spiritual relationship, so that if he have carnal intercourse with her, he sins as grievously as if she were his spiritual daughter. The reason of this is that the relations between priest and penitent are most intimate, and consequently in order to remove the occasion of sin this prohibition (*Decretals*) was made.

REPLY OBJ. 9: A spiritual father is so called from his likeness to a carnal father. Now as the Philosopher says (*Ethics* 8.2) a carnal father gives his child three things, *being, nourishment, and instruction*; and consequently a person's spiritual father is so called from one of these three things. Nevertheless he has not, through being his spiritual father, a spiritual relationship with him, unless he is like a carnal father as to generation, which is the way to being.

THIS SOLUTION may also be applied to the foregoing eighth objection.

Article 3

Whether Spiritual Relationship Is Contracted Between the Person Baptized and the Person Who Raises Him From the Sacred Font?

AD TERTIUM SIC PROCEDITUR. Videtur quod cognatio spiritualis non contrahatur inter suscipientem sacramentum baptismi et levantem de sacro fonte. Quia in generatione carnali contrahitur propinquitas solum ex parte eius ex cuius; semine generatur proles, non autem ex parte eius qui puerum natum suscipit. Ergo nec spiritualis cognatio contrahitur inter eum qui suscipit de sacro fonte et eum qui suscipitur.

PRAETEREA, ille qui in sacro fonte levat, *anadochus* a Dionysio dicitur, et ad eius officium spectat puerum instruere. Sed instructio non est suffiens causa spiritualis cognationis, ut dictum est. Ergo nulla cognatio contrahitur inter eum et illum qui de sacro fonte levatur.

PRAETEREA, potest contingere quod aliquis levet aliquem de sacro fonte antequam ipse sit baptizatus. Sed ex

OBJECTION 1: It would seem that spiritual relationship is not contracted between the person baptized and the person who raises him from the sacred font. For in carnal generation, carnal relationship is contracted only on the part of the person of whose seed the child is born, and not on the part of the person who receives the child after birth. Therefore, neither is spiritual relationship contracted between the receiver and the received at the sacred font.

OBJ. 2: Further, he who raises a person from the sacred font is called *anadochos* by Dionysius (*On the Ecclesiastical Hierarchies* 2), and it is part of his office to instruct the child. But instruction is not a sufficient cause of spiritual relationship, as stated above (A. 2). Therefore, no relationship is contracted between him and the person whom he raises from the sacred font.

OBJ. 3: Further, it may happen that someone raises a person from the sacred font before he himself is baptized.

hoc non contrahitur aliqua spiritualis cognatio: quia ille qui non est baptizatus, non est capax alicuius spiritualitatis. ergo aliquem levare de sacro fonte non sufficit ad spiritualem cognationem contrahendam.

Sed contra est definitio spiritualis cognationis supra inducta; et auctoritates quae ponuntur in littera.

Respondeo dicendum quod, sicut iri generatione carnali aliquis nascitur ex matre et patre, ita in generatione spirituali aliquis renascitur filius Dei sicut patris et Ecclesiae sicut matris. Sicut autem ille qui sacramentum confert, gerit personam Dei, cuius instrumentum et minister est; ita ille qui baptizatum suscipit de sacro fonte, aut confirmandum tenet, gerit personam Ecclesiae. Unde ad utrumque spiritualis cognatio contrahitur.

Ad primum ergo dicendum quod non tantum pater, ex cuius semine generatur proles, habet cognationem carnalem ad natum; sed etiam mater, quae materiam subministrat, et in cuius utero generatur. Et ita etiam anadochus, qui baptizandum vice totius Ecclesiae offert et suscipit, et confirmandum tenet, spiritualem cognationem contrahit.

Ad secundum dicendum quod non ratione instructionis debitae, sed ratione generationis spiritualis, ad quam cooperatur, cognationem spiritualem contrahit.

Ad tertium dicendum quod non-baptizatus non potest aliquem levare de sacro fonte: cum non sit membrum Ecclesiae, cuius typum gerit in baptismo suscipiens. Quamvis possit baptizare: quia est creatura Dei, cuius typum gerit baptizans. Nec tamen aliquam cognationem spiritualem contrahere potest: quia est expers spiritualis vitae, in quam homo primo per baptismum nascitur.

Now spiritual relationship is not contracted in such a case, since one who is not baptized is not capable of spirituality. Therefore, raising a person from the sacred font is not sufficient to contract a spiritual relationship.

On the contrary, There is the definition of spiritual relationship quoted above (A. 1), as also the authorities mentioned in the text (*Sentences* IV, D. 42).

I answer that, Just as in carnal generation a person is born of a father and mother, so in spiritual generation a person is born again a son of God as father, and of the Church as mother. Now, while he who confers the sacrament stands in the place of God, whose instrument and minister he is, he who raises a baptized person from the sacred font or holds the candidate for confirmation stands in the place of the Church. Therefore, spiritual relationship is contracted with both.

Reply Obj. 1: Not only the father, of whose seed the child is born, is related carnally to the child, but also the mother who provides the matter, and in whose womb the child is begotten. So too the godparent, who, in place of the Church, offers and raises the candidate for baptism and holds the candidate for confirmation, contracts spiritual relationship.

Reply Obj. 2: He contracts spiritual relationship not by reason of the instruction it is his duty to give, but on account of the spiritual birth in which he cooperates.

Reply Obj. 3: A person who is not baptized cannot raise anyone from the sacred font, since he is not a member of the Church whom the godparent in baptism represents, although he can baptize because he is a creature of God, whom the baptizer represents. And yet he cannot contract a spiritual relationship, since he is void of spiritual life to which man is first born by receiving baptism.

Article 4

Whether Spiritual Relationship Passes From Husband to Wife?

Ad quartum sic proceditur. Videtur quod cognatio spiritualis non transeat a viro in uxorem. Quia spiritualis unio et corporalis sunt disparatae et diversorum generum. Ergo, mediante carnali coniunctione, quae inter virum et uxorem est, non transitur ad spiritualem cognationem.

Praeterea, magis conveniunt in spirituali generatione, quae est causa spiritualis cognationis, pater et mater spiritualis quam vir qui est spiritualis pater et uxor. Sed pater et mater spiritualis nullam ex hoc spiritualem cognationem contrahunt. Ergo nec uxor contrahit aliquam spiritualem cognationem ex hoc quod vir eius fit pater spiritualis alicuius.

Objection 1: It would seem that spiritual relationship does not pass from husband to wife. For spiritual and bodily union are disparate and differ generically. Therefore, carnal union which is between husband and wife cannot be the means of contracting a spiritual relationship.

Obj. 2: Further, the godfather and godmother have more in common in the spiritual birth, that is the cause of spiritual relationship, than a husband who is godfather has with his wife. Now godfather and godmother do not hereby contract spiritual relationship. Therefore, neither does a wife contract a spiritual relationship through her husband being godfather to someone.

PRAETEREA, potest contingere quod vir est baptizatus et uxor non est baptizata: sicut quando unus est ab infidelitate conversus sine alterius coniugis conversione. Sed spiritualis cognatio non potest pervenire ad nonbaptizatum. Ergo non transit semper de viro ad uxorem.

PRAETEREA, vir et uxor possunt aliquem simul de fonte levare. Si ergo spiritualis cognatio a viro transiret in uxorem, sequeretur quod uterque coniugum esset bis pater et mater spiritualis eiusdem. Quod est inconveniens.

SED CONTRA, bona spiritualia magis multiplicabilia sunt quam corporalia. Sed consanguinitas corporalis viri transit ad uxorem per affinitatem. Ergo multo magis spiritualis cognatio.

RESPONDEO dicendum quod aliquis potest fieri alicuius compater dupliciter. Uno modo, per actum alterius, qui baptizat vel in baptismo suscipit filium eius. Et sic cognatio spiritualis non transit a viro in uxorem: nisi forte ille sit filius uxoris, quia tunc directe uxor contrahit cognationem spiritualem, sicut et vir.

Alio modo, per actum proprium: sicut cum levat filium alterius de sacro fonte. Et sic cognatio spiritualis transit ad uxorem quam iam carnaliter cognovit: non autem si nondum sit matrimonium consummatum, quia nondum effecti sunt *una caro*. Et hoc est per modum cuiusdam affinitatis. Unde etiam, pari ratione, videtur transire, ad mulierem quae est carnaliter cognita, quamvis non sit uxor.

Unde versus: *quae mihi, vel cuius natum mea fonte levavit: Haec mea commater, fieri mea non valet uxor. Si qua meae natum non ex me fonte levavit: Hanc post fata meae non inde vetabor habere.*

AD PRIMUM ergo dicendum quod ex hoc quod sunt diversorum generum unio corporalis et spiritualis, potest concludi quod una non est altera: non autem quod una non possit esse causa alterius, quia eorum quae sunt in diversis generibus, unum quandoque est causa alterius, vel per se vel per accidens.

AD SECUNDUM dicendum quod pater spiritualis: et mater spiritualis eidem non coniunguntur in generatione spirituali nisi per accidens: quia ad hoc unus per se sufficeret. Unde non oportet quod ex hoc aliqua cognatio spiritualis inter eos nascatur, quin possit esse inter eos matrimonium. Unde versus: *unus semper erit compatrum spiritualis: Alter carnalis, non fallit regula talis.* Sed per matrimonium fit vir et uxor una caro per se loquendo. Et ideo non est simile.

AD TERTIUM dicendum quod, si uxor non sit baptizata, non perveniet ad eam spiritualis cognatio propter hoc quod non est capax: non ex hoc quod non possit per matrimonium traduci spiritualis cognatio a viro in uxorem.

OBJ. 3: Further, it may happen that the husband is baptized and his wife not: for instance, when he is converted from unbelief without his wife being converted. Now spiritual relationship cannot be contracted by one who is not baptized. Therefore, it does not always pass from husband to wife.

OBJ. 4: Further, husband and wife together can raise a person from the sacred font, since no law forbids it. If, therefore, spiritual relationship passed from husband to wife, it would follow that each of them is twice godfather or godmother of the same individual, which is absurd.

ON THE CONTRARY, Spiritual goods are more communicable than bodily goods. But the bodily consanguinity of the husband passes to his wife by affinity. Much more, therefore, does spiritual relationship.

I ANSWER THAT, Someone may become co-parent with another in two ways. First, by the act of another, who baptizes the former's child, or raises him in baptism. In this way spiritual relationship does not pass from husband to wife, unless perchance it be his wife's child, for then she contracts spiritual relationship directly, even as her husband.

Second, by his own act, for instance, when he raises the other's child from the sacred font: and thus spiritual relationship passes to the wife if he has already had carnal knowledge of her, but not if the marriage be not yet consummated, since they are not as yet made *one flesh*. And this is by way of a kind of affinity; wherefore it would seem on the same grounds to pass to a woman of whom he has carnal knowledge, though she be not his wife.

Hence the verse: *I may not marry my own child's godmother, nor the mother of my godchild; but after the death of my wife, I may marry the godmother of my wife's child.*

REPLY OBJ. 1: From the fact that corporal and spiritual union differ generically we may conclude that the one is not the other, but not that the one cannot cause the other, since things of different genera sometimes cause one another either directly or indirectly.

REPLY OBJ. 2: The godfather and godmother of the same person are not united in that person's spiritual birth save accidentally, since one of them would be self-sufficient for the purpose. Hence it does not follow from this that any spiritual relationship results between them whereby they are hindered from marrying one another. Hence the verse: *of two co-parents one is always spiritual, the other carnal: this rule is infallible.* On the other hand, marriage by itself makes husband and wife one flesh; wherefore the comparison fails.

REPLY OBJ. 3: If the wife be not baptized, the spiritual relationship will not reach her, because she is not a fit subject, and not because spiritual relationship cannot pass from husband to wife through marriage.

AD QUARTUM dicendum quod, ex quo inter patrem spiritualem et matrem non contrahitur aliqua cognatio spiritualis, nihil prohibet quin vir et uxor simul aliquem de sacro fonte levarent. Nec est inconveniens quod uxor ex diversis causis efficiatur mater spiritualis eiusdem: sicut etiam potest esse quod est affinis et consanguinea eiusdem per carnalem propinquitatem.

REPLY OBJ. 4: Since no spiritual relationship results between godfather and godmother, nothing prevents husband and wife from raising together someone from the sacred font. Nor is it absurd that the wife become twice godmother of the same person from different causes, just as it is possible for her to be connected in carnal relationship both by affinity and consanguinity to the same person.

Article 5

Whether Spiritual Relationship Passes to the Godfather's Carnal Children?

AD QUINTUM SIC PROCEDITUR. Videtur quod non transeat ad filios carnales patris spiritualis. Quia spirituali cognationi non assignantur gradus. Essent autem gradus si transirent a patre in filium; quia persona generata *mutat gradum*, ut supra dictum est. Ergo non transit ad filios carnales patris spiritualis.

PRAETEREA, pater eodem gradu attinet filio, et frater fratri. Si ergo cognatio spiritualis transit a patre in filium, eadem ratione transibit a fratre in fratrem. Quod falsum est.

SED CONTRA est quod in littera probatur per auctoritatem.

RESPONDEO dicendum quod filius est *aliquid patris*, et non e converso, ut dicitur in VIII *Ethic.* Et ideo spiritualis cognatio transit a patre in filium, et non e converso.

Et sic patet quod sunt tres cognationes spirituales. Una quae dicitur 'spiritualis paternitas', quae est inter patrem spiritualem et filium spiritualem. Alia quae dicitur 'compaternitas', quae est inter patrem spiritualem et carnalem eiusdem. Tertia autem dicitur 'spiritualis fraternitas', quae est inter filium spiritualem et filios carnales eiusdem patris. Et quaelibet harum impedit matrimonium contrahendum et dirimit contractum.

AD PRIMUM ergo dicendum quod persona addita per carnis propagationem facit gradum respectu illius personae quae eodem genere attinet, non autem respectu eius quae attinet in alio genere: sicut filius attinet in eodem gradu uxori patris in quo et pater, quamvis alio genere attinentiae. Spiritualis autem cognatio est alterius generis quam carnalis. Et ideo non iri eodem gradu attinet filius spiritualis filio naturali patris sui spiritualis, in quo attinet ei pater eius, quo mediante cognatio spiritualis transit. Et ita non oportet quod spiritualis cognatio habeat gradum.

AD SECUNDUM dicendum quod frater non est aliquid fratris, sicut filius est *aliquid patris*. Sed uxor est aliquid viri, cum quo *effecta est unum corpus*. Et ideo a fra-

OBJECTION 1: It would seem that spiritual relationship does not pass to the godfather's carnal children. For no degrees are assigned to spiritual relationship. Yet there would be degrees if it passed from father to son, since the person begotten involves a *change of degree*, as stated above (Q. 55, A. 5). Therefore, it does not pass to the godfather's carnal sons.

OBJ. 2: Further, father and son are related in the same degree as brother and brother. If, therefore, spiritual relationship passes from father to son, it will equally pass from brother to brother: and this is false.

ON THE CONTRARY, This is proved by the authority quoted in the text (*Sentences* IV, D. 42).

I ANSWER THAT, A son is *something of his father* and not conversely (*Ethics* 8.12): wherefore spiritual relationship passes from a father to his carnal son and not conversely.

Thus it is clear that there are three spiritual relationships: one called 'spiritual fatherhood' between godfather and godchild; another called 'co-paternity' between the godparent and carnal parent of the same person; and the third is called 'spiritual brotherhood' between godchild and the carnal children of the same parent. Each of these hinders the contracting of marriage and voids the contract.

REPLY OBJ. 1: The addition of a person by carnal generation entails a degree with regard to a person connected by the same kind of relationship, but not with regard to one connected by another kind of relationship. Thus a son is connected with his father's wife in the same degree as his father, but by another kind of relationship. Now spiritual relationship differs in kind from carnal. Wherefore a godson is not related to his godfather's carnal son in the same degree as the latter's father is related to him, through whom the spiritual relationship is contracted. Consequently, it does not follow that spiritual relationship admits of degrees.

REPLY OBJ. 2: A man is not part of his brother as a son is *something of his father*. But a wife is part of her husband, since she is *made one with him in body*. Consequently, the

tre in fratrem non transit, sive sit ante genitus sive post fraternitatem spiritualem.

relationship does not pass from brother to brother, whether the brother be born before or after spiritual brotherhood.

QUESTION 57

LEGAL RELATIONSHIP WHICH IS BY ADOPTION

Deinde considerandum est de cognatione legali, quae est per adoptionem.

Circa quod quaeruntur tria.

Primo: quid sit adoptio.

Secundo: utrum ex ea contrahatur aliquod vinculum impediens matrimonium.

Tertio: inter quas personas contrahatur.

We must now consider legal relationship which is by adoption.

Under this head there are three points of inquiry:

(1) What is adoption?

(2) Whether one contracts through it a tie that is an impediment to marriage?

(3) Between which persons is this tie contracted?

Article 1

Whether Adoption Is Rightly Defined?

AD PRIMUM SIC PROCEDITUR. Videtur quod inconvenienter adoptio definiatur: *adoptio est extraneae personae in filium vel nepotem, vel deinceps, legitima assumptio.* Filius enim debet esse subditus patri. Sed quandoque ille qui adoptatur, non transit in potestatem patris adoptantis. Ergo non semper per adoptionem aliquis *in filium* assumitur.

PRAETEREA, *parentes debent filiis thesaurizare,* II Cor. 12. Sed pater adoptans non oportet quod semper adoptato thesaurizet: quia quandoque adoptatus non succedit in bonis adoptantis. Ergo adoptio non est assumptio alicuius *in filium.*

PRAETEREA, adoptio, per quam aliquis in filium assumitur, similatur generationi naturali, per quam naturaliter producitur filius. Ergo cui competit naturalis generatio filii, competit adoptio. Sed hoc est falsum: quia ille qui non est sui iuris, et qui est minor viginti quinque annis, et mulier, non possunt adoptare; qui tamen possunt filium naturaliter generare. Ergo adoptio non dicitur proprie assumptio alicuius in filium.

PRAETEREA, assumptio extraneae personae in filium videtur esse necessaria ad supplendum defectum naturalium filiorum. Sed ille qui non potest generare, ut spado vel frigidus, maxime patitur defectum in filiis naturalibus. Ergo ei maxime competit assumere aliquem in filium. Sed non competit ei adoptare. Ergo adoptio non est *assumptio alicuius in filium.*

PRAETEREA, in spirituali cognatione, ubi aliquis in filium assumitur sine carnis propagatione, potest indifferenter maior aetate effici pater minoris et e converso: quia iuvenis potest senem baptizare, et e converso. Si ergo per adoptionem aliquis assumitur in filium sine carnis propagatione, similiter posset indifferenter senior

OBJECTION 1: It would seem that adoption is not rightly defined: *adoption is the act by which a person lawfully takes for his child or grandchild and so on one who does not belong to him.* For the child should be subject to its father. Now, sometimes the person adopted does not come under the power of the adopter. Therefore, adoption is not always the taking of someone *as a child.*

OBJ. 2: Further, *parents should lay up for their children* (2 Cor 12:14). But the adoptive father does not always necessarily lay up for his adopted child, since sometimes the adopted does not inherit the goods of the adopter. Therefore, adoption is not the taking of someone *as a child.*

OBJ. 3: Further, adoption, whereby someone is taken as a child, is likened to natural procreation whereby a child is begotten naturally. Therefore, whoever is competent to beget a child naturally is competent to adopt. But this is untrue, since neither one who is not his own master, nor one who is not twenty-five years of age, nor a woman can adopt, and yet they can beget a child naturally. Therefore, properly speaking, adoption is not the taking of someone as a child.

OBJ. 4: Further, to take as one's child one who is not one's own seems necessary in order to supply the lack of children begotten naturally. Now one who is unable to beget through being a eunuch or impotent suffers especially from the absence of children of his own begetting. Therefore, he is especially competent to adopt someone as his child. But he is not competent to adopt. Therefore, adoption is not the *taking of someone as one's child.*

OBJ. 5: Further, in spiritual relationship, where someone is taken as a child without carnal procreation, it is of no consequence whether an older person become the father of a younger, or vice versa, since a youth can baptize an old man and vice versa. Therefore, if by adoption a person is taken as a child without being carnally begotten, it

iuniorem, vel minor seniorem adoptare. Quod non est verum. Et sic idem quod prius.

Praeterea, adoptatus non differt secundum aliquem gradum ab adoptante. Ergo quilibet adoptatus adoptatur in filium. Et sic inconvenienter dicitur quod adoptatur *in nepotem*.

Praeterea, adoptio ex dilectione procedit: unde et Deus dicitur nos per caritatem in filios adoptasse. Sed caritas maior habenda est ad proximos quam ad extraneos. Ergo non debet esse adoptio *extraneae personae*, sed magis propinquae.

Respondeo dicendum quod *ars imitatur naturam*, et supplet defectum naturae in illis in quibus natura deficit. Unde, sicut per naturalem generationem aliquis filium producit, ita per ius positivum, quod est ars boni et aequi, potest aliquis alium sibi assumere in filium, ad similitudinem filii naturalis, et ad supplendum filiorum deperditorum defectum, propter quod praecipue adoptio est introducta. Et quia assumptio importat terminum a quo, propter quod assumens non est assumptum, oportet quod ille qui assumitur in filium, sit persona extranea. Ergo, sicut naturalis generatio habet terminum ad quem, scilicet formam, quae est finis generationis; et terminum a quo, scilicet formam contrariam: ita generatio legalis habet terminum ad quem, filium vel nepotem; et terminum a quo, personam extraneam. Et sic patet quod praedicta assignatio comprehendit genus adoptionis, quia dicitur *legitima assumptio*; et terminum a quo, quia dicitur *extraneae personae*; et terminum ad quem, quia dicitur *in filium vel nepotem*.

Ad primum ergo dicendum quod filiatio adoptionis est quaedam imitatio filiationis naturalis. Et ideo duplex est adoptionis species. Una quae perfecte naturalem filiationem imitatur: et haec vocatur 'adrogatio', per quam traducitur adoptatus in potestatem adoptantis. Et sic adoptatus succedit patri adoptanti ex intestato: nec potest eum pater sine culpa privare quarta parte haereditatis. Sic autem adoptari non potest nisi ille qui est sui iuris, qui scilicet non habet patrem, aut, si habet, est emancipatus. Et haec adoptio non fit nisi auctoritate principis.

Alia adoptio est quae imitatur naturalem filiationem imperfecte: quae vocatur simplex 'adoptio', per quam adoptatus non transit in potestatem adoptantis. Unde magis est dispositio quaedam ad perfectam adoptionem quam adoptio perfecta. Et secundum hanc potest adoptari etiam ille qui non est sui iuris; et sine auctoritate principis, ex auctoritate magistratus. Et sic adoptatus; non succedit in bonis adoptantis: nec tenetur ei adoptans aliquid de bonis suis in testamento dimittere nisi velit.

Et per hoc patet solutio ad secundum.

would make no difference whether an older person adopted a younger, or a younger an older person; which is not true. Therefore, the same conclusion follows.

Obj. 6: Further, there is no difference of degree between adopted and adopter. Therefore, whoever is adopted is adopted as a child; and consequently it is not right to say that one may be adopted *as a grandchild*.

Obj. 7: Further, adoption is a result of love, wherefore God is said to have adopted us as children through charity. Now we should have greater charity towards those who are connected with us than towards strangers. Therefore, adoption should be not *of a stranger* but of someone connected with us.

I answer that, *Art imitates nature* and supplies the defect of nature when nature is deficient. Hence, just as a man begets by natural procreation, so by positive law (which is the art of what is good and just) one person can take to himself another as a child in likeness to one that is his child by nature, in order to take the place of the children he has lost, this being the chief reason why adoption was introduced. And since taking implies a term from which, for which reason the taker is not the thing taken, it follows that the person taken as a child must be a stranger. Accordingly, just as natural procreation has a term to which, namely, the form which is the end of generation, and a term from which, namely, the contrary form, so legal generation has a term to which, namely, a child or grandchild, and a term from which, namely, a stranger. Consequently, the above definition includes the genus of adoption, for it is described as a *lawful taking*, and the term wherefrom, since it is said to be the taking of *a stranger*, and the term whereto, because it says, *as a child or grandchild*.

Reply Obj. 1: The sonship of adoption is an imitation of natural sonship. Wherefore there are two species of adoption, one which imitates natural sonship perfectly, and this is called 'adrogation', whereby the person adopted is placed under the power of the adopter; and one who is thus adopted inherits from his adopted father if the latter die intestate, nor can his father legally deprive him of a fourth part of his inheritance. But no one can adopt in this way except one who is his own master, namely, one who has no father or, if he has, is of age. There can be no adoption of this kind without the authority of the sovereign.

The other kind of adoption imitates natural sonship imperfectly, and is called simple 'adoption', and by this the adopted does not come under the power of the adopter; so that it is a disposition to perfect adoption, rather than perfect adoption itself. In this way even one who is not his own master can adopt without the consent of the sovereign and with the authority of a magistrate; and one who is thus adopted does not inherit the estate of the adopter, nor is the latter bound to bequeath to him any of his goods in his will, unless he will.

This suffices for the reply to the second objection.

Ad tertium dicendum quod generatio naturalis ordinatur ad speciem consequendam: et ideo omnibus competit posse naturaliter generare in quibus natura speciei non est impedita. Sed adoptio ordinatur ad haereditatis successionem: et ideo illis solis competit qui habent potestatem disponendi de haereditate sua. Unde qui non est sui iuris, vel est minor vigintiquinque annis, aut mulier, non potest adoptare aliquem, nisi ex speciali concessione principis.

Ad quartum dicendum quod per eum qui habet impedimentum perpetuum ad generandum, non potest haereditas transire in posterum. Unde ex hoc ipso iam debetur illis qui succedere ei debent iure propinquitatis. Et ideo ei non competit adoptare: sicut nec naturaliter generare.

Et praeterea maior est dolor de filiis amissis quam de illis qui nunquam sunt habiti. Et ideo habentes impedimentum generationis non indigent solatio; contra carentiam filiorum sicut illi qui habuerunt et amiserunt; vel etiam qui habere potuerunt, sed aliquo impedimento accidentali carent.

Ad quintum dicendum quod spiritualis cognatio contrahitur per sacramentum quo fideles renascuntur in Christo, in quo non differt *masculus et femina, servus et liber*, iuvenis et senex. Et ideo indifferenter quilibet potest effici pater spiritualis alterius. Sed adoptio fit ad haereditatis successionem, et quandam subiectionem adoptati ad adoptantem. Non autem est conveniens quod antiquior iuveni in cura rei familiaris subdatur. Et ideo minor non potest adoptare seniorem: sed oportet, secundum leges, quod adoptatus sit in tantum adoptante iunior quod posset eius esse filius naturalis.

Ad sextum dicendum quod, sicut contingit amitti filios, ita et nepotes. Et ideo, cum adoptio sit inducta in solatium filiorum amissorum, sicut aliquis per adoptionem potest subrogari in locum filii, ita in locum nepotis et deinceps.

Ad septimum dicendum quod propinquus iure propinquitatis debet succedere. Et ideo non competit ei quod per adoptionem ad successionem deducatur. Et si aliquis propinquus cui non competat successio haereditatis, adoptetur, non adoptatur inquantum est propinquus, sed inquantum est extraneus a iure successionis in bonis adoptantis.

Reply Obj. 3: Natural procreation is directed to the production of the species; wherefore anyone in whom the specific nature is not hindered is competent to be able to beget naturally. But adoption is directed to hereditary succession, wherefore those alone are competent to adopt who have the power to dispose of their estate. Consequently, one who is not his own master, or who is less than twenty-five years of age, or a woman, cannot adopt anyone, except by special permission of the sovereign.

Reply Obj. 4: An inheritance cannot pass to posterity through one who has a perpetual impediment from begetting. Hence for this very reason it ought to pass to those who ought to succeed to him by right of relationship; and consequently he cannot adopt, as neither can he beget.

Moreover, sorrow for children lost is greater than for children one has never had. Wherefore those who are impeded from begetting need no solace for their lack of children as those who have had and have lost them, or could have had them but do not because of some accidental impediment.

Reply Obj. 5: Spiritual relationship is contracted through a sacrament whereby the faithful are born again in Christ, in whom there is no difference between *male and female, slave and free*, youth and old age (Gal 3:28). Therefore, anyone can indifferently become another's godfather. But adoption aims at hereditary succession and a certain subjection of the adopted to the adopter, and it is not fitting that older persons should be subjected to younger in the care of the household. Consequently, a younger person cannot adopt an older; but according to law the adopted person must be so much younger than the adopter that he might have been the child of his natural begetting.

Reply Obj. 6: One may lose one's grandchildren even as one may lose one's children. Thus, since adoption was introduced as a solace for children lost, just as someone may be adopted in place of a child, so may someone be adopted in place of a grandchild, and so on.

Reply Obj. 7: A relative ought to succeed by right of relationship; and therefore such a person is not competent to be chosen to succeed by adoption. And if a relative who is not competent to inherit the estate be adopted, he is adopted not as a relative, but as a stranger lacking the right of succeeding to the adopter's goods.

Article 2

Whether a Tie That Is an Impediment to Marriage Is Contracted Through Adoption?

AD SECUNDUM SIC PROCEDITUR. Videtur quod ex adoptione non contrahatur aliquod vinculum impediens matrimonium. Quia cura spiritualis est dignior quam cura corporalis. Sed ex hoc quod aliquis curae alicuius subiicitur spiritualiter, non contrahit aliquod propinquitatis vinculum: alias omnes qui habitant in parochia, essent propinqui sacerdotis, et cum filio eius non possent contrahere. Ergo nec adoptio, quae trahit adoptatum in curam adoptantis, hoc facere potest.

PRAETEREA, ex hoc quod aliquis alicui fit beneficus, non contrahitur aliquod propinquitatis vinculum. Sed nihil aliud est adoptio quam collatio cuiusdam beneficii. Ergo ex adoptione non fit aliquod propinquitatis vinculum.

PRAETEREA, pater naturalis principaliter filio providet in tribus, ut Philosophus dicit: quia scilicet ab ipso habet *esse, nutrimentum et disciplinam*. Haereditatis autem successio est posterius ad ista. Sed per hoc quod aliquis alicui providet in nutrimento et disciplina, non contrahitur aliquod propinquitatis vinculum: alias nutrientes et paedagogi et magistri essent propinqui, quod falsum est. Ergo nec per adoptionem, per quam aliquis succedit in haereditate alterius, contrahitur aliqua propinquitas.

PRAETEREA, sacramenta Ecclesiae non subduntur humanis legibus. Sed matrimonium est sacramentum Ecclesiae. Cum ergo adoptio sit inducta per legem humanam, videtur quod non possit impedire matrimonium aliquod vinculum ex adoptione contractum.

SED CONTRA: Cognatio matrimonium impedit. Sed ex adoptione quaedam cognatio causatur, scilicet legalis, ut patet per eius definitionem: est enim *legalis cognatio quaedam proximitas proveniens ex adoptione*. Ergo adoptio causat vinculum per quod matrimonium impeditur.

PRAETEREA, hoc idem habetur ex auctoritatibus in littera positis.

RESPONDEO dicendum quod lex divina illas praecipue personas a matrimonio exclusit quas necesse erat cohabitare: ne, ut Rabbi Moyses dicit, si ad eas liceret carnalis copula, facilis pateret concupiscentiae locus, ad quam reprimendam matrimonium est ordinatum. Et quia filius adoptatus conversatur in domo patris adoptantis sicut filius naturalis, ideo legibus humanis prohibitum est inter tales matrimonium contrahi. Et talis prohibitio est per Ecclesiam approbata: et inde habetur quod legalis cognatio matrimonium impediat.

ET PER HOC patet solutio ad prima tria: quia per omnia illa non inducitur talis cohabitatio quae possit fo-

OBJECTION 1: It would seem that there is not contracted through adoption a tie that is an impediment to marriage. For spiritual care is more excellent than corporeal care. But no tie of relationship is contracted through one's being subjected to another's spiritual care, else all those who dwell in the parish would be related to the parish priest, and would be unable to marry his son. Neither, therefore, can this result from adoption, which places the adopted under the care of the adopter.

OBJ. 2: Further, no tie of relationship results from persons conferring a benefit on another. But adoption is nothing but the conferring of a benefit. Therefore, no tie of relationship results from adoption.

OBJ. 3: Further, a natural father provides for his child chiefly in three things, as the Philosopher states (*Ethics* 8.11–12), namely, by giving him *being, nourishment, and education*; and hereditary succession is subsequent to these. Now no tie of relationship is contracted by one's providing for a person's nourishment and education, else a person would be related to his nurses, tutors, and masters, which is false. Therefore, neither is any relationship contracted through adoption, by which one inherits another's estate.

OBJ. 4: Further, the sacraments of the Church are not subject to human laws. Now marriage is a sacrament of the Church. Since, then, adoption was introduced by human law, it would seem that a tie contracted from adoption cannot be an impediment to marriage.

ON THE CONTRARY, Relationship is an impediment to marriage. Now a kind of relationship results from adoption, namely, legal relationship, as evidenced by its definition, for *legal relationship is a connection arising out of adoption*. Therefore, adoption results in a tie which is an impediment to marriage.

FURTHER, The same is proved by the authorities quoted in the text (*Sentences* IV, D. 42).

I ANSWER THAT, The divine law especially forbids marriage between those persons who have to live together, lest, as Rabbi Moses observes (*Guide for the Perplexed* 3.49), if it were lawful for them to have carnal intercourse, there should be more room for concupiscence, to the repression of which marriage is directed. And since the adopted child dwells in the house of his adopted father like one that is begotten naturally, human laws forbid the contracting of marriage between the like, and this prohibition is approved by the Church. Hence it is that legal adoption is an impediment to marriage.

THIS SUFFICES for the replies to the first three objections, because none of those things entails such a cohabita-

mentum concupiscentiae praestare. Et ideo ex eis non causatur propinquitas quae matrimonium impediat.

Ad quartum dicendum quod prohibitio legis humanae non sufficeret ad impedimentum matrimonii nisi interveniret Ecclesiae auctoritas, quae idem etiam interdicit.

tion as might be an incentive to concupiscence. Therefore, they do not cause a relationship that is an impediment to marriage.

Reply Obj. 4: The prohibition of a human law would not suffice to make an impediment to marriage, unless the authority of the Church intervenes by issuing the same prohibition.

Article 3

Whether Such Relationship Is Contracted Only Between the Adopting Father and the Adopted Child?

Ad tertium sic proceditur. Videtur quod talis cognatio non contrahatur nisi inter patrem adoptantem et filium adoptatum. Maxime enim videretur quod deberet contrahi inter patrem adoptantem et matrem naturalem adoptati: sicut accidit in cognatione spirituali. Sed inter tales nulla est cognatio legalis. Ergo nec inter alias personas praeter adoptantem et adoptatum.

Praeterea, cognatio impediens matrimonium est perpetuum impedimentum. Sed inter filium adoptatum et filiam naturalem adoptantis non est perpetuum impedimentum: quia, soluta adoptione per mortem adoptantis vel emancipationem adoptati, potest contrahere cum ea. Ergo cum ea non habuit aliquam propinquitatem quae matrimonium impediret.

Praeterea, cognatio spiritualis in nullam personam transit quae non possit ad aliquod sacramentum tenere vel suscipere: unde in non-baptizatum non transit. Sed mulier non potest adoptare, ut ex dictis patet. Ergo cognatio legalis non transit a viro in uxorem.

Praeterea, cognatio spiritualis est fortior quam legalis. Sed spiritualis non transit in nepotem. Ergo nec legalis.

Sed contra: Plus concordat cognatio legalis cum carnis coniunctione vel propagatione quam spiritualis. Sed spiritualis transit in alteram personam. Ergo et legalis.

Praeterea, ad hoc sunt auctoritates quae in littera ponuntur.

Respondeo dicendum quod triplex est legalis cognatio. Prima, quasi descendentium: quae contrahitur inter patrem adoptantem et filium adoptatum, et filium filii adoptivi, et nepotem, et sic deinceps. Secunda quae est inter filium adoptivum et filium naturalem. Tertia per modum cuiusdam affinitatis: quae est inter patrem adoptantem et uxorem filii adoptivi, vel e converso inter filium adoptatum et uxorem patris adoptantis.

Prima ergo cognatio et tertia perpetuo matrimonium impediunt. Secunda autem non nisi quandiu manet in

Objection 1: It would seem that a relationship of this kind is contracted only between the adopting father and the adopted child. For it would seem that it ought above all to be contracted between the adopting father and the natural mother of the adopted, as happens in spiritual relationship. Yet there is no legal relationship between them. Therefore, it is not contracted between any other persons besides the adopter and adopted.

Obj. 2: Further, the relationship that impedes marriage is a perpetual impediment. But there is not a perpetual impediment between the adopted son and the naturally begotten daughter of the adopter; because when the adoption terminates at the death of the adopter, or when the adopted comes of age, the latter can marry her. Therefore, he was not related to her in such a way as to prevent him from marrying her.

Obj. 3: Further, spiritual relationship passes to no person incapable of being a god-parent; wherefore it does not pass to one who is not baptized. Now a woman cannot adopt, as stated above (A. 1). Therefore, legal relationship does not pass from husband to wife.

Obj. 4: Further, spiritual relationship is stronger than legal. But spiritual relationship does not pass to a grandchild. Neither, therefore, does legal relationship.

On the contrary, Legal relationship is more in agreement with carnal union or procreation than spiritual relationship is. But spiritual relationship passes to another person. Therefore, legal relationship does so also.

Further, The same is proved by the authorities quoted in the text (*Sentences* IV, D. 42).

I answer that, Legal relationship is of three kinds. The first is in the descending order as it were, and is contracted between the adoptive father and the adopted child, the latter's child, grandchild, and so on; the second is between the adopted child and the naturally begotten child; the third is like a kind of affinity, and is between the adoptive father and the wife of the adopted son, or contrariwise between the adopted son and the wife of the adoptive father.

Accordingly, the first and third relationships are perpetual impediments to marriage: but the second is not,

potestate patris adoptantis. Unde, mortuo patre vel filio emancipato, potest contrahi inter eos matrimonium.

Ad primum ergo dicendum quod per generationem spiritualem non trahitur filius extra potestatem patris, sicut fit per adoptionem. Et sic filius spiritualis remanet filius utriusque simul, non autem filius adoptivus. Et ideo non contrahitur aliqua propinquitas inter patrem adoptantem et matrem vel patrem naturalem: sicut erat in cognatione spirituali.

Ad secundum dicendum quod cognatio legalis impedit matrimonium propter cohabitationem. Et ideo, quando solvitur necessitas cohabitationis, non est inconveniens si praedictum vinculum non maneat: sicut quando fuerit extra potestatem eiusdem patris. Sed pater adoptans et uxor eius semper quandam auctoritatem retinent super filium adoptatum et uxorem eius. Et propter hoc manet vinculum inter eos.

Ad tertium dicendum quod etiam mulier, ex concessione principis, adoptare potest. Unde et in ipsam transit cognatio legalis. Et praeterea, non est causa quare cognatio spiritualis non transit in non-baptizatum quia non potest tenere ad sacramentum: sed quia non est alicuius spiritualitatis capax.

Ad quartum dicendum quod per generationem spiritualem filius non ponitur in potestate et cura alterius patris spiritualis, sicut in cognatione legali. Oportet enim quod quidquid est in potestate filii, transeat in potestatem patris adoptantis. Unde, adoptato patre, adoptantur filii et nepotes qui sunt in potestate adoptati.

but only so long as the adopted person remains under the power of the adoptive father, wherefore when the father dies or when the child comes of age, they can be married.

Reply Obj. 1: By spiritual generation the son is not withdrawn from the father's power, as in the case of adoption, so that the godson remains the son of both at the same time, whereas the adopted son does not. Hence no relationship is contracted between the adoptive father and the natural mother or father, as was the case in spiritual relationship.

Reply Obj. 2: Legal relationship is an impediment to marriage on account of the parties dwelling together; hence when the need for dwelling together ceases, it is not unreasonable that the aforesaid tie cease, for instance, when he ceases to be under the power of the same father. But the adoptive father and his wife always retain a certain authority over their adopted son and his wife, wherefore the tie between them remains.

Reply Obj. 3: Even a woman can adopt by permission of the sovereign, wherefore legal relationship passes also to her. Moreover, the reason why spiritual relationship does not pass to a non-baptized person is not because such a person cannot be a god-parent, but because he is not a fit subject of spirituality.

Reply Obj. 4: By spiritual relationship the son is not placed under the power and care of the godfather as in legal relationship, because it is necessary that whatever is in the son's power pass under the power of the adoptive father. Therefore, if a father be adopted, the children and grandchildren who are in the power of the person adopted are adopted also.

QUESTION 58

VARIOUS IMPEDIMENTS

Deinde considerandum est de quinque impedimentis matrimonii simul: scilicet de impedimento frigiditatis, maleficii, furiae vel amentiae, incestus, et defectus aetatis.

Et circa hoc quaeruntur quinque:

Primo: utrum frigiditas matrimonium impediat.
Secundo: utrum maleficium.
Tertio: utrum furia vel amentia.
Quarto: utrum incestus.
Quinto: utrum defectus aetatis.

We must now consider five impediments to marriage: (1) Impotence; (2) Spell; (3) Frenzy or madness; (4) Incest; (5) Defective age.

Under this head there are five points of inquiry:

(1) Whether impotence is an impediment to marriage?
(2) Whether a spell is?
(3) Whether frenzy or madness is?
(4) Whether incest is?
(5) Whether defective age is?

Article 1

Whether Impotence Is an Impediment to Marriage?

AD PRIMUM SIC PROCEDITUR. Videtur quod frigiditas matrimonium contrahendum non impediat. Copula enim carnalis non est de essentia matrimonii: quia perfectiora sunt matrimonia pari voto continentium. Sed frigiditas nihil tollit de matrimonio nisi carnalem copulam. Ergo non est impedimentum dirimens matrimonium contractum.

PRAETEREA, sicut nimia frigiditas impedit carnalem copulam, ita nimia caliditas, quae hominem exsiccat. Sed caliditas non ponitur matrimonii impedimentum. Ergo nec frigiditas debet poni.

PRAETEREA, omnes senes sunt frigidi. Sed senes possunt matrimonium contrahere. Ergo frigiditas non impedit matrimonium.

PRAETEREA, si scit mulier virum esse frigidum quando cum eo contrahit, verum est matrimonium. Ergo frigiditas, quantum est de se, matrimonium non impedit.

PRAETEREA, contingit in aliquo esse siccitatem sufficienter moventem ad carnalem copulam cum aliqua corrupta, non autem cum aliqua virgine: quia cito calidum evaporat, ratione suae debilitatis, ut ad corrumpendum virginem non sufficiat. Et similiter est in aliquo sufficiens caliditas ad pulchram, quae magis concupiscentiam inflammat, quae non sufficienter movet ad turpem. Ergo videtur quod frigiditas, etsi impediat respectu unius, non tamen impedit simpliciter.

OBJECTION 1: It would seem that impotence is not an impediment to marriage. For carnal copulation is not essential to marriage, since marriage is more perfect when both parties observe continency by vow. But impotence deprives marriage of nothing save carnal copulation. Therefore, it is not a diriment impediment to the marriage contract.

OBJ. 2: Futhermore, just as extreme impotence impedes carnal intimacy, so also does extreme heat, which dries a man out. But heat is not counted among the impediments to marriage. Therefore, neither should impotence be counted.

OBJ. 3: Furthermore, all old men are impotent. But old men can contract marriage. Therefore, impotence does not impede marriage.

OBJ. 4: Further, if the woman knows the man to be impotent when she marries him, the marriage is valid. Therefore, frigidity, considered in itself, is not an impediment to marriage.

OBJ. 5: Further, calidity may prove a sufficient incentive to carnal intimacy with an experienced woman, but not with a virgin; for immediately the heat evaporates because of its own weakness, so that it is not sufficient for penetrating a virgin. And likewise, in a certain man there may be sufficient heat to move him with respect to a pretty girl, who inflames more his concupiscence, but not sufficient to move him toward an ugly girl. Therefore, it seems that impotence also may impede with respect to one person, but not simply speaking.

PRAETEREA, mulier est universaliter frigidior viro. Sed mulieres non impediuntur a matrimonio. Ergo nec viri frigidi.

SED CONTRA: Est quod dicitur Extra, *de Frigidis et Maleilc.: sicut puer, qui non potest reddere debitum, non est aptus coniugio, sic qui impotentes sunt, minime apti ad contrahenda matrimonia reputantur.* Tales autem sunt frigidi. Ergo, etc.

PRAETEREA, nullus potest se obligare ad impossibile. Sed in matrimonio homo se obligat ad carnalem copulam: quia ad hoc dat alteri sui corporis potestatem. Ergo frigidus, qui non potest carnaliter copulari, non potest matrimonium contrahere.

RESPONDEO dicendum quod in matrimonio est contractus quidam quo unus alteri obligatur ad debitum carnale solvendum. Unde, sicut in aliis contractibus non est conveniens obligatio si aliquis se obliget ad hoc quod non potest dare vel facere, ita non est conveniens matrimonio contractus si fiat ab aliquo qui debitum carnale solvere non possit. Et hoc impedimentum vocatur *impotentia coeundi*, nomine generali.

Quae quidem potest esse vel ex causa intrinseca et naturali; vel ex causa extrinseca accidentali, sicut per maleficium, de qua post dicetur. Si autem sit ex causa naturali, hoc potest esse dupliciter. Quia vel est temporalis, cui potest subveniri beneficio medicinae vel processu aetatis: et tunc non solvit matrimonium. Vel est perpetua. Et tunc solvit matrimonium: ita quod ille ex parte cuius allegatur impedimentum, perpetuo maneat absque spe coniugii, alius *nubat cui vult in Domino*.

Ad hoc autem cognoscendum, utrum sit impedimentum perpetuum vel non, Ecclesia tempus determinatum adhibuit in quo huius rei posset esse experimentum, scilicet triennium: ita quod si, post triennium, in quo fideliter ex utraque parte dederunt operam copulae carnali implendae, inveniatur matrimonium non esse consummatum, iudicio Ecclesiae dissolvitur.

Et tamen in hoc quandoque Ecclesia errat: quia per triennium quandoque non sufficienter experiri potest perpetuitas impotentiae. Unde, si Ecclesia se deceptam inveniat, per hoc quod ille in quo erat impedimentum, invenitur carnalem copulam cum alia vel cum eadem perfecisse, reintegrat matrimonium praecedens, et dirimit secundum, quamvis de eius licentia sit factum.

AD PRIMUM ergo dicendum quod, quamvis actus carnalis copulae non sit de essentia matrimonii, tamen potentia ad hoc est de eius essentia: quia per matrimonium datur utrique coniugum potestas in corpore alterius respectu carnalis copulae.

AD SECUNDUM dicendum quod caliditas superflua vix potest esse impedimentum perpetuum. Si tamen in-

OBJ. 6: Further, woman is more frigid, generally speaking, than man. But women are not debarred from marriage. Neither, therefore, should men be debarred on account of impotence.

ON THE CONTRARY, It is stated (*Decretals*): *just as a boy who is incapable of marital intercourse is unfit to marry, so also those who are impotent are deemed most unfit for the marriage contract.* Now persons affected with frigidity are the like. Therefore, etc.

FURTHER, No one can bind himself to the impossible. Now in marriage man binds himself to carnal copulation; because it is for this purpose that he gives the other party power over his body. Therefore, a frigid person, being incapable of carnal copulation, cannot marry.

I ANSWER THAT, In marriage there is a contract whereby one is bound to pay the other the marital debt: wherefore just as in other contracts, the bond is unfitting if a person bind himself to what he cannot give or do, so the marriage contract is unfitting, if it be made by one who cannot pay the marital debt. This impediment is called by the general name of *impotence as regards coition*.

It can arise either from an intrinsic and natural cause, or from an extrinsic and accidental cause, for instance, a spell, of which we shall speak later (A. 2). If it be due to a natural cause, this may happen in two ways. For either it is temporary, and can be remedied by medicine or by the course of time, and then it does not void a marriage: or it is perpetual and then it voids marriage, so that the party who labors under this impediment remains forever without hope of marriage, while the other may *marry to whom she will in the Lord* (1 Cor 7:45).

In order to ascertain whether the impediment be perpetual or not, the Church has appointed a fixed time, namely, three years, for putting the matter to a practical proof: and if after three years, during which both parties have honestly endeavored to fulfill their marital intercourse, the marriage remain unconsummated, the Church adjudges the marriage to be dissolved.

And yet the Church is sometimes mistaken in this, because three years are sometimes insufficient to prove impotence to be perpetual. Wherefore if the Church find that she has been mistaken, seeing that the subject of the impediment has completed carnal copulation with another or with the same person, she reinstates the former marriage and dissolves the subsequent one, although the latter has been contracted with her permission.

REPLY OBJ. 1: Although the act of carnal copulation is not essential to marriage, ability to fulfill the act is essential, because marriage gives each of the married parties power over the other's body in relation to marital intercourse.

REPLY OBJ. 2: Excessive calidity can scarcely be a perpetual impediment. If, however, it were to prove an imped-

veniretur quod per triennium impediret carnalem copulam, iudicaretur perpetuum. Tamen, quia frigiditas magis et frequentius impedit (tollit enim non solum commixtionem seminum, sed etiam vigorem membrorum, quo fit coniunctio corporum), ideo frigiditas magis hic ponitur impedimentum quam caliditas: cum omnis defectus naturalis ad frigiditatem reducatur.

Ad tertium dicendum quod senes, quamvis quandoque non habeant caliditatem sufficientem ad generandum, tamen habent caliditatem sufficientem ad carnalem copulam. Et ideo conceditur eis matrimonium secundum quod est in remedium: quamvis non competat eis secundum quod est in officium naturae.

Ad quartum dicendum quod in quolibet contractu hoc universaliter tenetur, quod ille qui est impotens ad solvendum aliquid, non reputatur idoneus ad contractum illum quo se obligat ad eius solutionem. Tamen potest impotens esse tripliciter, Uno modo, quia non potest solvere de iure. Et sic talis impotentia omnibus modis facit contractum esse nullum: sive sciat ille cum quo facit talis contractum hanc impotentiam, sive non. Alio modo, quia non sit solvendo de facto. Et tunc, si sciat ille cum quo contrahit hanc impotentiam et nihilominus contrahit, ostenditur quod alium finem ex contractu quaerit: et ideo contractus stat. Si autem nescit, tunc contractus nullus est.

Et ideo frigiditas, quae causat talem impotentiam ut homo non possit de facto solvere debitum; et conditio servitutis, per quam non potest homo de facto libere reddere; impediunt matrimonium quando alter coniugum ignorat hoc, quod alius non potest reddere debitum. Impedimentum autem per quod quis non potest de iure reddere debitum, ut consanguinitas, annullat contractum matrimonium sive sciat alter coniugum sive non. Et propter hoc Magister ponit quod haec duo faciunt personas *non omnino illegitimas*.

Ad quintum dicendum quod non potest esse perpetuum impedimentum naturale viro respectu unius personae et non respectu alterius. Sed, si non. possit implere carnalem actum cum virgine et possit cum corrupta, tunc medicinaliter aliquo instrumento posset claustra pudoris frangere et ei coniungi. Nec esset hoc contra matrimonium: quia non fieret ad delectationem, sed ad medicamentum.

Abominatio autem mulieris non est causa naturalis, sed: causa accidentalis extrinseca. Et ideo de ea idem est iudicium quod de maleficio, de quo post dicetur.

Ad sextum dicendum quod mas est agens in generatione, sed femina est patiens. Et ideo maior caliditas requiritur in viro ad opus generationis quam in muliere. Unde frigiditas, quae facit virum impotentem, non face-

iment to marital intercourse for three years, it would be adjudged to be perpetual. Nevertheless, since frigidity is a greater and more frequent impediment (for it not only hinders the mingling of seeds but also weakens the members which cooperate in the union of bodies), it is accounted an impediment rather than calidity, since all natural defects are reduced to frigidity.

Reply Obj. 3: Although old people have not sufficient calidity to procreate, they have sufficient to copulate. Wherefore they are allowed to marry insofar as marriage is intended as a remedy, although it does not befit them as fulfilling an office of nature.

Reply Obj. 4: In all contracts it is agreed on all hands that anyone who is unable to satisfy an obligation is unfit to make a contract which requires the fulfilling of that obligation. Now this inability is of two kinds. First, because a person is unable to fulfill the obligation *de jure*, and such inability renders the contract altogether void, whether the party with whom he contracts knows of this or not. Second, because he is unable to fulfill *de facto*; and then if the party with whom he contracts knows of this and, notwithstanding, enters the contract, this shows that the latter seeks some other end from the contract, and the contract stands. But if he does not know of it, the contract is void.

Consequently, frigidity which causes such an impotence that a man cannot *de facto* pay the marriage debt, as also the condition of slavery, whereby a man cannot *de facto* give his service freely, are impediments to marriage when the one married party does not know that the other is unable to pay the marriage debt. But an impediment whereby a person cannot pay the marriage debt *de jure*, for instance, consanguinity, voids the marriage contract, whether the other party knows of it or not. For this reason the Master holds (*Sentences* IV, D. 34) that these two impediments, frigidity and slavery, make it not altogether *unlawful for their subjects to marry*.

Reply Obj. 5: A man cannot have a perpetual natural impediment in regard to one person and not in regard to another. But if he cannot fulfill the carnal act with a virgin, while he can with one who is not a virgin, the hymeneal membrane may be broken by a medical instrument, and thus he may have carnal intimacy with her. Nor would this be contrary to nature, for it would be done not for pleasure but for medical purposes.

Dislike for a woman is not a natural cause, but an accidental extrinsic cause: and therefore we must form the same judgment in its regard as about spells, of which we shall speak further on (A. 2).

Reply Obj. 6: The male is the agent in procreation, and the female is the patient, wherefore greater calidity is required in the male than in the female for the act of procreation. Hence the frigidity which renders the man impotent

ret mulierem impotentem. Sed in muliere potest esse impedimentum naturale ex alia causa, scilicet arctatione. Et tunc idem est iudicium de arctatione mulieris et de frigiditate viri.

would not disable the woman. Yet there may be a natural impediment from another cause, namely stricture, and then we must judge of stricture in the woman in the same way as of frigidity in the man.

Article 2

Whether a Spell Can Be an Impediment to Marriage?

Ad secundum sic proceditur. Videtur quod maleficium non possit matrimonium impedire. Huiusmodi enim maleficia fiunt operatione daemonum. Sed daemones non habent potestatem ad impediendum matrimonii actum magis quam alios corporales actus: quos impedire non possunt, quia sic totum mundum perverterent, si comestionem et gressum et alia huiusmodi impedirent. Ergo per maleficia non potest impediri matrimonium.

Praeterea, opus Dei est fortius quam opus diaboli. Sed maleficium est opus diaboli. Ergo non potest impedire matrimonium, quod est opus Dei.

Praeterea, nullum impedimentum dirimit contractum matrimonium nisi sit perpetuum. Sed maleficium non potest esse impedimentum perpetuum: quia, cum diabolus non habeat potestatem nisi super peccatores, expulso peccato tolletur maleficium; vel etiam per aliud maleficium; vel per exorcismos Ecclesiae, qui sunt ordinati ad reprimendam vim daemonum. Ergo maleficium non potest impedire matrimonium.

Praeterea, carnalis copula non potest impediri nisi impediatur potentia generandi, quae est principium eius. Sed unius viri generativa potentia se habet ad omnes mulieres quasi aequaliter. Ergo per maleficium non potest esse impedimentum respectu unius nisi sit respectu omnium.

Sed contra: Est quod dicitur in *Decretis*, XXXIII, qu. 1: *si per sortiarias vel maleficas*, et infra: *si sanari non poterunt, separari valebunt*.

Praeterea, potestas daemonum est maior quam potestas hominis: Iob 41, *non est potestas super terram*, etc. Sed opere humano potest aliquis fieri impotens ad carnalem copulam per aliquam potestatem, vel castraturam, et ex hoc matrimonium impediri. Ergo multo fortius virtute daemonis hoc fieri potest.

Respondeo dicendum quod quidam dixerunt quod maleficium nihil erat in mundo nisi in aestimatione hominum, qui effectus naturales quorum causae surit occultae, maleficiis imputabant. Sed hoc est contra auctoritates Sanctorum, qui dicunt quod daemones habent

Objection 1: It would seem that a spell cannot be an impediment to marriage. For the spells in question are caused by the operation of demons. But the demons have no more power to prevent the marriage act than other bodily actions; and these they cannot prevent, for thus they would upset the whole world if they hindered eating and walking and the like. Therefore, they cannot hinder marriage by spells.

Obj. 2: Further, God's work is stronger than the devil's. But a spell is the work of the devil. Therefore, it cannot hinder marriage, which is the work of God.

Obj. 3: Further, no impediment, unless it be perpetual, voids the marriage contract. But a spell cannot be a perpetual impediment, for since the devil has no power over others than sinners, the spell will be removed by casting out sin, or by another spell, or by the exorcisms of the Church which are employed for the repression of the demon's power. Therefore, a spell cannot be an impediment to marriage.

Obj. 4: Further, carnal copulation cannot be hindered unless there be an impediment to the generative power which is its principle. But the generative power of one man is equally related to all women. Therefore, a spell cannot be an impediment in respect of one woman without being so also in respect of all.

On the contrary, It is stated in the *Decretals*: *if by sorcerers or witches*, and further on, *if they be incurable, they must be separated*.

Further, The demons' power is greater than man's: *there is no power upon earth that can be compared with him* (Job 41:24). Now through the action of man a person may be rendered incapable of carnal copulation by some power or by castration; and this is an impediment to marriage. Therefore, much more can this be done by the power of a demon.

I answer that, Some have asserted that witchcraft is nothing in the world but an imagining of men who ascribed to spells those natural effects the causes of which are hidden. But this is contrary to the authority of holy men, who state that the demons have power over men's bodies and

potestatem supra corpora et supra imaginationem hominum, quando a Deo permittuntur. Unde per eos malefici aliqua signa facere possunt.

Procedit autem haec opinio ex radice infidelitatis sive incredulitatis. Quia non credunt esse daemones nisi in aestimatione vulgi tantum: ut terrores quos sibi facit homo, ex sua aestimatione imputet daemoni; et quia etiam ex imaginatione vehementi aliquae figurae apparent in sensu tales quales homo cogitat, et tunc creduntur daemones videri. Sed haec vera fides repudiat: per quam angelos de caelo cecidisse et daemones esse credimus, et ex subtilitate suae naturae multa posse quae nos non possumus. Et illi qui eos ad faciendum talia inducunt, *malefici* vocantur.

Et ideo alii dixerunt quod per maleficia praestari potest impedimentum carnali copulae, sed nullum tale est perpetuum: unde non dirimit matrimonium contractum. Et dicunt iura quae hoc dicebant, esse revocata. Sed hoc est contra experimentum. Et contra nova iura, quae antiquis concordant.

Et ideo distinguendum est. Quia impotentia coeundi ex maleficio aut est perpetua: et tunc matrimonium dirimit. Aut non est perpetua: et tunc non dirimit. Et ad hoc experiendum eodem modo Ecclesia tempus praefixit, triennium scilicet, sicut et de frigiditate dictum est.

Tamen haec est differentia inter maleficium et frigiditatem: quia qui est impotens ex frigiditate, sicut est impotens ad unam, ita est ad aliam; et ideo, quando matrimonium dirimitur, non datur licentia ei ut alteri coniungatur. Sed ex maleficio homo potest esse impotens ad unam et non ad aliam: et ideo, quando iudicio Ecclesiae matrimonium dirimitur, utrique datur licentia ut alteram copulam quaerat.

Ad primum ergo dicendum quod, quia corruptio peccati prima, per quam homo factus est servus diaboli, in nos per actum generativae devenit, ideo maleficii potestas permittitur diabolo a Deo in hoc actu magis quam in aliis: sicut in serpentibus magis ostenditur; virtus maleficiorum, ut dicitur, quam in aliis animalibus, quia per serpentem diabolus mulierem tentavit.

Ad secundum dicendum quod opus Dei potest opere diaboli impediri divina permissione: non quod diabolus sit Deo fortior, ut per violentiam opera eius destruat.

Ad tertium dicendum quod maleficium est ita perpetuum quod non potest habere remedium humano opere: quamvis Deus possit remedium praestare, daemonem cogendo; vel etiam daemon desistendo. Non enim semper oportet ut id quod per maleficium factum est, possit per aliud maleficium destrui: ut ipsi male-

imaginations when God allows them: wherefore by their means wizards can work certain signs.

Now this opinion grows from the root of unbelief or incredulity, because they do not believe that demons exist save only in the imagination of the common people, who ascribe to the demon the terrors which a man conjures from his thoughts, and because, owing to a vivid imagination, certain shapes such as he has in his thoughts become apparent to the senses, and then he believes that he sees the demons. But such assertions are rejected by the true faith whereby we believe that angels fell from heaven, and that the demons exist, and that by reason of their subtle nature they are able to do many things which we cannot; and those who induce them to do such things are called *wizards*.

Therefore, others have maintained that witchcraft can set up an impediment to carnal copulation, but that no such impediment is perpetual: hence it does not void the marriage contract, and they say that the laws asserting this have been revoked. But this is contrary to experience, and to the new legislation which agrees with the old.

We must therefore draw a distinction: for the inability to copulate caused by witchcraft is either perpetual and then it voids marriage, or it is not perpetual and then it does not void marriage. And in order to put this to practical proof the Church has fixed the space of three years in the same way as we have stated with regard to frigidity (A. 1).

There is, however, this difference between a spell and frigidity, that a person who is impotent through frigidity is equally impotent in relation to one as to another, and consequently when the marriage is dissolved, he is not permitted to marry another woman, whereas through witchcraft a man may be rendered impotent in relation to one woman and not to another, and consequently when the Church adjudges the marriage to be dissolved, each party is permitted to seek another partner in marriage.

Reply Obj. 1: The first corruption of sin whereby man became the slave of the devil was transmitted to us by the act of the generative power, and for this reason God allows the devil to exercise his power of witchcraft in this act more than in others. Even so the power of witchcraft is made manifest in serpents more than in other animals according to Genesis 3, since the devil tempted the woman through a serpent.

Reply Obj. 2: God's work may be hindered by the devil's work with God's permission; yet it is not that the devil is stronger than God so as to destroy his works by violence.

Reply Obj. 3: Some spells are so perpetual that they can have no human remedy, although God might afford a remedy by coercing the demon, or the demon by desisting. For, as wizards themselves admit, it does not always follow that what was done by one kind of witchcraft can be destroyed by another kind, and even though it were possible

fici confitentur. Et tamen, si posset per maleficium remedium adhiberi, nihilominus perpetuum reputaretur: quia nullo modo debet aliquis daemonis auxilium per maleficium invocare.

Similiter non oportet quod, si propter peccatum aliquod diabolo data est potestas in aliquem quod, cessante peccato, cesset potestas. Quia poena interdum remanet culpa transeunte.

Similiter etiam exorcismi Ecclesiae non valent ad reprimendum daemones semper, quantum ad omnes molestias corporales, iudicio divino hoc exigente. Semper tamen valent contra illas infestationes daemonum contra quas principaliter instituta sunt.

Ad quartum dicendum quod maleficium quandoque potest praestare ad omnes impedimentum, quandoque ad unam tantum: quia diabolus voluntaria causa est, non ex necessitate naturae agens. Et praeterea impedimentum maleficii potest esse ex impressione daemonis in imaginatione hominis, ex qua tollitur viro concupiscentia movens ad talem mulierem, et non ad aliam.

to use witchcraft as a remedy, it would nevertheless be reckoned to be perpetual, since in no way ought one to invoke the demon's help by witchcraft.

Again, if the devil has been given power over a person on account of sin, it does not follow that his power ceases with the sin, because the punishment sometimes continues after the fault has been removed.

And again, the exorcisms of the Church do not always avail to repress the demons in all their molestations of the body, if God will it so, but they always avail against those assaults of the demons against which they are chiefly instituted.

Reply Obj. 4: Witchcraft sometimes causes an impediment in relation to all, sometimes in relation to one only: because the devil is a voluntary cause not acting from natural necessity. Moreover, the impediment resulting from witchcraft may result from an impression made by the demon on a man's imagination, whereby he is deprived of the concupiscence that moves him in regard to a particular woman and not to another.

Article 3

Whether Madness Is an Impediment to Marriage?

Ad tertium sic proceditur. Videtur quod furia non impediat matrimonium. Matrimonium enim spirituale, quod in baptismo contrahitur, dignius est quam carnale. Sed furiosi possunt baptizari. Ergo et matrimonium contrahere.

Praeterea, frigiditas impedit matrimonium inquantum impedit carnalem copulam. Quae non impeditur per furiam. Ergo nec matrimonium.

Praeterea, matrimonium non dirimitur nisi per aliquod Impedimentum perpetuum. Sed de furia non potest sciri quod sit impedimentum perpetuum. Ergo non dirimit matrimonium.

Praeterea, in versibus supradictis sufficienter continentur impedimenta dirimentia matrimonium. Sed ibi non fit mentio de furia. Ergo, etc.

Sed contra: Plus tollit usum rationis furia quam error. Sed error impedit matrimonium. Ergo et furia.

Praeterea, furiosi, non sunt idonei ad aliquem contractum faciendum. Sed matrimonium est contractus quidam. Ergo, etc.

Respondeo dicendum quod furia aut praecedit matrimonium, aut sequitur. Si sequitur, nullo modo dirimit matrimonium. Si autem praecedit, tunc aut furiosus habet lucida intervalla, aut non. Si habet, tunc, quamvis dum est in illo intervallo non sit tutum quod matrimo-

Objection 1: It would seem that madness is not an impediment to marriage. For spiritual marriage, which is contracted in baptism, is more excellent than carnal marriage. But mad persons can be baptized. Therefore, they can also marry.

Obj. 2: Further, frigidity is an impediment to marriage because it impedes carnal copulation, which is not impeded by madness. Therefore, neither is marriage impeded thereby.

Obj. 3: Further, marriage is not voided save by a perpetual impediment. But one cannot tell whether madness is a perpetual impediment. Therefore, it does not void marriage.

Obj. 4: Further, the impediments that hinder marriage are sufficiently contained in the verses given above (Q. 50). But they contain no mention of madness. Therefore, etc.

On the contrary, Madness removes the use of reason more than error does. But error is an impediment to marriage. Therefore, madness is also.

Further, Mad persons are not fit for making contracts. But marriage is a kind of contract. Therefore, etc.

I answer that, The madness is either previous or subsequent to marriage. If subsequent, it in no way voids the marriage, but if it be previous, then the mad person either has lucid intervals, or not. If he has, then although it is not safe for him to marry during that interval, since he would

nium contrahat, quia nescit prolem educare; tamen, si contrahit, est matrimonium. Si autem non habet, vel si quando non habet contrahit, tunc, quia non potest esse consensus ubi deest rationis usus, non erit verum matrimonium.

Ad primum ergo dicendum quod usus rationis non exigitur ad baptismum quasi causa ipsius, sicut exigitur ad matrimonium. Et ideo non est similis ratio. Tamen de baptismo furiosorum dictum est supra.

Ad secundum dicendum quod furia impedit matrimonium ratione suae causae, quae est consensus, quamvis non ratione actus, ut frigiditas. Sed tamen simul cum frigiditate Magister determinat, quia utrumque est quidam naturae defectus.

Ad tertium dicendum quod momentaneum impedimentum quod causam matrimonii, scilicet consensum, impedit, matrimonium totaliter tollit. Sed impedimentum quod impedit actum, oportet esse perpetuum ad hoc quod matrimonium tollat.

Ad quartum dicendum quod hoc impedimentum reducitur ad errorem: quia utrobique est defectus consensus ex parte rationis.

not know how to educate his children, yet if he marries, the marriage is valid. But if he has no lucid intervals, or marries outside a lucid interval, then, since there can be no consent without use of reason, the marriage will be invalid.

Reply Obj. 1: The use of reason is not necessary for baptism as its cause, in which way it is necessary for matrimony. Hence the comparison fails. We have, however, spoken of the baptism of mad persons (III, Q. 68, A. 12).

Reply Obj. 2: Madness impedes marriage on the part of the latter's cause which is the consent, although not on the part of the act as frigidity does. Yet the Master treats of it together with frigidity, because both are defects of nature (*Sentences* IV, D. 34).

Reply Obj. 3: A passing impediment which hinders the cause of marriage, namely, the consent, voids marriage altogether. But an impediment that hinders the act must be perpetual in order to void the marriage.

Reply Obj. 4: This impediment is reducible to error, since in either case there is lack of consent on the part of the reason.

Article 4

Whether Marriage Is Annulled by the Husband Committing Incest with His Wife's Sister?

Ad quartum sic proceditur. Videtur quod incestus quo quis cognoscit sororem uxoris suae, matrimonium non dirimat. Quia mulier non debet puniri pro peccato viri. Sed puniretur si matrimonium solveretur. Ergo, etc.

Praeterea, plus peccat qui propriam consanguineam cognoscit quam qui cognoscit consanguineam uxoris. Sed primum peccatum non impedit matrimonium. Ergo nec secundum.

Praeterea, si in poenam peccati hoc infligitur, videtur etiam si, mortua uxore, cum alia contrahat incestuosus, quod separari debeant. Quod non est verum.

Praeterea, hoc etiam impedimentum non connumeratur inter alia supra enumerata. Ergo non dirimit contractum matrimonium.

Sed contra: Est, quia per hoc quod cognoscit sororem uxoris, contrahitur affinitas ad uxorem. Sed affinitas dirimit matrimonium contractum. Ergo et incestus praedictus.

Praeterea, *in quo quis peccat, in hoc punitur.* Sed talis peccavit contra matrimonium. Ergo debet puniri quod matrimonio privetur.

Objection 1: It would seem that marriage is not annulled by the husband committing incest with his wife's sister. For the wife should not be punished for her husband's sin. Yet she would be punished if the marriage were annulled. Therefore, etc.

Obj. 2: Further, it is a greater sin to know one's own relative than to know the relative of one's wife. But the former sin is not an impediment to marriage. Therefore, neither is the second.

Obj. 3: Further, if this is inflicted as a punishment of the sin, it would seem, if the incestuous husband marry even after his wife's death, that they ought to be separated: which is not true.

Obj. 4: Further, this impediment is not mentioned among those enumerated above (Q. 50). Therefore, it does not void the marriage contract.

On the contrary, By knowing his wife's sister he contracts affinity with his wife. But affinity voids the marriage contract. Therefore, the aforesaid incest does also.

Further, *By whatsoever a man sins, by the same also is he punished.* Now such a man sins against marriage. Therefore, he ought to be punished by being deprived of marriage.

RESPONDEO dicendum quod, si aliquis cognoscit sororem aut aliam consanguineam uxoris suae ante matrimonium contractum, etiam post sponsalia, oportet matrimonium separari ratione affinitatis contractae.

Si autem post matrimonium contractum et consummatum, non debet totaliter matrimonium separari: sed vir amittit ius petendi debitum, nec potest sine peccato petere. Sed tamen debet reddere petenti: quia uxor non debet puniri de peccato viri.

Sed post mortem uxoris debet omnino manere absque spe coniugii: nisi cum eo dispensetur, propter fragilitatem suam, cui timetur de illicito coitu. Si tamen praeter dispensationem contrahat, peccat Contra statuta Ecclesiae faciens, non tamen matrimonium propter hoc separandum est.

ET PER HOC patet solutio ad obiecta. Quia incestus ponitur matrimonii impedimentum non tam ratione culpae, quam ratione affinitatis quam causat. Et ideo etiam non connumeratur aliis impedimentis, sed impedimento affinitatis includitur.

I ANSWER THAT, If a man has connection with the sister or other relative of his wife before contracting marriage, even after his betrothal, the marriage should be broken off on account of the resultant affinity.

If, however, the connection take place after the marriage has been contracted and consummated, the marriage must not be altogether dissolved: but the husband loses his right to marital intercourse, nor can he demand it without sin.

And yet he must grant it if asked, because the wife should not be punished for her husband's sin. But after the death of his wife he ought to remain without any hope of marriage, unless he receive a dispensation on account of his frailty through fear of unlawful intercourse. If, however, he marry without a dispensation, he sins by contravening the law of the Church, but his marriage is not for this reason to be annulled.

THIS SUFFICES for the replies to the objections, for incest is accounted an impediment to marriage not so much for its being a sin as on account of the affinity which it causes. For this reason it is not mentioned with the other impediments, but is included in the impediment of affinity.

Article 5

Whether Defective Age Is an Impediment to Marriage?

AD QUINTUM SIC PROCEDITUR. Videtur quod defectus aetatis non impediat matrimonium. Secundum enim leges pueri accipiunt tutorem usque ad vigesimum quintum annum. Ergo videtur quod usque ad tempus illud non sit confortata ratio ad consensum. Et ita videtur quod illud debeat esse tempus statutum ad matrimonia ineunda. Sed ante tempus illud matrimonium potest contrahi. Ergo defectus statutae aetatis non impedit matrimonium.

PRAETEREA, sicut vinculum religionis est perpetuum, ita et vinculum matrimonii. Sed ante decimum quartum annum non possunt facere professionem, secundum novam constitutionem. Ergo nec matrimonium contrahere, si defectus aetatis matrimonium impediret.

PRAETEREA, sicut consensus ad matrimonium requiritur ex parte viri, ita ex parte uxoris. Sed mulier ante decimum quartum annum potest contrahere matrimonium. Ergo et vir.

PRAETEREA, impotentia coeundi, nisi sit perpetua et ignorata, non impedit matrimonium. Sed defectus aetatis non est perpetuus nec ignoratus. Ergo non impedit matrimonium.

PRAETEREA, non continetur in aliquo praedictorum impedimentorum. Et ita non videtur esse matrimonii impedimentum.

OBJECTION 1: It would seem that deficient age is not an impediment to marriage. For, according to the laws, children are under the care of a guardian until their twenty-fifth year. Therefore, it would seem that before that age their reason is not sufficiently mature to give consent, and consequently that ought seemingly to be the age fixed for marrying. Yet marriage can be contracted before that age. Therefore, lack of the appointed age is not an impediment to marriage.

OBJ. 2: Further, just as the tie of religion is perpetual, so is the marriage tie. Now, according to the new legislation (*Decretals*), no one can be professed before the fourteenth year of age. Therefore, neither could a person marry if defective age were an impediment.

OBJ. 3: Further, just as consent is necessary for marriage on the part of the man, so is it on the part of the woman. Now a woman can marry before the age of fourteen. Therefore, a man can also.

OBJ. 4: Further, inability to copulate, unless it be perpetual and unknown, is not an impediment to marriage. But lack of age is neither perpetual nor unknown. Therefore, it is not an impediment to marriage.

OBJ. 5: Further, it is not included under any of the aforesaid impediments (Q. 50), and consequently would seem not to be an impediment to marriage.

SED CONTRA: Decretalis dicit quod *puer qui non potest reddere, debitum, non est aptus matrimonio*. Sed ante decimum quartum annum, ut in pluribus, non potest reddere debitum, ut in IX *de Animalibus* dicitur. Ergo, etc.

PRAETEREA, *omnium natura constantium positus est terminus. magnitudinis et augmenti*. Et ita videtur, cum matrimonium sit naturale, quod debeat habere determinatum tempus, per cuius defectum impediatur.

RESPONDEO dicendum quod matrimonium, cum fiat per modum contractus cuiusdam, ordinationi legis positivae subiacet, sicut et alii contractus. Unde secundum iura determinatum est quod, ante illud tempus discretionis quo uterque possit sufficienter de matrimonio deliberare et debitum sibi invicem reddere, matrimonia non contrahantur: et, si non ita facta fuerint, dirimuntur. Hoc autem tempus, ut in pluribus, est in masculis in quarto decimo anno, in femina autem in duodecimo anno: cuius ratio supra, dist. 27, dicta est.

Quia tamen praecepta iuris positivi sequuntur id quod in pluribus est, si aliquis ad perfectionem debitam ante tempus praedictum perveniat, ita quod vigor naturae et rationis *defectum aetatis suppleat*, matrimonium non dissolvitur. Et ideo, si contrahentes ante annos pubertatis, ante tempus praedictum carnaliter fuerint copulati, nihilominus matrimonium stat indissolubile.

AD PRIMUM ergo dicendum quod in illis ad quae natura inclinat, non exigitur tantus vigor rationis ad deliberandum sicut in aliis. Et ideo ante potest sufficienter deliberans in matrimonium consentire quam possit in contractibus aliis res suas sine tutore pertractare.

ET SIMILITER est dicendum ad secundum. Quia votum religionis est eorum quae sunt supra inclinationem naturae, quae maiorem difficultatem habent quam matrimonium.

AD TERTIUM dicendum quod mulier citius ad tempus pubertatis pervenit quam vir, ut dicitur in IX *de Animalibus*. Et ideo non est simile de utroque.

AD QUARTUM dicendum quod ex parte ista non solum est impedimentum propter impotentiam coeundi sed propter defectum rationis, quae adhuc non sufficit ad consensum illum rite faciendum qui perpetuo durare debet.

AD QUINTUM dicendum quod, sicut impedimentum quod est ex furia, reducitur ad impedimentum erroris, ita etiam impedimentum quod est ex defectu aetatis: quia homo nondum habet plenum usum liberi arbitrii.

ON THE CONTRARY, A Decretal says that *a boy who is incapable of marriage intercourse is unfit to marry*. But in the majority of cases he cannot pay the marriage debt before the age of fourteen (*On the Generation of Animals* VII). Therefore, etc.

FURTHER, *There is a fixed limit of size and growth for all things in nature*, according to the Philosopher (*On the Soul* 2.4): and consequently it would seem that, since marriage is natural, it must have a fixed age by defect of which it is impeded.

I ANSWER THAT, Since marriage is effected by way of a contract, it comes under the ordinance of positive law like other contracts. Consequently, according to law (*Decretals*) it is determined that marriage may not be contracted before the age of discretion when each party is capable of sufficient deliberation about marriage and of mutual fulfilment of the marriage debt, and that marriages otherwise contracted are void. Now for the most part this age is the fourteenth year in males and the twelfth year in women.

But since the ordinances of positive law are consequent upon what happens in the majority of cases, if anyone reach the required perfection before the aforesaid age, so that nature and reason are sufficiently developed to *supply the lack of age*, the marriage is not annulled. Wherefore if the parties who marry before the age of puberty have marital intercourse before the aforesaid age, their marriage is nonetheless perpetually indissoluble.

REPLY OBJ. 1: In matters to which nature inclines there is not required such a development of reason in order to deliberate, as in other matters: and therefore it is possible after deliberation to consent to marriage before one is able to manage one's own affairs in other matters without a guardian.

REPLY OBJ. 2: The same answer applies, since the religious vow is about matters outside the inclination of nature, and which offer greater difficulty than marriage.

REPLY OBJ. 3: It is said that woman comes to the age of puberty sooner than man does (*On the Generation of Animals* IX); hence there is no parallel between the two.

REPLY OBJ. 4: In this case there is an impediment not only as to inability to copulate, but also on account of the defect of the reason, which is not yet qualified to give rightly that consent which is to endure in perpetuity.

REPLY OBJ. 5: The impediment arising from defective age, like that which arises from madness, is reducible to the impediment of error; because a man has not yet the full use of his free-will.

QUESTION 59

DISPARITY OF WORSHIP AS AN IMPEDIMENT TO MATRIMONY

Deinde considerandum, est de disparitate cultus, quae matrimonium impedit.

Circa quod quaeruntur sex.

Primo: utrum fidelis possit contrahere matrimonium cum infideli.

Secundo: utrum inter infideles sit matrimonium.

Tertio: utrum coniux conversus ad fidem possit commanere cum infideli nolente converti.

Quarto: utrum possit uxorem infidelem relinquere.

Quinto: utrum, ea dimissa, possit aliam ducere.

Sexto: utrum propter alia peccata vir possit dimittere uxorem, sicut propter infidelitatem.

We must now consider disparity of worship as an impediment to marriage.

Under this head there are six points of inquiry:

(1) Whether a believer can marry an unbeliever?

(2) Whether there is marriage between unbelievers?

(3) Whether a husband, being converted to the faith, can remain with his wife if she be unwilling to be converted?

(4) Whether he may leave his unbelieving wife?

(5) Whether after putting her away he may take another wife?

(6) Whether a husband may put aside his wife on account of other sins as he may for unbelief?

Article 1

Whether a Believer Can Marry an Unbeliever?

AD PRIMUM SIC PROCEDITUR. Videtur quod fidelis possit matrimonium cum infideli contrahere. Quia Ioseph contraxit cum Aegyptia, et Esther cum Assuero. In utroque autem matrimonio fuit disparitas cultus: quia alter erat fidelis et alter infidelis. Ergo disparitas cultus praecedens matrimonium ipsum non impedit.

PRAETEREA, eadem est fides quam docet vetus et nova lex. Sed secundum veterem legem poterat esse matrimonium inter fidelem et infidelem, ut patet Deut. 21: *si, egressus ad pugnam, videris mulierem pulchram in medio captivorum et adamaveris eam, introeas ad eam dormiens cum ea, et erit tibi uxor.* Ergo et in nova lege licet.

PRAETEREA, sponsalia ad matrimonium ordinantur. Sed inter fidelem et infidelem possunt in aliquo casu contrahi sponsalia, cum conditione futurae conversionis. Ergo, sub eadem conditione, matrimonium potest contrahi inter eos.

PRAETEREA, omne impedimentum matrimonii est aliquo modo contra matrimonium. Sed infidelitas non est contraria matrimonio: quia matrimonium est in officium naturae, cuius dictamen fides excedit. Ergo disparitas fidei non impedit matrimonium.

PRAETEREA, disparitas fidei etiam quandoque est inter duos baptizatos: sicut quando aliquis post baptismum in haeresim labitur. Et si talis cum aliqua fide-

OBJECTION 1: It would seem that a believer can marry an unbeliever. For Joseph married an Egyptian woman, and Esther married Ahasuerus: and in both marriages there was disparity of worship, since one was an unbeliever and the other a believer. Therefore, disparity of worship previous to marriage is not an impediment to it.

OBJ. 2: Further, the old law teaches the same faith as the new. But according to the old law there could be marriage between a believer and an unbeliever, as evidenced by Deuteronomy 21:10: *if you go out to the fight and see in the number of the captives a beautiful woman and love her, and will have her to wife, you shall go in unto her, and shall sleep with her, and she shall be your wife.* Therefore, it is lawful also under the new law.

OBJ. 3: Further, betrothal is directed to marriage. Now there can be a betrothal between a believer and an unbeliever in the case where a condition is made of the latter's future conversion. Therefore, under the same condition there can be marriage between them.

OBJ. 4: Further, every impediment to marriage is in some way contrary to marriage. But unbelief is not contrary to marriage, since marriage fulfills an office of nature whose dictate faith surpasses. Therefore, disparity of worship is not an impediment to marriage.

OBJ. 5: Further, there is sometime disparity of worship even between two persons who are baptized, for instance, when a person falls into heresy after baptism. Yet if such

li contrahat, nihilominus est verum matrimonium. Ergo disparitas cultus matrimonium non impedit.

Sed contra: Est quod dicitur II Cor. 6: *quae conventio lucis ad tenebras?* Sed maxima conventio est inter virum et uxorem. Ergo ille qui est in luce fidei, non potest contrahere matrimonium cum illa quae est in tenebris infidelitatis.

Praeterea, Malach. 2 dicitur: *contaminavit ludas sanctificationem Domini, quoniam dilexit et habuit filiam dei alieni.* Sed hoc non esset si inter eos posset verum matrimonium contrahi. Ergo disparitas cultus matrimonium impedit.

Respondeo dicendum quod principalius matrimonii bonum est proles ad cultum Dei educanda. Cum autem educatio fiat communiter inter patrem et matrem, uterque secundum fidem intendit ad cultum Dei prolem educare. Et ideo, si sint diversae fidei, intentio unius alterius intentioni contraria erit. Et ita non potest inter eos esse conveniens matrimonium. Et propter hoc disparitas cultus praecederis impedit ipsum, ne contrahi possit.

Ad primum ergo dicendum quod in veteri lege de aliquibus infidelibus erat permissum quod cum eis possent inire coniugia, et de aliquibus prohibitum. Specialiter quidem prohibitum erat de infidelibus habitantibus in terra Chanaan: tum quia Dominus praeceperat eos occidi, propter eorum obstinationem; tum quia maius periculum imminebat ne coniuges aut filios ad idololatriam perverterent, quia filii Israel ad ritus et mores eorum proniores erant propter conversationem cum eis. Sed de aliis gentibus permisit: praecipue quia non poterat esse timor pertrahendi ad idololatriam. Et sic Ioseph et Moyses et Esther cum infidelibus matrimonia contraxerunt.

Sed in nova lege, quae per totum orbem diffunditur, similis ratio prohibendi est de omnibus infidelibus. Et ideo disparitas cultus praecedens matrimonium impedit contrahendum et dirimit contractum.

Ad secundum dicendum quod lex illa vel loquitur de aliis nationibus cum quibus licite poterant inire coniugia: vel loquitur quando illa captiva ad fidem et cultum Dei converti volebat.

Ad tertium dicendum quod eadem est habitudo praesentis ad praesens et futuri ad futurum. Unde sicut, quando matrimonium in praesenti contrahitur, requiritur unitas cultus in utroque contrahentium; ita ad sponsalia, quibus fit sponsio futuri matrimonii, sufficit conditio apposita, de futura unitate cultus.

Ad quartum dicendum quod iam ex dictis patet quod disparitas cultus contraria est matrimonio ratione principalioris boni ipsius, quod est bonum prolis.

a person marry a believer, it is nevertheless a valid marriage. Therefore, disparity of worship is not an impediment to marriage.

On the contrary, It is written: *what concord has light with darkness?* (2 Cor 6:14) Now there is the greatest concord between husband and wife. Therefore, one who is in the light of faith cannot marry one who is in the darkness of unbelief.

Further, It is written: *Judah has profaned the holiness of the Lord, which he loved, and has married the daughter of a strange god* (Mal 2:11). But such had not been the case if they could have married validly. Therefore, disparity of worship is an impediment to marriage.

I answer that, The chief good of marriage is the offspring to be brought up to the worship of God. Now since education is the work of father and mother in common, each of them intends to bring up the child to the worship of God according to their own faith. Consequently, if they be of different faiths, the intention of the one will be contrary to the intention of the other, and therefore there cannot be a fitting marriage between them. For this reason disparity of faith previous to marriage is an impediment to the marriage contract.

Reply Obj. 1: In the old law it was allowable to marry with certain unbelievers, and forbidden with others. It was, however, especially forbidden with regard to inhabitants of the land of Canaan, both because the Lord had commanded them to be slain on account of their obstinacy, and because it was fraught with a greater danger, namely, lest they should pervert to idolatry those whom they married or their children, since the Israelites were more liable to adopt their rites and customs through dwelling among them. But it was permitted in regard to other unbelievers, especially when there could be no fear of their being drawn into idolatry. And thus Joseph, Moses, and Esther married unbelievers.

But under the new law, which is spread throughout the whole world, the prohibition extends with equal reason to all unbelievers. Hence disparity of worship previous to marriage is an impediment to its being contracted and voids the contract.

Reply Obj. 2: This law either refers to other nations with whom they could lawfully marry, or to the case when the captive woman was willing to be converted to the faith and worship of God.

Reply Obj. 3: Present is related to present in the same way as future to future. Wherefore just as when marriage is contracted in the present, unity of worship is required in both contracting parties, so in the case of a betrothal, which is a promise of future marriage, it suffices to add the condition of future unity of worship.

Reply Obj. 4: It has been made clear that disparity of worship is contrary to marriage in respect of its chief good, which is the good of the offspring.

Ad quintum dicendum quod matrimonium est sacramentum: et ideo, quantum pertinet ad necessitatem, sacramenti, requirit paritatem quantum ad sacramentum fidei, scilicet baptismum, magis quam quantum ad interiorem fidem. Unde etiam hoc impedimentum non dicitur disparitas *fidei*, sed disparitas *cultus*, qui respicit exterius servitium, ut in III libro dictum est. Et propter hoc, si aliquis fidelis cum haeretica baptizata matrimonium contrahat, verum est matrimonium. Quamvis peccet contrahendo, si scit eam haereticam: sicut peccaret si cum excommunicata contraheret. Non tamen propter hoc matrimonium dirimeretur. Et e converso, si aliquis catechumenus, habens rectam fidem sed nondum baptizatus, cum aliqua fideli baptizata contraheret, non esset verum matrimonium.

Reply Obj. 5: Matrimony is a sacrament: and therefore so far as the sacramental essentials are concerned, it requires purity with regard to the sacrament of faith, namely, baptism, rather than with regard to interior faith. For which reason also this impediment is not called disparity of *faith*, but disparity of *worship* which concerns outward service, as stated above (*Sentences* III, D. 9, Q. 1, A. 1, q. 1). Consequently, if a believer marry a baptized heretic, the marriage is valid, although he sins by marrying her if he knows her to be a heretic: even so he would sin were he to marry an excommunicate woman, and yet the marriage would not be void. Whereas on the other hand, if a catechumen, having right faith but not having been baptized, were to marry a baptized believer, the marriage would not be valid.

Article 2

Whether There Can Be Marriage Between Unbelievers?

Ad secundum sic proceditur. Videtur quod inter infideles non possit esse matrimonium. Matrimonium enim est sacramentum Ecclesiae. Sed baptismus est *ianua sacramentorum*. Ergo infideles, qui non sunt baptizati, matrimonium contrahere non possunt, sicut nec alia sacramenta suscipere.

Praeterea, duo mala sunt magis impeditiva boni quam unum. Sed infidelitas unius tantum impedit bonum matrimonii. Ergo multo fortius infidelitas utriusque. Et ita inter infideles non potest esse matrimonium.

Praeterea, sicut inter infideles et fideles est disparitas cultus, ita interdum inter duos infideles: ut si unus sit gentilis et alter Iudaeus. Sed disparitas cultus impedit matrimonium, ut dictum est. Ergo ad minus inter infideles qui habent cultum disparem, non potest esse verum matrimonium.

Praeterea, in matrimonio est vera pudicitia. Sed, sicut dicit Augustinus, et habetur XXVIII, qu. 1, *non est vera pudicitia infidelis cum uxore sua*. Ergo nec verum matrimonium.

Praeterea, matrimonium verum excusat carnalem copulam a peccato. Sed hoc non potest facere matrimonium inter infideles contractum: quia *omnis vita infidelium peccatum est*, ut dicit Glossa Rom. 14. Ergo inter infideles non est verum matrimonium.

Sed contra: Est quod dicitur I Cor. 7: *si quis frater uxorem habeat infidelem* etc. Sed uxor non dicitur nisi propter matrimonium. Ergo matrimonium quod est inter infideles, est verum matrimonium.

Objection 1: It would seem that there can be no marriage between unbelievers. For matrimony is a sacrament of the Church. Now baptism is the *door of the sacraments*. Therefore, unbelievers, since they are not baptized, cannot marry any more than they can receive other sacraments.

Obj. 2: Further, two evils are a greater impediment to good than one. But the unbelief of only one party is an impediment to marriage. Much more, therefore, is the unbelief of both, and consequently there can be no marriage between unbelievers.

Obj. 3: Further, just as there is disparity of worship between believer and unbeliever, so can there be between two unbelievers, for instance, if one be a heathen and the other a Jew. Now disparity of worship is an impediment to marriage, as stated above (A. 1). Therefore, there can be no valid marriage at least between unbelievers of different worship.

Obj. 4: Further, in marriage there is real chastity. But according to Augustine (*On Adulterous Marriages* 1.18) *there is no real chastity between an unbeliever and his wife*, and these words are quoted in the *Decretals*. Neither, therefore, is there a true marriage.

Obj. 5: Further, true marriage excuses carnal intercourse from sin. But marriage contracted between unbelievers cannot do this, since *the whole life of unbelievers is a sin*, as a Gloss observes on Romans 14:23, *all that is not of faith is sin*. Therefore, there is no true marriage between unbelievers.

On the contrary, It is written: *if any brother has a wife that does not believe, and she consent to dwell with him, let him not put her away* (1 Cor 7:10). But she is not called his wife except by reason of marriage. Therefore, marriage between unbelievers is a true marriage.

PRAETEREA, remoto posteriori, non removetur prius. Sed matrimonium pertinet ad officium naturae: quae praecedit statum gratiae, cuius principium est fides. Ergo infidelitas non facit quin sit inter infideles matrimonium.

RESPONDEO dicendum quod matrimonium principaliter est institutum ad bonum prolis non tantum generandae, quia hoc sine matrimonio fieri posset, sed etiam promovendae ad perfectum statum: quia quaelibet res intendit effectum suum naturaliter perducere ad perfectum statum. Est autem in prole duplex perfectio consideranda: scilicet perfectio naturae, non solum quantum ad corpus sed etiam quantum ad animam, per ea quae sunt in lege naturae; et perfectio gratiae. Et prima perfectio est materialis et imperfecta respectu secundae. Et ideo, cum res quae sunt propter finem, sint proportionatae fini, matrimonium quod tendit in primam perfectionem, est imperfectum et materiale respectu illius quod tendit in perfectionem secundam. Et quia prima perfectio communis esse potest infidelibus et fidelibus, secunda autem est tantum fidelium, ideo inter infideles est quidem matrimonium, sed non perfectum ultima perfectione, sicut est inter fideles.

AD PRIMUM ergo dicendum quod matrimonium non tantum est institutum in sacramentum, sed in officium naturae. Et ideo, quamvis infidelibus non competat matrimonium secundum quod est sacramentum in dispensatione ministrorum Ecclesiae consistens, competit tamen eis inquantum est in officium naturae. Et tamen etiam matrimonium tale est aliquo modo sacramentum habitualiter: quamvis non actualiter, eo quod actu non contrahunt in fide Ecclesiae.

AD SECUNDUM dicendum quod disparitas cultus non impedit matrimonium ratione infidelitatis, sed ratione disparitatis in fide. Disparitas enim cultus non solum secundam perfectionem prolis impedit, sed etiam primam, dum parentes ad diversa prolem trahere intendunt. Quod non est quando uterque est infidelis.

AD TERTIUM dicendum quod inter infideles est matrimonium prout matrimonium est in officium naturae. Ea autem quae pertinent ad legem naturae, sunt determinabilia per ius positivum. Et ideo, si prohibentur ab aliquo iure positivo apud eos infideles contrahere matrimonium cum infidelibus alterius ritus, disparitas cultus impedit matrimonium inter eos. Ex iure enim divino non prohibentur: quia apud Deum non differt qualitercumque aliquis a fide deviet, quantum ad hoc quod est a gratia alienum esse. Similiter nec aliquo Ecclesiae statuto: quae non habet *de his quae foris sunt iudicare.*

FURTHER, The removal of what comes after does not imply the removal of what comes first. Now marriage belongs to an office of nature which precedes the state of grace, the principle of which is faith. Therefore, unbelief does not prevent the existence of marriage between unbelievers.

I ANSWER THAT, Marriage was instituted chiefly for the good of the offspring, not only as to its begetting—since this can be effected even without marriage—but also as to its advancement to a perfect state, because everything intends naturally to bring its effect to perfection. Now a twofold perfection is to be considered in the offspring. One is the perfection of nature, not only as regards the body but also as regards the soul, by those means which are of the natural law. The other is the perfection of grace: and the former perfection is material and imperfect in relation to the latter. Consequently, since those things which are for the sake of the end are proportionate to the end, the marriage that tends to the first perfection is imperfect and material in comparison with that which tends to the second perfection. And since the first perfection can be common to unbelievers and believers, while the second belongs only to believers, it follows that between unbelievers there is marriage indeed, but not perfected by its ultimate perfection as there is between believers.

REPLY OBJ. 1: Marriage was instituted not only as a sacrament, but also as an office of nature. And therefore, although marriage is not competent to unbelievers as a sacrament dependent on the dispensation of the Church's ministers, it is nevertheless competent to them as fulfilling an office of nature. And yet even a marriage of this kind is a sacrament after the manner of a habit, although it is not actually since they do not marry actually in the faith of the Church.

REPLY OBJ. 2: Disparity of worship is an impediment to marriage not by reason of unbelief, but on account of the difference of faith. For disparity of worship hinders not only the second perfection of the offspring, but also the first, since the parents endeavor to draw their children in different directions, which is not the case when both are unbelievers.

REPLY OBJ. 3: As already stated (ad 1) there is marriage between unbelievers insofar as marriage fulfills an office of nature. Now those things that pertain to the natural law are determinable by positive law: and therefore if any law among unbelievers forbid the contracting of marriage with unbelievers of a different rite, the disparity of worship will be an impediment to their intermarrying. They are not, however, forbidden by divine law, because before God, however much one may stray from the faith, this makes no difference to one's being removed from grace: nor is it forbidden by any law of the Church who has not *to judge of those who are without.*

Ad quartum dicendum quod pudicitiae et aliae virtutes infidelium dicuntur non esse verae, quia non possunt attingere finem verae virtutis, qui est vera felicitas: sicut dicitur non esse verum vinum quod non habet effectum vini.

Ad quintum dicendum quod infidelis cognoscens uxorem suam non peccat, si propter bonum prolis, aut fidei qua tenetur uxori, debitum reddat: cum hoc sit actus iustitiae et temperantiae, quae in delectabilibus tactus debitas circumstantias servat; sicut non peccat faciens alios actus politicarum virtutum. Nec dicitur *omnis vita infidelium peccatum* quia quolibet actu peccent: sed quia per id quod agunt a servitute peccati non possunt liberari.

Reply Obj. 4: The chastity and other virtues of unbelievers are said not to be real, because they cannot attain the end of real virtue, which is real happiness. Thus we say it is not a real wine if it has not the effect of wine.

Reply Obj. 5: An unbeliever does not sin in having intercourse with his wife if he pays her the marriage debt for the good of the offspring, or for the troth whereby he is bound to her: since this is an act of justice and of temperance which observes the due circumstance in pleasure of touch; even as neither does he sin in performing acts of other civic virtues. Again, the reason why the *whole life of unbelievers is said to be a sin* is not that they sin in every act, but because they cannot be delivered from the bondage of sin by that which they do.

Article 3

Whether the Husband, Being Converted to the Faith, May Remain with His Wife If She Be Unwilling to Be Converted?

Ad tertium sic proceditur. Videtur quod coniux conversus ad fidem non possit commanere cum uxore infideli nolente converti, cum qua in infidelitate contraxerat. Ubi enim est idem periculum, debet eadem cautela adhiberi. Sed propter periculum subversionis fidei prohibetur ne fidelis cum infideli contrahat. Cum ergo periculum sit si fidelis commaneat cum infideli cum qua prius contraxerat; et adhuc maius, quia neophyti facilius pervertuntur quam illi qui sunt nutriti in fide: videtur quod fidelis post conversionem non possit commanere cum uxore infideli.

Praeterea, XXVIII, qu. i, dicitur: *non potest infidelis in eius coniunctione permanere quae iam in Christianam translata est fidem*. Ergo fidelis habet necesse uxorem infidelem dimittere.

Praeterea, matrimonium quod inter fideles contrahitur, est perfectius quam illud quod contrahitur inter infideles. Sed si fideles contrahant in gradu prohibito, ab Ecclesia dissolvitur eorum matrimonium. Ergo et infidelium. Et ita vir fidelis non potest commanere cum uxore infideli, ad minus quando cum ea in infidelitate contraxit in gradu prohibito.

Praeterea, aliquis infidelis habet quandoque plures uxores, secundum ritum suae legis. Si ergo potest commanere cum illis cum quibus in infidelitate contraxit, videtur quod possit etiam post conversionem plures uxores retinere.

Praeterea, potest contingere quod, repudiata una uxore, aliam duxerit, et in illo matrimonio existens con-

Objection 1: It would seem that when a husband is converted to the faith he cannot remain with his wife who is an unbeliever and is unwilling to be converted, and whom he had married while he was yet an unbeliever. For where the danger is the same one should take the same precautions. Now a believer is forbidden to marry an unbeliever for fear of being turned away from the faith. Since, then, if the believer remain with the unbeliever whom he had married previously, the danger is the same (in fact greater, for neophytes are more easily perverted than those who have been brought up in the faith) it would seem that a believer, after being converted, cannot remain with an unbeliever.

Obj. 2: Further, *an unbeliever cannot remain united to her who has been received into the Christian faith* (*Decretals*). Therefore, a believer is bound to put away a wife who does not believe.

Obj. 3: Further, a marriage contracted between believers is more perfect than one contracted between unbelievers. Now, if believers marry within the degrees forbidden by the Church, their marriage is void. Therefore, the same applies to unbelievers, and thus a believing husband cannot remain with an unbelieving wife, at any rate if as an unbeliever he married her within the forbidden degrees.

Obj. 4: Further, sometimes an unbeliever has several wives recognized by his law. If, then, he can remain with those whom he married while yet an unbeliever, it would seem that even after his conversion he can retain several wives.

Obj. 5: Further, it may happen that after divorcing his first wife he has married a second, and that he is converted

vertatur. Videtur ergo quod, saltem in hoc casu, non possit cum uxore quam de novo habet, commanere.

SED CONTRA: Est quod Apostolus, I Cor: 7, consulit quod commaneant.

PRAETEREA, nullum impedimentum superveniens vero matrimonio tollit ipsum. Sed matrimonium erat verum quando uterque infidelis erat. Ergo, quando alter convertitur, non dirimitur per hoc matrimonium. Et ita videtur quod possit licite commanere.

RESPONDEO dicendum quod fides eius qui est in matrimonio, non solvit, sed perficit matrimonium. Unde, cum inter infideles sit verum matrimonium, ut ex dictis patet, per hoc quod alter eorum convertitur ad fidem, non ex hoc ipso vinculum matrimonii solvitur. Sed aliquando, vinculo matrimonii manente, solvitur matrimonium quantum ad cohabitationem et debiti solutionem. In quo pari passu currunt infidelitas et adulterium: quia utrumque est contra bonum prolis. Unde, sicut se habet in potestate dimittendi adulteram vel commanendi cum ea, ita se habet in potestate dimittendi infidelem vel commanendi cum ea. Potest enim vir innocens libere manere cum adultera spe correctionis non autem si in adulterii peccato fuerit obstinata, ne videatur *patronus turpitudinis*; quamvis, etiam cum spe correctionis, possit eam libere dimittere. Similiter fidelis conversus potest cum infideli manere cum spe conversionis, si eam in infidelitate obstinatam non viderit: et bene facit commanendo, tametsi non tenetur. Et de hoc est consilium Apostoli.

AD PRIMUM ergo dicendum quod facilius impeditur aliquid fiendum, quam destruatur quod ite factum est. Et ideo multa sunt quae impediunt matrimonium contrahendum si praecedant, quae tamen ipsum non possunt dissolvere si sequantur: sicut de affinitate patet. Et similiter dicendum est de disparitate cultus.

AD SECUNDUM dicendum, quod in primitiva Ecclesia, tempore Apostolorum, passim convertebantur ad fidem et Iudaei et gentiles. Et ideo tunc vir fidelis poterat habere probabilem spem de uxoris conversione, etiam si conversionem non promitteret. Postmodum autem, tempore procedente, Iudaei sunt magis obstinati quam gentiles: quia gentiles adhuc intrabant ad fidem, sicut tempore martyrum et temporibus Constantini Imperatoris et circa tempora illa. Et ideo tunc non erat tutum fideli cum uxore infideli Iudaea cohabitare, nec erat spes de conversione eius, sicut erat de conversione uxoris gentilis. Et ideo tunc fidelis conversus poterat cohabitare cum gentili, sed non cum Iudaea, nisi conversionem promitteret. Et secundum hoc loquitur decretum illud. Sed nunc pari passu ambulant utrique, scilicet gentiles et Iudaei: quia utrique obstinati sunt. Et ideo, nisi uxor infidelis converti velit, non permittetur ei cohabitare, sive sit gentilis sive Iudaea.

during this latter marriage. It would seem, therefore, that at least in this case he cannot remain with this second wife.

ON THE CONTRARY, The Apostle counsels him to remain (1 Cor 7:12).

FURTHER, No impediment that supervenes upon a true marriage dissolves it. Now it was a true marriage when they were both unbelievers. Therefore, when one of them is converted, the marriage is not annulled on that account; and thus it would seem that they may lawfully remain together.

I ANSWER THAT, The faith of a married person does not dissolve but perfects the marriage. Wherefore, since there is true marriage between unbelievers, as stated above (A. 2), the marriage tie is not broken by the fact that one of them is converted to the faith, but sometimes while the marriage tie remains, the marriage is dissolved as to cohabitation and marital intercourse, in which unbelief and adultery are on a par, since both are against the good of the offspring. Consequently, the husband has the same power to put away an unbelieving wife or to remain with her as he has to put away an adulterous wife or to remain with her. For an innocent husband is free to remain with an adulterous wife in the hope of her amendment, but not if she *be obstinate in her sin* of adultery, lest he seem to approve of her disgrace; although even if there be hope of her amendment he is free to put her away. In like manner, the believer after his conversion may remain with the unbeliever in the hope of her conversion, if he see that she is not obstinate in her unbelief, and he does well in remaining with her, though not bound to do so: and this is what the Apostle counsels (1 Cor 7:12).

REPLY OBJ. 1: It is easier to prevent a thing being done than to undo what is rightly done. Hence there are many things that impede the contracting of marriage if they precede it, which nevertheless cannot dissolve it if they follow it. Such is the case with affinity (Q. 55, A. 6): and it is the same with disparity of worship.

REPLY OBJ. 2: In the early Church at the time of the apostles, both Jews and gentiles were everywhere converted to the faith: and consequently the believing husband could then have a reasonable hope for his wife's conversion, even though she did not promise to be converted. Afterwards, however, as time went on the Jews became more obstinate than the gentiles, because the gentiles still continued to come to the faith, for instance, at the time of the martyrs, and in the Emperor Constantine's times and thereabouts. Wherefore it was not safe then for a believer to cohabit with an unbelieving Jewish wife, nor was there hope for her conversion as for that of a gentile wife. Consequently, then, the believer could, after his conversion, cohabit with his wife if she were a gentile, but not if she were a Jewess, unless she promised to be converted. This is the sense of that decree. Now, however, they are on a par, namely, gentiles and Jews, because both are obstinate; and therefore unless the unbelieving wife be willing to be converted, he is not allowed to cohabit with her, be she gentile or Jew.

Ad tertium dicendum quod infideles non baptizati non sunt adstricti statutis Ecclesiae, sed sunt adstricti statutis iuris divini. Et ideo, si contraxerunt aliqui infideles in gradibus prohibitis secundum legem divinam, Levit. 18, sive uterque sive alter ad fidem convertatur, non possunt in tali matrimonio commanere. Si autem contraxerunt in gradibus prohibitis per statutum Ecclesiae, possunt commanere, si uterque convertatur, vel si, uno converso, sit spes de conversione alterius.

Ad quartum dicendum quod habere plures uxores est contra legem naturae, cui etiam infideles sunt adstricti. Et ideo non est verum matrimonium infidelis nisi cum illa cum qua primo contraxit. Unde, si ipse cum omnibus suis uxoribus convertatur, potest cum prima commanere, et alias debet abiicere. Si autem prima converti noluerit, et aliqua aliarum convertatur, idem ius habet contrahendi cum illa de novo quod cum alia habet: de quo post dicetur.

Ad quintum dicendum quod repudium Uxoris est contra legem naturae. Unde infideli non licet uxorem repudiare. Et ideo, si convertatur postquam, una repudiata, alteram duxerit, idem iudicium est de hoc et de illo qui plures uxores habebat: quia tenetur primam, quam repudiaverat, accipere, si converti voluerit, et aliam abiicere.

Reply Obj. 3: Non-baptized unbelievers are not bound by the laws of the Church, but they are bound by the ordinances of the divine law. Hence unbelievers who have married within the degrees forbidden by the divine law, whether both or one of them be converted to the faith, cannot continue in a like marriage. But if they have married within the degrees forbidden by a commandment of the Church, they can remain together if both be converted, or if one be converted and there be hope of the other's conversion.

Reply Obj. 4: To have several wives is contrary to the natural law by which even unbelievers are bound. Wherefore an unbeliever is not truly married save to her whom he married first. Consequently, if he be converted with all his wives, he may remain with the first, and must put the others away. If, however, the first refuse to be converted, and one of the others be converted, he has the same right to marry her again as he would have to marry another. We shall treat of this matter further on (A. 5).

Reply Obj. 5: To divorce a wife is contrary to the law of nature, wherefore it is not lawful for an unbeliever to divorce his wife. Hence if he be converted after divorcing one and marrying another, the same judgment is to be pronounced in this case as in the case of a man who had several wives, because if he wish to be converted he is bound to take the first whom he had divorced and to put the other away.

Article 4

Whether a Believer Can, After His Conversion, Put Away His Unbelieving Wife If She Be Willing to Cohabit With Him Without Insult to the Creator?

Ad quartum sic proceditur. Videtur quod fidelis conversus non possit uxorem infidelem dimittere volentem cohabitare *sine contumelia Creatoris*. Maius enim est vinculum viri ad mulierem quam servi ad dominum. Sed servus conversus non absolvitur a servitutis vinculo: ut patet I Cor. 7, et I Tim. 6. Ergo et vir non potest uxorem infidelem dimittere.

Praeterea, nullus potest alteri praeiudicium facere sine consensu ipsius. Sed uxor infidelis habebat ius in corpore viri infidelis. Si ergo per hoc quod vir ad fidem convertitur, mulier praeiudicium pati posset, ut libere dimitteretur, non posset vir converti ad fidem sine consensu uxoris: sicut nec potest ordinari, nec vovere continentiam, sine consensu uxoris.

Praeterea, si aliquis contrahat cum ancilla scienter, sive sit servus sive liber, non propter diversam conditionem potest ipsam dimittere. Cum ergo vir, quando contraxit cum infideli, sciverit eam esse infidelem, vide-

Objection 1: It would seem that a believer, after his conversion, cannot put away his unbelieving wife if she be willing to cohabit with him *without insult to the Creator*. For the husband is more bound to his wife than a slave to his master. But a converted slave is not freed from the bond of slavery, as appears from 1 Corinthians 7:21 and 1 Timothy 6:1. Therefore, neither can a believing husband put away his unbelieving wife.

Obj. 2: Further, no one may act to another's prejudice without the latter's consent. Now the unbelieving wife had a right in the body of her unbelieving husband. If, then, her husband's conversion to the faith could be prejudicial to the wife, so that he would be free to put her away, the husband could not be converted to the faith without his wife's consent, even as he cannot receive orders or vow continence without her consent.

Obj. 3: Further, if a man, whether slave or free, knowingly marry a slavewoman, he cannot put her away on account of her different condition. Since, then, the husband, when he married an unbeliever, knew that she was an un-

tur a simili quod non possit eam dimittere propter infidelitatem.

PRAETEREA, pater tenetur ex debito procurare salutem prolis. Sed si discederet ab infideli uxore, filii communes matri remanerent, quia *partus sequitur ventrem*: et sic essent in periculo salutis. Ergo non potest uxorem infidelem licite dimittere.

PRAETEREA, adulter non potest adulteram dimittere, etiam postquam de adulterio poenitentiam egit. Ergo, si sit idem iudicium de adultero et infideli, nec infidelis infidelem, etiam postquam ad fidem est conversus.

SED CONTRA: Est quod Apostolus dicit, 1 Cor. 7.

PRAETEREA, adulterium spirituale est gravius quam carnale. Sed propter carnale adulterium vir potest relinquere uxorem quantum ad cohabitationem. Ergo inulto fortius propter infidelitatem, quae est adulterium spirituale.

RESPONDEO dicendum quod homini secundum aliam et aliam vitam diversa competunt et expediunt. Et ideo qui moritur priori vitae, non tenetur ad illa ad quae in priori vita tenebatur. Et inde est quod ille qui, in vita saeculari existens, aliqua vovit, non tenetur illa, quando mundo moritur vitam religiosam assumens, perficere. Ille autem qui ad baptismum accedit, regeneratur in Christo et priori vitae moritur: cum *generatio unius sit corruptio alterius*. Et ideo liberatur ab obligatione qua uxori tenebatur reddere debitum, et ei cohabitare non tenetur, quando converti non vult. Quamvis in aliquo casu libere id possit facere, sicut dictum est: sicut et religiosus potest libere perficere vota quae fecit in saeculo, si non sunt contra religionem suam, quamvis ad ea non teneatur, ut dictum est.

AD PRIMUM ergo dicendum quod servire non est aliquid incompetens Christianae religionis perfectioni, quae maxime humilitatem profitetur. Sed obligatio matrimonii aliquid derogat perfectioni vitae Christianae, cuius summum statum continentes possident. Et ideo non est simile de utroque.

Et praeterea unus coniugum non obligatur alteri quasi possessio eius, sicut domino servus, sed per modum societatis cuiusdam: quae non congrue est fidelis ad infidelem, ut patet II Cor. 6. Et ideo non est simile de servo et coniuge.

AD SECUNDUM dicendum quod uxor, non habebat ius in corpore viri nisi quandiu in vita illa manebat in qua contraxerant: quia etiam, mortuo viro, *uxor soluta est a lege viri*, ut patet Rom. 7. Et ideo si, postquam vir mutat vitam moriens priori vitae, ab ea discedat, nullum fit ei praeiudicium.

believer, it would seem that in like manner he cannot put her away on account of her unbelief.

OBJ. 4: Further, a father is duty-bound to work for the salvation of his children. But if he were to leave his unbelieving wife, the children of their union would remain with the mother, because *the offspring follows the womb*, and thus their salvation would be imperiled. Therefore, he cannot lawfully put away his unbelieving wife.

OBJ. 5: Further, an adulterous husband cannot put away an adulterous wife, even after he has done penance for his adultery. Therefore, if an adulterous and an unbelieving husband are to be judged alike, neither can the believer put aside the unbeliever, even after his conversion to the faith.

ON THE CONTRARY, There are the words of the Apostle in 1 Corinthians 7:15–16.

FURTHER, Spiritual adultery is more grievous than carnal. But a man can put his wife away as to cohabitation on account of carnal adultery. Much more, therefore, can he do so on account of unbelief, which is spiritual adultery.

I ANSWER THAT, Different things are competent and expedient to man according as his life is of one kind or of another. Wherefore he who dies to his former life is not bound to those things to which he was bound in his former life. Hence it is that he who vowed certain things while living in the world is not bound to fulfill them when he dies to the world by adopting the religious life. Now he who is baptized is regenerated in Christ and dies to his former life, since the *generation of one thing is the corruption of another*, and consequently he is freed from the obligation whereby he was bound to pay his wife the marriage debt, and is not bound to cohabit with her when she is unwilling to be converted, although in a certain case he is free to do so, as stated above (A. 3), just as a religious is free to fulfill the vows he took in the world if they be not contrary to his religious profession, although he is not bound to do so.

REPLY OBJ. 1: Bondage is not inconsistent with the perfection of the Christian religion, which makes a very special profession of humility. But the obligation to a wife, or the conjugal bond, is somewhat derogatory to the perfection of Christian life, the highest state of which is in the possession of the continent: hence the comparison fails.

Moreover, one married party is not bound to the other as the latter's possession, as a slave to his master, but by way of a kind of partnership, which is unfitting between unbeliever and believer, as appears from 2 Corinthians 6:15; hence there is no comparison between a slave and a married person.

REPLY OBJ. 2: The wife had a right in the body of her husband only as long as he remained in the life wherein he had married, since also when the husband dies the wife *is delivered from the law of her husband* (Rom 7:2). Wherefore if the husband leave her after he has changed his life by dying to his former life, this is in no way prejudicial to her.

Transiens autem ad religionem moritur tantum spirituali morte, non autem corporali. Et ideo, si matrimonium sit consummatum, non potest vir sine consensu uxoris ad religionem transire. Potest autem ante carnalem copulam, quando est tantum copula spiritualis. Sed ille qui ad baptismum accedit, corporaliter etiam *consepelitur Christo in mortem*. Et ideo a debito reddendo absolvitur, etiam post matrimonium consummatum.

Vel dicendum quod ex culpa sua uxor praeiudicium patitur, quae converti contemnit.

Ad tertium dicendum quod disparitas cultus facit personam simpliciter illegitimam: non autem conditio servitutis, sed solum quando ignorata est. Et ideo non est similis ratio de infideli et ancilla.

Ad quartum dicendum quod proles aut pervenit ad perfectam aetatem: et tunc poterit libere sequi patrem fidelem vel matrem infidelem. Vel est in minori aetate constitutus. Et tunc debet dari fideli, non obstante quod indiget matris obsequio ad educationem.

Ad quintum dicendum quod adulter per poenitentiam non transit ad aliam vitam, sicut infidelis per baptismum. Et ideo non est similis ratio.

Now he who goes over to the religious life dies but a spiritual death and not a bodily death. Wherefore if the marriage be consummated, the husband cannot enter religion without his wife's consent, whereas he can before carnal connection when there is only a spiritual connection. On the other hand, he who is baptized is even *corporeally buried together with Christ unto death*; and therefore he is freed from paying the marriage debt even after the marriage has been consummated.

We may also reply that it is through her own fault in refusing to be converted that the wife suffers prejudice.

Reply Obj. 3: Disparity of worship makes a person simply unfit for lawful marriage, whereas the condition of bondage does not, but only where it is unknown. Hence there is no comparison between an unbeliever and a slave-woman.

Reply Obj. 4: Either the child has reached a perfect age, and then it is free to follow either the believing father or the unbelieving mother, or else it is under age, and then it should be given to the believer notwithstanding that it needs the mother's care for its education.

Reply Obj. 5: By doing penance the adulterer does not enter another life, as does an unbeliever by being baptized. Hence the comparison fails.

Article 5

Whether the Believer Who Leaves His Unbelieving Wife Can Take Another Wife?

Ad quintum sic proceditur. Videtur quod fidelis discedens ab uxore infideli non possit aliam ducere in uxorem. Quia indissolubilitas est de ratione matrimonii: cum repudium uxoris sit contra legem naturae. Sed inter infideles erat verum matrimonium. Ergo nullo modo potest illud matrimonium solvi. Sed, manente vinculo matrimonii ad unam, non potest aliquis cum alia contrahere. Ergo fidelis discedens non potest cum alia contrahere.

Praeterea, crimen superveniens matrimonio non solvit matrimonium. Sed, si mulier velit cohabitare sine contumelia Creatoris, non est solutum vinculum matrimonii: quia vir non potest aliam ducere. Ergo peccatum uxoris quae non vult cohabitare sine contumelia. Creatoris, non solvit matrimonium, ut libere possit vir aliam uxorem ducere.

Praeterea, vir et uxor sunt pares in vinculo matrimonii. Cum ergo uxori infideli non liceat, vivente viro, alium virum ducere, videtur quod nec fideli liceat.

Praeterea, favorabilius est continentiae votum quam matrimonii contractus. Sed viro fideli uxoris infidelis non licet, ut videtur, votum continentiae emittere:

Objection 1: It would seem that the believer who leaves his unbelieving wife cannot take another wife. For indissolubility is of the nature of marriage, since it is contrary to the natural law to divorce one's wife. Now there was true marriage between them as unbelievers. Therefore, their marriage can in no way be dissolved. But as long as a man is bound by marriage to one woman he cannot marry another. Therefore, a believer who leaves his unbelieving wife cannot take another wife.

Obj. 2: Further, a crime subsequent to marriage does not dissolve the marriage. Now, if the wife be willing to cohabit without insult to the Creator, the marriage tie is not dissolved, since the husband cannot marry another. Therefore, the sin of the wife who refuses to cohabit without insult to the Creator does not dissolve the marriage so that her husband be free to take another wife.

Obj. 3: Further, husband and wife are equal in the marriage tie. Since, then, it is unlawful for the unbelieving wife to marry again while her husband lives, it would seem that neither can the believing husband do so.

Obj. 4: Further, the vow of continence is more favorable than the marriage contract. Now seemingly it is not lawful for the believing husband to take a vow of continence with-

quia tunc uxor fraudaretur matrimonio si postmodum converteretur. Ergo multo minus licet ei matrimonium contrahere cum alia.

PRAETEREA, filius qui remanet in infidelitate, patre converso, amittit ius paternae haereditatis: et tamen, si postea convertitur, redditur ei haereditas sua, etiam si alius in possessionem eius intravit. Ergo videtur a simili quod, si uxor infidelis post convertatur, quod sit sibi reddendus vir suus, etiam si cum alia contraxerit. Quod non posset esse si secundum matrimonium verum esset. Ergo non potest contrahere cum alia.

SED CONTRA: Matrimonium non est ratum sine sacramento baptismi. Sed quod non est ratum, potest dissolvi. Ergo matrimonium in infidelitate contractum potest dissolvi. Et ita, soluto matrimoniali vinculo, licet viro aliam ducere in uxorem.

PRAETEREA, vir non debet cohabitare uxori infideli nolenti cohabitare sine contumelia Creatoris. Si ergo non liceret ei aliam ducere, cogeretur continentiam servare. Quod videtur inconveniens: quia sic ex conversione sua incommodum reportaret.

RESPONDEO dicendum quod, quando alter coniugum ad fidem convertitur, altero in infidelitate manente, distinguendum est. Quia si infidelis vult cohabitare sine contumelia Creatoris, idest, sine hoc quod ad infidelitatem inducat, potest fidelis libere discedere, sed discedens non potest alteri nubere. Si autem infidelis non velit cohabitare sine contumelia Creatoris, in verba blasphemiae prorumpens et nomen Christi audire nolens, tunc, si ad infidelitatem pertrahere nitatur, vir fidelis discedens potest alteri per matrimonium copulari.

AD PRIMUM ergo dicendum quod matrimonium infidelium est imperfectum: sed matrimonium fidelium est perfectum, et ita est firmius. Semper autem firmius vinculum solvit minus firmum, si sit ei contrarium. Et ideo matrimonium quod post in fide Christi contrahitur, solvit matrimonium quod prius in infidelitate contractum fuerat. Unde matrimonium infidelium non est omnino firmum et ratum, sed ratificatur postmodum per fidem Christi.

AD SECUNDUM dicendum quod crimen uxoris nolentis cohabitare sine contumelia Creatoris, absolvit virum a servitute qua tenebatur uxori ut non posset ea vivente aliam ducere, sed nondum solvit matrimonium: quia, si blasphema illa converteretur antequam ille aliud matrimonium contraheret, redderetur ei vir suus. Sed solvitur per matrimonium sequens, ad quod pervenire

out the consent of his unbelieving wife, since then the latter would be deprived of marriage if she were afterwards converted. Much less, therefore, is it lawful for him to take another wife.

OBJ. 5: Further, the son who persists in unbelief after his father's conversion loses the right to inherit from his father: and yet if he be afterwards converted, the inheritance is restored to him even though another should have entered into possession thereof. Therefore, it would seem that in like manner, if the unbelieving wife be converted, her husband ought to be restored to her even though he should have married another wife: yet this would be impossible if the second marriage were valid. Therefore, he cannot take another wife.

ON THE CONTRARY, Matrimony is not ratified without the sacrament of baptism. Now what is not ratified can be annulled. Therefore, marriage contracted in unbelief can be annulled, and consequently, the marriage tie being dissolved, it is lawful for the husband to take another wife.

FURTHER, A husband ought not to cohabit with an unbelieving wife who refuses to cohabit without insult to the Creator. If, therefore, it were unlawful for him to take another wife he would be forced to remain continent, which would seem unreasonable, since then he would be at a disadvantage through his conversion.

I ANSWER THAT, When either husband or wife is converted to the faith, the other remaining in unbelief, a distinction must be made. For if the unbeliever be willing to cohabit without insult to the Creator—that is, without drawing the other to unbelief—the believer is free to part from the other, but by parting is not permitted to marry again. But if the unbeliever refuse to cohabit without insult to the Creator, by making use of blasphemous words and refusing to hear Christ's name, then if she strive to draw him to unbelief, the believing husband, after parting from her, may be united to another in marriage.

REPLY OBJ. 1: As stated above (A. 2), the marriage of unbelievers is imperfect, whereas the marriage of believers is perfect and consequently binds more firmly. Now the firmer tie always looses the weaker if it is contrary to it, and therefore the subsequent marriage contracted in the faith of Christ dissolves the marriage previously contracted in unbelief. Therefore, the marriage of unbelievers is not altogether firm and ratified, but is ratified afterwards by Christ's faith.

REPLY OBJ. 2: The sin of the wife who refuses to cohabit without insult to the Creator frees the husband from the tie whereby he was bound to his wife so as to be unable to marry again during her lifetime. It does not, however, dissolve the marriage at once, since if she were converted from her blasphemy before he married again, her husband would be restored to her. But the marriage is dissolved by the sec-

non posset vir fidelis nisi solutus a servitute uxoris per culpam eius.

Ad tertium dicendum quod, postquam fidelis contraxit, solutum est vinculum matrimonii ex utraque parte: quia matrimonium non claudicat quantum ad vinculum. Sed quandoque Claudicat quantum ad effectum. Unde in poenam uxoris infidelis ei indicitur quod non possit cum alio contrahere, magis quam virtute matrimonii praecedentis. Sed, si postea convertatur, potest ei concedi dispensative ut alteri nubat, si vir eius aliam uxorem duxit.

Ad quartum dicendum quod, si post conversionem viri sit aliqua probabilis spes de conversione uxoris, non debet votum continentiae vir emittere, nec ad aliud matrimonium transire: quia difficilius converteretur uxor viro suo sciens se privatam esse. Si autem non sit spes de conversione, potest ad sacros ordines vel ad religionem accedere, prius requisita uxore quod convertatur. Et tunc si, postquam vir sacros ordines suscepit, uxor convertatur, non est sibi vir suus reddendus: sed debet imputare sibi in poenam tardae conversionis quod viro suo privatur.

Ad quintum dicendum quod vinculum paternitatis non solvitur per disparem cultum, sicut vinculum matrimonii. Et ideo non est simile de haereditate et uxore.

ond marriage, which the believing husband would be unable to accomplish unless he were freed from his obligation to his wife by her own fault.

Reply Obj. 3: After the believer has married, the marriage tie is dissolved on either side, because the marriage is not imperfect as to the bond, although it is sometimes imperfect as to its effect. Hence it is in punishment of the unbelieving wife rather than by virtue of the previous marriage that she is forbidden to marry again. If, however, she be afterwards converted, she may be allowed by dispensation to take another husband, should her husband have taken another wife.

Reply Obj. 4: The husband ought not to take a vow of continence nor enter into a second marriage, if after his conversion there be a reasonable hope of the conversion of his wife, because the wife's conversion would be more difficult if she knew she was deprived of her husband. If, however, there be no hope of her conversion, he can take holy orders or enter religion, having first besought his wife to be converted. And then if the wife be converted after her husband has received holy orders, her husband must not be restored to her, but she must take it as a punishment of her tardy conversion that she is deprived of her husband.

Reply Obj. 5: The bond of fatherhood is not dissolved by disparity of worship, as the marriage bond is: wherefore there is no comparison between an inheritance and a wife.

Article 6

Whether Other Sins Dissolve Marriage?

Ad sextum sic proceditur. Videtur quod alia vitia solvant matrimonium sicut et infidelitas. Adulterium enim videtur esse directius contra matrimonium quam infidelitas. Sed infidelitas solvit matrimonium in aliquo casu, ut liceat ad aliud matrimonium transire. Ergo et adulterium idem facit.

Praeterea, sicut infidelitas est fornicatio spiritualis, ita et quodlibet peccatum. Si ergo propter hoc infidelitas matrimonium solvit quia est fornicatio spiritualis, pari ratione quodlibet peccatum matrimonium solvet.

Praeterea, Matth. 5 dicitur: *si dextra manus tua scandalizat te, abscide eam et proiice abs te*: et dicit Glossa quod *in manu et dextro oculo possunt accipi fratres, uxor, propinqui et filii*. Sed per quodlibet peccatum efficiuntur nobis impedimento. Ergo propter quodlibet peccatum potest matrimonium dissolvi.

Praeterea, avaritia idololatria est, ut dicitur Ephes. 5. Sed propter idololatriam potest mulier dimitti. Ergo, pari ratione, propter avaritiam. Et ita propter alia peccata quae sunt maiora quam avaritia.

Objection 1: It would seem that other sins besides unbelief dissolve marriage. For adultery is seemingly more directly opposed to marriage than unbelief is. But unbelief dissolves marriage in a certain case so that it is lawful to marry again. Therefore, adultery has the same effect.

Obj. 2: Further, just as unbelief is spiritual fornication, so is any kind of sin. If, then, unbelief dissolves marriage because it is spiritual fornication, for the same reason any kind of sin will dissolve marriage.

Obj. 3: Further, it is said: *if your right hand scandalize you, pluck it off and cast it from you* (Matt 5:29), and a Gloss of Jerome says that *by the hand and the right eye we may understand our brother, wife, relatives and children*. Now these become obstacles to us by any kind of sin. Therefore, marriage can be dissolved on account of any kind of sin.

Obj. 4: Further, covetousness is idolatry according to Ephesians 5:5. Now a wife may be put away on account of idolatry. Therefore, in like manner she can be put away on account of covetousness, as also on account of other sins graver than covetousness.

PRAETEREA, Magister hoc expresse dicit in littera.

SED CONTRA: Est quod dicitur Matth. 5: *qui dimiserit uxorem, excepta causa fornicationis, moechatur.*

PRAETEREA, secundum hoc tota die fierent divortia: cum raro inveniatur matrimonium in quo alter coniugum in peccatum non labatur.

RESPONDEO dicendum quod fornicatio corporalis et infidelitas specialem habent contrarietatem ad bona matrimonii, ut ex dictis patere potest. Unde specialem habent vim separandi matrimonia. Sed tamen intelligendum est quod matrimonium dupliciter solvitur. Uno modo, quantum ad vinculum. Et sic non potest solvi, postquam matrimonium est ratificatum, neque per infidelitatem neque per adulterium. Sed si non est ratificatum, solvitur vinculum, permanente infidelitate in altero coniugum, si alter conversus ad fidem ad aliud coniugium transeat. Non autem solvitur vinculum praedictum per adulterium: alias infidelis libere posset dare libellum repudii uxori adulterae, et, ea dimissa, aliam ducere; quod falsum est.

Alio modo solvitur matrimonium quantum ad actum. Et sic solvi potest tam per infidelitatem quam per fornicationem corporalem. Sed propter alia peccata non potest solvi matrimonium etiam quantum ad actum: nisi forte ad tempus se velit vir subtrahere a consortio uxoris ad castigationem eius, subtrahendo ei praesentiae suae solatium.

AD PRIMUM ergo dicendum quod, quamvis adulterium magis directe opponatur matrimonio inquantum est in officium naturae, quam infidelitas; tamen e converso est inquantum matrimonium est sacramentum Ecclesiae, ex quo habet perfectam firmitatem, inquantum significat indivisibilem coniunctionem Christi et Ecclesiae. Et ideo matrimonium quod non est ratum, magis potest solvi quantum ad vinculum per infidelitatem quam per adulterium.

AD SECUNDUM dicendum quod coniunctio prima animae ad Deum est per fidem. Et ideo per eam anima quasi desponsatur Deo: ut patet Osee 2, *sponsabo te mihi in fide.* Unde in sacra Scriptura specialiter per fornicationem idololatria et infidelitas designantur. Sed alia peccata magis remota significatione dicuntur spirituales fornicationes.

AD TERTIUM dicendum quod hoc intelligendum est quando mulier praestat magnam occasionem ruinae viro suo, ut vir probabiliter sibi de periculo timeat. Tunc enim vir potest se subtrahere ab eius conversatione, ut dictum est.

AD QUARTUM dicendum quod avaritia dicitur idololatria per quandam similitudinem servitutis: quia tam avarus quam idololatra *potius servit creaturae quam Creatori.* Non autem per similitudinem infidelitatis: quia

OBJ. 5: Further, the Master says this expressly (*Sentences* IV, D. 30).

ON THE CONTRARY, It is said: *whosoever shall put away his wife, excepting for the cause of fornication, makes her commit adultery* (Matt 5:32).

FURTHER, If this were true, divorces would be made all day long, since it is rare to find a marriage in which one of the parties does not fall into sin.

I ANSWER THAT, Bodily fornication and unbelief have a special contrariety to the goods of marriage, as stated above (A. 3). Hence they are specially effective in dissolving marriages. Nevertheless, it must be observed that marriage is dissolved in two ways. In one way as to the marriage tie, and thus marriage cannot be dissolved after it is ratified, neither by unbelief nor by adultery. But if it be not ratified, the tie is dissolved if the one party remain in unbelief and the other, being converted to the faith, has married again. On the other hand, the aforesaid tie is not dissolved by adultery, else the unbeliever would be free to give a bill of divorce to his adulterous wife, and having put her away, could take another wife, which is false.

In another way, marriage is dissolved as to the act, and thus it can be dissolved on account of either unbelief or fornication. But marriage cannot be dissolved even as to the act on account of other sins, unless perchance the husband wish to cease from intercourse with his wife in order to punish her by depriving her of the comfort of his presence.

REPLY OBJ. 1: Although adultery is opposed to marriage as fulfilling an office of nature more directly than unbelief, it is the other way about if we consider marriage as a sacrament of the Church, from which source it derives perfect stability inasmuch as it signifies the indissoluble union of Christ with the Church. Therefore, the marriage that is not ratified can be dissolved as to the marriage tie on account of unbelief rather than on account of adultery.

REPLY OBJ. 2: The primal union of the soul to God is by faith, and consequently the soul is thereby espoused to God as it were, according to Hosea 2:20, *I will espouse you to me in faith.* Hence in Sacred Scripture idolatry and unbelief are specially designated by the name of fornication: whereas other sins are called spiritual fornications by a more remote signification.

REPLY OBJ. 3: This applies to the case when the wife proves a notable occasion of sin to her husband, so that he has reason to fear his being in danger: for then the husband can withdraw from living with her, as stated above (A. 5).

REPLY OBJ. 4: Covetousness is said to be idolatry on account of a certain likeness of bondage, because both the covetous and the idolater *serve the creature rather than the Creator*; but not on account of likeness of unbelief, since

corruptio infidelitatis est in intellectu, sed avaritiae in affectu.

AD QUINTUM dicendum quod verba Magistri sunt accipienda de sponsalibus: quia propter crimen superveniens sponsalia solvi possunt.

Vel, si loquitur de matrimonio, intelligendum est de separatione a communi conversatione ad tempus, ut dictum est. Vel quando uxor non cum cohabitare nisi sub conditione peccandi, ut vult dicit, *non ero uxor tua nisi mihi de latrocinio divitias congreges*: tunc enim potius eam debet dimittere quam latrocinia exercere.

unbelief corrupts the intellect whereas covetousness corrupts the affections.

REPLY OBJ. 5: The words of the Master refer to betrothal, because a betrothal can be rescinded on account of a subsequent crime.

Or, if he is speaking of marriage, they must be referred to the severing of mutual companionship for a time, as stated above, or to the case when the wife is unwilling to cohabit except on the condition of sinning, for instance, if she were to say: *I will not remain your wife unless you amass wealth for me by theft*, for then he ought to leave her rather than thieve.

QUESTION 60

Deinde considerandum est de uxoricidio.
Circa quod quaeruntur duo.
Primo: utrum in aliquo casu liceat uxorem occidere.

Secundo: utrum uxoricidium matrimonium impediat.

We must now consider uxoricide.
Under this head there are two points of inquiry:
(1) Whether in a certain case it is lawful to kill one's wife?
(2) Whether uxoricide is an impediment to marriage?

Article 1

Whether It Is Lawful for a Man to Kill His Wife If She Be Discovered in the Act of Adultery?

AD PRIMUM SIC PROCEDITUR. Videtur quod liceat viro uxorem interficere in actu adulterii deprehensam. Lex enim divina praecipit adulteras lapidari. Sed ille qui legem divinam exequitur, non peccat. Ergo nec occidens propriam uxorem, si sit adultera.

PRAETEREA, illud quod licet legi, licet ei cui lex hoc committit. Sed legi licet interficere adulteram, aut quamlibet personam ream mortis. Cum ergo lex commiserit viro interfectionem uxoris in actu adulterii deprehensae, videtur quod ei liceat.

PRAETEREA, vir habet potestatem maiorem super uxorem adulteram quam super eum qui cum ea adulterium commisit. Sed si vir percutiat clericum quem cum propria uxore invenit, non est excommunicatus. Ergo videtur quod etiam liceat interficere propriam uxorem in adulterio deprehensam.

PRAETEREA, vir tenetur uxorem suam corrigere. Sed correctio fit per inflictionem iustae poenae. Cum ergo iusta poena adulterii sit mors, quia est capitale crimen, videtur quod liceat viro uxorem adulteram occidere.

SED CONTRA: In littera dicitur quod *Ecclesia Dei, quae nunquam constringitur legibus mundanis, gladium non habet nisi spiritualem.* Ergo videtur quod ei qui vult esse de Ecclesia, non sit licitus usus legis illius quae uxoricidium permittit.

PRAETEREA, vir et uxor ad paria iudicantur. Sed uxori non licet interficere virum in adulterio deprehensum. Ergo nec viro uxorem.

RESPONDEO dicendum quod virum interficere uxorem contingit dupliciter. Uno modo, per iudicium civi-

OBJECTION 1: It would seem lawful for a man to kill his wife if she be discovered in the act of adultery. For the divine law commanded adulterous wives to be stoned. Now it is not a sin to fulfill the divine law. Neither, therefore, is it a sin to kill one's own wife if she be an adulteress.

OBJ. 2: Further, that which the law can rightly do can be rightly done by one whom the law has commissioned to do it. But the law can rightly kill an adulterous wife or any other person deserving of death. Since, then, the law has commissioned the husband to kill his wife if she be discovered in the act of adultery, it would seem that he can rightly do so.

OBJ. 3: Further, the husband has greater power over his adulterous wife than over the man who committed adultery with her. Now, if the husband strike a cleric whom he found with his wife, he is not excommunicated. Therefore, it would seem lawful for him even to kill his own wife if she be discovered in adultery.

OBJ. 4: Further, the husband is bound to correct his wife. But correction is given by inflicting a just punishment. Since, then, the just punishment of adultery is death, because it is a capital sin, it would seem lawful for a husband to kill his adulterous wife.

ON THE CONTRARY, It is stated in the text (*Sentences* IV, D. 37) that *the Church of God is never bound by the laws of this world, for she has none but a spiritual sword.* Therefore, it would seem that he who wishes to belong to the Church cannot rightly take advantage of the law which permits a man to kill his wife.

FURTHER, Husband and wife are judged on a par. But it is not lawful for a wife to kill her husband if he be discovered in adultery. Neither, therefore, may a husband kill his wife.

I ANSWER THAT, It happens in two ways that a husband kills his wife. First, by a civil judgment; and thus there is no

447

le. Et sic non est dubium quod sine peccato potest vir, zelo iustitiae, non livore vindictae aut odii motus, uxorem adulteram iri iudicio saeculari accusare criminaliter de adulterio, et poenam mortis a lege statutam petere: sicut etiam licet aliquem accusare de homicidio aut de alio crimine. Non tamen talis accusatio potest fieri in iudicio ecclesiastico: quia Ecclesia non habet gladium materialem, ut in littera dicitur.

Alio modo potest eam per seipsum occidere, non in iudicio convictam. Et sic extra actum adulterii eam interficere, quantumcumque sciat eam adulteram, neque secundum leges civiles neque secundum legem conscientiae licet. Sed lex civilis quasi licitum computat quod in ipso actu eam interficiat, non quasi praecipiens, sed quasi poenam homicidii non infligens, propter maximum incitamentum quod habet vir in tali facto ad occisionem uxoris. Sed Ecclesia in hoc non est adstricta legibus humanis, ut iudicet eum sine reatu poenae aeternae, vel poenae ecclesiastico iudicio infligendae, ex hoc quod est sine reatu poenae infligendae per iudicium saeculare. Et ideo in nullo casu licet viro occidere uxorem propria auctoritate.

AD PRIMUM ergo dicendum quod poenam illam infligendam lex non commisit personis privatis, sed personis publicis, quae habent officium ad hoc deputatum. Vir autem non est iudex uxoris. Et ideo non potest eam interficere, sed coram iudice accusare.

AD SECUNDUM dicendum quod lex civilis non commisit viro occisionem uxoris quasi praecipiens: quia sic non peccaret, sicut nec peccat minister iudicis latronem occideris condemnatum ad mortem. Sed permisit, poenam non adhibens. Unde etiam difficultates quasdam apposuit, quibus retraherentur viri ab uxoricidio.

AD TERTIUM dicendum quod ex hoc non probatur quod sit licitum simpliciter: sed quantum ad immunitatem ab aliqua poena; quia etiam excommunicatio quaedam poena est.

AD QUARTUM dicendum quod duplex est congregatio: quaedam oeconomica, sicut familia aliqua; et quaedam politica, sicut civitas et regnum. Ille igitur qui praeest secundae congregationi, ut rex aut iudex, potest infligere poenam et corrigentem personam et exterminantem, ad purgationem communitatis cuius curam gerit. Sed ille qui praeest in prima congregatione, ut paterfamilias, non potest infligere nisi poenam corrigentem, quae non se extendit ultra terminos emendationis, quam transcendit poena mortis. Et ideo vir, qui sic praeest uxori, non potest ipsam interficere, sed alias castigare.

doubt that a husband, moved by zeal for justice and not by vindictive anger or hatred can, without sin, bring a criminal accusation of adultery upon his wife before a secular court, and demand that she receive capital punishment as appointed by the law; just as it is lawful to accuse a person of murder or any other crime. Such an accusation, however, cannot be made in an ecclesiastical court, because, as stated in the text (*Sentences* IV, D. 37), the Church does not wield a material sword.

Second, a husband can kill his wife himself without her being convicted in court, and thus to kill her outside of the act of adultery is not lawful, neither according to civil law nor according to the law of conscience, whatever evidence he may have of her adultery. The civil law, however, considers it as though it were lawful that he should kill her in the very act, not by commanding him to do so, but by not inflicting on him the punishment for murder, on account of the very great provocation which the husband receives by such a deed to kill his wife. But the Church is not bound in this matter by human laws, neither does she acquit him of the debt of eternal punishment, nor of such punishment as may be awarded him by an ecclesiastical tribunal for the reason that he is quit of any punishment to be inflicted by a secular court. Therefore, in no case is it lawful for a husband to kill his wife on his own authority.

REPLY OBJ. 1: The law has committed the infliction of this punishment not to private individuals, but to public persons, who are deputed to this by their office. Now the husband is not his wife's judge: wherefore he may not kill her, but may accuse her in the judge's presence.

REPLY OBJ. 2: The civil law has not commissioned the husband to kill his wife by commanding him to do so, for thus he would not sin, just as the judge's deputy does not sin by killing the thief condemned to death: but it has permitted this by not punishing it. For which reason it has raised certain obstacles to prevent the husband from killing his wife.

REPLY OBJ. 3: This does not prove that it is lawful simply, but that it is lawful as regards immunity from a particular kind of punishment, since excommunication is also a kind of punishment.

REPLY OBJ. 4: There are two kinds of community: the household, such as a family, and the civil community, such as a city or kingdom. Accordingly, he who presides over the latter kind of community, a king for instance, can punish an individual both by correcting and by exterminating him, for the betterment of the community with whose care he is charged. But he who presides over a community of the first kind can inflict only corrective punishment, which does not extend beyond the limits of amendment, and these are exceeded by the punishment of death. Therefore, the husband who exercises this kind of control over his wife may not kill her, but he may accuse or chastise her in some other way.

Article 2

Whether Uxoricide Is an Impediment to Marriage?

Ad secundum sic proceditur. Videtur quod uxoricidium non impediat matrimonium. Directius enim opponitur matrimonio adulterium quam homicidium. Sed adulterium non impedit matrimonium. Ergo nec uxoricidium.

Praeterea, gravius est peccatum occidere matrem quam uxorem: quia nunquam licet verberare matrem, licet autem verberare uxorem. Sed occisio matris non impedit matrimonium. Ergo nec uxoris occisio.

Praeterea, magis peccat qui uxorem alterius propter adulterium interficit quam uxorem propriam: inquantum minus habet de motivo, et minus ad eum spectat eius correctio. Sed qui alienam uxorem occidit non impeditur a matrimonio. Ergo nec ille qui propriam uxorem interficit.

Praeterea, remota causa removetur effectus. Sed peccatum homicidii potest per poenitentiam removeri. Ergo et impedimentum matrimonii quod ex eo causatur. Et ita videtur quod, post peractam poenitentiam, non prohibeatur matrimonium contrahere.

Sed contra: Est quod canon dicit: *interfectores suarum coniugum ad poenitentiam redigendi sunt, quibus penitus denegatur coniugium.*

Praeterea, in eo in quo quis peccat, debet etiam puniri. Sed peccat contra matrimonium qui uxorem occidit. Ergo debet puniri ut matrimonio privetur.

Respondeo dicendum quod uxoricidium ex statuto Ecclesiae matrimonium impedit. Sed quandoque impedit contrahendum et non dirimit contractum: quando scilicet vir propter adulterium aut propter odium occidit uxorem. Tamen, si timetur de incontinentia ipsius, potest cum eo dispensari per Ecclesiam, ut licite matrimonium contrahat.

Quandoque etiam dirimit contractum: ut quando aliquis interficit uxorem suam ut ducat eam cum qua moechatur. Tunc enim efficitur illegitima persona simpliciter ad contrahendum cum illa, ita quod, si de facto cum ea contraxerit, matrimonium dirimitur . Sed per hoc non efficitur simpliciter persona illegitima respectu aliarum mulierum. Unde, si cum alia contraxerit, quamvis peccet contra statutum Ecclesiae faciens, tamen matrimonium contractum non dirimitur propter hoc.

Ad primum ergo dicendum quod homicidium et adulterium in aliquo casu impediunt matrimonium contrahendum et dirimunt contractum: sicut de uxoricidio hic dicitur, et de adulterio supra habitum est.

Vel dicendum quod uxoricidium est contra substantiam coniugii, sed adulterium contra bonum fidei ei de-

Objection 1: It would seem that uxoricide is not an impediment to marriage. For adultery is more directly opposed to marriage than murder is. Now adultery is not an impediment to marriage. Neither, therefore, is uxoricide.

Obj. 2: Further, it is a more grievous sin to kill one's mother than one's wife, for it is never lawful to strike one's mother, whereas it is sometimes lawful to strike one's wife. But matricide is not an impediment to marriage. Neither, therefore, is uxoricide.

Obj. 3: Further, it is a greater sin for a man to kill another man's wife on account of adultery than to kill his own wife, inasmuch as he has less motive and is less concerned with her correction. But he who kills another man's wife is not hindered from marrying. Neither, therefore, is he who kills his own wife.

Obj. 4: Further, if the cause be removed, the effect is removed. But the sin of murder can be removed by repentance. Therefore, the consequent impediment to marriage can be removed also: and consequently it would seem that after he has done penance he is not forbidden to marry.

On the contrary, A Decretal says: *the slayers of their own wives must be brought back to penance, and they are absolutely forbidden to marry.*

Further, In whatsoever a man sins, in that same must he be punished. But he who kills his wife sins against marriage. Therefore, he must be punished by being deprived of marriage.

I answer that, By the Church's decree uxoricide is an impediment to marriage. Sometimes, however, it forbids the contracting of marriage without voiding the contract, for example, when the husband kills his wife on account of adultery or even through hatred; nevertheless, if there be fear lest he should prove incontinent, he may be dispensed by the Church so as to marry lawfully.

Sometimes it also voids the contract, as when a man kills his wife in order to marry her with whom he has committed adultery, for then the law declares him simply unfit to marry her, so that if he actually marry her his marriage is void. He is not however hereby rendered simply unfit by law in relation to other women: wherefore if he should have married another, although he sin by disobeying the Church's ordinance, the marriage is nevertheless not voided for this reason.

Reply Obj. 1: Murder and adultery in certain cases forbid the contracting of marriage and void the contract, as we say here in regard to uxoricide, and shall say further on (*Sentences* IV, Q. 62, A. 2) in regard to adultery.

We may also reply that uxoricide is contrary to the substance of wedlock, whereas adultery is contrary to the good

bitae. Sic adulterium non est magis contra matrimonium quam uxoricidium. Et ita ratio procedit ex falsis.

AD SECUNDUM dicendum quod, simpliciter loquendo, gravius peccatum est occidere matrem quam uxorem, et magis contra naturam: quia naturaliter homo matrem reveretur. Et ideo minus inclinatur ad interfectionem matris, et pronior est ad interfectionem uxoris. Ad cuius pronitatis repressionem, uxoricidis est matrimonium ab Ecclesia interdictum.

AD TERTIUM dicendum quod talis non peccat Contra matrimonium, sicut ille qui propriam uxorem interficit. Et ideo non est simile.

AD QUARTUM dicendum quod non est necessarium quod, deleta culpa, deleatur omnis poena: sicut de irregularitate patet. Non enim poenitentia restituit in pristinam dignitatem, quamvis possit restituere in pristinum statum gratiae, ut dictum est.

of fidelity due to marriage. Hence adultery is not more opposed to marriage than uxoricide, and the argument is based on a false premise.

REPLY OBJ. 2: Simply speaking, it is a more grievous sin to kill one's mother than one's wife, as also more opposed to nature, since a man reveres his mother naturally. Consequently, he is less inclined to matricide and more prone to uxoricide; and it is to repress this propensity that the Church has forbidden marriage to the man who has murdered his wife.

REPLY OBJ. 3: Such a man does not sin against marriage as he does who kills his own wife. Hence the comparison fails.

REPLY OBJ. 4: It does not follow that because guilt has been remitted, the entire punishment is remitted, as evidenced by irregularity. For repentance does not restore a man to his former dignity, although it can restore him to his former state of grace, as stated above (Q. 38, A. 1).

QUESTION 61

THE IMPEDIMENT TO MATRIMONY OF A SOLEMN VOW

Deinde considerandum est de impedimentis quae superveniunt matrimonio. Et primo, de impedimento quod supervenit matrimonio, scilicet de voto solemni; secundo, de impedimento quod supervenit matrimonio consummato, scilicet de fornicatione.

Circa primum quaeruntur tria.

Primo: utrum alter coniugum, altero invito, post carnalem copulam possit religionem intrare.

Secundo: utrum ante carnalem copulam possit intrare.

Tertio: utrum mulier possit nubere alteri, viro ante carnalem copulam religionem ingresso.

We must next consider the impediments which supervene to marriage. We shall consider: (1) The impediment which affects an unconsummated marriage, namely, a solemn vow; (2) The impediment which affects a consummated marriage, namely, fornication.

Under the first head there are three points of inquiry:

(1) Whether either party, after the marriage has been consummated, can enter religion without the other's consent?

(2) Whether they can enter religion before the consummation of the marriage?

(3) Whether the wife can take another husband if her former husband has entered religion before the consummation of the marriage?

Article 1

Whether One Party, After the Marriage Has Been Consummated, Can Enter Religion Without the Other's Consent?

AD PRIMUM SIC PROCEDITUR. Videtur quod alter coniugum, etiam post carnalem copulam, possit, altero invito, ad religionem transire. Quia lex divina magis debet spiritualibus favere quam lex humana. Sed. lex humana hoc permisit. Ergo multo fortius lex divina permittere debuit.

PRAETEREA, minus bonum non impedit maius bonum. Sed matrimonii status est minus bonum quam status religionis, ut patet I Cor. 7. Ergo per matrimonium non debet homo impediri quin possit ad religionem transire.

PRAETEREA, in qualibet religione fit quoddam spirituale matrimonium. Sed licet de leviori religione ad arctiorem transire. Ergo licet de matrimonio leviori, scilicet carnali, ad arctius, scilicet matrimonium religionis, transire, etiam invita uxore.

SED CONTRA: Est quod dicitur I Cor. 7, ut nec etiam ad tempus vacent orationi coniuges sine mutuo consensu, a matrimonio abstinentes.

PRAETEREA, nullus potest facere licite quod est in praeiudicium alterius, sine eius voluntate. Sed votum religionis emissum ab uno coniugum est in praeiudicium alterius: quia unus habet *potestatem corporis* alterius. Er-

OBJECTION 1: It would seem that even after the marriage has been consummated one consort can enter religion without the other's consent. For the divine law ought to be more favorable to spiritual things than human law. Now human law has allowed this. Therefore, much more should the divine law permit it.

OBJ. 2: Further, the lesser good does not hinder the greater. But the married state is a lesser good than the religious state, according to 1 Corinthians 7:38. Therefore, marriage ought not to hinder a man from being able to enter religion.

OBJ. 3: Further, in every form of religious life there is a kind of spiritual marriage. Now it is lawful to pass from a less strict religious order to one that is stricter. Therefore, it is also allowable to pass from a less strict—namely, a carnal—marriage to a stricter marriage, namely, that of the religious life, even without the wife's consent.

ON THE CONTRARY, Married persons are forbidden (1 Cor 7:5) to abstain without one another's consent, even for a time, from the use of marriage in order to have time for prayer.

FURTHER, No one can lawfully do that which is prejudicial to another without the latter's consent. Now the religious vow taken by one consort is prejudicial to the other, since the one has *power over* the other's *body*. Therefore,

go unus sine consensu alterius non potest votum religionis emittere.

RESPONDEO dicendum quod nullus potest facere oblationem Deo de alieno. Unde, cum per matrimonium iam consummatum sit corpus viri factum uxoris, non potest sine consensu eius Deo ipsum offerre per continentiae votum.

AD PRIMUM ergo dicendum quod lex humana considerabat matrimonium solum inquantum est in officium naturae. Sed lex divina secundum quod est sacramentum, ex quo habet omnimodam indivisibilitatem. Et ideo non est simile.

AD SECUNDUM dicendum quod non est inconveniens maius bonum impediri per minus bonum quod habet contrarietatem ad ipsum: sicut etiam bonum per malum impeditur.

AD TERTIUM dicendum quod in qualibet religione contrahitur matrimonium ad unam personam, scilicet ad Christum, cui tamen ad plura obligatur aliquis in una religione quam in alia. Sed matrimonium materiale et religionis non fiunt ad unam personam. Et ideo non est simile.

one of them cannot take a religious vow without the other's consent.

I ANSWER THAT, No one can make an offering to God of what belongs to another. Therefore, since by a consummated marriage the husband's body already belongs to his wife, he cannot by a vow of continence offer it to God without her consent.

REPLY OBJ. 1: Human law considers marriage merely as fulfilling an office of nature: whereas the divine law considers it as a sacrament, by reason of which it is altogether indissoluble. Hence the comparison fails.

REPLY OBJ. 2: It is not unreasonable that a greater good be hindered by a lesser which is contrary to it, just as good is hindered by evil.

REPLY OBJ. 3: In every form of religious life marriage is contracted with one person, namely Christ: to whom, however, a person contracts more obligations in one religious order than in another. But in carnal marriage and religious marriage the contract is not with the same person: wherefore that comparison fails.

Article 2

Whether Before the Marriage Has Been Consummated One Consort Can Enter Religion Without the Other's Consent?

AD SECUNDUM SIC PROCEDITUR. Videtur quod nec etiam ante carnalem copulam. Indivisibilitas enim matrimonii pertinet ad matrimonii sacramentum, inquantum scilicet significat perpetuam coniunctionem: Christi ad Ecclesiam. Sed ante carnalem copulam, post consensum per verba de praesenti expressum, est verum matrimonii sacramentum. Ergo non potest fieri divisio per hoc quod alter ad religionem intrat.

PRAETEREA, in ipso consensu per verba de praesenti expresso unus coniugum in alterum potestatem sui corporis transfert. Ergo statim potest exigere debitum, et alter tenetur reddere. Et ita non potest unus, invito altero, ad religionem transire.

PRAETEREA, Matth. 19: *quos Deus coniunxit, homo non separet.* Sed coniunctio quae est ante carnalem copulam divinitus facta est. Ergo non potest separari humana voluntate.

SED CONTRA est quod, secundum Hieronymum, Dominus Ioannem vocavit de nuptiis.

RESPONDEO dicendum quod ante carnalem copulam est inter coniuges tantum vinculum spirituale, sed postea etiam est inter eos vinculum carnale. Et ideo, sicut post carnalem copulam matrimonium solvitur per

OBJECTION 1: It would seem that even before the marriage has been consummated one consort cannot enter religion without the other's consent. For the indissolubility of marriage belongs to the sacrament of matrimony, namely, inasmuch as it signifies the union of Christ with the Church. Now marriage is a true sacrament before its consummation and after consent has been expressed in words of the present. Therefore, it cannot be dissolved by one of them entering religion.

OBJ. 2: Further, by virtue of the consent expressed in words of the present, the one consort has given power over his body to the other. Therefore, the one can forthwith ask for the marriage debt, and the other is bound to pay: and so the one cannot enter religion without the other's consent.

OBJ. 3: Further, Matthew 19:6 says: *what God has joined together, let no man put asunder.* But the union which precedes marital intercourse was made by God. Therefore, it cannot be dissolved by the will of man.

ON THE CONTRARY, According to Jerome (*Prologue on the Gospel of John*) our Lord called John from his wedding.

I ANSWER THAT, Before marital intercourse there is only a spiritual bond between husband and wife, but afterwards there is a carnal bond between them. Wherefore, just as after marital intercourse marriage is dissolved by carnal

mortem carnalem, ita per ingressum religionis ante copulam carnalem solvitur: quia religio est quaedam mors spiritualis, qua aliquis, saeculo moriens, vivit Deo.

Ad primum ergo dicendum quod matrimonium ante carnalem copulam significat illam coniunctionem quae est Christi ad animam per gratiam, quae quidem solvitur per dispositionem spiritualem contrariam, scilicet per peccatum. Sed per carnalem copulam significat coniunctionem ad Ecclesiam quantum ad assumptionem humanae naturae in unitate personae, quae omnino est indivisibilis.

Ad secundum dicendum quod ante carnalem copulam non est omnino translatum corpus unius sub potestate alterius, sed sub conditione si interea alter ad frugem melioris vitae non convolet. Sed per carnalem copulam completur dicta translatio: quia tunc intrat uterque in corporalem possessionem sibi traditae potestatis. Unde etiam ante carnalem copulam non statim tenetur reddere debitum post matrimonium contractum per verba de praesenti, sed datur ei tempus duorum mensium, propter tria. Primo, ut interim possit deliberare de transeundo ad religionem. Secundo, ut praeparentur quae sunt necessaria ad solemnitatem nuptiarum. Tertio, *ne vilem habeat maritus datam quam non suspiravit dilatam.*

Ad tertium dicendum quod coniunctio matrimonialis ante carnalem copulam est quidem perfecta quantum ad esse primum, sed non consummata quantum ad actum secundum, qui est operatio, et similatur possessioni corporali. Et ideo non omnimodam indivisibilitatem habet.

death, so by entering religion the bond which exists before the consummation of the marriage is dissolved, because religious life is a kind of spiritual death, whereby a man dies to the world and lives to God.

Reply Obj. 1: Before consummation, marriage signifies the union of Christ with the soul by grace, which is dissolved by a contrary spiritual disposition, namely, mortal sin. But after consummation it signifies the union of Christ with the Church, as regards the assumption of human nature into the unity of person, which union is altogether indissoluble.

Reply Obj. 2: Before consummation the body of one consort is not absolutely delivered into the power of the other, but conditionally, provided neither consort meanwhile seek the fruit of a better life. But by marital intercourse the aforesaid delivery is completed, because then each of them enters into bodily possession of the power transferred to him. Wherefore also before consummation they are not bound to pay the marriage debt forthwith after contracting marriage by words of the present, but a space of two months is allowed them for three reasons. First, that they may deliberate meanwhile about entering religion; second, to prepare what is necessary for the solemnization of the wedding. Third, *lest the husband think little of a gift he has not longed to possess* (Decretals).

Reply Obj. 3: The marriage union, before consummation, is indeed perfect as to its primary being, but is not finally perfect as to its second act, which is operation. It is like bodily possession, and consequently is not altogether indissoluble.

Article 3

Whether the Wife May Take Another Husband If Her Husband Has Entered Religion Before the Consummation of the Marriage?

Ad tertium sic proceditur. Videtur quod mulier non possit nubere alteri, viro ante carnalem copulam religionem ingresso. Quia illud quod cum matrimonio stare potest, non solvit matrimoniale vinculum. Sed adhuc manet vinculum matrimoniale inter eos qui pari voto religionem intrant. Ergo ex hoc quod unus intrat religionem, alter non absolvitur a vinculo matrimoniali. Sed quandiu manet vinculum matrimoniale ad unum, non potest nubere alteri. Ergo, etc.

Praeterea, vir post ingressum religionis potest ante professionem redire ad saeculum. Si ergo mulier posset alteri nubere, viro intrante religionem, et ipse posset alteram ducere rediens ad saeculum. Quod est absurdum.

Objection 1: It would seem that the wife may not take another husband if her husband has entered religion before the consummation of the marriage. For that which is consistent with marriage does not dissolve the marriage tie. Now the marriage tie still remains between those who equally take religious vows. Therefore, by the fact that one enters religion, the other is not freed from the marriage tie. But as long as she remains tied to one by marriage, she cannot marry another. Therefore, etc.

Obj. 2: Further, after entering religion and before making his profession the husband can return to the world. If, then, the wife can marry again when her husband enters religion, he also can marry again when he returns to the world: which is absurd.

PRAETEREA, per Decretalem novam professio ante annum emissa pro nulla reputatur. Ergo, si post talem professionem ad uxorem redeat, tenetur eum recipere. Ergo neque per introitum viri in religionem, neque per votum, datur mulieri potestas nubendi alteri.

SED CONTRA, nullus potest alterum obligare ad ea quae sunt perfectionis. Sed continentia est de his quae ad perfectionem pertinent. Ergo mulier non arctatur ad continentiam ex hoc quod vir religionem ingreditur. Et sic potest nubere.

RESPONDEO dicendum quod, sicut mors corporalis viri hoc modo vinculum matrimoniale solvit ut mulier *nubat cui vult*, secundum Apostoli sententiam; ita etiam post mortem spiritualem viri per religionis ingressum poterit cui voluerit nubere.

AD PRIMUM ergo dicendum quod, quando uterque pari voto continentiam vovet, tunc neuter coniugali vinculo abrenuntiat, et ideo adhuc manet. Sed quando unus tantum vovet, tunc, quantum est in se, abrenuntiat vinculo coniugali. Et ideo alter absolvitur a vinculo illo.

AD SECUNDUM dicendum quod non intelligitur mortuus saeculo per religionis ingressum quousque professionem emiserit. Et ideo usque ad tempus illud tenetur eum uxor sua expectare.

AD TERTIUM dicendum quod de professione sic emissa ante tempus determinatum a iure est idem iudicium quod de voto simplici. Unde, sicut post votum simplex viri mulier ei debitum reddere non tenetur, tamen ipsa non haberet potestatem alteri nubere, ita et hic.

OBJ. 3: Further, by a new decree (*Decretals*) a religious profession made before a year is considered none at all. Therefore, if he return to his wife after making such a profession, she is bound to receive him. Therefore, neither by her husband's entry into religion nor by his taking a vow does the wife receive the power to marry again.

ON THE CONTRARY, No one can bind another to those things which belong to perfection. Now continence is of those things that belong to perfection. Therefore, a wife is not bound to continence on account of her husband entering religion, and consequently she can marry.

I ANSWER THAT, Just as bodily death of the husband dissolves the marriage tie in such a way that the wife *may marry whom she will*, according to the statement of the Apostle (1 Cor 7:39); so too after the husband's spiritual death by entering religion, she can marry whom she will.

REPLY OBJ. 1: When both consorts take a like vow of continence, neither renounces the marriage tie, wherefore it still remains: but when only one takes the vow, then for his own part he renounces the marriage tie, wherefore the other is freed therefrom.

REPLY OBJ. 2: A person is not accounted dead to the world by entering religion until he makes his profession, and consequently his wife is bound to wait for him until that time.

REPLY OBJ. 3: We must judge of a profession thus made before the time fixed by law, as of a simple vow. Wherefore just as when the husband has taken a simple vow his wife is not bound to pay him the marriage debt, and yet has not the power to marry again, so is it in this case.

QUESTION 62

THE IMPEDIMENT THAT SUPERVENES TO MARRIAGE

Deinde considerandum est de impedimento quod supervenit matrimonio consummato, scilicet de fornicatione, quae impedit matrimonium praecedens quoad actum, durante vinculo matrimoniali.

Et circa hoc quaeruntur sex.

Primo: utrum liceat viro dimittere uxorem causa fornicationis.

Secundo: utrum ad hoc teneatur.

Tertio: utrum proprio iudicio eam dimittere possit.

Quarto: utrum vir et uxor quantum ad hoc sint aequalis conditionis.

Quinto: utrum post divortium debeant manere innupti.

Sexto: utrum post divortium possint reconciliari.

We must now consider the impediment that supervenes upon marriage after its consummation, namely, fornication, which is an impediment to a previous marriage as regards the act, although the marriage tie remains.

Under this head there are six points of inquiry:

(1) Whether it is lawful for a husband to put his wife away on account of fornication?

(2) Whether he is bound to do so?

(3) Whether he may put her away at his own judgment?

(4) Whether in this matter husband and wife are of equal condition?

(5) Whether, after being divorced, they must remain unmarried?

(6) Whether they can be reconciled after being divorced?

Article 1

Whether It Is Lawful for a Husband to Put Away His Wife on Account of Fornication?

AD PRIMUM SIC PROCEDITUR. Videtur quod propter fornicationem non liceat viro uxorem dimittere. *Non enim est malum pro malo reddendum.* Sed vir dimittens uxorem propter fornicationem, videtur malum pro malo reddere. Ergo hoc non licet.

PRAETEREA, maius peccatum est si uterque fornicetur quam si alter tantum. Sed si uterque fornicetur, non poterit propter hoc fieri divortium. Ergo nec si unus tantum fornicatus fuerit.

PRAETEREA, fornicatio spiritualis et quaedam alia peccata sunt graviora quam fornicatio carnalis. Sed propter illa non potest fieri separatio a toro. Ergo nec propter fornicationem carnalem.

PRAETEREA, vitium contra naturam magis remotum est a bonis matrimonii quam fornicatio, quae modo naturae fit. Ergo magis debuit poni causa separationis quam fornicatio.

SED CONTRA: Est quod dicitur Matth. 5.

PRAETEREA, illi qui frangit fidem, non tenetur aliquis servare fidem. Sed coniux fornicando fidem frangit quam alteri coniugi debet. Ergo alter potest alterum causa fornicationis dimittere.

RESPONDEO dicendum quod Dominus dimittere uxorem concessit propter fornicationem in poenam illius qui fidem fregit, et in favorem illius qui fidem ser-

OBJECTION 1: It would seem unlawful for a husband to put away his wife on account of fornication. *For we must not return evil for evil.* But the husband, by putting away his wife on account of fornication, seemingly returns evil for evil. Therefore, this is not lawful.

OBJ. 2: Further, the sin is greater if both commit fornication than if one only commits it. But if both commit fornication, they cannot be divorced on that account. Neither, therefore, can they be if only one commits fornication.

OBJ. 3: Further, spiritual fornication and certain other sins are more grievous than carnal fornication. But separation from bed cannot be motived by those sins. Neither, therefore, can it be done on account of fornication.

OBJ. 4: Further, a vice against nature is further removed from the marriage goods than fornication is, the manner of which is natural. Therefore, it ought to have been a cause of separation rather than fornication.

ON THE CONTRARY, There are the words of Matthew 5:32.

FURTHER, One is not bound to keep faith with one who breaks his faith. But a spouse by fornication breaks the faith due to the other spouse. Therefore, one can put the other away on account of fornication.

I ANSWER THAT, Our Lord permitted a man to put away his wife on account of fornication, in punishment of the unfaithful party and in favor of the faithful party, so that

vavit, ut non sit adstrictus ad reddendum debitum ei qui non servavit fidem. Et propter hoc excipiuntur septem casus in quibus non licet viro uxorem dimittere fornicantem, in quibus vel uxor a culpa immunis est, vel utrique aequaliter culpabiles sunt.

Primus est, si ipse vir similiter fornicatus fuerit. Secundus, si ipse uxorem prostituerit. Tertius, si uxor virum probabiliter mortuum credens propter longam eius absentiam, alteri nupserit. Quartus est, si latenter cognita est ab aliquo sub specie viri lectum subintrante. Quintus, si fuerit vi oppressa. Sextus, si reconciliavit eam sibi post adulterium perpetratum, carnaliter eam cognoscens. Septimus, si in matrimonio in infidelitate utriusque contracto vir dederit uxori libellum repudii et uxor alteri nupserit. Tunc enim, si uterque convertatur, tenetur eam vir recipere.

Ad primum ergo dicendum quod vir, si dimittat uxorem fornicantem livore vindictae, peccat. Si autem ad infamiam propriam cavendam, ne videatur particeps criminis; vel ad vitium uxoris corrigendum; vel ad vitandum prolis incertitudinem, non peccat.

Ad secundum dicendum quod divortium ex causa fornicationis fit uno accusante alium. Et quia nullus potest accusare qui in simili crimine existit, quando uterque fornicatur divortium celebrari non potest: quamvis magis peccetur contra matrimonium utroque fornicante quam altero tantum.

Ad tertium dicendum quod fornicatio directe est contra bona matrimonii: quia tollitur per eam certitudo prolis; et fides frangitur; et significatio non servatur, dum unus coniugum pluribus *carnem suam dividit*. Et ideo alia crimina, quamvis forte sint maiora fornicatione, non causant divortium.

Sed quia infidelitas, quae dicitur *spiritualis fornicatio*, etiam est contra matrimonii bonum quod est proles educanda ad cultum Dei, etiam ipsa facit divortium. Sed tamen aliter quam corporalis fornicatio. Quia propter unum actum fornicationis carnalis potest procedi ad divortium, non autem propter unum actum infidelitatis, sed propter consuetudinem, quae pertinaciam ostendit, in qua infidelitas perficitur.

Ad quartum dicendum quod etiam propter vitium contra naturam potest procedi ad divortium. Sed tamen non fit ita mentio de ipso, tum quia est passio innominabilis; tum quia rarius accidit; tum quia non ita causat incertitudinem prolis.

the latter is not bound to marital intercourse with the unfaithful one. There are, however, seven cases to be excepted in which it is not lawful to put away a wife who has committed fornication, in which either the wife is not to be blamed or both parties are equally blameworthy.

The first is if the husband also has committed fornication; the second is if he has prostituted his wife; the third is if the wife, believing her husband dead on account of his long absence, has married again; the fourth is if another man has fraudulently impersonated her husband in the marriage-bed; the fifth is if she be overcome by force; the sixth is if he has been reconciled to her by having carnal intercourse with her after she has committed adultery; the seventh is if both having been married in the state of unbelief, the husband has given his wife a bill of divorce and she has married again, for then if both be converted the husband is bound to receive her back again.

Reply Obj. 1: A husband sins if through vindictive anger he puts away his wife who has committed fornication, but he does not sin if he does so in order to avoid losing his good name, lest he seem to share in her guilt, or in order to correct his wife's sin, or in order to avoid the uncertainty of her offspring.

Reply Obj. 2: Divorce on account of fornication is effected by the one accusing the other. And since no one can accuse who is guilty of the same crime, a divorce cannot be pronounced when both have committed fornication, although marriage is more sinned against when both are guilty of fornication that when only one is.

Reply Obj. 3: Fornication is directly opposed to the good of marriage, since by it the certainty of offspring is destroyed, faith is broken, and marriage ceases to have its signification when the *body of one spouse is given* to several others. Wherefore other sins, though perhaps they be more grievous than fornication, are not motives for a divorce.

Since, however, unbelief, which is called *spiritual fornication*, is also opposed to the good of marriage consisting in the rearing of the offspring to the worship of God, it is also a motive for divorce, yet not in the same way as bodily fornication. For one may take steps for procuring a divorce on account of one act of carnal fornication; not, however, on account of one act of unbelief, but on account of inveterate unbelief, which is a proof of obstinacy, wherein unbelief is perfected.

Reply Obj. 4: Steps may be taken to procure a divorce on account also of a vice against nature: but this is not mentioned in the same way, both because it is an unmentionable passion, and because it does not so affect the certainty of offspring.

Article 2

Whether the Husband Is Bound by Precept to Put Away His Wife When She Is Guilty of Fornication?

Ad secundum sic proceditur. Videtur quod vir teneatur ex praecepto uxorem fornicantem dimittere. Vir enim, cum sit *caput uxoris*, tenetur uxorem corrigere. Sed separatio a toro est inducta ad correctionem uxoris fornicantis. Ergo tenetur eam a se separare.

Praeterea, qui consentit peccanti mortaliter, ipse etiam mortaliter peccat. Sed vir retinens uxorem fornicantem *consentire ei videtur*, ut in littera dicitur. Ergo peccat nisi eam a se eiiciat.

Praeterea, I Cor: 6 dicitur: *qui adhaeret meretrici, unum corpus efficitur.* Sed non potest aliquis simul esse *membrum meretricis et Christi*, ut ibidem dicitur. Ergo vir uxori fornicanti adhaerens membrum Christi esse desinit, mortaliter peccans.

Praeterea, sicut cognatio tollit vinculum matrimonii, ita fornicatio separat a toro. Sed postquam vir noverit consanguinitatem sui ad uxorem, peccat mortaliter cognoscens eam. Ergo et si cognoscit uxorem postquam scit ipsam esse fornicatam, mortaliter peccat.

Sed contra: Est quod dicit Glossa 1 Cor. 7, quod *Dominus permisit causa fornicationis uxorem dimittere.* Ergo non est in praecepto.

Praeterea, quilibet potest dimittere alteri quod in se peccavit. Sed uxor fornicando peccavit in virum. Ergo vir potest ei parcere, ut non dimittat eam.

Respondeo dicendum quod dimissio uxoris fornicantis introducta est ad corrigendum uxoris crimen per talem poenam. Poena autem corrigeris non requiritur ubi emendatio iam praecessit. Et ideo, si mulier de peccato poeniteat, vir non tenetur eam dimittere. Si autem non poeniteat, tenetur: ne peccato eius consentire videatur, dum correptionem debitam non apponit.

Ad primum ergo dicendum quod peccatum fornicationis in uxore potest corrigi non tantum tali poena, sed etiam verbis et verbere. Et ideo, si alias ad correctionem sit parata, non tenetur vir praedictam poenam ad eius correctionem adhibere.

Ad secundum dicendum quod tunc vir uxori consentire videtur quando eam tenet non cessantem a peccato praeterito. Si autem emendata fuerit, non ei consentit.

Ad tertium dicendum quod ex quo de peccato fornicationis poenituit, meretrix dici non potest. Et ideo vir ei se coniungendo membrum meretricis non fit.

Objection 1: It would seem that the husband is bound by precept to put away his wife who is guilty of fornication. For since the husband is the *head of his wife*, he is bound to correct his wife. Now separation from bed is prescribed as a correction of the wife who is guilty of fornication. Therefore, he is bound to separate from her.

Obj. 2: Further, he who consents with one who sins mortally is also guilty of mortal sin. Now the husband who retains a wife guilty of fornication *would seem to consent with her*, as stated in the text (*Sentences* IV, D. 35). Therefore, he sins unless he puts her away.

Obj. 3: Further, it is written: *he who is joined to a harlot is made one body* (1 Cor 6:16). Now a man cannot at once be a *member of a harlot and a member of Christ* (1 Cor 6:15). Therefore, the husband who is joined to a wife guilty of fornication ceases to be a member of Christ, sinning mortally.

Obj. 4: Further, just as relationship voids the marriage tie, so does fornication dissolve the marriage-bed. Now after the husband becomes cognizant of his consanguinity with his wife, he sins mortally if he has carnal intercourse with her. Therefore, he also sins mortally if he does so after knowing her to be guilty of fornication.

On the contrary, A Gloss on 1 Corinthians 7:11: *let not the husband put away his wife*, says that *our Lord permitted a wife to be put away on account of fornication.* Therefore, it is not a matter of precept.

Further, One can always pardon the sin that another has committed against oneself. Now the wife, by committing fornication, sinned against her husband. Therefore, the husband may spare her by not putting her away.

I answer that, The putting away of a wife guilty of fornication was prescribed in order that the wife might be corrected by means of that punishment. Now a corrective punishment is not required when amendment has already taken place. Wherefore, if the wife repent of her sin, her husband is not bound to put her away: whereas if she repent not, he is bound to do so, lest he seem to consent to her sin by not having recourse to her due correction.

Reply Obj. 1: The wife can be corrected for her sin of fornication not only by this punishment but also by words and blows; wherefore if she be ready to be corrected otherwise, her husband is not bound to have recourse to the aforesaid punishment in order to correct her.

Reply Obj. 2: The husband seems to consent with her when he retains her notwithstanding that she persists in her past sin: if, however, she has mended her ways, he does not consent with her.

Reply Obj. 3: She can no longer be called a harlot since she has repented of her sin. Wherefore her husband, by being joined to her, does not become a member of a harlot.

Vel dicendum quod non coniungitur ei quasi meretrici, sed quasi uxori.

Ad quartum dicendum quod non est simile. Quia consanguinitas facit ut non sit inter eos vinculum matrimoniale, et ideo carnalis copula esset illicita. Sed fornicatio non tollit vinculum praedictum. Et ideo actus remanet, quantum est de se, licitus: nisi per accidens illicitus fiat, inquantum vir consentire turpitudini uxoris videtur.

Ad quintum dicendum quod permissio illa est intelligenda per *prohibitionis privationem*. Et sic contra praeceptum non dividitur: quia etiam quod cadit sub praecepto non est prohibitum.

Ad sextum dicendum quod uxor non tantum peccat in virum, sed etiam in seipsam et in Deum. Et ideo vir non totaliter potest poenam dimittere, nisi emendatio sequatur.

We might also reply that he is joined to her not as a harlot but as his wife.

Reply Obj. 4: There is no parallel because the effect of consanguinity is that there cannot be no marriage tie between them, so that carnal intercourse between them becomes unlawful. Whereas fornication does not remove the said tie, so that the act remains, in itself, lawful, unless it become accidentally unlawful, insofar as the husband seems to consent to his wife's lewdness.

Reply Obj. 5: This permission is to be understood as an *absence of prohibition*: and thus it is not in contradistinction with a precept, for that which is a matter of precept is also not forbidden.

Reply Obj. 6: The wife sins not only against her husband, but also against herself and against God, wherefore her husband cannot entirely remit the punishment, unless amendment has followed.

Article 3

Whether the Husband Can on His Own Judgment Put Away His Wife on Account of Fornication?

Ad tertium sic proceditur. Videtur quod proprio iudicio possit vir: uxorem fornicantem dimittere. Sententiam enim a iudice latam absque alio iudicio exequi licet. Sed Deus, *iustus iudex*, dedit hanc sententiam ut propter fornicationem vir uxorem dimittere possit. Non ergo requiritur ad hoc aliud iudicium.

Praeterea, Matth. 1 dicitur quod *Ioseph, cum esset iustus, cogitavit occulte dimittere Mariam*. Ergo videtur quod occulte vir possit divortium celebrare absque iudicio Ecclesiae.

Praeterea, si vir post fornicationem uxoris cognitam debitum ei reddit, amittit actionem quam contra fornicariam habebat. Ergo denegatio debiti, quae ad divortium pertinet, debet Ecclesiae iudicium praecedere.

Praeterea, illud quod non potest probari, non debet ad Ecclesiae iudicium adduci. Sed fornicationis crimen non potest probari: quia *oculus adulteri observat caliginem*, ut dicitur Iob 24. Ergo non debet iudicio Ecclesiae praedictum divortium fieri.

Praeterea, accusationem debet inscriptio praecedere, qua aliquis se ad talionem obliget si in probatione deficiat. Sed hoc non potest esse in ista materia: quia, qualitercumque res iret, vir consequeretur intentum suum, sive ipse uxorem dimitteret, sive uxor eum. Ergo non debet ad iudicium Ecclesiae per accusationem adduci.

Objection 1: It would seem that the husband can on his own judgment put away his wife on account of fornication. For when sentence has been pronounced by the judge, it is lawful to carry it out without any further judgment. But God, *the just judge*, has pronounced this judgment, that a husband may put his wife away on account of fornication. Therefore, no further judgment is required for this.

Obj. 2: Further, it is stated that *Joseph, being a just man, thought to put Mary away privately* (Matt 1:19). Therefore, it would seem that a husband may privately pronounce a divorce without the judgment of the Church.

Obj. 3: Further, if after becoming cognizant of his wife's fornication a husband has marital intercourse with his wife, he forfeits the action which he had against the adulteress. Therefore, the refusal of the marriage debt, which pertains to a divorce, ought to precede the judgment of the Church.

Obj. 4: Further, that which cannot be proved ought not to be submitted to the judgment of the Church. Now the crime of fornication cannot be proved, since *the eye of the adulterer observes darkness* (Job 24:15). Therefore, the divorce in question ought not to be made on the judgment of the Church.

Obj. 5: Further, accusation should be preceded by inscription, whereby a person binds himself under the pain of retaliation if he fails to bring proof. But this is impossible in this matter, because then in every event the husband would obtain his end, whether he put his wife away, or his wife put him away. Therefore, she ought not to be summoned by accusation to receive the judgment of the Church.

PRAETEREA, plus tenetur homo uxori quam extraneo. Sed homo crimen alterius, etiam extranei, non debet Ecclesiae deferre nisi monitione praemissa in secreto, ut patet Matth. 18. Ergo multo minus potest crimen uxoris ad Ecclesiam deferre, si eam prius occulte non corripuerit.

SED CONTRA: Nullus debet seipsum vindicare. Sed si vir uxorem fornicantem proprio arbitrio dimitteret, ipse se vindicaret. Ergo hoc non debet fieri.

PRAETEREA, nullus in eadem causa est actor et iudex. Sed vir est actor impetens uxorem de offensa in se commissa. Ergo ipse non potest esse iudex. Et sic non debet eam proprio arbitrio dimittere.

RESPONDEO dicendum quod vir potest uxorem dimittere dupliciter. Uno modo, quantum ad torum tantum. Et sic potest eam dimittere, quam cito sibi constat de fornicatione uxoris, proprio arbitrio. Nec tenetur reddere debitum exigenti nisi per Ecclesiam compellatur. Et taliter reddens nullum praeiudicium sibi facit.

Alio modo, quantum ad torum et cohabitationem. Et hoc modo non potest dimitti nisi iudicio Ecclesiae. Et si alias dimissa fuerit, debet cogi ad cohabitandum: nisi possit ei vir in continenti fornicationem probare. Haec autem dimissio *divortium* dicitur. Et ideo concedendum est quod divortium non potest celebrari nisi iudicio Ecclesiae.

AD PRIMUM ergo dicendum quod sententia est applicatio iuris communis ad particulare factum. Unde Dominus ius promulgavit, secundum quod sententia in iudicio formari debet.

AD SECUNDUM dicendum quod , Ioseph voluit Virginem dimittere, non quasi suspectam de fornicatione, sed ob reverentiam sanctitatis eius, timens ei cohabitare.

Nec tamen est simile. Quia tunc ex adulterio non solum procedebatur ad divortium sed ulterius ad lapidationem. Non autem nunc, quando agitur in iudicio Ecclesiae.

AD TERTIUM patet solutio ex dictis.

AD QUARTUM dicendum quod quandoque vir, uxorem suspectam habens, ei insidiatur, et deprehendere potest eam cum testibus in crimine fornicationis. Et sic potest ad accusationem procedere.

Et praeterea, si de facto ipso non constat, possunt esse violentae suspiciones fornicationis, quibus probatis, videtur fornicatio probata esse: ut si inveniatur *solus cum sola*, horis et locis suspectis, et *nudus cum nuda*.

AD QUINTUM dicendum: quod maritus potest accusare uxorem de adulterio dupliciter. Uno modo, ad tori separationem, coram iudice spirituali. Et tunc inscriptio

OBJ. 6: Further, a man is more bound to his wife than to a stranger. Now a man ought not to refer to the Church the crime of another, even though he be a stranger, without previously admonishing him privately (Matt 18:15). Much less, therefore, may the husband bring his wife's crime before the Church unless he has previously rebuked her in private.

ON THE CONTRARY, No one should avenge himself. But if a husband were by his own judgment to put away his wife on account of fornication, he would avenge himself. Therefore, this should not be done.

FURTHER, No man is prosecutor and judge in the same cause. But the husband is the prosecutor by suing his wife for the offense she has committed against him. Therefore, he cannot be the judge, and consequently he cannot put her away on his own judgment.

I ANSWER THAT, A husband can put away his wife in two ways. First, as to bed only, and thus he may put her away on his own judgment as soon as he has evidence of her fornication: nor is he bound to pay her the marriage debt at her demand, unless he be compelled by the Church, and by paying it thus he in no way prejudices his own case.

Second, as to bed and cohabitation, and in this way she cannot be put away except at the judgment of the Church; and if she has been put away otherwise, he must be compelled to cohabit with her unless the husband can at once prove the wife's fornication. Now this putting away is called a *divorce*: and consequently it must be admitted that a divorce cannot be pronounced except at the judgment of the Church.

REPLY OBJ. 1: The sentence is an application of the general law to a particular fact. Wherefore God gave out the law according to which the sentence of the court has to be pronounced.

REPLY OBJ. 2: Joseph was minded to put away the Blessed Virgin not as suspected of fornication, but because in reverence for her sanctity, he feared to cohabit with her.

Moreover, there is no parallel because then the sentence at law was not only divorce but also stoning, but not now when the case is brought to the Church for judgment.

THE REPLY to the third objection is clear from what has been said.

REPLY OBJ. 4: Sometimes when the husband suspects his wife of adultery he watches her secretly, that together with witnesses he may discover her in the sin of fornication, and so proceed to accusation.

Moreover, if he cannot establish the fact, there can be forceful suspicions of fornication, which, when they are proved, it seems that fornication is proved, for example, if a man and a woman are found *alone together* at suspect times and places, and if they are found *naked together*.

REPLY OBJ. 5: A husband may accuse his wife of adultery in two ways. First, he may seek a separation from bed before a spiritual judge, and then there is no need for

debet fieri sine obligatione ad legem talionis: quia sic vir consequeretur intentum suum, ut probat obiectio. Alio modo, ad punitionem criminis in iudicio saeculari. Et sic oportet quod praecedat inscriptio per quam ad poenam talionis se obliget si in probatione deficiat.

AD SEXTUM dicendum quod, sicut decretalis dicit, tribus modis in criminibus procedi potest. Primo, *per inquisitionem*: quam debet praecedere *clamosa insinuatio*, quae locum accusationis tenet. Secundo, *per accusationem*: quam debet praecedere *inscriptio*. Tertio, *per denuntiationem*: quam debet praecedere *fraterna correctio*. Verbum ergo Domini intelligitur quando agitur per viam denuntiationis, non quando agitur per viam accusationis: quia tunc non agitur solum ad correctionem delinquentis, sed ad punitionem, propter bonum commune conservandum, quod, iustitia deficiente, periret.

an inscription to be made under the pain of retaliation, since thus the husband would gain his end, as the objection proves. Second, he may seek for the crime to be punished in a secular court, and then it is necessary for inscription to precede, whereby he binds himself under pain of retaliation if he fail to prove his case.

REPLY OBJ. 6: According to the *Decretals*, there are three modes of procedure in criminal cases. First, *by inquisition*, which should be preceded *by notoriety*; second, *by accusation*, which should be preceded *by inscription*; third, *by denunciation*, which should be preceded *by fraternal correction*. Accordingly, the saying of our Lord refers to the case where the process is by way of denunciation, and not by accusation, because then the end in view is not only the correction of the guilty party, but also his punishment, for the safeguarding of the common good, which would be destroyed if justice were lacking.

Article 4

Whether in a Case of Divorce Husband and Wife Should Be Judged on a Par with Each Other?

AD QUARTUM SIC PROCEDITUR. Videtur quod vir et uxor non debeant in causa divortii ad paria iudicari. Divortium enim conceditur in lege nova loco repudii, quod erat in lege veteri, ut patet Matth. 5. Sed in repudio vir et uxor non iudicabantur ad paria: quia vir poterat repudiare uxorem, et non e converso. Ergo nec in divortio debent ad paria iudicari.

PRAETEREA, plus est contra legem naturae quod uxor plures viros habeat quam quod vir plures mulieres: unde hoc quandoque licuit, illud vero, illud vero nunquam. Ergo plus peccat mulier in adulterio quam vir. Et ita non debent ad paria iudicari.

PRAETEREA, ubi est maius nocumentum proximi, ibi est maius peccatum. Sed plus nocet uxor adultera viro quam vir adulter uxori: quia adulterium uxoris facit incertitudinem prolis, non autem adulterium viri. Ergo maius est peccatum uxoris. Et sic non debent ad paria iudicari.

PRAETEREA, divortium inducitur ad crimen adulterii corrigendum. Sed magis pertinet ad virum, qui est *caput mulieris*, ut dicitur I Cor. 11, corrigere uxorem quam e converso. Ergo non debent in repudio ad paria iudicari, sed vir debet esse melioris conditionis.

SED CONTRA: Videtur quod in hoc uxor debeat esse melioris conditionis. Quia quanto est maior fragilitas in peccante, tanto magis est peccatum venia dignum. Sed

OBJECTION 1: It would seem that, in a case of divorce, husband and wife ought not to be judged on a par with each other. For divorce under the new law takes the place of the divorce recognized by the old law (Matt 5:31–32). Now, in the repudium husband and wife were not judged on a par with each other, since the husband could put away his wife, but not vice versa. Therefore, neither in divorce ought they to be judged on a par with each other.

OBJ. 2: Further, it is more opposed to the natural law that a wife have several husbands than that a husband have several wives: wherefore the latter has been sometimes lawful, but the former never. Therefore, the wife sins more grievously in adultery than the husband, and consequently they ought not to be judged on a par with each other.

OBJ. 3: Further, where there is greater injury to one's neighbor, there is a greater sin. Now the adulterous wife does a greater injury to her husband than does the adulterous husband to his wife, since a wife's adultery involves uncertainty of the offspring, whereas the husband's adultery does not. Therefore, the wife's sin is the greater, and so they ought not to be judged on a par with each other.

OBJ. 4: Further, divorce is prescribed in order to punish the crime of adultery. Now it belongs to the husband who is the *head of the wife* (1 Cor. 11:3) to correct his wife, rather than vice versa. Therefore, they should not be judged on a par with each other for the purpose of divorce, but the husband ought to have the preference.

ON THE CONTRARY, It would seem in this matter the wife ought to have the preference. For the more frail the sinner, the more is his sin deserving of pardon. Now there

in mulieribus est maior fragilitas quam in viris: ratione cuius dicit Chrysostomus quod propria passio mulierum est luxuria. Et Philosophus dicit, in VII *Ethic.*, quod *mulieres non dicuntur continentes*, proprie loquendo, propter facilem inclinationem ad concupiscentias: quia nec bruta animalia possunt continere, propter hoc quod non habent aliquid quod concupiscentiis obviare possit. Ergo mulieribus in poena divortii deberet magis parci.

Praeterea, vir ponitur caput mulieris ut ipsam corrigat. Ergo magis peccat quam mulier. Et sic debet magis puniri.

Respondeo dicendum quod in causa divortii vir et uxor ad paria iudicantur, ut idem sit licitum et illicitum uni quod alteri. Non tamen pariter iudicantur ad illa: quia causa divortii est maior in uno quam in alio, cum tamen in utroque sit sufficiens causa ad divortium. Divortium enim est poena adulterii inquantum est contra matrimonii bona.

Quantum autem ad bonum fidei, ad quam coniuges aequaliter sibi invicem tenentur, tantum peccat contra matrimonium adulterium unius sicut adulterium alterius: et haec causa in utroque sufficit ad divortium.

Sed quantum ad bonum prolis, plus peccat adulterium uxoris quam viri: et ideo maior causa divortii est iri uxore quam in viro. Et sic ad aequalia, sed non ex aequali causa, obligantur. Nec tamen iniuste: quia in utroque est causa sufficiens ad hanc poenam; sicut est etiam de duobus qui damnantur ad eiusdem mortis poenam, quamvis alius altero gravius peccaverit.

Ad primum ergo dicendum quod repudium non permittebatur nisi ad evitandum homicidium. Et quia in viris magis erat de hoc periculum quam in mulieribus, ideo viro permittebatur dimittere uxorem, non autem e converso, per legem repudii.

Ad secundum et tertium dicendum quod rationes illae procedunt secundum quod in comparatione ad bonum prolis maior sit causa divortii in uxore adultera quam in viro. Non tamen sequitur quod non iudicentur ad paria, ut ex dictis patet.

Ad quartum dicendum quod, quamvis vir sit caput mulieris quasi gubernator, non tamen quasi iudex ipsius: sicut nec e converso. Et ideo in his quae per iudicium facienda sunt, non plus potest vir in uxorem quam e converso.

Ad quintum dicendum quod in adulterio invenitur de ratione peccati idem quod est in fornicatione simplici, et adhuc plus, quod magis gravat, scilicet matrimonii laesio. Si ergo consideretur id quod est commune adul-

is greater frailty in women than in men, for which reason Chrysostom (Hom. 40 in the *Opus Imperfectum*) says that lust is a passion proper to women, and the Philosopher says (*Ethics* 7.7) that properly speaking *women are not said to be continent* on account of their being easily inclined to concupiscence, for neither can dumb animals be continent, because they have nothing to stand in the way of their desires. Therefore, women are rather to be spared in the punishment of divorce.

Further, The husband is placed as the head of the woman in order to correct her. Therefore, his sin is greater than the woman's and so he should be punished the more.

I answer that, In a case of divorce husband and wife are judged on a par with each other, in the sense that the same things are lawful or unlawful to the one as to the other: but they are not judged on a par with each other in reference to those things, since the reason for divorce is greater in one spouse than in the other, although there is sufficient reason for divorce in both. For divorce is a punishment of adultery insofar as it is opposed to the marriage goods.

Now as regards the good of fidelity to which husband and wife are equally bound towards each other, the adultery of one is as great a sin against marriage as the adultery of the other, and this is in either of them a sufficient reason for divorce.

But as regards the good of the offspring, the wife's adultery is a greater sin against marriage than the husband's, wherefore it is a greater reason for divorce in the wife than in the husband: and thus they are under an equal obligation, but not for equal reasons. Nor is this unjust, for on either hand there is sufficient reason for the punishment in question, just as there is in two persons condemned to the punishment of death, although one of them may have sinned more grievously than the other.

Reply Obj. 1: The only reason why divorce was permitted was to avoid murder. And since there was more danger of this in men than in women, the husband was allowed to put away his wife by a bill of divorce, but not vice versa.

Reply Obj. 2 and 3: These arguments are based on the fact that in comparison with the good of the offspring there is more reason for divorce in an adulterous wife than in an adulterous husband. It does not follow, however, that they are not judged on a par with each other.

Reply Obj. 4: Although the husband is the head of the wife, he is, as it were, her pilot, and is no more her judge than she is his. Consequently, in matters that have to be submitted to a judge, the husband has no more power over his wife, than she over him.

Reply Obj. 5: In adultery there is the same sinful character as in simple fornication, and something more which aggravates it, namely, the lesion to marriage. Accordingly, if we consider that which is common to adultery and for-

terio et fornicationi, peccatum viri et mulieris se habent ut excedentia et excessa: quia in mulieribus est plus de humore, et ideo sunt magis ducibiles a concupiscentiis; sed in viro est plus de calore, qui concupiscentiam excitat. Sed tamen, simpliciter loquendo, ceteris paribus, vir in simplici fornicatione plus peccat quam mulier: quia plus habet de rationis bono, quod praevalet quibuslibet motibus corporalium passionum.

Sed quantum ad laesionem matrimonii, quam adulterium fornicationi addit, ex qua divortium causatur, plus peccat mulier quam vir, ut ex dictis patet. Et quia hoc est gravius quam simplex fornicatio, ideo, simpliciter loquendo, plus peccat mulier adultera quam vir adulter ceteris paribus.

AD SEXTUM dicendum quod, quamvis regimen quod datur viro in mulierem sit quaedam circumstantia aggravans, tamen ex illa circumstantia quae in aliam speciem trahit, magis aggravatur peccatum: scilicet ex laesione matrimonii, quae trahit ad speciem iniustitiae, in hoc quod furtive aliena proles submittitur.

nication, the sin of the husband and that of the wife are compared the one to the other as that which exceeds to that which is exceeded, for in women the humors are more abundant, wherefore they are more inclined to be led by their concupiscences, whereas in man there is abundance of heat which excites concupiscence. Simply speaking, however, other things being equal, a man sins more grievously in simple fornication than a woman, because he has more of the good of reason, which prevails over all movements of bodily passions.

But as regards the lesion to marriage which adultery adds to fornication and for which reason it is an occasion for divorce, the woman sins more grievously than the man, as appears from what we have said above. And since it is more grievous than simple fornication, it follows that, simply speaking, the adulterous wife sins more grievously than the adulterous husband, other things being equal.

REPLY OBJ. 6: Although the control which the husband receives over his wife is an aggravating circumstance, nevertheless the sin is yet more aggravated by this circumstance which draws the sin to another species, namely, by the lesion to marriage, which becomes a kind of injustice through the fraudulent substitution of another's child.

Article 5

Whether a Husband Can Marry Again After Having a Divorce?

AD QUINTUM SIC PROCEDITUR. Videtur quod post divortium vir alteri nubere possit. Nullus enim tenetur ad perpetuam continentiam. Sed vir tenetur in aliquo casu uxorem fornicantem a se in perpetuum separare, ut patet ex dictis. Ergo videtur quod ad minus in tali casu alteram ducere possit.

PRAETEREA, peccanti non est danda maior occasio peccandi. Sed si ei qui propter culpam fornicationis dimittitur, non licet aliam copulam quaerere, datur sibi maior occasio peccandi: non enim est probabile quod qui in matrimonio non continuit, quod postea continere possit. Ergo videtur quod liceat ei ad aliam copulam transire.

PRAETEREA, uxor non tenetur viro nisi ad debitum reddendum et cohabitationem. Sed per divortium ab utroque absolvitur. Ergo omnino *soluta est a lege viri*. Ergo potest alteri nubere. Et eadem ratio est de viro.

PRAETEREA, Matth. 19 dicitur: *qui dimiserit uxorem et aliam duxerit, excepta causa fornicationis, moechatur.* Ergo videtur quod si, causa fornicationis dimissa uxore,

OBJECTION 1: It would seem that a husband can marry again after having a divorce. For no one is bound to perpetual continence. Now in some cases the husband is bound to put away his wife forever on account of fornication, as stated above (A. 2). Therefore, seemingly at least in this case he can marry again.

OBJ. 2: Further, a sinner should not be given a greater occasion of sin. But if she who is put away on account of the sin of fornication is not allowed to seek another marriage, she is given a greater occasion of sin: for it is improbable that one who was not continent during marriage will be able to be continent afterwards. Therefore, it would seem lawful for her to marry again.

OBJ. 3: Further, the wife is not bound to the husband save as regards the payment of the marriage debt and cohabitation. But she is freed from both obligations by divorce. Therefore, *she is loosed from the law of her husband* (Rom 7:2). Therefore, she can marry again; and the same applies to her husband.

OBJ. 4: Further, it is said: *whosoever shall put away his wife, except it be for fornication, and shall marry another commits adultery* (Matt 5:32). Therefore, it seems that he

aliam duxerit, non moechetur. Et ita erit verum matrimonium.

SED CONTRA: I Cor. 7: *praecipio non ego, sed Dominus, uxorem a viro non discedere: quod si discesserit, manere innuptam.*

PRAETEREA, nullus ex peccato debet *reportare commodum.* Sed reportaret si liceret adulterae ad aliud magis desideratum connubium transire: et esset occasio adulterandi volentibus alia matrimonia quaerere. Ergo non licet aliam copulam quaerere neque viro neque uxori.

RESPONDEO dicendum quod nihil adveniens supra matrimonium potest ipsum dissolvere. Et ideo adulterium non facit quin sit verum matrimonium. *Manet* enim, ut Augustinus dicit, *inter viventes coniugale vinculum, quod nec separatio nec cum alio iunctio potest auferre.* Et ideo non licet uni, altero vivente, ad aliam copulam transire.

AD PRIMUM ergo dicendum quod, quamvis per se nullus obligetur ad continentiam, tamen per accidens potest esse quod obligetur: sicut si uxor sua aegritudinem incurabilem incurrat, et talem quae carnalem copulam non patiatur. Et similiter etiam est si incorrigibiliter spirituali infirmitate, scilicet fornicatione, laboret.

AD SECUNDUM dicendum quod ipsa confusio quam reportat ex divortio, debet eam cohibere a peccato. Quod si cohibere non potest, minus malum est quod ipsa sola peccet quam quod vir peccati eius sit particeps.

AD TERTIUM dicendum quod, quamvis uxor post divortium non teneatur viro adultero ad debitum reddendum et cohabitandum, tamen adhuc manet vinculum matrimonii, ex quo ad hoc tenebatur. Et ideo non potest ad aliam copulam transire, viro vivente. Potest tamen continentiam vovere, viro invito: nisi videatur Ecclesia decepta fuisse per falsos testes sententiando de divortio; quia in tali casu, etiam si votum professionis emisisset, restitueretur viro et teneretur reddere debitum, sed non liceret ei exigere.

AD QUARTUM dicendum quod exceptio illa quae est in verbis Domini, refertur ad dimissionem uxoris. Et ideo obiectio ex falso intellectu procedit.

does not commit adultery if he marry again after putting away his wife on account of fornication, and consequently this will be a true marriage.

ON THE CONTRARY, It is written: *not I, but the Lord, commands that the wife depart not from her husband and, if she depart, that she remain unmarried* (1 Cor 7:10).

FURTHER, No one should *gain advantage* from sin. But the adulteress would if she were allowed to contract another and more desired marriage; and an occasion of adultery would be afforded those who wish to marry again. Therefore, it is unlawful both to the wife and to the husband to contract a second marriage.

I ANSWER THAT, Nothing supervenient to marriage can dissolve it: wherefore adultery does not make a marriage cease to be valid. For, according to Augustine (*On Marriage and Concupiscence* 1.10), *as long as they live they are bound by the marriage tie, which neither divorce nor union with another can destroy.* Therefore, it is unlawful for one to marry again while the other lives.

REPLY OBJ. 1: Although no one is absolutely bound to continence, he may be bound accidentally; for instance, if his wife should contract an incurable disease that is incompatible with carnal intercourse. And it is the same if she labor under a spiritual disease, namely fornication, so as to be incorrigible.

REPLY OBJ. 2: The very shame of having been divorced ought to keep her from sin: and if it cannot keep her from sin, it is a lesser evil that she alone should sin than that her husband take part in her sin.

REPLY OBJ. 3: Although after divorce the wife is not bound to her husband as regards paying him the marriage debt and cohabiting with him, the marriage tie remains by which she was bound to this, and consequently she cannot marry again during her husband's lifetime. She can, however, take a vow of continence against her husband's will, unless it seem that the Church has been deceived by false witnesses in pronouncing the divorce; for in that case, even if she has made her vow of profession she ought to be restored to her husband, and would be bound to pay the marriage debt, but it would be unlawful for her to demand it.

REPLY OBJ. 4: The exception expressed in our Lord's words refers to the putting away of the wife. Hence the objection is based on a false interpretation.

Article 6

Whether Husband and Wife May Be Reconciled After Being Divorced?

AD SEXTUM SIC PROCEDITUR. Videtur quod post divortium vir et uxor non possint reconciliari. Regula enim est in iure: *quod semel bene definitum est, nulla debet iteratione retractari.* Sed iudicio Ecclesiae definitum

OBJECTION 1: It would seem that husband and wife may not be reconciled after being divorced. For the law contains the rule: *that which has been once well decided must not be subsequently withdrawn* (*Decretals*). Now it has been

est quod debent separari. Ergo non possunt reconciliari ulterius.

PRAETEREA, si posset esse reconciliatio, praecipue videretur quod post poenitentiam uxoris vir teneatur eam recipere. Sed non tenetur: quia etiam uxor non potest pro exceptione proponere in iudicio suam poenitentiam contra virum accusantem de fornicatione. Ergo nullo modo potest esse reconciliatio.

PRAETEREA, si posset esse reconciliatio, videtur quod uxor adultera teneretur redire ad virum ipsam revocantem. Sed non tenetur: quia iam separati sunt iudicip Ecclesiae. Ergo, etc.

PRAETEREA, si liceret reconciliare uxorem adulteram, in illo casu praecipue deberet fieri quando vir post divortium invenitur adulterium committere. Sed in hoc casu uxor non potest cogere eum ad reconciliationem, cum iuste sit divortium celebratum. Ergo nullo modo potest reconciliari.

PRAETEREA, si vir adulter occulte dimittat per iudicium Ecclesiae uxorem convictam de adulterio, non videtur iuste factum divortium. Sed tamen vir non tenetur uxorem sibi reconciliare: quia uxor probare in iudicio adulterium viri non potest. Ergo multo minus quando divortium iuste est celebratum, reconciliatio fieri potest.

SED CONTRA: Est quod dicitur I Cor. 7: *quod si discesserit, manere innuptam, aut viro suo reconciliari.*

PRAETEREA, vir poterat eam non dimittere post fornicationem. Ergo, eadem ratione, potest eam reconciliare sibi.

RESPONDEO dicendum quod, si uxor post divortium de peccato poenitentiam agens emendata fuerit, potest eam sibi vir reconciliare. Si autem in peccato incorrigibilis maneat, non debet eam ad se assumere: eadem ratione qua non licebat eam nolentem a peccato desistere retinere.

AD PRIMUM ergo dicendum quod sententia Ecclesiae divortium Celebrantis non fuit cogens ad separationem, sed licentiam praebens. Et ideo absque retractatione praecedentis sententiae potest reconciliatio sequi.

AD SECUNDUM dicendum quod poenitentia uxoris debet inducere virum ut uxorem fornicantem non accuset aut dimittat: sed tamen non potest ad hoc cogi; nec potest per poenitentiam uxor eum ab accusatione repellere. Quia, cessante culpa et quantum ad actum et quantum ad maculam, adhuc manet aliquid de reatu; et cessante etiam reatu quantum ad Deum, adhuc manet reatus quoad poenam humano iudicio inferendam, quia homo non videt cor, sicut Deus.

decided by the judgment of the Church that they ought to be separated. Therefore, they cannot subsequently be reconciled.

OBJ. 2: Further, if it were allowable for them to be reconciled, the husband would seem bound to receive his wife, especially after she has repented. But he is not bound, for the wife, in defending herself before the judge, cannot allege her repentance against her husband's accusation of fornication. Therefore, in no way is reconciliation allowable.

OBJ. 3: Further, if reconciliation were allowable, it would seem that the adulterous wife is bound to return to her husband if her husband asks her. But she is not bound, since they are separated by the Church. Therefore, etc.

OBJ. 4: Further, if it were lawful to be reconciled to an adulterous wife, this would especially be the case when the husband is found to have committed adultery after the divorce. But in this case the wife cannot compel him to be reconciled, since the divorce has been justly pronounced. Therefore, she may in no way be reconciled.

OBJ. 5: Further, if a husband whose adultery is unknown put away his wife who is convicted of adultery by the sentence of the Church, the divorce would seem to have been pronounced unjustly. And yet the husband is not bound to be reconciled to his wife, because she is unable to prove his adultery in court. Much less, therefore, is reconciliation allowable when the divorce has been granted justly.

ON THE CONTRARY, It is written: *and if she depart, that she remain unmarried, or be reconciled to her husband* (1 Cor 7:11).

FURTHER, It is allowable for the husband not to put her away after fornication. Therefore, for the same reason he can be reconciled to her after divorce.

I ANSWER THAT, If the wife has mended her ways by repenting of her sin after the divorce, her husband may become reconciled to her; but if she remain incorrigible in her sin, he must not take her back, for the same reason which forbade him to retain her while she refused to desist from sin.

REPLY OBJ. 1: The sentence of the Church in pronouncing the divorce did not bind them to separate, but allowed them to do so. Therefore, reconciliation may be effected or ensue without any withdrawal of the previous sentence.

REPLY OBJ. 2: The wife's repentance should induce the husband not to accuse or put away the wife who is guilty of fornication. He cannot, however, be compelled to this course of action, nor can his wife oppose her repentance to his accusation, because although she is no longer guilty, neither in act nor in the stain of sin, there still remains something of the debt of punishment, and though this has been taken away in the sight of God, there still remains the debt of punishment to be inflicted by the judgment of man, because man sees not the heart as God does.

AD TERTIUM dicendum quod illud quod inducitur in favorem alicuius, non facit ei praeiudicium. Unde, cum divortium sit inductum in favorem viri, non aufert ei ius petendi debitum vel revocandi uxorem. Unde uxor tenetur reddere et ad eum redire si fuerit revocata, nisi de licentia eius votum continentiae emiserit.

AD QUARTUM dicendum quod propter adulterium quod vir prius innocens post divortium committit, secundum rigorem iuris non debet cogi ad recipiendum uxorem adulteram prius. Tamen secundum aequitatem iuris iudex ex officio suo debet eum cogere ut caveat periculo animae eius et scandalo aliorum, quamvis uxor non possit reconciliationem petere.

AD QUINTUM dicendum quod, si adulterium viri sit occultum, per hoc non aufertur ius excipiendi contra accusationem viri uxori adulterae, quamvis desit sibi probatio. Et ideo peccat vir divortium petens: et si post sententiam de divortio uxor petat debitum aut reconciliationem, vir tenetur ad utrumque.

REPLY OBJ. 3: That which is done in a person's favor does him no prejudice. Wherefore since the divorce has been granted in favor of the husband, it does not deprive him of the right of asking for the marriage debt, or of asking his wife to return to him. Hence his wife is bound to pay the debt, and to return to him if he ask her, unless with his consent she has taken a vow of continence.

REPLY OBJ. 4: According to strict law, a husband who was previously innocent should not be compelled to receive an adulterous wife on account of his having committed adultery after the divorce. But according to equity, the judge is bound by virtue of his office first of all to admonish him to beware of imperiling his own soul and of scandalizing others; although the wife may not herself seek reconciliation.

REPLY OBJ. 5: If the husband's adultery is secret, this does not deprive his adulterous wife of the right to allege it in self-defense, although she cannot prove it. Wherefore the husband sins by seeking a divorce, and if, after the sentence of divorce, his wife asks for the marriage debt or for a reconciliation, the husband is bound to both.

QUESTION 63

SECOND MARRIAGES

Consequenter considerandum est de secundis nuptiis.

Et circa hoc quaeruntur duo.
Primo: utrum sint licitae.
Secundo: utrum sint sacramentales.

In the next place we must consider second marriage.

Under this head there are two points of inquiry:
(1) Whether it is lawful?
(2) Whether it is a sacrament?

Article 1

Whether a Second Marriage Is Lawful?

AD PRIMUM SIC PROCEDITUR. Videtur quod secundae nuptiae non sint licitae. Quia iudicium de re debet esse secundum veritatem. Dicit autem Chrysostomus quod *secundum virum accipere est fornicatio secundum veritatem*. Quae non est licita. Ergo nec secundum matrimonium.

PRAETEREA, omne quod non est bonum, non est licitum. Sed Ambrosius dicit quod *duplex matrimonium non est bonum*. Ergo non est licitum.

PRAETEREA, nullus arceri debet ne intersit illis quae sunt honesta et licita. Sed sacerdotes arcentur ne intersint secundis nuptiis, ut in littera patet. Ergo non sunt licitae.

PRAETEREA, nullus reportat poenam nisi pro culpa. Sed pro secundis nuptiis aliquis reportat irregularitatis poenam. Ergo non sunt licitae.

SED CONTRA: Est quod Abraham legitur secundas nuptias contraxisse, Gen. 25.

PRAETEREA, I Tim. 5 dicit Apostolus: *volo autem iuniores*, scilicet viduas, *nubere, filios procreare*. Ergo secundae nuptiae sunt licitae.

RESPONDEO dicendum quod vinculum matrimoniale non durat nisi usque ad mortem: ut patet Rom. 7. Et ideo, moriente altero coniugum, vinculum matrimoniale cessat. Unde propter praecedens matrimonium non impeditur aliquis a secundo, mortuo coniuge. Et sic non solum secundae, sed tertiae et sic deinceps nuptiae sunt licitae.

AD PRIMUM ergo dicendum quod Chrysostomus loquitur quantum ad causam quae aliquando solet ad secundas nuptias incitare, scilicet concupiscentiam, quae etiam ad fornicationem incitat.

AD SECUNDUM dicendum quod secundum matrimonium dicitur non esse bonum, non quia sit illicitum,

OBJECTION 1: It would seem that a second marriage is unlawful. For we should judge of things according to truth. Now Chrysostom (Hom. 32 in the *Opus Imperfectum*) says that *to take a second husband is in truth fornication*, which is unlawful. Therefore, neither is a second marriage lawful.

OBJ. 2: Further, whatever is not good is unlawful. Now Ambrose (*On Widows*) says that *a second marriage is not good*. Therefore, it is unlawful.

OBJ. 3: Further, no one should be debarred from being present at such things as are becoming and lawful. Yet priests are debarred from being present at second marriages, as stated in the text (*Sentences* IV, D. 42). Therefore, they are unlawful.

OBJ. 4: Further, no one incurs a penalty save for sin. Now a person incurs the penalty of irregularity on account of being married twice. Therefore, a second marriage is unlawful.

ON THE CONTRARY, We read of Abraham having contracted a second marriage (Gen 25:1).

FURTHER, The Apostle says: *I will that the younger*, namely, widows, *should marry, bear children* (1 Tim 5:14). Therefore, second marriages are lawful.

I ANSWER THAT, The marriage tie lasts only until death (Rom 7:2), wherefore at the death of either spouse the marriage tie ceases: and consequently when one dies the other is not hindered from marrying a second time on account of the previous marriage. Therefore, not only second marriages are lawful, but even third and so on.

REPLY OBJ. 1: Chrysostom is speaking in reference to the cause which is wont at times to incite a person to a second marriage, namely, concupiscence, which incites also to fornication.

REPLY OBJ. 2: A second marriage is stated not to be good not because it is unlawful, but because it lacks the

sed quia caret illo honore significationis qui est in primis nuptiis, ut sit *una unius*, sicut est *in Christo et Ecclesia.*

AD TERTIUM dicendum quod homines divinis dediti non solum ab illicitis, sed etiam ab illis quae habent aliquam turpitudinis speciem, arcentur. Et ideo etiam arcentur a secundis nuptiis, quae carent honestate quae erat in primis.

AD QUARTUM dicendum quod irregularitas non semper inducitur propter culpam, sed propter defectum sacramenti. Et ideo ratio non est ad propositum.

honor of the signification which is in a first marriage, where *one husband has one wife*, as in the case *of Christ and the Church.*

REPLY OBJ. 3: Men who are consecrated to divine things are debarred not only from unlawful things, but even from things which have any appearance of turpitude; and consequently they are debarred from second marriages, which lack the decorum which was in a first marriage.

REPLY OBJ. 4: Irregularity is not always incurred on account of a sin, and may be incurred through a defect in a sacrament. Hence the argument is not to the point.

Article 2

Whether a Second Marriage Is a Sacrament?

AD SECUNDUM SIC PROCEDITUR. Videtur quod secundum matrimonium non sit sacramentum. *Qui enim iterat sacramentum, facit ei iniuriam.* Sed nulli sacramento facienda est iniuria. Ergo, si secundum matrimonium esset sacramentum, nullo modo esset iterandum.

PRAETEREA, in omni sacramento adhibetur aliqua benedictio. Sed in secundis nuptiis non adhibetur, ut in littera dicitur. Ergo non fit ibi aliquod sacramentum.

PRAETEREA, significatio est de essentia sacramenti. Sed in secundo matrimonio non salvatur significatio matrimonii: quia non est una unius, sicut *Christus et Ecclesia.* Ergo non est sacramentum.

PRAETEREA, unum sacramentum non impedit a susceptione alterius. Sed secundum matrimonium impedit a susceptione ordinis. Ergo non est sacramentum.

SED CONTRA: Coitus in secundis nuptiis excusatur a peccato sicut et in primis. Sed per tria bona matrimonii excusatur coitus matrimonialis, quae sunt *fides*, *proles* et *sacramentum*. Ergo secundum matrimonium est sacramentum.

PRAETEREA, ex secunda coniunctione viri ad mulierem non sacramentali non contrahitur irregularitas: sicut patet in fornicatione. Sed in secundis nuptiis contrahitur irregularitas. Ergo surit sacramentales.

RESPONDEO dicendum quod, ubicumque inveniuntur illa quae sunt de essentia sacramenti, ibi est verum sacramentum. Unde, cum in secundis nuptiis inveniantur omnia quae sunt de essentia sacramenti, quia debita materia, quam facit personarum legitimitas, et debita forma, scilicet expressio consensus interioris per verba de praesenti; constat quod etiam secundum matrimonium est sacramentum, sicut et primum.

AD PRIMUM ergo dicendum quod hoc intelligitur de sacramento quod inducit perpetuum effectum: tunc

OBJECTION 1: It would seem that a second marriage is not a sacrament. For *he who repeats a sacrament injures the sacrament.* But no sacrament should be done an injury. Therefore, if a second marriage were a sacrament, marriage ought in no way to be repeated.

OBJ. 2: Further, in every sacrament some kind of blessing is given. But no blessing is given in a second marriage, as stated in the text (*Sentences* IV, D. 42). Therefore, no sacrament is conferred therein.

OBJ. 3: Further, signification is essential to a sacrament. But the signification of marriage is not preserved in a second marriage, because there is not a union of only one woman with only one man, as in the case *of Christ and the Church.* Therefore, it is not a sacrament.

OBJ. 4: Further, one sacrament is not an impediment to receiving another. But a second marriage is an impediment to receiving orders. Therefore, it is not a sacrament.

ON THE CONTRARY, Marital intercourse is excused from sin in a second marriage even as in a first marriage. Now marital intercourse is excused (Q. 69, A. 1) by the marriage goods which are *fidelity*, *offspring*, and *sacrament*. Therefore, a second marriage is a sacrament.

FURTHER, Irregularity is not contracted through a second and non-sacramental union, such as fornication. Yet irregularity is contracted through a second marriage. Therefore, it is a sacramental union.

I ANSWER THAT, Wherever we find the essentials of a sacrament, there is a true sacrament. Wherefore, since in a second marriage we find all the essentials of the sacrament of marriage (namely, the due matter—which results from the parties having the conditions prescribed by law—and the due form, which is the expression of the inward consent by words of the present), it is clear that a second marriage is a sacrament even as a first.

REPLY OBJ. 1: This is true of a sacrament which causes an everlasting effect: for then, if the sacrament be repeated,

enim, si iteratur sacramentum, datur intelligi quod primum non fuit efficax, et sic fit primo iniuria; sicut patet in omnibus sacramentis quae imprimunt characterem. Sed illa sacramenta quae habent effectum non perpetuum, possunt iterari sine iniuria sacramenti: sicut patet de poenitentia. Et quia vinculum matrimoniale tollitur per mortem, nulla fit iniuria sacramento si mulier post mortem viri iterato nubat.

AD SECUNDUM dicendum quod secundum matrimonium, quamvis in se consideratum sit perfectum sacramentum, tamen in ordine ad primum consideratum habet aliquid de defectu sacramenti: quia non habet plenam significationem, cum non sit *una unius*, sicut est in matrimonio *Christi et Ecclesiae*. Et ratione huius defectus benedictio a secundis nuptiis subtrahitur.

Sed hoc est intelligendum quando secundae nuptiae sunt secundae et ex parte viri et ex parte mulieris, vel ex parte mulieris tantum. Si enim virgo contrahat cum illo qui habuit aliam uxorem, nihilominus nuptiae benedicuntur: salvatur enim aliquo modo significatio etiam in ordine ad primas nuptias; quia Christus, etsi unam Ecclesiam sponsam habeat, habet tamen plures personas desponsatas in una Ecclesia. Sed anima non potest esse sponsa alterius quam Christi: quia alias, cum daemone fornicatur, nec est ibi matrimonium spirituale. Et propter hoc, quando mulier secundo nubit, nuptiae non benedicuntur, propter defectum sacramenti.

AD TERTIUM dicendum quod significatio perfecta invenitur in secundo matrimonio secundum se considerato: non autem si consideretur in ordine ad praecederis matrimonium. Et sic habet defectum sacramentum.

AD QUARTUM dicendum quod secundum matrimonium impedit sacramentum ordinis quantum ad id quod habet de defectu sacramenti, et non inquantum est sacramentum.

it is implied that the first was not effective, and thus an injury is done to the first, as is clear in all those sacraments which imprint a character. But those sacraments which have not an everlasting effect can be repeated without injury to the sacrament, as in the case of penance. And, since the marriage tie ceases with death, no injury is done to the sacrament if a woman marry again after her husband's death.

REPLY OBJ. 2: Although the second marriage, considered in itself, is a perfect sacrament, yet if we consider it in relation to the first marriage, it is somewhat a defective sacrament because it has not its full signification, since there is not a union of *only one woman with only one man* as in the marriage *of Christ with the Church*. And on account of this defect the blessing is omitted in a second marriage.

This, however, refers to the case when it is a second marriage on the part of both man and woman, or on the part of the woman only. For if a virgin marry a man who has had another wife, the marriage is blessed nevertheless, because the signification is preserved to a certain extent even in relation to the former marriage: since though Christ has but one Church for his spouse, there are many persons espoused to him in the one Church. But the soul cannot be espoused to another besides Christ, because then it commits fornication with the devil, and neither is there a spiritual marriage. For this reason when a woman marries a second time, the marriage is not blessed on account of the defect in the sacrament.

REPLY OBJ. 3: The perfect signification is found in a second marriage considered in itself; not, however, if it be considered in relation to the previous marriage, and it is thus that it is a defective sacrament.

REPLY OBJ. 4: A second marriage, insofar as there is a defect in the sacrament, is an impediment to the sacrament of holy orders, but not insofar as it is a sacrament.

Question 64

The Payment of the Marriage Debt

Consequenter considerandum est de annexis matrimonio. Et primo, de debiti redditione; secundo, de pluralitate uxorum; tertio, de bigamia; quarto, de libello repudii; quinto, de filiis illegitime natis.

Circa primum quaeruntur septem.

Primo: utrum alter coniugum teneatur alteri debitum reddere.

Secundo: utrum debeat aliquando reddere non poscenti.

Tertio: utrum liceat mulieri menstruatae debitum petere.

Quarto: utrum mulier menstruata debeat reddere debitum petenti.

Quinto: utrum vir et uxor in hoc sint aequales.

Sexto: utrum unus sine consensu alterius possit votum emittere per quod redditio debiti impediatur.

Septimo: utrum tempus impediat debiti petitionem.

Octavo: utrum petens tempore sacro peccet mortaliter.

Nono: utrum reddere teneatur tempore festivo.

Decimo: utrum nuptiae sint interdicendae temporibus.

In the next place we must consider those things which are annexed to marriage: (1) The payment of the marriage debt; (2) Plurality of wives; (3) Bigamy; (4) The bill of divorce; (5) Illegitimate children.

Under the first head there are ten points of inquiry:

(1) Whether one spouse is bound to pay the marriage debt to the other?

(2) Whether one is sometimes bound to pay without being asked?

(3) Whether a wife may demand the debt during the menses?

(4) Whether she is bound to pay it at that time?

(5) Whether husband and wife are equal in this matter?

(6) Whether the one without the other's consent may take a vow that prohibits the payment of the debt?

(7) Whether it is forbidden to ask for the debt at any particular time?

(8) Whether it is a mortal sin to ask for it at a holy time?

(9) Whether it is an obligation to pay it at the time of a festival?

(10) Whether weddings should be forbidden at certain times?

Article 1

Whether Husband and Wife Are Mutually Bound to the Payment of the Marriage Debt?

Ad primum sic proceditur. Videtur quod alter coniugum non teneatur alteri ad redditionem debiti ex necessitate praecepti. Nullus enim prohibetur a sumptione Eucharistiae propter hoc quod praeceptum implet. Sed *ille qui uxori debitum reddit, non potest carnes Agni edere*, ut Hieronymus in littera dicit. Ergo reddere debitum non est de necessitate praecepti.

Praeterea, quilibet potest licite abstinere ab his quae sunt sibi nociva in persona. Sed aliquando reddere debitum poscenti esset personae nocivum, vel ratione infirmitatis, vel ratione solutionis iam factae. Ergo videtur quod licite possit debitum poscenti negari.

Praeterea, quicumque facit se impotentem ad faciendum id ad quod ex praecepto tenetur, peccat. Si er-

Objection 1: It would seem that husband and wife are not mutually bound, under the obligation of a precept, to the payment of the marriage debt. For no one is forbidden to receive the Eucharist on account of fulfilling a precept. Yet *he who has had intercourse with his wife cannot partake of the flesh of the Lamb*, according to Jerome as quoted in the text (*Homily on the Eating of the Lamb* 8; *Sentences* IV, D. 32). Therefore, the payment of the debt does not come under the obligation of a precept.

Obj. 2: Further, it is lawful to everyone to abstain from what is hurtful to his person. But it is sometimes harmful to a person to pay the debt when asked, whether on account of sickness, or because they have already paid it. Therefore, it would seem allowable to refuse the one who asks.

Obj. 3: Further, it is a sin to render oneself unfit to fulfill an obligation of precept. If, therefore, the payment of the

go aliquis ex necessitate praecepti tenetur ad reddendum debitum, videtur quod peccet si, ieiunando vel alias corpus suum attenuando, impotentem se reddat ad debiti solutionem. Quod non videtur verum.

PRAETEREA, matrimonium, secundum Philosophum, ordinatur ad procreationem prolis et educationem, et iterum ad communicationem vitae. Sed lepra est contra utrumque matrimonii finem: quia, cum sit morbus contagiosus, mulier leproso non tenetur cohabitare; similiter etiam morbus ille frequenter transmittitur ad prolem. Ergo videtur quod viro leproso uxor debitum reddere non tenetur.

SED CONTRA: Sicut servus est in potestate domini sui, ita et unus coniugum in potestate alterius, ut patet I Cor. 7. Sed servus tenetur ex necessitate praecepti domino suo debitum servitutis reddere, ut patet Rom. 13: *reddite omnibus debita, cui tributum tributum*, etc. Ergo et unus coniugum ex necessitate praecepti tenetur alteri debitum reddere.

PRAETEREA, matrimonium est ordinatum ad fornicationem vitandam, ut patet I Cor. 7. Sed hoc non posset per matrimonium fieri si unus alteri non teneretur debitum reddere quando concupiscentia infestatur. Ergo reddere debitum est de necessitate praecepti.

RESPONDEO dicendum quod matrimonium principaliter est institutum in officium naturae. Et ideo in actu ipsius servandus est naturae motus. Secundum quem nutritiva non ministrat generativae nisi illud quod superfluit ad conservationem individui: quia hic est ordo naturalis, ut prius aliquid in seipso perficiatur, et postmodum alteri de perfectione sua communicet. Hoc etiam ordo caritatis habet, quae naturam perficit. Et ideo, cum uxor in viro potestatem non habeat nisi quantum ad genetivam virtutem, non autem quantum ad ea quae sunt ad conservationem individui ordinata, vir tenetur uxori debitum reddere in his quae ad generationem prolis spectant, salva tamen prius personae incolumitate.

AD PRIMUM ergo dicendum quod aliquis implens aliquod praeceptum potest reddi inhabilis ad aliquod sacrum officium exequendum: sicut iudex qui hominem ad mortem condemnat praeceptum implens, irregularis efficitur. Similiter etiam ille qui praeceptum implens debitum solvit, redditur ineptus ad divina officia exequenda, non quod ille actus sit peccatum, sed ratione carnalitatis illius actus. Et sic, secundum quod Magister dicit, Hieronymus loquitur tantum de ministris Ecclesiae: non autem de aliis, qui sunt suo iudicio relinquendi; quia possunt et ex devotione dimittere, et sumere corpus Christi, absque peccato.

AD SECUNDUM dicendum quod uxor non habet potestatem in corpus viri nisi salva consistentia personae ipsius, ut dictum est. Unde, si ultra exigit, non est petitio

debt comes under the obligation of a precept, it would seem sinful to render oneself unfit for paying the debt by fasting or otherwise weakening the body: but apparently this is untrue.

OBJ. 4: Further, according to the Philosopher (*Ethics* 8.12), marriage is directed to the begetting and rearing of children, as well as to the community of life. Now leprosy is opposed to both these ends of marriage, for since it is a contagious disease, the wife is not bound to cohabit with a leprous husband; and besides, this disease is often transmitted to the offspring. Therefore, it would seem that a wife is not bound to pay the debt to a leprous husband.

ON THE CONTRARY, As the slave is in the power of his master, so is one spouse in the power of the other (1 Cor 7:4). But a slave is bound by an obligation of precept to pay his master the debt of his service, according to Romans 13:7: *render to all men their dues, tribute to whom tribute is due*. Therefore, husband and wife are mutually bound to the payment of the marriage debt.

FURTHER, Marriage is directed to the avoidance of fornication (1 Cor 7:2). But this could not be the effect of marriage, if the one were not bound to pay the debt to the other when the latter is troubled with concupiscence. Therefore, the payment of the debt is an obligation of precept.

I ANSWER THAT, Marriage was instituted especially as fulfilling an office of nature. Wherefore in its act the movement of nature must be observed, according to which the nutritive power administers to the generative power that alone which is in excess of what is required for the preservation of the individual: for the natural order requires that a thing should be first perfected in itself, and that afterwards it should communicate of its perfection to others. This is also the order of charity, which perfects nature. And therefore, since the wife has power over her husband only in relation to the generative power and not in relation to things directed to the preservation of the individual, the husband is bound to pay the debt to his wife in matters pertaining to the begetting of children, with due regard, however, to his own welfare.

REPLY OBJ. 1: It is possible through fulfilling a precept to render oneself unfit for the exercise of a sacred duty: thus a judge becomes irregular by sentencing a man to death. In like manner, he who pays the marriage debt in fulfillment of the precept becomes unfit for the exercise of divine offices not because the act in question is sinful, but on account of its carnal nature. And so, according to the Master (*Sentences* IV, D. 32), Jerome is speaking only of the ministers of the Church, and not of others who should be left to use their own discretion, because without sin they may either abstain out of reverence or receive Christ's body out of devotion.

REPLY OBJ. 2: The wife has no power over her husband's body except as is consistent with the welfare of his person, as stated above. Wherefore if she go beyond this in

debiti, sed iniusta exactio. Et propter hoc vir non tenetur ei satisfacere.

AD TERTIUM dicendum quod, si aliquis redditur impotens ad debitum solvendum ex causa ex matrimonio secuta, puta cum prius debitum reddidit et est impotens ad debitum solvendum ulterius, mulier non habet ius plus petendi: et in petendo ulterius se magis meretricem quam coniugem exhibet. Si autem reddatur impotens ex alia causa, si illa est licita, sic iterum non tenetur, nec potest mulier exigere. Si non est, tunc peccat, et peccatum uxoris, si propter hoc in fornicationem labatur, aliquo modo sibi imputatur. Et ideo debet, quantum potest, dare operam ut uxor contineat.

AD QUARTUM dicendum quod lepra solvit sponsalia, sed non matrimonium. Unde uxor etiam viro leproso tenetur reddere debitum. Non tamen tenetur ei cohabitare: quia non ita cito inficitur ex coitu sicut ex frequenti cohabitatione. Et quamvis generetur infirma proles, tamen melius est ei sic esse quam penitus non esse.

her demands, it is not a request for the debt, but an unjust exaction; and for this reason the husband is not bound to satisfy her.

REPLY OBJ. 3: If the husband be rendered incapable of paying the debt through a cause consequent upon marriage, for instance, through having already paid the debt and being unable to pay it, the wife has no right to ask again, and in doing so she behaves as a harlot rather than as a wife. But if he be rendered incapable through some other cause, then if this be a lawful cause, he is not bound, and she cannot ask, but if it be an unlawful cause, then he sins, and his wife's sin, should she fall into fornication on this account, is somewhat imputable to him. Hence he should endeavor to do his best that his wife may remain continent.

REPLY OBJ. 4: Leprosy voids a betrothal but not a marriage. Wherefore a wife is bound to pay the debt even to a leprous husband. But she is not bound to cohabit with him, because she is not so liable to infection from marital intercourse as from continual cohabitation; and although a sickly child may be generated, nevertheless it is better for it to exist so diseased than not to be at all.

Article 2

Whether a Husband Is Bound to Pay the Debt If His Wife Does Not Ask for It?

AD SECUNDUM SIC PROCEDITUR. Videtur quod vir non teneatur reddere debitum uxori non petenti. Praeceptum enim affirmativum non obligat nisi ad tempus determinatum. Sed tempus determinatum solutionis debiti non potest esse nisi quando petitur. Ergo alias solvere non tenetur.

PRAETEREA, de quolibet debemus praesumere meliora. Sed melius est etiam coniugibus continere quam matrimonio uti, Ergo, nisi expresse debitum petat, debet vir praesumere quod ei placeat continere. Et sic non tenetur debitum ei reddere.

PRAETEREA, sicut uxor habet potestatem in virum, ita dominus in servum. Sed domino non tenetur servus servire nisi quando sibi ab ipso imperatur. Nec ergo vir tenetur uxori reddere debitum nisi quando ab ea exigitur.

PRAETEREA, vir potest aliquando uxorem exigentem precibus a vertere ne exigat. Ergo multo magis potest non reddere si non exigat.

SED CONTRA: Per redditionem debiti medicamentum praestatur contra uxoris concupiscentiam. Sed medicus cui infirmus est commissus, tenetur morbo eius subvenire etiam si ipse non petat. Ergo vir uxori non petenti tenetur debitum reddere.

OBJECTION 1: It would seem that the husband is not bound to pay the marriage debt if his wife does not ask for it. For an affirmative precept is binding only at a certain time. But the time fixed for the payment of the debt can only be when it is asked for. Therefore, he is not bound to payment otherwise.

OBJ. 2: Further, we ought to presume the better things of everyone. Now, even for married people it is better to be continent than to make use of marriage. Therefore, unless she ask expressly for the debt, the husband should presume that it pleases her to be continent, and so he is not bound to pay her the debt.

OBJ. 3: Further, as the wife has power over her husband, so has a master over his slave. Now a slave is not bound to serve his master save when the latter commands him. Therefore, neither is a husband bound to pay the debt to his wife except when she demands it.

OBJ. 4: Further, the husband can sometimes request his wife not to exact the debt when she asks for it. Much more, therefore, may he not pay it when he is not asked.

ON THE CONTRARY, By the payment of the debt a remedy is afforded against the wife's concupiscence. Now a physician who has the care of a sick person is bound to remedy the disease without being asked. Therefore, the husband is bound to pay the debt to his wife, although she ask not for it.

PRAETEREA, praelatus tenetur correctionis remedium contra peccata subditorum adhibere etiam eis contradicentibus. Sed redditio debiti in viro est ordinata contra peccata uxoris. Ergo tenetur vir debitum reddere quandoque etiam non petenti.

RESPONDEO dicendum quod petere debitum est dupliciter. Uno modo, expresse: ut quando verbis invicem petunt. Alio modo est petitio debiti interpretativa: quando scilicet vir percipit per aliqua signa quod uxor vellet sibi debitum reddi, sed propter verecundiam tacet. Et ita; etiam si non expresse verbis debitum petat, tamen vir tenetur reddere quando expressa signa in uxore apparent voluntatis reddendi debiti.

AD PRIMUM ergo dicendum quod tempus determinatum non est quando petitur, sed quando timetur ex aliquibus signis periculum ad quod vitandum ordinatur debiti redditio, nisi tunc reddatur.

AD SECUNDUM dicendum quod vir potest talem praesumptionem habere de uxore quando in ea contraria signa non videt. Sed quando videt, esset stulta praesumptio.

AD TERTIUM dicendum quod dominus non ita verecundatur a servo petere debitum servitutis sicut uxor a viro debitum coniugii. Si tamen dominus non peteret, vel propter ignorantiam vel alia de causa, nihilominus servus teneretur implere si periculum immineret. Hoc enim est *non ad oculum servire*, quod Apostolus servis mandat.

AD QUARTUM dicendum quod non debet vir uxorem avertere ne petat debitum nisi propter aliquam rationabilem causam. Et tunc etiam non debet cum magna instantia averti, propter pericula imminentia.

FURTHER, A superior is bound to apply a remedy for the sins of his subjects even though they rebel against it. But the payment of the debt on the husband's part is directed against the sins of his wife. Therefore, sometimes the husband is bound to pay the debt to his wife even though she ask it not of him.

I ANSWER THAT, The debt may be demanded in two ways. First, explicitly, as when they ask one another by words; second, implicitly, as when the husband knows by certain signs that the wife would wish him to pay the debt, but is silent through shame. And so, even though she does not ask for the debt explicitly in words, the husband is bound to pay it whenever his wife shows signs of wishing him to do so.

REPLY OBJ. 1: The appointed time is not only when it is demanded but also when on account of certain signs there is fear of danger (to avoid which is the purpose of the payment of the debt) unless it be paid then.

REPLY OBJ. 2: The husband may presume this of his wife when he perceives in her no signs of the contrary; but it would be foolish of him to admit this presumption if he does see such signs.

REPLY OBJ. 3: The master is not ashamed to demand of his slave the duty of his service, as a wife is to ask the marriage debt of her husband. Yet if the master were not to demand it either through ignorance or some other cause, the slave would nevertheless be bound to fulfill his duty if some danger were threatening. For this is what is meant by *not serving to the eye* (Eph 6:6), which is the Apostle's command to servants.

REPLY OBJ. 4: A husband should not dissuade his wife from asking for the debt except for a reasonable cause; and even then he should not be too insistent, on account of the besetting danger.

Article 3

Whether It Is Licit for a Menstruating Woman to Request the Marriage Debt?

AD TERTIUM SIC PROCEDITUR. Videtur quod liceat mulieri menstruatae conjugale debitum petere. Sicut enim in lege mulier menstruata erat immunda, ita et vir fluxum seminis patiens. Sed vir seminifluus potest debitum petere. Ergo pari ratione et mulier menstruata.

PRAETEREA, major infirmitas est lepra quam passio menstruorum; et majorem, ut videtur, corruptionem causat in prole. Sed leprosa potest debitum petere. Ergo, etc.

PRAETEREA, si menstruatae non licet petere debitum, hoc non est nisi ratione defectus qui timetur in pro-

OBJECTION 1: In addition, it seems that it is licit for a menstruating woman to request the debt from her spouse. For under the old law, just as a menstruating woman was unclean, so also was a man suffering an outflowing of semen. But a man suffering in this way can request the debt. Therefore, by the same reasoning, a woman in menstruation can also.

OBJ. 2: Likewise, leprosy is a greater infirmity than suffering a menstrual period. And it causes, so it seems, a greater corruption in children. But a leper may request the debt. Therefore, etc.

OBJ 3: Further, if a menstruating woman is not permitted to request the debt, this is only because of a defect which

le. Sed si mulier sit sterilis, non timetur talis defectus. Ergo videtur quod saltem sterilis menstruata possit petere.

Sed contra, Levit. 18, 19: *ad mulierem quae patitur menstruum, non accedes*: ubi Augustinus: *cum sufficienter prohibuisset, hic etiam repetit, ne forte in superioribus videretur figurative accipiendum.*

Praeterea, Isa. 64, 6: *omnes justitiae vestrae quasi pannus menstruatae*; ubi Hieronymus: *tunc viri abstinere debent a mulieribus, quoniam concipiuntur membris damnati, caeci, claudi, leprosi; ut quia parentes non erubuerunt in conclavi commisceri, eorum peccata pateant cunctis, et apertius redarguantur in parvulis.* Et sic idem quod prius.

Respondeo dicendum quod accedere ad menstruatam in lege prohibitum erat duplici ratione: tum propter immunditiam; tum propter nocumentum quod in prole ex hujusmodi commixtione frequenter sequebatur. Et quo ad primum, praeceptum erat caeremoniale, sed quantum ad secundum erat morale: quia cum matrimonium sit ad bonum prolis principaliter ordinatum, ordinatus est omnis matrimonii usus quo bonum prolis impenditur; et ideo hoc praeceptum obligat etiam in nova lege propter secundam rationem, etsi non propter primam.

Fluxus tamen menstruorum potest esse naturalis et innaturalis. Naturalis quidem, quando scilicet mulieres patiuntur temporibus determinatis, quando sunt sanae. Innaturalis autem quando inordinate et quasi continue ex aliqua infirmitate fluxum sanguinis patiuntur. In fluxu ergo menstruorum innaturali non est prohibitum ad mulierem menstruatam accedere in lege nova: tum propter infirmitatem, quia mulier in tali statu concipere non potest; tum quia talis fluxus est perpetuus et diuturnus; unde oporteret quod vir perpetuo abstineret. Sed quando naturaliter mulier patitur fluxus menstruorum, potest concipere; et iterum talis fluxus non durat nisi ad modicum tempus. Unde prohibitum est ad talem accedere. Et similiter prohibitum est mulieri in tali fluxu debitum petere.

Ad primum dicendum, quod fluxus seminis in viro ex infirmitate procedit, nec semen sic fluens est aptum ad generationem; et praeterea talis passio est diuturna vel perpetua, sicut lepra. Unde non est similis ratio.

Et per hoc solvitur etiam secundum.

Ad tertium dicendum, quod quamdiu mulier menstrua patitur, non potest esse certum eam esse sterilem. Quaedam enim in juventute sunt steriles, quae pro-

is feared in the children. But if the woman were barren, such a defect would not be feared. Therefore, it seems that at least a barren woman may request the debt during menstruation.

On the contrary, Leviticus 18:19 says: *you shall not approach the woman who undergoes menstruation.* To which Augustine adds, *although he had sufficiently prohibited it, here again he repeats, so that it would not perhaps seem to be taken figuratively in higher things.*

Further, According to Isaiah 64:6: *all of your justices are like the rags of a menstruous woman.* About which Jerome says: *At that time men must abstain from their wives, since those damaged in their members are conceived—blind, lame, leprous—so that because the parents were not ashamed to commingle in their chamber, their sins might be evident to all, and more openly are they rebuked in their little ones.* And thus the same conclusion as above.

I answer that, It should be said that to approach a menstruating woman was prohibited under the law for two reasons: both because of uncleanness as well as because of the harm which frequently resulted in the children from this kind of commingling. And so as to the first, this precept was ceremonial, but as to the second, it was moral; for since matrimony is principally ordered to the good of offspring, the use of matrimony is ordered by what is employed for the good of offspring: and therefore this precept also obliges under the new law because of the second reason, even if not for the first.

The menstrual flow can, however, be natural or unnatural. It is natural when women suffer it at the determined times, when they are healthy. However, it is unnatural when they suffer a flow of blood inordinately and almost incessantly because of some infirmity. Therefore, in an unnatural menstrual flow it is not prohibited to approach the menstruating woman under the new law: both because of the infirmity, since a woman cannot conceive in such a state, and also since such an issue of blood is perpetual and long-lasting, whence it would be necessary for her husband to abstain perpetually. But when the woman naturally undergoes the menstrual flow, she can conceive; and again such a period does not last but a little time. Whence it is prohibited to approach such a one, and likewise it is prohibited for the woman in such a period to request the debt.

Reply Obj. 1: The flow of semen in a man proceeds from an infirmity, and semen flowing like that is not suitable for generation. Furthermore, such a condition is long-lasting or perpetual, like leprosy; whence there is no similar argument.

Reply Obj. 2: And by this answer the second objection is also resolved.

Reply Obj. 3: As long as a woman undergoes menstruation, one cannot be certain that she is barren. Certain women are barren in their youth who become fertile by the

cessu temporis sunt fecundae, et e converso, ut dicitur in 10 *de Animalibus.*

process of time, and vice versa, as is stated in Book 10 of the *History of Animals.*

Article 4

Whether a Menstruating Woman Ought to Render the Debt to a Husband Who Asks?

Ad quartum sic proceditur. Videtur quod mulier menstruata non debeat reddere debitum petenti. Levit. 20, dicitur quod si aliquis ad menstruatam accesserit, uterque morte est puniendus. Ergo videtur quod tam reddens quam exigens debitum mortaliter peccet.

Praeterea, Rom. 1, 32: *non solum qui faciunt, sed etiam qui consentiunt, digni sunt morte.* Sed exigens debitum scienter a menstruata mortaliter peccat. Ergo et mulier consentiens ei in redditione debiti.

Praeterea, furioso non est gladius reddendus, ne se vel alium interficiat. Ergo eadem ratione nec uxor tempore menstruorum debet viro corpus suum exponere, ne spiritualiter occidat.

Sed contra, 1 Corinth. 7, 4: *mulier sui corporis potestatem non habet, sed vir.* Ergo petenti viro mulier etiam menstruata debet debitum reddere.

Praeterea, mulier menstruata non debet esse viro peccandi occasio. Sed si viro petenti debitum, debitum ipsa non redderet, etiam tempore menstruorum, esset viro peccandi occasio: quia forte fornicaretur. Ergo, etc.

Respondeo dicendum quod circa hoc dixerunt quidam, quod mulier menstruata sicut non debet petere debitum, ita nec reddere. Sicut enim non tenetur reddere si haberet infirmitatem in propria persona, ex qua periculum ei immineret; ita non tenetur reddere ad vitandum periculum prolis. Sed ista opinio videtur derogare matrimonio, per quod datur omnimoda potestas viro in corpus mulieris quantum ad matrimonialem actum. Nec est simile de infirmitate corporis prolis et periculo proprii corporis; quia si mulier infirmatur, certissimum est quod ex carnali actu periculum ei imminet; non autem ita certum est de prole, quae forte nulla sequetur.

Et ideo alii dicunt, quod mulieri menstruatae nunquam licet petere debitum. Si tamen vir ejus petat; aut petit scienter, et tunc debet eum avertere precibus et monitis, tamen non ita efficaciter ut possit ei esse occasio in alias damnabiles corruptelas, si ad id pronus creda-

Objection 1: In addition, it seems that a menstruating wife should not render the debt to a husband who asks. In Leviticus 20:18, it says that if someone approaches a menstruating woman, both are to be punished by death. Therefore, it seems that a woman rendering the debt sins mortally as much as the one demanding the debt.

Obj. 2: Again, Romans 1:32 says: *not only they that do them, but also they who consent to them that do them, are worthy of death.* But someone who knowingly demands the debt of a menstruating woman sins mortally. Therefore, also the woman consenting to him in the rendering of the debt.

Obj. 3: Again, a sword is not to be handed over to a furious man, lest he might kill himself or another. Therefore, by the same reasoning neither should a woman expose her body to her husband in the time of menstruation, lest he should die spiritually.

On the contrary, 1 Corinthians 7:4 says: *the woman does not have power over her body, but the man does.* Therefore, the woman must render the debt to her husband requesting it even during the time of menstruation.

Further, A menstruating woman must not be an occasion of sin for her husband. But if the husband should ask for his rights and she should not render the debt even in the time of her menstruation, she would be an occasion of sin to her husband, for perhaps he would fall into fornication. Therefore, etc.

I answer that, On this matter certain ones have said that the menstruating woman should not render the debt, just as she should not request it. For just as she is not bound to render it if she has an infirmity in her own person from the fact that danger threatens her, so also she is not bound to render in order to avoid danger to the children. But this opinion detracts from matrimony, by which complete power is given to the man over the body of his wife with respect to the marital act. Nor is the infirmity of the body of the offspring similar to danger to one's own body, for if the woman is unwell, it is most certain that in the carnal act danger would threaten her; but it is not so certain about the children, who perhaps will not even follow.

And therefore, others say that the menstruating woman is never allowed to request the debt. If, however, her husband should ask, either he asks knowingly, and then she should turn him aside by entreaties and warnings, yet not so categorically that it might be an occasion to him for

tur: aut ignoranter; et mulier potest aliquam occasionem praetendere, vel infirmitatem allegare, ne debitum reddat, nisi periculum viro timeatur. Tamen finaliter, si vir non desistit a petitione, debet debitum reddere poscenti. Passionem vero suam non est tutum indicare, ne forte vir ex hoc ad eam abominationem concipiat, nisi de viri prudentia praesumatur.

AD PRIMUM ERGO DICENDUM, quod hoc intelligendum est quando uterque voluntarie consentit; non autem si mulier involuntaria et quasi coacta debitum reddat.

AD SECUNDUM DICENDUM, quod cum consensus non sit nisi voluntatis, non intelligitur mulier consentire peccato viri nisi voluntarie debitum reddat: quando enim est involuntaria, magis patitur quam consentiat.

AD TERTIUM DICENDUM, quod gladius furioso etiam esset reddendus quando majus periculum timeretur in non reddendo; et similiter est in proposito.

other condemnable seductions, if he is believed to be prone to that; or else he asks ignorantly, and the woman can give some pretext, or say that she is unwell, so as not to render the debt, unless danger is feared for her husband. However, ultimately, if the man does not cease to request it, she should render the debt when he asks. Indeed, it is not safe for her to indicate her own situation lest perhaps the man should conceive a loathing for her because of it, unless he is presumed a man of prudence.

REPLY OBJ. 1: This is to be understood when both consent voluntarily; not, however, if the woman should render the debt involuntarily, as though compelled.

REPLY OBJ. 2: Since consent only comes from the will, a woman is not understood to consent to the sin of her husband unless she renders the debt voluntarily: for when it is involuntary, she suffers it rather than consenting.

REPLY OBJ. 3: A sword would be given even to a furious man when greater danger would be feared if it were not given; and it is likewise in the case at hand.

Article 5

Whether Husband and Wife Are Equals in the Marriage Act?

AD QUINTUM SIC PROCEDITUR. Videtur quod vir et mulier non sint in actu matrimonii aequales. *Agens* enim *est nobilius patiente*: ut Augustinus dicit, XII *super Gen. ad litt.* Sed in actu coniugali vir se habet ut agens, et femina ut patiens. Ergo non sunt in actu illo aequales.

PRAETEREA, uxor non tenetur viro debitum reddere nisi petat. Vir autem tenetur uxori, ut dictum est. Ergo non sunt pares in actu matrimonii.

PRAETEREA, in matrimonio *mulier propter virum facta est*, ut patet Gen. 2: *faciamus ei adiutorium simile sibi*. Sed illud propter quod est alterum, semper est principalius. Ergo, etc.

PRAETEREA, matrimonium principaliter ordinatur ad actum coniugalem. Sed in matrimonio *vir est caput mulieris*, ut patet I Cor. 11. Ergo non sunt aequales in actu praedicto.

SED CONTRA: Est quod dicitur I Cor. 7: *vir non habet potestatem sui corporis*; et simile dicit de uxore. Ergo sunt aequales in actu matrimonii.

PRAETEREA, matrimonium est relatio aequiparentiae: cum sit coniunctio, ut dictum est. Ergo vir et uxor sunt aequales in actu matrimonii.

RESPONDEO dicendum quod duplex est aequalitas: scilicet quantitatis, et proportionis. Aequalitas quidem

OBJECTION 1: It would seem that husband and wife are not equals in the marriage act. For, according to Augustine, *the agent is more noble than the patient* (*On the Literal Meaning of Genesis* 12). But in the marriage act the husband is as agent and the wife as patient. Therefore, they are not equal in that act.

OBJ. 2: Further, the wife is not bound to pay her husband the debt without being asked; whereas he is so bound, as stated above (A. 1–2). Therefore, they are not equal in the marriage act.

OBJ. 3: Further, *the woman was made on the man's account* in reference to marriage, according to Genesis 2:18: *let us make him a help like unto himself*. But that on account of which another thing is, is always the principal. Therefore, etc.

OBJ. 4: Further, marriage is chiefly directed to the marriage act. But in marriage *the husband is the head of the wife* (Eph 5:22). Therefore, they are not equal in the aforesaid act.

ON THE CONTRARY, It is written: *the husband does not have power of his own body* (1 Cor 7:4), and the same is said of the wife. Therefore, they are equal in the marriage act.

FURTHER, Marriage is a relation of equiparence, since it is a kind of union, as stated above (Q. 44, A. 1, 3). Therefore, husband and wife are equal in the marriage act.

I ANSWER THAT, Equality is twofold: of quantity and of proportion. Equality of quantity is that which is observed

quantitatis est quae attenditur inter duas quantitates eiusdem mensurae, sicut bicubiti ad bicubitum. Sed aequalitas proportionis est quae attenditur inter duas proportiones eiusdem speciei, sicut dupli ad duplum. Loquendo ergo de prima aequalitate, vir et uxor non sunt aequales in matrimonio: neque quantum ad actum coniugalem, in quo id quod nobilius est viro debetur; neque quantum ad dispensationem domus, in qua uxor regitur et vir regit. Sed quantum ad secundam aequalitatem sunt aequales in utroque: quia sicut tenetur vir uxori in actu coniugali et dispensatione domus ad id quod viri est, ita uxor viro ad id quod uxoris est. Et secundum hoc dicitur in littera quod sunt aequales in reddendo et petendo debitum.

Ad primum ergo dicendum quod, quamvis agere sit nobilius quam pati, tamen eadem est proportio patientis ad patiendum et agentis ad agendum. Et secundum hoc est ibi; aequalitas proportionis.

Ad secundum dicendum quod hoc est per accidens. Vir enim, quia nobiliorem partem habet in actu coniugali, naturaliter habet quod non ita erubescat petere debitum sicut uxor. Et inde est quod non ita uxor tenetur reddere debitum non petenti viro sicut vir uxori.

Ad tertium dicendum quod ex hoc ostenditur quod non sunt aequales absolute: non autem quod non sint aequales secundum proportionem.

Ad quartum dicendum quod, quamvis caput sit principalius membrum, tamen, sicut membra tenentur capiti in officio suo, ita caput membris in suo. Et sic est ibi aequalitas proportionis.

between two quantities of the same measure, for instance, a thing two cubits long and another two cubits long. But equality of proportion is that which is observed between two proportions of the same kind, as double to double. Accordingly, speaking of the first equality, husband and wife are not equal in marriage: neither as regards the marriage act, wherein the more noble part is due to the husband, nor as regards the household management, wherein the wife is ruled and the husband rules. But with reference to the second kind of equality, they are equal in both matters, because just as in both the marriage act and in the management of the household the husband is bound to the wife in all things pertaining to the husband, so is the wife bound to the husband in all things pertaining to the wife. It is in this sense that it is stated in the text (*Sentences* IV, D. 32) that they are equal in paying and demanding the debt.

Reply Obj. 1: Although it is more noble to be active than passive, there is the same proportion between patient and passivity as between agent and activity; and accordingly there is equality of proportion between them.

Reply Obj. 2: This is accidental. For since the husband has the more noble part in the marriage act, it is natural that he should be less ashamed than the wife to ask for the debt. Hence it is that the wife is not bound to pay the debt to her husband without being asked, whereas the husband is bound to pay it to the wife.

Reply Obj. 3: This proves that they are not equal absolutely, but not that they are not equal in proportion.

Reply Obj. 4: Although the head is the principal member, yet just as the members are bound to the head in their own respective capacities, so is the head in its own capacity bound to the members: and thus there is equality of proportion between them.

Article 6

Whether Husband and Wife Can Take a Vow Contrary to the Marriage Debt Without Their Mutual Consent?

Ad sextum sic proceditur. Videtur quod vir et uxor possint votum emittere contra debitum matrimonii sine mutuo consensu. Vir enim et uxor aequaliter obligantur ad debiti solutionem, ut dictum est. Sed licitum est viro, etiam uxore prohibente, accipere crucem in subsidium Terrae Sanctae. Ergo etiam hoc licitum est uxori. Et ideo, cum per hoc votum redditio debiti impediatur, potest alter coniugum sine consensu alterius votum praedictum emittere.

Praeterea, non est expectandus in aliquo voto consensus alicuius qui non potest sine peccato dissentire. Sed unus coniugum non potest sine peccato dissentire quin alter continentiam voveat, vel simpliciter vel ad

Objection 1: It would seem that husband and wife may take a vow contrary to the marriage debt without their mutual consent. For husband and wife are equally bound to pay the debt, as stated above (A. 5). Now it is lawful for the husband, even if his wife be unwilling, to take the cross in defense of the Holy Land: and consequently this is also lawful to the wife. Therefore, since this prevents the payment of the debt, either husband or wife may without the other's consent take the aforesaid vow.

Obj. 2: Further, in taking a vow one should not await the consent of another who cannot dissent without sin. Now the husband or wife cannot without sin refuse their consent to the other's taking a vow of continence, whether

tempus: quia impedire profectum spiritualem est peccatum in Spiritum Sanctum. Ergo unus potest votum continentiae simpliciter vel ad tempus sine consensu alterius vovere.

PRAETEREA, sicut in actu matrimoniali requiritur debiti redditio, ita debiti petitio. Sed unus potest sine consensu alterius vovere quod debitum non petat: cum in hoc sit suae potestatis. Ergo, pari ratione, quod debitum non reddat.

PRAETEREA, nullus potest ex praecepto superioris cogi ad id quod non liceret sibi simpliciter vovere et facere: quia in illicitis non est obediendum. Sed praelatus superior posset praecipere viro ut uxori ad tempus debitum non redderet, occupando eum in aliquo servitio. Ergo hoc etiam ipse posset per se facere et vovere per quod a debiti redditione impediretur.

SED CONTRA: Est quod dicitur I Cor. 7: *ne fraudetis vos invicem, nisi ex communi consensu ad tempus*, ut vacetis orationi.

PRAETEREA, nullus potest facere votum de alieno. Sed *vir non habet potestatem sui corporis, sed uxor*. Ergo sine eius consensu non potest votum continentiae facere, vel simpliciter vel ad tempus.

RESPONDEO dicendum quod vovere voluntatis est: ut etiam ipsum nomen ostendit. Unde de illis tantum bonis potest esse votum quae nostrae subiacent voluntati. Qualia non sunt ea in quibus unus alteri tenetur. Et ideo in talibus non potest aliquis votum emittere sine consensu eius cui tenetur. Unde, cum coniuges sibi invicem teneantur in redditione debiti, per quam continentia impeditur, non potest unus absque consensu alterius continentiam vovere. Et si voverit, peccat: nec debet servare votum, sed agere poenitentiam de malo voto facto.

AD PRIMUM ergo dicendum quod satis probabile est quod uxor debeat velle continere ad tempus pro subveniendo necessitati Ecclesiae generalis. Et ideo in favorem negotii pro quo crux sibi datur, institutum est quod vir possit absque consensu uxoris crucem accipere: sicut etiam posset domino suo terreno, a quo feudum tenet, absque eius consensu militare. Nec tamen in hoc omnino subtrahitur uxori ius suum: quia uxor potest eum sequi. Nec est simile de uxore ad virum. Quia, cum vir debeat regere uxorem et non e converso, magis tenetur uxor sequi virum quam e converso. Et praeterea uxor cum maiori periculo castitatis discurreret per terras quam vir, et cum minori Ecclesiae utilitate. Et ideo uxor non potest huiusmodi votum facere sine viri consensu.

AD SECUNDUM dicendum quod alter coniugum dissentiens voto continentiae alterius non peccat: quia non

absolutely or for a time; because to prevent a person's spiritual progress is a sin against the Holy Spirit. Therefore, the one can take a vow of continence, either absolutely or for a time, without the other's consent.

OBJ. 3: Further, in the marriage act, the debt has to be demanded just as it has to be paid. Now the one can, without the other's consent, vow not to demand the debt, since in this he is within his own rights. Therefore, he can equally take a vow not to pay the debt.

OBJ. 4: Further, no one can be bound by the command of a superior to do what he cannot lawfully vow or do simply, since one must not obey in what is unlawful. Now the superior authority might command the husband not to pay the debt to his wife for a time by occupying him in some service. Therefore, he might of his own accord do or vow that which would hinder him from paying the debt.

ON THE CONTRARY, 1 Corinthians 7:5 says: *defraud not one another, except by consent, for a time, that you may give yourselves to prayer.*

FURTHER, No one can vow that which belongs to another. Now *the husband does not have power of his own body, but the wife* (1 Cor 7:4). Therefore, without her consent, the husband cannot take a vow of continence whether absolutely or for a time.

I ANSWER THAT, A vow is a voluntary act, as its very name implies: and consequently a vow can only be about those goods which are subject to our will, and those in which one person is bound to another do not come under this head. Therefore, in matters of this kind one person cannot take a vow without the consent of the one to whom he is bound. Consequently, since husband and wife are mutually bound as regards the payment of the debt, which is an obstacle to continence, the one cannot vow continence without the other's consent; and if he take the vow he sins, and must not keep the vow, but must do penance for an ill-taken vow (Q. 53, A. 1,4; Q. 61, A. 1).

REPLY OBJ. 1: It is sufficiently probable that the wife ought to be willing to remain continent for a time, in order to succor the need of the universal Church. Hence in favor of the business for which the cross is given to him, it is laid down that the husband may take the cross without his wife's consent, even as he might go fighting without the consent of his landlord whose land he has leased. And yet the wife is not entirely deprived of her right, since she can follow him. Nor is there a parallel between wife and husband: because, since the husband has to rule the wife and not vice versa, the wife is bound to follow her husband rather than the husband the wife. Moreover, there would be more danger to the wife's chastity as a result of wandering from country to country than to the husband's, and less profit to the Church. Wherefore the wife cannot take this vow without her husband's consent.

REPLY OBJ. 2: The one spouse, by refusing to consent to the other's vow of continence, does not sin, because the

dissentit ut bonum illius impediat, sed ne sibi praeiudicium generetur.

AD TERTIUM dicendum quod circa hoc est duplex opinio. Quidam enim dicunt quod unus absque consensu alterius potest vovere quod non petat debitum, non autem quod non reddat: quia in primo uterque est sui iuris, sed non in secundo. Sed quia, si alter nunquam peteret debitum, ex hoc alteri matrimonium onerosum redderetur, dum oporteret unum semper confusionem debiti petendi subire; ideo alii probabilius dicunt quod neutrum potest unus sine consensu alterius vovere.

AD QUARTUM dicendum quod, sicut mulier accipit potestatem in corpore viri salvo hoc in quo vir tenetur corpori suo, ita etiam salvo hoc in quo tenetur alii domino. Et ideo, sicut uxor non potest debitum petere a viro contra salutem sui corporis, ita nec ad impediendum hoc in quo domino tenetur; sed praeter hoc non potest dominus prohibere quin debitum reddat.

object of his dissent is to hinder not the other's good, but the harm to himself.

REPLY OBJ. 3: There are two opinions on this point. For some say that one can vow not to demand the debt without the other's consent, not, however, not to pay it, because in the former case they are both within their own rights, but not in the second. Seeing, however, that if one were never to ask for the debt, marriage would become too burdensome to the other who would always have to undergo the shame of asking for the debt, others assert with greater probability that neither vow can be lawfully taken by one spouse without the other's consent.

REPLY OBJ. 4: Just as the wife receives power over her husband's body without prejudice to the husband's duty to his own body, so also is it without prejudice to his duty to his master. Hence just as a wife cannot ask her husband for the debt to the detriment of his bodily health, so neither can she do this so as to hinder him in his duty to his master. And yet the master cannot for this reason prevent her from paying the debt.

Article 7

Whether It Is Forbidden to Demand the Debt on Holy Days?

AD SEPTIMUM SIC PROCEDITUR. Videtur quod temporibus sacris non debeat aliquis impediri quin debitum petat. Tunc enim est subveniendum morbo quando invalescit: Sed possibile est quod in die festo invalescat concupiscentia. Ergo tunc debet ei subveniri per debiti petitionem.

PRAETEREA, non est alia ratio quare non sit petendum debitum in diebus festivis nisi quia sunt orationi deputati. Sed in illis diebus sunt horae determinatae orationi. Ergo aliis horis liceret debitum petere.

SED CONTRA, sicut aliqua loca sunt sacra quiri deputata sunt sacris, ita aliqua tempora sunt sacra propter eandem rationem. Sed in loco sacro non licet petere debitum. Ergo nec in tempore, sacro.

RESPONDEO dicendum quod actus matrimonialis, quamvis culpa careat, tamen quia rationem deprimit propter carnalem delectationem, hominem reddit ineptum ad spiritualia. Et ideo iri diebus in quibus spiritualibus praecipue est vacandum, non licet petere debitum.

AD PRIMUM ergo dicendum quod tempore illo possunt alia; adhiberi ad concupiscentiam reprimendam: sicut oratio et multa huiusmodi, quae etiam illi adhibent qui perpetuo continent.

OBJECTION 1: It would seem that a person ought not to be forbidden to ask for the debt on holy days. For the remedy should be applied when the disease gains strength. Now concupiscence may possibly gain strength on a feast day. Therefore, the remedy should be applied then by asking for the debt.

OBJ. 2: Further, the only reason why the debt should not be demanded on feast days is because they are devoted to prayer. Yet on those days certain hours are appointed for prayer. Therefore, one may ask for the debt at some other time.

ON THE CONTRARY, Just as certain places are holy because they are devoted to holy things, so are certain times holy for the same reason. But it is not lawful to demand the debt in a holy place. Therefore, neither is it lawful at a holy time.

I ANSWER THAT, Although the marriage act is void of sin, nevertheless since it oppresses the reason on account of the carnal pleasure, it renders man unfit for spiritual things. Therefore, on those days when one ought especially to give one's time to spiritual things, it is not lawful to ask for the debt.

REPLY OBJ. 1: At such a time other means may be employed for the repression of concupiscence: for instance, prayer and many similar things, to which those who observe perpetual continence also have recourse.

AD PRIMUM dicendum quod, quamvis non teneatur omnibus horis orare, tamen tenetur tota die se conservare idoneum ad orandum.

REPLY OBJ. 2: Although one is not bound to pray at all hours, one is bound throughout the day to keep oneself fit for prayer.

Article 8

Whether It Is a Mortal Sin to Ask for the Debt at a Holy Time?

AD OCTAVUM SIC PROCEDITUR. Videtur quod petens in tempore sacro mortaliter peccet. Gregorius enim dicit, in I Dial., quod mulier quae in nocte cognita est a viro, mane ad processionem veniens a diabolo est arrepta. Sed hoc non esset nisi mortaliter peccasset. Ergo, etc.

PRAETEREA, quicumque facit contra praeceptum divinum, mortaliter peccat. Sed Dominus praecepit, Exodi 19, *nolite appropinquare uxoribus vestris*: quando scilicet erant legem accepturi. Ergo multo magis peccant mortaliter si tempore quo sacramentis novae legis intendendum est, cum uxoribus viri commisceantur.

SED CONTRA, nulla circumstantia aggravat in infinitum. Sed indebitum tempus est circumstantia quaedam. Ergo non aggravat in infinitum, ut faciat mortale quod alias esset veniale.

RESPONDEO dicendum quod debitum petere in die festivo non est circumstantia trahens in aliam speciem peccati. Unde non potest in infinitum aggravare. Et ideo non peccat mortaliter uxor vel vir si in die festo debitum petat. Sed tamen gravius est peccatum si sola delectationis causa petatur, quam si propter timorem quo quis sibi timet de lubrico carnis, debitum petat.

AD PRIMUM ergo dicendum quod non fuit punita mulier illa propter hoc quod debitum reddidit: sed quia postmodum se temere ad divina ingessit contra conscientiam.

AD SECUNDUM dicendum quod ex auctoritate illa non potest probari quod esset peccatum mortale, sed quod sit incongruum. Multa enim ad munditiam carnis pertinentia exigebantur de necessitate praecepti in veteri lege, quae carnalibus dabatur, quae in nova lege non exiguntur, quae est lex spiritus.

OBJECTION 1: It would seem that it is a mortal sin to ask for the debt at a holy time. For Gregory says (*Dialogues* 1) that the devil took possession of a woman who had intercourse with her husband at night and came in the morning to the procession. But this would not have happened had she not sinned mortally. Therefore, etc.

OBJ. 2: Further, whoever disobeys a divine command commits a mortal sin. Now the Lord commanded: *come not near your wives* (Exod 19:15), namely, when they were about to receive the law. Much more, therefore, do husbands sin mortally if they have intercourse with their wives at a time when they should be intent on the sacred observances of the new law.

ON THE CONTRARY, No circumstance aggravates infinitely. But undue time is a circumstance. Therefore, it does not aggravate a sin infinitely, so as to make mortal what was otherwise venial.

I ANSWER THAT, To ask for the debt on a feast day is not a circumstance drawing a sin into another species; wherefore it cannot aggravate infinitely. Consequently, a wife or husband does not sin mortally by asking for the debt on a feast day. It is, however, a more grievous sin to ask for the sake of mere pleasure than through fear of the weakness of the flesh.

REPLY OBJ. 1: This woman was punished not because she paid the debt, but because afterwards she rashly intruded into the divine service against her conscience.

REPLY OBJ. 2: The authority quoted shows not that it is a mortal sin but that it is unbecoming. For under the old law which was given to a carnal people, many things were required under an obligation of precept for the sake of bodily cleanness which are not required in the new law, which is the law of the spirit.

Article 9

Whether One Spouse Is Bound to Pay the Debt to the Other at a Festal Time?

AD NONUM SIC PROCEDITUR. Videtur quod non teneatur reddere tempore festivo. Quia peccantes et consentientes pariter puniuntur, ut patet Rom. 1. Sed ille qui

OBJECTION 1: It would seem that neither are they bound to pay the debt at a festal time. For those who commit a sin as well as those who consent to it are equally pun-

reddit debitum, consentit petenti, qui peccat. Ergo et ipse peccat.

PRAETEREA, ex praecepto affirmativo obligamur ad orandum, et ita ad aliquod tempus determinatum. Ergo pro tempore illo in quo quis orare tenetur, debitum reddere non debet: sicut nec eo tempore quo tenetur temporali domino ad speciale obsequium.

SED CONTRA est quod dicitur 1 Cor. 7: *nolite fraudari invicem, nisi communi consensu ad tempus,* etc. Ergo, quando petit, reddendum est ei.

RESPONDEO dicendum quod, cum mulier habeat potestatem in corpore viri quantum ad actum generationis spectat, et e converso, tenetur unus alteri debitum reddere quocumque tempore et quacumque hora, salva debita honestate quae in talibus exigitur; quia non oportet quod statim in publico reddat debitum.

AD PRIMUM ERGO DICENDUM quod iste, quantum in se est, non consentit, sed id quod ab eo exigitur invitus et Cum dolore reddit. Et ideo non peccat. Hoc enim est propter lubricum carnis divinitus ordinatum, ut semper petenti debitum reddatur, ne aliqua occasio peccati detur.

AD SECUNDUM DICENDUM quod non est aliqua hora ita determinata ad orandum quin possit postea recompensari in aliis horis. Et ideo obiectio non cogit.

ished (Rom 1:32). But the one who pays the debt consents with the one that asks, who sins. Therefore, he sins also.

OBJ. 2: Further, it is an affirmative precept that binds us to pray, and therefore we are bound to do so at a fixed time. Therefore, one ought not to pay the debt at a time when one is bound to pray, as neither ought one at a time when one is bound to fulfill a special duty towards a temporal master.

ON THE CONTRARY, It is written: *defraud not one another, except by consent, for a time* (1 Cor 7:5). Therefore, when one spouse asks, the other must pay.

I ANSWER THAT, Since the wife has power of her husband's body, and vice versa, with regard to the act of procreation, the one is bound to pay the debt to the other at any season or hour, with due regard to the decorum required in such matters, for this must not be done at once in public.

REPLY OBJ. 1: As far as he is concerned, he does not consent, but grants unwillingly and with grief that which is exacted of him; and consequently he does not sin. For it is ordained by God, on account of the weakness of the flesh, that the debt must always be paid to the one who asks, lest he be afforded an occasion of sin.

REPLY OBJ. 2: No hour is fixed for praying, but that compensation can be made at some other hour; wherefore the argument is not cogent.

Article 10

Whether Marriage Is Forbidden During Certain Periods?

AD DECEM SIC PROCEDITUR. Videtur quod nuptiae non sint interdicendae temporibus. Quia matrimonium sacramentum est. Sed in illis temporibus non interdicitur celebratio aliorum sacramentorum. Ergo nec celebratio matrimonii.

PRAETEREA, magis incompetens est diebus festis petitio debiti quam celebratio nuptiarum. Sed in diebus illis potest debitum peti. Ergo et nuptiae celebrari.

PRAETEREA, matrimonia quae fiunt contra statutum Ecclesiae, debent separari. Sed non separantur, si fiant nuptiae in talibus temporibus. Ergo non debet esse prohibitum per Ecclesiae statuta.

SED CONTRA est quod dicitur Eccles. 3, 5: *tempus amplexandi, et tempus longe fieri ab amplexibus.*

RESPONDEO dicendum quod quando novae sponsae traduntur, animus conjugum magis ex ipsa novitate ad curam carnalium occupatur et ideo in nuptiis consueverunt signa multa laetitiae dissolutae ostendi; et propter hoc illis temporibus in quibus homines praecipue debent se ad spiritualia elevare, prohibitum est nuptias ce-

OBJECTION 1: Again, it seems that weddings are not forbidden during certain periods. For matrimony is a sacrament. But in those times the celebration of the other sacraments is not forbidden. Therefore, neither should the celebration of matrimony.

OBJ. 2: Furthermore, the requesting of the debt is more unfitting for holy days than wedding celebrations. But in those days the marital debt can be requested. Therefore, so can weddings be celebrated.

OBJ. 3: Furthermore, marriages which happen against the statutes of the Church should be dissolved. But they are not dissolved if the wedding happens during such periods. Therefore, neither should they be prohibited by the statutes of the Church.

ON THE CONTRARY, There is what Ecclesiastes 3:5 says: *a time to embrace, and a time to be far from embraces.*

I ANSWER THAT, When new brides are given to their husbands, the souls of the spouses are more greatly occupied by the concern for carnal things in this very newness, and therefore in weddings many signs of wild rejoicing are wont to be shown; and because of this, in those times in which men should particularly elevate themselves to spir-

lebrari. Hoc autem est ab Adventu usque ad Epiphaniam propter communionem, quae secundum antiquos canones in nativitate fieri convenienter solet; et a septuagesima usque ad octavas Paschae, propter communionem Paschalem; et a tribus diebus ante Ascensionem usque ad octavas Pentecostes, propter praeparationem ad communionem illo tempore sumendam.

AD PRIMUM ERGO DICENDUM, quod celebratio matrimonii habet aliquam mundanam laetitiam et carnalem adjunctam, quod non est de aliis sacramentis. Et ideo non est simile.

AD SECUNDUM DICENDUM, quod non fit tanta distractio animorum in redditione vel petitione debiti, sicut in celebratione nuptiarum. Et ideo non est simile.

AD TERTIUM DICENDUM, quod cum tempus non sit de essentia matrimonii, si in tempore indebito contrahatur, nihilominus verum est sacramentum; nec separatur matrimonium simpliciter, sed ad tempus, ut poenitentiam agant de hoc quod statutum Ecclesiae sunt transgressi; et sic est intelligendum quod Magister dicit *Littera*, IV *Sentent.*, dist. xxxiii.

itual things, it is prohibited for weddings to be celebrated. Now this is from Advent until Epiphany because of the reception of communion, which, according to the ancient canons, is usually to be made appropriately during the period of the Nativity; and from Septuagesima until the octave of Easter, because of the Easter communion; and from three days before the Ascension until the octave of Pentecost, because of preparation for consuming communion at that time.

REPLY OBJ. 1: The celebration of matrimony has something of worldly and carnal rejoicing joined to it, which is not in the other sacraments. Therefore, it is not similar.

REPLY OBJ. 2: Such great distraction of souls does not occur in the rendering or requesting of the debt as in the celebration of a wedding, and therefore it is not similar.

REPLY OBJ. 3: Since time is not of the essence of matrimony, if it is contracted at an improper time, nevertheless it is a valid sacrament; nor are the contractants separated simply, but for a time, that they may do penance for having transgressed the statutes of the Church; and in this way what the Master says is to be understood (*Sentences* IV, Dist. 33).

QUESTION 65

BIGAMY

Deinde considerandum est de pluralitate uxorum. Circa quod quaeruntur quinque.

Primo: utrum habere plures uxores sit contra legem naturae.

Secundo: utrum aliquando fuerit licitum.

Tertio: utrum habere concubinam sit contra legem naturae.

Quarto: utrum accedere ad concubinam sit peccatum mortale.

Quinto: utrum aliquando licitum fuerit habere concubinam.

We must now consider the plurality of wives.

Under this head there are five points of inquiry:

(1) Whether it is against the natural law to have several wives?

(2) Whether this was ever lawful?

(3) Whether it is against the natural law to have a concubine?

(4) Whether it is a mortal sin to have intercourse with a concubine?

(5) Whether it was ever lawful to have a concubine?

Article 1

Whether It Is Against the Natural Law to Have Several Wives?

AD PRIMUM SIC PROCEDITUR. Videtur quod habere plures uxores non sit contra legem naturae. Consuetudo enim legi naturali non praeiudicat. Sed habere plures uxores *peccatum non erat quando mos erat*, ut ab Augustino habetur in littera. Ergo habere plures uxores non est contra legem naturae.

PRAETEREA, quicumque facit contra legem naturae, facit contra praeceptum: quia sicut lex scripta habet sua praecepta, ita et lex naturae. Sed Augustinus dicit quod habere plures uxores *non erat contra praeceptum, quia nulla lege erat prohibitum*. Ergo habere plures uxores non est contra legem naturae.

PRAETEREA, matrimonium principaliter ordinatur ad prolis procreationem. Sed unus potest ex pluribus prolem accipere, plures fecundando; Ergo non est contra legem naturae habere plures uxores.

PRAETEREA, *ius naturale est quod natura omnia animalia docuit*, ut in principio *Digestorum* dicitur. Sed natura non docuit hoc omnia animalia, quod sit una unius: cum unus mas in multis animalibus pluribus feminis coniungatur. Ergo non est contra legem naturae habere plures uxores.

PRAETEREA, secundum Philosophum, XV *de Animalibus*, in generatione prolis mas se habet ad feminam sicut agens ad patiens et artifex ad materiam. Sed non est contra ordinem naturae quod unum agens in plura patientia agat, aut unus artifex ex diversis materiis ope-

OBJECTION 1: It would seem that it is not against the natural law to have several wives. For custom does not prejudice the law of nature. But to have several wives *was not a sin when this was the custom*, according to Augustine as quoted in the text (*On the Good of Marriage* 15; *Sentences* IV, D. 33). Therefore, it is not contrary to the natural law to have several wives.

OBJ. 2: Further, whoever acts in opposition to the natural law disobeys a commandment, for the law of nature has its commandments even as the written law has. Now Augustine says that *it was not contrary to a commandment* to have several wives, *because by no law was it forbidden* (*On the Good of Marriage* 15; *The City of God* 15.38). Therefore, it is not against the natural law to have several wives.

OBJ. 3: Further, marriage is chiefly directed to the begetting of offspring. But one man may get children of several women by causing them to be pregnant. Therefore, it is not against the natural law to have several wives.

OBJ. 4: Further, *natural right is that which nature has taught all animals*, as stated at the beginning of the *Digests*. Now nature has not taught all animals that one male should be united to but one female, since with many animals the one male is united to several females. Therefore, it is not against the natural law to have several wives.

OBJ. 5: Further, according to the Philosopher (*On the Generation of Animals* 1.20), in the begetting of offspring the male is to the female as agent to patient, and as the craftsman is to his material. But it is not against the order of nature for one agent to act on several patients, or for one

retur. Ergo nec est contra legem naturae quod unus mas plures uxores habeat.

Sed contra: Illud praecipue videtur esse de iure naturali quod homini in sua institutione inditum est. Sed quod sit una unius in ipsa institutione humanae naturae est ei inditum, ut patet Gen: 2: *erunt duo in carne una*. Ergo est die lege naturae.

Praeterea, contra legem naturae est quod homo se ad impossibile obliget, et ut quod uni datum est alteri detur. Sed homo contrahens cum una uxore sui corporis potestatem sibi tradidit, ut necesse sit reddere debitum cum petierit. Ergo contra legem est si postea alteri potestatem sui corporis tradat; quia nemo posset simul utrique reddere debitum, si simul peterent.

Praeterea, de lege naturae est, *quod tibi non vis fieri, alteri ne feceris*. Sed vir nullo modo vellet quod uxor alium virum haberet. Ergo contra legem naturae faceret si uxorem aliam superinduceret.

Praeterea, quidquid est contra naturale desiderium, est contra legem naturae. Sed zelus viri ad uxorem, et uxoris ad virum, naturalis est: quia in omnibus invenitur. Ergo, cum zelus sit *amor non patiens consortium in amato*, videtur quod contra legem naturae sit quod plures uxores habeant unum virum.

Respondeo dicendum quod omnibus rebus naturalibus insunt quaedam principia quibus non solum operationes proprias efficere possunt, sed quibus etiam eas convenientes fini suo reddant: sive sint actiones quae consequantur rem aliquam ex natura sui generis, sive consequantur ex natura speciei; ut magneti competit ferri deorsum ex natura sui generis, et attrahere ferrum ex natura speciei. Sicut autem in rebus agentibus ex necessitate naturae sunt principia actionum ipsae formae, a quibus operationes propriae prodeunt convenientes fini; ita in his quae cognitionem participant, principia agendi sunt cognitio et appetitus. Unde oportet quod in vi cognitiva sit naturalis conceptio, et in vi appetitiva naturalis inclinatio, quibus operatio conveniens generi sive speciei reddatur competens fini. Sed quia homo inter cetera animalia rationem finis cognoscit et proportionem operationis ad finem, ideo naturalis conceptio ei indita qua dirigitur ad operandum, convenienter *lex naturalis* vel *ius naturale* dicitur. In ceteris autem *aestimatio naturalis* vocatur: bruta enim ex vi naturae impelluntur ad operandum convenientes actiones, magis quam regulentur, quasi proprio arbitrio agentia.

craftsman to work in several materials. Therefore, neither is it contrary to the law of nature for one husband to have many wives.

On the contrary, That which was instilled into man at the formation of human nature would seem especially to belong to the natural law. Now it was instilled into him at the very formation of human nature that one man should have one wife, according to Genesis 2:24: *they shall be two in one flesh*. Therefore, it is of natural law.

Further, It is contrary to the law of nature that man should bind himself to the impossible, and that what is given to one should be given to another. Now when a man contracts with a wife, he gives her the power of his body so that he is bound to pay her the debt when she asks. Therefore, it is against the law of nature that he should afterwards give the power of his body to another, because it would be impossible for him to pay both were both to ask at the same time.

Further, *Do not to another what you would not were done to yourself* (Tobias 4:16) is a precept of the natural law. But a husband would by no means be willing for his wife to have another husband. Therefore, he would be acting against the law of nature were he to have another wife in addition.

Further, Whatever is against the natural desire is contrary to the natural law. Now a husband's jealousy of his wife and the wife's jealousy of her husband are natural, for they are found in all. Therefore, since jealousy is *love impatient of sharing the beloved*, it would seem to be contrary to the natural law that several wives should share one husband.

I answer that, All natural things are imbued with certain principles whereby they are enabled not only to exercise their proper actions, but also to render those actions proportionate to their end, whether such actions belong to a thing by virtue of its generic nature, or by virtue of its specific nature: thus it belongs to a magnet to be borne downwards by virtue of its generic nature, and to attract iron by virtue of its specific nature. Now, just as in those things which act from natural necessity the principle of action is the form itself, whence their proper actions proceed proportionately to their end, so in things which are endowed with knowledge the principles of action are knowledge and appetite. Hence in the cognitive power there needs to be a natural concept, and in the appetitive power a natural inclination, whereby the action befitting the genus or species is rendered proportionate to the end. Now since man, of all animals, knows the aspect of the end, and the proportion of the action to the end, it follows that he is imbued with a natural concept, whereby he is directed to act in a befitting manner, and this is called *the natural law* or *the natural right*, but in other animals *the natural instinct*. For brutes are impelled by the force of nature to do befitting actions rather than guided to act on their own judgment.

Lex ergo naturalis nihil aliud est quam conceptio homini naturaliter indita qua dirigitur ad convenienter agendum in actionibus propriis: sive competant ei ex natura generis, ut generare, comedere, et huiusmodi; sive ex natura speciei, ut ratiocinari et huiusmodi. Omne autem illud quod actionem inconvenientem reddit fini quem natura ex opere aliquo intendit, contra legem naturae esse dicitur.

Potest autem actio non esse conveniens fini vel principali, vel secundario: et, sive sic sive sic, hoc contingit dupliciter. Uno modo, ex aliquo quod omnino impedit finem: ut nimia superfluitas aut defectus comestionis impedit salutem corporis, quasi principalem finem comestionis; et bonam habitudinem in negotiis exercendis, qui est finis secundarius. Alio modo, ex aliquo quod facit difficilem aut minus decentem perventionem ad finem principalem vel secundarium: sicut inordinata comestio quantum ad tempus indebitum. Si ergo sit inconveniens fini quasi omnino prohibens finem principalem, directe per legem naturae prohibetur primis praeceptis legis naturae, quae sunt in operabilibus sicut sunt communes conceptiones in speculativis. Si autem sit incompetens fini secundario quocumque modo, aut etiam principali ut faciens difficilem vel minus congruam perventionem ad ipsum, prohibetur non quidem primis praeceptis legis naturae, sed secundis, quae ex primis derivantur, sicut conclusiones in speculativis ex principiis per se notis fidem habent. Et sic dicta actio contra legem naturae esse dicitur.

Matrimonium ergo habet pro fine principali prolis procreationem et educationem: qui quidem finis competit homini secundum naturam sui generis; unde et *aliis animalibus est communis*, ut dicitur in VIII *Ethic*. Et sic bonum matrimonii assignatur proles. Sed pro fine secundario, ut dicit Philosophus, habet in hominibus solum communicationem operum quae sunt necessaria in vita. Et secundum hoc fidem sibi invicem debent, quae est unum de bonis matrimonii. Habet ulterius alium finem inquantum in fidelibus est, scilicet significationem Christi et Ecclesiae. Et sic bonum matrimonii dicitur sacramentum. Unde primus finis respondet matrimonio hominis inquantum est animal; secundus inquantum est homo; tertius inquantum est fidelis.

Pluralitas ergo uxorum neque totaliter tollit neque aliqualiter impedit primum finem: cum unus vir sufficiat pluribus uxoribus fecundandis, et educandis filiis ex eis natis. Sed secundum finem, etsi non totaliter tollit, tamen multum impedit: eo quod non facile potest esse pax in familia ubi uni viro plures uxores iunguntur, cum non possit unus vir sufficere ad satisfaciendum pluribus uxo-

Therefore, the natural law is nothing else than a concept naturally instilled into man whereby he is guided to act in a befitting manner in his proper actions, whether they are competent to him by virtue of his generic nature, as, for instance, to beget, to eat, and so on, or belong to him by virtue of his specific nature, as, for instance, to reason and so forth. Now, whatever renders an action improportionate to the end which nature intends to obtain by a certain work is said to be contrary to the natural law.

But an action may be improportionate either to the principal or to the secondary end, and in either case this happens in two ways. First, on account of something which wholly hinders the end; for instance, a very great excess or a very great deficiency in eating hinders both the health of the body, which is the principal end of food, and aptitude for conducting business, which is its secondary end. Second, on account of something that renders the attainment of the principal or secondary end difficult, or less satisfactory, for instance, eating inordinately at an undue time. Accordingly, if an action be improportionate to the end through altogether hindering the principal end directly, it is forbidden by the first precepts of the natural law, which hold the same place in practical matters as the general concepts of the mind in speculative matters. If, however, it be in any way improportionate to the secondary end, or again to the principal end, as rendering its attainment difficult or less satisfactory, it is forbidden, not indeed by the first precepts of the natural law, but by the second, which are derived from the first even as conclusions in speculative matters receive our assent by virtue of self-known principles: and thus the act in question is said to be against the law of nature.

Now marriage has for its principal end the begetting and rearing of children, and this end is competent to man according to his generic nature, wherefore it is *common to other animals* (*Ethics* 8.12), and thus it is that the offspring is assigned as a marriage good. But for its secondary end, as the Philosopher says (*Ethics* 8.12), it has among men alone the community of works that are a necessity of life, as stated above (Q. 41, A. 1). And in reference to this they owe one another fidelity, which is one of the goods of marriage. Furthermore, it has another end as regards marriage between believers, namely, the signification of Christ and the Church: and thus the sacrament is said to be a marriage good. Wherefore the first end corresponds to the marriage of man inasmuch as he is an animal; the second, inasmuch as he is a man; the third, inasmuch as he is a believer.

Accordingly, plurality of wives neither wholly destroys nor in any way hinders the first end of marriage, since one man is sufficient to get children of several wives, and to rear the children born of them. But though it does not wholly destroy the second end, it hinders it considerably, for there cannot easily be peace in a family where several wives are joined to one husband, since one husband cannot suffice to

ribus ad votum; et quia communicatio plurium in uno officio causat litem, sicut *figuli conrixantur ad invicem*, et similiter plures uxores unius viri. Tertium autem finem totaliter tollit: eo quod, sicut Christus est unus, ita Ecclesia una.

Et ideo patet ex dictis quod pluralitas uxorum quodammodo est contra legem naturae, et quodammodo non.

AD PRIMUM ergo dicendum quod consuetudo non praeiudicat legi naturae quantum ad prima praecepta ipsius, quae sunt quasi communes animi conceptiones in speculativis. Sed ea quae ex istis trahuntur ut conclusiones, *consuetudo auget*, ut Tullius dicit, in III *Rhetoric.*, et similiter minuit. Et huiusmodi est praeceptum legis naturae de unitate uxoris.

AD SECUNDUM dicendum quod, sicut Tullius dicit, *res a natura perfectas et a consuetudine approbatas legum metus et religio sanxit*. Unde patet quod illa quae lex naturalis dictat quasi ex primis principiis legis naturae derivata, non habent vim coactivam per modum praecepti absolute, nisi postquam lege divina et humana sancita sunt. Et hoc est quod dicit Augustinus, quod *non faciebant contra praeceptum, quia nulla lege erat prohibitum*.

AD TERTIUM patet solutio ex dictis.

AD QUARTUM dicendum quod ius naturale multipliciter accipitur. Primo enim aliquod ius dicitur naturale ex principio, quia natura est inditum. Et sic definit Tullius, in II *Rhetoric.*, dicens: *ius naturae est quod non opinio genuit, sed quaedam innata vis inseruit.*

Et quia etiam in rebus naturalibus dicuntur aliqui motus naturales, non quia sint ex principio intrinseco, sed quia sunt a principio superiori movente, sicut motus qui sunt in elementis ex impressione corporum caelestium, naturales dicuntur, ut Commentator dicit, in III *de Coelo et Mundo*; ideo ea quae sunt de iure divino, dicuntur esse de iure naturali, cum sint ex impressione et infusione superioris principii, scilicet Dei. Et sic accipitur ab Isidoro, qui dicit quod *ius naturale est quod in lege et in Evangelio continetur.*

Tertio, dicitur ius naturale non solum a principio, sed a natura, quia de naturalibus est. Et quia natura contra rationem dividitur, a qua homo est homo, ideo, strictissimo modo accipiendi ius naturale, illa quae ad homines tantum pertinent, etsi sint de dictamine naturalis rationis, non dicuntur esse de iure naturali; sed illa tantum quae naturalis ratio dictat de his quae sunt homini aliisque communia. Et sic datur dicta definitio, scilicet: *ius naturale est quod natura omnia animalia docuit.*

satisfy the requisitions of several wives, and again because the sharing of several in one occupation is a cause of strife: thus *potters quarrel with one another* (Aristotle, *Rhetoric* ii), and in like manner the several wives of one husband. The third end, it removes altogether, because as Christ is one, so also is the Church one.

It is therefore evident from what has been said that plurality of wives is in a way against the law of nature, and in a way not against it.

REPLY OBJ. 1: Custom does not prejudice the law of nature as regards the first precepts of the latter, which are like the general concepts of the mind in speculative matters. But those which are drawn like conclusions from these *custom enforces*, as Cicero declares (*On Rhetorical Invention* 2), or weakens. Such is the precept of nature in the matter of having one wife.

REPLY OBJ. 2: As Cicero says (*On Rhetorical Invention* 2), *fear of the law and religion have sanctioned those things that come from nature and are approved by custom*. Wherefore it is evident that those dictates of the natural law, which are derived from the first principles, as it were, of the natural law, have not the binding force of an absolute commandment, except when they have been sanctioned by divine or human law. This is what Augustine means by saying that *they did not disobey the commandments of the law, since it was not forbidden by any law*.

THE REPLY to the third objection follows from what has been said.

REPLY OBJ. 4: Natural right has several significations. First, a right is said to be natural by its principle because it is instilled by nature: and thus Cicero defines it (*On Rhetorical Invention* 2) when he says: *natural right is not the result of opinion but the product of an innate force*.

And since even in natural things certain movements are called natural, not because they are from an intrinsic principle, but because they are from a higher moving principle—thus the movements that are caused in the elements by the impress of heavenly bodies are said to be natural, as the Commentator states (*On Heaven and Earth* III, 28)—therefore those things that are of divine right are said to be of natural right, because they are caused by the impress and influence of a higher principle, namely God. Isidore takes it in this sense when he says (*Etymologies* 5) that *the natural right is that which is contained in the law and the Gospel*.

Third, right is said to be natural not only from its principle but also from its matter, because it is about natural things. And since nature is contradistinguished with reason, whereby man is a man, it follows that if we take natural right in its strictest sense, those things which are dictated by natural reason and pertain to man alone are not said to be of natural right, but only those which are dictated by natural reason and are common to man and other animals. Thus we have the aforesaid definition, namely: *natural right is what nature has taught all animals*.

Pluralitas ergo uxorum, quamvis non sit contra ius naturale tertio modo acceptum, est tamen contra ius naturale secundo modo acceptum: quia iure divino prohibetur. Et etiam contra ius naturale primo modo acceptum, ut ex dictis patet: quia natura dictat animali cuilibet secundum modum convenientem suae speciei. Unde etiam quaedam animalia, in quibus ad educationem prolis requiritur sollicitudo utriusque, scilicet maris et feminae, naturali instinctu servant coniunctionem unius ad unum: sicut patet in turture et columba et huiusmodi.

AD QUINTUM patet solutio ex dictis.

Sed quia rationes inductae in contrarium videntur ostendere quod pluralitas uxorum sit contra prima principia legis naturae, ideo ad eas respondendum.

AD SEXTUM dicendum quod natura humana absque omni defectu instituta est. Et ideo non solum sunt indita ei illa sine quibus matrimonii finis principalis esse non potest, sed etiam illa sine quibus secundarius finis matrimonii sine difficultate haberi non posset. Et hoc modo sufficit homini in ipsa sui institutione habere unam uxorem.

AD SEPTIMUM dicendum quod vir per matrimonium non dat sui corporis potestatem uxori quantum ad omnia, sed solum quantum ad illa quae matrimonium requirit. Non autem requirit matrimonium ut quolibet tempore uxori petenti vir debitum reddat, quantum ad id ad quod matrimonium principaliter est instituturn, scilicet bonum prolis, sed quantum sufficit ad impraegnationem. Requirit autem hoc matrimonium inquantum est ad remedium instituturn quod est secundarius ipsius finis, ut quolibet tempore debitum petenti reddatur. Et sic patet quod accipiens plures uxores non se obligat ad impossibile, considerato principali fine matrimonii. Et ideo pluralitas uxorum non est contra praecepta prima legis naturae.

AD OCTAVUM dicendum quod illud praeceptum legis naturae, *quod tibi non vis fieri, alteri ne feceris*, debet intelligi, *eadem proportione servata*: non enim, si praelatus non vult sibi resisti a subdito, ipse subdito resistere non debet. Et ideo non oportet quod, ex vi illius praecepti, quod si vir non vult quod uxor sua habeat alium virum, quod ipse non habeat aliam uxorem: quia unum virum habere plures uxores non est contra prima praecepta legis naturae, ut dictum est; sed unam uxorem habere plures viros est contra prima praecepta legis naturae, eo quod per hoc quantum ad aliquid totaliter tollitur, et quantum ad aliquid impeditur bonum prolis, quod est principalis matrimonii finis. In bono enim prolis intelligitur non solum procreatio, sed etiam educatio. Ipsa enim procreatio prolis, etsi non totaliter tollatur, quia contingit post impraegnationem primam iterum mulierem impraegnari, ut dicitur in IX *de*

Accordingly, plurality of wives, though not contrary to natural right taken in the third sense, is nevertheless against natural right taken in the second sense because it is forbidden by the divine law. It is also against natural right taken in the first sense, as appears from what has been said, for such is nature's dictate to every animal according to the mode befitting its nature. Wherefore also certain animals, the rearing of whose offspring demands the care of both (namely, the male and female), by natural instinct cling to the union of one with one, for instance, the turtle-dove, the dove, and so forth.

THE REPLY to the fifth objection is clear from what has been said.

Since, however, the arguments adduced on the contrary side would seem to show that plurality of wives is against the first principles of the natural law, we must reply to them.

REPLY OBJ. 6: Human nature was founded without any defect, and consequently it is endowed not only with those things without which the principal end of marriage is impossible of attainment, but also with those without which the secondary end of marriage could not be obtained without difficulty: and in this way it sufficed man when he was first formed to have one wife, as stated above.

REPLY OBJ. 7: In marriage the husband gives his wife power of his body not in all respects, but only in those things that are required by marriage. Now marriage does not require the husband to pay the debt every time his wife asks for it, if we consider the principal end for which marriage was instituted, namely, the good of the offspring, but only as far as is necessary for impregnation. But insofar as it is instituted as a remedy (which is its secondary end), marriage does require the debt to be paid at all times on being asked for. Hence it is evident that by taking several wives a man does not bind himself to the impossible, considering the principal end of marriage; and therefore plurality of wives is not against the first principles of the natural law.

REPLY OBJ. 8: This precept of the natural law, *do not to another what you would not were done to yourself*, should be understood with the provison that there be *equal proportion*. For if a superior is unwilling to be resisted by his subject, he is not therefore bound not to resist his subject. Hence it does not follow in virtue of this precept that as a husband is unwilling for his wife to have another husband, he must not have another wife: because for one man to have several wives is not contrary to the first principles of the natural law, as stated above: whereas for one wife to have several husbands is contrary to the first principles of the natural law, since thereby the good of the offspring which is the principal end of marriage is, in one respect, entirely destroyed, and in another respect hindered. For the good of the offspring means not only begetting, but also rearing. Now the begetting of offspring, though not wholly voided, since a woman may be impregnated a second time after

Animalibus; tamen multum impeditur, quia vix: potest accidere quin corruptio accidat quantum ad utrumque fetum vel quantum ad alterum. Sed educatio totaliter tollitur: quia ex hoc quod una mulier plures maritos haberet, sequeretur incertitudo prolis respectu patris, cuius cura necessaria est in educando. Et ideo nulla lege vel consuetudine est permissum unam mulierem habere plures viros, sicut e converso.

AD NONUM dicendum quod naturalis inclinatio in appetitiva sequitur naturalem conceptionem in cognitione. Et quia non ita est contra conceptionem naturalem quod vir habeat plures uxores sicut quod uxor habeat plures viros, ideo affectus uxoris non tantum, refugit consortium in viro sicut e converso. Et ideo tam in hominibus quam in aliis animalibus invenitur maior zelus maris ad feminam quam e converso.

impregnation has already taken place, as stated in *On the Generation of Animals* 7.4, is nevertheless considerably hindered, because this can scarcely happen without injury either to both fetuses or to one of them. But the rearing of the offspring is altogether destroyed, because as a result of one woman having several husbands there follows uncertainty of the offspring in relation to its father, whose care is necessary for its education. Wherefore the marriage of one wife with several husbands has not been sanctioned by any law or custom, whereas the converse has been.

REPLY OBJ. 9: The natural inclination in the appetitive power follows the natural concept in the cognitive power. And since it is not so much opposed to the natural concept for a man to have several wives as for a wife to have several husbands, it follows that a wife's love is not so averse to another sharing the same husband with her, as a husband's love is to another sharing the same wife with him. Consequently, both in man and in other animals the male is more jealous of the female, than vice versa.

Article 2

Whether It Was Ever Lawful to Have Several Wives?

AD SECUNDUM SIC PROCEDITUR. Videtur quod habere plures uxores non potuerit aliquando esse licitum. Quia secundum Philosophum, in V *Ethic.*, *ius naturale semper et ubique habet eandem potentiam*. Sed iure naturali prohibetur pluralitas uxorum, ut ex dictis patet. Ergo, sicut modo non licet, ita nec unquam licuit.

PRAETEREA, si aliquando licuit, hoc non fuit nisi quia vel per se licitum erat, vel per aliquam dispensationem licebat. Si primo modo, sic etiam nunc licitum esset. Si autem secundo modo, hoc esse non potest. Quia, secundum. Augustinum, *Deus, cum sit naturae Conditor, non facit aliquid contra rationes quas naturae inseruit*. Cum ergo naturae nostrae Deus inseruerit quod sit una unius, videtur quod ipse contra hoc nunquam dispensaverit.

PRAETEREA, si aliquid est licitum ex dispensatione, hoc non licet nisi illis quibus dispensatio fit. Non autem legitur aliqua dispensatio communis in lege cum omnibus facta. Cum ergo omnes communiter qui volebant plures uxores acciperent in veteri Testamento, nec ex hoc reprehendebantur in lege vel a prophetis, non videtur quod fuerit ex dispensatione licitum.

PRAETEREA, ubi est eadem causa dispensationis, debet eadem dispensatio fieri. Sed causa dispensationis non potest alia poni nisi multiplicatio prolis ad cultum

OBJECTION 1: It would seem that it can never have been lawful to have several wives. For, according to the Philosopher (*Ethics* 5.7), *the natural law has the same power at all times and places*. Now plurality of wives is forbidden by the natural law, as stated above (A. 1). Therefore, as it is unlawful now, it was unlawful at all times.

OBJ. 2: Further, if it was ever lawful, this could only be because it was lawful either in itself or by dispensation. If the former, it would also be lawful now; if the latter, this is impossible, for according to Augustine (*Against Faustus* 26.3), *as God is the founder of nature, he does nothing contrary to the principles which he has planted in nature*. Since, then, God has planted in our nature the principle that one man should be united to one wife, it would seem that he has never dispensed man from this.

OBJ. 3: Further, if a thing be lawful by dispensation, it is only lawful for those who receive the dispensation. Now we do not read in the law of a general dispensation having been granted to all. Since, then, in the Old Testament all who wished to do so, without any distinction, took to themselves several wives, nor were reproached on that account either by the law or by the prophets, it would seem that it was not made lawful by dispensation.

OBJ. 4: Further, where there is the same reason for dispensation, the same dispensation should be given. Now we cannot assign any other reason for dispensation than

Dei: quae etiam nunc necessaria est. Ergo adhuc dicta dispensatio duraret: praecipue cum non legatur revocata.

Praeterea, in dispensatione non debet praetermitti maius bonum propter minus bonum. Sed fides et sacramentum, quae non videntur posse servari in matrimonio quo unus pluribus uxoribus coniungitur, sunt meliora quam prolis multiplicatio. Ergo intuitu huius multiplicationis dispensatio praedicta fieri non debuisset.

Sed contra: Galat. 3 dicitur quod *lex propter praevaricatores posita est*, ut scilicet eos prohiberet. Sed lex vetus facit mentionem de pluralitate uxorum sine aliqua eius prohibitione, ut patet Deuteron. 21: *si habuerit homo duas uxores*, etc. Ergo habendo duas uxores non erant praevaricatores. Et ita erat licitum.

Praeterea, hoc idem videtur exemplo ex sanctis Patribus, qui plures leguntur habuisse uxores, cum Deo essent acceptissimi: sicut Iacob et David et plures alii. Ergo aliquando fuit licitum.

Respondeo dicendum quod, sicut ex dictis patet, pluralitas uxorum dicitur esse contra legem naturae, non quantum ad prima praecepta eius, sed quantum ad secunda, quae quasi conclusiones a primis praeceptis derivantur. Sed quia actus humanos variari oportet secundum diversas conditiones personarum et temporum et aliarum circumstantiarum, ideo conclusiones praedictae a primis legis naturae praeceptis non procedunt ut semper efficaciam habentes, sed in maiori parte: talis est enim tota materia moralis, ut patet per Philosophum, in libro *Ethicorum*. Et ideo, ubi eorum efficacia deficit, licite ea praetermitti possunt. Sed quia non est facile determinare huiusmodi varietates, ideo illi ex cuius auctoritate lex efficaciam habet, reservatur ut licentiam praebeat legem praetermittendi in illis casibus ad quos legis efficacia se non extendere debet. Et talis licentia *dispensatio* dicitur.

Lex autem de unitate uxoris non est humanitus, sed divinitus instituta: nec unquam verbo aut litteris tradita, sed cordi impressa, sicut et alia quae ad legem naturae qualitercumque pertinent. Et ideo in hoc a solo Deo dispensatio fieri potuit per inspirationem internam. Quae quidem principaliter sanctis patribus facta est, et per eorum exemplum ad alios derivata est, eo tempore quo oportebat praedictum naturae praeceptum praetermitti ut maior esset multiplicatio prolis ad cultum Dei educandae. Semper enim principalior finis magis observandus est quam secundarius. Unde, cum bonum prolis sit principalis matrimonii finis, ubi prolis multiplicatio necessaria erat, debuit negligi ad tempus impedimentum quod posset in secundariis finibus evenire, ad quod re-

the multiplying of the offspring for the worship of God, and this is necessary also now. Therefore, this dispensation would be still in force, especially as we read nowhere of its having been recalled.

Obj. 5: Further, in granting a dispensation, the greater good should not be overlooked for the sake of a lesser good. Now fidelity and the sacrament, which it would seem impossible to safeguard in a marriage where one man is joined to several wives, are greater goods than the multiplication of the offspring. Therefore, this dispensation ought not to have been granted with a view to this multiplication.

On the contrary, It is stated that the law *was set because of transgressors* (Gal 3:19), namely, in order to prohibit them. Now the old law mentions plurality of wives without any prohibition, as appears from Deuteronomy 21:15: *if a man have two wives*. Therefore, they were not transgressors through having two wives; and so it was lawful.

Further, This is confirmed by the example of the holy patriarchs, who are stated to have had several wives, and yet were most pleasing to God, for instance, Jacob, David, and several others. Therefore, at one time it was lawful.

I answer that, As stated above (A. 1), plurality of wives is said to be against the natural law not as regards its first precepts, but as regards the secondary precepts, which, like conclusions, are drawn from its first precepts. Since, however, human acts must vary according to the various conditions of persons, times, and other circumstances, the aforesaid conclusions do not proceed from the first precepts of the natural law, so as to be binding in all cases, but only in the majority. For such is the entire matter of ethics according to the Philosopher (*Ethics* 1.3, 7). Hence, when they cease to be binding, it is lawful to disregard them. But because it is not easy to determine the above variations, it belongs exclusively to him from whose authority he derives its binding force to permit the non-observance of the law in those cases to which the force of the law ought not to extend, and this permission is called a *dispensation*.

Now the law prescribing the one wife was framed not by man but by God, nor was it ever given by word or in writing, but was imprinted on the heart, like other things belonging in any way to the natural law. Consequently, a dispensation in this matter could be granted by God alone through an inward inspiration, vouchsafed originally to the holy patriarchs, and by their example continued to others, at a time when it was necessary that the aforesaid precept not be observed, in order to ensure the multiplication of the offspring educated in the worship of God. For the principal end is ever to be borne in mind before the secondary end. Wherefore, since the good of the offspring is the principal end of marriage, for a time it was necessary to disregard the impediment that might arise to the secondary ends, when

movendum praeceptum prohibens pluralitatem uxorum ordinatur, ut ex dictis patet.

AD PRIMUM ergo dicendum quod ius naturale semper et ubique, quantum est de se, habet eandem potentiam. Sed per accidens, propter aliquod impedimentum, quandoque et alicubi potest variari: sicut ibidem Philosophus exemplum ponit de aliis rebus naturalibus. Semper enim et ubique dextera est melior quam sinistra secundum naturam: sed per aliquod accidens contingit aliquem esse ambidextrum, quia natura nostra variabilis est. Et similiter etiam est de naturali iusto, ut ibidem Philosophus dicit.

AD SECUNDUM dicendum quod in *Decretali* quadam, *de Divortiis*, dicitur quod *numquam licuit alicui plures habere uxores sine dispensatione per divinam inspirationem habita*. Nec tamen talis dispensatio datur contra rationes quas Deus naturae inseruit, sed praeter eas: quia rationes illae non sunt ordinatae ad semper, sed in pluribus esse, ut dictum est; sicut etiam non est contra naturam quando aliqua accidunt in rebus naturalibus miraculose, praeter ea quae ut frequenter solent evenire.

AD TERTIUM dicendum quod qualis est lex, talis debet esse dispensatio legis. Et quia lex naturae non est litteris scripta sed est cordibus impressa, propter hoc non oportuit dispensationem eorum quae ad legem naturae pertinent lege scripta dari, sed per internam inspirationem fieri.

AD QUARTUM dicendum quod, veniente Christo, fuit tempus plenitudinis gratiae Christi, per quam cultus Dei in omnes gentes spirituali propagatione diffusus est. Et ideo non est eadem ratio dispensationis quae erat ante Christi adventum, quando cultus Dei carnali propagatione multiplicabatur et conservabatur.

AD QUINTUM dicendum quod proles quod est bonum matrimonii, includit fidem ad Deum servandam: quia secundum quod proles expectatur ad cultum Dei educanda, ponitur matrimonii bonum. Fides autem ad Deum servanda est potior quam fides uxori, quae ponitur bonum matrimonii; et quam significatio, quae pertinet ad sacramentum, quia significatio ad fidei cognitionem ordinatur. Et ideo non est inconveniens si propter bonum prolis aliquid detrahitur aliis duobus bonis.

Nec tamen omnino tolluntur. Quia et fides manet ad plures: et sacramentum aliquo modo. Quia, quamvis non significatur coniunctio Christi ad Ecclesiam inquantum est una, significatur tamen distinctio graduum in Ecclesia per pluralitatem uxorum, quae quidem non solum est in Ecclesia militante, sed etiam triumphante. Et ideo illorum matrimonia aliquo modo significabant

it was necessary for the offspring to be multiplied; because it was for the removal of this impediment that the precept forbidding a plurality of wives was framed, as stated above (A. 1).

REPLY OBJ. 1: The natural law, considered in itself, has the same force at all times and places; but accidentally on account of some impediment it may vary at certain times and places, as the Philosopher instances in the case of other natural things (*Ethics* 1.3, 7). For at all times and places the right hand is better than the left according to nature, but it may happen accidentally that a person is ambidextrous, because our nature is variable; and the same applies to the natural, just as the Philosopher states (*Ethics* 1.3, 7).

REPLY OBJ. 2: In the *Decretals*, it is asserted that *it was never lawful to have several wives without having a dispensation received through divine inspiration*. Nor is the dispensation thus granted a contradiction to the principles which God has implanted in nature, but an exception to them, because those principles are not intended to apply to all cases but to the majority, as stated. Even so, it is not contrary to nature when certain occurrences take place in natural things miraculously, by way of exception to more frequent occurrences.

REPLY OBJ. 3: Dispensation from a law should follow the quality of the law. Wherefore, since the law of nature is imprinted on the heart, it was not necessary for a dispensation from things pertaining to the natural law to be given under the form of a written law but by internal inspiration.

REPLY OBJ. 4: When Christ came, it was the time of the fullness of the grace of Christ, whereby the worship of God was spread abroad among all nations by a spiritual propagation. Hence there is not the same reason for a dispensation as before Christ's coming, when the worship of God was spread and safeguarded by a carnal propagation.

REPLY OBJ. 5: Offspring, considered as one of the marriage goods, includes the keeping of faith with God, because the reason why it is reckoned a marriage good is because it is awaited with a view to its being brought up in the worship of God. Now the faith to be kept with God is of greater import than the faith to be kept with a wife, which is reckoned a marriage good, and than the signification which pertains to the sacrament, since the signification is subordinate to the knowledge of faith. Hence it is not unfitting if something is taken from the two other goods for the sake of the good of the offspring.

Nor are they entirely done away with, since there remains faith towards several wives; and the sacrament remains after a fashion, for though it did not signify the union of Christ with the Church as one, nevertheless the plurality of wives signified the distinction of degrees in the Church, which distinction is not only in the Church Militant but also in the Church Triumphant. Consequently, their mar-

coniunctionem Christi ad Ecclesiam, non solum militantem, ut quidam dicunt, sed etiam triumphantem, in qua sunt *diversae mansiones*.

riages signified somewhat the union of Christ not only with the Church Militant, as some say, but also with the Church Triumphant, where there are *many mansions* (John 19:2).

Article 3

Whether It Is Against the Natural Law to Have a Concubine?

AD TERTIUM SIC PROCEDITUR. Videtur quod habere concubinam non sit contra legem naturae, Legis enim caeremonia non sunt de lege naturae. Sed fornicatio prohibetur, Act. 15, inter alia caeremonia legis quae ad tempus credentibus ex gentibus imponebantur. Ergo fornicatio simplex, quae est accessus ad concubinam, non est contra legem naturae.

PRAETEREA, ius positivum a naturali iure profectum est, ut Tullius dicit. Sed secundum ius positivum fornicatio simplex non prohibetur: immo potius in poenam secundum antiquas leges mulieres lupanaribus tradendae condemnabantur. Ergo habere concubinam non est contra legem naturae.

PRAETEREA, naturalis lex non prohibet quin illud quod datur simpliciter, possit dari ad tempus et secundum quid. Sed una mulier soluta potest dare viro soluto in perpetuum sui corporis potestatem, ut ea utatur licite cum voluerit. Ergo non est contra legem naturae si dederit ei potestatem sui corporis ad horam.

PRAETEREA, quicumque re sua utitur ut vult, nemini facit iniuriam. Sed ancilla est res domini. Ergo, si dominus ea utitur ad libitum, nulli facit iniuriam. Et ita habere concubinam non est contra legem naturae.

PRAETEREA, quilibet potest alteri dare quod suum est. Sed uxor habet potestatem in corpore viri, ut patet I Cor. 7. Ergo, si uxor velit, vir poterit alteri mulieri coniungi sine peccato.

SED CONTRA: Secundum omnes leges filii qui de concubina nascuntur, sunt vituperabiles. Sed hoc non esset nisi concubitus ex quo oriuntur esset naturaliter turpis. Ergo habere concubinam est contra legem naturae.

PRAETEREA, matrimonium est naturale. Sed hoc non esset si sine praeiudicio legis naturae homo posset coniungi mulieri praeter matrimonium. Ergo contra legem naturae est concubinam habere.

RESPONDEO dicendum quod illa actio dicitur esse contra legem naturae quae non est conveniens fini debito, sive quia non ordinatur in ipsum per actionem agentis, sive quia de se est improportionata illi fini. Finis autem quem natura ex concubitu intendit, est proles pro-

OBJECTION 1: It would seem that to have a concubine is not against the natural law. For the ceremonies of the law are not of the natural law. But fornication is forbidden (Acts 15:29) in conjunction with ceremonies of the law which for the time were being imposed on those who were brought to the faith from among the heathens. Therefore, simple fornication, which is intercourse with a concubine, is not against the natural law.

OBJ. 2: Further, positive law is an outcome of the natural law, as Cicero says (*On Invention* II). Now fornication was not forbidden by positive law; indeed, according to the ancient laws, women used to be sentenced to be taken to brothels. Therefore, it is not against the natural law to have a concubine.

OBJ. 3: Further, the natural law does not forbid ɪt which is given simply to be given for a time or under certain restrictions. Now one unmarried woman may give the power of her body perpetually to an unmarried man so that he may use her when he will. Therefore, it is not against the law of nature if she give him power of her body for a time.

OBJ. 4: Further, whoever uses his own property as he will injures no one. But a slavewoman is her master's property. Therefore, if her master use her as he will, he injures no one: and consequently it is not against the natural law to have a concubine.

OBJ. 5: Further, everyone may give his own property to another. Now the wife has power of her husband's body (1 Cor 7:4). Therefore, if his wife be willing, the husband can have intercourse with another woman without sin.

ON THE CONTRARY, According to all laws the children born of a concubine are children of shame. But this would not be so unless the union of which they are born were naturally shameful. Therefore, to have a concubine is against the law of nature.

FURTHER, As stated above (Q. 41, A. 1), marriage is natural. But this would not be so if, without prejudice to the natural law, a man could be united to a woman otherwise than by marriage. Therefore, it is against the natural law to have a concubine.

I ANSWER THAT, As stated above (A. 1), an action is said to be against the natural law if it is not in keeping with the due end intended by nature, whether through not being directed thereto by the action of the agent, or through being in itself improportionate to that end. Now the end which

creanda et educanda: et ut hoc bonum quaereretur, posuit delectationem in coitu, ut Constantinus dicit.

Quicumque ergo concubitu utitur propter delectationem quae in ipso est, non referendo in finem a natura intentum, contra naturam facit: et similiter etiam nisi sit talis concubitus qui ad illum finem convenienter ordinari possit. Et quia res a fine plerumque nominantur tanquam ab optimo, sicut coniunctio *matrimonii* a prolis bono nomen accepit, quod per matrimonium principaliter quaeritur; ita *concubinae* nomen illam coniunctionem exprimit qua solus concubitus propter seipsum quaeritur.

Et si etiam aliquis quandoque ex tali concubitu prolem quaerat, non tamen est conveniens ad prolis bonum, in quo non solum intelligitur ipsius procreatio, per quam proles esse accipit, sed etiam educatio et instructio, per quam accipit *nutrimentum* et *disciplinam* a parentibus, in quibus tribus parentes proli tenentur, secundum Philosophum, VIII *Ethic.*

Cum autem educatio et instructio proli a parentibus debeantur per longum tempus, exigit lex naturae ut pater et mater in longum tempus commaneant, ad subveniendum communiter proli. Unde aves quae communiter pullos nutriunt, ante completam nutritionem non separantur a mutua societate, quae incipit a concumbendo. Haec autem obligatio ad commanendum feminam marito matrimonium facit.

Et ideo patet quod accedere ad mulierem non iunctam sibi matrimonio, quae concubina vocatur, est contra legem naturae.

AD PRIMUM ergo dicendum quod in gentibus quantum ad multa lex naturae obfuscata erat. Unde accedere ad concubinam malum non reputabant, sed passim fornicatione quasi relicita utebantur: sicut et aliis quae erant contra caeremonias Iudaeorum, quamvis non essent contra legem naturae. Et ideo Apostoli immiscuerunt prohibitionem fornicationis caeremonialibus, propter discretionem quae erat in utroque inter Iudaeos et gentiles.

AD SECUNDUM dicendum quod ex praedicta obscuritate, scilicet in quam ceciderunt gentiles, Deo debitam gloriam non reddentes, ut dicitur Rom. i, lex illa processit, et non ex instinctu legis naturae. Unde, praevalente Christiana religione, lex ilia extirpata est.

AD TERTIUM dicendum quod in aliquibus, sicut nihil inconveniens sequitur si rem aliquam quam quis in

nature intends in sexual union is the begetting and rearing of the offspring, and that this good might be sought after, it attached pleasure to the union, as Augustine says (*On Marriage and Concupiscence* 1.8).

Accordingly, to make use of sexual intercourse on account of its inherent pleasure without reference to the end for which nature intended it is to act against nature, as also is it if the intercourse be not such as may fittingly be directed to that end. And since, for the most part, things are denominated from their end as being that which is of most consequence to them, just as the marriage union took its name from the good of the offspring (Q. 44, A. 2), which is the end chiefly sought after in *marriage*, so the name of *concubine* is expressive of that union where sexual intercourse is sought after for its own sake.

Moreover, even though sometimes a man may seek to have offspring of such an intercourse, this is not befitting to the good of the offspring, which signifies not only the begetting of children from which they take their being, but also their rearing and instruction, by which means they receive *nourishment* and *learning* from their parents, in respect of which three things the parents are bound to their children, according to the Philosopher (*Ethics* 8.11–12).

Now since the rearing and teaching of the children remain a duty of the parents during a long period of time, the law of nature requires the father and mother to dwell together for a long time, in order that together they may be of assistance to their children. Hence birds that unite together in rearing their young do not sever their mutual fellowship from the time when they first come together until the young are fully fledged. Now this obligation which binds the female and her mate to remain together constitutes matrimony.

Consequently, it is evident that it is contrary to the natural law for a man to have intercourse with a woman who is not married to him, which is the signification of a concubine.

REPLY OBJ. 1: Among the gentiles, the natural law was obscured in many points: and consequently they did not think it wrong to have intercourse with a concubine, and in many cases practiced fornication as though it were lawful, as also other things contrary to the ceremonial laws of the Jews, though not contrary to the law of nature. Wherefore the apostles inserted the prohibition of fornication among that of other ceremonial observances, because in both cases there was a difference of opinion between Jews and gentiles.

REPLY OBJ. 2: This law was the result of the darkness just mentioned, into which the gentiles had fallen by not giving due honor to God, as stated in Romans 1:21, and did not proceed from the instinct of the natural law. Hence, when the Christian religion prevailed, this law was abolished.

REPLY OBJ. 3: In certain cases no evil results ensue if a person surrenders his right to a thing, whether absolutely

potestate habet alteri simpliciter tradat, ita etiam nec si tradat ad tempus: et sic neutrum est contra legem naturae. Ita autem non est in proposito. Ideo ratio non sequitur.

Ad quartum dicendum quod iniuria iustitiae opponitur. Lex autem naturalis non solum prohibet iniustitiam, sed etiam opposita omnium virtutum: sicut contra legem naturae est ut aliquis immoderate comedat, quamvis talis, rebus utens suis, nulli iniuriam facit. Et praeterea ancilla, quamvis sit res domini ad obsequium, non est tamen res sua ad concubitum. Et iterum interest qualiter quisque re sua utatur. Facit etiam talis iniuriam proli procreandae, ad cuius bonum non sufficienter talis coniunctio ordinatur, ut dictum est.

Ad quintum dicendum quod mulier habet potestatem in corpore viri non simpliciter quantum ad omnia, sed solum quantum ad matrimonium. Et ideo non potest contra bonum matrimonii corpus viri alteri praebere.

or for a time, so that in neither case is the surrender against the natural law. But that does not apply to the case in point, wherefore the argument does not prove.

Reply Obj. 4: Injury is opposed to justice. Now the natural law forbids not only injustice, but also whatever is opposed to any of the virtues: for instance, it is contrary to the natural law to eat immoderately, although by doing so a man uses his own property without injury to anyone. Moreover, although a slavewoman is her master's property that she may serve him, she is not his to be a concubine. And again it depends how a person makes use of his property. For such a man does an injury to the offspring he begets, since such a union is not directed to its good, as stated above.

Reply Obj. 5: The wife has power of her husband's body not simply and in all respects, but only in relation to marriage, and consequently she cannot transfer her husband's body to another to the detriment of the good of marriage.

Article 4

Whether It Is a Mortal Sin to Have Intercourse With a Concubine?

Ad quartum sic proceditur. Videtur quod accedere ad concubinam non sit peccatum mortale. Maius enim peccatum est mendacium quam fornicatio simplex: quod patet ex hoc quod ludas, qui fornicationem non horruit cum Thamar committere, recusavit mendacium, dicens 1: *certe mendacii arguere nos non poterit.* Sed mendacium non est semper peccatum mortale. Ergo neque fornicatio simplex.

Praeterea, peccatum mortale morte puniri debet. Sed lex vetus non puniebat concubitum concubinae morte, nisi in aliquo casu, ut patet Deut. 22. Ergo non est peccatum mortale.

Praeterea, secundum Gregorium, peccata mortalia carnalia sunt minoris culpae quam spiritualia. Sed non omnis superbia aut avaritia est peccatum mortale, quae sunt spiritualia peccata. Ergo non omnis fornicatio, quae est peccatum carnale.

Praeterea, ubi est maius incitamentum, ibi est minus peccatum: quia magis peccat qui minori tentatione vincitur. Sed concupiscentia maxime instigat ad venerea. Ergo, cum actus gulae non semper sit peccatum mortale, nec fornicatio simplex erit mortale.

Sed contra: Nihil excludit a regno Dei nisi peccatum mortale. Sed fornicatores excluduntur a regno Dei, ut patet I ad Cor. 6. Ergo fornicatio simplex est peccatum mortale.

Praeterea, sola peccata mortalia crimina dicuntur. Sed fornicatio dicitur crimen: ut patet Tobiae 4, *at-*

Objection 1: It would seem that it is not a mortal sin to have intercourse with a concubine. For a lie is a greater sin than simple fornication: and a proof of this is that Judah, who did not abhor to commit fornication with Tamar, recoiled from telling a lie, saying: *surely she cannot charge us with a lie* (Gen 38:23). But a lie is not always a mortal sin. Neither, therefore, is simple fornication.

Obj. 2: Further, a mortal sin should be punished with death. But the old law did not punish with death intercourse with a concubine, save in a certain case (Deut 22:25). Therefore, it is not a mortal sin.

Obj. 3: Further, according to Gregory (*Morals on Job* 33.12), the sins of the flesh are less blameworthy than spiritual sins. Now pride and covetousness, which are spiritual sins, are not always mortal sins. Therefore, fornication, which is a sin of the flesh, is not always a mortal sin.

Obj. 4: Further, where the incentive is greater, the sin is less grievous, because he sins more who is overcome by a lighter temptation. But concupiscence is the greatest incentive to lust. Therefore, since lustful actions are not always mortal sins, neither is simple fornication a mortal sin.

On the contrary, Nothing but mortal sin excludes from the kingdom of God. But fornicators are excluded from the kingdom of God (1 Cor 6:9–10). Therefore, simple fornication is a mortal sin.

Further, Mortal sins alone are called crimes. Now all fornication is a crime, according to Tobit 4:13: *take heed to*

tende tibi ab omni fornicatione, et praeter uxorem tuam nunquam patiaris crimen scire.

Respondeo dicendum quod, sicut in Secunda Parte dictum est, illi actus ex suo genere sunt peccata mortalia per quos foedus amicitiae hominis ad Deum et hominis ad hominem violatur: haec enim sunt contra duo praecepta caritatis, quae est animae vita. Et ideo, cum concubitus fornicarius tollat debitam ordinationem parentis ad prolem, quam natura ex concubitu intendit, non est dubium quod fornicatio simplex de sui ratione est peccatum mortale, etiam si lex scripta non esset.

Ad primum ergo dicendum quod frequenter homo qui non vitat peccatum mortale, vitat aliquod peccatum veniale, ad quod non habet tantum incitamentum. Et ita etiam ludas mendacium vitavit, fornicationem non vitans. Quamvis illud mendacium perniciosum fuisset, iniuriam habens annexam, si promissum non reddidisset.

Ad secundum dicendum quod peccatum non dicitur mortale quia morte temporali puniatur, sed quia punitur aeterna. Unde etiam furtum, quod est peccatum mortale, et multa alia, interdum non puniuntur per leges temporali morte. Et similiter etiam est de fornicatione.

Ad tertium dicendum quod, sicut non quilibet motus superbiae est peccatum mortale, ita nec quilibet motus luxuriae: quia primi motus luxuriae et huiusmodi sunt peccata venialia, et etiam concubitus matrimonialis interdum. Tamen aliqui luxuriae actus sunt peccata, mortalia, aliquibus motibus superbiae venialibus existentibus: quia in verbis Gregorii inductis intelligitur comparatio vitiorum secundum genus, non quantum ad singulos actus.

Ad quartum dicendum quod illa circumstantia efficacior est ad gravandum quae magis appropinquat ad speciem peccati. Unde, quamvis fornicatio ex magnitudine incitamenti diminuatur, tamen ex materia circa quam est, gravitatem habet maiorem quam inordinata comestio: cum sit circa ea quae pertinent ad fovendum foedus societatis humanae. Et ideo ratio non sequitur.

keep yourself from all fornication, and beside your wife never endure to know crime. Therefore, etc.

I answer that, As we have already stated (*Sentences* II, D. 42, Q. 1, A. 4), those sins are mortal in their genus which violate the bond of friendship between man and God, and between man and man; for such sins are against the two precepts of charity, which is the life of the soul. Therefore, since the intercourse of fornication destroys the due relations of the parent with the offspring that is nature's aim in sexual intercourse, there can be no doubt that simple fornication by its very nature is a mortal sin, even though there were no written law.

Reply Obj. 1: It often happens that a man who does not avoid a mortal sin avoids a venial sin to which he has not so great an incentive. Thus, too, Judah avoided a lie while he avoided not fornication. Nevertheless, that would have been a pernicious lie, for it would have involved an injury if he had not kept his promise.

Reply Obj. 2: A sin is called mortal not because it is punished with temporal, but because it is punished with eternal death. Hence also theft, which is a mortal sin, and many other sins are sometimes not punished with temporal death by the law. The same applies to fornication.

Reply Obj. 3: Just as not every movement of pride is a mortal sin, so neither is every movement of lust, because the first movements of lust and the like are venial sins, even sometimes marriage intercourse. Nevertheless, some acts of lust are mortal sins, while some movements of pride are venial: since the words quoted from Gregory are to be understood as comparing vices in their genus and not in their particular acts.

Reply Obj. 4: A circumstance is the more effective in aggravating a sin according as it comes nearer to the nature of sin. Thus, although fornication is less grave on account of the greatness of its incentive, yet on account of the matter about which it is, it has a greater gravity than immoderate eating, because it is about those things which tighten the bond of human fellowship, as stated above. Hence the argument does not prove.

Article 5

Whether It Was Ever Lawful to Have a Concubine?

Ad quintum sic proceditur. Videtur quod aliquando licitum fuerit concubinam habere. Sicut enim habere unam uxorem est de lege naturae, ita non habere concubinam. Sed aliquando licuit plures uxores habere. Ergo et habere concubinam.

Objection 1: It would seem that it has been sometimes lawful to have a concubine. For just as the natural law requires a man to have but one wife, so does it forbid him to have a concubine. Yet at times it has been lawful to have several wives. Therefore, it has also been lawful to have a concubine.

Praeterea, non potest aliqua simul esse ancilla et uxor: unde secundum legem ex hoc ipso quod ancilla in matrimonium ducebatur, libera reddebatur. Sed aliqui amicissimi Deo leguntur ad suas accessisse ancillas; sicut Abraham et Iacob. Ergo illae non erant uxores. Et sic aliquando licuit concubinas habere.

Praeterea, illa quae in matrimonium ducitur, non potest eiici, et filius eius debet esse haereditatis particeps. Sed Abraham eiecit Agar, et filius eius non fuit haeres. Ergo non fuit uxor Abrahae.

Sed contra: Ea quae sunt contra praecepta Decalogi, nunquam licuerunt. Sed habere concubinam est contra praeceptum Decalogi, scilicet; *non moechaberis*. Ergo nunquam fuit licitum.

Praeterea, Ambrosius dicit, in libro *de Patriarchis*: *viro non licet quod mulieri non licet*. Sed nunquam licuit mulieri ad alium virum accedere, dimisso viro proprio. Ergo nec viro unquam licuit concubinam habere.

Respondeo dicendum quod Rabbi Moyses dicit quod ante tempus legis fornicatio non erat peccatum: quod probat ex hoc quod ludas cum Thamar concubuit. Sed ista ratio non cogit. Non enim necesse est filios Iacob a peccato excusari: cum accusati fuerint apud patrem *crimine pessimo*, et in Ioseph necem vel venditionem consenserint.

Et ideo dicendum est quod, cum habere concubinam non matrimonio iunctam sit contra legem naturae, nullo tempore secundum se licitum fuit, nec etiam ex dispensatione. Sicut enim ex dictis patet, concubitus cum ea quae non est matrimonio iuncta, non est convenient actus ad bonum prolis, quod est principalis finis matrimonii. Et ideo est contra prima praecepta legis naturae, quae dispensationem non recipiunt.

Unde ubicumque legitur in veteri Testamento aliquos concubinas habuisse quos necesse sit a peccato mortali excusari, oportet eas esse matrimonio iunctas, et tamen concubinas dici quia aliquid habebant de ratione uxoris et aliquid de ratione concubinae. Secundum enim quod matrimonium ordinatur ad suum principalem finem, qui est bonum prolis, uxor viro coniungitur insolubili coniunctione, vel saltem diuturna, ut ex dictis patet: et contra hoc non est aliqua dispensatio. Sed quantum ad secundum finem, qui est dispensatio familiae et communicatio operturi, uxor coniungitur viro ut socia. Sed hoc deerat in his quae concubinae nominantur. In hoc enim poterat esse dispensatio: eum sit secundarius matrimo-

Obj. 2: Further, a woman cannot be at the same time a slave and a wife; wherefore according to the law (Deut 21:11) a slavewoman gained her freedom by the very fact of being taken in marriage. Now we read that certain men who were most beloved of God, for instance, Abraham and Jacob, had intercourse with their bondswomen. Therefore, these were not wives, and consequently it was sometime lawful to have a concubine.

Obj. 3: Further, a woman who is taken in marriage cannot be cast out, and her son should have a share in the inheritance. Yet Abraham sent Hagar away, and her son was not his heir (Gen 21:14). Therefore, she was not Abraham's wife.

On the contrary, Things opposed to the precepts of the Decalogue were never lawful. Now to have a concubine is against a precept of the Decalogue, namely, *thou shalt not commit adultery*. Therefore, it was never lawful.

Further, Ambrose says in his book on the patriarchs (*On Abraham* 1.4): *what is unlawful to a wife is unlawful to a husband*. But it is never lawful for a wife to put aside her own husband and have intercourse with another man. Therefore, it was never lawful for a husband to have a concubine.

I answer that, Rabbi Moses says (*Guide for the Perplexed* 3.49) that before the time of the law fornication was not a sin; and he proved his assertion from the fact that Judah had intercourse with Tamar. But this argument is not conclusive. For there is no need to excuse Jacob's sons from mortal sin, since they were accused to their father of a *most wicked crime* (Gen 37:2), and consented kill Joseph and to sell him.

Wherefore we must say that since it is against the natural law to have a concubine outside wedlock, as stated above (A. 3), it was never lawful either in itself or by dispensation. For, as we have shown, intercourse with a woman outside wedlock is an action improportionate to the good of the offspring, which is the principal end of marriage: and consequently it is against the first precepts of the natural law which admit of no dispensation.

Hence wherever in the Old Testament we read of concubines being taken by such men as we ought to excuse from mortal sin, we must understand them to have been taken in marriage, and yet to have been called concubines, because they had something of the character of a wife and something of the character of a concubine. Insofar as marriage is directed to its principal end, which is the good of the offspring, the union of wife and husband is indissoluble or at least of a lasting nature, as shown above (A. 1), and in regard to this there is no dispensation. But in regard to the secondary end, which is the management of the household and community of works, the wife is united to the husband as his mate: and this was lacking in those who were known

nii finis. Et ex hac parte habebant aliquid simile concubinis, ratione cuius concubinae nominantur.

AD PRIMUM ergo dicendum quod habere plures uxores non est contra legis naturae prima praecepta, sicut habere concubinam. Et ideo ratio non sequitur.

AD SECUNDUM dicendum quod antiqui Patres, ea dispensatione qua plures uxores habebant, ad ancillas accedebant uxorio affectu. Erant enim uxores quantum ad principalem et primarium finem matrimonii. Sed non erant uxores quantum ad illam coniunctionem quae respicit secundarium finem, cui conditio servitutis opponitur, cum non possit simul esse socia et ancilla.

AD TERTIUM dicendum quod, sicut in lege Moysi per dispensationem licebat dare libellum repudii ad evitandum uxoricidium, ut dicetur; ita ex eadem dispensatione licuit Abrahae eiicere Agar, ad significandum mysterium quod Apostolus explicat, Galat. 4. Quod etiam ille filius haeres non fuit, ad mysterium pertinet, ut ibidem patet. Sicut etiam ad mysterium pertinet quod Esau, filius liberae, haeres non fuit: ut patet Rom. 9. Similiter etiam propter mysterium factum est ut filii Iacob ex ancillis et liberis nati haeredes essent, ut Augustinus dicit: quia Christo nascuntur in baptismo filii tam per bonos, quos liberae significant, quam per malos ministros, qui per ancillas significantur.

as concubines. For in this respect a dispensation was possible, since it is the secondary end of marriage. And from this point of view they bore some resemblance to concubines, and for this reason they were known as such.

REPLY OBJ. 1: As stated above (A. 1) to have several wives is not against the first precepts of the natural law as is to have a concubine; thus the argument does not follow.

REPLY OBJ. 2: The patriarchs of old, by virtue of the dispensation which allowed them several wives, approached their bondswomen with the disposition of a husband toward his wife. For these women were wives as to the principal and first end of marriage, but not as to the other union which regards the secondary end, to which bondage is opposed, since a woman cannot be at once mate and slave.

REPLY OBJ. 3: As in the Mosaic law it was allowable by dispensation to grant a bill of divorce in order to avoid uxoricide (as we shall state further on, Q. 67, A. 6), so by the same dispensation Abraham was allowed to send Agar away, in order to signify the mystery which the Apostle explains (Gal 4:22). Again, that this son did not inherit belongs to the mystery, as explained in the same place. Even so Esau, the son of a free woman, did not inherit (Rom 9:13). In like manner, on account of the mystery it came about that the sons of Jacob born of bond and free women inherited, as Augustine says (*Tractates on John* 11) because sons and heirs are born to Christ both of good ministers (denoted by the free woman) and of evil ministers (denoted by the slavewoman).

QUESTION 66

BIGAMY AND THE IRREGULARITY CONTRACTED THEREBY

Deinde considerandum est de bigamia et irregularitate ex ea contracta.

Circa quod quaeruntur quinque.

Primo: utrum illi bigamiae quae est ex hoc quod aliquis duas uxores successive habuerit, sit irregularitas annexa.

Secundo: utrum irregularitatem contrahat qui simul vel successive duas uxores habuit, unam de iure, aliam de facto.

Tertio: utrum irregularitas contrahatur ex hoc quod quis uxorem virginem non accepit.

Quarto: utrum bigamia per baptismum solvatur,

Quinto: utrum cum bigamo liceat dispensare.

In the next place we must consider bigamy and the irregularity contracted thereby.

Under this head there are five points of inquiry.

(1) Whether irregularity attaches to the bigamy that consists in having two successive wives?

(2) Whether irregularity is contracted by one who has two wives at once, one according to law, the other in fact?

(3) Whether irregularity is contracted by marrying one who is not a virgin?

(4) Whether bigamy is removed by baptism?

(5) Whether a dispensation can be granted to a bigamous person?

Article 1

Whether Irregularity Attaches to the Bigamy That Consists in Having Two Wives Successively?

AD PRIMUM SIC PROCEDITUR. Videtur quod illi bigamiae quae est ex hoc quod aliquis duas uxores successive habuit, non sit irregularitas annexa. Quia multitudo et unitas consequuntur ens. Ergo ens et non ens non faciunt multitudinem aliquam. Sed ille qui habet successive duas uxores, quando una est in esse, alia non est in esse. Ergo ex hoc non efficitur vir *non unius uxoris*, qui, secundum Apostolum, ab episcopatu prohibetur.

PRAETEREA, maius signum incontinentiae apparet in eo qui plures fornicarie cognoscit quam qui plures uxores successive habet. Sed ex primo non efficitur aliquis irregularis. Ergo nec ex secundo.

PRAETEREA, si bigamia irregularitatem causat, aut hoc est ratione sacramenti, aut ratione carnalis copulae. Sed non ratione primi: quia sic, si aliquis cum una contraxisset per verba de praesenti, et, ea mortua ante carnalem copulam subsecutam, duceret aliam, efficeretur irregularis; quod est contra decretalem Innocentii III. Nec iterum ratione secundi: quia secundum hoc etiam qui plures fornicario concubitu cognosceret, irregularis esset; quod falsum est. Ergo nullo modo bigamia irregularitatem causat.

RESPONDEO dicendum quod aliquis per sacramentum ordinis minister sacramentorum constituitur: et ille qui aliis sacramenta ministrare debet, nullum defectum

OBJECTION 1: It would seem that irregularity is not attached to the bigamy that consists in having two wives successively. For multitude and unity are consequent upon being. Since, then, non-being does not cause plurality, a man who has two wives successively, the one in being, the other in non-being, does not thereby become the husband *of more than one wife*, so as to be debarred, according to the Apostle (1 Tim 3:2; Titus 1:6), from the episcopate.

OBJ. 2: Further, a man who commits fornication with several women gives more evidence of incontinence than one who has several wives successively. Yet in the first case a man does not become irregular. Therefore, neither in the second should he become irregular.

OBJ. 3: Further, if bigamy causes irregularity, this is either because of the sacrament or because of the carnal intercourse. Now it is not on account of the former, for if a man had contracted marriage by words of the present and, his wife dying before the consummation of the marriage, he were to marry another, he would become irregular, which is against the decree of Innocent III (*Register*). Nor again is it on account of the second, for then a man who had committed fornication with several women would become irregular: which is false. Therefore, bigamy in no way causes irregularity.

I ANSWER THAT, By the sacrament of order a man is appointed to the ministry of the sacraments; and he who has to administer the sacraments to others must suffer from no

in sacramentis pati debet. Defectus autem in sacramento est quando sacramenti significatio integra non invenitur. Sacramentum autem matrimonii significat coniunctionem Christi ad Ecclesiam, quae est unius ad unam. Et ideo requiritur ad perfectam significationem sacramenti quod vir sit tantum unius vir, et uxor sit tantum unius uxor. Et ideo bigamia, quae hoc tollit, irregularitatem inducit.

Et sunt quattuor modi bigamiae. Primus est, cum quis plures habet uxores de iure successive. Secundus, cum simul habet plures, unam de iure, aliam de facto. Tertius, cum habet plures successive, unam de iure, aliam de facto. Quartus, quando viduam ducit uxorem. Et in omnibus his est irregularitas adiuncta.

Alia autem causa Consequens assignatur: quia in illis qui accipiunt sacramentum ordinis, maxima spiritualitas debet apparere; tum quia spiritualia ministrant, scilicet sacramenta; tum quia spiritualia docent; et in spiritualibus occupari debent. Unde, cum concupiscentia maxime spiritualitati repugnet, per quam *totus homo caro efficitur*, non debet aliquod signum concupiscentiae permanentis in eis apparere. Quod quidem apparet in bigamis, qui una uxore contenti esse noluerunt. Tamen prima ratio est melior.

AD PRIMUM ergo dicendum quod multitudo plurium uxorum simul existentium est multitudo simpliciter. Et ideo talis multitudo totaliter significationi sacramenti repugnat. Et propter hoc tollitur sacramentum. Sed multitudo uxorum successive est multitudo secundum quid. Et ideo non tollit significationem sacramenti totaliter: nec sacramentum evacuat quantum ad sui essentiam, sed quantum ad sui perfectionem. Quae requiritur in illis qui sunt sacramentorum dispensatores.

AD SECUNDUM dicendum quod, quamvis sit in fornicariis maioris concupiscentiae signum, non tamen concupiscentiae ita adhaerentis: quia per fornicationem unus alteri non in perpetuo obligatur. Et iterum non est defectus sacramenti.

AD TERTIUM dicendum quod, sicut dictum est, bigamia causat irregularitatem inquantum tollit perfectam significationem matrimonii, quae quidem consistit et in coniunctione animorum, quae fit per consensum, et in coniunctione corporum. Et ideo ratione utriusque simul oportet esse bigamiam quae irregularitatem faciat. Unde per decretalem Innocentii III derogatur ei quod Magister in littera dicit, scilicet quod solus consensus per verba de praesenti sufficit ad irregularitatem inducendam.

defect in the sacraments. Now, there is a defect in a sacrament when the entire signification of the sacrament is not found therein. And the sacrament of marriage signifies the union of Christ with the Church, which is the union of one with one. Therefore, the perfect signification of the sacrament requires the husband to have only one wife, and the wife to have but one husband; and consequently bigamy, which does away with this, causes irregularity.

And there are four kinds of bigamy: the first is when a man has several lawful wives successively; the second is when a man has several wives at once, one in law, the other in fact; the third, when he has several successively, one in law, the other in fact; the fourth, when a man marries a widow. Accordingly, irregularity attaches to all of these.

There is another consequent reason assigned: since those who receive the sacrament of order should be signalized by the greatest spirituality, both because they administer spiritual things, namely, the sacraments, and because they teach spiritual things and should be occupied in spiritual matters. Wherefore since concupiscence is most incompatible with spirituality, inasmuch as *it makes a man to be wholly carnal*, they should give no sign of persistent concupiscence, which does indeed show itself in bigamous persons, seeing that they were unwilling to be content with one wife. The first reason, however, is the better.

REPLY OBJ. 1: The multitude of several wives at the same time is a multitude simply, wherefore a multitude of this kind is wholly inconsistent with the signification of the sacrament, so that the sacrament is voided on that account. But the multitude of several successive wives is a multitude relatively, wherefore it does not entirely destroy the signification of the sacrament, nor does it void the sacrament in its essence but in its perfection, which is required of those who are the dispensers of sacraments.

REPLY OBJ. 2: Although those who are guilty of fornication give proof of greater concupiscence, theirs is not a so persistent concupiscence, since by fornication one party is not bound to the other forever; and consequently no defect attaches to the sacrament.

REPLY OBJ. 3: As stated above, bigamy causes irregularity because it destroys the perfect signification of the sacrament: which signification is seated both in the union of minds, as expressed by the consent, and in the union of bodies. Wherefore bigamy must affect both of these at the same time in order to cause irregularity. Hence the decree of Innocent III disposes of the statement of the Master (*Sentences* IV, D. 27), namely, that consent alone by words of the present is sufficient to cause irregularity.

Article 2

*Whether Irregularity Results From Bigamy When One Husband Has
Two Wives, One in Law, the Other in Fact?*

Ad secundum sic proceditur. Videtur quod irregularitas non sit annexa bigamiae quae contingit ex hoc quod homo habet duas uxores, simul vel successive, unam de iure, aliam de facto. Quia ubi nullum est sacramentum, non potest esse defectus sacramenti. Sed quando aliquis contrahit de facto cum aliqua et non de iure, non est ibi aliquod sacramentum: quia talis coniunctio non significat coniunctionem Christi ad Ecclesiam. Ergo, cum irregularitas non consequatur bigamiam nisi propter defectum sacramenti, videtur quod talem bigamiam irregularitas non consequatur.

Praeterea, aliquis accedens ad illam cum qua contrahit de facto et non de iure, committit fornicationem si non habeat aliam uxorem legitimam, vel adulterium si habeat aliam. Sed *dividere carnem suam in plures* per fornicationem vel adulterium non causat irregularitatem. Ergo nec dictus bigamiae modus.

Praeterea, contingit quod aliquis, antequam cognoscat carnaliter illam cum qua de iure contraxit, cum alia contrahat de facto non de iure, et eam carnaliter cognoscat, sive prima mortua sive vivente. Talis contraxit cum pluribus vel de iure vel de facto, et tamen non est irregularis, quia *carnem suam non divisit in plures*. Ergo ex praedicto modo bigamiae non contrahitur irregularitas.

Respondeo dicendum quod in secundis duobus modis bigamiae contrahitur irregularitas, quia, quamvis in altero non sit sacramentum, est tamen quaedam sacramenti similitudo. Unde isti duo modi sunt secundarii, et primus est principalis in irregularitate causanda.

Ad primum ergo dicendum quod, quamvis ibi non sit sacramentum, est tamen ibi aliqua similitudo sacramenti. Quae non est in fornicatione vel adulterino concubitu. Et ideo non est simile.

Et per hoc patet solutio ad secundum.

Ad tertium dicendum quod in tali casu non reputatur bigamus, quia primum matrimonium non habuit perfectam significationem suam. Tamen si per iudicium Ecclesiae compellatur ad primam redire et eam cognoscere, statim efficitur irregularis: quia irregularitatem non facit peccatura, sed imperfectio significationis.

Objection 1: It would seem that irregularity does not result from bigamy when one husband has two wives at the same time, one in law and one in fact. For when the sacrament is void there can be no defect in the sacrament. Now when a man marries a woman in fact but not in law there is no sacrament, since such a union does not signify the union of Christ with the Church. Therefore, since irregularity does not result from bigamy except on account of a defect in the sacrament, it would seem that no irregularity attaches to bigamy of this kind.

Obj. 2: Further, if a man has intercourse with a woman whom he has married in fact and not in law, he commits fornication if he has not a lawful wife, or adultery if he has. But a man does not become irregular by *dividing his flesh among several women* by fornication or adultery. Therefore, neither does he by the aforesaid kind of bigamy.

Obj. 3: Further, it may happen that a man, before knowing carnally the woman he has married in law, marries another in fact and not in law, and knows her carnally whether the former woman be living or dead. Now this man has contracted marriage with several women either in law or in fact, and yet he is not irregular, since *he has not divided his flesh among several women*. Therefore, irregularity is not contracted by reason of the aforesaid kind of bigamy.

I answer that, Irregularity is contracted in the two second kinds of bigamy, for although in the one there is no sacrament, there is a certain likeness to a sacrament. Wherefore these two kinds are secondary, and the first is the principal kind in causing irregularity.

Reply Obj. 1: Although there is no sacrament in this case, there is a certain likeness to a sacrament, whereas there is no such likeness in fornication or adultery. Hence the comparison fails.

This suffices for the reply to the second objection.

Reply Obj. 3: In this case the man is not reckoned a bigamist because the first marriage lacked its perfect signification. Nevertheless, if by the judgment of the Church he is compelled to return to his first wife and carnally to know her, he becomes irregular forthwith, because the irregularity is the result not of the sin, but of imperfect signification.

Article 3

Whether Irregularity is Contracted by Marrying One Who Is Not a Virgin?

AD TERTIUM SIC PROCEDITUR. Videtur quod non contrahatur irregularitas ex hoc quod aliquis ducit uxorem non virginem. Quia plus impeditur aliquis defectu proprio quam alieno. Sed si ipse contrahens non sit virgo, non fit irregularis. Ergo multo minus si uxor: eius virgo non sit.

PRAETEREA, potest esse quod aliquis defloravit aliquam et postea ducat eam in uxorem. Talis non videtur fieri irregularis: quia *non divisit carnem in plures*, nec etiam uxor eius. Sed tamen ducit corruptam in uxorem. Ergo talis modus bigamiae non causat irregularitatem.

PRAETEREA, nullus potest contrahere irregularitatem nisi voluntarius. Sed aliquis quandoque ducit uxorem non virginem involuntarius: ut quando credit eam virginem esse et postea invenit eam corruptam fuisse cognoscens eam. Ergo talis modus non semper facit irregularitatem.

PRAETEREA, corruptio sequens matrimonium est vituperabilior quam praecedens. Sed si uxor, postquam est consummatum matrimonium, ab alio cognoscatur, non efficitur vir irregularis: alias puniretur pro peccato uxoris. Et potest etiam esse, postquam hoc sciat, quod reddat ei debitum poscenti, antequam de adulterio accusata condemnetur. Ergo videtur quod ille modus bigamiae non causet irregularitatem.

SED CONTRA est quod Gregorius dicit: *praecipimus ne unquam illicitas ordinationes facias: ne bigamum, aut qui virginem non est sortitus in uxorem, aut ignorantem litteras, aut qualibet parte corporis vitiatum, vel poenitentiae vel curiae aut cuilibet conditioni obnoxium, ad sacros ordines permittas accedere.*

RESPONDEO dicendum quod in coniunctione Christi et Ecclesiae unitas ex utraque parte invenitur. Et ideo, sive divisio carnis inveniatur ex parte viri sive ex parte uxoris, est defectus sacramenti. Sed tamen diversimode: quia ex parte viri requiritur quod aliam non duxerit in uxorem, non quod sit virgo; sed ex parte uxoris requiritur quod etiam sit virgo.

Cuius ratio a Decretistis assignatur, quia episcopus significat Ecclesiam militantem, cuius curam gerit, in qua sunt multae corruptiones: sed sponsa significat Christum, qui virgo fuit. Et ideo ex parte sponsae requiritur virginitas, sed non ex parte sponsi, ad hoc quod aliquis episcopus fieri possit, Sed haec ratio est expresse contra Apostolum, Ephes. 5: *viri, diligite uxores vestras, sicut et Christus Ecclesiam*: ex quo apparet quod uxor si-

OBJECTION 1: It would seem that irregularity is not contracted by marrying one who is not a virgin. For a man's own defect is a greater impediment to him than the defect of another. But if the man himself who marries is not a virgin, he does not become irregular. Therefore, much less does he if his wife is not a virgin.

OBJ. 2: Further, it may happen that a man marries a woman after corrupting her. Now, seemingly, such a man does not become irregular, since *he has not divided his flesh among several*, nor has his wife done so, and yet he marries a woman who is not a virgin. Therefore, this kind of bigamy does not cause irregularity.

OBJ. 3: Further, no man can become irregular except voluntarily. But sometimes a man involuntarily marries one who is not a virgin, for instance, when he thinks her a virgin and afterwards, by knowing her carnally, finds that she is not. Therefore, this kind does not always cause irregularity.

OBJ. 4: Further, unlawful intercourse after marriage is more guilty than before marriage. Now if a wife, after the marriage has been consummated, has intercourse with another man, her husband does not become irregular, otherwise he would be punished for his wife's sin. Moreover, it might happen that, after knowing of this, he pays her the debt at her asking before she is accused and convicted of adultery. Therefore, it would seem that this kind of bigamy does not cause irregularity.

ON THE CONTRARY, Gregory says (*Register* 2.37): *we command you never to make unlawful ordinations, nor to admit to holy orders a bigamist, or one who has married a woman that is not a virgin, or one who is unlettered, or one who is deformed in his limbs, or bound to do penance or to perform some civil duty, or who is in any state of subjection.*

I ANSWER THAT, In the union of Christ with the Church, unity is found on either side. Consequently, whether we find division of the flesh on the part of the husband, or on the part of the wife, there is a defect of sacrament. There is, however, a difference, because on the part of the husband it is required that he should not have married another wife, but not that he should be a virgin, whereas on the part of the wife it is also required that she be a virgin.

The reason assigned by those versed in the *Decretals* is because the bridegroom signifies the Church Militant which is entrusted to the care of a bishop, and in which there are many corruptions, while the spouse signifies Christ who was a virgin: wherefore virginity on the part of the bride, but not on the part of the bridegroom, is required in order that a man be made a bishop. This reason, however, is expressly contrary to the words of the Apostle:

gnificat Ecclesiam, et sponsus Christum. Et iterum: *quia vir est caput mulieris, sicut Christus Ecclesiae.*

Et ideo alii dicunt quod per sponsum significatur Christus, per sponsam Ecclesia triumphans, in qua *non est aliqua macula.* Christus autem primo habuit synagogam, quasi concubinam. Et sic non tollitur aliquid de perfectione significationis sacramenti si sponsus prius habuit.

Sed hoc est valde absurdum. Quia, sicut est una fides antiquorum et modernorum, ita una Ecclesia. Unde, illi qui tempore synagogae Deo serviebant, ad unitatem Ecclesiae, in qua Deo servimus, pertinebant. Et praeterea hoc est expresse contra illud quod habetur Ierem. 3 et Ezech. 16 et Osee 2, ubi expresse fit mentio de desponsatione synagogae. Unde non fuit sicut concubina, sed sicut uxor. Et praeterea secundum hoc fornicatio esset sacramentum illius coniunctionis: quod est absurdum. Et ideo gentilitas, priusquam desponsaretur a Christo in fide Ecclesiae, corrupta fuit a diabolo per idololatriam.

Et ideo aliter dicendum, quod defectus in ipso sacramento causat irregularitatem. Corruptio autem carnis extra matrimonium contingens quae praecessit matrimonium, nullum defectum facit in sacramento ex parte illius in quo est corruptio, sed facit defectum ex parte alterius; quia actus contrahentis matrimonium non cadit supra seipsum, sed supra alterum; et ideo ex termino specificatur, qui etiam est respectu illius actus quasi materia sacramenti. Unde, si mulier esset ordinis susceptiva, sicut vir efficitur irregularis ex hoc quod ducit in uxorem corruptam, non autem ex hoc quod corruptus contrahit; ita fieret mulier irregularis si contraheret cum corrupto, non autem si contraheret corrupta; nisi in alio matrimonio prius corrupta fuisset.

ET PER HOC patet solutio ad primum.

AD SECUNDUM dicendum quod in tali casu sunt diversae opiniones. Tamen probabilius est quod non sit irregularis: quia *carnem suam non divisit in plures.*

AD TERTIUM dicendum quod irregularitas non est poena inflicta, sed defectus quidam sacramenti. Et ideo non oportet quod semper sit voluntaria bigamia ad hoc quod irregularitatem causet. Et ideo ille qui uxorem ducit corruptam quam virginem credit, irregularis est eam cognoscens.

AD QUARTUM dicendum quod, si mulier fornicetur post matrimonium contractum, non efficitur ex hoc vir irregularis, nisi post corruptionem adulterinam eam iterato cognoscat: quia alias corruptio uxoris nullo modo cadit sub actu matrimoniali viri. Sed si etiam per ius

husbands, love your wives, as Christ also loved the Church (Eph 5:25), which show that the bride signifies the Church, and the bridegroom Christ; and again he says: *because the husband is the head of the wife, as Christ is the head of the Church* (Eph 5:23).

Wherefore others say that Christ is signified by the bridegroom, and that the bride signifies the Church Triumphant in which *there is no stain.* Also that the synagogue was first united to Christ as a concubine; so that the sacrament loses nothing of its signification if the bridegroom previously had a concubine.

But this is most absurd, since just as the faith of ancients and of moderns is one, so is the Church one. Wherefore those who served God at the time of the synagogue belonged to the unity of the Church in which we serve God. Moreover, this is expressly contrary to Jeremiah 3:14, Ezekial 16:8, and Hosea 2:16, where the espousals of the synagogue are mentioned explicitly: so that she was not as a concubine but as a wife. Again, according to this, fornication would be the sacred sign of that union, which is absurd. Wherefore heathendom, before being espoused to Christ in the faith of the Church, was corrupted by the devil through idolatry.

Hence we must say otherwise that irregularity is caused by a defect in the sacrament itself. Now when corruption of the flesh occurs outside wedlock on account of a preceding marriage, it causes no defect in the sacrament on the part of the person corrupted, but it causes a defect in the other person, because the act of one who contracts marriage terminates not in himself but in the other party, wherefore it takes its species from its term, which, moreover, in regard to that act is like the matter of the sacrament. Consequently, if a woman were able to receive holy orders, just as her husband becomes irregular through marrying one who is not a virgin, but not through his not being a virgin when he marries, so also would a woman become irregular if she were to marry a man who is not a virgin, but not if she were no longer a virgin when she married—unless she had been corrupted by reason of a previous marriage.

THIS SUFFICES for the reply to the first objection.

REPLY OBJ. 2: In this case opinions differ. It is, however, more probable that he is not irregular, because *he has not divided his flesh among several women.*

REPLY OBJ. 3: Irregularity is not the infliction of a punishment, but the defect of a sacrament. Consequently, it is not always necessary for bigamy to be voluntary in order to cause irregularity. Hence a man who marries a woman thinking her to be a virgin, whereas she is not, becomes irregular by knowing her carnally.

REPLY OBJ. 4: If a woman commits fornication after being married, her husband does not become irregular on that account, unless he again knows her carnally after she has been corrupted by adultery, since otherwise the corruption of the wife in no way affects the marriage act of

compellatur ei reddere debitum vel ex conscientia propria, illa petente debitum, ante condemnationem adulterii, irregularis efficitur. Quamvis de hoc sint opiniones: sed hoc quod dictum est, est probabilius; quia hic non quaeritur quid sit peccatum, sed significatio tantum.

the husband. But if he should be compelled to render the debt to her by right, or because of his own conscience, if she should ask for the debt before her condemnation as an adulterer, he would become irregular; although about this opinions vary. However, what we have said is more probable, since here it is not a question of sin, but of signification only.

Article 4

Whether Bigamy Is Removed by Baptism?

AD QUARTUM SIC PROCEDITUR. Videtur quod bigamia per baptismum solvatur. Dicit enim Hieronymus, super Epistolam ad Titum, quod, si quis ante baptismum plures uxores habuit, vel unam ante et aliam post, non est bigamus. Ergo bigamia per baptismum solvitur.

PRAETEREA, qui facit quod maius est, facit quod minus est. Sed baptismus tollit omne peccatum, quod est gravius quam irregularitas. Ergo tollit bigamiae irregularitatem.

PRAETEREA, baptismus tollit omnem poenam ex actu provenientem. Sed irregularitas bigamiae est huiusmodi. Ergo, ect.

PRAETEREA, bigamus est irregularis inquam tum deficit a repraesentatione Christi. Sed per baptismum plene Christo conformamur. Ergo solvitur illa irregularitas.

PRAETEREA, sacramenta novae legis sunt magis efficacia quam sacramenta veteris legis. Sed sacramenta veteris legis solvebant irregularitates, ut in principio Libri dictum est a Magistro. Ergo et baptismus, qui est efficacissimum sacramentum in nova lege, solvit irregularitatem ex bigamia contractam.

SED CONTRA: Est quod Augustinus dicit: *acutius intelligunt qui nec eum qui catechumenus aut paganus habuit alteram, ordinandum censuerunt: quia de sacramento agitur, non de peccato.*

PRAETEREA, sicut idem dicit, *femina, si catechumena vel pagana vitiata est, non potest inter Dei virgines post baptismum velari.* Ergo, eadem ratione, nec bigamus ante baptismum ordinari.

RESPONDEO dicendum quod baptismus solvit culpas, et non solvit coniugia. Unde, cum ex ipso coniugio sequatur irregularitas, per baptismum tolli non potest, ut Augustinus dicit.

OBJECTION 1: It would seem that bigamy is removed by baptism. For Jerome says in his commentary on the Epistle to Titus (on Titus 1:6: *the husband of one wife*) that if a man has had several wives before receiving baptism, or one before and another after baptism, he is not a bigamist. Therefore, bigamy is removed by baptism.

OBJ. 2: Further, he who does what is more, does what is less. Now baptism removes all sin, and sin is a greater thing than irregularity. Therefore, it removes irregularity.

OBJ. 3: Further, baptism takes away all punishment resulting from an act. Now such is the irregularity of bigamy. Therefore, etc.

OBJ. 4: Further, a bigamist is irregular because he is deficient in the representation of Christ. Now by baptism we are fully conformed to Christ. Therefore, this irregularity is removed.

OBJ. 5: Further, the sacraments of the new law are more efficacious than the sacraments of the old law. But the sacraments of the old law removed irregularities, according to the Master's statement (*Sentences* 4). And therefore baptism, being the most efficacious of the sacraments of the new law, removes the irregularity consequent upon bigamy.

ON THE CONTRARY, Augustine says: *those understand the question more correctly who maintain that a man who has married a second wife, though he was a catechumen or even a pagan at the time, cannot be ordained, because it is a question of a sacrament, not of a sin* (*On the Good of Marriage* 18).

FURTHER, According to the same authority, *a woman who has been corrupted while a catechumen or a pagan cannot after baptism be consecrated among God's virgins* (*On the Good of Marriage* 18). Therefore, in like manner one who was a bigamist before baptism cannot be ordained.

I ANSWER THAT, Baptism removes sin, but does not dissolve marriage. Therefore, since irregularity results from marriage, it cannot be removed by baptism, as Augustine says (*On the Good of Marriage* 18).

AD PRIMUM ergo dicendum quod in casu isto non tenetur Hieronymi opinio: nisi forte velimus eum exponere quod loquitur quantum ad faciliorem dispensationem.

AD SECUNDUM dicendum quod non oportet ut quod facit maius faciat minus, nisi sit ad illud ordinatum. Et hoc deficit in proposito: quia baptismus ad irregularitatem tollendam non ordinatur.

AD TERTIUM dicendum quod hoc intelligendum est de poenis quae consequuntur ex actuali peccato quasi inflictae, non infligendae. Non enim aliquis per baptismum virginitatem recuperat. Et similiter nec carnis indivisionem.

AD QUARTUM dicendum quod baptismus conformat Christo quantum ad virtutem mentis: sed non quantum ad statum carnis, qui consideratur in virginitate vel indivisione carnis.

AD QUINTUM dicendum quod illae irregularitates ex levibus causis non perpetuis erant contractae. Et ideo etiam per illa sacramenta auferri poterant. Et iterum, erant ad hoc ordinata. Non autem baptismus ad hoc ordinatur.

REPLY OBJ. 1: In this case Jerome's opinion is not to be held: unless perhaps he wished to explain that he means that a dispensation should be more easily granted.

REPLY OBJ. 2: It does not follow that what does a greater thing does a lesser, unless it be directed to the latter. This is not so in the case in point, because baptism is not directed to the removal of an irregularity.

REPLY OBJ. 3: This must be understood of punishments consequent upon actual sin, which are, or have yet to be, inflicted: for one does not recover virginity by baptism, nor again undivision of the flesh.

REPLY OBJ. 4: Baptism conforms a man to Christ as regards the virtue of the mind, but not as to the condition of the body, which is effected by virginity or division of the flesh.

REPLY OBJ. 5: Those irregularities were contracted through slight and temporary causes, and consequently they could be removed by those sacraments. Moreover, the latter were ordained for that purpose, whereas baptism is not.

Article 5

Whether It Is Lawful for a Bigamist to Receive a Dispensation?

AD QUINTUM SIC PROCEDITUR. Videtur quod cum bigamo non liceat dispensare. Quia Extra, *de Bigamis*, dicitur: *cum clericis qui, inquantum in ipsis fuit, secundas sibi mulieres coniunxerunt matrimonialiter, tanquam cum bigamis, non licet dispensare.*

PRAETEREA, contra ius divinum non licet dispensare. Sed omnia quae in canone dicuntur, ad ius divinum pertinent. Cum ergo Apostolus in Scriptura canonica dicat, *oportet episcopum unius uxoris virum esse*, videtur quod in hoc non possit dispensari.

PRAETEREA, nullus potest dispensare in his quae sunt de necessitate sacramenti. Sed non esse irregularem est de necessitate sacramenti ordinis: cum significatio, quae est sacramento essentialis, desit. Ergo non potest in hoc dispensari.

PRAETEREA, quod rationabiliter factum est, non potest rationabiliter mutari. Si ergo potest rationabiliter dispensari cum bigamo, irrationabiliter est ei adiuncta irregularitas. Quod est inconveniens.

SED IN CONTRARIUM: Est quod Lucius Papa dispensavit cum episcopo Panormitano, qui erat bigamus.

PRAETEREA, Martinus Papa dicit: *lector, si viduam uxorem accipiat, in lectoratu permaneat, aut, si necessi-*

OBJECTION 1: It would seem unlawful for a bigamist to be granted a dispensation. For it is said (*Decretals*): *it is not lawful to grant a dispensation to clerics who, as far as they could do so, have taken to themselves a second wife.*

OBJ. 2: Further, it is not lawful to grant a dispensation from the divine law. Now whatever is in the canonical writings belongs to the divine law. Since, then, in canonical Scripture the Apostle says: *a bishop ought to be the husband of one wife* (1 Tim 3:2), it would seem that a dispensation cannot be granted in this matter.

OBJ. 3: Further, no one can receive a dispensation in what is essential to a sacrament. But it is essential to the sacrament of order that the recipient be not irregular, since the signification which is essential to a sacrament is lacking in one who is irregular. Therefore, he cannot be granted a dispensation in this.

OBJ. 4: Further, what is reasonably done cannot be reasonably undone. If, therefore, a bigamist can lawfully receive a dispensation, it was unreasonable that he should be irregular: which is inadmissible.

ON THE CONTRARY, Pope Lucius granted a dispensation to the bishop of Palermo, who was a bigamist (*Decretals*).

FURTHER, Pope Martin (*Martinus Bracarensis*: cap. xliii) says: *if a lector marry a widow, let him remain a lec-*

tas fuerit, subdiaconus fiat: nihil autem supra. Similiter si bigamus fuerit. Ergo ad minus usque ad subdiaconatum cum eo dispensari potest.

Respondeo dicendum quod bigamiae non est adiuncta irregularitas de iure naturali, sed de iure positivo. Nec iterum est de essentialibus ordinis quod aliquis non sit bigamus: quod patet ex hoc quod, si aliquis bigamus ad ordines accedit, characterem accipit. Et ideo Papa potest dispensare in tali irregularitate totaliter: sed episcopus quantum ad minores ordines. Et quidam dicunt quod etiam quantum ad maiores in illis qui volunt Deo in religione servire, propter vitandum religiosorum discursum.

Ad primum ergo dicendum quod per illam Decretalem ostenditur eadem esse difficultas dispensandi in illis qui de facto cum pluribus contraxerunt, ac si de iure contraxissent: non quod subtrahatur simpliciter potestas Papae dispensandi in talibus.

Ad secundum dicendum quod hoc est verum quantum ad ea quae sunt de iure naturali, et quantum ad ea quae sunt de necessitate sacramentorum et fidei: sed in aliis, quae sunt de institutione Apostolorum, cum Ecclesia habeat nunc eandem potestatem statuendi et destituendi quam tunc habuit, potest per eum qui primatum in Ecclesia tenet, dispensari.

Ad tertium dicendum quod non quaelibet significatio est de essentia sacramenti, sed tantum illa quae pertinet ad officium sacramenti. Et talis non tollitur per irregularitatem.

Ad quartum dicendum quod in particularibus non potest inveniri ratio quae omnibus competat aequaliter, propter eorum diversitatem. Et ideo quod universaliter statutum est rationabiliter consideratis his quae in plurimis accidunt, potest etiam per dispensationem rationabiliter removeri in aliquo casu determinato.

tor, or if there be need for it, he may receive the subdiaconate, but no higher order: and the same applies if he should be a bigamist. Therefore, he may at least receive a dispensation as far as the subdiaconate.

I answer that, Irregularity attaches to bigamy not by natural, but by positive law; nor again is it one of the essentials of holy orders that a man be not a bigamist, which is evident from the fact that if a bigamist present himself for holy orders, he receives the character. Wherefore the Pope can dispense altogether from such an irregularity; but a bishop, only as regards the minor orders, though some say that in order to prevent religious wandering abroad he can dispense from it as regards the major orders in those who wish to serve God in religion.

Reply Obj. 1: This Decretal shows that there is the same difficulty against granting a dispensation in those who have married several wives in fact, as if they had married them in law; but it does not prove that the Pope has no power to grant a dispensation in such cases.

Reply Obj. 2: This is true as regards things belonging to the natural law, and those which are essential to the sacraments and to faith. But in those which owe their institution to the apostles, since the Church has the same power now as then of setting up and of putting down, she can grant a dispensation through him who holds the primacy.

Reply Obj. 3: Not every signification is essential to a sacrament, but that alone which belongs to the sacramental effect, and this is not removed by irregularity.

Reply Obj. 4: In particular cases there is no *ratio* that applies to all equally, on account of their variety. Hence what is reasonably established for all, in consideration of what happens in the majority of cases, can be with equal reason done away in a certain definite case.

QUESTION 67

THE BILL OF DIVORCE

Deinde considerandum est de libello repudii. Circa quod quaeruntur septem.

Primo: utrum inseparabilitas matrimonii sit de lege naturae.

Secundo: utrum repudiare uxorem possit esse licitum per dispensationem.

Tertio: utrum sub lege Moysi fuerit licitum.

Quarto: utrum liceret uxori repudiatae alium accipere.

Quinto: utrum liceret viro repudiatam a se iterum ducere.

Sexto: utrum causa repudii fuerit odium uxoris.

Septimo: utrum causae repudii deberent in libello scribi.

We must now consider the bill of divorce. Under this head there are seven points of inquiry:

(1) Whether the indissolubility of marriage is of natural law?

(2) Whether by dispensation it may become lawful to put away a wife?

(3) Whether it was lawful under the Mosaic law?

(4) Whether a wife who has been divorced may take another husband?

(5) Whether the husband can marry again the wife whom he has divorced?

(6) Whether the cause of divorce was hatred of the wife?

(7) Whether the reasons for divorce had to be written on the bill?

Article 1

Whether Inseparableness of the Wife Is of Natural Law?

AD PRIMUM SIC PROCEDITUR. Videtur, quod inseparabilitas uxoris non sit de lege naturae. Lex enim naturae communis est apud omnes. Sed nulla lege praeter legem Christi fuit prohibitum uxorem dimittere. Ergo inseparabilitas uxoris non est de lege naturae.

PRAETEREA, sacramenta non sunt de lege naturae. Sed inseparabilitas matrimonii ad sacramenti bonum pertinet. Ergo non est de lege naturae.

PRAETEREA, coniunctio viri et feminae in matrimonio ordinatur principaliter ad prolis generationem et educationem et instructionem. Sed haec omnia aliquo certo tempore consummantur. Ergo post illud tempus licet uxorem dimittere sine aliquo praeiudicio legis naturae.

PRAETEREA, ex matrimonio principaliter quaeritur bonum prolis. Sed inseparabilitas est contra bonum prolis: quia, ut tradunt physici, aliquis vir non potest ex aliqua femina prolem accipere qui tamen ex alia accipere posset, et quae etiam ab alio viro impraegnaretur. Ergo inseparabilitas matrimonii magis est contra legem naturae quam de lege naturae.

SED CONTRA: Illud praecipue est de lege naturae quod natura bene instituta accepit in sui principio. Sed

OBJECTION 1: It would seem that inseparableness of the wife is not of natural law. For the natural law is the same for all. But no law save Christ's has forbidden the divorcing of a wife. Therefore, inseparableness of a wife is not of natural law.

OBJ. 2: Further, the sacraments are not of the natural law. But the indissolubility of marriage is one of the marriage goods. Therefore, it is not of the natural law.

OBJ. 3: Further, the union of man and woman in marriage is chiefly directed to the begetting, rearing, and instruction of the offspring. But all things are complete by a certain time. Therefore, after that time it is lawful to put away a wife without prejudice to the natural law.

OBJ. 4: Further, the good of the offspring is the principal end of marriage. But the indissolubility of marriage is opposed to the good of the offspring, because according to philosophers, a certain man cannot beget offspring of a certain woman, and yet he might beget of another, even though she may have had intercourse with another man. Therefore, the indissolubility of marriage is against rather than according to the natural law.

ON THE CONTRARY, Those things which were assigned to nature when it was well established in its beginning be-

inseparabilitas matrimonii est huiusmodi, ut patet Matth. 19. Ergo est de lege naturae.

PRAETEREA, de lege naturae est quod homo Deo non contrarietur. Sed homo quodammodo contrarius esset Deo si separaret *quos Deus coniunxit*. Cum ergo ex hoc instituta sit inseparabilitas matrimonii, Matth. 19, videtur quod sit de lege naturae.

RESPONDEO dicendum quod matrimonium ex intentione naturae ordinatur ad educationem prolis non solum ad aliquod tempus, sed per totam vitam prolis. Unde de lege naturae est quod *parentes filiis thesaurizent*, et filii parentum haeredes sint. Et ideo, cum proles sit commune bonum viri et uxoris, oportet eorum societatem perpetuo permanere indivisam secundum legis naturae dictamen. Et sic inseparabilitas matrimonii est de lege naturae.

AD PRIMUM ergo dicendum quod sola lex Christi *ad perfectum* humanum genus adduxit, reducens in statum novitatis naturae. Unde et in lege Moysi et in legibus humanis non potuit totum auferri quod contra legem naturae erat. Hoc enim *soli legi spiritus* et vitae reservatum est.

AD SECUNDUM dicendum quod inseparabilitas competit matrimonio secundum quod est signum perpetuae coniunctionis Christi et Ecclesiae; et secundum quod est in officium naturae ad bonum prolis ordinatum, ut dictum est. Sed quia separatio matrimonii magis directe repugnat significationi quam prolis bono, cui consequenter repugnat, ut dictum est; inseparabilitas matrimonii magis in bono sacramenti intelligitur quam in bono prolis. Quamvis in utroque intelligi possit. Et secundum quod pertinet ad bonum prolis, erit de lege naturae: non autem secundum quod pertinet ad bonum sacramenti.

AD TERTIUM patet solutio ex dictis.

AD QUARTUM dicendum quod matrimonium principaliter ordinatur ad bonum commune ratione principalis finis, qui est bonum prolis: quamvis etiam ratione finis secundarii ordinetur ad bonum matrimonium contrahentis, prout per se est in remedium concupiscentiae. Et ideo in legibus matrimonii magis attenditur quid omnibus expediat quam quid uni competere possit. Quamvis ergo matrimonii inseparabilitas impediat bonum prolis in aliquo homine, tamen est conveniens ad bonum prolis simpliciter. Et propter hoc ratio non sequitur.

long especially to the law of nature. Now the indissolubility of marriage is one of these things, according to Matthew 19:4–6. Therefore, it is of natural law.

FURTHER, It is of natural law that man should not oppose himself to God. Yet man would, in a way, oppose himself to God if he were to sunder *what God has joined together* (Matt 19:6). Since, then, the indissolubility of marriage is instituted by this passage, it would seem that it is of natural law.

I ANSWER THAT, By the intention of nature marriage is directed to the rearing of the offspring not merely for a time, but throughout the whole life. Hence it is of natural law that *parents should lay up for their children*, and that children should be their parents' heirs (2 Cor 12:14). Therefore, since the offspring is the common good of husband and wife, the dictate of the natural law requires the latter to live together forever inseparably: and so the indissolubility of marriage is of natural law.

REPLY OBJ. 1: Christ's law alone brought mankind *to perfection* (Heb 7:19) by bringing man back to the state of the newness of nature. Wherefore neither Mosaic nor human laws could remove all that was contrary to the law of nature, for this was reserved exclusively to *the law of the spirit of life* (Rom 8:2).

REPLY OBJ. 2: Indissolubility belongs to marriage insofar as the latter is a sign of the perpetual union of Christ with the Church, and insofar as it fulfills an office of nature that is directed to the good of the offspring, as stated above. But since divorce is more directly incompatible with the signification of the sacrament than with the good of the offspring, with which it is consequently incompatible, as stated above (Q. 65, A. 2), the indissolubility of marriage is implied in the good of the sacrament rather than in the good of the offspring, although it may be connected with both. And insofar as it is connected with the good of the offspring, it is of the natural law, but not as connected with the good of the sacrament.

THE REPLY to the third objection may be gathered from what has been said.

REPLY OBJ. 4: Marriage is chiefly directed to the common good in respect of its principal end, which is the good of the offspring; although in respect of its secondary end it is directed to the good of the contracting party, insofar as it is by its very nature a remedy for concupiscence. Hence marriage laws consider what is expedient for all rather than what may be suitable for one. Therefore, although the indissolubility of marriage may hinder the good of the offspring with regard to some individual, it is proportionate with the good of the offspring absolutely speaking: and for this reason the argument does not follow.

Article 2

Whether It May Have Been Lawful by Dispensation to Put Away a Wife?

AD SECUNDUM SIC PROCEDITUR. Videtur quod uxorem dimittere per dispensationem esse licitum non potuerit. Illud enim quod est in matrimonio contra bonum prolis, est contra prima praecepta legis naturae, quae indissolubilia sunt. Sed dimissio uxoris est huiusmodi, ut ex dictis patet. Ergo, etc.

PRAETEREA, concubina differt ab uxore praecipue in hoc quod non est inseparabiliter iuncta. Sed habere concubinas fuit indispensabile. Ergo et dimittere uxorem.

PRAETEREA, homines ita sunt modo receptibiles dispensationis sicut olim fuerunt. Sed modo non potest dispensari cum aliquo ut uxorem dimittat. Ergo nec olim.

SED CONTRA, Agar cognita est ab Abraham uxorio affectu, ut dictum est. Sed ipse eam praecepto divino eiecit, et non peccavit. Ergo potuit per dispensationem fieri licitum quod homo uxorem dimitteret.

RESPONDEO dicendum quod dispensatio in praeceptis, praecipue quae sunt aliquo modo legis naturae, est sicut mutatio cursus rei naturalis. Qui quidem mutari dupliciter potest. Uno modo, ex aliqua causa naturali, per quam alia causa naturalis impeditur a cursu suo: sicut est in omnibus quae in minori parte casualiter accidunt in natura. Sed per hunc modum non variatur cursus rerum naturalium quae sunt semper, sed quae sunt frequenter. Alio modo per causam penitus supernaturalem: sicut in miraculis accidit. Et hoc modo potest mutari cursus naturalis non solum qui est ordinatus ut sit frequenter, sed qui est ordinatus etiam ut sit semper: ut patet in statione solis tempore Iosue, et reditu eiusdem tempore Ezechiae, et de eclipsi miraculosa tempore passionis Christi.

Haec autem ratio dispensationis in praeceptis legis naturae quandoque est in causis inferioribus. Et sic dispensatio cadere potest supra secunda praecepta legis naturae: non autem supra prima, quia illa sunt quasi semper existentia: ut dictum est de pluralitate uxorum, et de huiusmodi. Aliquando autem est tantum in causis superioribus. Et tunc potest dispensatio esse divinitus etiam contra prima praecepta legis naturae, ratione alicuius mysterii divini significandi vel ostendendi: sicut patet de dispensativo praecepto Abrahae facto de occisione filii innocentis. Tales autem dispensationes non fiunt communiter ad omnes, sed ad aliquas singulares personas: sicut etiam in miraculis accidit.

OBJECTION 1: It seems that it could not be lawful by dispensation to put away a wife. For in marriage anything that is opposed to the good of the offspring is against the first precepts of the natural law, which admit of no dispensation. Now such is the putting away of a wife, as stated above (A. 1). Therefore, etc.

OBJ. 2: Further, a concubine differs from a wife especially in the fact that she is not inseparably united. But by no dispensation could a man have a concubine. Therefore, by no dispensation could he put his wife away.

OBJ. 3: Further, men are as fit to receive a dispensation now as of old. But now a man cannot receive a dispensation to divorce his wife. Neither, therefore, could he before.

ON THE CONTRARY, Abraham carnally knew Hagar with the disposition of a husband towards his wife, as stated above (Q. 65, A. 1). Now by divine command he sent her away, and yet sinned not. Therefore, it could be lawful by dispensation for a man to put away his wife.

I ANSWER THAT, In the commandments, especially those which in some way are of natural law, a dispensation is like a change in the natural course of things: and this course is subject to a twofold change. First, by some natural cause whereby another natural cause is hindered from following its course: it is thus in all things that happen by chance less frequently in nature. In this way, however, there is no variation in the course of those natural things which happen always, but only in the course of those which happen frequently. Second, by a cause altogether supernatural, as in the case of miracles: and in this way there can be a variation in the course of nature not only in the course which is appointed for the majority of cases, but also in the course which is appointed for all cases, as instanced by the sun standing still at the time of Joshua, and by its turning back at the time of Ezekiel, and by the miraculous eclipse at the time of Christ's Passion.

In like manner, the reason for a dispensation from a precept of the law of nature is sometimes found in the lower causes, and in this way a dispensation may bear upon the secondary precepts of the natural law, but not on the first precepts, because these are always existent, as it were, as stated above in reference to the plurality of wives and so forth (Q. 65, A. 1). But sometimes this reason is found in the higher causes, and then a dispensation may be given by God even from the first precepts of the natural law, for the sake of signifying or showing some divine mystery, as instanced in the dispensation vouchsafed to Abraham in the slaying of his innocent son. Such dispensations, however, are not granted to all generally, but to certain individual persons, as also happens in regard to miracles.

Si ergo inseparabilitas matrimonii inter prima praecepta legis naturae contineatur, solum hoc secundo modo sub dispensatione cadet. Si autem sit inter secunda praecepta legis naturae, etiam primo modo cadere potuit sub dispensatione: Videtur autem magis inter secunda praecepta legis naturae contineri. Inseparabilitas enim matrimonii non ordinatur ad prolis bonum, quod est principalis matrimonii finis, nisi quantum ad hoc quod per parentes filiis provideri debet in totam vitam per debitam praeparationem eorum quae sunt .necessaria in vita. Huiusmodi autem rerum appropriatio non est de prima intentione naturae, secundum quam omnia sunt communia. Et ideo non videtur contra primam intentionem naturae dimissio uxoris esse: et per consequens nec contra prima praecepta, sed contra secunda, legis naturae. Unde etiam primo modo sub dispensatione videtur posse cadere.

AD PRIMUM ergo dicendum quod in bono prolis, secundum quod est de prima intentione naturae, intelligitur procreatio et nutritio et instructio quousque proles ad perfectam aetatem ducatur. Sed quod ei provideatur in posterum per haereditatis et aliorum bonorum dimissionem, videtur pertinere ad secundam legis naturae intentionem.

AD SECUNDUM dicendum quod habere concubinam est contra bonum prolis quantum ad id quod natura in eo de prima intentione intendit, scilicet educationem et instructionem, quae requirit diuturnam commansionem parentum, quod non est in concubina, quae ad tempus assumitur. Et ideo non est simile. Tamen quantum ad secundam dispensationem, etiam habere concubinam sub dispensatione cadere potest: ut patet Osee 1.

AD TERTIUM dicendum quod inseparabilitas, quamvis sit de secunda intentione matrimonii prout est in officium naturae, tamen est de prima intentione ipsius prout est sacramentum Ecclesiae. Et ideo, ex quo institutum est ut sit Ecclesiae sacramentum, manente tali institutione non potest sub dispensatione cadere: nisi forte secundo modo dispensationis.

Accordingly, if the indissolubility of marriage is contained among the first precepts of the natural law, it could only be a matter of dispensation in this second way; but if it is one of the second precepts of the natural law, it could be a matter of dispensation even in the first way. Now it would seem to belong rather to the secondary precepts of the natural law. For the indissolubility of marriage is not directed to the good of the offspring, which is the principal end of marriage, except insofar as parents have to provide for their children for their whole life by due preparation of those things that are necessary in life. Now this preparation does not pertain to the first intention of nature, in respect of which all things are common. And therefore it would seem that to put away one's wife is not contrary to the first intention of nature, and consequently that it is contrary not to the first but to the second precepts of the natural law. Therefore, seemingly it can be a matter of dispensation even in the first way.

REPLY OBJ. 1: The good of the offspring, insofar as it belongs to the first intention of nature, includes procreation, nourishment, and instruction, until the offspring comes to perfect age. But that provision be made for the children by bequeathing to them the inheritance or other goods belongs seemingly to the second intention of the natural law.

REPLY OBJ. 2: To have a concubine is contrary to the good of the offspring in respect of nature's first intention in that good, namely, the rearing and instruction of the child, for which purpose it is necessary that the parents remain together permanently; which is not the case with a concubine, since she is taken for a time. Hence the comparison fails. But in respect of nature's second intention, even to have a concubine may be a matter of dispensation, as evidenced by Hosea 1.

REPLY OBJ. 3: Although indissolubility belongs to the second intention of marriage as fulfilling an office of nature, it belongs to its first intention as a sacrament of the Church. Hence, from the moment it was made a sacrament of the Church, and as long as it remains such, it cannot be a matter of dispensation, except perhaps by the second kind of dispensation.

Article 3

Whether It Was Lawful to Divorce a Wife Under the Mosaic Law?

AD TERTIUM SIC PROCEDITUR. Videtur quod sub lege Moysi fuerit licitum uxorem dimittere. Unus enim modus consentiendi est non prohibere, cum prohibere possit. Consentire autem illicito est illicitum. Cum ergo Moyses non prohibuerit uxoris repudium; nec peccave-

OBJECTION 1: It would seem that it was lawful to divorce a wife under the Mosaic law. For one way of giving consent is to refrain from prohibiting when one can prohibit. It is also unlawful to consent to what is unlawful. Since, then, the Mosaic law did not forbid the putting away

rit, quia *lex sancta est*, ut dicitur Rom. 7: videtur quod repudium fuerit aliquando licitum.

PRAETEREA, prophetae locuti sunt *Spiritu Sancto inspirante*, ut patet II Petr. I. Sed Malach. 2 dicitur: *si odio habueris eam, dimitte eam.* Ergo, cum illud quod Spiritus Sanctus inspirat, non sit illicitum, videtur quod repudium uxoris non semper fuerit illicitum.

PRAETEREA, Chrysostomus dicit quod, sicut Apostoli permiserunt secundas nuptias, ita Moyses permisit libellum repudii. Sed secundae nuptiae non sunt peccatum. Ergo nec repudium uxoris sub lege Moysi.

SED CONTRA: Est quod Dominus dicit, quod libellus repudii datus est a Moyse Iudaeis *propter duritiam cordis eorum.* Sed duritia cordis eorum non excusabat eos a peccato. Ergo nec lex de libello repudii.

PRAETEREA, Chrysostomus dicit, super Matth., quod *Moyses, dando libellum repudii, non iustitiam Dei monstravit: ut quasi per legem agentibus peccatum non videatur esse peccatum.*

RESPONDEO dicendum quod circa hoc est duplex opinio. Quidam enim dicunt quod illi qui sub lege uxorem, dato libello repudii, dimittebant, non excusabantur a peccato, quamvis excusarentur a poena secundum legem infligenda. Et propter hoc dicitur Moyses libellum repudii permisisse. Et sic ponunt quattuor modos permissionis. Unus, per privationem praeceptionis: ut, quando maius bonum non praecipitur, minus bonum permitti dicitur; sicut Apostolus, non praecipiendo virginitatem, matrimonium permisit, I Cor. 7.

Secundus, per privationem prohibitionis: sicut venialia dicuntur permissa, quia non sunt prohibita. Tertius, per privationem cohibitionis: et sic peccata omnia dicuntur permitti a Deo, inquantum non impedit, cum impedire possit. Quartus, per privationem punitionis. Et sic libellus repudii lege permissus fuit: non quidem propter aliquod maius bonum consequendum, sicut fuit dispensatio de pluribus uxoribus habendis; sed propter maius malum cohibendum, scilicet uxoricidium, ad quod Iudaei proni erant propter corruptionem irascibilis; sicut permissum fuit eis extraneis faenerari propter corruptionem aliquam in concupiscibili, ne scilicet fratribus suis faenerarentur; et sicut, propter corruptionem suspicionis in rationali, fuit permissum sacrificium zelotypiae, ne sola suspicio apud eos iudicium corrumperet.

Sed quia lex vetus, quamvis gratiam non conferret, tamen ad hoc data erat ut peccatum ostenderet, ut communiter sancti dicunt; ideo aliis videtur quod, si repu-

of a wife and did no wrong by not forbidding it, for *the law is holy* (Rom 7:12), it would seem that divorce was at one time lawful.

OBJ. 2: Further, the prophets spoke *inspired by the Holy Spirit*, according to 2 Peter 1:21. Now it is written: *if you should hate her, put her away* (Mal 2:16). Since, then, that which the Holy Spirit inspires is not unlawful, it would seem that it was not always unlawful to divorce a wife.

OBJ. 3: Further, Chrysostom (Hom. 32 in the *Opus Imperfectum*) says that even as the apostles permitted second marriages, so Moses allowed the bill of divorce. But second marriages are not sinful. Therefore, neither was it sinful under the Mosaic law to divorce a wife.

ON THE CONTRARY, Our Lord said that Moses granted the Jews the bill of divorce *by reason of the hardness of their heart* (Matt 19:8). But their hardness of heart did not excuse them from sin. Neither, therefore, did the law about the bill of divorce.

FURTHER, Chrysostom says (Hom. 32 in the *Opus Imperfectum*) that *Moses, by granting the bill of divorce, did not indicate the justice of God, but deprived their sin of its guilt, for while the Jews acted as though they were keeping the law, their sin seemed to be no sin.*

I ANSWER THAT, On this point there are two opinions. For some say that under the law those who put away their wives after giving them a bill of divorce were not excused from sin, although they were excused from the punishment which they should have suffered according to the law: and that for this reason Moses is stated to have permitted the bill of divorce. Accordingly, they reckon four kinds of permission: one by absence of precept, so that when a greater good is not prescribed, a lesser good is said to be permitted: thus the Apostle permitted marriage by not prescribing virginity (1 Cor 7).

The second is by absence of prohibition: thus venial sins are said to be permitted because they are not forbidden. The third is by absence of prevention, and thus all sins are said to be permitted by God insofar as he does not prevent them whereas he can. The fourth is by omission of punishment, and in this way the bill of divorce was permitted in the law, not indeed for the sake of obtaining a greater good, as was the dispensation to have several wives, but for the sake of preventing a greater evil, namely, uxoricide, to which the Jews were prone on account of the corruption of their irascible appetite. Even so they were allowed to lend money for usury to strangers on account of corruption in their concupiscible appetite, lest they should exact usury of their brethren; and again on account of the corruption of suspicion in the reason, they were allowed the sacrifice of jealousy, lest mere suspicion should corrupt their judgment.

But because the old law, though it did not confer grace, was given that it might indicate sin, as the saints are agreed in saying, others are of opinion that if it had been a sin for a

diando uxorem peccassent, hoc saltem eis per legem aut prophetas indicari debuisset: Isaiae 58, *annuntia populo meo scelera eorum*. Alias viderentur nimis esse neglecti, si ea quae necessaria sunt ad salutem, quae non cognoscebant, nunquam eis nuntiata fuissent. Quod non potest dici: cum iustitia legis, tempore suo observata, vitam meretur aeternam. Et propter hoc dicunt quod, quamvis repudiare uxorem per se sit malum, tamen ex permissione divina licitum fiebat. Et hoc confirmant auctoritate Chrysostomi, qui dicit quod *a peccato abstulit culpam* Legislator quando permisit repudium.

Et quamvis hoc probabiliter dicatur, tamen primum communius sustinetur. Ideo ad utrasque rationes respondendum est.

AD PRIMUM ergo dicendum quod aliquis qui potest prohibere, non peccat si a prohibitione abstineat non sperans correctionem, sed maius malum aestimans ex tali prohibitione occasionem sumere. Et sic accidit Moysi. Unde, divina auctoritate fretus, libellum repudii non prohibuit.

AD SECUNDUM dicendum quod prophetae, *Spiritu Sancto inspirati*, non dicebant dimittendam esse uxorem quasi Spiritus Sancti praeceptum sit: sed quasi permissum, ne aliqua peiora fierent.

AD TERTIUM dicendum quod illa permissionis similitudo non est intelligenda quantum ad omnia, sed solum quantum ad causam eandem, quia utraque permissio ad vitandam turpitudinem facta est.

AD QUARTUM dicendum quod, quamvis duritia cordis non excusaret a peccato, tamen permissio ex duritia facta excusat. Quaedam enim prohibentur sanis quae non prohibentur infirmis corporaliter, nec tamen infirmi peccant permissione sibi facta utentes.

AD QUINTUM dicendum quod aliquod bonum potest intermitti dupliciter. Uno modo, propter aliquod maius bonum consequendum. Et tunc intermissio illius boni ex ordine ad maius bonum accipit honestatem: sicut intermittebatur singularitas uxoris honeste a Iacob propter bonum prolis. Alio modo bonum aliquod intermittitur ad vitandum maius malum. Et tunc, si auctoritate eius qui dispensare potest hoc fiat, reatum talis boni intermissio non habet, sed honestatem etiam non acquirit. Et sic indivisibilitas matrimonii in lege Moysi intermittebatur propter maius malum vitandum, scilicet uxoricidium: Et ideo Chrysostomus dicit quod *a peccato abstulit culpam*. Quamvis enim inordinatio maneret in repudio, ex quo peccatum dicitur; tamen reatum poenae non habebat, neque temporalis neque perpetuae, inquantum divina dispensatione fiebat. Et sic erat ab eo culpa ablata. Et ideo etiam ipse ibidem dicit quod *permissum est repudium, mulum quidem, tamen licitum*. Quod quidem

man to put away his wife, this ought to have been indicated to him, at least by the law or the prophets: *show my people their wicked doings* (Isa 58:1): else they would seem to have been neglected if those things which are necessary for salvation and which they knew not were never made known to them: and this cannot be admitted, because the righteousness of the law observed at the time of the law would merit eternal life. For this reason they say that although to put away one's wife is wrong in itself, it nevertheless became lawful by God's permitting it, and they confirm this by the authority of Chrysostom, who says (Hom. 32 in the *Opus Imperfectum*) that the Lawgiver by permitting divorce *removed the guilt from the sin*.

Although this opinion has some probability, the former is more generally held: wherefore we must reply to the arguments on both sides.

REPLY OBJ. 1: He who can forbid does not sin by omitting to forbid if he has no hope of correcting, but fears by forbidding to furnish the occasion of a greater evil. Thus it happened to Moses: wherefore acting on divine authority he did not forbid the bill of divorce.

REPLY OBJ. 2: The prophets, *inspired by the Holy Spirit*, said that a wife ought to be put away not as though this were a command of the Holy Spirit, but as being permitted lest greater evils should be perpetrated.

REPLY OBJ. 3: This likeness of permission must not be applied to every detail, but only to the cause which was the same in both cases, since both permissions were granted in order to avoid some form of wickedness.

REPLY OBJ. 4: Although their hardness of heart did not excuse them from sin, the permission given on account of that hardness excused them. For certain things are forbidden those who are healthy in body which are not forbidden the sick, and yet the sick sin not by availing themselves of the permission granted to them.

REPLY OBJ. 5: A good may be omitted in two ways. First, in order to obtain a greater good, and then the omission of that good becomes virtuous by being directed to a greater good; thus Jacob rightly omitted to have only one wife on account of the good of offspring. In another way a good is omitted in order to avoid a greater evil, and then if this is done with the authority of one who can grant a dispensation, the omission of that good is not sinful, and yet it does not also become virtuous. In this way the indissolubility of marriage was suspended in the law of Moses in order to avoid a greater evil, namely, uxoricide. Hence Chrysostom says that *he removed the guilt from the sin*. For though divorce remained inordinate, for which reason it is called a sin, it did not incur the debt of punishment, either temporal or eternal, insofar as it was done by divine permission: and thus its guilt was taken away from it. And therefore he says again (Hom. 32 in the *Opus Imperfectum*) that *divorce was permitted, an evil indeed, yet lawful*. Those who

illi qui sunt de prima opinione, referunt ad hoc tantum quod non habebat reatum temporalis poenae.

hold the first opinion understand by this only that divorce incurred the debt of temporal punishment.

Article 4

Whether It Was Lawful for a Divorced Wife to Have Another Husband?

AD QUARTUM SIC PROCEDITUR. Videtur quod liceret uxori repudiatae alium virum habere. Quia in repudio magis erat iniquitas viri repudiantis quam uxoris repudiatae. Sed vir poterat sine peccato aliam ducere uxorem. Ergo uxor sine peccato alium virum ducere poterat.

PRAETEREA, Augustinus dicit de duabus uxoribus quod, *quando mos erat, peccatum non era*t. Sed tempore legis veteris erat talis consuetudo quod repudiata alium virum ducebat: ut patet Deuteron. 24, *cum egressa virum alterum duceret*, etc. Ergo non peccabat alteri viro se iungendo.

PRAETEREA, Dominus, Matth. 5, iustitiam novi Testamenti ostendit superabundantem esse respectu iustitiae veteris Testamenti. Hoc autem dicit ad iustitiam novi Testamenti per superabundantiam pertinere quod uxor repudiata non ducit alterum virum. Ergo in veteri lege licebat.

SED CONTRA: Est quod dicitur Matth. 5: *qui dimissam duxerit, moechatur*. Sed moechia nunquam fuit iri veteri lege licita. Ergo nec uxori repudiatae licuit alium virum habere.

PRAETEREA, Deuteron. 24 dicitur quod *mulier repudiata quae alium virum duceret, polluta erat et abominabilis facta coram Domino*. Ergo peccabat alium virum ducendo.

RESPONDEO dicendum quod, secundum primam opinionem, post repudium uxor peccabat alteri viro coniuncta: quia adhuc matrimonium primum non erat solutum. *Mulier enim, quanto tempore vivit, alligata est legi viri*, ut patet Rom. 7: non autem poterat simul plures viros habere. Sed secundum aliam opinionem, sicut licebat ex dispensatione divina viro uxorem repudiare, ita uxori alium virum ducere. Quia inseparabilitas matrimonii ex causa divinae dispensationis tollebatur: qua inseparabilitate manente intelligitur verbum Apostoli.

UT ERGO ad utrasque rationes respondeamus:

AD PRIMUM dicendum quod viro licebat plures uxores simul habere secundum dispensationem divinam. Et ideo, una dimissa, etiam matrimonio non soluto, poterat

OBJECTION 1: It would seem that it was lawful for a divorced wife to have another husband. For in divorce the husband did a greater wrong by divorcing his wife than the wife by being divorced. But the husband could without sin marry another wife. Therefore, the wife could without sin marry another husband.

OBJ. 2: Further, Augustine, speaking about bigamy, says (*On the Good of Marriage* 15, 18) that *when it was the manner it was no sin*. Now at the time of the old law it was the custom for a wife after divorce to marry another husband: *when she is departed and marries another husband* (Deut 24:2). Therefore, the wife did not sin by marrying another husband.

OBJ. 3: Further, our Lord showed that the justice of the New Testament is superabundant in comparison with the justice of the Old Testament (Matt 5). Now he said that it belongs to the superabundant justice of the New Testament that the divorced wife marry not another husband (Matt 5:32). Therefore, it was lawful in the old law.

OBJ. 4: On the contrary are the words of Matthew 5:32: *he that shall marry her that is put away commits adultery*. Now adultery was never permitted in the old law. Therefore, it was not lawful for the divorced wife to have another husband.

OBJ. 5: Further, it is written that a divorced woman who marries another husband is *defiled, and is become abominable before the Lord* (Deut 24:3). Therefore, she sinned by marrying another husband.

I ANSWER THAT, According to the first above mentioned opinion (A. 3), she sinned by marrying another husband after being divorced, because her first marriage still held good. For *the woman while her husband lives is bound to the law of her husband* (Rom 7:2): and she could not have several husbands at one time. But according to the second opinion, just as it was lawful by virtue of the divine dispensation for a husband to divorce his wife, so could the wife marry another husband, because the indissolubility of marriage was removed by reason of the divine dispensation: and as long as that indissolubility remains, the saying of the Apostle holds.

ACCORDINGLY, to reply to the arguments on either side:

REPLY OBJ. 1: It was lawful for a husband to have several wives at one time by virtue of the divine dispensation: wherefore, having put one away, he could marry another

aliam ducere. Sed nunquam uxori licuit habere plures viros. Et ideo non est simile.

Ad secundum dicendum quod in illo verbo Augustini *mos* non ponitur pro consuetudine, sed pro actu honesto: secundum quod a *more* aliquis dicitur *morigeratus*, quia est bonorum morum; vel sicut a *more* philosophia *moralis* nominatur.

Ad tertium dicendum quod Dominus, Matth. 5, ostendit novam legem abundare per consilia ad veterem, non solum quantum ad ea quae lex vetus licita faciebat, sed etiam quantum ad ea quae in veteri lege illicita erant sed a multis licita putabantur per non rectam praeceptorum expositionem: sicut patet de odio inimici. Et ita est etiam de repudio.

Ad quartum dicendum quod verbum Domini intelligitur quantum ad tempus novae legis, in quo dicta permissio est sublata.

Et sic etiam intelligitur quoddam verbum Chrysostomi, qui dicit quod *qui secundum legem dimittit uxorem, quattuor facit iniquitates: quia quoad Deum existit homicida*, inquantum habet propositum occidendi uxorem nisi eam dimitteret; et quia dimittit non fornicantem, in quo solo casu lex Evangelii uxorem dimittere permittit; *et similiter quia facit eam adulteram; et illum cui copulatur.*

Ad quintum dicendum quod quaedam Interlinearis dicit: *polluta est et abominabilis* scilicet illius iudicio qui quasi pollutam eam prius dimisit. Et sic non oportet quod sit polluta simpliciter.

Vel dicitur polluta eo modo quo immundus dicebatur qui mortuum tangebat vel leprosum, non immunditia culpae, sed cuiusdam irregularitatis legalis. Unde et sacerdoti non licebat viduam aut repudiatam ducere in uxorem.

even though the former marriage were not dissolved. But it was never lawful for a wife to have several husbands. Wherefore the comparison fails.

Reply Obj. 2: In this saying of Augustine, *manner* does not signify custom but good manners; in the same sense a person is said to have 'manners' because he has good manners; and 'moral' philosophy takes its name from the same source.

Reply Obj. 3: Our Lord shows the superabundance of the new law over the old in respect of the counsels, not only as regards those things which the old law permitted, but also as regards those things which were forbidden in the old law, and yet were thought by many to be permitted on account of the precepts being incorrectly explained—for instance, that of the hatred towards our enemies—and so is it in the matter of divorce.

Reply Obj. 4: The saying of our Lord refers to the time of the new law, when the aforesaid permission was recalled.

In the same way we are to understand the statement of Chrysostom (Hom. 12 in the *Opus Imperfectum*) who says that *a man who divorces his wife according to the law is guilty of four crimes: for in God's sight he is a murderer*, insofar as he has the purpose of killing his wife unless he divorce her; *and because he divorces her without her having committed fornication*, in which case alone the law of the Gospel allows a man to put away his wife; *and again, because he makes her an adulteress, and the man whom she marries an adulterer.*

Reply Obj. 5: A interlinear Gloss observes here: *she is defiled and abominable, namely, in the judgment of him who first put her away as being defiled*, and consequently it does not follow that she is defiled absolutely speaking.

Or she is said to be defiled just as a person who had touched a dead or leprous body was said to be unclean with the uncleanness, not of sin, but of a certain legal irregularity. Wherefore a priest could not marry a widow or a divorced woman.

Article 5

Whether a Husband Could Lawfully Take Back the Wife He Had Divorced?

Ad quintum sic proceditur. Videtur quod licebat viro repudiatam a se accipere. Licet enim corrigere quod male factum est. Sed male factum erat quod vir uxorem repudiabat. Ergo licebat hoc corrigere reducendo uxorem ad se.

Praeterea, semper licuit peccanti indulgere: cum sit morale praeceptum, quod in omni lege manet. Sed vir accipiendo repudiatam ei peccanti indulgebat. Ergo hoc licitum erat.

Objection 1: It would seem that a husband could lawfully take back the wife he had divorced. For it is lawful to undo what was badly done. But for the husband to divorce his wife was badly done. Therefore, it was lawful for him to undo it by taking back his wife.

Obj. 2: Further, it has always been lawful to be indulgent to the sinner because this is a moral precept, which remains in every law. Now the husband, by taking back the wife he had divorced, was indulgent to one who had sinned. Therefore, this also was lawful.

Praeterea, Deuteron. 24, ponitur pro causa quare non possit accipi iterum, *quia polluta est*. Sed repudiata non polluitur nisi alterum virum ducendo. Ergo saltem antequam alium virum duceret, licebat eam accipere.

Sed contra est quod dicitur Deuteron. 24, quod *non poterat prior maritus accipere eam*, etc.

Respondeo dicendum quod in lege de libello repudii duo erant permissa, scilicet dimittere uxorem, et uxorem dimissam alteri iungi; et duo praecepta, scilicet scriptura libelli repudii, et quod iterum maritus repudians eam accipere non possit. Quod quidem, secundum eos qui primam opinionem tenent, factum fuit in poenam mulieris quae alteri nupsit et in hoc peccato polluta est. Sed secundum alios, ut vir non de facili uxorem repudiaret, quam postea nullo modo recuperare posset.

Ad primum ergo dicendum quod ad illius mali impedimentum quod committebat aliquis repudiando uxorem, ordinabatur quod vir uxorem repudiatam assumere iterato non posset, ut patet ex dictis. Et ideo divinitus ordinatum fuit.

Ad secundum dicendum quod semper licuit indulgere peccanti quantum ad rancorem cordis: sed non quantum ad poenam divinitus taxatam.

Ad tertium dicendum quod in hoc est duplex opinio. Quidam enim dicunt quod licuit repudiatam viro reconciliari nisi matrimonio alteri viro esset iuncta. Tunc enim, propter adulterium, cui se mulier voluntarie subdidit, in poenam dabatur ei quod ad priorem virum non rediret.

Sed quia lex universaliter prohibet, ideo dicunt alii quod etiam antequam alteri nuberet, non poterat revocari, ex quo repudiata erat: quia pollutio non intelligitur quantum ad culpam, sed ut dictum est.

Obj. 3: Further, the reason given for its being unlawful to take back a divorced wife was *because she is defiled* (Deut 24:4). But the divorced wife is not defiled except by marrying another husband. Therefore, at least it was lawful to take back a divorced wife before she married again.

On the contrary, Deuteronomy 24:4 says that *the former husband cannot take her again.*

I answer that, In the law concerning the bill of divorce two things were permitted: namely, for the husband to put away the wife, and for the divorced wife to take another husband; and two things were commanded, namely, that the bill of divorce should be written, and second, that the husband who divorced his wife could not take her back. According to those who hold the first opinion (A. 3) this was done in punishment of the woman who married again, and that it was by this sin that she was defiled: but according to the others it was done that a husband might not be too ready to divorce his wife if he could in no way take her back afterwards.

Reply Obj. 1: In order to prevent the evil committed by a man in divorcing his wife, it was ordered that the husband could not take back his divorced wife, as stated above: and for this reason it was ordered by God.

Reply Obj. 2: It was always lawful to be indulgent to the sinner as regards the unkindly feelings of the heart, but not as regards the punishment appointed by God.

Reply Obj. 3: There are two opinions on this point. For some say that it was lawful for a divorced wife to be reconciled to her husband unless she were joined in marriage to another husband. For then, on account of the adultery to which she had voluntarily yielded, it was assigned to her in punishment that she should not return to her former husband.

Since, however, the law makes no distinction in its prohibition, others say that from the moment that she was put away she could not be taken back, even before marrying again, because the defilement must be understood not in reference to sin, but as explained above (A. 4).

Article 6

Whether the Reason for Divorce Was Hatred for the Wife?

Ad sextum sic proceditur. Videtur quod causa repudii fuerit odium uxoris: secundum hoc quod dicitur Malach. 2: *si odio habueris eam, dimitte illam*.

Praeterea, Deuteron. 24 dicitur: *cum non invenerit gratiam in oculis eius propter aliquam foeditatem*, etc. Ergo idem quod prius.

Objection 1: It would seem that the reason for divorce was hatred for the wife. For it is written: *if you should hate her, put her away* (Mal 2:16). Therefore, etc.

Obj. 2: Further, it is written: *if she find not favor in his eyes, for some uncleanness* (Deut 24:1). Therefore, the same conclusion follows as before.

SED CONTRA: Sterilitas et fornicatio magis contrariantur matrimonio quam odium. Ergo illa potius debuerunt esse causa repudii quam odium.

PRAETEREA, odium potest causari ex virtute eius qui odio habetur. Si ergo odium est sufficiens causa, tunc mulier posset repudiari propter virtutem suam. Quod est absurdum.

PRAETEREA, Deuteron. 22 dicitur: *si duxerit vir uxorem suam et postea odio habuerit*, et obiecerit ei stuprum ante coniugium, si in probatione defecerit, *verberabitur, et centum siclis argenti condemnabitur, et non poterit eam dimittere omni tempore vitae suae.* Ergo odium non est sufficiens causa repudii.

RESPONDEO dicendum quod causa permissionis repudiandi uxorem fuit vitatio uxoricidii, ut sancti communiter dicunt. Proxima autem causa homicidii est odium. Et ideo proxima causa repudii est odium. Sed odium ex aliqua causa causatur, sicut et amor. Et ideo oportet etiam alias causas repudii ponere remotas, quae erant causa odii.

Dicit autem Augustinus, in Glossa Deuteron. 24: *multae erant in lege causae dimittendi uxorem. Solam Christus fornicationem excipit: ceteras molestias iubet pro fide et castitate coniugii sustinere.* Hae autem causae intelliguntur foeditates in corpore, puta infirmitas, vel aliqua notabilis macula; vel in anima, sicut fornicatio, vel aliquod huiusmodi quod in moribus inhonestatem facit.

Sed quidam has causas magis coarctant, satis probabiliter dicentes quod non licebat uxorem repudiare nisi propter aliquam causam post matrimonium supervenientem; nec propter quamlibet talem, sed propter illas solum quae possunt bonum prolis impedire; vel in corpore, ut sterilitas aut lepra aut aliquid huiusmodi; vel in anima, ut si esset malorum morum, quos filii ex conversatione ad ipsam imitarentur.

Sed quaedam Glossa super illud Deuteron. 22, *cum non invenerit gratiam* etc., videtur magis arctare, scilicet ad peccatum: cum dicit ibi *per foeditatem peccatum intelligit.* Sed peccatum Glossa nominat non solum in moribus animae, sed etiam in natura corporis.

SIC ERGO prima duo concedimus.

AD TERTIUM dicendum quod sterilitas et alia huiusmodi sunt causa odii. Et sic sunt causae remotae.

AD QUARTUM dicendum quod propter virtutem non est aliquis odibilis per se loquendo: quia bonitas est causa amoris. Et ideo ratio non sequitur.

AD QUINTUM dicendum quod dabatur in poenam viri quod non posset in perpetuum repudiare uxorem in casu illo: sicut etiam in alio casu, quando puellam defloraverat.

OBJ. 3: On the contrary, barrenness and fornication are more opposed to marriage than hatred. Therefore, they ought to have been reasons for divorce rather than hatred.

OBJ. 4: Further, hatred may be caused by the virtue of the person hated. Therefore, if hatred is a sufficient reason, a woman could be divorced on account of her virtue, which is absurd.

OBJ. 5: Further, *if a man marry a wife and afterwards hate her, and seek occasions to put her away* (Mal 2:16), alleging that she was not a virgin when he married her, should he fail to prove this, *he shall be beaten, and shall be fined a hunded shekels of silver, and he shall be unable to put her away all the days of his life* (Deut 22:13–19). Therefore, hatred is not a sufficient reason for divorce.

I ANSWER THAT, It is the general opinion of holy men that the reason for permission being given to divorce a wife was the avoidance of uxoricide. Now the proximate cause of murder is hatred: wherefore the proximate cause of divorce was hatred. But hatred proceeds, like love, from a cause. Wherefore we must assign to divorce certain remote causes which were a cause of hatred.

For Augustine says in his Gloss (*On the Lord's Sermon on the Mount* 1.14): *in the law there were many causes for divorcing a wife; Christ admitted none but fornication, and he commands other grievances to be borne for conjugal fidelity and chastity.* Such causes are imperfections either of body, as sickness or some notable deformity, or in soul, as fornication or the like which amounts to moral depravity.

Some, however, restrict these causes within narrower limits, saying with sufficient probability that it was not lawful to divorce a wife except for some cause subsequent to the marriage; and that not even then could it be done for any such cause, but only for such as could hinder the good of the offspring, whether in body as barrenness, or leprosy and the like, or in soul, for instance, if she were a woman of wicked habits which her children through continual contact with her would imitate.

There is, however, a Gloss on Deuteronomy 24:1: *if . . . she find not favor in his eyes*, which would seem to restrict them yet more, namely to sin, by saying that there *uncleanness* denotes sin: but *sin* in the Gloss refers not only to the morality of the soul but also to the condition of the body.

ACCORDINGLY, we grant the first two objections.

REPLY OBJ. 3: Barrenness and other like things are causes of hatred, and so they are remote causes of divorce.

REPLY OBJ. 4: No one is hateful on account of virtue as such, because goodness is the cause of love. Wherefore the argument does not hold.

REPLY OBJ. 5: The husband was punished in that case by being unable to put away his wife forever, just as in the case when he had corrupted a maid (Deut 22:28–30).

Article 7

Whether the Causes of Divorce Had to Be Written in the Bill?

Ad septimum sic proceditur. Videtur quod causae repudii debebant in libello scribi. Quia per libellum repudii scriptum a poena legis absolvebatur. Sed hoc omnino videtur iniustum nisi causis sufficientibus repudii assignatis. Ergo oportebat illas scribere in libello.

Praeterea, ad nihil aliud illa scriptura valere videbatur nisi ut causae repudii ostenderentur. Ergo, si non inscribebantur, frustra libellus ille tradebatur sibi.

Praeterea, hoc Magister dicit in littera.

Sed contra, causae repudii aut erant sufficientes, aut non. Si sufficientes, praecludebatur mulieri via ad secundas nuptias, quae ei secundum legem concedebantur. Si autem insufficientes, ostendebatur iniustum repudium: et sic repudium fieri non poterat. Ergo nullo modo causae repudii ibi inscribebantur.

Respondeo dicendum quod causae repudii in speciali non scribebantur in libello, sed in generali, ut ostenderetur iustum repudium. Sed secundum Iosephum, ut mulier, habens libellum conscriptum de repudio, alteri nubere posset: alias enim ei; traditum non fuisset. Unde secundum eum erat scriptura talis: *promitto tibi quod nunquam tecum conveniam.*

Sed secundum Augustinum, ideo libellus scribebatur *ut, mora interveniente, et consilio scribarum dissuadente, vir a proposito repudiandi desisteret.*

Et per hoc patet solutio ad obiecta.

Objection 1: It would seem that the causes of divorce had to be written in the bill. For the husband was absolved from the punishment of the law by the written bill of divorce. But this would seem altogether unjust, unless sufficient causes were alleged for a divorce. Therefore, it was necessary for them to be written in the bill.

Obj. 2: Further, seemingly this document was of no use except to show the causes for divorce. Therefore, if they were not written down, the bill was delivered for no purpose.

Obj. 3: Further, the Master says that it was so in the text (*Sentences* IV, D. 33).

On the contrary, The causes for divorce were either sufficient or not. If they were sufficient, the wife was debarred from a second marriage, though this was allowed her by the law. If they were insufficient, the divorce was proved to be unjust, and therefore could not be effected. Therefore, the causes for divorce were by no means particularized in the bill.

I answer that, The causes for divorce were not particularized in the bill, but were indicated in a general way, so as to prove the justice of the divorce. According to Josephus (*Antiquities of the Jews* 4.6) this was in order that the woman, having the written bill of divorce, might take another husband, else she would not have been believed. Wherefore according to him it was written in this wise: *I promise never to have you with me again.*

But according to Augustine (*Against Faustus*, 19.26) the bill was put into writing *in order to cause a delay, and that the husband might be dissuaded by the counsel of the notaries to refrain from his purpose of divorce.*

This suffices for the replies to the objections.

QUESTION 68

ILLEGITIMATE CHILDREN

Deinde considerandum est de filiis illegitime natis. Et circa hoc quaeruntur tria.

Primo: utrum filii qui nascuntur extra verum matrimonium, sint illegitimi.

Secundo: utrum illegitimi filii debeant ex hoc damnum reportare.

Tertio: utrum possint legitimari.

We must now consider children of illegitimate birth. Under this head there are three points of inquiry:

(1) Whether those born out of true marriage are illegitimate?

(2) Whether children should suffer any loss through being illegitimate?

(3) Whether they can be legitimized?

Article 1

Whether Children Born out of True Marriage Are Illegitimate?

AD PRIMUM SIC PROCEDITUR. Videtur quod filii qui nascuntur extra verum matrimonium, non sint illegitimi. Quia secundum legem natus legitimus filius dicitur. Sed quilibet filius nascitur secundum legem, ad minus naturae, quae fortissima est. Ergo quilibet filius est legitimus.

PRAETEREA, communiter dicitur quod legitimus filius est *qui est de legitimo matrimonio natus, vel de eo quod in facie Ecclesiae legitimum reputatur.* Sed contingit quandoque quod aliquod matrimonium legitimum reputatur in facie Ecclesiae quod habet impedimentum ne sit verum matrimonium, et tamen a contrahentibus in facie Ecclesiae scitur. Et si occulte nubant et impedimentum nesciant, legitimum videtur in facie Ecclesiae, ex quo per Ecclesiam non prohibentur. Ergo filii extra verum matrimonium nati non sunt illegitimi.

SED CONTRA, illegitimum dicitur quod est contra legem. Sed illi qui nascuntur extra matrimonium, nascuntur contra legem. Ergo sunt illegitimi.

RESPONDEO dicendum quod quadruplex est status filiorum. Quidam enim sunt naturales et legitimi: sicut illi qui nascuntur ex legitimo matrimonio. Quidam naturales et non legitimi: ut filii qui nascuntur ex simplici fornicatione. Quidam legitimi et non naturales: sicut filii adoptivi. Quidam nec legitimi nec naturales: sicut spurii nati de adulterio vel de stupro; tales enim nascuntur et contra legem positivam, et expresse contra legem naturae. Et sic concedendum est quosdam filios esse illegitimos.

AD PRIMUM ergo dicendum quod, quamvis illi qui nascuntur ex illicito coitu, nascuntur secundum naturam quae communis est homini et omnibus animalibus,

OBJECTION 1: It would seem that children born out of true marriage are legitimate. For he that is born according to law is called a legitimate son. Now everyone is born according to law, at least the law of nature, which has more force than any other. Therefore, every child is to be called legitimate.

OBJ. 2: Further, it is the common saying that a legitimate child *is one born of a legitimate marriage, or of a marriage that is deemed legitimate in the eyes of the Church.* Now it happens sometimes that a marriage is deemed legitimate in the eyes of the Church, whereas there is some impediment affecting its validity: which impediment may be known to the parties who marry in the presence of the Church, or they may marry in secret and be ignorant of the impediment, in which case their marriage would seem legitimate in the eyes of the Church for the very reason that it is not prevented by the Church. Therefore, children born out of true marriage are not illegitimate.

ON THE CONTRARY, 'Illegitimate' is that which is against the law. Now those who are born out of wedlock are born contrary to the law. Therefore, they are illegitimate.

I ANSWER THAT, Children are of four conditions. Some are natural and legitimate, for instance, those who are born of a true and lawful marriage; some are natural and illegitimate, as those who are born of fornication; some are legitimate and not natural, as adopted children; some are neither legitimate nor natural; such are those born of adultery or incest, for these are born not only against the positive law, but against the express natural law. Hence we must grant that some children are illegitimate.

REPLY OBJ. 1: Although those who are born of an unlawful intercourse are born according to the nature common to man and all animals, they are born contrary to

tamen nascuntur contra legem naturae quae est propria hominibus: quia fornicatio et adulterium et huiusmodi sunt contra legem naturae. Et ideo tales secundum nullam legem sunt legitimi.

AD SECUNDUM dicendum quod ignorantia excusat illicitum coitum a peccato nisi sit affectata. Unde illi qui conveniunt bona fide in facie Ecclesiae, quamvis sit impedimentum, dum tamen ignorent, non peccant, nec filii sunt illegitimi. Si autem sciant, quamvis Ecclesia sustineat, quae ignorat impedimentum, non excusantur a peccato, nec filii ab illegitimitate. Si autem nesciant et in occulto contrahant, non excusantur: quia talis ignorantia videtur affectata.

the law of nature which is proper to man: since fornication, adultery, and the like are contrary to the law of nature. Hence the like are not legitimate by any law.

REPLY OBJ. 2: Ignorance, unless it be affected, excuses unlawful intercourse from sin. Wherefore those who contract together in good faith in the presence of the Church although there be an impediment, of which, however, they are ignorant, sin not, nor are their children illegitimate. If, however, they know of the impediment, although the Church upholds their marriage because she knows not of the impediment, they are not excused from sin, nor do their children avoid being illegitimate. Neither are they excused if they know not of the impediment and marry secretly, because such ignorance would appear to be affected.

Article 2

Whether Children Should Suffer Any Loss Through Being Illegitimate?

AD SECUNDUM SIC PROCEDITUR. Videtur quod illegitimi filii non debeant ex hoc aliquod damnum reportare. Quia filius non debet puniri pro peccato patris: ut patet per sententiam Domini, Ezech. 18. Sed quod iste nascatur ex illicito coitu, non est peccatum proprium, sed peccatum patris. Ergo ex hoc non debet aliquod damnum incurrere.

PRAETEREA, iustitia humana est exemplata a divina. Sed Deus aequaliter largitur bona naturalia legitimis et illegitimis filiis. Ergo et secundum iura humana filii illegitimi debent legitimis aequiparari.

SED CONTRA est quod dicitur Genes. 25, quod *Abraham dedit omnia bona sua Isaac, et filiis concubinarum largitus est munera*. Et tamen illi non erant ex illicito coitu nati. Ergo multo magis debent illi qui ex illicito coitu nascuntur, hoc damnum reportare quod non succedant in bonis paternis.

RESPONDEO dicendum quod aliquis dicitur damnum ex aliquo incurrere dupliciter. Uno modo, per hoc quod ei subtrahitur quod ei erat debitum. Et sic filius illegitimus nullum damnum incurrit. Alio modo, per: hoc quod ei aliquid non est debitum quod alias poterat esse ei debitum. Et sic filius illegitimus damnum incurrit duplex: unum, quia non admittitur ad actus legitimos, sicut ad officia et dignitates, quae requirunt quandam honestatem in illis qui hoc exercent; aliud damnum incurrit quia non succedit in hereditate paterna.

Sed tamen naturales filii succedere possunt in sexta parte tantum. Spurii autem in nulla parte: quamvis ex iure naturali parentes eis in necessariis providere teneantur. Unde pertinet ad sollicitudinem episcopi ut utrumque parentum cogat ad hoc quod eis provideant.

OBJECTION 1: It would seem that children ought not to suffer any loss through being illegitimate. For a child should not be punished on account of his father's sin, according to the Lord's saying (Ezech. 18:20). But it is not his own but his father's fault that he is born of an unlawful union. Therefore, he should not incur a loss on this account.

OBJ. 2: Further, human justice is copied from divine. Now God confers natural goods equally on legitimate and illegitimate children. Therefore, illegitimate should be equal to legitimate children according to human laws.

ON THE CONTRARY, It is stated that *Abraham gave all his possessions to Isaac, and that to the children of the concubines he gave gifts* (Gen 25:5): and yet the latter were not born of an unlawful intercourse. Much more, therefore, ought those born of an unlawful intercourse to incur loss by not inheriting their father's property.

I ANSWER THAT, A person is said to incur a loss for some cause in two ways: First, because he is deprived of his due, and thus an illegitimate child incurs no loss. Second, because something is not due to him which might have been due otherwise, and thus an illegitimate son incurs a twofold loss. First, because he is excluded from legitimate acts such as offices and dignities, which require a certain respectability in those who perform them. Second, he incurs a loss by not succeeding to his father's inheritance.

Nevertheless, natural sons can inherit a sixth only, whereas spurious children cannot inherit any portion, although by natural law their parents are bound to provide for their needs. Hence it is part of a bishop's care to compel both parents to provide for them.

Ad primum ergo dicendum quod incurrere damnum hoc secundo modo non est poena. Et ideo non dicimus quod sit poena alicui quod non succedit in regno aliquo per hoc quod non est filius regis. Et similiter non est poena quod alicui qui non est legitimus, non debeantur ea quae sunt legitimorum filiorum.

Ad secundum dicendum quod coitus illegitimus non est contra legem inquantum est actus generativae virtutis, sed inquantum ex prava voluntate procedit. Et ideo filius illegitimus non incurrit damnum in his quae acquiruntur per naturalem originem, sed in his quae per voluntatem fiunt vel possidentur.

Reply Obj. 1: To incur a loss in this second way is not a punishment. Hence we do not say that a person is punished by not succeeding to the throne through not being the king's son. In like manner, it is no punishment to an illegitimate child that he has no right to that which belongs to the legitimate children.

Reply Obj. 2: Illegitimate intercourse is contrary to the law not as an act of the generative power, but as proceeding from a wicked will. Hence an illegitimate son incurs a loss not in those things which come to him by his natural origin, but in those things which are dependent on the will for being done or possessed.

Article 3

Whether an Illegitimate Son Can Be Legitimized?

Ad tertium sic proceditur. Videtur quod filius illegitimus non possit legitimari. Quantum enim distat legitimus ab illegitimo, tantum e converso illegitimus a legitimo. Sed legitimus nunquam fit illegitimus. Ergo illegitimus nunquam fit legitimus.

Praeterea, coitus illegitimus causat illegitimum filium. Sed coitus illegitimus nunquam fit legitimus. Ergo nec filius illegitimus legitimari potest.

Sed contra, quod per legem inducitur, per legem revocari potest. Sed illegitimitas filiorum est per legem positivam inducta. Ergo potest filius illegitimus legitimari ab eo qui habet auctoritatem legis.

Respondeo dicendum quod filius illegitimus potest legitimari, non ut fiat de legitimo coitu natus, quia coitus ille transivit, et nunquam potest fieri legitimus ex quo semel fuit illegitimus: sed dicitur legitimari inquantum damna quae illegitimus filius incurrit, subtrahuntur per legis auctoritatem.

Et sunt sex modi legitimandi. Duo secundum canones: scilicet cum quis ducit in uxorem illam ex qua filium illegitimum generavit, si non fuit adulterium; et per specialem indulgentiam et dispensationem Domini Papae.

Quattuor autem alii modi sunt secundum leges. Primus est si pater filium naturalem curiae Imperatoris offerat: ex hoc enim ipso legitimatur, propter curiae honestatem. Secundus, si pater testamento nominet eum legitimum heredem, et filius postmodum testamentum Imperatori offerat. Tertius est si nullus sit filius legitimus, et ipsemet filius se principi offerat. Quartus, si pater iri

Objection 1: It would seem that an illegitimate son cannot be legitimized. For the legitimate child is as far removed from the illegitimate as the illegitimate from the legitimate. But a legitimate child is never made illegitimate. Neither, therefore, is an illegitimate child ever made legitimate.

Obj. 2: Further, illegitimate intercourse begets an illegitimate child. But illegitimate intercourse never becomes legitimate. Neither, therefore, can an illegitimate son become legitimate.

On the contrary, What is done by the law can be undone by the law. Now the illegitimacy of children is an effect of positive law. Therefore, an illegitimate child can be legitimized by one who has legal authority.

I answer that, An illegitimate child can be legitimized not so that he be born of a legitimate intercourse, because this intercourse is a thing of the past and can never be legitimized from the moment that it was once illegitimate. But the child is said to be legitimized insofar as the losses which an illegitimate child ought to incur are withdrawn by the authority of the law.

There are six ways of becoming legitimate: two according to the canons (*Decretals*), namely, when a man marries the woman of whom he has an unlawful child (if it were not a case of adultery); and by special indulgence and dispensation of the lord Pope.

The other four ways are according to the laws: (1) if the father offer his natural son to the emperor's court, for by this very fact the son is legitimate on account of the reputation of the court; (2) if the father designate him in his will as his legitimate heir, and the son afterwards offer the will to the emperor; (3) if there be no legitimate son and the son himself offer himself to the emperor; (4) if the father desig-

publico instrm mento, vel cum trium testium subscriptione, eum legitimum nominet nec adiiciat *naturalem*.

AD PRIMUM ergo dicendum quod alicui potest sine iniustitia gratia fieri: sed non potest aliquis damnificari nisi pro culpa. Et ideo magis potest illegitimus fieri legitimus quam e converso. Etsi enim legitimus aliquando hereditate privatur pro culpa, non tamen dicitur illegitimus filius: quia generationem legitimam habuit.

AD SECUNDUM dicendum quod actus illegitimus habet defectum intra se inseparabilem, quo legi opponitur: et ideo non potest fieri legitimus. Nec est simile de filio illegitimo, qui non habet huiusmodi defectum.

nate him as legitimate in a public document or in a document signed by three witnesses, without calling him *natural*.

REPLY OBJ. 1: A favor may be bestowed on a person without injustice, but a person cannot be damnified except for a fault. Hence an illegitimate child can be legitimized rather than vice versa; for although a legitimate son is sometimes deprived of his inheritance on account of his fault, he is not said to be illegitimate, because he was legitimately begotten.

REPLY OBJ. 2: Illegitimate intercourse has an inherent inseparable defect whereby it is opposed to the law: and consequently it cannot be legitimized. Nor is there any comparison with an illegitimate child who has no such defect.